Gas-Phase Ion and Neutral Thermochemistry

Journal of Physical and Chemical Reference Data

David R. Lide, Jr., Editor

Editorial Board

Term ending 31 December 1988
William A. Goddard III, Ronald A. Phaneuf, Alfons Weber
Term ending 31 December 1989
Mostafa A. El-Sayed, Glen A. Slack, Barry N. Taylor
Term ending 31 December 1990
Sidney C. Abrahams, Carlos M. Bowman, Malcolm W. Chase, Jr.

Management Board

David R. Lide, Jr., Charles R. Bertsch, John T. Scott

Editorial Staff at NBS: Julian M. Ives, Joan Sauerwein
Editorial Staff at AIP: Kathleen Strum, Managing Editor; Susan A. Walsh, Chief Copy Editor; Thomas J. Buckley, Copy Editor

The Journal of Physical and Chemical Reference Data (ISSN 0047-2689) is published quarterly by the American Chemical Society (1155 16th St., N. W., Washington, DC 20036-9976) and the American Institute of Physics (335 E. 45th St., New York, NY 10017-3483) for the National Bureau of Standards. Second-class postage paid at Washington, DC and additional mailing offices. POSTMASTER: Send address changes to *Journal of Physical and Chemical Reference Data*, Membership and Subscription Services, P. O. Box 3337, Columbus, Ohio 43210.

The objective of the Journal is to provide critically evaluated physical and chemical property data, fully documented as to the original sources and the criteria used for evaluation. Critical reviews of measurement techniques, whose aim is to assess the accuracy of available data in a given technical area, are also included. The Journal is not intended as a publication outlet for original experimental measurements such as those that are normally reported in the primary research literature, nor for review articles of a descriptive or primarily theoretical nature.

Supplements to the Journal are published at irregular intervals and are not included in subscriptions to the Journal. They contain compilations which are too lengthy for a journal format.

The Editor welcomes appropriate manuscripts for consideration by the Editorial Board. Potential contributors who are interested in preparing a compilation are invited to submit an outline of the nature and scope of the proposed compilation, with criteria for evaluation of the data and other pertinent factors, to:

David R. Lide, Jr., Editor
J. Phys. Chem. Ref. Data
National Bureau of Standards
Gaithersburg, MD 20899

One source of contributions to the Journal is The National Standard Reference Data System (NSRDS), which was established in 1963 as a means of coordinating on a national scale the production and dissemination of critically evaluated reference data in the physical sciences. Under the Standard Reference Data Act (Public Law 90-396) the National Bureau of Standards of the U.S. Department of Commerce has the primary responsibility in the Federal Government for providing reliable scientific and technical reference data. The Office of Standard Reference Data of NBS coordinates a complex of data evaluation centers, located in university, industrial, and other Government laboratories as well as within the National Bureau of Standards, which are engaged in the compilation and critical evaluation of numerical data on physical and chemical properties retrieved from the world scientific literature. The participants in this NBS-sponsored program, together with similar groups under private or other Government support which are pursuing the same ends, comprise the National Standard Reference Data System.

The primary focus of the NSRDS is on well-defined physical and chemical properties of well-characterized materials or systems. An effort is made to assess the accuracy of data reported in the primary research literature and to prepare compilations of critically evaluated data which will serve as reliable and convenient reference sources for the scientific and technical community.

Information for Contributors

Manuscripts submitted for publication must be prepared in accordance with *Instructions for Preparation of Manuscripts for the Journal of Physical and Chemical Reference Data*, available on request from the Editor.

New and renewal subscriptions should be sent with payment to the Office of the Controller at the American Chemical Society, 1155 Sixteenth Street, N.W., Washington, DC 20036-9976. **Address changes**, with at least six weeks advance notice, should be sent to *Journal of Physical and Chemical Reference Data*, Membership and Subscription Services, American Chemical Society, P.O. Box 3337, Columbus, OH 43210. Changes of address must include both old and new addresses and ZIP codes and, if possible, the address label from the mailing wrapper of a recent issue. Claims for missing numbers will not be allowed: if loss was due to failure of the change-of-address notice to be received in the time specified; if claim is dated (a) North America: more than 90 days beyond issue date, (b) all other foreign: more than one year beyond issue date.

Members of AIP member and affiliate societies requesting member subscription rates should direct subscriptions, renewals, and address changes to American Institute of Physics, Dept. S/F, 335 E. 45th St., NY 10017-3483.

Subscription Prices (1988) (not including supplements)	U.S.A.	Foreign (surface mail)	Optional air freight Europe Mideast N. Africa	Asia and Oceania
Members (of ACS, AIP, or affiliated society)	$ 60.00	$ 70.00	$ 80.00	$ 80.00
Regular rate	$265.00	$275.00	$285.00	$285.00

Rates above do not apply to nonmember subscribers in Japan, who must enter subscription orders with Maruzen Company Ltd., 3-10 Nihonbashi 2-chome, Chuo-ku, Tokyo 103, Japan. Tel: (03) 272-7211.

Back numbers are available at a cost of $75 per single copy and $295 per volume.

Orders for reprints, supplements, and back numbers should be addressed to the American Chemical Society, 1155 Sixteenth Street, N. W., Washington, DC 20036-9976. Prices for reprints and supplements are listed at the end of this issue.

Copying Fees: The code that appears on the first page of articles in this journal gives the fee for each copy of the article made beyond the free copying permitted by AIP. (See statement under "Copyright" elsewhere in this journal.) If no code appears, no fee applies. The fee for pre-1978 articles is $0.25 per copy. With the exception of copying for advertising and promotional purposes, the express permission of AIP is not required provided the fee is paid through the *Copyright Clearance Center, Inc. (CCC), 21 Congress Street, Salem, MA 01970*. Contact the CCC for information on how to report copying and remit payment.

Microfilm subscriptions of the *Journal of Physical and Chemical Reference Data* are available on 16 mm and 35 mm. This journal also appears in Sec. I of *Current Physics Microform* (CPM) along with 26 other journals published by the American Institute of Physics and its member societies. A *Microfilm Catalog* is available on request.

Copyright 1988 by the U.S. Secretary of Commerce; copyright assigned to the American Institute of Physics (AIP) and the American Chemical Society (ACS). Individual teachers, students, researchers, and libraries acting for them are permitted to make copies of articles in this journal for their own use in research or teaching, including multiple copies for classroom or library reserve use, provided such copies are not sold. Copying for sale is subject to payment of copying fees. (See "Copying Fees" paragraph elsewhere in this journal.) Permission is granted to quote from this journal with the customary acknowledgment of the source. To reprint a figure, table, or other excerpt requires in addition the consent of one of the original authors and notification to AIP. Reproduction for advertising or promotional purposes, or republication in any form, is permitted only under license from AIP, which will normally require that the permission of one of the authors also be obtained. Direct inquiries to Office of Rights and Permissions, American Institute of Physics, 335 East 45th Street, New York, NY 10017-3483. The right of the U.S. Government to unrestricted copying for its own use of copyrighted material originating in its laboratories or under its contracts is specifically recognized.

Journal of
Physical and Chemical Reference Data

Volume 17, 1988
Supplement No. 1

Gas-Phase Ion and Neutral Thermochemistry

Sharon G. Lias
Center for Chemical Physics, National Bureau of Standards,
Gaithersburg, Maryland 20899

John E. Bartmess
Department of Chemistry, The University of Tennessee,
Knoxville, Tennessee 37996-1600

Joel F. Liebman
Department of Chemistry, University of Maryland,
Baltimore County Campus, Baltimore, Maryland 21228

John L. Holmes
Department of Chemistry, University of Ottawa,
Ottawa, Ontario K1N 9B4, Canada

Rhoda D. Levin
Center for Chemical Physics, National Bureau of Standards,
Gaithersburg, Maryland 20899

and

W. Gary Mallard
Center for Chemical Physics, National Bureau of Standards,
Gaithersburg, Maryland 20899

Published by the **American Chemical Society**
and the **American Institute of Physics** for
the **National Bureau of Standards**

Copyright © 1988 by the U.S. Secretary of Commerce on behalf of the United States. This copyright will be assigned to the American Institute of Physics and the American Chemical Society, to whom all requests regarding reproduction should be addressed.

Library of Congress Catalog Card Number 88-70606

International Standard Book Number
0-88318-562-8

American Institute of Physics, Inc.

335 East 45th Street

New York, New York 10017-3483

Printed in the United States of America

Foreword

The *Journal of Physical and Chemical Reference Data* is published jointly by the American Institute of Physics and the American Chemical Society for the National Bureau of Standards. Its objective is to provide critically evaluated physical and chemical property data, fully documented as to the original sources and the criteria used for evaluation. One of the principal sources of material for the journal is the National Standard Reference Data System (NSRDS), a program coordinated by NBS for the purpose of promoting the compilation and critical evaluation of property data.

The regular issues of the *Journal of Physical and Chemical Reference Data* are published quarterly and contain compilations and critical data reviews of moderate length. Longer monographs, volumes of collected tables, and other material unsuited to a periodical format are published separately as *Supplements to the Journal*. This tabulation, "Gas-Phase Ion and Neutral Thermochemistry", by Sharon G. Lias, John E. Bartmess, Joel F. Liebman, John L. Holmes, Rhoda D. Levin, and W. Gary Mallard, is presented as Supplement No. 1 to Volume 17 of the *Journal of Physical and Chemical Reference Data*.

David R. Lide, Jr., Editor
Journal of Physical and Chemical Reference Data

Gas-Phase Ion and Neutral Thermochemistry

Sharon G. Lias
Center for Chemical Physics, National Bureau of Standards, Gaithersburg, Maryland 20899

John E. Bartmess
Department of Chemistry, The University of Tennessee, Knoxville, Tennessee 37996-1600

Joel F. Liebman
Department of Chemistry, University of Maryland, Baltimore County Campus, Baltimore, Maryland 21228

John L. Holmes
Department of Chemistry, University of Ottawa, Ottawa, Ontario K1N 9B4, Canada

Rhoda D. Levin
Center for Chemical Physics, National Bureau of Standards, Gaithersburg, Maryland 20899

and

W. Gary Mallard
Center for Chemical Physics, National Bureau of Standards, Gaithersburg, Maryland 20899

Critically evaluated data on heats of formation of positive and negative ions in the gas phase are compiled and presented in these tables (GIANT tables), along with auxiliary information on ionization energies, proton affinities, electron affinities and acidities, as well as relevant thermochemistry of related neutral species. The literature coverage is through the middle of 1986. The criteria used in carrying out evaluations of data are described, and a short discussion is presented of special concerns for the thermochemistry of charged species.

Key words: acidity; anion; basicity; cation; Franck-Condon principle; electron affinity; heats of formation; ion/molecule equilibrium; ionization energy; negative ion; proton affinity.

Contents

1. Introduction 5
   1.1. History 5
   1.2. Definitions 5
   1.3. Scope, Limitations to Coverage, and Organization......... 6
   1.4. Literature References.................................... 7
   1.5. Units 7
   1.6. Ion Thermochemistry at Finite Temperatures............... 8
        1.6.1. Thermochemical Conventions for the Electron 8
        1.6.2. Thermochemistry of Positive Ions at Finite
               Temperatures 10
        1.6.3. Thermochemistry of Negative Ions at Finite
               Temperatures 12
2. Positive Ions... 12
   2.1. The Evaluation of Experimentally-Determined Ionization
        Energies: The Franck-Condon Principle 12
   2.2. Interpretation of Appearance Energies 13
   2.3. Experimental Techniques.................................. 14
        2.3.1. Optical Spectroscopy 14
        2.3.2. Beam Studies Involving Laser Photoionization 14
        2.3.3. Determination of Ionization/Appearance Energies by
               Threshold Techniques 14
        2.3.4. Photoelectron Spectroscopy 15
        2.3.5. Ion/Molecule Equilibrium Constant Determinations. 15
        2.3.6. Ion/Molecule Bracketing Experiments 16
        2.3.7. Onsets of Endothermic Reactions................... 16
        2.3.8. Other Techniques.................................. 16
   2.4. Reliability of Ionization Energy Data and Criteria for
        Evaluation... 16
        2.4.1. Comparisons between Results of Different Techniques ... 16
        2.4.2. Reliability of Data; Error Limits 17
   2.5. Trends in the Data 18
        2.5.1. Estimation Schemes for Heats of Formation of Cations... 18
        2.5.2. Correlations of Ionization Energies with Proton
               Affinities, Substituent Constants 19
3. Negative Ions... 25
   3.1. Aims 25
   3.2. Experimental Techniques.................................. 26
        3.2.1. Laser Photoelectron Spectroscopy [LPES].......... 26
        3.2.2. Laser Photodetachment [LPD] 26
        3.2.3. Photodetachment [PD] 26
        3.2.4. Photodissociation [PDis].......................... 26
        3.2.5. Ion/Molecule Reaction Equilibrium Constant
               Determinations [IMRE, Kine, TDEq, TDAs] 26
        3.2.6. Ion/Molecule Reaction Bracketing [IMRB] 27
        3.2.7. Electron Impact Appearance Potentials [EIAP]..... 27
        3.2.8. Neutral Beam Ionization/Appearance Potentials
               [NBIP/NBAP]....................................... 28
        3.2.9. Photoionization [PI].............................. 28
        3.2.10. Endothermic Reaction Energy, Including Charge
                Transfer [Endo, EnCT, CIDT] 28
        3.2.11. Surface Ionization (Magnetron) [SI] 28
        3.2.12. Electron Swarm [ES] 28
        3.2.13. Lattice Energy [Latt] 28
        3.2.14. Kinetic Branching Methods [Bran, CIDC] 29
        3.2.15. Electron Transmission Spectroscopy [ETS] 29

		3.2.16. Electron Capture Detector [ECD]	29
		3.2.17. Mobility of Ions in a Gas [Mobl]	29
		3.2.18. Laser Optogalvanic Photodetachment Spectroscopy [LOG]	29
	3.3.	Thermochemical Cycles	29
	3.4.	Priority of Data	30
4.	Thermochemistry of Neutral Species		30
	4.1.	Literature Sources	31
		4.1.1. Organic Compounds	31
		4.1.2. Inorganic Compounds	31
		4.1.3. Specialized Classes of Compounds and Radicals	31
		4.1.4. Other Literature Sources	31
	4.2.	Conventions Used and Assumptions Made	32
	4.3.	Use of Condensed Phase Heats of Formation	32
	4.4.	Estimated Heats of Formation	32
		4.4.1. Estimates from Data on Isomeric Species	32
		4.4.2. Summing of Increments	33
5.	Summary of Conventions Used in Tables		34
	5.1.	Positive Ion Table (Table 1)	34
	5.2.	Negative Ion Table (Table 2)	34
	5.3.	References to Tables 1 and 2	36
6.	Acknowledgements		36
7.	References to Introduction		37

List of Tables
Tables in Introductory Text

1.6.1.1.	Summary of assumptions about electron thermochemistry in data compilations	9
2.5.1.1.	Estimation scheme of Holmes, Fingas and Lossing: $\Delta_f H(M^+)$ kcal/mol $= A - Bn + C/n$	19
2.5.1.2.	Estimation scheme of Bachiri, Mouvier, Carlier, and DuBois: $\log_{10}\{[IP(R_1XR_2) - IP_\infty]/(IP_0 - IP_\infty)\} = 0.106[I(R_1) + I(R_2)]$	20
2.5.1.3.	Comparison of ionization energies/heats of formation with estimated values predicted from estimation schemes	20
2.5.2.1.	The relationship between proton affinity, ionization energy, and hydrogen affinity for homologous series	23
5.2.	Acronyms, abbreviations and symbols used in negative ion table	35

Tables of Data

1.	Ionization energies and related heats of formation of positive ions	40
2.	Acidities, electron affinities, and heats of formation of anions	647
	References to Tables 1 and 2	797

1. Introduction

1.1. History

This publication is the direct linear descendant of two earlier compilations of evaluated heats of formation of ions derived from ionization potential and appearance potential data, both carried out under the auspices of the National Bureau of Standards. The first such volume, "Ionization Potentials, Appearance Potentials, and Heats of Formation of Gaseous Positive Ions" by J. L. Franklin, J. G. Dillard, H. M. Rosenstock, J. T. Herron, K. Draxl, and F. H. Field[1] appeared in 1969, and included all data on threshold energies for formation of positive ions which had appeared in the literature through mid-1966. That book, although woefully out-of-date now, is still occasionally referred to in the mass spectrometric literature, and is one of the most widely cited publications in the history of mass spectrometry. In 1977, H. M. Rosenstock, K. Draxl, B. W. Steiner, and J. T. Herron published an update, "Energetics of Gaseous Ions," which covered the literature through mid-1971[2]; the scope of the work was also extended to cover data on anions. In both of these books, the data for the threshold energies for formation of ions (ionization potentials and appearance potentials) were evaluated where possible, and where thermochemical data for relevant neutral species were available, values for heats of formation of the corresponding ions were derived.

In 1982, two of the present authors published an extensive compilation of *unevaluated* ionization potential and appearance potential data ("Ionization Potential and Appearance Potential Measurements, 1971–1981")[3] which covered the literature from the 1971 cut-off date of the 1977 book through mid-1981.

Since the mid-1970's, much information about ion thermochemistry has been derived from determinations of the equilibrium constants of ion/molecule reactions, a type of data which was not covered in the earlier compilations. Much of the work on equilibria of positive ions involves proton transfer reactions. These data have been compiled and evaluated by some of the present authors[4].

1.2. Definitions

The *heat of formation of a positive ion in the gas phase* is obtained by taking the heat of formation of the corresponding neutral species and adding the energy required to remove an electron, the so-called adiabatic ionization potential or, more correctly, the *adiabatic ionization energy*, IP_a (sometimes designated IE, or, in the older literature, I):

$$M \xrightarrow{IP_a} M^+ + e \qquad (1)$$

$$\Delta_f H(M^+) = \Delta_f H°(M) + IP_a - \Delta_f H(e) \qquad (2)$$

As discussed in Sec. 1.6.2., Eq. (2) is rigorously correct only at absolute zero. According to the convention adopted in this work for dealing with the thermochemistry of the electron (the "ion convention", sometimes called the "stationary electron convention", see Sec. 1.6.1.) "298 K heats of formation" of positive ions are often derived by simply adding the 0 K value for the ionization energy to the 298 K heat of formation of the molecule. The assumptions inherent in this treatment are discussed in Secs. 1.6.1. and 1.6.2. The user of these tables is cautioned that there is an alternate convention for dealing with the thermochemistry of the electron, which results in numerically different values for heats of formation for ions than those given here; details are discussed in Sec. 1.6.1.

The *vertical ionization energy* is the energy change corresponding to formation of the ion in a configuration which is effectively the same as that of the equilibrium geometry of the ground state neutral molecule. See Sec. 2.1. for a more complete discussion.

Accepting the simplifications described and justified in Sec. 1.6., determination of the heat of formation of a *molecular ion* is, in principle, straightforward, requiring only a value for the heat of formation of the corresponding neutral molecule and a reliable value for the adiabatic ionization energy. Many positive ions of interest, however, do not have stable neutral molecular counterparts. These include many of the ions which originate by fragmentation of a molecular ion, *fragment ions*:

$$AB^+ \rightarrow A^+ + B + e \qquad (3)$$

Heats of formation of fragment ions, A^+, are usually based on mass spectrometric determinations of the energy required to generate the ion from the neutral precursor molecule. This energy is called the "appearance potential" or, more correctly, the *"appearance energy"*, AP:

$$AB \xrightarrow{AP} A^+ + B + e \qquad (4)$$

In the case that there is no potential barrier in the reaction coordinate, and little or no kinetic shift (see Sec. 2.2.), the onset energy for formation of A^+ corresponds approximately to the enthalpy change of reaction 4. Under these conditions, the heat of formation of A^+ is usually assumed to be given by:

$$\Delta_f H(A^+) = \Delta_f H°(AB) - \Delta_f H°(B) + AP \qquad (5)$$

where, according to the ion convention, the term accounting for the electron has been taken to be zero. For a discussion of a more exact treatment of the energetics of ionic fragmentation processes, see Sec. 1.6.2.

Stable cations formed in the gas phase also include ions formed by protonating a neutral molecule:

$$BH^+ + M \rightarrow MH^+ + B \qquad (6)$$

In practice, heats of formation of most *protonated molecules* are derived from experiments in which the equilibrium constant of a proton transfer reaction such as 6 is determined (given that a heat of formation of a reference BH^+ ion is available from appearance potential determinations). Formally, the relationship between the heat of formation of MH^+ and its neutral counterpart, M, is defined in terms of a quantity called the *proton affinity, PA*. The proton affinity is the negative of the enthalpy change of the hypothetical protonation reaction:

$$M + H^+ \xrightarrow{-PA} MH^+ \quad (7)$$

$$\Delta_f H(MH^+) = \Delta_f H°(M) + \Delta_f H(H^+) - PA \quad (8)$$

The term proton affinity, as universally used, is a quantity defined at 298 K (and therefore not strictly analogous to the adiabatic ionization energy, which is the 0 K enthalpy change of reaction 1). (The Gibbs energy change associated with reaction 7 is called the *gas basicity, GB*, of molecule M.) At 298 K, the heat of formation of the proton, using the ion ("stationary electron") convention, is 365.7 kcal/mol, 1530.0 kJ/mol.

The *electron affinity (EA)* of a molecule is, for *negative ions* or *anions*, the quantity which is analogous to the ionization energy for positive ions. That is, the electron affinity is equal to the energy difference between the heat of formation of a neutral species and the *heat of formation of the negative ion* of the same structure. The electron affinity is defined as the negative of the 0 K enthalpy change for the electron attachment reaction:

$$M + e \xrightarrow{-EA_a} M^- \quad (9)$$

The *gas phase acidity* (or merely, acidity) of a molecule AH, $\Delta_{acid} G(AH)$, is the Gibbs energy change of the reaction:

$$AH \rightarrow A^- + H^+ \quad (10)$$

usually defined at 298 K. The enthalpy change of reaction 10, $\Delta_{acid} H$, is, of course, the proton affinity of the anion. The Gibbs energy change of the reaction:

$$AH + B^- \rightarrow BH + A^- \quad (11)$$

is called the *relative acidity* of species AH and BH.

1.3. Scope, Limitations to Coverage, and Organization

The intent of the present effort is to give (a) the "best" available experimentally-determined values for ionization potentials, electron affinities, acidities or proton affinities of molecules or molecular fragments, and (b) the heats of formation of the corresponding positive and negative ions. Also included are values for the heats of formation of the relevant neutral species which were used to obtain the heats of formation of the ions. Appearance energies are not specifically listed here, although heats of formation of ions derived from such data are given where the accuracy is sufficiently great to warrant inclusion.

In evaluating heats of formation of ions for the present work, all data presented in the previous compilations[1,2,3,4] have been considered, along with data from the more recent literature, 1981–1986. In addition, thermochemical information about ions derived from ion/molecule equilibrium constant determinations has been fully utilized, both in evaluations of ionization potential/appearance potential, proton affinity, acidity, and electron affinity data, and in deriving values for heats of formation of ions for which no other information is available.

Because the values for the heats of formation of ions are, of course, dependent on the larger corpus of thermochemical data on uncharged species, the values for heats of formation of relevant neutral species which were utilized are included as an intrinsic part of the tables.

The user familiar with the previous compilations in this series will note that the format of the present work is considerably different from that of its predecessors. In all three previous volumes, *all* ionization energy or appearance energy data pertaining to a particular ionic species were displayed, so that the books served as complete summaries and guides to the literature. Because of the increasing volume of such an archive with time, such a display is no longer practical for the positive ion data. Furthermore, because the general quality of mass spectrometric measurements has increased greatly over the last decade, display of some of the now out-of-date early data is no longer even desirable for ionization potentials/appearance potentials.

On the other hand, there has been a tremendous increase in the number of anions for which some thermochemical information is known, and this publication presents the first extensive evaluated compilation of those data. The table of anion thermochemistry (Table 2), therefore, includes both as *complete* a collection as possible of the literature data, and an assignment where possible of the "best" value for the thermochemistry.

Because earlier volumes in this series[1,2] were devoted to deriving values for *heats of formation* of ions, this work has been defined in the same way. It should be emphasized that in Table 1 (the positive ion table) molecules for which heats of formation are not known or have not been estimated are not included, even if the corresponding ionization energies or proton affinities are known. On the other hand, Table 2 (the negative ion table) presents a complete archive of data on electron affinities and gas phase acidities, whether or not the thermochemistry of relevant neutral species is available; the evaluation of the scale of gas phase acidities will, however, be the subject of a separate publication[5]. The total archive of ionization energy and appearance energy data will be published separately[6], as will the updated scales of gas phase basicities/proton affinities[7].

Another consequence of defining this work in terms of thermochemical data is that the abundant data on excited states of ions from photoelectron spectroscopy are not included here. The combined bibliographies of this work and its predecessors, however, do include the entire corpus of literature of photoelectron spectroscopy, since values for the *lowest* ionization energy derived from photoelectron experiments are included. Also not included are data on multiply charged ions.

Thermochemical information about ion/molecule clusters has been published in a recent compilation[8], and is not specifically included here, although some information derived from the enthalpy changes associated with the association of the first solvent molecule have been used in evaluating certain heats of formation.

At this writing, publications are beginning to appear in increasing numbers giving quantum mechanical calculations of very high accuracy on the thermochemical properties of ions, especially small ions[9,10]. The present work includes *only* data derived from experimental determinations. However, conclusions derived from some high level calculations have been taken into account in the evaluation of data for particular species.

The solution phase reduction potentials of a variety of species have been correlated with gas phase electron affinities (EAs), and values for a large number of EAs have been extrapolated from such correlations. More recent determinations of accurate gas phase data have shown that such relationships hold only for limited classes of compounds, so that the solution phase data can be taken only as an approximate guide to predicting electron affinities. Thus, any electron affinity values derived from reduction potentials have been omitted from this compilation. Such values were included in a recent compilation of anion data[11].

This compilation also does not attempt to cover negative electron affinities — cases where the electron in the highest occupied molecular orbital is unbound (resonance states), and therefore the lifetime of the anion with respect to autodetachment is on the order of microseconds, at most. Electron transmission spectrometry[12] is used to determine thermochemical data for such species. Brief mention is made for certain small molecules and elements for which the anion is known to be unbound, to differentiate from cases for which there is just no data available.

The data on positive ions and on negative ions are not interdependent, and have been evaluated separately. Data on the positive ions were collected and evaluated at the National Bureau of Standards (ionization energies, equilibrium constant data) and the University of Ottawa (appearance energies), while information concerning the negative ions was handled at the University of Tennessee. The data on cations and anions are presented in two separate tables.

Since heats of formation of ions are derived using data on heats of formation of neutral molecules and radicals, data on the thermochemistry of uncharged species are an integral part of this work. Although only experimentally-determined values for heats of formation of neutral species were utilized in the 1977 evaluation, estimation schemes for arriving at thermochemical information are now widely accepted and used. Estimated heats of formation are included for many species for which no experimental data are available. These estimations, and a literature search for thermochemical data not available in compilations, were performed primarily at the University of Maryland, Baltimore County Campus.

1.4. Literature References

With respect to ionization energies, appearance energies, or proton affinities, the present publication gives specific citations only to publications which were not included in the previous compilations[1,2,3,4]. The bibliography includes *all* references which have appeared since the previous publications[1,2,3,4] even if the data from a particular paper are not given here because of a lack of information about the thermochemistry of relevant neutral molecules. When no literature reference is given for these kinds of data in the positive ion table, it should be assumed that the primary reference can be obtained from the secondary sources, references 1, 2, 3, or 4. When the source of the data on ion thermochemistry is a recent paper which was not included in any of these previous compilations, the reference is specifically cited in a footnote. The literature citations for which a specific column is provided in Table 1 refer only to the source of the data on the thermochemistry of the neutral species.

In Table 2, specific citations are given for the data on both the ion thermochemistry and the relevant neutral thermochemistry.

1.5. Units

Information is displayed in the tables using different units, dictated by the current practices for reporting data of a particular kind. For example, ionization energy and electron affinity values are usually reported in electron volts, and that is the unit used here for these data. Heats of formation of positive ions are given here in both kcal/mol and kJ/mol. The reason for this duplication is simply that both units are extensively used in the literature, and users of these tables will be about equally divided between those who prefer kilocalories and those who prefer kilojoules. Furthermore, because of the duplication in units, the data can always be displayed as they appeared in the original paper, a practice which helps in elimination of transcribing errors. While the same statements certainly apply to data on negative ions, the amount of information which needs to be displayed in Table 2 is sufficiently great that including the same information twice, in two sets of units, would crowd the page too much; therefore, the negative ion heats of formation and acidities are given only in the SI unit, kJ/mol.

The conversion factors which were used in this work are: 1 electron volt (eV) = 23.06036 kilocalories/mole = 96.4845 kilojoules/mole; 1 kilocalorie/mole = 4.184 kilojoules/mole.

1.6. Ion Thermochemistry at Finite Temperatures

The auxiliary thermochemical information required for citation of ion heats of formation—heats of formation of relevant neutral species—is available mostly for species at 298 K. These thermochemical data are correct for use in deriving ion heats of formation from equilibrium constant determinations, i.e., for treatment of data derived from processes occurring at temperatures other than 0 K. However, strictly speaking, the ionization energy and the electron affinity of a molecule are quantities which correspond to processes occurring at 0 K. As mentioned above in Sec. 1.2., a rigorously correct treatment of heats of formation of ions requires explicit treatment of the differences in thermochemical values at 0 K and at higher temperatures. This section describes the principles involved in such a correct treatment, considers the simplifications which are often made in the literature, and specifies how data have been treated in this work.

1.6.1. Thermochemical Conventions for the Electron

We are concerned with the way in which the enthalpies of formation of the chemical species, M^+ and M^-, are *defined*, particularly at temperatures other than 0 K. The enthalpy of formation of any chemical species is always taken as the difference between the enthalpy of the compound and the sum of the enthalpies of the elements of which it is composed. However, in the case of an ion, M^+ or M^-, a special problem arises—one must explicitly take into account the enthalpy of the electron in some way.

There are two conventions for dealing with the thermochemistry of the electron, one used predominantly by thermodynamicists[13,14,15] and one adopted by scientists studying ion physics/chemistry[16,17]. The thermodynamicists' convention, commonly called the "thermal electron convention" or merely the "electron convention", defines the electron as a standard *chemical element* and treats its thermochemistry accordingly. The mass spectrometrists' convention, known as the "stationary electron convention" or the "ion convention", defines the electron as a *sub-atomic particle*. Because of differences in the treatment of the thermochemistry under these two definitions, except at absolute zero values cited for the enthalpies of formation of ions in certain thermochemical compilations such as the JANAF tables[13] or the NBS Tables of Chemical Thermodynamic Properties[14] differ from those cited here, or in most mass spectrometric literature, by 1.481 kcal/mol, 6.197 kJ/mol. Our values are lower for positive ions and higher for negative ions. Problems arise when users unknowingly mix inconsistent values for heats of formation in the same equation.

There is considerable confusion and misunderstanding of the basic assumptions and treatment of the thermochemistry of the electron in the two approaches. Many scientists who regularly use one or the other convention in their work can not clearly explain the differences. Indeed, some hold that the two ways of dealing with the thermochemistry of the electron are not merely two conventions, but two scientifically different concepts, one of which must be incorrect. The discussion which follows is an attempt to present the question of how the electron is treated in a thermochemical equation in as simple and straightforward a manner as possible, in the hope that some of the confusion will be dispelled and the identity of the two treatments as *conventions* will become clear. This discussion is also intended to justify the choice of the usual mass spectrometrists' convention for use in these tables.

The relationships between the various quantities which must be considered are shown in the thermochemical cycles:

$$M_{0\,K} \xrightarrow{IP} M^+_{0\,K} + e_{0\,K} \quad (12a)$$
$$A \downarrow \qquad B \downarrow \qquad C \downarrow$$
$$M_{298\,K} \xrightarrow{\Delta H_I} M^+_{298\,K} + e_{298\,K} \quad (12b)$$

and

$$M_{0\,K} + e_{0\,K} \xrightarrow{-EA} M^-_{0\,K} \quad (13a)$$
$$A \downarrow \qquad C \downarrow \qquad D \downarrow$$
$$M_{298\,K} + e_{298\,K} \xrightarrow{\Delta H_{EA}} M^-_{298\,K} \quad (13b)$$

where A, B, C, and D are the integrated heat capacities for the various indicated species, e.g., A is the energy required to raise M from 0 K to 298 K, and ΔH_I and ΔH_{EA} are the 298 K enthalpies of reaction. This discussion will be concerned with the standard temperature, 298 K, but the arguments can obviously be extended to any other temperature.

At 0 K, the heat of formation of the electron is zero and the heats of formation of the ions are exactly equal to the 0 K heat of formation of the molecule M plus the energy difference between M and the corresponding ion:

$$\Delta_f H(M^+)_{0\,K} = \Delta_f H°(M)_{0\,K} + IP_a \quad (14)$$

$$\Delta_f H(M^-)_{0\,K} = \Delta_f H°(M)_{0\,K} - EA \quad (15)$$

At absolute zero, there is no difference between the two conventions.

When the temperature is raised to 298 K, the heats of formation of M^+ and M^- will be related to the heat of formation of M at 298 K through the enthalpy changes of reactions 12b and 13b:

$$\Delta_f H(M^+)_{298\,K} = \Delta_f H°(M)_{298\,K} - \Delta_f H(e)_{298\,K} + \Delta H_I \quad (16)$$

$$\Delta_f H(M^-)_{298\,K} = \Delta_f H°(M)_{298\,K} + \Delta_f H(e)_{298\,K} + \Delta H_{EA} \quad (17)$$

The enthalpy changes of reaction at 298 K are related to the 0 K ionization energy and electron affinity through the relationships:

$$\Delta H_I = IP_a + (C + B - A) \quad (18)$$

$$\Delta H_{EA} = -EA - (C + A - D) \quad (19)$$

If the electron is defined to be a chemical element (the "electron convention"), its heat of formation by definition is zero at all temperatures in its standard state. Thermodynamicists start from this assumption and then make a second one, that an electron gas can be treated as an ideal gas following Boltzmann statistics; this second assumption is used to calculate the integrated heat capacity of the electron, C. In many thermodynamics data compilations, the integrated heat capacity terms for M and the corresponding ion, M^+ or M^-, are taken to be approximately equal for many ions, i.e. $A = B = D$. (See Sec. 1.6.2. for a discussion of this assumption.) Under this set of assumptions, Eqs. (16) and (17) can be written:

$$\Delta_f H(M^+)_{298\ K} = \Delta_f H°(M)_{298\ K} + [IP_a + C] \quad (20)$$

$$\Delta_f H(M^-)_{298\ K} = \Delta_f H°(M)_{298\ K} - [EA - C] \quad (21)$$

(where the term $\Delta_f H(e)_{298\ K}$ has been taken to be equal to zero and the quantity in brackets is the assumed enthalpy change of reaction at 298 K). What most often causes confusion for non-thermodynamicists is the de facto assignment of the integrated heat capacity of the electron, C, to the ion M^+ or M^-, rather than to the electron in going from 0 K to 298 K. This is required if the heat of formation of the electron is constrained to be zero at all temperatures. It is questionable whether an ion is any more "ideal" than an electron, due to the Coulombic forces between the particles, but this assignment is a necessity if the original assumptions are carried through the argument.

In contrast, the standard treatment of ion heats of formation followed in almost the entire corpus of literature on ion physics/chemistry essentially assumes that:

$$\Delta_f H(M^+)_{298\ K} = \Delta_f H°(M)_{298\ K} + [IP_a + B - A] \quad (22)$$

$$\Delta_f H(M^-)_{298\ K} = \Delta_f H°(M)_{298\ K} + [-EA - A + D] \quad (23)$$

(where the expressions in brackets are assumed to be equal to the enthalpy change of reaction at 298 K, and the quantities A, B, and D are often, but not always, taken to be equal). Since this is equivalent to taking a value of zero for the integrated heat capacity of the electron (the term C in Eqs. (18) and (19)), this way of treating the thermochemistry of the electron has come to be known as the "stationary electron" convention. The use of this term has unfortunately led to the widespread conception that this convention defines the ionization process as producing an electron which has no thermal energy at 298 K. Since this is not the case, it is preferable to choose another designation for the convention. In this publication we will adopt the term originally suggested by Syverud[18] for the mass spectrometrists' convention, "ion convention".

At 298 K, the integrated heat capacity of an ideal Boltzmann gas is 1.481 kcal/mol, 6.197 kJ/mol. The relationship between 298 K heats of formation of ions in the ion convention (IC) and the thermodynamicists' convention (TC) is:

$$\Delta_f H(M^+)_{298\ K}(IC) = \Delta_f H(M^+)_{298\ K}(TC) - 6.197\ kJ/mol \quad (24)$$

$$\Delta_f H(M^-)_{298\ K}(IC) = \Delta_f H(M^-)_{298\ K}(TC) + 6.197\ kJ/mol \quad (25)$$

Table 1.6.1.1. summarizes the assumptions made in the two conventions and the data compilations where they are used.

TABLE 1.6.1.1. Summary of assumptions about electron thermochemistry in data compilations.

Convention	Compilation	Convention Includes $H_T - H_0$ for Species: M^+ or M^-	e	Value of C, kJ/mol
Thermal electron	JANAF Tables[13]	Yes[a] Yes[a]	Yes	6.197
Thermal electron	Gurvich et al[15]	Yes[a] Yes[a]	Yes	6.197
Thermal electron (Modified)	TN270[14]	No No	Yes	6.197
Ion convention	This work, Refs. 1–4	Yes[a] Yes[a]	No	0
Ion convention	Some papers	No No	No	0

[a]When sufficient information is available. See discussion in Sec. 1.6.2.

The objection has been made that the mass spectrometrists' convention is scientifically incorrect because the electron actually does have thermal energy at 298 K. Note, however, that the values derived in the mass spectrometrists' convention for the heats of formation of the ions are numerically identical to those one would obtain if one assigned the thermal energy of the electron *to the electron* rather than to the enthalpy of formation of the accompanying ion (as is done in the thermodynamicists' convention). That is, in Eqs. (16) and (17) if one assigns a value of C to $\Delta_f H(e)_{298\ K}$ and takes the value for the enthalpy change of reaction from Eqs. (18) and (19), one obtains:

$$\Delta_f H(M^+)_{298\ K} = \Delta_f H°(M)_{298\ K} - C + IP_a + (C + B - A) \quad (26)$$

$$\Delta_f H(M^-)_{298\ K} = \Delta_f H°(M)_{298\ K} + C - EA - (C + A - D) \quad (27)$$

which are identical to expressions 22 and 23. Although this is a nonstandard treatment, it is possible to justify using a special convention for the thermochemical properties of the electron, since this species is not normally considered to be a chemical element; a stronger justification is found by considering that the use of the standard treatment for an element in this case results in heats of formation for a large body of molecular species — ions — which reflect an arbitrary temperature dependence which can not be experimentally measured or verified at the present time.

In fact, the mass spectrometrists' convention for treating the electron was not derived from a conscious treatment of the electron as having a non-zero heat of formation at 298 K. Indeed, earlier discussions of this convention[16,17,18] have centered mainly on the reluctance to assign a purely arbitrary temperature dependence to ionization or electron attachment events and a recognition that absolute values of the various parameters, ΔH_I, ΔH_{EA}, B, D, and especially C were not available. The enthalpy changes of reactions 12b and 13b are not directly measured by any currently-available experimental techniques, and can not be said to be known within ±6.197 kJ/mol. As will be discussed below, accurate values for the integrated heat capacities of ions M^+ and M^- are not available except for a few small species, and the assumption that $(B - A)$ and $(A - D)$ are exactly equal to zero is often not warranted (see Sec. 1.6.2.). Most important, however, the value chosen for the integrated heat capacity of the electron, C, is completely arbitrary. To quote from the 1985 edition of the JANAF thermochemical tables[13c]:

"As shown by Sommerfeld[19], the electron gas is a degenerate Fermi-Dirac gas and its properties will differ from the classical (Boltzmann) gas. These deviations will increase as the temperature decreases or as the density increases. Due to the low mass of the electron, these departures from classical behavior will persist to higher temperatures and lower densities than for atomic systems. Under conditions of 1 atm pressure, Gordon[20] showed that the deviation of the Fermi-Dirac gas from the Boltzmann gas is negligible above 1250 K. Below this temperature the deviation between classical and quantum statistics will be significant.

Despite these known deviations we have chosen to present the classical (Boltzmann) values here since the primary purpose of this table is to serve as a reference state for the calculation of tables of thermodynamic properties for atomic and molecular ions..... Therefore, although this ideal-gas table has the formalism of 1 bar as the standard reference state, it should not be applied to real systems where the electron partial pressure exceeds 10^{-6} bar."

That is, the authors of the JANAF tables[13] recognize that the standard thermodynamicists' convention for dealing with the electron does involve a completely arbitrary assumption about the value assigned to the enthalpy of the electron (as does the mass spectrometrists' convention when expressed by Eqs. (22) and (23)—but not in the assumptions built into the equivalent Eqs. (26) and (27)). Syverud[18], in an unpublished discussion of conventions for treating the thermochemical properties of the electron, cites a value of approximately 3.3 kJ/mol, 0.8 kcal/mol for the value of C derived from a quantum chemical calculation (source not quoted). Furthermore, while the rationale for the thermodynamicists' convention is that the values "correspond to a meaningful thermal process"[21], the use of that convention is excluded for a substantial set of possible thermal conditions.

The mass spectrometrists' approach to the problem recognizes that the specific inclusion of the term for the enthalpy of the electron in deriving ion heats of formation is not physically meaningful if it is based on the assumption that an electron gas can be treated like an ideal gas. In fact, at this time neither the enthalpy changes of reactions 12b and 13b nor the enthalpy of the electron are established; a solution is to adopt a convention (the "ion convention") which sidesteps the problem, that is, in which the enthalpy change of reaction and the enthalpy of the electron need not be known or assumed. If, in the future, information about the integrated heat capacities of the electron and the ions does become available, the values for heats of formation of ions can be fine-tuned; however, in the meantime, there is no real problem with using data in the present form as long as internal consistency is maintained.

It will be noted that in the tables, the symbol $\Delta_f H$ rather than $\Delta_f H°$ is used to denote the standard heats of formation of the ions. This convention has been adopted here to emphasize that the heats of formation are referred to the ion convention rather than the electron convention used by thermodynamicists.

1.6.2. Thermochemistry of Positive Ions at Finite Temperatures

Molecular ions. Using the ion convention (also known as the stationary electron convention, see Sec. 1.6.1.) the heat of formation of molecular ion M^+ at temperature T can be defined in terms of the heat of formation of the corresponding neutral species, M, at temperature T, and a quantity labelled ΔH_I, the gas phase enthalpy change of ionization, which represents the energy required to bring about ionization at temperature T:

$$\Delta_f H(M^+)_T = \Delta_f H°(M)_T + \Delta H_I \quad (28)$$

In applying Eq. (28), the value for ΔH_I is usually taken to be exactly equal to the adiabatic ionization potential. Although the use of the ion convention obviates the necessity of assigning an exact value to the increase in the ionization energy at temperature T due to energy imparted to the electron, the assumption that ΔH_I is the same as IP_a is still not correct. The adiabatic ionization energy of a molecule is the energy difference between the lowest rotational and vibrational levels of the ground state of the molecule and the lowest rotational and vibrational levels of the electronic ground state of the ion, i.e., the difference between the heats of formation of the molecule and the corresponding ion at absolute zero. The adiabatic ionization energy—the quantity obtained from analysis of a Rydberg series (Sec. 2.3.1.) or from determinations of an ionization onset energy (Sec. 2.3.3.) — is a measure of the $0 \rightarrow 0$ transition, and does not depend on the temperature at which the determination is made.

However, it is a common practice to derive "298 K heats of formation" of positive ions by simply adding the 0 K value for the ionization energy to the 298 K heat of formation of the molecule. This practice probably gains impetus from the fact that much of the available thermochemical data for chemical compounds (particularly for organic and other large polyatomic compounds) correspond to values for heats of formation at 298 K.

The relationship between the enthalpy change associated with ionization at temperature T, ΔH_I, and the adiabatic ionization energy is shown in thermochemical cycle 12, and given explicitly in Eq. 18. When using the ion convention for dealing with thermochemistry of the electron (Sec. 1.6.1.), the integrated heat capacity of the electron (the quantity C in the cycle) can be ignored, and the relationship between the adiabatic ionization energy and the enthalpy change of ionization at temperature T is given by:

$$\Delta H_I = IP_a + B - A \qquad (29)$$

That is, IP_a and ΔH_I are the same only when the integrated heat capacities of the neutral molecule, M, and the ion, M^+, are identical over this temperature range. An analysis[22] of the differences between integrated heat capacities of M and M^+ for various molecules demonstrated that (a) there will be no discernable differences between the translational and rotational heat capacities of M and M^+, (b) that differences arising from a splitting of degenerate energy levels in multiplet ground states of M or M^+ will never be larger than 0.009 eV at temperatures in the 300–400 K range, and (c) when the frequency of a particular vibration changes upon ionization, there will be a difference between the integrated heat capacities of M and M^+. However, even this contribution will usually be sufficiently small that a significant error will not be introduced if it is ignored. For example, the lowest ionization energy of ethylene corresponds to removal of an electron from the C–C pi bond, which leads to a lowering of the frequency of the symmetric C–C stretch from 1623 to 1230 cm^{-1} and a reduction in the frequency of the twisting around the C–C bond from 1027 to 430 cm^{-1}. Although these differences in vibrational frequencies are significant, the predicted effect on the 298 K enthalpy of ionization is to raise it above the value for the adiabatic ionization potential by only 0.0069 eV, i.e. only the most accurate experimental measurements would detect an increment of this size. Thus for most species, the simplifying assumption that the adiabatic ionization energy and the 298 K enthalpy of ionization, ΔH_I, are approximately the same:

$$IP_a \sim \Delta H_I \qquad (30)$$

will not introduce significant errors in the 298 K heats of formation of molecular radical cations.

In this compilation, most values of heats of formation of molecular ions correspond to 298 K. Most of these were obtained by simply adding the value for the adiabatic ionization energy to the 298 K heat of formation of the neutral species, that is, the assumption stated in Eq. (30) was usually made. Of course, a rigorously correct treatment would require calculating exact values for integrated heat capacities A and B from complete sets of vibrational frequencies for the molecule and the ion. This complete procedure has been applied to only a few of the species listed in this compilation. Vibrational frequencies for most of the ions are not available, and the correction would simply cancel out if one made the often-used assumption that the vibrational frequencies of the ion and its neutral counterpart are the same. Whenever the original authors carried out such a complete analysis (a routine procedure only for photoelectron-photoion coincidence studies), the results of that analysis are included here, and both 0 K and 298 K values for the ion heat of formation are given. In addition, for those diatomic and triatomic and other small molecules for which values for the 0 K heats of formation as well as the vibrational frequencies of the molecule[23] and the ion[24] were readily available, the heats of formation of the ion at absolute zero and at 298 K were derived by the more correct procedure. In the course of this work, we did not, however, carry out a comprehensive literature search for sets of vibrational frequencies, but only made use of readily available compilations[23,24].

Fragment ions. Analogous arguments can be applied to the use of appearance energies for the derivation of heats of formation of fragment ions, A^+, at temperature T in Eq. (5). If there are no complicating factors (see Sec. 2.2.), the appearance energy, AP, corresponds to the enthalpy change for the fragmentation reaction 4, and can be used to derive a value for the heat of formation of the fragment ion, A^+. Correctly, a 0 K heat of formation of A^+ must be obtained using 0 K heats of formation of AB and B in the calculation, and this heat of formation can then be corrected to some other temperature, T, taking into account the vibrational frequencies of the ion and appropriate thermodynamic functions of the elements.

For the most common experimental techniques (energy selected electron impact, photoionization mass spectroscopy, etc.) for measuring the appearance energy of a fragment ion starting from a molecule or radical at temperature, T, the major problem is to identify the internal energies of the reaction products. This matter has been discussed at length by Traeger and McLaughlin[25]. At *onset* the products of the unimolecular decomposition will be formed with zero translational energy with respect to the center of mass (provided that the fragmentation does not involve a reverse energy barrier) and a center of mass translational energy the same as that of the precursor molecule. The products thus are at a translational quasi-temperature, T^*. In principle, if the observational time scale of the experiment and the sensitivity of the ion detector are great enough, then the observed appearance energy approaches that for products having 0 K internal energy (i.e., all internal energy modes have contributed to reaching the transition state). Traeger and McLaughlin[25] showed that for the molecule AB:

$$AP_T(\exp) = \Delta_f H[A^+ + B + e]_T - \Delta_f H°[AB]_T \\ + 5/2 RT - \int C_p[A^+ + B + e]dT \quad (31)$$

In effect, this equation corrects the observed threshold energy for the fragmentation process to an effective 0 K value by adding the thermal rotational and vibrational energy contained in AB to the onset.

Most heats of formation of fragment ions are derived making the simplifying assumption that the last two terms of Eq. (31) will cancel one another. That is, values for heats of formation of fragment ions at 298 K derived from appearance potential data are more often obtained by simply using an observed onset energy and 298 K heats of formation of relevant neutral species in Eq. (5). When such a value for a heat of formation has been reported in the literature, the value is given here as it appeared in the original paper, with only the imposed requirement that the thermochemistry of the relevant neutral species employed must be internally consistent with the values of those species used in this publication. Where the original authors have used a more sophisticated analysis, such as that represented by Eq. (31), or that routinely used in the interpretation of photoelectron-photoion data, both 0 K and 298 K values of the ion are cited. The user should be cautioned that the 298 K value assigned to a heat of formation of a fragment ion may differ by as much as 3 or 4 kcal/mol, 12–18 kJ/mol, depending on which of these treatments has been used. For example, Baer and Brand[26], and Lossing[27] determined the appearance energies for formation of $C_4H_7^+$ ions in C_5H_{10} isomers. Although the appearance energies reported in the two studies were almost identical, the 298 K values for heats of formation of the $C_4H_7^+$ ions derived by Baer and Brand[26], using a complete treatment of the temperature dependence of the heat of formation, are higher than the values derived by Lossing[27] by 4.3 kcal/mol, 18 kJ/mol.

1.6.3. Thermochemistry of Negative Ions at Finite Temperatures

The electron affinity is a quantity which is analogous to the ionization energy. That is, the electron affinity is a 0 K quantity which corresponds to the transition from the ground state of the neutral species to the ground state of the anion. Thus, the heat of formation of an anion at 298 K can not rigorously be taken as the heat of formation of the corresponding neutral species (298 K) minus the (positive) electron affinity (0 K) without some estimate of the temperature dependence of the electron affinity. Although the use of the ion convention ("stationary electron" convention) allows one to ignore the integrated heat capacity of the electron, a term for correcting for the integrated heat capacity of the anion from 0 K to 298 K is required. Statistical mechanics permits a calculation of this quantity if the structure and vibrational frequencies of the anion are known. However, at present the necessary data are not readily available for most anions, and therefore this correction is generally ignored in this work.

Under the assumption that the temperature dependence of the electron affinity and that of the ionization energy of the H atom are equal, one can relate the (298 K) gas phase acidity, Eq. (10), to the (0 K) electron affinity:

$$\Delta_{acid}H(AH) = D(A-H) - EA_{0K}(A) + IP_{0K}(H) \quad (32)$$

There is not extensive data on the validity of this assumption, although it appears to hold[13] to ±2 kJ/mol for Cl^- and OH^-.

2. Positive Ions

In the discussion which follows, a brief description of the Franck-Condon principle along with a discussion of the implications for an analysis of data obtained from experimental determinations of ionization energies will be given in Sec. 2.1. In Sec. 2.2., special problems in the interpretation of appearance potential data will be summarized, followed in Sec. 2.3. by short descriptions of the various experimental techniques used in obtaining the data given here, with attention to intrinsic experimental problems which may affect the reliability of data. Section 2.4. will give a discussion of the rationale used in evaluating ionization energy and appearance energy data from the various approaches, and a description of the conventions and symbols used in the tables. Finally, Sec. 2.5. summarizes a few of the regular trends observed in the data, and describes schemes for estimating data on heats of formation of positive ions.

Detailed discussions of the ionization process and of the experimental techniques used in studying ion chemistry, as well as of thermodynamics, are available in many books and reviews. Therefore, no attempt will be made to present a comprehensive discussion or review of these subjects. Rather, attention will be given only to those aspects which have a bearing on the evaluation of data on ionization energies, appearance energies, or ion/molecule equilibrium constants.

2.1. The Evaluation of Experimentally-Determined Ionization Energies:

The Franck-Condon Principle

Ionization of a molecule by photoionization or by electron impact is governed by the Franck-Condon principle, which states that the most probable ionizing transition will be that in which the positions and momenta of the nuclei are unchanged[28,29]. Thus, when the equilibrium geometries of an ion and its corresponding neutral species are closely similar, the energy dependence of the onset of ionization will be a sharp step function leading to the ion vibrational ground state. However, when the equilibrium geometry of the ion involves a significant change in one or more bond lengths/angles from that of the neutral species, the transition to the lowest vibrational level of the ion is no longer the most intense, and the maximum transition probability (the vertical ionization energy) will favor population of a higher vibrational level of the ion; if the geometry change is great, it is possible that the transition to the lowest vibrational level of the ion will not even be observed. These situations are illustrated for hypothetical diatomic species in Fig. 1.

In evaluating ionization energy data, the shapes of photoelectron bands are useful indicators as to which of the situations pictured in Fig. 1 prevails for the particular molecule. A sharp onset indicates that the equilibrium geometries of ion and neutral are quite similar, and that photoionization or electron impact determinations of the ionization threshold are likely to be free of complications. When an ionization process proceeds according to the second situation pictured in the figure, the *onset* of the photoelectron band is observed approximately at the adiabatic ionization energy; adiabatic ionization energies derived from observation of the onsets of photoelectron bands are usually in excellent agreement with adiabatic ionization energies obtained from analyses of Rydberg series or from the most reliable threshold determinations.

When the equilibrium geometry of the ion is very different from that of the corresponding neutral molecule and the lowest vibrational level is not populated in ionization by photon absorption or electron impact, it has been shown that values for the adiabatic ionization energies can be obtained by determining the equilibrium constant for charge transfer to another molecule of known ionization energy:

$$A^+ + B \rightleftharpoons B^+ + A \qquad (33)$$

The enthalpy change for this reaction, which (Sec. 2.3.5.) is obtained from the equilibrium constant determination, is just the difference between the enthalpies of ionization, ΔH_I, of species A and B. As shown above (Sec. 1.6.) this difference is likely to be quite close to the difference in the adiabatic ionization energies:

$$\Delta H(33) = [\Delta H_I(B) - \Delta H_I(A)] \sim [IP_a(B) - IP_a(A)] \quad (34)$$

In such determinations, the ions are at thermal equilibrium with their surroundings, and one measures the thermochemical properties of the ions in their equilibrium geometries.

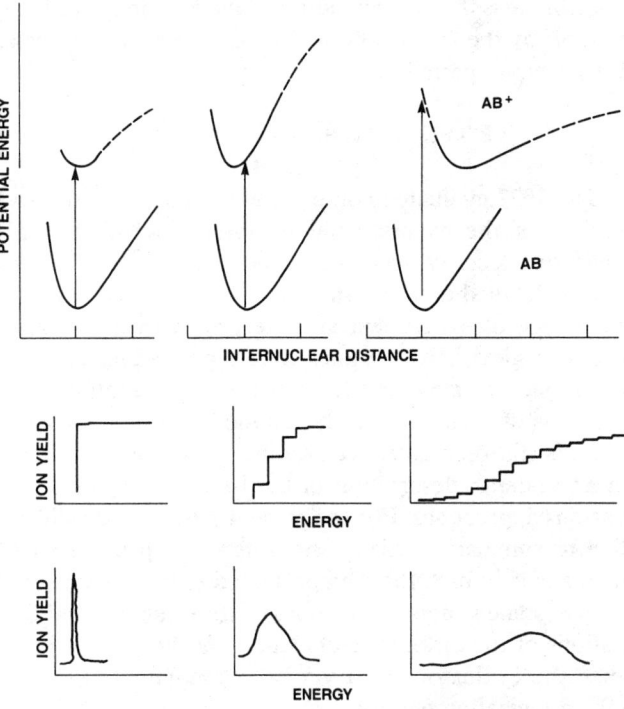

Fig. 1. Potential energy curves for hypothetical diatomic molecule AB, and the corresponding positive ion, AB$^+$ for the cases in which the equilibrium internuclear distance is (a) the same, (b) slightly different, or (c) greatly different. Below the potential energy curves are hypothetical probabilities for ionization as a function of energy for cases (a), (b), and (c), and, at bottom, shapes of observed photoelectron bands for the three corresponding cases.

2.2. Interpretation of Appearance Energies

In the discussion above, the appearance energy for formation of a fragment ion (reaction 4) was defined, and Eqs. (5) and (31), for obtaining values for the heat of formation of the fragment ion, were derived, with the proviso that the equations were valid only when there is no potential barrier in the reaction coordinate, and no significant "kinetic shift" associated with the determination.

The "kinetic shift"[2,30,31] is the term applied to describe the experimental observation of ionization onsets which are higher than the thermodynamic onset energy due to the fact that the apparatus samples the (fragmenting) ions at a certain time (usually around 10^{-5} s) after ionization has occurred, when ions undergoing a slow fragmentation process have not yet had time to dissociate. One approach for getting around this problem is an analysis based on the determination of the so-called rate-energy curve for a given fragmentation, in which the rate constant of the dissociating ion is derived as a function of energy. This kind of information is derived by analysis of the data from an elegant technique which is, moreover, capable of delivering very accurate thermochemical information for fragmentation processes, photoelectron-photoion coincidence spectroscopy (PEPICO)[32]. Another approach to detecting a barrier in the reaction coordinate is the determination of the kinetic energy carried off by the fragment ion. Studies of metastable peaks, for example, permit such an evaluation[33].

2.3. Experimental Techniques

The 1977 evaluated compilation included an extensive review of the experimental techniques which provide ionization energy and appearance energy data, along with a detailed description of how the data derived from each type of experiment are interpreted to give ionization energies[2,31]. Although technological advances have been made in mass spectrometric instrumentation since that review was written, the detailed presentation given there is still recommended reading for anyone interested in an in-depth description of the basic principles of the various approaches. For the present purposes, it will suffice to summarize briefly the different types of experiments from which the data presented here originate, and to give some general indications of the strengths and limitations of the different techniques, and how these influence the evaluator in arriving at a recommended value for an ionization energy.

2.3.1. Optical Spectroscopy

The identification of a Rydberg series in an atomic or molecular spectrum leads to a value for the ionization energy; in cases where the analysis of the spectrum is straightforward, the spectroscopic ionization energy values are highly accurate. The determination of atomic ionization energies through optical spectroscopy is a highly developed field which has been extensively reviewed. A large fraction of atomic ionization energies listed here are from expert evaluations of atomic spectra[34]. In the evaluation of ionization energies of atoms and diatomic molecules, spectroscopic ionization energies have been chosen where they are available. For polyatomic species, a value derived from an analysis of the optical spectrum has been given great weight, unless several determinations from other highly reliable techniques are in conflict with the spectroscopic value. As pointed out by Rosenstock[2,31], the evaluation of molecular Rydberg series is not always straightforward, and reported spectroscopic ionization energies of polyatomic species may disagree with values derived from ionization onset determinations or the onsets of photoelectron bands due to complications in the analysis of vibrational and rotational structure.

2.3.2. Beam Studies Involving Laser Photoionization

In the years since the cut-off date of the literature search for the previous volume of this series[2], several highly accurate ionization energy values have been reported based on multi-photon ionization of vibrationally-cooled species in a molecular beam[35]. In these studies, a vibrationally and rotationally cooled beam of molecules is raised to a specific excited state by irradiation with a tunable laser; while this excitation energy is held constant, a second independently tunable laser is used to ionize the beam of excited molecules, with the photon energy being tuned through the ionization onset. The excitation laser is then tuned to a different transition, and the ionization scan is repeated. In this way, the entire Franck-Condon accessible region of the intermediate electronic state is mapped out, insuring that the molecular geometry corresponding to the adiabatic ionization energy is accessed. Since every intermediate vibronic state leads to an independent value of the ionization threshold, the experiment contains an internal consistency check.

2.3.3. Determination of Ionization/Appearance Energies by Threshold Techniques

In the several techniques which fall under this heading, the onset of ionization or of the appearance of a particular fragment ion is detected as a function of the energy of the ionizing agent, either photons or an electron beam. The most obvious problem which must be considered with regard to this technique is the accurate characterization of the energy of the ionizing medium, photons or electrons. When ionization is brought about by photon absorption, this is usually not a problem; monochromators capable of delivering photons with a high energy resolution are available. The most sophisticated photoionization experiments involve detection of energy-selected electrons; in the so-called "threshold photoelectron spectroscopy" technique, only those photoelectrons which correspond to essentially zero energy of ejection are detected.

In the past, many experimental determinations of ionization onsets were carried out in instruments in which ionization was effected by bombarding the sample of interest with an electron beam in which the electrons had a known energy. This technique, called "electron ionization" or in the older literature, "electron impact", resulted in many determinations which were unreliable because of the energy spread of the electrons in a conventional beam. Several approaches have been utilized to overcome this problem; the most successful has been the use of a so-called "electron monochromator", in which the energy of the electron beam is narrowly defined by passing the beam through electron energy selectors of various designs[31,36,37,38,39]. Results obtained using electron beams with well-defined energies are in excellent agreement with analogous results derived from determinations of photoionization thresholds. At this writing, reliable data on ion thermochemistry are being obtained from experiments of this sort. Although studies are still being published which report ionization energy and appearance energy data from less accurate electron ionization techniques, the intent of the authors of those studies is rarely to examine the thermochemistry of the ionization process.

In the powerful threshold technique known as photoelectron-photoion coincidence (PEPICO)[32], the thermochemistry and detailed mechanism of an ionic fragmentation process can be mapped out very accurately. Ejected electrons which originated with "zero" kinetic energy are matched with their corresponding positive ions. At energies where parent ions, M^+, are undergoing dissociation to form one or more fragment ions, one obtains the relative probabilities for the formation of the daughter ions from parent ions of known energy (i.e. the breakdown curve). The ions can be detected at differing times after the ionization event for the determination of the time dependence of the dissociation process. The complete interpretation of such data requires a modeling of the dissociation using statistical theories of unimolecular decomposition (i.e. quasi-equilibrium/RRKM theory)[40,41]. As pointed out by Dannacher in a recent review[32], in spite of its great strengths, this technique has not been widely utilized, possibly because of the intricate instrumentation required, the complexity of the data analysis, and the fact that each determination requires the investment of a great amount of time on the part of the experimentalist.

To summarize, intrinsic problems associated with threshold determinations of ionization energies are: a) the difficulty of detecting the onset when there is a large change of molecular geometry in the ionization process, as discussed in Sec. 2.1.; and, b) the observation of ionization at energies below the adiabatic ionization energy when there is a significant population of vibrationally excited molecules in the system ("hot bands").

2.3.4. Photoelectron Spectroscopy

It is also possible to determine the energy change associated with ionization process 1 by effecting ionization with a photon of well-defined energy and measuring the energy of the ejected electrons:

$$M + h\nu \rightarrow M^+ + e \quad (35)$$

where
$$KE(e) = h\nu - I - E^*(\text{vib,rot}) \quad (36)$$

(where $E^*(\text{vib,rot})$ is the internal energy of M^+ and I is the binding energy of the electron).

The most widely-used technique of this type is conventional photoelectron spectroscopy[42] in which the photon sources are usually the helium resonance lines of 58.4331 nm (21.218 eV) or 30.3781 nm (40.813 eV); some work is done with neon resonance lines (73.589 nm and 74.370 nm, 16.848 and 16.671 eV) or other intense monochromatic sources. In such an experiment, the ejected electrons will have differing energies depending on the distribution of energy levels in the M^+ ions formed; a map of the abundances of the electron as a function of energy is called the photoelectron *spectrum*. As described in Sec. 2.1., the shapes of the photoelectron bands will reflect not only the energy differences in the different states of M^+ but the $M \rightarrow M^+$ transition probabilities as governed by the Franck-Condon principle. In cases where the equilibrium geometry of the ion and the corresponding neutral are the same or are similar, it is found that the observed onset of the first photoelectron band is usually a reliable indicator of the adiabatic ionization potential (see Fig. 1).

2.3.5. Ion/Molecule Equilibrium Constant Determinations

This evaluation takes into account (although previous works in the series did not) all information on ion thermochemistry generated by ion/molecule equilibrium constant determinations.

An ion/molecule equilibrium:

$$A^+ + B \rightleftharpoons C^+ + D \quad (37)$$

is established in a high pressure mass spectrometer[43], flow tube[44], or ion cyclotron resonance spectrometer[45], and the equilibrium constant is determined by observing the relative abundances of the two ions, A^+ and C^+, after a large number of collisions:

$$K_{eq} = \frac{[C^+][D]}{[A^+][B]} \quad (38)$$

The neutral reactants, B and D, are present in great abundance compared to the ionic reactants, and therefore, the ratio [D]/[B] does not change as equilibrium is established. A single measurement leads to a value for the Gibbs energy change of reaction 37 at the temperature of the measurement, while a series of measurements at different temperatures permits an experimental evaluation of the entropy and enthalpy changes associated with the reaction:

$$-RT \ln K_{eq} = \Delta G = \Delta H - T\Delta S \quad (39)$$

In practice, many studies have been published in which measurements were made at a single temperature, the (usually small) entropy change for the reaction was estimated from statistical mechanical considerations (usually just from consideration of changes in symmetry numbers), and the corresponding enthalpy change was derived from these two pieces of information.

Published ion/molecule equilibrium studies involving cations provide data on charge transfer (reaction 33), proton transfer (reaction 6), and hydride or halide transfer equilibria:

$$R_1^+ + R_2X \rightleftharpoons R_2^+ + R_1X \quad (40)$$

(where X is H, F, Cl, Br, or I). Studies of hydride transfer and halide transfer equilibria have led to quantitative information about the relative heats of formation of alkyl carbocations. These data were used to supplement information from appearance potential determinations in evaluating heats of formation of alkyl carbocations.

Most ion/molecule equilibrium studies involving positive ions have been devoted to the derivation of an extensive (more than 100 kcal/mol in length) scale of relative proton affinities (see Eqs. (7) and (8)). The results were mainly derived from interlocking ladders of enthalpy changes for reaction 6. These data have recently been evaluated to establish internal consistency[4]. Most of the values for heats of formation of protonated molecules given in this evaluation are taken from that publication. When this is the case, no specific literature reference is given, it being understood that the source is the evaluated compilation[4].

As noted above (reaction 33), in determinations of charge transfer equilibrium constants, the difference in the ionization energies of two reacting molecules is obtained. A thermochemical ladder of relative ionization energies determined in this way[22] closely reproduces the equivalent scale of spectroscopic ionization energies, thus demonstrating the reliability of the approach for deriving information on relative ionization energies. The most useful application of this approach for ionization energy data has proved to be the determination of ionization energies for species which undergo a large change of geometry upon ionization (case 3 in Fig. 1), and which therefore exhibit very slow onsets of ionization as a function of energy. For example, the only reliable data on the adiabatic ionization energies of n-alkanes[46] and of alkyl hydrazines[47,48] come from thermochemical ladders established through equilibrium constant determinations.

The main uncertainty associated with this technique, aside from the necessity of relating the thermochemical ladder to a reliable comparison standard, is the temperature of the reacting system. However, the reproduction of relative spectroscopic ionization energies through equilibrium measurements[22] demonstrates that this is not a serious problem.

2.3.6. Ion/Molecule Bracketing Experiments

There are some ion/molecule systems for which an equilibrium can not be established in an ion source, either because one of the relevant neutral species is unstable (e.g. a radical or unstable molecule) or because of competing reactions in the system. In such cases, it is sometimes possible to obtain an experimental estimate of the enthalpy change of a particular reaction (charge transfer, proton transfer, hydride transfer, etc.) by use of a technique known as "bracketing" in which the ion of interest is reacted with a series of molecules chosen for variations in the relevant thermochemical parameter (proton affinity, ionization energy, etc.). The occurrence, and sometimes the rate constant, of reaction is monitored as a function of the parameter of interest; the approximate onset energy is usually assumed to lie on the energy scale at a point where the rate of reaction becomes very slow. Few data in this work are derived from such measurements, but in cases where heats of formation are derived from this kind of experiment, a specific comment describes the experiment.

2.3.7. Onsets of Endothermic Reactions

Several pieces of data given here have been derived from an analysis of the enthalpy changes of endothermic ion/molecule reactions. Although some such information has been obtained from straightforward kinetic treatments (Arrhenius plots) of the temperature dependences of the rate constants of endothermic ion/molecule reactions[49,50] recent quantitative studies[51,52,53] cover a much broader energy range by generating a beam of energy- and mass-selected ions which is focussed into a collision chamber containing the reactant gas; product ions are detected as a function of the energy of the ions in the beam.

2.3.8. Other Techniques

Essentially all of the ionization potentials and heats of formation of positive ions included in this evaluation have been derived from results obtained using the experimental approaches listed above. Several additional techniques (Auger electron spectroscopy, Penning ionization, Born-Haber cycle calculations, and analyses of so-called charge transfer spectra) were described in the Introduction to the 1977 compilation[2,31] but are not widely used for the quantitative determination of data of interest to this compilation. Such data, when available, have been taken into account in the evaluation, except for ionization energies derived from charge transfer spectra. The latter technique is mainly used for obtaining values for ionization potentials of compounds of low vapor pressure. Since the cut-off date for inclusion of literature in the 1977 volume, numerous quantitative determinations of ionization energies for such species, mainly by photoelectron spectroscopy or by ion/molecule equilibrium constant determinations, have appeared in the literature. These have made the charge transfer spectra data obsolete for many species. Since it is generally seen that the gas phase ionization potentials derived from charge transfer spectra may be very inaccurate, all these data have been ignored in the present volume.

2.4. Reliability of Ionization Energy Data and Criteria for Evaluation

2.4.1. Comparisons between Results of Different Techniques

The data on ionization energies summarized here are derived from the different types of measurements described above, and are consequently of widely varying quality, not only because the accuracies of the measurement techniques differ, but also because of differences in the focusses of the research in which the measurements were made. For example, many of the ionization energies reported for inorganic species were never intended by the original authors to be quantitative ionization energy measurements, but are simply qualitative indicators of whether or not a given ion observed in the vapor over a heated Knudsen cell has been formed by electron impact ionization of the corresponding neutral species (in which case it exhibits an onset at a relatively low energy) or through fragmentation of a molecular ion (which would correspond to a higher onset energy). In these experiments, error limits of 0.5 to 1 eV are commonly cited by the original authors. Similarly, most photoelectron spectroscopic studies are carried out for the purpose of examining molecular orbital energy levels; thermochemistry is not a concern, and often, although the accuracy of the measurements is very high, only vertical ionization energies, which are not necessarily related to thermochemical onsets, are reported.

Because many of the values for ionization energies given here are derived from evaluations of several different determinations carried out using different techniques, there is no specific indication in Table 1 of an experimental method associated with a particular value. In carrying out the evaluation, an attempt was made to integrate the entire corpus of information about any given ion, giving weight to various determinations depending on the nature of the ionization onset, the measurement techniques used, the attention to detail by the original authors, and so forth. Usually (but not always) a spectroscopically-determined ionization energy was considered more reliable than a contradictory value obtained by observation of an ionization threshold. A value obtained from an observed ionization onset using photoionization or an electron monochromator was considered more reliable than an onset obtained using less accurate techniques. In all of these cases, an observed onset of a photoelectron band was given great weight in carrying out the analysis, with values from any of the above three techniques being downgraded if they did not match the photoelectron onset (unless, of course, the differences could be rationalized in terms of the principles outlined above).

As mentioned above, many photoelectron spectroscopy studies do not cite values for adiabatic ionization potentials. In these cases, where the authors have provided a figure showing the photoelectron spectrum, it is usually possible to estimate from the figure the value for the adiabatic onset; where adiabatic ionization energies have been obtained in this way, a specific comment to that effect is made.

Data derived from ion/molecule equilibrium constant determinations have been utilized as an aid in evaluating information obtained from other sources. For example, where scales of relative ionization energies were available from equilibrium constant determinations, internal consistency with these scales was required in the assigned ionization energy or heat of formation values. Where this was not possible, a specific comment spells out the discrepancy. As described in Sec. 2.3.5., ionization energy values derived from equilibrium constant determinations provide the only values for ionization energies of species which undergo large changes of geometry upon ionization such as normal alkanes with six or more C–atoms[46], or hydrazines[47,48]. When an ionization energy has been obtained solely from this approach, the source of the data is indicated in a comment, and the identity of the reference compound is given.

Heats of formation of protonated molecules derived from the evaluated proton affinity scale[4] are taken from that publication. More recent data are included, with the internal consistency requirement rigorously maintained. The value for the corresponding proton affinity of the molecule is given in a comment. Note that to locate a value for a *proton affinity*, one must look under the empirical formula of the corresponding *protonated molecule*, i.e. the proton affinity of methane is located by looking under CH_5. When data from recent publications are given, the literature source is specifically cited.

2.4.2. Reliability of Data; Error Limits

Ionization Energies. The experimentally-determined ionization energies collected here display widely varying uncertainties, ranging from ±0.0001 eV or smaller for some spectroscopic or multiphoton-laser determinations to ±1 eV for measurements carried out on the vapor above a heated Knudsen cell. The error limits associated with a particular ionization energy are specifically listed when the original work(s) gave an estimate of this quantity. In other cases, the error limits are indicated by the number of significant figures displayed; in these cases, it can be assumed that the error limits are five times the last significant figure displayed.

Some of the ionization energy values are shown enclosed in parentheses. Data enclosed in parentheses are considered not to be firmly established for one of three reasons:

(1) The measurement itself must be considered unreliable (as in, for example, threshold determinations in which the energy spread of the electrons was not well defined).

(2) The relevant ionization energy has been determined more than once but with poor agreement between the different results, and there is no auxiliary information available which allows a choice between the divergent values. In such cases, the evaluation gives either (a) the value determined by the most reliable technique, or (b) an average of two or more values determined by the same technique, with error limits indicating the scatter in the data. In a very few cases where the scatter in the reported values is very great or where the value obtained by the "most reliable" technique appears to be specious, no evaluated ionization energy is cited, but a note is included which lists the various determined values.

(3) Parentheses are also used to indicate data which are unevaluated. That is, when a particular molecule has been studied only once, and additional information which would permit one to judge the reliability of the data is unavailable, the ionization energy is given exactly as it appears in the original reference but is enclosed in

parentheses. Many of these untested determinations are undoubtedly reliable; the cited error limits and the number of significant figures shown in the table will give an indication of the probable reliability of the technique by which such a value was obtained.

As described above, some ionization energy values were obtained by reading onsets of photoelectron bands in figures reproduced in papers, where the original authors did not assign a numerical value to the band onset. In every such case, a specific comment is made indicating that the value has been derived from a figure. The accuracy with which such onsets can be read should be assumed to be not better than 0.1–0.2 eV, except where the authors have given an enlarged view of the band onset, in which case, an additional significant figure is cited. When a figure was not given, the lowest vertical ionization potential from the original paper is cited as the upper limit to the adiabatic ionization energy.

Heats of Formation. The cited heats of formation of ions necessarily reflect both the uncertainties in the ionization (or appearance) energy values and the uncertainties in the heats of formation of the relevant neutral species. Values of ionic heats of formation which are not firmly established - either because of a poorly established ionization/appearance energy or because of large uncertainties in the heat of formation of the neutral species - are shown enclosed in parentheses.

Although the values which were used for heats of formation of neutral species will be discussed separately in Sec. 4, it should be emphasized here that many of these data are based on estimates. Some of the estimation schemes for particular classes of compounds are sophisticated and well-documented, and can be considered to lead to values for heats of formation which are as reliable as most experimental data. Other estimations have been carried out by various authors with varying degrees of attention to complexities, or in some cases, with little or no documentation about how the estimate was accomplished. A large fraction of the estimates used were made specifically for this publication, and even among this fraction, there is a broad spectrum of quality depending on the size of the network of related information which was available. Rather than try to sort out and make judgments about the quality of each estimate of the heat of formation of a neutral molecule, the policy has been followed of enclosing in parentheses each ion heat of formation based on an estimated value for the heat of formation of relevant neutral molecules or radicals; this practice is not meant to disparage the quality of the estimated data, but simply to alert the reader to the fact that it is being used. As a first approximation, the user can assume that the reliability of an estimate varies inversely with the complexity of the molecule.

2.5. Trends in the Data
2.5.1. Estimation Schemes for Heats of Formation of Cations

Within the past few years, a sufficient amount of reliable information on ionization energies and heats of formation of many classes of positive ions has become available so that regular trends as a function of molecular size and structure can be discerned. These can be used to develop empirical schemes for estimating ionization energies and/or heats of formation of cations. Since ionization energies for a homologous series do not have a linear dependence on molecular size, values for heats of formation of ions can not be reproduced satisfactorily by simple additivity systems like those in widespread use for the prediction of thermochemical data for neutral molecules. The predictive schemes put forward to date utilize equations which are empirical.

One series of several papers[54,55,56,57] presents a scheme which is designed to predict values for the heat of formation of positive ions at 298 K from equations of the form:

$$\Delta_f H(M^+) = A - Bn + C/n \quad (41)$$

where A, B, and C are constants derived from the data for any particular series, and n is the total number of *atoms* in the molecule. The parameters derived in the paper of Holmes, Fingas, and Lossing[54] for predicting heats of formation of the parent ions of several common classes of compounds are listed in Table 2.5.1.1.

This method works because to an excellent approximation, the ionization energies of a homologous series vary linearly as n^{-1}, as expressed in the term C/n in Eq. (41). The other two terms, A and Bn, reflect the additive nature of heats of formation of neutral molecules. Also, for molecules in which there is multiple substitution by characteristic groups on charge-bearing atoms or at the position of charge delocalized pi-electron systems, good straight-line relationships exist between ionic heats of formation and the logarithm of the number of atoms (i.e. ion size). Such correlations permit reasonably accurate estimates of ion enthalpies of formation[54,55,56,57].

Bachiri, Mouvier, Carlier, and DuBois[58] have advanced a scheme for the estimation of ionization energies of alkenes, alkynes, aldehydes, ketones, alcohols, ethers, mercaptans, and thioethers. Their empirical equation takes the form:

$$\log_{10} \frac{IP(R_1XR_2) - IP_\infty}{IP_0 - IP_\infty} = 0.106[I(R_1) + I(R_2)] \quad (42)$$

where X is a functional group (i.e. $-CH=CH-$ or $>C=CH_2$ for alkenes, $-O-$ for alcohols and ethers, $>C=O$ for aldehydes and ketones, etc.), R_1 and R_2 are the attached alkyl groups, IP_0 is the ionization potential of the reference compound for which $R_1 = R_2 = H$. IP_∞ in Eq. (42) is a constant for each compound type. (A modification of this scheme which does away with the need for the parameter IP_∞ has also been put forward recently[59]). Table 2.5.1.2. lists the constants for the alkyl substituent groups and the different compound types (modified slightly from the values given in the original publication to predict adiabatic rather than vertical ionization energies).

TABLE 2.5.1.1. Estimation scheme[c] of Holmes, Fingas, and Lossing[54]:
$\Delta_f H(M^+) \text{kcal/mol} = A - Bn + C/n$

Compound Type	A	B (kcal/mol[a])	C	Correction Terms
Alkanes	224	2.2	298	For each branch: −3
1-Alkenes	231.6	1.61	110	For each branch on C-2: −13
				For each remote branch: −2.5
x-Alkenes	219.6	1.61	110	For each branch on =C: −13
				For each branch elsewhere: −2.5
				One cis correction: +1
				Two cis corrections at one double bond: +3
				If one group is t-butyl: +4
				If both groups are t-butyl: +10
1-Alkynes	278	1.57	110	For each branch: −4
2-Alkynes	260	1.58	110	For each branch: −4
3-Alkynes	257	1.57	110	For each branch: −4
4-Alkynes	257	1.57	110	For each branch: −4
5-Alkynes	256	1.57	110	For each branch: −4
Alkanols	175	1.59	216	For each branch adjacent to −OH: −6
				For each branch elsewhere: −2
Aliphatic ethers	157	1.41	368	For each branch adjacent to −O−: −6
				For each branch elsewhere: −3
				[b]Asymmetry correction per carbon: +1
Aliphatic	188	1.65	135	For each branch adjacent to C=O: −5
				For each branch elsewhere: −3
Aliphatic ketones	166	1.78	252	For each branch adjacent to C=OD: −3.5
				[b]Asymmetry correction per carbon: +1.5
Alkanoic acids	142	1.90	112	For each branch adjacent to C=O: −3.5
				For each branch elsewhere: −1.5
Chloroalkanes	236	1.98	57	For each branch adjacent to halogen: −5
				For each branch elsewhere: −3
Bromoalkanes	219	1.40	115	For each branch adjacent to halogen: −5
				For each branch elsewhere: −3
Iodoalkanes	222	1.69	44	For each branch adjacent to halogen: −5

[a]Constants are given here in the units used in the original paper[54].
[b]Asymmetry correction for ethers and ketones having different numbers of C-atoms on either side of the functional group is based on the smallest numbers of C-atoms which must be transferred to give the most symmetrical species, e.g. for methyl pentyl ketone, +3 kcal/mol.
[c]n is the total number of atoms in the molecule.

A comparison of ionization energy values[58] or heats of formation of cations[54] predicted from expressions 41 or 42 with the corresponding evaluated experimental values is given in Table 2.5.1.3. For both predictive schemes, the agreement between estimated values and experiment is generally quite good — good enough to inspire confidence in the use of the equations for filling in blanks in the data series.

As pointed out in one of the papers advancing these empirical estimation schemes[54] the equations are "not only useful for predicting new $\Delta_f H$ values, but also for revealing misfits which could indicate incorrect values for $\Delta_f H°$(Neutral) or the ionization energy, or, more interestingly, an ion structure having special stabilizing or destabilizing properties." In fact, the trends described by these equations were routinely examined in evaluating the data for just these reasons.

2.5.2. Correlations of Ionization Energies with Proton Affinities or Substituent Constants

The proton affinity of molecule M, defined by Eq. 7, is equal to the M–H$^+$ bond energy of the MH$^+$ ion. The M$^+$–H bond energy is called the *hydrogen affinity* (*HA*) of M$^+$:

$$M^+ + H \xrightarrow{-HA} MH^+ \quad (43)$$

Consider the thermodynamic cycle, constructed from reactions 7 and 43:

$$\begin{array}{ccccc} M & + & H^+ & \xrightarrow{-PA} & MH^+ \\ \downarrow IP(M) & & \downarrow -IP(H) & & \downarrow \\ M^+ & + & H & \xrightarrow{-HA} & MH^+ \end{array} \quad (44)$$

From cycle 44 we write:

$$PA(M) = HA(M^+) + IP(H) - IP(M)$$
$$= HA(M^+) + 13.6\,\text{eV} - IP(M) \quad (45)$$

If the hydrogen affinity were a constant for a given compound type, the proton affinity values would vary linearly with the ionization potentials for a homologous

TABLE 2.5.1.2. Estimation scheme of Bachiri, Mouvier, Carlier, and DuBois[58]:

$$\log_{10} \frac{IP(R_1XR_2) - IP_\infty}{IP_0 - IP_\infty} = 0.106[I(R_1) + I(R_2)]$$

X		IP_0(eV)	IP_∞(eV)
−C≡C−	(Alkynes)	11.400	6.577
−HC=CH−	(Alkenes)	10.507	6.849
>C=CH$_2$	(Alkenes, gem)	10.737	6.814
−(C=O)−H	(Aldehydes except CH$_2$O)	12.063	3.575
>C=O	(Ketones)	13.334	3.936
−OH	(Alcohols)	12.607	(3.7)
−O−	(Ethers)	12.612	5.483
−S−	(H$_2$S, Thiols, Thioethers)	10.473	5.725

R	I
H	0 (Convention)
Methyl	1 (Convention)
Ethyl	1.166
n-Propyl	1.271
i-Propyl	1.291
n-Butyl	1.330
s-Butyl	1.400
i-Butyl	1.358
t-Butyl	1.394
n-Pentyl	1.340
i-Pentyl	1.389
neo-Pentyl	1.369
t-Pentyl	1.479
s-Pentyl [-CH(C$_2$H$_5$)$_2$]	1.462
n-Hexyl	1.355
t-Hexyl [-C(CH$_3$)$_2$(n-C$_3$H$_7$)]	1.524
t-Hexyl [-C(CH$_3$)$_2$(i-C$_3$H$_7$)]	1.570
neo-Hexyl [-CH$_2$CH$_2$C(CH$_3$)$_3$]	1.360

TABLE 2.5.1.3. Comparison of ionization energies/heats of formation with estimated values predicted from estimation schemes[a]

Compound	IP (eV)	Δ_fH/(Ion) (kJ/mol)	Holmes et al.[54] IP (eV)	Holmes et al.[54] Δ_fH(Ion) (kJ/mol)	Bachiri et al.[58] IP (eV)	Bachiri et al.[58] Δ_fH(Ion) (kJ/mol)
Alkynes						
CH$_3$C≡CH	10.36	1186	[10.34]	1184	10.36	[1184]
C$_2$H$_5$C≡CH	10.178	1147	[10.13]	1142	10.21	[1151]
n-C$_3$H$_7$C≡CH	10.05	1113	[10.04]	1113	10.11	[1121]
n-C$_4$H$_9$C≡CH	(9.95)	(1079)	[10.02]	1088	10.06	[1092]
n-C$_5$H$_{11}$C≡CH	(10.04)	(1071)	[9.93]	1063	10.06	[1075]
n-C$_6$H$_{13}$C≡CH	(9.95)	(1038)	[9.93]	1038	10.04	[1046]
i-C$_3$H$_7$C≡CH	9.97	1096	[9.95]	1096	10.10	[1109]
i-C$_3$H$_7$C≡CCH$_3$	9.31	996	[9.32]	996	9.33	[996]
t-C$_4$H$_9$C≡CH	(9.80)	(1050)	[9.80]	1050	10.01	[1071]
CH$_3$C≡CCH$_3$	9.562	1068	[9.55]	1067	9.54	[1067]
C$_2$H$_5$C≡CCH$_3$	9.44	1038	[9.43]	1038	9.42	[1038]
n-C$_3$H$_7$C≡CCH$_3$	9.366	1013	[9.37]	1013	9.35	[1013]
n-C$_4$H$_9$C≡CCH$_3$	(9.33)	(983)	[9.37]	987	9.31	[983]
n-C$_5$H$_{11}$C≡CCH$_3$	9.31	962	[9.32]	962	9.30	[958]
n-C$_6$H$_{11}$C≡CCH$_3$	(9.30)	(941)	[9.28]	941	9.29	[941]
C$_2$H$_5$C≡CC$_2$H$_5$	9.323	1004	[9.28]	1000	9.31	[1004]
n-C$_3$H$_7$C≡CC$_2$H$_5$	(9.26)	(975)	[9.24]	975	9.24	[975]
n-C$_4$H$_9$C≡CC$_2$H$_5$	9.22	954	[9.19]	950	9.20	[950]
n-C$_5$H$_{11}$C≡CC$_2$H$_5$	9.20	929	[9.19]	929	9.19	[929]
n-C$_6$H$_{13}$C≡CC$_2$H$_5$	9.19	908	[9.19]	908	9.18	[908]

TABLE 2.5.1.3. Comparison of ionization energies/heats of formation with estimated values[a] — Continued

	IP (eV)	$\Delta_f H$(Ion) (kJ/mol)	Holmes et al.[54] IP (eV)	$\Delta_f H$(Ion) (kJ/mol)	Bachiri et al.[58] IP (eV)	$\Delta_f H$(Ion) (kJ/mol)
Compound						
Alkenes						
$CH_3CH=CH_2$	9.73	958	[9.73]	958	9.71	[958]
$C_2H_5CH=CH_2$	9.58	925	[9.59]	925	9.60	[925]
$n-C_3H_7CH=CH_2$	9.52	895	[9.54]	900	9.53	[895]
$n-C_4H_9CH=CH_2$	9.44	870	[9.48]	874	9.49	[874]
$n-C_5H_{11}CH=CH_2$	9.44	849	[9.45]	849	9.49	[853]
$n-C_6H_{13}CH=CH_2$	9.43	828	[9.41]	828	9.48	[833]
$i-C_3H_7CH=CH_2$	8.96	812	[8.94]	812	8.92	[808]
$t-C_4H_9CH=CH_2$	9.45	849	[9.43]	853	9.45	[853]
$(C_2H_5)_2C=CH_2$	9.06	820	[9.06]	820	9.03	[816]
$E-CH_3CH=CHCH_3$	9.100	866	[9.12]	866	9.09	[866]
$E-C_2H_5CH=CHCH_3$	9.036	840	[9.05]	841	9.00	[837]
$E-n-C_3H_7CH=CHCH_3$	(8.97)	(812)	[8.99]	816	8.95	[812]
$i-C_3H_7CH=CHCH_3$	8.97	803	[8.96]	803	8.94	[803]
$E/Z-n-C_4H_9CH=CHCH_3$	(8.84)	(782)	[8.92]	791	8.92	[791]
$E-n-C_5H_{11}CH=CHCH_3$	8.85	757	[8.97]	766	8.91	[761]
$C_2H_5CH=CHC_2H_5$	8.96	812	[8.94]	812	8.92	[808]
$(CH_3)_2C=C(CH_3)_2$	8.27	728	[8.04]	707	8.23	[724]
Alcohols						
CH_3OH	10.85	845	[10.82]	845	10.68	[828]
C_2H_5OH	10.47	774	[10.45]	774	10.40	[770]
$n-C_3H_7OH$	10.22	732	[10.20]	728	10.23	[732]
$n-C_4H_9OH$	10.06	695	[10.03]	695	10.14	[703]
$n-C_5H_{11}OH$	10.00	669	[9.96]	661	10.12	[678]
$n-C_6H_{13}OH$	(9.89)	(640)	[9.86]	636	10.10	[661]
$i-C_3H_7OH$	10.12	703	[10.10]	703	10.20	[711]
$s-C_4H_9OH$	9.88	661	[9.96]	669	10.03	[674]
$i-C_4H_9OH$	10.09	690	[10.03]	686	10.09	[690]
$t-C_4H_9OH$	9.97	648	[9.90]	644	10.09	[661]
Ethers						
CH_3OCH_3	10.025	782	[9.94]	774	9.86	[766]
$C_2H_5OCH_3$	9.72	720	[9.77]	715	9.69	[717]
$n-C_3H_7OCH_3$	—	—	9.58			
$i-C_3H_7OCH_3$	(9.42)	657	[9.41]	657	9.56	[669]
$n-C_4H_9OCH_3$	(9.54)	(661)	[9.32]	640	9.52	[661]
$n-C_3H_7OC_2H_5$	(9.45)	(640)	[9.46]	640	9.42	[636]
$C_2H_5OC_2H_5$	9.51	665	[9.56]	669	9.52	[665]
$n-C_4H_9OC_2H_5$	9.36	611	[9.36]	611	9.36	[611]
$t-C_4H_9OCH_3$	9.41	619	[9.26]	602	9.46	[623]
Aldehydes						
CH_3CHO	10.229	821	[10.21]	820	10.23	[820]
C_2H_5CHO	9.953	773	[9.97]	774	9.96	[774]
$n-C_3H_7CHO$	9.84	741	[9.82]	741	9.80	[736]
$n-C_4H_9CHO$	9.74	711	[9.76]	711	9.71	[707]
$n-C_5H_{11}CHO$	9.67	686	[9.66]	685	9.69	[688]
$i-C_3H_7CHO$	9.705	721	[9.69]	719	9.77	[727]
$i-C_4H_9CHO$	9.70	699	[9.71]	700	9.67	[695]
$s-C_4H_9CHO$	(9.59)	(690)	[9.58]	690	9.61	[692]
$t-C_4H_9CHO$	9.50	674	[9.45]	669	9.62	[686]
$neo-C_5H_{11}CHO$	(9.61)	(661)	[9.61]	661	9.65	[665]
Ketones						
CH_3COCH_3	9.705	719	[9.77]	724	9.704	[761]
$C_2H_5COCH_3$	9.51	678	[9.53]	680	9.48	[675]
$n-C_3H_7COCH_3$	9.38	644	[9.40]	646	9.33	[639]
$n-C_4H_9COCH_3$	9.35	628	[9.26]	619	9.26	[619]
$C_2H_5COC_2H_5$	9.31	640	[9.32]	642	9.26	[636]

TABLE 2.5.1.3. Comparison of ionization energies/heats of formation with estimated values[a] — Continued

Compound	IP (eV)	$\Delta_f H$/(Ion) (kJ/mol)	Holmes et al.[54] IP (eV)	$\Delta_f H$(Ion) (kJ/mol)	Bachiri et al.[58] IP (eV)	$\Delta_f H$(Ion) (kJ/mol)
Ketones – Continued						
n-$C_3H_7COC_2H_5$	9.12	598	[9.25]	611	9.12	[598]
n-$C_4H_9COC_2H_5$	(9.02)	(573)	[9.14]	586	9.05	[577]
i-$C_3H_7COCH_3$	9.30	636	[9.21]	628	9.31	[636]
i-$C_3H_7COC_2H_5$	(9.10)	(594)	[9.15]	598	9.10	[590]
(i-$C_3H_7)_2CO$	8.95	552	[8.92]	548	8.94	[552]
s-$C_4H_9COCH_3$	9.21	598	[9.24]	602	9.17	[594]
i-$C_4H_9COCH_3$	9.30	607	[9.43]	619	9.22	[602]
t-$C_4H_9COCH_3$	9.11	590	[9.14]	590	9.17	[594]
neo-$C_5H_{11}COCH_3$	(9.23)	(573)	[9.29]	577	9.21	[569]

[a]In these lists, values obtained through the use of the estimation scheme of Holmes et al[58] are *heats of formation* of ions at 298 K. The scheme of Bachiri et al[58] predicts *ionization energies*. For purposes of comparison, both quantities are given here, the conversion being made using standard heats of formation of corresponding neutral molecules from Table 1. The derived quantity is enclosed in brackets. Parentheses indicate a quantity which is not well established (see conventions for Table 1).

series, the slope of the plot would be -1 and the intercept would be $[HA(M^+) + 13.6 \text{ eV}]$.

It has been observed[45a,60,61] that the value which can be assigned to the M^+–H bond strength (i.e. the HA) is indeed often approximately constant for a homologous series, at least over a limited range. For instance, it was reported[62] that linear plots of PA versus IP for primary, secondary, and tertiary amines display the same slope, but have different intercepts (i.e. different values of HA). However, a detailed statistical analysis[63] of the relationships between proton affinities and ionization potentials for many different compound types (alcohols, ethers, primary-, secondary- and tertiary-amines, nitriles, mercaptans, sulfides, aldehydes, ketones, carboxylic acids, esters, amides, and atoms) demonstrated that only the parent radical cations of sulfides and mercaptans displayed a characteristic (constant) value of the hydrogen affinity. For other compound types, it was concluded that the hydrogen affinity itself varies linearly with the ionization energy:

$$HA(M^+) = c + d \, IP(M) \quad (46)$$

Several series of compounds for which reliable evaluated ionization energy and proton affinity data are both available are summarized in Table 2.5.2.1. along with values for the hydrogen affinities. The published analysis utilized vertical ionization energies corresponding to the orbital of the site of protonation, and a proton affinity scale which, although internally consistent, was constricted in length (due to the incorrect assumption in early equilibrium studies using ICR that the operating temperature was 300 K rather than 320 K) and related to an absolute standard whose proton affinity value has now been revised downward by 3 kcal/mol. Repeating that statistical analysis, but using instead the thermochemically more meaningful adiabatic ionization energies which relate to the M^+–H bond strengths, and the evaluated scale of proton affinities[4], it is seen that Eq. (46) does hold for alcohols, aldehydes, ketones, primary amines, cyclic ethers and esters. In the series of aliphatic ethers, thioethers, and secondary and tertiary amines, values of the hydrogen affinity appear to decrease slightly with decreasing ionization energy, but the differences are too small to be meaningful (i.e. the slope of a plot of Eq. (46) is -0.7 or greater), and the assumption that the hydrogen affinity is constant will be approximately valid. The hydrogen affinities of mercaptans and of aromatic amines are indeed constant. Substituting Eq. (46) into Eq. (45), we derive an expression which permits the estimation of an unknown proton affinity/ionization energy when one of these two parameters is known:

$$PA_1 - PA_2 = (d-1)(IP_1 - IP_2) = K(IP_1 - IP_2) \quad (47)$$

where $K = (d-1)$ is the slope of a plot of PA versus IP for a compound series:

$$PA_x = C + K \, IP_x \quad (48)$$

Values for C and K derived from the statistical analysis of the data are given in Table 2.5.2.1. for those compound types for which sufficient information was available to make a meaningful analysis.

Attention has also been given to relating ionization energies and proton affinities of various series of compounds to the appropriate Taft substituent constants[64,65,66,67]. It has been shown that the adiabatic ionization energies of compounds RX (where R is an alkyl group) correlate linearly with $\sigma^*(R)$ and $\sigma_I(R)$ (measures of the polarizability and electron-releasing and donating ability of R) for constant electron-withdrawing group X. This is easily understood in terms of a lowering of the energy required to remove an electron with increasing electron-donating ability of the groups, R.

TABLE 2.5.2.1. The relationship between proton affinity, ionization energy, and hydrogen affinity for homologous series

$$PA(M) = C + K \cdot IP(M)$$
$$HA(M^+) = c + d \cdot IP(M)$$
$$(C - c = 1312 \text{ kJ/mol}, d - K = 1.00)$$

	kJ/mol		
	IP	PA	HA
Alcohols: $K = -0.54$, $C = 1335$ kJ/mol			
CH_3OH	1047	761	494
C_2H_5OH	1010	788	485
n-C_3H_7OH	986	798	472
n-C_4H_9OH	971	800	456
i-C_4H_9OH	974	805	464
i-C_3H_7OH	976	800	464
s-C_4H_9OH	953	799	439
t-C_4H_9OH	958	810	460
Acyclic Ethers: ($K = -0.77$, $C = 1548$ kJ/mol)			
CH_3OCH_3	967	804	460
$C_2H_5OCH_3$	938	822	448
$C_2H_5OC_2H_5$	918	838	444
$(n$-$C_3H_7)_2O$	895	846	427
$(n$-$C_4H_9)_2O$	910	852	448
$(s$-$C_4H_9)_2O$	879	874	439
t-$C_4H_9OCH_3$	<908	846	<444
Cyclic Ethers: ($K = -0.40$, $C = 1192$ kJ/mol)			
c-C_2H_4O	1020	786	494
c-C_3H_6O	933	824	448
c-C_4H_8O	908	832	427
c-$C_5H_{10}O$	892	836	414
Aldehydes: ($K = -0.50$, $C = 1276$ kJ/mol)			
CH_3CHO	987	781	456
C_2H_5CHO	960	793	444
n-C_3H_7CHO	949	801	439
i-C_3H_7CHO	936	806	431
i-C_4H_9CHO	936	806	431
Ketones: ($K = -0.39$, $C = 1188$ kJ/mol)			
CH_3COCH_3	936	823	448
$C_2H_5COCH_3$	917	836	444
$C_2H_5COC_2H_5$	898	843	427
i-$C_3H_7COCH_3$	897	851	435
$(i$-$C_3H_7)_2CO$	864	857	410
t-$C_4H_9COCH_3$	879	846	414
$(t$-$C_4H_9)_2CO$	836	864	389
Primary Amines: ($K = -0.59$, $C = 1406$ kJ/mol)			
CH_3NH_2	866	896	448
$C_2H_5NH_2$	855	908	452
n-$C_3H_7NH_2$	847	912	448
i-$C_3H_7NH_2$	841	915	444
n-$C_4H_9NH_2$	841	914	444
s-$C_4H_9NH_2$	839	923	448
i-$C_4H_9NH_2$	839	915	444
t-$C_4H_9NH_2$	833	924	444
n-$C_5H_{11}NH_2$	836	916	439

TABLE 2.5.2.1. The relationship between proton affinity, ionization energy, and hydrogen affinity for homologous series—Continued

$$PA(M) = C + C \cdot IP(M)$$
$$HA(M^+) = c + d \cdot IP(M)$$
$$(C - c = 1312 \text{ kJ/mol}, d - K = 1.00)$$

	kJ/mol		
	IP	PA	HA
Secondary Amines: ($K = -0.72$, $C = 1502$ kJ/mol, $HA = 397$ kJ/mol)			
$(CH_3)_2NH$	794	923	406
$(CH_3)(C_2H_5)NH$	786	932	406
$(C_2H_5)_2NH$	773	945	406
$(n-C_3H_7)_2NH$	756	952	397
$(i-C_3H_7)_2NH$	746	963	397
$(n-C_4H_9)_2NH$	742	956	385
$(s-C_4H_9)_2NH$	736	966	389
$(i-C_4H_9)_2NH$	754	956	397
Tertiary Amines: ($K = -0.83$, $C = 1573$ kJ/mol, $HA = 385$ kJ/mol)			
$(CH_3)_3N$	754	942	385
$(CH_3)_2(C_2H_5)N$	747	952	385
$(CH_3)(C_2H_5)_2N$	723	962	372
$(C_2H_5)_3N$	723	972	385
$(n-C_3H_7)_3N$	715	979	381
Aromatic Amines: ($K = -1.0$, $C = 1636$ kJ/mol, $HA = 305$ kJ/mol)			
$C_6H_5NH_2$	741	877	305
$C_6H_5N(CH_3)_2$	687	935	310
$3-(CH_3)C_6H_4N(CH_3)_2$	677	939	305
$4-(CH_3)C_6H_4N(CH_3)_2$	669	944	301
$3,5-(CH_3)_2C_6H_3N(CH_3)_2$	671	950	301
$C_6H_5N(C_2H_5)_2$	674	952	314
Mercaptans: ($K = -0.98$, $C = 1678$ kJ/mol, $HA = 381$ kJ/mol)			
CH_3SH	911	784	381
C_2H_5SH	896	798	381
$n-C_3H_7SH$	887	802	377
$i-C_3H_7SH$	882	812	381
$t-C_4H_9SH$	871	824	381
Thioethers: ($K = -0.83$, $C = 1531$ kJ/mol, $HA = 360$ kJ/mol)			
CH_3SCH_3	838	839	364
$C_2H_5SCH_3$	824	851	364
$(C_2H_5)_2S$	813	858	360
$(n-C_3H_7)_2S$	801	864	351
$(i-C_3H_7)_2S$	796	877	360
$(n-C_4H_9)_2S$	793	873	356
$(t-C_4H_9)_2S$	779	890	356
Nitriles:			
CH_3CN	1177	788	653
C_2H_5CN	1142	806	636
$n-C_3H_7CN$	1129	810	628
$i-C_3H_7CN$	1133	813	632
Esters: ($K = -0.58$, $C = 1401$ kJ/mol)			
$HCOOCH_3$	1043	790	523
$HCOOC_2H_5$	1024	808	519
$HCOO(n-C_3H_7)$	1015	813	515
$HCOO(i-C_3H_7)$	1008	820	515
$HCOO(n-C_4H_9)$	1013	815	515
CH_3COOCH_3	991	828	506
$CH_3COOC_2H_5$	966	840	494
$CH_3COO(n-C_3H_7)$	969	839	494

TABLE 2.5.2.1. The relationship between proton affinity, ionization energy, and hydrogen affinity for homologous series—Continued

$$PA(M) = C + K \cdot IP(M)$$
$$HA(M^+) = c + d \cdot IP(M)$$
$$(C - c = 1312 \text{ kJ/mol}, d - K = 1.00)$$

	kJ/mol		
	IP	PA	HA
Esters: ($K = -0.58$, $C = 1401$ kJ/mol)			
$C_2H_5COOCH_3$	979	838	506
n-$C_3H_7COOCH_3$	971	837	498
i-$C_3H_7COOCH_3$	951	843	481
t-$C_4H_9COOCH_3$	955	849	490
Acids:			
CH_3COOH	1028	796	510
C_2H_5COOH	1015	802	506

3. Negative Ions

The previous publication of evaluated heats of formation of ions, "Energetics of Gaseous Ions"[2], contains ionization/appearance potential data for over 4000 species leading to evaluated heats of formation for more than 600 positive ions. By contrast, that volume contains thermochemical data for only 117 anions, including only 12 organic (C, H containing) anions. These statistics reflect the relative importance of studies on cation versus anion thermochemistry at the time of the cut-off for the literature search for that volume, 1971.

The large discrepancy in the numbers of early studies on anions as compared to cations is easy to rationalize. Most neutral species display a much lower cross section for production of anions than for cation production, with the necessary consequence that conventional electron impact mass spectrometry is much more adaptable to studies of positive ions. Similarly, the presence of excess energy in a cation can cause fragmentation, with the identities of the fragment cations providing useful structural information. In contrast, loss of an electron from a bound anion to form the corresponding neutral species is often energetically preferred to a dissociation process producing a fragment anion. Thus, the "cation bias" of much of gaseous ion thermochemistry until the last decade is understandable.

The renaissance in gas phase anion chemistry and thermochemistry came about with the development of chemical ionization mass spectrometry as a commonly-used technique. Anions are often more useful than cations for analytical work in that they can originate with less internal energy. In a proton transfer reaction leading to an anion product, the new bond which is formed—with its share of the excess energy of reaction—is in the departing neutral species (reaction 11) while in the analogous reaction involving cations (reaction 6), the new bond is in the ion. Likewise, thermal electron attachment to those species which form stable radical anions is considerably faster than particle transfer, so that the chemical ionization step can be much more sensitive.

3.1. Aims

The compilation of anion thermochemistry in this work has slightly different aims than the companion cation compilation, in that the latter presents only the "best" available values for the ionization energy/heat of formation of a given structure. A complete archive of the literature having to do with cations has not been given, because the previous compilations[1,2,3,4] have summarized the literature exhaustively. Although there have been a number of compilations concerned with the thermochemistry of anions in the last few years[11,68-75] these have not presented data which are critically evaluated, i.e., the best values are not assigned, save for atomic ions[70]. The advances in the last decade in ion/molecule chemistry and in such techniques as photoelectron and photodetachment spectrometry have resulted in a tremendous increase in the number of chemical structures for which some anionic thermochemistry is known. This publication therefore includes a collection of the literature data which is as complete as possible, and an assignment of the "best" value for the thermochemistry where sufficient information is available.

The thermochemical parameters of critical interest in this compilation are the heat of formation of the anion and the electron affinity of the radical or neutral molecule corresponding to the anion. In order to properly evaluate these, however, data on the energetics of chemical processes involving the anions (Brønsted basicity of the anion, parameters for solvation by neutral species, etc.) are also included. The extensive thermochemical ladders of relative acidities, electron affinities, solvation thermochemistry, and similar data derived from chemical equilibria have provided a powerful tool for evaluating the thermochemistry of anions: chemical intuition. The use of structure-reactivity relationships allows the examination of the structure of an acid and a prediction about what its acidity, and therefore anion heat of formation, should be. The extra thermodynamic techniques such as linear free energy and enthalpy relationships often allow prediction of expected values accurate to better than a kJ/mol. Although results derived from such relationships can not always be trusted in cases of unusual structures, they nevertheless provide a reasonable rationale for assigning "best" values in many cases.

A problem that has become increasingly important recently is the question of the thermochemistry of the allied neutral species. As indicated below in the section on thermochemical relationships, the limiting factor in deriving anion thermochemical data is often the reliability of the data on the related thermochemistry of the neutral species (heats of formation, bond strengths). The information generated by the field of ion chemistry has outpaced the availability of neutral thermochemical data in recent years. In many cases, the best values for certain bond strengths are derived from data on the thermochemical properties of ions, rather than the other way around.

3.2. Experimental Techniques

Detailed descriptions of the various techniques used to obtain anion thermochemical data will not be presented here, since these are well documented in the literature by their practitioners. Brief descriptions of each technique follow, with comments about accuracy and limitations. The phrase in square brackets following the name is the acronym used in the database to refer to the method.

3.2.1. Laser Photoelectron Spectroscopy [LPES]

A fixed frequency laser (commonly 2.54 eV photons) is used to irradiate a beam of anions, and the energies of the detached electrons are analyzed[70]. The method often provides information on the vibrational states of the neutral and ionic species as well. However, the assignment of the (0–0) threshold can be complicated by these states. The precision is commonly better than 0.2 kJ/mol, and can be much better.

3.2.2. Laser Photodetachment [LPD]

In this technique, which may be considered the converse of photoelectron spectroscopy, the laser wavelength is varied to determine the threshold for detachment of a (presumably) thermal electron[71] from an anion. This experiment has usually been carried out in an ICR ion trap, with the decrease in the ICR signal of the ion as the detected quantity; the lower power of variable wavelength lasers often requires a longer irradiation period than with the ion beam in photoelectron spectroscopy. Precision is ca. 1-4 kJ/mol. The detection of the true threshold is often complicated by a gradual onset, although the general theory of the onset has been worked out[68,69]. This method actually yields the vertical detachment energy, which is equated with the electron affinity. This assumption is usually valid, but fails for molecules for which the geometries of the anion and neutral are considerably different (i.e., for which there is poor Franck-Condon overlap). A notable case is CF_3^-, where the photodetachment value is larger than the adiabatic value by 0.8 eV[77].

A recent determination of the spectrum of the hydroxide anion is at a resolution of ca. 2 J/mol[70] while coaxial LPD for O^- furnishes a resolution of 0.006 cm^{-1}, or 0.07 J/mol[76]!

3.2.3. Photodetachment [PD]

Early photodetachment experiments were carried out using an arc lamp and a monochromator to irradiate the ICR cell[71]. Precision was lower than with the laser experiment.

3.2.4. Photodissociation [PDis]

Irradiation of anions does not always yield electron detachment as the first threshold process since bond cleavage may also be an allowed process. The wavelength threshold for such a process can provide information on the heat of formation of the anion, if the heats of formation of the products are known.

3.2.5. Ion/Molecule Equilibrium Constant Determinations [IMRE,Kine,TDEq,TDAs]

As discussed in Sec. 2.3.5., this evaluation takes into account (although previous works in the series did not) all information on ion thermochemistry generated by ion/molecule equilibrium constant determinations. In the case of anions, ion/molecule equilibrium studies on electron transfer reactions:

$$A^- + B \rightleftharpoons B^- + A \qquad (49)$$

lead to scales of relative electron affinities.

$$K_{eq} = \frac{[B^-][A]}{[A^-][B]} \qquad (50)$$

while equilibrium constants for hydride or halide transfer reactions:

$$A + BY^- \rightleftharpoons B + AY^- \qquad (51)$$

(where Y is H, F, Cl, Br, or I) lead to thermochemical ladders of relative acidities or halide affinities. Other scales of anionic thermochemistry are derived from equilibrium constants for solvation equilibria:

$$Y^- + X \rightleftharpoons [X \cdot \cdot Y^-] \qquad (52)$$

Further, if the forward and reverse rate constants for a reaction are known, then the equilibrium constant, and thus ΔG, can be calculated from kinetic data [Kine].

The bulk of the available data on anion thermochemistry in the past decade has been derived from ion/molecule equilibrium constant determinations and photoelectron/photodetachment spectroscopy. Extensive scales, spanning an energy range of nearly 400 kJ/mol, have been determined for proton transfer (leading to relative Brønsted acidities of molecules), electron transfer, and halide transfer reactions.

In general, the free energy changes associated with such equilibria are measured to a precision of ca. 0.5 kJ/mol. The absolute uncertainty of anion heats of formation derived from such results is usually on the order of 5–10 kJ/mol, and depends on the accuracy of the method of "anchoring" the resulting scales of relative thermochemical values.

There remain at present several points of uncertainty regarding these data. There is an active debate[78] about the actual temperature of the ions in an ICR cell. Although some early results indicated that effective ion temperatures could be as much as several hundred degrees above ambient[78], the accuracy of the kinetic rate constant "thermometer" used as the basis of that judgement was not established. Comparisons of equilibrium constant data obtained in ICR cells with data derived from other sources indicate that the effective ion temperatures in ICR cells are not more than 10 degrees higher than measured gas temperatures in the cells[22,78].

The measured equilibrium constant data lead directly to values of free energies, which require some knowledge of the entropy changes of the processes under consideration in order to derive the desired enthalpy changes. Entropy changes have been obtained either through statistical mechanical calculations[79,80], or by measuring equilibrium constants as a function of temperature [TDEq = temperature dependent equilibrium constant], leading through a van't Hoff treatment of the results to experimental values for the entropy and enthalpy changes. Finally, the dynamic range (i.e. ion trapping time) of all the mass spectrometric techniques now in use for ion/molecule equilibrium constant determinations is such that the maximum free energy change which can be determined for particle transfer reactions is no greater than ca. 30–40 kJ/mol at most, and often only 10 kJ/mol at room temperature. The dynamic range for determinations of thermochemical parameters of association reactions is much greater [TDAs = temperature dependent association].

There have been questions raised regarding the accuracy of this method, since alcohol bond strengths derived in this way were consistently 9 kJ/mol smaller than accepted values. It was originally thought that this discrepancy was due to the temperature problem alluded to above[78], because the acidity scale measured in the ICR spectrometer[80] was compressed relative to that determined by pulsed high pressure mass spectrometry[79]. If the equilibria established in the reaction cell of the ICR spectrometer were actually at a higher temperature than the value which was used to convert K_{eq} to $\Delta(\Delta_{acid}G)$, then the calculated free energy scale from ICR experiments would be compressed. However, the gas phase basicity scales measured by ICR and by high pressure mass spectrometric methods agree quite well[4]. In addition, Taft[81] has recently redetermined many of the relative acidities that make up the thermochemical ladder, and finds that the region of the acidity scale from trifluoroethanol to acetone has a larger range than the original work indicated. These results have been confirmed in the laboratory of one of the present authors[82]. The region of the acidity scale from trifluoroethanol up to methanol has therefore been adjusted to include these new data. The data affected by this revision are still referred to by the original literature reference, e.g. 79BAR/SCO, and the original values are still displayed, but the method is denoted IMRE°. The revised values are *preferred* in the evaluation.

3.2.6. Ion/Molecule Reaction Bracketing [IMRB]

For most of the techniques currently used for studying thermal ion/molecule reaction equilibria and kinetics, ions can only be examined for, at most, several thousand collisions with the reactive neutral gas. Thus, any reaction more endothermic than a few kcal/mol can not be observed on the time scale of the presently used techniques. In the observation of a series of reactions for which the functional groups present at the reactive site of the molecule are always the same, and the energy of the reaction is being varied by changing some distant substituent, then if the rate constant falls to less than the observable rate over some small energy range, it is a fair assumption that the reaction pathway has become endothermic at that point. From this, an estimate of the thermoneutral (equilibrium) point may be made. This technique must be applied with caution, because the mechanism of the observed reaction may not be the same for the entire series of molecules, so that apparent variations in reactivity may not actually reflect the thermochemistry of the assumed reaction.

3.2.7. Electron Impact Appearance Potentials [EIAP]

Since a bound anion must be thermochemically more stable than the combined energies of the free electron plus the neutral species, simple attachment of electrons, even thermal ones, in general results in rapid autodetachment. In certain cases, however, the excited anion state can fragment to yield either an anion plus a neutral species (dissociative attachment), or an anion plus a cation (ion pair production). The latter process has not been well studied save for relatively small species, and is not at present a source of much thermochemical data. On the other hand, a considerable amount of thermochemical data has been derived from experiments in which the onset energy for dissociative attachment is measured. A complication in the interpretation of such onsets involves the unknown internal energy of both the anionic and neutral fragments. A particularly useful case is where two onsets are observed, with the fragments differing only in the identity of the species associated with the electron:

$$AB + e \rightarrow A^- + B\cdot \qquad (53)$$

$$\rightarrow A\cdot + B^- \qquad (54)$$

If the electron affinity of one of the product species is known, that of the other can be inferred from the known electron affinity and the difference in the onset energies for the two channels.

Most workers have not used monoenergetic electron beams, so the precision in the energy onsets is generally larger than 0.1 eV (10 kJ/mol). The resulting anion heats of formation include that uncertainty plus the uncertainties in the heats of formation of the associated reactant and neutral species. A few retarding potential difference measurements have been carried out, to improve the accuracy of such results.

3.2.8. Neutral Beam Ionization/Appearance Potentials [NBIP/NBAP]

Collision of a neutral species with an energetic particle of low ionization potential, such as an alkali atom, can result in electron transfer, giving an alkali cation and an anion[83]. The electron affinity of the neutral species is equal to the translational energy of the alkali atom less its ionization potential. Determinations of electron affinities by this method have the advantage that one obtains values for the true electron affinity: electron attachment to a neutral species, rather than detachment from an anion. Certain anions can be produced by this technique which are not accessible via electron impact due to low energy exit channels, e.g. CCl_4^-. Due to the limited energy resolution of the neutral alkali beam, the precision of this technique is not high, typically 20 kJ/mol. The onset energies of fragment ions can also provide useful thermochemical information, if the thermochemistry of the co-produced neutral species is known.

Normally this technique results in a determination of the adiabatic electron affinity, but for a sufficiently fast beam of neutral species, the onset corresponds to the vertical attachment energy of the electron, which, in contrast to detachment methods, is smaller than the adiabatic value.

3.2.9. Photoionization [PI]

This technique involves production of cation-anion pairs by vacuum ultraviolet photons. It has been used primarily for small molecules (O_2, F_2, etc.). The difference in onset for dissociative ion pair production and dissociative ionization

$$AB + h\nu \rightarrow A^- + B^+ \qquad (55)$$

$$AB + h\nu \rightarrow A\cdot + B^+ + e \qquad (56)$$

corresponds to the electron affinity of A.

3.2.10. Endothermic Reaction Energy, Including Charge Transfer [Endo,EnCT,CIDT]

If an ion/molecule reaction is appreciably endothermic at thermal (room temperature) energies, it is not observable by present techniques. For some processes it is possible to increase the rate by increasing the translational energy of the reactants so that products can be observed. Assuming that all the translational energy is available to bring about the reaction through the intermediacy of a long-lived complex in which energy is statistically distributed, the onset energy for observation of a given reaction can be taken as the threshold for the process, and thermochemistry assigned accordingly. Here the acronym "Endo" describes the use of such onset energies for deriving thermochemical data, "EnCT" the use of such onsets in charge transfer processes.

A variant is the case of collision of a *non-reactive* species, which serves only to provide the energy necessary for the negative ion to fragment or detach the electron. This is termed the "Collision Induced Dissociation Threshold" method [CIDT].

3.2.11. Surface Ionization (Magnetron) [SI]

The production of ions on a surface can yield thermochemical data if a number of parameters are known, including the work function of the surface. A common version of this experiment, the Magnetron technique[84] [Surface Ionization, SI], lacks mass analysis, and therefore many of the values for thermochemical parameters resulting from this method correspond to anions of uncertain identity. Precision is thought to be several tenths of a volt (>20 kJ/mol).

3.2.12. Electron Swarm [ES]

In this technique[85], the electron affinity of a neutral species (usually a closed shell molecule) is calculated by a statistical method, using the rate of electron attachment, the autodetachment lifetime, and the vibrational frequencies of the species. The attachment rate is measured in a drift tube — electron swarm experiment, and extrapolated to thermal energy. The autodetachment lifetime is taken from results of beam experiments. The precision is probably a few tenths of an eV (30-40 kJ/mol) at best.

3.2.13. Lattice energy [Latt]

The heat of formation of an anion can be derived from a Born-Haber cycle using the lattice energy and heat of formation of a crystal and the thermochemistry of the appropriate gas phase cation. This method is not especially accurate relative to more recent techniques, but for some singly charged inorganic anions it provides the only data available.

3.2.14. Kinetic Branching Methods [Bran, CIDC]

If certain ion/molecule complexes are subjected to collision induced dissociation (CID), the weakest bond between the two species in the complex is the most likely one to break. If the functional groups forming the bond are identical, with the acids differing only in distant substitution, then either species has a chance to acquire the proton on breakup of the complex. The branching ratio in the reaction:

$$ROH\cdots{}^-OR' \xrightarrow{M} ROH + R'O^- \quad (57a)$$
$$\phantom{ROH\cdots{}^-OR'} \xrightarrow{M} RO^- + R'OH \quad (57b)$$

has been shown to reflect the relative acidities of the two species[87]. Once the sensitivity of this branching ratio for compounds of known acidity has been established, then CID of clusters with one compound of known acidity and one unknown can lead to an estimate for the acidity of the unknown species. This appears to be reliable to 1–2 kJ/mol in determining relative acidities. This approach has some limitations. First, values for the gas phase acidities for several members of the series must first be known from other sources for proper calibration. Further, the temperature of the reacting system is not defined, and so problems may arise in interpretation for systems with significant entropy changes. The general method has also been applied to the estimation of relative electron affinities[87] for complexes of aromatic radical anions with aromatic molecules.

The excited intermediate complex can be prepared other ways than by collision. If an ion/molecule reaction is sufficiently exothermic, and has more than one available reaction channel, then the branching ratio of products formed on breakup of the complex can reflect product stabilities. This assumption has been used to estimate the acidities of the simple alkanes[88] since many of the localized carbanions from those compounds do not appear to be bound with respect to electron loss. Such ions exist only in ion/molecule complexes, where the cluster energy may serve to prevent electron detachment before reaction.

3.2.15. Electron Transmission Spectroscopy [ETS]

In this technique, the scattering angles of a monoenergetic electron beam impacting on a gas at less than the ionization threshold are determined. The presence of resonances in the spectrum implies electron capture to produce a temporary state, followed by autodetachment. This is the principal technique for measurement of negative electron affinities. Occasionally, a series of resonances can be extrapolated to below zero electron energy to give an estimate of a positive electron affinity[11].

3.2.16. Electron Capture Detector [ECD]

An electron capture detector for a gas chromatograph, when operated in a variable temperature pulse sampling mode, can provide data on electron capture/detachment ratios. These can be converted into electron affinities. Use of the method is limited to the determination of electron affinities in the 0.2–0.8 eV (20–80 kJ/mol) range. The precision of such measurements is commonly quoted as less than 1 kJ/mol[89].

3.2.17. Mobility of Ions in a Gas [Mobl]

If the mobility of an ion in a gas can be measured in response to a weak electric field, the potential well depth, corresponding to $\Delta_{\text{aff}}H$, for the ion associating with the neutral gas can be determined.

3.2.18. Laser Optogalvanic Photodetachment Spectroscopy [LOG]

The gas of interest is subjected to an electrical discharge, and the discharge region is probed by a laser. The LOG[90] spectrum is recorded by scanning the wavelength of the laser, and monitoring laser-induced changes in the discharge impedance. The spectrum produced will be similar to the laser absorption spectrum but relative intensities of spectral features may be very different. The method is particularly suitable for detecting unstable (radical) species.

3.3. Thermochemical Cycles

The relationships between the different quantities measured in the above experimental techniques can be exploited to derive additional thermochemical information. In Table 2, such derivations have been made wherever possible. In the table, the quantities which have been *derived* from the experimentally-determined value are indicated by superscripted letters, which correspond to the various types of derivation described here, while the quantity actually determined in the reported experiment is given without any superscripted letter. A list of the various approaches to derivation and their corresponding superscript letters is given in the Table in Sec. 5.2.

The *heat of formation of an anion* can be derived from the heat of formation of the acid, its gas phase acidity, the heat of formation of the proton:

$$\Delta_f H(A^-) = \Delta_{\text{acid}} H(AH) - \Delta_f H(H^+) + \Delta_f H°(AH) \quad (58)$$

The quantity $\Delta_f H°(AH)$ is lacking in many cases where acidities are now available; various group additivity estimation schemes (see below, and Sec. 4.) have been employed to fill in this information.

As discussed in Sec. 1.6.3., the calculation of the anion heat of formation as the heat of formation of the neutral species less the electron affinity:

$$\Delta_f H(A^-) = \Delta_f H°(A) - EA(A) \quad (59)$$

is not, strictly speaking, correct, since for most of the species given here the heat of formation of the neutral species is a 298 K value, while the electron affinity is a threshold 0 K value. The preference is for anion heats of formation calculated by Eq. 58.

In an inversion of the bond strength/electron affinity Eq. 32 for calculating acidities, a known acidity and bond strength can yield an *electron affinity*.

$$EA(A) = BDE(A-H) + IP(H·) - \Delta_{acid}H(AH) \quad (60)$$

Based on the temperature cancellation effect, this should correspond to the 0 K value. This is also an adiabatic value, which can be less than the vertical electron affinity obtained from the optical techniques if the geometries of the neutral and anion differ appreciably.

The difference between the anion and neutral heats of formation (at 298 K) give a 298 K electron affinity:

$$EA(A) = \Delta_f H°(A) - \Delta_f H(A^-) \quad (61)$$

If the geometry change is small, this should be a reasonable approximation to the 0 K value.

Gas phase acidities, taken as the enthalpy of acidity, can be calculated from the homolytic bond strength of the acidity site, the electron affinity of the resulting radical, and the ionization energy of the hydrogen atom:

$$\Delta_{acid}H(AH) = BDE(A-H) - EA(A) + IP(H) \quad (62)$$

The last is common to all acids, and is very accurately known (1311.98 kJ/mol), and does not present a limitation in determining the values. A more valid concern is the temperature of definition for these terms. The acidity and bond strength are commonly taken as 298 K values, while the electron affinity and ionization potential are threshold values defined at 0 K. The cancellation necessary for this equation to be considered valid is discussed in Sec. 1.6.3.

Sometimes a heat of formation of an anion or an electron affinity value may be known without a value for the bond strength being available. The *acidity of the conjugate acid* can be derived in those cases from the acid heat of formation:

$$\Delta_{acid}H(AH) = \Delta_f H(A^-) + \Delta_f H(H^+) - \Delta_f H°(AH) \quad (63)$$

While the primary goal of this work is not to obtain values for *homolytic bond strengths*, such values can be derived from gas phase acidities and electron affinities in cases where they are not known from more conventional sources.

$$BDE(A-H) = \Delta_{acid}H(AH) + EA(A) - IP(H·) \quad (64)$$

$$BDE(A-H) = \Delta_f H°(AH) - \Delta_f H°(A) - \Delta_f H°(H) \quad (65)$$

3.4. Priority of Data

At the present time, the heat of formation of an anion in the gas phase is not directly measurable, since gas phase plasma calorimetry is not a known technique. Likewise, direct measurement of an electron affinity, in the sense of exothermic electron attachment to a neutral, is not feasible in a calorimetric sense, although the combination of attachment and detachment rate constants can be used. The electron affinity and anionic heat of formation are available from either thermochemical cycles, based on other known and measurable quantities, or by reasonable assumptions about the reversibility of processes such as electron detachment from anions.

For electron affinities, we adopt the following order of priority for the evaluation of "best" values. There are exceptions in many cases to this order, where a given method is known not to be suitable. The user should be aware of the difference between adiabatic and vertical values that these techniques yield.

Laser photoelectron spectroscopy
Laser photodetachment
Photodetachment
From bond strengths and gas phase acidities
Neutral beam ionization/appearance potentials
Electron impact appearance potentials
Ion/molecule bracketing reactions
Electron swarm

For gas phase acidities, the following priorities are assigned to data sources:

Direct gas phase equilibrium constant determinations
Kinetic methods for gas phase acidities:branching ratios in collisional dissociation and ion/molecule complex breakup.
From bond strengths and electron affinities
Ion/molecule bracketing reactions (using either the heat of formation of the anion or of the acid as the unknown quantity).

4. Thermochemistry of Neutral Species

Tables 1 and 2 display values for heats of formation of the neutral gas phase molecules which are "related" to the archived ions. In Table 1, which is concerned with cation thermochemistry, the "related" neutral species is either (a) the neutral molecule which corresponds to the ion plus an electron (for ionization potential data) or (b) the molecule which has one less proton than the ion of interest (for proton affinity data). In Table 2, concerned with anion thermochemistry, the term "related" means that the neutral is formed from the ion either by loss of an electron (electron affinity) or gaining of a proton (gas phase acidity). For every case, the identity of the neutral molecule corresponding to the displayed heat of formation is made unambiguous.

4.1. Literature Sources

Values for the heats of formation of neutral molecules were taken from the experimental literature whenever possible. If a value for a particular compound was available from an evaluated data compilation, this value was generally selected for inclusion here. The primary compilations which were used were as follows.

4.1.1. Organic Compounds

J. B. Pedley and J. Rylance, "Sussex-N. P. L. Computer Analysed Thermochemical Data: Organic and Organometallic Compounds," University of Sussex (1977). The numerous data from this evaluated compilation[91] of 298 K heats of formation of gas phase organic compounds are identified by the squib 77PED/RYL. A second edition of this work (86PED/NAY) has appeared[92], but regrettably, was available to the authors of the current compilation too late to obviate an extensive literature search for heats of formation from the primary literature to cover the period 1976-mid-1986. Since the updated compilation of Pedley, Naylor and Kirby[92] (which is complete only through 1982) became available only as this work was nearing completion, references to 77PED/RYL or to recent primary literature have been retained even in cases where the data are given in 86PED/NAY.

4.1.2. Inorganic Compounds

(1) D. D. Wagman, W. H. Evans, V. B. Parker, R. H. Schumm, I. Halow, S. M. Bailey, K. L. Churney, and R. L. Nuttall, "The NBS Tables of Chemical Thermodynamic Properties: Selected Values for Inorganic and C_1 and C_2 Organic Substances in SI Units," J. Phys. Chem. Ref. Data, Vol. 11, Suppl. 2 (1982), hereafter referred to as 82TN270, from the original publication of this compilation[14] as a series of NBS Technical Notes called the 270-series. (It should be noted that when this source is used in Table 2, both the value and an associated error limit are given, while only the former is given in Table 1.)

(2) (a) D. R. Stull and H. Prophet, "JANAF Thermochemical Tables," NSRDS-NBS 37 (1971); (b) M. W. Chase, J. C. Curnutt, H. Prophet, R. A. McDonald, and A. N. Syverud, "JANAF Thermochemical Tables," 1975 Supplement, J. Phys. Chem. Ref. Data 2, 1 (1975); (c) M. W. Chase, Jr., J. L. Curnutt, J. R. Downey, Jr., R. A. McDonald, A. N. Syverud, and E. A. Valenzuela, J. Phys. Chem. Ref. Data, 11, 695 (1982). Information from these sources[13] is referenced as 71JANAF, 75JANAF, or 82JANAF. An updated composite edition[13c] of this compilation was in press at the time this work was being prepared, but was not actually available until these tables were near completion. A few values for heats of formation from the updated version have been inserted here where warranted by changes in recommended values, but an exhaustive check of the new publication was not made.

(3) L. V. Gurvich, I. V. Veits, V. A. Medvedev, G. A. Khachkuruzov, V. S. Yungman, G. A. Bergman, et al, "Termodinamicheskie Svoistva Individual'nykh Veshchestv" (Thermodynamic Properties of Individual Substances); V. P. Glushko, Gen. Ed., Vols. 1 through 4 (in 8 parts), (1978-1982), Izdatel'stvo "Nauka" Moscow. These volumes[15] are collectively cited as 82TPIS.

4.1.3. Specialized Classes of Compounds and Radicals

In addition, various literature compilations which cover well-defined, but restricted, classes of compounds such as nitriles, organometallic compounds, free radicals, or strained hydrocarbons were utilized. The preferential use of data compilations as sources of experimental data recognizes that these data have been evaluated for internal consistency insofar as possible.

Many values for heats of formation of free radicals were taken from the review of McMillen and Golden[93]. With respect to the alkyl radicals, however, a recent re-evaluation of data from the literature has led to the suggestion that C-H bond energies in alkanes should be revised upwards[94]. The heats of formation of these radicals are still a matter of controversy at this writing. Values cited in the tables are based on the following revised[94] C-H bond strengths: Primary C-H bond (101 kcal/mol, 422 kJ/mol); Secondary C-H bond (99 kcal/mol, 415 kJ/mol); Tertiary C-H bond (95 kcal/mol, 398 kJ/mol).

The corresponding values for the heats of formation of the alkyl radicals are in some cases (e.g. t-butyl radical) entirely consistent with the differences between well-established heats of formation of the corresponding alkyl cations and experimental ionization energy values, but there are also cases for which the relevant values show inconsistencies. These are pointed out in Table 1 by a specific comment.

4.1.4. Other Literature Sources

Experimental information about heats of formation of species not included in evaluated compilations was generally obtained from primary literature sources. When more than one value for a heat of formation was available from such unevaluated primary sources, and no supplementary information was available which would allow an educated choice, the most recent value was usually arbitrarily chosen in the possibly naive expectation that "improved instrumentation" as well as a greater (historical) awareness of the problems inherent in an analysis of the thermochemistry of the particular species would lead to a more reliable value.

Care was taken in utilizing these data from unrelated literature sources to be aware of ambiguities in thermochemical reference states. Values for heats of formation derived from heats of reaction (e.g. hydrolysis, bromination) were used in preference to directly-determined heats of combustion because of the inherent problems associated with numbers derived from relatively small differences between two large numbers. In many cases, heats of formation of neutral species were derived using well-established ionization energies or proton affinity values in combination with well-established heats of formation of relevant ions; these values are identified by an explanatory sentence in the comment field.

4.2. Conventions Used and Assumptions Made

Implicitly, in assigning gas phase heats of formation to the neutral species, the compounds are assumed to be ideal gases at S. T. P. Whenever sufficient information is readily available, values for heats of formation at both 0 and 298 K are given. In some cases, the 0 K value has been obtained by combining the 298 K values from a preferred literature source (i.e., an evaluated compilation) with the 298—0 K difference taken from another reference. In other cases, this difference was calculated from experimental or estimated extrathermodynamic quantities such as vibrational frequencies and the appropriate elemental thermochemical functions. Another approach was to use isoelectronic or isostructural analogies (e.g., data for O_3 may be compared with that on NO_2^- and neutral NO_2).

4.3. Use of Condensed Phase Heats of Formation

Numerous methods exist for measuring and interpreting experimental heats of sublimation and heats of vaporization. Where available, such measurements were used to translate condensed phase data into gas phase values for heats of formation. In such cases, the cited reference is the source of the condensed phase heat of formation data, although the bibliography includes the references from which the information about heats of sublimation or vaporization were obtained.

In most cases, data on heats of sublimation (and the associated methodologies for translating condensed phase heats of formation to gas phase values at 298 K) are from the recent publication[95], 87CHI, for organic compounds.

Regrettably, while work on this publication was in progress no such single literature source for heats of vaporization was available, although such a compilation has since appeared[96]. In fact, however, experimental data on heats of vaporization do not exist for numerous species of interest here, either because of experimental difficulties associated with such determinations (i.e. lack of adequate volatility, purity, or thermal stability) or perhaps because of a lack interest in, or availability of, the compound.

Estimation methods for heats of vaporization and sublimation have been described in the literature[95,97]. Some require auxiliary experimental data (e.g. critical constants). Other such estimation methods can be applied only to well-defined classes of compounds. For heats of vaporization, these estimates are usually reliable to approximately 4 kJ/mol (1 kcal/mol). In presenting data on heats of formation incorporating the use of such estimated heats of vaporization, a choice had to be made of whether to cite the source of the experimental heat of formation of the liquid or the paper from which the method for estimating the heat of vaporization was obtained; the experimental work is given as the primary citation. For heats of sublimation, no generally accurate estimation approaches exist. Thermochemical values obtained using estimated heats of sublimation are clearly labelled as estimates in the tables.

4.4. Estimated Heats of Formation

Estimates were also made for heats of formation of neutral molecules and radicals for which no experimental data were available. Several estimation approaches were utilized and are now briefly described. The relationships between the various estimation approaches have been described in a recent review[98].

4.4.1. Estimates from Data on Isomeric Species

One approach utilizes experimental information about isoenergetic processes for the formation of two or more isomeric species in a particular reaction. That is, given a pair of isomers for which information about the heat of formation is available for only one of the pair, an estimate of the thermochemistry of the second compound can be based on the casual and generally rather reliable assumption that if two isomers are formed in comparable yield in a particular process then their Gibbs energies and enthalpies of formation are generally comparable. Likewise, though less reliable, one may assert if one isomer is formed in higher yield, then this is the more stable product. Estimates made in this way often include the assumption that heats of vaporization and of solution are also comparable for the relevant pair of isomers; this will be a valid approximation except when there are great differences in the extent of hydrogen bonding (such as might exist for isomeric alcohols and ethers), and even in these cases, approximate corrections (such as assuming constant H-bond strengths) can be made.

In estimating thermochemical data from known information about an isomeric species, a common assumption made is that $\Delta(\Delta_f H) = \Delta(\Delta_f G)$ for the pair of isomers (i.e. $\Delta(\Delta_f S)$ is negligible). A related approach examines experimentally-determined reaction rates and/or kinetic activation energies. The thermochemical estimate is based on the assumption that the structural effects on rates and equilibria will vary in a parallel manner, and that thermodynamic and kinetic control of arbitrary reactions result in the same products. While not in fact absolutely true, experience has shown this to be a useful assumption for predicting substituent effects for numerous homologous series.

Another approach to estimating heats of formation is based on the assumption that $\Delta(\Delta_f H)$ can be equated with ΔE_{tot} for two isomers, where ΔE_{tot} is the difference in total energies of the two species calculated by quantum mechanics. For this assumption, as well as all other estimation approaches in this study employing results from quantum mechanics, ab initio calculations were given preference over results from any of the plethora of semi-empirical methods in the literature. (The reader should note that heats of formation from MNDO and from molecular mechanical calculations were occasionally used, however). Care was explicitly taken to contrast only species studied with the same basis set and degree of geometry optimization. Implicit, however, are the requirements that both the zero-point energy and 0 K – 298 K corrections are essentially identical for a pair of isomers. These last assumptions are surprisingly valid where sufficient experimental data are available to test them.

All values for heats of formation based on these approaches are labelled as estimates (EST) in the Tables.

4.4.2. Summing of Increments

There remain three related approaches which were employed to estimate heats of formation of molecules here. The best characterized is Benson's "group increment" approach[99] in which the molecule of interest is defined as a collection of groups, and a "group" is then defined as a polyvalent atom (ligancy ≥ 2) with all of its associated ligands in the molecule. The heat of formation of the molecule is obtained by summing the contributions of the heats of formation of the various groups, correcting for various higher order interactions and "correction" terms. These corrections include the presence of gauche configurations in substituted alkanes, gem-substitution of large and/or polar groups, and the presence of rings that are strained because of heteroatoms and/or are not six-membered. These group energies and the various corrections have been obtained using both statistical analysis and by chemical intuition, and for "reasonable" molecules generally give reasonable results. Estimates using this approach are better defined, though not necessarily of better quality, than the others.

Because this approach is now very common in the chemical literature, many of the papers included here which are primarily concerned with aspects of ion chemistry (e.g. ionization energy, gas phase basicity or acidity determinations) include estimates of heats of formation of relevant neutral species based on this approach; rather than cite the work of the authors who made the (rather standard) estimate, these values, when they were used, have been labelled as estimates. In Table 2 estimates utilizing this approach are labelled "Est", but are accompanied by error bars.

A related approach takes advantage of regularities in trends in heats of formation of different homologous series of compounds. As an example of how this approach works, if it is observed that the heats of formation of several RXR compounds differ from those of RYR compounds by some approximately constant increment, then this difference is defined as a "correction term" for deriving heats of formation of any –Y– compound from the heat of formation of the corresponding –X– compound (or vice versa)[100]. The unknown heat of formation is taken to the be the sum of the known heat of formation and the suitable correction term associated with the exchange of the substituent and parent components. One may also derive correction terms from suitable bond energies, e.g., assume that the O–H bond energy in all carboxylic acids is the same. This approach is more commonly used in anion chemistry and is designated as Est2 in Table 2 (but as EST without a special designator in Table 1).

The final estimation approach used here is commonly called "macroincrementation"[101,102], and, as the name implies, involves building up the molecule of interest by adding increments (as in the Benson approach), but with the difference that the incremental heats of formation are specifically derived from thermochemical data for molecules or large ("macro") molecular fragments which incorporate factors which need to be considered, such as resonance, strain energy, steric effects, etc. This approach assumes that "if for each of two sets of molecules the total number of bonds, atoms and structural types is the same, then the total heat of formation of each set of molecules is the same. Then, if all but one of the heats of formation are available, the remaining one can be estimated by simple arithmetic." Macroincrementation maximizes the direct use of chemical intuition with regard to electronic and/or steric effects, as well as the direct use of available experimental data. The majority of estimates for organic compounds in Table 1 were made using this approach.

The heats of formation of only a few inorganic or organometallic compounds were estimated. Where estimates were made, it generally was assumed that the heat of ligand exchange was negligible, i.e. the heats of reaction of the following generic reactions for suitably similar ligands (L_1 and L_2) could be taken to be zero:

$$M-L_1 + L_2 \rightleftharpoons M-L_2 + L_1 \quad (66)$$

$$L_1-M-L_1 + L_2-M-L_2 \rightleftharpoons 2(L_1-M-L_2) \quad (67)$$

Likewise, simple additive assumptions were made as to heats of vaporization and sublimation and the 0 K – 298 K energy differences.

5. Summary of Conventions Used in Tables

In an attempt to present as much information as possible in Tables 1 and 2, while keeping the pages uncluttered, it was sometimes necessary to resort to the use of bold face, italic typefaces, asterisks, etc. to convey additional information. The various conventions are summarized below. The user is particularly cautioned that these conventions are different for Table 1 and Table 2. In particular, italicized numbers have different meanings in Table 1 (zero Kelvin heats of formation) and Table 2 (a hydride or halide affinity, and information relating to thermochemistry of neutral species).

5.1. Positive Ion Table (Table 1)

Value underscored: A well-established value of an ionization energy or ion heat of formation.

Value enclosed in parentheses: A value of an ionization energy or heat of formation which is not well established, or not evaluated, for one of the following reasons: (1) Only one determination of the ionization energy has been reported, and there are no auxiliary data which would permit one to judge its accuracy; (2) The heat of formation of relevant neutral species is/are not well established; (3) Two or more contradictory values for the ionization energy or appearance energy have been reported, and while one value has been selected, there is sufficient doubt that one can not regard the selected value as well-established. (For data falling under category (3), an explanatory comment is always included.)

Value given in italics: Thermochemical data corresponding to a temperature of absolute zero.

Literature citations: In Table 1, there is no column giving references to the source of ionization energy/appearance energy data. Such data are always taken from the earlier compilations[1,2,3,4] unless specifically noted in a comment. When data are from the 1981–1986 primary literature, the reference is always specifically mentioned in the comment, and is specifically given in the bibliography. Heats of formation derived from proton affinity data (and the proton affinity data themselves) are taken from the evaluated compilation[4] or from more recent literature, which will always be specifically cited in the comment and listed in the bibliography.

Sort scheme: Data are sorted by empirical formula ordered according to the so-called Hill scheme, which is the same sort scheme used by Chemical Abstracts. Formulas are written as $C_nH_mX_xY_y...$, where the primary sort is ordered by n, the number of carbon atoms, and the first sub-sort is ordered according to m, the number of H atoms. All other atoms in the molecule (X, Y, etc) are ordered alphabetically, and the various sub-subsorts follow accordingly. Any molecules which do not contain carbon appear according to a strictly alphabetical sort.

Proton affinity data: To locate the proton affinity of a molecule, look under the empirical formula of the protonated molecule, i.e. the proton affinity of CH_4 appears under CH_5.

Estimated heats of formation of neutral molecules: The literature citation column contains the acronym EST for estimated values.

5.2 Negative Ion Table (Table 2)

Chemical species: Each entry is headed by an empirical formula of the relevant anion, with the atoms ordered according to the Hill formulation. Below this there appears a structural representation of the anion where this can be conveniently represented on one line; the last-listed atom is usually the atom judged to carry the negative charge (insofar as this can be ascertained). These formulas may contain simplifying abbreviations in common use by organic chemists, for example "Me" for CH_3, "Et" for C_2H_5, "Pr" for C_3H_7, "COT" for cyclooctatetraene, or "Ph" for phenyl. For chemical species which have structures which are too complex to be represented by a semi-structural formulation, a name is given. The names chosen for inclusion are easily recognizable by most chemists, or at least can be readily located in standard texts.

Units: In Table 2, all data are presented in kJ/mol, except the values for electron affinities, which (as specifically indicated) are given in electron volts.

Presentation of Data: Each line presents data from a different reference, which is cited at the end of the line. The value (or values) which results (or result) from a primary experimental measurement will appear without an affiliated superscript alphabetic letter. These letters point out data which have been derived from the experimental result; the derivations are described in Sec. 3.3., and summarized (along with their alphabetic identifiers) in Table 5.2. The data in the Table are divided into columns as follows:

Ion $\Delta_f H(A)$; EA(A) $\Delta_{acid}H(AH)$; $\Delta_{acid}G(AH)$; Method; Comment; Reference
    or   eV   or   or
  [X··Y$^-$] $\Delta_{aff}H(X··Y^-)$ $\Delta_{aff}G(X·Y^-)$

Ion: The chemical formula of the anion of interest.

$\Delta_f H(A^-)$ or $[X··Y^-]$: The second column presents the heat of formation of the listed anion in kJ/mol. The column heading specifies that the data correspond to anion A^- which may also be represented as $[X··Y^-]$. The second designation is included for the cases where the heat of formation of the anion has been derived from data on the clustering of anion Y^- to neutral molecule X (see reaction 52). For example, data on the heat of formation of AlF_4^- ($X··Y^-$) is derived from information on the fluoride affinity of AlF_3 (that is, AlF_3 is X and F^- is Y^-).

EA(A): The electron affinity of neutral species A is listed in this column in electron volts.

$\Delta_{acid}H(AH)$ or $\Delta_{aff}H(X \cdot\cdot Y^-)$ and $\Delta_{acid}G(AH)$ or $\Delta_{aff}G(X \cdot\cdot Y^-)$: The fourth and fifth columns serve double purposes, with normal typefaced data representing the enthalpy change (fourth column) or Gibbs energy change (fifth column), respectively, of reaction 10 for the species AH leading to a value for the heat of formation of anion A^-. Data given in italics represent enthalpy changes for reaction 52, that is the *affinity* of molecule X for anion Y^-. These have been derived either from direct determinations of equilibrium constants for reaction 52, or from equilibrium constants for Y^- transfer reaction 51 which yield scales of relative Y^--affinities.

Method: This column gives an acronym to indicate the experimental technique used in determining a particular piece of data. These are discussed in detail in Sec. 3.2. For quick reference, an alphabetized summary of the acronyms with their definitions, and the locations of the relevant discussions, is given in Table 5.2. This table also includes other acronyms, abbreviations, and symbols used in Table 2 for ready reference.

Comment: Where necessary for clarity, details of a particular experiment are given as a comment. In this column, there also appears information about auxiliary thermochemistry concerning neutral species. All data pertaining to neutral species appear in a different italicized typeface.

Reference: The squib given in this column refers to the article in which the primary datum reported on a particular line was reported. The complete reference can be found in the bibliography for Tables 1 and 2.

Thermochemistry of neutral species: The relevant heats of formation of neutral species and accompanying references are given in the top line of the "Comment" column. All data and the references pertaining to neutral molecules are presented in a different italicized typeface, so that they will not be mistaken for data concerning the anion.

Sort scheme: Data are sorted by empirical formula using the same sort scheme as that used for the Positive Ion Table. This is the Hill (or Chemical Abstracts) scheme.

Acidity data: Data on the acidity of a given neutral species is given under the empirical formula of the conjugate base, i.e. the acidity of CH_3OH is found under CH_3O^-.

Asterisk in left hand margin: Due to the comprehensive nature of the Negative Ion compilation, there can be numerous entries in Table 2 for a given quantity associated with a particular negative ion, unlike the convention adopted for the cation table, where only one value of an ionization energy/heat of formation is given. A special indication must be given, therefore, to denote the preferred value. Any line with an asterisk in the left margin contains the selected "best" value for a given piece of data pertaining to that ion. There may be more than one line thus marked for a given anion, since the best values for an acidity value and an electron affinity value may be from different sources. (The quantity without a superscripted letter is the primary piece of information for any given line.)

Absence of asterisk in margin: If no line is marked as preferred in the data collected for an ion, then no definitive evaluation could be made. Some preference should be given to the first reference cited in such cases, but this is a qualitative judgement on the part of the compiler, and should not be given undue weight.

Superscript "o" after method acronym [IMRE]: Original data which were re-evaluated to take into account new results which expanded a portion of the acidity[81,82] scale; corrected values are shown above "original" data, with original reference cited for both values.

Primary data originating from cited experimental reference: In Table 2, on any given line (which presents information derived from a single paper) items which were *derived* from the primary experimental data using the relationships listed in Sec. 3.3. and summarized in Table 5.2., have a superscripted letter indicating the relationship used to derive the value (see Table 5.2.). The primary data do not display a superscript.

TABLE 5.2. Acronyms, abbreviations and symbols used in Negative Ion Table

BDE(A-H):	Bond dissociation energy of A-H bond
Bran:	Branching ratio in an exothermic reaction (see Sec. Sec. 3.2.14.)
Calc:	Calculation
CIDC:	Collision-induced dissociation of cluster ion-branching ratio (see Sec. 3.2.7.)
CIDT:	Collision induced dissociation threshold (see Sec. 3.2.10.)
Def:	Defined
EA(A):	Electron affinity of A.
ECD:	Electron capture detector (see Sec. 3.2.16.)
EIAP:	Electron impact appearance potentials (see Sec. 3.2.7.)
EnCT:	Endothermic charge transfer threshold (see Sec. 3.2.10.)
Endo:	Endothermic reaction threshold energy (see Sec. 3.2.10.)
ES:	Electron swarm (see Sec. 3.2.12.)
Est:	Estimate, based on addition of increments
Est2:	Estimate, based on thermochemistry of analogous compounds
ETS:	Electron transmission spectroscopy (see Sec. 3.2.15.)
IMRB:	Ion/molecule reaction—bracketing (see Sec. 3.2.6.)
IMRE:	Ion/molecule reaction equilibrium constant determination (see Sec. 3.2.5.)
Kine:	Attachment/detachment rate ratio (see Sec. 3.2.5.)
Latt:	Lattice energy calculation (see Sec. 3.2.13.)
LOG:	Laser optogalvanic spectroscopy
LPD:	Laser photodetachment (see Sec. 3.2.2.)
LPES:	Laser photoelectron spectroscopy (see Sec. 3.2.1.)
Mobl:	Mobility of ion in gas (see Sec. 3.2.17.)
NBAP:	Neutral beam appearance potential (see Sec. 3.2.8.)
NBIP:	Neutral beam ionization potential (see Sec. 3.2.8.)
PD:	Photodetachment (see Sec. 3.2.3.)
PDis:	Photodissociation (see Sec. 3.2.4.)

TABLE 5.2. Acronyms, abbreviations and symbols used in Negative Ion Table — Continued

PI:	Photoionization (see Sec. 3.2.9.)
PLA:	Plasma absorption
SI:	Surface ionization (Magnetron) (see Sec. 3.2.11.)
TDAs:	Temperature dependent association equilibrium constant determination (see Sec. 3.2.5.)
TDEq:	Temperature dependent equilibrium constant determination (see Sec. 3.2.5.)
$\Delta_f H(A^-)$:	Heat of formation of A^-
$\Delta_{aff} H(X\cdot\cdot Y^-)$:	Enthalpy of association of neutral X to anion Y^-, the affinity of X for Y^-
$\Delta_{aff} G(X\cdot\cdot Y^-)$:	Gibbs energy of association of neutral X to anion Y^-
$\Delta_{acid} H(AH)$:	Acidity of molecule AH; see definition below under f

Single letter codes which define chemical reaction types (superscripts)

a: $\Delta_f H(A^-) = \Delta_{acid} H(AH) - \Delta_f H°(AH) + \Delta_f H(H^+)$
b: $\Delta_f H(A^-) = \Delta_f H°(A) - EA(A)$
c: $\Delta_f H(X\cdot\cdot Y^-) = -\Delta_{aff} H(X\cdot\cdot Y^-) + \Delta_f H°(X) + \Delta_f H(Y^-)$
d: $EA(A) = \Delta_{acid} H(AH) - IP(H^+) - BDE(A-H)$
e: $BDE(A-H) = \Delta_{acid} H(AH) - IP(H^+) + EA(A)$
f: $\Delta_{acid} H(AH) = \Delta_f H(A^-) + \Delta_f H(H^+) - \Delta_f H°(AH)$
g: $\Delta_{Rxn} H = \Delta_{Rxn} G + T\Delta_{Rxn} S$
h: $\Delta_{Rxn} G = \Delta_{Rxn} H - T\Delta_{Rxn} S$
i: $EA(A) = \Delta_f H°(A) - \Delta_f H(A^-)$
j: $\Delta_{aff} H(X\cdot\cdot Y^-) = \Delta_f H°(X) + \Delta_f H(Y^-) - \Delta_f H(X\cdot\cdot Y^-)$

5.3. References to Tables 1 and 2

The bibliography given at the back of the volume includes (a) references to the sources data having a bearing on the thermochemistry of the positive ions given in Table 1 (including ionization potentials, appearance potentials, proton affinities, and other related information) *except when those references appeared in the bibliographies of references 1 through 4*; (b) references to the sources of *all* data on the thermochemistry of negative ions from Table 2; and (c) references to the sources of the data on the thermochemistry of neutral molecules.

The references are identified in the tables, and in the bibliography, by a squib, made up of the year of the publication, the first three letters of the surname of the first author, followed by a slash and the first three letters of the surname of the second author. Example: A publication by J. B. Pedley and J. Rylance which appeared in 1977 would be designated by 77PED/RYL.

The references given in the bibliography are sorted according to these squibs, that is, first according to year, and then alphabetically according to the first three letters of the names of the first two authors. Example: Within the papers which appeared during a given year, reference to a paper by "Beauchamp and Armentrout" (BEA/ARM) would precede a reference to a paper by "Beach and Jackson" (BEA/JAC), which in turn would appear above a reference to "Beauchamp and Schwarz" (BEA/SCH). Note that papers of a given first author do not necessarily follow one another in the listing.

6. Acknowledgements

This work was initiated by Henry M. Rosenstock in the late 1970's. Until his death in 1982, Dr. Rosenstock was the guru of the project, assembling the current list of collaborators, participating vigorously in planning sessions, and, on occasion, engaging in scientific discussions which sometimes had the distinct character of teaching seminars, with Henry Rosenstock making certain that the rest of us clearly understood the science associated with our data evaluation project. There is no question that the quality of the evaluations reported here has been substantially improved by the interactions of the authors with this distinguished scientist.

The authors also acknowledge the contributions of the original group, D. Sims, S. S. Shroyer, and W. J. Webb, who started work on this project under Dr. Rosenstock's direction in 1978. Much of the literature search for the years 1971–1977 was completed by this team, as was the abstracting of data for the years 1971–72.

John Holmes especially wishes to record the contributions of Fred Lossing to this formidable task; his unquenchable enthusiasm and countless stimulating discussions over the past 15 or more years are most gratefully acknowledged.

At the National Bureau of Standards, Kathy Maugh, Jose Portal, Carol Martin, Clairemarie Lanthier, Kathy Whalen, and Elizabeth Rogers have helped in abstracting data from the literature, retrieving Chemical Abstracts Registry Numbers, proofreading, and numerous other tasks necessary to the completion of the project. Kathy Whalen and Elizabeth Rogers were responsible for affixing the drawings of molecules to the camera-ready pages. The careful, detailed work of all of these collaborators is acknowledged with thanks. We should also mention the help received from Julian Ives and Connie Seymour on preparation of the camera-ready copy.

Dr. Stephen E. Stein has collaborated with one of the present authors (W. G. M.) to develop a searchable PC version of this work, which can be purchased through the Office of Standard Reference Data.

Mahnaz Motevalli-Aliabadi of the University of Maryland, Baltimore County Campus, participated in the task of estimating heats of formation of neutral molecules during the early part of the project. Clairemarie Lanthier also provided estimations.

The molecular representations for the camera-ready copy were drawn by Andrea Fladager Buckley and Frances Baldwin.

The list of professional colleagues who have contributed data in preprint form or who have critically examined these tables and contributed advice, or pointed out errors is so long that a complete accounting is impossible. However, special mention should go to Dr. Charles DePuy of the University of Colorado for consultations on the table of anion thermochemistry. Dr. Malcolm Chase (NBS), editor of the JANAF tables, consulted with us about the discussion given here on the thermochemical conventions for the electron. Drs.

Eugene Domalski, Arthur Greenberg, Wing Tsang, and Deborah Van Vechten were frequently consulted about all aspects of that part of the project involving compilation of thermochemistry of neutral species. Dr. Pierre Ausloos critically reviewed the work several times during the five year period, and also contributed expert evaluations of thermochemical data from time to time. Also, we thank the three reviewers who provided thoughtful, informative, helpful comments on the manuscript; one of these, Dr. David A. Dixon, took the trouble to discuss the publication with us in some depth.

The project was carried out under the joint sponsorship of the Office of Standard Reference Data and the Center for Chemical Physics, National Bureau of Standards. We would like to acknowledge the support of Dr. David R. Lide, Director of OSRD, and Dr. Pierre Ausloos, Director of CCP, as well as Dr. Howard White, program manager in the Office of Standard Reference Data.

6. References to Introduction

[1] J. L. Franklin, J. G. Dillard, H. M. Rosenstock, J. T. Herron, K. Draxl, and F. H. Field, *Ionization Potentials, Appearance Potentials, and Heats of Formation of Gaseous Positive Ions*, Nat. Stand. Ref. Data Ser., Nat. Bur. Stand. (U. S.) **26**, (1969).

[2] H. M. Rosenstock, K. Draxl, B. W. Steiner, and J. T. Herron, "Energetics of Gaseous Ions," J. Phys. Chem. Ref. Data, Vol. **6**, Suppl. 1 (1977).

[3] R. D. Levin and S. G. Lias, *Ionization Potential and Appearance Potential Measurements, 1971-1981*, Nat. Stand. Ref. Data Ser., Nat. Bur. Stand. (U. S.) **71**, (1982).

[4] S. G. Lias, J. F. Liebman, and R. D. Levin, "Evaluated Gas Phase Basicities and Proton Affinities of Molecules; Heats of Formation of Protonated Molecules," J. Phys. Chem. Ref. Data, Vol. **13**, 695 (1984).

[5] J. E. Bartmess, to be published.

[6] S. G. Lias and R. D. Levin, to be published.

[7] S. G. Lias, J. F. Liebman, and R. D. Levin, to be published.

[8] R. G. Keesee and A. W. Castleman, Jr., "Thermochemical Data on Gas-Phase Ion-Molecule Association and Clustering Reactions," J. Phys. Chem. Ref. Data **15**, 1011 (1986).

[9] D. A. Dixon and S. G. Lias, "Absolute Values of Gas Phase Proton Affinities and Basicities of Molecules: A Comparison between Theory and Experiment," Chapter 7 in *Molecular Structure and Energetics, Vol. 2* (J. F. Liebman and A. Greenberg, Editors), VCH Publishers, Inc.: Deerfield Beach, Fla., 1987, p. 269.

[10] J. E. Del Bene, "Quantum Chemical Reaction Enthalpies," Chapter 9 in *Molecular Structure and Energetics, Vol. 1* (J. F. Liebman and A. Greenberg, editors), VCH Publishers, Inc.: Deerfield Beach, Fla., 1986, p. 319.

[11] A.A. Christodoulides; D.L. McCorkle, L.G. Christophorou, "Electron Affinities of Atoms, Molecules, and Radicals", Ch. 13 in *Electron-Molecule Interactions and Their Applications, Vol. 2*, Academic Press: New York, 1984, pp, 423-641.

[12] K. D. Jordan and P. D. Burrow, "Studies of the Temporary Anion States of Unsaturated Hydrocarbons by Electron Transmission Spectroscopy," Acc. Chem. Res. **11**, 341 (1978).

[13] (a) D. R. Stull and H. Prophet, "JANAF Thermochemical Tables," Nat. Stand. Ref. Data Ser. (U. S.) **37**, (1971); (b) M. W. Chase, J. L. Curnutt, A. T. Hu, H. Prophet, A. N. Syverud, and L. C. Walker, "JANAF Thermochemical Tables, 1974 Supplement," J. Phys. Chem. Ref. Data 3, 311 (1974); (c) M. W. Chase, Jr., C. A. Davies, J. R. Downey, Jr., D. J. Frurip, R. A. McDonald, and A. N. Syverud, "JANAF Thermochemical Tables, Third Edition, Parts I and II," J. Phys. Chem. Ref. Data **14**, Suppl. 1 (1985).

[14] D. D. Wagman, W. H. Evans, V. B. Parker, R. H. Schumm, I. Halow, S. M. Bailey, K. L. Churney, and R. L. Nuttall, "The NBS Tables of Chemical Thermodynamic Properties: Selected Values for Inorganic and C_1 and C_2 Organic Substances in SI Units," J. Phys. Chem. Ref. Data **11**, Suppl. 2 (1982).

[15] L. V. Gurvich, I. V. Veits, V. A. Medvedev, G. A. Khachkuruzov, V. S. Yungman, G. A. Bergman, et al., *Termodinamicheskie Svoistva Individual'nykh Veshchestv* (Thermodynamic Properties of Individual Substances); V. P. Glushko, Gen. Ed., Vols. 1 through 4 (in 8 parts), (1978-1982), Izdatel'stvo "Nauka" Moscow.

[16] S. G. Lias, "Thermochemistry of Polyatomic Cations," in *Kinetics of Ion-Molecule Reactions*, (P. Ausloos, Editor), New York: Plenum, 1979, p. 223.

[17] H. M. Rosenstock, "Standard States in Gas Phase Ion Thermochemistry," in *Kinetics of Ion-Molecule Reactions*, (P. Ausloos, Editor), Plenum: New York, 1979, p. 246.

[18] A. N. Syverud, personal communication (1978).

[19] A. Sommerfeld, Z. Physik **47**, 1 (1928).

[20] A. R. Gordon, J. Chem. Phys. **4**, 678 (1936).

[21] W. H. Evans, personal communication to H. M. Rosenstock (1976).

[22] S. G. Lias and P. Ausloos, "Ionization Energies of Organic Compounds by Equilibrium Measurements," J. Am. Chem. Soc. **100**, 6027 (1978).

[23] (a) T. Shimanouchi, "Tables of Molecular Vibrational Frequencies. Consolidated Volume I," Nat. Stand. Ref. Data Ser., Nat. Bur. Stand. (U. S.) **39**, (1972); (b) T. Shimanouchi, "Tables of Molecular Vibrational Frequencies. Consolidated Volume II," J. Phys. Chem. Ref. Data **6**, 993 (1977); (c) T. Shimanouchi, "Tables of Molecular Vibrational Frequencies, Part 9," J. Phys. Chem. Ref. Data **7**, 1323 (1978); (d) T. Shimanouchi, "Tables of Molecular Vibrational Frequencies, Part 10," J. Phys. Chem. Ref. Data **9**, 1149 (1980).

[24] M. E. Jacox, "Ground State Vibrational Energy Levels of Polyatomic Transient Molecules," J. Phys. Chem. Ref. Data **13**, 945 (1984).

[25] J. C. Traeger and R. G. McLaughlin, "Absolute Heats of Formation for Gas Phase Cations," J. Am. Chem. Soc. **103**, 3647 (1981).

[26] W. A. Brand and T. Baer, J. Am. Chem. Soc. **106**, 3154 (1984).

[27] F. P. Lossing, Can. J. Chem. **50**, 3973 (1972).

[28] J. Franck, "Elementary Processes of Photochemical Reactions," Trans. Faraday Soc. **21**, 536 (1926).

[29] (a) E. U. Condon, "Nuclear Motions Associated with Electron Transitions in Diatomic Molecules," Phys. Rev. **32**, 858 (1928); (b) E. U. Condon, "The Franck-Condon Principle and Related Topics," Am. J. Phys. **15**, 365 (1947).

[30] W. A. Chupka, "Effect of Unimolecular Decay Kinetics on the Interpretation of Appearance Potentials," J. Chem. Phys. **30**, 191 (1959).

[31] H. M. Rosenstock, "The Measurement of Ionization and Appearance Potentials," Int. J. Mass Spectrom. Ion Phys. **20**, 139 (1976).

[32] J. Dannacher, "The Study of Ionic Fragmentation by Photoelectron-Photoion Coincidence Spectroscopy," Org. Mass Spectrom. **19**, 253 (1984).

[33] J. L. Holmes, "Assigning Structures to Ions in the Gas Phase," Org. Mass Spectrom. **20**, 169 (1985).

[34] C. E. Moore, "Ionization Potentials and Ionization Limits Derived from the Analyses of Optical Spectra," Nat. Stand. Ref. Data Ser., Nat. Bur. Stand. (U. S.) **34**, (1970).

[35] S. Leutwyler, M. Hofmann, H.-P. Harri, and E. Schumacher, "The Ionization Potentials of the Alkali Dimers Na_2, NaK, and K_2," Chem. Phys. Lett. **77**, 257 (1981) and references cited therein.

[36] K. Maeda, G. P. Semeluk, and F. P. Lossing, "A Two-Stage Double Hemispherical Electron Energy Selector," Int. J. Mass Spectrom. Ion Phys. **1**, 395 (1968).

[37] E. M. Clarke, "Ionization Probability Curves Using an Electron Selector," Can. J. Phys. **32**, 764 (1954).

[38] P. Marmet, and L. Kerwin, "An Improved Electrostatic Electron Selector," Can. J. Phys. **38**, 787 (1960).

[39] P. Marmet and J. D. Morrison, "Secondary Reactions in the Ion Chamber of a Mass Spectrometer," J. Chem. Phys. **36**, 1238 (1962).

[40] H. M. Rosenstock and M. Krauss, *Mass Spectrometry of Organic Ions*, Chapter 1, New York: Academic Press (1963).

[41] H. M. Rosenstock, M. B. Wallenstein, A. L. Wahrhaftig and H. Eyring, Proc. Natl. Acad. Sci. U. S., **38**, 667 (1952).

[42] (a) C. R. Brundle and A. D. Baker, *Electron Spectroscopy: Theory, Techniques and Applications*, New York: Academic Press, 1977; (b) J. W. Rabalais, *Principles of Ultraviolet Photoelectron Spectroscopy*, New York: Wiley-Interscience, 1977; (c) J. H. D. Eland, *Photoelectron Spectroscopy: An Introduction to Ultraviolet Photoelectron Spectroscopy in the Gas Phase*, New York: John Wiley & Sons, 1974; (d) D. W. Turner, C. Baker, A. D. Baker, and C. R. Brundle, *Molecular Photoelectron Spectroscopy*, New York: Wiley-Interscience, 1970.

[43] (a) P. Kebarle, "Higher-Order Reaction-Ion Clusters and Ion Solvation," Chapter 7 in *Ion-Molecule Reactions* (J. L. Franklin, Editor), New York: Plenum Press, 1972; (b) P. Kebarle, "Ion Thermochemistry and Solvation from Gas Phase Ion Equilibria," Ann. Rev. Phys. Chem. **28**, 445 (1977).

[44] (a) E. E. Ferguson, "Flowing Afterglow Studies," Chapter 8 in *Ion Molecule Reactions* (J. L. Franklin, Editor), New York: Plenum Press, 1972; (b) D. K. Bohme, "The Kinetics and Energetics of Proton Transfer," in *Interactions between Ions and Molecules*, (P. Ausloos, Editor), New York: Plenum Press, 1975, p. 504.

[45] (a) J. L. Beauchamp, "Ion Cyclotron Resonance Spectroscopy," Ann. Rev. Phys. Chem. **22**, 527 (1971); (b) R. W. Taft, "Gas Phase Proton Transfer Equilibria," in *Proton Transfer Reactions*, (E. F. Caldin and V. Gold, Editors), New York: John Wiley & Sons, 1975, p. 31; (c) D. H. Aue and M. T. Bowers, "Stabilities of Positive Ions from Equilibrium Gas Phase Basicity Measurements," in *Gas Phase Ion Chemistry*, (M. T. Bowers, Editor), New York: Academic Press, 1979, p. 1; (d) C. R. Moylan and J. I. Brauman, "Gas Phase Acid-Base Chemistry," Ann. Rev. Phys. Chem. **34**, 187 (1983).

[46] (a) S. G. Lias, P. Ausloos, and Z. Horvath, "Charge Transfer Reactions in Alkane and Cycloalkane Systems. Estimated Ionization Potentials," Int. J. Chem. Kinetics **8**, 725 (1976); (b) M. Meot-Ner (Mautner), L. W. Sieck, and P. Ausloos, "Ionization of Normal Alkanes: Enthalpy, Entropy, Structural, and Isotope Effects," J. Am. Chem. Soc. **103**, 5342 (1981).

[47] M. Meot-Ner (Mautner), S. F. Nelsen, M. R. Willi, and T. B. Frigo, "Special Effects of an Unusually Large Neutral to Radical Cation Geometry Change. Adiabatic Ionization Energies and Proton Affinities of Alkylhydrazines," J. Am. Chem. Soc. **106**, 7384 (1984).

[48] S. F. Nelsen, "Hydrazine-Hydrazine Cation Electron Transfer Reactions," in *Molecular Structure and Energetics, Volume 3*, (J. F. Liebman and A. Greenberg, Editors), VCH Publishers, Inc.: Deerfield Beach, Fla., 1986, p. 1.

[49] K. Hiroaka, "Endothermic Ion-Molecule Reactions: The Reactions of H_3O^+ and H_3S^+ with Isobutane," Int. J. Mass Spectrom. Ion Phys. **27**, 139 (1978).

[50] S. G. Lias, "Thermochemical Information from Ion-Molecule Rate Constants," in Ion Cyclotron Resonance Spectrometry II, Berlin: Springer-Verlag (1982), p. 409.

[51] (a) P. B. Armentrout and J. L. Beauchamp, "Ion Beam Studies of the Reactions of Atomic Cobalt Ions with Alkanes: Determination of Metal-Hydrogen and Metal-Carbon Bond Energies and an Examination of the Mechanism by which Transition Metals Cleave Carbon-Carbon Bonds," J. Am. Chem. Soc. **103**, 784 (1981); (b) P. B. Armentrout, L. F. Halle, and J. L. Beauchamp, "Reaction of Cr^+, Mn^+, Fe^+, Co^+, and Ni^+ with O_2 and N_2O. Examination of the Translational Energy Dependence of the Cross Sections of Endothermic Reactions," J. Chem. Phys. **76**, 2449 (1982); and references cited therein.

[52] E. Murad, "Abstraction Reactions of Ca^+ and Sr^+ Ions," J. Chem. Phys. **78**, 6611 (1983) and references cited therein.

[53] W. S. Koski, "Reactions of Electronically Excited Positive Ions," in *Interactions between Ions and Molecules*, (P. Ausloos, ed.) New York and London: Plenum (1975), p. 215, and references cited therein.

[54] J. L. Holmes, M. Fingas, and F. P. Lossing, "Towards a General Scheme for Estimating the Heats of Formation of Organic Ions in the Gas Phase. Part I. Odd-Electron Cations," Can. J. Chem. **59**, 80 (1981).

[55] J. L. Holmes and F. P. Lossing, "Towards a General Scheme for Estimating the Heats of Formation of Organic Ions in the Gas Phase. Part II. The Effect of Substitution at Charge-Bearing Sites," Can. J. Chem. **60**, 2365 (1982).

[56] J. L. Holmes and F. P. Lossing, "The Need for Adequate Thermochemical Data for the Interpretation of Fragmentation Mechanisms and Ion Structure Assignments," Int. J. Mass Spectrom. Ion Phys. **47**, 133 (1983).

[57] F. P. Lossing and J. L. Holmes, "Stabilization Energy and Ion Size in Carbocations in the Gas Phase," J. Am. Chem. Soc. **106**, 6917 (1984).

[58] M. Bachiri, G. Mouvier, P. Carlier, and J. E. Dubois, "Evaluation-Quantitative des Effets de Substituants sur les Premiers Potentiels d'Ionisation de Composes Monofonctionnels Aliphatiques," J. Chim. Phys. **77**, 899 (1980).

[59] J. F. Liebman, unpublished results, derived from his earlier equations discussed in *Structural Thermochemistry and Reactivity of Ions*, P. Ausloos and S. G. Lias, Editors, Amsterdam, D. Reidel, 371 (1987).

[60] S. G. Lias and P. Ausloos in "Ion-Molecule Reactions: Their Role in Radiation Chemistry," Washington: Am. Chem. Soc. (1975), pp. 91-95.

[61] S. G. Lias, J.-A. A. Jackson, H. Argentar, and J. F. Liebman, "Substituted N,N-Dialkylanilines: Relative Ionization Energies and Proton Affinities through Determination of Ion-Molecule Reaction Equilibrium Constants," J. Org. Chem. **50**, 333 (1985).

[62] D. H. Aue, H. M. Webb, and M. T. Bowers, "Quantitative Relative Gas Phase Basicities of Alkylamines: Correlations with Solution Basicity," J. Am. Chem. Soc. **94**, 4726 (1972).

[63] I. Koppel, U. Molder, and R. Pikver, "On Relationship Between Ionization Potentials and Proton Affinities in Gas Phase," Org. Reactivity (Engl. Ed.) **17**, 457 (1980).

[64] L. S. Levitt and H. F. Widing, "The Alkyl Inductive Effect. Calculation of Inductive Substituent Parameters," Prog. Phys. Org. Chem. **12**, 119 (1977).

[65] I. A. Koppel and U. H. Molder, "The Dependence of Ionization Potentials and Proton Affinities on Structure. II. Proton Affinities. Correlations with Substituent Constants and Polarizability," Org. Reactivity **20**, 3 1983).

[66] I. A. Koppel and U. H. Molder, "Internal Substituent Parameters and Correlation of Proton Affinities," Org. Reactivity (Engl. Ed.) **21**, 213 (1984).

[67] I. A. Koppel, U. H. Molder, and R. I. Pikver, "The Dependence of Ionization Potentials and Proton Affinties on Structure. I. Ionization Potentials. Correlations with Substituent Constants and Polarizability," Org. Reactivity (Engl. Ed.) **18**, 380 (1981).

[68] R. D. Mead, A. E. Stevens, W. C. Lineberger, *Gas Phase Ion Chemistry*, Vol. 3, M.T. Bowers, Ed. Academic Press, Orlando, FL, 1984; Ch. **22** "Photodetachment in Negative Ion Beams".

[69] P. S. Drzaic, J. Marks, J. I. Brauman *Gas Phase Ion Chemistry*, Vol. 3, M.T. Bowers, Ed. Academic Press, Orlando, FL, (1984); Ch. **21** "Electron Photodetachment from Gas Phase Molecular Anions".

[70] H. Hotop and W. C. Lineberger, "Binding Energies in Atomic Negative Ions: II," J. Phys. Chem. Ref. Data **14**, 731 (1985).

[71] T. M. Miller, *Adv. Electron. Electron Phys.* 1981 **55**, 119.

[72] R. R. Corderman and W.C. Lineberger *Ann. Rev. Phys. Chem.* **30**, 347 (1979).

[73] R. C. Dunbar *Gas Phase Ion Chemistry*, Vol. **2**, M.T. Bowers, Ed. Academic Press, Orlando, FL, (1979).

[74] R. S. Berry and S. Leach, *Adv. Electron. Electron Phys.* **57**, 1 (1982).

[75] P. Kebarle and S. Chowdhury, "Electron Affinities and Electron Transfer Reactions", Chem. Rev. **87**, 513 (1987).

[76] D. M. Neumark, K. R. Lykke, T. Andersen and W. C. Lineberger, "Laser Photodetachment Measurement of the Electron Affinity of Atomic Oxygen," Phys. Rev. **A32**, 1890 (1985).

[77] J. H. Richardson, L. M. Stephenson and J. I. Brauman, "Photodetachment of Electrons from Trifluoromethyl and Trifluorosilyl Ions; the Electron Affinities of CF_3 and SiF_3," Chem. Phys. Lett. **30**, 17 (1975).

[78] J. E. Bartmess in "Structure/Thermochemistry and Reactivity of Ions" (P. Ausloos and S. G. Lias, Editors), Amsterdam: D. Reidel (1987).

[79] J. B. Cumming and P. Kebarle, "Summary of Gas Phase Measurements Involving Acids, AH. Entropy Changes in Proton Transfer Reactions Involving Negative Ions. Bond Dissociation Energies D(A-H) and Electron Affinities, EA(A)," Can. J. Chem. **56**, 1 (1978).

[80] J. E. Bartmess, J. A. Scott, and R. T. McIver, Jr., "The Gas Phase Acidity Scale from Methanol to Phenol," J. Am. Chem. Soc. **101**, 6047 (1979).
[81] R. W. Taft, personal communication.
[82] J. E. Bartmess, to be published.
[83] K. Lacmann and D. R. Herschbach, "Collisional Excitation and Ionization of K Atoms by Diatomic Molecules: Role of Ion-pair States," Chem. Phys. Lett. **6**, 106 (1970).
[84] F. M. Page and G. C. Goode, "Negative Ions and the Magnetron," New York: Wiley (1969).
[85] L. G. Christophorou, P. M. Collins and J. C. Carter, "Electron Attachment in the Field of the Ground and Excited States of the Azulene Molecule," J. Chem. Phys. **52**, 4413 (1970).
[86] G. S. A. McLuckey, D. Cameron and R. G. Cooks, "Proton Affinities from the Dissociation of Proton Bound Dimers," J. Am. Chem. Soc. **103**, 1313 (1981); (b) Boand, R. Houriet, and T. Gaumann, "The Gas Phase Acidity of Aliphatic Alcohols," J. Am. Chem. Soc. **105**, 2203 (1983).
[87] D. J. Burinsky, E. K. Fukuda and J. E. Campana, "Electron Affinities from Dissociations of Mixed Negative Ion Dimers," J. Am. Chem. Soc. **106**, 2770 (1984).
[88] C. H. DePuy, V. M. Bierbaum and R. Damrauer, "Relative Gas Phase Acidities of the Alkanes," J. Am. Chem. Soc. **106**, 4051 (1984).
[89] E. C. M. Chen and W. E. Wentworth, J. Phys. Chem. **87**, 45 (1983).
[90] C. R. Webster, I. S. McDermid, and C. T. Rettner, "Laser Optogalvanic Photodetachment Spectroscopy: A New Technique for Studying Photodetachment Thresholds with Application to I^-," J. Chem. Phys. **78**, 646 (1983).
[91] J. B. Pedley and J. Rylance, *Sussex-N. P. L. Computer Analysed Thermochemical Data: Organic and Organometallic Compounds*, University of Sussex (1977).
[92] J. B. Pedley, R. D. Naylor, and S. P. Kirby, *Thermochemical Data of Organic Compounds*, Second Edition, London/New York: Chapman and Hall (1986).
[93] D. F. McMillen and D. M. Golden, *The Annual Review of Physical Chemistry*, Vol. 33, Annual Reviews, Palo Alto, CA (1982).
[94] W. Tsang, "The Stability of Alkyl Radicals," J. Am. Chem. Soc. **107**, 2872 (1985).
[95] J. S. Chickos, "Heats of Sublimation" in *Molecular Structure and Energetics*, Vol. 2 (J. F. Liebman and A. Greenberg, Editors), VCH Publishers, Deerfield Beach 67 (1987).
[96] V. Majer and V. Svoboda, *Enthalpies of Vaporization of Organic Compounds: A Critical Review and Data Compilation*, Oxford: Blackwell Scientific Publications, 1985.
[97] J. S. Chickos, A. S. Hyman, L. H. Ladon, and J. F. Liebman, J. Org. Chem. **46**, 4294 (1981).
[98] J. F. Liebman and D. Van Vechten, "Universality: The Differences and Equivalences of Heats of Formation, Strain Energy, and Resonance Energy," in *Molecular Structure and Energetics*, Vol. 2, 315 (J. F. Liebman and A. Greenberg, Editors), VCH Publishers, Deerfield Beach (1987).
[99] (a) S. W. Benson and J. H. Buss, "Additivity Rules for the Estimation of Molecular Properties. Thermodynamic Properties," J. Chem. Phys. **29**, 546 (1958); (b) S. W. Benson, *Thermochemical Kinetics: Methods for the Estimation of Thermochemical Data and Rate Parameters*, 2nd Ed. John Wiley & Sons, New York (1976).
[100] For a recent example, see: K. Bystrom, "Enthalpies of Combustion, Vaporization and Formation for Di-n-propyldiazene N-oxide and Di-t-butyldiazene N-oxide," J. Chem. Thermodyn. **13**, 139 (1981).
[101] H. M. Rosenstock, J. Dannacher, and J. F. Liebman, "The Role of Excited Electronic States in Ion Fragmentation: $C_6H_6^+$," Radiat. Phys. Chem. **20**, 7 (1982).
[102] J. F. Liebman, "Macroincrementation Reactions: A Holistic Estimation Approach for the Properties of Organic Compounds," in *Molecular Structure and Energetics*, Vol. 3 (J. F. Liebman and A. Greenberg, Editors), VCH Publishers, Deerfield Beach 262 (1986).

Table 1. Positive Ion Table

ION / Neutral	Ionization potential eV	$\Delta_f H$(Ion) kcal/mol	$\Delta_f H$(Ion) kJ/mol	$\Delta_f H$(Neutral) kcal/mol	$\Delta_f H$(Neutral) kJ/mol	Neutral reference	CAS registry number
Ac$^+$							
Ac	5.17±0.12	216	905	97	406	82TN270	7440-34-8
Ag$^+$							
Ag	7.576	242.7	1015.6	68.0	284.6	82TN270	7440-22-4
		242.6	1015.1	67.9	284.1		
	See also: 80KRA.						
AgAl$^+$							
AgAl	(7.8±0.5)	(287)	(1200)	107	448	79HUB/HER	12379-67-8
	0 K values.						
AgBr$^+$							
AgBr	≤9.59	≤246	≤1028	25	103	79HUB/HER	7785-23-1
	0 K values.						
AgCl$^+$							
AgCl	(≤10.08)	(≤255)	(≤1065)	22	93	79HUB/HER	7783-90-6
	0 K values.						
AgF$^+$							
AgF	(11.0±0.3)	(256)	(1071)	2	10	79HUB/HER	7775-41-9
	0 K values.						
AgH$^+$							
AgH	(9.2)	(280)	(1170)	67	282	79HUB/HER	
	$\Delta_f H$(Ion) from onset of endothermic reaction (86ELK/ARM). 0 K value.						
	IP is $\Delta_f H$(Ion) - $\Delta_f H$(Neutral).						
Ag$_2^+$							
Ag$_2$	(7.35)	(267)	(1119)	98.0	410.0	82TN270	12187-06-3
		(268)	(1120)	98	411		
Al$^+$							
Al	5.986	216.3	904.9	78.2	327.3	85JANAF	7429-90-5
		216.8	907.3	78.8	329.7		
AlAu$^+$							
AuAl	(7.6±0.3)	(263)	(1101)	88	368	79HUB/HER	12250-38-3
	0 K values.						
AlBO$_2^+$							
AlBO$_2$	(9.5±0.5)	(90)	(376)	−129±4	−541±17	71JANAF	
AlBr$^+$							
AlBr	(9.3)	(218.3)	(913.2)	3.8±3.0	15.9±12.6	85JANAF	22359-97-3
		(220.0)	(920.4)	5.5±3.0	23.1±12.5		

Table 1. Positive Ion Table - Continued

ION / Neutral	Ionization potential eV	$\Delta_f H$(Ion) kcal/mol	$\Delta_f H$(Ion) kJ/mol	$\Delta_f H$(Neutral) kcal/mol	$\Delta_f H$(Neutral) kJ/mol	Neutral reference	CAS registry number
$AlBr_3^+$							
$AlBr_3$	(10.4)	(142)	(593)	−98.1	−410.4	85JANAF	7727-15-3
		(147)	(616)	−92.5	−387.2		
	IP is onset of photoelectron band.						
$AlCl^+$							
$AlCl$	9.4	204	855	−12.3	−51.5	85JANAF	13595-81-8
		204	855	−12.3	−51.7		
$AlClF^+$							
$AlClF$	(7.9±1.0)	(66)	(276)	−117	−489	85JANAF	
		(65)	(271)	−117	−488		
$AlCl_3^+$							
$AlCl_3$	(12.01)	(137)	(574)	−140	−585	85JANAF	7446-70-0
		(138)	(576)	−139	−583		
AlF^+							
AlF	9.73±0.01	160.9	673.1	−63.5±0.8	−265.7±3.4	79HUB/HER	13595-82-9
		160.9	673.9	−63.5±0.8	−265.6±3.4		
	IP from 84DYK/KIR.						
AlF_2^+							
AlF_2	(8.1)	(8)	(33)	−179	−749	81WOO	13569-23-8
	IP from 85JANAF.						
AlF_3^+							
AlF_3	≤15.45	≤67	≤282	−289	−1209	85JANAF	7784-18-1
		≤68	≤285	−288	−1206		
	IP from 84DYK/KIR.						
AlI^+							
AlI	(9.3±0.3)	(230.7)	(965.3)	16.3±1	68.0±4.2	85JANAF	29977-41-1
		(231.0)	(966.6)	16.6±1	69.3±4.2		
AlI_3^+							
AlI_3	(9.1)	(160)	(670)	−49	−208	82TN270	7784-23-8
	IP is onset of photoelectron band.						
AlO^+							
AlO	9.46±0.06	234.1	979.6	16.0±2	66.9±8	85JANAF	14457-64-8
		234.2	979.7	16.0±2	67.0±8		
	IP from 82ARM/HAL. See also: 80MUR/HIL, 81KAP/STA.						
AlO_2^+							
AlO_2	(10.0±1.0)	(200)	(835)	−31	−130	82KAS/CHE	11092-32-3
AlP^+							
AlP	(8.4±0.4)	(295)	(1232)	101	422	79HUB/HER	20859-73-8
	0 K values.						

Table 1. Positive Ion Table - Continued

ION / Neutral	Ionization potential eV	$\Delta_f H$(Ion) kcal/mol	$\Delta_f H$(Ion) kJ/mol	$\Delta_f H$(Neutral) kcal/mol	$\Delta_f H$(Neutral) kJ/mol	Neutral reference	CAS registry number
$AlSe^+$							
AlSe	(8.3±0.5) 0 K values.	(243)	(1016)	52	215	79HUB/HER	23330-87-2
Al_2^+							
Al_2	(5.4±1.0)	(240.9) (240.8)	(1008.0) (1007.3)	116.4±0.8 116.2±0.8	487.0±3.5 486.3±3.5	85JANAF	32752-94-6
$Al_2Br_6^+$	(10.97)	(21)	(87)	−232	−971	82TN270	18898-34-5
$Al_2Cl_6^+$	(12.18)	(−28)	(−116)	−309	−1291	82TN270	13845-12-0
Al_2O^+							
Al_2O	(7.7±0.2)	(144) (145)	(603) (605)	−33±5 −33	−140±22 −138	82KAS/CHE	12004-36-3
$Al_2O_2^+$	(9.9±0.5)	(131)	(551)	−97±12	−404±48	82KAS/CHE	12252-63-0
Am^+							
Am	5.99 See also: 81CHE/GAB.	206	862	68	284	85KLE/WAR	7440-35-9
Ar^+							
Ar	15.75973±0.00001 See also: 81KIM/KAT.	363.42 363.42	1520.57 1520.57	0	0	*DEF	7440-37-1
ArH^+							
ArH		277	1159				
	From proton affinity of Ar (RN 7440-37-1). PA = 88.6 kcal/mol, 371. kJ/mol.						
$ArHe^+$							
ArHe	15.735 $\Delta_f H$(Ion) from 81DAB/HER. 0 K values.	362.8	1518.0	−0.055	−0.23	79HUB/HER	12254-69-2

Table 1. Positive Ion Table - Continued

ION Neutral	Ionization potential eV	$\Delta_f H$(Ion) kcal/mol	$\Delta_f H$(Ion) kJ/mol	$\Delta_f H$(Neutral) kcal/mol	$\Delta_f H$(Neutral) kJ/mol	Neutral reference	CAS registry number
$ArHg^+$							
ArHg	(10.217±0.012)	(250.6)	(1048.6)	15.0	62.8	84BOU/BRA	87193-95-1
	IP from 85LIN/BRO.						
$ArKr^+$							
ArKr	13.484±0.015	310.6	1299.7	−0.3	−1.3	79HUB/HER	51184-77-1
	IP from 82DEH/PRA. 0 K values.						
$ArNe^+$							
ArNe	15.685±0.004	361.6	1512.9	−0.10	−0.43	76BOB/BAR	12301-65-4
	IP from 82PRA/DEH2. 0 K values.						
$ArXe^+$							
ArXe	11.968±0.012	275.7	1153.4	−0.32	−1.35	76BOB/BAR	58206-67-0
	IP from 82DEH/PRA. See also: 85PRA/DEH, 85PRA/DEH2. 0 K values.						
Ar_2^+							
Ar_2	14.501±0.025	334.2	1398.1	−0.24	−1.01	79HUB/HER	12595-59-4
	IP from 82DEH/PRA2. See also: 81DEH/POL, 82LEV/LIA. 0 K values.						
As^+							
As	9.7883±0.0002	298.0	1246.9	72.3	302.5	82TN270	7440-38-2
		297.7	1245.8	72.0	301.4		
$AsBr_3^+$							
$AsBr_3$	(10.0)	(200)	(835)	−31	−130	82TN270	7784-33-0
		(205)	(858)	−25.5	−106.9		
	IP is onset of photoelectron band.						
$AsClO^+$							
AsOCl	(11.1)	(249)	(1040)	−7	−31	83BIN	14525-25-8
	IP from 83BIN.						
$AsCl_3^+$							
$AsCl_3$	(10.55±0.025)	(181)	(756)	−63	−262	82TN270	7784-34-1
		(181)	(758)	−62	−260		
	See also: 83OZG.						
AsF_3^+							
AsF_3	(12.84±0.05)	(108)	(453)	−188	−786	82TN270	7784-35-2
		(109)	(457)	−187	−782		
AsF_3H^+							
F_3AsH		23	96				
	From proton affinity of AsF_3 (RN 7784-35-2). PA = 155 kcal/mol, 648 kJ/mol.						
AsH_3^+							
AsH_3	9.89	244	1020	16	66	82TN270	7784-42-1
		246	1028	18	74		
	See also: 82ELB/DIE.						

Table 1. Positive Ion Table − Continued

ION / Neutral	Ionization potential eV	$\Delta_f H$(Ion) kcal/mol	$\Delta_f H$(Ion) kJ/mol	$\Delta_f H$(Neutral) kcal/mol	$\Delta_f H$(Neutral) kJ/mol	Neutral reference	CAS registry number
AsH_4^+							
AsH_4		202	846				
From proton affinity of AsH_3 (RN 7784-42-1). PA = 179.2 kcal/mol, 750 kJ/mol.							
As_2^+							
As_2	(10.1±0.2)	(278)	(1165)	45.5±0.7	190.4±2.9	73BEN/MAR	23878-46-8
		(278)	(1164)	45.5±0.7	190.4±2.9		
See also: 85HIR/STR.							
As_4^+							
As_4	(9.07±0.07)	(244)	(1019)	34	144	82TN270	12187-08-5
See also: 85HIR/STR.							
$As_4O_6^+$							
As_4O_6	(9.6)	(−68)	(−283)	−289	−1209	82TN270	12505-67-8
IP is onset of photoelectron band.							
Au^+							
Au	9.225	300	1256	87	366	82TN270	7440-57-5
		300.2	1256.0	87.5	365.9		
AuB^+							
AuB	(8.7±0.5)	(337)	(1411)	137	572	79HUB/HER	12408-81-0
0 K values.							
$AuCe^+$							
AuCe	(6.0±0.3)	(248)	(1036)	109	457	82TN270	12408-82-1
		(248)	(1039)	110	460		
$AuHo^+$							
AuHo	(6.2±0.5)	(242)	(1013)	99.1	414.5	82TN270	12044-80-3
		(243)	(1016)	100	418		
$AuLa^+$							
AuLa	(5.9±0.5)	(247)	(1033)	111	464	82TN270	12429-32-2
		(247)	(1035)	111	466		
$AuNd^+$							
AuNd	(5.8±0.8)	(228)	(955)	94	395	82TN270	12429-33-3
		(229)	(957)	95	397		
$AuPr^+$							
AuPr	(5.4±0.8)	(224)	(937)	99	416	82TN270	12429-34-4
		(224)	(939)	100	418		

Table 1. Positive Ion Table – Continued

ION / Neutral	Ionization potential eV	$\Delta_f H$(Ion) kcal/mol	kJ/mol	$\Delta_f H$(Neutral) kcal/mol	kJ/mol	Neutral reference	CAS registry number
$AuSi^+$							
AuSi	(9.5±0.5)	(340)	(1422)	(121)	(505)	79HUB/HER	12256-53-0
	0 K values.						
Au_2^+							
Au_2	(9.5±0.3)	(343)	(1433)	123.5	516.7	79HUB/HER	12187-09-6
		(341)	(1427)	122.0	510.4		
B^+							
B	8.29808±0.00002	<u>325.9</u>	<u>1363.3</u>	134.5	562.7	82TN270	7440-42-8
		<u>324.7</u>	<u>1358.2</u>	133.3	557.6		
BBr_2H^+							
$BHBr_2$	(10.92±0.02)	(227)	(949)	−25±5	−105±21	71JANAF	13709-65-4
		(231)	(966)	−21±5	−88±21		
	IP from 81FRO/KIR.						
BBr_3^+							
BBr_3	(10.51±0.02)	(194)	(810)	−49±0.2	−204±1	71JANAF	10294-33-4
BCl^+							
BCl	(10.2)	(269.0)	(1125.5)	33.8	141.4	85JANAF	20583-55-5
		(268.3)	(1122.5)	33.1	138.4		
	$\Delta_f H$(Ion) from appearance potential (18.37±0.02 eV) in BCl_3.						
	Cited ionization potential is difference between heats of formation of ion and neutral.						
$BClF_2^+$							
$BClF_2$	(13.06±0.11)	(88)	(370)	−213	−890	82TN270	14720-30-0
BCl_2^+							
BCl_2	(7.8)	(159)	(664)	−20±15	−83±63	71JANAF	13842-52-9
	$\Delta_f H$(Ion) from appearance potential (12.30±0.02 eV) in BCl_3.						
	Cited ionization potential is difference between heats of formation of ion and neutral.						
BCl_2F^+							
BCl_2F	(12.18±0.10)	(130)	(544)	−151	−631	82TN270	14720-31-1
BCl_2H^+							
$HBCl_2$	(11.91±0.02)	(215)	(901)	−59.3±1	−248.1±4	71JANAF	10325-39-0
		(216)	(904)	−58.6±1	−245.2±4		
	IP from 81FRO/KIR.						
BCl_3^+							
BCl_3	11.60±0.02	171	715	−96	−404	82TN270	10294-34-5
		171	716	−96	−403		
BF^+							
BF	11.12±0.01	229	957	−27.7	−115.8	79HUB/HER	13768-60-0
		228	954	−28.4	−118.8		
	IP from 83DYK/KIR.						

Table 1. Positive Ion Table – Continued

ION Neutral	Ionization potential eV	$\Delta_f H$(Ion) kcal/mol	 kJ/mol	$\Delta_f H$(Neutral) kcal/mol	 kJ/mol	Neutral reference	CAS registry number
BFS^+							
FBS	(10.90±0.01)	(165)	(690)	−86	−362	*EST	83995-89-5
	IP from 84COO/KRO.						
BF_2^+							
BF_2	(9.4)	(75)	(314)	−141.0±3	−589.9±12	71JANAF	
	From appearance potential of 15.81±0.04 eV in BF_3. IP is $\Delta_f H$(Ion) - $\Delta_f H$(Neutral).						
BF_2H^+							
HBF_2	(13.60±0.05)	(138)	(578)	−175.4±0.8	−733.8±3.3	71JANAF	13709-83-6
		(139)	*(582)*	*−174.5±0.8*	*−730.1±3.3*		
	IP from 81CHO/KIR.						
BF_3^+							
BF_3	15.56±0.03	87.1	364.3	−271.7	−1137.0	82TN270	7637-07-2
		87.8	*367.3*	*−271.0*	*−1134.0*		
	See also: 84FAR/SRI, 84DEH/PAR, 81ASB/SVE, 81KIM/KAT.						
BH^+							
BH	9.77±0.05	331.1	1385.4	105.8±2.0	442.7±8.4	85JANAF	13766-26-2
		330.3	*1382.2*	*105.0±2.0*	*439.5±8.4*		
BHO_2^+							
BHO_2	(12.6±0.2)	(156)	(654)	−134	−562	82TN270	13460-50-9
BHS^+							
HBS	11.11±0.03	(268)	(1122)	12±10	50±42	78JANAF	14457-85-3
BH_2^+							
BH_2	(9.8±0.2)	(274)	(1146)	48±15	201±63	71JANAF	14452-64-3
BH_3^+							
BH_3	12.3±0.1	(308)	(1287)	24	100	82TN270	13283-31-3
BI_3^+							
BI_3	(9.25±0.03)	(230)	(964)	17.0	71.1	82TN270	13517-10-7
		(231)	*(967)*	*18*	*75*		
BKO_2^+							
KBO_2	(8.62±0.14)	(38)	(160)	−161±2	−672±10	85FAR/SRI	
	See also: 85FAR/SRI.						
$BLiO^+$							
LiBO	7.7±0.5	(136)	(568)	−42	−175	*EST	77965-53-8
	IP from 85NEU.						
$BLiO_2^+$							
$LiBO_2$	(9.8±0.5)	(66)	(274)	−160	−671	71JANAF	
	IP from 85NEU.						

Table 1. Positive Ion Table − Continued

ION / Neutral	Ionization potential eV	$\Delta_f H$(Ion) kcal/mol	$\Delta_f H$(Ion) kJ/mol	$\Delta_f H$(Neutral) kcal/mol	$\Delta_f H$(Neutral) kJ/mol	Neutral reference	CAS registry number
$BNaO_2^+$							
$NaBO_2$	(9.18±0.10)	(58)	(242)	−154	−644	82TN270	
		(59)	(244)	−153	−642		
BO^+							
BO	13.0±0.3	(300)	(1254)	0	0	83PED/MAR	12505-77-0
		(299)	(1251)	−1	−3		
	See also: 79BAG/NIK, 85NEU.						
BO_2^+							
BO_2	(13.5±0.3)	(240)	(1003)	−72	−300	82TN270	13840-88-5
	IP from 79BAG/NIK.						
BSe^+							
BSe	(10.3)	(315)	(1320)	78	326	79HUB/HER	29750-36-5
	0 K values.						
$B_2Cl_2^+$							
B_2Cl_2		(223)	(934)				
	From appearance potential (17.24±0.03 eV) in B_2Cl_4 assumed to give $B_2Cl_2^+$ + 2Cl.						
$B_2Cl_3^+$							
B_2Cl_3		120	502				
	From appearance potential of 11.52±0.02 eV in B_2Cl_4. 0 K values.						
$B_2Cl_4^+$							
B_2Cl_4	10.32±0.02	121	506	−117	−490	82TN270	13701-67-2
		121	506	−117	−490		
$B_2F_3^+$							
B_2F_3		−7	−28				
	From appearance potential of 15.40±0.01 eV in B_2F_4. 0 K values.						
$B_2F_4^+$							
B_2F_4	12.07±0.01	−66	−275	−344	−1440	82TN270	13965-73-6
		−65	−272	−343	−1437		
$B_2H_6^+$							
(diborane structure)	11.38±0.03	271	1134	8.5	35.6	82TN270	19287-45-7
		275	1149	12.3	51.4		
	See also: 81ASB/SVE, 81KIM/KAT.						
$B_2H_7^+$							
(diborane·H^+ structure)		228	955				
	From proton affinity of Diborane(6). (RN 19287-45-7). PA = ~146 kcal/mol, ~611 kJ/mol.						

Table 1. Positive Ion Table – Continued

ION / Neutral	Ionization potential eV	$\Delta_f H$(Ion) kcal/mol	$\Delta_f H$(Ion) kJ/mol	$\Delta_f H$(Neutral) kcal/mol	$\Delta_f H$(Neutral) kJ/mol	Neutral reference	CAS registry number
$B_2O_2^+$ O=BB=O	13.58 IP from 84RUS/CUR. See also: 79BAG/NIK.	204	854	−109±2	−456±8	71JANAF	13766-28-4
$B_2O_3^+$ B_2O_3	13.5±0.15 *IP from 79BAG/NIK.*	110 *110*	460 *462*	−201.3 *−201*	−842.1 *−841*	79BAG/NIK	1303-86-2
$B_3F_3O_3^+$	(13.9±0.1)	(−244)	(−1024)	−565±1	−2365±4	71JANAF	13703-95-2
$B_3H_3O_3^+$	(13.5±0.5)	(20)	(85)	−291	−1218	71JANAF	289-56-5
$B_3H_6N_3^+$	9.88±0.02	106 *112*	441 *467*	−122.3 *−116.2*	−511.8 *−486.2*	82TN270	6569-51-3
$B_3H_7N_3^+$		49	206				
	From proton affinity of borazine (RN 6569-51-3). PA = 194.1 kcal/mol, 812 kJ/mol.						
$B_4H_{10}^+$	10.76±0.04	264	1104	16	66	82TN270	18283-93-7
$B_4H_{11}^+$		237	993				
	From proton affinity of B_4H_{10} (RN 18283-93-7). PA = ~144 kcal/mol, ~602 kJ/mol.						

Table 1. Positive Ion Table – Continued

ION Neutral	Ionization potential eV	$\Delta_f H$(Ion) kcal/mol	$\Delta_f H$(Ion) kJ/mol	$\Delta_f H$(Neutral) kcal/mol	$\Delta_f H$(Neutral) kJ/mol	Neutral reference	CAS registry number
$B_5H_9^+$	9.90±0.04	246 *253*	1028 *1057*	17.5 *24.4*	73.2 *102.1*	82TN270	19624-22-7
$B_5H_{10}^+$		214	896				

From proton affinity of B_5H_9 (RN 19624-22-7). PA = 169 kcal/mol, 707 kJ/mol.

$B_5H_{11}^+$	(10.1)	(257)	(1078)	24.6	103.3	82TN270	18433-84-6

IP is onset of photoelectron band.

$B_6H_{10}^+$	(9.0)	(230)	(963)	23	95	82TN270	2377-80-2

IP is onset of photoelectron band.

$B_{10}H_{14}^+$	9.88±0.03	235 *247*	985 *1031*	7.6 *18.7*	31.6 *78.1*	82TN270	17702-41-9
Ba^+ Ba	5.212	163 *163*	683 *684*	43 *43*	180 *181*	82TN270	7440-39-3
$BaBr^+$ BaBr	(5.0)	(88.9) *(91.0)*	(371.8) *(380.8)*	−26.4±10.0 *−24.3±10.0*	−111±41 *−102±41*	85JANAF	14832-97-4
$BaBr_2^+$ $BaBr_2$	(8.5)	(90) *(93)*	(377) *(391)*	−106 *−102*	−443 *−429*	82EMO/KIE	10553-31-8

IP is onset of photoelectron band (79LEE/POT). See also: 82EMO/KIE, 79LEE/POT2.

Table 1. Positive Ion Table - Continued

ION / Neutral	Ionization potential eV	$\Delta_f H$(Ion) kcal/mol	kJ/mol	$\Delta_f H$(Neutral) kcal/mol	kJ/mol	Neutral reference	CAS registry number
BaCl⁺							
BaCl	5.01±0.010	81	340	−34	−143	85JANAF	14832-99-6
		82	*341*	*−34*	*−142*		
BaCl₂⁺							
BaCl₂	(9.4)	(97)	(405)	−120	−502	82EMO/KIE	10361-37-2
	IP is onset of photoelectron band (79LEE/POT, 79LEE/POT2). See also: 82EMO/KIE. 0 K values.						
BaF⁺							
BaF	(4.8±0.3)	(34)	(144)	−77	−324	82TN270	13966-70-6
		(34)	*(142)*	*−77*	*−326*		
BaHO⁺							
BaOH	4.35±0.3	45	189	−55±4	−230±17	81MUR	12009-08-4
	IP from 81MUR. See also: 81FAR/SRI.						
BaH₂O₂⁺							
Ba(OH)₂	(8)	(44)	(186)	−140	−586	82TN270	17194-00-2
	IP from 81FAR/SRI.						
BaI⁺							
BaI	(5.0±0.3)	(105.2)	(440.0)	−10.1±20.1	−42.4±84	85JANAF	12524-20-8
		(105.9)	*(443.1)*	*−9.4±20.1*	*−39.3±84*		
BaI₂⁺							
BaI₂	(8.24)	(116)	(487)	−74	−308	82EMO/KIE	13718-50-8
		(117)	*(490)*	*−73*	*−305*		
	IP is onset of photoelectron band (79LEE/POT, 79LEE/POT2). See also: 82EMO/KIE.						
BaO⁺							
BaO	6.91±0.06	129.8	542.9	−29.6±2	−123.8±8	85JANAF	1304-28-5
		130.3	*545.1*	*−29.1±2*	*−121.6±8*		
	See also: 81MUR.						
BaO₄W⁺							
BaWO₄	(9.8±0.5)	(−181)	(−757)	−407	−1703	76DEL/HAL	
Be⁺							
Be	9.322	<u>292.5</u>	<u>1223.7</u>	77.5	324.3	82TN270	7440-41-7
		<u>*291.5*</u>	<u>*1219.4*</u>	*76.5*	*320.0*		
BeCl₂⁺							
BeCl₂	(11.15)	(171)	(717)	−86	−359	82TN270	7787-47-5
	IP is onset of photoelectron band (79LEE/POT2).						

Table 1. Positive Ion Table – Continued

ION / Neutral	Ionization potential eV	$\Delta_f H$(Ion) kcal/mol	$\Delta_f H$(Ion) kJ/mol	$\Delta_f H$(Neutral) kcal/mol	$\Delta_f H$(Neutral) kJ/mol	Neutral reference	CAS registry number
BeF^+				−40.6±2	−169.9±8	85JANAF	13597-96-1
BeF				−41.2±2	−172.2±8		

A value of 168 kcal/mol, 703 kJ/mol is obtained for the enthalpy of formation of BeF^+ based on experimental ionization potential values of 9.1±0.5 or 9.3±1.0 eV; the enthalpy of formation based on an appearance potential of 15.4±0.4 eV in BeF_2 is 147 kcal/mol, 615 kJ/mol.

ION / Neutral	Ionization potential eV	$\Delta_f H$(Ion) kcal/mol	$\Delta_f H$(Ion) kJ/mol	$\Delta_f H$(Neutral) kcal/mol	$\Delta_f H$(Neutral) kJ/mol	Neutral reference	CAS registry number
BeF_2^+							
BeF_2	(14.6±0.5)	(147)	(615)	−190	−794	82TN270	7787-49-7
BeH^+							
BeH	8.21±0.04	272	1136	82	344	79HUB/HER	13597-97-2
		271	1132	81.2	339.8		
BeO^+							
BeO	(10.1±0.4)	(265.5)	(1110.9)	32.6±3	136.4±13	85JANAF	1304-56-9
		(264.9)	(1108.5)	32.0±3	134.0±13		
Be_2O^+							
Be_2O	(10.5±0.5)	(227)	(950)	−15±10	−63±42	71JANAF	12009-99-3
$Be_2O_2^+$							
$(BeO)_2$	(10.8±0.7)	(151)	(632)	−98±12	−410±50	71JANAF	70478-90-9
$Be_3O_3^+$							
$(BeO)_3$	(10.9±0.6)	(−1)	(−2)	−252±9	−1054±38	71JANAF	61279-73-0
$Be_4O_4^+$							
$(BeO)_4$	(11.0)	(−126)	(−529)	−380±12	−1590±50	71JANAF	61279-74-1
$Be_5O_5^+$							
$(BeO)_5$	(~11)	(~−251)	(~−1052)	−505±23	−2113±95	71JANAF	61279-75-2
$Be_6O_6^+$							
$(BeO)_6$	(~11)	(~−239)	(~−1000)	−492±22	−2061±92	71JANAF	61279-76-3
Bi^+							
Bi	7.289	218	910	49	207	82TN270	7440-69-9
		217.7	910.7	49.6	207.4		
$BiCl_3^+$							
$BiCl_3$	(10.4)	(176)	(738)	−64	−266	82TN270	7787-60-2
		(177)	(739)	−63	−264		

IP is onset of photoelectron band (83NOV/POT). See also: 83OZG.

ION / Neutral	Ionization potential eV	$\Delta_f H$(Ion) kcal/mol	$\Delta_f H$(Ion) kJ/mol	$\Delta_f H$(Neutral) kcal/mol	$\Delta_f H$(Neutral) kJ/mol	Neutral reference	CAS registry number
BiH_3^+							
BiH_3	(10.1)	(288)	(1204)	55	230	64GUN	18288-22-7

Table 1. Positive Ion Table - Continued

ION Neutral	Ionization potential eV	$\Delta_f H$(Ion) kcal/mol	kJ/mol	$\Delta_f H$(Neutral) kcal/mol	kJ/mol	Neutral reference	CAS registry number
BiO$^+$							
BiO	(9.0±0.5)	(236)	(989)	29±3	121±13	83PED/MAR	1332-64-5
		(236)	(988)	29	120		
BiS$^+$							
BiS	(8.7±0.5)	(243)	(1017)	42	178	79HUB/HER	12048-34-9
	0 K values.						
BiTe$^+$							
BiTe	(8.4±0.5)	(235)	(983)	41	173	79HUB/HER	12010-57-0
	0 K values.						
Bi$_2^+$							
Bi$_2$	(7.3±0.5)	(221)	(924)	53	220	82TN270	12187-12-1
		(221)	(926)	53.1	222.2		
Bk$^+$							
Bk	6.30±0.09	219	918	74	310	85KLE/WAR	7440-40-6
Br$^+$							
Br	11.814	299.2	1251.7	26.7	111.9	82BAU/COX	10097-32-2
		300.6	1257.8	28.2	117.9		
	See also: 81KIM/KAT.						
BrCa$^+$							
CaBr	5.54	123	513	−5	−21	79HUB/HER	10024-43-8
	IP from 84MEY/SCH. 0 K values.						
BrCl$^+$							
BrCl	11.01	257	1077	4	15	82TN270	13863-41-7
		259	1084	5	22		
	IP from 84DYK/JOS.						
BrCl$_5$N$_3$P$_3^+$	(9.83±0.1)	(52)	(218)	−174	−730	*EST	14740-93-3
BrCs$^+$							
CsBr	7.72±0.05	130	545	−48	−200	84PAR/WEX	7787-69-1
		133	554	−45.5±1.8	−190.4±7.5		
BrF$^+$							
BrF	11.77±0.01	257.4	1077.1	−14.0±0.4	−58.5±1.7	85JANAF	13863-59-7
		259.3	1084.8	−12.1±0.4	−50.8±1.7		
	See also: 84DYK/JOS.						

Table 1. Positive Ion Table - Continued

ION / Neutral	Ionization potential eV	$\Delta_f H$(Ion) kcal/mol	$\Delta_f H$(Ion) kJ/mol	$\Delta_f H$(Neutral) kcal/mol	$\Delta_f H$(Neutral) kJ/mol	Neutral reference	CAS registry number
BrF_3^+							
BrF_3	(12.15±0.04)	(219)	(917)	−61.1	−255.6	82TN270	7787-71-5
		(222)	(928)	−58.4	−244.4		
BrF_5^+							
BrF_5	(13.17±0.01)	(201)	(842)	−103	−429	82TN270	7789-30-2
		(205)	(858)	−99	−413		
BrH^+							
HBr	11.66±0.03	260	1089	−9	−36	82TN270	10035-10-6
		262	1096	−7	−29		

IP from 79HUB/HER, 77ROS/DRA, 82LEV/LIA. See also: 81KIM/KAT.

BrH_2^+							
H_2Br		218	911				

From proton affinity of HBr (RN 10035-10-6) (84POL/MUN, 85MCM/KEB).
PA = 139 kcal/mol, 582 kJ/mol.

BrH_3Si^+							
SiH_3Br	10.6	(226)	(945)	−19±4	−78±17	82JANAF	13465-73-1

IP is onset of photoelectron band.

BrI^+							
IBr	9.790±0.004	235.5	985.4	9.8	40.8	82TN270	7789-33-5
		237.7	994.4	11.9	49.8		

See also: 84DYK/JOS, 71POT/PRI.

$BrIn^+$							
InBr	(9.09)	(202)	(845)	−8	−32	79HUB/HER	14280-53-6
		(204)	(854)	−6	−23		
BrK^+							
KBr	7.85±0.1	138	577	−43	−180	82TN270	7758-02-3
		140	586	−41	−171		
$BrLi^+$							
LiBr	(8.7)	(164)	(685)	−37±3	−154±13	71JANAF	7550-35-8
		(166)	(693)	−35±3	−146±13		

IP is onset of photoelectron band.

$BrNO^+$							
NOBr	10.17±0.03	254	1063	20	82	82BAU/COX	13444-87-6
$BrNa^+$							
NaBr	8.31±0.1	157	659	−34	−143	82TN270	7647-15-6
		160	668	−32	−134		
BrO^+							
BrO	(10.2)	(265)	(1110)	30.1	125.8	82TN270	14380-62-2
		(267)	(1118)	31.9	133.5		

IP is onset of photoelectron band.

Table 1. Positive Ion Table – Continued

ION Neutral	Ionization potential eV	$\Delta_f H$(Ion) kcal/mol	kJ/mol	$\Delta_f H$(Neutral) kcal/mol	kJ/mol	Neutral reference	CAS registry number
$BrRb^+$ RbBr	7.94±0.03	139 *142*	583 *592*	−43.7 *−41.4*	−182.8 *−173.4*	82TN270	7789-39-1
$BrSi^+$ SiBr	(7.3)	(224.6) *(225.9)*	(939.6) *(945.1)*	56.3±11.0 *57.6±11.0*	235.3±46.0 *240.8±46.0*	85JANAF	14791-57-2
$BrSr^+$ SrBr	(5.5)	(106) *(108)*	(442) *(450)*	−21±10 *−19.2±10*	−89±42 *−80.4±42*	85JANAF	14519-13-2
$BrTl^+$ TlBr	9.14±0.02 See also: 83BAN/BRI.	202 *204*	844 *853*	−9 *−7*	−38 *−29*	82TN270	7789-40-4
Br_2^+ Br_2	10.515±0.005	250 *253*	1046 *1061*	7.4 *11*	31.0 *46*	82BAU/COX	7726-95-6
	Cited IP leads to Br_2^+ $(^2\Pi_{3/2\,g})$; formation of Br_2^+ $(^2\Pi_{1/2\,g})$ requires 10.865±0.005 eV. IP from 84VAN/DEL2, 84DYK/JOS, 77ROS/DRA. See also: 81KIM/KAT.						
Br_2Ca^+ $CaBr_2$	≤9.68 IP is onset of photoelectron band (79LEE/POT2).	≤130 *≤134*	≤545 *≤560*	−93 *−89±2*	−389 *−374±9*	82TPIS	7789-41-5
$Br_2Cl_4N_3P_3^+$	(9.80±0.1)	(63)	(265)	−163	−681	*EST	15964-99-5
$Br_2F_4N_3P_3^+$	(10.63±0.03) IP from 81CLA/SOW.	(−135)	(−563)	−380	−1589	*EST	29871-63-4
Br_2Fe^+ $FeBr_2$	(10.7±0.5)	(237)	(991)	−10±0.5	−41±2	71JANAF	7789-46-0
Br_2Ge^+ $GeBr_2$	(9.60±0.05) IP from 82JON/VAN.	(206)	(863)	−15	−63	82TN270	24415-00-7

Table 1. Positive Ion Table – Continued

| ION | Ionization potential | $\Delta_f H$(Ion) | | $\Delta_f H$(Neutral) | | Neutral | CAS registry |
Neutral	eV	kcal/mol	kJ/mol	kcal/mol	kJ/mol	reference	number
$Br_2H_2Si^+$							
SiH_2Br_2	(10.7)	(201)	(842)	−45±4	−190±17	82JANAF	13768-94-0
	IP is onset of photoelectron band.						
Br_2Hg^+							
$HgBr_2$	10.560±0.003	223	934	−20±2	−85±8	71JANAF	7789-47-1
	Cited ionization potential (83LIN/TZE) refers to formation of $HgBr_2^+$ ($^2\Pi_{3/2\,g}$).						
	IP for formation of $HgBr_2^+$ ($^2\Pi_{1/2\,g}$) is 10.8846±0.0012 eV. See also: 81LEE/POT.						
$Br_2Li_2^+$							
(Li₂Br₂ ring structure)	(≤10.05±0.08)	(≤112)	(≤469)	−120	−501	81LIN/BES	12380-84-6
Br_2Mg^+							
$MgBr_2$	10.47	169	708	−72	−302	82TPIS	7789-48-2
		173	*723*	*−69±4*	*−287±15*		
	IP is onset of photoelectron band (79LEE/POT2).						
Br_2OS^+							
$SOBr_2$	(10.1)	(204)	(851)	−29	−123	82TN270	507-16-4
		(209)	*(872)*	*−24*	*−102*		
	IP is onset of photoelectron band.						
Br_2Pb^+							
$PbBr_2$	9.6	(196)	(822)	−25±1	−104±6	75JANAF	10031-22-8
	IP is onset of photoelectron band (84NOV/POT2, 82LEV/LIA).						
$Br_2S_2^+$							
S_2Br_2	(9.23±0.03)	(221)	(923)	8	33	82TN270	13172-31-1
	IP from 81KAU/VAH.						
Br_2Se^+							
$SeBr_2$	9.07	204	854	−5	−21	82TN270	22987-45-7
Br_2Sn^+							
$SnBr_2$	9.0	201	839	−7	−29	82TPIS	10031-24-0
	IP is onset of photoelectron band (84NOV/POT2, 82LEV/LIA).						
Br_2Sr^+							
$SrBr_2$	(9.11)	(114)	(477)	−96	−402	82TPIS	10476-81-0
		(118)	*(492)*	*−92±3*	*−387±11*		
	IP is onset of photoelectron band (79LEE/POT2). See also: 82EMO/KIE.						

Table 1. Positive Ion Table – Continued

ION / Neutral	Ionization potential eV	$\Delta_f H$(Ion) kcal/mol	$\Delta_f H$(Ion) kJ/mol	$\Delta_f H$(Neutral) kcal/mol	$\Delta_f H$(Neutral) kJ/mol	Neutral reference	CAS registry number
$Br_3Cl_3N_3P_3^+$	(9.72±0.1)	(73)	(306)	−151	−632	*EST	16032-52-3
$Br_3F_3N_3P_3^+$	(10.37±0.03) IP from 81CLA/SOW.	(−74)	(−311)	−314	−1312	*EST	67336-18-9
Br_3Ga^+ / $GaBr_3$	10.40	170	710	−70	−293	82TN270	13450-88-9
Br_3In^+ / $InBr_3$	(10.0) IP is onset of photoelectron band.	(163)	(683)	−67	−282	82TN270	13465-09-3
Br_3La^+ / $LaBr_3$	(9.85) IP is onset of photoelectron band (83RUS/GOO).	(87)	(364)	−140±2	−586±7	78TPIS	13536-79-3
Br_3OP^+ / $POBr_3$	10.75±0.02	151 / *161*	632 / *673*	−97 / *−87*	−405 / *−364*	71JANAF	7789-59-5
Br_3P^+ / PBr_3	9.7 IP is onset of photoelectron band.	(190) / *(196)*	(797) / *(821)*	−33 / *−27*	−139 / *−115*	82TN270	7789-60-8
$Br_4Cl_2N_3P_3^+$	(9.60±0.1)	(82)	(343)	−139	−583	*EST	15965-00-1
Br_4Hf^+ / $HfBr_4$	(10.9) IP is onset of photoelectron band.	(87)	(365)	−164	−687	81SPE	13777-22-5
Br_4Sn^+ / $SnBr_4$	10.6 IP is onset of photoelectron band.	169 / *177*	708 / *739*	−75 / *−68*	−315 / *−284*	82TN270	7789-67-5

Table 1. Positive Ion Table - Continued

ION / Neutral	Ionization potential eV	$\Delta_f H$(Ion) kcal/mol	$\Delta_f H$(Ion) kJ/mol	$\Delta_f H$(Neutral) kcal/mol	$\Delta_f H$(Neutral) kJ/mol	Neutral reference	CAS registry number
Br_4Ti^+							
$TiBr_4$	10.3	(90)	(376)	−148±1	−618±5	71JANAF	7789-68-6
	IP is onset of photoelectron band.						
Br_4Zr^+							
$ZrBr_4$	(10.7)	(93)	(387)	−154±2	−645±8	78JANAF	13777-25-8
	IP is onset of photoelectron band.						
$Br_5ClN_3P_3^+$	(9.47±0.1)	(91)	(380)	−128	−534	*EST	15608-37-4
Br_5W^+							
WBr_5	(8.3±0.2)	(144)	(602)	−48±5	−199±21	71JANAF	13470-11-6
		(153)	(638)	−39	−163		
$Br_6N_3P_3^+$	9.62±0.03	(82)	(343)	−140	−585	*EST	13701-85-4
	IP from 81CLA/SOW.						
$Br_9Re_3^+$	(8.4)	(125)	(521)	−69	−289	82TN270	33517-16-7
	IP is onset of photoelectron band.						
C^+							
C	11.260	431.0	1803.2	171.3	716.7	82TN270	7440-44-0
		429.7	1797.6	170.0	711.2		
CBr^+							
CBr	(10.43±0.02)	(362.5)	(1516.7)	122.0±15	510.4±63	85JANAF	
		(363.4)	(1520.6)	122.9±15	514.3±63		
$CBrClF_2^+$							
CF_2BrCl	(≤11.83)	(≤168)	(≤703)	−105±2	−438±8	78KUD/KUD	353-59-3
$CBrCl_3^+$							
CCl_3Br	(10.6)	(234)	(980)	−10.2±0.6	−42.7±2.4	77PED/RYL	75-62-7
	IP is onset of photoelectron band (81NOV/CVI3).						

Table 1. Positive Ion Table - Continued

ION / Neutral	Ionization potential eV	$\Delta_f H$(Ion) kcal/mol	kJ/mol	$\Delta_f H$(Neutral) kcal/mol	kJ/mol	Neutral reference	CAS registry number
$CBrF_3^+$							
CF_3Br	11.4	108	450	−155	−650	78KUD/KUD	75-63-8
		111	*463*	*−152*	*−637*		
\multicolumn{8}{l}{IP is onset of photoelectron band. See also: 82BOC/WIT.}
$CBrN^+$							
BrCN	11.84±0.01	316	1323	43±1	181±4	77PED/RYL	506-68-3
$CBr_2Cl_2^+$							
CCl_2Br_2	(10.4)	(242)	(1012)	2±2	9±8	78KUD/KUD	594-18-3
\multicolumn{8}{l}{IP is onset of photoelectron band.}
$CBr_2F_2^+$							
CF_2Br_2	11.07±0.03	165	689	−91±2	−379±8	78KUD/KUD	75-61-6
CBr_2O^+							
$COBr_2$	(10.8)	(222)	(929)	−27±0.5	−113±2	77PED/RYL	593-95-3
\multicolumn{8}{l}{IP is onset of photoelectron band.}
CBr_3^+							
CBr_3	(8.2)	(239)	(1000)	49.6	207.5	*EST	
\multicolumn{8}{l}{From appearance potential (10.47±0.02 eV) in CBr_4; IP is $\Delta_f H$(Ion) - $\Delta_f H$(Neutral).}
CBr_3F^+							
$CFBr_3$	10.67±0.01	190	793	−56±2	−236±8	78KUD/KUD	353-54-8
CBr_4^+							
CBr_4	(10.31±0.02)	(258)	(1079)	20.1±0.8	83.9±3.4	84BIC/MIN	558-13-4
		(265)	*(1109)*	*27.2*	*113.8*		
CCe^+							
CCe	(7.5±1.0)	(336)	(1406)	163	682	82TN270	12011-58-4
CCl^+							
CCl	(8.9±0.2)	(297)	(1243)	(92)	(384)		
\multicolumn{8}{l}{$\Delta_f H$(Ion) from appearance potential determination. $\Delta_f H$(Neutral) is $\Delta_f H$(Ion) - IP. IP from 82HEP/TRE.}
$CClF^+$							
CClF	(10.7)	(243)	(1017)	−5±7	−20±29	85LIA/KAR	1691-88-9
\multicolumn{8}{l}{$\Delta_f H$(Ion) from appearance potential determinations. IP is $\Delta_f H$(Ion)-$\Delta_f H$(Neutral). See: 85LIA/KAR (re-evaluated here).}
$CClF_2^+$							
$CClF_2$	(8.3)	126	528	−66	−275	*EST	1691-89-0
\multicolumn{8}{l}{Cited heat of formation based on observation of near-thermoneutral reaction: $(C_2H_5^+ + CF_2Cl_2 \rightarrow CF_2Cl^+ + C_2H_5Cl)$. Value based on appearance potential of ion (11.99 eV) in CF_2Cl_2 is 133 kcal/mol, 556 kJ/mol. IP is $\Delta_f H$(Ion) - $\Delta_f H$(Neutral).}

Table 1. Positive Ion Table — Continued

ION / Neutral	Ionization potential eV	$\Delta_f H$(Ion) kcal/mol	$\Delta_f H$(Ion) kJ/mol	$\Delta_f H$(Neutral) kcal/mol	$\Delta_f H$(Neutral) kJ/mol	Neutral reference	CAS registry number
$CClF_3^+$ / CF_3Cl	12.39	116 / 117	485 / 491	−169.7±0.6 / −168	−710.0±2.3 / −704	77PED/RYL	75-72-9

See also: 85KIS/MOR.

| $CClN^+$ / $ClCN$ | 12.34±0.01 | 318 / 317 | 1329 / 1328 | 33.0 / 32.8 | 138.0 / 137.3 | 77PED/RYL | 506-77-4 |

Cited ionization potential corresponds to the formation of $CNCl^+(^2\Pi_{3/2})$. Formation of $CNCl^+(^2\Pi_{1/2})$ requires 12.37 eV.

| $CClNO^+$ / $ClNCO$ | (10.72±0.01) | (253) | (1057) | 5.5 | 23.0 | 83DEW/RZE | 13858-09-8 |

| CCl_2^+ / CCl_2 | 10.36 | 278 | 1163 | 39 | 163 | 85LIA/KAR | 1605-72-7 |

$\Delta_f H$(Ion) from appearance potential determinations.
Cited IP is $\Delta_f H$(Ion) − $\Delta_f H$(Neutral). See 85LIA/KAR.

| CCl_2F^+ / CCl_2F | (8.0) | (168) | (703) | −17.5 | −73 | *EST | 1691-90-3 |

From observation of near-thermoneutral reaction: ($C_2H_5^+ + CF_2Cl_2 \rightarrow CCl_2F^+ + C_2H_5F$) (77LIA/AUS). Appearance potential determinations lead to values of 175 kcal/mol, 732 kJ/mol, for the heat of formation of this ion. IP is $\Delta_f H$(Ion) − $\Delta_f H$(Neutral).

| $CCl_2F_2^+$ / CF_2Cl_2 | 11.75±0.04 | 157 / 158 | 656 / 661 | −114.1±1.3 / −113 | −477.5±5.6 / −473 | 77PED/RYL | 75-71-8 |

See also: 85KIS/MOR.

| CCl_2O^+ / $COCl_2$ | (11.4) | (210) / (211) | (880) / (882) | −53 / −52 | −220 / −218 | 82BAU/COX | 75-44-5 |

IP is onset of photoelectron band.

| CCl_2S^+ / $CSCl_2$ | 9.61±0.02 | 215 | 900 | −6 | −27 | 79JOS | 463-71-8 |

| CCl_3^+ / CCl_3 | (7.8) | (199) | (831) | 19 | 79 | 82MCM/GOL | 3170-80-7 |

$\Delta_f H$(Ion) is based on the observation of the reaction ($H_3O^+ + CFCl_3 \rightarrow CCl_3^+ + HF + H_2O$) and lack of occurrence of (sec-$C_3H_7^+ + CFCl_3 \rightarrow CCl_3^+ + C_3H_7F$) which brackets the heat of formation between 197 and 200 kcal/mol, 824 and 837 kJ/mol (77LIA/AUS). IP is $\Delta_f H$(Ion) − $\Delta_f H$(Neutral). Experimental value: 8.28 eV.

| CCl_3F^+ / $CFCl_3$ | 11.77±0.02 | 207 / 208 | 868 / 871 | −64±2 / −63 | −268±8 / −265 | 77PED/RYL | 75-69-4 |

See also: 85KIS/MOR.

Table 1. Positive Ion Table - Continued

ION / Neutral	Ionization potential eV	$\Delta_f H$(Ion) kcal/mol	$\Delta_f H$(Ion) kJ/mol	$\Delta_f H$(Neutral) kcal/mol	$\Delta_f H$(Neutral) kJ/mol	Neutral reference	CAS registry number
CCl_4^+							
CCl_4	11.47±0.01	241	1010	−23.2±0.7	−97.1±3	77PED/RYL	56-23-5
		242	*1012*	*−22.7*	*−95.0*		
	See also: 82VON/ASB, 81KIM/KAT.						
CCo^+							
CCo		(364)	(1524)				
	$\Delta_f H$(Ion) from photodissociation onset to give Co^+ (86HET/FRE).						
CF^+							
CF	9.11±0.01	271.1	1134.2	61.0±2	255.2±8	85JANAF	3889-75-6
		270.2	*1130.6*	*60.1±2*	*231.6±8*		
	IP from 84DYK/LEW. See also: 82HEP/TRE.						
CFN^+							
FCN	13.32±0.01	316	1321	9±4	36±17	71JANAF	1495-50-7
CFO^+							
FCO	8.76±0.32	(160)	(669)	−42±4	−175±16	81DYK/JON2	
	IP from 81DYK/JON2.						
CF_2^+							
CF_2	11.42±0.01	214	897	−49±3	−205±12	85LIA/KAR	2154-59-8
CF_2O^+							
COF_2	13.03	147	617	−153	−640	77PED/RYL	353-50-4
		148	*620*	*−152*	*−637*		
CF_2S^+							
CSF_2	(10.45±0.01)	(157)	(658)	−84	−350	79JOS	420-32-6
	See also: 85BIN/GRO.						
CF_2Se^+							
$CSeF_2$	(9.6±0.2)	(154)	(646)	−67	−280	*EST	54393-39-4
	IP from 85BIN/GRO, 84BOC/AYG.						
CF_3^+							
CF_3	(≤8.9)	(95.4)	(399.0)	−110	−460	86TSA	2264-21-3
		(96.1)	*(402.0)*	*−109*	*−457*		
	$\Delta_f H$(Ion) from appearance potential determinations (82BOM/DAN). See also: 81BER/BEA, 83WAN/LER. IP estimated in 81LOG/TAK.						
CF_3I^+							
CF_3I	10.23	95	397	−141±5	−590±21	78KUD/KUD	2314-97-8
	See also: 81BER/BEA, 84BAN/YAT.						
CF_3NO^+							
CF_3NO	(10.5±0.1)	(116)	(484)	−126	−529	*EST	334-99-6

Table 1. Positive Ion Table – Continued

ION / Neutral	Ionization potential eV	$\Delta_f H$(Ion) kcal/mol	$\Delta_f H$(Ion) kJ/mol	$\Delta_f H$(Neutral) kcal/mol	$\Delta_f H$(Neutral) kJ/mol	Neutral reference	CAS registry number
CF_4^+							
CF_4				−223.4±0.1	−934.5±0.4	77PED/RYL	75-73-0
				−221.6	−927		

The stable region of the CF_4^+ ground state is not accessible by a vertical transition from the CF_4 molecule; no CF_4^+ ions have been experimentally observed. The onset of the photoelectron spectrum is at ~15.3 eV(81BIE/ASB, 84CAR/FAH, 85NOV/POT). A value of < 14.7 eV was suggested in 77ROS/DRA. See also: 75LLO/ROB, 85KIS/MOR.

ION / Neutral	Ionization potential eV	$\Delta_f H$(Ion) kcal/mol	$\Delta_f H$(Ion) kJ/mol	$\Delta_f H$(Neutral) kcal/mol	$\Delta_f H$(Neutral) kJ/mol	Neutral reference	CAS registry number
CF_4O^+							
CF_3OF	(13.0)	(112)	(469)	−188	−785	69STU/WES	373-91-1

IP is onset of photoelectron band.

ION / Neutral	IP eV	$\Delta_f H$(Ion) kcal/mol	kJ/mol	$\Delta_f H$(Neutral) kcal/mol	kJ/mol	Neutral reference	CAS
CF_5N^+							
CF_3NF_2	(11.9)	(105)	(440)	−169±0.5	−708±2	77PED/RYL	335-01-3

IP from 82BUR/PAW.

ION / Neutral	IP eV	$\Delta_f H$(Ion) kcal/mol	kJ/mol	$\Delta_f H$(Neutral) kcal/mol	kJ/mol	Neutral reference	CAS
CFe^+							
FeC		(358)	(1499)				

$\Delta_f H$(Ion) from photodissociation onset to give Fe^+ (86HET/FRE).

ION / Neutral	IP eV	$\Delta_f H$(Ion) kcal/mol	kJ/mol	$\Delta_f H$(Neutral) kcal/mol	kJ/mol	Neutral reference	CAS
CGe^+							
GeC	(10.3±0.3)	(388)	(1622)	150	628	79HUB/HER	12334-26-8

0 K values.

ION / Neutral	IP eV	$\Delta_f H$(Ion) kcal/mol	kJ/mol	$\Delta_f H$(Neutral) kcal/mol	kJ/mol	Neutral reference	CAS
CH^+							
CH	10.64±0.01	387.8	1622.4	142.4	595.8	79HUB/HER	3315-37-5
		387.0	1619.1	141.6	592.5		

See also: 83PLE/MAR.

ION / Neutral	IP eV	$\Delta_f H$(Ion) kcal/mol	kJ/mol	$\Delta_f H$(Neutral) kcal/mol	kJ/mol	Neutral reference	CAS
$CHBrCl_2^+$							
$CHBrCl_2$	10.6	233	974	−12	−49	78KUD/KUD	75-27-4

IP is onset of photoelectron band (81NOV/CVI3).

ION / Neutral	IP eV	$\Delta_f H$(Ion) kcal/mol	kJ/mol	$\Delta_f H$(Neutral) kcal/mol	kJ/mol	Neutral reference	CAS
$CHBrF_3^+$							
CF_3BrH		73	305				

From proton affinity of $CBrF_3$(RN 75-63-8) (85MCM/KEB) re-evaluated relative to CO standard (84LIA/LIE). PA = 137.5 kcal/mol, 575.3 kJ/mol.

ION / Neutral	IP eV	$\Delta_f H$(Ion) kcal/mol	kJ/mol	$\Delta_f H$(Neutral) kcal/mol	kJ/mol	Neutral reference	CAS
$CHBrN^+$							
BrCNH		231	965				

From proton affinity of BrCN (RN 506-68-3). PA = 178.3 kcal/mol, 746 kJ/mol.

ION / Neutral	IP eV	$\Delta_f H$(Ion) kcal/mol	kJ/mol	$\Delta_f H$(Neutral) kcal/mol	kJ/mol	Neutral reference	CAS
$CHBr_2^+$							
$CHBr_2$	(7.4)	(224)	(936)	54	227	82MCM/GOL	14362-13-1

Ion heat of formation from appearance potential (10.70±0.02 eV) in $CHBr_3$. Cited ionization potential is difference between this heat of formation and that of neutral. Experimental determinations of this ionization potential gave values of 8.13±0.16 eV (77ROS/DRA), 8.41±0.03 eV (V) (84AND/DYK3).

Table 1. Positive Ion Table - Continued

ION Neutral	Ionization potential eV	$\Delta_f H$(Ion) kcal/mol	$\Delta_f H$(Ion) kJ/mol	$\Delta_f H$(Neutral) kcal/mol	$\Delta_f H$(Neutral) kJ/mol	Neutral reference	CAS registry number
$CHBr_2Cl^+$ $CHClBr_2$	10.59±0.01	246	1031	2±2	9±8	78KUD/KUD	124-48-1

IP (77ROS/DRA) in good agreement with onset of photoelectron band (81NOV/CVI3).

$CHBr_3^+$ $CHBr_3$	10.48±0.02	247.4	1035.0	5.7±1.1	23.8±4.5	84BIC/MIN	75-25-2

See also: 82VON/ASB.

$CHCl^+$ $CHCl$	9.84	298	1247	71	297	85LIA/KAR	2108-20-5

$\Delta_f H$(Ion) derived from hydrogen affinity considerations. IP is $\Delta_f H$(Ion)-$\Delta_f H$(Neutral).

$CHClF^+$ $CClFH$	(8.81±0.02)	(178)	(743)	(−25)	(−105)		33272-71-8

$\Delta_f H$(Ion) from observation of: (CF_2Cl^+ + $CHFCl_2$ → $CHFCl^+$ + CF_2Cl_2)
and non-observation of: ($C_2H_5^+$ + $CHFCl_2$ → $CHFCl^+$ + C_2H_5Cl)(77LIA/AUS).
Appearance potential determinations lead to a value of 205 kcal/mol, 858 kJ/mol.
IP from 84AND/DYK.

$CHClF_2^+$ CHF_2Cl	(12.2)	(166)	(694)	−115.6±0.5	−483.5±2.2	77PED/RYL	75-45-6

See also: 81NOV/CVI3.

$CHClF_3^+$ CF_3ClH		60	251				

From proton affinity of CF_3Cl(RN 75-72-9) (85MCM/KEB)
re-evaluated relative to CO standard(84LIA/LIE). PA = 136 kcal/mol, 569 kJ/mol.

$CHClN^+$ $ClCNH$		224	937				

From proton affinity of ClCN (RN 506-77-4). PA = 174.8 kcal/mol, 731 kJ/mol (86MAR/TOP).

$CHCl_2^+$ $CHCl_2$	(8.1)	(212)	(887)	26±1	108±4	83WEI/BEN	3474-12-2

$\Delta_f H$(Ion) from appearance potential (11.49±0.02 eV) in CCl_3H. Cited
IP is difference between heats of formation of ion and neutral.
An experimental determination of the IP gave a value of 8.32 eV(84AND/DYK)
which would correspond to a $\Delta_f H$(Radical) of 20 kcal/mol, 84 kJ/mol.

$CHCl_2F^+$ $CHFCl_2$	(11.5)	(198)	(829)	−67±2	−281±8	78KUD/KUD	75-43-4

IP is onset of photoelectron band (82LEV/LIA, 81NOV/CVI3).

$CHCl_3^+$ $CHCl_3$	11.37±0.02	237 238	992 997	−25.0±0.5 −23.8	−104.8±2 −99.7	77PED/RYL	67-66-3

See also: 82VON/ASB, 81KIM/KAT.

Table 1. Positive Ion Table – Continued

| ION | Ionization potential | $\Delta_f H$(Ion) | | $\Delta_f H$(Neutral) | | Neutral | CAS registry |
Neutral	eV	kcal/mol	kJ/mol	kcal/mol	kJ/mol	reference	number
$CHCo^+$							
CHCo		(325)	(1361)				
	$\Delta_f H$(Ion) from photodissociation onset to give Co^+ (86HET/FRE).						
CHF^+							
CHF	(10.49)	(268)	(1121)	26±3	109±12	85LIA/KAR	13453-52-6
	$\Delta_f H$(Ion) from hydrogen affinity considerations. IP is $\Delta_f H$(Ion)-$\Delta_f H$(Neutral)(85LIA/KAR).						
$CHFN^+$							
FCNH		(224)	(934)				
	$\Delta_f H$(Ion) from core binding energies of isoelectronic neutral HNCO (84BEA/EYE).						
$CHFO^+$							
HFCO	(12.37±0.02)	(195)	(817)	−90	−377	71JANAF	1493-02-3
CHF_2^+							
CHF_2	(8.78)	(146)	(611)	−57±1	−237±5	83PIC/ROD	2670-13-5
	Heat of formation of ion derived from observed ion-molecule reactions (74BLI/MCM, 77LIA/AUS); cited ionization potential is the difference between the heats of formation of the ion and the radical.						
CHF_2O^+							
F_2COH		52	219				
	From proton affinity of CF_2O (RN 353-50-4). PA = 160.5 kcal/mol, 671.5 kJ/mol.						
CHF_3^+							
CHF_3	13.86	154	642	−166±2	−695±8	78KUD/KUD	75-46-7
		156	649	−164	−688		
	See also: 81BIE/ASB, 85NOV/POT, 82BOC/WIT.						
CHF_3I^+							
CF_3IH		(78)	(326)				
	From proton affinity of CF_3I (RN 2314-97-8) (85MCM/KEB) re-evaluated relative to CO standard (84LIA/LIE). PA = 146.7 kcal/mol, 614 kJ/mol.						
CHF_3NO^+							
CF_3NHO		(70)	(294)				
	From the proton affinity of CF_3NO (RN 334-99-6). PA = 70. kcal/mol, 294. kJ/mol.						
CHF_4^+							
F_3CFH		17	70				
	From proton affinity of CF_4 (RN 75-73-0). PA = ~126 kcal/mol, ~527 kJ/mol.						
CHF_4N^+							
CHF_2NF_2	(11.5)	(156)	(655)	−109	−455	*EST	24708-53-0
	IP from 82BUR/PAW.						
$CHFe^+$							
CHFe		(322)	(1349)				
	$\Delta_f H$(Ion) from photodissociation onset to give Fe^+ (86HET/FRE).						

Table 1. Positive Ion Table - Continued

ION / Neutral	Ionization potential eV	$\Delta_f H$(Ion) kcal/mol	$\Delta_f H$(Ion) kJ/mol	$\Delta_f H$(Neutral) kcal/mol	$\Delta_f H$(Neutral) kJ/mol	Neutral reference	CAS registry number
CHI_3^+							
CHI_3	9.25±0.02	241	1010	28±5	118±21	78KUD/KUD	75-47-8
		244	1019	30	127		
CHN^+							
HCN	13.60±0.01	346	1447	32.3	135.1	82TN270	74-90-8
		346	1448	32.4	135.5		

See also: 82KRE/SCH, 81KIM/KAT.

HNC	(12.5±0.1)	(336)	(1407)	48±2	201±8	82PAU/HEH	6914-07-4

IP by charge exchange bracketing of HNC^+ ions generated in CH_3NC(78BIE/JON).
See also: 80MCL/MCG.

$CHNO^+$							
HNCO	11.61±0.03	243	1015	−25±3	−105±13	86SPI/PER	75-13-8
HCNO	(10.83)	(302)	(1263)	52	218	*EST	506-85-4
$CHNS^+$							
HNCS	9.94±0.02	260	1087	31	128	82TN270	3129-90-6
CHO^+							
HCO	8.10±0.05	197.3	825.6	10.7	44.8	77BEC/LIP	17030-74-9

$\Delta_f H$(Ion) from appearance potential measurements (85TRA2).
See also: 76GUY/CHU, 84WAN/CAP, 80DYK/JON.

COH		(230)	(963)				

$\Delta_f H$(Ion) from correlation with oxygen 1s binding energy (85MCM/KEB2). See also: 85WAG/KEM, 83BUR/MOM.

$CHOS^+$							
COSH		181	757				

From proton affinity of COS (RN 463-58-1) (85MCM/KEB, 85MCM/KEB2) re-evaluated relative to CO standard (84LIA/LIE). PA = 150.7 kcal/mol, 631 kJ/mol.

$CHOSe^+$							
COSeH		230	962				

From proton affinity of COSe (RN 1603-84-5) (85KAR). PA = 152. kcal/mol, 637. kJ/mol.

CHO_2^+							
COOH		141	589				2564-86-5

$\Delta_f H$(Ion) from appearance potential in HCOOH.

CHP^+							
HCP	(10.79±0.01)	(289)	(1208)	40±15	167±63	71JANAF	6829-52-3

Table 1. Positive Ion Table - Continued

ION / Neutral	Ionization potential eV	$\Delta_f H$(Ion) kcal/mol	$\Delta_f H$(Ion) kJ/mol	$\Delta_f H$(Neutral) kcal/mol	$\Delta_f H$(Neutral) kJ/mol	Neutral reference	CAS registry number
CHS^+ / HCS	>(7.3)	243 / *243*	1018 / *1018*	≤73 / *≤74*	≤305 / *≤310*	83BUT/BAE	

$\Delta_f H$(Ion) from appearance potential determinations in thiirane (RN 420-12-2) (82BUT/BAE) in good agreement with value derived from proton affinity of CS (RN 2944-05-0) (85SMI/ADA). PA = 188.2 kcal/mol, 787 kJ/mol. IP is $\Delta_f H$(Ion)-$\Delta_f H$(Neutral). See also: 82KUT/EDW, 82KUT/EDW.

ION / Neutral	Ionization potential eV	$\Delta_f H$(Ion) kcal/mol	$\Delta_f H$(Ion) kJ/mol	$\Delta_f H$(Neutral) kcal/mol	$\Delta_f H$(Neutral) kJ/mol	Neutral reference	CAS registry number
CHS_2^+ / HSCS		229	959				

From proton affinity of CS_2(RN 75-15-0), re-evaluated. PA = 164.4 kcal/mol, 688. kJ/mol. See also: 85MCM/KEB, 85WEI/PLA.

ION / Neutral	Ionization potential eV	$\Delta_f H$(Ion) kcal/mol	$\Delta_f H$(Ion) kJ/mol	$\Delta_f H$(Neutral) kcal/mol	$\Delta_f H$(Neutral) kJ/mol	Neutral reference	CAS registry number
$CHTi^+$ / TiCH		*(289)*	*(1209)*				

$\Delta_f H$(Ion) from onset of endothermic reaction (86ELK/ARM). 0 K value.

ION / Neutral	Ionization potential eV	$\Delta_f H$(Ion) kcal/mol	$\Delta_f H$(Ion) kJ/mol	$\Delta_f H$(Neutral) kcal/mol	$\Delta_f H$(Neutral) kJ/mol	Neutral reference	CAS registry number
CHV^+ / VCH		*(307)*	*(1283)*				

$\Delta_f H$(Ion) from onset energy of endothermic reaction (84ARI/ARM, 85ELK/ARM, 86ARI/ARM). 0 K value.

ION / Neutral	Ionization potential eV	$\Delta_f H$(Ion) kcal/mol	$\Delta_f H$(Ion) kJ/mol	$\Delta_f H$(Neutral) kcal/mol	$\Delta_f H$(Neutral) kJ/mol	Neutral reference	CAS registry number
CH_2^+ / CH_2	10.396±.003	331 / *331*	1386 / *1386*	93 / *93*	390 / *390*	82TN270	60528-76-9

$\Delta_f H$(Ion) from appearance potential determination (83PLE/MAR).

ION / Neutral	Ionization potential eV	$\Delta_f H$(Ion) kcal/mol	$\Delta_f H$(Ion) kJ/mol	$\Delta_f H$(Neutral) kcal/mol	$\Delta_f H$(Neutral) kJ/mol	Neutral reference	CAS registry number
CH_2Br^+ / CH_2Br	(7.9)	(224)	(937)	42	174	82MCM/GOL	16519-97-4

Heat of formation of ion from appearance potential (11.35±0.02) in CH_2Br_2. Cited ionization potential is $\Delta_f H$(Ion) - $\Delta_f H$(Neutral). An experimental value of 8.61±0.01 eV has been reported for the ionization potential (84AND/DYK3).

ION / Neutral	Ionization potential eV	$\Delta_f H$(Ion) kcal/mol	$\Delta_f H$(Ion) kJ/mol	$\Delta_f H$(Neutral) kcal/mol	$\Delta_f H$(Neutral) kJ/mol	Neutral reference	CAS registry number
CH_2BrCl^+ / CH_2ClBr	10.77±0.01	259	1084	11±2	45±8	78KUD/KUD	74-97-5

IP from 77ROS/DRA, 81NOV/CVI3.

ION / Neutral	Ionization potential eV	$\Delta_f H$(Ion) kcal/mol	$\Delta_f H$(Ion) kJ/mol	$\Delta_f H$(Neutral) kcal/mol	$\Delta_f H$(Neutral) kJ/mol	Neutral reference	CAS registry number
$CH_2Br_2^+$ / CH_2Br_2	10.50±0.02	242	1013	0±1	0±4	EST	74-95-3

See also: 82VON/ASB.

ION / Neutral	Ionization potential eV	$\Delta_f H$(Ion) kcal/mol	$\Delta_f H$(Ion) kJ/mol	$\Delta_f H$(Neutral) kcal/mol	$\Delta_f H$(Neutral) kJ/mol	Neutral reference	CAS registry number
CH_2Cl^+ / CH_2Cl	(8.6)	(229.2) / *(229.9)*	(959.0) / *(962.1)*	31	130	83WEI/BEN	6806-86-6

$\Delta_f H$(Ion) from appearance potential determinations. Cited ionization potential is difference in heats of formation of ion and radical; an experimental determination of the ionization potential gives 8.75±0.01 eV(84AND/DYK) which would correspond to a radical heat of formation of 27 kcal/mol, 115 kJ/mol.

Table 1. Positive Ion Table - Continued

ION Neutral	Ionization potential eV	$\Delta_f H$(Ion) kcal/mol	$\Delta_f H$(Ion) kJ/mol	$\Delta_f H$(Neutral) kcal/mol	$\Delta_f H$(Neutral) kJ/mol	Neutral reference	CAS registry number
CH_2ClF^+							
CH_2FCl	11.71±0.01	208	869	−62±2	−261±8	78KUD/KUD2	593-70-4
	IP from 84AND/DYK.						
$CH_2Cl_2^+$							
CH_2Cl_2	11.32±0.01	238	997	−22.9±0.2	−95.7±0.8	77PED/RYL	75-09-2
		240	1003	−21.2	−88.8		
	See also: 82VON/ASB, 81KIM/KAT.						
$CH_2Cl_4Si^+$							
Cl_3SiCH_2Cl	(10.7)	(116)	(486)	−130	−546	*EST	1558-25-4
	IP is onset of photoelectron band (81ZYK/KHV).						
CH_2Co^+							
$CH_2=Co$		(290)	(1213)				
	$\Delta_f H$(Ion) from onset of endothermic reaction and photodissociation (81ARM/HAL, 81ARM/BEA2, 86HET/FRE). 0 K values.						
CH_2Cr^+							
$CH_2=Cr$		(292)	(1223)				
	$\Delta_f H$(Ion) from onset of endothermic reaction (86ELK/ARI). See also: 81ARM/HAL, 81HAL/ARM. 0 K values.						
CH_2F^+							
CH_2F	9.05±0.01	199	833	−8±2	−33±8	82MCM/GOL	3744-29-4
	IP from 84AND/DYK. $\Delta_f H$(Ion) evaluated from observed ion-molecule reactions (77LIA/AUS).						
$CH_2F_2^+$							
CH_2F_2	12.71	185	773	−108±2	−453±8	78KUD/KUD	75-10-5
	See also: 81BIE/ASB.						
$CH_2F_3^+$							
F_2CHFH		53	220				
	From proton affinity of CF_3H (RN 75-46-7). PA = 147 kcal/mol, 615 kJ/mol.						
$CH_2F_3O_3S^+$							
$CF_3SO_3H_2$		(−85)	(−356)				
	From proton affinity of CF_3SO_3H (RN 1493-13-6). PA = (169) kcal/mol, (707) kJ/mol.						
CH_2Fe^+							
$CH_2=Fe$		(292)	(1222)				
	$\Delta_f H$(Ion) from photodissociation onset to give Fe^+ (86HET/FRE). See also: 81ARM/HAL, 84JAC/JAC.						
$CH_2I_2^+$							
CH_2I_2	9.46±0.02	246	1031	28±5	118±21	78KUD/KUD	75-11-6
		249	1040	30	127		
CH_2Mn^+							
$CH_2=Mn$		(237)	(992)				65127-77-7
	$\Delta_f H$(Ion) from onset of endothermic reaction (81ARM/HAL). 0 K values.						

Table 1. Positive Ion Table - Continued

ION / Neutral	Ionization potential eV	$\Delta_f H$(Ion) kcal/mol	$\Delta_f H$(Ion) kJ/mol	$\Delta_f H$(Neutral) kcal/mol	$\Delta_f H$(Neutral) kJ/mol	Neutral reference	CAS registry number
CH_2N^+							
HCNH		226	947				

From proton affinity of HCN (RN 74-90-8) (PA = 171 kcal/mol, 717 kJ/mol) and HNC (RN 6914-07-4) (PA = 190 kcal/mol, 796 kJ/mol).

CNH_2		(265)	(1109)				

$\Delta_f H$(Ion) from appearance potential determinations (84BUR/HOL).

CH_2NO^+							
H_2NCO		167	700				

From proton affinity of HNCO (RN 75-13-8) (PA = 173 kcal/mol, 725 kJ/mol).

$CH_2N_2^+$							
CH_2N_2	8.999±0.001	263	1098	55±4	230±17	78VOG/WIL	334-88-3
H_2NCN	(10.4)	(272)	(1137)	32	134	77PED/RYL	420-04-2

IP is onset of photoelectron band.

(diazirine)	(10.3)	(301)	(1259)	63.3±2.7	264.8±11	72LAU/OKA	157-22-2

$CH_2N_4^+$							
(tetrazole)	(10.95)	(333)	(1392)	80±1	335±4	77PED/RYL	288-94-8

IP is onset of photoelectron band (82LEV/LIA, 81PAL/SIM).

CH_2Ni^+							
$CH_2=Ni$		(285)	(1193)				60187-22-6

$\Delta_f H$(Ion) from onset of endothermic reaction (81ARM/HAL). 0 K values.

CH_2O^+							
CH_2O	10.874±0.002	<u>224.8</u>	<u>940.5</u>	−26.0±0.2	−108.7±0.7	77PED/RYL	50-00-0
		<u>225.8</u>	<u>944.5</u>	−25.0	−104.7		

See also: 81BOM/DAN, 76GUY/CHU, 80VON/BIE, 84WAN/CAP, 81KIM/KAT.

HCOH		230	962				

$\Delta_f H$(Ion) from appearance potential measurement (83BUR/MOM).

$CH_2O_2^+$							
HCOOH	11.33±0.01	170.7	714.3	−90.5±0.1	−378.8±0.5	78CHA/ZWO	64-18-6

See also: 80VON/BIE, 81KIM/KAT.

$C(OH)_2$		175	732				71946-83-3

$\Delta_f H$(Ion) from appearance potential determinations (82BUR/HOL, 83BUR/MOM).

Table 1. Positive Ion Table - Continued

ION / Neutral	Ionization potential eV	$\Delta_f H$(Ion) kcal/mol	$\Delta_f H$(Ion) kJ/mol	$\Delta_f H$(Neutral) kcal/mol	$\Delta_f H$(Neutral) kJ/mol	Neutral reference	CAS registry number
CH_2S^+							
CH_2S	9.34±0.01	240	1006	25	105	82ROY/MCM	865-36-1

See also: 83ERM/AKO, 82KUT/EDW.

HCSH		(270)	(1130)				

$\Delta_f H$(Ion) from appearance potential determination (82KUT/EDW). 0 K values.

CH_2Se^+							
CH_2Se	(8.95)	(245)	(1024)	38	160	*EST	6596-50-5

IP from 84BOC/AYG.

CH_2Ti^+							
$CH_2=Ti$		(277)	(1158)				

$\Delta_f H$(Ion) from onset of endothermic reaction (86ELK/ARM). 0 K value.

CH_2V^+							
$CH_2=V$		(295)	(1234)				

$\Delta_f H$(Ion) from onset energy of endothermic reaction (84ARI/ARM, 85ELK/ARM, 86ARI/ARM). 0 K value.

CH_3^+							
CH_3	9.84±0.01	261.3±0.4	1093.3±1.7	34.8±0.3	145.8±1	81HEN/KNO	2229-07-4
		_262_	_1098_	_35.6_	_149.0_		

$\Delta_f H$(Ion) from appearance potential determinations (81TRA/MCL). See also: 83PLE/MAR.

$CH_3BBr_2^+$							
CH_3BBr_2	10.60	197	824	-48	-199	82HOL/SMI	17933-16-3

$CH_3BCl_2^+$							
CH_3BCl_2	(11.51)	(185)	(774)	-81	-337	82HOL/SMI	7318-78-7

$CH_3BF_2^+$							
CH_3BF_2	(12.54±0.03)	(90)	(377)	-199	-833	82HOL/SMI	373-64-8

CH_3BO^+							
BH_3CO	11.14±0.02	230	964	-27	-111	82TN270	13205-44-2
		232	970	_-25.0_	_-104.8_		

CH_3Br^+							
CH_3Br	10.541±0.003	234	979	-9.1±0.3	-38.1±1.3	84BIC/MIN	74-83-9
		238	994	_-5.5_	_-23.0_		

Cited IP leads to $CH_3Br^+(^2E_{3/2})$; formation of $CH_3Br^+(^2E_{1/2})$ requires 10.857 eV. IPs from 82BAI/CON,82LEV/LIA,77ROS/DRA,82VON/ASB,81HOL/FIN,84AND/DYK3,81KIM/KAT,77KAR/JAD.

CH_2BrH		(237)	(990)				

$\Delta_f H$(Ion) from appearance potential determination (83HOL/LOS2).

CH_3BrHg^+							
CH_3HgBr	(9.9)	(224)	(937)	-4±0.7	-18±3	77PED/RYL	506-83-2

IP is onset of photoelectron band.

Table 1. Positive Ion Table – Continued

ION Neutral	Ionization potential eV	$\Delta_f H$(Ion) kcal/mol	$\Delta_f H$(Ion) kJ/mol	$\Delta_f H$(Neutral) kcal/mol	$\Delta_f H$(Neutral) kJ/mol	Neutral reference	CAS registry number
CH_3Cd^+							
CH_3Cd		(213)	(891)				
\multicolumn{8}{l}{From appearance potential (9.69 eV) in $(CH_3)_2Cd$.}
CH_3Cl^+							
CH_3Cl	11.22±0.01	239	1000	−19.6±0.1	−82.0±0.5	79KUD/KUD	74-87-3
		241	1009	−17.5	−73.4		
\multicolumn{8}{l}{See also: 81KIM/KAT, 77KAR/JAD.}
CH_2ClH		(246)	(1029)				
\multicolumn{8}{l}{$\Delta_f H$(Ion) from appearance potential determination (83HOL/LOS2).}
CH_3ClHg^+							
CH_3HgCl	(10.5)	(230)	(962)	−12±0.7	−51±3	77PED/RYL	115-09-3
\multicolumn{8}{l}{IP is onset of photoelectron band (77ROS/DRA, 81BAI/CHI2).}
CH_3ClO^+							
CH_3OCl	(10.39±0.02)	(226)	(944)	−14	−58	*EST	593-78-2
\multicolumn{8}{l}{IP from 81COL/FRO.}
$CH_3ClO_2S^+$							
CH_3SO_2Cl	11.3	(173)	(722)	−88	−368	*EST	124-63-0
\multicolumn{8}{l}{IP is onset of photoelectron band.}
$CH_3Cl_2N^+$							
CH_3NCl_2	9.52	(264)	(1104)	44	185	*EST	7651-91-4
$CH_3Cl_2OP^+$							
CH_3POCl_2	10.91	119	497	−133±6	−556±25	77PED/RYL	676-97-1
\multicolumn{8}{l}{IP from 80ZVE/VIL, 82LEV/LIA.}
$CH_3Cl_2P^+$							
CH_3PCl_2	(9.5)	(168)	(703)	−51	−214	*EST	676-83-5
\multicolumn{8}{l}{IP is onset of photoelectron band.}
$CH_3Cl_3Si^+$							
CH_3SiCl_3	(11.36±0.03)	(131)	(547)	−131	−549	81BEL/PER	75-79-6
CH_3Co^+							
CH_3Co	(7.0±0.3)	(257)	(1075)	(96)	(400)	81ARM/BEA	76826-90-9
\multicolumn{8}{l}{$\Delta_f H$(Ion) from onset of endothermic reaction (81ARM/HAL). IP from 81ARM/BEA. 0 K values.}
CH_3Cr^+							
CH_3Cr	(7.2)	(257)	(1074)	90	375	86ELK/ARI	
\multicolumn{8}{l}{$\Delta_f H$(Ion) from onset of endothermic reaction (86ELK/ARI).}
\multicolumn{8}{l}{See also: 81ARM/HAL. 0 K values. IP is $\Delta_f H$(Ion) - $\Delta_f H$(Neutral).}
CH_3F^+							
CH_3F	12.47±0.02	228	956	−59	−247	85LIA/KAR	593-53-3
\multicolumn{8}{l}{See also: 81BIE/ASB, 81KIM/KAT, 77KAR/JAD.}

Table 1. Positive Ion Table - Continued

ION Neutral	Ionization potential eV	$\Delta_f H$(Ion) kcal/mol	$\Delta_f H$(Ion) kJ/mol	$\Delta_f H$(Neutral) kcal/mol	$\Delta_f H$(Neutral) kJ/mol	Neutral reference	CAS registry number
CH_3F^+							
CH_2FH		217	908				

$\Delta_f H$(Ion) from appearance potential determination (83HOL/LOS2).

$CH_3F_2^+$							
FCH_2FH		110	462				

From proton affinity of CH_2F_2 (RN 75-10-5). PA = 147 kcal/mol, 615 kJ/mol.

$CH_3F_2P^+$							
CH_3PF_2	(9.8)	(68)	(285)	-158	-661	*EST	753-59-3

IP is onset of photoelectron band.

$CH_3F_2Si^+$							
CH_3SiF_2		23	95				

From appearance potential (11.70±0.03) of ion in $(CH_3)_2SiF_2$.

$CH_3F_3Si^+$							
CH_3SiF_3	12.48±0.04	-8	-33	-296	-1237	71JANAF	373-74-0

CH_3Fe^+							
CH_3Fe	(8.1)	(257)	(1075)	71	298	86ELK/ARI	

$\Delta_f H$(Ion) from onset of endothermic reaction (86ELK/ARI). See also: 81ARM/HAL, 84JAC/JAC. IP is $\Delta_f H$(Ion) - $\Delta_f H$(Neutral). 0 K values.

CH_3Hg^+							
CH_3Hg		221	926				
		225	942				

From appearance potential (10.10±0.02 eV) in $(CH_3)_2Hg$.

CH_3HgI^+							
CH_3HgI	(9.0)	(213)	(891)	5.3±0.4	22.4±1.9	77PED/RYL	143-36-2

IP is onset of photoelectron band.

CH_3I^+							
CH_3I	9.538	223.6	935.7	3.7±0.2	15.4±0.9	77PED/RYL	74-88-4
		226	945	6	25		

See: 78LIA/AUS, 83POW, 81KIM/KAT, 77KAR/JAD.

CH_3Mn^+							
CH_3Mn		(223)	(934)				

$\Delta_f H$(Ion) from onset of endothermic reaction (86ARM). See also: 81ARM/HAL. 0 K values.

$CH_3Mn_2^+$							
CH_3Mn_2		(261)	(1090)				

$\Delta_f H$(Ion) from onset of endothermic reaction (86ARM). 0 K values.

CH_3N^+							
$CH_2=NH$	(9.9)	(260)	(1090)	32	135	78DEF/HEH	2053-29-4

IP is onset of photoelectron band (82SCH/SCH, 86WER).

$HCNH_2$		258	1079				35430-17-2

$\Delta_f H$(Ion) from appearance potential determinations (84BUR/HOL).

Table 1. Positive Ion Table – Continued

ION / Neutral	Ionization potential eV	$\Delta_f H$(Ion) kcal/mol	$\Delta_f H$(Ion) kJ/mol	$\Delta_f H$(Neutral) kcal/mol	$\Delta_f H$(Neutral) kJ/mol	Neutral reference	CAS registry number
CH_3NO^+							
$HCONH_2$	10.16±0.06	190	794	−44	−186	69BEN/CRU	75-12-7

See also: 81KIM/KAT, 81ASB/SVE, 81HEN/ISA.

$CH_2=NOH$	10.11	(240)	(1004)	7	29	*EST	75-17-2

IP is onset of photoelectron band (82FRO/LAU, 84DOG/POU).

CH_3NO	9.3	231	967	17±0.7	70±3	73BAT/MIL	865-40-7

IP is onset of photoelectron band (82CHO/FRO, 82FRO/LAU).

ION / Neutral	IP eV	$\Delta_f H$(Ion) kcal/mol	kJ/mol	$\Delta_f H$(Neutral) kcal/mol	kJ/mol	Neutral reference	CAS
$CH_3NO_2^+$							
CH_3NO_2	11.02±0.04	236	987	−17.9±0.2	−74.8±1.0	77PED/RYL	75-52-5

See also: 83GIL/HSI, 83OGD/SHA, 81ALL/MIG, 81ASB/SVE, 81KIM/KAT.

CH_3ONO	10.38±0.03	223	935	−15.9±0.2	−66.5±0.9	74BAT/CHR	624-91-9

IP from 83GIL/HSI, 83GIL/HSI2, 80MEI/HSI, 83OGD/SHA.

$CH_3NO_3^+$							
CH_3ONO_2	(11.53±0.01)	(237)	(990)	−29±1	−122±4	77PED/RYL	598-58-3

CH_3NS^+							
$HCSNH_2$	8.69	(210)	(877)	9	39	*EST	115-08-2

See also: 81HEN/ISA.

$CH_3N_2^+$							
CH_3N_2		216	902				

From appearance energy and from proton affinity of CH_2N_2 (RN 334-88-3)(PA = 205 kcal/mol, 858 kJ/mol).

H_2NCNH		(234)	(978)				

From core binding energy of isoelectronic CH_3CN (84BEA/EYE). PA of H_2NCN = (164) kcal/mol, (686) kJ/mol.

$CH_3N_3^+$							
CH_3N_3	9.81±0.02	293	1227	67	280	69BEN/CRU	624-90-8

See also: 81BOC/DAM.

CH_3Ni^+							
CH_3Ni		(265)	(1109)				63583-16-4

$\Delta_f H$(Ion) from onset of endothermic reaction (81ARM/HAL, 86ELK/ARI). 0 K values.

CH_3O^+							
CH_2OH	7.56±0.01	168	703	−6.2±1.5	−25.9±6	82MCM/GOL	17691-31-5

$\Delta_f H$(Ion) from proton affinity of formaldehyde. PA = 171.7 kcal/mol, 718 kJ/mol.
$\Delta_f H$(Ion) from appearance potential measurements is 169 kcal/mol, 709 kJ/mol.
(82MAC, 83HOL/LOS2, 84LOS/HOL). IP from 84DYK/ELL2.

CH_3O	(8.6)	(201)	(842)	3.7±0.7	15.5±2.9	74BAT/CHR	2143-68-2

The reaction: $HCO^+ + H_2 \rightarrow CH_3O^+$ is 3.9 kcal/mol, 16.3 kJ/mol, exothermic (77HIR/KEB). A value of 247 kcal/mol, 1034 kJ/mol, has been reported for $^3CH_3O^+$ (84BUR/HOL2) in agreement with 87FER/RON. IP is $\Delta_f H$(Ion) − $\Delta_f H$(Neutral).

Table 1. Positive Ion Table – Continued

ION Neutral	Ionization potential eV	$\Delta_f H$(Ion) kcal/mol	$\Delta_f H$(Ion) kJ/mol	$\Delta_f H$(Neutral) kcal/mol	$\Delta_f H$(Neutral) kJ/mol	Neutral reference	CAS registry number
$CH_3O_2^+$							
$HC(OH)_2$		96	403				

From proton affinity of HCOOH (RN 64-18-6) and appearance potential determinations (84HOL/LOS). PA = 178.8 kcal/mol, 748 kJ/mol.

CH_2OOH		(185)	(774)				

$\Delta_f H$(Ion) from 87FER/RON.

$CH_3O_3^+$							
$C(OH)_3$		37	155				

$\Delta_f H$(Ion) from appearance potential determinations (82HOL/LOS2).

CH_3S^+							
CH_2SH		206	862				20879-50-9
		208	870				

Heat of formation of ion from appearance potential determinations (83BUT/BAE, 82LEV/LIA). See also: 83ERM/AKO, 83HOL/LOS2.

CH_3S	(8.06±0.1)	(215)	(901)	29.4±2.1	123.0±8.8	82MCM/GOL	7175-75-9

Collisional activation results (79DIL/MCL) indicate that this structure is a stable triplet; ab initio calculations predict its heat of formation to be ~10 kcal/mol above that of CH_2SH^+, in agreement with the experimentally obtained value given here.

$CH_3S_2^+$							
CH_3SS	(8.0)	200	835	16	69	86HAW/GRI	
		201	839				

$\Delta_f H$(Ion) from appearance potential determination (83BUT/BAE).
IP is $\Delta_f H$(Ion) - $\Delta_f H$(Neutral).

CH_3Sc^+							
CH_3Sc	(5.1)	(212)	(887)	93	391	86SUN/ARI	

$\Delta_f H$(Ion) from onset of endothermic reaction (84TOL/BEA).
See also: 87SUN/ARI. IP is $\Delta_f H$(Ion) - $\Delta_f H$(Neutral). 0 K values.

CH_3Se^+							
CH_2SeH		219	916				

From proton affinity of CH_2Se (RN 6596-50-5)(85KAR). PA = 185 kcal/mol, 774 kJ/mol.

CH_3Ti^+							
CH_3Ti	(6.3)	(248)	(1039)	(102)	(426)	86ELK/ARI	

$\Delta_f H$(Ion) from onset of endothermic reaction (86ELK/ARM).
IP is $\Delta_f H$(Ion) - $\Delta_f H$(Neutral). 0 K values.

CH_3V^+							
CH_3V	(6.6)	(263)	(1102)	111	463	86ARI/ARM	

$\Delta_f H$(Ion) from onset energy of endothermic reaction (84ARI/ARM, 85ELK/ARM, 86ARI/ARM). IP is $\Delta_f H$(Ion) - $\Delta_f H$(Neutral). 0 K values.

Table 1. Positive Ion Table - Continued

ION / Neutral	Ionization potential eV	$\Delta_f H$(Ion) kcal/mol	$\Delta_f H$(Ion) kJ/mol	$\Delta_f H$(Neutral) kcal/mol	$\Delta_f H$(Neutral) kJ/mol	Neutral reference	CAS registry number
CH_3Xe^+							
CH_3Xe		(210)	(877)				

$\Delta_f H$(Ion) derived from results of 86HOV/MCM.

CH_3Zn^+							
CH_3Zn	(7.2)	(213)	(890)	(47)	(197)		

From appearance potential (10.22±0.02 eV) in $(CH_3)_2Zn$.
Value from onset of endothermic reaction (86GEO/ARM) is in agreement.
IP is $\Delta_f H$(Ion) - $\Delta_f H$(Neutral). 0 K values.

CH_4^+							
CH_4	12.51	271	1132	-17.8±0.1	-74.5±0.4	77PED/RYL	74-82-8
		272	1140	-16.0	-66.8		

See also: 83PLE/MAR, 81KIM/KAT, 84CHA/HIL.

CH_4Br^+							
CH_3BrH		191	800				

From proton affinity of CH_3Br (RN 74-83-9). PA = 165.7 kcal/mol, 693 kJ/mol.

CH_4Cl^+							
CH_3ClH		183	767				

From proton affinity of CH_3Cl (RN 74-87-3). PA = ~163 kcal/mol, ~682 kJ/mol.

CH_4ClN^+							
CH_3NHCl	(9.19±0.02)	(230)	(964)	18	77	*EST	6154-14-9

$CH_4Cl_2Si^+$							
CH_3SiHCl_2	(11.47)	(168)	(705)	-96±2	-402±8	81BEL/PER	20156-50-7

CH_4F^+							
CH_3FH		(162)	(678)				

From proton affinity of CH_3F (RN 593-53-3). PA = 145 kcal/mol, 605 kJ/mol
(86MCM/KEB, 85MCM/KEB3).

CH_4I^+							
CH_3IH		(198)	(830)				

From proton affinity of CH_3I (RN 74-88-4). PA = ~171 kcal/mol, ~715 kJ/mol.

CH_4N^+							
CH_2NH_2	6.1	(178)	(745)	38±2	159±8	81GRI/LOS	54088-53-8

$\Delta_f H$(Ion) from appearance potential determinations (81LOS/LAM).
See also: 81GRI/LOS, 84LOS/HOL, 82MAC, 83BUR/CAS.

CH_3NH	(6.7)	(199)	(833)	43.6±3.0	182.4±12.5	78SEN/FRA	49784-84-1

$\Delta_f H$(Ion) from appearance potential determinations (84LOS/HOL). IP is $\Delta_f H$(Ion) - $\Delta_f H$(Neutral).

CH_4NO^+							
$HC(OH)NH_2$		123	514				

From proton affinity of $HCONH_2$ (RN 75-12-7). PA = 198.4 kcal/mol, 830 kJ/mol.

Table 1. Positive Ion Table - Continued

ION / Neutral	Ionization potential eV	$\Delta_f H$(Ion) kcal/mol	$\Delta_f H$(Ion) kJ/mol	$\Delta_f H$(Neutral) kcal/mol	$\Delta_f H$(Neutral) kJ/mol	Neutral reference	CAS registry number
$CH_4NO_2^+$							
CH_3NOOH		169	705				
From proton affinity of CH_3NO_2 (RN 75-52-5). PA = 179.2 kcal/mol, 750 kJ/mol.							
CH_3ONHO		157	658				
From proton affinity of CH_3ONO (RN 624-91-9). PA = 192.5 kcal/mol, 805 kJ/mol.							
$CH_4N_2^+$							
(E)-$CH_3N=NH$	8.8±0.1	(248)	(1037)	45±2	188±8	*EST	26981-93-1
$CH_4N_2O^+$							
$(NH_2)_2CO$	9.7	165	690	−58.8±0.5	−245.9±2.1	77PED/RYL	57-13-6
See also: 82BIE/ASB.							
$CH_4N_2S^+$							
$(NH_2)_2CS$	7.9	188	785	5±0.5	23±2	82TOR/SAB	62-56-6
CH_4O^+							
CH_3OH	10.85±0.01	202.0	845.3	−48.2±0.1	−201.6±0.2	77PED/RYL	67-56-1
		204.6	856.2	−45.6	−190.7		
See also: 82MIS/POK, 80VON/BIE, 82ALL/MIG, 84BOW/MAC, 81KIM/KAT, 80BAC/MOU, 77KAR/JAD.							
CH_2OH_2		195±2	815±8				25765-84-8
$\Delta_f H$(Ion) from appearance potential measurements (82HOL/LOS).							
CH_4S^+							
CH_3SH	9.44±0.005	212.3	888.2	−5.5±0.1	−22.9±0.6	77PED/RYL	74-93-1
		214.8	899.0	−2.9	−12.1		
IP from 83BUT/BAE, 81KIM/KAT, 82KUT/EDW.							
CH_2SH_2		219	916				63933-47-1
		221	925				
$\Delta_f H$(Ion) from appearance potential determination (83HOL/LOS2).							
$CH_4S_2^+$							
$CH_2(SH)_2$	(9.42)	(225)	(942)	8±2	33±8	78BEN	6725-64-0
CH_4Sc^+							
CH_3ScH		(214)	(895)				
$\Delta_f H$(Ion) from onset of endothermic reaction (84TOL/BEA). See also: 86ELK/ARI.							
CH_5^+							
CH_5		216	905				
From proton affinity of CH_4. (RN 74-82-8) See also: 85MCM/KEB. PA = 131.6 kcal/mol, 551. kJ/mol.							
CH_5As^+							
CH_3AsH_2	(8.5)	(207)	(868)	11	48	*EST	593-52-2
IP is onset of photoelectron band (82ELB/DIE).							

Table 1. Positive Ion Table - Continued

ION / Neutral	Ionization potential eV	$\Delta_f H$(Ion) kcal/mol	$\Delta_f H$(Ion) kJ/mol	$\Delta_f H$(Neutral) kcal/mol	$\Delta_f H$(Neutral) kJ/mol	Neutral reference	CAS registry number
CH_5N^+							
CH_2NH_3		(≤201)	(≤841)				

The reaction c-$C_3H_6^+$ + NH_3 → $CH_2NH_3^+$ + C_2H_4 is at least 15 kcal/mol exothermic (84LIA/BUC). See also: 83HOL/LOS2, 72GRO.

CH_3NH_2	8.97±0.02	201	842	−5.5±0.1	−23.0±0.4	77PED/RYL	74-89-5

See also: 81KIM/KAT, 82BIE/ASB, 82ELB/DIE.

CH_5NO^+							
CH_3ONH_2	9.55	(214)	(895)	−6±2	−26±8	69BEN/CRU	67-62-9

IP from 83MOL/PIK. See also: 81KIM/KAT.

CH_3NHOH	(9.0)	(196)	(818)	−12±2	−50±8	69BEN/CRU	593-77-1

IP is onset of photoelectron band.

$CH_5N_3^+$							
$(NH_2)_2C=NH$	(9.10±0.05)	(218)	(910)	8	32	82JOS	113-00-8
CH_5O^+							
CH_3OH_2		136	567				

From proton affinity of CH_3OH (RN 67-56-1). PA = 181.9 kcal/mol, 761 kJ/mol.

CH_5P^+							
CH_3PH_2	9.12±0.07	(206)	(862)	−4	−18	*EST	593-54-4

See also: 82COW/KEM, 82ELB/DIE.

CH_5S^+							
CH_3SH_2		173	723				

From proton affinity of CH_3SH (RN 74-93-1). PA = 187.4 kcal/mol, 784 kJ/mol.

CH_6N^+							
CH_3NH_3	(4.3±0.1)	(146)	(611)				

$\Delta_f H$(Ion) from proton affinity of CH_3NH_2 (RN 74-89-5). PA = 214.1 kcal/mol, 896 kJ/mol.
IP estimated from neutralized ion-beam spectroscopy data (85JEO/RAK).

$CH_6N_2^+$							
CH_3NHNH_2	7.67±0.02	199	835	22.6±0.1	94.6±0.6	77PED/RYL	60-34-4

IP from charge transfer equilibrium constant determinations (84MAU/NEL) is in agreement. See also: 81KIM/KAT.

CH_6P^+							
CH_3PH_3		158	658				

From proton affinity of CH_3PH_2 (RN 593-54-4). PA = 204.1 kcal/mol, 854 kJ/mol.

CH_6Si^+							
CH_3SiH_3	10.7	240	1003	−7±1	−29±4	86DON/WAL	992-94-9
$CH_7N_2^+$							
$CH_3NH_2NH_2$		(174)	(729)				

From proton affinity of CH_3NHNH_2 (RN 60-34-4). PA = (214.1) kcal/mol, (896) kJ/mol.

Table 1. Positive Ion Table – Continued

ION / Neutral	Ionization potential eV	$\Delta_f H$(Ion) kcal/mol	kJ/mol	$\Delta_f H$(Neutral) kcal/mol	kJ/mol	Neutral reference	CAS registry number
CH_8BN^+							
$CH_3NH_2BH_3$	(9.66±0.01)	(210)	(878)	−13±1	−54±4	80TEL/RAB	1722-33-4
CIN^+							
ICN	10.87±0.02	305	1274	53.9	225.5	82TN270	506-78-5
		305	1275	54.0	226.1		
CI_4^+							
CI_4	8.95	142	596	−64	−268	78KUD/KUD	507-25-5
	IP is onset of photoelectron band (82JON/DEL).						
CIr^+							
IrC	(9.5±1)	(400)	(1670)	180	753	79HUB/HER	12385-37-4
	0 K values.						
CKN^+							
KCN	(9.3±0.3)	(236)	(988)	22	91	82TN270	151-50-8
		(236)	(987)	21	90		
CN^+							
CN	(14.09)	(428.9)	(1794.6)	104.0±2	435.1±10	85JANAF	57-12-5
		(429.3)	(1796.3)	104.4±2	436.8±10		
	$\Delta_f H$(Ion) from appearance potential measurements. IP cited is $\Delta_f H$(Ion)-$\Delta_f H$(Neutral).						
CNO^+							
NCO	(11.76±0.01)	(308)	(1289)	37±3	154±14	70OKA	
	IP from 83DYK/JON.						
CN_2O^+							
ONCN	10.93	300.9	1259.0	48.85±0.03	204.4±0.1	84NAD/REI	4343-68-4
	IP from 81JON/MOO. See also: 81KIM/KAT.						
CN_4^+							
$N\equiv CN_3$	(≤10.98±0.02)	(≤361)	(≤1512)	108±5	453±20	69OKA/MEL	764-05-6
CO^+							
CO	14.0139	<u>296.74</u>	<u>1241.59</u>	−26.42	−110.53	82TN270	630-08-0
		<u>295.97</u>	<u>1238.32</u>	−27.20	−113.80		
	See also: 81KIM/KAT.						
COS^+							
COS	11.1736±0.0015	224	936	−34	−142	77PED/RYL	463-58-1
		224	936	−34	−142		
	Cited ionization potential corresponds to formation of $COS^+(^2\Pi_{3/2})$. Formation of $COS^+(^2\Pi_{1/2})$ requires 11.2204±0.0015 eV. IP from 81ONO/OSU, 80DEL/HUB.						
$COSe^+$							
COSe	10.36±0.01	(222)	(928)	−17	−72	*EST	1603-84-5

Table 1. Positive Ion Table - Continued

ION / Neutral	Ionization potential eV	$\Delta_f H$(Ion) kcal/mol	$\Delta_f H$(Ion) kJ/mol	$\Delta_f H$(Neutral) kcal/mol	$\Delta_f H$(Neutral) kJ/mol	Neutral reference	CAS registry number
CO_2^+							
CO_2	13.773±0.002	223.6	935.4	−94.05	−393.51	82TN270	124-38-9
		223.7	935.7	−93.96	−393.14		
See also: 81KIM/KAT.							
CP^+							
CP	(10.5±0.5)	(365)	(1529)	123	516	79HUB/HER	12326-85-1
CRh^+							
CRh	(8.9±0.5)	(370)	(1550)	165±1	692±4	84SHI/GIN	12127-42-3
0 K values. See also: 81HAQ/GIN.							
CS^+							
CS	11.33±0.01	327	1368	64	267		2944-05-0
		324	1356	63	262		
Heat of formation of ion from appearance potentials in CS_2 of 13.64±0.02 eV (to give $CS^+ + S^-$) and 15.75±0.02 eV (to give $CS^+ + S$). $\Delta_f H$(Neutral) = $\Delta_f H$(Ion) - IP, in good agreement with 79HUB/HER.							
CS_2^+							
CS_2	10.0685±0.0020	260	1088	28±0.2	117±1	77PED/RYL	75-15-0
		260	1088	28	117		
See also: 81KIM/KAT.							
CSe_2^+							
CSe_2	9.258±0.0002	275	1149	61±5	256±20	82PIL/SKI	506-80-9
CSi_2^+							
Si_2C	(9.2±0.4)	(344)	(1440)	132	552	82TN270	12070-04-1
		(343)	(1437)	131	549		
CV^+							
CV		(360)	(1506)				
$\Delta_f H$(Ion) from onset energy of endothermic reaction (84ARI/ARM, 85ELK/ARM). 0 K value.							
C_2^+							
C_2	12.11	478	1998	198.8	831.9	79HUB/HER	12070-15-4
		476	1992	196.8	823.4		
IP from 79HUB/HER.							
C_2BrI^+							
BrC≡CI	(9.34)	(276.56)	(1157.15)	61.18	255.98	84DEW/HEA	26395-29-9
$C_2Br_2^+$							
BrC≡CBr	9.67	285	1192	61.8	258.6	83DEW/HEA	624-61-3
$C_2Br_2F_4^+$							
$(CF_2Br)_2$	(11.1)	(67)	(282)	−189±1	−789±4	83KOL/PAP	124-73-2
IP is onset of photoelectron band.							

Table 1. Positive Ion Table - Continued

ION / Neutral	Ionization potential eV	$\Delta_f H$(Ion) kcal/mol	$\Delta_f H$(Ion) kJ/mol	$\Delta_f H$(Neutral) kcal/mol	$\Delta_f H$(Neutral) kJ/mol	Neutral reference	CAS registry number
$C_2Br_2O_2^+$							
BrCOCOBr	(10.49±0.1)	(180)	(752)	−62	−260	*EST	15219-34-8
C_2Ce^+							
C_2Ce	(5.6±0.5)	(265)	(1110)	136	570	82TN270	12012-32-7
		(265)	*(1109)*	*136*	*569*		
$C_2ClF_3^+$							
C_2F_3Cl	9.81±0.03	(89)	(374)	−137±2	−573±8	77PED/RYL	79-38-9
		(90)	*(377)*	*−136*	*−570*		
$C_2ClF_5^+$							
CF_3CF_2Cl	(12.6)	(23)	(98)	−267±1	−1118±4	81BUC/FOR	76-15-3
	IP is onset of photoelectron band.						
C_2ClI^+							
$ClC\equiv CI$	(9.44)	(271.94)	(1137.79)	54.25	226.98	84DEW/HEA	25604-71-1
$C_2Cl_2^+$							
$ClC\equiv CCl$	10.09	283	1183	50±10	209±42	71JANAF	7572-29-4
		282	*1180*	*49±10*	*205±42*		
	See: 81BOC/RIE, 82MAI/THO, 83KLA/MAI.						
$C_2Cl_2F_2^+$							
$CF_2=CCl_2$	9.65±0.03	142	593	−81±3	−338±11	83KOL/PAP	79-35-6
$CFCl=CFCl$	(10.2±0.1)	(157)	(657)	−78	−327	82TN270	598-88-9
$C_2Cl_2F_4^+$							
$(CF_2Cl)_2$	12.2	60	252	−221±1	−925±4	83KOL/PAP	76-14-2
$C_2Cl_2O^+$							
$Cl_2C=C=O$	9.0	(191)	(799)	−16	−69	*EST	4591-28-0
	IP is onset of photoelectron band (81BOC/HIR, 82LEV/LIA).						
$C_2Cl_2O_2^+$							
$(COCl)_2$	10.91±0.05	173	724	−79±1	−329±5	77PED/RYL	79-37-8
	See also: 81KIM/KAT.						
$C_2Cl_3F_3^+$							
CF_3CCl_3	11.5	92	385	−173±2	−725±10	83KOL/PAP	354-58-5
	IP is onset of photoelectron band (81DUM/DUP). See also: 77ROS/DRA.						
$CFCl_2CF_2Cl$	11.99±0.02	103	430	−174±0.7	−727±3	83KOL/PAP	76-13-1
$C_2Cl_3N^+$							
CCl_3CN	11.89	(294)	(1229)	20	82	*EST	545-06-2
	IP from 83MOL/PIK2.						

Table 1. Positive Ion Table - Continued

ION / Neutral	Ionization potential eV	$\Delta_f H$(Ion) kcal/mol	$\Delta_f H$(Ion) kJ/mol	$\Delta_f H$(Neutral) kcal/mol	$\Delta_f H$(Neutral) kJ/mol	Neutral reference	CAS registry number
$C_2Cl_4^+$							
C_2Cl_4	9.32	212	888	−3±0.5	−11±2	83KOL/PAP	127-18-4
		212	889	−2	−10		
See also: 82VON/ASB, 81KIM/KAT.							
$C_2Cl_4F_2^+$							
$CFCl_2CFCl_2$	11.3	135	563	−126±2	−527±10	83KOL/PAP	76-12-0
IP is onset of photoelectron band (81DUM/DUP).							
$C_2Cl_4O^+$							
CCl_3COCl	(11.0)	(198)	(828)	−56±2	−236±9	77PED/RYL	76-02-8
IP is onset of photoelectron band (81KIM/KAT).							
$C_2Cl_6^+$							
CCl_3CCl_3	11.1	220	921	−36±1	−150±5	83KOL/PAP	67-72-1
IP is onset of photoelectron band (81KIM/KAT). See also: 82LEV/LIA.							
$C_2F_2^+$							
FC≡CF	11.18	(263)	(1100)	5±5	21±21	71JANAF	689-99-6
See also: 81BIE/ASB.							
$C_2F_2O_2^+$							
FCOCOF	(12.20±0.02)	(107)	(449)	−174	−728	*EST	359-40-0
$C_2F_3^+$							
C_2F_3	(10.2)	(189)	(791)	−45.9±2.0	−192.0±8.4	83SPY/SAU	
From appearance potentials of 15.84±0.02 eV in C_2F_4 and 15.4±0.1 eV in C_2F_3Cl. IP is $\Delta_f H$(Ion) - $\Delta_f H$(Neutral).							
$C_2F_3N^+$							
CF_3CN	13.86	200	837	−119.4±0.3	−499.8±1.2	77PED/RYL	353-85-5
IP from 81ASB/SVE. See also: 83MOL/PIK2.							
$C_2F_4^+$							
C_2F_4	10.12±0.02	75	316	−158±0.7	−659±3	83KOL/PAP	116-14-3
		76	319	−157	−657		
See also: 81BIE/VON, 81BIE/ASB.							
$C_2F_5^+$							
C_2F_5		(0)	(0)	−213±1	−893±4	82MCM/GOL	3369-48-0
Appearance potentials of this ion in C_2F_6 (15.46 eV), C_2F_5I (11.71 eV); C_3F_8 (13.32 eV), and n-C_4F_{10} (13.05 eV) lead to estimated values for the heat of formation of 15 kcal/mol, 5 kcal/mol, -5 kcal/mol and -14 kcal/mol, respectively. See: 80ING/HAN.							
$C_2F_5I^+$							
C_2F_5I	(10.66±0.1)	(6)	(25)	−240±1	−1004±4	81BUC/FOR	354-64-3

Table 1. Positive Ion Table - Continued

ION / Neutral	Ionization potential eV	$\Delta_f H$(Ion) kcal/mol	$\Delta_f H$(Ion) kJ/mol	$\Delta_f H$(Neutral) kcal/mol	$\Delta_f H$(Neutral) kJ/mol	Neutral reference	CAS registry number
$C_2F_6^+$							
C_2F_6	(13.4)	(−12)	(−50)	−321	−1343	75CHE/ROD	76-16-4
		(−10)	(−41)	−319	−1334		
IP is onset of photoelectron band. (80ING/HAN).							
$C_2F_7N^+$							
$(CF_3)_2NF$	(11.6)	(−10)	(−44)	−278	−1163	*EST	359-62-6
IP from 82BUR/PAW.							
C_2H^+							
C_2H	(11.7)	(405)	(1693)	135±1	565±4	82MCM/GOL	2122-48-7
		(404)	(1689)	134	560		
Heat of formation of ion from appearance potential measurement; IP given is $\Delta_f H$(Ion) − $\Delta_f H$(Neutral).							
C_2HBr^+							
$HC\equiv CBr$	10.31±0.02	297.0	1242.4	59.2	247.7	75OKA	593-61-3
IP from 77ALL/KLO. See also: 82LEV/LIA.							
$C_2HBrClF_3^+$							
$CF_3CHClBr$	11.0	86	361	−167±1	−700±4	83KOL/PAP	151-67-7
IP is onset of photoelectron band (81DUM/DUP).							
C_2HBrO^+							
$CHBr=C=O$	(≤9.10)	(≤207)	(≤868)	−2	−10	*EST	78957-22-9
IP from 81BOC/HIR.							
C_2HCl^+							
$HC\equiv CCl$	10.58±0.02	305	1276	61	255	70KLO/PAS	593-63-5
IP from 77ALL/KLO. See also: 84MAI/THO.							
$C_2HClF_2^+$							
$CF_2=CHCl$	9.80±0.04	150	629	−76	−316	82TN270	359-10-4
$C_2HClF_3O^+$							
$CF_3C(OH)Cl$		4	14				
From proton affinity of CF_3COCl (RN 354-32-5)(85MCM/KEB, 85MCM/KEB2). PA = 161.2 kcal/mol, 674 kJ/mol.							
C_2HClO^+							
$CHCl=C=O$	(≤9.3)	(≤201)	(≤840)	−14	−57	*EST	29804-89-5
See also: 81BOC/HIR.							
$C_2HCl_2F_3^+$							
CF_3CHCl_2	11.5	88	370	−177±2	−740±10	83KOL/PAP	306-83-2
IP is onset of photoelectron band (81DUM/DUP).							
$CF_2ClCHFCl$	≤12.00	≤104	≤434	−173±2	−724±10	83KOL/PAP	354-23-4

Table 1. Positive Ion Table – Continued

ION Neutral	Ionization potential eV	$\Delta_f H$(Ion) kcal/mol	 kJ/mol	$\Delta_f H$(Neutral) kcal/mol	 kJ/mol	Neutral reference	CAS registry number
$C_2HCl_3^+$							
C_2HCl_3	9.47±0.01	214	895	−4.5±0.7	−19±3	85PAP/KOL	79-01-6
		215	*898*	*−4*	*−16*		
See also: 82VON/ASB, 81KIM/KAT.							
$C_2HCl_3N^+$							
CCl_3CNH		209	876				
From proton affinity of CCl_3CN (RN 545-06-2). PA = 175.8 kcal/mol, 735.5 kJ/mol.							
$C_2HCl_3O^+$							
CCl_3CHO	(10.5)	(195)	(816)	−47	−197	82TN270	75-87-6
IP is onset of photoelectron band (81KIM/KAT). See also: 85GUI/PFI2.							
$CHCl_2COCl$	(11.0)	(196)	(820)	−58±2	−241±9	77PED/RYL	79-36-7
IP is onset of photoelectron band.							
$C_2HCl_5^+$							
$CHCl_2CCl_3$	(11.0)	(220)	(919)	−34±2	−143±7	78GUN/HEA	76-01-7
IP is onset of photoelectron band (81KIM/KAT).							
C_2HF^+							
$HC{\equiv}CF$	11.26	285	1193	26	107	80STA/VOG	2713-09-9
See also: 81BIE/ASB.							
$C_2HF_3^+$							
C_2HF_3	10.14	117	487	−117±2	−491±8	77PED/RYL	359-11-5
See also: 81BIE/VON, 81BIE/ASB.							
$C_2HF_3N^+$							
CF_3CNH		82	343				
From proton affinity of CF_3CN (RN 353-85-5) (85MCM/KEB, 85MCM/KEB2). PA = 164.3 kcal/mol, 687. kJ/mol.							
$C_2HF_3O_2^+$							
CF_3COOH	11.46	18	75	−246.3±0.3	−1030.7±1	77PED/RYL	76-05-1
See also: 81ASB/SVE.							
$C_2HF_4O^+$							
$CF_3C(OH)F$				−44	−182		
From proton affinity of CF_3COF (RN 354-34-7). PA = 160.2 kcal/mol, 670 kJ/mol.							
C_2HN^+							
$HCCN$		(366)	(1531)				
$\Delta_f H$(Ion) from appearance potential determinations. See also: 85HAR/MCI. 0 K values.							
$C_2HN_2^+$							
$NCCNH$		277	1161				
From proton affinity of $NCCN$ (RN 460-19-5) (87DEA/MAU). PA = 162 kcal/mol, 678 kJ/mol.							

Table 1. Positive Ion Table - Continued

ION / Neutral	Ionization potential eV	$\Delta_f H$(Ion) kcal/mol	$\Delta_f H$(Ion) kJ/mol	$\Delta_f H$(Neutral) kcal/mol	$\Delta_f H$(Neutral) kJ/mol	Neutral reference	CAS registry number
C_2HO^+							
HCCO	(9.5)	(262)	(1096)	42.4±2.1	177.4±8.8	*EST	51095-15-9
	Heat of formation from appearance potential determination (84LOS/HOL).						
	IP is $\Delta_f H$(Ion) - $\Delta_f H$(Neutral).						
C_2HV^+							
VC_2H		(303)	(1268)				
	$\Delta_f H$(Ion) from onset energy of endothermic reaction (84ARI/ARM, 85ELK/ARM). 0 K value.						
$C_2H_2^+$							
C_2H_2	11.400±0.002	<u>317.4</u>	<u>1327.9</u>	54.5±0.25	228.0±1	77PED/RYL	74-86-2
		<u>317.5</u>	<u>1328.5</u>	54.7	228.6		
	See also: 81KIM/KAT, 82HAY/IWA.						
$C_2H_2Br_2^+$							
(E)-CHBr=CHBr	9.51±0.04	(245)	(1024)	25	106	*EST	590-12-5
	An IP of 9.30±0.02 has also been reported (72CHA/FRO).						
(Z)-BrCH=CHBr	9.63±0.01	247	1035	25	106	*EST	590-11-4
	An IP of 9.32±0.02 eV has also been reported (72CHA/FRO).						
$CBr_2=CH_2$	9.78±0.01	(247)	(1034)	21	90	*EST	593-92-0
	See also: 82VON/ASB.						
$C_2H_2Br_2F_2^+$							
CF_2BrCH_2Br	10.83±0.01	147	614	−103±5	−431±20	83KOL/PAP	75-82-1
$C_2H_2ClN^+$							
CH_2ClCN	11.95±0.01	(296)	(1239)	21	86	*EST	107-14-2
$C_2H_2Cl_2^+$							
$CH_2=CCl_2$	9.79±0.04	226	947	0.5±0.2	2.3±0.7	77PED/RYL	75-35-4
		228	953	2.0	8.4		
	See also: 82VON/ASB, 81KIM/KAT.						
(Z)-CHCl=CHCl	9.66±0.01	224	936	1±0.2	4±1	83KOL/PAP	156-59-2
		225	942	2	10		
	See also: 82VON/ASB, 81KIM/KAT.						
(E)-CHCl=CHCl	9.65±0.02	224	937	1±0.2	6±1	83KOL/PAP	156-60-5
		225	942	3	11		
	See also: 82VON/ASB, 81KIM/KAT.						
$C_2H_2Cl_2F_2^+$							
CF_2ClCH_2Cl	≤11.8	≤142	≤596	−130±2	−543±10	83KOL/PAP	1649-08-7
	IP from 81DUM/DUP.						
$C_2H_2Cl_2O^+$							
$CHCl_2CHO$	10.5	(199)	(833)	−43±5	−180±20	*EST	79-02-7
	IP is onset of photoelectron band (81KIM/KAT).						

Table 1. Positive Ion Table - Continued

ION / Neutral	Ionization potential eV	$\Delta_f H$(Ion) kcal/mol	$\Delta_f H$(Ion) kJ/mol	$\Delta_f H$(Neutral) kcal/mol	$\Delta_f H$(Neutral) kJ/mol	Neutral reference	CAS registry number
$C_2H_2Cl_2O^+$							
$CH_2ClCOCl$	(11.0)	(195)	(815)	−59±2	−246±9	77PED/RYL	79-04-9
IP is onset of photoelectron band.							
$C_2H_2Cl_3O_2^+$							
$CCl_3C(OH)_2$		76	318				
From proton affinity of CCl_3COOH (RN 76-03-9)(PA = 183.5 kcal/mol, 768 kJ/mol).							
$C_2H_2Cl_4^+$							
CH_2ClCCl_3	(11.1)	(220)	(919)	−36±0.2	−152±1	83KOL/PAP	630-20-6
IP is onset of photoelectron band (81KIM/KAT).							
$(CHCl_2)_2$	(≤11.62)	(≤232)	(≤971)	−36±1	−150±5	77PED/RYL	79-34-5
IP from 81KIM/KAT.							
$C_2H_2F^+$							
CH_2CF		227	951				
From appearance potential of 13.56 eV in C_2H_3F in agreement with value from proton affinity of HCCF (PA = 165 kcal/mol, 689 kJ/mol). See also: 85HEI/BAR, 84BEA/EYE.							
$C_2H_2F_2^+$							
$CH_2=CF_2$	10.29±0.01	155	648	−82±2	−345±10	76WIL/LEB	75-38-7
		157	*655*	*−81*	*−338*		
See also: 81BIE/VON, 81BIE/ASB.							
(Z)-CHF=CHF	10.23	165	690	−71	−297	80STA/VOG	1630-77-9
See also: 81BIE/VON, 81BIE/ASB, 79JOC/LOH, 81MAI/THO2.							
(E)-CHF=CHF	10.21	165	692	−70	−293	80STA/VOG	1630-78-0
See also: 81BIE/VON, 81BIE/ASB, 79JOC/LOH.							
$C_2H_2F_3^+$							
CHF_2CHF		(79)	(332)				
From proton affinity of $CF_2=CHF$ (RN 359-11-5). PA = ~169 kcal/mol, ~707 kJ/mol.							
CF_3CH_2	(10.6±0.1)	(120)	(506)	−124±2	−517±8	82MCM/GOL	3248-58-6
$C_2H_2F_3I^+$							
CF_3CH_2I	9.998	75	316	−155±1	−649±4	83KOL/PAP	353-83-3
$C_2H_2F_3NO^+$							
CF_3CONH_2	(10.8)	(49)	(206)	−200	−836	*EST	354-38-1
IP from 81ASB/SVE.							
$C_2H_2F_3O^+$							
CF_3CHOH		12	49				
From proton affinity of CF_3CHO (RN 75-90-1). PA = 165.1 kcal/mol, 691 kJ/mol.							
$C_2H_2F_3O_2^+$							
$CF_3C(OH)_2$		−50	−208				
From proton affinity of CF_3COOH (RN 76-05-1). PA = 169.0 kcal/mol, 707 kJ/mol.							

Table 1. Positive Ion Table - Continued

ION / Neutral	Ionization potential eV	$\Delta_f H$(Ion) kcal/mol	$\Delta_f H$(Ion) kJ/mol	$\Delta_f H$(Neutral) kcal/mol	$\Delta_f H$(Neutral) kJ/mol	Neutral reference	CAS registry number
$C_2H_2I_2^+$							
(Z)-CHI=CHI	(8.6)	(248)	(1037)	49.5±0.3	207.2±1.1	77PED/RYL	590-26-1
	IP is onset of photoelectron band.						
(E)-CHI=CHI	(8.6)	(248)	(1037)	49.5±0.3	207.2±1.1	77PED/RYL	590-27-2
	IP is onset of photoelectron band.						
$C_2H_2N^+$							
CH_2CN	(10.0)	(290)	(1214)	59±2	245±10	82MCM/GOL	2932-82-3
	$\Delta_f H$(Ion) from appearance potential measurements (77ROS/DRA, 85HAR/MCI)						
	IP cited is $\Delta_f H$(Ion)-$\Delta_f H$(Neutral). See also: 82ALL/MIG.						
$C_2H_2N_2Se^+$	(8.9)	(290)	(1212)	84	353	*EST	26223-16-5
	IP from 80BOC/AYG, 82LEV/LIA.						
$C_2H_2N_4^+$	(9.14)	(322)	(1346)	111	464	82JOS	290-96-0
$C_2H_2O^+$							
HC≡COH		247	1033				
	$\Delta_f H$(Ion) from appearance potential determination (86BAA/WEI).						
CH_2CO	9.61±0.02	210.2	879.6	−11.4±0.6	−47.7±2.5	71NUT/LAU	463-51-4
		210.9	*882.7*	*−10.7*	*−44.6*		
	See also: 81BOC/HIR.						
$C_2H_2O_2^+$							
$(CHO)_2$	10.1	182	763	−50.6±0.2	−211.9±0.8	77PED/RYL	107-22-2
	IP is onset of photoelectron band (80VON/BIE, 81KIM/KAT).						
$C_2H_2O_4^+$							
HOOCCOOH	(10.8)	(74)	(310)	−175±0.7	−732±3	77PED/RYL	144-62-7
	IP is onset of photoelectron band.						
$C_2H_2S^+$							
$CH_2=C=S$	(8.77)	(242)	(1011)	39	165	*EST	18282-77-4
		(234)	*(979)*				
	Cited IP is onset of photoelectron band (77ROS/SOL). Heat of formation of ion from appearance potential in CH_3SSCH_3 (83BUT/BAE). $\Delta_f H$(Neutral) is ($\Delta_f H$(Ion) - IP).						

Table 1. Positive Ion Table - Continued

ION Neutral	Ionization potential eV	$\Delta_f H$(Ion) kcal/mol	 kJ/mol	$\Delta_f H$(Neutral) kcal/mol	 kJ/mol	Neutral reference	CAS registry number
$C_2H_2S_2^+$							
(structure: 4-membered ring with two S)	(8.5)	(258)	(1080)	62	260	*EST	7092-01-5
IP is onset of photoelectron band (83SCH/SCH).							
$C_2H_2Se^+$							
$CH_2=C=Se$	8.7	(256)	(1071)	55	232	*EST	61134-37-0
IP is onset of photoelectron band (80BOC/AYG).							
$C_2H_3^+$							
C_2H_3	8.9	265.9 267.9	1112 1120.9	63.4±1 62.7	265.3±4 262.2	85KIE/WEI	2669-89-8
Heat of formation of ion from appearance potential measurement; IP from J.L. Beauchamp, personal communication.							
$C_2H_3Br^+$							
C_2H_3Br	9.80±0.02	244.9 248.5	1024.8 1039.7	18.9±0.5 22.5	79.3±1.9 94.2	77PED/RYL	593-60-2
See also: 82VON/ASB, 83CAM/CIU, 84MIL/BAE.							
$C_2H_3BrHg^+$							
$CH_2=CHHgBr$	(9.8)	(256)	(1072)	30	126	*EST	16188-37-7
IP is onset of photoelectron band (81BAI/CHI).							
$C_2H_3BrO^+$							
CH_3COBr	10.4±0.1	194	813	−45.5±0.1	−190.4±0.5	77PED/RYL	506-96-7
IP is onset of photoelectron band (82LEV/LIA, 81KIM/KAT).							
$C_2H_3BrO_2^+$							
$CH_2BrCOOH$	(10.4)	(145)	(608)	−94.4±1.5	−395±6	*EST	79-08-3
IP is onset of photoelectron band.							
$C_2H_3Cl^+$							
C_2H_3Cl	9.99±0.02	236 238	987 995	5±0.5 7	23±2 31	83KOL/PAP	75-01-4
See also: 83CAM/CIU, 82VON/ASB, 81KIM/KAT.							
$C_2H_3ClF_2^+$							
CH_3CF_2Cl	11.98±0.01	149.7	626.2	−126.6±1.2	−529.7±5.0	78PAP/KOL	75-68-3
$C_2H_3ClN^+$							
$ClCH_2CNH$		207	865				
From proton affinity of $ClCH_2CN$ (RN 107-14-2). PA = 179.5 kcal/mol, 751 kJ/mol.							
$C_2H_3ClO^+$							
CH_3COCl	10.85±0.05	192 194	804 813	−58±0.2 −56	−243±1 −234	77PED/RYL	75-36-5
See: 81KIM/KAT							

Table 1. Positive Ion Table - Continued

ION / Neutral	Ionization potential eV	$\Delta_f H$(Ion) kcal/mol	kJ/mol	$\Delta_f H$(Neutral) kcal/mol	kJ/mol	Neutral reference	CAS registry number
$C_2H_3ClO^+$							
CH_2ClCHO	10.48±0.03	(195)	(816)	−47±4	−195±15	*EST	107-20-0
See: 81KIM/KAT.							
$C_2H_3ClO_2^+$							
$CH_2ClCOOH$	(10.7)	(143)	(597)	−104±2	−435±9	77PED/RYL	79-11-8
IP is onset of photoelectron band.							
$C_2H_3Cl_3^+$							
$CHCl_2CH_2Cl$	11.0	218	912	−36±0.5	−149±2	77PED/RYL	79-00-5
IP is onset of photoelectron band (81KIM/KAT).							
CH_3CCl_3	(11.0)	(219)	(916)	−34.6±0.1	−144.9±0.6	83KOL/PAP	71-55-6
IP is onset of photoelectron band (81KIM/KAT).							
$C_2H_3Cl_3O^+$							
CCl_3CH_2OH	(10.94)	(182)	(763)	(−70)	(−293)	*EST	115-20-8
IP from 83KOP/MOL.							
$C_2H_3Cl_3Si^+$							
$CH_2=CHSiCl_3$	(≤11.0)	(≤144)	(≤603)	−109	−458	*EST	75-94-5
IP from 81KHV/ZYK.							
$C_2H_3F^+$							
C_2H_3F	10.363±0.015	205.8	861.1	−33.2±0.4	−138.8±1.7	76WIL/LEB	75-02-5
See also: 81BIE/VON, 81BIE/ASB.							
$C_2H_3FO^+$							
CH_3COF	11.51±0.02	159	667	−106±0.7	−444±3	77PED/RYL	557-99-3
See: 81KIM/KAT.							
$C_2H_3F_2^+$							
CH_2FCHF		130	543				
From proton affinity of (E)-CHF=CHF (RN 1630-78-0). PA = 166 kcal/mol, 694 kJ/mol.							
CH_3CF_2	(7.92)	(109)	(458)	−72±2	−303±8	82MCM/GOL	40640-67-3
Value of $\Delta_f H$(Ion) from appearance potential determination (84HEI/BAR, 85HEI/BAR); value from proton affinity of $CH_2=CF_2$ (RN 75-38-7) = 108 kcal/mol, 451 kJ/mol. PA = 176 kcal/mol, 736 kJ/mol.							
$C_2H_3F_3^+$							
CH_3CF_3	12.9±0.1	118	496	−179±0.7	−749±3	83KOL/PAP	420-46-2
		122	509	−176	−736		
IP from 73GOL/KOR.							
$C_2H_3F_3O^+$							
CF_3CH_2OH	11.49	53	221	−212±1	−888±5	77PED/RYL	75-89-8
IP from 83KOP/MOL.							
$C_2H_3I^+$							
$CH_2=CHI$	9.30	(246)	(1027)	31	130	*EST	593-66-8

Table 1. Positive Ion Table – Continued

ION / Neutral	Ionization potential eV	$\Delta_f H$(Ion) kcal/mol	$\Delta_f H$(Ion) kJ/mol	$\Delta_f H$(Neutral) kcal/mol	$\Delta_f H$(Neutral) kJ/mol	Neutral reference	CAS registry number
$C_2H_3N^+$							
CH_3CN	12.194±0.005	299	1251	18±0.2	74±1	83AN/MAN	75-05-8
		300	*1258*	*19*	*81*		
IP from 81RID/RAY. See also: 82CHE/LAP, 84OHN/MAT, 82ALL/MIG, 81KIM/KAT, 85HAR/MCI.							
CH_2CNH		(240)	(1004)				
		(242)	*(1011)*				
From appearance potential determinations.							
CH_3NC	11.24	300	1257	41±0.2	173±1	83AN/MAN	593-75-9
		302	*1262*	*43*	*178*		
See also: 82CHE/LAP, 81BEV/SAN, 85HAR/MCI.							
$C_2H_3NO^+$							
CH_3NCO	(10.67±0.02)	(215)	(899)	−31	−130	75COM/DES	624-83-9
$C_2H_3NS^+$							
CH_3SCN	(9.96±0.05)	(268)	(1121)	38	160	82TN270	556-64-9
CH_3NCS	(9.25±0.03)	(245)	(1023)	31	131	82TN270	556-61-6
		(247)	*(1032)*	*33*	*140*		
$C_2H_3N_3^+$							
1H-1,2,3-triazole	10.06	291	1218	59	247	82JOS	288-36-8
See: 81PAL/SIM.							
1H-1,2,4-triazole	(9.8)	(272)	(1140)	46±0.5	194±2	85FAO/AKA	288-88-0
IP is onset of photoelectron band (81PAL/SIM).							
$C_2H_3O^+$							
CH_3CO	7.0	156	653	−6±0.5	−24±2	82MCM/GOL	15762-07-9

$\Delta_f H$(Ion) at 298 K from 82TRA/MCL, 84LIA/LIE, and 81LIF/TZI. See also: 84LOS/HOL, 83LIF/BER. Value derived from proton affinity of ketene is 157 kcal/mol, 657 kJ/mol. PA = 198.0 kcal/mol, 828 kJ/mol. IP cited is $\Delta_f H$(Ion)-$\Delta_f H$(Neutral). Experimentally determined IP of this radical is 8.05±0.17 eV. See also: 82BUR/HOL2.

$CH_2=COH$		(192)	(803)				

$\Delta_f H$(Ion) from appearance potential determinations (82HOL/LOS, 82HOL/LOS2, 83BUR/HOL2).

oxirane (radical)		(201)	(841)				31586-84-2

$\Delta_f H$(Ion) from appearance potential measurements. See also: 83BUR/HOL2.

Table 1. Positive Ion Table – Continued

ION / Neutral	Ionization potential eV	$\Delta_f H$(Ion) kcal/mol	$\Delta_f H$(Ion) kJ/mol	$\Delta_f H$(Neutral) kcal/mol	$\Delta_f H$(Neutral) kJ/mol	Neutral reference	CAS registry number
$C_2H_3O_2I^+$							
CH_2ICOOH	(9.6)	(327)	(1367)	105	441	*EST	64-69-7

IP is onset of photoelectron band.

$C_2H_3S^+$							
CH_3CS		204	853				

From proton affinity of $CH_2=C=S$ (RN 18282-77-4) (83CAS/KIM). PA = 201.2 kcal/mol, 842 kJ/mol. Original authors recommend value of 210 kcal/mol, 879 kJ/mol, using $\Delta_f H(CH_2=C=S) = 46$ kcal/mol, 196 kJ/mol, from MNDO calculation.

$C_2H_3V^+$							
VC_2H_3		(266)	(1115)				

$\Delta_f H$(Ion) from onset energy of endothermic reaction (84ARI/ARM, 85ELK/ARM). 0 K value.

$C_2H_4^+$							
C_2H_4	10.507±0.004	<u>254.8</u> 256.8	<u>1066</u> 1074	12.5±0.2 14.5	52.2±1 60.7	77PED/RYL	74-85-1

See also: 81KIM/KAT, 84POL/TRE.

$C_2H_4BrCl^+$							
CH_2BrCH_2Cl	10.67±0.03	225	942	−21±1	−87±5	83KOL/PAP	107-04-0

See: 81KIM/KAT.

$CH_3CHClBr$	10.37	219±1	918±5	−20±1	−83±5	83KOL/PAP	593-96-4
$C_2H_4BrF^+$							
CH_2FCH_2Br	≤10.57	(≤184)	(≤769)	−60±5	−251±20	83KOL/PAP	762-49-2
$C_2H_4Br_2^+$							
CH_2BrCH_2Br	10.37	230	962	−9±0.2	−39±1	83KOL/PAP	106-93-4

See: 78GAN/PEE, 81KIM/KAT, 77STA/WIE.

CH_3CHBr_2	10.17	226	944	−9±1	−37±6	83KOL/PAP	557-91-5
$C_2H_4Cl^+$							
CH_3CHCl		(199)	(832)				

From appearance potential (11.20 eV) in CH_3CHCl_2.

CH_2ClCH_2		(204)	(855)				

From appearance potential (11.47 eV) in CH_2ClCH_2Cl.

$C_2H_4ClO_2^+$							
$CH_2ClC(OH)_2$		79	332				

From proton affinity of $CH_2ClCOOH$ (RN 79-11-8). PA = 182.4 kcal/mol, 763 kJ/mol.

$C_2H_4Cl_2^+$							
CH_3CHCl_2	11.06	224 *229*	936 *959*	−31±0.7 *−26*	−131±3 *−108*	83KOL/PAP	75-34-3

See also: 81KIM/KAT.

Table 1. Positive Ion Table – Continued

ION / Neutral	Ionization potential eV	$\Delta_f H$(Ion) kcal/mol	kJ/mol	$\Delta_f H$(Neutral) kcal/mol	kJ/mol	Neutral reference	CAS registry number
$C_2H_4Cl_2^+$							
CH_2ClCH_2Cl	11.04	222	931	−32±0.2	−134±1	83KOL/PAP	107-06-2
		225	942	−29	−123		
See also: 81KIM/KAT.							
$C_2H_4Cl_2O^+$							
CH_3OCHCl_2	(10.6)	(191)	(800)	−53	−222	*EST	4885-02-3
IP is onset of photoelectron band (80VER/SAL).							
$C_2H_4Cl_3O^+$							
$CCl_3CH_2OH_2$		118	495				
From proton affinity of CCl_3CH_2OH (RN 115-20-8). PA = 177.4 kcal/mol, 742 kJ/mol.							
$C_2H_4F^+$							
CH_3CHF	7.93	157	659	−26	−106		
$\Delta_f H$(Ion) from proton affinity of C_2H_3F (RN 75-02-5). PA = 175 kcal/mol, 732 kJ/mol.							
$\Delta_f H$(Neutral) = IP − $\Delta_f H$(Ion).							
$C_2H_4FO_2^+$							
$CH_2FC(OH)_2$		42	176				
From proton affinity of CH_2FCOOH (RN 144-49-0). PA = 183.5 kcal/mol, 768. kJ/mol.							
$C_2H_4F_2^+$							
CH_3CHF_2	11.87±0.03	154	644	−120±1	−501±6	75CHE/ROD	75-37-6
IP from 84HEI/BAR, 85HEI/BAR.							
$C_2H_4F_3N^+$							
$CF_3CH_2NH_2$	(9.8±0.1)	(58)	(244)	(−167)	(−701)	*EST	753-90-2
IP is average of values from 83MOL/PIK3, 79AUE/BOW.							
$C_2H_4F_3O^+$							
$CF_3CH_2OH_2$		−16	−65				
From proton affinity of CF_3CH_2OH (RN 75-89-8). See also: 85MCM/KEB. PA = 169.0 kcal/mol, 707 kJ/mol.							
$C_2H_4Fe^+$							
$H_2C\overset{Fe}{-\!\!-\!\!-}CH_2$		(256)	(1071)				
$\Delta_f H$(Ion) from 84JAC/JAC.							
$C_2H_4I_2^+$							
CH_2ICH_2I	(9.4)	(233)	(973)	15.8±0.3	66.3±1.4	77PED/RYL	624-73-7
IP is onset of photoelectron band.							
$C_2H_4N^+$							
CH_3CNH		195	817				
From proton affinity of CH_3CN (RN 75-05-8). PA = 188.2 kcal/mol, 787 kJ/mol.							

Table 1. Positive Ion Table – Continued

ION Neutral	Ionization potential eV	$\Delta_f H$(Ion) kcal/mol kJ/mol	$\Delta_f H$(Neutral) kcal/mol kJ/mol	Neutral reference	CAS registry number
$C_2H_4N^+$					
CH$_3$NCH		205 860			
From proton affinity of CH$_3$NC (RN 593-75-9) (86KNI/FRE, 86MAU/KAR). PA = 201.4 kcal/mol, 843 kJ/mol.					
$C_2H_4NO^+$					
CH$_3$NHCO		150 628			
From proton affinity of CH$_3$NCO (RN 624-83-9)(85KAR/STE). PA = 184.5 kcal/mol, 772. kJ/mol.					
$C_2H_4NS^+$					
CH$_3$SCNH		212 886			
From proton affinity of CH$_3$SCN (RN 556-64-9) (85KAR/STE). PA = 192. kcal/mol, 804. kJ/mol.					
CH$_3$NCSH		204 853			
From proton affinity of CH$_3$NCS (RN 556-61-6) (85KAR/STE). PA = 193.0 kcal/mol, 807.5 kJ/mol.					
$C_2H_4N_2^+$					
CH$_2$=NN=CH$_2$	(8.95)	(264) (1104)	58 241	82JOS	503-27-5
See also: 84KIR/POP.					
$C_2H_4N_2O_2^+$					
NH$_2$COCONH$_2$	(9.41)	(121) (505)	−96±1 −403±5	77PED/RYL	471-46-5
$C_2H_4N_3^+$					
(1H-1,2,4-triazole structure)		199 835			
From proton affinity of 1H-1,2,4-Triazole (RN 288-88-0) (86MAU/LIE). PA = 212.4 kcal/mol, 889. kJ/mol.					
$C_2H_4N_4^+$					
NCN=C(NH$_2$)$_2$	(8.4)	(230) (963)	36 153	77PED/RYL	10191-60-3
IP is onset of photoelectron band (80KLA/BUT).					
$C_2H_4O^+$					
CH$_3$CHO	10.229±0.0007	196.3 821.1 198.9 831.9	−39.6±0.1 −165.8±0.4 −37.0 −155.0	77PED/RYL	75-07-0
See also: 82JOH/POW, 72POT/SOR, 81ELS/ALL, 81KIM/KAT, 77STA/WIE.					
CH$_2$=CHOH	9.14	181 757	−30 −125	82HOL/LOS3	557-75-5
From 82HOL/LOS3, 84ALB/ALL.					
CH$_3$COH		(207) (865)			
$\Delta_f H$(Ion) from appearance potential determinations (83TER/WEZ).					

Table 1. Positive Ion Table – Continued

ION / Neutral	Ionization potential eV	$\Delta_f H$(Ion) kcal/mol	$\Delta_f H$(Ion) kJ/mol	$\Delta_f H$(Neutral) kcal/mol	$\Delta_f H$(Neutral) kJ/mol	Neutral reference	CAS registry number
$C_2H_4O^+$							
(oxirane)	10.566±0.01	231.0	966.8	−12.6±0.1	−52.6±0.6	77PED/RYL	75-21-8
		234.1	*979.4*	*−9.6*	*−40.1*		
See also: 82JOH/POW, 81KIM/KAT, 82BIE/ASB.							
$C_2H_4OS^+$							
CH_3COSH	10.00±0.02	189	790	−42±2	−175±8	77PED/RYL	507-09-5
(thiirane S-oxide)	9.2	(205)	(858)	−7	−30	*EST	7117-41-1
IP is onset of photoelectron band.							
$C_2H_4OS_2^+$							
(1,3-dithietane 1-oxide)	(8.8)	(199)	(831)	−4	−18	*EST	58816-63-0
IP is onset of photoelectron band (82BLO/COR).							
$C_2H_4O_2^+$							
$HCOOCH_3$	10.815±0.005	164.4	688.0	−85.0±0.2	−355.5±0.7	77PED/RYL	107-31-3
See also: 81KIM/KAT, 85CAN/HAM.							
CH_3COOH	10.66±0.02	142.5	596.4	−103.3±0.1	−432.1±0.4	78CHA/ZWO	64-19-7
		145.9	*610.4*	*−99.9±0.1*	*−418.1±0.4*		
See also: 81HOL/FIN, 80VON/BIE, 81KIM/KAT.							
$CH_2C(OH)_2$		120	503				
$\Delta_f H$(Ion) from appearance potential determinations.							
$HOCH=CHOH$	(9.62±0.10)	(146)	(612)	−76	−316	*EST	
IP from 86TUR/HAV3.							
CH_3OCOH		158	661				
$\Delta_f H$(Ion) from appearance potential of metastable ion (83TER/WEZ).							
$CH_2CO(H_2O)$		(138)	(579)				
$\Delta_f H$(Ion) from appearance potential determinations (86POS/RUT).							
$C_2H_4O_2S^+$							
(thiirane 1,1-dioxide)	(10.3)	(177)	(741)	−60	−253	*EST	1782-89-4
IP is onset of photoelectron band.							

Table 1. Positive Ion Table - Continued

ION / Neutral	Ionization potential eV	$\Delta_f H$(Ion) kcal/mol	$\Delta_f H$(Ion) kJ/mol	$\Delta_f H$(Neutral) kcal/mol	$\Delta_f H$(Neutral) kJ/mol	Neutral reference	CAS registry number
$C_2H_4O_2S_2^+$							
(structure: 1,3-dithietane 1,1-dioxide)	(9.4) IP is onset of photoelectron band (82BLO/COR).	(159)	(666)	−58	−241	*EST	60743-07-9
(structure: 1,3-dithietane 1,3-dioxide)	(8.6) IP is onset of photoelectron band (82BLO/COR).	(167)	(700)	−31	−130	*EST	60743-08-0
$C_2H_4O_3^+$							
(1,3,2-dioxathiolane / 1,3-dioxolane related)	(10.1) IP is onset of photoelectron band.	(183)	(765)	−50	−209	82CRE	289-14-5
$C_2H_4O_3S_2^+$							
(structure)	(9.6) IP is onset of photoelectron band (82BLO/COR).	(137)	(573)	−84	−353	*EST	60743-10-4
$C_2H_4O_4S_2^+$							
(structure)	(10.6) IP is onset of photoelectron band (82BLO/COR).	(107)	(447)	−138	−576	*EST	21511-46-6
$C_2H_4S^+$							
CH_3CHS	8.98±0.02 See also: 83BUT/BAE2.	218	910	11	44	79JOS	6851-93-0
(thiirane)	9.051±0.006 See also: 82BUT/BAE, 83BUT/BAE2.	228 / 231	955 / 967	19.6±0.3 / 22.4	82.1±1.2 / 93.7	77PED/RYL	420-12-2
$C_2H_4S_2^+$							
(1,3-dithietane)	(8.5) IP is onset of photoelectron band (82BLO/COR).	(218)	(914)	22	94	*EST	287-53-6

Table 1. Positive Ion Table - Continued

ION / Neutral	Ionization potential eV	Δ_fH(Ion) kcal/mol	kJ/mol	Δ_fH(Neutral) kcal/mol	kJ/mol	Neutral reference	CAS registry number
$C_2H_4S_3^+$	(≤8.72)	(≤196)	(≤818)	−5	−23	*EST	289-16-7
$C_2H_4Sc^+$		(215)	(899)				

Δ_fH(Ion) from onset of endothermic reaction (84TOL/BEA). See also: 86ELK/ARI.

$C_2H_4Se^+$ $CH_3CH=Se$	(8.3)	(219)	(915)	27	114	*EST	67281-48-5

IP is onset of photoelectron band (84BOC/AYG).

$C_2H_5^+$ C_2H_5	8.13	215.6±1.0	902±4	28	118	84CAO/BAC	14936-94-8
		_218.5±1.0_	_914±4_	_31_	_130_		

Heat of formation of ion from appearance potential measurements (See: 81TRA/MCL, 80BAE, 82DYK/JON2, 82ROS/BUF). IP given is Δ_fH(Ion) − Δ_fH(Neutral). Δ_fH(Neutral) based on D[C-H] = 100.5 kcal/mol.
Experimental IP of radical ≤8.26±0.02 eV.(84DYK/ELL).

$C_2H_5Br^+$ C_2H_5Br	10.28	222.2	929.6	−14.9±0.2	−62.3±1.0	77PED/RYL	74-96-4
		_227.4_	_951.5_	_−9.6±0.2_	_−40.4±1.0_		

See also: 81KIM/KAT, 85OHN/IMA.

$C_2H_5BrO^+$ CH_2BrCH_2OH(gauche)	(≤10.75)	(≤196)	(≤820)	(−52)	(−217)	*EST	540-51-2

See also: 84KOB, 81KIM/KAT, 85OHN/IMA.

CH_2BrCH_2OH(trans)	(≤10.65)	(≤194)	(≤811)	(−52)	(−217)	*EST	540-51-2

See also: 84KOB, 81KIM/KAT, 85OHN/IMA.

$C_2H_5Cl^+$ C_2H_5Cl	10.97±0.02	226	946	−26.8±0.1	−112.1±0.5	77PED/RYL	75-00-3
		_230_	_961_	_−23.3_	_−97.6_		

See also: 83OHN/IMA, 81KIM/KAT.

CH_3CHClH		227	951				

Δ_fH(Ion) from appearance potential determination (83HOL/BUR).

$C_2H_5ClHg^+$ C_2H_5HgCl	9.9	212	888	−16±1	−67±4	80TEL/RAB	107-27-7

IP is onset of photoelectron band (81BAI/CHI2).

Table 1. Positive Ion Table - Continued

ION Neutral	Ionization potential eV	$\Delta_f H$(Ion) kcal/mol	$\Delta_f H$(Ion) kJ/mol	$\Delta_f H$(Neutral) kcal/mol	$\Delta_f H$(Neutral) kJ/mol	Neutral reference	CAS registry number
$C_2H_5ClO^+$							
C_2H_5OCl	(10.13±0.02)	(212)	(886)	−22	−91	*EST	624-85-1
	IP from 81COL/FRO.						
CH_2ClCH_2OH	(10.52)	(181)	(756)	−62	−259	*EST	107-07-3
	IP is onset of photoelectron band (81KIM/KAT, 85OHN/IMA). See also: 84KOB.						
CH_3OCH_2Cl	(10.2)	(184)	(769)	−51	−215	*EST	107-30-2
	IP is onset of photoelectron band (80VER/SAL).						
$C_2H_5ClS^+$							
CH_3SCH_2Cl	(≤7.74)	(≤157)	(≤657)	−22	−90	*EST	2373-51-5
$C_2H_5Cl_2P^+$							
$C_2H_5PCl_2$	9.3	153	638	−62±4	−259±18	80TEL/RAB	1498-40-4
	IP is onset of photoelectron band (83ZVE/BAZ, 82LEV/LIA).						
$C_2H_5Cl_3Si^+$							
$C_2H_5SiCl_3$	(10.74±0.04)	(122)	(509)	−126±6	−527±25	80TEL/RAB	115-21-9
$CH_3SiCl_2(CH_2Cl)$	(10.4)	(129)	(538)	−111	−465	*EST	1558-33-4
	IP is onset of photoelectron band (81ZYK/KHV).						
$C_2H_5F^+$							
C_2H_5F	(11.6)	(205)	(856)	−63±0.5	−263±2	75CHE/ROD	353-36-6
	IP is onset of photoelectron band (81BIE/ASB). See also: 81KIM/KAT.						
$C_2H_5FO^+$							
CH_2FCH_2OH	(10.66)	(146)	(612)	−100	−417	*EST	371-62-0
	IP from 83KOP/MOL.						
$C_2H_5F_2N^+$							
$CF_2HCH_2NH_2$	(9.4)	(326)	(1366)	110	462	*EST	430-67-1
	IP from 79AUE/BOW.						
$C_2H_5F_2O^+$							
$CF_2HCH_2OH_2$		34	144				
	From proton affinity of CF_2HCH_2OH (RN 359-13-7). PA = 176.2 kcal/mol, 737 kJ/mol.						
$C_2H_5F_3N^+$							
$CF_3CH_2NH_3$		−4	−18				
	From proton affinity of $CF_3CH_2NH_2$ (RN 753-90-2). PA = 202.5 kcal/mol, 847 kJ/mol.						
$C_2H_5I^+$							
C_2H_5I	9.346	213.3	891.9	−2.2±0.2	−9.0±0.9	77PED/RYL	75-03-6
		216.9	907.8	1.6	6.9		
	See: 78LIA/AUS, 83OHN/IMA, 81KIM/KAT.						

Table 1. Positive Ion Table — Continued

ION / Neutral	Ionization potential eV	$\Delta_f H$(Ion) kcal/mol	$\Delta_f H$(Ion) kJ/mol	$\Delta_f H$(Neutral) kcal/mol	$\Delta_f H$(Neutral) kJ/mol	Neutral reference	CAS registry number
$C_2H_5IO^+$							
gauche-ICH_2CH_2OH	9.73	(186)	(778)	−38	−161	*EST	624-76-0
trans-ICH_2CH_2OH	9.60	(183)	(765)	−38	−161	*EST	624-76-0
$C_2H_5N^+$							
$CH_2=NCH_3$	(9.4)	(234)	(979)	17	72	69BEN/CRU	1761-67-7
IP is onset of photoelectron band. See also: 86WER.							
$CH_3CH=NH$	(9.6)	(222)	(930)	2±4	8±17	79ELL/EAD	20729-41-3
IP is onset of photoelectron band (86LAF/GON).							
$CH_2=CHNH_2$	(8.20)	(196)	(820)	7	29	81ELL/DIX	593-67-9
IP from 84ALB/ALL2.							
aziridine (H-N△)	9.2±0.1	242	1014	30.2±0.2	126.5±0.9	77PED/RYL	151-56-4
See also: 82BIE/ASB.							
$C_2H_5NO^+$							
CH_3CONH_2	9.65±0.03	165	693	−57.0±0.2	−238.3±0.8	77PED/RYL	60-35-5
See also: 81ASB/SVE.							
(E)-$CH_3CH=NOH$	(10.0)	(226)	(945)	−4.7±2	−20±8	69BEN/CRU	107-29-9
IP is onset of photoelectron band.							
$HCONHCH_3$	9.79	(181)	(758)	−45±0.7	−187±3	*EST	123-39-7
See also: 81KIM/KAT.							
$C_2H_5NO_2^+$							
NH_2CH_2COOH	8.8	109	458	−93±1	−391±5	77NGA/SAB	56-40-6
See also: 83CAN/HAM.							
$C_2H_5NO_2$	10.88±0.05	226.5	947.5	−24.4±0.1	−102.2±0.6	77PED/RYL	79-24-3
See also: 81KIM/KAT.							
C_2H_5ONO	(10.53±0.01)	(218)	(913)	−25	−103	74BAT/CHR	109-95-5
$C_2H_5NO_3^+$							
$C_2H_5ONO_2$	(11.22)	(222)	(928)	−36.8±0.2	−154.1±1.0	77PED/RYL	625-58-1
$C_2H_5NS^+$							
CH_3CSNH_2	8.33	194	814	2±0.2	10±1	82TOR/SAB2	62-55-5
$C_2H_5N_2^+$							
$NCCH_2NH_3$		194	812				
From proton affinity of $NCCH_2NH_2$ (RN 540-61-4). PA = 197.4 kcal/mol, 826 kJ/mol.							

Table 1. Positive Ion Table - Continued

ION / Neutral	Ionization potential eV	$\Delta_f H$(Ion) kcal/mol	$\Delta_f H$(Ion) kJ/mol	$\Delta_f H$(Neutral) kcal/mol	$\Delta_f H$(Neutral) kJ/mol	Neutral reference	CAS registry number

$C_2H_5O^+$

CH$_3$CHOH

| | 6.7 | 139 | 583 | −16±1 | −66±4 | 82MCM/GOL | 17104-36-8 |

$\Delta_f H$(Ion) from proton affinity of acetaldehyde (RN 75-07-0). PA = 186.6 kcal/mol, 781 kJ/mol. The IP given is $\Delta_f H$(Ion) - $\Delta_f H$(Neutral). See also: 82MAC, 84LOS/HOL.

CH$_3$OCH$_2$

| | 6.94 | (157) | (657) | −3±1 | −13±4 | 82MCM/GOL | 16520-04-0 |
| | | (165) | (690) | | | | |

$\Delta_f H$(Ion) at 0 K from appearance potential determination (82MAC, 84BUT/HOL). See also: 84BOW/MAC.

CH$_2$=CHOH$_2$

| | | 148 | 619 | | | | |

$\Delta_f H$(Ion) from appearance potential determination (82BUR/TER2).

(oxirane)H$^+$

| | | 165 | 691 | | | | |

From proton affinity of oxirane (RN 75-21-8). PA = 187.9 kcal/mol, 786 kJ/mol.

$C_2H_5O_2^+$

CH$_3$C(OH)$_2$

| | | 72 | 302 | | | | |

From proton affinity of CH$_3$COOH (RN 64-19-7). See also: 84HOL/LOS. 85AUD/MIL. PA = 190.2 kcal/mol, 796. kJ/mol.

HC(OH)OCH$_3$

| | | 92 | 386 | | | | |

From proton affinity of HCOOCH$_3$ (RN 107-31-3). PA = 188.4 kcal/mol, 788. kJ/mol. (86KNI/FRE, 84LIA/LIE).

$C_2H_5P^+$

(phosphirane H)

| | (9.4±0.1) | (200) | (838) | −16±0.5 | −69±2 | *EST | 6569-82-0 |

$C_2H_5S^+$

CH$_3$CHSH

| | | 197 | 823 | | | | 58794-14-2 |
| | | 200 | 836 | | | | |

$\Delta_f H$(Ion) from appearance potential determinations (83BUT/BAE).

CH$_3$SCH$_2$

| | | (194) | (812) | | | | 31533-72-9 |

$\Delta_f H$(Ion) from appearance potential determinations. See also: 83ERM/AKO. 0 K values.

(thiirane)H$^+$

| | | 191 | 798 | | | | |

From proton affinity of thiirane (RN 420-12-2). PA = 194.6 kcal/mol, 814 kJ/mol.

Table 1. Positive Ion Table — Continued

ION / Neutral	Ionization potential eV	$\Delta_f H$(Ion) kcal/mol	$\Delta_f H$(Ion) kJ/mol	$\Delta_f H$(Neutral) kcal/mol	$\Delta_f H$(Neutral) kJ/mol	Neutral reference	CAS registry number
$C_2H_6^+$							
C_2H_6	11.52±0.01	245.6	1028	−20.1±0.05	−84.0±0.2	77PED/RYL	74-84-0
		249.3	*1043*	*−16.4*	*−68.4*		
	See also: 81KIM/KAT, 84CHA/HIL.						
$C_2H_6BBr^+$							
$(CH_3)_2BBr$	10.25	192	804	−44	−185	82HOL/SMI	5158-50-9
$C_2H_6BCl^+$							
$(CH_3)_2BCl$	(10.2)	(173)	(725)	−62	−259	82HOL/SMI	1803-36-7
	IP is onset of photoelectron band.						
$C_2H_6BCl_2N^+$							
$(CH_3)_2NBCl_2$	9.56	125	521	−96±1	−401±4	77PED/RYL	1113-31-1
$C_2H_6B_4^+$	(9.77)	(236.3)	(988.6)	11.0±2.9	45.9±12.1	85GAL/TAM	20693-67-8
$C_2H_6Br^+$							
C_2H_5BrH		(180)	(753)				
	From proton affinity of C_2H_5Br (RN 74-96-4). PA = ~171 kcal/mol, ~715 kJ/mol.						
$C_2H_6BrSi^+$							
$(CH_3)_2SiBr$		146	612				
		151	*633*				
	$\Delta_f H$(Ion) from appearance potential determination (84SZE/BAE).						
$C_2H_6Cd^+$							
$(CH_3)_2Cd$	(8.56±0.02)	(223)	(932)	25.3±0.3	105.8±1.3	77PED/RYL	506-82-1
$C_2H_6Cl^+$							
C_2H_5ClH		170	711				
	From proton affinity of C_2H_5Cl (RN 75-00-3). PA = 169 kcal/mol, 707 kJ/mol.						
CH_3ClCH_3		(177)	(743)				24400-15-5
	Derived (85SHA/HOJ).						
$C_2H_6ClN^+$							
$(CH_3)_2NCl$	8.75	(221)	(925)	19	81	*EST	1585-74-6
$C_2H_6ClP^+$							
$(CH_3)_2PCl$	(8.7)	(163)	(681)	−38	−158	*EST	811-62-1
	IP is onset of photoelectron band (82LEV/LIA, 86BOC/BAN).						
$C_2H_6Cl_2NOP^+$							
$(CH_3)_2NPOCl_2$	(9.5)	(86)	(361)	−133	−556	*EST	677-43-0
	IP is onset of photoelectron band.						

Table 1. Positive Ion Table - Continued

ION / Neutral	Ionization potential eV	$\Delta_f H$(Ion) kcal/mol	$\Delta_f H$(Ion) kJ/mol	$\Delta_f H$(Neutral) kcal/mol	$\Delta_f H$(Neutral) kJ/mol	Neutral reference	CAS registry number
$C_2H_6Cl_2NP^+$							
$(CH_3)_2NPCl_2$	(8.9)	(171)	(716)	−34	−143	*EST	683-85-2
	IP is onset of photoelectron band.						
$C_2H_6Cl_2Si^+$							
$(CH_3)_2SiCl_2$	(10.7)	(137)	(574)	−109	−458	81BEL/PER	75-78-5
	IP is onset of photoelectron band.						
$C_2H_6Cl_2Sn^+$							
$(CH_3)_2SnCl_2$	(10.43)	(174)	(727)	−67	−279	*EST	753-73-1
$C_2H_6F^+$							
CH_3FCH_3		(147)	(614)				
	$\Delta_f H$(Ion) derived from results of 86HOV/MCM.						
C_2H_5FH		138	577				
	From proton affinity of C_2H_5F (RN 75-02-5). PA = 165 kcal/mol, 690 kJ/mol.						
$C_2H_6FN^+$							
$CH_2FCH_2NH_2$	(9.1)	(155)	(650)	−55	−229	*EST	406-34-8
	IP from 79AUE/BOW.						
$C_2H_6FP^+$							
$(CH_3)_2PF$	(8.8)	(112)	(468)	−91	−381	*EST	507-15-3
	IP is onset of photoelectron band.						
$C_2H_6FSi^+$							
$(CH_3)_2SiF$		86	359				
	From appearance potential (10.70±0.04 eV) of ion in $(CH_3)_3SiF$.						
$C_2H_6F_2N^+$							
$CF_2HCH_2NH_3$		269	1124				
	From proton affinity of $CF_2HCH_2NH_2$ (RN 430-67-1). PA = 207.5 kcal/mol, 868 kJ/mol.						
$C_2H_6F_2Si^+$							
$(CH_3)_2SiF_2$	11.03±0.03	42	177	−212	−887	77MUR/BEA	353-66-2
$C_2H_6Hg^+$							
$(CH_3)_2Hg$	(9.10±0.05)	(232)	(972)	22.5±0.2	94.0±1.0	77PED/RYL	593-74-8
		(237)	(991)	27.0	113.3		
$C_2H_6I^+$							
C_2H_5IH		(188)	(785)				
	From proton affinity of C_2H_5I (RN 75-03-6). PA = ~176 kcal/mol, ~736 kJ/mol.						
$C_2H_6N^+$							
CH_2NHCH_3	5.9	166	695	30	126	83BUR/CAS	31277-24-4
	$\Delta_f H$(Ion) from appearance potential determination(81LOS/LAM); IP derived (81GRI/LOS, 83BUR/CAS).						
CH_3CHNH_2	5.7	157	657	26	109	83BUR/CAS	30208-36-7
	$\Delta_f H$(Ion) from appearance potential determination(81LOS/LAM); IP derived(83BUR/CAS).						

Table 1. Positive Ion Table - Continued

ION / Neutral	Ionization potential eV	$\Delta_f H$(Ion) kcal/mol	$\Delta_f H$(Ion) kJ/mol	$\Delta_f H$(Neutral) kcal/mol	$\Delta_f H$(Neutral) kJ/mol	Neutral reference	CAS registry number
$C_2H_6N^+$							
$(CH_3)_2N$	(5.17)	(154)	(644)	35±2	145±8	82MCM/GOL	15337-44-7

$\Delta_f H$(Ion) from appearance potential measurement. IP cited is $\Delta_f H$(Ion) - $\Delta_f H$(Neutral).

aziridine·H⁺		180	755				

From proton affinity of aziridine (RN 151-56-4). PA = 215.7 kcal/mol, 902 kJ/mol.

ION / Neutral	IP eV	$\Delta_f H$(Ion) kcal/mol	$\Delta_f H$(Ion) kJ/mol	$\Delta_f H$(Neutral) kcal/mol	$\Delta_f H$(Neutral) kJ/mol	Neutral reference	CAS registry number
$C_2H_6NO^+$							
$CH_3C(OH)NH_2$		103	429				

From proton affinity of CH_3CONH_2 (RN 60-35-5). PA = 206.2 kcal/mol, 863 kJ/mol.

$HC(OH)NHCH_3$		115	481				

From proton affinity of $HCONHCH_3$ (RN 123-39-7). PA = 205.8 kcal/mol, 861 kJ/mol.

ION / Neutral	IP eV	$\Delta_f H$(Ion) kcal/mol	$\Delta_f H$(Ion) kJ/mol	$\Delta_f H$(Neutral) kcal/mol	$\Delta_f H$(Neutral) kJ/mol	Neutral reference	CAS registry number
$C_2H_6NO_2^+$							
NH_3CH_2COOH		61	254				

From proton affinity of NH_2CH_2COOH (RN 56-40-6). PA = 211.6 kcal/mol, 885 kJ/mol.

C_2H_5ONHO		144	602				

From proton affinity of C_2H_5ONO (RN 109-95-5). PA = 197.3 kcal/mol, 825.5 kJ/mol.

C_2H_5NOOH		157	655				

From proton affinity of $C_2H_5NO_2$ (RN 79-24-3). PA = 184.8 kcal/mol, 773 kJ/mol.

ION / Neutral	IP eV	$\Delta_f H$(Ion) kcal/mol	$\Delta_f H$(Ion) kJ/mol	$\Delta_f H$(Neutral) kcal/mol	$\Delta_f H$(Neutral) kJ/mol	Neutral reference	CAS registry number
$C_2H_6N_2^+$							
(E)-$CH_3N=NCH_3$	8.45±0.05	231	964	36	149	82PAM/ROG	4143-41-3
$C_2H_6N_2O^+$							
(E)-$CH_3NN(O)CH_3$	(9.7)	(238)	(997)	15	61	*EST	54168-20-6

IP is onset of photoelectron band.

$CH_3NHCONH_2$	(≤9.66)	(≤164)	(≤688)	-58	-244	*EST	598-50-5
$(CH_3)_2NNO$	8.69	200	835	-0.7±2	-3±8	67KOR/PEP	62-75-9
$C_2H_6N_2O_2^+$							
$(CH_3)_2NNO_2$	(9.53)	(219)	(914)	-1±0.8	-5±3	77PED/RYL	4164-28-7
(E)-$(CH_3NO)_2$	(≤8.68)	(≤217)	(≤908)	17±0.2	71±1	73BAT/MIL	37765-15-4
$C_2H_6O^+$							
C_2H_5OH	10.47±0.02	185.3	775.4	-56.1±0.1	-234.8±0.2	77PED/RYL	64-17-5
		189.5	*793.1*	*-51.9*	*-217.1*		

See also: 82MIS/POK, 72POT/SOR, 80VON/BIE, 84BOW/MAC, 83OHN/IMA, 81KIM/KAT, 80BAC/MOU, 74BET/BAK.

Table 1. Positive Ion Table - Continued

ION Neutral	Ionization potential eV	$\Delta_f H$(Ion) kcal/mol kJ/mol		$\Delta_f H$(Neutral) kcal/mol kJ/mol		Neutral reference	CAS registry number
$C_2H_6O^+$							
$(CH_3)_2O$	10.025±0.025	187.2	783.3	−44.0±0.1	−184.0±0.5	77PED/RYL	115-10-6
		191.5	*801.0*	*−39.7*	*−166.3*		
	IP from 84BUT/HOL. See also: 84BOW/MAC, 81KIM/KAT, 80BAC/MOU, 82BIE/ASB.						
$C_2H_4OH_2$		175	732				60786-90-5
	$\Delta_f H$(Ion) from appearance potential measurements (85BUR/HOL). See also: 82HOL/LOS, 82BUR/HOL). The authors propose the structure $C_2H_3..H^+..OH_2$ for the ion. See also: 81TER/HEE.						
$C_2H_6OS^+$							
$(CH_3)_2SO$	(9.01)	(172)	(718)	−36.2±0.2	−151.3±0.8	77PED/RYL	67-68-5
		(176)	*(738)*	*−31.4*	*−131.5*		
	See: 81KIM/KAT.						
$C_2H_6O_2^+$							
$HOCH_2CH_2OH$	10.16	142	593	−92.6±0.4	−387.6±1.7	77PED/RYL	107-21-1
	IP from 82HOL/LOS2. See also: 80VON/BIE, 81KIM/KAT.						
$(CH_3O)_2$	9.1	180	752	−30.0±0.3	−125.7±1.3	77PED/RYL	690-02-8
	IP is onset of photoelectron band (81KIM/KAT, 82LEV/LIA).						
$C_2H_6O_2S^+$							
$(CH_3)_2SO_2$	(10.3)	(148)	(621)	−89±0.7	−373±3	77PED/RYL	67-71-0
		(154)	*(644)*	*−84*	*−350*		
	IP is onset of photoelectron band.						
$C_2H_6O_3S^+$							
$(CH_3O)_2SO$	(9.9)	(113)	(472)	−115±0.5	−483±2	77PED/RYL	616-42-2
	IP is onset of photoelectron band.						
$C_2H_6P^+$							
(phosphiranium structure)		158	660				
	From proton affinity of phosphirane (RN 6569-82-0). PA = 191.4 kcal/mol, 801 kJ/mol.						
$C_2H_6S^+$							
C_2H_5SH	9.285±0.005	203	850	−11.1±0.1	−46.3±0.6	77PED/RYL	75-08-1
		207	*867*	*−7.0*	*−29.5*		
	See also: 83OHN/IMA, 81KIM/KAT.						
$(CH_3)_2S$	8.69±0.01	191	801	−9.0±0.1	−37.5±0.5	77PED/RYL	75-18-3
		195	*817*	*−5.1*	*−21.3*		
	See also: 81KIM/KAT.						
$C_2H_6SSi^+$							
$(CH_3)_2Si=S$		(203)	(848)				1111-83-7
	$\Delta_f H$(Ion) from appearance potential determination (81GUS/VOL).						

Table 1. Positive Ion Table - Continued

ION Neutral	Ionization potential eV	$\Delta_f H$(Ion) kcal/mol	kJ/mol	$\Delta_f H$(Neutral) kcal/mol	kJ/mol	Neutral reference	CAS registry number
$C_2H_6S_2^+$							
$(CH_3S)_2$	(7.4±0.3)	(165±4) (169)	(690±15) (707)	−5.8±0.2 −1.6	−24.2±1.0 −6.8	77PED/RYL	624-92-0
	colspan="7"	Adiabatic ionization potential determined from consideration of dissociation rates; experimentally observed onset of ionization, 8.33 eV, is much higher because of change in the CSSC bond angle upon ionization from 90° to 180°. (83BUT/BAE). See also: 81KIM/KAT.					
$C_2H_6S_3^+$							
CH_3SSSCH_3	(8.73±0.03)	(199)	(831)	−3	−11	*EST	3658-80-8
$C_2H_6Sc^+$							
C_2H_5ScH		(205)	(858)				
		$\Delta_f H$(Ion) from onset of endothermic reaction (84TOL/BEA).					
$(CH_3)_2Sc$		189	791				
		$\Delta_f H$(Ion) from onset of endothermic reaction (84TOL/BEA). See also: 86ELK/ARI.					
$C_2H_4ScH_2$		(218)	(912)				
		$\Delta_f H$(Ion) from onset of endothermic reaction (84TOL/BEA).					
$C_2H_6Se^+$							
$(CH_3)_2Se$	8.40±0.01	(198)	(827)	4	17	*EST	593-79-3
		IP from 84BOC/AYG, 82LEV/LIA.					
$C_2H_6Se_2^+$							
$(CH_3Se)_2$	(8.1)	(197)	(826)	11	44	*EST	7101-31-7
		IP is onset of photoelectron band (84BOC/AYG).					
$C_2H_6Si^+$							
$CH_2=CHSiH_3$	10.1	234	978	1±3	4±13	80TEL/RAB	7291-09-0
		IP is onset of photoelectron band.					
$C_2H_6Zn^+$							
$(CH_3)_2Zn$	(9.00±0.02)	(220)	(919)	12.1±0.3	50.6±1.3	77PED/RYL	544-97-8
$C_2H_7^+$							
C_2H_7		202	845				
		From proton affinity of C_2H_6 (RN 74-84-0). See also: 85MCM/KEB. PA = 143.6 kcal/mol, 601 kJ/mol.					
$C_2H_7As^+$							
$(CH_3)_2AsH$	(8.1)	(194)	(813)	7	31	*EST	593-57-7
		IP is onset of photoelectron band (82ELB/DIE).					
$C_2H_7BO_2^+$							
$(CH_3O)_2BH$	(9.7±1.0)	(85)	(355)	−138.8±0.4	−580.7±1.7	77PED/RYL	4542-61-4

Table 1. Positive Ion Table - Continued

ION / Neutral	Ionization potential eV	$\Delta_f H$(Ion) kcal/mol	$\Delta_f H$(Ion) kJ/mol	$\Delta_f H$(Neutral) kcal/mol	$\Delta_f H$(Neutral) kJ/mol	Neutral reference	CAS registry number
$C_2H_7B_4^+$		(170)	(710)				

From proton affinity of 1,6-dicarbahexaborane(6) (RN 20693-67-8). PA = 207. kcal/mol, 866. kJ/mol.

$C_2H_7B_5^+$	10.54	240.5	1006.3	-2.5 ± 2.6	-10.6 ± 10.9	85GAL/TAM	20693-69-0
$C_2H_7ClO^+$ $(CH_3)_2OHCl$	(10.4)	(167)	(698)	-73	-305	82TN270	24521-77-5

IP is onset of photoelectron band.

$C_2H_7FN^+$ $CH_2FCH_2NH_3$		99	413				

From proton affinity of $CH_2FCH_2NH_2$ (RN 406-34-8). PA = 212.3 kcal/mol, 888 kJ/mol.

$C_2H_7Hg^+$ $(CH_3)_2HgH$		(202)	(846)				

From proton affinity of CH_3HgCH_3 (RN 593-74-8). PA = ~186 kcal/mol, ~778 kJ/mol.

$C_2H_7N^+$ $C_2H_5NH_2$	8.86±0.02	193	807	-11.3 ± 0.2	-47.5 ± 0.7	77PED/RYL	75-04-7

See also: 83OHN/IMA, 81KIM/KAT.

$(CH_3)_2NH$	8.23±0.08	185	776	-4.4 ± 0.1	-18.5 ± 0.4	77PED/RYL	124-40-3

See also: 81KIM/KAT.

$C_2H_7NO^+$ $NH_2CH_2CH_2OH$	8.96	158	662	-48	-202	77REI/PRA	141-43-5

IP from 83KOP/MOL, 83MOL/PIK3, in agreement with onset of photoelectron band (81KIM/KAT).

CH_3NHOCH_3	8.92	(197)	(824)	-9	-37	*EST	1117-97-1

IP from 83MOL/PIK.

$C_2H_7N_2^+$ CH_3NNHCH_3		194	813				

From proton affinity of (E)-$CH_3N=NCH_3$ (RN 4143-41-3). PA = 206.9 kcal/mol, 866 kJ/mol.

$C_2H_7O^+$ $C_2H_5OH_2$		121	507				

From proton affinity of C_2H_5OH (RN 64-17-5). PA = 188.3 kcal/mol, 788 kJ/mol.

$(CH_3)_2OH$		130	542				

From proton affinity of $(CH_3)_2O$ (RN 115-10-6). PA = 192.1 kcal/mol, 804 kJ/mol.

Table 1. Positive Ion Table — Continued

ION / Neutral	Ionization potential eV	$\Delta_f H$(Ion) kcal/mol	$\Delta_f H$(Ion) kJ/mol	$\Delta_f H$(Neutral) kcal/mol	$\Delta_f H$(Neutral) kJ/mol	Neutral reference	CAS registry number
$C_2H_7OS^+$							
$(CH_3)_2SOH$		118	495				

From proton affinity of $(CH_3)_2SO$ (RN 67-68-5). PA = 211.3 kcal/mol, 834 kJ/mol.

$C_2H_7O_3P^+$							
$(CH_3O)_2PHO$	(10.53)	(43)	(179)	(−200)	(−837)	*EST	868-85-9

IP from 80ZVE/VIL.

$C_2H_7P^+$							
$(CH_3)_2PH$	8.47±0.07	(181)	(757)	−14	−60	*EST	676-59-5

See also: 82COW/KEM.

$C_2H_7S^+$							
$C_2H_5SH_2$		164	686				

From proton affinity of C_2H_5SH (RN 75-08-1). PA = 190.8 kcal/mol, 798 kJ/mol.

| $(CH_3)_2SH$ | | 156 | 653 | | | | |

From proton affinity of $(CH_3)_2S$ (RN 75-18-3). PA = 200.6 kcal/mol, 839 kJ/mol.

$C_2H_7S_2^+$							
CH_3SSHCH_3		(164)	(686)				

From proton affinity of CH_3SSCH_3 (RN 624-92-0). PA = ~196 kcal/mol, ~820 kJ/mol.

$C_2H_8B_5^+$

	(195)	(816)				

From proton affinity of 2,4-dicarbaheptabornane(7) (RN 20693-69-0).
PA = 168. kcal/mol, 703. kJ/mol.

$C_2H_8N^+$							
$C_2H_5NH_3$		137	574				

From proton affinity of $C_2H_5NH_2$ (RN 75-04-7). PA = 217.0 kcal/mol, 908. kJ/mol.

| $(CH_3)_2NH_2$ | | 141 | 588 | | | | |

From proton affinity of $(CH_3)_2NH$ (RN 124-40-3). PA = 220.6 kcal/mol, 923. kJ/mol.

$C_2H_8NO^+$							
$H_3N(CH_2)_2OH$		96	402				

From proton affinity of $NH_2(CH_2)_2OH$ (RN 141-43-5). PA = 221.3 kcal/mol, 926. kJ/mol.

$C_2H_8N_2^+$							
$H_2NCH_2CH_2NH_2$	(8.6)	(194)	(812)	−4.3±0.5	−17.8±2.1	77PED/RYL	107-15-3

IP is onset of photoelectron band (81KIM/KAT).

| $(CH_3)_2NNH_2$ | 7.28±0.04 | 188 | 786 | 20±0.5 | 84±2 | 77PED/RYL | 57-14-7 |

IP from charge transfer equilibrium constant determination. Reference standard:
IP ($C_6H_5N(CH_3)_2$) = 7.12 eV (84MAU/NEL). See also: 81KIM/KAT.

Table 1. Positive Ion Table – Continued

ION Neutral	Ionization potential eV	$\Delta_f H$(Ion) kcal/mol	$\Delta_f H$(Ion) kJ/mol	$\Delta_f H$(Neutral) kcal/mol	$\Delta_f H$(Neutral) kJ/mol	Neutral reference	CAS registry number
$C_2H_8N_2^+$							
$C_2H_5NHNH_2$				16±0.2	69±1	*EST	624-80-6

A value of 8.12 eV has been reported for the adiabatic IP of this compound. Values of IP's of hydrazines determined by threshold measurements are usually significantly higher than the adiabatic value because of the large geometry change associated with ionization.

$(CH_3NH)_2$				22±1	92±4	77PED/RYL	540-73-8

Values of 7.75 and 8.22 eV have been reported for the adiabatic IP of this compound. Reported values of IP's of hydrazines determined by threshold measurements are usually significantly higher than the adiabatic value because of the large geometry change associated with ionization. See also: 81KIM/KAT.

$C_2H_8P^+$							
$(CH_3)_2PH_2$		134	559				

From proton affinity of $(CH_3)_2PH$ (RN 676-59-5). PA = 216.3 kcal/mol, 905 kJ/mol.

$C_2H_8Si^+$							
$C_2H_5SiH_3$	(10.18±0.05)	(262)	(1095)	27±3	113±13	80TEL/RAB	2814-79-1
$(CH_3)_2SiH_2$	10.3	215	899	−23±1	−95±4	86DON/WAL	1111-74-6
$C_2H_9N_2^+$							
$H_2NCH_2CH_2NH_3$		135	567				

From proton affinity of $H_2NCH_2CH_2NH_2$ (RN 107-15-3). PA = 225.9 kcal/mol, 945 kJ/mol.

$(CH_3)_2NHNH_2$		166	694				

From proton affinity of $(CH_3)_2NNH_2$ (RN 57-14-7). PA = 219.9 kcal/mol, 920 kJ/mol (84MAU/NEL).

$C_2H_{10}BN^+$							
$((CH_3)_2NH)(BH_3)$	(9.39±0.01)	(202)	(847)	−14±1	−59±4	80TEL/RAB	74-94-2
$C_2H_{12}B_{10}^+$	(10.19)	(191)	(800)	−44±2	−183±8	82PIL/SKI	16986-24-6
	(10.2)	(175)	(733)	−60±2	−251±8	82PIL/SKI	20644-12-6

IP is onset of photoelectron band.

$C_2I_2^+$							
IC≡CI	(9.03)	(269.57)	(1127.90)	61.34	256.64	84DEW/HEA	624-74-8

Table 1. Positive Ion Table - Continued

ION / Neutral	Ionization potential eV	$\Delta_f H$(Ion) kcal/mol	$\Delta_f H$(Ion) kJ/mol	$\Delta_f H$(Neutral) kcal/mol	$\Delta_f H$(Neutral) kJ/mol	Neutral reference	CAS registry number
C_2La^+							
LaC$_2$	(5.4±0.3)	(266)	(1113)	141±2	592±6	81GIN/PEL	12071-15-7
		(266)	*(1112)*	*141*	*591*		
C_2N^+							
CCN	12.0	(410)	(1715)	133	556	85JANAF	12327-12-7

$\Delta_f H$(Ion) from appearance potential measurements (83SMI, 85HAR/MCI).
IP cited is $\Delta_f H$(Ion) - $\Delta_f H$(Neutral).

CNC		(387)	(1620)				

$\Delta_f H$(Ion) from appearance potential measurements (85HAR/MCI).

$C_2N_2^+$							
NCCN	13.37±0.01	381.6	1596.7	73.3±0.2	306.7±0.7	77PED/RYL	460-19-5
		381.1	*1594.8*	*72.8*	*304.8*		

See also: 83SMI.

$C_2N_2O^+$							
NCNCO	(11.49±0.02)	(296)	(1238)	31	129	*EST	22430-66-6
$C_2N_2S_2^+$							
(SCN)$_2$	(10.5)	(326)	(1363)	84±1	350±6	77PED/RYL	505-14-6

IP is onset of photoelectron band.

C_2Sc^+							
C$_2$Sc	7.7±0.2	325	1360	147±3	617±12	81HAQ/GIN	12175-91-6
		324	*1357*	*147*	*614*		

See also: 81HAQ/GIN.

C_2Si^+							
(C≡C / Si cyclic)	(10.2±0.5)	(382)	(1599)	147	615	82TN270	12071-27-1
		(381)	*(1594)*	*146*	*610*		
C_2Th^+							
C$_2$Th	(6.4±0.5)	(321)	(1341)	173	724	82TN270	12071-31-7
C_2V^+							
C$_2$V		(335)	(1401)				

$\Delta_f H$(Ion) from onset energy of endothermic reaction (84ARI/ARM, 85ELK/ARM). 0 K value.

C_2Y^+							
C$_2$Y	6.7±0.3	297	1243	143	597	82TN270	12071-35-1
		296	*1240*	*142*	*594*		
C_3^+							
C$_3$	(12.1±0.3)	(479)	(2004)	200±4	837±17	83RAK/BOH	12075-35-3

Table 1. Positive Ion Table - Continued

ION / Neutral	Ionization potential eV	$\Delta_f H$(Ion) kcal/mol	kJ/mol	$\Delta_f H$(Neutral) kcal/mol	kJ/mol	Neutral reference	CAS registry number
C_3BrN^+							
BrC≡CCN	(10.71±0.02)	(350)	(1466)	103±5	433±20	79BUC/VOG	3114-46-3
	See also: 84KUH/MAI.						
C_3ClN^+							
ClC≡CCN	10.95±0.02	334	1396	81±5	339±20	79BUC/VOG	2003-31-8
C_3FN^+							
CF≡CCN	(11.51±0.02)	(305)	(1278)	40±12	167±50	79BUC/VOG	32038-83-8
$C_3F_3N^+$							
$CF_2=CFCN$	(10.6±0.1)	(139)	(584)	−105±0.7	−439±3	71JANAF	433-43-2
$C_3F_3N_3^+$	(11.3)	(131)	(548)	−129	−542	*EST	675-14-9
	IP is onset of photoelectron band (81ASB/SVE).						
$C_3F_4^+$							
$CF_2=C=CF_2$	(10.88)	(109)	(456)	−142	−594	86SMA	461-68-7
$C_3F_6^+$							
$CF_3CF=CF_2$	10.60±0.03	−24	−102	−269	−1125	75CHE/ROD	116-15-4
	IP from 81BER/BOM.						
	11.18±0.03	24	101	−234	−978	81BOM/BER	931-91-9
	IP from 81BER/BOM.						
$C_3F_6O^+$							
$(CF_3)_2CO$	(11.44)	(−70)	(−293)	−334	−1397	72GOR	684-16-2
$C_3F_8^+$							
C_3F_8	13.38	−118	−492	−426±2	−1783±7	77PED/RYL	76-19-7
$C_3F_9N^+$							
$(CF_3)_3N$	11.7	(−168)	(−703)	−438	−1832	*EST	432-03-1
	IP is onset of photoelectron band (82ELB/DIE, 82BUR/PAW).						
C_3H^+							
HCCC		(381)	(1593)				
	From proton affinity of C_3 (RN 12075-35-3). PA = ~185 kcal/mol, ~774 kJ/mol.						
$C_3HF_3^+$							
$CF_3C≡CH$	(11.96±0.02)	(177)	(741)	−99	−413	86SMA	661-54-1
	See also: 81BIE/ASB.						

Table 1. Positive Ion Table – Continued

ION Neutral	Ionization potential eV	Δ_fH(Ion) kcal/mol kJ/mol		Δ_fH(Neutral) kcal/mol kJ/mol		Neutral reference	CAS registry number
$C_3HF_5N^+$							
C_2F_5CNH		−21	−86				
From proton affinity of C_2F_5CN (RN 422-04-8). PA = 167.1 kcal/mol, 699 kJ/mol.								
$C_3HF_6O^+$							
$(CF_3)_2COH$		−118	−495				
From proton affinity of $(CF_3)_2CO$ (RN 684-16-2) (85MCM/KEB, 85MCM/KEB2) re-evaluated relative to CO standard (84LIA/LIE). PA = 150.0 kcal/mol, 628. kJ/mol.								
$C_3HF_8N^+$							
$(CF_3)_2NCHF_2$	(11.7)	(−110)	(−461)	−380	−1590	*EST	73563-15-2
IP from 82BUR/PAW.							
C_3HN^+							
$HC{\equiv}CCN$	11.64±0.01	352	1474	84	351	85HAR	1070-71-9
C_3HNO^+							
$NCCH{=}C{=}O$	(≤10.07)	(≤256)	(≤1073)	24	101	*EST	
IP from 81BOC/HIR.							
C_3HO^+							
$HC{\equiv}C{-}C{=}O$		232	971				
From appearance potential determinations (83TER/HOL).								
$C_3H_2^+$							
$HC{\equiv}CCH$		(330±3)	(1381±12)				2008-19-7
$C_3H^+ + H_2 \rightarrow C_3H_2^+ + H$ is ~1 kcal/mol endothermic. (84SMI/ADA).							
(cyclopropenylidene)		281±3	1176±12				75123-91-0
From appearance potentials in CH_3CCX compounds. (84HOL/SZU).							
$C_3H_2F_2^+$							
$CF_2{=}C{=}CH_2$	(9.79±0.03)	(178)	(743)	−48	−202	86SMA	430-64-8
$C_3H_2F_4O^+$							
$(CHF_2)_2CO$	(10.7)	(15)	(61)	−232±4	−971±16	*EST	360-52-1
IP is onset of photoelectron band.							
$C_3H_2F_6O^+$							
$CF_3CH(OH)CF_3$	11.94	(−92)	(−384)	−367±2	−1536±8	*EST	920-66-1
IP from 83KOP/MOL.							
$C_3H_2F_7N^+$							
$(CF_2H)_2NCF_3$	(11.4)	(−60)	(−250)	−323	−1350	*EST	73551-02-7
IP from 82BUR/PAW.							
$C_3H_2N^+$							
$HCCCNH$		269	1127.5				
From proton affinity of $HC{\equiv}CCN$ (RN 1070-71-9) (87DEA/MAU, 85KNI/FRE). PA = 180. kcal/mol, 753.5 kJ/mol.							

Table 1. Positive Ion Table – Continued

ION / Neutral	Ionization potential eV	$\Delta_f H$(Ion) kcal/mol	$\Delta_f H$(Ion) kJ/mol	$\Delta_f H$(Neutral) kcal/mol	$\Delta_f H$(Neutral) kJ/mol	Neutral reference	CAS registry number
$C_3H_2N_2^+$							
$CH_2(CN)_2$	(12.70) IP from 83MOL/PIK2.	(356)	(1491)	63.5±0.4	265.5±1.5	77PED/RYL	109-77-3
$C_3H_2N_2O_3^+$							
(hydantoin structure)	(10.67)	(134)	(559)	−112	−470	*EST	120-89-8
$C_3H_2O^+$							
HC≡CCHO	(10.8) IP from 80VON/BIE. See also: 79CAR/MOU.	(276)	(1157)	27	115	*EST	624-67-9
$CH_2=C=C=O$	9.12±0.05 IP from 83TER/HOL. See also: 85MCN/SUF.	(233)	(975)	23	95	*EST	61244-93-7
(cyclopropenone)	(9.47)	(251)	(1052)	33±2	138±8	*EST	2961-80-0
$C_3H_2OS_2^+$							
(1,3-dithiol-2-one)	(8.6) IP is onset of photoelectron band (83SCH/SCH).	(195)	(815)	−3.6±1.2	−15.0±5.1	77PED/RYL	2314-40-1
$C_3H_2O_2^+$							
HC≡CCOOH	(10.45) IP is onset of photoelectron band (80VON/BIE).	(213)	(891)	−28	−117	*EST	471-25-0
$C_3H_2O_3^+$							
(vinylene carbonate)	(9.8) IP is onset of photoelectron band.	(126)	(527)	−100±5	−419±21	77PED/RYL	872-36-6
$C_3H_2S_3^+$							
(1,3-dithiole-2-thione)	8.26	251	1050	60.5±2	253±7	77PED/RYL	930-35-8

Table 1. Positive Ion Table - Continued

ION / Neutral	Ionization potential eV	$\Delta_f H$(Ion) kcal/mol	$\Delta_f H$(Ion) kJ/mol	$\Delta_f H$(Neutral) kcal/mol	$\Delta_f H$(Neutral) kJ/mol	Neutral reference	CAS registry number
$C_3H_3^+$							
$CH_2C\equiv CH$	8.68	282	1179	82	343		2932-78-7

$HCCCH^+ + H_2 \rightarrow CH_2C\equiv CH^+ + H$ is 4 kcal/mol endothermic (84SMI/ADA); value derived from appearance potential measurements is 281±3 kcal/mol; 1176 kJ/mol. $\Delta_f H$(Neutral) = $\Delta_f H$(Ion) - IP.

cyclo-C_3H_3	6.6	257	1075	105±4	440±17	82MCM/GOL	28933-84-8

Heat of formation of ion from appearance potential measurements; IP given is $\Delta_f H$(Ion) - $\Delta_f H$(Neutral).

ION / Neutral	IP eV	$\Delta_f H$(Ion) kcal/mol	kJ/mol	$\Delta_f H$(Neutral) kcal/mol	kJ/mol	Neutral reference	CAS registry number
$C_3H_3Cl^+$							
$CH_2=C=CHCl$	(9.57)	(263)	(1102)	43	179	*EST	3223-70-9
$CH_3C\equiv CCl$	9.82	(276)	(1153)	49±4	206±15	*EST	7747-84-4
$CH_2ClC\equiv CH$	10.68	(285)	(1192)	39	162	*EST	624-65-7

See also: 81ZVE/ERM, 82BIE/ASB.

$C_3H_3F_3^+$							
CH_2CHCF_3	(10.9)	(104)	(438)	−147±2	−614±7	77PED/RYL	32718-30-2
$C_3H_3F_3O^+$							
CH_3COCF_3	10.67	(52)	(217)	−194	−812	*EST	421-50-1
$C_3H_3F_3O_2^+$							
$HCOOCH_2CF_3$	(11.31)	(5)	(18)	−256	−1073	*EST	32042-38-9
$C_3H_3F_4O^+$							
$(CF_2H)_2COH$		−32	−134				

From proton affinity of CF_2HCOCF_2H (RN 360-52-1). PA = 170 kcal/mol, 711 kJ/mol.

$C_3H_3F_5O^+$							
$C_2F_5CH_2OH$	(11.2)	(−55)	(−229)	−313±0.7	−1310±3	77PED/RYL	422-05-9

IP is onset of photoelectron band.

$C_3H_3F_6N^+$							
$(CF_2H)_3N$	(11.2)	(−7)	(−29)	−265	−1110	*EST	73551-03-8

IP from 82BUR/PAW.

$C_3H_3F_6O^+$							
$(CF_3)_2CHOH_2$		−180	−755				

From proton affinity of $(CF_3)_2CHOH$ (RN 920-66-1). PA = 165.0 kcal/mol, 690 kJ/mol.

$C_3H_3N^+$							
CH_2CHCN	10.91±0.01	296	1237	44	184	82CHU/NGU	107-13-1

See also: 84OHN/MAT, 81KIM/KAT.

Table 1. Positive Ion Table - Continued

ION / Neutral	Ionization potential eV	$\Delta_f H$(Ion) kcal/mol	$\Delta_f H$(Ion) kJ/mol	$\Delta_f H$(Neutral) kcal/mol	$\Delta_f H$(Neutral) kJ/mol	Neutral reference	CAS registry number
$C_3H_3NO^+$							
$CH_2=CHNCO$	(9.3)	(208)	(872)	−6	−25	*EST	3555-94-0
	IP is onset of photoelectron band.						
$HC\equiv CCONH_2$	(9.85)	(244)	(1023)	17	73	*EST	7341-96-0
	IP is onset of photoelectron band (81ASB/SVE).						
(isoxazole)	9.93±0.05	248	1037	19	79	78MCC/HAM	288-14-2
	IP from 81BOU/HOP.						
(oxazole)	(9.6)	(217)	(910)	−4±0.2	−16±1	78MCC/HAM	288-42-6
$C_3H_3NS^+$							
(isothiazole)	(9.55)	(261)	(1090)	40	169	*EST	288-16-4
(thiazole)	(≤9.50)	(≤256)	(≤1070)	37±2	153±10	*EST	288-47-1
$C_3H_3N_2^+$							
$NCCH_2CNH$		254	1061				
	From proton affinity of $CH_2(CN)_2$ (RN 109-77-3). PA = 175.6 kcal/mol, 735 kJ/mol.						
$C_3H_3N_3^+$							
(1,2,4-triazine)	(9.3)	(314)	(1313)	99	416	*EST	289-96-3
	IP is onset of photoelectron band (83GLE/SPA).						
(1,3,5-triazine)	(9.2)	(292)	(1222)	80	334	*EST	290-38-0
	IP is onset of photoelectron band.						

Table 1. Positive Ion Table – Continued

ION / Neutral	Ionization potential eV	$\Delta_f H$(Ion) kcal/mol	$\Delta_f H$(Ion) kJ/mol	$\Delta_f H$(Neutral) kcal/mol	$\Delta_f H$(Neutral) kJ/mol	Neutral reference	CAS registry number
$C_3H_3N_3^+$ (1,2,4-triazine)	10.03±0.05	285	1194	54±0.2	226±1	82BYS	290-87-9
See also: 84SHA/URA.							
$C_3H_3N_3O_2^+$ (cyanuric acid)	(10.59)	(181)	(756)	−64	−266	*EST	
IP from 81AJO/CAS2.							
(isomer)	10.18	(181)	(756)	−54	−226	*EST	
IP from 81AJO/CAS2, 77ROS/DRA.							
$C_3H_3O^+$							
$CH_2=CHCO$	(7.0)	(179)	(751)	17	72	82MCM/GOL	72241-20-4
IP is $\Delta_f H$(Ion) − $\Delta_f H$(Neutral). $\Delta_f H$(Ion) from appearance potential determination.							
$HC\equiv CCH_2O$		227	950				92056-62-7
$\Delta_f H$(Ion) from appearance potential determination (84LOS/HOL).							
$C_3H_4^+$							
$CH_2=C=CH_2$	9.69±0.01	269	1126	45.6±.2	190.6±1	77PED/RYL	463-49-0
		271	1134	47.7	199.5		
See also: 81KIM/KAT, 84MOM/BUR.							
$CH_3C\equiv CH$	10.36±0.01	283.5	1186.2	44.6±.5	186.6±2	77PED/RYL	74-99-7
		285.5	1194.5	46.6	195.1		
See also: 81KIM/KAT, 84MOM/BUR.							
(cyclopropene)	9.67±0.01	289	1210	66±0.7	277±3	77PED/RYL	2781-85-3
$C_3H_4F_3O^+$							
$CH_3C(OH)CF_3$		−3	−11				
From proton affinity of CH_3COCF_3 (RN 421-50-1). PA = 174.2 kcal/mol, 729 kJ/mol.							
$C_3H_4F_3O_2^+$							
$HC(OH)CH_2CF_3$		−70	−294				
From proton affinity of $HCOOCH_2CF_3$ (RN 32042-38-9). PA = 179.4 kcal/mol, 751 kJ/mol.							

Table 1. Positive Ion Table - Continued

| ION | Ionization potential | Δ_fH(Ion) | | Δ_fH(Neutral) | | Neutral | CAS registry |
Neutral	eV	kcal/mol	kJ/mol	kcal/mol	kJ/mol	reference	number
$C_3H_4F_3O_2^+$							
$CF_3C(OH)CH_3$		−55	−231				

From proton affinity of CF_3COOCH_3 (RN 431-47-0). PA = 178.8 kcal/mol, 748 kJ/mol.

| $C_3H_4N^+$ | | | | | | | |
| CH_2CHCNH | (7.37) | 220 | 920 | 50±2 | 209±10 | 82MCM/GOL | 74738-52-6 |

From proton affinity of $CH_2=CHCN$ (RN 107-13-1). PA = 189.7 kcal/mol, 794. kJ/mol.
IP cited is Δ_fH(Ion) - Δ_fH(Neutral).

| $C_3H_4NO^+$ | | | | | | | |
| CH_3COCNH | | 181 | 759 | | | | |

From proton affinity of CH_3COCN (RN 631-57-2). PA = 179.5 kcal/mol, 751. kJ/mol (86MAR/TOP).

| | | 182 | 761 | | | | |

From proton affinity of isooxazole (RN 288-14-2). PA = 202.7 kcal/mol, 848 kJ/mol.

| | | 154 | 643 | | | | |

From proton affinity of oxazole (RN 288-42-6). PA = 208.2 kcal/mol, 871 kJ/mol.

| $C_3H_4NO_2^+$ | | | | | | | |
| $CH_3COOCNH$ | | 138 | 576 | | | | |

From proton affinity of CH_3OOCCN (86MAR/TOP). PA = 179.5 kcal/mol, 751. kJ/mol.

| $C_3H_4NS^+$ | | | | | | | |
| | | 189 | 791 | | | | |

From proton affinity of thiazole (RN 288-47-1). PA = 213.2 kcal/mol, 892 kJ/mol.

$C_3H_4N_2^+$							
	9.25±0.01	258	1077	44±0.5	185±2	80SAB	288-13-1
		261	1093	48	201		

IP from 86MAI/OLE.

| | 8.81±0.01 | 238 | 995 | 35±0.5 | 145±2 | 80SAB | 288-32-4 |
| | | 242 | 1011 | 38 | 161 | | |

IP from 86MAI/OLE.

Table 1. Positive Ion Table — Continued

ION / Neutral	Ionization potential eV	$\Delta_f H$(Ion) kcal/mol	$\Delta_f H$(Ion) kJ/mol	$\Delta_f H$(Neutral) kcal/mol	$\Delta_f H$(Neutral) kJ/mol	Neutral reference	CAS registry number
$C_3H_4N_3^+$							
(1,3,5-triazine radical)		219	915				
From proton affinity of 1,3,5-triazine (RN 290-87-9). PA = 201.1 kcal/mol, 841 kJ/mol.							
$C_3H_4O^+$							
$CH_3CH=C=O$	8.95	181	759	−25	−105	80DEM/WUL	6004-44-0
IP from 81BOC/HIR.							
$CH_2=CHCHO$	10.103±0.006	215	898	−18	−77	79VAJ/HAR	107-02-8
See also: 80VON/BIE, 81KIM/KAT, 78VAN/OSK.							
$HC\equiv CCH_2OH$	10.51	(253)	(1060)	11	46	*EST	107-19-7
IP from 83KOP/MOL, 80VON/BIE.							
$HC\equiv COCH_3$	9.48	(236)	(989)	18	74	*EST	6443-91-0
IP from 86HOL/LOS.							
(cyclopropanone)	(9.1±0.1)	(214)	(894)	4	16	76ROD/CHA	5009-27-8
$C_3H_4OS_2^+$							
(1,3-dithiolan-2-one)	(9.2)	(182)	(762)	−30±1	−126±5	77PED/RYL	2080-58-2
IP is onset of photoelectron band.							
$C_3H_4O_2^+$							
$CH_2=CHCOOH$	10.60	167	699	−77	−324	80VIL/PER	79-10-7
See also: 78VAN/OSK.							
CH_3COCHO	9.60±0.06	156	655	−65±1	−271±5	77PED/RYL	78-98-8
See also: 81KIM/KAT.							
(β-propiolactone)	(9.70±0.01)	(156)	(653)	−67.6±0.2	−282.9±0.8	77PED/RYL	57-57-8

Table 1. Positive Ion Table - Continued

ION / Neutral	Ionization potential eV	$\Delta_f H$(Ion) kcal/mol	$\Delta_f H$(Ion) kJ/mol	$\Delta_f H$(Neutral) kcal/mol	$\Delta_f H$(Neutral) kJ/mol	Neutral reference	CAS registry number
$C_3H_4O_2S^+$							
(thiolactone structure)	(8.6)	(129)	(538)	−70	−292	*EST	20628-59-5
IP is onset of photoelectron band.							
$C_3H_4O_3^+$							
(ethylene carbonate structure)	(10.4)	(117)	(491)	−122±1	−512±4	83CAL	96-49-1
$CH_3COCOOH$	9.9	97	407	−131	−548	83TER/WEZ	127-17-3
IP is onset of photoelectron band.							
$C_3H_4S^+$							
$CH_2=CHCH=S$	(8.3)	(223)	(934)	32	133	*EST	53439-64-8
IP from 82BOC/MOH.							
$CH_3SC\equiv CH$	(8.3)	(247)	(1036)	56	235	*EST	10152-75-7
IP is onset of photoelectron band (81BOC/RIE).							
$C_3H_4S_3^+$							
(1,3-dithiolane-2-thione)	(8.40)	(216)	(904)	22.4±0.5	93.8±2.2	77PED/RYL	822-38-8
$C_3H_5^+$							
$CH_2CH=CH_2$	8.13	<u>226.0</u>	<u>945.6</u>	39	161	84HOL/LOS	1981-80-2
		228.9	*957.7*	*41*	*173*		
ΔH_f(Ion) from appearance potential measurements. (See also: 84TRA, 82MAC).							
For IP determination, see also 83KAG/UJS. For $\Delta_f H$(Neutral), 81TSA							
recommends 43 kcal/mol, 179 kJ/mol and 82MCM/GOL recommends 40 kcal/mol, 167 kJ/mol.							
CH_3CCH_2		231	969				
$\Delta_f H$(Ion) from appearance potential determinations (83BUR/HOL).							
(cyclopropenyl)H⁺	8.18±0.03	255	1069	66.9	279.9	82MCM/GOL	2417-82-5
IP from 85DYK/ELL.							
$C_3H_5Br^+$							
$CH_3CH=CHBr$	(9.30±0.05)	(224)	(938)	10±1	41±4	77PED/RYL	41407-21-0
$CH_2=CHCH_2Br$	10.06	243	1018	11.4±0.6	47.7±2.4	84TRA	106-95-6
See also: 82BIE/ASB.							

Table 1. Positive Ion Table — Continued

ION / Neutral	Ionization potential eV	$\Delta_f H$(Ion) kcal/mol	$\Delta_f H$(Ion) kJ/mol	$\Delta_f H$(Neutral) kcal/mol	$\Delta_f H$(Neutral) kJ/mol	Neutral reference	CAS registry number
$C_3H_5BrO^+$							
CH_3COCH_2Br	(9.73)	(181)	(758)	−43±2	−181±8	77PED/RYL	598-31-2
	IP from 84OLI/GUE.						
$C_3H_5Cl^+$							
$CH_2=CHCH_2Cl$	9.9	227	949	−1.3±0.6	−5.6±2.4	84TRA	107-05-1
	IP is onset of photoelectron band (82BIE/ASB). See also: 82LEV/LIA, 81ZVE/ERM.						
$C_3H_5ClN^+$							
$ClCH_2CH_2CNH$		188	787				
	From proton affinity of $ClCH_2CH_2CN$ (RN 542-76-7). PA = 187.5 kcal/mol, 784.5 kJ/mol.						
$C_3H_5ClO^+$							
CH_3COCH_2Cl	9.91±0.03	(175)	(731)	−54	−225	*EST	78-95-5
	See also: 84OLI/GUE.						
(epoxide)-CH_2Cl	(10.2)	(209)	(876)	−26±1	−108±4	77PED/RYL	106-89-8
	IP is onset of photoelectron band.						
$C_3H_5ClO_2^+$							
$ClH_2CCOOCH_3$	(10.3)	(138)	(577)	−100	−417	*EST	96-34-4
	IP is onset of photoelectron band (85CAN/HAM).						
$C_3H_5F^+$							
$CH_2=CHCH_2F$	10.11	196	819	−37	−156	82DOL/MED	818-92-8
$C_3H_5FO^+$							
CH_3COCH_2F	(9.9)	(136)	(572)	−92	−383	*EST	430-51-3
	See also: 84OLI/GUE.						
$C_3H_5F_2O^+$							
$(CFH_2)_2COH$		52	219				
	From proton affinity of CFH_2COCFH_2 (RN 453-14-5). PA = 187 kcal/mol, 782 kJ/mol.						
$C_3H_5F_3O^+$							
$CF_3CH_2OCH_3$	10.53	(35)	(147)	−208	−869	*EST	460-43-5
	IP from 83MOL/PIK.						
$C_3H_5I^+$							
CH_2CHCH_2I	9.298	238.2	996.6	23.8	99.5	84TRA	556-56-9
$C_3H_5IO^+$							
CH_3COCH_2I	(9.3)	(183)	(767)	−31±1	−130±5	77PED/RYL	3019-04-3
	IP is onset of photoelectron band (84OLI/GUE).						

Table 1. Positive Ion Table - Continued

ION Neutral	Ionization potential eV	$\Delta_f H$(Ion) kcal/mol	$\Delta_f H$(Ion) kJ/mol	$\Delta_f H$(Neutral) kcal/mol	$\Delta_f H$(Neutral) kJ/mol	Neutral reference	CAS registry number
$C_3H_5N^+$							
C_2H_5CN	11.84±0.02 See also: 82CHE/LAP, 81KIM/KAT.	285	1194	12.3±0.1	51.5±0.5	82CHU/NGU	107-12-0
C_2H_5NC	11.2±0.1 IP from 82CHE/LAP, 77ROS/DRA.	292	1222	33.8±1	141.4±4.2	77BAG/COL	624-79-3
(E)-CH_2=CHCH=NH	(9.65) IP is onset of photoelectron band (82SCH/SCH).	(249)	(1043)	27	112	*EST	73311-40-7
H_2C-CH $\;\;\;\;\;\;\;\;\;\;\;\;\parallel$ H_2C-N	(9.30) IP from 83DAM/BOC.	(265)	(1108)	50	211	*EST	6788-85-8
(azabicyclic structure)	(≤9.76±0.22)	(≤300)	(≤1256)	75	314	*EST	19540-05-7
$C_3H_5NO^+$							
C_2H_5NCO	(10.1) IP is onset of photoelectron band.	(196)	(819)	−37	−155	*EST	109-90-0
$NCCH_2OCH_3$	10.75 IP from 83MOL/PIK.	(240)	(1002)	−8	−35	*EST	1738-36-9
$CH_2CHCONH_2$	9.5 IP is onset of photoelectron band (78VAN/OSK).	(172)	(722)	−47	−195	*EST	79-06-1
$C_3H_5NOS^+$							
(thiazolidinone)	(9.2) IP is onset of photoelectron band (80AND/DEV).	(177)	(743)	−35	−145	*EST	2682-49-7
$C_3H_5NO_2^+$							
(oxazolidinone)	(9.6) IP is onset of photoelectron band (80AND/DEV).	(139)	(582)	−82	−344	*EST	497-25-6

Table 1. Positive Ion Table - Continued

ION / Neutral	Ionization potential eV	$\Delta_f H$(Ion) kcal/mol	$\Delta_f H$(Ion) kJ/mol	$\Delta_f H$(Neutral) kcal/mol	$\Delta_f H$(Neutral) kJ/mol	Neutral reference	CAS registry number
$C_3H_5NSSe^+$							
(2-selenoxo-thiazolidine)	7.3	(155)	(650)	−13	−54	*EST	63369-86-8

IP is onset of photoelectron band (80AND/DEV).

$C_3H_5NS_2^+$							
(2-thioxo-thiazolidine)	≤8.25	(≤161)	(≤672)	−30	−124	*EST	96-53-7

IP from 80AND/DEV, 82LEV/LIA.

$C_3H_5N_2^+$							
(imidazole·)		177	740				

From proton affinity of imidazole (RN 288-32-4) (86MAU/LIE, 84FLA/MAQ, 86TAF/ANV).
PA = 223.4 kcal/mol, 935. kJ/mol.

| (pyrazole·) | | 197 | 825 | | | | |

From proton affinity of pyrazole (RN 288-13-1) (86MAU/LIE, 84FLA/MAQ).
PA = 212.8 kcal/mol, 890. kJ/mol.

$C_3H_5O^+$							
C_2H_5CO	(5.7)	141	591	10±1	43±4	82MCM/GOL	15843-24-0

$\Delta_f H$(Ion) from appearance potential measurements (85TRA) and from proton affinity of $CH_3CH=CO$ (RN 6004-44-0). PA = 199.4 kcal/mol, 834 kJ/mol. IP given is $\Delta_f H$(Ion) − $\Delta_f H$(Neutral).

| $CH_2CHCHOH$ | | 153 | 642 | | | | |

From proton affinity of $CH_2=CHCHO$ (RN 107-02-8). PA = 193.9 kcal/mol, 811 kJ/mol.

$C_3H_6^+$							
$CH_3CH=CH_2$	9.73±0.02	229	959	4.8±0.2	20.2±0.4	77PED/RYL	115-07-1

See also: 81KIM/KAT.

| (cyclopropane) | 9.86 | 240 | 1004 | 12.7±.2 | 53.3±0.5 | 77PED/RYL | 75-19-4 |
| | | 244 | 1022 | 16.9 | 70.9 | | |

IP from 84LIA/BUC. See also: 81KIM/KAT.

$C_3H_6Br_2^+$							
$CH_2BrCHBrCH_3$	10.1	216	903	−17±0.2	−71±1	77PED/RYL	78-75-1

IP is onset of photoelectron band (81KIM/KAT).

| $CH_2BrCH_2CH_2Br$ | ≤10.26 | (≤220) | (≤919) | −17 | −71 | *EST | 109-64-8 |

Table 1. Positive Ion Table - Continued

ION / Neutral	Ionization potential eV	$\Delta_f H$(Ion) kcal/mol	$\Delta_f H$(Ion) kJ/mol	$\Delta_f H$(Neutral) kcal/mol	$\Delta_f H$(Neutral) kJ/mol	Neutral reference	CAS registry number
$C_3H_6Cl_2^+$							
$CH_3CHClCH_2Cl$	(10.87±0.05)	(212)	(886)	−38.9±0.3	−162.6±0.3	77PED/RYL	78-87-5
$CH_2ClCH_2CH_2Cl$	10.85±0.05	212	887	−38±2	−160±8	77PED/RYL	142-28-9
$C_3H_6FO^+$							
$CH_3C(OH)CH_2F$		82	344				
From proton affinity of CH_3COCH_2F (RN 430-51-3). PA = 192.0 kcal/mol, 803. kJ/mol.							
$C_3H_6F_2^+$							
$(CH_3)_2CF_2$	(11.42±0.02)	(138)	(578)	−125±3	−524±13	82DOL/MED	420-45-1
$C_3H_6F_3N^+$							
$CF_3CH_2CH_2NH_2$	(9.3)	(40)	(166)	−175	−731	*EST	460-39-9
IP from 79AUE/BOW							
$CF_3N(CH_3)_2$	(9.2)	(25)	(104)	−187	−784	*EST	677-41-8
IP from 79AUE/BOW.							
$C_3H_6N^+$							
C_2H_5CNH		185	775				
From proton affinity of C_2H_5CN (RN 107-12-0). PA = 192.6 kcal/mol, 806 kJ/mol.							
C_2H_5NCH		196	819				
From proton affinity of C_2H_5NC (RN 624-79-3) (86MAU/KAR). PA = 203.7 kcal/mol, 852. kJ/mol.							
$HCCCH_2NH_3$		208	870				
From proton affinity of $HC\equiv CCH_2NH_2$ (RN 2450-71-7). PA = 210.8 kcal/mol, 882 kJ/mol.							
1-azabicyclo[1.1.0]butane·H⁺		(229)	(957)				
From proton affinity of 1-azabicyclo[1.1.0]butane (RN 19540-05-7). PA = (212) kcal/mol, (887) kJ/mol.							
$C_3H_6N_2^+$							
$(CH_3)_2NC\equiv N$	(9.0)	(241)	(1007)	33	139	*EST	1467-79-4
IP is onset of photoelectron band.							
3,3-dimethyldiazirine	(≤9.76)	(≤267)	(≤1118)	42	176	*EST	5161-49-9

J. Phys. Chem. Ref. Data, Vol. 17, Suppl. 1, 1988

Table 1. Positive Ion Table — Continued

ION / Neutral	Ionization potential eV	$\Delta_f H$(Ion) kcal/mol	$\Delta_f H$(Ion) kJ/mol	$\Delta_f H$(Neutral) kcal/mol	$\Delta_f H$(Neutral) kJ/mol	Neutral reference	CAS registry number
$C_3H_6N_2O^+$	(8.9)	(163)	(683)	−42	−176	*EST	120-93-4
	IP is onset of photoelectron band (80AND/DEV).						
$C_3H_6N_2S^+$	8.15	210	880	22	94	*EST	96-45-7
$C_3H_6N_2Se^+$	(7.0)	(192)	(803)	31	128	*EST	33251-51-3
	IP is onset of photoelectron band (80AND/DEV).						
$C_3H_6O^+$							
C_2H_5CHO	9.953±0.005	184.7	772.9	−44.8±0.4	−187.4±1.5	77PED/RYL	123-38-6
	See also: 81ELS/ALL, 85TRA, 81KIM/KAT, 77STA/WIE.						
$(CH_3)_2CO$	9.705	171.9	719.2	−51.9±0.1	−217.2±0.4	76CHA/ZWO	67-64-1
	See also: 72POT/SOR, 81KIM/KAT, 77STA/WIE.						
$CH_2=CHCH_2OH$	9.67±0.05	193	809	−30±0.5	−124±2	77PED/RYL	107-18-6
	See also: 83BOM/DAN, 82HOL/BUR.						
(E)-$CH_3CH=CHOH$	8.64±0.02	159	665	−40	−169	84TUR2	57642-95-2
	$\Delta_f H$(Ion) from appearance potential determinations. (82HOL/LOS3, 82HOL/BUR). IP from 84TUR2. $\Delta_f H$(Neutral) is $\Delta_f H$(Ion) - IP. (See 84TUR2).						
(Z)-$CH_3CH=CHOH$	8.70±0.03	159	665	−42	−174	84TUR2	57642-96-3
	$\Delta_f H$(Ion) from appearance potential determinations. (82HOL/LOS3, 82HOL/BUR) IP from 84TUR2. $\Delta_f H$(Neutral) is $\Delta_f H$(Ion) - IP. (See 84TUR2).						
$CH_2=C(OH)CH_3$	8.67±0.05	158	661	−42	−176	84TUR/HAN	74324-85-9
	$\Delta_f H$(Ion) from appearance potential determinations 82HOL/LOS3. (See also: 82LIF2). IP from 84TUR/HAN.						
$CH_2=CHOCH_3$	(8.93±0.02)	(182)	(762)	−24±2	−100±7	*EST	107-25-5
(oxetane)	9.668±0.005	203.7	852.3	−19.2±0.1	−80.5±0.6	77PED/RYL	503-30-0
	See also: 79AUE/BOW.						

Table 1. Positive Ion Table - Continued

ION Neutral	Ionization potential eV	$\Delta_f H$(Ion) kcal/mol	$\Delta_f H$(Ion) kJ/mol	$\Delta_f H$(Neutral) kcal/mol	$\Delta_f H$(Neutral) kJ/mol	Neutral reference	CAS registry number
$C_3H_6O^+$							
(methyloxirane)	10.22±0.02 See also: 81KIM/KAT, 79AUE/BOW.	213	891	−22.6±0.1	−94.7±0.6	77PED/RYL	75-56-9
(cyclopropanol)	(9.10) IP from 83BOM/DAN. See also: 82HOL/BUR.	(188)	(785)	−22	−93	*EST	16545-68-9
$C_3H_6OS^+$							
$CH_3C(=O)SCH_3$	(9.5) IP is onset of photoelectron band.	(182)	(761)	−37	−156	*EST	1534-08-3
(1,3-oxathiolane)	(8.1) IP is onset of photoelectron band (83JOR/CAR).	(231)	(966)	44	184	*EST	5684-29-7
(thietane-S-oxide)	(8.5) IP is onset of photoelectron band (83JOR/CAR).	(184)	(769)	−12	−51	*EST	13153-11-2
(2-hydroxythietane)	(8.3) IP is onset of photoelectron band (83JOR/CAR).	(137)	(572)	−55	−229	*EST	50879-06-6
$C_3H_6O_2^+$							
C_2H_5COOH	10.525±0.003 See also: 81HOL/FIN, 81KIM/KAT.	136	567	−107±0.5	−448±2	77PED/RYL	79-09-4
$HCOOC_2H_5$	10.61±0.01	(153)	(637)	−92	−387	*EST	109-94-4
CH_3COOCH_3	10.27±0.02 See also: 85CAN/HAM.	139	581	−98.0±0.2	−410.0±0.8	77PED/RYL	79-20-9
$CH_2=C(OH)OCH_3$	From appearance potential determination.	114	477				4453-91-2
$CH_3CH=C(OH)_2$	From appearance potential determinations.	104	437				
$CH_3C(OH)OCH_2$	Estimated in 86BUR/HOL.	(127)	(533)				

Table 1. Positive Ion Table - Continued

ION Neutral	Ionization potential eV	$\Delta_f H$(Ion) kcal/mol	 kJ/mol	$\Delta_f H$(Neutral) kcal/mol	 kJ/mol	Neutral reference	CAS registry number
$C_3H_6O_2^+$							
(1,2-dioxolane)	(≤9.86)	(≤203)	(≤847)	−25	−104	*EST	4362-13-4
(1,3-dioxolane)	(9.9)	(157)	(658)	−71.1±0.1	−297.5±0.6	77PED/RYL	646-06-0
	IP is onset of photoelectron band.						
$C_3H_6O_2S^+$							
$(CH_3O)_2CS$	(8.7)	(121)	(504)	−80	−335	*EST	1115-13-5
	IP is onset of photoelectron band.						
$C_3H_6O_3^+$							
$CH_3OCOOCH_3$	(10.5)	(103)	(432)	−139	−581	*EST	616-38-6
	IP is onset of photoelectron band.						
(1,3,5-trioxane)	(10.3)	(126)	(528)	−111.4±0.1	−465.9±0.3	77PED/RYL	110-88-3
	IP is onset of photoelectron band.						
$C_3H_6O_3P^+$							
(2,6,7-trioxa-1-phosphabicyclo[2.2.1]heptane)		25	105				
	From proton affinity of 2,6,7-trioxa-1-phosphabicyclo[2.2.1]heptane (RN 279-53-8). PA = 194.0 kcal/mol, 812. kJ/mol.						
$C_3H_6S^+$							
$(CH_3)_2CS$	≤8.60±0.05	≤196	≤821	−2	−9	79JOS	4756-05-2
$CH_2=CHCH_2SH$	9.25	(228)	(956)	15±2	64±9	*EST	870-23-5
$CH_2=CHSCH_3$	8.2	(207)	(865)	18±0.2	74±1	*EST	1822-74-8
	IP is onset of photoelectron band.						
(thietane)	8.69	214.9 219.5	899.1 918.4	14.5 19.1	60.7 79.9	77PED/RYL	287-27-4
	Results from 83BUT/BAE2. See also: 79AUE/BOW.						

Table 1. Positive Ion Table - Continued

ION / Neutral	Ionization potential eV	$\Delta_f H$(Ion) kcal/mol	$\Delta_f H$(Ion) kJ/mol	$\Delta_f H$(Neutral) kcal/mol	$\Delta_f H$(Neutral) kJ/mol	Neutral reference	CAS registry number
$C_3H_6S^+$							
(methylthiirane)	8.7	212	885	11±0.5	46±2	77PED/RYL	1072-43-1

IP is onset of photoelectron band. See also: 79AUE/BOW.

$C_3H_6S_2^+$							
CH_3CSSCH_3	(8.1)	(211)	(882)	24±3	100±13	*EST	2168-84-5

IP is onset of photoelectron band.

| (1,2-dithiolane) | (7.6) | (170) | (712) | −5 | −21 | *EST | 557-22-2 |

IP is onset of photoelectron band (80BOC/STE).

| (1,3-dithiolane) | 8.6 | (201) | (840) | 2 | 10 | *EST | 4829-04-3 |

IP is onset of photoelectron band.

$C_3H_6S_3^+$							
$(CH_3S)_2CS$	(7.9)	(203)	(851)	21	89	*EST	2314-48-9

IP is onset of photoelectron band.

| (1,3,5-trithiane) | (7.7) | (190) | (797) | 13 | 54 | *EST | 291-21-4 |

IP is onset of photoelectron band. (81BOC/SCH).

$C_3H_7^+$							
n-C_3H_7	8.09±0.01	211	881	24.0±0.5	100.5±2.1	85TSA	2143-61-5
		214	*896*	*27*	*115*		

IP from 85DYK/ELL. See also: 84SCH/HOU. $\Delta_f H$(Neutral) based on D[C-H] = 100.5 kcal/mol.

| iso-C_3H_7 | 7.36±0.02 | 190.9 | 798.9 | 22.3±0.6 | 93.3±2.5 | 85TSA | 19252-53-0 |
| | | *195.3* | *817.1* | *25.6* | *107.0* | | |

Heat of formation of ion from appearance potential measurements (80BAE, 82ROS/BUF, 81TRA/MCL). IP from 85DYK/ELL. See also: 83BRA/BAE2. $\Delta_f H$(Neutral) based on D[C-H] = 99 kcal/mol. PA ($CH_3CH=CH_2$) = 179.5 kcal/mol, 751. kJ/mol.

| (c-C_3H_6)H^+ | | 198.5 | 831 | | | | |

From proton affinity of c-C_3H_6. (RN 75-19-4). PA = 179.8 kcal/mol, 752 kJ/mol.

Table 1. Positive Ion Table – Continued

ION / Neutral	Ionization potential eV	$\Delta_f H$(Ion) kcal/mol	kJ/mol	$\Delta_f H$(Neutral) kcal/mol	kJ/mol	Neutral reference	CAS registry number
$C_3H_7Br^+$							
n-C_3H_7Br	10.18±0.01	214	898	−20.2±0.1	−84.5±0.5	77PED/RYL	106-94-5
		221	*926*	*−13*	*−56*		
	See also: 81KIM/KAT.						
iso-C_3H_7Br	10.07±0.01	209	873	−23.4±0.2	−98.3±0.9	80TRA	75-26-3
		215	*901*	*−17*	*−70*		
	See also: 81KIM/KAT.						
$C_3H_7Cl^+$							
n-C_3H_7Cl	10.82±0.03	218	911	−31.6±0.1	−132.4±0.6	77PED/RYL	540-54-5
	See also: 81KIM/KAT.						
iso-C_3H_7Cl	10.78±0.02	214	895	−34.6±0.1	−145.0±0.6	80TRA	75-29-6
	See also: 81KIM/KAT.						
$C_3H_7ClHg^+$							
n-C_3H_7HgCl	≤10.15	≤213	≤891	−21±2	−88±8	80TEL/RAB	2440-40-6
	IP from 81BAI/CHI2.						
iso-C_3H_7HgCl	≤9.80	≤206	≤863	−20±2	−83±8	80TEL/RAB	30615-19-1
	IP from 81BAI/CHI2.						
$C_3H_7ClO^+$							
$ClCH_2OC_2H_5$	10.30	(184)	(771)	−53	−223	*EST	3188-13-4
	IP from 83MOL/PIK.						
$C_3H_7F^+$							
n-C_3H_7F	(11.3)	(192)	(804)	−68±0.5	−286±2	77PED/RYL	460-13-9
	IP is onset of photoelectron band.						
iso-C_3H_7F	(11.08±0.02)	(185)	(776)	−70±0.5	−293±2	77PED/RYL	420-26-8
$C_3H_7F_3N^+$							
$CF_3NH(CH_3)_2$		−15	−65				
	From proton affinity of $CF_3N(CH_3)_2$ (RN 677-41-8). PA = 193.8 kcal/mol, 811 kJ/mol.						
$CF_3CH_2CH_2NH_3$		−20	−82				
	From proton affinity of $CF_3CH_2CH_2NH_2$ (RN 460-39-9). PA = 210.6 kcal/mol, 881 kJ/mol.						
$CF_3CH_2NH_2CH_3$		−11	−47				
	From proton affinity of $CF_3CH_2NHCH_3$ (RN 2730-67-8). PA = 209.8 kcal/mol, 878 kJ/mol.						
$C_3H_7I^+$							
n-C_3H_7I	9.269	206	862	−7.8±0.4	−32.5±1.7	77PED/RYL	107-08-4
		211	*884*	*−2.4±0.5*	*−10.2±2*		
	See: 82ROS/BUF, 83BRA/BAE2, 81KIM/KAT.						

Table 1. Positive Ion Table - Continued

ION / Neutral	Ionization potential eV	$\Delta_f H$(Ion) kcal/mol	kJ/mol	$\Delta_f H$(Neutral) kcal/mol	kJ/mol	Neutral reference	CAS registry number
$C_3H_7I^+$							
iso-C_3H_7I	9.175	202	844	−9.9±0.4	−41.6±1.7	77PED/RYL	75-30-9
		207	*865*	*−4.8±0.5*	*−20.1±2*		
	See: 82ROS/BUF, 83BRA/BAE2, 81KIM/KAT.						
$C_3H_7N^+$							
$CH_2=CHCH_2NH_2$	8.76	(213)	(893)	11	48	*EST	107-11-9
	See also: 79AUE/BOW.						
azetidine (NH)	(8.3)	(215)	(898)	24±1	99±4	*EST	503-29-7
	IP from 79AUE/BOW.						
N-methylaziridine (CH_3)	(8.7)	(230)	(964)	30±0.5	127±2	*EST	1072-44-2
	IP from 79AUE/BOW. See also: 86CAU/DIV.						
2-methylaziridine	(9.0)	(230)	(961)	22±1	91±6	*EST	75-55-8
	IP from 79AUE/BOW.						
cyclopropylamine (NH_2)	(8.7)	(219)	(916)	18.4±0.1	77.0±0.6	77PED/RYL	765-30-0
	IP is onset of photoelectron band (81KIM/KAT). See also: 79AUE/BOW.						
$C_3H_7NO^+$							
$HCON(CH_3)_2$	9.13±0.02	165	689	−45.8±0.4	−191.7±1.7	77PED/RYL	68-12-2
	See also: 82BIE/ASB, 81HEN/ISA.						
$(CH_3)_2C=NOH$	(9.1)	(195)	(815)	−15±3	−63±12	*EST	127-06-0
	IP is onset of photoelectron band.						
$CH_3CONHCH_3$	9.3	158	661	−56	−236	*EST	79-16-3
	IP is onset of photoelectron band.						
$C_3H_7NO_2^+$							
n-$C_3H_7NO_2$	10.81±0.03	220	919	−29.7±0.1	−124.0±0.6	77PED/RYL	108-03-2
	See also: 81KIM/KAT.						
i-$C_3H_7NO_2$	10.71±0.05	214	894	−33.2±0.2	−139.0±0.9	77PED/RYL	79-46-9
	See also: 81KIM/KAT.						
n-C_3H_7ONO	(10.34±0.01)	(210)	(879)	−28±1	−119±4	74BAT/CHR	543-67-9

Table 1. Positive Ion Table - Continued

ION / Neutral	Ionization potential eV	$\Delta_f H$(Ion) kcal/mol	$\Delta_f H$(Ion) kJ/mol	$\Delta_f H$(Neutral) kcal/mol	$\Delta_f H$(Neutral) kJ/mol	Neutral reference	CAS registry number
$C_3H_7NO_2^+$							
i-C_3H_7ONO	(10.23±0.01)	(204)	(854)	−32±1	−133±4	74BAT/CHR	541-42-4
$H_2NCH_2CH_2COOH$	(8.8)	(101)	(425)	−101±0.5	−424±2	83SKO/SAB	28854-76-4
	IP is onset of photoelectron band (83CAN/HAM).						
CH_3NHCH_2COOH	(8.4)	(106)	(443)	−88±0.2	−367±1	78SAB/LAF	107-97-1
	IP is onset of photoelectron band (83CAN/HAM).						
L-$CH_3CH(NH_2)COOH$	8.88	106	442	−99±1	−415±4	77NGA/SAB	56-41-7
	See also: 83CAN/HAM.						
$NH_2COOC_2H_5$	(10.15)	(127)	(533)	−107	−446	75BER/BOU	51-79-6
	IP is onset of photoelectron band.						
$NH_2CH_2COOCH_3$	(9.1)	(121)	(505)	−89	−373	*EST	616-34-2
	IP is onset of photoelectron band (83CAN/HAM).						
$C_3H_7NO_2S^+$							
L-HSCH$_2$CH(NH$_2$)COOH	(9.5)	(128)	(534)	−92	−383	*EST	3374-22-9
	IP from 83CAN/HAM.						
$C_3H_7NO_3^+$							
n-$C_3H_7ONO_2$	(11.07±0.02)	(214)	(894)	−41.6±0.3	−173.9±1.3	77PED/RYL	627-13-4
L-HOCH$_2$CH(NH$_2$)COOH	(8.7)	(67)	(278)	−134	−561	*EST	302-84-1
	IP is onset of photoelectron band(83CAN/HAM).						
$C_3H_7NS^+$							
HCSN(CH$_3$)$_2$	(≤8.2)	(≤201)	(≤840)	12	49	*EST	758-16-7
	IP from 81HEN/ISA.						
$C_3H_7N_2^+$							
H$_3$N(CH$_2$)$_2$CN		180	755				
	From proton affinity of H$_2$N(CH$_2$)$_2$CN (RN 151-18-8). PA = 207.0 kcal/mol, 866. kJ/mol.						
CH$_3$NH$_2$CH$_2$CN		185	775				
	From proton affinity of CH$_3$NHCH$_2$CN (RN 5616-32-0). PA = 206.0 kcal/mol, 862. kJ/mol.						
(CH$_3$)$_2$NCNH		194	811				
	From proton affinity of (CH$_3$)$_2$NCN (RN 1467-79-4) (86MAR/TOP). PA = 205.0 kcal/mol, 858 kJ/mol.						
$C_3H_7O^+$							
n-C_3H_7O	(9.20±0.05)	(202)	(847)	−10	−41	82MCM/GOL	16499-18-6
i-C_3H_7O	(9.20±0.05)	(197)	(825)	−15	−63	82MCM/GOL	3958-66-5

Table 1. Positive Ion Table - Continued

ION / Neutral	Ionization potential eV	$\Delta_f H$(Ion) kcal/mol kJ/mol	$\Delta_f H$(Neutral) kcal/mol kJ/mol	Neutral reference	CAS registry number
$C_3H_7O^+$					
C_2H_5CHOH		131 550			

From proton affinity of C_2H_5CHO (RN 123-38-6). PA = 189.6 kcal/mol, 793. kJ/mol. $C_3H_7O^+$ formed in n-C_3H_7OH with appearance potential of 10.71 eV is probably the same species. See also: 82MAC.

$(CH_3)_2COH$		117 490			

From proton affinity of $(CH_3)_2CO$ (RN 67-64-1). PA = 196.7 kcal/mol, 823 kJ/mol. See also: 84LOS/HOL.

$C_2H_5OCH_2$		(142) (593)			

$\Delta_f H$(Ion) from appearance potential determination. See also: 82MAC.

CH_3CHOCH_3		134 562			

From proton affinity of $CH_2=CHOCH_3$ (RN 107-25-5). PA = 207.4 kcal/mol, 868 kJ/mol. See also: 82MAC.

(oxetane)·H^+		149 625			

From proton affinity of oxetane (RN 503-30-0). PA = 196.9 kcal/mol, 824 kJ/mol.

(methyloxirane)·H^+		148 620			

From proton affinity of methyloxirane (RN 75-56-9). PA = 194.7 kcal/mol, 815 kJ/mol.

$C_3H_7OS^+$					
$CH_3C(SH)OCH_3$		125 522			

From proton affinity of $CH_3C(=S)OCH_3$ (RN 21119-13-1) (83CAS/KIM). PA = 203.7 kcal/mol, 852. kJ/mol.

$CH_3C(OH)SCH_3$		106 443			

From proton affinity of $CH_3C(=O)SCH_3$ (RN 1534-08-3) (83CAS/KIM). PA = 199.7 kcal/mol, 836. kJ/mol.

$C_3H_7O_2^+$					
$C_2H_5C(OH)_2$		67 280			

From proton affinity of C_2H_5COOH (RN 79-09-4). PA = 191.8 kcal/mol, 802 kJ/mol.

$HC(OH)OC_2H_5$		80 335			

From proton affinity of $HCOOC_2H_5$ (RN 109-94-4). PA = 193.1 kcal/mol, 808 kJ/mol.

$CH_3C(OH)OCH_3$		69 288			

From proton affinity of CH_3COOCH_3 (RN 79-20-9). PA = 197.8 kcal/mol, 828. kJ/mol.

$CH(OCH_3)_2$		97 406			4483-45-8

From appearance potential determination (82HOL/LOS2).

Table 1. Positive Ion Table – Continued

ION / Neutral	Ionization potential eV	$\Delta_f H$(Ion) kcal/mol	$\Delta_f H$(Ion) kJ/mol	$\Delta_f H$(Neutral) kcal/mol	$\Delta_f H$(Neutral) kJ/mol	Neutral reference	CAS registry number
$C_3H_7O_3^+$							
$CH_3OC(OH)OCH_3$		27	111				

From proton affinity of $CH_3OCOOCH_3$ (RN 616-38-6). PA = 200.2 kcal/mol, 838. kJ/mol.

| $C_3H_7O_3P^+$ | | | | | | | |
| (cyclic structure: O,O-ring P–OCH₃) | (9.06±0.1) | (45) | (186) | −164 | −688 | *EST | 3741-36-4 |

See also: 82WOR/HAR.

| $C_3H_7S^+$ | | | | | | | |
| (thietane)H⁺ | | (179) | (749) | | | | |

From proton affinity of thietane (RN 287-27-4). PA = (201.3) kcal/mol, (842) kJ/mol.

| (2-methylthiirane)H⁺ | | (176) | (737) | | | | |

From proton affinity of 2-methylthiirane (RN 1072-43-1). PA = (200.6) kcal/mol, (839) kJ/mol.

| $C_3H_7S_2^+$ | | | | | | | |
| $CH_3C(SH)SCH_3$ | | 182 | 763 | | | | |

From proton affinity of $CH_3C(=S)SCH_3$ (RN 2168-84-5). PA = 207.3 kcal/mol, 867. kJ/mol.

| $C_3H_8^+$ | | | | | | | |
| C_3H_8 | 10.95±0.05 | 227.5 | 951.5 | −25.0±0.1 | −104.5±0.3 | 77PED/RYL | 74-98-6 |

See also: 81KIM/KAT.

| $C_3H_8Cl^+$ | | | | | | | |
| $CH_3ClC_2H_5$ | | (164) | (688) | | | | |

$\Delta_f H$(Ion) from equilibrium constant determination (85SHA/HOJ).

| $C_3H_8Cl_2Si^+$ | | | | | | | |
| $(CH_3)_2SiCl(CH_2Cl)$ | (9.2) | (126) | (527) | −86 | −361 | *EST | 1719-57-9 |

IP is onset of photoelectron band (81ZYK/KHV).

| $C_3H_8N^+$ | | | | | | | |
| $CH_3CH_2CHNH_2$ | | 152 | 636 | | | | |

$\Delta_f H$(Ion) from appearance potential measurements (81LOS/LAM).

| $CH_3CHCH_2NH_2$ | | (161) | (673) | | | | |

From proton affinity of $CH_2=CHCH_2NH_2$ (RN 107-11-9). PA = 215.6 kcal/mol, 903 kJ/mol.

ION	Ionization potential	$\Delta_f H$(Ion)		$\Delta_f H$(Neutral)		Neutral	CAS registry
Neutral	eV	kcal/mol	kJ/mol	kcal/mol	kJ/mol	reference	number

$C_3H_8N^+$

$(CH_3)_2CNH_2$ (5.4)   (141)   (590)   (17)   (69)   81LOS/LAM   26374-12-9

$\Delta_f H$(Ion) from appearance potential measurements (81LOS/LAM). IP derived (83BUR/CAS). Value derived from proton affinity of $CH_2=C(CH_3)NH_2$ (PA = 226.3 kcal/mol, 947 kJ/mol) and $(CH_3)_2C=NH_2$ (PA = 221 kcal/mol, 925 kJ/mol) is 147 kcal/mol, 615 kJ/mol. (84LIA/LIE).

$CH_3CH_2NHCH_2$ 156   653

$\Delta_f H$(Ion) from appearance potential measurements (81LOS/LAM).

$CH_3CHNHCH_3$ (147)   (615)

$\Delta_f H$(Ion) from appearance potential measurements (81LOS/LAM).

$CH_2N(CH_3)_2$ 5.7   (158)   (661)   (26)   (109)   81GRI/LOS   30208-47-0

$\Delta_f H$(Ion) from appearance potential measurements (81LOS/LAM), IP derived (81GRI/LOS, 83BUR/CAS, 81LOG/TAK).

(azetidine)·H^+ (167)   (698)

From proton affinity of azetidine. (RN 503-29-7). PA = 222.8 kcal/mol, 932. kJ/mol.

(c-$C_3H_5NH_2$)·H^+ 169   707

From proton affinity of c-$C_3H_5NH_2$ (RN 765-30-0). PA = 215.2 kcal/mol, 900 kJ/mol.

(N-methylaziridine)·H^+ 174   730

From proton affinity of N-methylaziridine (RN 1072-44-2). PA = 221.6 kcal/mol, 927. kJ/mol.

(2-methylaziridine)·H^+ (168)   (704)

From proton affinity of 2-methylaziridine (RN 75-55-8). PA = (219.2) kcal/mol, (917) kJ/mol.

$C_3H_8NO^+$

$HC(OH)N(CH_3)_2$ 108   454

From proton affinity of $HCON(CH_3)_2$ (RN 68-12-2). PA = 211.4 kcal/mol, 884 kJ/mol.

$C_3H_8NO_2^+$

i-C_3H_7ONHO 132   552

From proton affinity of i-C_3H_7ONO (RN 541-42-4). PA = 201.9 kcal/mol, 845 kJ/mol.

$CH_3CH(NH_3)COOH$ 52   216

From proton affinity of L-alanine (RN 56-41-7). PA = 214.8 kcal/mol, 899. kJ/mol.

Table 1. Positive Ion Table – Continued

ION / Neutral	Ionization potential eV	$\Delta_f H$(Ion) kcal/mol	$\Delta_f H$(Ion) kJ/mol	$\Delta_f H$(Neutral) kcal/mol	$\Delta_f H$(Neutral) kJ/mol	Neutral reference	CAS registry number
$C_3H_8NO_2^+$							
$CH_3NH_2CH_2COOH$		59	248				
From proton affinity of sarcosine (RN 107-97-1). PA = 218.7 kcal/mol, 915. kJ/mol.							
$C_3H_8NO_3^+$							
$HOCH_2CH(NH_3)COOH$		15	62				
From proton affinity of L-serine (RN 302-84-1). PA = 216.8 kcal/mol, 907. kJ/mol.							
$C_3H_8N_2^+$							
(pyrazolidine)	(≤7.90)	(≤216)	(≤903)	34	141	*EST	504-70-1
(1,2-dimethyldiaziridine)	(8.7)	(259)	(1082)	58	243	*EST	6794-95-2
IP is onset of photoelectron band.							
$C_3H_8N_2O^+$							
$(CH_3NH)_2CO$	(≤9.23)	(≤155)	(≤649)	−58	−242	*EST	96-31-1
$(CH_3)_2NCONH_2$	(≤8.96)	(≤149)	(≤622)	−58	−242	*EST	598-94-7
$C_3H_8N_2S^+$							
$(CH_3NH)_2CS$	(≤8.08±0.03)	(≤194)	(≤814)	8	34	*EST	534-13-4
$C_3H_8O^+$							
$n\text{-}C_3H_7OH$	10.22±0.03	175	731	−60.9±0.2	−254.8±1.	77PED/RYL	71-23-8
		181	*756*	*−55.1*	*−230.4*		
See also: 84BOW/MAC, 81KIM/KAT, 80BAC/MOU.							
$iso\text{-}C_3H_7OH$	10.12±0.08	168	704	−65.1±0.1	−272.5±0.4	77PED/RYL	67-63-0
		174	*729*	*−59.2*	*−247.7*		
See also: 72POT/SOR, 81KIM/KAT, 80BAC/MOU, 84BOW/MAC.							
$C_2H_5OCH_3$	9.72	172	721	−51.7±0.1	−216.4±0.6	77PED/RYL	540-67-0
IP from 81HOL/FIN, 84BOW/MAC, 81KIM/KAT, 80BAC/MOU, 82LEV/LIA, 79AUE/BOW.							
$CH_2CH_2CH_2OH_2$		171	714				
From appearance potential determinations (84HOL/MOM).							
$CH_2CHCH_2HOH_2$		172	721				
From appearance potential determinations (84HOL/MOM). Authors propose that ion is proton-bound dimer of water and allyl radical.							

Table 1. Positive Ion Table – Continued

ION / Neutral	Ionization potential eV	$\Delta_f H$(Ion) kcal/mol	kJ/mol	$\Delta_f H$(Neutral) kcal/mol	kJ/mol	Neutral reference	CAS registry number
$C_3H_8O_2^+$							
$(CH_3O)_2CH_2$	9.5	136	568	−83.2±0.2	−348.2±0.7	77PED/RYL	109-87-5
	IP from 82HOL/LOS2. See also: 81JOR, 82ZVE/VIL, 81KIM/KAT.						
$HOCH_2CH_2OCH_3$	9.6	134	562	−87	−364	*EST	109-86-4
	IP is onset of photoelectron band (83BIE/MOR, 81KIM/KAT).						
$C_3H_8O_3P^+$							
[2-methoxy-1,3,2-dioxaphospholane structure]		−11	−48				
	From proton affinity of 2-methoxy-1,3,2-dioxaphospholane (RN 3741-36-4). PA = 212.7 kcal/mol, 890 kJ/mol.						
$C_3H_8S^+$							
$n\text{-}C_3H_7SH$	9.195±0.005	195.8	819.2	−16.2±0.1	−67.9±0.6	77PED/RYL	107-03-9
	See also: 81KIM/KAT.						
$iso\text{-}C_3H_7SH$	9.14	193	806	−18.2±0.1	−76.2±0.6	77PED/RYL	75-33-2
	See: 81KIM/KAT.						
$C_2H_5SCH_3$	8.54±0.1	183	764	−14.2±0.3	−59.6±1.1	77PED/RYL	624-89-5
	See also: 79AUE/BOW.						
$C_3H_8S_2^+$							
$CH_3SCH_2SCH_3$	(8.4)	(195)	(815)	1±2	5±8	*EST	1618-26-4
	IP is onset of photoelectron band.						
$C_3H_8Sc^+$							
$C_2H_4ScH(CH_3)$		(197)	(824)				
	$\Delta_f H$(Ion) from 84TOL/BEA.						
$C_3H_8Si^+$							
$(CH_3)_2Si=CH_2$	7.71±0.03	183	765	5	21	86WAL	4112-23-6
	IP from 82DYK/JOS. See also: 81KOE/MCK.						
$C_3H_9^+$							
C_3H_9		191	797				
	From proton affinity of C_3H_8. (RN 74-98-6). PA = 150 kcal/mol, 628 kJ/mol.						
$C_3H_9Al^+$							
$(CH_3)_3Al$	(≤9.76)	(≤206)	(≤861)	−19±3	−81±11	77PED/RYL	75-24-1
$C_3H_9As^+$							
$(CH_3)_3As$	(8.2)	(192)	(804)	3±2	13±10	77PED/RYL	593-88-4
	IP is onset of photoelectron band (82ELB/DIE).						
$C_3H_9AsO_3^+$							
$As(OCH_3)_3$	(7.93)	(51)	(215)	−131±0.5	−550±2	77PED/RYL	6596-95-8

Table 1. Positive Ion Table - Continued

ION / Neutral	Ionization potential eV	$\Delta_f H$(Ion) kcal/mol	$\Delta_f H$(Ion) kJ/mol	$\Delta_f H$(Neutral) kcal/mol	$\Delta_f H$(Neutral) kJ/mol	Neutral reference	CAS registry number
$C_3H_9B^+$	(9.5)	(190)	(794)	−29±2	−123±10	77PED/RYL	593-90-8
$(CH_3)_3B$		*(196)*	*(820)*	*−23*	*−97*		

IP is onset of photoelectron band.

$C_3H_9BO_3^+$	(10.0)	(15)	(65)	−215±0.5	−900±2	77PED/RYL	121-43-7
$B(OCH_3)_3$							

IP is onset of photoelectron band.

$C_3H_9BS_3^+$	(8.74)	(164)	(687)	−37±0.7	−156±3	77PED/RYL	997-49-9
$B(SCH_3)_3$							

$C_3H_9BrPb^+$	(≤9.30)	(≤229)	(≤956)	14	59	85DEW/HOL	6148-48-7
$(CH_3)_3PbBr$							

$C_3H_9BrSi^+$	10.0	(161)	(672)	−70±1	−293±4	77PED/RYL	2857-97-8
$(CH_3)_3SiBr$		*(169)*	*(707)*	*−61±0.8*	*−258±4*		

IP is onset of photoelectron band.

$C_3H_9BrSn^+$	(9.4)	(184)	(769)	−33±1	−138±6	77PED/RYL	1066-44-0
$(CH_3)_3SnBr$							

$C_3H_9ClGe^+$	(9.2)	(148)	(620)	−64±3	−268±13	80TEL/RAB	1529-47-1
$(CH_3)_3GeCl$							

IP is onset of photoelectron band. See also: 79DRA/GLA2.

$C_3H_9ClSi^+$	(10.15)	(149)	(625)	−85	−354	81BEL/PER	75-77-4
$(CH_3)_3SiCl$		*(156)*	*(654)*	*−78*	*−325*		

IP is onset of photoelectron band. See also: 84SZE/BAE, 81ZYK/KHV.

$C_3H_9ClSn^+$	(9.90)	(185)	(773)	−43	−182	*EST	1066-45-1
$(CH_3)_3SnCl$							

IP from 82LEV/LIA.

$C_3H_9FN^+$		87	365				
$CH_2FCH_2CH_2NH_3$							

From proton affinity of $CH_2FCH_2CH_2NH_2$ (RN 462-41-9). PA = 217.8 kcal/mol, 911. kJ/mol.

$C_3H_9FSi^+$	10.31±0.04	112	468	−126	−527	77MUR/BEA	420-56-4
$(CH_3)_3SiF$							

$C_3H_9Ga^+$	(8.9)	(195)	(817)	−10±1	−42±6	77PED/RYL	1445-79-0
$(CH_3)_3Ga$							

IP is onset of photoelectron band.

Table 1. Positive Ion Table - Continued

ION / Neutral	Ionization potential eV	$\Delta_f H$(Ion) kcal/mol	$\Delta_f H$(Ion) kJ/mol	$\Delta_f H$(Neutral) kcal/mol	$\Delta_f H$(Neutral) kJ/mol	Neutral reference	CAS registry number
$C_3H_9Ge^+$							
$(CH_3)_3Ge$		180	754				
$\Delta_f H$(Ion) from appearance potential determinations. Proton affinity of $(CH_3)_2Ge=CH_2$ (RN 82064-99-1) = 204.9 kcal, 857. kJ/mol.							
$C_3H_9N^+$							
$n-C_3H_7NH_2$	8.78±0.02	186	777	−16.8±0.1	−70.2±0.4	77PED/RYL	107-10-8
	See also: 81KIM/KAT.						
$iso-C_3H_7NH_2$	8.72±0.03	181	758	−20.0±0.1	−83.8±0.5	77PED/RYL	75-31-0
	See also: 81KIM/KAT.						
$(CH_3)(C_2H_5)NH$	(8.15)	(177)	(740)	−11±0.5	−46±2	*EST	624-78-2
	IP from 79AUE/BOW.						
$(CH_3)_3N$	7.82±0.06	175	731	−5.7±0.1	−23.7±0.6	77PED/RYL	75-50-3
	See also: 81KIM/KAT, 82ELB/DIE.						
$C_3H_9NO^+$							
$NH_2(CH_2)_3OH$	(9.0)	(156)	(650)	−52	−218	*EST	156-87-6
	IP is onset of photoelectron band.						
$CH_3OCH_2CH_2NH_2$	(8.9)	(161)	(675)	−44±0.7	−184±3	*EST	109-85-3
	IP is onset of photoelectron band.						
$CH_3ON(CH_3)_2$	≤8.78	(≤194)	(≤810)	−9	−37	*EST	5669-39-6
	IP from 83MOL/PIK. See also: 82LEV/LIA.						
$C_3H_9N_3Si^+$							
$(CH_3)_3SiN_3$	(≤9.7±0.1)	(≤241)	(≤1007)	17±2	71±8	80TEL/RAB	4648-54-8
$C_3H_9O^+$							
$n-C_3H_7OH_2$		114	476				
	From proton affinity of $n-C_3H_7OH$ (RN 71-23-8). PA = 190.8 kcal/mol, 798. kJ/mol.						
$i-C_3H_7OH_2$		109	457				
	From proton affinity of $i-C_3H_7OH$ (RN 67-63-0). PA = 191.2 kcal/mol, 800. kJ/mol.						
$C_2H_5OHCH_3$		118	492				
	From proton affinity of $C_2H_5OCH_3$ (RN 540-67-0). PA = 196.4 kcal/mol, 822. kJ/mol.						
$C_3H_9OP^+$							
$(CH_3)_3PO$	(9.5)	(115)	(482)	−104±2	−434±8	77PED/RYL	676-96-0
	IP is onset of photoelectron band.						
$C_3H_9O_2^+$							
$HOCH_2CH_2OHCH_3$		96	402				
	From proton affinity of $HOCH_2CH_2OCH_3$ (RN 109-86-4) (78TAF/TAA). PA = 182.6 kcal/mol, 764. kJ/mol.						

Table 1. Positive Ion Table - Continued

ION / Neutral	Ionization potential eV	Δ_fH(Ion) kcal/mol	Δ_fH(Ion) kJ/mol	Δ_fH(Neutral) kcal/mol	Δ_fH(Neutral) kJ/mol	Neutral reference	CAS registry number
$C_3H_9O_3P^+$							
$P(OCH_3)_3$	(8.50)	(29)	(123)	−167±5	−697±20	77PED/RYL	121-45-9

See also: 81CHA/FIN, 82WOR/HAR, 77COW/GOO.

$C_3H_9O_3PS^+$							
$(CH_3O)_3PS$	(≤9.16)	(≤28)	(≤117)	−183	−767	*EST	152-18-1

$C_3H_9O_4P^+$							
$(CH_3O)_3PO$	9.99	(−34)	(−143)	−265	−1107	*EST	512-56-1

See also: 81CHA/FIN.

$C_3H_9P^+$							
$(CH_3)_3P$	8.06±0.05	162	677	−24±1	−101±5	77PED/RYL	594-09-2

See also: 82IKU/KEB, 82COW/KEM, 82ELB/DIE, 82BAN/CHA2.

$C_3H_9Pb^+$							
$(CH_3)_3Pb$		200	840				

Δ_fH(Ion) from appearance potential determinations. Proton affinity of $(CH_3)_2Pb=CH_2$ (RN 82065-01-8) = 223.9 kcal/mol, 937. kJ/mol.

$C_3H_9S^+$							
n-$C_3H_7SH_2$		158	660				

From proton affinity of n-C_3H_7SH (RN 107-03-9). PA = 191.6 kcal/mol, 802 kJ/mol.

i-$C_3H_7SH_2$		153	642				

From proton affinity of i-C_3H_7SH (RN 75-33-2). PA = 194.1 kcal/mol, 812 kJ/mol.

$CH_3SHC_2H_5$		148	619				

From proton affinity of $CH_3SC_2H_5$ (RN 624-89-5). PA = 203.5 kcal/mol, 851 kJ/mol.

$C_3H_9Sb^+$							
$(CH_3)_3Sb$	(7.7)	(185)	(775)	8±6	32±25	77PED/RYL	594-10-5

IP is onset of photoelectron band(82ELB/DIE).

$C_3H_9Si^+$							
$(CH_3)_3Si$	(6.5)	(150)	(630)	−0.8±2	−3±8	86DON/WAL	16571-41-8
		(157)	(656)	6	26		

Δ_fH(Ion) from appearance potential determinations (84SZE/BAE, 84SZE/BAE2). IP is Δ_fH(Ion)−Δ_fH(Neutral).

$C_3H_9Sn^+$							
$(CH_3)_3Sn$	(7.10±0.05)	(181)	(759)				

Δ_fH(Ion) from appearance potential determinations. Proton affinity of $(CH_3)_2Sn=CH_2$ (RN 82065-00-7) = 215.8 kcal/mol, 903. kJ/mol.

$C_3H_{10}As^+$							
$(CH_3)_3AsH$		155	650				

From proton affinity of $(CH_3)_3As$ (RN 593-88-4). PA = 213.4 kcal/mol, 893 kJ/mol.

ION / Neutral	Ionization potential eV	$\Delta_f H$(Ion) kcal/mol	kJ/mol	$\Delta_f H$(Neutral) kcal/mol	kJ/mol	Neutral reference	CAS registry number
$C_3H_{10}N^+$							
n-$C_3H_7NH_3$		131	548				
From proton affinity of n-$C_3H_7NH_2$ (RN 107-10-8). PA = 217.9 kcal/mol, 912. kJ/mol.							
i-$C_3H_7NH_3$		127	531				
From proton affinity of i-$C_3H_7NH_2$ (RN 75-31-0). PA = 218.6 kcal/mol, 915. kJ/mol.							
$(CH_3)(C_2H_5)NH_2$		132	552				
From proton affinity of $(CH_3)(C_2H_5)NH$ (RN 624-78-2). PA = 222.8 kcal/mol, 932. kJ/mol.							
$(CH_3)_3NH$		135	564				
From proton affinity of $(CH_3)_3N$ (RN 75-50-3). PA = 225.1 kcal/mol, 942. kJ/mol.							
$C_3H_{10}NO^+$							
$NH_3(CH_2)_3OH$		85	356				
From proton affinity of $NH_2(CH_2)_3OH$ (RN 156-87-6). PA = 228.6 kcal/mol, 956.5 kJ/mol.							
$CH_3OCH_2CH_2NH_3$		98	412				
From proton affinity of $CH_3OCH_2CH_2NH_2$ (RN 109-85-3). PA = 223.3 kcal/mol, 934 kJ/mol.							
$C_3H_{10}N_2^+$							
$(CH_3)_2NNH(CH_3)$				21	87	69BEN/CRU	1741-01-1
A value of 7.93 eV has been reported for the adiabatic IP of this compound. Reported values of IP's of hydrazines determined by threshold measurements are usually significantly higher than the adiabatic value because of the large geometry change associated with ionization.							
$C_3H_{10}OP^+$							
$(CH_3)_3POH$		124	518				
From proton affinity of $(CH_3)_3PO$ (RN 676-96-0) (84BOL/HOU). PA = 217.1 kcal/mol, 908. kJ/mol.							
$C_3H_{10}O_3P^+$							
$HP(OCH_3)_3$		−22	−92				
From proton affinity of $P(OCH_3)_3$ (RN 121-45-9). PA = 220.6 kcal/mol, 923. kJ/mol.							
$C_3H_{10}O_3PS^+$							
$(CH_3O)_3PSH$		−32	−134				
From proton affinity of $(CH_3O)_3PS$ (RN 152-18-1). PA = 214.5 kcal/mol, 897. kJ/mol.							
$C_3H_{10}O_4P^+$							
$(CH_3O)_3POH$		−111	−464				
From proton affinity of $(CH_3O)_3PO$ (RN 512-56-1). PA = 212.0 kcal/mol, 887. kJ/mol.							
$C_3H_{10}P^+$							
$(CH_3)_3PH$		114	479				
From proton affinity of $(CH_3)_3P$ (RN 594-09-2). PA = 227.1 kcal/mol, 950. kJ/mol.							

Table 1. Positive Ion Table - Continued

ION / Neutral	Ionization potential eV	$\Delta_f H$(Ion) kcal/mol	$\Delta_f H$(Ion) kJ/mol	$\Delta_f H$(Neutral) kcal/mol	$\Delta_f H$(Neutral) kJ/mol	Neutral reference	CAS registry number
$C_3H_{10}Si^+$							
$(CH_3)_3SiH$	9.9	189	792	−39±1	−163±4	86DON/WAL	993-07-7
	IP from 81HOT.						
$C_3H_{10}Sn^+$							
$(CH_3)_3SnH$	(≤9.9)	(≤228)	(≤955)	0±2	0±8	80TEL/RAB	1631-73-8
$C_3H_{11}N_2^+$							
$NH_2(CH_2)_3NH_3$		124	518				
	From proton affinity of $NH_2(CH_2)_3NH_2$ (RN 109-76-2). PA = 234.1 kcal/mol, 979. kJ/mol.						
$C_3H_{12}BN^+$							
$(CH_3)_3NBH_3$	(9.28±0.2)	(194)	(810)	−20	−85	82TN270	75-22-9
		(203)	(848)	−11	−47		
$C_3H_{12}B_3N_3^+$							
(isomer 1)	(9.1±0.15)	(−13)	(−55)	−223	−933	70FIN/GAR	1004-35-9
(isomer 2)	(9.07)	(−8)	(−33)	−217±1	−908±4	80TEL/RAB	5314-85-2
C_3IN^+							
$IC≡CCN$	(10.18±0.02)	(347)	(1451)	112±10	469±40	79BUC/VOG	2003-32-9
	See also: 84KUH/MAI.						
C_3La^+							
LaC_3	(6.8±0.5)	(336)	(1404)	179±1	748±1	81GIN/PEL	12602-63-0
$C_3N_2O^+$							
$(CN)_2CO$	(≤12.56)	(≤349)	(≤1459)	59±1	247±6	77PED/RYL	1115-12-4
$C_3O_2^+$							
C_3O_2	10.60	222	929	−22±0.5	−94±2	71JANAF	504-64-3
C_4^+							
C_4	(12.6)	(522)	(2187)	232±8	971±33	71JANAF	12184-80-4
$C_4Cl_2Hg^+$							
$(ClC≡C)_2Hg$	9.58±0.02	(373)	(1559)	152	635	*EST	64771-59-1
	IP is onset of photoelectron band (81FUR/PIA).						

Table 1. Positive Ion Table - Continued

ION / Neutral	Ionization potential eV	$\Delta_f H$(Ion) kcal/mol	kJ/mol	$\Delta_f H$(Neutral) kcal/mol	kJ/mol	Neutral reference	CAS registry number
$C_4Cl_2O_2^+$							
[structure: cyclobutenedione with two Cl]	(9.5)	(204)	(856)	−14	−61	*EST	2892-63-9
	IP is onset of photoelectron band (81BOC/RIE).						
$C_4F_2O_3^+$							
[structure: difluoromaleic anhydride]	(11.45)	(79)	(330)	−185	−775	*EST	669-78-3
	IP from 81ASB/SVE.						
$C_4F_4O_2^+$							
[structure: tetrafluorocyclobutanedione]	10.05±0.1	(47)	(199)	−184	−771	*EST	663-45-6
	IP is onset of photoelectron band (85GLE/SCH, 85ALB/HEL).						
$C_4F_6^+$							
$CF_2=CFCF=CF_2$	(9.5)	(−5)	(−21)	−224	−938	68LAC/SKI	685-63-2
$C_4F_6O^+$							
$(CF_3)_2C=C=O$	(10.67)	(−95)	(−398)	−341	−1427	*EST	
	IP is onset of photoelectron band (83GLE/SAA).						
[structure: perfluorocyclobutanone]	(10.7)	(−30)	(−124)	−276	−1157	*EST	699-35-4
	IP is onset of photoelectron band (85GLE/SCH).						
$C_4F_6S^+$							
$(CF_3)_2C=C=S$	(9.4)	(−71)	(−295)	−287	−1202	*EST	7445-60-5
	IP is onset of photoelectron band (83GLE/SAA).						
$C_4F_6S_2^+$							
[structure: bis(trifluoromethyl)dithietene]	9.6	(37)	(154)	−185	−772	*EST	360-91-8
	IP is onset of photoelectron band (83SCH/SCH, 83JIA/MOH).						
$C_4F_8^+$							
(Z)-2-C_4F_8	(11.1)	(−126)	(−526)	−382	−1597	70BEN/O'N	1516-65-0
	IP is onset of photoelectron band.						
(E)-2-C_4F_8	(11.0)	(−129)	(−540)	−383	−1601	70BEN/O'N	1516-64-9
	IP is onset of photoelectron band.						

Table 1. Positive Ion Table - Continued

ION / Neutral	Ionization potential eV	Δ_fH(Ion) kcal/mol	Δ_fH(Ion) kJ/mol	Δ_fH(Neutral) kcal/mol	Δ_fH(Neutral) kJ/mol	Neutral reference	CAS registry number
$C_4FeI_2O_4^+$ $Fe(CO)_4I_2$	(8.4) IP is onset of photoelectron band.	(42)	(174)	−152±2	−636±9	82PIL/SKI	14911-55-8
C_4HCl^+ $CH\equiv CC\equiv CCl$	(9.72±0.02)	(345)	(1443)	121±0.5	505±2	*EST	6089-44-7
$C_4HCoO_4^+$ $HCo(CO)_4$	(8.2) IP is onset of photoelectron band.	(53)	(222)	−136±0.5	−569±2	77PED/RYL	16842-03-8
$C_4HF_7N^+$ $n\text{-}C_3F_7CNH$		−110	−460				
	From proton affinity of n-C_3F_7CN (RN 375-00-8). PA = 167.4 kcal/mol, 700. kJ/mol.						
$C_4HF_9O^+$ $(CF_3)_3COH$	12.25 IP from 83KOP/MOL.	(−266)	(−1115)	(−549)	(−2297)	*EST	2378-02-1
$C_4HNiO_4^+$ $HNi(CO)_4$		(43)	(179)				
	From proton affinity of $Ni(CO)_4$ (RN 13463-39-3). PA = (180) kcal/mol, (753) kJ/mol.						
$C_4H_2^+$ $HC\equiv CC\equiv CH$	10.180±0.003 See also: 80MAI/THO.	340	1422	105	440	85STE/FAH	460-12-8
$C_4H_2Br_2S^+$ (2,5-dibromothiophene)	(≤8.49)	(≤233)	(≤976)	38	157	*EST	3141-27-3
(3,4-dibromothiophene)	(≤8.94)	(≤246)	(≤1028)	39	165	*EST	3141-26-2
$C_4H_2Cl_2S^+$ (2,5-dichlorothiophene)	(8.60±0.05)	(213)	(890)	14	60	*EST	3172-52-9
$C_4H_2F_4^+$ $CF_2CHCHCF_2$	(10.6±0.1)	(82)	(343)	−163	−680	*EST	407-70-5

Table 1. Positive Ion Table – Continued

ION / Neutral	Ionization potential eV	$\Delta_f H$(Ion) kcal/mol	$\Delta_f H$(Ion) kJ/mol	$\Delta_f H$(Neutral) kcal/mol	$\Delta_f H$(Neutral) kJ/mol	Neutral reference	CAS registry number
$C_4H_3BrS^+$							
2-bromothiophene	8.6	(231)	(966)	33	136	*EST	1003-09-4
	IP is onset of photoelectron band.						
3-bromothiophene	8.812±0.005	(236)	(986)	33	136	*EST	872-31-1
$C_4H_3ClS^+$							
2-chlorothiophene	8.89±0.05	(225)	(941)	20	83	*EST	96-43-5
$C_4H_3F_9N^+$							
$(CF_3)_3CNH_3$		(−329)	(−1375)				
	From proton affinity of $(CF_3)_3CNH_2$ (RN 2809-92-9). PA = (191.5) kcal/mol, (801.) kJ/mol.						
$C_4H_3IS^+$							
2-iodothiophene	≤8.46	(≤242)	(≤1010)	46	194	*EST	3437-95-4
3-iodothiophene	(≤8.46)	(≤241)	(≤1010)	46	194	*EST	10486-61-0
$C_4H_3N^+$							
$CH_2=C=CHCN$	(10.1)	(259)	(1084)	26	110	*EST	1001-56-5
	IP is onset of photoelectron band.						
$CH_3C\equiv CCN$	10.78±0.02	(329)	(1378)	81±0.7	338±3	*EST	13752-78-8
$C_4H_3NO_3^+$							
2-nitrofuran	(≤9.75±0.05)	(≤218)	(≤910)	−7	−31	*EST	609-39-2

Table 1. Positive Ion Table - Continued

ION / Neutral	Ionization potential eV	$\Delta_f H$(Ion) kcal/mol	kJ/mol	$\Delta_f H$(Neutral) kcal/mol	kJ/mol	Neutral reference	CAS registry number
$C_4H_2F_9N^+$							
$(CF_3)_3CNH_2$	(10.4)	(−263)	(−1100)	−503	−2104	*EST	2809-92-9
	IP from 79AUE/BOW.						
$C_4H_2F_9O^+$							
$(CF_3)_3COH_2$		−346	−1449				
	From proton affinity of $(CF_3)_3COH$ (RN 2378-02-1). PA = 163.1 kcal/mol, 682. kJ/mol.						
$C_4H_2I_2S^+$							
2,5-diiodothiophene	≤8.28	(≤256)	(≤1072)	65	273	*EST	625-88-7
3,4-diiodothiophene	(≤8.45)	(≤263)	(≤1099)	68	284	*EST	19259-08-6
$C_4H_2N_2^+$							
(Z)-CH(CN)CH(CN)	(11.15)	(338)	(1416)	81.3±0.5	340.2±1.9	77PED/RYL	928-53-0
(E)-CH(CN)CH(CN)	11.16±0.03	338	1417	81	340	82CHU/NGU	764-42-1
$C_4H_2O_2^+$							
cyclobutenedione	(≤9.79)	(≤239)	(≤1002)	14	57	*EST	32936-74-6
$C_4H_2O_3^+$							
maleic anhydride	(10.8)	(154)	(644)	−95±1	−398±5	77PED/RYL	108-31-6
	IP is onset of photoelectron band (81KIM/KAT).						
$C_4H_3^+$							
$HCCCCH_2$		(291)	(1217)				
	From proton affinity of HC≡CC≡CH (RN 460-12-8) (87DEA/MAU). PA = 180 kcal/mol, 753 kJ/mol.						

Table 1. Positive Ion Table - Continued

ION Neutral	Ionization potential eV	$\Delta_f H$(Ion) kcal/mol	kJ/mol	$\Delta_f H$(Neutral) kcal/mol	kJ/mol	Neutral reference	CAS registry number
$C_4H_4^+$							
$CH_2=C=C=CH_2$	(9.15) See also: 85DEW/TIE.	(294)	(1232)	83	349	82ROS/DAN	2873-50-9
$CH_2=CHC\equiv CH$	9.58±0.02	(294)	(1229)	73	305	69STU/WES	689-97-4
methylenecyclopropene	8.15	(289)	(1209)	101	423	87STA/NOR	4095-06-1
	Heat of formation of ion from appearance potential measurements (82ROS/DAN); $\Delta_f H$(Neutral) is $\Delta_f H$(Ion) - IP (87STA/NOR).						
$C_4H_4N_2^+$							
$NCCH_2CH_2CN$	12.1±0.25 IP from 82CHE/LAP.	329	1377	50.1±0.1	209.7±0.6	77PED/RYL	110-61-2
pyridazine	(8.64)	(266)	(1112)	66.5±0.2	278.3±1	77PED/RYL	289-80-5
pyrimidine	9.23 See also: 83PIA/KEL.	260	1087	47.0±0.2	196.6±0.9	77PED/RYL	289-95-2
pyrazine	9.29±0.01 See also: 83PIA/KEL.	261	1092	46.8±0.3	196.0±1.3	77PED/RYL	290-37-9
$C_4H_4N_2O^+$							
pyridazine N-oxide	(8.89±0.02)	(252)	(1056)	47	198	*EST	1457-42-7
pyrimidine N-oxide	(8.80±0.02)	(231)	(966)	28	117	*EST	17043-94-6
2-pyrimidinone	(10.06±0.05)	(221)	(924)	−11	−47	*EST	557-01-7

Table 1. Positive Ion Table – Continued

ION Neutral	Ionization potential eV	$\Delta_f H$(Ion) kcal/mol	 kJ/mol	$\Delta_f H$(Neutral) kcal/mol	 kJ/mol	Neutral reference	CAS registry number
$C_4H_4N_2O^+$							
(pyrazine N-oxide)	(9.0)	(235)	(984)	28	116	*EST	2423-65-6
IP is onset of photoelectron band.							
$C_4H_4N_2O_2^+$							
(uracil)	(9.2)	(140)	(585)	−72±0.5	−303±2	77NAB/SAB	66-22-8
IP is onset of photoelectron band. See also: 81YU/ODO.							
(2-nitropyrrole)	(9.30±0.05)	(237)	(990)	23	93	*EST	5919-26-6
$C_4H_4N_2O_3^+$							
(barbituric acid)	(10.20)	(103)	(430)	−132	−554	72DOM	67-52-7
$C_4H_4O^+$							
$CH_3CH=C=C=O$	8.68±0.05	(215)	(900)	15	63	*EST	78957-08-1
IP from 83TER/HOL. See also: 79HOL/TER, 81MOH/HIR.							
$(CH_2)_2C=C=O$		198	828				
From appearance potential determination (82BUR/HOL).							
$CH_2=CHCH=C=O$	8.29±0.05	(195)	(817)	4	17	*EST	50888-73-8
IP from 79TER/BUR. See also: 82BUR/HOL, 81MOH/HIR, 79HOL/TER, 85MCN/SUF, 81BOC/HIR.							
$CH_2=C=CHCHO$	(9.5)	(236)	(987)	18	75	*EST	53268-92-1
$\Delta_f H$(Ion) from 82BUR/HOL. IP from 79HOL/TER.							
$HC{\equiv}CCH_2CHO$	(9.85)	(247)	(1034)	20	84	*EST	52844-23-2
IP estimated in 82BUR/HOL.							
$CH_3C{\equiv}CCHO$	10.20±0.02	(253)	(1057)	17	73	*EST	1119-19-3
IP from 79CAR/MOU. See also: 79TER/BUR, 82BUR/HOL, 79HOL/TER.							
$CH_3COC{\equiv}CH$	10.17±0.02	(250.18)	(1046.75)	15.6±.2	65.5±1	85FUC	1423-60-5
IP from 79CAR/MOU. See also: 79TER/BUR, 82BUR/HOL, 79HOL/TER.							
$CH_2=C=C=CHOH$		222	931				
From appearance potential determination (82BUR/HOL).							

Table 1. Positive Ion Table - Continued

ION Neutral	Ionization potential eV	$\Delta_f H$(Ion) kcal/mol	$\Delta_f H$(Ion) kJ/mol	$\Delta_f H$(Neutral) kcal/mol	$\Delta_f H$(Neutral) kJ/mol	Neutral reference	CAS registry number

$C_4H_4O^+$

HC≡CCH=CHOH
| | | 220 | 922 | | | | 59095-55-5 |

From appearance potential determination (82BUR/HOL).

$CH_2=C(OH)C≡CH$
| | (8.92) | (226) | (944) | 20±2 | 83±7 | 86TUR/HAV2 | |

$\Delta_f H$(Ion) from appearance potential determination (86TUR/HAV2).
See also: 82BUR/HOL, 79HOL/TER.

HC≡COCH=CH_2
| | 9.40 | (273) | (1142) | 56 | 235 | *EST | |

IP from 82BUR/HOL. See also: 79HOL/TER.

(furan)
|  | 8.883±0.003 | 196.5 | 822.3 | −8.3±0.1 | −34.8±0.4 | 77PED/RYL | 110-00-9 |

See also: 82BUR/HOL, 82KOB/KUB, 79HOL/TER, 81GAL/KLA, 81KIM/KAT, 82BIE/ASB, 80TED/VID, 83BOC/ROT, 83ZYK/ERC, 82KLA/SAB.

(cyclobutenone)
| 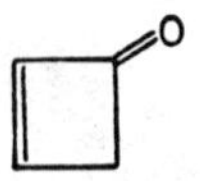 | (9.3) | (223) | (933) | 8 | 33 | *EST | 32264-87-2 |

From appearance potential determination; kinetic energy release = 0.19 eV (82BUR/HOL).
IP from 79HOL/TER.

(methylcyclopropenone)
| 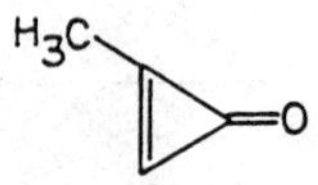 | 9.15±0.05 | (240) | (1004) | 29 | 121 | *EST | 4883-96-9 |

See also: 79TER/BUR, 82BUR/HOL, 79HOL/TER.

(cyclopropylidene ketene)
| 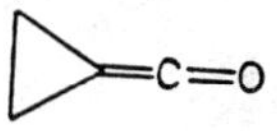 | (8.78) | (222) | (931) | 20 | 84 | *EST | |

IP from 81BOC/HIR.

(cyclopropanecarboxaldehyde)
| 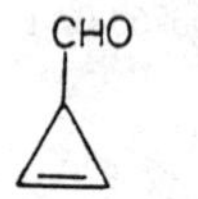 | (9.6) | (235) | (983) | 14 | 58 | *EST | 36998-21-7 |

IP from 79HOL/TER.

$C_4H_4O_2^+$

HC≡CCOOCH$_3$
| | (10.3) | (214) | (894) | −24 | −100 | *EST | 922-67-8 |

IP is onset of photoelectron band (82BIE/ASB).

(1,4-dioxin)
| 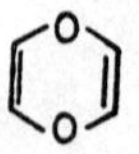 | (7.75±0.02) | (152) | (633) | −27±1 | −115±5 | *EST | 290-67-5 |

Table 1. Positive Ion Table - Continued

ION / Neutral	Ionization potential eV	$\Delta_f H$(Ion) kcal/mol	kJ/mol	$\Delta_f H$(Neutral) kcal/mol	kJ/mol	Neutral reference	CAS registry number
$C_4H_4O_2^+$							
(cyclobutanedione)	(9.4)	(178)	(745)	−39	−163	*EST	33689-28-0
	IP is onset of photoelectron band.						
(β-propiolactone, methylene)	(9.6±0.02)	(176)	(736)	−45.5±0.1	−190.3±0.4	77PED/RYL	674-82-8
	IP from 84OLI/FLE.						
$C_4H_4O_3^+$							
(maleic anhydride)	(10.6)	(119)	(498)	−125	−525	77PED/RYL	108-30-5
	IP is onset of photoelectron band (81KIM/KAT).						
$C_4H_4O_4^+$							
(E)-$HO_2CCH=CHCO_2H$	(10.7)	(85)	(352)	−162±0.6	−680±3	77PED/RYL	110-17-8
	IP is onset of photoelectron band.						
$C_4H_4S^+$							
(thiophene)	8.87±0.04	232	971	27.5±0.1	115.0±0.4	81KUD/KUD3	110-02-1
	See also: 80TED/VID, 83BOC/ROT, 81GAL/KLA, 82KLA/SAB.						
$C_4H_4S_2^+$							
(1,4-dithiin)	(7.7)	(233)	(976)	56±3	233±13	*EST	290-79-9
	IP is onset of photoelectron band.						
$C_4H_5^+$							
$CH_2=CCH=CH_2$		(246)	(1029)				62698-26-4
	From appearance potential measurements (84LOS/HOL).						
$CH\equiv CCHCH_3$	7.97	257	1074	73	305	82MCM/GOL	3315-42-2
	From appearance potential measurements (84LOS/HOL).						
$CH_3C\equiv CCH_2$	7.95	252	1056	69	289	82MCM/GOL	64235-83-2
	From appearance potential measurements (84LOS/HOL).						

Table 1. Positive Ion Table – Continued

ION / Neutral	Ionization potential eV	$\Delta_f H$(Ion) kcal/mol	kJ/mol	$\Delta_f H$(Neutral) kcal/mol	kJ/mol	Neutral reference	CAS registry number
$C_4H_5^+$							
(methylcyclopropenyl, CH₃ on cyclopropene)		(237)	(992)				60824-24-0
From appearance potential measurements (84LOS/HOL).							
$C_4H_5ClO^+$							
(E)-CH₃CH=CHCOCl	(9.4)	(216)	(906)	−0.2	−1	*EST	625-35-4
IP is onset of photoelectron band (81MOH/HIR).							
$C_4H_5F_3O_2^+$							
CF₃COOC₂H₅	(11.0)	(5)	(19)	−249	−1042	*EST	383-63-1
IP is onset of photoelectron band.							
$C_4H_5F_4O_2^+$							
CF₃C(OH)OCH₂CH₂F		−105	−441				
From proton affinity of CF₃COOCH₂CH₂F (RN 1683-88-1). PA = 178.6 kcal/mol, 747. kJ/mol.							
$C_4H_5F_6O^+$							
(CF₃)₂C(CH₃)OH₂		−192	−805				
From proton affinity of (CF₃)₂C(CH₃)OH (RN 1515-14-6). PA = 167.0 kcal/mol, 699. kJ/mol.							
$C_4H_5N^+$							
CH₂=CHCH₂CN	10.20±0.05	273	1140	37±0.5	156±2	77PED/RYL	109-75-1
See also: 84OHN/MAT.							
CH₂C(CH₃)CN	10.34	269	1128	31	130	80WIL/BAE	126-98-7
(E)-CH₃CH=CHCN	(≤10.23±0.05)	(≤272)	(≤1137)	36	150	82CHU/NGU	627-26-9
pyrrole	8.208±0.005	215.2	900.2	25.9±0.1	108.3±0.4	80WIL/BAE	109-97-7
See also: 81GAL/KLA, 82BIE/ASB, 80TED/VID, 82KLA/SAB.							
cyclopropanecarbonitrile	10.25	280	1172	44±0.2	183±1	82FUC/HAL	5500-21-0

Table 1. Positive Ion Table - Continued

ION Neutral	Ionization potential eV	$\Delta_f H$(Ion) kcal/mol kJ/mol	$\Delta_f H$(Neutral) kcal/mol kJ/mol	Neutral reference	CAS registry number

$C_4H_5N_2^+$

|  | | 216   906 | | | |

From proton affinity of pyridazine (RN 289-80-5). PA = 215.7 kcal/mol, 902 kJ/mol.

|  | | 202   846 | | | |

From proton affinity of pyrimidine (RN 289-95-2). PA = 210.8 kcal/mol, 882. kJ/mol.

|  | | 203   852 | | | |

From proton affinity of pyrazine (RN 290-37-9). PA = 209.0 kcal/mol, 874. kJ/mol.

$C_4H_5N_2O^+$

| 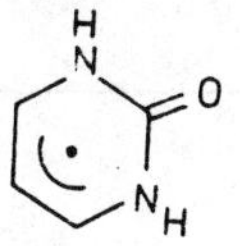 | | 146   613 | | | |

From proton affinity of 2(1H)-pyrimidinone (RN 557-01-7). PA = ~208 kcal/mol, ~870 kJ/mol.

$C_4H_5N_2O_2^+$

| 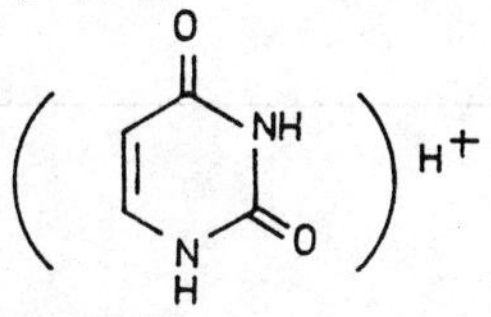 | | (85)   (357) | | | |

From proton affinity of uracil (RN 66-22-8). PA = ~208 kcal/mol, ~870 kJ/mol.

$C_4H_5N_2S_2^+$

| 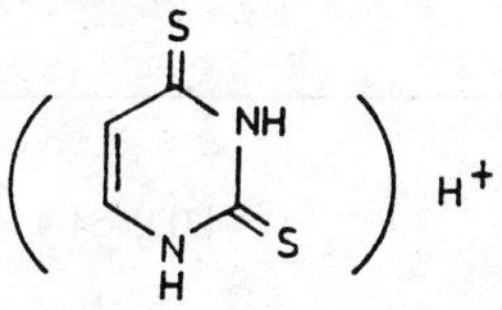 | | (200)   (836) | | | |

From proton affinity of dithiouracil (RN 2001-93-6). PA = ~217 kcal/mol, ~907 kJ/mol.

$C_4H_5N_3^+$

| 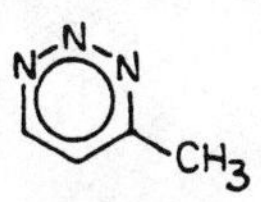 | (≤9.7) | (≤313)   (≤1311) | 90   375 | *EST | 77202-08-5 |

IP from 83GLE/SPA.

|  | (9.1) | (301)   (1258) | 91   380 | *EST | 86402-30-4 |

IP is onset of photoelectron band (83GLE/SPA).

Table 1. Positive Ion Table - Continued

ION Neutral	Ionization potential eV	$\Delta_f H$(Ion) kcal/mol	kJ/mol	$\Delta_f H$(Neutral) kcal/mol	kJ/mol	Neutral reference	CAS registry number
$C_4H_5N_3^+$							
3-methyl-1,2,4-triazine	(8.6) (IP is onset of photoelectron band.)	(268)	(1123)	70	293	*EST	24108-33-6
3-methyl-1,2,4,5-tetrazine	(≤9.31)	(≤285)	(≤1191)	70	293	*EST	21134-95-2
3-methyl-1,2,4,5-tetrazine isomer	(≤9.35)	(≤286)	(≤1195)	70	293	*EST	21134-96-3
$C_4H_5N_3O^+$							
cytosine	(8.45)	(181)	(756)	−14±2	−59±10	80SAB2	71-30-7
$C_4H_5O^+$		165	691				

From proton affinity of furan (RN 110-00-9). PA = 192.2 kcal/mol, 804. kJ/mol.

$C_4H_5O_2^+$							
$CH_3C(OH)=CHCO$		110	461				43115-54-4

From appearance potential of 10.24 eV in $CH_3COCH_2COCH_3$.

$C_4H_5S^+$		197	826				

From proton affinity of thiophene (RN 110-02-1) (86MAU, 84LIA/LIE). PA = 195.8 kcal/mol, 819. kJ/mol.

$C_4H_6^+$							
$CH_2=C=CHCH_3$	(9.03)	(247)	(1033)	38.8±0.1	162.3±0.5	77PED/RYL	590-19-2

Table 1. Positive Ion Table - Continued

ION / Neutral	Ionization potential eV	$\Delta_f H$(Ion) kcal/mol	$\Delta_f H$(Ion) kJ/mol	$\Delta_f H$(Neutral) kcal/mol	$\Delta_f H$(Neutral) kJ/mol	Neutral reference	CAS registry number
$C_4H_6^+$							
$CH_3C\equiv CCH_3$	9.562±0.005	<u>255.2</u>	<u>1068</u>	34.7±0.2	145.4±0.8	77PED/RYL	503-17-3
(cyclobutadiene)	9.43	255	1067	37.5±0.4	156.7±1.5	77PED/RYL	822-35-5
(methylenecyclopropane)	(9.57) See also: 81KIM/KAT.	(269)	(1124)	48±0.5	201±2	77PED/RYL	6142-73-0
(bicyclobutane)	8.700±0.005 IP from 83BOM/DAN3.	253	1057	51.9±0.2	217.2±0.8	77PED/RYL	157-33-5
$C_4H_6Cl_2Si^+$							
$CH_2=CHSiCl_2CH=CH_2$	(≤10.8) IP from 81KHV/ZYK.	(≤192)	(≤802)	−57	−240	*EST	1745-72-8
(silacyclopentene)	≤9.65 See also: 81KHV/ZYK.	(≤143)	(≤598)	−80	−333	*EST	872-46-8
$C_4H_6F_3O_2^+$							
$CF_3C(OH)OC_2H_5$		−68	−284				
From proton affinity of $CF_3COOC_2H_5$ (RN 383-63-1). PA = 184.6 kcal/mol, 772. kJ/mol.							
$C_4H_6N^+$							
$(CH_3)_2CCN$	(8.2) IP is onset of photoelectron band.	(229)	(960)	40.3±2.2	168.6±9.2	82MCM/GOL	3225-31-8
(pyrroline)		184	769				
From proton affinity of pyrroline (RN 109-97-7). PA = 207.6 kcal/mol, 868 kJ/mol.							
(cyclopropylcarbonitrile) H^+		214	895				
From proton affinity of cyclopropylcarbonitrile (RN 5500-21-0). PA = 195.4 kcal/mol, 817.5 kJ/mol.							

Table 1. Positive Ion Table – Continued

ION / Neutral	Ionization potential eV	$\Delta_f H$(Ion) kcal/mol	kJ/mol	$\Delta_f H$(Neutral) kcal/mol	kJ/mol	Neutral reference	CAS registry number
$C_4H_6NO_2{}^+$							
(NCCOOC$_2$H$_5$)H		134	562				
From proton affinity of NCCOOC$_2$H$_5$ (RN 623-49-4). PA = 179.5 kcal/mol, 751. kJ/mol.							
$C_4H_6N_2{}^+$							
1-methylimidazole	(≤8.66)	≤236	≤986	36	150	*EST	616-47-7
2-methylimidazole	(≤8.50)	≤225	≤942	29	122	*EST	693-98-1
$C_4H_6N_2S^+$							
1-methyl-5-mercaptopyrazole	≤9.1 IP from 83GUI/PFI.	(≤265)	(≤1107)	55	229	*EST	
1-methyl-3-mercaptopyrazole	(≤8.6) IP from 83GUI/PFI.	(≤251)	(≤1049)	52	219	*EST	79208-64-3
$C_4H_6N_3O^+$							
(cytosine)H$^+$		128	535				
From proton affinity of cytosine (RN 71-30-7). PA = 223.8 kcal/mol, 936. kJ/mol.							
$C_4H_6O^+$							
C$_2$H$_5$CH=C=O	8.80 IP from 81BOC/HIR.	(171)	(714)	−32	−135	*EST	20334-52-5
(CH$_3$)$_2$C=C=O	(8.45) IP from 81BOC/HIR.	(163)	(681)	−32±1	−134±4	80DEM/WUL	598-26-5
(E)-CH$_3$CH=CHCHO	9.73±0.01 See also: 78VAN/OSK.	200	835	−24.8±0.4	−103.6±1.5	79VAJ/HAR	4170-30-3
CH$_2$=C(CH$_3$)CHO	(9.86) IP from 86HOL/LOS.	(199)	(834)	−28	−117	79VAJ/HAR	78-85-3

Table 1. Positive Ion Table - Continued

ION Neutral	Ionization potential eV	$\Delta_f H$(Ion) kcal/mol	kJ/mol	$\Delta_f H$(Neutral) kcal/mol	kJ/mol	Neutral reference	CAS registry number
$C_4H_6O^+$							
$CH_2=CHCOCH_3$	9.64	(189)	(792)	−33	−138	79VAJ/HAR	78-94-4
	See also: 80TER/HEE, 82MOR/MER.						
$CH_3C\equiv COCH_3$	(8.79)	(206)	(860)	2.9	12.1	*EST	13169-01-2
	IP from 86HOL/LOS.						
$CH_2=CHCH=CHOH(E)$	(8.51±0.03)	(175)	(733)	−21±1	−88±5	86TUR/HAV	70411-98-2
	IP from 86TUR/HAV, 86TUR/HAV3. See also: 80TER/HEE.						
$CH_2=CHCH=CHOH(Z)$	(8.47±0.03)	(174)	(728)	−21±2	−89±9	86TUR/HEE	70415-58-6
	IP from 86TUR/HAV, 86TUR/HAV3. See also: 80TER/HEE.						
$CH_2=C=CHCH_2OH$	(8.74)	(206)	(861)	4.3	18.0	*EST	18913-31-0
	IP from 80TER/HEE.						
$HC\equiv CCH_2CH_2OH$	(9.66)	(226)	(945)	3.2	13.4	*EST	927-74-2
	IP from 86HOL/LOS.						
$CH_3C\equiv CCH_2OH$	(9.78)	(227)	(948)	1.1	4.6	*EST	764-01-2
	IP from 86HOL/LOS.						
$HC\equiv CCH(CH_3)OH$	(10.15)	(236)	(987)	2	8	*EST	2028-63-9
$CH_2=CHC(OH)=CH_2$	8.68±0.03	182	761	−18	−76	84TUR	59120-04-6
	$\Delta_f H$(Ion) from appearance potential determination(80TER/HEE). IP from 84TUR.						
$CH_2=C=CHOCH_3$	(8.64)	(207)	(866)	7.7	32.2	*EST	13169-00-1
	IP from 86HOL/LOS, onset of photoelectron band (86KAM/BOS).						
$HC\equiv CCH_2OCH_3$	(9.78)	(240)	(1005)	14.7	61.5	*EST	627-41-8
	IP from 86HOL/LOS.						
$CH_2=CHOCH=CH_2$	(8.7)	(197)	(824)	−3	−13	*EST	109-93-3
	$\Delta_f H$(Ion) from appearance potential determination (81HOL/BUR). IP is $\Delta_f H$(Ion) − $\Delta_f H$(Neutral).						
(2,5-dihydrofuran)	9.14±0.02	195	816	−16±1	−66±3	81ALL/GLA	1708-29-8
(cyclobutanone)	9.354	(194)	(814)	−21	−89	*EST	1191-95-3

Table 1. Positive Ion Table - Continued

ION / Neutral	Ionization potential eV	$\Delta_f H$(Ion) kcal/mol	$\Delta_f H$(Ion) kJ/mol	$\Delta_f H$(Neutral) kcal/mol	$\Delta_f H$(Neutral) kJ/mol	Neutral reference	CAS registry number
$C_4H_6O^+$							
(epoxide-CH=CH$_2$)	9.52	(222)	(928)	2	10	*EST	930-22-3
	IP from 86HOL/LOS.						
$C_4H_6OSi^+$							
(furan-SiH$_3$)	(<8.0)	(<183)	(<765)	-2	-7	*EST	73726-79-1
	IP is onset of photoelectron band (83ZYK/ERC).						
$C_4H_6O_2^+$							
(Z)-CH$_3$CH=CHCOOH	(10.08)	(150)	(626)	-83	-346	*EST	503-64-0
(E)-CH$_3$CH=CHCOOH	(9.9)	(145)	(605)	-84	-350	*EST	107-93-7
	IP is onset of photoelectron band (78VAN/OSK, 81MOH/HIR).						
CH$_2$=CHCH$_2$COOH	(9.75)	(141)	(589)	-84	-352	*EST	625-38-7
	IP is onset of photoelectron band (81MOH/HIR).						
CH$_2$=C(CH$_3$)COOH	(10.15)	(146)	(610)	-88	-369	84BOU/HOP	3724-65-0
CH$_3$CO$_2$CH=CH$_2$	9.19	137	572	-75.3±0.1	-314.9±0.5	77PED/RYL	108-05-4
	"Doubtful" IP value reported in K. Watanabe, T. Nakayama, and J. R. Mottl, J. Quant. Spectrosc. Radiat. Transfer 2, 369 (1962) is in good agreement with onset of photoelectron band (78VAN/OSK). See also: 82LEV/LIA.						
CH$_2$=CHCOOCH$_3$	(9.9)	(154)	(643)	-75	-312	80VIL/PER	96-33-3
	IP is onset of photoelectron band (78VAN/OSK). See also: 82LEV/LIA.						
(CH$_3$CO)$_2$	9.24±0.04	135	564	-78.2±0.3	-327.1±1.1	77PED/RYL	431-03-8
	See also: 80VON/BIE, 81KIM/KAT.						
(3,6-dihydro-1,2-dioxin)	(9.5)	(224)	(938)	5	21	*EST	18715-02-1
	IP is onset of photoelectron band (81KIM/KAT).						
(1,4-dioxin)	(8.07±0.02)	(131)	(549)	-55	-230	*EST	543-75-9

Table 1. Positive Ion Table – Continued

ION Neutral	Ionization potential eV	$\Delta_f H$(Ion) kcal/mol	$\Delta_f H$(Ion) kJ/mol	$\Delta_f H$(Neutral) kcal/mol	$\Delta_f H$(Neutral) kJ/mol	Neutral reference	CAS registry number
$C_4H_6O_2^+$ (cyclopropane-COOH)	10.64	(167)	(699)	−78	−328	*EST	1759-53-1
$C_4H_6O_2S^+$ $(CH_2=CH)_2SO_2$	10.59±0.03	208	871	−36±0.9	−151±4	77PED/RYL	77-77-0
(2,5-dihydrothiophene 1,1-dioxide)	(10.0)	(169)	(709)	−61±0.7	−256±3	77PED/RYL	77-79-2
	IP is onset of photoelectron band (82LEV/LIA, 84AIT/GOS).						
$C_4H_6O_3^+$ $(CH_3CO)_2O$	(10.0)	(95)	(398)	−135.6±0.3	−567.3±1.3	77PED/RYL	108-24-7
	IP is onset of photoelectron band (81BOC/HIR).						
(propylene carbonate)	(10.52)	(103)	(432)	−139±0.5	−583±2	77PED/RYL	108-32-7
$C_4H_6O_4^+$ $CH_3OCOCOOCH_3$	(10.0)	(69)	(289)	−162	−676	76ANT/CAR	553-90-2
	IP is onset of photoelectron band.						
$C_4H_6S^+$ $(CH_2=CH)_2S$	(8.25±0.01)	(232)	(970)	42±2	174±9	*EST	627-51-0
(2,5-dihydrothiophene)	(8.4)	(215)	(897)	20.8±0.3	87.0±1.1	81KUD/KUD3	1708-32-3
	IP is onset of photoelectron band.						
$C_4H_6S_2^+$ $CH_3SC{\equiv}CSCH_3$	(7.8)	(238)	(995)	58	242	*EST	59507-56-1
	IP is onset of photoelectron band (81BOC/RIE).						
(3,4-dimethyl-1,2-dithiete)	(8.0)	(231)	(966)	46	194	*EST	74378-81-7
	IP is onset of photoelectron band (83SCH/SCH).						

Table 1. Positive Ion Table - Continued

ION Neutral	Ionization potential eV	$\Delta_f H$(Ion) kcal/mol	kJ/mol	$\Delta_f H$(Neutral) kcal/mol	kJ/mol	Neutral reference	CAS registry number
$C_4H_6S_3^+$							
(structure)	(8.2)	(208)	(869)	19±0.7	78±3	77PED/RYL	1748-15-8
	IP is onset of photoelectron band.						
$C_4H_7^+$							
$CH_3CHCH=CH_2$	(7.49±0.02)	202	845	31.7	132.6	87LIA/AUS	65338-31-0
		206	863	35.7	149.4		
	IP from 84SCH/HOU2. Value of $\Delta_f H$(Ion) from proton affinity of						
	1,3-butadiene (RN 106-99-0). PA = 190 kcal/mol, 795 kJ/mol (87LIA/AUS). See also: 86TRA.						
$CH_2C(CH_3)=CH_2$	7.90±0.02	(211)	(883)	29	121	87LIA/AUS	15157-95-6
	IP from 84SCH/HOU2.						
(1-methylcyclopropene)H^+		(218)	(912)				65338-31-0
	From proton affinity of 1-methylcyclopropene (RN 3100-04-7). PA = (206) kcal/mol,						
	(862) kJ/mol.						
CH_3CCHCH_3		(213)	(893)				
		(217)	(908)				
	From proton affinity of 2-butyne. (RN 503-17-3).						
	PA = 188 kcal/mol, 787 kJ/mol (87LIA/AUS).						
$CH_2=CHCH_2CH_2$	8.04	(231)	(968)	46	191	84SCH/HOU2	2154-62-3
	IP from 84SCH/HOU2.						
(cyclobutane)H^+	7.54±0.02	(225)	(941)	51.2	214.2	82MCM/GOL	4548-06-5
	IP from 84SCH/HOU2. Value of $\Delta_f H$(Ion) formed by protonation of cyclobutene						
	(RN 822-35-5) = 212 kcal/mol, 888 kJ/mol.						
$C_4H_7F_3O^+$							
$CF_3CH_2OC_2H_5$	10.27	(21)	(86)	−216	−905	*EST	461-24-5
	IP from 83MOL/PIK.						
$C_4H_7IO_2^+$							
$CH_3CHICOOCH_3$	(9.1)	(122)	(510)	−88	−368	*EST	56905-18-1
	IP from 83BUR/HOL3.						
$C_4H_7N^+$							
$n-C_3H_7CN$	(11.2)	(266)	(1112)	7	31	82CHU/NGU	109-74-0
	IP is onset of photoelectron band (84OHN/MAT, 81KIM/KAT). See also: 82CHE/LAP.						
$n-C_3H_7NC$	(11.8)	(302)	(1262)	29.5	123.4	*EST	627-36-1
	IP from 82CHE/LAP.						

Table 1. Positive Ion Table - Continued

ION / Neutral	Ionization potential eV	$\Delta_f H$(Ion) kcal/mol	$\Delta_f H$(Ion) kJ/mol	$\Delta_f H$(Neutral) kcal/mol	$\Delta_f H$(Neutral) kJ/mol	Neutral reference	CAS registry number
$C_4H_7N^+$							
iso-C_3H_7CN	(11.3)	(266)	(1115)	5.8±0.2	24.5±0.7	77PED/RYL	78-82-0
	IP is onset of photoelectron band (84OHN/MAT, 81KIM/KAT).						
(3-pyrroline)	(8.0)	(210)	(882)	26±0.7	110±3	*EST	109-96-6
	IP is onset of photoelectron band.						
(N-vinylaziridine)	(8.2)	(251)	(1048)	61	257	*EST	
	IP from 81MUL/PRE.						
$C_4H_7NO^+$							
(2-pyrrolidinone)	(9.2)	(161)	(675)	−51	−213	77PED/RYL	616-45-5
	IP is onset of photoelectron band (80AND/DEV).						
$C_4H_7NO_2^+$							
$CH_2=CHCH_2CH_2ONO$	(9.7)	(224)	(939)	0.7	3	*EST	67428-02-8
	IP is onset of photoelectron band.						
$C_4H_7NO_3^+$							
$CH_3CONHCH_2COOH$	(9.4)	(72)	(303)	−144	−604	*EST	543-24-8
	IP is onset of photoelectron band (83CAN/HAM).						
$C_4H_7NS^+$							
(pyrrolidine-2-thione)	(8.14)	(192)	(801)	4	16	*EST	2295-35-4
	IP is onset of photoelectron band (80AND/DEV).						
$C_4H_7NSe^+$							
(pyrrolidine-2-selone)	7.6	(196)	(819)	21	86	*EST	23164-74-1
	IP is onset of photoelectron band (80AND/DEV).						

Table 1. Positive Ion Table - Continued

ION Neutral	Ionization potential eV	$\Delta_f H$(Ion) kcal/mol kJ/mol		$\Delta_f H$(Neutral) kcal/mol kJ/mol		Neutral reference	CAS registry number
$C_4H_7N_2^+$							
(1-methylimidazole structure)		(173)	(723)				
From proton affinity of 1-methylimidazole (RN 616-47-7). PA = 228.9 kcal/mol, 958. kJ/mol.							
(4-methylimidazole structure)		(170)	(713)				
From proton affinity of 4-methylimidazole (RN 822-36-6). PA = 224.4 kcal/mol, 939. kJ/mol.							
$C_4H_7N_3S^+$							
(triazole-SCH₃ structure)	≤8.33 IP from 83GUI/PFI.	(≤250)	(≤1047)	58	243	*EST	36811-14-0
(triazole-SCH₃ structure)	≤8.65 IP from 83GUI/PFI.	(≤258)	(≤1077)	58	243	*EST	35262-23-8
(dimethyl triazole-thione structure)	(7.4) IP from 83GUI/PFI.	(259)	(1084)	88	370	*EST	64808-28-2
$C_4H_7O^+$							
(E)-$CH_3CHCHCHOH$		141	591				
From proton affinity of (E)-$CH_3CH=CHCHO$ (RN 4170-30-3). PA = 199.7 kcal/mol, 835.5 kJ/mol.							
$CH_2C(CH_3)CHOH$		142	596				
From proton affinity of $CH_2=C(CH_3)CHO$ (RN 78-85-3). PA = 195.2 kcal/mol, 817. kJ/mol.							
$CH_2CHC(OH)CH_3$		133	554				
From proton affinity of $CH_2=CHCOCH_3$ (RN 78-94-4). PA = 200.2 kcal/mol, 838. kJ/mol.							
(tetrahydrofuran structure)		141	589				
From proton affinity of 2,3-dihydrofuran (RN 1191-99-7) (86BOU/DJA). PA = 206.8 kcal/mol, 865 kJ/mol.							

Table 1. Positive Ion Table - Continued

ION / Neutral	Ionization potential eV	$\Delta_f H$(Ion) kcal/mol	$\Delta_f H$(Ion) kJ/mol	$\Delta_f H$(Neutral) kcal/mol	$\Delta_f H$(Neutral) kJ/mol	Neutral reference	CAS registry number

$C_4H_7O^+$

(tetrahydrofuran structure)

| 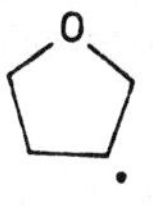 | | 152 | 634 | | | | |

From proton affinity of 2,5-dihydrofuran (RN 1708-29-8) (86BOU/DJA).
PA = 198.4 kcal/mol, 830. kJ/mol.

$C_4H_7O_2^+$

(Z)-$CH_3CH=CHC(OH)_2$

| | | 78 | 327 | | | | |

From proton affinity of (Z)-$CH_3CH=CHCOOH$ (RN 503-64-0)(84BOU/HOP).
PA = 199.7 kcal/mol, 836. kJ/mol.

$CH_3C(CH_2)C(OH)_2$

| | | 81 | 338 | | | | |

From proton affinity of $CH_3C(=CH_2)COOH$ (RN 3724-65-0)(84BOU/HOP).
PA = 196.8 kcal/mol, 823. kJ/mol.

$CH_2=CHC(OH)OCH_3$

| | | 92 | 386 | | | | |

$\Delta_f H$(Ion) from appearance potential determination (83BUR/HOL3).

$CH_3CO_2CHCH_3$

| | | 94 | 392 | | | | |

From proton affinity of $CH_3CO_2CH=CH_2$ (RN 108-05-4) (86MAU). PA = 196.7 kcal/mol, 823. kJ/mol.

$CH_3CHCOOCH_3$

| | | 115 | 480 | | | | |

$\Delta_f H$(Ion) from appearance potential determination (83BUR/HOL3).

$CH_3COC(OH)CH_3$

| | | 93 | 388 | | | | |

From proton affinity of $(CH_3CO)_2$ (RN 431-03-8). PA = 194.8 kcal/mol, 815. kJ/mol.

(1,4-dioxane structure)

| 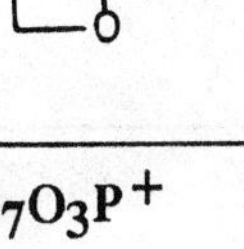 | | 126 | 529 | | | | |

From proton affinity of dihydro-1,4-dioxin (RN 543-75-9) (86BOU/HAN).
PA = 198.4 kcal/mol, 830. kJ/mol.

(oxetane-OCH_3 structure)

| 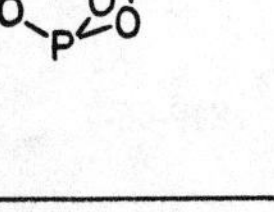 | | 108 | 450 | | | | |

$\Delta_f H$(Ion) from appearance potential determination (83BUR/HOL3).

$C_4H_7O_3P^+$

| | (9.42±0.1) | (89) | (371) | −129 | −538 | *EST | 280-45-5 |

Table 1. Positive Ion Table − Continued

ION / Neutral	Ionization potential eV	$\Delta_f H$(Ion) kcal/mol	$\Delta_f H$(Ion) kJ/mol	$\Delta_f H$(Neutral) kcal/mol	$\Delta_f H$(Neutral) kJ/mol	Neutral reference	CAS registry number

$C_4H_7S^+$

		237	992				39925-70-7
		214	*895*				

$\Delta_f H$(Ion) from appearance potential in tetrahydrothiophene (83BUT/BAE2).

$C_4H_8^+$

1-C_4H_8	9.58±0.02	221	924	−0.1±0.1	−0.4±0.5	77PED/RYL	106-98-9
	See also: 83HOL/LOS, 86TRA.						
(Z)-2-C_4H_8	9.108±0.008	208	871	−1.9±0.1	−7.8±0.5	77PED/RYL	590-18-1
	IP from 78LIA/AUS. See also: 81KIM/KAT, 86TRA.						
(E)-2-C_4H_8	9.100±0.008	207	866	−2.9±0.2	−12.2±0.5	77PED/RYL	624-64-6
	IP from 78LIA/AUS. See also: 81KIM/KAT, 86TRA.						
iso-C_4H_8	9.239±0.003	209	874	−4.0±0.1	−16.9±0.6	77PED/RYL	115-11-7
	See also: 83HOL/LOS, 81KIM/KAT, 86TRA.						
☐	(9.92±0.05)	(235)	(985)	6.8±0.2	28.4±0.5	77PED/RYL	287-23-0
▷−CH_3	(9.46)	(224)	(938)	5.5	23	77PED/RYL	594-11-6

$C_4H_8Br_2^+$

$CH_3CHBrCHBrCH_3$-(R,R(±))	(≤10.12)	(≤206)	(≤860)	−28	−116	*EST	598-71-0
$CH_3CHBrCHBrCH_3$-(R,S)	(≤10.16)	(≤207)	(≤864)	−28	−116	*EST	5780-13-2
$BrCH_2CH_2CH_2CH_2Br$	(10.15)	(210)	(880)	−24	−99	77PED/RYL	110-52-1
	IP from 77STA/WIE.						

$C_4H_8F_3N^+$

$CF_3CH_2CH_2CH_2NH_2$	(9.1)	(29)	(123)	−180	−755	*EST	819-46-5
	IP from 79AUE/BOW.						
$(CH_3)_2NCH_2CF_3$	(8.42)	(27)	(112)	−167	−700	81LOG/TAK	819-06-7
	IP from 81LOG/TAK. See also: 79AUE/BOW.						

Table 1. Positive Ion Table – Continued

ION / Neutral	Ionization potential eV	$\Delta_f H$(Ion) kcal/mol	$\Delta_f H$(Ion) kJ/mol	$\Delta_f H$(Neutral) kcal/mol	$\Delta_f H$(Neutral) kJ/mol	Neutral reference	CAS registry number
$C_4H_8F_3O^+$							
$C_2H_5OCH_2CF_3$		−37	−154				

From proton affinity of $C_2H_5OCH_2CF_3$ (RN 461-24-5). PA = 186.4 kcal/mol, 780. kJ/mol.

$C_4H_8N^+$							
n-C_3H_7CNH		179	751				

From proton affinity of n-C_3H_7CN (RN 109-74-0). PA = 193.7 kcal/mol, 810. kJ/mol.

i-C_3H_7CNH		177	740				

From proton affinity of i-C_3H_7CN (RN 78-82-0). PA = 194.3 kcal/mol, 813. kJ/mol.

i-C_3H_7NCH		186	778				

From proton affinity of i-C_3H_7NC (RN 598-45-8) (86MAU/KAR). PA = 206. kcal/mol, 862. kJ/mol.

$C_4H_8NO_4^+$							
HOOCCH$_2$CH(NH$_3$)COOH		−44	−184				

From proton affinity of L-aspartic acid (RN 617-45-8). PA = 216.7 kcal/mol, 907. kJ/mol.

$C_4H_8N_2^+$							
(CH$_3$)$_2$NCH$_2$CN	(8.72±0.05)	(228)	(953)	27	112	*EST	926-64-7

See also: 83MOL/PIK2.

$C_4H_8N_2OS^+$							
(CH$_3$)$_2$NCSOCNH$_2$	(≤8.21)	(≤171)	(≤714)	−19	−78	*EST	41168-96-1

IP from 81HEN/ISA.

(CH$_3$)$_2$NCOCSNH$_2$	≤8.37	(≤168)	(≤704)	−25	−104	*EST	18138-14-2

IP from 81HEN/ISA.

$C_4H_8N_2O_2^+$							
CH$_3$NHCOCONHCH$_3$	(9.33)	(121)	(504)	−95	−396	*EST	615-35-0

$C_4H_8N_2S^+$	(7.7)	(201)	(842)	24	99	*EST	13431-10-2

IP is onset of photoelectron band (80AND/DEV).

$C_4H_8N_2S_2^+$							
CH$_3$NHCSCSNHCH$_3$	≤8.23	(≤163)	(≤684)	−26	−110	*EST	120-79-6

IP from 81HEN/ISA.

$C_4H_8N_4^+$							
NCN=C(NHCH$_3$)$_2$	(8.5)	(234)	(977)	38	157	*EST	31857-31-5

IP is onset of photoelectron band (80KLA/BUT).

Table 1. Positive Ion Table – Continued

ION / Neutral	Ionization potential eV	$\Delta_f H$(Ion) kcal/mol	$\Delta_f H$(Ion) kJ/mol	$\Delta_f H$(Neutral) kcal/mol	$\Delta_f H$(Neutral) kJ/mol	Neutral reference	CAS registry number
$C_4H_8O^+$							
n-C_3H_7CHO	9.84±0.02	177	742	−49.6±0.4	−207.5±1.5	77PED/RYL	123-72-8

See also: 81ELS/ALL, 83MCA/HUD, 81KIM/KAT, 86TRA/MCA.

iso-C_3H_7CHO	9.705±0.005	172	721	−51.5±0.1	−215.6±0.6	77PED/RYL	78-84-2

See also: 83MCA/HUD, 86TRA/MCA.

$C_2H_5COCH_3$	9.51±0.04	162	677	−57.5±0.1	−240.8±0.6	77PED/RYL	78-93-3

See also: 72POT/SOR, 85TRA, 81KIM/KAT.

$CH_3CH_2CH=CHOH$	(8.34±0.05)	(150)	(628)	−42	−177	*EST	56640-69-8

$\Delta_f H$(Ion) from appearance potential determinations. IP is $\Delta_f H$(Ion) − $\Delta_f H$(Neutral) (83HOL/LOS). See also: 83MCA/HUD.

(E)-$CH_3CH=CHCH_2OH$	(9.13±0.02)	(173)	(726)	−37	−155	*EST	

IP from 86TRA/MCA. See also: 83MCA/HUD.

$CH_2=CHCH_2CH_2OH$	(9.56±0.05)	(184)	(770)	−36	−152	*EST	627-27-0

IP from 83HOL/LOS.

CH_3CHCH_2CHOH		(165)	(690)				

Based on appearance energy measurements of metastable processes (83MCA/HUD).

$CH_2=C(CH_3)CH_2OH$	(9.26±0.02)	(176)	(734)	−38	−159	*EST	513-42-8

IP is average of values from 83HOL/LOS and 86TRA/MCA.

$(CH_3)_2C=CHOH$	(8.27±0.05)	(145)	(607)	−46	−192	*EST	56640-70-1

$\Delta_f H$(Ion) from appearance potential determinations.
IP is $\Delta_f H$(Ion) − $\Delta_f H$(Neutral)(83HOL/LOS).

$CH_2CH(CH_3)CHOH$		(154)	(644)				

Based on appearance energy measurements of metastable processes (83MCA/HUD).

$CH_3CH_2C(OH)=CH_2$	(8.36±0.05)	(150)	(628)	−43	−179	*EST	61923-55-5

$\Delta_f H$(Ion) from appearance potential determinations.
IP is $\Delta_f H$(Ion) − $\Delta_f H$(Neutral)(83HOL/LOS). See also:83MCA/HUD.

$CH_3C(OH)=CHCH_3$		139	581				21411-38-1

$\Delta_f H$(Ion) from appearance potential determinations. See also: 83MCA/HUD.

$CH_2=CHCH(OH)CH_3$	9.50±0.05	(180)	(756)	−38	−161	*EST	598-32-3

IP from 83MCA/HUD, 83HOL/LOS, 86TRA/MCA.

$CH_3C(OH)CH_2CH_2$		(147)	(613)				

Based on appearance energy measurements of metastable processes (83MCA/HUD).

$CH_2=CHCH_2OCH_3$	(9.56)	(195)	(817)	−25	−105	*EST	627-40-7

IP from 86HOL/LOS.

Table 1. Positive Ion Table – Continued

ION / Neutral	Ionization potential eV	$\Delta_f H$(Ion) kcal/mol	$\Delta_f H$(Ion) kJ/mol	$\Delta_f H$(Neutral) kcal/mol	$\Delta_f H$(Neutral) kJ/mol	Neutral reference	CAS registry number
$C_4H_8O^+$							
$CH_2=CHOC_2H_5$	(8.8) IP from 86HOL/LOS. See also: 82MOR/MER.	(169)	(708)	−34	−141	77PED/RYL	109-92-2
$CH_2=C(CH_3)OCH_3$	(8.64) IP from 82HOL/LOS2.	(164)	(688)	−35	−146	*EST	116-11-0
(tetrahydrofuran)	9.41±0.02 See also: 81KIM/KAT.	173	724	−44.0±0.2	−184.2±0.7	77PED/RYL	109-99-9
(cyclobutanol)	9.25 IP from 83MCA/HUD, 86TRA/MCA.	(181)	(756)	−32	−136	*EST	2919-23-5
(2,2-dimethyloxirane)	(10.00)	(198)	(830)	−32	−135	*EST	558-30-5
(2,3-dimethyloxirane)	(9.98)	(199)	(832)	−31	−131	*EST	21490-63-1
(ethyloxirane)	(10.15)	(206)	(864)	−28	−115	*EST	106-88-7
$C_4H_8OS^+$							
$CH_3COSC_2H_5$	(9.2) IP is onset of photoelectron band.	(158)	(660)	−54±0.2	−228±1	66WAD	625-60-5
(1,4-oxathiane)	(8.67)	(164)	(688)	−36	−149	*EST	15980-15-1
(tetrahydrothiophene-1-oxide)	8.5 IP is onset of photoelectron band.	(161)	(674)	−35	−146	*EST	1600-44-8

Table 1. Positive Ion Table – Continued

ION / Neutral	Ionization potential eV	$\Delta_f H$(Ion) kcal/mol	$\Delta_f H$(Ion) kJ/mol	$\Delta_f H$(Neutral) kcal/mol	$\Delta_f H$(Neutral) kJ/mol	Neutral reference	CAS registry number
$C_4H_8O_2^+$							
n-C_3H_7COOH	10.17±0.05	121	507	−113±1	−473±4	82BUT/FRA	107-92-6
		127	*533*	*−107*	*−447*		
	See also: 82BUT/FRA, 81HOL/FIN.						
iso-C_3H_7COOH	10.33±0.03	(123)	(517)	−115	−480	*EST	79-31-2
HCOOCH$_2$CH$_2$CH$_3$	10.52±0.02	132	553	−110	−462	77PED/RYL	110-74-7
HCOOCH(CH$_3$)$_2$	10.44±0.05	(144)	(602)	−97	−405	*EST	625-55-8
CH$_3$COOC$_2$H$_5$	10.01±0.05	125	523	−106.1±0.1	−443.9±0.4	77PED/RYL	141-78-6
		131	*548*	*−99.9±0.1*	*−418.0±0.4*		
	IP from 82FRA/FRA2.						
C$_2$H$_5$COOCH$_3$	10.15±0.03	(131)	(547)	−103	−432	*EST	554-12-1
CH$_3$CH$_2$CH=C(OH)$_2$		97	405				12542-32-4
	From appearance potential of 10.14 eV in (C$_2$H$_5$)$_2$CHCOOH (RN 88-09-5).						
(CH$_3$)$_2$C=C(OH)$_2$		92	387				
	From appearance potentials of 10.02 eV in C$_2$H$_5$C(CH$_3$)$_2$COOH (RN 595-37-9) and 9.96 eV in n-C$_3$H$_7$C(CH$_3$)$_2$COOH (RN 1185-39-3).						
CH$_2$=C(OH)OC$_2$H$_5$		104	433				
	From appearance potential of 10.06 eV in n-C$_3$H$_7$COOC$_2$H$_5$ (RN 105-54-4) and 9.96 eV in n-C$_5$H$_{11}$COOC$_2$H$_5$ (RN 123-66-0).						
CH$_3$CH=C(OH)OCH$_3$		99	413				
	From appearance potential of 9.81 eV in sec-C$_4$H$_9$COOCH$_3$ (RN 868-57-5).						
CH$_3$COCH$_2$OCH$_3$	≤9.66	(≤143)	(≤598)	−80	−334	*EST	5878-19-3
	IP from 84OLI/GUE.						
(1,3-dioxane)	(≤10.0)	(≤195)	(≤816)	−36	−149	*EST	5703-46-8
(1,4-dioxane)	9.8	145	608	−81±0.2	−338±1	82BYS/MAN	505-22-6
	See also: 84ASF/ZYK.						

Table 1. Positive Ion Table - Continued

ION / Neutral	Ionization potential eV	$\Delta_f H$(Ion) kcal/mol	$\Delta_f H$(Ion) kJ/mol	$\Delta_f H$(Neutral) kcal/mol	$\Delta_f H$(Neutral) kJ/mol	Neutral reference	CAS registry number

$C_4H_8O_2^+$

1,4-dioxane

| 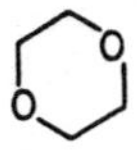 | 9.19±0.01 | 136 | 571 | −75.5±0.2 | −316.0±0.7 | 82BYS/MAN | 123-91-1 |
| | | 144 | 602 | −68.2±0.2 | −285.3±0.8 | | |

IP from 82FRA/FRA. See also: 81KIM/KAT, 73GOL/KOR, 82BIE/ASB.

$C_4H_8O_2S^+$

tetrahydrothiophene-1,1-dioxide

| 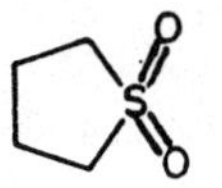 | (9.8) | (138) | (577) | −88 | −369 | *EST | 126-33-0 |

IP is onset of photoelectron band. See also: 84AIT/GOS.

2,3-dimethylthiirane-1,1-dioxide

| 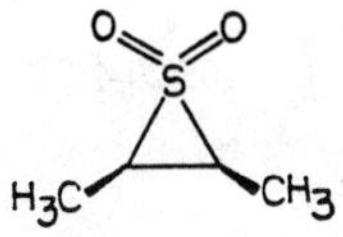 | (9.5) | (142) | (593) | −77 | −324 | *EST | 54697-52-8 |

IP is onset of photoelectron band.

$C_4H_8O_3^+$

$(CH_3)_2COHCOOH$

| | ≤10.9 | (≤96) | (≤404) | −155 | −648 | *EST | 594-61-6 |

IP from 73GOL/KOR.

$C_4H_8O_3P^+$

| 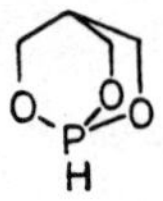 | | 30 | 126 | | | | |

From proton affinity of 2,6,7-trioxa-1-phosphabicyclo[2.2.2]octane (RN 280-45-5). PA = 207.1 kcal/mol, 866.5 kJ/mol.

| 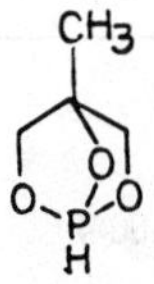 | | 13 | 55 | | | | |

From proton affinity of 4-methyl-2,6,7-trioxa-1-phosphabicyclo[2.2.1]heptane (RN 61580-09-4). PA = 198.1 kcal/mol, 829. kJ/mol.

$C_4H_8O_4^+$

| 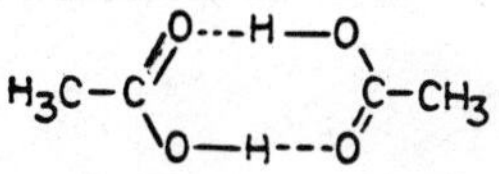 | (≤10.6) | (≤22) | (≤94) | −222 | −929 | *EST | 6993-75-5 |

$C_4H_8S^+$

| $CH_3SCH_2CH=CH_2$ | 8.6 | (210) | (880) | 12±2 | 50±9 | *EST | 10152-76-8 |
| $CH_2=CHSC_2H_5$ | (8.21±0.01) | (201) | (840) | 11±1 | 48±6 | *EST | 627-50-9 |

Table 1. Positive Ion Table - Continued

ION / Neutral	Ionization potential eV	$\Delta_f H$(Ion) kcal/mol	kJ/mol	$\Delta_f H$(Neutral) kcal/mol	kJ/mol	Neutral reference	CAS registry number
$C_4H_8S^+$							
(tetrahydrothiophene)	8.47	187.1	782.8	−8.2±0.2	−34.1±0.9	81KUD/KUD3	110-01-0
		193.8	*810.8*	*−1.5*	*−6.2*		
	Results from 83BUT/BAE2.						
$C_4H_8S_2^+$							
(Z)-$CH_3SCH=CHSCH_3$	(≤7.80)	(≤203)	(≤849)	23	96	*EST	764-44-3
(E)-$CH_3SCH=CHSCH_3$	(≤7.85)	(≤204)	(≤853)	23	96	*EST	764-45-4
$CH_2=C(SCH_3)_2$	(≤8.2)	(≤212)	(≤887)	23	96	*EST	51102-74-0
(1,2-dithiane)	8.1	(178)	(746)	−9	−36	*EST	505-20-4
	IP is onset of photoelectron band.						
(1,3-dithiane)	8.2	(188)	(786)	−1	−5	*EST	505-23-7
	IP is onset of photoelectron band.						
(1,4-dithiane)	(8.4)	(193)	(805)	−1	−5	*EST	505-29-3
	IP is onset of photoelectron band.						
$C_4H_8S_4^+$							
(1,2,4,5-tetrathiane)	(7.8)	(197)	(825)	17	72	*EST	2373-00-4
	IP is onset of photoelectron band (81BOC/SCH).						
$C_4H_8Sc^+$							
((E)-$CH_3CH=CHCH_3$)Sc		(191)	(799)				
	$\Delta_f H$(Ion) from onset of endothermic reaction (84TOL/BEA).						
(methylcyclopropane-Sc)		(179)	(749)				
	$\Delta_f H$(Ion) from onset of endothermic reaction (84TOL/BEA).						

Table 1. Positive Ion Table – Continued

ION / Neutral	Ionization potential eV	$\Delta_f H$(Ion) kcal/mol	$\Delta_f H$(Ion) kJ/mol	$\Delta_f H$(Neutral) kcal/mol	$\Delta_f H$(Neutral) kJ/mol	Neutral reference	CAS registry number
$C_4H_9{}^+$							
n-C_4H_9	8.02	(203)	(849)	18	74	*EST	2492-36-6
	IP from 84SCH/HOU. Error limits +0.04-0.1. $\Delta_f H$(Neutral) based on D[C-H] = 100.5 kcal/mol.						
sec-C_4H_9	7.25±0.02	183	766	17.0±0.4	71.0±1.6	85TSA	4630-45-9
	IP from 84SCH/HOU. Heat of formation of ion at 298 K from appearance potential measurements (81TRA). $\Delta_f H$(Neutral) based on D[C-H] = 99 kcal/mol. $\Delta_f H$(Ion) - IP leads to $\Delta_f H$(Neutral) = 16 kcal/mol, 66 kJ/mol.						
iso-C_4H_9	7.93	(199)	(832)	16	70	81TSA	65114-21-8
	IP from 84SCH/HOU. Error limits +0.03-0.1. $\Delta_f H$(Neutral) based on D[C-H] = 100.5 kcal/mol.						
tert-C_4H_9	6.70±0.03	165.8	693.7	11.0±0.6	46.2±2.5	85TSA	1605-73-8
	Same value is obtained for heat of formation of ion from appearance potential measurements (81TRA/MCL). Neutral $\Delta_f H$ based on D[C-H] = 95.5 kcal/mol. $\Delta_f H$(Ion) - IP leads to $\Delta_f H$(Neutral) = 11.3 kcal/mol, 47.2 kJ/mol.						
$C_4H_9Br^+$							
n-C_4H_9Br	10.13	208	870	−25.6±0.3	−107.1±1.3	77PED/RYL	109-65-9
	See: 81KIM/KAT.						
sec-C_4H_9Br	9.98±0.01	201	842	−28.9±0.1	−120.9±0.4	77PED/RYL	78-76-2
	See also: 81TRA, 81KIM/KAT.						
iso-C_4H_9Br	10.09±0.02	(205)	(858)	−27	−115	*EST	78-77-3
	See: 81KIM/KAT.						
tert-C_4H_9Br	9.92±0.03	197	824	−32	−133	79WIB/SQU	507-19-7
	See: 81KIM/KAT.						
$C_4H_9Cl^+$							
n-C_4H_9Cl	10.67±0.03	209	874	−36.9±0.2	−154.5±1	78SEL/STR	109-69-3
	See also: 81KIM/KAT.						
sec-C_4H_9Cl	10.53	204	855	−38±2	−161±8	77PED/RYL	78-86-4
	See also: 81KIM/KAT.						
iso-C_4H_9Cl	10.66±0.03	208	869	−38±2	−159±8	77PED/RYL	513-36-0
	See also: 81KIM/KAT.						
tert-C_4H_9Cl	10.61±0.03	201	842	−43.5±0.3	−182.1±1.2	77PED/RYL	507-20-0
	See also: 81KIM/KAT.						
$C_4H_9ClHg^+$							
n-C_4H_9HgCl	≤10.08	(≤206)	(≤864)	−26	−109	*EST	543-63-5
	IP from 81BAI/CHI2.						
sec-C_4H_9HgCl	9.5	(194)	(814)	−25	−103	*EST	38455-12-8
	IP is onset of photoelectron band (81BAI/CHI2).						

Table 1. Positive Ion Table - Continued

ION / Neutral	Ionization potential eV	$\Delta_f H$(Ion) kcal/mol	$\Delta_f H$(Ion) kJ/mol	$\Delta_f H$(Neutral) kcal/mol	$\Delta_f H$(Neutral) kJ/mol	Neutral reference	CAS registry number
$C_4H_9ClHg^+$							
iso-C_4H_9HgCl	≤10.04 IP from 81BAI/CHI2.	(≤204)	(≤852)	−28	−117	*EST	27151-74-2
tert-C_4H_9HgCl	≤9.52 IP from 81BAI/CHI2.	(≤198)	(≤830)	−21	−89	*EST	38442-51-2
$C_4H_9ClO^+$							
tert-C_4H_9OCl	≤9.91 IP from 81COL/FRO.	≤188	≤788	−40	−168	68WAL/PAP	507-40-4
$C_4H_9Cl_2P^+$							
tert-$C_4H_9PCl_2$	(9.0) IP is onset of photoelectron band.	(136)	(570)	−71	−298	*EST	25979-07-1
$C_4H_9F_2P^+$							
tert-$C_4H_9PF_2$	(9.2) IP is onset of photoelectron band.	(34)	(143)	−178	−745	*EST	29149-32-4
$C_4H_9F_3N^+$							
$CF_3CH_2NH(CH_3)_2$				−17	−69		
	From proton affinity of $CF_3CH_2N(CH_3)_2$ (RN 819-06-7). PA = 215.0 kcal/mol, 900. kJ/mol.						
$CF_3CH_2CH_2CH_2NH_3$				−29	−122		
	From proton affinity of $CF_3CH_2CH_2CH_2NH_2$ (RN 819-46-5). PA = 214.3 kcal/mol, 897 kJ/mol.						
$C_4H_9I^+$							
n-C_4H_9I	9.229 See: 81KIM/KAT.	(200)	(838)	−12	−52	*EST	542-69-8
sec-C_4H_9I	9.09±0.02 See also: 81TRA, 81KIM/KAT.	(195)	(815)	−15	−62	*EST	513-48-4
iso-C_4H_9I	9.202 See also: 81KIM/KAT.	(197)	(826)	−15	−62	*EST	513-38-2
tert-C_4H_9I	9.02±0.03 See also: 81KIM/KAT.	191	798	−17.2±0.5	−72.0±2.2	77PED/RYL	558-17-8
$C_4H_9N^+$							
$CH_2=C(CH_3)CH_2NH_2$	(8.8) IP from 79AUE/BOW.	(207)	(866)	5	21	*EST	2878-14-0
(E)-$CH_3CH=NC_2H_5$	(9.29) See also: 79AUE/BOW.	(218)	(914)	4±0.2	18±1	*EST	1190-79-0

Table 1. Positive Ion Table – Continued

ION / Neutral	Ionization potential eV	$\Delta_f H$(Ion) kcal/mol	$\Delta_f H$(Ion) kJ/mol	$\Delta_f H$(Neutral) kcal/mol	$\Delta_f H$(Neutral) kJ/mol	Neutral reference	CAS registry number
$C_4H_9N^+$							
pyrrolidine	(8.0)	(184)	(771)	−0.8±0.1	−3.4±0.6	77PED/RYL	123-75-1
	IP from 79AUE/BOW. Predicted $\Delta_f H$(Ion) based on hydrogen affinities of homologous series is 186 kcal/mol, 778 kJ/mol corresponding to IP of 8.1 eV.						
2,2-dimethylaziridine	(8.94)	(222)	(929)	16±0.5	66±2	*EST	2658-24-4
$C_4H_9NO^+$							
tert-C_4H_9NO	(7.5)	(163)	(681)	−10±1	−43±6	74CHO/MEN	917-95-3
	IP is onset of photoelectron band.						
$CH_3CON(CH_3)_2$	8.81	147	617	−56	−233	78BEA/LEE	127-19-5
(E)-$CH_3(CH_2)_2CH=NOH$	(9.5)	(203)	(849)	−16	−68	*EST	110-69-0
	IP is onset of photoelectron band.						
morpholine	(8.2)	(201)	(842)	12	51	*EST	110-91-8
$C_4H_9NOS^+$							
$(CH_3)_3CNSO$	(10.0)	(166)	(695)	−65	−270	*EST	38662-39-4
	IP is onset of photoelectron band.						
$C_4H_9NO_2^+$							
$H_2NCH_2CH_2CH_2COOH$	(8.7)	(95)	(398)	−105±0.5	−441±2	83SKO/SAB	56-12-2
	IP is onset of photoelectron band (83CAN/HAM).						
$C_2H_5CH(NH_2)COOH$	(8.70)	(97)	(402)	−104±2	−437±10	*EST	80-60-4
$H_2NCH_2COOC_2H_5$	(8.8)	(107)	(447)	−96	−402	*EST	459-73-4
n-$C_4H_9NO_2$	(10.71±0.01)	(213)	(889)	−34.4±0.3	−143.9±1.4	77PED/RYL	627-05-4
sec-$C_4H_9NO_2$	(10.71±0.01)	(208)	(870)	−39.1±0.4	−163.6±1.6	77PED/RYL	600-24-8
$C_4H_9NO_2S^+$							
L-$CH_3SCH_2CH(NH_2)COOH$	(8.4)	(99)	(412)	−95	−398	*EST	1187-84-9
	IP is onset of photoelectron band (83CAN/HAM).						

Table 1. Positive Ion Table - Continued

ION / Neutral	Ionization potential eV	$\Delta_f H$(Ion) kcal/mol	$\Delta_f H$(Ion) kJ/mol	$\Delta_f H$(Neutral) kcal/mol	$\Delta_f H$(Neutral) kJ/mol	Neutral reference	CAS registry number
$C_4H_9NO_3^+$							
L-$CH_3CH(OH)CH(NH_2)COOH$	(≤10.2)	(≤94)	(≤392)	−141	−592	*EST	72-19-5

IP from 83CAN/HAM.

$C_4H_9N_2^+$							
$NCCH_2NH(CH_3)_2$		(188)	(788)				

From proton affinity of $NCCH_2N(CH_3)_2$ (RN 926-64-7). PA = 211.1 kcal/mol, 883. kJ/mol.

$C_4H_9N_2O_3^+$							
L-$H_2NCOCH_2CH(NH_3)COOH$		5	19				

From proton affinity of L-asparagine (RN 3130-87-8). PA = 219.8 kcal/mol, 920. kJ/mol.

$C_4H_9O^+$							
n-C_4H_9O	(9.22)	(196)	(820)	−17	−69	82MCM/GOL	21576-64-7
n-C_3H_7CHOH		124	521				

From proton affinity of n-C_3H_7CHO (RN 123-72-8). PA = 191.5 kcal/mol, 801. kJ/mol.

i-C_3H_7CHOH		121	508				

From proton affinity of i-C_3H_7CHO (RN 78-84-2). PA = 192.6 kcal/mol, 806. kJ/mol.

$(CH_3)(C_2H_5)COH$		109	455				

From proton affinity of $CH_3COC_2H_5$ (RN 78-93-3). PA = 199.8 kcal/mol, 836. kJ/mol. See 82MAC for appearance potential determination.

$C_2H_5OCHCH_3$		125	521				

From proton affinity of $C_2H_5OCH=CH_2$ (RN 109-92-2). PA = 207.4 kcal/mol, 868. kJ/mol (86BOU/DJA). See also: 82MAC.

$(CH_3)_2COCH_3$		(114)	(477)				

From appearance potential determination (82MAC).

(tetrahydrofuran)·H^+		123	514				

From proton affinity of tetrahydrofuran (RN 109-99-9). PA = 198.8 kcal/mol, 831. kJ/mol.

$C_4H_9O_2^+$							
1HOH(O-n-C_3H_7)		61	256				

From proton affinity of HCOO(n-C_3H_7) (RN 110-74-7). PA = 194.2 kcal/mol, 812.5 kJ/mol.

Table 1. Positive Ion Table - Continued

ION / Neutral	Ionization potential eV	$\Delta_f H$(Ion) kcal/mol kJ/mol	$\Delta_f H$(Neutral) kcal/mol kJ/mol	Neutral reference	CAS registry number

$C_4H_9O_2^+$

HCOH(O-i-C_3H_7)   73   305
From proton affinity of HCOOCH(CH_3)$_2$ (RN 625-55-8). PA = 196.0 kcal/mol, 820. kJ/mol.

CH_3COH(O-C_2H_5)   59   247
From proton affinity of CH_3COOC_2H_5 (RN 141-78-6). PA = 200.7 kcal/mol, 840. kJ/mol.

C_2H_5COH(O-CH_3)   62   260
From proton affinity of C_2H_5COOCH_3 (RN 554-12-1). PA = 200.2 kcal/mol, 838. kJ/mol.

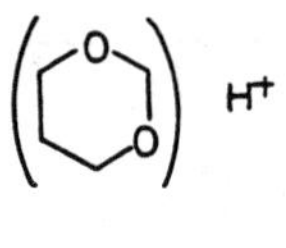

(1,3-dioxane)H^+ 86   360
From proton affinity of 1,3-dioxane (RN 505-22-6). PA = 198.8 kcal/mol, 832. kJ/mol.

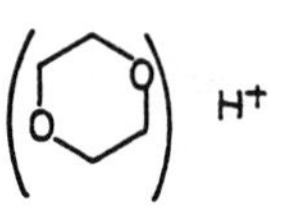

(1,4-dioxane)H^+ 96   403
From proton affinity of 1,4-dioxane (RN 123-91-1). PA = 193.8 kcal/mol, 811. kJ/mol.

$C_4H_9O_2S^+$

C_2H_5S(OCH_3)COH   64   269
From proton affinity of C_2H_5S(OCH_3)CO (RN 38103-96-7). PA = 201.0 kcal/mol, 841. kJ/mol.

$C_4H_9O_3^+$

C(OCH_3)$_3$ 53   223
From appearance potential of 10.22 eV in CH(OCH_3)$_3$, and appearance potential of 9.86 eV in CH_3C(OCH_3)$_3$ (82HOL/LOS2).

C_2H_5OC(OH)OCH_3 22   90
From proton affinity of C_2H_5OCOOCH_3 (RN 623-53-0). PA = 202.7 kcal/mol, 848 kJ/mol.

$C_4H_9O_3P^+$

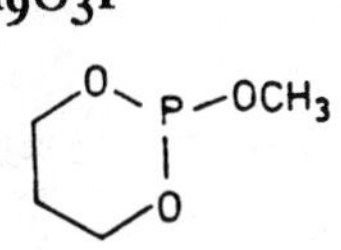

(cyclic P(OCH_3) with O,O ring)   (8.74±0.1)   (26)   (110)   −175   −733   *EST   31121-06-9

ION / Neutral	Ionization potential eV	$\Delta_f H$(Ion) kcal/mol	kJ/mol	$\Delta_f H$(Neutral) kcal/mol	kJ/mol	Neutral reference	CAS registry number
$C_4H_9S^+$							
(tetrahydrothiophene)H$^+$		153	640				

From proton affinity of tetrahydrothiophene (RN 110-01-0) (83CAS/KIM). PA = 204.6 kcal/mol, 856. kJ/mol.

$C_4H_{10}^+$							
n-C_4H_{10}	10.53±0.10	213	889	−30.2±0.1	−126.5±0.4	77PED/RYL	106-97-8

IP based on charge transfer equilibrium constant in cyclopentane: n-butane system. IP (c-C_5H_{10}) = 10.51 eV (81MAU/SIE). Threshold value = 10.55 eV. See also: 81KIM/KAT.

iso-C_4H_{10}	10.57	(212)	(885)	−32.1±0.1	−134.5±0.5	77PED/RYL	75-28-5

See also: 81KIM/KAT.

$C_4H_{10}Cd^+$							
$(C_2H_5)_2Cd$	(8.0)	(210)	(877)	25±0.7	105±3	77PED/RYL	592-02-9

IP is onset of photoelectron band.

$C_4H_{10}Cl^+$							
$(CH_3)_2CHClCH_3$		(150)	(628)				

From equilibrium constant determination (85SHA/HOJ).

$C_4H_{10}Cl_2Si^+$							
$(CH_3)_3SiCHCl_2$	(9.7)	(163)	(683)	−60	−253	*EST	5926-38-5

IP is onset of photoelectron band (81ZYK/KHV).

$(CH_3)_2Si(CH_2Cl)_2$	(9.7)	(165)	(689)	−59	−247	*EST	2917-46-6

IP is onset of photoelectron band (81ZYK/KHV).

$C_4H_{10}Hg^+$							
$(C_2H_5)_2Hg$	≤8.45	≤212	≤887	17.3±0.2	72.3±0.8	77PED/RYL	627-44-1

$C_4H_{10}N^+$							
$CH_2C(CH_3)CH_2NH_3$		(152)	(638)				

From proton affinity of $CH_2=C(CH_3)CH_2NH_2$ (RN 2878-14-0). PA = (218.2) kcal/mol, (913.) kJ/mol.

$CH_3CHN(CH_3)_2$		153	639				

From proton affinity of $(CH_3)_2NCH=CH_2$ (RN 5763-87-1). PA = 227.8 kcal/mol, 953. kJ/mol.

$CH_3CHNHC_2H_5$		147	616				

From proton affinity of $CH_3CH=NC_2H_5$ (RN 1190-79-0). PA = 222.7 kcal/mol, 932. kJ/mol.

Table 1. Positive Ion Table - Continued

ION / Neutral	Ionization potential eV	$\Delta_f H$(Ion) kcal/mol	$\Delta_f H$(Ion) kJ/mol	$\Delta_f H$(Neutral) kcal/mol	$\Delta_f H$(Neutral) kJ/mol	Neutral reference	CAS registry number
$C_4H_{10}N^+$							
pyrrolidine·H⁺		140	585				

From proton affinity of pyrrolidine (RN 123-75-1). PA = 225.2 kcal/mol, 942. kJ/mol.

$C_4H_{10}NO^+$							
$CH_3C(OH)N(CH_3)_2$		94	392				

From proton affinity of $CH_3CON(CH_3)_2$ (RN 127-19-5) (86TAF/GAL). PA = 216.2 kcal/mol, 905. kJ/mol.

| n-C_3H_7NHCHOH | | 95 | 395 | | | | |

From proton affinity of n-C_3H_7NHCHO (RN 6281-94-3). PA = (210.0) kcal/mol, (879.) kJ/mol.

| morpholine·H⁺ | | 158 | 663 | | | | |

From proton affinity of morpholine (RN 110-91-8). PA = 219.4 kcal/mol, 918. kJ/mol.

$C_4H_{10}NO_2^+$							
t-C_4H_9ONHO		119	497				

From proton affinity of t-C_4H_9ONO (RN 540-80-7). PA = 205.7 kcal/mol, 861. kJ/mol.

$C_4H_{10}NO_3^+$							
$CH_3CH(OH)CH(NH_3)COOH$		(6)	(23)				

From proton affinity of L-threonine (RN 72-19-5). PA = 218.6 kcal/mol, 915. kJ/mol.

$C_4H_{10}N_2^+$							
$(CH_3)_2NN=CHCH_3$	(7.54)	(176)	(736)	2	9	80LEB/MAS	7422-90-4
piperazine	(≤8.72)	(≤207)	(≤866)	6±0.2	25±1	*EST	110-85-0

$C_4H_{10}N_2O^+$							
$(CH_3)_2NCONHCH_3$	(≤8.80)	(≤146)	(≤609)	−57	−240	*EST	632-14-4

$C_4H_{10}O^+$							
n-C_4H_9OH	10.06±0.03	166	696	−65.7±0.1	−275.0±0.4	77PED/RYL	71-36-3

See also: 81KIM/KAT, 80BAC/MOU, 84BOW/MAC.

| sec-C_4H_9OH | 9.88 | 158 | 660 | −70.5±0.1 | −295.0±0.4 | 77PED/RYL | 78-92-2 |

IP from 81HOL/FIN, 84BOW/MAC. See also: 80BAC/MOU.

Table 1. Positive Ion Table – Continued

ION Neutral	Ionization potential eV	$\Delta_f H$(Ion) kcal/mol kJ/mol		$\Delta_f H$(Neutral) kcal/mol kJ/mol		Neutral reference	CAS registry number
$C_4H_{10}O^+$							
iso-C_4H_9OH	10.12±0.04 IP from 81HOL/FIN, 84BOW/MAC, 77ROS/DRA.	166	692	−67.8±0.1	−283.6±0.4	77PED/RYL	78-83-1
tert-C_4H_9OH	9.97±0.02 See also: 84BOW/MAC.	155	650	−74.7±0.7	−312.5±2.9	77PED/RYL	75-65-0
$(C_2H_5)_2O$	9.51±0.03 See also: 81KIM/KAT, 80BAC/MOU, 84BOW/MAC.	159	666	−60.1±0.1	−251.7±0.3	77PED/RYL	60-29-7
n-$C_3H_7OCH_3$	(9.42) IP from 84BOW/MAC. See also: 80BAC/MOU.	(160)	(671)	−56.8±0.1	−237.9±0.5	77PED/RYL	557-17-5
i-$C_3H_7OCH_3$	9.42 IP from 81HOL/FIN, 84BOW/MAC.	157	657	−60.2±0.2	−252.0±0.9	77PED/RYL	598-53-8
$C_4H_{10}OS^+$							
$(CH_3CH_2)_2SO$	≤8.76	≤153	≤640	−49.1±0.4	−205.6±1.5	77PED/RYL	70-29-1
$C_4H_{10}O_2^+$							
n-C_4H_9OOH	(9.36±0.03) IP from 77ASH/BUR.	(166)	(696)	−49	−207	*EST	4813-50-7
tert-C_4H_9OOH	(≤10.24)	(≤178)	(≤744)	−58±1	−244±6	77PED/RYL	75-91-2
$HOCH_2CH_2CH_2OCH_3$	(9.3) IP is onset of photoelectron band (83BIE/MOR).	(122)	(509)	−93	−388	*EST	1320-67-8
$HOCH_2CH_2OC_2H_5$	(9.6) IP is onset of photoelectron band (81KIM/KAT).	(126)	(528)	−95	−398	*EST	110-80-5
$CH_3OCH_2CH_2OCH_3$	(9.3) IP is onset of photoelectron band (83BAK/ARM, 81KIM/KAT).	(133)	(557)	−81	−340	67LOU/LAI	110-71-4
$CH_3CH(OCH_3)_2$	(9.65±0.03)	(129)	(541)	−93.1±0.2	−389.7±0.8	77PED/RYL	534-15-6
$C_4H_{10}O_2S^+$							
$(C_2H_5)_2SO_2$	(9.96±0.03)	(127)	(532)	−103±0.7	−429±3	77PED/RYL	597-35-3
$C_4H_{10}O_3^+$							
$CH(OCH_3)_3$	(9.5) IP from 82HOL/LOS2.	(89)	(372)	−130±0.2	−545±1	77PED/RYL	149-73-5
$C_4H_{10}O_3P^+$							
(cyclic O–P(–OCH_3) structure)		(−29)	(−121)				

From proton affinity of 2-methoxy-1,3,2-dioxaphosphorinane (RN 31121-06-9).
PA = 219.4 kcal/mol, 918. kJ/mol.

Table 1. Positive Ion Table – Continued

ION Neutral	Ionization potential eV	$\Delta_f H$(Ion) kcal/mol	$\Delta_f H$(Ion) kJ/mol	$\Delta_f H$(Neutral) kcal/mol	$\Delta_f H$(Neutral) kJ/mol	Neutral reference	CAS registry number
$C_4H_{10}O_3S^+$							
$(C_2H_5O)_2SO$	(9.68)	(91)	(382)	-132 ± 0.5	-552 ± 2	77PED/RYL	623-81-4
$C_4H_{10}S^+$							
n-C_4H_9SH	9.14 ± 0.02	190	794	-21.1 ± 0.3	-88.1 ± 1.2	77PED/RYL	109-79-5
sec-C_4H_9SH	(9.10)	(187)	(781)	-23.2 ± 0.2	-96.9 ± 0.8	77PED/RYL	513-53-1
iso-C_4H_9SH	(9.12)	(187)	(783)	-23.3 ± 0.2	-97.3 ± 0.8	77PED/RYL	513-44-0
tert-C_4H_9SH	(9.03)	(182)	(762)	-26.2 ± 0.2	-109.6 ± 0.8	77PED/RYL	75-66-1
n-$C_3H_7SCH_3$	(8.8 ± 0.2)	(183)	(767)	-19.6 ± 0.2	-82.2 ± 0.9	77PED/RYL	3877-15-4
iso-$C_3H_7SCH_3$	(8.7 ± 0.2)	(179)	(748)	-21.6 ± 0.2	-90.5 ± 0.7	77PED/RYL	
$(C_2H_5)_2S$	8.43 ± 0.01	174	729	-20 ± 0.2	-84 ± 1	77PED/RYL	352-93-2
		181	757	-13	-56		
$C_4H_{10}SSi^+$							
$(C_2H_5)_2Si=S$		(188)	(787)				

$\Delta_f H$(Ion) from appearance potential determination (81GUS/VOL).

$(H_3C)_2Si$ (cyclic with S)	(8.25 ± 0.03)	(193)	(806)	(2)	(10)	81GUS/VOL	77205-52-8

IP from 81GUS/VOL

$C_4H_{10}S_2^+$							
$(C_2H_5S)_2$	$\leq8.27\pm0.03$	≤173	≤723	-17.8 ± 0.3	-74.7 ± 1.1	77PED/RYL	110-81-6

Dialkyl disulfides undergo a change in the dihedral CSSC angle from 90° to 180°.
upon ionization; adiabatic ionization potentials are probably well below the
the experimentally observed ionization onset.

$CH_3SCH_2CH_2SCH_3$	(≤8.64)	(≤190)	(≤797)	-9	-37	*EST	6628-18-8
$C_4H_{10}Sc^+$							
$HScCH(CH_3)C_2H_5$		(195)	(816)				

$\Delta_f H$(Ion) from onset of endothermic reaction (84TOL/BEA).

$CH_3ScC_3H_7$		(174)	(728)				

$\Delta_f H$(Ion) from onset of endothermic reaction (84TOL/BEA).

$C_2H_4Sc(CH_3)_2$		(175)	(732)				

$\Delta_f H$(Ion) from onset of endothermic reaction (84TOL/BEA).

$(CH_3CH=CH_2)ScH(CH_3)$		(184)	(770)				

$\Delta_f H$(Ion) from onset of endothermic reaction (84TOL/BEA).

Table 1. Positive Ion Table - Continued

ION / Neutral	Ionization potential eV	$\Delta_f H$(Ion) kcal/mol	$\Delta_f H$(Ion) kJ/mol	$\Delta_f H$(Neutral) kcal/mol	$\Delta_f H$(Neutral) kJ/mol	Neutral reference	CAS registry number
$C_4H_{10}Sc^+$ $(CH_3CH=CHCH_3)ScH_2$		(195)	(816)				
$\Delta_f H$(Ion) from onset of endothermic reaction (84TOL/BEA).							
$C_4H_{10}Se^+$ $(C_2H_5)_2Se$	(8.3±0.3)	(178)	(743)	−14±1	−58±5	77PED/RYL	627-53-2
$C_4H_{10}Zn^+$ $(C_2H_5)_2Zn$	(≤8.6)	(≤212)	(≤888)	14±0.7	58±3	77PED/RYL	557-20-0
$C_4H_{11}^+$ $((CH_3)_3CH)H$		170	712				
From proton affinity of iso-C_4H_{10}. (RN 75-28-5). PA = 163.3 kcal/mol, 683. kJ/mol.							
$C_4H_{11}ClO_3Si^+$ $(CH_3O)_3SiCH_2Cl$	(10.0)	(4)	(17)	−226	−948	*EST	5926-26-1
IP is onset of photoelectron band (81ZYK/KHV).							
$C_4H_{11}ClSi^+$ $(CH_3)_3SiCH_2Cl$	(9.4)	(159)	(667)	−57	−240	*EST	2344-80-1
IP is onset of photoelectron band (81ZYK/KHV, 82LEV/LIA).							
$C_4H_{11}N^+$							
n-$C_4H_9NH_2$	8.71±0.03	179	748	−22±0.2	−92±1	77PED/RYL	109-73-9
See also: 81KIM/KAT, 79AUE/BOW.							
sec-$C_4H_9NH_2$	(8.70)	(176)	(734)	−25.0±0.2	−104.8±0.9	77PED/RYL	13952-84-6
iso-$C_4H_9NH_2$	(8.70)	(177)	(741)	−23.6±0.1	−98.8±0.4	77PED/RYL	78-81-9
tert-$C_4H_9NH_2$	(8.64)	(170)	(713)	−28.9±0.1	−120.9±0.4	77PED/RYL	75-64-9
$(C_2H_5)_2NH$	8.01±0.01	167	700	−17.4±0.5	−72.6±2	77PED/RYL	109-89-7
$C_2H_5N(CH_3)_2$	(7.74±0.05)	(167)	(701)	−11	−48	*EST	598-56-1
IP is onset of photoelectron band. See also: 81LOG/TAK, 79AUE/BOW.							
$C_4H_{11}NO^+$ $(CH_3)_2NCH_2CH_2OH$	(8.2)	(140)	(587)	−49	−204	81LOS/LAM	108-01-0
IP is onset of photoelectron band (82LEV/LIA, 86VOR/BRO).							
$C_4H_{11}N_2^+$ (piperazine)H^+		147	617				
From proton affinity of piperazine (RN 110-85-0). PA = 224.2 kcal/mol, 938. kJ/mol.							

Table 1. Positive Ion Table - Continued

ION / Neutral	Ionization potential eV	$\Delta_f H$(Ion) kcal/mol	$\Delta_f H$(Ion) kJ/mol	$\Delta_f H$(Neutral) kcal/mol	$\Delta_f H$(Neutral) kJ/mol	Neutral reference	CAS registry number

$C_4H_{11}N_2^+$

(HN-HN)C(CH_3)(C_2H_5) · H⁺   (182)   (764)

From proton affinity of 3-ethyl-3-methyldiaziridine (RN 4901-75-1).
PA = (214.9) kcal/mol, (899) kJ/mol.

$C_4H_{11}O^+$

   n-$C_4H_9OH_2$ 109   456

From proton affinity of n-C_4H_9OH (RN 71-36-3). PA = 191.1 kcal/mol, 799.5 kJ/mol.

   sec-$C_4H_9OH_2$ (101)   (421)

From proton affinity of sec-C_4H_9OH (RN 78-92-2) (78PAU/KIM).
PA = (195) kcal/mol, (816) kJ/mol.

   iso-$C_4H_9OH_2$ 105   441

From proton affinity of iso-C_4H_9OH (RN 78-83-1) (78TAF/TAA).
PA = 192.4 kcal/mol, 805. kJ/mol.

   tert-$C_4H_9OH_2$ 97   408

From proton affinity of tert-C_4H_9OH (RN 75-65-0). PA = 193.7 kcal/mol, 810. kJ/mol.

   $(C_2H_5)_2OH$ 105   440

From proton affinity of $(C_2H_5)_2O$ (RN 60-29-7) (86KNI/FRE, 86MAU/LIE).
PA = 200.2 kcal/mol, 838 kJ/mol.

$C_4H_{11}O_2^+$

   $HO(CH_2)_4OH_2$ 52   216

From proton affinity of $HO(CH_2)_4OH$ (RN 110-63-4). PA = (212) kcal/mol, (887) kJ/mol.

   $CH_3OCH_2CH_2OHCH_3$

    80   333

From proton affinity of $CH_3OCH_2CH_2OCH_3$ (RN 110-71-4). PA = 204.9 kcal/mol, 857. kJ/mol.

$C_4H_{11}O_3P^+$

Neutral	IP (eV)	$\Delta_f H$(Ion) kcal/mol	kJ/mol	$\Delta_f H$(Neut) kcal/mol	kJ/mol	Ref	CAS
$OPH(OC_2H_5)_2$	(10.31)	(19)	(79)	−219	−916	*EST	762-04-9

See also: 80ZVE/VIL.

$C_4H_{11}P^+$

Neutral	IP (eV)	$\Delta_f H$(Ion) kcal/mol	kJ/mol	$\Delta_f H$(Neut) kcal/mol	kJ/mol	Ref	CAS
tert-$C_4H_9PH_2$	(8.9)	(181)	(757)	−24	−102	*EST	2501-94-2

IP is onset of photoelectron band.

| $(C_2H_5)_2PH$ | (8.69) | (176) | (736) | −24 | −102 | *EST | 627-49-6 |

$C_4H_{11}S^+$

   $(C_2H_5)_2SH$ 141   588

From proton affinity of $(C_2H_5)_2S$ (RN 352-93-2). PA = 205.0 kcal/mol, 858. kJ/mol.

Table 1. Positive Ion Table - Continued

ION / Neutral	Ionization potential eV	$\Delta_f H$(Ion) kcal/mol	$\Delta_f H$(Ion) kJ/mol	$\Delta_f H$(Neutral) kcal/mol	$\Delta_f H$(Neutral) kJ/mol	Neutral reference	CAS registry number
$C_4H_{11}S^+$							
tert-$C_4H_9SH_2$		143	596				

From proton affinity of t-C_4H_9SH (RN 75-66-1). PA = 196.9 kcal/mol, 824. kJ/mol.

| sec-$C_4H_9SH_2$ | | (148) | (621) | | | | |

From proton affinity of sec-C_4H_9SH (RN 513-53-1) (78PAU/KIM). PA = (194.0) kcal/mol, (812.) kJ/mol.

| $C_4H_{11}SSi^+$ | | | | | | | |
| $(C_2H_5)_2SiSH$ | | (157) | (657) | | | | |

$\Delta_f H$(Ion) from appearance potential determination (81GUS/VOL).

$C_4H_{12}BClN_2^+$							
$B(N(CH_3)_2)_2Cl$	8.08	106	445	−80±1	−335±5	77PED/RYL	6562-41-0
$C_4H_{12}ClN_2OP^+$							
$((CH_3)_2N)_2POCl$	(8.61)	(75)	(316)	−123	−515	*EST	1605-65-8
$C_4H_{12}ClN_2P^+$							
$((CH_3)_2N)_2PCl$	(7.6)	(127)	(531)	−48	−202	*EST	3348-44-5

IP is onset of photoelectron band.

| $C_4H_{12}F_4N_5P_3^+$ | | | | | | | |
| 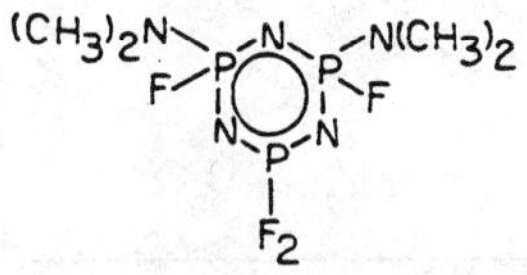 (structure shown) | (8.96) | (−169) | (−706) | −375.5 | −1571 | *EST | 30004-14-9 |

IP from 81CLA/SOW.

$C_4H_{12}Ge^+$							
$(CH_3)_4Ge$	9.33±0.05	198	828	−17±2	−72±9	77PED/RYL	865-52-1
$C_4H_{12}N^+$							
n-$C_4H_9NH_3$		122	524				

From proton affinity of n-$C_4H_9NH_2$ (RN 109-73-9). PA = 218.4 kcal/mol, 914. kJ/mol.

| sec-$C_4H_9NH_3$ | | 120 | 502 | | | | |

From proton affinity of sec-$C_4H_9NH_2$ (RN 13952-84-6). PA = 220.5 kcal/mol, 922. kJ/mol.

| iso-$C_4H_9NH_3$ | | 123 | 515 | | | | |

From proton affinity of iso-$C_4H_9NH_2$ (RN 78-81-9). PA = 218.8 kcal/mol, 915. kJ/mol.

| tert-$C_4H_9NH_3$ | | 116 | 485 | | | | |

From proton affinity of tert-$C_4H_9NH_2$ (RN 75-64-9). PA = 220.8 kcal/mol, 924. kJ/mol.

| $(C_2H_5)_2NH_2$ | | 125 | 512 | | | | |

From proton affinity of $(C_2H_5)_2NH$ (RN 109-89-7). PA = 225.9 kcal/mol, 945. kJ/mol.

Table 1. Positive Ion Table - Continued

ION / Neutral	Ionization potential eV	$\Delta_f H$(Ion) kcal/mol	$\Delta_f H$(Ion) kJ/mol	$\Delta_f H$(Neutral) kcal/mol	$\Delta_f H$(Neutral) kJ/mol	Neutral reference	CAS registry number
$C_4H_{12}N^+$							
$(CH_3)_2(C_2H_5)NH$		127	531				
From proton affinity of $(CH_3)_2(C_2H_5)N$ (RN 598-56-1). PA = 227.5 kcal/mol, 952. kJ/mol.							
$C_4H_{12}NO^+$							
$NH_3(CH_2)_4OH$		75	312				
From proton affinity of $NH_2(CH_2)_4OH$ (RN 13325-10-5). PA = 233.8 kcal/mol, 978. kJ/mol.							
$C_4H_{12}NO_2P^+$							
$(CH_3O)_2PN(CH_3)_2$	(8.1)	(71)	(296)	−116	−486	*EST	597-07-9
IP is onset of photoelectron band (82WOR/HAR).							
$C_4H_{12}N_2^+$							
$(CH_3)_2NN(CH_3)_2$	(6.87)	(175)	(732)	16	69	61GOW/JON	6415-12-9
IP from charge transfer equilibrium constant determination (86RUM). Reference standard: $IP(C_6H_5N(CH_3)_2) = 7.12$ eV. See also: 84MAU/NEL.							
$C_4H_{12}N_2S_2^+$							
$(CH_3)_2NSSN(CH_3)_2$	(7.2)	(163)	(683)	−3	−12	*EST	928-05-2
IP is onset of photoelectron band (81BOC/SCH).							
$C_4H_{12}N_4^+$							
(E)-$(CH_3)NN=NN(CH_3)_2$	(7.0)	(227)	(948)	65±0.7	273±3	77PED/RYL	6130-87-6
IP is onset of photoelectron band.							
$C_4H_{12}OSi^+$							
$(CH_3)_3SiOCH_3$	9.61	(110)	(459)	−112±2	−468±8	*EST	1825-61-2
IP from 83MOL/PIK.							
$C_4H_{12}Pb^+$							
$(CH_3)_4Pb$	(8.50)	(229)	(956)	33±1	136±4	82PIL/SKI	75-74-1
$C_4H_{12}Si^+$							
$(CH_3)_4Si$	9.80±0.04	170	711	−55.7±0.7	−233.0±2.9	83STE2	75-76-3
		178	*743*	*−48*	*−202*		
$(C_2H_5)_2SiH_2$	(9.8)	(182)	(763)	−44±1	−183±6	77PED/RYL	542-91-6
$C_4H_{12}SiS^+$							
$(CH_3)_3SiSCH_3$	(8.4)	(128)	(534)	−66	−276	*EST	3908-55-2
IP is onset of photoelectron band.							
$C_4H_{12}Sn^+$							
$(CH_3)_4Sn$	8.89±0.05	200	838	−5±0.5	−20±2	77PED/RYL	594-27-4

Table 1. Positive Ion Table - Continued

ION Neutral	Ionization potential eV	$\Delta_f H$(Ion) kcal/mol	$\Delta_f H$(Ion) kJ/mol	$\Delta_f H$(Neutral) kcal/mol	$\Delta_f H$(Neutral) kJ/mol	Neutral reference	CAS registry number
$C_4H_{13}N_2^+$							
$NH_2(CH_2)_4NH_3$		115	483				
From proton affinity of $NH_2(CH_2)_4NH_2$ (RN 110-60-1). PA = 237.6 kcal/mol, 994 kJ/mol.							
$(CH_3)_2NNH(CH_3)_2$		157	658				
From proton affinity of $(CH_3)_2NN(CH_3)_2$ (RN 6415-12-9) (84MAU/NEL). PA = 224.8 kcal/mol, 941. kJ/mol.							
$C_4H_{13}OSi^+$							
$(CH_3)_3Si(OH)CH_3$		(51)	(213)				
From proton affinity of $(CH_3)_3SiOCH_3$ (RN 1825-61-2). PA = ~203 kcal/mol, ~849 kJ/mol.							
$C_4H_{14}N_3OP^+$							
$((CH_3)_2N)_2(NH_2)PO$	(8.60±0.05)	(83)	(348)	−115	−482	*EST	3732-86-3
$C_4H_{15}N_3OP^+$							
$((CH_3)_2N)_2(NH_2)POH$		26	109				
From proton affinity of $((CH_3)_2N)_2(NH_2)PO$ (RN 3732-86-3) (85BOL/HOU). PA = 224.4 kcal/mol, 939. kJ/mol.							
$C_4H_{15}OSi_2^+$							
$((CH_3)_2SiH)_2OH$		(6)	(26)				
From proton affinity of $((CH_3)_2SiH)_2O$ (RN 3277-26-7). PA = ~203 kcal/mol, ~849 kJ/mol.							
$C_4I_4S^+$	(≤8.27)	(≤302)	(≤1262)	111	464	*EST	19259-11-1
C_4La^+							
LaC_4	(4.7±0.5)	(288)	(1207)	180±2	754±8	81GIN/PEL	12603-31-5
$C_4N_2^+$							
NCC≡CCN	11.81±0.01	400	1673	128	534	82CHU/NGU	1071-98-3
See also: 82MAI/MIS.							
$C_4N_2O^+$							
$(NC)_2C=C=O$	(10.56)	(300)	(1255)	56.5	236	*EST	4361-47-1
IP is onset of photoelectron band (80HOT/NEI).							

Table 1. Positive Ion Table - Continued

ION / Neutral	Ionization potential eV	$\Delta_f H$(Ion) kcal/mol	$\Delta_f H$(Ion) kJ/mol	$\Delta_f H$(Neutral) kcal/mol	$\Delta_f H$(Neutral) kJ/mol	Neutral reference	CAS registry number
$C_4N_2S^+$							
$(NC)_2C=C=S$	(9.94)	(339)	(1419)	110	460	80SCH/SCH2	54856-36-9
IP is onset of photoelectron band (80SCH/SCH2).							
$C_4NiO_4^+$							
$Ni(CO)_4$	8.27±0.04	48	200	−143±1	−598±4	77PED/RYL	13463-39-3
See also: 86REU/WAN.							
C_4Sc^+							
ScC_4	(6.7±1.0)	(339)	(1418)	184±4	772±18	81HAQ/GIN	12547-95-4
IP from 81HAQ/GIN.							
$C_5BrMnO_5^+$							
$Mn(CO)_5Br$	8.4	(−16)	(−65)	−209±1	−876±5	82CON/ZAF	14516-54-2
IP is onset of photoelectron band.							
$C_5BrO_5Re^+$							
$Re(CO)_5Br$	8.5	(−9)	(−38)	−205±1	−858±5	83ALT/CON	14220-21-4
IP is onset of photoelectron band.							
$C_5ClMnO_5^+$							
$Mn(CO)_5Cl$	8.6	(−21)	(−88)	−219±2	−918±10	82CON/ZAF	14100-30-2
IP is onset of photoelectron band.							
$C_5ClO_5Re^+$							
$Re(CO)_5Cl$	8.55	(−12)	(−52)	−210±4	−877±18	83ALT/CON	14099-01-5
IP is onset of photoelectron band.							
$C_5FeO_4S^+$							
$Fe(CO)_4CS$	(7.8)	(65)	(273)	−115	−480	*EST	66517-47-3
IP is onset of photoelectron band (82BOH/GLE).							
$C_5FeO_5^+$							
$Fe(CO)_5$	7.96±0.01	10	43	−173±2	−725±7	82PIL/SKI	13463-40-6
See also: 83HAR/OHN.							
$C_5HFeO_5^+$							
$HFe(CO)_5$		(−10)	(−40)				
From proton affinity of $Fe(CO)_5$ (RN 13463-40-6). PA = ~202 kcal/mol, ~845 kJ/mol.							
$C_5HMnO_5^+$							
$Mn(CO)_5H$	8.5±0.1	19	80	−177±2	−740±10	82CON/ZAF	16972-33-1
$C_5HN_3^+$							
$C(CN)_2=CHCN$	(~11.55)	(390)	(1632)	124	518	82CHU/NGU	997-76-2
$C_5H_2MnO_5^+$							
$H_2Mn(CO)_5$		(−12)	(−51)				
From proton affinity of $HMn(CO)_5$ (RN 16972-33-1). PA = (201) kcal/mol, (841) kJ/mol.							

Table 1. Positive Ion Table - Continued

ION Neutral	Ionization potential eV	$\Delta_f H$(Ion) kcal/mol	$\Delta_f H$(Ion) kJ/mol	$\Delta_f H$(Neutral) kcal/mol	$\Delta_f H$(Neutral) kJ/mol	Neutral reference	CAS registry number
$C_5H_2O_3^+$							
(cyclopentenetrione structure)	(9.3) IP is onset of photoelectron band (82GLE/DOB).	(144)	(603)	−70	−294	*EST	15548-56-8
$C_5H_3Cl^+$							
$CH_3C{\equiv}CC{\equiv}CCl$	9.19±0.01 IP from 84KLA/KUH.	(321)	(1342)	110±0.2	459±1	*EST	
$C_5H_3NO^+$							
(furan-2-carbonitrile)	(≤9.47±0.05)	(≤243)	(≤1018)	25	104	*EST	617-90-3
$C_5H_3NS^+$							
(thiophene-2-carbonitrile)	(9.83±0.05)	(293)	(1226)	66	278	*EST	1003-31-2
$C_5H_4^+$							
$CH_2{=}C{=}C{=}C{=}CH_2$	(8.67)	(315)	(1318)	115	481	*EST	21986-03-8
$CH{\equiv}CCH_2C{\equiv}CH$	10.1 IP from 83HOL.	(338)	(1413)	105	439	*EST	24442-69-1
$CH_3C{\equiv}CC{\equiv}CH$	9.4 IP from 81FOR/MAI. See also: 81MAI.	(318)	(1332)	101	425	*EST	4911-55-1
$C_5H_4BrN^+$							
2-bromopyridine	9.65±0.05	(261)	(1092)	38	161	*EST	109-04-6
3-bromopyridine	(9.75±0.1)	(263)	(1102)	38	161	*EST	626-55-1
4-bromopyridine	9.94±0.05	(268)	(1120)	38	161	*EST	1120-87-2

Table 1. Positive Ion Table – Continued

ION / Neutral	Ionization potential eV	$\Delta_f H$(Ion) kcal/mol	kJ/mol	$\Delta_f H$(Neutral) kcal/mol	kJ/mol	Neutral reference	CAS registry number
C$_5$H$_4$ClN$^+$							
2-chloropyridine	9.0	(232)	(971)	25	103	*EST	109-09-1
	IP is onset of photoelectron band (81MOD/DIS2).						
3-chloropyridine	9.1	(236)	(986)	26	108	*EST	626-60-8
	IP is onset of photoelectron band (81MOD/DIS2).						
4-chloropyridine	9.5	(245)	(1025)	26	108	*EST	626-61-9
	IP is onset of photoelectron band (81MOD/DIS2).						
C$_5$H$_4$ClN$_4$$^+$							
6-chloropurine·H$^+$		(200)	(839)				
	From proton affinity of 6-chloropurine (RN 87-42-3). PA = ~208 kcal/mol, ~870 kJ/mol.						
C$_5$H$_4$FN$^+$							
2-fluoropyridine	(9.4)	(201)	(839)	−16	−68	*EST	372-48-5
	IP is onset of photoelectron band (83PIA/KEL).						
C$_5$H$_4$N$_2$$^+$							
cyclopentadienyldiazo	(8.09±0.01)	(277)	(1161)	91±4	380±16	*EST	1192-27-4
C$_5$H$_4$N$_2$O$_2$$^+$							
3-nitropyridine	(10.3±0.1)	(270)	(1130)	33	136	*EST	2530-26-9
4-nitropyridine	(10.4)	(273)	(1140)	33	137	*EST	1122-61-8

Table 1. Positive Ion Table — Continued

ION Neutral	Ionization potential eV	$\Delta_f H$(Ion) kcal/mol	$\Delta_f H$(Ion) kJ/mol	$\Delta_f H$(Neutral) kcal/mol	$\Delta_f H$(Neutral) kJ/mol	Neutral reference	CAS registry number
$C_5H_4N_2O_3{}^+$ (3-nitropyridine N-oxide)	(9.03±0.02)	(222)	(930)	14	59	*EST	1124-82-9
$C_5H_4N_4{}^+$ (purine)	(≤9.52±0.03)	(≤275)	(≤1149)	55	230	*EST	120-73-0
$C_5H_4N_4O^+$ (hypoxanthine)	(≤8.55±0.03)	(≤209)	(≤875)	12	50	77PED/RYL	68-94-0
$C_5H_4O^+$ (cyclopentadienone)	(9.49)	(211)	(881)	−8±8	−35±35	*EST	13177-38-3
$C_5H_4OS^+$ (2-thiophenecarboxaldehyde)	(≤9.37±0.05)	(≤222)	(≤928)	6	24	*EST	98-03-3
$C_5H_4O_2{}^+$ (4H-pyran-4-one)	9.35±0.05	(176)	(733)	−40	−169	*EST	108-97-4
$C_5H_4O_2{}^+$ (4-cyclopentene-1,3-dione)	(9.6)	(168)	(704)	−53	−222	*EST	930-60-9

IP is onset of photoelectron band (82GLE/DOB).

Table 1. Positive Ion Table - Continued

ION / Neutral	Ionization potential eV	$\Delta_f H$(Ion) kcal/mol	$\Delta_f H$(Ion) kJ/mol	$\Delta_f H$(Neutral) kcal/mol	$\Delta_f H$(Neutral) kJ/mol	Neutral reference	CAS registry number
$C_5H_4O_2^+$							
furan-2-CHO	9.21±0.01	176	738	−36±1	−151±5	77PED/RYL	98-01-1
$C_5H_4O_3^+$							
furan-2-COOH	(≤9.16±0.05)	(≤118)	(≤493)	−93±0.7	−391±3	77PED/RYL	488-93-7
methyl maleic anhydride	(10.7)	(140)	(585)	−106.9±0.6	−447.2±2.5	77PED/RYL	616-02-4
	IP is onset of photoelectron band (81KIM/KAT).						
$C_5H_4S^+$							
cyclopentadienethione	(8.4)	(239)	(1000)	45	190	*EST	77825-99-1
	IP is onset of photoelectron band (81SCH/SCH).						
$C_5H_5^+$							
HC≡CCHCH=CH$_2$	7.88	271	1132	89	372	82MCM/GOL	50706-18-8
	IP from 84LOS/HOL.						
cyclopentadienyl	8.41	(252)	(1052)	58±1	241±6	82MCM/GOL	62744-94-9
vinylcyclopropenyl		(242)	(1012)				
	From appearance energy from $C_6H_5CH_2^+$ precursor, 3.55 eV (78MCC/FRE).						
$C_5H_5BrN^+$							
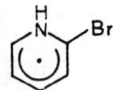		189	793				
	From proton affinity of 2-bromopyridine (RN 109-04-6).						

Table 1. Positive Ion Table - Continued

ION / Neutral	Ionization potential eV	$\Delta_f H$(Ion) kcal/mol kJ/mol	$\Delta_f H$(Neutral) kcal/mol kJ/mol	Neutral reference	CAS registry number

C₅H₅BrN⁺

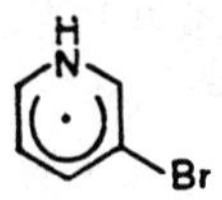

3-bromopyridinium: 189 791
From proton affinity of 3-bromopyridine (RN 626-55-1).

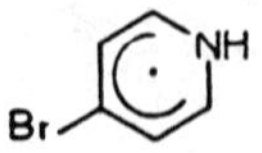

4-bromopyridinium: 186 779
From proton affinity of 4-bromopyridine (RN 1120-87-2).

C₅H₅Br₃Ti⁺

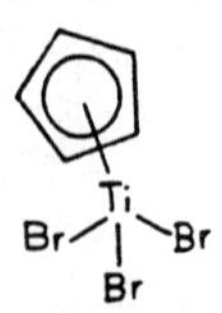

(9.1) (102) (428)   −108 −450   *EST   12240-42-5
IP is onset of photoelectron band (84TER/LOU).

C₅H₅ClN⁺

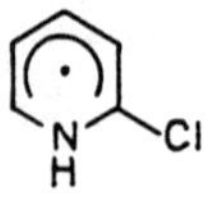

2-chloropyridinium: 176 736
From proton affinity of 2-chloropyridine (RN 109-09-1). PA = 214.4 kcal/mol, 897. kJ/mol.

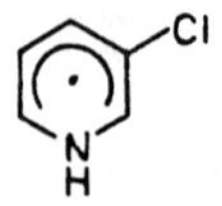

3-chloropyridinium: 177 739
From proton affinity of 3-chloropyridine (RN 626-60-8). PA = 214.8 kcal/mol, 899. kJ/mol.

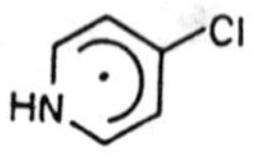

4-chloropyridinium: 174 727
From proton affinity of 4-chloropyridine (RN 626-61-9). PA = 217.8 kcal/mol, 911 kJ/mol.

C₅H₅Cl₃Ti⁺

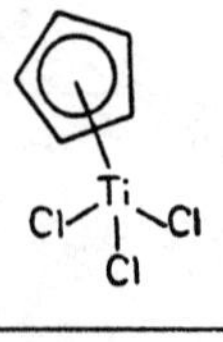

(9.1) (76) (319)   −133±3 −559±12   77PED/RYL   1270-98-0
IP is onset of photoelectron band (84TER/LOU).

Table 1. Positive Ion Table - Continued

ION / Neutral	Ionization potential eV	$\Delta_f H$(Ion) kcal/mol kJ/mol	$\Delta_f H$(Neutral) kcal/mol kJ/mol	Neutral reference	CAS registry number

$C_5H_5FN^+$

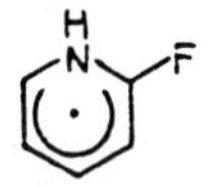

2-fluoropyridine (N-H, F at 2)
                139 581
From proton affinity of 2-fluoropyridine (RN 372-48-5). PA = 210.6 kcal/mol, 881 kJ/mol.

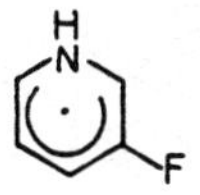

3-fluoropyridine
                138 577
From proton affinity of 3-fluoropyridine (RN 372-47-4). PA = 214.3 kcal/mol, 897. kJ/mol.

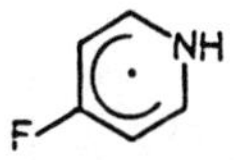

4-fluoropyridine
                135 567
From proton affinity of 4-fluoropyridine (RN 694-52-0). PA = 216.6 kcal/mol, 906. kJ/mol.

$C_5H_5F_3O_2^+$

| $CF_3COH=CHCOCH_3$ | (9.5) | (−20.7) (−86.7) | −239.8 −1003.3 | 84ERA/KOL | 367-57-7 |

IP is onset of photoelectron band.

$C_5H_5N^+$

|  pyridine | 9.25 | 247 1032 | 33±0.2 140±1 | 79KUD/KUD3 | 110-86-1 |

See also: 83PIA/KEL, 82LIF, 81KIM/KAT.

$C_5H_5NO^+$

| 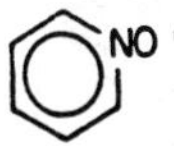 pyridine-NO | 8.38±0.02 | (207) (869) | 14 61 | *EST | 694-59-7 |

| 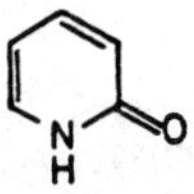 2-pyridone | (8.4) | (176) (733) | −18±0.5 −77±2 | 82SUR/ELS | 142-08-5 |

IP is onset of photoelectron band.

| 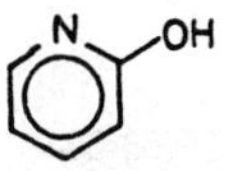 2-hydroxypyridine | 8.6 | (179) (750) | −19±0.5 −80±2 | 82SUR/ELS | 109-10-4 |

IP is onset of photoelectron band.

Table 1. Positive Ion Table - Continued

ION / Neutral	Ionization potential eV	$\Delta_f H$(Ion) kcal/mol	kJ/mol	$\Delta_f H$(Neutral) kcal/mol	kJ/mol	Neutral reference	CAS registry number
$C_5H_5NO^+$							
3-hydroxypyridine	(≤9.15±0.03)	(≤200)	(≤839)	−11±0.5	−44±2	82SUR/ELS	109-00-2
4-hydroxypyridine	9.75±0.11	(215)	(900)	−10±0.5	−41±2	82SUR/ELS	626-64-2
$C_5H_5NO_2^+$							
2-hydroxypyridine N-oxide	(8.90±0.05)	(167)	(699)	−38	−160	*EST	
3-hydroxypyridine N-oxide	(8.60±0.05)	(168)	(706)	−30	−124	*EST	6602-28-4
4-hydroxypyridine N-oxide	(8.18±0.05)	(160)	(668)	−29	−121	*EST	6890-62-6
$C_5H_5NS^+$							
2-thiopyridone	(7.7) IP is onset of photoelectron band.	(220)	(921)	43	178	*EST	2637-34-5
2-mercaptopyridine	≤8.7 IP from 81DRE/BEC, 82LEV/LIA.	(≤230)	(≤963)	30	124	*EST	73018-10-7
3-mercaptopyridine	(≤8.89±0.03)	(≤239)	(≤999)	34	141	*EST	16133-26-9

Table 1. Positive Ion Table - Continued

ION / Neutral	Ionization potential eV	$\Delta_f H$(Ion) kcal/mol	$\Delta_f H$(Ion) kJ/mol	$\Delta_f H$(Neutral) kcal/mol	$\Delta_f H$(Neutral) kJ/mol	Neutral reference	CAS registry number
$C_5H_5NS^+$ (4-mercaptopyridine)	≤9.25±0.03	(≤247)	(≤1033)	34	141	*EST	4556-23-4
$C_5H_5N_2O_2^+$ (4-nitropyridine·H+)		190	795				

From proton affinity of 4-nitropyridine (RN 1122-61-8). PA = 208.5 kcal/mol, 872. kJ/mol.

$C_5H_5N_4^+$ (9H-purine·H+)		201	843				

From proton affinity of 9H-purine (RN 120-73-0). PA = 219.3 kcal/mol, 917.5 kJ/mol.

$C_5H_5N_4O^+$ (hypoxanthine·H+)		(161)	(673)				

From proton affinity of hypoxanthine (RN 68-94-0). PA = ~217 kcal/mol, ~907 kJ/mol.

$C_5H_5N_5^+$ (adenine)	(7.8)	(229)	(960)	49±2	207±8	83KIR/DOM	73-24-5

IP is onset of photoelectron band.

$C_5H_5N_5O^+$ (guanine)	(7.85)	(181)	(759)	0.5	2	77PED/RYL	73-40-5
$C_5H_6^+$							
$CH_2=C=CHCH=CH_2$	(8.88)	(265)	(1108)	60	251	*EST	10563-01-6
(Z)-$CH_3CH=CHC\equiv CH$	9.14±0.04	272	1138	61±1	256±6	78SHA	1574-40-9
(E)-$CH_3CH=CHC\equiv CH$	(9.05)	(270)	(1130)	61±0.7	257±3	78SHA	2004-69-5
$CH_2=CHC\equiv CCH_3$	9.00±0.01	(267)	(1118)	(60)	(250)	*EST	646-05-9

Table 1. Positive Ion Table - Continued

ION Neutral	Ionization potential eV	$\Delta_f H$(Ion) kcal/mol	$\Delta_f H$(Ion) kJ/mol	$\Delta_f H$(Neutral) kcal/mol	$\Delta_f H$(Neutral) kJ/mol	Neutral reference	CAS registry number
$C_5H_6^+$							
$CH_2=C(CH_3)C\equiv CH$	9.23±0.01	275	1148	62	258	77LEB/RYA	78-80-8
(cyclopentadiene)	8.56±0.01	229	957	31±1	131±4	77PED/RYL	542-92-7
(cyclopropyl-C≡CH)	(8.7)	(275)	(1152)	75	313	*EST	6746-94-7
IP is onset of photoelectron band.							
(bicyclic structure)	(8.0)	(264)	(1103)	79	331	*EST	5164-35-2
(tetrahedral structure)	9.74	308	1291	84±1	351±4	85WIB/DAI	35634-10-7
IP from 85HON/HUB.							
$C_5H_6N^+$							
(protonated pyridine)		178	746				
From proton affinity of pyridine (RN 110-86-1). PA = 220.8 kcal/mol, 924 kJ/mol.							
$C_5H_6NO^+$							
(protonated pyridine-N-oxide)		160	669				
From proton affinity of pyridine-N-oxide (RN 694-59-7). PA = 220.3 kcal/mol, 922. kJ/mol.							
$C_5H_6N_2^+$							
(2-aminopyridine)	(8.0)	(213)	(890)	28±0.2	118±1	84BIC/PIL	504-29-0
IP is onset of photoelectron band (82LEV/LIA, 82GUI/KHA).							

Table 1. Positive Ion Table - Continued

ION / Neutral	Ionization potential eV	$\Delta_f H$(Ion) kcal/mol	$\Delta_f H$(Ion) kJ/mol	$\Delta_f H$(Neutral) kcal/mol	$\Delta_f H$(Neutral) kJ/mol	Neutral reference	CAS registry number
$C_5H_6N_2^+$							
3-aminopyridine	(8.1) IP is onset of photoelectron band.	(221)	(926)	34±0.5	144±2	84BIC/PIL	462-08-8
4-aminopyridine	(8.4) IP is onset of photoelectron band. Value of $\Delta_f H$(Ion) predicted from hydrogen affinity considerations: 214 kcal/mol, 895 kJ/mol, corresponding to IP of 7.9 eV.	(225)	(940)	31±0.2	130±1	84BIC/PIL	504-24-5
$C_5H_6N_2O^+$							
2-aminopyridine N-oxide	(8.04±0.05)	(197)	(825)	12	49	*EST	14150-95-9
3-aminopyridine N-oxide	(8.21±0.05)	(204)	(853)	15	61	*EST	1657-32-5
4-aminopyridine N-oxide	(7.67±0.05)	(191)	(797)	14	57	*EST	3535-75-9
$C_5H_6N_2O_2^+$							
thymine	(8.8) IP from onset of photoelectron band.	(124)	(520)	−79±1	−329±4	77NAB/SAB	65-71-4
$C_5H_6N_2O_2S^+$							
1,3-dimethyl-2-thiohydantoin	8.6	(152)	(635)	−47	−195	*EST	21035-65-4

Table 1. Positive Ion Table - Continued

ION Neutral	Ionization potential eV	Δ_fH(Ion) kcal/mol	kJ/mol	Δ_fH(Neutral) kcal/mol	kJ/mol	Neutral reference	CAS registry number
$C_5H_6N_2O_3^+$ (1,3-dimethyl parabanic acid)	10.19 IP from 85ROT/BOC.	(≤124)	(≤519)	−111	−464	*EST	5176-82-9
$C_5H_6N_5^+$ (adenine·H$^+$)		191	802				
From proton affinity of adenine (RN 73-24-5). PA = 223.5 kcal/mol, 935. kJ/mol.							
$C_5H_6N_5O^+$ (guanine·H$^+$)		(143)	(599)				
From proton affinity of guanine (RN 73-40-5). PA = ~223 kcal/mol, ~933 kJ/mol.							
$C_5H_6O^+$ (2H-pyran)	8.4 IP from 86SPI/GRU.	(192)	(803)	−2±1	−7±5	*EST	289-65-6
(cyclopent-2-enone)	≤9.34±0.02	(≤196)	(≤823)	−19	−78	*EST	930-30-3
(2-methylfuran)	8.39±0.01 IP from 78LIA/AUS, 77ROS/DRA. See also: 83ZYK/ERC, 86SPI/GRU.	(174)	(730)	−19	−80	*EST	534-22-5
(3-methylfuran)	(8.64) IP from 86SPI/GRU.	(182)	(763)	−17	−71	*EST	930-27-8

Table 1. Positive Ion Table – Continued

ION / Neutral	Ionization potential eV	$\Delta_f H$(Ion) kcal/mol	$\Delta_f H$(Ion) kJ/mol	$\Delta_f H$(Neutral) kcal/mol	$\Delta_f H$(Neutral) kJ/mol	Neutral reference	CAS registry number
$C_5H_6OS^+$							
2-methoxythiophene	(7.8)	(131)	(547)	−49	−206	*EST	16839-97-7
IP is onset of photoelectron band (85BAJ/HUM).							
$C_5H_6OS_2^+$							
4,5-dimethyl-1,3-dithiol-2-one	(≤8.5)	(≤177)	(≤740)	−19	−80	*EST	49675-88-9
IP from 83SCH/SCH.							
$C_5H_6O_3^+$							
$CH_3(CO)_3CH_3$	(≤9.52)	(≤115)	(≤482)	−104	−437	*EST	921-11-9
$C_5H_6S^+$							
2-methylthiophene	8.61±0.02	218	914	20.0±0.2	83.5±0.8	77PED/RYL	554-14-3
3-methylthiophene	(8.40)	(213)	(893)	19.7±0.2	82.6±0.8	77PED/RYL	616-44-4
2H-thiopyran	(7.9)	(224)	(940)	42±2	178±8	*EST	289-70-3
IP is onset of photoelectron band.							
$C_5H_6Si^+$							
silabenzene	(7.8)	(197)	(824)	17	71	83GOR/BOU	289-77-0
IP is onset of photoelectron band (84BOC/ROS).							
$C_5H_7^+$							
$CH_2=CHCHCH=CH_2$	(7.25)	(220)	(922)	53	222	69GOL/BEN	14362-08-4
See also: 80WOL/HOL.							
$HC≡CC(CH_3)_2$	(7.44)	(234)	(981)	63	263	76LOS/TRA	56897-57-5
See also: 80WOL/HOL.							

ION Neutral	Ionization potential eV	$\Delta_f H$(Ion) kcal/mol	kJ/mol	$\Delta_f H$(Neutral) kcal/mol	kJ/mol	Neutral reference	CAS registry number
$C_5H_7^+$							
cyclopentadienyl	7.00	199	833	38	159	70FUR/GOL	54846-63-8

Proton affinity of cyclopentadiene (RN 542-92-7) (PA = 199.6 kcal/mol, 835. kJ/mol) leads to $\Delta_f H$(Ion) = 197 kcal/mol, 826 kJ/mol. IP from 80WOL/HOL.

ION Neutral	Ionization potential eV	$\Delta_f H$(Ion) kcal/mol	kJ/mol	$\Delta_f H$(Neutral) kcal/mol	kJ/mol	Neutral reference	CAS registry number
$C_5H_7N^+$							
1-methylpyrrole	7.94±0.02	207.6	869.2	24.6±0.1	103.1±0.5	77PED/RYL	96-54-8
2-methylpyrrole	(7.78±0.01)	(197)	(825)	18±0.2	74±1	*EST	636-41-9

ION Neutral	Ionization potential eV	$\Delta_f H$(Ion) kcal/mol	kJ/mol	$\Delta_f H$(Neutral) kcal/mol	kJ/mol	Neutral reference	CAS registry number
$C_5H_7N_2^+$							
2-pyridinamine		170	711				

From proton affinity of 2-pyridinamine (RN 504-29-0). PA = 223.8 kcal/mol, 936. kJ/mol.

| 3-pyridinamine | | 179 | 747 | | | | |

From proton affinity of 3-pyridinamine (RN 462-08-8). PA = 221.0 kcal/mol, 925. kJ/mol.

| 4-pyridinamine | | (169) | (706) | | | | |

From proton affinity of 4-pyridinamine (RN 504-24-5). PA = (230) kcal/mol, (962) kJ/mol.

ION Neutral	Ionization potential eV	$\Delta_f H$(Ion) kcal/mol	kJ/mol	$\Delta_f H$(Neutral) kcal/mol	kJ/mol	Neutral reference	CAS registry number
$C_5H_7N_3^+$							
4,5-dimethyltriazine	(≤9.5)	(≤302)	(≤1263)	83	346	*EST	86402-31-5

IP from 83GLE/SPA.

| 3,6-dimethyltriazine | (≤9.5) | (≤300) | (≤1257) | 81 | 340 | *EST | 77202-09-6 |

IP from 83GLE/SPA.

ION / Neutral	Ionization potential eV	$\Delta_f H$(Ion) kcal/mol	$\Delta_f H$(Ion) kJ/mol	$\Delta_f H$(Neutral) kcal/mol	$\Delta_f H$(Neutral) kJ/mol	Neutral reference	CAS registry number
$C_5H_7N_3^+$							
3,5-dimethyl-1,2,4-triazine	(≤9.02)	(≤268)	(≤1123)	60	253	*EST	24108-34-7
5,6-dimethyl-1,2,4-triazine	(≤9.15)	(≤274)	(≤1145)	63	262	*EST	21134-90-7
$C_5H_7O^+$							
$(CH_3)_2C=CHCO$		(138)	(577)				44391-34-6

$\Delta_f H$(Ion) from appearance potential determination (85ALA/ATT).

		140	587				
2-methylfuran radical							

From proton affinity of 2-methylfuran (RN 534-22-5) (85HOU/ROL, 86MAU/LIE, 86SAN/BAL). PA = 206.2 kcal/mol, 863. kJ/mol.

		145	606				
3-methylfuran radical							

From proton affinity of 3-methylfuran (RN 930-27-8) (85HOU/ROL). PA = 204.0 kcal/mol, 853. kJ/mol.

$C_5H_7S^+$

		180	754				

From proton affinity of 2-methylthiophene (RN 554-14-3) (86MAU). PA = 205.4 kcal/mol, 859. kJ/mol.

$C_5H_8^+$							
$CH_2=C=CHCH_2CH_3$	9.22	246	1030	33.6±0.2	140.7±0.6	77PED/RYL	591-95-7
(Z)-$CH_2=CHCH=CHCH_3$	8.63±0.03 IP from 81MAS/MOU.	218	914	19.4±0.2	81.1±1.0	77PED/RYL	1574-41-0
(E)-$CH_2=CHCH=CHCH_3$	8.59±0.02 IP from 81MAS/MOU.	216	905	18.2±0.1	76.3±0.6	77PED/RYL	2004-70-8
$CH_2=CHCH_2CH=CH_2$	(9.62±0.02)	(247)	(1034)	25.3±0.2	105.7±0.6	77PED/RYL	591-93-5
$CH_3CH=C=CHCH_3$	(8.7) IP is onset of photoelectron band.	(232)	(972)	31.8±0.2	133.1±0.7	77PED/RYL	591-96-8

Table 1. Positive Ion Table - Continued

ION / Neutral	Ionization potential eV	$\Delta_f H$(Ion) kcal/mol	$\Delta_f H$(Ion) kJ/mol	$\Delta_f H$(Neutral) kcal/mol	$\Delta_f H$(Neutral) kJ/mol	Neutral reference	CAS registry number
$C_5H_8{}^+$							
$CH_2=C(CH_3)CH=CH_2$	8.84±0.01 See also: 81MAS/MOU.	221.8	927.9	17.9±.2	75±1	77PED/RYL	78-79-5
$C_3H_7C\equiv CH$	10.05 IP from 81HOL/FIN.	266	1114	34.4±1	144±4	79ROG/DAG	627-19-0
$C_2H_5C\equiv CCH_3$	9.44±0.01	248	1039	30.6±1	128±4	79ROG/DAG	627-21-4
$(CH_3)_2CHC\equiv CH$	9.97 IP from 81HOL/FIN.	262	1098	32.5	136	69BEN/CRU	598-23-2
cyclopentene	9.01±0.02 See also: 81KIM/KAT.	216	905	8.6	36	82ALL/DOD	142-29-0
methylenecyclobutane	9.16±0.02	241	1008	29.6±.2	124±1	78LEB/TSV	1120-56-5
vinylcyclopropane	(8.7)	(236)	(988)	35.6±.2	149±1	77PED/RYL	693-86-7
bicyclo[2.1.0]pentane	(8.7±0.1)	(238)	(997)	37.8	158	82WIB/WEN	185-94-4
spiropentane	(9.65)	(272)	(1139)	49.7	208	82WIB/WEN	311-75-1
bicyclopropylidene	9.26 See also: 86GLE/KRE.	258	1078	44.2±0.2	185.1±0.7	77PED/RYL	157-40-4

Table 1. Positive Ion Table – Continued

ION / Neutral	Ionization potential eV	$\Delta_f H$(Ion) kcal/mol	$\Delta_f H$(Ion) kJ/mol	$\Delta_f H$(Neutral) kcal/mol	$\Delta_f H$(Neutral) kJ/mol	Neutral reference	CAS registry number
$C_5H_8Br_2^+$							
trans-1,2-dibromocyclopentane	10.06	(218)	(913)	−14	−58	*EST	10230-26-9
cis-1,2-dibromocyclopentane	(10.02±0.02)	(217)	(909)	−14	−58	*EST	33547-17-0
$C_5H_8F_3O_2^+$							
$CF_3C(OH)O(n-C_3H_7)$				−74	−311		
From proton affinity of $CF_3COO(n-C_3H_7)$ (RN 383-66-4).							
$C_5H_8N_2^+$							
1,2-dimethylimidazole	(≤8.38)	(≤224)	(≤936)	30	127	*EST	1739-84-0
2,3-diazabicyclo[2.2.2]oct-2-ene	8.45±0.04	244	1022	49±0.7	207±3	80ENG	2721-32-6
$C_5H_8N_2O^+$							
(N-oxide)	(9.2)	(243)	(1015)	30.55±0.3	127.8±1.4	83BYS	22509-00-8
IP is onset of photoelectron band.							
$C_5H_8O^+$							
(E)-$CH_3CH_2CH=CHCHO$	(9.70)	(194)	(810)	−30	−126	83HOL	764-39-6
$CH_3CH=C(CH_3)CHO$	(9.60)	(188)	(787)	−33	−139	83HOL	497-03-0
$C_2H_5COCH=CH_2$	(9.50)	(186)	(781)	−33	−136	83HOL	1629-58-9
(E)-$CH_3CH=CHC(=O)CH_3$	(9.39)	(175)	(732)	−42	−174	84BOU/HOP	625-33-2
$CH_2=C(CH_3)C(=O)CH_3$	(9.50)	(177)	(741)	−42	−176	84BOU/HOP	814-78-8

Table 1. Positive Ion Table - Continued

ION Neutral	Ionization potential eV	$\Delta_f H$(Ion) kcal/mol kJ/mol		$\Delta_f H$(Neutral) kcal/mol kJ/mol		Neutral reference	CAS registry number
$C_5H_8O^+$							
(E)-$CH_3OCH=CHCH=CH_2$	(8.03)	(222)	(931)	37	156	*EST	10034-09-0
3,4-dihydro-2H-pyran	8.34±0.01	162	679	−29.9±0.4	−125.2±1.5	77PED/RYL	110-87-2
cyclopentanone	9.25±0.01 See also: 82BIE/ASB.	167	698	−46±0.5	−194±2	77PED/RYL	120-92-3
cyclopropyl methyl ketone	9.46	190	794	−28±0.2	−119±1	83FUC/SMI	765-43-5
$C_5H_8OS^+$							
(Z)-$CH_3C(=S)CH=C(OH)CH_3$	(8.4) IP is onset of photoelectron band (81JOR/CAR).	(160)	(670)	−33	−140	*EST	73059-87-7
(Z)-$CH_3C=(SH)CHC(=O)CH_3$	(≤8.73) IP from 81JOR/CAR.	(≤168)	(≤702)	−33	−140	*EST	65581-04-6
tetrahydrothiopyran-3-one	(8.90±0.05)	(168)	(704)	−37±0.7	−155±3	77PED/RYL	1072-72-6
$C_5H_8O_2^+$							
$C_2H_5CH=CHCOOH$	(10.14)	(144)	(601)	−90±2	−377±8	*EST	626-98-2
$(CH_3)_2C=CHCOOH$	(9.63)	(124)	(519)	−98	−410	*EST	541-47-9
$CH_3CH=C(CH_3)COOH$	(9.50)	(121)	(507)	−98	−410	*EST	13201-46-2
$CH_2=C(C_2H_5)COOH$	(10.06)	(139)	(582)	−93	−389	*EST	3586-58-1
$CH_2=C(CH_3)CH_2COOH$	(9.52)	(128)	(536)	−92	−383	*EST	53774-20-2

GAS-PHASE ION AND NEUTRAL THERMOCHEMISTRY

Table 1. Positive Ion Table – Continued

ION / Neutral	Ionization potential eV	$\Delta_f H$(Ion) kcal/mol	kJ/mol	$\Delta_f H$(Neutral) kcal/mol	kJ/mol	Neutral reference	CAS registry number
$C_5H_8O_2^+$							
$CH_3CH=CHCH_2COOH$	(9.41)	(126)	(527)	−91	−381	*EST	1617-32-9
$CH_2=CHCOOC_2H_5$	(>10.3) IP from 82MOR/MER.	(>147)	(>617)	−90	−377	*EST	140-88-5
$CH_2=C(CH_3)COOCH_3$	(9.7) IP is onset of photoelectron band(78VAN/OSK).	(141)	(588)	−83	−348	80VIL/PER	80-62-6
$CH_3COCH_2COCH_3$	8.85±0.02 Enol form, $CH_3COCH=C(OH)CH_3$, is preferred.	112	470	−92±0.2	−384±1	79HAC/PIL	123-54-6
$CH_2=C(CH_3)OC(=O)CH_3$	9.1 IP is onset of photoelectron band (78VAN/OSK). See also: 82LEV/LIA.	126	529	−83	−349	77PED/RYL	591-87-7
(dioxepine structure)	≤9.54 IP from 82ZVE/VIL.	(≤163)	(≤682)	−57	−238	*EST	5417-32-3
(cyclobutane-COOH structure)	(10.35)	(154)	(645)	−85	−354	*EST	3721-95-7
$C_5H_8Si^+$							
(silacyclohexadiene structure)	(9.1) IP is onset of photoelectron band (84BOC/ROS).	(238)	(997)	28	119	*EST	81200-77-3
$C_5H_9^+$							
$CH_2=CHCHCH_2CH_3$	(7.30)	(193)	(810)	25	106	76LOS/TRA	17829-37-7
$CH_3CHCH=CHCH_3$	(7.07) Heat of formation of ion from proton affinity of (E)-1,3-pentadiene (RN 2004-70-8). PA = (201.8) kcal/mol, (844.) kJ/mol.	(182)	(763)	(22)	(92)	76LOS/TRA	51685-67-7
$CH_3CH=CC_2H_5$	From proton affinity of 2-pentyne (RN 627-21-4). PA = (196) kcal/mol, (820) kJ/mol.	200	838				
$(CH_3)_2CCH=CH_2$	(7.13) Heat of formation of ion from proton affinity of 2-methyl-1,3-butadiene (RN 78-79-5). PA = (200.4) kcal/mol, (838.) kJ/mol. See also: 85LAD/HAR.	(183)	(767)	19	81	76LOS/TRA	29791-12-6

ION Neutral	Ionization potential eV	$\Delta_f H$(Ion) kcal/mol kJ/mol		$\Delta_f H$(Neutral) kcal/mol kJ/mol		Neutral reference	CAS registry number
$C_5H_9^+$							
$(CH_3)_2CHC=CH_2$		(200)	(838)				

From proton affinity of 3-methyl-1-butyne (RN 598-23-2). PA = (198) kcal/mol, (828) kJ/mol.

$CH_3CH=C(CH_3)CH_2$		190	797				60288-51-9

Heat of formation of ion from appearance potential measurements (84LOS/HOL).

[cyclopentyl]	7.21	191.4	800.8	24±1	102±4	82MCM/GOL	3889-74-5

Value of $\Delta_f H$(Ion) from hydride and chloride transfer equilibrium constant determinations (76SOL/FIE, 85SHA/SHA), and from proton affinity of cyclopentene (84LIA/LIE). PA = 183.4 kcal/mol, 767.5 kJ/mol. IP from 79HOU. $\Delta_f H$(Ion)-IP leads to $\Delta_f H$(Neutral) = 25 kcal/mol, 105 kJ/mol.

[methylcyclobutene]H^+		(193)	(807)				53249-17-5

From proton affinity of 1-methylcyclobutene (RN 1489-60-7). PA = 201 kcal/mol, 841 kJ/mol.

[vinylcyclopropane]H^+		204	852				

From proton affinity of vinylcyclopropane (RN 693-86-7). PA = 197.6 kcal/mol, 827. kJ/mol.

[3,3-dimethylcyclopropene]H^+		(213)	(890)				63974-90-3

From proton affinity of 3,3-dimethylcyclopropene (RN 3907-06-0). PA = 203 kcal/mol, 849 kJ/mol.

ION Neutral	Ionization potential eV	$\Delta_f H$(Ion) kcal/mol kJ/mol		$\Delta_f H$(Neutral) kcal/mol kJ/mol		Neutral reference	CAS registry number
$C_5H_9Br^+$							
cyclopentyl-Br	(9.94±0.02)	(213)	(891)	−16	−68	*EST	137-43-9
$C_5H_9BrO^+$							
$(CH_3)_2CBrCOCH_3$	(9.35)	(154)	(646)	−61	−256	*EST	

IP from 84BOU/DAG.

$C_5H_9I^+$							
cyclopentyl-I	9.07	(206)	(861)	−3	−14	*EST	1556-18-9

Table 1. Positive Ion Table - Continued

ION / Neutral	Ionization potential eV	$\Delta_f H$(Ion) kcal/mol	kJ/mol	$\Delta_f H$(Neutral) kcal/mol	kJ/mol	Neutral reference	CAS registry number
$C_5H_9N^+$							
n-C_4H_9NC	(11.1)	(280)	(1173)	24±0.5	102±2	*EST	2769-64-4
$(CH_3)_2NCH_2C\equiv CH$	(8.17)	(242)	(1013)	54±1	225±5	*EST	7223-38-3
	See also: 81LOG/TAK.						
(tetrahydropyridine, NH)	(8.0)	(201)	(845)	17	73	74PIH/TAS	694-05-3
	IP is onset of photoelectron band.						
(N-methyl pyrroline)	(≤8.21±0.05)	(≤216)	(≤907)	27±0.5	115±2	*EST	554-15-4
(N-propenyl aziridine, E)	(7.9)	(224)	(939)	42	177	*EST	
	IP is onset of photoelectron band (81MUL/PRE).						
(N-propenyl aziridine, Z)	(8.0)	(227)	(949)	42	177	*EST	
	IP from 81MUL/PRE.						
$C_5H_9NO^+$							
n-C_4H_9NCO	(10.14±0.05)	(186)	(776)	−48	−202	*EST	111-36-4
tert-C_4H_9CNO	≤9.55±0.005	(≤223)	(≤931)	2	10	*EST	27143-81-3
(cyclopentanone oxime)	(8.92±0.03)	(193)	(809)	−12	−52	*EST	1192-28-5
	IP from 79GOL/KUL.						
(N-methyl-2-pyrrolidinone)	≤9.17	≤161	≤674	−50	−211	77PED/RYL	872-50-4
	IP from 85TRE/RAD.						
(N-methyl-3-pyrrolidinone)	(8.3)	(165)	(691)	−26	−110	*EST	68165-06-0
	IP is onset of photoelectron band.						

Table 1. Positive Ion Table - Continued

ION / Neutral	Ionization potential eV	$\Delta_f H$(Ion) kcal/mol	$\Delta_f H$(Ion) kJ/mol	$\Delta_f H$(Neutral) kcal/mol	$\Delta_f H$(Neutral) kJ/mol	Neutral reference	CAS registry number
$C_5H_9NO_2^+$							
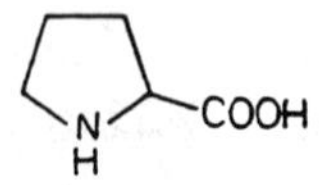 (proline)	(8.3)	(104)	(435)	−87±1	−366±4	78SAB/LAF	609-36-9

IP is onset of photoelectron band (83CAN/HAM).

$C_5H_9NO_3^+$							
$CH_3CONHCH(CH_3)COOH$	(9.2)	(62)	(260)	−150	−628	*EST	97-69-8

IP is onset of photoelectron band (83CAN/HAM).

| 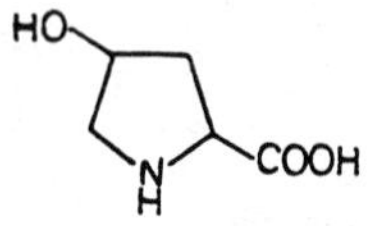 (hydroxyproline) | (≤9.1) | (≤87) | (≤362) | −123 | −516 | 77PED/RYL | 51-35-4 |

IP from 83CAN/HAM.

$C_5H_9O^+$

$CH_3C(OH)C(CH_2)CH_3$

| | | 121 | 507 | | | | |

From proton affinity of $CH_3C(=O)C(=CH_2)CH_3$ (RN 814-78-8) (84BOU/HOP). PA = 202.4 kcal/mol, 847. kJ/mol.

$(E)-CH_3CHCHC(OH)CH_3$

| | | 117 | 491 | | | | |

From proton affinity of $(E)-CH_3CH=CHC(=O)CH_3$ (RN 625-33-2) (84BOU/HOP). PA = 206.7 kcal/mol, 865. kJ/mol.

| 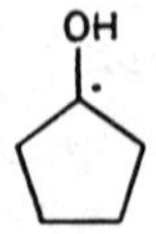 | | 121 | 506 | | | | |

From proton affinity of cyclopentanone (RN 120-92-3). PA = 198.8 kcal/mol, 832. kJ/mol.

| 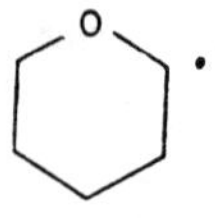 | | 129 | 539 | | | | |

From proton affinity of 3,4-dihydro-4H-pyran (RN 110-87-2) (86BOU/HAN). PA = 206.9 kcal/mol, 866. kJ/mol.

| 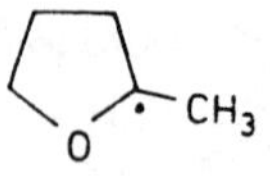 | | 121 | 507 | | | | |

From proton affinity of 2-methyl-4,5-dihydrofuran (RN 1487-15-6) (86BOU/DJA). PA = 215.6 kcal/mol, 902. kJ/mol.

Table 1. Positive Ion Table – Continued

ION / Neutral	Ionization potential eV	$\Delta_f H$(Ion) kcal/mol kJ/mol	$\Delta_f H$(Neutral) kcal/mol kJ/mol	Neutral reference	CAS registry number
$C_5H_9O^+$					
3-methyl-tetrahydrofuran radical		132 552			
From proton affinity of 3-methyl-4,5-dihydrofuran (RN 557-31-3) (86BOU/DJA). PA = 207.0 kcal/mol, 866. kJ/mol.					
1-cyclopropyl-1-hydroxyethyl		133 555			
From proton affinity of 1-cyclopropylethanone (RN 765-43-5). PA = 205.1 kcal/mol, 858. kJ/mol.					
$C_5H_9O_2^+$					
$CH_3C(OH)CHC(OH)CH_3$		66 277			
From proton affinity of $CH_3COCH=C(OH)CH_3$ (RN 123-54-6). PA = 207.8 kcal/mol, 869. kJ/mol.					
cyclopropyl-C(OCH_3)(OH)		89 373			
From proton affinity of methylcyclopropane carboxylate (RN 2868-37-3). PA = 202.9 kcal/mol, 849. kJ/mol.					
$C_5H_9O_3P^+$					
4-methyl-2,6,7-trioxa-1-phosphabicyclo	(9.2)	(76) (317)	−136 −571	*EST	1449-91-8
IP is onset of photoelectron band. (77COW/GOO).					
$C_5H_{10}^+$					
1-C_5H_{10}	9.52±0.02	214 897 221.5 926.9	−5.1±0.1 −21.4±0.4 2.0 8.4	84WIB/WAS	109-67-1
See also: 83HOL/LOS, 86TRA, 84BRA/BAE.					
2-(Z)-C_5H_{10}	9.036±0.005	202.0 845.3	−6.3±0.1 −26.5±0.4	84WIB/WAS	627-20-3
See also: 86TRA.					
2-(E)-C_5H_{10}	9.036±0.005	200.8 840.3 208.0 870.1	−7.5±0.1 −31.5±0.4 −0.4 −1.7	84WIB/WAS	646-04-8
See also: 84BRA/BAE.					
$(CH_3)_2CHCH=CH_2$	9.52±0.02	213 891 220.3 921.6	−6.5±0.2 −27.4±0.6 0.7 3.1	77PED/RYL	563-45-1
See also: 84BRA/BAE.					
$C_2H_5C(CH_3)=CH_2$	9.13±0.03	202 845 209.3 875.8	−8.5±0.2 −35.6±0.7 −1.2 −5.1	77PED/RYL	563-46-2
See also: 86TRA, 84BRA/BAE.					

Table 1. Positive Ion Table - Continued

ION Neutral	Ionization potential eV	$\Delta_f H$(Ion) kcal/mol	kJ/mol	$\Delta_f H$(Neutral) kcal/mol	kJ/mol	Neutral reference	CAS registry number
$C_5H_{10}^+$							
$(CH_3)_2C=CHCH_3$	8.68±0.01	190	795	−10.1±0.1	−42.1±0.6	77PED/RYL	513-35-9
		197.4	825.8	−2.8	−11.6		
	See also: 86TRA, 84BRA/BAE.						
cyclopentane	10.51±0.05	224	936	−18.7±0.2	−78.4±0.8	77PED/RYL	287-92-3
		231.8	969.8	−10.6	−44.2		
	See also: 81MAU/SIE, 81KIM/KAT, 86TRA, 84BRA/BAE.						
methylcyclobutane	(9.60)	(221)	(923)	−0.7	−3	*EST	598-61-8
ethylcyclopropane	(9.50)	(218)	(912)	−1	−5	77PED/RYL	1191-96-4
1,1-dimethylcyclopropane	(9.08)	(207)	(868)	−2	−8	77PED/RYL	1630-94-0
	See also: 81PLE/VIL.						
cis-1,2-dimethylcyclopropane	(9.76±0.02)	(225)	(942)	0	0	77PED/RYL	930-18-7
trans-1,2-dimethylcyclopropane	(9.73±0.02)	(223)	(934)	−1	−5	77PED/RYL	2402-06-4
$C_5H_{10}Br_2^+$							
$Br(CH_2)_5Br$	(≤10.23)	(≤207)	(≤868)	−28	−119	*EST	111-24-0
$C_5H_{10}ClN^+$							
N-chloropiperidine	(8.5)	(208)	(871)	12	51	*EST	2156-71-0
	IP is onset of photoelectron band.						

Table 1. Positive Ion Table - Continued

ION / Neutral	Ionization potential eV	$\Delta_f H$(Ion) kcal/mol	$\Delta_f H$(Ion) kJ/mol	$\Delta_f H$(Neutral) kcal/mol	$\Delta_f H$(Neutral) kJ/mol	Neutral reference	CAS registry number
$C_5H_{10}N^+$							
n-C_4H_9CNH		174	728				

From proton affinity of n-C_4H_9CN (RN 110-59-8). PA = 194.0 kcal/mol, 812. kJ/mol.

t-C_4H_9CNH		169	709				

From proton affinity of t-C_4H_9CN (86MAR/TOP, 86MAU/KAR). PA = 195.7 kcal/mol, 819. kJ/mol.

t-C_4H_9NCH		178	744				

From proton affinity of t-C_4H_9NC (RN 7188-38-7) (86MAU/KAR). PA = 207.5 kcal/mol, 868 kJ/mol.

$C_5H_{10}NO^+$							
(2-methoxy pyrrolidine)		103	433				

From proton affinity of 2-methoxy-1-pyrroline (RN 5264-35-7). PA = 225.9 kcal/mol, 945. kJ/mol.

(1-methyl-2-hydroxypyrrolidine)		98	412				

From proton affinity of 1-methyl-2-pyrrolidinone (RN 872-50-4). PA = 216.8 kcal/mol, 907. kJ/mol.

$C_5H_{10}NO_2^+$							
(L-proline)H^+		58	243				

From proton affinity of L-proline (RN 609-36-9). PA = 220.2 kcal/mol, 921. kJ/mol.

$C_5H_{10}NO_3^+$							
$CH_3C(OH)NHCH_2COOCH_3$		8	34				

From proton affinity of $CH_3CONHCH_2COOCH_3$. PA = 217.7 kcal/mol, 911. kJ/mol.

$C_5H_{10}NO_4^+$							
L-HOOC$(CH_2)_2$CH(NH_3)COOH		29	121				

From proton affinity of L-HOOC$(CH_2)_2$CH(NH_2)COOH (RN 617-65-2). PA = 216.5 kcal/mol, 906. kJ/mol.

$C_5H_{10}N_2^+$							
(1-methyl pyrazolidine)	(≤8.78)	(≤264)	(≤1108)	62	261	*EST	6794-96-3

Table 1. Positive Ion Table — Continued

ION / Neutral	Ionization potential eV	$\Delta_f H$(Ion) kcal/mol	kJ/mol	$\Delta_f H$(Neutral) kcal/mol	kJ/mol	Neutral reference	CAS registry number
$C_5H_{10}N_2S^+$							
H₃CN⌐NCH₃ (=S) [1,3-dimethyl-2-thione]	≤7.95 See also: 80AND/DEV.	(≤208)	(≤869)	24	102	*EST	13461-16-0
HN⌐N-C₂H₅ (=S)	(7.7) IP is onset of photoelectron band (80AND/DEV).	(194)	(813)	17	70	*EST	29704-02-7
$C_5H_{10}N_4^+$							
$NCN=C(N(CH_3)_2)(NHCH_3)$	(8.2) IP is onset of photoelectron band (80KLA/BUT).	(227)	(950)	38	159	*EST	17686-53-2
$C_5H_{10}O^+$							
$n\text{-}C_4H_9CHO$	9.74±0.04 See also: 81HOL/FIN.	169	709	−55.1±0.5	−230.5±2	77PED/RYL	110-62-3
$sec\text{-}C_4H_9CHO$	(9.59±0.01)	(165)	(689)	−56	−236	*EST	96-17-3
$iso\text{-}C_4H_9CHO$	9.70±0.02 See also: 81HOL/FIN.	(167)	(699)	−57	−237	*EST	590-86-3
$tert\text{-}C_4H_9CHO$	9.50	(161)	(673)	−58	−244	*EST	630-19-3
$n\text{-}C_3H_7COCH_3$	9.38±0.01 See also: 84OLI/GUE.	154.4	645.9	−61.9±0.2	−259.1±0.8	77PED/RYL	107-87-9
$(C_2H_5)_2CO$	9.31±0.01 See also: 81HOL/FIN.	153.0	639.9	−61.7±0.2	−258.4±0.7	77PED/RYL	96-22-0
$iso\text{-}C_3H_7COCH_3$	9.30±0.01	151.8	634.9	−62.7±0.2	−262.4±0.8	77PED/RYL	563-80-4
$CH_2=CHCH_2CH_2CH_2OH$	(9.42±0.05) IP from 83HOL/LOS.	(176)	(737)	−41	−172	*EST	821-09-0
$CH_2=CHC(CH_3)_2OH$	(≤9.90)	(≤198)	(≤830)	−30	−125	84GUB/GER	115-18-4
$CH_2=CHCH_2CH(OH)CH_3$	(9.38±0.05) IP from 83HOL/LOS.	(171)	(717)	−45	−188	*EST	625-31-0
$CH_2=CHCH(OH)CH_2CH_3$	9.40±0.05 IP from 83HOL/LOS. See also: 84ZWI/HAR.	(173)	(725)	−43	−182	*EST	616-25-1

Table 1. Positive Ion Table – Continued

ION / Neutral	Ionization potential eV	$\Delta_f H$(Ion) kcal/mol	kJ/mol	$\Delta_f H$(Neutral) kcal/mol	kJ/mol	Neutral reference	CAS registry number
$C_5H_{10}O^+$							
$CH_2=CHOCH(CH_3)_2$	(≤8.90)	(≤164)	(≤685)	−42±1	−174±5	81TRO/NED	926-65-8
tetrahydropyran	9.25±0.01 See also: 81KIM/KAT.	160	669	−53.3±0.2	−223.0±0.7	77PED/RYL	142-68-7
cyclopentanol	9.72 IP from 85TRA.	166	695	−58.0±0.3	−242.6±1.2	77PED/RYL	96-41-3
$C_5H_{10}OS^+$							
$CH_3COCH_2SCH_2CH_3$	(≤8.72) IP from 84OLI/GUE.	(≤153)	(≤638)	−49	−203	*EST	20996-62-7
$C_5H_{10}O_2^+$							
$n\text{-}C_4H_9COOH$	(≤10.53)	(≤126)	(≤526)	−117±0.5	−490±2	77PED/RYL	109-52-4
$iso\text{-}C_4H_9COOH$	(≤10.51)	(≤119)	(≤499)	−123±1	−515±6	77PED/RYL	503-74-2
$tert\text{-}C_4H_9COOH$	(10.08) IP from 81HOL/FIN.	(110)	(460)	−122	−512	*EST	75-98-9
$HCOO(CH_2)_3CH_3$	10.50±0.02	(139)	(583)	−103	−430	*EST	592-84-7
$CH_3COOCH_2CH_2CH_3$	10.04±0.03	(123)	(515)	−109	−454	*EST	109-60-4
$CH_3COOCH(CH_3)_2$	9.99±0.03	115	482	−115.1±0.1	−481.5±0.6	77PED/RYL	108-21-4
$C_2H_5COOC_2H_5$	(10.00±0.02)	(120)	(501)	−111±0.5	−464±2	77PED/RYL	105-37-3
$n\text{-}C_3H_7COOCH_3$	10.07±0.03	(124)	(520)	−108	−452	*EST	623-42-7
$iso\text{-}C_3H_7COOCH_3$	9.86 IP from 83BUR/HOL3.	118	495	−109±0.2	−456±1	83FUC/SMI	547-63-1
1,3-dioxepane	(≤9.75)	(≤190)	(≤797)	−34	−144	*EST	505-63-5

Table 1. Positive Ion Table - Continued

ION / Neutral	Ionization potential eV	$\Delta_f H$(Ion) kcal/mol	kJ/mol	$\Delta_f H$(Neutral) kcal/mol	kJ/mol	Neutral reference	CAS registry number
$C_5H_{10}O_2^+$							
(1,3-dioxepane)	(9.45)	(135)	(565)	−83±0.5	−347±2	77PED/RYL	505-65-7
(2-methyl-1,3-dioxane)	(≤10.03) IP from 84ASF/ZYK	(≤136)	(≤570)	−95.1±0.07	−397.8±2.9	77PED/RYL	626-68-6
(4-methyl-1,3-dioxane)	(≤10.04) IP from 84ASF/ZYK.	(≤141)	(≤592)	−90.1±0.7	−376.9±3.1	77PED/RYL	1120-97-4
(2,2-dimethyl-1,3-dioxolane)	(9.2) IP is onset of photoelectron band.	(120)	(502)	−92±0.2	−386±1	*EST	2916-31-6
$C_5H_{10}O_2S^+$							
(1,3-dioxa-6-thiacycloheptane)	8.67±0.05 IP from 72CON/COL.	128	537	−72	−300	72CON/COL	2094-92-0
$C_5H_{10}O_3P^+$		19	80				
	From proton affinity of 4-methyl-2,6,7-trioxa-1-phosphabicyclo[2.2.2]octane (RN 1449-91-8). PA = 210.0 kcal/mol, 879. kJ/mol.						
$C_5H_{10}S^+$							
$CH_2=CHCH_2SC_2H_5$	(8.51±0.01)	(200)	(839)	4±0.7	18±3	77PED/RYL	5296-62-8
(tetrahydro-2H-thiopyran)	(8.2) IP is onset of photoelectron band (80SAR/WOR, 82LEV/LIA).	(174)	(730)	−15.2±0.2	−63.5±0.7	77PED/RYL	1613-51-0

Table 1. Positive Ion Table – Continued

ION / Neutral	Ionization potential eV	$\Delta_f H$(Ion) kcal/mol	$\Delta_f H$(Ion) kJ/mol	$\Delta_f H$(Neutral) kcal/mol	$\Delta_f H$(Neutral) kJ/mol	Neutral reference	CAS registry number
$C_5H_{10}S_5^+$							
(1,3,5,7,9-pentathiecane)	(7.6)	(197)	(823)	22	90	*EST	2372-99-8

IP is onset of photoelectron band (81BOC/SCH).

$C_5H_{11}^+$							
1-C_5H_{11}	(7.85)	(194)	(812)	13	56	*EST	2672-01-7

$\Delta_f H$(Neutral) based on D[C-H] = 100.5 kcal/mol. IP estimated by J.L. Holmes, personal communication.

$CH_3CH_2CH_2CHCH_3$	(7.1)	(175)	(732)	12	50	*EST	2492-34-4

Cited ionization potential is difference between heats of formation of ion and neutral. $\Delta_f H$(Neutral) based on D[C-H] = 99 kcal/mol. Experimental value = 7.41 eV.

$(CH_3)_2CCH_2CH_3$	6.6	158±1	661±4	6.5	27	*EST	4348-35-0

$\Delta_f H$(Ion) from hydride transfer equilibrium constant determinations (75SOL/FIE, 76GOR/MUN). $\Delta_f H$(Neutral) based on D[C-H] = 95.5 kcal/mol. IP given is $\Delta_f H$(Ion) -$\Delta_f H$(Neutral). Experimental IP of radical = 6.65 eV (86KRU/BEA).

$(CH_3)_3CCH_2$	7.88±0.05	(190)	(795)	8	33	*EST	3744-21-6

IP from 84SCH/HOU. $\Delta_f H$(Neutral) based on D[C-H] = 100.5 kcal/mol.

$C_5H_{11}Br^+$							
n-$C_5H_{11}Br$	10.09±0.02	202	844	−30.8±0.3	−129.1±1.4	77PED/RYL	110-53-2
$(CH_3)_3CCH_2Br$	10.04	196	822	−35	−147	81HOL/FIN	630-17-1
$C_5H_{11}ClHg^+$							
n-$C_5H_{11}HgCl$	≤9.99	(≤200)	(≤835)	−31	−129	*EST	544-15-0

IP from 81BAI/CHI2.

iso-$C_5H_{11}HgCl$	≤9.95	(≤197)	(≤823)	−33	−137	*EST	17774-08-2

IP from 81BAI/CHI2.

$C_5H_{11}I^+$							
n-$C_5H_{11}I$	9.201	(195)	(816)	−17	−72	*EST	628-17-1
$(CH_3)_2C(C_2H_5)I$	(8.93)	(184)	(769)	−22	−93	*EST	594-38-7
$CH_2ICH_2CH(CH_3)_2$	9.192	(193)	(807)	−19	−80	*EST	541-28-6
$C_5H_{11}N^+$							
$C_2H_5CH=NC_2H_5$	(8.7)	(201)	(839)	0	0	69BEN/CRU	18328-91-1

IP is onset of photoelectron band.

$(CH_3)_2C=NC_2H_5$	(8.83)	(195)	(816)	−9±2	−36±9	*EST	15673-04-8

See also: 79AUE/BOW.

Table 1. Positive Ion Table – Continued

ION / Neutral	Ionization potential eV	$\Delta_f H$(Ion) kcal/mol	kJ/mol	$\Delta_f H$(Neutral) kcal/mol	kJ/mol	Neutral reference	CAS registry number
$C_5H_{11}N^+$							
$(CH_3)_2NCH_2CH=CH_2$	7.84	195	813	14	57	70BEN/O'N	2155-94-4
	See also: 81LOG/TAK.						
piperidine	8.05±0.05	174	728	−11.7±0.4	−48.9±1.5	77PED/RYL	110-89-4
	See also: 82ROZ/HOU.						
N-methylpyrrolidine	(≤8.41±0.02)	(≤193)	(≤809)	−0.5±0.5	−2±2	*EST	120-94-5
	$\Delta_f H$(Ion) from hydrogen affinities of homologues, 178 kcal/mol; 746 kJ/mol; corresponding IP, 7.8 eV.						
1,2,2-trimethylaziridine	(≤8.68±0.02)	(≤201)	(≤842)	1	5	*EST	23132-47-0
$C_5H_{11}NO^+$							
$(CH_3)_2NCH_2COCH_3$	(7.71)	(135)	(567)	−42	−177	81LOG/TAK	15364-56-4
	IP from 81LOG/TAK. See also: 84OLI/GUE.						
$C_5H_{11}NO_2^+$							
$H_2N(CH_2)_4COOH$	(≤9.4)	(≤107)	(≤447)	−110±.7	−460±3	83SKO/SAB	660-88-8
n-$C_3H_7CH(NH_2)COOH$	(8.53)	(87)	(364)	−110±2	−459±10	*EST	6600-40-4
L-iso-$C_3H_7CH(NH_2)COOH$	(8.71)	(92)	(385)	−108.8±0.2	−455.1±1.0	77PED/RYL	72-18-4
$(CH_3)_2NCH_2COOCH_3$	(7.96)	(98)	(411)	−85	−357	81LOG/TAK	7148-06-3
	IP from 81LOG/TAK.						
$C_5H_{11}NO_2S^+$							
L-$CH_3SCH_2CH_2CH(NH_2)COOH$	(8.3)	(92)	(387)	−99±1	−414±4	81SAB/MIN	59-51-8
	IP is onset of photoelectron band (83CAN/HAM).						
$C_5H_{11}N_2O_3^+$							
L-$H_2NCO(CH_2)_2CH(NH_3)COOH$		73	304				
	From proton affinity of L-$H_2NCO(CH_2)_2CH(NH_2)COOH$ (RN 585-21-7). PA = 218.4 kcal/mol, 914. kJ/mol.						

Table 1. Positive Ion Table - Continued

ION / Neutral	Ionization potential eV	$\Delta_f H$(Ion) kcal/mol	$\Delta_f H$(Ion) kJ/mol	$\Delta_f H$(Neutral) kcal/mol	$\Delta_f H$(Neutral) kJ/mol	Neutral reference	CAS registry number

$C_5H_{11}O^+$

$i\text{-}C_3H_7C(OH)CH_3$
    102   427
From proton affinity of $i\text{-}C_3H_7COCH_3$ (RN 563-80-4). PA = 201.1 kcal/mol, 841. kJ/mol.

$n\text{-}C_4H_9CHOH$
    118   493
From proton affinity of $n\text{-}C_4H_9CHO$ (RN 110-62-3). PA = 192.6 kcal/mol, 806. kJ/mol.

$(CH_3)_2COC_2H_5$
    (104)   (435)
From appearance potential determination (82MAC).

$(C_2H_5)_2COH$
    102   429
From proton affinity of $(C_2H_5)_2CO$ (RN 96-22-0). PA = 201.4 kcal/mol, 843. kJ/mol.

$C_2H_5OCHCH_2CH_3$
    (114)   (476)
From proton affinity of $C_2H_5OCH=CHCH_3$ (86BOU/DJA). PA = (210.) kcal/mol, (880.) kJ/mol.

$C_2H_5O(H)CH_2CHCH_2$
    (132)   (552)
From proton affinity of $C_2H_5OCH_2CH=CH_2$.

(tetrahydropyran)H^+
    113   472
From proton affinity of tetrahydropyran (RN 142-68-7). PA = 199.7 kcal/mol, 835.5 kJ/mol.

(2-methyltetrahydrofuran)H^+
    110   461
From proton affinity of 2-methyltetrahydrofuran (RN 96-47-9). PA = 203.6 kcal/mol, 852. kJ/mol.

$C_5H_{11}O_2^+$

$HC(OH)(O\text{-}n\text{-}C_4H_9)$
    68   285
From proton affinity of $HCOO(n\text{-}C_4H_9)$ (RN 592-84-7). PA = 194.8 kcal/mol, 815. kJ/mol.

$n\text{-}C_3H_7C(OH)(OCH_3)$
    57   241
From proton affinity of $C_3H_7COOCH_3$ (RN 623-42-7). PA = 200.1 kcal/mol, 837. kJ/mol.

$CH_3C(OH)(O\text{-}C_3H_7)$
    57   237
From proton affinity of $CH_3COOC_3H_7$ (RN 109-60-4). PA = 200.6 kcal/mol, 839. kJ/mol.

$i\text{-}C_3H_7C(OH)OCH_3$
    55   231
From proton affinity of $i\text{-}C_3H_7COOCH_3$ (RN 547-63-7). PA = 201.6 kcal/mol, 843. kJ/mol.

Table 1. Positive Ion Table - Continued

ION Neutral	Ionization potential eV	$\Delta_f H$(Ion) kcal/mol	$\Delta_f H$(Ion) kJ/mol	$\Delta_f H$(Neutral) kcal/mol	$\Delta_f H$(Neutral) kJ/mol	Neutral reference	CAS registry number
$C_5H_{11}O_3P^+$	(8.7)	(22)	(93)	−178	−746	*EST	33892-95-4

IP is onset of photoelectron band (81ARS/ZVE).

$C_5H_{12}^+$							
n-C_5H_{12}	10.35±0.01	204 *211*	852 *884*	−35.0±0.1 *−27.3±0.1*	−146.5±0.4 *−114.2±0.4*	77PED/RYL	109-66-0

See also: 81MAU/SIE, 82LIA, 81KIM/KAT.

| iso-C_5H_{12} | ≤10.22 | ≤199
≤207 | ≤832
≤867 | −36.7±0.1
−28.4 | −153.8±0.5
−118.8 | 77PED/RYL | 78-78-4 |

IP from 81TRA. See also: 81KIM/KAT.

| neo-C_5H_{12} | ≤10.21±0.04 | ≤195
≤203 | ≤818
≤850 | −40.0±0.1
−32.4 | −167.4±0.7
−135.6 | 77PED/RYL | 463-82-1 |

See also: 81KIM/KAT.

$C_5H_{12}Cl^+$							
$(CH_3)_3CClCH_3$		(137)	(572)				

From equilibrium constant determination (85SHA/HOJ).

$C_5H_{12}N^+$							
$(CH_3)_2CNHC_2H_5$		(128)	(534)				

From proton affinity of $(CH_3)_2C=NC_2H_5$ (RN 15673-04-8). PA = (229.5) kcal/mol, (960.) kJ/mol.

| $CH_3CH_2CHN(CH_3)_2$ | | 142 | 596 | | | | |

From proton affinity of $CH_3CH=CHN(CH_3)_2$ (RN 6163-56-0). PA = 229.4 kcal/mol, 960. kJ/mol.

| piperidine·H^+ | | 128 | 535 | | | | |

From proton affinity of piperidine (RN 110-89-4). PA = 226.4 kcal/mol, 947. kJ/mol.

| N-methylpyrrolidine·H^+ | | 136 | 571 | | | | |

From proton affinity of N-methylpyrrolidine (RN 120-94-5). PA = 228.7 kcal/mol, 957. kJ/mol.

$C_5H_{12}NO_2^+$							
$(CH_3)_2NC(OH)OC_2H_5$		43	180				

From proton affinity of $(CH_3)_2NCOOC_2H_5$ (RN 687-48-9). PA = 213.7 kcal/mol, 894. kJ/mol.

Table 1. Positive Ion Table – Continued

ION Neutral	Ionization potential eV	$\Delta_f H$(Ion) kcal/mol kJ/mol		$\Delta_f H$(Neutral) kcal/mol kJ/mol		Neutral reference	CAS registry number
$C_5H_{12}NO_2^+$							
L-i-C_3H_7CH(NH_3)COOH		40	167				
From proton affinity of L-i-C_3H_7CH(NH_2)COOH (RN 72-18-4). PA = 217.0 kcal/mol, 908. kJ/mol.							
$C_5H_{12}NO_2P^+$							
[cyclic phosphite with N(CH$_3$)$_2$]	7.8	(50)	(208)	−130	−545	*EST	17454-25-0
IP from 81ARS/ZVE.							
$C_5H_{12}NO_2S^+$							
L-$CH_3SCH_2CH_2$CH(NH_3)COOH		45	190				
From proton affinity of L-$CH_3SCH_2CH_2$CH(NH_2)COOH (RN 59-51-8). PA = 221.4 kcal/mol, 926. kJ/mol.							
$C_5H_{12}N_2^+$							
[1,2-dimethylpyrazolidine]	6.66	(180)	(754)	27	111	*EST	38704-89-1
IP from charge transfer equilibrium constant determination (86RUM). Reference standard: IP ($C_6H_5N(CH_3)_2$) = 7.12 eV. See also: 84NEL.							
$C_5H_{12}N_2O^+$							
(($CH_3)_2$N)$_2$CO	≤8.64	(≤142)	(≤595)	−57	−238	*EST	632-22-4
$C_5H_{12}N_2S^+$							
(($CH_3)_2$N)$_2$CS	(7.5)	(184)	(769)	11±0.5	45±2	82INA/MUR2	2782-91-4
IP is onset of photoelectron band. See also: 85ROT/BOC.							
$C_5H_{12}O^+$							
n-C_5H_{11}OH	10.00±0.03	160	668	−70.9±0.4	−296.7±1.6	77PED/RYL	71-41-0
IP from 77ASH/BUR. See also: 80BAC/MOU.							
CH_3CH_2CH(CH_3)CH_2OH	(9.86)	(155)	(649)	−72.2±0.3	−302.0±1.4	77PED/RYL	137-32-6
IP from 81HOL/FIN.							
n-C_3H_7CH(OH)CH_3	(9.78±0.03)	(151)	(630)	−75.0±0.2	−313.8±0.8	77PED/RYL	6032-29-7
IP from 77ASH/BUR, 84BOW/MAC.							
($C_2H_5)_2$CHOH	9.78	150	628	−75.4±0.2	−315.5±0.9	77PED/RYL	584-02-1
IP from 81HOL/FIN, 84BOW/MAC. See also: 77ASH/BUR.							
($CH_3)_2$CHCH(OH)CH_3	(10.01)	(155)	(650)	−75.4±0.3	−315.7±1.1	77PED/RYL	598-75-4
IP from 84BOW/MAC.							

Table 1. Positive Ion Table - Continued

ION Neutral	Ionization potential eV	$\Delta_f H$(Ion) kcal/mol	$\Delta_f H$(Ion) kJ/mol	$\Delta_f H$(Neutral) kcal/mol	$\Delta_f H$(Neutral) kJ/mol	Neutral reference	CAS registry number
$C_5H_{12}O^+$							
$C_2H_5C(CH_3)_2OH$	9.80	147	615	−79.1±0.3	−330.8±1.3	77PED/RYL	75-85-4
	IP from 84BOW/MAC, 82LEV/LIA.						
n-$C_4H_9OCH_3$	(9.54)	(158)	(662)	−61.7±0.3	−258.1±1.1	77PED/RYL	628-28-4
	IP from 81HOL/FIN.						
n-$C_3H_7OC_2H_5$	(9.45±0.1)	(153)	(640)	−65.0±0.2	−272.2±1	77PED/RYL	628-32-0
	IP cited in 81HOL/FIN.						
tert-$C_4H_9OCH_3$	(9.24)	(145)	(608)	−67.8±0.2	−283.6±1	77PED/RYL	1634-04-4
	IP from 84BOW/MAC. See also: 80BAC/MOU.						
$C_5H_{12}O_2^+$							
n-$C_3H_7CH(CH_3)OOH$							
	(9.35±0.03)	(159)	(666)	−56	−236	*EST	14018-58-7
	IP from 77ASH/BUR.						
$CH_3O(CH_2)_3OCH_3$	(9.3)	(126)	(526)	−89	−371	*EST	17081-21-9
	IP is onset of photoelectron band (83BIE/MOR).						
n-$C_5H_{11}OOH$	(9.50±0.03)	(167)	(698)	−52	−219	*EST	74-80-6
	IP from 77ASH/BUR.						
$C_5H_{12}O_3^+$							
$CH_3C(OCH_3)_3$	(9.65)	(82)	(343)	−140±0.5	−588±2	77PED/RYL	1445-45-0
	IP from 82HOL/LOS2.						
$C_5H_{12}S^+$							
n-$C_3H_7SC_2H_5$	(8.50±0.05)	(171)	(715)	−25.0±0.2	−104.7±0.7	77PED/RYL	4110-50-3
$(CH_3)_3CSCH_3$	(8.38±0.05)	(164)	(687)	−29.0±0.2	−121.3±0.7	77PED/RYL	6163-64-0
$C_2H_5S(iso-C_3H_7)$							
	(8.35±0.01)	(165)	(689)	−28±0.6	−117±2	77PED/RYL	5145-99-3
$C_5H_{12}S_2^+$							
$C_2H_5SCH_2SC_2H_5$	(8.22±0.02)	(179)	(750)	−10	−43	*EST	4396-19-4
$C_5H_{12}Si^+$							
$CH_2=CHSi(CH_3)_3$	(9.5)	(190)	(794)	−29	−123	*EST	754-05-2
	IP is onset of photoelectron band (81KHV/ZYK, 82LEV/LIA).						
⟨▱-Si(CH₃)₂⟩	8.83±0.07	184	769	−19.8	−82.8	81GUS/VOL2	2295-12-7
	See also: 82DYK/JOS, 81KOE/MCK, 81GUS/VOL2.						

Table 1. Positive Ion Table – Continued

ION / Neutral	Ionization potential eV	$\Delta_f H$(Ion) kcal/mol	$\Delta_f H$(Ion) kJ/mol	$\Delta_f H$(Neutral) kcal/mol	$\Delta_f H$(Neutral) kJ/mol	Neutral reference	CAS registry number
$C_5H_{12}Sn^+$							
$CH_2=CHSn(CH_3)_3$	(≤9.7)	(≤246)	(≤1028)	22±3	92±13	77PED/RYL	754-06-3
$C_5H_{13}N^+$							
$n-C_5H_{11}NH_2$	(8.67) IP from 79AUE/BOW.	(174)	(726)	−26	−110	*EST	110-58-7
$tert-C_5H_{11}NH_2$	(8.46±0.1)	(165)	(689)	−30	−127	*EST	594-39-8
$neo-C_5H_{11}NH_2$	(8.54±0.1)	(166)	(692)	−31	−132	*EST	5813-64-9
$(C_2H_5)_2(CH_3)N$	(7.50±0.1) IP from 79AUE/BOW.	(156)	(654)	−17	−70	*EST	616-39-7
$(CH_3)_2(i-C_3H_7)N$	(7.3)	(150)	(628)	−18	−76	*EST	996-35-0

$\Delta_f H$(Ion) from hydrogen affinities of homologous series. IP cited is $\Delta_f H$(Ion)-$\Delta_f H$(Neutral). See also: 84NEL.

ION / Neutral		kcal/mol	kJ/mol				
$C_5H_{13}N_2O^+$							
$[(CH_3)_2N]_2COH$		88	367				

From proton affinity of $[(CH_3)_2N]_2C=O$ (RN 632-22-4) (86TAF/GAL). PA = 221.1 kcal/mol, 925. kJ/mol.

$C_5H_{13}O^+$							
$neo-C_5H_{11}OH_2$		97	406				

From proton affinity of $neo-C_5H_{11}OH$ (RN 75-84-3) (78TAF/TAA). PA = 193.6 kcal/mol, 810. kJ/mol.

$C_2H_5OH(i-C_3H_7)$		94	393				

From proton affinity of $C_2H_5O(i-C_3H_7)$ (RN 625-54-7). PA = 203.5 kcal/mol, 851. kJ/mol.

$t-C_4H_9OHCH_3$		96	400				

From proton affinity of $t-C_4H_9OCH_3$ (RN 1634-04-4). PA = 202.2 kcal/mol, 846. kJ/mol.

$C_5H_{14}N^+$							
$n-C_5H_{11}NH_3$		121	504				

From proton affinity of $n-C_5H_{11}NH_2$ (RN 110-58-7). PA = 218.9 kcal/mol, 916. kJ/mol.

$tert-C_5H_{11}NH_3$		112	468				

From proton affinity of $tert-C_5H_{11}NH_2$ (RN 594-39-8). PA = 222.3 kcal/mol, 930. kJ/mol.

$neo-C_5H_{11}NH_3$		115	481				

From proton affinity of $neo-C_5H_{11}NH_2$ (RN 5813-64-9). PA = 219.3 kcal/mol, 917.5 kJ/mol.

Table 1. Positive Ion Table - Continued

ION / Neutral	Ionization potential eV	$\Delta_f H$(Ion) kcal/mol kJ/mol	$\Delta_f H$(Neutral) kcal/mol kJ/mol	Neutral reference	CAS registry number
$C_5H_{14}N^+$					
$(C_2H_5)(i\text{-}C_3H_7)NH_2$		113 474			
	From proton affinity of $(C_2H_5)(i\text{-}C_3H_7)NH$ (RN 19961-27-4). PA = 227.4 kcal/mol, 951. kJ/mol.				
$(CH_3)(C_2H_5)_2NH$		119 498			
	From proton affinity of $(CH_3)(C_2H_5)_2N$ (RN 616-39-7). PA = 230.0 kcal/mol, 962. kJ/mol.				
$(CH_3)_2(i\text{-}C_3H_7)NH$		118 493			
	From proton affinity of $(CH_3)_2(i\text{-}C_3H_7)N$ (RN 996-35-0). PA = 229.8 kcal/mol, 961. kJ/mol.				
$C_5H_{14}N_2^+$					
$(C_2H_5)(CH_3)NN(CH_3)_2$	(8.18)	(201) (839)	12 50	*EST	50599-41-2
	Reported values of IP's of hydrazines determined by threshold measurements are usually significantly higher than the adiabatic value because of the large geometry change associated with ionization. See also: 84NEL.				
$((CH_3)_2N)_2CH_2$	(7.74±0.05)	(174) (729)	-4.2±0.3 -17.6±1.4	77PED/RYL	51-80-9
	See also: 81LOG/TAK.				
$C_5H_{14}N_2OP^+$					
2,5-dimethyl-1,3,2-diazaphospholidine-2-oxide · H⁺		42 176			
	From proton affinity of 2,5-dimethyl-1,3,2-diazaphospholidine-2-oxide (RN 16606-18-1) (84MAU/NEL). PA = 224.8 kcal/mol, 941. kJ/mol.				
$C_5H_{14}N_3^+$					
$[(CH_3)_2N]_2CNH_2$		192 803			
	From proton affinity of $[(CH_3)_2N]_2C=NH$ (RN 31081-16-0) (86TAF/GAL). PA = 241.0 kcal/mol, 1008. kJ/mol.				
$C_5H_{14}Si^+$					
$(CH_3)_3SiC_2H_5$	(9.6)	(164) (685)	-58 -241	*EST	3439-38-1
$C_5H_{14}Sn^+$					
$(CH_3)_3SnC_2H_5$	(8.6)	(191) (800)	-7±0.7 -30±3	77PED/RYL	3531-44-0
	IP is onset of photoelectron band.				
$C_5H_{15}N_2^+$					
$NH_2(CH_2)_5NH_3$		110 461			
	From proton affinity of $NH_2(CH_2)_5NH_2$ (RN 462-94-2). PA = 238.1 kcal/mol, 996. kJ/mol.				

Table 1. Positive Ion Table - Continued

ION / Neutral	Ionization potential eV	$\Delta_f H$(Ion) kcal/mol	$\Delta_f H$(Ion) kJ/mol	$\Delta_f H$(Neutral) kcal/mol	$\Delta_f H$(Neutral) kJ/mol	Neutral reference	CAS registry number
$C_5H_{15}N_2^+$ $(CH_3)_2NH(CH_2)_3NH_2$		118	494				
From proton affinity of $(CH_3)_2N(CH_2)_3NH_2$ (RN 109-55-7). Data re-evaluated. PA = 241. kcal/mol, 1006. kJ/mol.							
$C_5H_{15}Si_2^+$ $(CH_3)_3SiSi(CH_3)_2$		117	489				
$\Delta_f H$(Ion) from appearance potential determination (84SZE/BAE, 84SZE/BAE2). 0 K values.							
$C_5H_{15}Ta^+$ $Ta(CH_3)_5$	8.25	241	1007	51±6	212±26	82PIL/SKI	53378-72-6
IP is onset of photoelectron band (75GAL/WIL, 82LEV/LIA).							
$C_5H_{16}NSi^+$ $(CH_3)_3SiNH(CH_3)_2$		(81)	(336)				
From proton affinity of $(CH_3)_3SiN(CH_3)_2$ (RN 18135-05-2). PA = (226) kcal/mol, (946) kJ/mol.							
$C_5IMnO_5^+$ $Mn(CO)_5I$	(8.1)	(−13)	(−52)	−199±1	−834±5	82CON/ZAF	14879-42-6
IP is onset of photoelectron band.							
$C_5N_2OS_2^+$	≤9.94	(≤294)	(≤1229)	65	270	*EST	934-31-6
IP from 83SCH/SCH.							
$C_5N_4^+$ $C(CN)_4$	(13.94)	(482)	(2018)	161±2	673±9	82CHU/NGU	24331-09-7
$C_6BrF_5^+$	9.57±0.02	51	211	−170±4	−712±17	77KRE/PRI	344-04-7
$C_6ClF_5^+$	(9.72±0.02)	(30)	(128)	−194±3	−810±11	77PED/RYL	344-07-0

Table 1. Positive Ion Table - Continued

ION / Neutral	Ionization potential eV	$\Delta_f H$(Ion) kcal/mol	$\Delta_f H$(Ion) kJ/mol	$\Delta_f H$(Neutral) kcal/mol	$\Delta_f H$(Neutral) kJ/mol	Neutral reference	CAS registry number
$C_6Cl_4O_2^+$	9.74	180	754	-44.4 ± 2.8	-185.7 ± 11	77PED/RYL	118-75-2
	IP from 81SAT/SEK.						
$C_6Cl_6^+$	8.98	196.4	821.7	-10.7	-44.7	83PLA/SIM	118-74-1
	IP from 81SAT/SEK. See also: 81RUS/KLA, 81KIM/KAT.						
$C_6CrO_6^+$ $Cr(CO)_6$	8.142 ± 0.017	-29	-122	-217.0 ± 0.3	-908 ± 1.2	77PED/RYL	13007-92-6
	See also: 82HUB/LIC, 85DAS/NIS.						
$C_6F_3MnO_5^+$ $CF_3Mn(CO)_5$	8.8	-128	-537	-331 ± 1	-1386 ± 4	82CON/ZAF	13601-14-4
	IP is onset of photoelectron band.						
$C_6F_4O_2^+$	(10.7)	(52)	(216)	-195.0 ± 9.9	-816 ± 41	*EST	527-21-9
	IP is onset of photoelectron band.						
$C_6F_5I^+$	9.54	87	362	-133 ± 3	-558 ± 13	77PED/RYL	827-15-6
	See also: 81BIE/ASB.						
$C_6F_6^+$ $CF_3C\equiv CC\equiv CCF_3$	(10.99 ± 0.01)	(78)	(326)	-175	-734	77PRA/HUB	10524-09-1
(hexafluorobenzene)	9.906	2	10	-226 ± 2	-946 ± 8	79PRI/SAP	392-56-3
	IP from 81BIE/ASB. A value of 9.91 eV is assigned to the ionization potential at 300 K based on determinations of charge transfer equilibrium constants (reference standard, ionization potential of $C_6H_5CF_3$ = 9.685 eV). See also: 81MAI/THO.						
(hexafluorocyclobutadiene dimer)	10.08 ± 0.05	62	260	-170	-713	77PRA/HUB	6733-01-3

Table 1. Positive Ion Table - Continued

ION / Neutral	Ionization potential eV	$\Delta_f H$(Ion) kcal/mol	$\Delta_f H$(Ion) kJ/mol	$\Delta_f H$(Neutral) kcal/mol	$\Delta_f H$(Neutral) kJ/mol	Neutral reference	CAS registry number
$C_6F_{12}^+$ (perfluorocyclohexane)	(13.2)	(−262)	(−1095)	−566±2	−2369±8	79PRI/SAP	355-68-0
$C_6HCl_5^+$ (pentachlorobenzene)	(8.9)	(195.7)	(818.7)	−9.6±2.1	−40.0±8.7	85PLA/SIM2	608-93-5

IP is onset of photoelectron band (81RUS/KLA3).

$C_6HCrO_6^+$ / $HCr(CO)_6$		(−31)	(−131)				

From proton affinity of $Cr(CO)_6$ (RN 13007-92-6). PA = (180) kcal/mol, (753) kJ/mol.

$C_6HF_5^+$ (pentafluorobenzene)	9.63	29	123	−193±2	−806±7	77PED/RYL	363-72-4

Ionization potential from charge transfer equilibrium constant determinations (standard: $C_6H_5CF_3$, 9.685 eV)(78LIA/AUS). Value of 9.64 eV reported from photoelectron spectroscopy measurement. See also: 81BIE/ASB.

$C_6HF_5O^+$ (pentafluorophenol)	9.20±0.02	−17	−69	−229±0.5	−957±2	77PED/RYL	771-61-9

$C_6HF_6^+$		−38	−159				

From proton affinity of C_6F_6 (RN 392-56-3). PA = 177.7 kcal/mol, 743. kJ/mol.

$C_6HMoO_6^+$ / $HMo(CO)_6$		−38	−160				

From proton affinity of $Mo(CO)_6$ (RN 13939-06-5). PA = (185) kcal/mol, (774) kJ/mol.

$C_6HO_6V^+$ / $HV(CO)_6$		(−33)	(−138)				

From proton affinity of $V(CO)_6$ (RN 20644-87-5). PA = (194.5) kcal/mol, (814) kJ/mol.

$C_6HO_6W^+$ / $HW(CO)_6$		−30	−127				

From proton affinity of $W(CO)_6$ (RN 14040-11-0). PA = (184) kcal/mol, (770) kJ/mol.

Table 1. Positive Ion Table - Continued

ION Neutral	Ionization potential eV	$\Delta_f H$(Ion) kcal/mol	kJ/mol	$\Delta_f H$(Neutral) kcal/mol	kJ/mol	Neutral reference	CAS registry number
$C_6H_2^+$							
HC≡CC≡CH	(9.50)	(375)	(1569)	155	652	*EST	3161-99-7
$C_6H_2Cl_4^+$							
1,2,3,4-tetrachlorobenzene	(8.9)	(199.1)	(833.3)	−6.1	−25.4	85PLA/SIM	634-66-2
IP is onset of photoelectron band (81RUS/KLA3).							
1,2,3,5-tetrachlorobenzene	(9.0)	(199)	(833)	−8.3	−34.9	85PLA/SIM	634-90-2
IP is onset of photoelectron band (81RUS/KLA3).							
1,2,4,5-tetrachlorobenzene	8.9	197.4	826.1	−7.8	−32.6	83PLA/SIM	95-94-3
IP is onset of photoelectron band (81RUS/KLA3, 81KIM/KAT).							
$C_6H_2Cl_4O_2^+$							
tetrachlorohydroquinone	(8.30±0.05)	(104)	(437)	−87	−364	77PED/RYL	87-87-6
$C_6H_2F_4^+$							
1,2,3,4-tetrafluorobenzene	9.53±0.01	(68)	(281)	−152±0.2	−638±1	*EST	551-62-2
Ionization potential from charge transfer equilibrium constant determinations (standard: IP of $C_6H_5CF_3$, 9.685 eV)(78LIA/AUS). Value of ionization potential from photoelectron spectroscopy, 9.56 eV. See also: 81BIE/ASB.							
1,2,3,5-tetrafluorobenzene	9.53±0.01	(63)	(262)	−157±0.2	−657±1	*EST	2367-82-0
Ionization potential from charge transfer equilibrium constant determinations (standard: ionization potential of $C_6H_5CF_3$, 9.685 eV)(78LIA/AUS). Value of ionization potential from photoionization, 9.55 eV; from photoelectron spectroscopy, 9.56 eV. See also: 81BIE/ASB.							
1,2,4,5-tetrafluorobenzene	9.35±0.01	61	255	−155±1	−647±3	78HAR/HEA	327-54-8
Ionization potential from charge transfer equilibrium constant determinations (standard: ionization potential of $C_6H_5CF_3$, 9.685 eV)(78LIA/AUS). Value of IP from photoelectron spectroscopy, 9.36 eV (82LEV/LIA, 81BIE/ASB).							

Table 1. Positive Ion Table - Continued

ION / Neutral	Ionization potential eV	$\Delta_f H$(Ion) kcal/mol	$\Delta_f H$(Ion) kJ/mol	$\Delta_f H$(Neutral) kcal/mol	$\Delta_f H$(Neutral) kJ/mol	Neutral reference	CAS registry number
$C_6H_2F_5^+$ (pentafluorobenzene cation)				−7	−29		

From proton affinity of C_6HF_5 (RN 363-72-4). PA = 179.9 kcal/mol, 753. kJ/mol.

$C_6H_2N_2S^+$ (2,5-dicyanothiophene)	≤9.76 IP from 83BOC/ROT.	(≤319)	(≤1337)	94	395	*EST	18853-40-2
(3,4-dicyanothiophene)	(≤10.20) IP from 83BOC/ROT.	(≤331)	(≤1384)	96	400	*EST	18853-32-2
$C_6H_3Cl_2NOS^+$ (3,5-dichlorophenyl-N-sulfinyl)	(≤9.46) IP from 82LOU/VAN.	(≤197)	(≤826)	−21	−87	*EST	
$C_6H_3Cl_3^+$ (1,2,3-trichlorobenzene)	9.18 IP from 81RUS/KLA3.	209.8	877.6	−1.9	−8.1	85PLA/SIM	87-61-6
(1,2,4-trichlorobenzene)	9.04 IP from 81RUS/KLA3	210	880	1.9	8.1	85PLA/SIM	120-82-1
(1,3,5-trichlorobenzene)	9.32±0.02	215	899	0	0	82SHA	108-70-3

IP from 81RUS/KLA(3), onset of photoelectron band (81KIM/KAT). See also: 82MAI/THO2.

ION Neutral	Ionization potential eV	$\Delta_f H$(Ion) kcal/mol	$\Delta_f H$(Ion) kJ/mol	$\Delta_f H$(Neutral) kcal/mol	$\Delta_f H$(Neutral) kJ/mol	Neutral reference	CAS registry number
$C_6H_3F_3^+$							
1,2,3-trifluorobenzene	(9.7) IP from 81BIE/ASB.	(107)	(448)	−117	−488	*EST	1489-53-8
1,2,4-trifluorobenzene	9.30±0.05 IP from charge transfer equilibrium constant determinations (standard: IP of $C_6H_5CF_3$, 9.685 eV)(78LIA/AUS) and from photoelectron spectroscopy (81BIE/ASB, 77ROS/DRA).	(96)	(401)	−119	−496	*EST	367-23-7
1,3,5-trifluorobenzene	9.64 See also: 81BIE/ASB.	(100)	(418)	−122±0.7	−512±3	*EST	372-38-3
$C_6H_3F_4^+$							
(1,2,3,4-$C_6F_4H_2$)H+	From proton affinity of 1,2,3,4-$C_6F_4H_2$ (RN 551-62-2). PA = 181.1 kcal/mol, 758. kJ/mol.	32	134				
1,2,3,5-$C_6F_4H_2$·H	From proton affinity of 1,2,3,5-$C_6F_4H_2$ (RN 2367-82-0). PA = 180.6 kcal/mol, 756. kJ/mol.	28	117				
1,2,4,5-$C_6F_4H_2$·H	From proton affinity of 1,2,4,5-$C_6F_4H_2$ (RN 327-54-8). PA = 179.7 kcal/mol, 752. kJ/mol.	31	131				
$C_6H_3MnO_5^+$ $CH_3(CO)_5Mn$	(8.4) IP is onset of photoelectron band.	(14)	(57)	−180±1	−753±4	82CON/ZAF	13601-24-6
$C_6H_3N_3O_6^+$ 1,3,5-trinitrobenzene	(10.96±0.02)	(268)	(1119)	15±0.5	62±2	77PED/RYL	99-35-4

Table 1. Positive Ion Table – Continued

ION / Neutral	Ionization potential eV	$\Delta_f H$(Ion) kcal/mol	$\Delta_f H$(Ion) kJ/mol	$\Delta_f H$(Neutral) kcal/mol	$\Delta_f H$(Neutral) kJ/mol	Neutral reference	CAS registry number
$C_6H_3O_5Re^+$							
$(CO)_5CH_3Re$	8.5	14	60	−182±1	−760±6	82PIL/SKI	14524-92-6
	IP is onset of photoelectron band.						
$C_6H_4^+$							
(Z)-HC≡CCH=CHC≡CH	(9.10±0.02)	(333)	(1394)	123	516	*EST	16668-67-0
(E)-HC≡CCH=CHC≡CH	(9.07±0.02)	(334)	(1400)	125	525	*EST	16668-68-1
benzyne	8.6	313	1311	115	481	80POL/HEH	462-80-6
		316	*1321*	*118*	*492*		
	$\Delta_f H$(Ion) from 80ROS/STO2. Cited IP = $\Delta_f H$(Ion) − $\Delta_f H$(Neutral); a value of 8.95 eV has been estimated (80ROS/STO2). See also: 82ROS/DAN, 85DEW/TIE.						
$C_6H_4Br^+$							
bromobenzene	9.04	298	1247	89.6	374.9	77NUY/MES	2973-43-5
	$\Delta_f H$(Ion) from 77NUY/MES. IP is $\Delta_f H$(Ion)−$\Delta_f H$(Neutral).						
$C_6H_4BrNOS^+$							
4-Br-C₆H₄-N=S=O	(≤8.91)	(≤203)	(≤851)	−2	−9	*EST	26516-62-1
	IP from 82LOU/VAN.						
$C_6H_4BrN_2^+$							
4-Br-C₆H₄-N=N·	(8.18)	(276)	(1155)	87	366	*EST	
	$\Delta_f H$(Ion) from 77NUY/MES. IP is $\Delta_f H$(Ion) − $\Delta_f H$(Neutral).						
$C_6H_4Br_2^+$							
1,2-dibromobenzene	8.8	(234)	(981)	31.5	132	*EST	583-53-9
	IP is onset of photoelectron band.						
1,3-dibromobenzene	8.85	235	985	31	131	83DEW/HEA	108-36-1
	IP is onset of photoelectron band.						

Table 1. Positive Ion Table - Continued

ION / Neutral	Ionization potential eV	$\Delta_f H$(Ion) kcal/mol	$\Delta_f H$(Ion) kJ/mol	$\Delta_f H$(Neutral) kcal/mol	$\Delta_f H$(Neutral) kJ/mol	Neutral reference	CAS registry number
$C_6H_4Br_2^+$ 1,4-dibromobenzene	8.7 IP is onset of photoelectron band.	(232)	(970)	31	131	*EST	106-37-6
$C_6H_4ClF^+$ 2-chlorofluorobenzene	9.18±0.01 See also: 78LIA/AUS.	(181)	(756)	−31	−130	*EST	348-51-6
3-chlorofluorobenzene	9.21±0.01	(179)	(749)	−33	−140	*EST	625-98-9
4-chlorofluorobenzene	9.01±0.01 IP from 78LIA/AUS.	(174)	(728)	−34	−141	*EST	352-33-0
$C_6H_4ClNOS^+$	(8.8) IP is onset of photoelectron band (82LOU/VAN).	(188)	(787)	(−15)	(−62)		
$C_6H_4ClNO_2^+$ 3-chloronitrobenzene	(9.92±0.1)	(238)	(995)	9.1±2.0	38.1±8.4	*EST	121-73-3
4-chloronitrobenzene	9.96±0.1	(239)	(999)	9.1±2.0	38.1±8.4	*EST	100-00-5

Table 1. Positive Ion Table - Continued

ION / Neutral	Ionization potential eV	$\Delta_f H$(Ion) kcal/mol	$\Delta_f H$(Ion) kJ/mol	$\Delta_f H$(Neutral) kcal/mol	$\Delta_f H$(Neutral) kJ/mol	Neutral reference	CAS registry number
$C_6H_4Cl_2^+$							
1,2-dichlorobenzene	9.08±0.01	217.3	909.1	7.9	33.0	84PLA/SIM	95-50-1

IP from charge transfer equilibrium constant determination (78LIA/AUS). See also: 81RUS/KLA2, 81KIM/KAT.

1,3-dichlorobenzene	9.11±0.01	216.8	907.1	6.7	28.1	84PLA/SIM	541-73-1

IP from charge transfer equilibrium constant determination (78LIA/AUS). See also: 82LEV/LIA, 81RUS/KLA2, 81KIM/KAT.

1,4-dichlorobenzene	8.89±0.01	210.9	882.3	5.9	24.6	84PLA/SIM	106-46-7

IP from 81RUS/KLA2 (onset of photoelectron band), and 78LIA/AUS (charge transfer equilibrium constant determination). See also: 81KIM/KAT.

ION / Neutral	Ionization potential eV	$\Delta_f H$(Ion) kcal/mol	$\Delta_f H$(Ion) kJ/mol	$\Delta_f H$(Neutral) kcal/mol	$\Delta_f H$(Neutral) kJ/mol	Neutral reference	CAS registry number
$C_6H_4Cl_2O^+$							
2,6-dichlorophenol	(8.65±0.02)	(174)	(729)	−25	−106	82SHA	87-65-0

$C_6H_4FNO_2^+$							
2-fluoronitrobenzene	(≤9.86)	(≤199)	(≤833)	−28	−118	*EST	1493-27-2
3-fluoronitrobenzene	9.88	(198)	(827)	−30	−126	*EST	402-67-5
4-fluoronitrobenzene	9.90	(197)	(824)	−31	−131	*EST	350-46-9

$C_6H_4F_2^+$							
1,2-difluorobenzene	(9.28±0.01)	(144)	(602)	−70.2±0.2	−293.8±1.0	77PED/RYL	367-11-3

Ionization potential from charge transfer equilibrium constant determinations (standard: ionization potential of $C_6H_5CF_3$, 9.685 eV). Value of ionization potential from Rydberg series and from photoelectron spectroscopy (81BIE/ASB) = 9.30 eV.

Table 1. Positive Ion Table - Continued

ION / Neutral	Ionization potential eV	$\Delta_f H$(Ion) kcal/mol	$\Delta_f H$(Ion) kJ/mol	$\Delta_f H$(Neutral) kcal/mol	$\Delta_f H$(Neutral) kJ/mol	Neutral reference	CAS registry number
$C_6H_4F_2^+$							
1,3-difluorobenzene	9.33±0.01	141	591	−73.9±0.3	−309.2±1.1	77PED/RYL	372-18-9

Ionization potential from charge transfer equilibrium constant determinations (standard: ionization potential of $C_6H_5CF_3$, 9.685 eV). Value of ionization potential from Rydberg series, 9.35 eV, from photoelectron spectroscopy, 9.32 eV. See also: 81BIE/ASB.

1,4-difluorobenzene	9.14±0.01	137	575	−73.3±0.3	−306.6±1.1	77PED/RYL	540-36-3

Ionization potential from charge transfer equilibrium constant determinations (standard: ionization potential of $C_6H_5CF_3$, 9.685 eV). Value of ionization potential from Rydberg series, 9.18 eV, from photoionization and photoelectron spectroscopy, 9.14 eV (81BIE/ASB).

$C_6H_4F_3^+$							
1,3,5-isomer		62	261				

From proton affinity of 1,3,5-$C_6F_3H_3$ (RN 372-38-3). PA = 181. kcal/mol, 757. kJ/mol.

1,2,4-isomer		69	289				

From proton affinity of 1,2,4-$C_6F_3H_3$ (RN 367-23-7). PA = 181.4 kcal/mol, 759. kJ/mol.

$C_6H_4F_3N^+$							
4-(trifluoromethyl)pyridine	(≤10.1)	(≤105)	(≤438)	−128	−536	*EST	3796-24-5

$C_6H_4F_3NO^+$							
4-(trifluoromethyl)pyridine N-oxide	(≤8.90)	(≤58)	(≤243)	−147	−616	*EST	

$C_6H_4FeO_4^+$							
(ethylene)Fe(CO)$_4$	(7.6)	(46)	(192)	−129±2	−541±10	82PIL/SKI	32799-25-0

IP is onset of photoelectron band.

Table 1. Positive Ion Table - Continued

ION Neutral	Ionization potential eV	$\Delta_f H$(Ion) kcal/mol kJ/mol		$\Delta_f H$(Neutral) kcal/mol kJ/mol		Neutral reference	CAS registry number
$C_6H_4I_2^+$							
(1,4-diiodobenzene)	8.45	(252)	(1056)	58	241	*EST	624-38-4
	IP is onset of photoelectron band.						
$C_6H_4MnO_5^+$							
$CH_3MnH(CO)_5$		3	11				
	From proton affinity of $CH_3Mn(CO)_5$ (RN 13601-24-6). PA = 183 kcal/mol, 766 kJ/mol.						
$C_6H_4NO_2^+$							
(nitrobenzene radical)	(9.06)	(283)	(1183)	74	309	*EST	2395-99-5
	IP from 77NUY/MES.						
$C_6H_4N_2^+$							
(2-cyanopyridine)	10.12	301	1260	67±0.5	281±2	84BIC/PIL	100-70-9
(3-cyanopyridine)	(10.0)	(297)	(1243)	66±0.5	278±2	84BIC/PIL	100-54-9
	IP is onset of photoelectron band.						
(4-cyanopyridine)	(9.9)	(296)	(1239)	68±0.2	284±1	84BIC/PIL	100-48-1
	IP is onset of photoelectron band.						
$C_6H_4N_2O^+$							
(2-cyanopyridine N-oxide)	(8.96±0.02)	(256)	(1069)	49	204	*EST	2402-98-4
(3-cyanopyridine N-oxide)	(≤8.93±0.02)	(≤254)	(≤1064)	48	202	*EST	14906-64-0

Table 1. Positive Ion Table – Continued

ION / Neutral	Ionization potential eV	$\Delta_f H$(Ion) kcal/mol	kJ/mol	$\Delta_f H$(Neutral) kcal/mol	kJ/mol	Neutral reference	CAS registry number
$C_6H_4N_2O^+$							
(4-cyanopyridine N-oxide)	8.95±0.02	(255)	(1068)	49	204	*EST	14906-59-3
(benzofurazan)	(9.37)	(288)	(1205)	72±0.5	301±2	80ARS	273-09-6
$C_6H_4N_2O_4^+$							
(1,2-dinitrobenzene)	(≤10.71)	(≤267)	(≤1119)	21±0.5	86±2	76FER/PIA	528-29-0
(1,3-dinitrobenzene)	10.43±0.02	255	1065	14±0.2	59±1	76FER/PIA	99-65-0
(1,4-dinitrobenzene)	10.3±0.1	251	1051	14±0.7	57±3	76FER/PIA	100-25-4
$C_6H_4N_2Se^+$							
(benzoselenadiazole) IP is onset of photoelectron band.	(8.5)	(292)	(1223)	96	403	*EST	273-92-7
$C_6H_4N_3O_2^+$							
(4-nitrobenzenediazonium) IP from 77NUY/MES.	(7.89)	(258)	(1079)	76	318	*EST	

Table 1. Positive Ion Table – Continued

ION / Neutral	Ionization potential eV	$\Delta_f H$(Ion) kcal/mol	$\Delta_f H$(Ion) kJ/mol	$\Delta_f H$(Neutral) kcal/mol	$\Delta_f H$(Neutral) kJ/mol	Neutral reference	CAS registry number
$C_6H_4N_4^+$ (pyrazino-pyrazine)	(8.9)	(295)	(1233)	89	374	*EST	255-53-8

IP is onset of photoelectron band (84GLE/SPA2).

$C_6H_4O^+$ (cyclopentadienyl ketene)	8.2	(214)	(895)	25±1	104±6	*EST	4727-22-4

IP is onset of photoelectron band (79SCH/SCH, 81BOC/HIR).

$C_6H_4O_2^+$ (p-benzoquinone)	10.04±0.18	202	846	−29±1	−123±4	77PED/RYL	106-51-4

See also: 83BOC/MOH.

(o-benzoquinone)	(9.3)	(189)	(791)	−25±1	−106±4	*EST	583-63-1

IP is onset of photoelectron band.

$C_6H_4O_3^+$	(9.0)	(119)	(498)	−88	−370	*EST	81640-31-5

IP is onset of photoelectron band (81BEC/HOF).

$C_6H_5^+$ (phenyl radical)	8.25	269.3 / 272.8	1126.9 / 1141.3	79±1	329±4	82MCM/GOL	2396-01-2

$\Delta_f H$(Ion) from appearance potential measurements(86MAL/LIF). See also: 83DAN/ROS, 85MAL/ARA, 76BAE/TSA, 84LIF/MAL, 80ROS/STO, 81PRA/CHU, 84GEF/LIF, 85DUN, 74BEA, 84PAN/BAE, 85PAN/BAE, 85PAN/BAE2, 86NIS/DAS and 84BUR/HOL.
IP given is $\Delta_f H$(Ion) - $\Delta_f H$(Neutral). Experimental IP of radical = 8.1-8.2 eV.

$C_6H_5BCl_2^+$ (phenyl-BCl_2)	(9.3)	(151)	(631)	−64±0.5	−266±2	77PED/RYL	873-51-8

IP is onset of photoelectron band.

Table 1. Positive Ion Table — Continued

ION / Neutral	Ionization potential eV	$\Delta_f H$(Ion) kcal/mol	$\Delta_f H$(Ion) kJ/mol	$\Delta_f H$(Neutral) kcal/mol	$\Delta_f H$(Neutral) kJ/mol	Neutral reference	CAS registry number
$C_6H_5Br^+$ (bromobenzene)	8.98±0.02	232 / 237	971 / 993	24.9±0.7 / 30.1±0.7	104.3±3.1 / 126.1±3.1	77PED/RYL	108-86-1

IP from 78LIA/AUS, 82LEV/LIA, onset of photoelectron band in 81KIM/KAT.
See also: 82VON/ASB, 83KLA/KOV, 86FUJ/OHN.

| $C_6H_5BrHg^+$ (C$_6$H$_5$—HgBr) | (9.1) | (248) | (1037) | 38 | 159 | *EST | 1192-89-8 |

IP is onset of photoelectron band (81BAI/CHI).

| $C_6H_5Cl^+$ (chlorobenzene) | 9.06±0.02 | 222 | 929 | 13.0±0.2 | 54.4±0.9 | 85PLA/SIM | 108-90-7 |

See also: 78LIA/AUS, 81RUS/KLA2, 82VON/ASB, 83KLA/KOV, 81KIM/KAT, 86FUJ/OHN.

| $C_6H_5ClHg^+$ (C$_6$H$_5$—HgCl) | 9.14±0.04 | 240.5 | 1006.2 | 29.7 | 124.3 | 85DEW/GRA | 100-56-1 |

See also: 81BAI/CHI.

| $C_6H_5ClO^+$ (3-chlorophenol) | (8.65) | (163) | (682) | −37±2 | −153±9 | 77PED/RYL | 108-43-0 |

IP from 85OIK/ABE.

| (4-chlorophenol) | (≤8.69) | (≤165) | (692) | −35±2 | −146±9 | 77PED/RYL | 106-48-9 |

| (cyclopentadienyl acid chloride) | (8.9) | (194) | (813) | −11 | −46 | *EST | 78957-21-8 |

IP is onset of photoelectron band (81BOC/HIR).

Table 1. Positive Ion Table – Continued

ION / Neutral	Ionization potential eV	$\Delta_f H$(Ion) kcal/mol	$\Delta_f H$(Ion) kJ/mol	$\Delta_f H$(Neutral) kcal/mol	$\Delta_f H$(Neutral) kJ/mol	Neutral reference	CAS registry number
$C_6H_5Cl_2N^+$ 2,6-dichloroaniline	(7.60±0.02)	(182)	(763)	7	30	*EST	608-31-1
$C_6H_5Cl_3Si^+$ phenyltrichlorosilane IP from 84VES/HAR.	(9.10)	(115)	(481)	−95	−397	*EST	98-13-5
$C_6H_5F^+$ fluorobenzene See also: 81BIE/ASB, 81KIM/KAT, 86FUJ/OHN.	9.200±0.005	184.4	771.6	−27.7±0.3	−116.0±1.4	77PED/RYL	462-06-6
$C_6H_5FO^+$ 2-fluorophenol IP from 85OIK/ABE.	8.68±0.02	(131)	(548)	−69	−289	*EST	367-12-4
3-fluorophenol IP from 85OIK/ABE.	8.73±0.02	(131)	(547)	−71	−295	*EST	372-20-3
4-fluorophenol IP is onset of photoelectron band.	(8.5)	(126)	(529)	−70	−291	*EST	371-41-5
$C_6H_5F_2^+$ (from 1,2-difluorobenzene) From proton affinity of 1,2-difluorobenzene (RN 367-11-3). PA = 181.8 kcal/mol, 761. kJ/mol.		114	475				
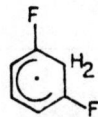 (from 1,3-difluorobenzene) From proton affinity of 1,3-difluorobenzene (RN 372-18-9) (82MAS/BOH). PA = 181.9 kcal/mol, 761. kJ/mol.		110	460				

Table 1. Positive Ion Table – Continued

ION / Neutral	Ionization potential eV	$\Delta_f H$(Ion) kcal/mol	$\Delta_f H$(Ion) kJ/mol	$\Delta_f H$(Neutral) kcal/mol	$\Delta_f H$(Neutral) kJ/mol	Neutral reference	CAS registry number

$C_6H_5F_2^+$

| 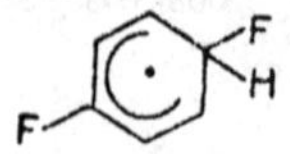 | | 111 | 465 | | | | |

From proton affinity of 1,4-difluorobenzene (RN 540-36-3). PA = 181.2 kcal/mol, 758. kJ/mol.

$C_6H_5F_3N^+$

| 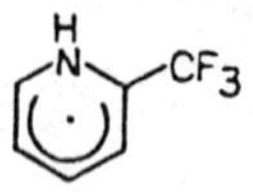 | | 27 | 113 | | | | |

From proton affinity of 2-trifluoromethylpyridine (RN 368-48-9). PA = 211.5 kcal/mol, 885. kJ/mol.

| 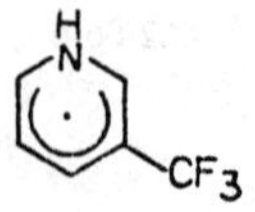 | | 25 | 104 | | | | |

From proton affinity of 3-trifluoromethylpyridine (RN 3796-23-4). PA = 212.6 kcal/mol, 889. kJ/mol.

| 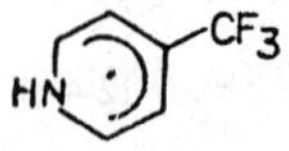 | | 25 | 104 | | | | |

From proton affinity of 4-trifluoromethylpyridine (RN 3796-24-5). PA = 212.8 kcal/mol, 890. kJ/mol.

$C_6H_5F_3Si^+$

| 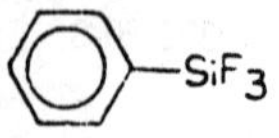 | (9.18) | (−50) | (−207) | −261 | −1093 | *EST | 368-47-8 |

IP from 84VES/HAR.

$C_6H_5FeIO_3^+$

| 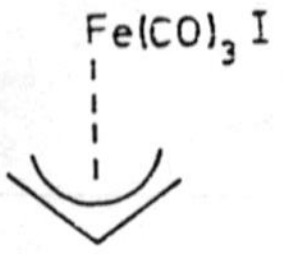 | 8.17 | 106 | 444 | −82±3 | −344±11 | 82PIL/SKI | 12189-10-5 |

IP is onset of photoelectron band (82LOU/HAR).

$C_6H_5I^+$

|  | 8.685 | 240 | 1003 | 39.4±1.4 | 164.9±5.9 | 77PED/RYL | 591-50-4 |
| | | 243 | 1019 | 43.2±1.4 | 180.9±5.9 | | |

See also: 83KLA/KOV, 83DAN/ROS, 81KIM/KAT, 86FUJ/OHN.

Table 1. Positive Ion Table - Continued

ION / Neutral	Ionization potential eV	$\Delta_f H$(Ion) kcal/mol	$\Delta_f H$(Ion) kJ/mol	$\Delta_f H$(Neutral) kcal/mol	$\Delta_f H$(Neutral) kJ/mol	Neutral reference	CAS registry number
$C_6H_5NO^+$ (nitrosobenzene)	(8.09)	(235)	(982)	48±1	201±4	75CHO/GOL	586-96-9
$C_6H_5NOS^+$ (N-sulfinylaniline)	(8.8)	(196)	(819)	−7	−30	*EST	1122-83-4
	IP is onset of photoelectron band (82LOU/VAN).						
$C_6H_5NO_2^+$ (nitrobenzene)	9.86±0.02	243	1019	16.1±0.2	67.6±1	77PED/RYL	98-95-3
		250	1045	22	92		
	See also: 83KLA/KOV, 81KIM/KAT, 81ALL/MIG, 82ALL/MIG, 73GOL/KOR.						
	0 K values from 84PAN/BAE, 85PAN/BAE2.						
$C_6H_5NO_3^+$ (2-nitrophenol)	(9.1)	(187)	(780)	−23	−98	*EST	88-75-5
	IP is onset of photoelectron band.						
(3-nitrophenol)	(9.0)	(181)	(757)	−27	−111	*EST	554-84-7
	IP is onset of photoelectron band.						
(4-nitrophenol)	(9.1)	(182)	(762)	−28	−116	*EST	100-02-7
	IP is onset of photoelectron band.						
$C_6H_5N_2^+$ (protonated 2-pyridinecarbonitrile)		225	943				
	From proton affinity of 2-pyridinecarbonitrile. (RN 100-70-9).						
	208.1 kcal/mol, 871. kJ/mol.						

Table 1. Positive Ion Table – Continued

ION / Neutral	Ionization potential eV	$\Delta_f H$(Ion) kcal/mol	$\Delta_f H$(Ion) kJ/mol	$\Delta_f H$(Neutral) kcal/mol	$\Delta_f H$(Neutral) kJ/mol	Neutral reference	CAS registry number

$C_6H_5N_2^+$

(3-pyridinecarbonitrile, protonated, H on ring N)
| 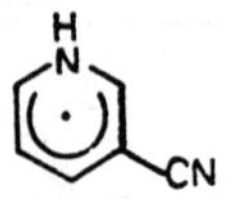 | | 222 | 932 | | | | |

From proton affinity of 3-pyridinecarbonitrile (RN 100-54-9).
PA = 209.3 kcal/mol, 876. kJ/mol.

(4-pyridinecarbonitrile, protonated)
| 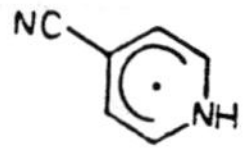 | | 223 | 934 | | | | |

From proton affinity of 4-pyridinecarbonitrile (RN 100-48-1).
PA = 210.3 kcal/mol, 880 kJ/mol.

$C_6H_5N_3^+$

(phenyl azide)
| 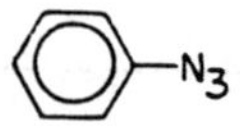 | (8.4) | (286) | (1195) | 92 | 385 | 29ROT/MUE | 622-37-7 |

IP is onset of photoelectron band.

(benzotriazole)
| 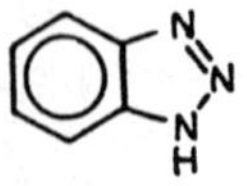 | (9.20±0.05) | (295) | (1236) | 83 | 348 | 61ZIM/GEI | 95-14-7 |

$C_6H_5O^+$

(phenoxy)
| 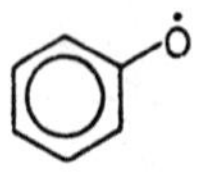 | (8.56) | (208) | (870) | 11.4 | 48 | 82MCM/GOL | 2122-46-5 |
| | | (212) | (888) | | | | |

$\Delta_f H$(Ion) from appearance potential determinations (84LOS/HOL). IP from 80DEW/DAV. See also: 84PAN/BAE, 85PAN/BAE, 85PAN/BAE2, 86DAS/GIL.

$C_6H_5S^+$

(phenylthio)
| 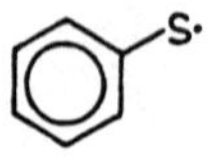 | (8.63±0.10) | (254) | (1063) | 55±2 | 230±8 | 82MCM/GOL | 4985-62-0 |

$C_6H_6^+$

$CH_2=C=CHCH=C=CH_2$
| | (8.53) | (295) | (1234) | 98 | 411 | 82ROS/DAN | 29776-96-3 |
| | | (299) | (1251) | 102 | 428 | | |

$HC\equiv CCH_2CH=C=CH_2$
| | (9.40) | (316) | (1321) | 99 | 414 | 82ROS/DAN | 33142-15-3 |
| | | (320) | (1339) | 103 | 432 | | |

IP from 82ROS/DAN (onset of photoelectron band).

Table 1. Positive Ion Table - Continued

ION / Neutral	Ionization potential eV	$\Delta_f H$(Ion) kcal/mol	$\Delta_f H$(Ion) kJ/mol	$\Delta_f H$(Neutral) kcal/mol	$\Delta_f H$(Neutral) kJ/mol	Neutral reference	CAS registry number
$C_6H_6^+$							
HC≡CCH=CHCH=CH$_2$	(9.20)	(299)	(1253)	87	365	82ROS/DAN	10420-90-3
		(303)	(1270)	91	382		
IP from 82ROS/DAN.							
CH$_2$=CHC≡CCH=CH$_2$	(8.50±0.02)	(280)	(1172)	84	352	82ROS/DAN	821-08-9
		(284)	(1189)	88	369		
See also: 85DEW/TIE.							
HC≡CC≡CC$_2$H$_5$	(9.41)	(312)	(1306)	95	398	82ROS/DAN	4447-21-6
		(316)	(1323)	99	415		
IP from 82ROS/DAN.							
HC≡CCH$_2$C≡CCH$_3$	(9.50)	(317)	(1328)	98	411	82ROS/DAN	10420-91-4
		(321)	(1345)	102	428		
IP from 82ROS/DAN (onset of photoelectron band).							
HC≡CCH$_2$CH$_2$C≡CH	9.90	327	1369	99	414	82ROS/DAN	628-16-0
		331	1387	103	432		
See also: 82ROS/DAN.							
CH$_3$C≡CC≡CCH$_3$	8.92±0.05	296	1238	90	377	82ROS/DAN	2809-69-0
		299	1255	94	394		
See also: 82ROS/DAN.							
benzene	9.2459±0.0002	233.2	975.8	19.8±0.1	82.9±0.3	77PED/RYL	71-43-2
		237.2	992.6	24.0±0.2	100.4±1		
IP from 84GRU/WHE. IP at 298 K = 9.225±0.005 (78LIA/AUS). See also: 81KIM/KAT, 81KIM/KAT, 84HOW/GON.							
5-methylene-1,3-cyclopentadiene	(8.36)	(246)	(1030)	53.5	223.8	84ROT	497-20-1
		(251)	(1048)	57.8	241.9		
1,2-dimethylenecyclobutene	(8.80)	(283)	(1184)	80.4	335.5	86ROT/LEN	5291-90-7
		(286)	(1198)	83	349		

Table 1. Positive Ion Table - Continued

ION / Neutral	Ionization potential eV	$\Delta_f H$(Ion) kcal/mol	$\Delta_f H$(Ion) kJ/mol	$\Delta_f H$(Neutral) kcal/mol	$\Delta_f H$(Neutral) kJ/mol	Neutral reference	CAS registry number

$C_6H_6^+$

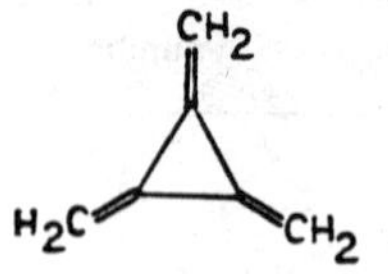

[3,4-dimethylene-1-methylenecyclopropane structure]

(8.80) | (298) | (1245) | 95 | 396 | 82ROS/DAN | 3227-90-5
  | (302) | (1263) | 99 | 414 | |

IP from 82ROS/DAN (onset of photoelectron band).

[bicyclopropenyl / Dewar benzene-like structure]

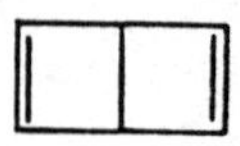

(9.0) | (294) | (1232) | 87 | 364 | 82ROS/DAN | 5649-95-6
  | (298) | (1250) | 91 | 382 | |

IP from 82ROS/DAN (onset of photoelectron band).

[benzvalene structure]

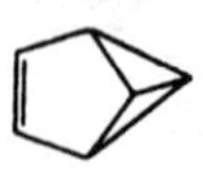

8.1 | (274) | (1144) | 87 | 363 | 82ROS/DAN | 659-85-8
  | (278) | (1163) | 91 | 381 | |

IP from 82ROS/DAN (onset of photoelectron band).

$C_6H_6Br^+$

[protonated bromobenzene structure]

  | 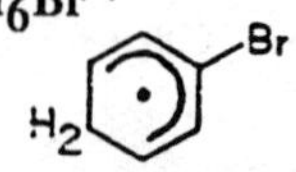 208 | 871 | | | |

From proton affinity of C_6H_5Br (RN 108-86-1). PA = 182.4 kcal/mol, 763. kJ/mol.

$C_6H_6Cl^+$

[protonated chlorobenzene structure]

  | 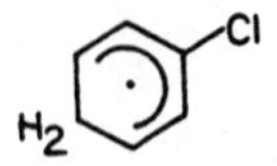 196 | 821 | | | |

From proton affinity of C_6H_5Cl (RN 108-90-7). PA = 181.7 kcal/mol, 760. kJ/mol.

$C_6H_6ClN^+$

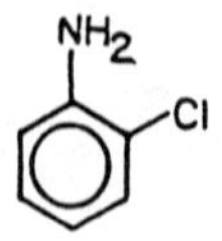

[2-chloroaniline structure]

(8.50) | (211) | (881) | 15 | 61 | *EST | 95-51-2

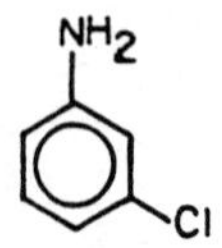

[3-chloroaniline structure]

(8.09±0.1) | (200) | (836) | 13 | 55 | *EST | 108-42-9

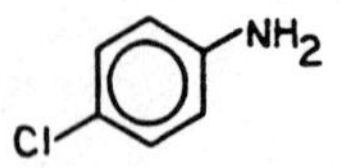

[4-chloroaniline structure]

(≤8.18) | (≤202) | (≤844) | 13 | 55 | *EST | 106-47-8

Table 1. Positive Ion Table - Continued

ION / Neutral	Ionization potential eV	$\Delta_f H$(Ion) kcal/mol	$\Delta_f H$(Ion) kJ/mol	$\Delta_f H$(Neutral) kcal/mol	$\Delta_f H$(Neutral) kJ/mol	Neutral reference	CAS registry number
$C_6H_6F^+$							
fluorobenzene (H₂ adduct)		155	650				

From proton affinity of C_6H_5F (RN 462-06-6). PA = 182.6 kcal/mol, 764. kJ/mol.

$C_6H_6FN^+$							
2-fluoroaniline	(≤8.18)	(≤164)	(≤683)	−25	−106	*EST	348-54-9
3-fluoroaniline	(≤8.32)	(≤165)	(≤691)	−27	−112	*EST	372-19-0
4-fluoroaniline	(≤8.18)	(≤163)	(≤680)	−26	−109	*EST	371-40-4

$C_6H_6Hg^+$							
$(CH_3C{\equiv}C)_2Hg$	8.98±0.07	(323)	(1351)	116	485	*EST	64705-15-3

IP is onset of photoelectron band (81FUR/PIA).

$C_6H_6N^+$							
anilino radical	(8.26±0.1)	(247)	(1034)	57±2	237±8	82MCM/GOL	2835-77-0

$C_6H_6NO^+$							
nitrosobenzene (protonated)		209	874				

From proton affinity of nitrosobenzene (RN 586-96-9). PA = 204.8 kcal/mol, 857. kJ/mol.

| | | (156) | (654) | | | | |

From proton affinity of 4-pyridinecarboxaldehyde (RN 872-85-5). PA = (215.2) kcal/mol, (900.) kJ/mol.

Table 1. Positive Ion Table - Continued

ION Neutral	Ionization potential eV	Δ_fH(Ion) kcal/mol kJ/mol		Δ_fH(Neutral) kcal/mol kJ/mol		Neutral reference	CAS registry number
$C_6H_6NO_2^+$ (phenyl-N(O)OH)		189	789				
	From proton affinity of nitrobenzene (RN 98-95-3). PA = 193.4 kcal/mol, 809. kJ/mol.						
$C_6H_6N_2^+$ (diimino-cyclohexadiene)	(9.36±0.03)	(294)	(1229)	78±1	326±5	*EST	4377-73-5
$C_6H_6N_2O_2^+$ (2-nitroaniline)	8.27±0.01	206	862	15±1	64±4	77PED/RYL	88-74-4
(3-nitroaniline)	8.31±0.02	207	864	15±0.5	62±2	83NIS/SAK	99-09-2
(4-nitroaniline)	8.34±0.01	205	860	13±0.5	55±2	83NIS/SAK	100-01-6
$C_6H_6N_4^+$ (6-methylpurine)	(8.9)	(248)	(1037)	43	178	*EST	2004-03-7
	IP is onset of photoelectron band.						
$C_6H_6O^+$ (phenol)	8.47	173 175	722 732	−23.0±0.2 −20.4	−96.3±0.8 −85.2	78KUD/KUD	108-95-2
	IP from 84FRA/FRA. See also: 84FUK/YOS, 83KLA/KOV, 81KIM/KAT.						

Table 1. Positive Ion Table – Continued

ION Neutral	Ionization potential eV	$\Delta_f H$(Ion) kcal/mol	$\Delta_f H$(Ion) kJ/mol	$\Delta_f H$(Neutral) kcal/mol	$\Delta_f H$(Neutral) kJ/mol	Neutral reference	CAS registry number
$C_6H_6OS^+$							
2-acetylthiophene	(9.20±0.05)	(206)	(862)	−6	−26	*EST	88-15-3
3-acetylthiophene	(9.32±0.05)	(209)	(875)	−6	−24	*EST	1468-83-3
$C_6H_6O_2^+$							
catechol	(8.15) IP is onset of photoelectron band.	(123)	(514)	−65±1	−272±5	79KUD/KUD	120-80-9
resorcinol	(8.2) IP is onset of photoelectron band.	(123)	(514)	−65.6±0.5	−274.7±2.1	79KUD/KUD	108-46-3
hydroquinone	7.95±0.03 IP from 85OIK/ABE.	121	505	−63±0.5	−262±2	79KUD/KUD	123-31-9
2-cyclohexene-1,4-dione	(9.77) IP is onset of photoelectron band (85GLE/JAH).	(205)	(859)	−20	−84	*EST	4505-38-8
bicyclic diketone	(9.4) IP is onset of photoelectron band (81BEC/HOF).	(170)	(713)	−46	−194	*EST	29798-87-6
$C_6H_6O_3^+$							
methyl 2-furoate	(≤9.00±0.05)	(≤110)	(≤463)	−97	−405	80BAL/LEB	611-13-2

Table 1. Positive Ion Table — Continued

ION / Neutral	Ionization potential eV	$\Delta_f H$(Ion) kcal/mol	$\Delta_f H$(Ion) kJ/mol	$\Delta_f H$(Neutral) kcal/mol	$\Delta_f H$(Neutral) kJ/mol	Neutral reference	CAS registry number
$C_6H_6O_4^+$ (dimethyl squarate, H_3CO, H_3CO substituted cyclobutenedione)	≤9.20	(≤107)	(≤447)	−105	−441	*EST	5222-73-1
$C_6H_6S^+$ (PhSH)	8.30±0.02	218	913	26.9±0.2	112.4±0.8	77PED/RYL	108-98-5

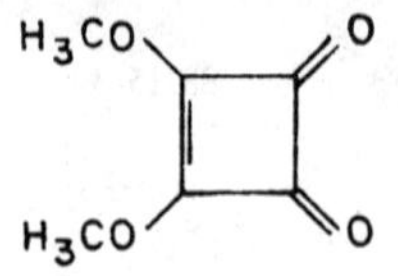

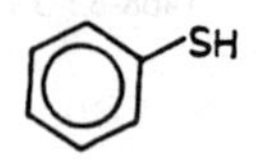

See also: 82CAR/KIB, 81KIM/KAT.

$C_6H_6Se^+$ (PhSeH)	(≤7.7)	(≤217)	(≤906)	39	163	*EST	645-96-5

IP is onset of photoelectron band (81BAK/ARM).

$C_6H_7^+$

(protonated benzene)

		204	854				

From proton affinity of benzene. (RN 71-43-2). PA = 181.3 kcal/mol, 759. kJ/mol.

$(HC\equiv CCH_2CH_2C\equiv CH)H$

		269	1124				

From proton affinity of $HC\equiv C(CH_2)_2C\equiv CH$ (RN 628-16-0) (85LIA/AUS). PA = 196 kcal/mol, 819 kJ/mol.

$(CH_3C\equiv CC\equiv CCH_3)H$

		260	1087				

From proton affinity of $CH_3C\equiv CC\equiv CCH_3$ (RN 2809-69-0) (85LIA/AUS). PA = 196 kcal/mol, 819 kJ/mol.

$C_6H_7BrN^+$ (protonated 3-bromoaniline)

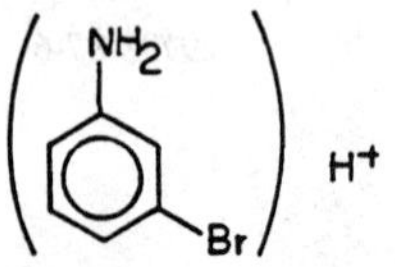		183	767				

From proton affinity of 3-$BrC_6H_4NH_2$ (RN 591-19-5).

$C_6H_7Br_3Ti^+$ (methylcyclopentadienyl titanium tribromide)

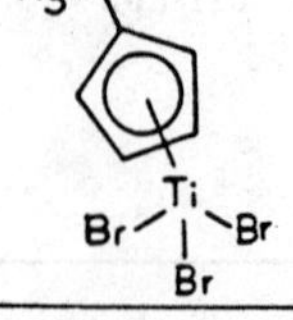	(8.6)	(80)	(337)	−118	−493	*EST	1277-45-8

IP is onset of photoelectron band (84TER/LOU).

Table 1. Positive Ion Table - Continued

ION / Neutral	Ionization potential eV	$\Delta_f H$(Ion) kcal/mol kJ/mol	$\Delta_f H$(Neutral) kcal/mol kJ/mol	Neutral reference	CAS registry number

$C_6H_7ClN^+$

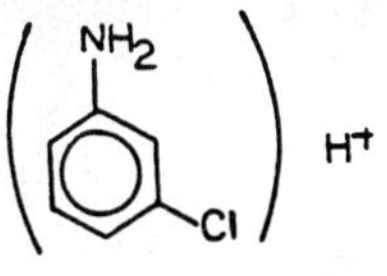

(3-ClC$_6$H$_4$NH$_2$)·H⁺ — 172   718
From proton affinity of 3-ClC$_6$H$_4$NH$_2$ (RN 108-42-9). PA = 207.2 kcal/mol, 867. kJ/mol.

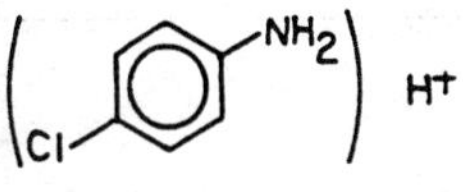

(4-ClC$_6$H$_4$NH$_2$)·H⁺ — 170   712
From proton affinity of 4-ClC$_6$H$_4$NH$_2$ (RN 106-47-8). PA = 208.6 kcal/mol, 873. kJ/mol.

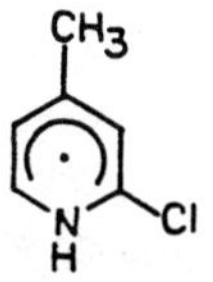

(2-chloro-4-methylpyridine)·H⁺ — (163) (681)
From proton affinity of 2-chloro-4-methylpyridine (RN 3678-62-4). (218.6) kcal/mol, (915.) kJ/mol.

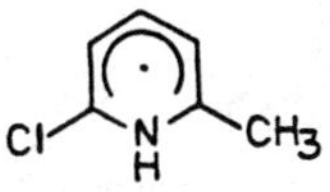

(2-chloro-6-methylpyridine)·H⁺ — (161) (675)
From proton affinity of 2-chloro-6-methylpyridine (RN 18368-63-3). PA = (219) kcal/mol, (916) kJ/mol.

$C_6H_7ClNO^+$

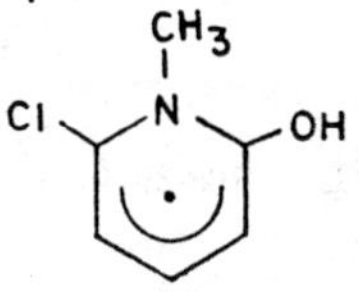

(6-chloro-1-methyl-2(1H)pyridinone)·H⁺ — 127   531
From proton affinity of 6-chloro-1-methyl-2(1H)pyridinone (RN 17228-63-6). PA = 217.8 kcal/mol, 911. kJ/mol.

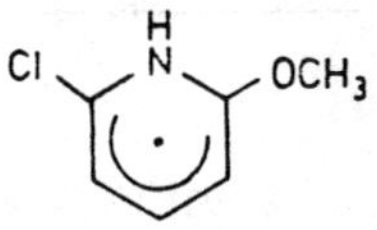

(2-chloro-6-methoxypyridine)·H⁺ — 129   538
From proton affinity of 2-chloro-6-methoxypyridine (RN 17228-64-7). PA = 215.9 kcal/mol, 903. kJ/mol.

$C_6H_7Cl_3Ti^+$

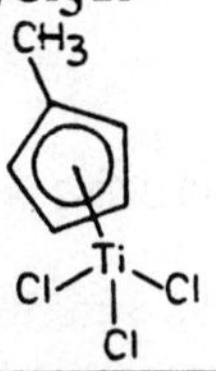

(methylcyclopentadienyl)TiCl$_3$ — (9.1)   (66)   (276)   −144   −602   *EST   1282-31-1
IP is onset of photoelectron band (84TER/LOU).

$C_6H_7FN^+$

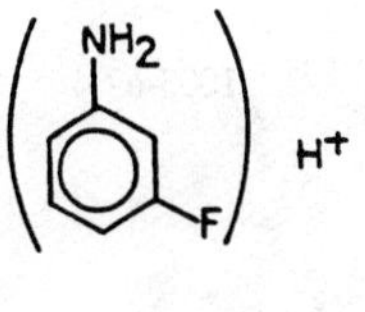

(3-F-C$_6$H$_4$NH$_2$)·H⁺ — 132   552
From proton affinity of 3-fluorobenzeneamine (RN 372-19-0). PA = 207.0 kcal/mol, 866. kJ/mol.

Table 1. Positive Ion Table - Continued

ION / Neutral	Ionization potential eV	$\Delta_f H$(Ion) kcal/mol	$\Delta_f H$(Ion) kJ/mol	$\Delta_f H$(Neutral) kcal/mol	$\Delta_f H$(Neutral) kJ/mol	Neutral reference	CAS registry number
$C_6H_7FN^+$ (4-fluorobenzeneamine)H⁺		132	550				
From proton affinity of 4-fluorobenzeneamine (RN 371-40-4). PA = 208.1 kcal/mol, 871. kJ/mol.							
$C_6H_7N^+$							
aniline	7.720±0.002	198	829	20.8±0.2	87.1±0.8	77PED/RYL	62-53-3
IP from 84SMI/HAG. See also: 83KLA/KOV, 81KIM/KAT, 85MEE/SEK, 85HAG/SMI.							
2-methylpyridine	9.02±0.03	232	969	23.7±0.2	99.2±0.7	77PED/RYL	109-06-8
See also: 81KIM/KAT.							
3-methylpyridine	9.04±0.03	234	979	25.4±0.1	106.4±0.5	77PED/RYL	108-99-6
See also: 81MOD/DIS2, 81KIM/KAT.							
4-methylpyridine	9.04±0.03	233	976	24.8±0.3	103.8±1.2	77PED/RYL	108-89-4
$C_6H_7NO^+$							
2-methylpyridine N-oxide	≤8.21±0.02	(≤194)	(≤811)	5	19	*EST	931-19-1
3-methylpyridine N-oxide	(≤8.20±0.02)	(≤195)	(≤817)	6	26	*EST	1003-73-2
4-methylpyridine N-oxide	8.12±0.02	(193)	(807)	6	24	*EST	1003-67-4

Table 1. Positive Ion Table - Continued

ION / Neutral	Ionization potential eV	$\Delta_f H$(Ion) kcal/mol	$\Delta_f H$(Ion) kJ/mol	$\Delta_f H$(Neutral) kcal/mol	$\Delta_f H$(Neutral) kJ/mol	Neutral reference	CAS registry number
$C_6H_7NO^+$							
2-methoxypyridine	(8.7) IP is onset of photoelectron band.	(189)	(787)	−12	−52	*EST	1628-89-3
3-methoxypyridine	(9.34±0.02)	(211)	(885)	−4	−16	*EST	7295-76-3
4-methoxypyridine	(9.58±0.02)	(218)	(911)	−3	−13	*EST	620-08-6
1-methyl-2-pyridone	(8.2) IP is onset of photoelectron band. See also: 81DRE/BEC.	(169)	(706)	−20±2	−85±10	*EST	694-85-9
1-methyl-4-pyridone	(≤8.20±0.03)	(≤186)	(≤778)	−3±2	−13±8	*EST	695-19-2
2-methyl-6-hydroxypyridine	(8.33)	(163)	(684)	−29±0.7	−120±3	82SUR/ELS	73229-70-6
2-methyl-5-hydroxypyridine	(9.15±0.05)	(194)	(813)	−17±0.7	−70±3	82SUR/ELS	1121-78-4
$C_6H_7NO_2^+$							
2-methoxypyridine N-oxide	(7.5) IP is onset of photoelectron band.	(151)	(631)	−22	−93	*EST	1122-96-9

ION / Neutral	Ionization potential eV	$\Delta_f H$(Ion) kcal/mol	kJ/mol	$\Delta_f H$(Neutral) kcal/mol	kJ/mol	Neutral reference	CAS registry number
$C_6H_7NO_2^+$							
2-methoxypyridine N-oxide	(8.21±0.05)	(158)	(660)	−32	−132	*EST	20773-98-2
3-methoxypyridine N-oxide	(8.40±0.05)	(171)	(714)	−23	−96	*EST	14906-61-7
$C_6H_7NS^+$							
2-aminothiophenol	(7.6) IP is onset of photoelectron band (82ZVE/ASH).	(203)	(849)	28	116	*EST	137-07-5
2-(methylthio)pyridine	(8.24±0.03) See also: 81DRE/BEC.	(223)	(933)	33	138	*EST	18438-38-5
3-(methylthio)pyridine	(≤8.41±0.03)	(≤231)	(≤966)	37	155	*EST	18794-33-7
4-(methylthio)pyridine	(≤8.73±0.03)	(≤238)	(≤997)	37	155	*EST	22581-72-2
1-methyl-2(1H)-pyridinethione	(7.69±0.03) See also: 81DRE/BEC.	(218)	(912)	41	170	*EST	2044-27-1
1-methyl-4(1H)-pyridinethione	7.54±0.02	(239)	(999)	65	272	*EST	6887-59-8

Table 1. Positive Ion Table – Continued

ION Neutral	Ionization potential eV	$\Delta_f H$(Ion) kcal/mol	$\Delta_f H$(Ion) kJ/mol	$\Delta_f H$(Neutral) kcal/mol	$\Delta_f H$(Neutral) kJ/mol	Neutral reference	CAS registry number
$C_6H_7NSe^+$							
1-methyl-2(1H)-pyridineselone	≤7.22 IP from 81DRE/BEC.	(≤224)	(≤937)	57	240	*EST	2240-85-9
$C_6H_7N_2O_2^+$							
(4-O_2N-C_6H_4-NH_2)H^+		172	719				
From proton affinity of 4-$NO_2C_6H_4NH_2$ (RN 100-01-6) (84ROL/HOU). PA = 207.0 kcal/mol, 866. kJ/mol.							
$C_6H_7N_4^+$							
(6-methylpurine)H^+		185	775				
From proton affinity of 6-methylpurine (RN 2004-03-7). PA = (223) kcal/mol, (933) kJ/mol.							
$C_6H_7O^+$							
phenol·H (protonated phenol)		146	613				
From proton affinity of C_6H_5OH (RN 108-95-2). PA = 196.3 kcal/mol, 821. kJ/mol.							
$(HC\equiv CCH_2)_2OH$		(246)	(1031)				
From proton affinity of $(HC\equiv CCH_2)_2O$ (RN 6921-27-3). PA = 190.8 kcal/mol, 798. kJ/mol.							
$C_6H_7P^+$							
phenylphosphine	(8.47±0.01) See also: 81CAB/COW2.	(226)	(945)	31	128	*EST	638-21-1
$C_6H_8^+$							
(E)-CH_2=C=CHCH=CHCH$_3$	(8.32)	(244)	(1020)	52	217	*EST	20130-95-4
(Z)-CH_2=CHCH=CHCH=CH_2	8.31±0.01	233	973	41	171	70BEN/O'N	2612-46-6
(E)-CH_2=CHCH=CHCH=CH_2	8.28±0.02	(231)	(965)	40	166	*EST	821-07-8
		(237)	(991)	46	192		
CH_3CH=C=CHCH=CH_2	(8.56)	(250)	(1048)	53	222	*EST	33755-64-5

Table 1. Positive Ion Table - Continued

ION / Neutral	Ionization potential eV	$\Delta_f H$(Ion) kcal/mol	$\Delta_f H$(Ion) kJ/mol	$\Delta_f H$(Neutral) kcal/mol	$\Delta_f H$(Neutral) kJ/mol	Neutral reference	CAS registry number
$C_6H_8^+$							
$CH_2=C=C(CH_3)CH=CH_2$	(8.54)	(249)	(1040)	52	216	*EST	25054-29-9
$CH_2=C=CHC(CH_3)=CH_2$	(8.54)	(249)	(1040)	52	216	*EST	14763-81-6
$C_2H_5C{\equiv}CCH=CH_2$	(8.91±0.01)	(260)	(1090)	55	230	*EST	13721-54-5
$CH_3C{\equiv}CC(CH_3)=CH_2$	(8.72±0.01)	(253)	(1058)	52	217	*EST	926-55-6
1,3-cyclohexadiene	8.25±0.02 See also: 81KIM/KAT.	215.6 / 221.3	902.3 / 926.1	25.4±0.1 / 31.1±0.1	106.3±0.5 / 130.1±0.5	77PED/RYL	592-57-4
1,4-cyclohexadiene	8.82±0.02 See also: 81KIM/KAT.	229 / 235	959 / 985	25.8±0.5 / 32.0±0.5	107.9±2 / 133.9±2	77SHA/GOL	628-41-1
methylcyclopentadiene (1)	8.40±0.05	(217)	(907)	23	97	*EST	96-39-9
methylcyclopentadiene (2)	8.45±0.05	(218)	(911)	23	96	*EST	3727-31-9
methylenecyclopentene	(8.40)	(223)	(931)	29	121	*EST	930-26-7
1,2-bis(methylene)cyclobutane	(8.4) IP is onset of photoelectron band.	(242)	(1011)	48	201	80GAJ	14296-80-1

Table 1. Positive Ion Table – Continued

ION / Neutral	Ionization potential eV	$\Delta_f H$(Ion) kcal/mol kJ/mol	$\Delta_f H$(Neutral) kcal/mol kJ/mol	Neutral reference	CAS registry number
$C_6H_8^+$					
1,3-bis(methylene)cyclobutane	(8.7) (254) (1063) IP is onset of photoelectron band.		54 224	80GAJ	2045-78-5
cyclobutylacetylene	(9.6) (284) (1188) IP is onset of photoelectron band.		63 262	*EST	50786-62-4
bicyclopropylidene	(8.5) (280) (1170) IP is onset of photoelectron band.		84 350	*EST	27567-82-4
bicyclo structure	(9.1) (271) (1135) IP is onset of photoelectron band.		61 257	80ROT/KLA	3097-63-0
tricyclic structure	(≤9.43) (≤272) (≤1138)		54.5 228.0	85SVY/IOF	287-12-7
$C_6H_8Cl_2S_2^+$					
dichloro dithia bicyclic	(7.8) (158) (660) IP is onset of photoelectron band (83JOR/MCC).		−22 −93	*EST	74796-12-6
$C_6H_8F_2S^+$					
thiane=CF$_2$	(9.34) (129) (538) IP from 80SAR/WOR.		−87 −363	*EST	77471-71-7
$C_6H_8N^+$					
$(HC\equiv CCH_2)_2NH_2$		262 1098 From proton affinity of $(HC\equiv CCH_2)_2NH$ (RN 6921-28-4). PA = 216.1 kcal/mol, 904. kJ/mol.			

Table 1. Positive Ion Table – Continued

ION / Neutral	Ionization potential eV	$\Delta_f H$(Ion) kcal/mol	kJ/mol	$\Delta_f H$(Neutral) kcal/mol	kJ/mol	Neutral reference	CAS registry number

$C_6H_8N^+$

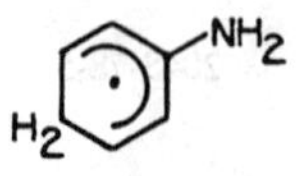

[aniline radical cation, H₂·—C₆H₄—NH₂]
  177 740
From proton affinity of $C_6H_5NH_2$ (RN 62-53-3). PA = 209.5 kcal/mol, 876. kJ/mol.

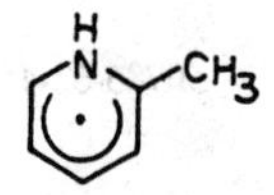

[2-methylpyridine, N–H, ·, CH₃]
  164 688
From proton affinity of 2-methylpyridine (RN 109-06-8). PA = 225.0 kcal/mol, 942. kJ/mol.

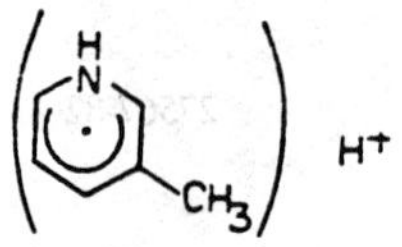

[(3-methylpyridine)H⁺]
  167 698
From proton affinity of 3-methylpyridine (RN 108-99-6). PA = 224.1 kcal/mol, 938. kJ/mol.

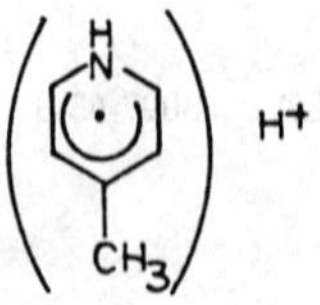

[(4-methylpyridine)H⁺]
  165 692
From proton affinity of 4-methylpyridine (RN 108-89-4). PA = 225.2 kcal/mol, 942. kJ/mol.

$C_6H_8NO^+$

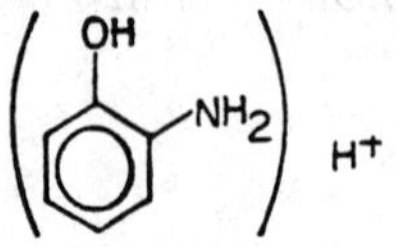

[(2-HOC₆H₄NH₂)H⁺]
  131 547
From proton affinity of 2-$HOC_6H_4NH_2$. PA = 214.2 kcal/mol, 896. kJ/mol.

[3-(OH)C₆H₄NH₂]
  130 545
From proton affinity of 3-$(OH)C_6H_4NH_2$ (RN 591-27-5). PA = 214.2 kcal/mol, 896. kJ/mol.

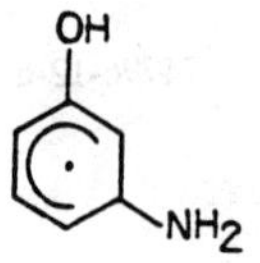

[2-methoxypyridine, N–H, ·, OCH₃]
  131 550
From proton affinity of 2-methoxypyridine (RN 1628-89-3). PA = 221.9 kcal/mol, 928. kJ/mol.

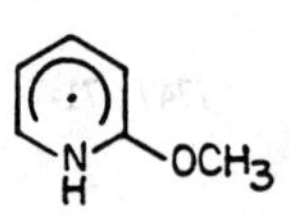

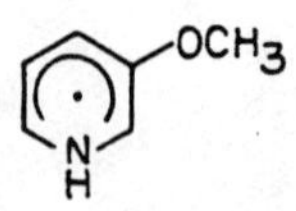

[3-methoxypyridine, N–H, ·, OCH₃]
  138 579
From proton affinity of 3-methoxypyridine (RN 7295-76-3). PA = 223.6 kcal/mol, 935. kJ/mol.

Table 1. Positive Ion Table – Continued

ION / Neutral	Ionization potential eV	$\Delta_f H$(Ion) kcal/mol	$\Delta_f H$(Ion) kJ/mol	$\Delta_f H$(Neutral) kcal/mol	$\Delta_f H$(Neutral) kJ/mol	Neutral reference	CAS registry number

$C_6H_8NO^+$

4-methoxypyridine (protonated) | | 135 | 565 | | | | |

From proton affinity of 4-methoxypyridine (RN 620-08-6). PA = 227.6 kcal/mol, 952. kJ/mol.

1-methyl-2-hydroxypyridine | | 125 | 524 | | | | |

From proton affinity of 1-methyl-2-pyridinone (RN 694-85-9). PA = 220.2 kcal/mol, 921. kJ/mol.

$C_6H_8NS^+$

2-(methylthio)pyridine (protonated) | | 177 | 739 | | | | |

From proton affinity of 2-(methylthio)pyridine (RN 18438-38-5). PA = 222.0 kcal/mol, 929. kJ/mol.

4-(methylthio)pyridine (protonated) | | (177) | (742) | | | | |

From proton affinity of 4-(methylthio)pyridine (RN 22581-72-2). PA = (225.5) kcal/mol, (943.) kJ/mol.

$C_6H_8N_2^+$

1,2-diaminobenzene	7.2	(188)	(787)	22±1	92±5	*EST	95-54-5
See also: 81NEL/GRE.							
1,3-diaminobenzene	7.14	(186)	(777)	21	88	*EST	108-45-2
1,4-diaminobenzene	6.87±0.05	(181)	(760)	23	97	*EST	106-50-3
See also: 81CAB/COW2.							
2-(methylamino)pyridine	(8.26±0.05)	(220)	(924)	30	127	*EST	4597-87-9

Table 1. Positive Ion Table - Continued

ION / Neutral	Ionization potential eV	$\Delta_f H$(Ion) kcal/mol	kJ/mol	$\Delta_f H$(Neutral) kcal/mol	kJ/mol	Neutral reference	CAS registry number
$C_6H_8N_2^+$							
3-(methylamino)pyridine	(8.53±0.05)	(231)	(965)	34	142	*EST	18364-47-1
4-(methylamino)pyridine	(8.75±0.05)	(233)	(972)	31	128	*EST	1121-58-0
phenylhydrazine				48.6±0.2	203.5±0.8	77PED/RYL	100-63-0

Values of 7.64 and 7.74 have been reported for the adiabatic IP of this compound. Reported values of IP's of hydrazines determined by threshold measurements are usually significantly higher than the adiabatic value because of the large geometry change associated with ionization.

2,6-dimethylpyrazine	(8.80)	(270)	(1128)	67±0.7	279±3	*EST	108-50-9
$C_6H_8N_2O^+$							
2-(methylamino)pyridine N-oxide	(7.67±0.05)	(188)	(787)	11	47	*EST	54818-70-1
3-(methylamino)pyridine N-oxide	(7.97±0.05)	(198)	(829)	14	60	*EST	54818-71-2
4-(methylamino)pyridine N-oxide	(7.45±0.05)	(185)	(775)	13	56	*EST	1122-92-5
$C_6H_8O^+$ $HC{\equiv}CCOCH_2CH_2CH_3$	(10.00±0.04) IP from 86TUR/HAV2.	(233)	(975)	2.5	10.5	*EST	

Table 1. Positive Ion Table – Continued

ION / Neutral	Ionization potential eV	$\Delta_f H$(Ion) kcal/mol	kJ/mol	$\Delta_f H$(Neutral) kcal/mol	kJ/mol	Neutral reference	CAS registry number
$C_6H_8O^+$							
cyclohex-2-enone	9.23±0.05	(185)	(775)	−28±0.7	−116±3	*EST	930-68-7
cyclohex-3-enone	(≤9.42)	(≤185)	(≤773)	−33±0.7	−136±3	*EST	4096-34-8
2,3-dimethylfuran	(8.25±0.10) IP from 85GRU/SPI.	(166)	(694)	−24	−102	*EST	
2,4-dimethylfuran	(8.39±0.10) IP from 85GRU/SPI.	(166)	(694)	−28	−116	*EST	3710-43-8
2,5-dimethylfuran	(8.25±0.10) IP from 85GRU/SPI.	(165)	(690)	−25	−106	*EST	625-86-5
2-ethylfuran	(8.45±0.05)	(171)	(715)	−24	−100	*EST	3208-16-0
2-oxabicyclo[2.2.2]oct-5-ene	(≤9.44±0.02)	(≤207)	(≤867)	−11	−44	*EST	6705-50-6
$C_6H_8O_2^+$							
3-hydroxycyclohex-2-enone	9.52±0.05	(141)	(589)	−79	−330	*EST	504-02-9

Table 1. Positive Ion Table — Continued

ION / Neutral	Ionization potential eV	$\Delta_f H$(Ion) kcal/mol	$\Delta_f H$(Ion) kJ/mol	$\Delta_f H$(Neutral) kcal/mol	$\Delta_f H$(Neutral) kJ/mol	Neutral reference	CAS registry number
$C_6H_8O_2S^+$	<9.6	(<187)	(<784)	−34	−142	*EST	84451-42-3
	IP is onset of photoelectron band (84AIT/GOS).						
$C_6H_8P_2^+$	≤8.78	(≤237)	(≤990)	34	143	*EST	78550-67-1
	IP from 81CAB/COW2.						
$C_6H_8S^+$							
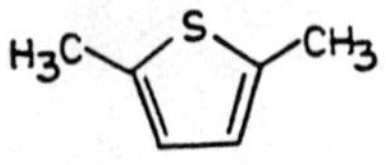 2,5-dimethylthiophene	(8.10)	(199)	(832)	12	50	*EST	638-02-8
	See also: 83BOC/ROT.						
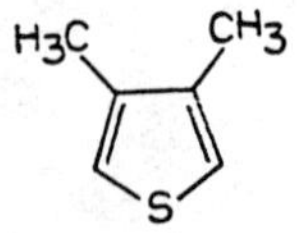 3,4-dimethylthiophene	(≤8.55)	(≤209)	(≤875)	12	50	*EST	632-15-5
	IP from 83BOC/ROT.						
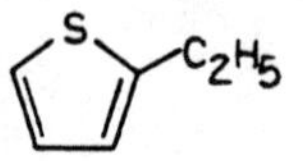 2-ethylthiophene	(8.67±0.05)	(215)	(898)	15	61	*EST	872-55-9
$C_6H_8Si^+$ phenylsilane	(9.09)	(236)	(988)	27	111	*EST	694-53-1
$C_6H_9^+$ $CH_3C\equiv CC(CH_3)_2$		216	904				77920-98-0

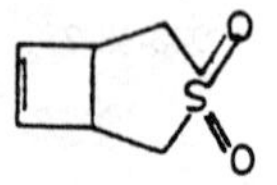

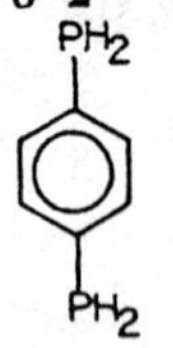

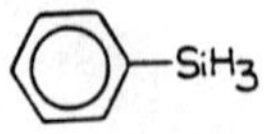

From appearance potential measurements (84LOS/HOL).

$C_6H_9^+$ (cyclohexenyl)

191   800

From proton affinities of 1,3-c-C_6H_8 (RN 592-57-4) PA = (200) kcal/mol, (837) kJ/mol and 1,4-c-C_6H_8 (RN 628-41-1) (83GAU/HOU) PA = (200) kcal/mol, (837) kJ/mol. Value derived from appearance potential measurements (84LOS/HOL) is the same.

Table 1. Positive Ion Table – Continued

ION / Neutral	Ionization potential eV	$\Delta_f H$(Ion) kcal/mol	$\Delta_f H$(Ion) kJ/mol	$\Delta_f H$(Neutral) kcal/mol	$\Delta_f H$(Neutral) kJ/mol	Neutral reference	CAS registry number
$C_6H_9^+$							
1-methylcyclopentenyl radical		190	795				72026-92-7
From appearance potential measurements (84LOS/HOL).							
1,3-dimethylcyclobutenyl cation		(202)	(845)				
From proton affinity of 1-methyl-3-methylenecyclobutene. (RN 15082-13-0). PA = (212) kcal/mol, (887) kJ/mol.							
trimethylcyclopropenyl cation		199	833				26827-04-3
From appearance potential measurements (84LOS/HOL).							
$C_6H_9Br^+$							
bromobicyclo	(9.5)	(235)	(983)	16	66	*EST	77379-00-1
IP is onset of photoelectron band (84DEL/ABE).							
$C_6H_9ClHg^+$							
cyclohexenyl-HgCl	(8.8)	(212)	(887)	9	38	*EST	10080-39-4
IP is onset of photoelectron band (81BAI/CHI).							
$C_6H_9Cl_2P^+$							
$(CH_3)_3CC\equiv CPCl_2$	(≤9.58)	(≤211)	(≤883)	−10	−41	*EST	77376-08-0
IP from 81CAB/COW.							
$C_6H_9I^+$							
iodobicyclo	(8.8)	(233)	(976)	30	127	*EST	74725-75-0
IP is onset of photoelectron band (84DEL/ABE).							
$C_6H_9N^+$							
(E)-$(CH_3)_2NCH=CHC\equiv CH$	(7.7)	(260)	(1087)	82±1	344±6	*EST	2206-24-8

ION / Neutral	Ionization potential eV	$\Delta_f H$(Ion) kcal/mol	$\Delta_f H$(Ion) kJ/mol	$\Delta_f H$(Neutral) kcal/mol	$\Delta_f H$(Neutral) kJ/mol	Neutral reference	CAS registry number
$C_6H_9N^+$							
2,4-dimethylpyrrole	(7.54±0.02)	(184)	(767)	10	40	*EST	625-82-1
2,5-dimethylpyrrole	(≤7.69)	(≤187)	(≤782)	9.5±0.2	39.8±0.8	77PED/RYL	625-84-3
2-ethylpyrrole	(7.97±0.05)	(197)	(823)	13	54	*EST	1551-06-0

$C_6H_9N_2^+$

1,2-$C_6H_4(NH_2)_2 \cdot H^+$ — 175 — 732
From proton affinity of 1,2-$C_6H_4(NH_2)_2$ (RN 95-54-5). PA = 212.8 kcal/mol, 890. kJ/mol.

1,3-$C_6H_4(NH_2)_2 \cdot H^+$ — 164 — 688
From proton affinity of 1,3-$C_6H_4(NH_2)_2$ (RN 108-45-2). PA = 222.4 kcal/mol, 930.5 kJ/mol.

1,4-$C_6H_4(NH_2)_2 \cdot H^+$ — 173 — 723
From proton affinity of 1,4-$C_6H_4(NH_2)_2$ (RN 106-50-3). PA = 215.9 kcal/mol, 903. kJ/mol.

ION / Neutral	Ionization potential eV	$\Delta_f H$(Ion) kcal/mol	$\Delta_f H$(Ion) kJ/mol	$\Delta_f H$(Neutral) kcal/mol	$\Delta_f H$(Neutral) kJ/mol	Neutral reference	CAS registry number
$C_6H_9N_3^+$							
3,5,6-trimethyl-1,2,4-triazine	≤9.4 IP from 83GLE/SPA.	(≤267)	(≤1118)	50	211	*EST	33209-85-7
3,5,6-trimethyl-1,2,4-triazine (isomer)	(≤8.84)	(≤274)	(≤1146)	70	293	*EST	24108-36-9

Table 1. Positive Ion Table – Continued

ION Neutral	Ionization potential eV	$\Delta_f H$(Ion) kcal/mol kJ/mol	$\Delta_f H$(Neutral) kcal/mol kJ/mol	Neutral reference	CAS registry number

$C_6H_9O^+$

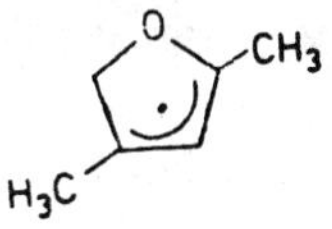

2,4-dimethylfuran

                     125   523

From proton affinity of 2,4-dimethylfuran (RN 3710-43-8) (85HOU/ROL).
PA = 213.0 kcal/mol, 819. kJ/mol.

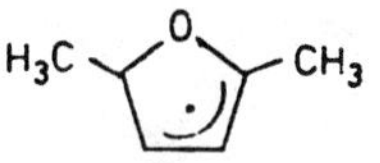

2,5-dimethylfuran

                     131   550

From proton affinity of 2,5-dimethylfuran (RN 625-86-5) (85HOU/ROL, 86MAU).
PA = 209.0 kcal/mol, 874. kJ/mol.

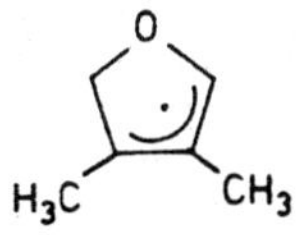

3,4-dimethylfuran

                     133   556

From proton affinity of 3,4-dimethylfuran (RN 20843-07-6) (85HOU/ROL).
PA = 207.1 kcal/mol, 867. kJ/mol.

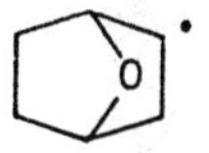

bicyclo[2.2.1]hept-2-ene, 7-oxa-

                     155   649

From proton affinity of bicyclo[2.2.1]hept-2-ene, 7-oxa- (RN 6705-50-6)
(86HOU/SCH). PA = 200.0 kcal/mol, 837. kJ/mol.

$C_6H_9O_2^+$

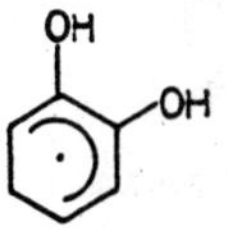

1,2-cyclohexanedione

                     92   384

From proton affinity of 1,2-cyclohexanedione (RN 765-87-7) (83MAU).
PA = 203.9 kcal/mol, 853. kJ/mol.

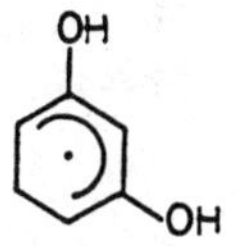

1,3-cyclohexanedione

                     76   318

From proton affinity of 1,3-cyclohexanedione (RN 504-02-9). PA = 210.8 kcal/mol, 882. kJ/mol.

$C_6H_{10}^+$

$CH_2=C=CHCH_2C_2H_5$

| | (9.00±0.05) | (237) | (990) | 29 | 122 | *EST | 592-44-9 |

(E)-$CH_2=CHCH=CHC_2H_5$

| | 8.51 | (210) | (878) | 14 | 57 | *EST | 20237-34-7 |

IP from 81MAS/MOU.

(Z)-$CH_2=CHCH_2CH=CHCH_3$

| | (9.04±0.05) | (227) | (950) | 19 | 80 | *EST | 7318-67-4 |

(E)-$CH_2=CHCH_2CH=CHCH_3$

| | (8.98±0.05) | (225) | (940) | 18 | 74 | *EST | 7319-00-8 |

ION / Neutral	Ionization potential eV	$\Delta_f H$(Ion) kcal/mol	$\Delta_f H$(Ion) kJ/mol	$\Delta_f H$(Neutral) kcal/mol	$\Delta_f H$(Neutral) kJ/mol	Neutral reference	CAS registry number
$C_6H_{10}{}^+$							
$CH_2=CHCH_2CH_2CH=CH_2$	9.29±0.05	234	980	20.1±0.1	84.1±0.6	77PED/RYL	592-42-7
$CH_3CH=C=CHC_2H_5$	(8.76±0.05)	(228)	(955)	26	110	*EST	592-49-4
(Z),(Z)-$CH_3CH=CHCH=CHCH_3$	(8.27) See also: 81MAS/MOU.	(203)	(850)	12	52	*EST	6108-61-8
(E),(Z)-$CH_3CH=CHCH=CHCH_3$	8.24±0.02 See also: 81MAS/MOU.	(202)	(844)	12	49	*EST	5194-50-3
(E),(E)-$CH_3CH=CHCH=CHCH_3$	8.18±0.06 See also: 81MAS/MOU.	(199)	(832)	11	43	*EST	5194-51-4
$CH_2=C=CHCH(CH_3)_2$	(9.06±0.05)	(236)	(987)	27	113	*EST	13643-05-5
$CH_2=C=C(CH_3)C_2H_5$	(8.74±0.05)	(227)	(951)	26	108	*EST	7417-48-3
$(CH_3)_2C=CHCH=CH_2$	8.25 IP from 81MAS/MOU, 82LEV/LIA.	(201)	(839)	10	43	70BEN/O'N	926-56-7
(Z)-$CH_2=CHC(CH_3)=CHCH_3$	8.42 IP from 81MAS/MOU.	(205)	(859)	11	47	*EST	2787-43-1
(E)-$CH_2=CHC(CH_3)=CHCH_3$	(8.38) IP from 81MAS/MOU.	(204)	(852)	10	43	*EST	2787-45-3
(E)-$CH_2=C(CH_3)CH=CHCH_3$	8.43 IP from 81MAS/MOU.	(205)	(856)	10	43	*EST	926-54-5
$CH_2=C(CH_3)CH_2CH=CH_2$	(9.16±0.05)	(228)	(956)	17	72	*EST	763-30-4
$CH_2=CHCH(CH_3)CH=CH_2$	(9.40±0.05)	(235)	(985)	19	78	*EST	1115-08-8
$(CH_3)_2C=C=CHCH_3$	8.64±0.05	(222)	(930)	23	96	*EST	3043-33-2
$CH_2=C(CH_3)C(CH_3)=CH_2$	8.71 See also: 81MAS/MOU.	211	884	10±0.2	44±1	77PED/RYL	513-81-5

Table 1. Positive Ion Table - Continued

ION / Neutral	Ionization potential eV	$\Delta_f H$(Ion) kcal/mol	$\Delta_f H$(Ion) kJ/mol	$\Delta_f H$(Neutral) kcal/mol	$\Delta_f H$(Neutral) kJ/mol	Neutral reference	CAS registry number
$C_6H_{10}^+$							
$C_2H_5C(=CH_2)CH=CH_2$	(8.79±0.02) See also: 81MAS/MOU.	(216)	(904)	13	56	*EST	3404-63-5
$C_4H_9C\equiv CH$	(9.95±0.05) See 81HOL/FIN.	(258)	(1082)	29±0.2	122±1	79ROG/DAG	693-02-7
$C_3H_7C\equiv CCH_3$	9.366±0.005	242	1012	26±0.5	108±2	79ROG/DAG	764-35-2
$C_2H_5C\equiv CC_2H_5$	9.323±0.005	240	1005	25±0.5	106±2	79ROG/DAG	928-49-4
$(CH_3)_2CHCH_2C\equiv CH$	(9.83±0.05)	(254)	(1064)	28	116	*EST	7154-75-8
$CH_3CH_2CH(CH_3)C\equiv CH$	9.79±0.05	253	1058	27±0.2	113±1	79ROG/DAG	922-59-8
$(CH_3)_3CC\equiv CH$	(9.80±0.05) See also: 81CAB/COW, 85ORL/BOG.	(251)	(1051)	25±0.7	106±3	77KUP/SHI	917-92-0
$(CH_3)_2CHC\equiv CCH_3$	9.31±0.05	(238)	(995)	23	97	*EST	21020-27-9
cyclohexene	8.945±0.01 See also: 81KIM/KAT.	205.2	858.4	−1.1±0.1	−4.6±0.5	77PED/RYL	110-83-8
1-methylcyclopentene	8.55±0.05	196	821	−1±0.2	−4±1	82ALL/DOD	693-89-0
3-methylcyclopentene	8.95±0.01	208	871	2±0.5	7±2	79FUC/PEA	1120-62-3
methylenecyclopentane	8.55±0.01	200	837	3±0.5	12±2	82ALL/DOD	1528-30-9
ethylidenecyclobutane	(8.70±0.05)	(221)	(925)	21	86	*EST	1528-21-8

Table 1. Positive Ion Table - Continued

ION Neutral	Ionization potential eV	$\Delta_f H$(Ion) kcal/mol	kJ/mol	$\Delta_f H$(Neutral) kcal/mol	kJ/mol	Neutral reference	CAS registry number
$C_6H_{10}^+$							
cyclobutyl-CH=CH₂	(≤9.44)	(≤242)	(≤1010)	24	99	*EST	2597-49-1
cyclopropyl-C(CH₃)=CH₂	(8.66±0.05)	(222)	(930)	22	94	82KOZ/MAS	4663-22-3
trimethylcyclopropene	(8.58±0.05) See also: 81PLE/VIL.	(239)	(1001)	41	173	*EST	3664-56-0
bicyclo[2.1.0]pentane methyl	(9.16±0.02)	(220.4)	(922.1)	9.2±0.1	38.3±0.4	77PED/RYL	285-58-5
bicyclo[2.2.0]	(9.0) IP is onset of photoelectron band.	(237)	(993)	30	125	82WIB/WEN	186-04-9
bicyclo[2.1.1]	(9.7) IP is onset of photoelectron band (84DEL/PIG).	(239)	(1000)	15.3	64.0	82WIB/WEN	285-86-9
bicyclopropylidene	(8.9) IP is onset of photoelectron band (82SPA/GLE).	(236)	(988)	31±1	129±4	77PED/RYL	5685-46-1
spiro	(9.1) IP is onset of photoelectron band.	(250)	(1045)	40	167	*EST	157-45-9

Table 1. Positive Ion Table – Continued

ION / Neutral	Ionization potential eV	$\Delta_f H$(Ion) kcal/mol	kJ/mol	$\Delta_f H$(Neutral) kcal/mol	kJ/mol	Neutral reference	CAS registry number
$C_6H_{10}Br_2^+$							
(1,2-dibromocyclohexane)	10.02±0.02	(206)	(863)	−25	−104	*EST	7429-37-0
(1,2-dibromocyclohexane isomer)	(9.94±0.02)	(204)	(855)	−25	−104	*EST	19246-38-9
$C_6H_{10}F_3O_2^+$ $CF_3C(OH)O(n\text{-}C_4H_9)$		−79	−332				

From proton affinity of $CF_3COO(n\text{-}C_4H_9)$ (RN 367-64-6). PA = 185.8 kcal/mol, 777. kJ/mol.

$C_6H_{10}N^+$							
(2,5-dimethylpyrrole, protonated)		157	656				

From proton affinity of 2,5-dimethylpyrrole (RN 625-84-3) (86MAU/LIE). PA = 218.2 kcal/mol, 913. kJ/mol.

$C_6H_{10}N_2^+$							
	(7.79±0.04)	(218)	(913)	38	161	77OTH/OLS	3310-62-1
$C_6H_{10}N_2O^+$							
	(≤9.30±0.03)	(≤237)	(≤990)	22.08±.44	92.38±1.84	83BYS	25926-96-9
$C_6H_{10}N_2S^+$							
	(7.9)	(208)	(869)	26	107	*EST	75899-43-3

IP is onset of photoelectron band (80KLA/BUT).

Table 1. Positive Ion Table - Continued

ION / Neutral	Ionization potential eV	$\Delta_f H$(Ion) kcal/mol	kJ/mol	$\Delta_f H$(Neutral) kcal/mol	kJ/mol	Neutral reference	CAS registry number
$C_6H_{10}N_2S_2{}^+$							
(H$_3$C-N, N-CH$_3$ dithione ring)	≤7.82 IP from 81HEN/ISA.	(≤236)	(≤986)	55	232	*EST	78134-03-9
$C_6H_{10}N_3O_2{}^+$							
(L-histidine structure)	From proton affinity of L-histidine. PA = 231.9 kcal/mol, 970. kJ/mol.	103	431				
$C_6H_{10}O^+$							
(E)-n-C$_3$H$_7$CH=CHCHO	(9.65)	(187)	(782)	−36	−149	*EST	505-57-7
CH$_3$CH$_2$CH=C(CH$_3$)CHO	(9.54)	(181)	(758)	−39	−162	*EST	623-36-9
CH$_3$CH=C(C$_2$H$_5$)CHO	(9.53)	(181)	(757)	−39	−162	*EST	19780-25-7
iso-C$_3$H$_7$COCH=CH$_2$	(9.39)	(177)	(741)	−39	−165	*EST	1606-47-9
(E)-CH$_3$CH=CHC(=O)C$_2$H$_5$	(9.32)	(175)	(730)	−40	−169	*EST	2497-21-4
CH$_3$CH=C(CH$_3$)C(=O)CH$_3$	(9.35)	(172)	(719)	−44	−183	*EST	565-62-8
(CH$_3$)$_2$C=CHC(=O)CH$_3$	9.08±0.03	(165)	(693)	−44	−183	*EST	141-79-7
(cyclohexanone)	9.14±0.01 See also: 86SPA/RAD.	157	656	−54±0.5	−226±2	77PED/RYL	108-94-1
(4-methyl-3,4-dihydro-2H-pyran)	(8.88) IP from 84ALA/RYE.	(173)	(724)	−32	−133	*EST	2270-61-3

Table 1. Positive Ion Table – Continued

ION / Neutral	Ionization potential eV	$\Delta_f H$(Ion) kcal/mol	kJ/mol	$\Delta_f H$(Neutral) kcal/mol	kJ/mol	Neutral reference	CAS registry number
$C_6H_{10}O^+$							
(cyclohexene oxide)	(9.82) IP from 84ALA/RYE.	(197)	(822)	−30	−125	*EST	286-20-4
(2-oxabicyclo structure)	(≤9.57±0.02)	(≤177)	(≤740)	−44	−183	74PIH/TAS	279-49-2
$C_6H_{10}OS^+$ $CH_3SC(CH_3)=CHC(=O)CH_3$	(8.15) IP is onset of photoelectron band (81JOR/CAR).	(152)	(636)	−36	−150	*EST	60887-86-7
$C_6H_{10}OSi^+$ (2-(dimethylsilyl)furan)	≤8.62 IP from 83ZYK/ERC.	(≤165)	(≤689)	−34	−143	*EST	13271-68-6
$C_6H_{10}O_2^+$ (E)-$CH_3CH=CHCOOC_2H_5$	(≤10.11)	(≤143)	(≤599)	−90±0.5	−376±2	77PED/RYL	623-70-1
(bicyclic diperoxide)	(8.6) IP is onset of photoelectron band (84GLE/DOB).	(163)	(683)	−35	−147	*EST	51272-66-3
(cyclic dioxolane)	8.4 IP is onset of photoelectron band.	(159)	(663)	−35	−147	*EST	280-53-5
$C_6H_{10}O_3P^+$ (2,8,9-trioxa-1-phosphaadamantane)		−14	−58				

From proton affinity of 2,8,9-trioxa-1-phosphaadamantane (RN 281-33-4).
PA = 213.8 kcal/mol, 894. kJ/mol.

Table 1. Positive Ion Table - Continued

ION Neutral	Ionization potential eV	Δ_fH(Ion) kcal/mol kJ/mol		Δ_fH(Neutral) kcal/mol kJ/mol		Neutral reference	CAS registry number
$C_6H_{10}O_4^+$							
$C_2H_5OCOCOOC_2H_5$	(9.8) IP is onset of photoelectron band.	(49)	(206)	−177±2	−740±9	77PED/RYL	95-92-1
$C_6H_{10}S^+$							
(thiacyclohexane=CH₂)	9.22 IP from 80SAR/WOR.	(221)	(923)	8	34	*EST	50550-56-6
$C_6H_{11}^+$							
$CH_3CH=CHC(CH_3)_2$		(169)	(706)				
From proton affinity of $CH_3CH=CHC(CH_3)=CH_2$. (RN 1118-58-7). PA = (207.9) kcal/mol, (870.) kJ/mol.							
$C_2H_5C(CH_3)CH=CH_2$		(170)	(712)				
From proton affinity of $CH_3CH=C(CH_3)CH=CH_2$. (RN 4549-74-0). PA = (205.7) kcal/mol, (860.6) kJ/mol.							
$(CH_3)_2CC(CH_3)=CH_2$		(174)	(728)				
From proton affinity of $CH_2=C(CH_3)C(CH_3)=CH_2$. (RN 513-81-5). PA = (202.1) kcal/mol, (846.) kJ/mol.							
(cyclohexyl cation)		(175)	(733)	18	77	81TSA	3170-58-9
From proton affinity of cyclohexene (RN 110-83-8). PA = (189) kcal/mol, (792) kJ/mol.							
(methylcyclopentyl radical cation)		167	698				
From proton affinities of methylenecyclopentane (RN 1528-30-9) PA = 200.8 kcal/mol, 840. kJ/mol and 1-methylcyclopentene (RN 693-89-0), PA = 196.9 kcal/mol, 824. kJ/mol, and from hydride and chloride transfer equilibrium constant determinations (76SOL/FIE, 76GOR/MUN, 85SHA/SHA).							
(methylcyclopentyl isomer)		(179)	(747)				
From appearance potential measurements (81HER/SIC).							
(1,2-dimethylcyclobutene·H⁺)		(182)	(762)				
From proton affinity of 1,2-dimethylcyclobutene. (RN 1501-58-2). PA = (201) kcal/mol, (841) kJ/mol.							

Table 1. Positive Ion Table - Continued

ION / Neutral	Ionization potential eV	$\Delta_f H$(Ion) kcal/mol kJ/mol	$\Delta_f H$(Neutral) kcal/mol kJ/mol	Neutral reference	CAS registry number

$C_6H_{11}^+$

▷–Ċ(CH₃)₂

| 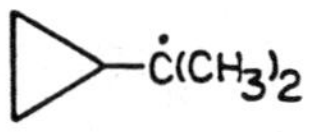 | | 179   750 | | | |

From proton affinity of 2-cyclopropylpropene (RN 4663-22-3). PA = 209.0 kcal/mol, 874. kJ/mol.

(▷(CH=CH₂)(CH₃))H⁺

| 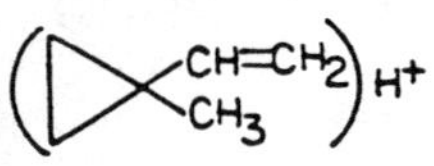 | | (181)   (756) | | | |

From proton affinity of 1-methyl-1-vinylcyclopropane (RN 16906-27-7). PA = (206) kcal/mol, (862) kJ/mol.

(H₃C–▷(CH₃)(CH₃))H⁺

| 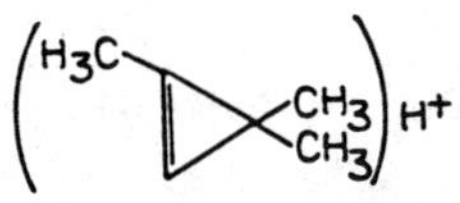 | | (193)   (808) | | | |

From proton affinity of 1,3,3-trimethylcyclopropene. (RN 3664-56-0). PA = (214) kcal/mol, (895) kJ/mol.

$C_6H_{11}Br^+$

cyclohexyl-Br

| 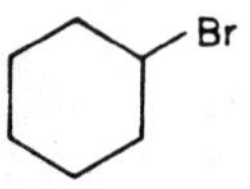 | (9.85±0.01) | (200)   (835) | −27   −115 | *EST | 108-85-0 |

$C_6H_{11}Cl^+$

cyclohexyl-Cl

| 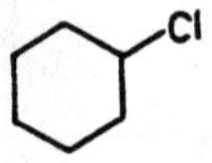 | (10.10±0.01) | (194)   (810) | −39±1   −164±4 | 77PED/RYL | 542-18-7 |

$C_6H_{11}ClHg^+$

cyclohexyl-HgCl

| 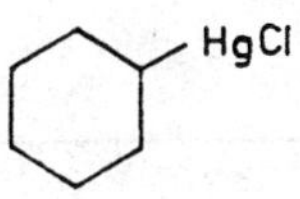 | 9.2 | (188)   (787) | −24   −101 | *EST | 24371-94-6 |

IP is onset of photoelectron band (81BAI/CHI2).

$C_6H_{11}F_3NO^+$

$CF_3C(OH)NH(n\text{-}C_4H_9)$

| | | −54   −226 | | | |

From proton affinity of $CF_3CONH(n\text{-}C_4H_9)$ (RN 400-59-9). PA = 203.6 kcal/mol, 852. kJ/mol.

Table 1. Positive Ion Table - Continued

ION / Neutral	Ionization potential eV	$\Delta_f H$(Ion) kcal/mol	kJ/mol	$\Delta_f H$(Neutral) kcal/mol	kJ/mol	Neutral reference	CAS registry number
$C_6H_{11}I^+$ (cyclohexyl iodide)	9.003	195	818	−12±1	−51±4	77PED/RYL	626-62-0
$C_6H_{11}N^+$							
(E)-$CH_3CH=CHCH=NC_2H_5$	(8.9) IP is onset of photoelectron band.	(225)	(941)	20±1	82±6	*EST	3653-19-8
$(CH_2=CHCH_2)_2NH$	(8.2) IP is onset of photoelectron band.	(224)	(937)	35±1	146±6	*EST	124-02-7
N-methyl-tetrahydropyridine	(≤8.67±0.05)	(≤219)	(≤914)	19±2	78±10	*EST	694-55-3
1-(1-butenyl)aziridine (Z)	(7.9) IP from onset of photoelectron band (81MUL/PRE).	(220)	(919)	38	157	*EST	
1-(1-butenyl)aziridine (E)	(7.7) IP is onset of photoelectron band (81MUL/PRE, 81MUL/PRE2).	(215)	(900)	38	157	*EST	
1-(2-methylpropenyl)aziridine	(7.6) IP is onset of photoelectron band (81MUL/PRE, 81MUL/PRE2).	(220)	(919)	44	186	*EST	
$C_6H_{11}NO^+$							
caprolactam	(9.07±0.02)	(150)	(629)	−58.8±0.3	−246.2±1.2	77PED/RYL	105-60-2
cyclohexanone oxime	(8.97±0.03) IP from 79GOL/KUL.	(186)	(779)	−21	−86	*EST	100-64-1

Table 1. Positive Ion Table - Continued

ION / Neutral	Ionization potential eV	$\Delta_f H$(Ion) kcal/mol	$\Delta_f H$(Ion) kJ/mol	$\Delta_f H$(Neutral) kcal/mol	$\Delta_f H$(Neutral) kJ/mol	Neutral reference	CAS registry number
$C_6H_{11}NO^+$							
1-methyl-2-piperidone	≤8.92 IP from 85TRE/RAD.	≤149	≤624	−57±0.7	−237±3	77PED/RYL	931-20-4
H₃C—N(ring)=O (1-methyl-4-piperidone)	(8.3) IP from 80SAR/WOR. See also: 86SPA/RAD.	(155)	(648)	−37	−153	*EST	1445-73-4
$C_6H_{11}NOS^+$							
cyclohexyl-N=S=O	(≤10.0)	(≤169)	(≤707)	−62	−258	*EST	30980-11-1
$C_6H_{11}O^+$							
$(CH_3)_2CCHC(OH)CH_3$		(112)	(470)				
From proton affinity of $(CH_3)_2C=CHC(=O)CH_3$ (RN 141-79-7). PA = (210) kcal/mol, (877) kJ/mol.							
$(CH_2CHCH_2)_2OH$		158	661				
From proton affinity of $(CH_2=CHCH_2)_2O$ (RN 557-40-4). PA = 200.4 kcal/mol, 838. kJ/mol.							
cyclohexanol-OH (protonated cyclohexanone)		111	466				
From proton affinity of cyclohexanone (RN 108-94-1) (86SAN/BAL). PA = 201.4 kcal/mol, 843. kJ/mol.							
(7-oxa-bicyclo[2.2.1]heptane)H⁺		119	498				
From proton affinity of bicyclo[2.2.1]heptane, 7-oxa- (RN 279-49-2). PA = 203 kcal/mol, 849 kJ/mol.							
$C_6H_{11}O_2^+$							
$CH_3C(OH)CH_2CH_2COCH_3$		64	269			83MAU	
From proton affinity of $CH_3COCH_2CH_2COCH_3$ (RN 110-13-4). PA = 213.2 kcal/mol, 892. kJ/mol.							
$C_6H_{11}P^+$							
$(CH_3)_3CC\equiv CPH_2$	≤9.05 IP from 81CAB/COW.	(≤246)	(≤1028)	37	155	*EST	77376-07-9

Table 1. Positive Ion Table - Continued

ION / Neutral	Ionization potential eV	$\Delta_f H$(Ion) kcal/mol	kJ/mol	$\Delta_f H$(Neutral) kcal/mol	kJ/mol	Neutral reference	CAS registry number
$C_6H_{12}^+$							
1-C_6H_{12}	9.44±0.04	207.7	869.0	−10.0±0.2	−41.8±1	81WIB/WAS	592-41-6
(Z)-2-C_6H_{12}	(8.97±0.01)	(195.5)	(817.8)	−11.4±0.2	−47.7±1	81WIB/WAS	7688-21-3
(E)-2-C_6H_{12}	(8.97±0.01)	(194.5)	(814.0)	−12.3±0.2	−51.5±1	81WIB/WAS	4050-45-7
(Z)-3-C_6H_{12}	(8.95±0.01)	(195.2)	(816.7)	−11.2±0.2	−46.8±0.8	81WIB/WAS	7642-09-3
(E)-3-C_6H_{12}	8.96±0.02	194.5	813.9	−12.1±0.2	−50.6±1	81WIB/WAS	13269-52-8
$C_2H_5CH_2C(CH_3)=CH_2$	(9.08±0.01)	(195)	(817)	−14.2±0.3	−59.4±1	77PED/RYL	763-29-1
$C_2H_5CH(CH_3)CH=CH_2$	(9.44) IP from 81HOL/FIN.	(206)	(861)	−11.8±0.4	−49.5±1.5	77PED/RYL	29564-68-9
$(CH_3)_2CHCH_2CH=CH_2$	(9.45±0.01)	(206)	(861)	−12±0.5	−51±2	77PED/RYL	691-37-2
$(C_2H_5)_2C=CH_2$	(9.06±0.02)	(196)	(818)	−13.4±0.3	−56.0±1	77PED/RYL	760-21-4
$(CH_3)_2CHC(CH_3)=CH_2$	(9.07±0.01)	(194)	(812)	−15.1±0.2	−63.3±0.8	77PED/RYL	563-78-0
$(CH_3)_3CCH=CH_2$	9.45±0.01	203	851	−14.5±0.2	−60.7±0.9	77PED/RYL	558-37-2
(Z)-$CH_3CH=C(CH_3)C_2H_5$	(8.58) IP from 81HOL/FIN.	(183)	(766)	−14.9±0.4	−62.3±1	77PED/RYL	922-61-2
(Z)-$(CH_3)_2CHCH=CHCH_3$	(8.98±0.01)	(193)	(809)	−13.7±0.2	−57.5±1	77PED/RYL	691-38-3
(E)-$(CH_3)_2CHCH=CHCH_3$	(8.97±0.01)	(192)	(804)	−14.7±0.3	−61.5±1	77PED/RYL	674-76-0
$(CH_3)_2C=CHC_2H_5$	(8.58) IP from 81HOL/FIN.	(182)	(761)	−16.0±0.3	−66.8±1	77PED/RYL	625-27-4
$(CH_3)_2C=C(CH_3)_2$	8.27±0.01	174	729	−16.6±0.2	−69.3±0.8	77PED/RYL	563-79-1
⌬ (cyclohexane)	9.86±0.03	198	828	−29.5±0.1	−123.3±0.3	77PED/RYL	110-82-7

From charge transfer equilibria relative to fluorobenzenes; data re-interpreted. (82SIE/MAU; 82LIA). Threshold measurement leads to IP = 9.88 eV. See also: 81KIM/KAT.

Table 1. Positive Ion Table - Continued

ION / Neutral	Ionization potential eV	$\Delta_f H$(Ion) kcal/mol	$\Delta_f H$(Ion) kJ/mol	$\Delta_f H$(Neutral) kcal/mol	$\Delta_f H$(Neutral) kJ/mol	Neutral reference	CAS registry number
$C_6H_{12}^+$							
methylcyclopentane	9.85±0.03	202	844	−25.3±0.1	−105.9±0.4	77PED/RYL	96-37-7

From charge transfer equilibrium constant relative to cyclohexane (76LIA/AUS).

| | (8.90) | (197) | (825) | −8.0 | −33.5 | | *EST |

IP from 85LAD/HAR.

| $C_6D_{12}^+$ | | | | | | | |
| cyclohexane-d_{12} | 9.89 | | | | | | 1735-17-7 |

From charge transfer equilibria relative to fluorobenzenes; data re-interpreted. (82SIE/MAU; 82LIA). Threshold measurement leads to IP = 9.88 eV.

| $C_6H_{12}N^+$ | | | | | | | |
| $(CH_2CHCH_2)_2NH_2$ | | 175 | 735 | | | | |

From proton affinity of $(CH_2=CHCH_2)_2NH$ (RN 124-02-7). PA = 224.7 kcal/mol, 940. kJ/mol.

| $C_6H_{12}NO^+$ | | | | | | | |
| 2-methoxypiperidine | | 96 | 400 | | | | |

From proton affinity of 2,3,4,5-tetrahydro-6-methoxypyridine (RN 53687-79-9). PA = 228.1 kcal/mol, 954. kJ/mol.

| | | 90 | 376 | | | | |

From proton affinity of 1-methylpiperidine-2-one (RN 931-20-4). PA = 219.3 kcal/mol, 917.5 kJ/mol.

| $C_6H_{12}NO_3^+$ | | | | | | | |
| $CH_3C(OH)NHCH(CH_3)COOCH_3$ | | −4 | −18 | | | | |

From proton affinity of $CH_3CONHCH(CH_3)COOCH_3$. (RN 3619-02-1). PA = 224.5 kcal/mol, 939. kJ/mol.

| $C_6H_{12}N_2^+$ | | | | | | | |
| | (8.2) | (225) | (941) | 36±0.7 | 150±3 | 80ENG | 54166-22-2 |

IP is onset of photoelectron band.

Table 1. Positive Ion Table — Continued

ION / Neutral	Ionization potential eV	$\Delta_f H$(Ion) kcal/mol	$\Delta_f H$(Ion) kJ/mol	$\Delta_f H$(Neutral) kcal/mol	$\Delta_f H$(Neutral) kJ/mol	Neutral reference	CAS registry number
$C_6H_{12}N_2^+$							
(pyrrolizidine-diN structure)	(7.87) IP from 82LEV/LIA. See also: 84NEL.	(219)	(915)	37	156	*EST	5397-67-1
(bicyclic diN structure)	≤8.24	(≤210)	(≤878)	20	83	*EST	280-28-4
(DABCO)	7.197±0.001 IP from 84SMI/HAG2.	187	784	21±2	89±7	71RAP/WES	280-57-9
$C_6H_{12}N_2O_2^+$ $(CH_3)_2NCOCON(CH_3)_2$	9.02 IP from 82LEV/LIA, 85ROT/BOC.	(132)	(554)	−76	−316	*EST	1608-14-6
$C_6H_{12}N_2S^+$ H_3CN-NCH_3 (C=S)	(7.3) IP is onset of photoelectron band.	(192)	(802)	23	98	*EST	16597-35-6
$C_6H_{12}N_2S_2^+$ $(CH_3)_2NC(=S)C(=S)N(CH_3)_2$	≤7.75 IP from 81HEN/ISA.	(≤222)	(≤930)	43	182	*EST	35840-78-9
$C_6H_{12}N_3OP^+$ (cage structure)	≤8.89 IP from 82COW/LAT.	(≤190)	(≤794)	−15	−64	*EST	71771-37-4
(P=O cage structure)	≤8.19±0.10 IP from 82COW/LAT.	(≤151)	(≤631)	−38	−159	*EST	53597-70-9

Table 1. Positive Ion Table – Continued

ION / Neutral	Ionization potential eV	$\Delta_f H$(Ion) kcal/mol	kJ/mol	$\Delta_f H$(Neutral) kcal/mol	kJ/mol	Neutral reference	CAS registry number
$C_6H_{12}N_3P^+$	≤8.05±0.10 IP from 82COW/LAT.	(≤227)	(≤952)	42	175	*EST	53597-69-6
$C_6H_{12}N_3PS^+$	≤8.02±0.10 IP from 82COW/LAT.	(≤205)	(≤857)	20	83	*EST	56796-56-6
	≤8.43±0.10 IP from 82COW/LAT.	(≤237)	(≤991)	43	178	*EST	
$C_6H_{12}N_4^+$	(≤8.53) See also: 82COW/LAT.	(≤244)	(≤1022)	47±0.7	199±3	77PED/RYL	100-97-0
$C_6H_{12}O^+$							
n-C_5H_{11}CHO	9.67±0.05	164	686	−59	−247	78TRC	66-25-1
n-C_3H_7CH(CH_3)CHO	(9.70)	(163)	(679)	−61	−257	*EST	123-15-9
$(C_2H_5)_2$CHCHO	(9.54) IP from 81HOL/FIN.	(158)	(663)	−61	−257	*EST	97-96-1
C_2H_5CH(CH_3)CH_2CHO	(9.68) IP from 81HOL/FIN.	(161)	(676)	−62	−258	*EST	15877-57-3
neo-C_5H_{11}CHO	9.61±0.01	(158)	(658)	−64	−269	*EST	2987-16-8
n-C_4H_9COCH$_3$	9.35±0.02	150	624	−66±0.2	−278±1	77PED/RYL	591-78-6
n-C_3H_7COC_2H_5	9.12±0.02 See also: 81HOL/FIN.	143	601	−67±0.2	−279±1	77PED/RYL	589-38-8
sec-C_4H_9COCH$_3$	9.21±0.01 IP from 81HOL/FIN, 82LEV/LIA, 84BOU/FLA.	(144)	(602)	−69	−287	*EST	565-61-7
iso-C_4H_9COCH$_3$	9.30±0.01	(145)	(610)	−69	−287	*EST	108-10-1

Table 1. Positive Ion Table - Continued

ION Neutral	Ionization potential eV	$\Delta_f H$(Ion) kcal/mol	$\Delta_f H$(Ion) kJ/mol	$\Delta_f H$(Neutral) kcal/mol	$\Delta_f H$(Neutral) kJ/mol	Neutral reference	CAS registry number
$C_6H_{12}O^+$							
tert-$C_4H_9COCH_3$	9.11±0.02	141	589	−69.3±0.2	−289.8±0.9	77PED/RYL	75-97-8
iso-$C_3H_7COC_2H_5$	9.10±0.01	141	592	−68.3±0.2	−286.1±0.9	77PED/RYL	565-69-5
cyclohexanol (OH)	(9.75) IP from 83RAB/SEL.	(155.5)	(650.7)	−69.3±0.2	−290.0±0.9	85WIB/WAS	108-93-0
$C_6H_{12}O_2^+$							
$CH_3(CH_2)_4COOH$	≤10.12 IP from 81HOL/FIN.	≤111	≤463	−122.8±0.4	−513.6±1.6	77PED/RYL	142-62-1
$CH_3COO(CH_2)_3CH_3$	10.0	114	479	−116.1±0.1	−485.6±0.5	77PED/RYL	123-86-4
$CH_3COOCH(CH_3)C_2H_5$	9.90 IP from 82GRE/MCC.	109	454	−120	−501	82GRE/MCC	105-46-4
$CH_3(CH_2)_3COOCH_3$	(10.4±0.2)	(127)	(532)	−112.7±0.3	−471.5±1.4	77PED/RYL	624-24-8
tert-$C_4H_9COOCH_3$	(9.90±0.04)	(111)	(464)	−117±0.2	−491±1	77PED/RYL	598-98-1
(1,3-dioxocane)	(≤9.29)	(≤178)	(≤746)	−36	−150	*EST	6572-89-0
(2,2-dimethyl-1,3-dioxane)	≤9.84 IP from 84ASF/ZYK.	(≤124)	(≤519)	−103	−430	77PED/RYL	695-30-7
(2,6-dimethyl-1,3-dioxane)	(≤9.90) IP from 84ASF/ZYK.	(≤127)	(≤530)	−102±1	−425±4	77PED/RYL	766-20-1
(4,4-dimethyl-1,3-dioxane)	≤9.80 IP from 84ASF/ZYK.	(≤124)	(≤521)	−102	−425	*EST	766-15-4

Table 1. Positive Ion Table – Continued

ION / Neutral	Ionization potential eV	$\Delta_f H$(Ion) kcal/mol	$\Delta_f H$(Ion) kJ/mol	$\Delta_f H$(Neutral) kcal/mol	$\Delta_f H$(Neutral) kJ/mol	Neutral reference	CAS registry number
$C_6H_{12}O_2^+$	(8.53)	(156)	(653)	−41	−170	78GRE/LIE	35856-82-7
$C_6H_{12}O_2Si^+$	≤9.59 IP from 81KHV/ZYK.	(≤39)	(≤163)	−182	−762	*EST	61667-33-2
$C_6H_{12}O_4^+$	(≤10.4)	(≤10)	(≤40)	−230	−963	*EST	
$C_6H_{12}S_3^+$	(8.0) IP is onset of photoelectron band.	(178)	(746)	−6	−26	*EST	2765-04-0
	8.0 IP is onset of photoelectron band.	(151)	(633)	−33	−139	*EST	38348-31-1
$C_6H_{12}Se_3^+$	(7.7) IP is onset of photoelectron band (84BOC/AYG).	(211)	(882)	33	139	*EST	15732-69-1
$C_6H_{12}Si^+$	≤9.0	(≤182)	(≤760)	−26	−108	*EST	16054-12-9
$C_6H_{13}^+$ 1-C_6H_{13}	7.92±0.06 $\Delta_f H$(Neutral) based on D[C-H] = 100.5 kcal/mol.	(191)	(800)	8	33	*EST	2679-29-0

Table 1. Positive Ion Table - Continued

ION / Neutral	Ionization potential eV	$\Delta_f H$(Ion) kcal/mol	$\Delta_f H$(Ion) kJ/mol	$\Delta_f H$(Neutral) kcal/mol	$\Delta_f H$(Neutral) kJ/mol	Neutral reference	CAS registry number
$C_6H_{13}^+$							
2-C_6H_{13}	7.0	(168)	(704)	7	29	*EST	2493-44-9
	$\Delta_f H$(Neutral) based on D[C-H] = 99 kcal/mol.						
n-$C_3H_7C(CH_3)_2$		152	636				21058-26-4
	From hydride transfer equilibrium constant (75SOL/FIE and 76GOR/MUN); Heat of formation relative to $\Delta_f H$(tert-$C_4H_9^+$).						
$(CH_3)_2CHC(CH_3)_2$		150	628				24436-98-4
	From hydride transfer equilibrium constant (75SOL/FIE and 76GOR/MUN); Heat of formation relative to $\Delta_f H$(tert-$C_4H_9^+$).						
$(C_2H_5)_2(CH_3)C$		152	638				23088-03-1
	From proton affinity of $CH_3CH = C(CH_3)C_2H_5$. (RN 922-61-2). PA = 198.2 kcal/mol, 829. kJ/mol.						
cyclohexane-H^+		(167)	(700)				
	From proton affinity of cyclohexane. (RN 110-82-7). PA = (169) kcal/mol, (707) kJ/mol.						
$C_6H_{13}ClHg^+$							
n-$C_6H_{13}HgCl$	≤9.96	(≤194)	(≤811)	-36	-150	*EST	17774-09-3
	IP from 81BAI/CHI2.						
$C_6H_{13}I^+$							
n-$C_6H_{13}I$	9.179	190	794	-22	-92	81HOL/FIN	638-45-9
$C_6H_{13}N^+$							
n-$C_3H_7CH=NC_2H_5$	(9.00)	(203)	(847)	-5	-21	*EST	1611-12-7
	See also: 79AUE/BOW.						
(iso-C_3H_7)CH=NC_2H_5	(8.7)	(192)	(805)	-8	-34	*EST	1743-56-2
	IP is onset of photoelectron band.						
n-$C_3H_7N=CHCH_2CH_3$	(8.55±0.2)	(192)	(802)	-5	-23	*EST	7707-70-2
n-$C_3H_7N=C(CH_3)_2$	(8.31±0.2)	(178)	(742)	-14±2	-60±8	*EST	22023-64-9
iso-$C_3H_7N=CHCH_2CH_3$	(8.50±0.2)	(186)	(780)	-10	-40	69BEN/CRU	28916-23-6
$(CH_3)_2NCH=CHC_2H_5$	≤7.57	(≤174)	(≤730)	0	0	*EST	14548-12-0
	IP from 81MUL/PRE2.						

Table 1. Positive Ion Table - Continued

ION / Neutral	Ionization potential eV	$\Delta_f H$(Ion) kcal/mol	$\Delta_f H$(Ion) kJ/mol	$\Delta_f H$(Neutral) kcal/mol	$\Delta_f H$(Neutral) kJ/mol	Neutral reference	CAS registry number
$C_6H_{13}N^+$							
$(CH_3)_2NCH=C(CH_3)_2$	≤8.15 IP from 81MUL/PRE2.	(≤189)	(≤791)	1	5	*EST	6906-32-7
azepane	(≤8.41±0.02)	(≤183)	(≤767)	−10	−44	*EST	111-49-9
cyclohexylamine	(8.62±0.24) See also: 79AUE/BOW.	(174)	(727)	−25±0.2	−105±1	79STE	108-91-8
1-methylpiperidine	7.74 See also: 82ROZ/HOU, 80SAR/WOR, 86SPA/RAD, 86CAU/DIV.	(166)	(697)	−12±1	−50±4	*EST	626-67-5
2-methylpiperidine	7.76±0.05 See also: 82ROZ/HOU.	159	664	−20.2±0.2	−84.4±1.0	77PED/RYL	109-05-7
3-methylpiperidine	7.94±0.05 See also: 82ROZ/HOU.	(164)	(685)	−19±0.4	−81±2	*EST	626-56-2
4-methylpiperidine	8.01±0.05 See also: 82ROZ/HOU.	(166)	(692)	−19±0.4	−81±2	*EST	626-58-4
$C_6H_{13}NO^+$							
2-aminocyclohexanol	(≤9.49)	(≤186)	(≤777)	−33	−139	*EST	6982-39-4
$CH_3CON(C_2H_5)_2$	(8.60±0.02)	(130)	(543)	−69	−287	*EST	685-91-6

Table 1. Positive Ion Table - Continued

ION / Neutral	Ionization potential eV	$\Delta_f H$(Ion) kcal/mol	kJ/mol	$\Delta_f H$(Neutral) kcal/mol	kJ/mol	Neutral reference	CAS registry number
$C_6H_{13}NO_2{}^+$							
n-$C_4H_9CH(NH_2)COOH$	(8.52)	(82)	(343)	−114±2	−479±10	*EST	327-57-1
sec-$C_4H_9CH(NH_2)COOH$	(8.66)	(83)	(349)	−116±2	−487±10	*EST	73-32-5
iso-$C_4H_9CH(NH_2)COOH$	(8.51)	(80)	(333)	−117±0.7	−488±3	77PED/RYL	61-90-5
$C_6H_{13}N_2{}^+$							
(pyrazine)H^+		158	661				

From proton affinity of 1,4-diazabicyclo[2.2.2]octane (RN 280-57-9).
PA = 229.0 kcal/mol, 958. kJ/mol.

$C_6H_{13}O^+$							
t-$C_4H_9C(OH)CH_3$		94	394				

From proton affinity of t-$C_4H_9COCH_3$ (RN 75-97-8). PA = 202.3 kcal/mol, 846. kJ/mol.

(oxepane)H^+		(161)	(674)				

From proton affinity of oxepane (RN 592-90-5). PA = (202) kcal/mol, (845) kJ/mol.

$C_6H_{13}O_2{}^+$							
t-$C_4H_9C(OH)OCH_3$		46	191				

From proton affinity of t-$C_4H_9COOCH_3$ (RN 598-98-1). PA = 202.8 kcal/mol, 848.5 kJ/mol.

$C_6H_{13}O_3P^+$							
(cyclic phosphite isomer 1)	(8.34±0.1)	(11)	(45)	−182	−760	*EST	7735-82-2
(cyclic phosphite isomer 2)	(8.69±0.1)	(19)	(78)	−182	−760	*EST	41821-91-4

Table 1. Positive Ion Table — Continued

ION / Neutral	Ionization potential eV	$\Delta_f H$(Ion) kcal/mol	$\Delta_f H$(Ion) kJ/mol	$\Delta_f H$(Neutral) kcal/mol	$\Delta_f H$(Neutral) kJ/mol	Neutral reference	CAS registry number
$C_6H_{13}SSi^+$		(162)	(679)				79126-87-7

$\Delta_f H$(Ion) from appearance potential determination (81GUS/VOL).

$C_6H_{14}^+$							
n-C_6H_{14}	10.13	194	810	−39.9±0.1	−167.1±0.4	74SCO	110-54-3
		202	847	−31.1±0.1	−130.1±0.4		

From charge transfer equilibrium constant determinations relative to fluorobenzenes; data re-interpreted (81MAU/SIE; 82LIA). Threshold measurement leads to IP = 10.2 eV.

$(CH_3)_2CH(CH_2)_2CH_3$	(10.12)	(191)	(802)	−41.6±0.2	−173.8±0.9	74SCO	107-83-5
		(201±0.2)	(842±0.9)	−32.2±0.2	−134.6±0.9		
$(C_2H_5)_2CHCH_3$	(10.08)	(191)	(801)	−40.9±0.2	−171.3±0.9	74SCO	96-14-0
		(201)	(841)	−31.5±0.2	−131.9±0.9		
$(CH_3)_2CHCH(CH_3)_2$	(10.02)	(189)	(791)	−42.1±0.2	−176.2±0.9	74SCO	79-29-8
		(199)	(832)	−32.3±0.2	−135.1±0.9		
$(CH_3)_3CCH_2CH_3$	(10.06)	(188)	(787)	−43.9±0.2	−183.9±0.9	74SCO	75-83-2
		(198)	(827)	−34.3±0.2	−143.5±0.9		

$C_6H_{14}Hg^+$							
$(n-C_3H_7)_2Hg$	(≤8.29)	(≤200)	(≤836)	9±2	36±6	77PED/RYL	628-85-3
$(iso-C_3H_7)_2Hg$	(≤8.03)	(≤195)	(≤815)	10±1	40±6	77PED/RYL	1071-39-2

$C_6H_{14}N^+$							
$n-C_3H_7CHNHC_2H_5$		(135)	(566)				

From proton affinity of $n-C_3H_7CH=NC_2H_5$ (RN 1611-12-7). PA = (225.3) kcal/mol, (943) kJ/mol.

$(CH_3)_2NC(CH_3)CH_2CH_3$		129	539				

From proton affinity of $(CH_3)_2NC(CH_3)=CHCH_3$ (RN 52113-79-8). PA = 237 kcal/mol, 992 kJ/mol.

cyclohexyl-$NH_2 \cdot H^+$		120	500				

From proton affinity of cyclohexanamine (RN 108-91-8). PA = 221.2 kcal/mol, 925.5 kJ/mol.

Table 1. Positive Ion Table - Continued

ION / Neutral	Ionization potential eV	$\Delta_f H$(Ion) kcal/mol	$\Delta_f H$(Ion) kJ/mol	$\Delta_f H$(Neutral) kcal/mol	$\Delta_f H$(Neutral) kJ/mol	Neutral reference	CAS registry number
$C_6H_{14}N^+$							
1-methylpiperidine + H$^+$		124	519				

From proton affinity of 1-methylpiperidine (RN 626-67-5). PA = 229.7 kcal/mol, 961 kJ/mol.

$C_6H_{14}NO_2^+$							
L-C_2H_5CH(CH$_3$)CH(NH$_3$)COOH		30	127				

From proton affinity of L-C_2H_5CH(CH$_3$)CH(NH$_2$)COOH (RN 73-32-5). PA = 218.9 kcal/mol, 916. kJ/mol.

L-(CH$_3$)$_2$CHCH$_2$CH(NH$_3$)COOH		31	130				

From proton affinity of L-(CH$_3$)$_2$CHCH$_2$CH(NH$_2$)COOH (RN 61-90-5). PA = 218.1 kcal/mol, 912.5 kJ/mol.

ION / Neutral	Ionization potential eV	$\Delta_f H$(Ion) kcal/mol	$\Delta_f H$(Ion) kJ/mol	$\Delta_f H$(Neutral) kcal/mol	$\Delta_f H$(Neutral) kJ/mol	Neutral reference	CAS registry number
$C_6H_{14}N_2^+$							
(E)-(C$_3$H$_7$)$_2$NN	(8.1)	(199)	(833)	12±1	51±4	80ENG	55204-42-7

IP is onset of photoelectron band.

(Z)-iso-(C$_3$H$_7$)$_2$NN	(≤8.24)	(≤210)	(≤879)	20	84	*EST	23201-84-5
(E)-(iso-C$_3$H$_7$)$_2$NN	(8.0)	(193)	(808)	9±0.5	36±2	80ENG	15464-00-3

IP is onset of photoelectron band.

1,2-dimethylhexahydropyridazine	6.54	(167)	(699)	16	68	*EST	26163-37-1

IP from charge transfer equilibrium constant determinations (84MAU/NEL). Reference standard: IP (C$_6$H$_5$N(CH$_3$)$_2$) = 7.12 eV.) See also: 82LEV/LIA, 84NEL, 80SCH/THO.

pyrrolidine-N(CH$_3$)$_2$	(≤7.97)	(≤207)	(≤865)	23	96	*EST	53779-90-1

Reported values of IP's of hydrazines determined by threshold measurements are usually significantly higher than the adiabatic value because of the large geometry change associated with ionization. See also: 82LEV/LIA, 84NEL.

ION / Neutral	Ionization potential eV	$\Delta_f H$(Ion) kcal/mol	$\Delta_f H$(Ion) kJ/mol	$\Delta_f H$(Neutral) kcal/mol	$\Delta_f H$(Neutral) kJ/mol	Neutral reference	CAS registry number
$C_6H_{14}N_2O_2^+$							
L-H$_2$N(CH$_2$)$_4$CH(NH$_2$)COOH	(8.6)	(74)	(308)	−125	−522	*EST	56-87-1

IP is onset of photoelectron band (83CAN/HAM).

$C_6H_{14}O^+$							
n-C_6H_{13}OH	(9.89±0.03)	(153)	(639)	−75.3±0.3	−315.1±1.4	77PED/RYL	111-27-3

IP from 77ASH/BUR.

Table 1. Positive Ion Table - Continued

ION Neutral	Ionization potential eV	$\Delta_f H$(Ion) kcal/mol	 kJ/mol	$\Delta_f H$(Neutral) kcal/mol	 kJ/mol	Neutral reference	CAS registry number
$C_6H_{14}O^+$							
n-C_4H_9CH(OH)CH_3	(9.80±0.03) IP from 77ASH/BUR.	(146)	(612)	−80	−334	84WIB/WAS	626-93-7
C_2H_5CH(OH)C_3H_7	(9.63±0.03) IP from 77ASH/BUR.	(143)	(597)	−79	−332	*EST	623-37-0
n-$C_5H_{11}OCH_3$	(≤9.67) IP from 80BAC/MOU.	(≤157)	(≤656)	−66	−277	*EST	628-80-8
$(CH_3)_2CHCH_2CH_2OCH_3$	(≤9.65) IP from 80BAC/MOU.	(≤154)	(≤646)	−68	−285	*EST	626-91-5
$(CH_3)_3CCH_2OCH_3$	(≤9.41) IP from 80BAC/MOU.	(≤146)	(≤611)	−71	−297	*EST	1118-00-9
n-$C_4H_9OC_2H_5$	9.36 IP from 81HOL/FIN. See also: 82AUD/BOU, 80BAC/MOU.	146	609	−70	−294	81HOL/FIN	628-81-9
sec-$C_4H_9OC_2H_5$	(9.32) IP from 81HOL/FIN. See also: 82AUD/BOU.	(140)	(587)	−75	−312	81HOL/FIN	2679-87-0
$(CH_3)_2CHCH_2OC_2H_5$	(9.30) IP from 82AUD/BOU.	(140)	(585)	−75	−312	*EST	627-02-1
tert-$C_4H_9OC_2H_5$	(≤9.39±0.015)	(≤139)	(≤582)	(−77)	(−324)	*EST	637-92-3
(n-$C_3H_7)_2O$	9.27±0.05 See also: 80BAC/MOU.	144	601	−70±0.5	−293±2	77PED/RYL	111-43-3
(iso-$C_3H_7)_2O$	9.20±0.05 See also: 80BAC/MOU.	136	569	−76.2±0.4	−318.8±1.8	77PED/RYL	108-20-3
$C_6H_{14}OS^+$							
(n-$C_3H_7)_2SO$	(≤8.60)	(≤137)	(≤575)	−60.9±0.4	−254.9±1.5	77PED/RYL	4253-91-2
$[(CH_3)_2CH]_2SO$	(≤8.46)	(≤134)	(≤562)	−61	−254	*EST	2211-89-4
$C_6H_{14}O_2^+$							
n-C_4H_9CH(CH_3)OOH	9.25±0.03 IP from 77ASH/BUR.	(152)	(636)	−61	−256	*EST	24254-55-5
n-C_6H_{13}OOH	(9.47±0.03) IP from 77ASH/BUR.	(162)	(677)	−57	−237	*EST	4312-76-9
(iso-$C_3H_7O)_2$	(≤9.16)	(≤147)	(≤614)	−65	−270	74BAT/CHR	16642-57-2

Table 1. Positive Ion Table – Continued

ION Neutral	Ionization potential eV	$\Delta_f H$(Ion) kcal/mol kJ/mol	$\Delta_f H$(Neutral) kcal/mol kJ/mol	Neutral reference	CAS registry number
$C_6H_{14}O_2^+$					
$CH_3CH(OC_2H_5)_2$	≤9.78	≤117 ≤490	−108.4±0.6 −453.5±2.4	77PED/RYL	105-57-7
	IP from 82ZVE/VIL.				
$C_6H_{14}O_3^+$					
$CH_3OCH_2CH_2OCH_2CH_2OCH_3$	≤9.8	(≤107) (≤448)	−119 −498	*EST	111-96-6
	IP from 83BAK/ARM.				
$C_6H_{14}O_3P^+$					
(structure: 2-eq-methoxy-4,6-dimethyl-1,3,2-dioxaphosphorinane)		−42 −176			
	From proton affinity of 2-eq-methoxy-4,6-dimethyl-1,3,2-dioxaphosphorinane (RN 7735-82-2). PA = 226.2 kcal/mol, 946 kJ/mol.				
(structure: 2-ax-methoxy-4,6-dimethyl-1,3,2-dioxaphosphorinane)		−41 −171			
	From proton affinity of 2-ax-methoxy-4,6-dimethyl-1,3,2-dioxaphosphorinane (RN 41821-91-4). PA = 225 kcal/mol, 941 kJ/mol.				
$C_6H_{14}S^+$					
$(n-C_3H_7)_2S$	8.30±0.02	161 676	−29.9±0.2 −125.3±0.8	77PED/RYL	111-47-7
$(i-C_3H_7)_2S$	8.0	(150) (630)	−33.9±0.2 −141.9±0.9	77PED/RYL	625-80-9
	IP is onset of photoelectron spectrum. See also: 82HIR/MOH.				
$C_6H_{14}S_2^+$					
$(n-C_3H_7S)_2$	(≤8.62)	(≤171) (≤714)	−28.0±0.3 −117.3±1.1	77PED/RYL	629-19-6
	Dialkyl disulfides undergo a change in the CSSC bond angle from 90° to 180° upon ionization; adiabatic ionization potentials are probably well below the experimentally observed ionization onset.				
$(i-C_3H_7S)_2$	≤8.51	(≤164) (≤688)	−32 −133	*EST	4253-89-8
	Dialkyl disulfides undergo a change in the CSSC bond angle from 90° to 180° upon ionization; adiabatic ionization potentials are probably well below the experimentally observed ionization onset.				
$C_6H_{14}Si^+$					
$(C_2H_5)_2Si=CHCH_3$		(201) (839)			2372-29-4
	$\Delta_f H$(Ion) from appearance potential determination (81GUS/VOL).				
(cyclohexyl-Si(CH$_3$)$_2$)	(9.0)	(164) (686)	−43±3 −182±12	77PED/RYL	1072-54-4
	IP is onset of photoelectron band. See also: 81GUS/VOL2.				

Table 1. Positive Ion Table - Continued

ION / Neutral	Ionization potential eV	$\Delta_f H$(Ion) kcal/mol	$\Delta_f H$(Ion) kJ/mol	$\Delta_f H$(Neutral) kcal/mol	$\Delta_f H$(Neutral) kJ/mol	Neutral reference	CAS registry number
$C_6H_{14}Si^+$							
1,1,2-trimethylsilacyclobutane	8.59±0.03 IP from 81GUS/VOL2.	(167)	(699)	−31	−130	81GUS/VOL2	30681-90-4
1,1,3-trimethylsilacyclobutane	(8.67±0.03) IP from 81GUS/VOL2.	(170)	(709)	−30	−127	81GUS/VOL2	2295-13-8
$C_6H_{15}B^+$							
$(C_2H_5)_3B$	9.6	(186)	(777)	−36±1	−149±6	77PED/RYL	97-94-9
$C_6H_{15}BO_3^+$							
$B(OC_2H_5)_3$	(10.13)	(−6)	(−25)	−239±0.5	−1002±2	77PED/RYL	150-46-9
$C_6H_{15}N^+$							
$n\text{-}C_6H_{13}NH_2$	(8.63±0.05) See also: 79AUE/BOW.	(167)	(700)	−32±0.7	−133±3	*EST	111-26-2
$(n\text{-}C_3H_7)_2NH$	7.84±0.02	153	640	−27.7±0.1	−116.0±1.4	77PED/RYL	142-84-7
$(iso\text{-}C_3H_7)_2NH$	(7.73±0.03)	(144)	(602)	−34.4±0.1	−144.0±0.4	77PED/RYL	108-18-9
$n\text{-}C_4H_9N(CH_3)_2$	≤8.35 IP from 84NEL.	(≤172)	(≤722)	−20	−84	*EST	927-62-8
$i\text{-}C_4H_9N(CH_3)_2$	≤8.31 IP from 84NEL.	(≤170)	(≤711)	−22	−91	*EST	
$t\text{-}C_4H_9N(CH_3)_2$	≤8.08 IP from 84NEL.	(≤166)	(≤694)	−21	−86	*EST	918-02-5
$(C_2H_5)_3N$	7.50	151	631	−22.1±0.1	−92.8±0.6	77PED/RYL	121-44-8

IP values of 7.11 and 7.20 eV have also been reported; selected value gives hydrogen affinity value consistent with other tertiary amine ions.

$C_6H_{15}NO_3^+$							
$N(CH_2CH_2OH)_3$	(7.9) IP is onset of photoelectron band.	(49)	(205)	−133±0.7	−558±3	82MIN/SAB	102-71-6
$C_6H_{15}N_2^+$							
hexahydro-1,2-dimethylpyridazine		152	637				

From proton affinity of hexahydro-1,2-dimethylpyridazine (RN 26163-37-1) (84MAU/NEL). PA = 229.8 kcal/mol, 961. kJ/mol.

Table 1. Positive Ion Table - Continued

ION Neutral	Ionization potential eV	$\Delta_f H$(Ion) kcal/mol	 kJ/mol	$\Delta_f H$(Neutral) kcal/mol	 kJ/mol	Neutral reference	CAS registry number
$C_6H_{15}N_2O_2^+$							
L-$H_3N(CH_2)_4CH(NH_2)COOH$		11	45				
From proton affinity of L-$H_2N(CH_2)_4CH(NH_2)COOH$ (RN 56-87-1). PA = 230.3 kcal/mol, 963.5 kJ/mol.							
$C_6H_{15}N_3^+$							
(1,3,5-trimethylhexahydro-1,3,5-triazine)	7.6	185	772	9.4	39	69BEN/CRU	108-74-7
IP is onset of photoelectron band (86BEC/HUN).							
$C_6H_{15}O^+$							
$(n-C_3H_7)_2OH$		93	391				
From proton affinity of $(n-C_3H_7)_2O$ (RN 111-43-3). PA = 202.3 kcal/mol, 846. kJ/mol.							
$(i-C_3H_7)_2OH$		84	350				
From proton affinity of $(i-C_3H_7)_2O$ (RN 108-20-3). PA = 206.0 kcal/mol, 862. kJ/mol.							
$C_2H_5OH(t-C_4H_9)$		83	347				
From proton affinity of $C_2H_5O(t-C_4H_9)$ (RN 637-92-3). PA = 205.3 kcal/mol, 859. kJ/mol.							
$C_6H_{15}OSi^+$							
$(CH_3)_2COSi(CH_3)_3$		40	168				
From proton affinity of $CH_2=C(CH_3)OSi(CH_3)_3$ (RN 1833-53-0). PA = 221. kcal/mol, 925. kJ/mol.							
$C_6H_{15}O_2^+$							
$CH_3OH(CH_2)_4OCH_3$		46	194				
From proton affinity of $CH_3O(CH_2)_4OCH_3$ (RN 13179-96-9). PA = 221.8 kcal/mol, 928. kJ/mol.							
$C_6H_{15}O_3^+$							
$(CH_3OCH_2CH_2)_2OH$		27	114				
From proton affinity of $CH_3(OCH_2CH_2)_2OCH_3$ (RN 111-96-6). PA = 219.4 kcal/mol, 918. kJ/mol.							
$C_6H_{15}O_3P^+$							
$(C_2H_5O)_3P$	(8.4)	(0.6)	(2.5)	−193±1	−808±5	80TEL/RAB	122-52-1
IP is onset of photoelectron band (81ARS/ZVE, 81CHA/FIN, 82LEV/LIA).							
$C_6H_{15}O_3PS^+$							
$(C_2H_5O)_3PS$	(8.49±0.02)	(−35)	(−148)	−231	−967	*EST	126-68-1

Table 1. Positive Ion Table - Continued

ION / Neutral	Ionization potential eV	$\Delta_f H$(Ion) kcal/mol	$\Delta_f H$(Ion) kJ/mol	$\Delta_f H$(Neutral) kcal/mol	$\Delta_f H$(Neutral) kJ/mol	Neutral reference	CAS registry number
$C_6H_{15}O_3PSe^+$							
$(C_2H_5O)_3PSe$	(<7.9)	(<-27)	(<-113)	-209	-875	*EST	2651-89-0
	IP from 81ZVE/VIL.						
$C_6H_{15}O_4P^+$							
$(C_2H_5O)_3PO$	(9.79)	(-58)	(-242)	-284±1	-1187±6	77PED/RYL	78-40-0
	See also: 81CHA/FIN.						
$C_6H_{15}P^+$							
$(C_2H_5)_3P$	8.15±0.11	(134)	(561)	-54	-225	*EST	554-70-1
	See also: 77COW/GOO, 69BOG/GRI, 79AUE/BOW.						
$C_6H_{15}S^+$							
$(n-C_3H_7)_2SH$		129	541				
	From proton affinity of $(n-C_3H_7)_2S$ (RN 111-47-7). PA = 206.5 kcal/mol, 864. kJ/mol.						
$(i-C_3H_7)_2SH$		122	511				
	From proton affinity of $(i-C_3H_7)_2S$ (RN 625-80-9). PA = 209.6 kcal/mol, 877. kJ/mol.						
$C_6H_{15}Sb^+$							
$(C_2H_5)_3Sb$	(9.2±0.3)	(224)	(937)	12±3	49±11	82TN270	617-85-6
$C_6H_{16}N^+$							
$n-C_6H_{13}NH_3$		116	484				
	From proton affinity of $n-C_6H_{13}NH_2$ (RN 111-26-2). PA = 218.9 kcal/mol, 916. kJ/mol.						
$(n-C_3H_7)_2NH_2$		110	462				
	From proton affinity of $(n-C_3H_7)_2NH$ (RN 142-84-7). PA = 227.5 kcal/mol, 952. kJ/mol.						
$(i-C_3H_7)_2NH_2$		101	423				
	From proton affinity of $(i-C_3H_7)_2NH$ (RN 108-18-9). PA = 230.2 kcal/mol, 963. kJ/mol.						
$(CH_3)_2(tert-C_4H_9)NH$		109	457				
	From proton affinity of $(CH_3)_2(tert-C_4H_9)N$ (RN 918-02-5). PA = 232.0 kcal/mol, 971. kJ/mol.						
$(C_2H_5)_3NH$		111	465				
	From proton affinity of $(C_2H_5)_3N$ (RN 121-44-8). PA = 232.3 kcal/mol, 972. kJ/mol.						
$C_6H_{16}NO^+$							
$NH_3(CH_2)_6OH$		(68)	(285)				
	From proton affinity of $NH_2(CH_2)_6OH$ (RN 4048-33-3). PA = (231.0) kcal/mol, (966.5) kJ/mol.						

Table 1. Positive Ion Table - Continued

ION / Neutral	Ionization potential eV	$\Delta_f H$(Ion) kcal/mol	$\Delta_f H$(Ion) kJ/mol	$\Delta_f H$(Neutral) kcal/mol	$\Delta_f H$(Neutral) kJ/mol	Neutral reference	CAS registry number
$C_6H_{16}N_2^+$							
$(CH_3)_2NCH_2CH_2N(CH_3)_2$	7.59±0.3	170	713	-4.7	-19.7	81LOG/TAK	110-18-9
		IP from 81LOG/TAK, 82LEV/LIA.					
$(C_2H_5)_2NN(CH_3)_2$	≤8.10	(≤196)	(≤819)	9	37	*EST	21849-74-1

Reported values of IP's of hydrazines determined by threshold measurements are usually significantly higher than the adiabatic value because of the large geometry change associated with ionization. See also: 82LEV/LIA, 84NEL.

$(n-C_3H_7)(CH_3)NN(CH_3)_2$	(6.63)	(160)	(671)	7	31	*EST	60678-65-1

IP from charge transfer equilibrium determinations (84MAU/NEL). Reference standard: IP ($C_6H_5N(CH_3)_2$ = 7.12 eV.) See also: 84NEL.

$(C_2H_5)(CH_3)NN(CH_3)(C_2H_5)$	6.75	(164)	(686)	8	35	*EST	23337-93-1

IP from charge transfer equilibrium constant determinations (86RUM). See also: 82LEV/LIA, 84NEL.

$C_6H_{16}N_3P^+$

(cyclic structure with CH_3, P-N(CH_3)_2, CH_3)	(7.1)	(159)	(666)	-4	-19	*EST	6069-38-1

IP is onset of photoelectron band (82WOR/HAR).

$C_6H_{16}OP^+$

$(C_2H_5)_3POH$		70	292				

From proton affinity of $(C_2H_5)_3PO$ (RN 597-50-2) (85BOL/HOU). PA = 222.6 kcal/mol, 931. kJ/mol.

$C_6H_{16}O_4P^+$

$HOP(OC_2H_5)_3$		-135	-565				

From proton affinity of $OP(OC_2H_5)_3$ (RN 78-40-0). PA = (217) kcal/mol, (910) kJ/mol.

$C_6H_{16}P^+$

$(C_2H_5)_3PH$		80	336				

From proton affinity of $(C_2H_5)_3P$ (RN 554-70-1). PA = (231.7) kcal/mol, (969.) kJ/mol.

$C_6H_{16}Si^+$

$(C_2H_5)_3SiH$	9.5	171	716	-48±4	-201±15	77PED/RYL	617-86-7

See also: 81HOT.

Table 1. Positive Ion Table - Continued

ION / Neutral	Ionization potential eV	$\Delta_f H$(Ion) kcal/mol	$\Delta_f H$(Ion) kJ/mol	$\Delta_f H$(Neutral) kcal/mol	$\Delta_f H$(Neutral) kJ/mol	Neutral reference	CAS registry number
$C_6H_{16}Si_2^+$							
(H$_3$C)$_2$Si-SiCH$_2$-Si(CH$_3$)$_2$	(8.56±0.07) See also: 81KHV/ZYK.	(125)	(525)	−72±3	−301±14	77PED/RYL	1627-98-1
$C_6H_{16}Sn^+$							
(C$_2$H$_5$)$_3$SnH	(≤9.1)	(≤210)	(≤878)	0±2	0±8	80TEL/RAB	997-50-2
i-C$_3$H$_7$Sn(CH$_3$)$_3$	8.2 IP is onset of photoelectron band.	(178)	(744)	−11±1	−47±5	77PED/RYL	3531-46-2
$C_6H_{17}NSi^+$							
(CH$_3$)$_2$NCH$_2$Si(CH$_3$)$_3$	7.61 See also: 81LOG/TAK.	(126)	(527)	−49	−207	*EST	18182-40-6
$C_6H_{17}N_2^+$							
NH$_3$(CH$_2$)$_6$NH$_2$		106	442				
From proton affinity of NH$_2$(CH$_2$)$_6$NH$_2$ (RN 124-09-4). PA = 237.7 kcal/mol, 994.4 kJ/mol.							
(n-C$_3$H$_7$)(CH$_3$)HNN(CH$_3$)$_2$		145	605				
From proton affinity of (n-C$_3$H$_7$)(CH$_3$)NN(CH$_3$)$_2$ (RN 60678-65-1) (84MAU/NEL). PA = 229.1 kcal/mol, 959. kJ/mol.							
(CH$_3$)$_2$NH(CH$_2$)$_2$N(CH$_3$)$_2$		121	507				
From proton affinity of (CH$_3$)$_2$N(CH$_2$)$_2$N(CH$_3$)$_2$ (RN 110-18-9) re-evaluated. PA = 240 kcal/mol, 1003 kJ/mol.							
$C_6H_{17}N_3OP^+$		37	154				
From proton affinity of 1,3,2-Diazaphospholidine-2-amine,N,N',1,3-tetramethyl-2-oxide- (RN 7778-06-5) (85BOL/HOU). PA = 226.9 kcal/mol, 949. kJ/mol.							
$C_6H_{18}BN_3^+$							
B(N(CH$_3$)$_2$)$_3$	7.60	116	487	−59	−246	82HOL/SMI	4375-83-1
$C_6H_{18}NSi^+$							
(CH$_3$)$_3$SiCH$_2$NH(CH$_3$)$_2$		85	354				
From proton affinity of (CH$_3$)$_3$SiCH$_2$N(CH$_3$)$_2$ (RN 18182-40-6). PA = 231.5 kcal/mol, 968. kJ/mol.							

ION Neutral	Ionization potential eV	$\Delta_f H$(Ion) kcal/mol	kJ/mol	$\Delta_f H$(Neutral) kcal/mol	kJ/mol	Neutral reference	CAS registry number
$C_6H_{18}N_3OP^+$							
$((CH_3)_2N)_3PO$	7.82	66	277	−114	−477	69BEN/CRU	630-31-9
	IP is onset of photoelectron band. (82LEV/LIA, 82WOR/HAR). See also: 82COW/LAT.						
$C_6H_{18}N_3P^+$							
$((CH_3)_2N)_3P$	6.75	(124)	(517)	−32	−134	69BEN/CRU	1608-26-0
	IP is onset of photoelectron band (82LEV/LIA, 82WOR/HAR, 77COW/GOO). See also: 82COW/LAT.						
$C_6H_{18}N_3PS^+$							
$SP[N(CH_3)_2]_3$	≤8.63±0.10	(≤162)	(≤677)	−37	−156	*EST	3732-82-9
	IP from 82COW/LAT.						
$C_6H_{18}N_3P_3^+$	(8.35±0.05)	(64)	(268)	−129±5	−538±23	77PED/RYL	6607-30-3
$C_6H_{18}OSi_2^+$							
$((CH_3)_3Si)_2O$	9.64±0.01	36 (48)	153 (202)	−186±1 −174	−777±6 −728	77PED/RYL	107-46-0
	IP from 83MOL/PIK, 85SEE/MOL.						
$C_6H_{18}Si_2^+$							
$(CH_3)_6Si_2$	8.27±0.05	110 122	459 513	−81±2 −68±2	−339±8 −285±8	81WAL	1450-14-2
	IP from 84SZE/BAE, 81SZE/KOR. See also: 81KHV/ZYK, 85MOC/WOR.						
$C_6H_{18}Sn_2^+$							
$((CH_3)_3Sn)_2$	(7.8)	(173)	(726)	−6±2	−27±8	77PED/RYL	661-69-8
	IP is onset of photoelectron band (85GRA/BER, 81SZE/KOR). See also: 85MOC/WOR.						
$C_6H_{18}W^+$							
$(CH_3)_6W$	(8.3)	(376)	(1572)	185±8	772±35	82PIL/SKI	36133-73-0
	IP is onset of photoelectron band (82LEV/LIA, 75GAL/WIL).						
$C_6H_{19}NSi_2^+$							
$((CH_3)_3Si)_2NH$	≤8.55	≤83	≤348	−114±1	−477±6	77PED/RYL	999-97-3
	IP from 83MOL/PIK3.						
$C_6H_{19}N_3P^+$							
$HP(N(CH_3)_2)_3$		113	472				
	From proton affinity of $P(N(CH_3)_2)_3$ (RN 1608-26-0). PA = 220.9 kcal/mol, 924. kJ/mol.						
$C_6H_{19}OSi_2^+$							
$((CH_3)_3Si)_2OH$		(−23)	(−96)				
	From proton affinity of $((CH_3)_3Si)_2O$ (RN 107-46-0). PA = (203) kcal/mol, (849) kJ/mol.						

Table 1. Positive Ion Table - Continued

ION / Neutral	Ionization potential eV	$\Delta_f H$(Ion) kcal/mol	$\Delta_f H$(Ion) kJ/mol	$\Delta_f H$(Neutral) kcal/mol	$\Delta_f H$(Neutral) kJ/mol	Neutral reference	CAS registry number
$C_6MoO_6^+$ / $Mo(CO)_6$	8.227±0.011	−28 / −29	−118 / −121	−218 / −219	−912 / −915	77ROS/DRA	13939-06-5
See also: 82HUB/LIC.							
$C_6N_4^+$ / $(NC)_2CC(CN)_2$	11.77±0.01	440	1842	169±1	706±6	77PED/RYL	670-54-2
$C_6O_6V^+$ / $V(CO)_6$	7.52	−31	−128	−204±7	−854±29	67BID/MCI	20644-87-5
$C_6O_6W^+$ / $W(CO)_6$	8.20	−23	−96	−212±1	−887±4	84ALT/CON2	14040-11-0
IP from 82HUB/LIC, 77ROS/DRA.							
$C_7ClF_5O^+$	(9.8)	(−3)	(−13)	−229	−959	*EST	2251-50-5
IP is onset of photoelectron band (81MEE/WAH).							
$C_7F_3MnO_6^+$ / $CF_3COMn(CO)_5$	(8.5)	(−164)	(−688)	−360±1	−1508±6	82CON/ZAF	14099-62-8
IP is onset of photoelectron band.							
$C_7F_8^+$	(9.9)	(−56)	(−232)	−284±2	−1187±8	77PED/RYL	434-64-0
$C_7HF_5O_2^+$	(9.2)	(−62)	(−260)	−274±1	−1148±4	77PED/RYL	602-94-8
IP is onset of photoelectron band (81MEE/WAH).							
$C_7H_3F_5^+$	(9.4)	(15)	(64)	−201.5±0.4	−842.9±1.8	77PED/RYL	771-56-2
Value of IP from charge transfer equilibrium constant determinations is 9.63 eV.							

Table 1. Positive Ion Table - Continued

ION Neutral	Ionization potential eV	$\Delta_f H$(Ion) kcal/mol	kJ/mol	$\Delta_f H$(Neutral) kcal/mol	kJ/mol	Neutral reference	CAS registry number
$C_7H_4FN^+$							
2-fluorobenzonitrile	(9.78)	(231)	(965)	5	21	*EST	394-47-8
3-fluorobenzonitrile	(9.79)	(231)	(966)	5	21	*EST	403-54-3
4-fluorobenzonitrile	(9.74)	(229)	(957)	4	17	*EST	1194-02-1
$C_7H_4F_4^+$							
1-CF₃-4-F-benzene	9.98 IP from 82CAB/COW.	(41)	(171)	−189±0.3	−792±1	*EST	402-44-8
$C_7H_4N_2O_2^+$							
3-nitrobenzonitrile	(10.29±0.1)	(286)	(1197)	49	204	*EST	619-24-9
4-nitrobenzonitrile	(10.23±0.1)	(284)	(1189)	48	202	*EST	619-72-7
$C_7H_4S_3^+$							
benzodithiole-thione	(7.9) IP is onset of photoelectron band.	(242)	(1013)	60±1	251±5	72GEI/RAU	3354-42-5
benzodithiole-thione isomer	(8.14)	(246)	(1027)	57.8±0.4	242.0±1.7	77PED/RYL	934-36-1

Table 1. Positive Ion Table - Continued

ION / Neutral	Ionization potential eV	$\Delta_f H$(Ion) kcal/mol	$\Delta_f H$(Ion) kJ/mol	$\Delta_f H$(Neutral) kcal/mol	$\Delta_f H$(Neutral) kJ/mol	Neutral reference	CAS registry number
$C_7H_5BrO^+$							
Br-C₆H₄-CHO (benzoyl bromide)	(9.65) IP from 79MCL/TRA. See also: 84GAN/LIV.	(211)	(882)	−12	−49	79MCL/TRA	618-32-6
Br-C₆H₄-CHO (4-bromobenzaldehyde)	≤9.22 IP from 85GAL/GER.	(≤209)	(≤874)	−4	−16	*EST	1122-91-4
$C_7H_5BrO_2^+$							
Br-C₆H₄-COOH	(9.72±0.2)	(155)	(648)	−69±1	−290±5	77PED/RYL	586-76-5
$C_7H_5ClO^+$							
Cl-C₆H₄-CHO	9.59±0.02 IP from 85GAL/GER, 77ROS/DRA.	(205)	(856)	−16	−69	*EST	104-88-1
C₆H₅-COCl	9.54 IP is onset of photoelectron band (84GAN/LIV, 81MEE/WAH). See also: 80GOF/YAR, 79MCL/TRA.	195	817	−25±1	−103±4	75MOS/PRI	98-88-4
$C_7H_5Cl_2^+$							
C₆H₅-ĊCl₂	$\Delta_f H$(Ion) from chloride transfer equilibrium constant determinations (85SHA/SHA).	(197)	(824)				
$C_7H_5Cl_3^+$							
C₆H₅-CCl₃	≤9.60 IP from 81ZVE/ERM.	(≤219)	(≤915)	−3	−11	*EST	98-07-7

Table 1. Positive Ion Table - Continued

ION / Neutral	Ionization potential eV	$\Delta_f H$(Ion) kcal/mol	$\Delta_f H$(Ion) kJ/mol	$\Delta_f H$(Neutral) kcal/mol	$\Delta_f H$(Neutral) kJ/mol	Neutral reference	CAS registry number
$C_7H_5FO^+$							
C₆H₅C(O)F	9.78 IP from 79MCL/TRA, 84GAN/LIV.	(153)	(639)	−73	−305	*EST	455-32-3
4-F-C₆H₄-CHO	≤9.60 IP from 85GAL/GER.	(≤167)	(≤700)	−54	−226	*EST	459-57-4
$C_7H_5FO_2^+$							
3-F-C₆H₄-COOH	(9.91±0.2)	(111)	(466)	−117	−490	*EST	455-38-9
4-F-C₆H₄-COOH	(9.91±0.2)	(111)	(461)	−118±1	−495±3	77PED/RYL	456-22-4
$C_7H_5F_3^+$							
C₆H₅-CF₃	9.685±0.004 See also: 81BER/BOM.	80.1	335.4	−143.2±0.2	−599.0±0.9	77PED/RYL	98-08-8
$C_7H_5N^+$							
C₆H₅-NC	(9.4) IP is onset of photoelectron band.	(289)	(1208)	72±2	301±7	*EST	931-54-4
C₆H₅-CN	9.62 See also: 83KLA/KOV, 81KIM/KAT.	274	1147	52	219	82CHU/NGU	100-47-0

Table 1. Positive Ion Table - Continued

ION / Neutral	Ionization potential eV	$\Delta_f H$(Ion) kcal/mol kJ/mol		$\Delta_f H$(Neutral) kcal/mol kJ/mol		Neutral reference	CAS registry number
$C_7H_5NO^+$							
Ph-C≡NO	(8.96±0.02)	(275)	(1148)	68	283	*EST	873-67-6
Ph-N=C=O	(8.8) IP is onset of photoelectron band.	(206)	(862)	3	13	*EST	103-71-9
$C_7H_5NO_3^+$							
O_2N-C6H4-CHO	10.27±0.01 See also: 85GAL/GER.	(249)	(1043)	12	52	*EST	555-16-8
$C_7H_5NO_4^+$							
3-NO_2-C6H4-COOH	(10.31±0.2)	(143)	(600)	−94.3±0.3	−394.7±1.3	77PED/RYL	121-92-6
4-O_2N-C6H4-COOH	10.18±0.2	141	589	−93.7±0.4	−392.2±1.5	77PED/RYL	62-23-7
$C_7H_5N_2^+$							
7-azaindole	8.11±0.01 IP from 84FUK/YOS.	(238)	(995)	51	213	*EST	
$C_7H_5N_3O_6^+$							
2,4,6-trinitrotoluene	(10.59±0.04)	(252)	(1054)	8±0.5	32±2	77PEL	118-96-7

Table 1. Positive Ion Table - Continued

ION Neutral	Ionization potential eV	$\Delta_f H$(Ion) kcal/mol kJ/mol		$\Delta_f H$(Neutral) kcal/mol kJ/mol		Neutral reference	CAS registry number
$C_7H_5O^+$ (phenyl–CO)		168±1	705±6				2652-65-5

From appearance potential measurements (79MCL/TRA, 82BUR/HOL2. See also: 85TAJ/TOB.

ION Neutral	Ionization potential eV	$\Delta_f H$(Ion) kcal/mol kJ/mol		$\Delta_f H$(Neutral) kcal/mol kJ/mol		Neutral reference	CAS registry number
$C_7H_6^+$ (fulvenylidene, =C=CH₂)	(8.29)	(275)	(1150)	84±2	350±10	*EST	27041-32-3
(benzvalene/bicyclic)	(≤8.82)	(≤292)	(≤1223)	89±1	372±4	73BIL/CHO	4646-69-9
$C_7H_6BrNS^+$ (2-bromothiobenzamide)	(8.5)	(232)	(972)	36	152	*EST	30216-44-5

IP from 81GRU.

| $C_7H_6Cl^+$ (PhCHCl) | | (209) | (873) | | | | |

$\Delta_f H$(Ion) from chloride transfer equilibrium constant determinations (85SHA/SHA); $\Delta_f H(C_6H_5CCl_2H)$ estimated as 3 kcal/mol, 13 kJ/mol.

$C_7H_6ClNOS^+$							
(4-chloro-2-methyl-N-sulfinylaniline)	(8.5)	(166)	(694)	−30	−126	*EST	
(3-chloro-2-methyl-N-sulfinylaniline)	(≤9.23)	(≤184)	(≤769)	−29	−122	*EST	

IP is onset of photoelectron band (82LOU/VAN).

IP from 82LOU/VAN.

Table 1. Positive Ion Table - Continued

ION / Neutral	Ionization potential eV	$\Delta_f H$(Ion) kcal/mol	$\Delta_f H$(Ion) kJ/mol	$\Delta_f H$(Neutral) kcal/mol	$\Delta_f H$(Neutral) kJ/mol	Neutral reference	CAS registry number
$C_7H_6ClNS^+$							
(2-chlorobenzothioamide)	8.8 IP from 81GRU.	(226)	(948)	24	99	*EST	15717-17-6
$C_7H_6ClO^+$							
(4-Cl-C$_6$H$_4$-CHOH)		149	623				

From proton affinity of 4-ClC$_6$H$_4$CHO (RN 104-88-1). PA = 200.2 kcal/mol, 838. kJ/mol.

$C_7H_6F^+$							
(o-F-C$_6$H$_4$-CH$_2\cdot$)		(170)	(710)				40880-01-1

$\Delta_f H$(Ion) from chloride-transfer equilibrium constants (85SHA/SHA); $\Delta_f H$(o-C$_6$H$_4$FCH$_2$Cl) estimated as -43.5 kcal/mol, -182 kJ/mol.

| (m-F-C$_6$H$_4$-CH$_2\cdot$) | | (173) | (725) | | | | 2599-73-7 |

$\Delta_f H$(Ion) from chloride-transfer equilibrium constants (85SHA/SHA); $\Delta_f H$(m-C$_6$H$_4$FCH$_2$Cl) estimated as -43.5 kcal/mol, -182 kJ/mol.

| (p-F-C$_6$H$_4$-CH$_2\cdot$) | | (166) | (696) | | | | 2194-09-4 |

$\Delta_f H$(Ion) from chloride-transfer equilibrium constants (85SHA/SHA); $\Delta_f H$(o-C$_6$H$_4$FCH$_2$Cl) estimated as -43.5 kcal/mol, -182 kJ/mol.

$C_7H_6FO^+$							
(3-F-C$_6$H$_4$-CHOH)		113	472				

From proton affinity of 3-FC$_6$H$_4$CHO (RN 456-48-4). PA = 196.4 kcal/mol, 822. kJ/mol.

| (4-F-C$_6$H$_4$-CHOH) | | 110 | 462 | | | | |

From proton affinity of 4-FC$_6$H$_4$CHO (RN 459-57-4). PA = 199.2 kcal/mol, 833. kJ/mol.

ION Neutral	Ionization potential eV	$\Delta_f H$(Ion) kcal/mol	kJ/mol	$\Delta_f H$(Neutral) kcal/mol	kJ/mol	Neutral reference	CAS registry number
$C_7H_6FeO_3^+$	8.04	100	417	−86±2	−359±9	82PIL/SKI	12078-32-9
IP is onset of photoelectron band. See also: 82GRE/KEL.							
$C_7H_6INS^+$	8.5	(246)	(1030)	50	210	*EST	81568-85-6
IP from 81GRU.							
$C_7H_6N^+$		222	929				
From proton affinity of C_6H_5CN (RN 100-47-0). PA = 195.9 kcal/mol, 820. kJ/mol.							
		231	965				
From proton affinity of C_6H_5NC (RN 931-54-4). (86MAU/KAR). PA = 207 kcal/mol, 866 kJ/mol.							
$C_7H_6N_2^+$	(8.61±0.05)	(252)	(1053)	53	222	*EST	2237-30-1
	(8.17)	(240)	(1004)	52	216	*EST	873-74-5
IP is onset of photoelectron band (81MOD/DIS).							
	(8.35)	(253)	(1060)	60.8±1.1	254.2±4.6	85FAO/AKA	271-44-3
	(8.0)	(228)	(957)	44±2	185±10	*EST	51-17-2
IP is onset of photoelectron band.							

Table 1. Positive Ion Table - Continued

ION / Neutral	Ionization potential eV	$\Delta_f H$(Ion) kcal/mol	$\Delta_f H$(Ion) kJ/mol	$\Delta_f H$(Neutral) kcal/mol	$\Delta_f H$(Neutral) kJ/mol	Neutral reference	CAS registry number
$C_7H_6N_4^+$							
2-methylpteridine	(8.8)	(283)	(1182)	80	333	*EST	6499-38-3

IP is onset of photoelectron band (84GLE/SPA2).

$C_7H_6O^+$							
benzaldehyde	9.49±0.02	210	879	−9±0.5	−37±2	77PED/RYL	100-52-7

IP from 79MCL/TRA. See also: 83KLA/KOV, 85GAL/GER.

2,4,6-cycloheptatrien-1-one	8.90±0.02	215	903	10±0.7	44±3	77PED/RYL	539-80-0

$C_7H_6O_2^+$							
2-hydroxy-2,4,6-cycloheptatrien-1-one	(9.86±0.02)	(191)	(797)	−36.8±0.2	−154.0±0.9	77PED/RYL	533-75-5
benzoic acid	(9.47)	(148)	(620)	−70.3±0.4	−294.1±1.6	77PED/RYL	65-85-0

IP from onset of photoelectron band (83KLA/KOV). See also: 81MEE/WAH.

4-hydroxybenzaldehyde	(9.32±0.02)	(159)	(666)	−56±2	−233±8	*EST	
2-methyl-2,5-cyclohexadiene-1,4-dione	9.78±0.02	188	789	−37.1±2.0	−155±9	*EST	553-97-9
1,3-benzodioxole	(8.0)	(150)	(629)	−34±0.7	−143±3	77PED/RYL	274-09-9

IP is onset of photoelectron band.

Table 1. Positive Ion Table - Continued

ION / Neutral	Ionization potential eV	$\Delta_f H$(Ion) kcal/mol	$\Delta_f H$(Ion) kJ/mol	$\Delta_f H$(Neutral) kcal/mol	$\Delta_f H$(Neutral) kJ/mol	Neutral reference	CAS registry number
$C_7H_6O_2^+$							
(bicyclic dione)	(9.64) IP from 85GLE/JAH.	(232)	(971)	10	41	*EST	53735-22-1
(cyclohexene dione)	(8.4) IP is onset of photoelectron band.	(175)	(731)	−19	−79	*EST	17994-26-2
$C_7H_7^+$							
(tropyl radical)	6.24±0.01	203 / 208	849 / 872	59	247	82MCM/GOL	3551-27-7

$\Delta_f H$(Ion) from appearance potential measurements (83BOM/DAN, 83BOM/DAN2); Heat of formation of radical derived from $\Delta_f H(C_7H_7^+)$-IP; 82MCM/GOL cite 65±2 kcal/mol, 271±8 kJ/mol.

(benzyl radical)	7.20±0.02	215 / 219	899 / 917	49 / 53	204 / 223	81TSA	2154-56-5

$\Delta_f H$(Ion) from chloride transfer equilibrium constants (81SEN/KEB) is in agreement.

$C_7H_7Br^+$							
(benzyl bromide)	9.0 IP is onset of photoelectron band.	(224)	(935)	16±0.5	67±2	76ASH	100-39-0
(o-bromotoluene)	8.58±0.1 See also: 85BAI/MIS.	(213)	(890)	15	62	*EST	95-46-5
(m-bromotoluene)	8.79±0.02	(217)	(909)	15	61	*EST	591-17-3
(p-bromotoluene)	8.67±0.01 IP from 82LEV/LIA, 78LIA/AUS, 77ROS/DRA. See also: 85BAI/MIS.	(217)	(908)	17	71	*EST	106-38-7

Table 1. Positive Ion Table - Continued

ION / Neutral	Ionization potential eV	$\Delta_f H$(Ion) kcal/mol	$\Delta_f H$(Ion) kJ/mol	$\Delta_f H$(Neutral) kcal/mol	$\Delta_f H$(Neutral) kJ/mol	Neutral reference	CAS registry number
$C_7H_7BrO^+$							
4-bromoanisole (H₃CO–C₆H₄–Br)	(8.11)	(177)	(739)	−10	−43	*EST	104-92-7
$C_7H_7BrS^+$							
4-bromothioanisole (H₃CS–C₆H₄–Br)	(7.5) IP is onset of photoelectron band (81BAK/ARM).	(201)	(843)	28	119	*EST	104-95-0
$C_7H_7Cl^+$							
benzyl chloride (C₆H₅–CH₂Cl)	9.14±0.01 See also: 81ZVE/ERM, 81KIM/KAT.	215	899	4±0.7	17±3	76ASH	25168-05-2
2-chlorotoluene	(8.83±0.02) See also: 85BAI/MIS.	(208)	(871)	4	18	*EST	95-49-8
3-chlorotoluene	(8.83±0.02)	(208)	(870)	4	18	*EST	108-41-8
4-chlorotoluene	8.69±0.02 See also: 85BAI/MIS.	(205)	(856)	4	18	*EST	106-43-4
2-chloronorbornadiene	≤8.77 IP from 83HOU/RON.	(≤256)	(≤1071)	54	225	*EST	2294-41-9
$C_7H_7ClHg^+$							
4-methylphenylmercuric chloride (H₃C–C₆H₄–HgCl)	(8.7) IP is onset of photoelectron band (81FUR/PIA).	(223)	(931)	22	92	*EST	539-43-5

Table 1. Positive Ion Table - Continued

ION / Neutral	Ionization potential eV	$\Delta_f H$(Ion) kcal/mol	kJ/mol	$\Delta_f H$(Neutral) kcal/mol	kJ/mol	Neutral reference	CAS registry number
$C_7H_7ClO^+$							
3-chlorobenzyl alcohol	(8.51) IP from 83RUS/FRE.	(166)	(697)	−30	−124	83RUS/FRE	873-63-2
4-chlorobenzyl alcohol	(8.58) IP from 83RUS/FRE.	(167)	(698)	−31	−130	83RUS/FRE	873-76-7
2-chloroanisole	(8.42) IP from 83RUS/FRE.	(169)	(707)	−25	−105	83RUS/FRE	766-51-8
4-chloroanisole	(7.79) IP from 83RUS/FRE.	(153)	(641)	−26	−111	83RUS/FRE	623-12-1
$C_7H_7F^+$							
2-fluorotoluene	8.91±0.01 See also: 78LIA/AUS.	(170)	(711)	−36	−149	*EST	95-52-3
3-fluorotoluene	8.91±0.01	(170)	(710)	−36	−150	*EST	352-70-5
4-fluorotoluene	8.79±0.01 See also: 78LIA/AUS.	167	700	−35.2±0.3	−147.5±1.2	77PED/RYL	352-32-9
$C_7H_7FO^+$							
2-fluoroanisole	8.41 IP from 85OIK/ABE.	(130)	(544)	−64	−267	*EST	456-49-5

Table 1. Positive Ion Table - Continued

ION / Neutral	Ionization potential eV	$\Delta_f H$(Ion) kcal/mol	$\Delta_f H$(Ion) kJ/mol	$\Delta_f H$(Neutral) kcal/mol	$\Delta_f H$(Neutral) kJ/mol	Neutral reference	CAS registry number
$C_7H_7F_3N^+$ 3-CF₃-C₆H₄-NH₂ (protonated)		19	81				

From proton affinity of 3-CF₃C₆H₄NH₂ (RN 98-16-8). PA = 204.2 kcal/mol, 854. kJ/mol.

$C_7H_7I^+$							
2-iodomethylpyridine (CH₂I-pyridine)	(8.6)	(223)	(933)	25±1	103±4	76ASH	620-05-3
2-iodotoluene	(8.62±0.01)	(231)	(965)	32±1	133±6	77PED/RYL	615-37-2
See also: 85BAI/MIS.							
3-iodotoluene	(8.61±0.03)	(231)	(965)	32±1	134±6	77PED/RYL	625-95-6
4-iodotoluene	(8.50±0.01)	(225)	(942)	29±1	122±6	77ROS/DRA	624-31-7
See also: 85BAI/MIS.							

$C_7H_7N^+$							
2-vinylpyridine	(8.6)	(246)	(1030)	48	200	*EST	100-69-6
IP is onset of photoelectron band (81MOD/DIS2).							
4-vinylpyridine	(8.9)	(254)	(1061)	48	202	*EST	100-43-6
IP is onset of photoelectron band (81MOD/DIS2).							
pyridine-fused cyclobutene	(≤9.11)	(≤270)	(≤1129)	60	250	*EST	56911-25-2
IP from 79AUE/BOW.							

Table 1. Positive Ion Table - Continued

ION / Neutral	Ionization potential eV	$\Delta_f H$(Ion) kcal/mol	$\Delta_f H$(Ion) kJ/mol	$\Delta_f H$(Neutral) kcal/mol	$\Delta_f H$(Neutral) kJ/mol	Neutral reference	CAS registry number
$C_7H_7N^+$ (pyridine fused cyclobutene)	(≤9.37)	(≤276)	(≤1156)	60	252	*EST	56911-27-4
IP from 79AUE BOW. $\Delta_f H$(Ion) estimated from hydrogen affinities of pyridine ions = 268 kcal/mol, 1121 kJ/mol. Corresponding IP = 9.02 eV.							
$C_7H_7NO^+$ (2-aminotropone)	(9.43±0.02)	(227)	(949)	9.4±0.6	39.5±2.5	77PED/RYL	6264-93-3
benzamide	9.45	194	811	−24±0.2	−101±1	82TOR/SAB2	55-21-0
2-acetylpyridine	(8.9)	(200)	(838)	−5	−21	*EST	1122-62-9
IP is onset of photoelectron band (81MOD/DIS2).							
3-acetylpyridine	(9.1)	(204)	(852)	−6	−26	*EST	
IP is onset of photoelectron band (81MOD/DIS2).							
4-acetylpyridine	(9.3)	(208)	(871)	−6	−26	*EST	1122-54-9
IP is onset of photoelectron band (81MOD/DIS2).							
4-nitroso-toluene	(8.79±0.1)	(216)	(903)	13.2±1	55±4	*EST	623-11-0
$C_7H_7NOS^+$ (2-methylphenyl-N-sulfinylamine)	(8.75)	(187)	(782)	−15	−62	*EST	
IP is onset of photoelectron band (82LOU/VAN).							

Table 1. Positive Ion Table - Continued

ION / Neutral	Ionization potential eV	$\Delta_f H$(Ion) kcal/mol	$\Delta_f H$(Ion) kJ/mol	$\Delta_f H$(Neutral) kcal/mol	$\Delta_f H$(Neutral) kJ/mol	Neutral reference	CAS registry number
$C_7H_7NOS^+$ / 4-methyl-N-sulfinylaniline	(≤8.84) IP from 82LOU/VAN.	(≤190)	(≤795)	−14	−58	*EST	
$C_7H_7NO_2^+$ / 2-aminobenzoic acid	(7.6) IP is onset of photoelectron band (81MEE/WAH).	(104)	(435)	−71±0.5	−298±2	77NAB/SAB	118-92-3
3-aminobenzoic acid	(7.8) IP is onset of photoelectron band (81MEE/WAH).	(111)	(463)	−69±1	−289±4	77NAB/SAB	99-05-8
4-aminobenzoic acid	(7.8) IP is onset of photoelectron band (81MEE/WAH). See also: 84TOB/TAJ.	(110)	(458)	−70±1	−294±4	77NAB/SAB	150-13-0
2-nitrotoluene	9.45±0.04 IP from 82LEV/LIA, 82BAL/CAR. See also: 73GOL/KOR.	231	965	13	53	77PED/RYL	88-72-2
3-nitrotoluene	(9.48±0.02)	(226)	(946)	7	31	77PED/RYL	99-08-1
4-nitrotoluene	(9.4) IP is onset of photoelectron band.	(224)	(938)	7±1	31±4	77PED/RYL	99-99-0
$C_7H_7NO_3^+$ / 2-nitroanisole	(8.8) IP is onset of photoelectron band.	(186)	(779)	−17	−70	*EST	91-23-6

Table 1. Positive Ion Table - Continued

ION / Neutral	Ionization potential eV	$\Delta_f H$(Ion) kcal/mol	$\Delta_f H$(Ion) kJ/mol	$\Delta_f H$(Neutral) kcal/mol	$\Delta_f H$(Neutral) kJ/mol	Neutral reference	CAS registry number
$C_7H_7NO_3^+$							
3-methoxy-nitrobenzene	(8.7) IP is onset of photoelectron band.	(179)	(749)	−22	−90	*EST	555-03-3
4-methoxy-nitrobenzene	(8.79)	(182)	(760)	−21	−88	*EST	100-17-4
$C_7H_7NS^+$							
benzenecarbothioamide	(8.8) IP from 81GRU.	(234)	(980)	31.3±0.3	131.0±1.3	82TUR/SAB2	2227-79-4
$C_7H_7N_2^+$							
3-cyanobenzenamine · H+		218	912				
From proton affinity of 3-cyanobenzenamine (RN 2237-30-1). PA = 200.7 kcal/mol, 840. kJ/mol.							
indazole · H		208	870				
From proton affinity of indazole (RN 271-44-3) (84FLA/MAQ). PA = 218 kcal/mol, 914 kJ/mol.							
benzimidazole · H		181	757				
From proton affinity of benzimidazole (RN 51-17-2) (83CAT/ELG, 84FLA/MAQ). PA = 227 kcal/mol, 958 kJ/mol.							
$C_7H_7N_2O^+$							
4-methoxyphenyldiazonium	(7.28) IP from 77NUY/MES.	(178)	(746)	11	44	*EST	17333-79-8

GAS–PHASE ION AND NEUTRAL THERMOCHEMISTRY

Table 1. Positive Ion Table – Continued

ION / Neutral	Ionization potential eV	$\Delta_f H$(Ion) kcal/mol	kJ/mol	$\Delta_f H$(Neutral) kcal/mol	kJ/mol	Neutral reference	CAS registry number
$C_7H_7O^+$							
PhĊHOH		157	655				

From proton affinity of benzaldehyde (RN 100-52-7). PA = 200.2 kcal/mol, 838. kJ/mol.

| | | 176 | 735 | | | | 65108-16-9 |

From appearance potential determinations (83RUS/FRE).

| | | 174 | 728 | | | | 65108-08-9 |

From appearance potential determinations (83RUS/FRE).

| | | 175 | 731 | | | | 29180-18-5 |

$\Delta_f H$(Ion) from appearance potential determinations (83RUS/FRE). Value derived from proton affinity of 4-methylene-2,5-cyclohexadiene-1-one is (153) kcal/mol, (641) kJ/mol, a serious discrepancy. PA = (222) kcal/mol, (929) kJ/mol.

| anisole·+ | (8.32) | (202) | (845) | 10 | 42 | *EST | 2396-03-4 |

IP from 77NUY/MES.

| | | 157 | 656 | | | | |

From proton affinity of 2,4,6-cycloheptatrien-1-one. PA = 219 kcal/mol, 918 kJ/mol (RN 539-80-0) and appearance potential determinations (83RUS/FRE).

$C_7H_7O_2^+$

| PhĊ(OH)$_2$ | | 97 | 407 | | | | |

From proton affinity of benzoic acid (RN 65-85-0). PA = 198.2 kcal/mol, 829. kJ/mol.

Table 1. Positive Ion Table - Continued

ION / Neutral	Ionization potential eV	$\Delta_f H$(Ion) kcal/mol	$\Delta_f H$(Ion) kJ/mol	$\Delta_f H$(Neutral) kcal/mol	$\Delta_f H$(Neutral) kJ/mol	Neutral reference	CAS registry number
$C_7H_8^+$							
HC≡C(CH$_2$)$_3$C≡CH	(9.85) IP from 78TRA/MCL.	(322)	(1346)	94.7	396	58BEN/BUS	2396-63-6
(cycloheptatriene)	8.29 IP from 78TRA/MCL.	235 / 240	982 / 1004	43.7±0.2 / 48.7	182.8±1 / 203.8	77PED/RYL	544-25-2
(toluene)	8.82±0.01 See also: 82SEL/HEL, 81KIM/KAT, 78LIA/AUS, 84HOW/GON.	215 / 221	901 / 924	12.0±0.1 / 17.5	50.1±0.3 / 73.3	77PED/RYL	108-88-3
(methylenecyclohexadiene)	7.9 IP from 85BAL/HAS. See also: 82BUR/TER, 82BAR.	223	934	41	172	85BAL/HAS	20679-59-8
(methylenecyclohexadiene isomer)	(8.6) IP from 82BAR.	(233)	(975)	35±3	146±13	82BAR	3217-87-6
(norbornadiene)	8.35 IP from 78TRA/MCL. See also: 83HOU/RON, 82BIE/ASB, 85OHN/ISH.	250	1046	57±1	240±4	80ROG/CHO	121-46-0
(methylenebicyclic)	8.8 IP from 85BAL/HAS.	288	1206	85	357	85BAL/HAS	67254-49-3
(quadricyclane)	(7.8) IP is onset of photoelectron band.	(260)	(1086)	80±1	333±4	80ROG/CHO	278-06-8

Table 1. Positive Ion Table - Continued

ION / Neutral	Ionization potential eV	$\Delta_f H$(Ion) kcal/mol	$\Delta_f H$(Ion) kJ/mol	$\Delta_f H$(Neutral) kcal/mol	$\Delta_f H$(Neutral) kJ/mol	Neutral reference	CAS registry number
$C_7H_8{}^+$ (spiro cyclopentadiene-cyclopropane)	(8.14)	(250)	(1045)	62	260	*EST	765-46-8

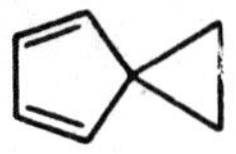

$C_7H_8Br^+$

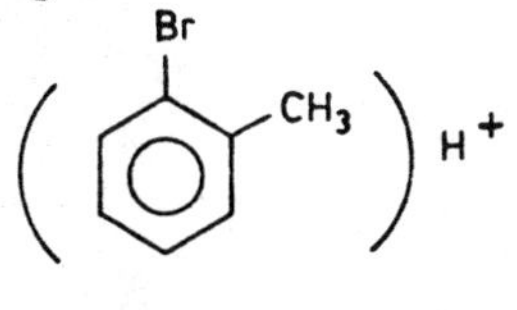

(2-bromotoluene)H^+ — 193, 809
From proton affinity of 1,2-$C_6H_4(CH_3)$Br (RN 95-46-5) (82MAS/BOH).
PA = 187.2 kcal/mol, 783. kJ/mol.

(3-bromotoluene)H^+ — 191, 801
From proton affinity of 1,3-$C_6H_4(CH_3)$Br (RN 591-17-3) (82MAS/BOH).
PA = 188.8 kcal/mol, 790. kJ/mol.

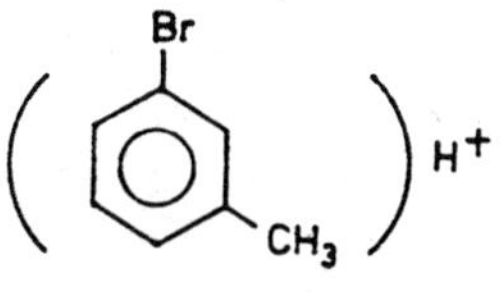

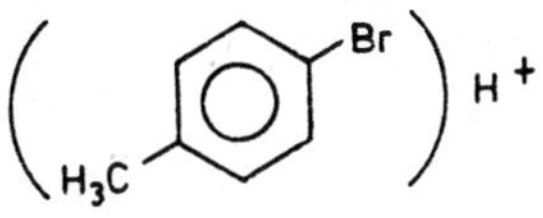

(4-bromotoluene)H^+ — 196, 818
From proton affinity of 1,4-$C_6H_4(CH_3)$Br (RN 106-38-7) (82MAS/BOH).
PA = 187.2 kcal/mol, 783. kJ/mol.

$C_7H_8Cl^+$

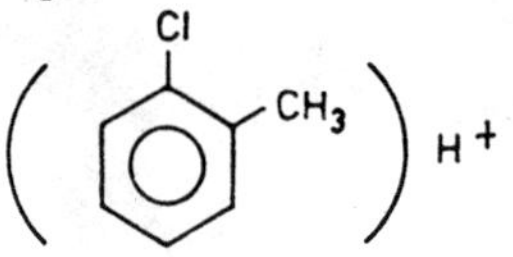

(2-chlorotoluene)H^+ — 186, 777
From proton affinity of 1,2-$C_6H_4(CH_3)$Cl (RN 95-49-8) (82MAS/BOH).
PA = 184.3 kcal/mol, 771. kJ/mol.

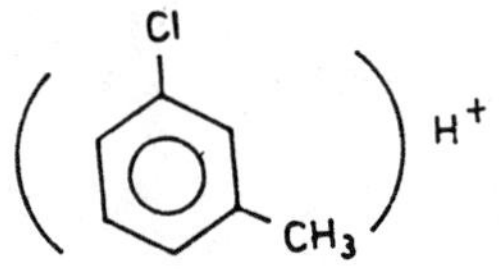

(3-chlorotoluene)H^+ — 181, 758
From proton affinity of 1,3-$C_6H_4(CH_3)$Cl (RN 108-41-8) (82MAS/BOH).
PA = 188.9 kcal/mol, 790. kJ/mol.

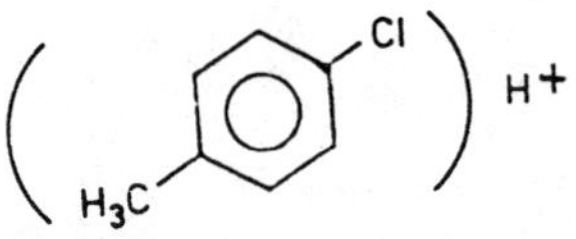

(4-chlorotoluene)H^+ — 189, 792
From proton affinity of 1,4-$C_6H_4(CH_3)$Cl (RN 106-43-4) (82MAS/BOH).
PA = 180.6 kcal/mol, 756. kJ/mol.

$C_7H_8Cl_2Si^+$

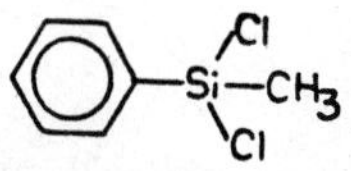

(PhSi(CH$_3$)Cl$_2$) — (8.97), (132), (551), −75, −314, *EST, 149-74-6
IP from 84VES/HAR.

Table 1. Positive Ion Table – Continued

ION / Neutral	Ionization potential eV	$\Delta_f H$(Ion) kcal/mol kJ/mol	$\Delta_f H$(Neutral) kcal/mol kJ/mol	Neutral reference	CAS registry number

$C_7H_8F^+$

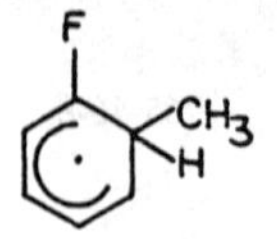

2-fluoromethylbenzene cation: 143 599
From proton affinity of 2-$FC_6H_4CH_3$ (RN 95-52-3) (82MAS/BOH).
PA = 187.0 kcal/mol, 782. kJ/mol.

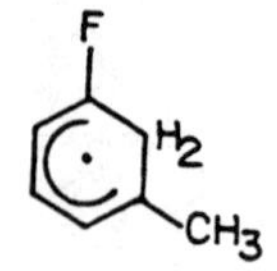

3-fluoromethylbenzene cation: 140 587
From proton affinity of 3-$FC_6H_4CH_3$ (RN 352-70-5) (82MAS/BOH).
PA = 189.5 kcal/mol, 793. kJ/mol.

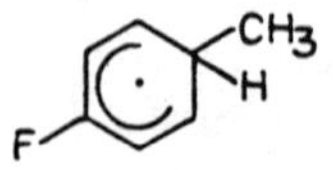

4-fluoromethylbenzene cation: 149 625
From proton affinity of 4-$FC_6H_4CH_3$ (RN 352-32-9) (82MAS/BOH).
PA = 180.9 kcal/mol, 757. kJ/mol.

$C_7H_8F_2Si^+$

| 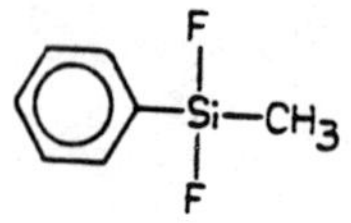 | (8.97) | (29) (122) | −178 −743 | *EST | 328-57-4 |

IP from 84VES/HAR.

$C_7H_8I^+$

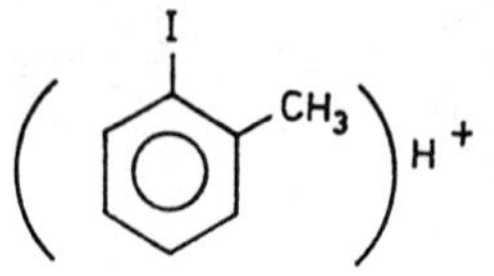

209 875
From proton affinity of 2-$IC_6H_4CH_3$ (RN 615-37-2) (82MAS/BOH).
PA = 188.4 kcal/mol, 788. kJ/mol.

$C_7H_8N^+$

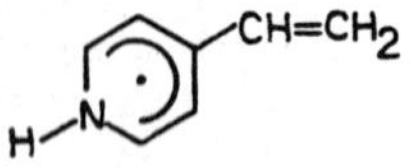

(191) (798)
From proton affinity of 4-vinylpyridine (RN 100-43-6). PA = (223.2) kcal/mol, (934) kJ/mol.

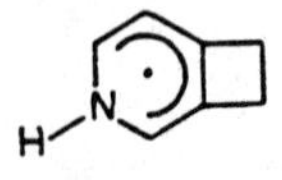

(202) (846)
From proton affinity of 3,4-cyclobutenopyridine (RN 56911-27-4).
PA = (225.9) kcal/mol, (945) kJ/mol.

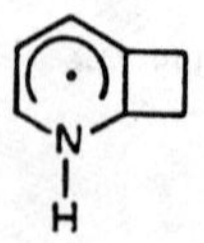

(200) (838)
From proton affinity of 2,3-cyclobutenopyridine. PA = (223.3) kcal/mol, (934) kJ/mol.

Table 1. Positive Ion Table - Continued

ION / Neutral	Ionization potential eV	$\Delta_f H$(Ion) kcal/mol	$\Delta_f H$(Ion) kJ/mol	$\Delta_f H$(Neutral) kcal/mol	$\Delta_f H$(Neutral) kJ/mol	Neutral reference	CAS registry number

$C_7H_8NO^+$

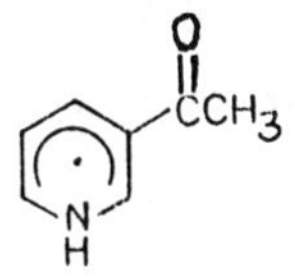

3-acetylpyridinium (protonated 3-acetylpyridine): 142, 595.
From proton affinity of 1-(3-pyridinyl)-ethanone (RN 350-03-8).
PA = 217.2 kcal/mol, 909 kJ/mol.

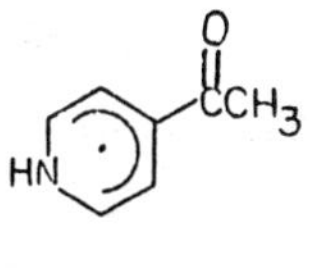

4-acetylpyridinium (protonated 4-acetylpyridine): 142, 594.
From proton affinity of 1-(4-pyridinyl)-ethanone (RN 1122-54-9).
PA = 217.4 kcal/mol, 910. kJ/mol.

$C_7H_8NO_2^+$

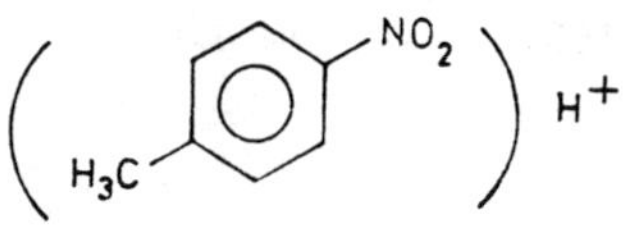

(4-nitrotoluene)H^+: 176, 738.
From proton affinity of 4-nitrotoluene (RN 99-99-0) (84ROL/HOU).
PA = 196.8 kcal/mol, 823. kJ/mol.

$C_7H_8N_2O_2^+$

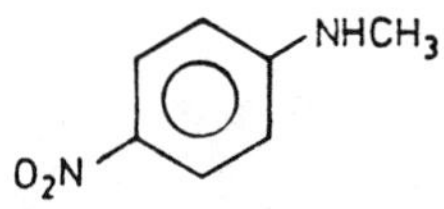

N-methyl-4-nitroaniline: (8.1), (201), (843), 15, 61, *EST, 100-15-2.
IP is onset of photoelectron band.

$C_7H_8O^+$

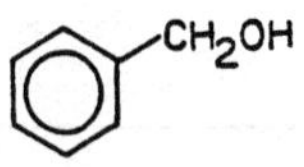

benzyl alcohol: (8.5), (172), (720), −24.0, −100.4, 77PED/RYL, 100-51-6.
See also: 82DES/DUT, 83RUS/FRE. IP is onset of photoelectron band (86BAL/JON).

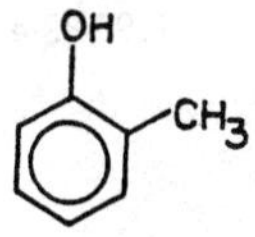

2-methylphenol (o-cresol): 8.14, 158, 661, −30, −124, 79KUD/KUD, 95-48-7.
IP from 83RUS/FRE.

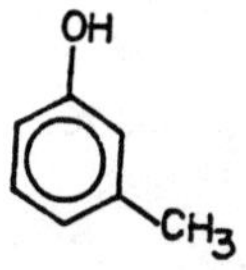

3-methylphenol (m-cresol): 8.29, 160, 668, −31.6±0.3, −132.3±1.2, 79KUD/KUD, 108-39-4.
IP from 85OIK/ABE, 83RUS/FRE.

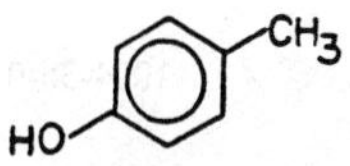

4-methylphenol (p-cresol): 8.13, 157, 659, −29.9, −125.1, 79KUD/KUD, 106-44-5.
IP from 83RUS/FRE.

Table 1. Positive Ion Table – Continued

ION Neutral	Ionization potential eV	$\Delta_f H$(Ion) kcal/mol	kJ/mol	$\Delta_f H$(Neutral) kcal/mol	kJ/mol	Neutral reference	CAS registry number
$C_7H_8O^+$							
(cyclohepta-2,4-dienone)	(8.24) IP from 83RUS/FRE.	(188)	(788)	−1.7	−7.1	83RUS/FRE	1121-65-9
(anisole)	8.21±0.02 See also: 83KLA/KOV.	173	724	−16.2±0.3	−68.0±1.1	77PED/RYL	100-66-3
(bicyclic ketone)	(≤8.86)	(≤197)	(≤826)	−7	−29	*EST	694-98-4
(bicyclic ketone)	(≤9.25)	(≤210)	(≤877)	−4	−15	*EST	694-71-3
(dimethyl tricyclic ketone)	(8.9) IP is onset of photoelectron band (84GLE/HAI).	(251)	(1049)	45	190	*EST	3350-02-5
$C_7H_8OS^+$							
(methyl phenyl sulfoxide)	(8.5) IP is onset of photoelectron band.	(191)	(800)	−5	−20	*EST	1193-82-4
$C_7H_8O_2^+$							
(4-methoxyphenol)	(7.50)	(115)	(482)	−58	−242	*EST	150-76-5
(2,6-dimethyl-4H-pyran-4-one)	(9.03) IP from 85GRU/SPI	(152)	(636)	−56	−235	*EST	1004-36-0

Table 1. Positive Ion Table - Continued

ION / Neutral	Ionization potential eV	$\Delta_f H$(Ion) kcal/mol	$\Delta_f H$(Ion) kJ/mol	$\Delta_f H$(Neutral) kcal/mol	$\Delta_f H$(Neutral) kJ/mol	Neutral reference	CAS registry number
$C_7H_8O_2^+$							
4,6-dimethyl-2H-pyran-2-one	(8.51) IP from 85GRU/SPI	(135)	(564)	−61	−257	*EST	675-09-2
bicyclic diketone	(9.4) IP is onset of photoelectron band (85GLE/JAH).	(168)	(702)	−49	−205	*EST	60582-65-2
bicyclic diketone	(9.26) IP is onset of photoelectron band (80FRO/WES).	(161)	(674)	−52	−219	*EST	27943-47-1
$C_7H_8O_2S^+$							
methyl phenyl sulfone	(9.5) IP is onset of photoelectron band (81MOH/JIA).	(159)	(663)	−60.6±0.7	−253.4±3.0	77PED/RYL	3112-85-4
$C_7H_8S^+$							
thioanisole	7.94±0.02	206	864	23.4±0.3	97.8±1.2	77PED/RYL	100-68-5
benzyl mercaptan	(8.5) IP is onset of photoelectron band.	(218)	(914)	22±0.7	94±3	77PED/RYL	100-53-8
2-methylthiophenol	(≤8.31)	(≤211)	(≤881)	19	79	*EST	137-06-4
3-methylthiophenol	(≤8.44)	(≤214)	(≤893)	19	79	*EST	108-40-7

Table 1. Positive Ion Table - Continued

ION / Neutral	Ionization potential eV	$\Delta_f H$(Ion) kcal/mol	$\Delta_f H$(Ion) kJ/mol	$\Delta_f H$(Neutral) kcal/mol	$\Delta_f H$(Neutral) kJ/mol	Neutral reference	CAS registry number

$C_7H_8S^+$

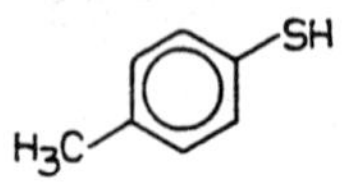

4-methylbenzenethiol (H₃C-C₆H₄-SH): (8.0), (203), (851), 19, 79, *EST, 106-45-6
IP is onset of photoelectron band.

$C_7H_8Se^+$

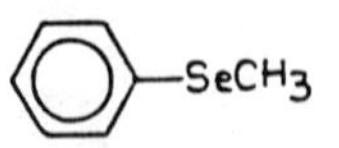

phenyl methyl selenide (C₆H₅-SeCH₃): (7.4), (207), (867), 36, 153, *EST, 4346-64-9
IP is onset of photoelectron band (81BAK/ARM).

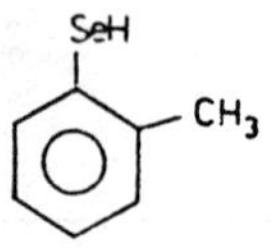

2-methylbenzeneselenol: ≤8.4, (≤225), (≤940), 31, 130, *EST, 37773-21-0
IP from 81BAK/ARM.

$C_7H_9^+$

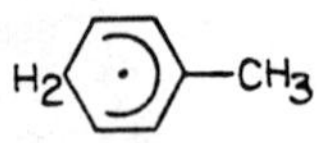

protonated toluene: 188, 786
From proton affinity of $C_6H_5CH_3$ (RN 108-88-3). PA = 189.8 kcal/mol, 794. kJ/mol.

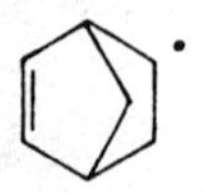

protonated norbornadiene: 220, 919
From proton affinity of 2,5-norbornadiene (RN 121-46-0) (86HOU/SCH). PA = 203.4 kcal/mol, 851. kJ/mol.

$C_7H_9Br^+$

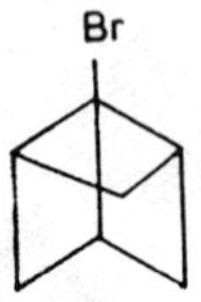

bromo compound 1: (8.7), (261), (1091), 60, 252, *EST, 59346-69-9
IP is onset of photoelectron band (84ABE/DEL).

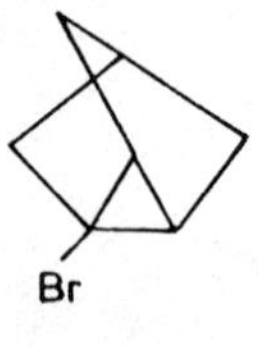

bromo compound 2: (8.55), (218), (912), 21, 87, *EST, 31991-53-4
IP is onset of photoelectron band (85DEL/PIG).

Table 1. Positive Ion Table — Continued

ION / Neutral	Ionization potential eV	$\Delta_f H$(Ion) kcal/mol	$\Delta_f H$(Ion) kJ/mol	$\Delta_f H$(Neutral) kcal/mol	$\Delta_f H$(Neutral) kJ/mol	Neutral reference	CAS registry number
$C_7H_9I^+$	(8.6)	(273)	(1143)	75	313	*EST	74725-76-1

IP is onset of photoelectron band (84ABE/DEL).

$C_7H_9N^+$							
benzylamine (CH₂NH₂)	8.64±0.05	219	918	20±0.7	84±3	77CAR/LAY	100-46-9

See also: 79AUE/BOW.

| N-methylaniline (NHCH₃) | 7.33±0.02 | 189 | 792 | 20 | 85 | 78COL/BEN | 100-61-8 |

See also: 84MAU/NEL, 83KLA/KOV.

o-toluidine (NH₂, CH₃)	7.44±0.02	(185)	(773)	13±0.2	55±1	*EST	95-53-4
m-toluidine (NH₂, CH₃)	7.50±0.02	(186)	(778)	13±0.4	54±2	*EST	108-44-1
p-toluidine (NH₂, CH₃)	(7.24±0.02)	(180)	(753)	13	54	*EST	106-49-0
2,3-dimethylpyridine	(8.85±0.02)	(220)	(922)	16.3	68.3	77PED/RYL	583-61-9

$\Delta_f H$(Ion) predicted from hydrogen affinities of pyridines: 224 kcal/mol, 937 kJ/mol. Corresponding IP = 9.01 eV. See also: 79AUE/BOW.

| 2,4-dimethylpyridine | (8.85±0.03) | (219) | (918) | 15.3 | 63.9 | 77PED/RYL | 108-47-4 |

Table 1. Positive Ion Table - Continued

ION / Neutral	Ionization potential eV	$\Delta_f H$(Ion) kcal/mol	$\Delta_f H$(Ion) kJ/mol	$\Delta_f H$(Neutral) kcal/mol	$\Delta_f H$(Neutral) kJ/mol	Neutral reference	CAS registry number

$C_7H_9N^+$

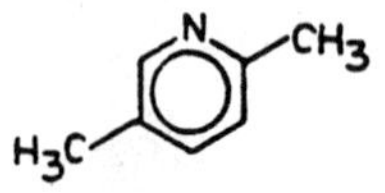

2,5-dimethylpyridine: (≤8.80±0.05) (≤219) (≤916) 15.9±0.2 66.5±1.0 77PED/RYL 589-93-5
$\Delta_f H$(Ion) predicted from hydrogen affinities of pyridines: 223 kcal/mol, 933 kJ/mol. Corresponding IP = 8.98eV. See also: 79AUE/BOW.

2,6-dimethylpyridine: 8.86±0.03 218 913 14.0±0.4 58.7±1.6 77PED/RYL 108-48-5
See also: 81KIM/KAT.

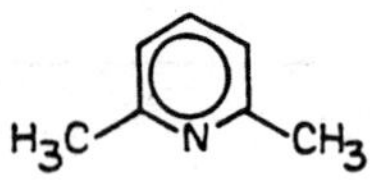

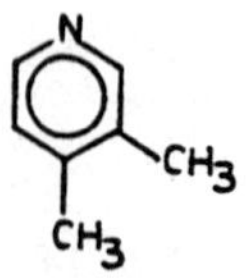

3,4-dimethylpyridine: (≤9.15) (≤228) (≤953) 16.7±0.2 70.1±1.1 77PED/RYL 583-58-4
$\Delta_f H$(Ion) predicted from hydrogen affinities of pyridines: 224 kcal/mol, 937 kJ/mol. Corresponding IP = 8.98eV. See also: 79AUE/BOW.

3,5-dimethylpyridine: (≤9.25) (≤231) (≤965) 17.4±0.2 72.8±0.9 77PED/RYL 591-22-0
$\Delta_f H$(Ion) predicted from hydrogen affinities of pyridines: 226 kcal/mol, 946 kJ/mol. Corresponding IP = 9.05 eV.

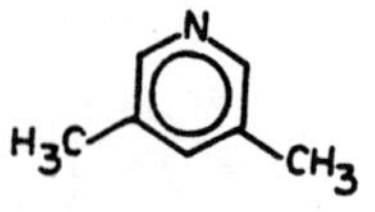

$C_7H_9NO^+$

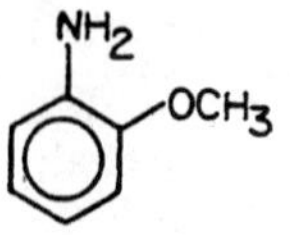

2-methoxyaniline: (7.46±0.1) (158) (663) −14 −57 *EST 90-04-0

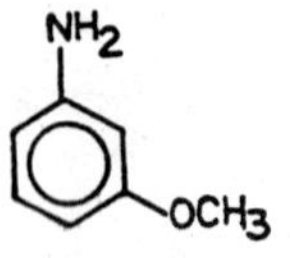

3-methoxyaniline: (7.76±0.1) (163) (682) −16 −67 *EST 536-90-3

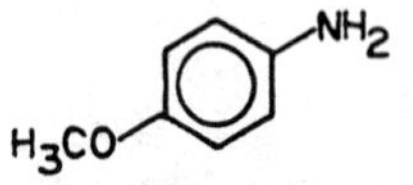

4-methoxyaniline: (7.44) (158) (660) −14 −58 *EST 104-94-9

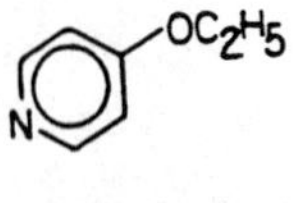

3-ethoxypyridine: (≤9.25±0.03) (≤202) (≤845) −11 −47 *EST 33399-46-1

Table 1. Positive Ion Table - Continued

ION / Neutral	Ionization potential eV	$\Delta_f H$(Ion) kcal/mol	$\Delta_f H$(Ion) kJ/mol	$\Delta_f H$(Neutral) kcal/mol	$\Delta_f H$(Neutral) kJ/mol	Neutral reference	CAS registry number

$C_7H_9N_2O_2^+$

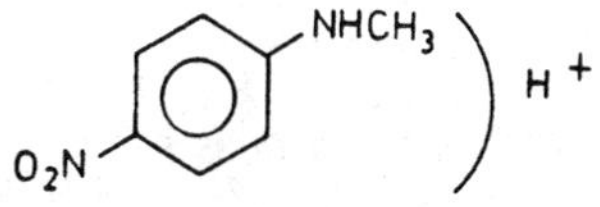

O₂N-C₆H₄-NHCH₃·H⁺ : 167 / 700

From proton affinity of N-methyl-4-nitroaniline (RN 100-23-2) (84ROL/HOU). PA = 212.9 kcal/mol, 891. kJ/mol.

$C_7H_9O^+$

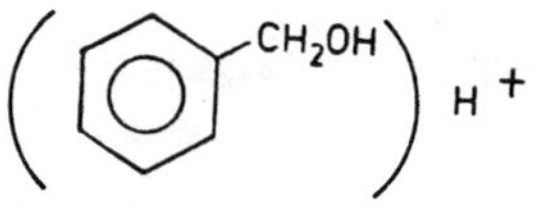

C₆H₅CH₂OH·H⁺ : 153 / 641

From proton affinity of $C_6H_5CH_2OH$ (RN 100-51-6) (78TAF/TAA). PA = 188.5 kcal/mol, 789. kJ/mol.

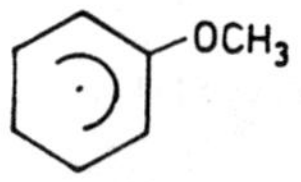

C₆H₅OCH₃ : 149 / 624

From proton affinity of $C_6H_5OCH_3$ (RN 100-66-3). PA = 200.3 kcal/mol, 838. kJ/mol.

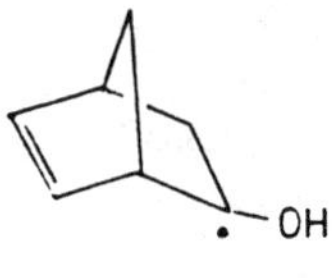

bicyclo[2.2.1]hept-2-ene-5-ol : 157 / 655

From proton affinity of bicyclo[2.2.1]hept-2-ene-5-one (RN 694-98-4). (86HOU/SCH). PA = 202.1 kcal/mol, 846. kJ/mol.

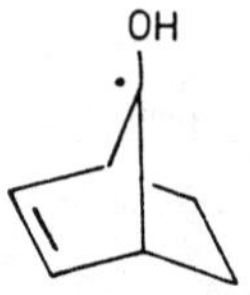

bicyclo[2.2.1]hept-2-ene-7-ol : 164 / 686

From proton affinity of bicyclo[2.2.1]hept-2-ene-7-one (RN 694-71-3). (86HOU/SCH). PA = 198.1 kcal/mol, 829. kJ/mol.

$C_7H_{10}^+$

Neutral	IP (eV)	$\Delta_f H$(Ion) kcal/mol	$\Delta_f H$(Ion) kJ/mol	$\Delta_f H$(Neutral) kcal/mol	$\Delta_f H$(Neutral) kJ/mol	Neutral reference	CAS registry number
$(CH_2=CH)_3CH$	(≤9.5) IP from 83GLE/HAI.	(≤265)	(≤1108)	46	191	*EST	26456-63-3
$(E,E)-CH_2=CHCH=CHCH=CHCH_3$	7.96±0.02	(215)	(901)	32±1	133±4	*EST	17679-93-5
$C_2H_5C\equiv CC(CH_3)=CH_2$	(8.66±0.01)	(247)	(1033)	47	197	*EST	23056-94-2
$(E)-HC\equiv CC(C_2H_5)=CHCH_3$	(8.70±0.01)	(247)	(1031)	46	192	*EST	14272-82-3
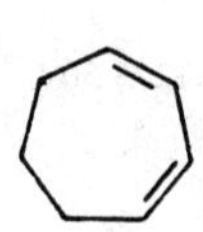 cycloheptatriene	≤8.31±0.03	≤214	≤896	22.5±0.2	94.2±0.9	77PED/RYL	4054-38-0

Table 1. Positive Ion Table — Continued

ION / Neutral	Ionization potential eV	$\Delta_f H$(Ion) kcal/mol	kJ/mol	$\Delta_f H$(Neutral) kcal/mol	kJ/mol	Neutral reference	CAS registry number
$C_7H_{10}{}^+$							
cycloheptadiene	(8.85±0.03)	(232)	(970)	28	116	76JEN	7161-35-5
5,5-dimethylcyclopentadiene	8.2 IP is onset of photoelectron band (85GUI/PFI3).	(206)	(860)	16	69	*EST	4125-18-2
cyclopropyl methyl allene	(8.83)	(257)	(1075)	53	223	82KOZ/MAS	51549-86-1
norcarene	(≤8.69)	(≤227)	(≤951)	27	113	*EST	2566-57-6
bicyclo[3.2.0]	(9.37)	(250)	(1046)	34	142	*EST	4927-03-1
norbornene	8.82±0.03 See also: 83HOU/RON.	225	941	21±1	90±4	80ROG/CHO	498-66-8
tricyclic	8.72 IP is onset of photoelectron band (85DEL/PIG).	245.5	1027.1	44.4	185.8	85SVY/IOF	287-13-8
tricyclic	(8.7) IP is onset of photoelectron band (84ABE/DEL).	(260)	(1089)	60	250	*EST	51273-50-8

Table 1. Positive Ion Table - Continued

ION Neutral	Ionization potential eV	$\Delta_f H$(Ion) kcal/mol kJ/mol	$\Delta_f H$(Neutral) kcal/mol kJ/mol	Neutral reference	CAS registry number

$C_7H_{10}{}^+$

norbornadiene: (8.72) (221) (926)   20±1   85±4   80ROG/CHO   279-19-6
IP is onset of photoelectron band (85DEL/PIG).

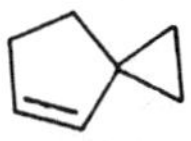

spiro compound: (≤8.48) (≤236) (≤986)   40   168   *EST   52708-23-3

$C_7H_{10}F_2{}^+$

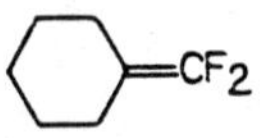

cyclohexylidene=CF$_2$: 8.84 (103) (433) −100 −420 *EST 696-32-2
IP from 80SAR/WOR.

$C_7H_{10}N^+$

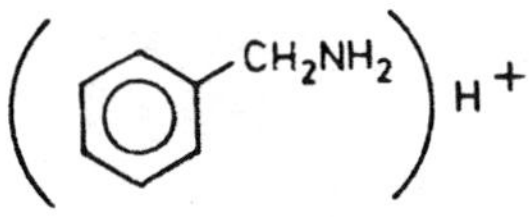

(C$_6$H$_5$CH$_2$NH$_2$)H$^+$:   169   707
From proton affinity of $C_6H_5CH_2NH_2$ (RN 100-46-9). PA = 216.8 kcal/mol, 907. kJ/mol.

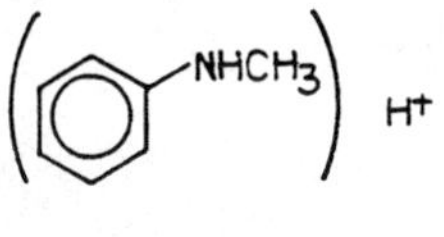

(C$_6$H$_5$NHCH$_3$)H$^+$:   168   703
From proton affinity of $C_6H_5NHCH_3$ (RN 100-61-8). PA = 218.1 kcal/mol, 912.5 kJ/mol.

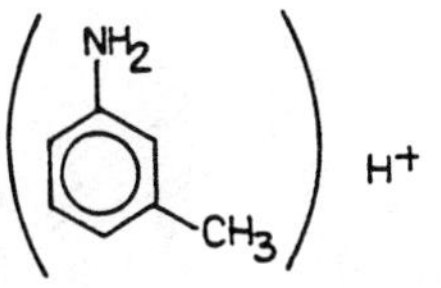

(3-CH$_3$C$_6$H$_4$NH$_2$)H$^+$:   165   690
From proton affinity of 3-$CH_3C_6H_4NH_2$ (RN 108-44-1). PA = 213.4 kcal/mol, 893. kJ/mol.

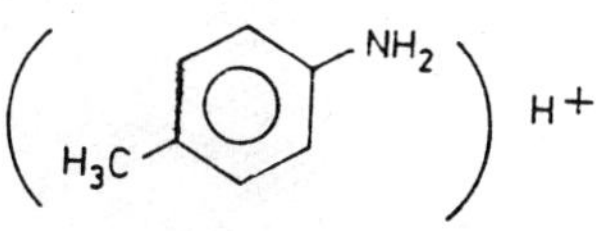

(4-CH$_3$C$_6$H$_4$NH$_2$)H$^+$:   165   690
From proton affinity of 4-$CH_3C_6H_4NH_2$ (RN 106-49-0). PA = 213.7 kcal/mol, 894. kJ/mol.

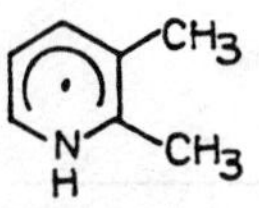

2,3-dimethylpyridine·H$^+$:   156   652
From proton affinity of 2,3-dimethylpyridine (RN 583-61-9). PA = 226.2 kcal/mol, 946. kJ/mol.

Table 1. Positive Ion Table - Continued

ION Neutral	Ionization potential eV	$\Delta_f H$(Ion) kcal/mol kJ/mol	$\Delta_f H$(Neutral) kcal/mol kJ/mol	Neutral reference	CAS registry number

$C_7H_{10}N^+$

| | | 153   643 | | | |

From proton affinity of 2,4-dimethylpyridine (RN 108-47-4). PA = 227.3 kcal/mol, 951. kJ/mol.

| | | 156   651 | | | |

From proton affinity of 2,5-dimethylpyridine (RN 589-93-5). PA = 226.2 kcal/mol, 946. kJ/mol.

| | | 152   634 | | | |

From proton affinity of 2,6-dimethylpyridine (RN 108-48-5). PA = 228.2 kcal/mol, 955. kJ/mol.

| | | 157   654 | | | |

From proton affinity of 3,4-dimethylpyridine (RN 583-58-4). PA = 226.0 kcal/mol, 946. kJ/mol.

| | | 158   661 | | | |

From proton affinity of 3,5-dimethylpyridine (RN 591-22-0). PA = 225.5 kcal/mol, 943. kJ/mol.

| | | 159   665 | | | |

From proton affinity of 2-ethylpyridine (RN 100-71-0). PA = 226.2 kcal/mol, 946. kJ/mol.

| | | 162   679 | | | |

From proton affinity of 3-ethylpyridine (RN 536-78-7). PA = 223.9 kcal/mol, 937. kJ/mol.

| | | (161) (672) | | | |

From proton affinity of 4-ethylpyridine (RN 536-75-4). PA = (224.6) kcal/mol, (940) kJ/mol.

Table 1. Positive Ion Table - Continued

ION / Neutral	Ionization potential eV	$\Delta_f H$(Ion) kcal/mol kJ/mol	$\Delta_f H$(Neutral) kcal/mol kJ/mol	Neutral reference	CAS registry number

$C_7H_{10}NO^+$

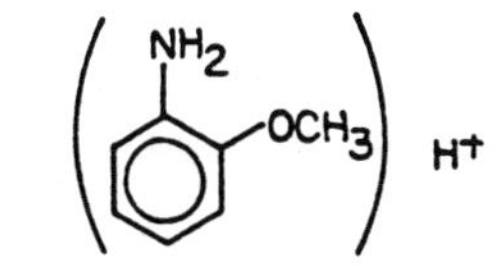

(2-methoxyaniline)·H⁺ — 137 575
From proton affinity of 2-$CH_3OC_6H_4NH_2$ (RN 90-04-0). PA = 214.7 kcal/mol, 898. kJ/mol.

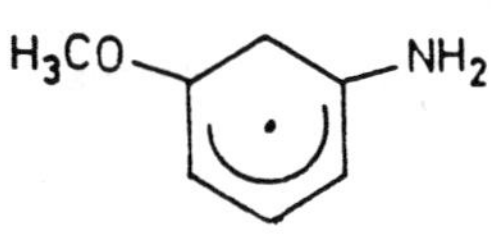

(3-methoxyaniline radical cation) — 132 553
From proton affinity of 3-$CH_3OC_6H_4NH_2$ (RN 536-90-3). PA = 217.6 kcal/mol, 910. kJ/mol.

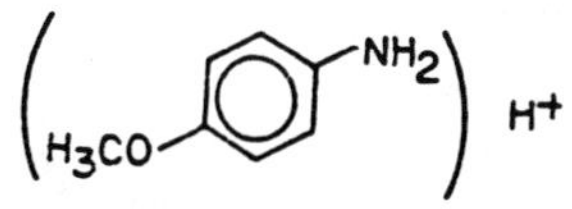

(4-methoxyaniline)·H⁺ — 137 575
From proton affinity of 4-$CH_3OC_6H_4NH_2$ (RN 104-94-9). PA = 214.3 kcal/mol, 897. kJ/mol.

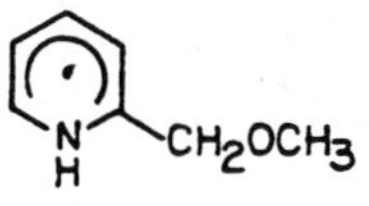

(2-methoxymethylpyridine)·H⁺ — (134) (563)
From proton affinity of pyridine,2-methoxymethyl (RN 23579-92-2). PA = (226.0) kcal/mol, (945.) kJ/mol.

$C_7H_{10}NS^+$

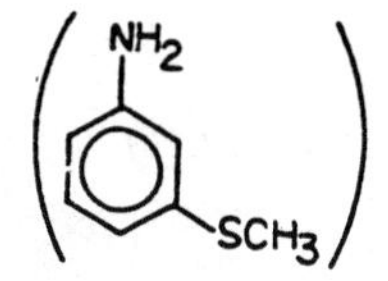

(3-methylthiobenzenamine)·H⁺ — 176 735
From proton affinity of 3-methylthiobenzenamine (RN 1783-81-9). PA = 214.5 kcal/mol, 897. kJ/mol.

$C_7H_{10}N_2^+$

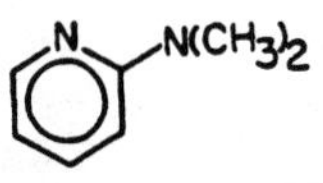 2-(dimethylamino)pyridine	7.75±0.15	(211)	(880)	32	132	*EST	5683-33-0
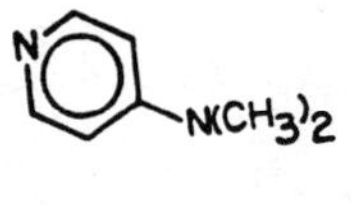 3-(dimethylamino)pyridine	(≤7.82)	(≤214)	(≤898)	34	144	84BIC/PIL	1122-58-3

$C_7H_{10}N_2O^+$

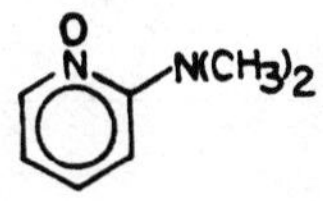 2-(dimethylamino)pyridine N-oxide	(7.62±0.05)	(191)	(798)	15	63	*EST	3618-79-9

Table 1. Positive Ion Table - Continued

ION / Neutral	Ionization potential eV	$\Delta_f H$(Ion) kcal/mol	$\Delta_f H$(Ion) kJ/mol	$\Delta_f H$(Neutral) kcal/mol	$\Delta_f H$(Neutral) kJ/mol	Neutral reference	CAS registry number
$C_7H_{10}N_2O^+$							
[3-dimethylamino-pyridine N-oxide]	(7.85±0.05)	(197)	(824)	16	67	*EST	36100-40-0
[4-dimethylamino-pyridine N-oxide]	(7.0) IP is onset of photoelectron band.	(178)	(746)	17	71	*EST	1005-31-8
$C_7H_{10}O^+$							
[dicyclopropyl ketone]	(9.1)	(249)	(1041)	39	163	*EST	1121-37-5
[norcamphor]	8.94±0.02 See also: 80FRO/WES.	166	695	−40±0.7	−168±3	78STE2	497-38-1
[2-norbornanone isomer]	≤9.01±0.02	≤176	≤735	−32±0.7	−134±3	78STE2	10218-02-7
$C_7H_{10}S^+$							
[2-propylthiophene]	(≤8.6±0.2)	(≤208)	(≤870)	10	40	*EST	1551-27-5
$C_7H_{11}^+$							
[norbornene·H⁺]	6.84	186	777	28	117	DERIVED	30967-37-4

IP from 79HOU. $\Delta_f H$ of $C_7H_{11}^+$ from PA of norbornene, 187 kcal/mol, 784 kJ/mol; PA = 199.9 kcal/mol, 836. kJ/mol. From hydride transfer equilibria relative to $\Delta_f H$(t-$C_4H_9^+$), 185 kcal/mol, 773 kJ/mol (76SOL/FIE, 85SHA/SHA); from chloride transfer equilibria 185.8 kcal/mol, 777.4 kJ/mol (85SHA/SHA). Cited $\Delta_f H$ of radical = $\Delta_f H(C_7H_{11}^+)$ - IP.

Table 1. Positive Ion Table – Continued

ION / Neutral	Ionization potential eV	$\Delta_f H$(Ion) kcal/mol	$\Delta_f H$(Ion) kJ/mol	$\Delta_f H$(Neutral) kcal/mol	$\Delta_f H$(Neutral) kJ/mol	Neutral reference	CAS registry number
$C_7H_{11}Br^+$ (1-bromonorbornane)	9.55	(209)	(874)	–11	–47	*EST	13474-70-9

IP is onset of photoelectron band (84DEL/ABE, 85HON/HEI2).

| $C_7H_{11}Cl^+$ $(CH_3)_3CCH=C=CHCl$ | 9.05 | (228) | (954) | 19 | 81 | *EST | 65388-53-6 |

IP is onset of photoelectron band (85ELS/VER).

| $C_7H_{11}ClN^+$ (3-chloro-1-azabicyclo[2.2.2]oct-2-ene · H⁺) | | (167) | (697) | | | | |

From proton affinity of 3-chloro-1-azabicyclo[2.2.2]oct-2-ene
PA = (224.0) kcal/mol, (937.) kJ/mol.

| $C_7H_{11}I^+$ | | | | | | | |
| 1-iodonorbornane | (8.8) | (206) | (863) | 3 | 14 | *EST | 930-80-3 |

IP is onset of photoelectron band (84DEL/ABE).

| 2-iodonorbornane (exo) | (9.00) | (210) | (878) | 2 | 10 | *EST | 57173-48-5 |

IP from 84HON/HEI.

| 2-iodonorbornane (endo) | 9.00 | (211) | (882) | 3 | 14 | *EST | 30983-85-8 |

IP from 84HON/HEI.

$C_7H_{11}N^+$							
1-azabicyclo[2.2.2]oct-2-ene	(8.02)	(222)	(930)	37	156	*EST	13929-94-7
2-azabicyclo[2.2.2]oct-2-ene (NH)	(≤8.35±0.05)	(≤218)	(≤913)	26	107	*EST	3693-58-1

Table 1. Positive Ion Table - Continued

ION Neutral	Ionization potential eV	$\Delta_f H$(Ion) kcal/mol	$\Delta_f H$(Ion) kJ/mol	$\Delta_f H$(Neutral) kcal/mol	$\Delta_f H$(Neutral) kJ/mol	Neutral reference	CAS registry number
$C_7H_{11}NO^+$							

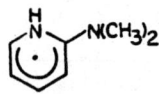

| | (≤8.2) | (≤161) | (≤675) | −28 | −116 | *EST | 3731-38-2 |

IP from 79AUE/BOW.

$C_7H_{11}N_2^+$

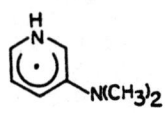

| | | 168 | 703 | | | | |

From proton affinity of N,N-dimethyl-2-pyridinamine (RN 5683-33-0).
PA = 229.2 kcal/mol, 959. kJ/mol.

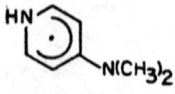

| | | (174) | (726) | | | | |

From proton affinity of N,N-dimethyl-3-pyridinamine (RN 18437-57-5).
PA = (229.9) kcal/mol, (962) kJ/mol.

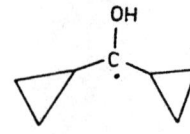

| | | 163 | 684 | | | | |

From proton affinity of N,N-dimethyl-4-pyridinamine (RN 1122-58-3).
(86TAF/GAL, 77ARN/CHA). PA = 236.6 kcal/mol, 990. kJ/mol.

$C_7H_{11}O^+$

| | | 194 | 812 | | | | |

From proton affinity of dicyclopropylmethanone (RN 1121-37-5). PA = 210.7 kcal/mol, 881.5 kJ/mol.

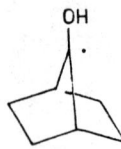

| | | 123 | 514 | | | | |

From proton affinity of bicyclo[2.2.1]heptan-2-one (RN 497-38-1) (86HOU/SCH).
PA = 202.6 kcal/mol, 848. kJ/mol.

| | | 134 | 561 | | | | |

From proton affinity of bicyclo[2.2.1]heptan-7-one (RN 10218-02-7) (86HOU/SCH).
PA = 199.5 kcal/mol, 835. kJ/mol.

$C_7H_{12}^+$
(E)-$CH_3CH_2CH_2CH=CHCH=CH_2$

| | (8.47) | (204) | (852) | 8 | 35 | *EST | 2384-92-1 |

IP from 81MAS/MOU.

Table 1. Positive Ion Table - Continued

ION / Neutral	Ionization potential eV	$\Delta_f H$(Ion) kcal/mol	kJ/mol	$\Delta_f H$(Neutral) kcal/mol	kJ/mol	Neutral reference	CAS registry number
$C_7H_{12}^+$							
(E),(E)-$CH_3CH_2CH=CHCH=CHCH_3$							
	≤8.17	(≤194)	(≤812)	6	24	*EST	2384-94-3
	IP from 81MAS/MOU.						
(3-methylcyclohexene)	8.89±0.01	(196)	(822)	−9	−36	*EST	591-48-0
	See also: 83BRO/BUS.						
(E)-$(CH_3)_2CHCH=CHCH=CH_2$							
	≤8.47	(≤202)	(≤847)	7	30	*EST	32763-70-5
	IP from 81MAS/MOU.						
(E)-$C_2H_5C(CH_3)=CHCH=CH_2$							
	(8.19)	(195)	(814)	6	24	*EST	4842-93-7
	IP from 81MAS/MOU.						
(E)-$CH_3CH=C(CH_3)C(CH_3)=CH_2$							
	(8.28)	(194)	(813)	3	14	*EST	1625-49-6
	IP from 81MAS/MOU.						
$CH_2=C(CH_3)C(C_2H_5)=CH_2$							
	(8.65)	(205)	(860)	6	25	*EST	14145-44-9
	IP from 81MAS/MOU.						
n-$C_5H_{11}C≡CH$	(10.04)	(256)	(1073)	25±0.7	104±3	79ROG/DAG	628-71-7
	From plot of trends in IP's of 1-alkynes, an IP of ~9.95 eV would be predicted.						
n-$C_4H_9C≡CCH_3$	(9.33±0.01)	(235)	(985)	20±0.5	85±2	79ROG/DAG	1119-65-9
n-$C_3H_7C≡CC_2H_5$	(9.26±0.01)	(233)	(976)	20	83±2	79ROG/DAG	2586-89-2
(tert-C_4H_9)$C≡CCH_3$	(9.276±0.10)	(235)	(984)	21	89	*EST	999-78-0
	See also: 85ORL/BOG.						
(cycloheptene)	(8.91±0.04)	(203)	(850)	−2.2±0.2	−9.4±0.9	77PED/RYL	628-92-2
(methylenecyclohexane)	8.93±0.01	200	837	−6±1	−25±4	79FUC/PEA	1192-37-6
	IP from 80SAR/WOR. See also: 86SPA/RAD.						

Table 1. Positive Ion Table – Continued

ION / Neutral	Ionization potential eV	$\Delta_f H$(Ion) kcal/mol	$\Delta_f H$(Ion) kJ/mol	$\Delta_f H$(Neutral) kcal/mol	$\Delta_f H$(Neutral) kJ/mol	Neutral reference	CAS registry number
$C_7H_{12}{}^+$							
1-methylcyclohexene	8.67±0.02	189.6	793.3	−10.3±0.2	−43.2±0.7	77PED/RYL	591-49-1
4-methylcyclohexene	(8.91±0.01)	(197)	(824)	−9	−36	*EST	591-47-9
1-ethylcyclopentene	(8.53±0.01)	(192)	(801)	−5±0.7	−22±3	82ALL/DOD	2146-38-5
3-ethylcyclopentene	8.88±0.01	202	843	−3	−14	82ALL/DOD	694-35-9
bicyclo[4.1.0]	(9.03±0.02)	(209)	(873)	0.5±0.5	2±2	77PED/RYL	286-08-8
norbornane	9.77±0.03	213	894	−12±1	−49±4	80ROG/CHO	279-23-2
$C_7H_{12}BrN^+$							
3-bromoquinuclidine	(≤8.5) IP from 79AUE/BOW.	(≤197)	(≤823)	1	3	*EST	
$C_7H_{12}ClN^+$							
3-chloroquinuclidine	(≤8.8) IP from 79AUE/BOW.	(≤192)	(≤805)	−11	−44	*EST	42332-45-6

Table 1. Positive Ion Table - Continued

ION / Neutral	Ionization potential eV	$\Delta_f H$(Ion) kcal/mol	kJ/mol	$\Delta_f H$(Neutral) kcal/mol	kJ/mol	Neutral reference	CAS registry number
$C_7H_{12}F_2N^+$ 3,3-difluoro-1-azabicyclo[2.2.2]octane · H⁺		(43)	(179)				
From proton affinity of 3,3-difluoro-1-azabicyclo[2.2.2]octane. PA = (221.8) kcal/mol, (928.) kJ/mol.							
$C_7H_{12}N^+$ 1-azabicyclo[2.2.2]oct-2-ene · H⁺		(175)	(730)				
From proton affinity of 1-azabicyclo[2.2.2]oct-2-ene (RN 13929-94-7). PA = (228.5) kcal/mol, (956.) kJ/mol.							
$C_7H_{12}NO^+$ 1-azabicyclo[2.2.2]octan-3-one · H⁺		(116)	(486)				
From proton affinity of 1-azabicyclo[2.2.2]octan-3-one (RN 3731-38-2). PA = (221.9) kcal/mol, (928) kJ/mol.							
$C_7H_{12}O^+$ cycloheptanone	≤9.14	≤152	≤634	−59.1±0.4	−247.5±1.8	77PED/RYL	502-42-1
cyclohexanecarboxaldehyde	(9.6±0.1)	(165)	(691)	−56.2	−235.1	82SPL/CAL	2043-61-0
IP from 82SPL/CAL.							
$C_7H_{12}OSi^+$ 2-(trimethylsilyl)furan	(8.1)	(134)	(563)	−52	−219	*EST	1578-33-2
IP is onset of photoelectron band (83ZYK/ERC).							
2-(ethyldimethylsilyl)furan	≤8.53	(≤151)	(≤630)	−46	−193	*EST	13271-69-7
IP from 83ZYK/ERC.							

ION Neutral	Ionization potential eV	$\Delta_f H$(Ion) kcal/mol kJ/mol	$\Delta_f H$(Neutral) kcal/mol kJ/mol	Neutral reference	CAS registry number
$C_7H_{12}O_2^+$ (bicyclic peroxide structure)	(8.5)	(161) (673)	−35 −147	*EST	68525-35-9

IP is onset of photoelectron band (84GLE/DOB).

| $C_7H_{12}SSi^+$ (2-trimethylsilylthiophene) | (8.1) | (173) (726) | −13 −56 | *EST | 18245-28-8 |

IP is onset of photoelectron band (83VES/HAR).

| $C_7H_{13}^+$ | | | | | |
| $(CH_3)_2CCHC(CH_3)_2$ | | (157) (655) | | | 60602-30-4 |

From proton affinity of $(CH_3)_2C=CHC(CH_3)=CH_2$. (RN 1000-86-8).
PA = (213.1) kcal/mol, (892.) kJ/mol.

| methylcyclohexyl cation (1-) | | 157 655 | | | 16998-65-5 |

From proton affinity of 1-methylcyclohexene. (RN 591-49-1). PA = 198.8 kcal/mol, 832. kJ/mol.

| methylcyclohexyl cation (2-) | | (169) (708) | | | 41771-02-2 |

From appearance potential measurements (81HER/SIC).

| methylcyclohexyl cation (3-) | | (173) (722) | | | 61838-22-0 |

From appearance potential measurements (81HER/SIC).

| methylcyclohexyl cation (4-) | | (172) (720) | | | 21029-96-9 |

From appearance potential measurements (81HER/SIC).

| 1,2-dimethylcyclopentene·H$^+$ | | 158 660 | | | |

From proton affinity of 1,2-dimethylcyclopentene. (RN 765-47-9). PA = 198.1 kcal/mol, 829. kJ/mol.

Table 1. Positive Ion Table - Continued

ION / Neutral	Ionization potential eV	$\Delta_f H$(Ion) kcal/mol	$\Delta_f H$(Ion) kJ/mol	$\Delta_f H$(Neutral) kcal/mol	$\Delta_f H$(Neutral) kJ/mol	Neutral reference	CAS registry number
$C_7H_{13}BrN^+$							
(3-bromo-1-azabicyclo[2.2.2]octane)·H⁺		139	583				

From proton affinity of 3-bromo-1-azabicyclo[2.2.2]octane. PA = (227.1) kcal/mol, (950.) kJ/mol.

$C_7H_{13}ClN^+$							
(3-chloro-1-azabicyclo[2.2.2]octane)·H⁺		(129)	(541)				

From proton affinity of 3-chloro-1-azabicyclo[2.2.2]octane (RN 42332-45-6). PA = (225.8) kcal/mol, (945.) kJ/mol.

$C_7H_{13}FN^+$							
(3-fluoro-1-azabicyclo[3.2.1]octane)·H⁺		(160)	(670)				

From proton affinity of 3-fluoro-1-azabicyclo[3.2.1]octane. PA = (228.1) kcal/mol, (954.) kJ/mol.

$C_7H_{13}N^+$							
H₃C—N=piperidine=CH₂	(≤8.36)	(≤204)	(≤855)	11	48	*EST	13669-28-8

IP from 80SAR/WOR.

	(7.1)	(197)	(823)	33	138	*EST	81156-87-8

IP is onset of photoelectron band (81MUL/PRE2).

	(6.9)	(192)	(803)	33	137	*EST	81156-88-9

IP is onset of photoelectron band (81MUL/PRE2).

	(7.4)	(170)	(710)	−1.0±0.3	−4.2±1.2	77PED/RYL	100-76-5

IP is onset of photoelectron band.

	(≤8.22±0.05)	(≤187)	(≤782)	−3	−11	*EST	280-38-6

ION / Neutral	Ionization potential eV	$\Delta_f H$(Ion) kcal/mol	kJ/mol	$\Delta_f H$(Neutral) kcal/mol	kJ/mol	Neutral reference	CAS registry number
$C_7H_{13}N^+$							
(bicyclic amine, NH₂ equatorial)	(8.33) IP from 79AUE/BOW.	(185)	(776)	−7±0.2	−28±1	*EST	31002-73-0
(bicyclic amine, NH₂ other)	(8.41) IP from 79AUE/BOW.	(186)	(779)	−8±0.2	−32±1	*EST	7242-92-4
$C_7H_{13}NO^+$							
cycloheptanone oxime	(8.88±0.03) IP from 79GOL/KUL.	(179)	(749)	−26	−108	*EST	2158-31-8
$C_7H_{14}^+$							
1-C_7H_{14}	(9.44)	(202.8)	(848.9)	−14.8	−61.9	84WIB/WAS	592-76-7
2-C_7H_{14}	(8.84±0.02) IP from 77ASH/BUR.	(187)	(782)	−17	−71	84WIB/WAS	592-77-8
3-C_7H_{14}	(8.92) IP from 81HOL/FIN.	(189)	(790)	−17	−71	84WIB/WAS	14686-14-7
$(CH_3)_3CCH_2CH=CH_2$	9.40±0.01	197	823	−20.0±0.2	−83.8±0.8	77PED/RYL	762-62-9
$n\text{-}C_4H_9C(CH_3)=CH_2$	(9.04±0.01)	(190)	(796)	−18	−76	*EST	6094-02-6
$(CH_3)_2CHCH_2C(CH_3)=CH_2$	(9.03±0.01)	(188)	(787)	−20.0±0.3	−83.8±1.4	77PED/RYL	2213-32-3
$(CH_3)_3CC(CH_3)=CH_2$	(9.02±0.01)	(187.5)	(784.4)	−20.4±0.3	−85.5±1.4	77PED/RYL	594-56-9
(Z)-$(CH_3)_2CHCH_2CH=CHCH_3$	(8.92±0.01)	(187)	(782)	−19	−78	*EST	13151-17-2
(E)-$(CH_3)_2CHCH_2CH=CHCH_3$	(8.92±0.01)	(186)	(779)	−20	−82	*EST	7385-82-2
(E)-$C_2H_5CH(CH_3)CH=CHCH_3$	(8.91±0.01)	(186)	(778)	−20	−82	*EST	3683-22-5
$C_3H_7CH=C(CH_3)_2$	(8.62) IP from 81HOL/FIN.	(179)	(748)	−20	−84	*EST	2738-19-4

Table 1. Positive Ion Table – Continued

ION / Neutral	Ionization potential eV	$\Delta_f H$(Ion) kcal/mol	$\Delta_f H$(Ion) kJ/mol	$\Delta_f H$(Neutral) kcal/mol	$\Delta_f H$(Neutral) kJ/mol	Neutral reference	CAS registry number
$C_7H_{14}^+$							
$C_2H_5C(CH_3)=C(CH_3)_2$	(8.21±0.01)	(168)	(702)	−21	−90	*EST	10574-37-5
(Z)-$(CH_3)_3CCH=CHCH_3$	(8.92±0.01)	(188)	(788)	−17.4±0.3	−72.6±1.4	77PED/RYL	762-63-0
(E)-$(CH_3)_3CCH=CHCH_3$	(8.91±0.01)	(184)	(771)	−21.3±0.3	−88.8±1.1	77PED/RYL	690-08-4
cycloheptane	9.97	202	844	−28.3±0.1	−118.2±0.6	77PED/RYL	291-64-5

300 K ionization energy from charge transfer equilibrium constants relative to cyclohexane and cyclohexane-d_{12} = 9.99 eV. (82SIE/MAU).

methylcyclohexane	9.64	185	775	−37.0±0.2	−154.7±1.0	77PED/RYL	108-87-2

IP from charge transfer equilibrium constant determinations (82SIE/MAU; 82LIA). Reference IP's, fluorobenzenes. Threshold determination gives IP = 9.76±0.03 eV.

1,2-dimethylcyclopentane (cis)	(9.92±0.05)	(198)	(828)	−30.9±0.3	−129.5±1.3	77PED/RYL	1192-18-3

IP from 81HER/SIC.

1,2-dimethylcyclopentane (trans)	(9.95±0.05)	(197)	(823)	−32.7±0.3	−136.7±1.1	77PED/RYL	822-50-4

IP from 81HER/SIC.

ethylcyclopentane	(10.12±0.02)	(203)	(850)	−30.3±0.2	−126.7±0.9	77PED/RYL	1640-89-7

$C_7H_{14}N^+$

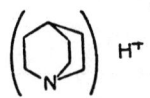 H^+

| | | 132 | 551 | | | | |

From proton affinity of 1-azabicyclo[2.2.2]octane (RN 100-76-5). (86TAF/GAL). PA = 233.1 kcal/mol, 975. kJ/mol.

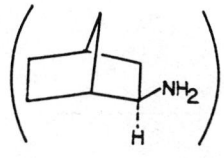 H^+

| | | 137 | 574 | | | | |

From proton affinity of bicyclo[2.2.1]heptan-2-amine,endo (RN 31002-73-0). PA = (221.7) kcal/mol, (927.) kJ/mol.

Table 1. Positive Ion Table - Continued

ION / Neutral	Ionization potential eV	$\Delta_f H$(Ion) kcal/mol	$\Delta_f H$(Ion) kJ/mol	$\Delta_f H$(Neutral) kcal/mol	$\Delta_f H$(Neutral) kJ/mol	Neutral reference	CAS registry number

$C_7H_{14}N^+$

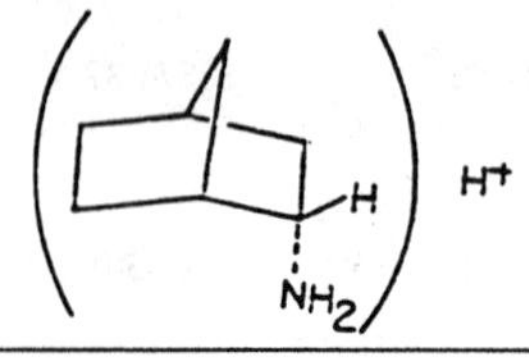

bicyclo[2.2.1]heptan-2-amine, exo · H⁺ : 136 kcal/mol, 570 kJ/mol
From proton affinity of bicyclo[2.2.1]heptan-2-amine,exo (RN 7242-92-4). PA = (221.7) kcal/mol, (927.) kJ/mol.

$C_7H_{14}N_2^+$

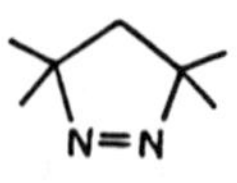	(≤8.63)	(≤208)	(≤872)	9.4±0.8	39.3±3.6	80ENG	2721-31-5
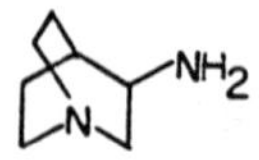	(≤8.0) IP from 79AUE/BOW.	(≤188)	(≤785)	4	17	*EST	6238-14-8
	≤8.02 IP from 82LEV/LIA. See also: 84NEL.	(≤215)	(≤898)	30	124	*EST	6523-29-1
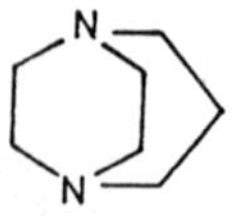	≤7.43	(≤192)	(≤802)	20	85	*EST	283-47-6
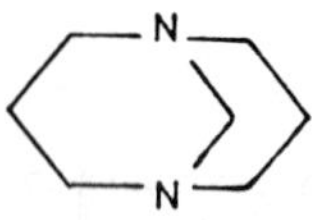	≤7.75	(≤191)	(≤800)	12	52	*EST	281-17-4
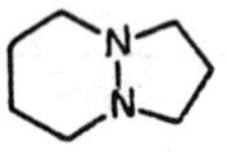	(7.63) IP from 82LEV/LIA. See also: 84NEL.	(204)	(853)	28	117	*EST	5721-43-7

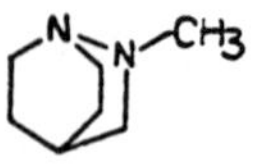

$C_7H_{14}N_2S^+$

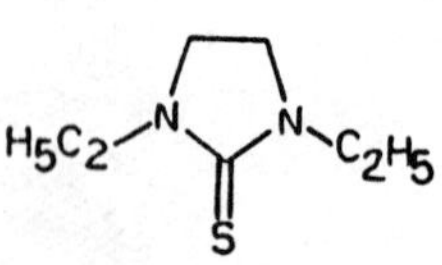

	(7.5) IP is onset of photoelectron band (80AND/DEV).	(177)	(742)	4	18	*EST	30826-80-3

Table 1. Positive Ion Table – Continued

ION / Neutral	Ionization potential eV	$\Delta_f H$(Ion) kcal/mol	kJ/mol	$\Delta_f H$(Neutral) kcal/mol	kJ/mol	Neutral reference	CAS registry number
$C_7H_{14}O^+$							
n-C_6H_{13}CHO	(9.65±0.02)	(159)	(667)	−63±1	−264±4	77PED/RYL	111-71-7
$(CH_3)_2$CHCH(C_2H_5)CHO	(9.44) IP from 81HOL/FIN.	(149)	(624)	−69	−287	*EST	26254-92-2
n-C_5H_{11}COCH$_3$	9.30±0.01	142	596	−72	−301	75TRC	110-43-0
n-C_4H_9COC$_2H_5$	(9.22±0.04) IP is average of values from 81HOL/FIN, 86TRA/MCA.	(141)	(590)	−71	−299	75TRC	106-35-4
$(n-C_3H_7)_2$CO	9.10±0.04	138	578	−72	−300	75TRC	123-19-3
$(CH_3)_2$CHCH$_2$CH$_2$COCH$_3$	(9.28±0.01)	(140)	(587)	−74	−308	*EST	110-12-3
$CH_3(CH_2)_2CH(CH_3)COCH_3$	(9.20±0.02) IP is average of values from 81HOL/FIN, 86TRA/MCA.	(139)	(581)	−73	−307	*EST	2550-21-2
neo-C_5H_{11}COCH$_3$	(9.23±0.01)	(137)	(571)	−76	−319	*EST	590-50-1
$C_2H_5C(CH_3)_2COCH_3$	(9.02±0.01)	(133)	(555)	−75	−315	*EST	20669-04-9
(iso-$C_3H_7)_2$CO	8.95±0.01	132	552	−74.4±0.3	−311.3±1.1	77PED/RYL	565-80-0
1-methylcyclohexanol (OH, CH$_3$)	(9.8±0.2)	(140)	(588)	−86	−358	85WIB/WAS	590-67-0
$C_7H_{14}O_2^+$							
2,2,4-trimethyl-1,3-dioxane	≤9.63 IP from 84ASF/ZYK.	≤111	≤463	−111	−466	77PED/RYL	696-79-7
cis-1,2-dimethoxycyclopentane	(8.6) IP is onset of photoelectron band.	(113)	(472)	−86	−358	*EST	61011-51-6
trans-1,2-dimethoxycyclopentane	(8.7) IP is onset of photoelectron band.	(115)	(481)	−86	−358	*EST	29887-56-7

Table 1. Positive Ion Table – Continued

ION / Neutral	Ionization potential eV	$\Delta_f H$(Ion) kcal/mol	kJ/mol	$\Delta_f H$(Neutral) kcal/mol	kJ/mol	Neutral reference	CAS registry number
$C_7H_{14}O_2^+$							
(2,2,4,4-tetramethyl-1,3-dioxolane structure)	8.9	(139)	(583)	−66	−276	*EST	22431-90-9

IP is onset of photoelectron band.

$C_7H_{15}^+$							
1-C_7H_{15}		(183)	(766)	4	15	*EST	

From appearance potential measurements (82MAC). $\Delta_f H$(Neutral) based on D[C-H] = 100.5 kcal/mol.

2-C_7H_{15}	(6.95)	(162)	(678)	2	8	*EST	

From appearance potential measurements (82MAC). IP is $\Delta_f H$(Ion) - $\Delta_f H$(Neutral). $\Delta_f H$(Neutral) based on D[C-H] = 99 kcal/mol.

$(CH_3)_2CCH_2CH_2CH_2CH_3$		147	615				40626-78-6

From appearance potential measurement (84LOS/HOL).

$(CH_3)_2CCH_2CH(CH_3)_2$		148.4	620.9				35443-14-2

From hydride transfer equilibrium constant determinations relative to $\Delta_f H$(tert-$C_4H_9^+$) (76MAU/SOL).

$(C_2H_5)_3C$		150.6	630.1				28013-53-8

From hydride transfer equilibrium constant determinations relative to $\Delta_f H$(tert-$C_4H_9^+$) (76MAU/SOL).

$(CH_3)_3CC(CH_3)_2$		144.5	604.5				24436-96-2

From hydride transfer equilibrium constant determinations relative to $\Delta_f H$(tert-$C_4H_9^+$) (76MAU/SOL).

$C_7H_{15}ClN^+$							
(piperidine, 2-chloromethyl-1-methyl, H^+)		(115)	(481)				

From proton affinity of Pyrrolidine, 2-chloromethyl-1-methyl- (RN 49665-74-9). PA = (227.6) kcal/mol, (952.) kJ/mol.

$C_7H_{15}N^+$							
(E)-$C_2H_5C(N(CH_3)_2)=CHCH_3$	(≤7.61)	(≤173)	(≤724)	−2	−10	*EST	32317-47-8

IP from 81MUL/PRE2.

(1,2-dimethylpiperidine structure)	(7.63)	(157)	(658)	−19	−78	*EST	671-36-3

IP from 82ROZ/HOU.

Table 1. Positive Ion Table - Continued

ION / Neutral	Ionization potential eV	$\Delta_f H$(Ion) kcal/mol	$\Delta_f H$(Ion) kJ/mol	$\Delta_f H$(Neutral) kcal/mol	$\Delta_f H$(Neutral) kJ/mol	Neutral reference	CAS registry number
$C_7H_{15}N^+$							
1,3-dimethylpiperidine	(7.76) IP from 82ROZ/HOU.	(160)	(669)	−19	−80	*EST	695-35-2
1,4-dimethylpiperidine	(7.79) IP from 82ROZ/HOU.	(161)	(672)	−19	−80	*EST	695-15-8
2,6-dimethylpiperidine	(7.93) IP from 82ROZ/HOU.	(155)	(648)	−28	−117	*EST	766-17-6
3,3-dimethylpiperidine	(8.05) IP from 82ROZ/HOU.	(160)	(670)	−26	−107	*EST	1193-12-0
$C_7H_{15}N_2^+$							
(3-amino-1-azabicyclo[2.2.2]octane)H$^+$		138	577				

From proton affinity of 3-amino-1-azabicyclo[2.2.2]octane (RN 6238-14-8). PA = (231.8) kcal/mol, (970) kJ/mol.

| (2-methyl-1,2-diazabicyclo[2.2.2]octane)H$^+$ | | 165 | 690 | | | | |

From proton affinity of 2-methyl-1,2-diazabicyclo[2.2.2]octane (RN 6523-29-1). (84MAU/NEL). PA = 230.4 kcal/mol, 964. kJ/mol.

| $C_7H_{15}O^+$ | | | | | | | |
| $(i-C_3H_7)_2COH$ | | 87 | 363 | | | | |

From proton affinity of $(i-C_3H_7)_2CO$ (RN 565-80-0). PA = 204.9 kcal/mol, 857. kJ/mol.

$C_7H_{16}^+$							
$n-C_7H_{16}$	9.92±0.05	184	770	−44.8±0.1	−187.5±0.5	74SCO	142-82-5
		194	811	−34.8±0.1	−145.7±0.5		

This value of IP from charge transfer equilibrium constant determinations (76LIA/AUS, 82LIA).

Table 1. Positive Ion Table - Continued

ION Neutral	Ionization potential eV	$\Delta_f H$(Ion) kcal/mol	$\Delta_f H$(Ion) kJ/mol	$\Delta_f H$(Neutral) kcal/mol	$\Delta_f H$(Neutral) kJ/mol	Neutral reference	CAS registry number

$C_7H_{16}N^+$
  $(CH_3)_2NC(C_2H_5)_2$

| | | 127 | 531 | | | | |

From proton affinity of (E)-$(CH_3)_2NC(C_2H_5)=CHCH_3$ (RN 78733-73-0).
PA = 236.4 kcal/mol, 989. kJ/mol.

$C_7H_{16}N_2^+$

|  (cyclohexyl)-NN(CH_3)_2 | (6.83) | (170) | (710) | 12 | 51 | *EST | 49840-60-0 |

IP from 86RUM. See also: 84NEL.

| 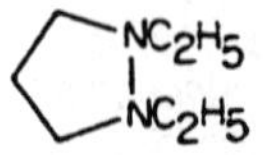 (pyrrolidine with two NC_2H_5) | (≤8.06) | (≤198) | (≤828) | 12 | 50 | *EST | 22825-58-7 |

See also: 84NEL.

| 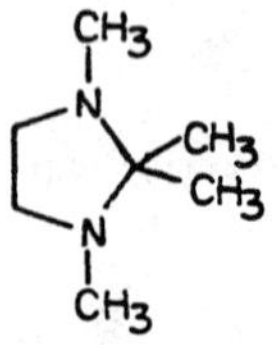 (imidazolidine trimethyl structure) | (7.2) | (196) | (822) | 30 | 127 | *EST | 33709-65-8 |

IP is onset of photoelectron band (82WOR/HAR).

$C_7H_{16}O^+$

| n-C_7H_{15}OH | (9.84±0.03) | (147) | (614) | −80.2±0.4 | −335.5±1.5 | 77PED/RYL | 111-70-6 |

IP from 77ASH/BUR.

| $CH_3(CH_2)_4CHOHCH_3$ | (9.70±0.03) | (139) | (582) | −85 | −354 | 84WIB/WAS | 543-49-7 |

IP from 77ASH/BUR.

| $CH_3(CH_2)_3CHOHCH_2CH_3$ | 9.68±0.03 | 139 | 580 | −85 | −354 | 84WIB/WAS | 589-82-2 |

IP from 77ASH/BUR.

| $CH_3(CH_2)_2CHOH(CH_2)_2CH_3$ | (9.61±0.03) | (137) | (573) | −85 | −354 | 84WIB/WAS | 589-55-9 |

IP from 77ASH/BUR.

| n-$C_5H_{11}OC_2H_5$ | (≤9.49) | (≤144) | (≤602) | −75 | −314 | *EST | 17952-11-3 |

IP from 80BAC/MOU.

| (i-C_3H_7)O(t-C_4H_9) | (≤9.20) | (≤131) | (≤548) | −81 | −339 | *EST | 17348-59-3 |

IP from 79AUE/BOW. Authors suggest that adiabatic IP is lower than cited vertical value by 25-29 kJ/mol, 6-7 kcal/mol.

Table 1. Positive Ion Table – Continued

ION / Neutral	Ionization potential eV	$\Delta_f H$(Ion) kcal/mol	$\Delta_f H$(Ion) kJ/mol	$\Delta_f H$(Neutral) kcal/mol	$\Delta_f H$(Neutral) kJ/mol	Neutral reference	CAS registry number
$C_7H_{16}O_2^+$							
n-C_7H_{15}OOH	(9.48±0.03)	(150)	(626)	−69	−289	*EST	764-81-8
	IP from 77ASH/BUR.						
n-C_5H_{11}CH(CH_3)OOH	(9.30±0.03)	(148)	(621)	−66	−276	*EST	762-46-9
	IP from 77ASH/BUR.						
$C_7H_{17}N^+$							
$(C_2H_5)_2$(n-C_3H_7)N	(7.67)	(150)	(626)	−27	−114	*EST	4458-31-5
	IP from 79AUE/BOW. Ion heat of formation predicted from hydrogen affinities of tertiary amine ions: 146 kcal/mol, 611 kJ/mol, corresponding to IP of 7.50 eV.						
$C_7H_{17}O^+$							
(i-C_3H_7)OH(t-C_4H_9)		(76)	(317)				
	From proton affinity of (i-C_3H_7)O(t-C_4H_9) (RN 17348-59-3). PA = (208.8) kcal/mol, (874.) kJ/mol.						
$C_7H_{17}O_2^+$							
$CH_3OH(CH_2)_5OCH_3$		40	167				
	From proton affinity of $CH_3O(CH_2)_5OCH_3$ (RN 111-89-7). PA = 221.8 kcal/mol, 928. kJ/mol.						
$C_7H_{18}N^+$							
n-$C_7H_{15}NH_3$		111	463				
	From proton affinity of n-$C_7H_{15}NH_2$ (RN 111-68-2). PA = 219.0 kcal/mol, 916. kJ/mol.						
$(CH_3)_2$(neo-C_5H_{11})NH		108	450				
	From proton affinity of $(CH_3)_2$(neo-C_5H_{11})N (RN 10076-31-0). PA = 229.9 kcal/mol, 962. kJ/mol.						
$(C_2H_5)_2$(n-C_3H_7)NH		(106)	(445)				
	From proton affinity of $(C_2H_5)_2$(n-C_3H_7)N (RN 4458-31-5). PA = (232.0) kcal/mol, (971.) kJ/mol.						
$C_7H_{18}N_2^+$							
$(CH_3)_2N(CH_2)_3N(CH_3)_2$	(7.6)	(168)	(704)	−7	−29	*EST	110-95-2
	IP is onset of photoelectron spectrum (81LIV/ROB).						
$(C_2H_5)_2NN(CH_3)(C_2H_5)$	(8.02)	(189)	(791)	4	17	*EST	50599-43-4
	Reported values of IP's of hydrazines determined by threshold measurements are usually significantly higher than the adiabatic value because of the large geometry change associated with ionization. See also: 84NEL, 79NEL/KES.						

Table 1. Positive Ion Table - Continued

ION / Neutral	Ionization potential eV	$\Delta_f H$(Ion) kcal/mol	$\Delta_f H$(Ion) kJ/mol	$\Delta_f H$(Neutral) kcal/mol	$\Delta_f H$(Neutral) kJ/mol	Neutral reference	CAS registry number
$C_7H_{18}N_2^+$							
$(n-C_4H_9)(CH_3)NN(CH_3)_2$	(6.63)	(156)	(652)	3	12	*EST	52598-10-4

IP from charge transfer equilibrium constant determination (84MAU/NEL). See also: 80NEL/KES, 84NEL.

$(t-C_4H_9)(CH_3)NN(CH_3)_2$	(6.80)	(159)	(667)	3	11	*EST	60678-73-1

IP from charge transfer equilibrium constant determination (84MAU/NEL).

ION / Neutral	IP eV	$\Delta_f H$(Ion) kcal/mol	kJ/mol	$\Delta_f H$(Neutral) kcal/mol	kJ/mol	Neutral reference	CAS registry number
$C_7H_{18}Si^+$							
$(CH_3)_3CSi(CH_3)_3$	(9.34±0.06)	(170)	(713)	−45	−188	72TRI/ALL	5037-65-0
$C_7H_{18}Si_2^+$							
$CH_2=CHSi(CH_3)_2Si(CH_3)_3$	(≤8.56)	(≤138)	(≤577)	−60	−249	*EST	1112-06-7

IP from 81KHV/ZYK.

$C_7H_{18}Sn^+$							
$(C_2H_5)_3(CH_3)Sn$	(≤8.95)	(≤152)	(≤638)	−54±1	−226±4	80TEL/RAB	2097-60-1
$(CH_3)_3(tert-C_4H_9)Sn$	(8.0)	(168)	(705)	−16±1	−67±6	77PED/RYL	3531-47-3

IP is onset of photoelectron band.

$C_7H_{19}NSi^+$							
$(CH_3)_3SiN(C_2H_5)_2$	(7.68)	(97)	(406)	−80±2	−335±8	80TEL/RAB	996-50-9

IP from 83MOL/PIK3.

$C_7H_{19}N_2^+$							
$H_3N(CH_2)_7NH_2$		100	419				

From proton affinity of $H_2N(CH_2)_7NH_2$ (RN 646-19-5). PA = 238. kcal/mol, 996. kJ/mol.

$(CH_3)_2NH(CH_2)_3N(CH_3)_2$		116	484				

From proton affinity of $(CH_3)_2N(CH_2)_3N(CH_3)_2$ (RN 110-95-2). PA = 243. kcal/mol, 1017. kJ/mol.

$(n-C_4H_9)(CH_3)NHN(CH_3)_2$		139	580				

From proton affinity of $(n-C_4H_9)(CH_3)NN(CH_3)_2$ (RN 52598-10-4). (84MAU/NEL). PA = 230.0 kcal/mol, 962. kJ/mol.

$(t-C_4H_9(CH_3)NHN(CH_3)_2$		139	582				

From proton affinity of $(t-C_4H_9)(CH_3)NN(CH_3)_2$ (RN 60678-73-1). (84MAU/NEL). PA = 229.3 kcal/mol, 959. kJ/mol.

Table 1. Positive Ion Table – Continued

ION / Neutral	Ionization potential eV	$\Delta_f H$(Ion) kcal/mol	$\Delta_f H$(Ion) kJ/mol	$\Delta_f H$(Neutral) kcal/mol	$\Delta_f H$(Neutral) kJ/mol	Neutral reference	CAS registry number
$C_7H_{20}NSi^+$ $(CH_3)_3Si(CH_2)_2NH(CH_3)_2$		79	332				

From proton affinity of $(CH_3)_3Si(CH_2)_2N(CH_3)_2$ (RN 23138-94-5). (84MAU/NEL). PA = 231.8 kcal/mol, 970. kJ/mol.

ION / Neutral	IP eV	$\Delta_f H$(Ion) kcal/mol	$\Delta_f H$(Ion) kJ/mol	$\Delta_f H$(Neutral) kcal/mol	$\Delta_f H$(Neutral) kJ/mol	Neutral reference	CAS registry number
$C_8Co_2O_8^+$	(8.12±0.22)	(−96)	(−402)	−283±2	−1185±8	82PIL/SKI	10210-68-1
$C_8F_{12}Mo_2O_8^+$	8.07	(−818)	(−3421)	−1004	−4200	*EST	36608-07-8

IP is onset of photoelectron band (82BAN/PEL).

| $C_8F_{18}O^+$ $(n-C_4F_9)_2O$ | 12.68 | −658.5 | −2755.2 | −950.9±1 | −3978.6±3 | 77PED/RYL | 308-48-5 |

IP from 83MOL/PIK.

$C_8H_2^+$ CH≡CC≡CC≡CH	(9.09±0.02)	(416)	(1741)	207	864	*EST	6165-96-4
$C_8H_3F_5^+$	(9.18±0.02)	(35)	(145)	−177	−741	*EST	653-34-9
$C_8H_4Cl_2OS^+$	≤9.00	(≤205)	(≤857)	−3	−11	*EST	30834-33-4

IP from 82BEN/DUR.

| $C_8H_4F_6^+$ | 10.57 | (−61) | (−255) | −305 | −1275 | *EST | 402-31-3 |

IP from 82CAB/COW.

Table 1. Positive Ion Table — Continued

ION / Neutral	Ionization potential eV	$\Delta_f H$(Ion) kcal/mol	$\Delta_f H$(Ion) kJ/mol	$\Delta_f H$(Neutral) kcal/mol	$\Delta_f H$(Neutral) kJ/mol	Neutral reference	CAS registry number
$C_8H_4N_2^+$							
1,2-dicyanobenzene	9.9 IP is onset of photoelectron band.	(316)	(1323)	88±0.5	368±2	80SAT/SAK	91-15-6
1,3-dicyanobenzene	10.2 IP is onset of photoelectron band.	(322)	(1347)	87±0.5	363±2	80SAT/SAK	626-17-5
1,4-dicyanobenzene	10.10	318	1331	85±0.5	357±2	80SAT/SAK	623-26-7
$C_8H_4O_2^+$							
benzocyclobutenedione	≤9.23	(≤237)	(≤992)	24	101	*EST	6383-11-5
$C_8H_4O_3^+$							
phthalic anhydride	(10.0) IP is onset of photoelectron band.	(142)	(594)	−89±0.5	−371±2	77PED/RYL	85-44-9
$C_8H_5BrOS^+$							
2-bromobenzothiophene S-oxide	≤9.10 IP from 82BEN/DUR.	(≤225)	(≤941)	15	63	*EST	57147-27-0
3-bromobenzothiophene S-oxide	≤8.95 IP from 82BEN/DUR.	(≤221)	(≤927)	15	63	*EST	57147-26-9

Table 1. Positive Ion Table – Continued

ION / Neutral	Ionization potential eV	$\Delta_f H$(Ion) kcal/mol	kJ/mol	$\Delta_f H$(Neutral) kcal/mol	kJ/mol	Neutral reference	CAS registry number
C$_8$H$_5$BrO$_2$S$^+$							
2-bromobenzothiophene 1,1-dioxide	≤9.10 IP from 82BEN/DUR.	(≤171)	(≤715)	−39	−163	*EST	5350-05-0
3-bromobenzothiophene 1,1-dioxide	≤9.40 IP from 82BEN/DUR.	(≤178)	(≤744)	−39	−163	*EST	16957-97-4
C$_8$H$_5$Cl$^+$							
4-chlorophenylacetylene	(8.6) IP is onset of photoelectron band.	(264)	(1104)	65	274	*EST	873-73-4
C$_8$H$_5$ClOS$^+$							
2-chlorobenzothiophene 1-oxide	≤9.10 IP from 82BEN/DUR.	(≤212)	(≤888)	2	10	*EST	57147-28-1
3-chlorobenzothiophene 1-oxide	≤8.95 IP from 82BEN/DUR.	(≤209)	(≤874)	2	10	*EST	63724-95-8
C$_8$H$_5$ClO$_2$S$^+$							
2-chlorobenzothiophene 1,1-dioxide	≤9.25 IP from 82BEN/DUR.	(≤162)	(≤676)	−52	−216	*EST	10133-41-2
3-chlorobenzothiophene 1,1-dioxide	≤9.45 IP from 82BEN/DUR.	(≤166)	(≤696)	−52	−216	*EST	21211-29-0

Table 1. Positive Ion Table - Continued

ION / Neutral	Ionization potential eV	$\Delta_f H$(Ion) kcal/mol	$\Delta_f H$(Ion) kJ/mol	$\Delta_f H$(Neutral) kcal/mol	$\Delta_f H$(Neutral) kJ/mol	Neutral reference	CAS registry number
$C_8H_5F_3O^+$ (PhC(=O)CF₃)	(9.72) IP from 79MCL/TRA.	(61)	(256)	−163	−682	*EST	434-45-7
$C_8H_5MnO_3^+$ ((CO)₃Mn(C₅H₅))	(7.6) IP is onset of photoelectron band (81CAL/HUB). See also: 86LIC/KEL.	(61)	(257)	−114±2	−476±8	77PED/RYL	12079-65-1
$C_8H_5NO^+$ (NC-C₆H₄-CHO)	≤10.10 IP from 85GAL/GER.	(≤258)	(≤1081)	25	107	*EST	105-07-7
$C_8H_5NO_2^+$ (NC-C₆H₄-COOH)	(10.0) IP from 84TOB/TAJ.	(193)	(807)	−38	−158	*EST	619-65-8
$C_8H_6^+$ (E),(E)-HC≡CCH=CHCH=CHC≡CH	(7.8) IP from 74KOP/SCH.	(278)	(1161)	98	409	*EST	53477-04-6
(Ph-C≡CH)	8.81±0.04 See also: 80BOC/AYG, 74KOP/SCH, 81ELB/LIE.	276	1156	73±0.5	306±2	85DAV/ALL	536-74-3
(benzocyclobutadiene)	(≤7.5) IP is onset of photoelectron band.	(≤291)	(≤1218)	118	494	85DEW/MER	4026-23-7
$C_8H_6Br_2^+$ (dibromocubane)	(9.0) IP is onset of photoelectron band (85HON/HEI).	(358)	(1496)	150	628	*EST	59346-70-2

Table 1. Positive Ion Table - Continued

ION / Neutral	Ionization potential eV	$\Delta_f H$(Ion) kcal/mol	$\Delta_f H$(Ion) kJ/mol	$\Delta_f H$(Neutral) kcal/mol	$\Delta_f H$(Neutral) kJ/mol	Neutral reference	CAS registry number

$C_8H_6Cl^+$

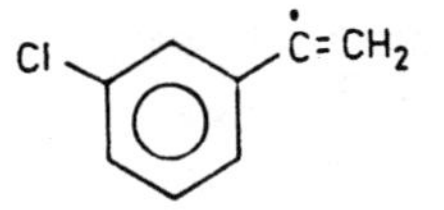

3-Cl-C₆H₄-Ċ=CH₂ : 235   984
From proton affinity of 3-ClC₆H₄C≡CH (RN 766-83-6). (85MAR/MOD).
PA = 196.1 kcal/mol, 820. kJ/mol.

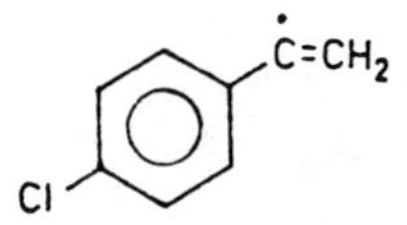

4-Cl-C₆H₄-Ċ=CH₂ : 232   970
From proton affinity of 4-ClC₆H₄C≡CH (RN 873-73-4). (85MAR/MOD).
PA = 199.4 kcal/mol, 834. kJ/mol.

$C_8H_6ClN^+$

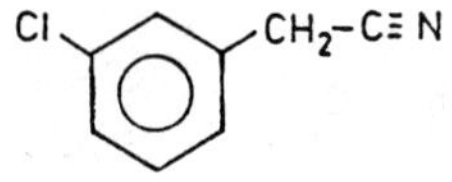

3-Cl-C₆H₄-CH₂-C≡N : (9.48±0.05) (256) (1071) 37 156 *EST

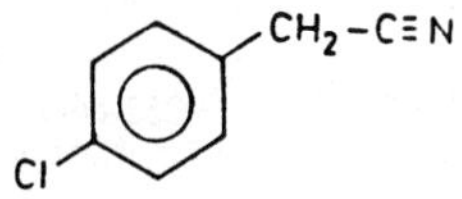

4-Cl-C₆H₄-CH₂-C≡N : (9.43±0.05) (255) (1066) 37 156 *EST

$C_8H_6Cl_2^+$

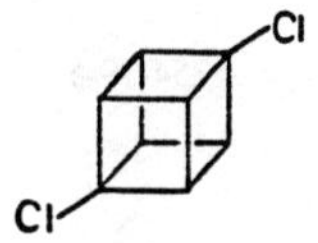

dichlorocubane: (9.15) (337) (1411) 126 528 *EST
IP is onset of photoelectron band (85HON/HEI).

$C_8H_6F^+$

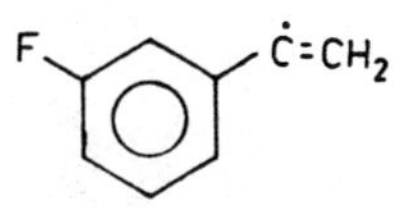

3-F-C₆H₄-Ċ=CH₂ : 196   819
From proton affinity of 3-FC₆H₄C≡CH (RN 2561-17-3). (85MAR/MOD).
PA = 195.4 kcal/mol, 818. kJ/mol.

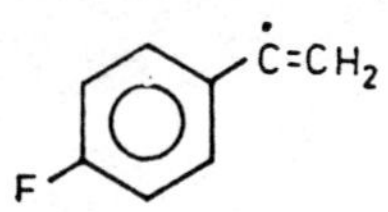

4-F-C₆H₄-Ċ=CH₂ : 190   797
From proton affinity of 4-FC₆H₄C≡CH (RN 766-98-3). (85MAR/MOD).
PA = 200.8 kcal/mol, 840. kJ/mol.

ION Neutral	Ionization potential eV	$\Delta_f H$(Ion) kcal/mol kJ/mol		$\Delta_f H$(Neutral) kcal/mol kJ/mol		Neutral reference	CAS registry number
$C_8H_6F_3O^+$ 4-CF$_3$C$_6$H$_4$ĊHOH		2	10				
	From proton affinity of 4-CF$_3$C$_6$H$_4$CHO (RN 455-19-6). PA = 191.9 kcal/mol, 799. kJ/mol.						
$C_8H_6I_2^+$ (diiodocubane)	(8.7)	(379)	(1587)	179	748	*EST	
	IP is onset of photoelectron band (85HON/HEI).						
$C_8H_6NO^+$ [4-(CN)C$_6$H$_4$CHO]H$^+$		204	855				
	From proton affinity of 4-(CN)C$_6$H$_4$CHO (RN 105-07-7). PA = 187.0 kcal/mol, 782. kJ/mol.						
$C_8H_6N_2^+$ (cinnoline)	(8.2)	(270)	(1129)	81±2	338±10	*EST	253-66-7
	IP is onset of photoelectron band.						
(1,5-naphthyridine)	(8.8)	(267)	(1116)	64	267	*EST	254-79-5
	IP is onset of photoelectron band.						
(1,6-naphthyridine)	(9.0)	(271)	(1135)	64	267	*EST	253-72-5
	IP is onset of photoelectron band.						
(1,7-naphthyridine)	(8.99)	(271)	(1134)	64	267	*EST	253-69-0
	IP is onset of photoelectron band.						
(1,8-naphthyridine)	(8.8)	(267)	(1116)	64	267	*EST	254-60-4

Table 1. Positive Ion Table - Continued

ION / Neutral	Ionization potential eV	$\Delta_f H$(Ion) kcal/mol	$\Delta_f H$(Ion) kJ/mol	$\Delta_f H$(Neutral) kcal/mol	$\Delta_f H$(Neutral) kJ/mol	Neutral reference	CAS registry number
$C_8H_6N_2^+$							
(phthalazine)	(8.4) IP is onset of photoelectron band.	(274)	(1148)	81	338	*EST	253-52-1
(2,6-naphthyridine)	(≤8.8) IP is onset of photoelectron band.	(267)	(1116)	64	267	*EST	253-50-9
(2,7-naphthyridine)	(8.8) IP is onset of photoelectron band.	(267)	(1116)	64	267	*EST	253-45-2
(quinazoline)	9.00±0.02	(269)	(1125)	61	257	*EST	253-82-7
(quinoxaline)	9.01±0.02	271	1131	63±1	262±4	81STE/BAR	91-19-0
$C_8H_6N_2O_2^+$							
(4-nitrophenylacetonitrile)	(10.11±0.04)	(274)	(1146)	41±1	171±4	*EST	555-21-5
$C_8H_6N_2Se^+$							
(2-phenyl-1,3,4-selenadiazole)	(8.1) IP is onset of photoelectron band (80BOC/AYG).	(295)	(1234)	108.1±2	452.3±8	73ARS/SHA	25660-64-4
$C_8H_6N_4^+$							
(2,2'-bipyrimidine)	(8.3) IP is onset of photoelectron band (82BAR/CAU).	(293)	(1227)	102	426	*EST	34671-83-5

Table 1. Positive Ion Table - Continued

ION / Neutral	Ionization potential eV	$\Delta_f H$(Ion) kcal/mol	$\Delta_f H$(Ion) kJ/mol	$\Delta_f H$(Neutral) kcal/mol	$\Delta_f H$(Neutral) kJ/mol	Neutral reference	CAS registry number
$C_8H_6O_2S^+$	(9.1)	(166)	(694)	−44	−184	*EST	825-44-5

IP is onset of photoelectron band (82BEN/DUR).

$C_8H_6O_4^+$ (1,3-benzenedicarboxylic acid)	(9.98±0.2)	(64)	(267)	−166±0.5	−696±2	77PED/RYL	121-91-5
(1,4-benzenedicarboxylic acid)	(9.86±0.2)	(55)	(233)	−172±0.7	−718±3	77PED/RYL	100-21-0

$C_8H_6S^+$ (benzothiophene)	8.13±0.015	227	950	40±0.2	166±1	79SAB	95-15-8
(isobenzothiophene)	(7.75)	(228)	(954)	49	206	*EST	270-82-6

$C_8H_6S_2^+$	(7.99)	(243)	(1017)	59	246	*EST	3172-56-3

$C_8H_7^+$		239	998				

From proton affinity of $C_6H_5C{\equiv}CH$ (RN 536-74-3). (85MAR/MOD).
PA = 200.2 kcal/mol, 838. kJ/mol.

Table 1. Positive Ion Table – Continued

ION / Neutral	Ionization potential eV	$\Delta_f H$(Ion) kcal/mol	$\Delta_f H$(Ion) kJ/mol	$\Delta_f H$(Neutral) kcal/mol	$\Delta_f H$(Neutral) kJ/mol	Neutral reference	CAS registry number
$C_8H_6N_4^+$							
4,4'-bipyrimidine	(9.0)	(309)	(1294)	102	426	*EST	2426-94-0
	IP is onset of photoelectron band (82BAR/CAU).						
2,2'-bipyrimidine	(9.0)	(306)	(1278)	98	410	*EST	28648-89-7
	IP is onset of photoelectron band (82BAR/CAU).						
5,5'-bipyrimidine	(9.0)	(306)	(1278)	98	410	*EST	56598-46-0
	IP is onset of photoelectron band (82BAR/CAU).						
$C_8H_6O^+$							
phenylketene (Ph-CH=C=O)	(≤8.17)	(≤194)	(≤813)	6	25	80DEM/WUL	3496-32-0
phenoxyacetylene (Ph-O-C≡CH)	(8.7)	(266)	(1113)	65	274	*EST	4279-76-9
benzofuran	8.37±0.015	199	833	6±2	26±10	77PED/RYL	271-89-6
$C_8H_6O_2^+$							
terephthalaldehyde	(10.13±0.01)	(196)	(820)	−37.6±2	−157±8	*EST	623-27-8
bicyclo[4.2.0]octa-3,7-diene-2,5-dione	(9.64)	(222)	(927)	−1	−3	*EST	77627-49-7
	IP is onset of photoelectron band (85GLE/JAH).						

Table 1. Positive Ion Table - Continued

ION Neutral	Ionization potential eV	$\Delta_f H$(Ion) kcal/mol	$\Delta_f H$(Ion) kJ/mol	$\Delta_f H$(Neutral) kcal/mol	$\Delta_f H$(Neutral) kJ/mol	Neutral reference	CAS registry number
$C_8H_7Br^+$ bromocubane	(8.76)	(351)	(1470)	149	625	*EST	59346-69-9

IP is onset of photoelectron band (85HON/HEI, 84ABE/DEL).

$C_8H_7ClHg^+$ styryl-HgCl	8.3	(232)	(971)	41	170	*EST	36525-03-8

IP is onset of photoelectron band (81BAI/CHI).

$C_8H_7ClO^+$ 3-chloroacetophenone	(9.51±0.1)	(191)	(801)	−28±2	−117±8	*EST	99-02-5
4-chloroacetophenone	(8.9)	(177)	(742)	−28±2	−117±8	*EST	99-91-2

IP is onset of photoelectron band. See also: 85GAL/GER, 82PFI/GER, 77ROS/DRA.

$C_8H_7FO^+$ 3-fluoroacetophenone	(9.76±0.1)	(158)	(662)	−67±2	−280±8	*EST	455-36-7
4-fluoroacetophenone	(9.57±0.2)	(154)	(643)	−67±2	−280±8	*EST	403-42-9

$C_8H_7I^+$ iodocubane	(8.6)	(362)	(1515)	164	685	*EST	74725-77-2

IP is onset of photoelectron band (84ABE/DEL).

Table 1. Positive Ion Table - Continued

ION Neutral	Ionization potential eV	$\Delta_f H$(Ion) kcal/mol	kJ/mol	$\Delta_f H$(Neutral) kcal/mol	kJ/mol	Neutral reference	CAS registry number
$C_8H_7N^+$							
(benzyl cyanide, C6H5-CH2-CN)	(9.34)	(260)	(1087)	44.5	186	*EST	140-29-4
(2-methylbenzonitrile)	9.38	(259)	(1083)	43	178	*EST	529-19-1
(3-methylbenzonitrile)	9.34	(259)	(1084)	44	183	*EST	620-22-4
(4-methylbenzonitrile)	9.32	(258)	(1081)	44	182	*EST	104-85-8
(indole)	7.761±0.001 IP from 85HAG/IVA. See also: 79COR.	216	906	38±1	157±5	77PED/RYL	120-72-9
(2,3-dihydroindolizine)	7.26	243	1015	75.2	314.6	79COR	274-40-8
(norbornadiene carbonitrile)	(≤9.26) IP from 83HOU/RON.	(≤302)	(≤1265)	89	372	*EST	39863-20-2
$C_8H_7NO^+$							
(4-methoxybenzonitrile, H_3CO-C6H4-CN)	(8.6) IP is onset of photoelectron band (81MOD/DIS).	(213)	(892)	15	62	*EST	874-90-8

Table 1. Positive Ion Table – Continued

ION Neutral	Ionization potential eV	$\Delta_f H$(Ion) kcal/mol kJ/mol	$\Delta_f H$(Neutral) kcal/mol kJ/mol	Neutral reference	CAS registry number
$C_8H_7NO^+$					
(furan-pyrrole)	(6.95) IP is onset of photoelectron band (81GAL/KLA).	(182) (760)	21 89	*EST	63122-43-0
$C_8H_7NO_3^+$					
O_2N-C$_6H_4$-CO-CH$_3$	≤9.98 IP from 85GAL/GER.	(≤206) (≤861)	−24 −102	*EST	100-19-6
$C_8H_7NS^+$					
(thiophene-pyrrole)	(7.1) IP is onset of photoelectron band (81GAL/KLA).	(221) (924)	57 239	*EST	52707-46-7
$C_8H_7N_2^+$					
(cinnoline)H$^+$	From proton affinity of cinnoline (RN 253-66-7). PA = 223.2 kcal/mol, 934. kJ/mol.	(223) (934)			
(quinoxaline)H$^+$	From proton affinity of quinoxaline (RN 91-19-0). PA = 214.4 kcal/mol, 897. kJ/mol.	(214) (895)			
$C_8H_8^+$					
(cyclooctatetraene)	8.01±0.04 See also: 78FU/DUN.	256 1070	71.1±0.3 297.6±1.3	77PED/RYL	629-20-9
(cyclooctatriene-yne)	(8.5) IP is onset of photoelectron band (85MEI/KON).	(287) (1201)	91 381	85KOL/MEI	
(cyclooctatriene-yne isomer)	(8.2) IP is onset of photoelectron band (85MEI/KON).	(281) (1176)	92 385	85KOL/MEI	68344-46-7

Table 1. Positive Ion Table - Continued

ION / Neutral	Ionization potential eV	Δ_fH(Ion) kcal/mol	kJ/mol	Δ_fH(Neutral) kcal/mol	kJ/mol	Neutral reference	CAS registry number
$C_8H_8^+$							
(cyclooctadiyne)	(8.9)	(321)	(1346)	116	487	78LEU/WIR	49852-40-6
(p-xylylene)	(7.5)	(221)	(927)	48±4	203±17	81POL/RAI	502-86-3
	IP is onset of photoelectron band. See also: 82DEW.						
styrene (Ph-CH=CH₂)	8.43±0.06	230	961	35.3±0.2	147.7±0.7	77PED/RYL	100-42-5
	IP from 78FU/DUN, 81KIM/KAT.						
(benzocyclobutene)	(≤8.66±0.03)	(≤248)	(≤1037)	48±1	201±4	81ROT/SCH	694-87-1
(cyclooctatetraene)	8.23	263	1100	73	306	76ALL	500-24-3
	See also: 82HAS/NEU, 83GLE/BOH.						
(norbornadiene-CH₂)	(8.5)	(274)	(1145)	78	325	*EST	37846-63-2
	IP is onset of photoelectron band. See also: 85MAR/MAY.						
(cubane)	(8.5)	(345)	(1444)	149±1	622±4	77PED/RYL	277-10-1
	Values for this IP of 8.74, 8.64 (77ROS/DRA), 8.46 (82LEV/LIA) and 8.56 eV (83LIF/EAT) have been reported.						
(pentalene derivative)	(8.18)	(285)	(1189)	96	400	81GOD/SCH	20656-23-9

Table 1. Positive Ion Table - Continued

ION / Neutral	Ionization potential eV	$\Delta_f H$(Ion) kcal/mol	$\Delta_f H$(Ion) kJ/mol	$\Delta_f H$(Neutral) kcal/mol	$\Delta_f H$(Neutral) kJ/mol	Neutral reference	CAS registry number

$C_8H_8Br^+$

3-BrC$_6$H$_4$ĊH-CH$_3$

| 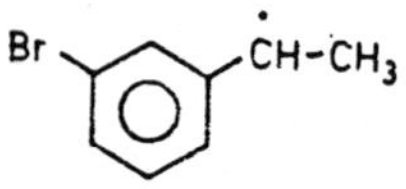 | | 199 | 831 | | | | |

From proton affinity of 3-BrC$_6$H$_4$CH=CH$_2$ (RN 2039-86-3) (84HAR/HOU).
PA = 197.4 kcal/mol, 826. kJ/mol.

4-BrC$_6$H$_4$ĊH-CH$_3$

| 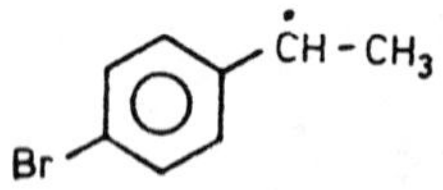 | | 195 | 815 | | | | |

From proton affinity of 4-BrC$_6$H$_4$CH=CH$_2$ (RN 2039-82-9) (84HAR/HOU).
PA = 201.3 kcal/mol, 842. kJ/mol.

$C_8H_8ClN^+$

N-(4-chlorophenyl)aziridine

| 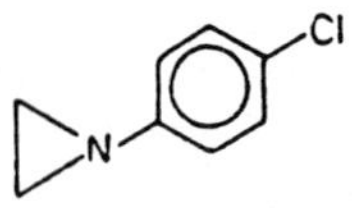 | ≤8.3 | (≤255) | (≤1067) | 64 | 266 | *EST | 28192-05-4 |

IP from 82CRI/LIC.

$C_8H_8FN^+$

N-(4-fluorophenyl)aziridine

| 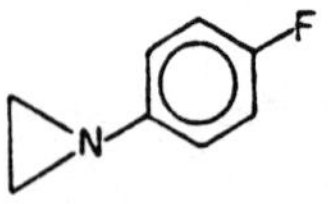 | (≤8.2) | (≤213) | (≤890) | 24 | 99 | *EST | 698-53-3 |

IP from 82CRI/LIC.

$C_8H_8N_2O_2^+$

N-(4-nitrophenyl)aziridine

| 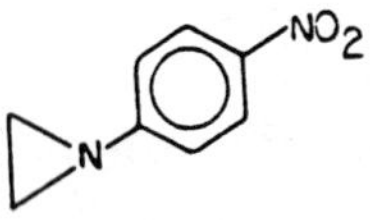 | (≤8.9) | (≤273) | (≤1142) | 68 | 283 | *EST | 30855-79-9 |

IP from 82CRI/LIC.

$C_8H_8N_4^+$

2,3-dimethylpyrazine[b]

| 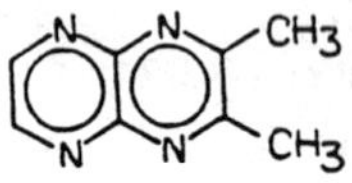 | (≤8.9) | (≤275) | (≤1151) | 70 | 292 | *EST | 6499-39-4 |

IP from 84GLE/SPA2.

$C_8H_8O^+$

C$_6$H$_5$CH$_2$CHO

| 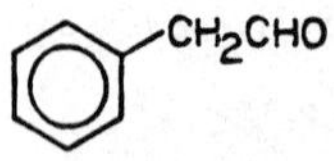 | (8.80) | (190) | (796) | −13 | −53 | *EST | 122-78-1 |

See also: 81DAL/NIB.

Table 1. Positive Ion Table - Continued

ION / Neutral	Ionization potential eV	$\Delta_f H$(Ion) kcal/mol	$\Delta_f H$(Ion) kJ/mol	$\Delta_f H$(Neutral) kcal/mol	$\Delta_f H$(Neutral) kJ/mol	Neutral reference	CAS registry number
$C_8H_8O^+$							
H₃C–C₆H₄–CHO (p-tolualdehyde)	9.33±0.05	(197)	(825)	−18	−75	*EST	104-87-0
See also: 85GAL/GER.							
C₆H₅–CO–CH₃ (acetophenone)	9.29±0.03	194	810	−20.7±0.4	−86.6±1.5	77PED/RYL	98-86-2
See also: 81DAL/NIB, 79MCL/TRA, 85GAL/GER, 78CEN/FRA, 82PFI/GER.							
C₆H₅–C(OH)=CH₂		(175)	(731)				4383-15-7
$\Delta_f H$(Ion) from appearance potential determination (81DAL/NIB).							
C₆H₅–CH=CHOH	(8.71±0.1)	(194)	(812)	−7	−28	*EST	4365-04-2
IP from 81DAL/NIB.							
2,3-dihydrobenzofuran	(7.65)	(163)	(683)	−13	−55	*EST	496-16-2
IP is onset of photoelectron band (81BAK/ARM). See also: 82LEV/LIA.							
$C_8H_8O_2^+$							
3-hydroxyacetophenone	(8.67±0.05)	(137)	(573)	−63±2	−264±8	*EST	
4-hydroxyacetophenone	(8.70±0.03)	(138)	(575)	−63±2	−264±8	*EST	
C₆H₅–CH₂COOH (phenylacetic acid)	(8.26)	(114)	(478)	−76	−319	*EST	103-82-2
IP is onset of photoelectron band (83KLA/KOV). See also: 81MEE/WAH.							

Table 1. Positive Ion Table – Continued

ION / Neutral	Ionization potential eV	$\Delta_f H$(Ion) kcal/mol	kJ/mol	$\Delta_f H$(Neutral) kcal/mol	kJ/mol	Neutral reference	CAS registry number
$C_8H_8O_2^+$							
2-methylbenzoic acid	(9.1) IP from 81MEE/WAH.	(133)	(558)	−76.5±0.2	−320±1	76COL/JIM	118-90-1
3-methylbenzoic acid	(9.43±0.2) See also: 81MEE/WAH.	(139)	(581)	−79±0.2	−329±1	76COL/JIM	99-04-7
4-methylbenzoic acid	(9.23±0.2) See also: 81MEE/WAH.	(134)	(558)	−79±0.2	−332±1	76COL/JIM	99-94-5
phenyl acetate	(8.6±0.05)	(131)	(550)	−66.8±0.3	−279.7±1.1	77PED/RYL	122-79-2
methyl benzoate	9.32±0.03 IP from 79MCL/TRA. See also: 81MEE/WAH, 82CAB/COW.	146	611	−69±2	−288±7	77PED/RYL	93-58-3
4-methoxybenzaldehyde	(8.43) See also: 85GAL/GER.	(145)	(610)	−49±1	−203±5	77PED/RYL	123-11-5
2,5-dimethyl-1,4-benzoquinone	9.58	(176)	(737)	−45	−187	*EST	137-18-8
bicyclo[4.2.0]octa-dienedione	(9.3) IP is onset of photoelectron band 85GLE/JAH.	(218)	(910)	3	13	*EST	77627-56-6

Table 1. Positive Ion Table - Continued

ION / Neutral	Ionization potential eV	$\Delta_f H$(Ion) kcal/mol	$\Delta_f H$(Ion) kJ/mol	$\Delta_f H$(Neutral) kcal/mol	$\Delta_f H$(Neutral) kJ/mol	Neutral reference	CAS registry number
$C_8H_8O_2^+$ (methylnorbornene dione)	(8.1) IP is onset of photoelectron band.	(160)	(669)	−27	−113	*EST	60526-48-9
$C_8H_8O_2Si^+$ (di-2-furylsilane)	(8.2) IP is onset of photoelectron band (83ZYK/ERC).	(178)	(743)	−11	−48	*EST	87027-12-1
$C_8H_8O_3^+$ (3-methoxybenzoic acid)	(9.06±0.2)	(102)	(428)	−107±0.2	−446±1	78COL/JIM	586-38-9
(4-methoxybenzoic acid)	(9.04±0.2)	(100)	(420)	−108±0.2	−452±1	78COL/JIM	100-09-4
(dimethyl trione)	(8.4) IP is onset of photoelectron band (81BEC/HOF).	(80)	(334)	−114	−476	*EST	81640-32-6
$C_8H_8S_2^+$ (benzodithiane)	(≤7.91) IP from 82BRE/SCH.	(≤219)	(≤916)	37	153	*EST	6247-55-8
$C_8H_8S_4^+$ (dithienyl disulfide)	(7.5) IP is onset of photoelectron band (83BOC/ROT).	(246)	(1032)	74	308	*EST	

Table 1. Positive Ion Table – Continued

ION / Neutral	Ionization potential eV	$\Delta_f H$(Ion) kcal/mol	$\Delta_f H$(Ion) kJ/mol	$\Delta_f H$(Neutral) kcal/mol	$\Delta_f H$(Neutral) kJ/mol	Neutral reference	CAS registry number

$C_8H_9^+$

C₆H₅ĊH–CH₃ : (6.9), (199), (831), 39.6±1.5, 165.7±6.3, 81ROB/STE, 2348-51-8

$\Delta_f H$(Ion) from proton affinity of $C_6H_5CH=CH_2$ PA = 202.0 kcal/mol, 845. kJ/mol, and from hydride transfer equilibrium constant determinations (85SHA/SHA). IP is $\Delta_f H$(Ion) - $\Delta_f H$(Neutral).

2-CH₃C₆H₄CH₂· : 7.07, (203), (849), 40, 167, 86HAY/KRU, 2348-48-3

IP from 86HAY/KRU. $\Delta_f H$(Ion) from chloride transfer equilibrium constants (85SHA/SHA). $\Delta_f H$(2-CH₃C₆H₄CH₂Cl) estimated as -3.6 kcal/mol, -15.0 KJ/mol.

3-CH₃C₆H₄CH₂· : 7.12, (204), (855), 40, 167, 86HAY/KRU, 2348-47-2

IP from 86HAY/KRU. $\Delta_f H$(Ion) from chloride transfer equilibrium constants (85SHA/SHA); $\Delta_f H$(3-CH₃C₆H₄CH₂Cl) estimated as -3.8 kcal/mol, -15.9 kJ/mol.

4-CH₃C₆H₄CH₂· : 6.96, (200), (837), 40, 167, 86HAY/KRU, 2348-52-9

IP from 86HAY/KRU. $\Delta_f H$(Ion) from chloride transfer equilibrium constants (85SHA/SHA); $\Delta_f H$(4-CH₃C₆H₄CH₂Cl) estimated as -3.8 kcal/mol, -15.0 KJ/mol.

$C_8H_9Cl^+$

3-CH₃C₆H₄CH₂Cl : (8.82±0.03), (200), (835), -4, -16, *EST, 620-19-9

4-CH₃C₆H₄CH₂Cl : (8.79±0.03), (199), (832), -4, -16, *EST, 104-82-5

$C_8H_9N^+$

C₆H₅CH=N–CH₃ : 8.77, (246), (1031), 44±2, 185±10, *EST, 622-29-7

N-phenylaziridine : (8.0), (256), (1070), 71, 298, *EST, 696-18-4

IP from 82ROZ/HOU2, 82CRI/LIC.

Table 1. Positive Ion Table – Continued

ION / Neutral	Ionization potential eV	$\Delta_f H$(Ion) kcal/mol	$\Delta_f H$(Ion) kJ/mol	$\Delta_f H$(Neutral) kcal/mol	$\Delta_f H$(Neutral) kJ/mol	Neutral reference	CAS registry number
$C_8H_9N^+$							
indoline	(7.15±0.02)	(212)	(888)	47	198	*EST	496-15-1
2,3-dihydro-1H-pyrindine	≤9.15	(≤238)	(≤994)	27	111	*EST	

IP from 79AUE/BOW. Ion heat of formation predicted from hydrogen affinities of pyridines: 234 kcal/mol, 979 kJ/mol, corresponding to IP of 9.0 eV.

6,7-dihydro-5H-[1]pyrindine	≤9.19	(≤239)	(≤1000)	27	113	*EST	

IP from (79AUE/BOW). Ion heat of formation predicted from hydrogen affinities of pyridines: 234 kcal/mol, 979 kJ/mol, corresponding to IP of 9.0 eV.

ION / Neutral	Ionization potential eV	$\Delta_f H$(Ion) kcal/mol	$\Delta_f H$(Ion) kJ/mol	$\Delta_f H$(Neutral) kcal/mol	$\Delta_f H$(Neutral) kJ/mol	Neutral reference	CAS registry number
$C_8H_9NO^+$							
	(7.28)	(212)	(888)	44	186	*EST	65194-06-1
	7.89	(207)	(866)	25	105	*EST	3376-23-6
acetanilide	(8.30)	(161)	(672)	−31±0.2	−129±1	77PED/RYL	103-84-4

Values reported for this ionization potential range from 8.18 eV to 8.60 eV.

p-aminoacetophenone	(7.8±0.1)	(159)	(666)	−21	−87	*EST	99-92-3

See also: 85GAL/GER.

ION / Neutral	Ionization potential eV	$\Delta_f H$(Ion) kcal/mol	$\Delta_f H$(Ion) kJ/mol	$\Delta_f H$(Neutral) kcal/mol	$\Delta_f H$(Neutral) kJ/mol	Neutral reference	CAS registry number
$C_8H_9NOS^+$							
3,5-dimethylphenyl-N-sulfinylamine	(8.2)	(166)	(695)	−23	−96	*EST	

IP is onset of photoelectron band (82LOU/VAN).

Table 1. Positive Ion Table - Continued

ION Neutral	Ionization potential eV	$\Delta_f H$(Ion) kcal/mol kJ/mol		$\Delta_f H$(Neutral) kcal/mol kJ/mol		Neutral reference	CAS registry number
$C_8H_9NO_2{}^+$							
[4-(methylamino)benzoic acid]	(7.3) IP is onset of photoelectron band (81MEE/WAH).	(99)	(412)	−70	−292	*EST	10541-83-0
[methyl 4-aminobenzoate]	(7.7) IP is onset of photoelectron band (81MEE/WAH).	(109)	(455)	−69	−288	*EST	619-45-4
[2,6-dimethylnitrobenzene]	9.17±0.015	(221)	(925)	10	40	*EST	81-20-9
[2,4-dimethylnitrobenzene]	(9.1) IP is onset of photoelectron band.	(215)	(898)	5	20	*EST	89-87-2
[2-ethylnitrobenzene]	(9.39) IP from 82BAL/CAR.	(219)	(917)	3±2	11±7	77PED/RYL	612-22-6
[3-ethylnitrobenzene]	(9.64) IP from 82BAL/CAR.	(224)	(937)	2	7	*EST	7369-50-8
[4-ethylnitrobenzene]	(9.71) IP from 82BAL/CAR.	(225)	(943)	2±2	7±7	77PED/RYL	100-12-9
$C_8H_9N_2{}^+$							
[1-methyl-1H-indazole, protonated]		204	852				

From proton affinity of 1-methyl-1H-indazole (RN 13436-48-1) (84FLA/MAQ).
PA = (221) kcal/mol, (925) kJ/mol.

Table 1. Positive Ion Table – Continued

ION / Neutral	Ionization potential eV	$\Delta_f H$(Ion) kcal/mol	$\Delta_f H$(Ion) kJ/mol	$\Delta_f H$(Neutral) kcal/mol	$\Delta_f H$(Neutral) kJ/mol	Neutral reference	CAS registry number

$C_8H_9N_2^+$

2-methyl-2H-indazole (protonated)

| 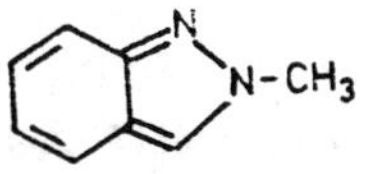 | | 218 | 913 | | | | |

From proton affinity of 2-methyl-2H-indazole (RN 4838-00-0) (84FLA/MAQ). PA = (224) kcal/mol, (939) kJ/mol.

$C_8H_9O^+$

4-CH_3-C_6H_4-ĊHOH

| 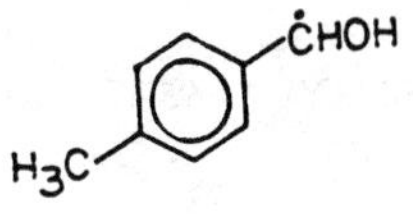 | | 144 | 603 | | | | |

From proton affinity of 4-$(CH_3)C_6H_4$CHO (RN 104-87-0). PA = 203.7 kcal/mol, 852. kJ/mol.

C_6H_5-C(OH)-CH_3

| 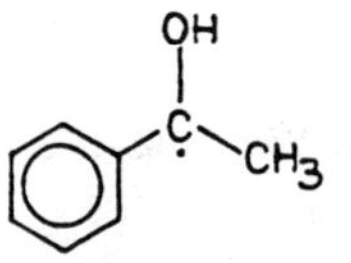 | | 140 | 584 | | | | |

From proton affinity of $C_6H_5COCH_3$ (RN 98-86-2). PA = 205.4 kcal/mol, 859. kJ/mol.

$C_8H_9O_2^+$

4-H_3CO-C_6H_4-ĊHOH

| 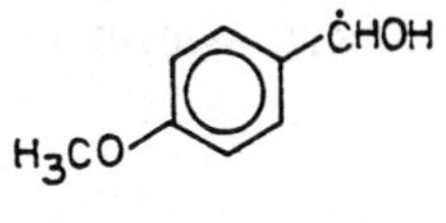 | | 104 | 434 | | | | |

From proton affinity of 4-$(CH_3O)C_6H_4$CHO (RN 123-11-5). PA = 213.5 kcal/mol, 893. kJ/mol.

C_6H_5-C(OH)-OCH_3

| 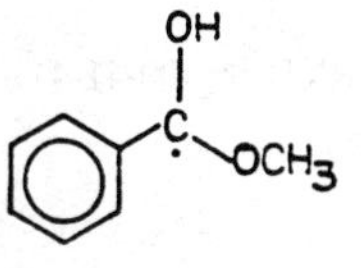 | | 94 | 395 | | | | |

From proton affinity of $C_6H_5COOCH_3$ (RN 93-58-3). PA = 203.7 kcal/mol, 852. kJ/mol.

$C_8H_{10}^+$

(E)-$CH_2=CHCH=CHCH=CHCH=CH_2$

| | 7.79±0.02 | (235) | (981) | 55 | 229 | *EST | 3725-31-3 |

IP from 84HOL, 77ROS/DRA.

$CH_2=C(CH_3)C\equiv CC(CH_3)=CH_2$

| | (8.95±0.1) | (324) | (1357) | 118 | 494 | 77LEB/RYA | 3725-05-1 |

cyclooctatriene

|  | (7.9) | (226) | (945) | 44 | 183 | 69BEN/CRU | 1871-52-9 |

cyclooctatetraene (1,3,5-cyclooctatriene isomer)

|  | (8.5) | (243) | (1017) | 47 | 197 | *EST | 3725-30-2 |

Table 1. Positive Ion Table - Continued

ION / Neutral	Ionization potential eV	$\Delta_f H$(Ion) kcal/mol	$\Delta_f H$(Ion) kJ/mol	$\Delta_f H$(Neutral) kcal/mol	$\Delta_f H$(Neutral) kJ/mol	Neutral reference	CAS registry number

$C_8H_{10}^+$

| cyclooctatetraene | (8.90) | (276) | (1158) | 71 | 299 | 78LEU/WIR | 68177-00-4 |

| o-xylene | 8.56±0.01 | 201.7 | 843.9 | 4.3±0.1 | 18.0±0.5 | 77PED/RYL | 95-47-6 |

Value derived from charge transfer equilibrium constant determinations (78LIA/AUS) is in agreement. See: 84HOW/GON.

| m-xylene | 8.56±0.01 | 202 | 843 | 4.1±0.1 | 17.3±0.6 | 77PED/RYL | 108-38-3 |

Value derived from charge transfer equilibrium constant determinations (78LIA/AUS) is in agreement. See: 84HOW/GON.

| p-xylene | 8.44±0.01 | 199 | 832 | 4.3±0.2 | 18.0±0.9 | 77PED/RYL | 106-42-3 |

IP at 298 K from charge transfer equilibrium constant determinations (78LIA/AUS) is 8.52 eV. See: 84HOW/GON.

| ethylbenzene | 8.77±0.01 | 209 | 875 | 7.0±0.1 | 29.2±0.5 | 77PED/RYL | 100-41-4 |

Value derived from charge transfer equilibrium constant determinations (78LIA/AUS) is in agreement. See also: 83KLA/KOV, 82SEL/HEL, 84HOW/GON.

| 6,6-dimethylfulvene | (≤8.03) | (≤217) | (≤909) | 32.1±1.3 | 134.4±5.4 | 77PED/RYL | 2175-91-9 |

| 1,2-dimethyl-3-methylenecyclopropene | (8.4) | (320) | (1340) | 127 | 530 | *EST | |

IP is onset of photoelectron band (82SPA/KOR).

| bicyclo[4.2.0]octa-2,4-diene | (7.6) | (224) | (938) | 49 | 205 | *EST | 3725-28-8 |

IP is onset of photoelectron band (81GLE/GUB2).

Table 1. Positive Ion Table – Continued

ION / Neutral	Ionization potential eV	$\Delta_f H$(Ion) kcal/mol	kJ/mol	$\Delta_f H$(Neutral) kcal/mol	kJ/mol	Neutral reference	CAS registry number

$C_8H_{10}^+$

|  | (8.5) | (230) | (964) | 34 | 144 | 76ALL | 657-23-8 |

IP is onset of photoelectron band. See also: 82HAS/NEU.

| 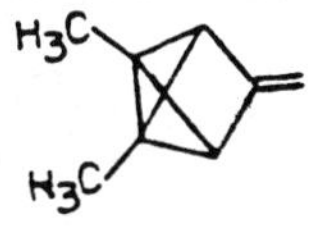 | (8.0) | (273) | (1141) | 88 | 369 | *EST | 63001-13-8 |

IP is onset of photoelectron band (84GLE/HAI).

|  | (8.4) | (242) | (1012) | 48.1 | 201.3 | 81GOD/SCH | 765-72-0 |

IP is onset of photoelectron band.

| 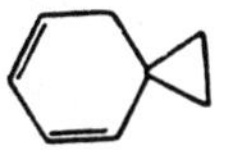 | (≤7.89) | (≤242) | (≤1012) | 60 | 251 | *EST | 53143-64-9 |

|  | (8.20) | (246) | (1029) | 57 | 238 | *EST | 15439-15-3 |

$C_8H_{10}Br^+$

| 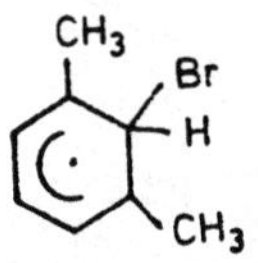 | | 178 | 743 | | | | |

From proton affinity of 1,3,2-$C_6H_3(CH_3)_2Br$ (RN 576-22-7). PA = (199) kcal/mol, (832) kJ/mol.

$C_8H_{10}N^+$

| 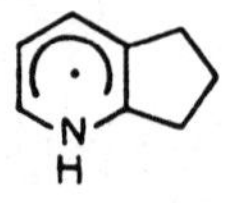 | | 166 | 695 | | | | |

From proton affinity of 2,3-cyclopentenopyridine. PA = (225.8) kcal/mol, (945.) kJ/mol.

| 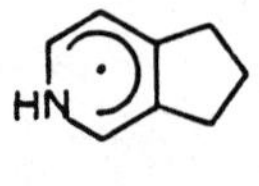 | | 166 | 696 | | | | |

From proton affinity of 3,4-cyclopentenopyridine. PA = (226.8) kcal/mol, (949.) kJ/mol.

Table 1. Positive Ion Table - Continued

ION / Neutral	Ionization potential eV	$\Delta_f H$(Ion) kcal/mol	$\Delta_f H$(Ion) kJ/mol	$\Delta_f H$(Neutral) kcal/mol	$\Delta_f H$(Neutral) kJ/mol	Neutral reference	CAS registry number
$C_8H_{10}N^+$ (2,3-dihydroindole·H⁺)		186	779				

From proton affinity of 2,3-dihydroindole (RN 496-15-1) (85BOL/HOU). PA = 226.7 kcal/mol, 949. kJ/mol.

$C_8H_{10}NO_2^+$ (2,4-dimethylnitrobenzene·H⁺)		153	641				

From proton affinity of $1,3,4\text{-}C_6H_3(CH_3)_2NO_2$ (RN 89-87-2) (84ROL/HOU). PA = 199.8 kcal/mol, 836. kJ/mol.

$C_8H_{10}N_2O_2^+$ (4-nitro-N,N-dimethylaniline)	(7.6±0.1)	(191)	(801)	16.1±0.4	67.3±1.8	84FUR/MUR	100-23-2

$C_8H_{10}O^+$ (methylcycloheptatrienone)	8.23	(146)	(611)	−44	−183	*EST	42104-03-0

IP from 83RUS/FRE.

(2,3-dimethylphenol)	(8.26)	(153)	(640)	−37.6±0.3	−157.2±1.4	77PED/RYL	526-75-0

IP from 83RUS/FRE.

(2,4-dimethylphenol)	(8.0)	(146)	(609)	−38.9±0.2	−162.9±0.9	77PED/RYL	105-67-9

IP is onset of photoelectron band.

(2,6-dimethylphenol)	8.05±0.02	147	615	−38.7±0.2	−161.8±1.0	77PED/RYL	576-26-1

(3,4-dimethylphenol)	(8.09)	(149)	(624)	−37.4±0.3	−156.6±1.1	77PED/RYL	95-65-8

IP from 83RUS/FRE.

Table 1. Positive Ion Table – Continued

ION / Neutral	Ionization potential eV	$\Delta_f H$(Ion) kcal/mol	kJ/mol	$\Delta_f H$(Neutral) kcal/mol	kJ/mol	Neutral reference	CAS registry number
$C_8H_{10}O^+$							
4-ethylphenol (HO–C₆H₄–C₂H₅)	(7.84) IP from 83RUS/FRE.	(146)	(612)	−34.4±0.2	−144.1±1.0	77PED/RYL	123-07-9
benzyl methyl ether (C₆H₅–CH₂OCH₃)	8.85±0.03	186	780	−18	−74	73BIL/CHO	538-86-3
2-methylanisole	7.90	(157)	(657)	−25	−105	*EST	578-58-5
3-methylanisole	(8.0) IP is onset of photoelectron band.	(160)	(668)	−25±1	−104±5	77PED/RYL	100-84-5
4-methylanisole	7.9 IP is onset of photoelectron band.	(158)	(662)	−24	−100	*EST	104-93-8
phenetole (C₆H₅–OC₂H₅)	8.13±0.02	163	683	−24.3±0.1	−101.7±0.5	77PED/RYL	103-73-1
2-methoxynorbornadiene	(≤8.05) IP from 83HOU/RON.	(≤207)	(≤865)	21	88	*EST	74437-38-0
$C_8H_{10}OS^+$							
2-methoxythioanisole	(≤8.05)	(≤172)	(≤720)	−14	−57	*EST	2388-73-0

Table 1. Positive Ion Table - Continued

ION / Neutral	Ionization potential eV	$\Delta_f H$(Ion) kcal/mol	kJ/mol	$\Delta_f H$(Neutral) kcal/mol	kJ/mol	Neutral reference	CAS registry number
$C_8H_{10}OS^+$							
4-(methylthio)anisole (H₃CS-C₆H₄-OCH₃)	≤7.80	(≤168)	(≤703)	−12	−50	*EST	1879-16-9
ethyl phenyl sulfoxide (C₆H₅-S(O)-C₂H₅)	(≤8.75) IP from 81MOH/JIA.	(≤193)	(≤809)	−8	−35	*EST	4170-80-3
methyl p-tolyl sulfoxide (CH₃-C₆H₄-S(O)-CH₃)	(≤8.70) IP from 81MOH/JIA.	(≤193)	(≤808)	−7.6	−31.8	*EST	934-72-5
$C_8H_{10}O_2^+$							
1,2-dimethoxybenzene	(7.8) IP is onset of photoelectron band.	(127)	(530)	−53±0.7	−223±3	77PED/RYL	91-16-7
1,3-dimethoxybenzene	(7.8) IP is onset of photoelectron band.	(122)	(511)	−58	−242	*EST	151-10-0
1,4-dimethoxybenzene	7.53 IP from 85OIK/ABE, 82LEV/LIA.	(118)	(493)	−56	−234	*EST	150-78-7
1,2-dicyclopropyl-1,2-ethanedione	(8.8) IP is onset of photoelectron band.	(173)	(724)	−30	−125	*EST	15940-88-2
bicyclo[4.2.0]octane-2,5-dione	(9.1) IP is onset of photoelectron band (85GLE/JAH).	(154)	(645)	−56	−233	*EST	54338-82-8

Table 1. Positive Ion Table – Continued

ION / Neutral	Ionization potential eV	$\Delta_f H$(Ion) kcal/mol	$\Delta_f H$(Ion) kJ/mol	$\Delta_f H$(Neutral) kcal/mol	$\Delta_f H$(Neutral) kJ/mol	Neutral reference	CAS registry number
$C_8H_{10}O_2{}^+$							
(bicyclic diketone)	(≤9.33) IP is onset of photoelectron band.	(≤138)	(≤576)	−77	−324	*EST	
(bicyclic diketone)	(8.7) IP is onset of photoelectron band.	(127)	(532)	−73	−307	*EST	74896-14-3
(dimethyl bicyclic diketone)	(9.14) IP is onset of photoelectron band (81BEC/HOF).	(139)	(582)	−72	−300	*EST	29978-55-0
$C_8H_{10}O_2S^+$							
PhSO$_2$C$_2$H$_5$	(9.4) IP from 81MOH/JIA.	(150)	(628)	−67	−279	*EST	599-70-2
$C_8H_{10}O_3S^+$							
(cyclic sulfone ketone)	(9.5) IP is onset of photoelectron band (84AIT/GOS).	(160)	(668)	−60	−249	*EST	
$C_8H_{10}S^+$							
PhSC$_2$H$_5$	7.88±0.02	200	837	18.4±0.6	77.0±2.6	77PED/RYL	622-38-8
PhCH$_2$SCH$_3$	(8.42)	(213)	(892)	19.0±0.7	79.5±2.9	77PED/RYL	766-92-7
3-CH$_3$-C$_6$H$_4$-SCH$_3$	(≤8.00)	(≤200)	(≤838)	16	66	*EST	4886-77-5

Table 1. Positive Ion Table - Continued

ION Neutral	Ionization potential eV	$\Delta_f H$(Ion) kcal/mol	$\Delta_f H$(Ion) kJ/mol	$\Delta_f H$(Neutral) kcal/mol	$\Delta_f H$(Neutral) kJ/mol	Neutral reference	CAS registry number

$C_8H_{10}S^+$

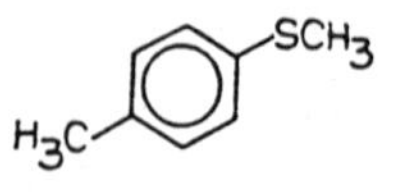

4-methylthioanisole: 7.5, (189), (790), 16, 66, *EST, 623-13-2
IP is onset of photoelectron band.

$C_8H_{10}S_2^+$

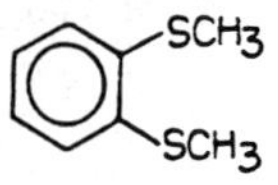

1,2-bis(methylthio)benzene: 7.7, (206), (864), 29, 121, *EST, 2388-68-3
IP is onset of photoelectron band (81TRA/RED, 82LEV/LIA).

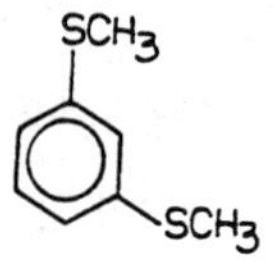

1,3-bis(methylthio)benzene: (≤8.0), (≤211), (≤885), 27, 113, *EST, 2388-69-4

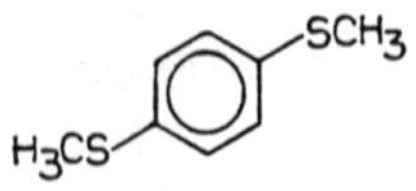

1,4-bis(methylthio)benzene: (7.3), (195), (817), 27, 113, *EST, 699-20-7
IP is onset of photoelectron band.

$C_8H_{10}Se^+$

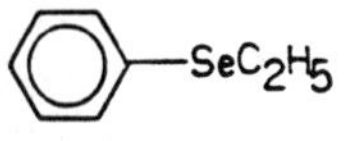

phenyl ethyl selenide: (7.6), (207), (865), 31, 132, *EST, 17774-38-8
IP is onset of photoelectron band (81BAK/ARM).

2-methylphenyl methyl selenide: (7.5), (200), (837), 27, 113, *EST, 1528-88-7
IP is onset of photoelectron band (81BAK/ARM).

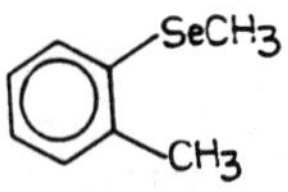

$C_8H_{11}^+$

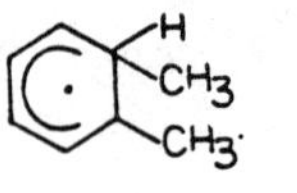

177, 739
From proton affinity of 1,2-$C_6H_4(CH_3)_2$ (RN 95-47-6). PA = 193.3 kcal/mol, 809. kJ/mol.

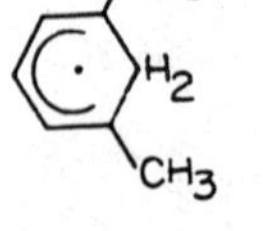

174, 727
From proton affinity of 1,3-$C_6H_4(CH_3)_2$ (RN 108-38-3). PA = 195.9 kcal/mol, 820. kJ/mol.

Table 1. Positive Ion Table - Continued

ION / Neutral	Ionization potential eV	$\Delta_f H$(Ion) kcal/mol	kJ/mol	$\Delta_f H$(Neutral) kcal/mol	kJ/mol	Neutral reference	CAS registry number

$C_8H_{11}^+$

1,4-dimethyl (H transferred): 178, 745
From proton affinity of 1,4-$C_6H_4(CH_3)_2$ (RN 106-42-3). PA = 192.0 kcal/mol, 803. kJ/mol.

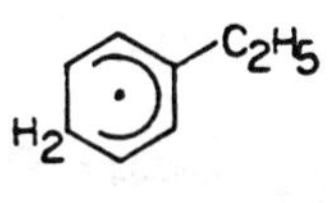

Ethylbenzene-derived: 181, 757
From proton affinity of $C_6H_5C_2H_5$ (RN 100-41-4). PA = 191.6 kcal/mol, 802. kJ/mol.

$C_8H_{11}BrO^+$

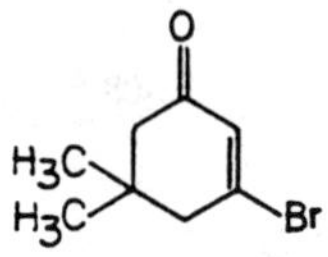

3-bromo-5,5-dimethylcyclohex-2-enone: (≤9.35) (≤180) (≤755) −35 −147 *EST 13271-49-3
IP from 82PFI/GER.

$C_8H_{11}ClO^+$

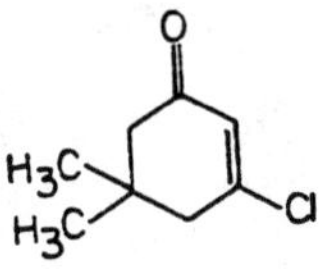

3-chloro-5,5-dimethylcyclohex-2-enone: (9.35) (170) (713) −45 −189 *EST 17530-69-7
IP from 82PFI/GER.

$C_8H_{11}ClSi^+$

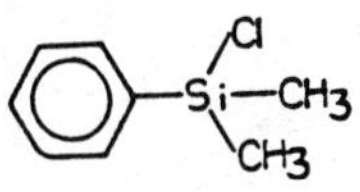

chlorodimethylphenylsilane: (8.93) (156) (652) −50 −210 *EST 768-33-2
IP from 84VES/HAR.

$C_8H_{11}N^+$

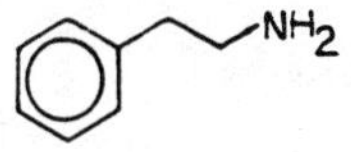

2-phenylethylamine: (8.5) (212) (885) 16 65 *EST 64-04-0
IP is onset of photoelectron band.

N-ethylaniline: (≤7.67) (≤190) (≤796) 13±1 56±6 77PED/RYL 103-69-5
IP from 82ROZ/HOU2.

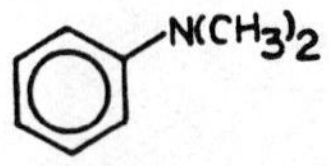

N,N-dimethylaniline: 7.12±0.02 188 788 24±0.7 101±3 82FUR/SAK 121-69-7

Table 1. Positive Ion Table – Continued

ION / Neutral	Ionization potential eV	$\Delta_f H$(Ion) kcal/mol	$\Delta_f H$(Ion) kJ/mol	$\Delta_f H$(Neutral) kcal/mol	$\Delta_f H$(Neutral) kJ/mol	Neutral reference	CAS registry number
$C_8H_{11}N^+$							
2-(methylamino)toluene	(7.27)	(182)	(759)	14	58	*EST	611-21-2
3-(methylamino)toluene	(7.26)	(180)	(753)	13	53	*EST	696-44-6
4-(methylamino)toluene	(7.13)	(177)	(741)	13	53	*EST	623-08-5
2,3-dimethylaniline	≤7.77±0.05	(≤186)	(≤777)	6	27	*EST	87-59-2
2,4-dimethylaniline	(≤7.65±0.05)	(≤182)	(≤761)	5	23	*EST	95-68-1
2,5-dimethylaniline	7.2	(172)	(718)	5	23	*EST	95-78-3

IP is onset of photoelectron band.

2,6-dimethylaniline	7.33±0.05	(175)	(734)	6±0.2	27±1	*EST	87-62-7
3,4-dimethylaniline	(≤7.68±0.05)	(≤183)	(≤764)	5	23	*EST	95-64-7

Table 1. Positive Ion Table - Continued

ION / Neutral	Ionization potential eV	$\Delta_f H$(Ion) kcal/mol	$\Delta_f H$(Ion) kJ/mol	$\Delta_f H$(Neutral) kcal/mol	$\Delta_f H$(Neutral) kJ/mol	Neutral reference	CAS registry number

$C_8H_{11}N^+$

3,5-dimethylaniline

| 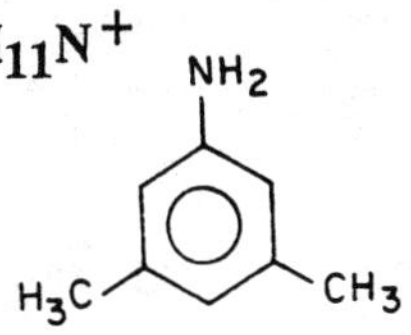 | 7.2 | (171) | (716) | 5 | 21 | *EST | 108-69-0 |

IP is onset of photoelectron band.

2,4,6-trimethylpyridine

| 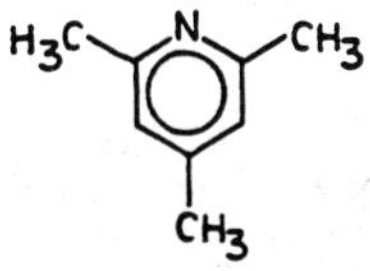 | (≤8.9±0.1) | (≤210) | (≤879) | 5 | 20 | *EST | 108-75-8 |

$C_8H_{11}N_2O_2^+$

(N,N-dimethyl-4-nitroaniline)H⁺

| 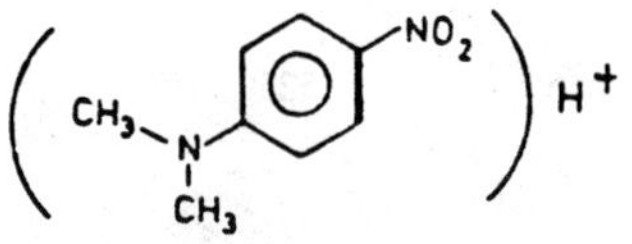 | | 167 | 699 | | | | |

From proton affinity of N,N-dimethyl-4-nitroaniline (RN 100-23-2) (84ROL/HOU).
PA = 214.6 kcal/mol, 898. kJ/mol.

$C_8H_{11}P^+$

phenyl-P(CH₃)₂

| 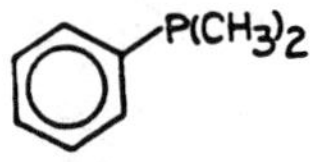 | 7.58±0.05 | (184) | (771) | 10 | 40 | *EST | 672-66-2 |

$C_8H_{12}^+$

(E),(E)-CH₃CH=C(CH₃)CH=CHCH=CH₂

| | (≤8.01) | (≤208) | (≤872) | 24 | 99 | *EST | 58434-77-8 |

CH₂=CHCH=CHCH(CH₃)CH=CH₂

| | (8.4±0.1) | (226) | (945) | 32.2 | 134.7 | *EST | 925-52-0 |

IP from 84GRO/GRO.

n-C₄H₉C≡CCH=CH₂

| | (8.83±0.01) | (248) | (1038) | 44±2 | 186±7 | 78SHA | 17679-92-4 |

(E)-n-C₄H₉CH=CHC≡CH

| | (8.87±0.01) | (248) | (1040) | 44 | 184 | *EST | 42104-42-7 |

n-C₃H₇C≡CC(CH₃)=CH₂

| | (8.62±0.01) | (241) | (1008) | 42 | 176 | *EST | 17669-40-8 |

(C₂H₅)₂C=CHC≡CH

| | (8.54±0.01) | (240) | (1004) | 43 | 180 | *EST | 2750-71-2 |

1,3,5-cyclooctatriene

| 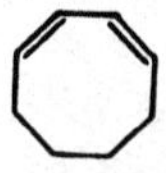 | (8.4) | (213) | (891) | 19 | 81 | 82KOZ/MAS | 1700-10-3 |

Table 1. Positive Ion Table - Continued

ION Neutral	Ionization potential eV	$\Delta_f H$(Ion) kcal/mol kJ/mol		$\Delta_f H$(Neutral) kcal/mol kJ/mol		Neutral reference	CAS registry number
$C_8H_{12}^+$							
(cycloocta-1,3-diene)	(8.5)	(221)	(925)	25±2	105±8	*EST	1073-07-0
(cycloocta-1,5-diene)	(8.9)	(219)	(917)	14.0±0.3	58.6±1.2	77PED/RYL	111-78-4
(E,Z-cyclooctadiene)	(8.2) IP is onset of photoelectron band.	(218)	(912)	29	121	*EST	5259-71-2
(cyclooctyne)	(8.9)	(248)	(1041)	43±1	182±3	75ALL/MEY	1781-78-8
cyclohexyl-C≡CH	(≤9.92)	(≤257)	(≤1076)	28±1	119±3	75ALL/MEY	931-48-6
cyclohexyl-CH=CH₂	(8.93±0.02) See also: 84GRO/GRO.	(221)	(927)	15.6±0.3	65.1±1.2	77PED/RYL	100-40-3
1-isopropenylcyclopentene	(8.60±0.01)	(219)	(917)	21	87	*EST	37689-19-3
isopropenylcyclopentane	(8.89±0.02)	(227)	(950)	22	92	*EST	14564-97-7

Table 1. Positive Ion Table - Continued

ION / Neutral	Ionization potential eV	$\Delta_f H$(Ion) kcal/mol	$\Delta_f H$(Ion) kJ/mol	$\Delta_f H$(Neutral) kcal/mol	$\Delta_f H$(Neutral) kJ/mol	Neutral reference	CAS registry number
$C_8H_{12}^+$							
1,2,3-trimethylcyclopentadiene	(7.96±0.05)	(192)	(804)	9	36	*EST	3853-27-8
trimethylcyclopentadiene	(8.0±0.1)	(195)	(818)	11	46	*EST	4249-09-6
1,2-divinylcyclobutane	(≤9.22) IP from 81BIS/GLE.	(≤252)	(≤1056)	39.8±0.8	166.5±3.5	77PED/RYL	16177-46-1
1,3-divinylcyclobutane	(≤9.20) IP from 81BIS/GLE.	(≤246)	(≤1031)	34.3±0.8	143.5±3.4	77PED/RYL	6553-48-6
1,3-dimethylenecyclobutane	(8.9) IP is onset of photoelectron band (81BIS/GLE).	(247)	(1035)	42	176	*EST	77614-53-0
1,2-dimethylenecyclobutane	(8.9) IP is onset of photoelectron band (81BIS/GLE).	(247)	(1035)	42	176	*EST	77614-67-6
dicyclopropylmethylene	8.08	(237)	(993)	51	213	*EST	822-93-5
norbornene	(8.92) See also: 82HAS/NEU.	(211)	(881)	4.9±0.2	20.5±0.8	77PED/RYL	931-64-6

Table 1. Positive Ion Table - Continued

ION / Neutral	Ionization potential eV	$\Delta_f H$(Ion) kcal/mol	kJ/mol	$\Delta_f H$(Neutral) kcal/mol	kJ/mol	Neutral reference	CAS registry number
$C_8H_{12}^+$							
(norbornane with =CH₂)	≤9.02	≤220	≤920	12	50	79AUE/BOW	497-35-8
(bicyclic with =CH₂)	(≤9.40)	(≤231.2)	(≤967.2)	14±1	60±3	77KOZ/BYC	31463-35-1
See also: 85MAR/MAY.							
	(≤8.95)	(≤234)	(≤980)	28	116	*EST	50695-42-6
	(≤9.39)	(≤244)	(≤1022)	28	116	*EST	50895-58-4
	(≤9.18)	(≤264)	(≤1102)	52±2	216±8	73ENG/AND2	28636-10-4
	(≤9.23)	(≤259)	(≤1084)	46±2	193±7	73ENG/AND2	13027-75-3
	(9.4)	(238)	(997)	21±3	90±14	81GOD/SCH2	250-21-5
IP is onset of photoelectron band.							
	(≤8.44)	(≤228)	(≤954)	33	140	*EST	7647-57-6

Table 1. Positive Ion Table - Continued

ION Neutral	Ionization potential eV	$\Delta_f H$(Ion) kcal/mol kJ/mol	$\Delta_f H$(Neutral) kcal/mol kJ/mol	Neutral reference	CAS registry number
$C_8H_{12}^+$					
(bicyclic structure)	(8.65)	(233) (975)	33 140	*EST	14783-50-7
(bicyclic structure)	(8.4) IP is onset of photoelectron band.	(266) (1112)	72 302	*EST	21426-37-9
(bicyclic structure)	(8.8) IP is onset of photoelectron band.	(275) (1151)	72 302	*EST	25399-32-0
$C_8H_{12}Cr_2O_8^+$					
(Cr complex)	(8.0) IP is onset of photoelectron band.	(−290) (−1212)	−474±7 −1984±28	82PIL/SKI	15020-15-2
$C_8H_{12}Mo_2O_8^+$					
(Mo complex)	6.54 IP from 84LIC/BLE.	(−280) (−1175)	−432±2 −1806±10	81CAV/CON	14221-06-8
$C_8H_{12}N^+$					
(3-ethylaniline)·H⁺		158 662 From proton affinity of 3-$C_2H_5C_6H_4NH_2$ (RN 587-02-0). PA = 214.0 kcal/mol, 895. kJ/mol.			
(N-ethylaniline)·H⁺		157 658 From proton affinity of $C_6H_5NHC_2H_5$ (RN 103-69-5). PA = 221.8 kcal/mol, 928. kJ/mol.			
(N,N-dimethylaniline)·H⁺		166 696 From proton affinity of $C_6H_5N(CH_3)_2$ (RN 121-69-7). PA = 223.4 kcal/mol, 935. kJ/mol.			

Table 1. Positive Ion Table - Continued

ION / Neutral	Ionization potential eV	$\Delta_f H$(Ion) kcal/mol	$\Delta_f H$(Ion) kJ/mol	$\Delta_f H$(Neutral) kcal/mol	$\Delta_f H$(Neutral) kJ/mol	Neutral reference	CAS registry number
$C_8H_{12}N^+$ 2-isopropylpyridine		152	635				

From proton affinity of 2-isopropylpyridine (RN 75981-47-4). PA = 227.2 kcal/mol, 951. kJ/mol.

$C_8H_{12}N_4^+$ (E)-(NCC(CH$_3$)$_2$)$_2$N$_2$	(9.2)	(271)	(1134)	59±0.4	246±1.8	84LEB/GUT	34241-39-9

IP is onset of photoelectron band.

$C_8H_{12}O^+$ 4,4-dimethylcyclohex-2-enone	(≤9.24)	(≤171)	(≤718)	−42	−174	*EST	4694-17-1

IP from 82PFI/GER.

2-tert-butylfuran	(8.38)	(157)	(656)	−37	−153	*EST	7040-43-9

IP from 83ZYK/ERC.

bicyclic ketone	(8.8)	(148)	(619)	−55±1	−230±5	77PED/RYL	2716-23-6

IP is onset of photoelectron band (81CAR/GAN).

2-methoxynorbornene	(≤8.15)	(≤173)	(≤724)	−15	−62	*EST	17190-90-8

IP from 83HOU/RON.

$C_8H_{12}OP^+$ (CH$_3$)$_2$(C$_6$H$_5$)P(OH)		82	341				

From proton affinity of (CH$_3$)$_2$(C$_6$H$_5$)PO (RN 10311-08-7) (86TRA/MUN). PA = 216 kcal/mol, 904 kJ/mol.

$C_8H_{12}OS^+$	(8.0)	(125)	(523)	−60	−249	*EST	76698-82-3

IP is onset of photoelectron band (81JOR/CAR).

Table 1. Positive Ion Table - Continued

ION / Neutral	Ionization potential eV	$\Delta_f H$(Ion) kcal/mol	$\Delta_f H$(Ion) kJ/mol	$\Delta_f H$(Neutral) kcal/mol	$\Delta_f H$(Neutral) kJ/mol	Neutral reference	CAS registry number
$C_8H_{12}OS^+$	(7.8)	(120)	(504)	−60	−249	*EST	
	IP is onset of photoelectron band (81JOR/CAR).						
$C_8H_{12}O_2^+$	≤8.80	≤129	≤541	−74±0.5	−308±2	77PED/RYL	933-52-8
	See also: 84OLI/FLE.						
	(≤9.45)	(≤149)	(≤625)	−68±3	−287±13	*EST	3471-13-4
	IP from 82PFI/GER.						
	(8.62)	(120)	(502)	−79	−330	82MOR/MER	
	IP from 82MOR/MER.						
	(9.28±0.05)	(145)	(608)	−68.5±3	−287±12	*EST	126-81-8
$C_8H_{12}O_2S^+$	(≤9.2)	(≤139)	(≤584)	−73	−304	*EST	
	IP from 84AIT/GOS.						
	(9.05)	(136)	(569)	−73	−304	*EST	
	IP is onset of photoelectron band (84AIT/GOS).						
$C_8H_{12}O_3^+$	(8.6)	(69)	(288)	−129	−542	*EST	
	IP from 82MOR/MER.						

Table 1. Positive Ion Table — Continued

ION / Neutral	Ionization potential eV	$\Delta_f H$(Ion) kcal/mol	$\Delta_f H$(Ion) kJ/mol	$\Delta_f H$(Neutral) kcal/mol	$\Delta_f H$(Neutral) kJ/mol	Neutral reference	CAS registry number

$C_8H_{12}P^+$

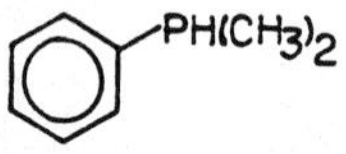

C₆H₅–PH(CH₃)₂ : 156, 651
From proton affinity of $C_6H_5P(CH_3)_2$ (RN 672-66-2). PA = 229.6 kcal/mol, 961. kJ/mol.

$C_8H_{12}S^+$

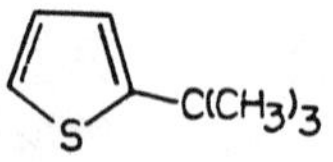

2-tert-butylthiophene: (8.32), (194), (812), 2, 9, *EST, 1689-78-7
IP is onset of photoelectron band (83VES/HAR).

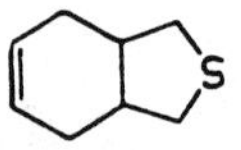

(bicyclic thiolane): (8.0), (192), (804), 8, 32, *EST
IP is onset of photoelectron band (84AIT/GOS).

$C_8H_{12}Si^+$

$(CH_2=CH)_4Si$: (9.3), (229), (958), 15, 61, 85GAD/GUB, 1112-55-6
IP is onset of photoelectron band.

C₆H₅–Si(CH₃)₂H : (8.92±0.15), (203), (848), −3, −13, *EST, 766-77-8

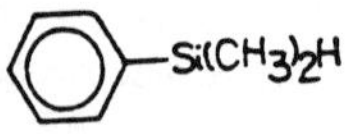

$C_8H_{12}Sn^+$

$Sn(CH=CH_2)_4$: (8.4), (277), (1162), 84, 352, *EST, 1112-56-7
IP is onset of photoelectron band (81NOV/CVI).

$C_8H_{13}^+$

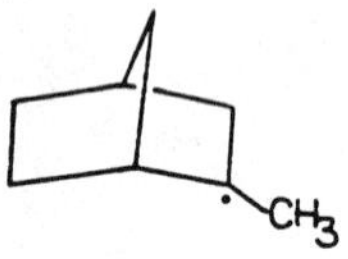

(2-methylnorbornyl cation): 171, 717, 3197-78-2
From proton affinities of 2-methylenebicyclo[2.2.1]heptane PA = (207) kcal/mol, (866) kJ/mol, (RN 497-35-8), 2-methylbicyclo[2.2.1]hept-2-ene PA = 206 kcal/mol, 862 kJ/mol, (RN 694-92-8) and hydride and chloride transfer equilibrium constants. (76SOL/FIE, 85SHA/SHA).

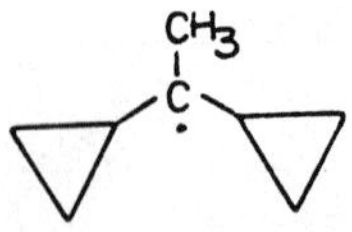

(dicyclopropyl methyl cation): 200, 837, 50555-45-8
From proton affinity of 1,1-dicyclopropylethylene (RN 822-93-5). PA = 216.5 kcal/mol, 906. kJ/mol.

Table 1. Positive Ion Table – Continued

ION / Neutral	Ionization potential eV	$\Delta_f H$(Ion) kcal/mol	$\Delta_f H$(Ion) kJ/mol	$\Delta_f H$(Neutral) kcal/mol	$\Delta_f H$(Neutral) kJ/mol	Neutral reference	CAS registry number

$C_8H_{13}Br^+$

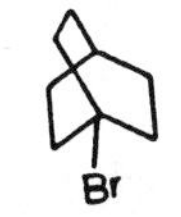

(9.4±0.1) (194) (812) −23 −95 *EST 7697-09-8
IP is onset of photoelectron band (84DEL/ABE).

$C_8H_{13}I^+$

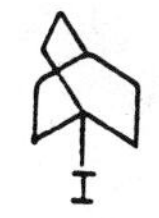

(8.7) (192) (805) −8 −34 *EST 931-98-6
IP is onset of photoelectron band (84DEL/ABE).

$C_8H_{13}NO^+$

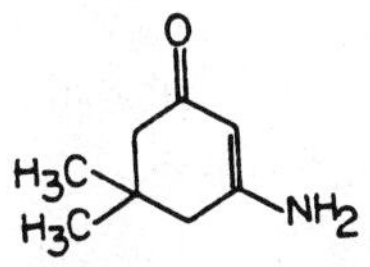

(≤8.55) (≤150) (≤628) −47 −197 *EST 873-95-0
IP from 82PFI/GER.

$C_8H_{13}O^+$

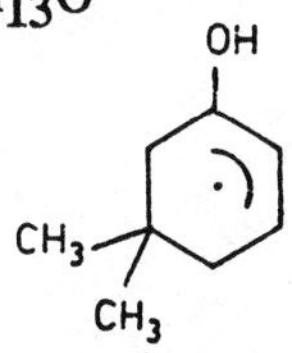

116   487
From proton affinity of 5,5-dimethylcyclohex-2-ene-1-one PA = 207.6 kcal/mol, 869. kJ/mol (86TAF/GAL).

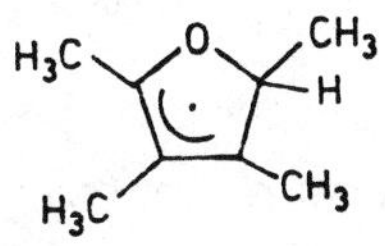

106   444
From proton affinity of 2,3,4,5-tetramethylfuran (RN 10599-58-3) (85HOU/ROL). PA = 217.6 kcal/mol, 910. kJ/mol.

$C_8H_{14}^+$

(E)-$CH_3CH_2CH_2CH_2CH=CHCH=CH_2$
(8.45) (198) (830) 4 15 *EST 39491-65-1
IP from 81MAS/MOU.

(E)-$CH_2=CHCH_2CH=CH(CH_2)_2CH_3$
(8.96) (215) (897) 8 32 *EST 53793-31-0
IP from 84HOL.

(E),(E)-$CH_3CH_2CH_2CH=CHCH=CHCH_3$
(8.13) (188) (786) 0.5 2 *EST 60919-80-4
IP from 81MAS/MOU.

(E)-$CH_3CH_2CH_2C(CH_3)=CHCH=CH_2$
(8.02) (185) (776) 0.5 2 *EST 40095-05-4
IP from 81MAS/MOU.

Table 1. Positive Ion Table - Continued

ION / Neutral	Ionization potential eV	$\Delta_f H$(Ion) kcal/mol	$\Delta_f H$(Ion) kJ/mol	$\Delta_f H$(Neutral) kcal/mol	$\Delta_f H$(Neutral) kJ/mol	Neutral reference	CAS registry number

$C_8H_{14}^+$

(Z)-(CH$_3$)$_3$CCH=CHCH=CH$_2$
 (8.46)   (199)   (833)   4   17   *EST   59697-92-6
 IP from 81MAS/MOU.

(E)-(CH$_3$)$_3$CCH=CHCH=CH$_2$
 (8.43)   (197)   (823)   2   10   *EST   36320-14-6
 IP from 81MAS/MOU.

(CH$_3$)$_2$C=CHCH=C(CH$_3$)$_2$
 (7.67)   (171)   (716)   −6   −24   *EST   764-13-6
 IP from 81MAS/MOU.

(Z),(Z)-(CH$_3$CH=C(CH$_3$))$_2$
 (8.1)   (182)   (761)   −5   −20   *EST   21293-01-6
 IP is onset of photoelectron band (84HON/ZHO).

(E),(E)-(CH$_3$CH=C(CH$_3$))$_2$
 (7.8)   (177)   (740)   −3   −12   *EST   18265-39-9
 IP is onset of photoelectron band (84HON/ZHO).

(E),(Z)-(CH$_3$CH=C(CH$_3$))$_2$
 (8.0)   (181)   (756)   −4   −16   *EST   2417-88-1
 IP is onset of photoelectron band (84HON/ZHO).

C$_2$H$_5$C(=CH$_2$)C(=CH$_2$)C$_2$H$_5$
 (8.58)   (199)   (834)   1   6   *EST   16356-05-1
 IP from 81MAS/MOU.

Neutral	IP (eV)	$\Delta_f H$(Ion) kcal/mol	kJ/mol	$\Delta_f H$(Neutral) kcal/mol	kJ/mol	Neutral reference	CAS registry
1-C$_8$H$_{14}$	(9.95±0.02)	(248)	(1041)	19±1	81±4	79ROG/DAG	629-05-0
n-C$_5$H$_{11}$C≡CCH$_3$	9.31±0.01	230	962	15±0.2	64±2	79ROG/DAG	2809-67-8
C$_4$H$_9$C≡CC$_2$H$_5$	9.22±0.01	228	953	15±0.5	63±2	79ROG/DAG	15232-76-5
n-C$_3$H$_7$C≡CC$_3$H$_7$	9.20±0.01	226	948	14±0.5	60±2	79ROG/DAG	1942-45-6
cyclooctene	8.82	196.9	824.0	−6.5±0.3	−27.0±1.1	77PED/RYL	931-88-4
ethylidenecyclohexane	8.44±0.05	174	726	−21	−88	76JEN	1003-64-1

Table 1. Positive Ion Table - Continued

ION Neutral	Ionization potential eV	$\Delta_f H$(Ion) kcal/mol	kJ/mol	$\Delta_f H$(Neutral) kcal/mol	kJ/mol	Neutral reference	CAS registry number
$C_8H_{14}^+$							
cyclohexenyl-C_2H_5	(8.48±0.01)	(180)	(755)	−15.2±0.2	−63.4±1	77PED/RYL	1453-24-3
cyclohexenyl-CH_2CH_3	(8.83±0.01)	(191)	(799)	−13	−53	*EST	2808-71-1
cyclohexenyl-C_2H_5	(8.88±0.01)	(192)	(804)	−13	−53	*EST	3742-42-5
cyclopentenyl-C_3H_7	(8.48±0.01)	(186)	(779)	−9	−39	*EST	3074-61-1
cyclopentenyl-C_3H_7	(8.84±0.02)	(196)	(819)	−8	−34	*EST	34067-75-9
cyclopentenyl-$CH(CH_3)_2$	8.81 IP from 84HOL.	(193)	(807)	−10	−43	*EST	4276-45-3
H_3C–CH_3 bicyclic	(8.8) IP is onset of photoelectron band (82SPA/GLE).	(222)	(931)	20	82	*EST	59020-33-6
bicyclic	(9.6) IP is onset of photoelectron band.	(220)	(921)	−1.2	−5	81MAI/SCH	7078-34-4

Table 1. Positive Ion Table — Continued

ION / Neutral	Ionization potential eV	$\Delta_f H$(Ion) kcal/mol	kJ/mol	$\Delta_f H$(Neutral) kcal/mol	kJ/mol	Neutral reference	CAS registry number
$C_8H_{14}^+$							
(bicyclic)	9.43±0.02	194	813	−23±1	−97±4	81GOD/SCH	280-33-1
(spiro)	(≤9.46)	(≤221)	(≤925)	3	12	*EST	185-65-9
(spiro)	(9.45)	(225)	(941)	7	29	*EST	175-56-4
$C_8H_{14}ClN^+$							
(N-Cl bicyclic)	(≤8.55) IP from 82NEL/GAN.	(≤190)	(≤795)	−7	−30	*EST	
$C_8H_{14}ClNO^+$							
(NOH, Cl cyclooctane)	(9.19±0.03) IP from 79GOL/KUL.	(178)	(747)	−33	−140	*EST	10499-33-9
$C_8H_{14}N^+$							
(3-methyl-1-azabicyclo[2.2.2]oct-2-ene)H$^+$		(164)	(687)				

From proton affinity of 1-azabicyclo[2.2.2]oct-2-ene,3-methyl-.
PA = (231.0) kcal/mol, (966.5) kJ/mol.

| | | (156) | (651) | | | | |

From proton affinity of 1-azabicyclo[2.2.2]octane, 3-methylene-.
PA = (230.1) kcal/mol, (963.) kJ/mol.

Table 1. Positive Ion Table - Continued

ION / Neutral	Ionization potential eV	$\Delta_f H$(Ion) kcal/mol	$\Delta_f H$(Ion) kJ/mol	$\Delta_f H$(Neutral) kcal/mol	$\Delta_f H$(Neutral) kJ/mol	Neutral reference	CAS registry number
$C_8H_{14}N_2^+$							
(2,3-diazabicyclic dimethyl structure)	(7.8) IP is onset of photoelectron band.	(202)	(846)	22±1	93±5	80ENG	49570-30-1
(diazabicyclic structure)	≤7.75	(≤190)	(≤795)	11	47	*EST	281-29-8
$C_8H_{14}O^+$							
n-C_3H_7CH=C(CH_3)C(=O)CH_3	(9.22)	(159)	(666)	−54	−224	*EST	39899-08-6
(cyclooctanone)	9.08 See also: 86SPA/RAD.	144	604	−65±1	−272±5	77PED/RYL	502-49-8
(bicyclic ether, isomer 1)	(9.0) IP is onset of photoelectron band (83TUR/HAN).	(149)	(624)	−58	−244	*EST	
(bicyclic ether, isomer 2)	(9.0) IP is onset of photoelectron band (83TUR/HAN).	(148)	(620)	−59	−248	*EST	
$C_8H_{14}OSi^+$							
(furyl diethylsilane)	(8.1) IP is onset of photoelectron band (83ZYK/ERC).	(129)	(540)	−58	−241	*EST	13271-67-5
$C_8H_{14}O_2^+$							
(H_3C-dihydropyran-OC_2H_5)	(≤8.6) IP from 82MOR/MER.	(≤86)	(≤358)	−113	−471	82MOR/MER	

Table 1. Positive Ion Table - Continued

ION / Neutral	Ionization potential eV	$\Delta_f H$(Ion) kcal/mol	kJ/mol	$\Delta_f H$(Neutral) kcal/mol	kJ/mol	Neutral reference	CAS registry number
$C_8H_{14}O_2^+$	(≤9.2) IP from 84GLE/DOB.	(≤177)	(≤741)	−35	−147	*EST	69492-24-6
$C_8H_{15}^+$ $(CH_3)_2C=C(CH_3)C(CH_3)_2$		(152)	(636)				
	From proton affinity of $(CH_3)_2C=C(CH_3)C(CH_3)=CH_2$ PA = (210.6) kcal/mol, (881.) kJ/mol.						
$C_8H_{15}N^+$	≤7.50 IP from 81MUL/PRE2.	(≤170)	(≤711)	−3	−12	*EST	13815-46-8
	(6.7) IP is onset of photoelectron band (81MUL/PRE2).	(153)	(642)	−1	−4	*EST	13937-89-8
	(6.8) IP is onset of photoelectron band (81MUL/PRE2).	(160)	(671)	4	15	*EST	2403-57-8
	(≤7.48) IP from 81MUL/PRE2.	(≤193)	(≤809)	21	87	*EST	
$C_8H_{15}NO^+$	(8.80±0.03) IP from 79GOL/KUL.	(171)	(717)	−32	−132	*EST	1074-51-7
$C_8H_{15}N_3^+$	(≤8.08)	(≤212)	(≤889)	26	109	*EST	38705-10-1

Table 1. Positive Ion Table – Continued

ION / Neutral	Ionization potential eV	$\Delta_f H$(Ion) kcal/mol	$\Delta_f H$(Ion) kJ/mol	$\Delta_f H$(Neutral) kcal/mol	$\Delta_f H$(Neutral) kJ/mol	Neutral reference	CAS registry number
$C_8H_{15}O^+$		98	410				

From proton affinity of cyclohexylethanone (RN 823-76-7). PA = 202.4 kcal/mol, 847. kJ/mol.

ION / Neutral	Ionization potential eV	$\Delta_f H$(Ion) kcal/mol	$\Delta_f H$(Ion) kJ/mol	$\Delta_f H$(Neutral) kcal/mol	$\Delta_f H$(Neutral) kJ/mol	Neutral reference	CAS registry number
$C_8H_{15}O_2^+$		51	212				

From proton affinity of methylcyclohexane carboxylate (RN 4630-82-4). PA = 203.7 kcal/mol, 852. kJ/mol.

ION / Neutral	Ionization potential eV	$\Delta_f H$(Ion) kcal/mol	$\Delta_f H$(Ion) kJ/mol	$\Delta_f H$(Neutral) kcal/mol	$\Delta_f H$(Neutral) kJ/mol	Neutral reference	CAS registry number
$C_8H_{16}^+$							
1-C_8H_{16}	9.43±0.01	198	829	−19.4±0.2	−81.2±1	77PED/RYL	111-66-0
(Z)-2-C_8H_{16}	8.91±0.01	(184)	(767)	−22	−91	*EST	7642-04-8
(E)-2-C_8H_{16}	8.91±0.01	(183)	(765)	−23	−95	*EST	13389-42-9
(Z)-3-C_8H_{16}	8.85±0.01	(183)	(764)	−21	−90	*EST	14850-22-7
(E)-3-C_8H_{16}	8.85±0.01	(181)	(759)	−23	−95	*EST	14919-01-8
(Z)-4-C_8H_{16}	8.84±0.01	(182)	(763)	−21	−90	*EST	7642-15-1
(E)-4-C_8H_{16}	8.83±0.01	(181)	(758)	−22	−94	*EST	14850-23-8
$(C_2H_5)_2C=CHC_2H_5$	(8.48±0.01)	(171)	(715)	−25	−103	*EST	16789-51-8
$C_2H_5CH_2C(CH_3)=C(CH_3)_2$	(8.19±0.01)	(162)	(680)	−26	−110	*EST	7145-20-2
(Z)-$(CH_3)_2CHCH=CHCH(CH_3)_2$	(8.85±0.01)	(179)	(749)	−25	−105	*EST	10557-44-5
(E)-$(CH_3)_2CHCH=CHCH(CH_3)_2$	(8.84±0.01)	(178)	(743)	−26	−110	*EST	692-70-6
(Z)-$C_2H_5C(CH_3)=C(CH_3)C_2H_5$	(8.17±0.01)	(162)	(678)	−26	−110	*EST	19550-87-9
(E)-$C_2H_5C(CH_3)=C(CH_3)C_2H_5$	(8.16±0.01)	(162)	(677)	−26	−110	*EST	19550-88-0
(tert-$C_4H_9)CH_2C(CH_3)=CH_2$	(8.91±0.01)	(179)	(749)	−26.4±0.2	−110.4±1	77PED/RYL	107-39-1
$(C_2H_5)_2C=C(CH_3)_2$	8.17±0.01	(162)	(678)	−26	−110	*EST	19780-67-7

Table 1. Positive Ion Table - Continued

ION Neutral	Ionization potential eV	$\Delta_f H$(Ion) kcal/mol	$\Delta_f H$(Ion) kJ/mol	$\Delta_f H$(Neutral) kcal/mol	$\Delta_f H$(Neutral) kJ/mol	Neutral reference	CAS registry number
$C_8H_{16}^+$							
$(CH_3)_2CHC(CH_3)=C(CH_3)_2$	(8.17±0.01)	(160)	(670)	−28	−118	*EST	565-77-5
cyclooctane	9.76	195	817	−29.7±0.2	−124.4±0.9	77PED/RYL	292-64-8

IP from charge transfer equilibrium constant determinations (82SIE/MAU, 82LIA). Reference IP's, fluorobenzenes. Photoelectron spectroscopy IP = 9.74±0.05 (79GOL/KUL).

1,1-dimethylcyclohexane	9.42	174	728	−43.2±0.5	−180.9±1.9	77PED/RYL	590-66-9

IP from charge transfer equilibrium constant determinations (82SIE/MAU, 82LIA). Reference IP's, fluorobenzenes.

cis-1,2-dimethylcyclohexane	9.41	174	728	−43.0±0.4	−179.9±1.8	77PED/RYL	6876-23-9

IP from charge transfer equilibrium constant determinations (82SIE/MAU, 82LIA). Reference IP's, fluorobenzenes. Electron impact IP = 9.89 eV (81HER/SIC).

trans-1,2-dimethylcyclohexane	(<9.78)	(<184)	(<771)	−41.1±0.4	−172.3±1.8	77PED/RYL	2207-01-4

IP from 81HER/SIC.

cis-1,3-dimethylcyclohexane	9.53	178	743	−42.2±0.4	−176.5±1.7	77PED/RYL	2207-03-6

IP from charge transfer equilibrium constant determinations (82SIE/MAU, 82LIA). Reference IP's, fluorobenzenes. Electron impact IP = 9.89 eV (81HER/SIC).

trans-1,3-dimethylcyclohexane	(<9.98)	(<186)	(<778)	−44.1±0.4	−184.6±1.7	77PED/RYL	638-04-0

IP from 81HER/SIC.

cis-1,4-dimethylcyclohexane	9.56	176	738	−44.1±0.4	−184.5±1.7	77PED/RYL	2207-04-7

IP from charge transfer equilibrium constant determinations (82SIE/MAU, 82LIA). Reference IP's, fluorobenenes. Threshold photoionization value of IP = 9.67 eV.

trans-1,4-dimethylcyclohexane	(<9.93)	(<187)	(<781)	−42.2±0.4	−176.6±1.7	77PED/RYL	624-29-3

IP from 81HER/SIC.

Table 1. Positive Ion Table – Continued

ION / Neutral	Ionization potential eV	$\Delta_f H$(Ion) kcal/mol	$\Delta_f H$(Ion) kJ/mol	$\Delta_f H$(Neutral) kcal/mol	$\Delta_f H$(Neutral) kJ/mol	Neutral reference	CAS registry number

$C_8H_{16}^+$

cyclohexyl–C_2H_5 9.54   178.8   748.1   −41.2±0.1   −172.4±0.6   77PED/RYL   1678-91-7

IP from charge transfer equilibrium constant determinations (82SIE/MAU, 82LIA). Reference IP's, fluorobenzenes.

cyclopentyl–$CH_2CH_2CH_3$ (10.00±0.04)   (195)   (817)   −35.3±0.2   −147.8±0.6   77PED/RYL   2040-96-2

$C_8H_{16}N^+$

(3-methyl-1-azabicyclo[2.2.2]octane)H^+ (126)   (528)

From proton affinity of 3-methyl-1-azabicyclo[2.2.2]octane (RN 695-88-5).
PA = (231.7) kcal/mol, (969.) kJ/mol.

$C_8H_{16}NO^+$

(cis-3-aminobicyclo[2.2.2]octan-2-ol)H^+ 84   353

From proton affinity of cis-3-aminobicyclo[2.2.2]octan-2-ol (RN 17997-65-8).
PA = 223.9 kcal/mol, 937. kJ/mol.

(trans-3-aminobicyclo[2.2.2]octan-2-ol)H^+ 86   359

From proton affinity of trans-3-aminobicyclo[2.2.2]octan-2-ol (RN 40335-14-6).
PA = 220.6 kcal/mol, 923. kJ/mol.

$C_8H_{16}N_2^+$

(diazabicyclic)   7.0   (174)   (729)   13   54   *EST

IP is onset of photoelectron band (85HON/YAN).

$C_8H_{16}N_2O^+$

(tetramethyl cyclic azoxy)   (≤9.13±0.03)   (≤204)   (≤854)   −6.33±0.55   −26.48±0.3   83BYS   54143-34-9

$C_8H_{16}O^+$

n-$C_6H_{13}COCH_3$ 9.40±0.03   140   586   −77   −321   75TRC   111-13-7

n-$C_4H_9COCH_2CH_2CH_3$ (9.10±0.05)   (133)   (558)   −76   −320   75TRC   589-63-9

Table 1. Positive Ion Table - Continued

ION Neutral	Ionization potential eV	$\Delta_f H$(Ion) kcal/mol	$\Delta_f H$(Ion) kJ/mol	$\Delta_f H$(Neutral) kcal/mol	$\Delta_f H$(Neutral) kJ/mol	Neutral reference	CAS registry number
$C_8H_{16}O^+$							
tert-C_4H_9CO(iso-C_3H_7)	(8.80±0.01)	(122)	(510)	−80.8±0.3	−338.3±1.2	77PED/RYL	5857-36-3
$C_8H_{16}O_2^+$							
cis-1,2-dimethoxycyclohexane	(8.7) IP is onset of photoelectron band.	(104)	(435)	−97	−404	*EST	29887-60-3
trans-1,2-dimethoxycyclohexane	(8.6) IP is onset of photoelectron band.	(102)	(426)	−97	−404	*EST	30363-80-5
3,3,6,6-tetramethyl-1,2-dioxane	9.2 IP is onset of photoelectron band.	(135)	(567)	−77	−321	*EST	22431-89-6
$C_8H_{16}O_2Si^+$							
1,1-diethoxy-1-silacyclopent-3-ene	≤9.44 IP from 81KHV/ZYK.	(≤52)	(≤216)	−166	−695	*EST	67059-49-8
$C_8H_{16}O_4^+$							
12-crown-4	(8.8) IP is onset of photoelectron band (83BAK/ARM, 82LEV/LIA).	(52)	(218)	−151±0.5	−631±2	82BYS/MAN	294-93-9
$C_8H_{16}Si^+$							
1,1-diethyl-1-silacyclopent-3-ene	(≤8.89) IP from 81KHV/ZYK.	(≤175)	(≤734)	−30	−124	*EST	69657-20-1
$C_8H_{17}^+$							
$(CH_3)_2CCH_2CH_2CH_2CH_2CH_3$		139	582				40626-79-7
	From appearance potential measurement (84LOS/HOL).						

Table 1. Positive Ion Table – Continued

ION Neutral	Ionization potential eV	$\Delta_f H$(Ion) kcal/mol kJ/mol		$\Delta_f H$(Neutral) kcal/mol kJ/mol		Neutral reference	CAS registry number
$C_8H_{17}N^+$							
cyclohexyl-N(CH₃)₂	(7.5) IP is onset of photoelectron band.	(148)	(618)	−25	−106	*EST	98-94-2
1,2,6-trimethylpiperidine	(7.77) IP from 82ROZ/HOU.	(148)	(620)	−31	−130	*EST	2439-13-6
1,3,5-trimethylpiperidine	(7.66) IP from 82ROZ/HOU.	(152)	(637)	−24	−102	*EST	16544-52-8
1,3,5-trimethylpiperidine isomer	(7.63) IP from 82ROZ/HOU.	(149)	(625)	−27	−111	*EST	14446-76-5
1,4,4-trimethylpiperidine	(7.77) IP from 82ROZ/HOU.	(148)	(621)	−31	−129	*EST	1003-84-5
$C_8H_{17}O_4^+$							
12-crown-4·H⁺	From proton affinity of 1,4,7,10-tetraoxacyclododecane (12-Crown-4) (RN 294-93-9). PA = 221.6 kcal/mol, 927. kJ/mol.			−7	−29		
$C_8H_{18}^+$							
n-C_8H_{18}	(9.82) IP from charge transfer equilibrium constant determinations (81MAU/SIE, 82LIA). Reference IP's, fluorobenzenes.	(177) *(188)*	(739) *(786)*	−49.8 *−38.6*	−208.5 *−161.4*	74SCO	111-65-9
(CH₃)₂CH(CH₂)₄CH₃	9.84 IP from charge transfer equilibrium constant determinations (81MAU/SIE, 82LIA). Reference IP's, fluorobenzenes.	176 *187*	734 *784*	−51.4±0.3 *−39.6±0.3*	−215.1±1.4 *−165.9±1.4*	74SCO	592-27-8
(CH₃)₃CC(CH₃)₃	9.8 IP is onset of photoelectron band (81SZE/KOR, 81KIM/KAT).	(172)	(720)	−53.9±0.3	−225.7±1.1	77PED/RYL	594-82-1

ION Neutral	Ionization potential eV	$\Delta_f H$(Ion) kcal/mol	$\Delta_f H$(Ion) kJ/mol	$\Delta_f H$(Neutral) kcal/mol	$\Delta_f H$(Neutral) kJ/mol	Neutral reference	CAS registry number
$C_8H_{18}{}^+$ $(CH_3)_2CHCH_2C(CH_3)_3$	9.86	(171)	(714)	−57	−238	*EST	540-84-1
$C_8H_{18}ClP^+$ (tert-C_4H_9)$_2$PCl	(8.0) IP is onset of photoelectron band.	(112)	(469)	−72	−303	*EST	13716-10-4
$C_8H_{18}FP^+$ (tert-C_4H_9)$_2$PF	(8.2) IP is onset of photoelectron band.	(63)	(265)	−126	−526	*EST	29146-24-5
$C_8H_{18}Hg^+$ (n-C_4H_9)$_2$Hg	(≤8.35)	(≤185)	(≤774)	−8±2	−32±8	77PED/RYL	629-35-6
(iso-C_4H_9)$_2$Hg	(≤8.30)	(≤182)	(≤763)	−9±2	−38±8	77PED/RYL	24470-76-6

$C_8H_{18}N^+$

	108	450				

From proton affinity of N,N-dimethylcyclohexanamine (RN 98-94-2) (86TAF/GAL). PA = 232.7 kcal/mol, 974. kJ/mol.

	(109)	(457)				

From proton affinity of N,3,5-trimethylpiperidine PA = (230) kcal/mol, (962) kJ/mol, (RN 14446-76-5) (84HOP/JAH).

ION Neutral	IP eV	$\Delta_f H$(Ion) kcal/mol	$\Delta_f H$(Ion) kJ/mol	$\Delta_f H$(Neutral) kcal/mol	$\Delta_f H$(Neutral) kJ/mol	Neutral reference	CAS registry number
$C_8H_{18}NO^+$ (tert-C_4H_9)$_2$NO	(6.77)	(126)	(527)	−30±3	−126±13	*EST	2406-25-9
$C_8H_{18}NO_2P^+$	(≤8.52) IP from 82WOR/HAR.	(≤71)	(≤295)	−126	−527	*EST	
$C_8H_{18}N_2{}^+$ (E)-(tert-C_4H_9N)$_2$	(7.7) IP is onset of photoelectron band.	(169)	(707)	−9±0.7	−36±3	80ENG	927-83-3

Table 1. Positive Ion Table – Continued

ION / Neutral	Ionization potential eV	$\Delta_f H$(Ion) kcal/mol	$\Delta_f H$(Ion) kJ/mol	$\Delta_f H$(Neutral) kcal/mol	$\Delta_f H$(Neutral) kJ/mol	Neutral reference	CAS registry number
$C_8H_{18}N_3OP^+$	(≤8.14±0.10) IP from 82COW/LAT.	(≤88)	(≤367)	−100	−418	*EST	15199-21-0
$C_8H_{18}N_3P^+$	(≤7.71±0.10) IP from 82COW/LAT.	(≤177)	(≤739)	−1	−5	*EST	14418-26-9
$C_8H_{18}N_3PS^+$	(≤8.14±0.10) IP from 82COW/LAT.	(≤164)	(≤688)	−23	−97	*EST	15199-22-1
$C_8H_{18}O^+$							
$(n-C_4H_9)_2O$	≤9.43 IP from 80BAC/MOU. Value derived from hydrogen affinity considerations: 9.37 eV.	≤138	≤577	−80	−333	77PED/RYL	142-96-1
$(sec-C_4H_9)_2O$	(9.11) IP from 81HOL/FIN.	(122)	(509)	−88±0.5	−370±2	77PED/RYL	6863-58-7
$(tert-C_4H_9)_2O$	8.81 See also: 80BAC/MOU.	117	488	−87±0.2	−362±1	77PED/RYL	6163-66-2
$C_8H_{18}OS^+$							
$[(CH_3)_3C]_2SO$	8.0 IP is onset of photoelectron band.	(113)	(471)	−72	−301	*EST	2211-92-9
$C_8H_{18}O_2^+$							
$(tert-C_4H_9O)_2$	(8.4) IP is onset of photoelectron band.	(111)	(461)	−83±0.7	−349±3	77PED/RYL	110-05-4
$C_8H_{18}O_2S^+$							
$(iso-C_4H_9)_2SO_2$	(9.54±0.05)	(92)	(384)	−128±0.7	−536±3	77PED/RYL	10495-45-1
$C_8H_{18}O_4^+$							
$(CH_3O(CH_2)_2OCH_2)_2$	(≤9.8) IP from 83BAK/ARM.	(≤69)	(≤289)	−157	−656	*EST	112-49-2
$C_8H_{18}S^+$							
$(n-C_4H_9)_2S$	(8.2) IP is onset of photoelectron band.	(149)	(624)	−40.0±0.3	−167.3±1.1	77PED/RYL	544-40-1
$(iso-C_4H_9)_2S$	8.36±0.05	150	628	−43±0.5	−179±2	77PED/RYL	592-65-4

Table 1. Positive Ion Table – Continued

ION / Neutral	Ionization potential eV	$\Delta_f H$(Ion) kcal/mol	$\Delta_f H$(Ion) kJ/mol	$\Delta_f H$(Neutral) kcal/mol	$\Delta_f H$(Neutral) kJ/mol	Neutral reference	CAS registry number
$C_8H_{18}S^+$							
(tert-C_4H_9)$_2$S	(8.0)	(139)	(582)	−45.1±0.2	−188.9±0.7	77PED/RYL	107-47-1
	IP is onset of photoelectron band.						
$C_8H_{18}SSi^+$							
(C_2H_5)$_2$Si(CH$_3$)–S–CH(CH$_3$) (ring)	(7.92±0.03)	(165)	(691)	(−17)	(−73)	81GUS/VOL	
	IP from 81GUS/VOL.						
$C_8H_{18}S_2^+$							
(n-C_4H_9S)$_2$	(≤8.51)	(≤158)	(≤663)	−38±0.7	−158±3	77PED/RYL	629-45-8
	Dialkyl disulfides undergo a change in the CSSC bond angle from 90° to 180° upon ionization; adiabatic ionization potentials are probably well below the the experimentally observed ionization onset.						
(tert-C_4H_9S)$_2$	(7.7)	(130)	(542)	−48±0.7	−200±3	77PED/RYL	110-06-5
	IP is onset of photoelectron band. Dialkyl disulfides undergo a change in the CSSC bond angle from 90° to 180° upon ionization; adiabatic ionization potentials are probably well below the experimentally observed ionization onset.						
$C_8H_{18}Si_2^+$							
$CH_2=CH[Si(CH_3)_2]_2CH=CH_2$	(≤8.63)	(≤166)	(≤694)	−33	−139	*EST	
	IP from 81KHV/ZYK.						
$C_8H_{19}ClNP^+$							
$(CH_3)_3CP(Cl)NHC(CH_3)_3$	(≤8.75)	(≤145)	(≤606)	−57	−238	*EST	
	IP from 85ELB/ELL.						
$C_8H_{19}N^+$							
n-$C_8H_{17}NH_2$	(8.5)	(155)	(648)	−41	−172	*EST	111-86-4
	IP from 79AUE/BOW.						
(n-C_4H_9)$_2$NH	(7.69±0.03)	(140)	(585)	−37.4±0.3	−156.6±1.3	77PED/RYL	111-92-2
	Ion heat of formation predicted from hydrogen affinities of secondary amines: 143 kcal/mol, 598 kJ/mol, corresponding to IP of 7.8 eV.						
(sec-C_4H_9)$_2$NH	(7.63)	(138)	(579)	−38	−157	*EST	626-23-3
	IP from 79AUE/BOW.						
(i-C_4H_9)$_2$NH	(7.81)	(137)	(574)	−43±2	−179±8	73PEP/GAF	110-96-3
	IP from 79AUE/BOW.						

Table 1. Positive Ion Table - Continued

| ION | Ionization potential | $\Delta_f H$(Ion) | | $\Delta_f H$(Neutral) | | Neutral | CAS registry |
Neutral	eV	kcal/mol	kJ/mol	kcal/mol	kJ/mol	reference	number
$C_8H_{19}N_2OP^+$							
(cyclic structure) P—N(CH(CH$_3$)$_2$)$_2$	(≤7.74) IP from 82WOR/HAR.	(≤79)	(≤330)	−100	−417	*EST	
$C_8H_{19}O^+$							
(n-C$_4$H$_9$)$_2$OH		82	345				
From proton affinity of (n-C$_4$H$_9$)$_2$O (RN 142-96-1). PA = 203.7 kcal/mol, 852. kJ/mol.							
(sec-C$_4$H$_9$)$_2$OH		68	286				
From proton affinity of (sec-C$_4$H$_9$)$_2$O (RN 6863-58-7). PA = 209.0 kcal/mol, 874. kJ/mol.							
$C_8H_{19}O_4^+$							
CH$_3$(OCH$_2$CH$_2$)$_2$O(H)CH$_2$CH$_2$OCH$_3$		−15	−64				
From proton affinity of CH$_3$(OCH$_2$CH$_2$)$_3$OCH$_3$ (RN 112-49-2). PA = 224.1 kcal/mol, 938. kJ/mol.							
$C_8H_{19}P^+$							
(tert-C$_4$H$_9$)$_2$PH	(7.9) IP is onset of photoelectron band.	(132)	(551)	−50	−211	*EST	819-19-2
$C_8H_{19}S^+$							
(n-C$_4$H$_9$)$_2$SH		117	490				
From proton affinity of (n-C$_4$H$_9$)$_2$S (RN 544-40-1). PA = 208.7 kcal/mol, 873. kJ/mol.							
(t-C$_4$H$_9$)$_2$SH		108	451				
From proton affinity of (t-C$_4$H$_9$)$_2$S (RN 107-47-1). PA = 212.8 kcal/mol, 890. kJ/mol.							
$C_8H_{20}Ge^+$							
(C$_2$H$_5$)$_4$Ge	8.9 IP is onset of photoelectron band.	(167)	(698)	−38±2	−161±8	77PED/RYL	597-63-7
$C_8H_{20}N^+$							
n-C$_8$H$_{17}$NH$_3$		(104)	(436)				
From proton affinity of n-C$_8$H$_{17}$NH$_2$ (RN 111-86-4). PA = 220.4 kcal/mol, 922. kJ/mol.							
(n-C$_4$H$_9$)$_2$NH$_2$		100	417				
From proton affinity of (n-C$_4$H$_9$)$_2$NH (RN 111-92-2). PA = 228.4 kcal/mol, 956. kJ/mol.							
(sec-C$_4$H$_9$)$_2$NH$_2$		(97)	(407)				
From proton affinity of (sec-C$_4$H$_9$)$_2$NH (RN 626-23-3), re-evaluated (84HOP/JAH). PA = (230.9) kcal/mol, (966) kJ/mol.							

Table 1. Positive Ion Table - Continued

ION Neutral	Ionization potential eV	$\Delta_f H$(Ion) kcal/mol	$\Delta_f H$(Ion) kJ/mol	$\Delta_f H$(Neutral) kcal/mol	$\Delta_f H$(Neutral) kJ/mol	Neutral reference	CAS registry number
$C_8H_{20}N^+$							
(iso-C_4H_9)$_2$NH$_2$		94	395				
From proton affinity of (iso-C_4H_9)$_2$NH (RN 110-96-3). PA = 228.6 kcal/mol, 956. kJ/mol.							
(tert-C_4H_9)$_2$NH$_2$		91	382				
From proton affinity of (tert-C_4H_9)$_2$NH (RN 21981-37-3). PA = 233.2 kcal/mol, 976. kJ/mol.							
(i-C_3H_7)$_2$(C_2H_5)NH		(97)	(406)				
From proton affinity of (i-C_3H_7)$_2$(C_2H_5)N (RN 7087-68-5). PA = 235.3 kcal/mol, 984. kJ/mol.							
(CH_3)$_3$C(CH_2)$_2$NH(CH_3)$_2$		(100)	(417)				
From proton affinity of (CH_3)$_3$C(CH_2)$_2$N(CH_3)$_2$ (RN 15673-04-8). PA = 230.4 kcal/mol, 964. kJ/mol.							
$C_8H_{20}N_2^+$							
(C_2H_5)$_2$NN(C_2H_5)$_2$	(6.50)	(149)	(625)	−0.5	−2	*EST	4267-00-9
IP from charge transfer equilibrium constant determination (84MAU/NEL). Reference standard: IP (C_6H_5N(CH_3)$_2$) = 7.12 eV). See also: 84NEL.							
(i-C_3H_7)$_2$NN(CH_3)$_2$	(6.53)	(153)	(639)	2	9	*EST	60678-72-0
IP from charge transfer equilibrium constant determination (86RUM).							
(i-C_3H_7)(CH_3)NN(CH_3)(i-C_3H_7)	(6.58)	(154)	(645)	2	10	*EST	60678-71-9
IP from charge transfer equilibrium constant determination (86RUM). See also: 84NEL.							
$C_8H_{20}N_3P^+$							
[structure: P—N(CH(CH$_3$)$_2$)$_2$ with cyclic NH–P–NH]	(≤7.40)	(≤136)	(≤568)	−35	−146	*EST	
IP from 82WOR/HAR.							
$C_8H_{20}N_4^+$							
(N_2(C_2H_5)$_2$)$_2$	(≤7.1)	(≤213)	(≤890)	49	205	70BEN/O'N	13304-29-5
$C_8H_{20}O_4Si^+$							
(C_2H_5O)$_4$Si	(≤9.77)	(≤−93)	(≤−388)	−318±5	−1331±21	80TEL/RAB	78-10-4
$C_8H_{20}Pb^+$							
(C_2H_5)$_4$Pb	(11.1)	(282)	(1180)	26±1	109±5	77PED/RYL	78-00-2

Table 1. Positive Ion Table - Continued

ION Neutral	Ionization potential eV	$\Delta_f H$(Ion) kcal/mol	 kJ/mol	$\Delta_f H$(Neutral) kcal/mol	 kJ/mol	Neutral reference	CAS registry number
$C_8H_{20}Si^+$							
$(C_2H_5)_4Si$	(8.9)	(142)	(594)	−63±4	−265±15	77PED/RYL	631-36-7
$C_8H_{20}Sn^+$							
$(C_2H_5)_4Sn$	(8.1)	(176)	(737)	−11±0.7	−45±3	77PED/RYL	597-64-8
	IP is onset of photoelectron band.						
$C_8H_{21}N_2^+$							
$(CH_3)_2NH(CH_2)_4N(CH_3)_2$		108	450				
	From proton affinity of $(CH_3)_2N(CH_2)_4N(CH_3)_2$ (RN 111-51-3). PA = 246. kcal/mol, 1029. kJ/mol.						
$(C_2H_5)_2NHN(C_2H_5)_2$		135	564				
	From proton affinity of $(C_2H_5)_2NN(C_2H_5)_2$ (RN 4267-00-9) (84MAU/NEL). PA = 230.4 kcal/mol, 964. kJ/mol.						
$C_8H_{22}NSi^+$							
$(CH_3)_3Si(CH_2)_3NH(CH_3)_2$		75	312				
	From proton affinity of $(CH_3)_3Si(CH_2)_3N(CH_3)_2$ (RN 28247-29-2). 231.8 kcal/mol, 970. kJ/mol.						
$(CH_3)_2(tert-C_4H_9)SiNH(CH_3)_2$		68	283				
	From proton affinity of $(CH_3)_2(tert-C_4H_9)SiN(CH_3)_2$ (RN 66365-05-7). PA = 229.7 kcal/mol, 961. kJ/mol.						
$C_8H_{24}N_4Mo^+$							
$((CH_3)_2N)_4Mo$	(≤5.30)	(≤153)	(≤642)	31±2	131±8	81CAV/CON	
$C_8H_{24}O_2Si_3^+$							
$[(CH_3)_3SiO]_2Si(CH_3)_2$	(≤10.04)	(≤−99)	(≤−412)	−330±3	−1381±12	77PED/RYL	107-51-7
	IP from 82ERM/KIR.						
$C_8H_{24}Si_3^+$							
$Si_3(CH_3)_8$	(7.7)	(65)	(273)	−112±4	−470±17	77PED/RYL	3704-44-7
	IP is onset of photoelectron band.						
$C_9Fe_2O_9^+$	(7.91±0.01)	(−136)	(−571)	−319±6	−1334±23	77PED/RYL	15321-51-4

Table 1. Positive Ion Table - Continued

ION / Neutral	Ionization potential eV	$\Delta_f H$(Ion) kcal/mol	$\Delta_f H$(Ion) kJ/mol	$\Delta_f H$(Neutral) kcal/mol	$\Delta_f H$(Neutral) kJ/mol	Neutral reference	CAS registry number
$C_9H_5ClCrO_3^+$	(7.00±0.1)	(74)	(311)	−87±1	−364±6	77PED/RYL	12082-03-0
$C_9H_6CrO_3^+$	7.0	(78)	(325)	−84±2	−350±9	77PED/RYL	12082-08-5

IP is onset of photoelectron band. See also: 82GUI/PFI.

$C_9H_6F_3^+$		83	347				

From proton affinity of 3-$CF_3C_6H_4C\equiv CH$ (RN 705-28-2) (85MAR/MOD).
PA = 192.9 kcal/mol, 807. kJ/mol.

$C_9H_6OS^+$	(8.5)	(222)	(930)	26	110	*EST	10095-83-7

IP is onset of photoelectron band (84GLE/BIS).

$C_9H_6O_2^+$	(8.65)	(190)	(795)	−10	−40	*EST	18895-06-2

IP is onset of photoelectron band (84GLE/BIS).

	(8.8)	(167)	(699)	−36	−150	*EST	16214-27-0

IP is onset of photoelectron band.

$C_9H_6S_3^+$	(7.8)	(253)	(1060)	74±2	311±10	72GEI/RAU	3445-76-9

IP is onset of photoelectron band.

Table 1. Positive Ion Table - Continued

ION / Neutral	Ionization potential eV	$\Delta_f H$(Ion) kcal/mol	$\Delta_f H$(Ion) kJ/mol	$\Delta_f H$(Neutral) kcal/mol	$\Delta_f H$(Neutral) kJ/mol	Neutral reference	CAS registry number
$C_9H_7BrO_2^+$ (2-bromocinnamic acid)	(8.80) IP from 84SCH.	(152)	(638)	−50	−211	*EST	
$C_9H_7ClO_2^+$ (2-chlorocinnamic acid)	(8.85) IP from 84SCH.	(147)	(615)	−57	−239	*EST	4513-41-1
$C_9H_7FO_2^+$ (2-fluorocinnamic acid)	(9.00) IP from 84SCH.	(103)	(430)	−105	−438	*EST	451-69-4
$C_9H_7IO_2^+$ (2-iodocinnamic acid)	(8.55) IP from 84SCH.	(160)	(668)	(−37)	(−156)	*EST	90276-19-0
$C_9H_7MnO_3^+$ (methylcyclopentadienyl Mn tricarbonyl)	(7.4) IP is onset of photoelectron band (81CAL/HUB, 81CAL/LIC).	(47)	(196)	−124	−518	*EST	12108-13-3
$C_9H_7N^+$ (quinoline)	8.62±0.01	249	1043	50±0.2	211±1	79VIS	91-22-5
(isoquinoline)	8.53±0.03	247	1031	50±0.2	208±1	79VIS/WIL	119-65-3

Table 1. Positive Ion Table - Continued

ION Neutral	Ionization potential eV	$\Delta_f H$(Ion) kcal/mol	$\Delta_f H$(Ion) kJ/mol	$\Delta_f H$(Neutral) kcal/mol	$\Delta_f H$(Neutral) kJ/mol	Neutral reference	CAS registry number
$C_9H_7NO^+$							
quinoline N-oxide	8.00±0.02	(215)	(903)	31	131	*EST	1613-37-2
4-cyanoacetophenone	(≤9.82) IP from 85GAL/GER.	(≤237)	(≤991)	11	44	*EST	1443-80-7
isoquinoline N-oxide	(7.9) IP is onset of photoelectron band.	(213)	(890)	31	128	*EST	1532-72-5
$C_9H_8^+$							
(1-propynyl)benzene	8.41 See also: 81ELB/LIE.	(258)	(1079)	64	268	85DAV/ALL	673-32-5
2-methylphenylacetylene	(≤8.61±0.02)	(≤264)	(≤1105)	65	274	*EST	766-47-2
3-methylphenylacetylene	(≤8.63±0.02)	(≤264)	(≤1106)	65	273	*EST	766-82-5
4-methylphenylacetylene	8.3 IP is onset of photoelectron band.	(257)	(1075)	65	274	*EST	766-97-2
indene	8.14±0.01	227	948	39±0.2	163±1	80KUD/KUD	95-13-6

Table 1. Positive Ion Table - Continued

ION / Neutral	Ionization potential eV	$\Delta_f H$(Ion) kcal/mol	$\Delta_f H$(Ion) kJ/mol	$\Delta_f H$(Neutral) kcal/mol	$\Delta_f H$(Neutral) kJ/mol	Neutral reference	CAS registry number
$C_9H_8^+$	(7.99)	(271)	(1134)	87	363	*EST	14867-83-5
$C_9H_8Cl_2^+$	(8.7)	(234)	(979)	33	140	*EST	2415-80-7

IP is onset of photoelectron band.

$C_9H_8F_3^+$

          43   182

From proton affinity of 3-$CF_3C_6H_4CH=CH_2$ (RN 402-24-4) (84HAR/HOU).
PA = 194.6 kcal/mol, 814. kJ/mol.

$C_9H_8MnO_3^+$

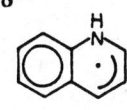

          (44)   (183)

From proton affinity of η^5-methylcyclopentadienyl-(RN 12108-13-3).
PA = (200.6) kcal/mol, (839.) kJ/mol.

$C_9H_8N^+$

          190   793

From proton affinity of quinoline (RN 91-22-5). PA = (226.5) kcal/mol, 948. kJ/mol.

          190   793

From proton affinity of isoquinoline (RN 119-65-3). PA = 225.9 kcal/mol, 945. kJ/mol.

$C_9H_8NO^+$

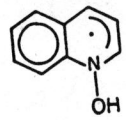

          172   721

From proton affinity of quinoline-1-oxide (RN 1613-37-2). PA = 224.6 kcal/mol, 940. kJ/mol.

Table 1. Positive Ion Table - Continued

ION / Neutral	Ionization potential eV	$\Delta_f H$(Ion) kcal/mol	kJ/mol	$\Delta_f H$(Neutral) kcal/mol	kJ/mol	Neutral reference	CAS registry number
$C_9H_8N_2^+$ (aziridinyl-phenyl-CN)	(≤8.5) IP from 82CRI/LIC.	(≤299)	(≤1251)	103	431	*EST	30855-80-2
$C_9H_8OS^+$ (2-methyl benzothiophene S-oxide)	(≤8.75) IP from 82BEN/DUR.	(≤203)	(≤848)	1	4	*EST	33945-86-7
(3-methyl benzothiophene S-oxide)	(8.2) IP is onset of photoelectron band (82BEN/DUR).	(190)	(795)	1	4	*EST	51500-43-7
$C_9H_8O_2^+$ (cis-cinnamic acid)	(8.90±0.05) IP from 84SCH.	(155)	(649)	−50	−210	*EST	102-94-3
(trans-cinnamic acid)	(9.00±0.05) IP from 84SCH.	(153)	(641)	−54	−227	77PED/RYL	140-10-3
	(≤9.38) IP from 85GLE/JAH.	(≤249)	(≤1043)	33	138	*EST	94499-50-0
	(≤8.65) IP from 78MAR/SCH.	(≤193)	(≤809)	−6	−26	*EST	
	(≤8.90) IP from 78MAR/SCH.	(≤204)	(≤854)	−1	−5	*EST	

Table 1. Positive Ion Table — Continued

ION / Neutral	Ionization potential eV	$\Delta_f H$(Ion) kcal/mol	$\Delta_f H$(Ion) kJ/mol	$\Delta_f H$(Neutral) kcal/mol	$\Delta_f H$(Neutral) kJ/mol	Neutral reference	CAS registry number
$C_9H_8O_2^+$	(8.1) IP is onset of photoelectron band.	(199)	(834)	12	52	*EST	60526-40-1
$C_9H_8O_2S^+$ (2-methyl benzothiophene dioxide)	(≤9.10) IP from 82BEN/DUR.	(≤158)	(≤662)	−52	−216	*EST	6224-55-1
(3-methyl benzothiophene dioxide)	(≤9.20) IP from 82BEN/DUR.	(≤160)	(≤672)	−52	−216	*EST	6406-91-3
$C_9H_8O_3^+$ (o-hydroxycinnamic acid)	(8.50±0.05) IP from 84SCH.	(93)	(389)	−103	−431	84SCH	614-60-8
$C_9H_9^+$		227	951				

From proton affinity of 4-$CH_3C_6H_4C\equiv CH$ (RN 766-97-2) (85MAR/MOD).
PA = 203.8 kcal/mol, 853. kJ/mol.

		(217)	(907)				

$\Delta_f H$(Ion) from appearance potential determination in $C_6H_5C(CH_3)=CH_2$ (85HON/SEG); structure may be indanyl or vinyltropylium.

| $C_9H_9BrO_2S^+$ | ≤8.92 IP from 84CAU/FUR. | (≤174) | (≤727) | −32 | −134 | *EST | |

ION Neutral	Ionization potential eV	$\Delta_f H$(Ion) kcal/mol	$\Delta_f H$(Ion) kJ/mol	$\Delta_f H$(Neutral) kcal/mol	$\Delta_f H$(Neutral) kJ/mol	Neutral reference	CAS registry number
$C_9H_9Cl^+$ (cyclopropyl-chlorobenzene)	(≤8.64)	(≤228)	(≤953)	28	119	*EST	1798-84-1
$C_9H_9ClO_2S^+$ (4-chlorostyryl methyl sulfone)	≤8.94 IP from 84CAU/FUR.	(≤162)	(≤679)	−44	−184	*EST	
$C_9H_9FO_2S^+$ (4-fluorostyryl methyl sulfone)	(≤9.05) IP from 84CAU/FUR.	(≤145)	(≤607)	−64	−266	*EST	
$C_9H_9N^+$ (4-methylbenzyl cyanide)	(9.16±0.06)	(248)	(1037)	36.6	153	*EST	
(2-methylindole)	(7.44±0.015)	(203)	(850)	32	132	*EST	95-20-5
(3-methylindole)	(7.54±0.01)	(205)	(859)	32	132	*EST	83-34-1
(4-methylindole)	(7.60±0.015)	(207)	(865)	32	132	*EST	16096-32-5
(6-methylindole)	(7.54±0.015)	(205)	(859)	32	132	*EST	3420-02-8

Table 1. Positive Ion Table – Continued

ION / Neutral	Ionization potential eV	$\Delta_f H$(Ion) kcal/mol	$\Delta_f H$(Ion) kJ/mol	$\Delta_f H$(Neutral) kcal/mol	$\Delta_f H$(Neutral) kJ/mol	Neutral reference	CAS registry number
$C_9H_9N^+$							
7-methylindole	(7.53±0.015)	(205)	(859)	32	132	*EST	933-67-5
2-methylisoindole	(≤7.12)	(≤214)	(≤895)	50	208	*EST	33804-84-1
$C_9H_9NO^+$							
2,6-dimethylbenzonitrile N-oxide	(8.4) IP is onset of photoelectron band.	(249)	(1042)	55	232	*EST	19111-74-1
4-methoxybenzyl cyanide	(8.77±0.05)	(209)	(876)	7.1	30	*EST	104-47-2
$C_9H_9NO_4S^+$							
4-nitrostyryl methyl sulfone	(≤9.62) IP from 84CAU/FUR.	(≤181)	(≤758)	−41	−170	*EST	
$C_9H_9O^+$							
4-methoxy-α-methylstyrene cation		193	806				
From proton affinity of 4-$CH_3OC_6H_4C\equiv CH$ (RN 768-60-5) (85MAR/MOD). PA = 210.1 kcal/mol, 879. kJ/mol.							
$C_9H_{10}^+$							
β-methylstyrene (cis)	8.15 IP from 78FU/DUN and onset of photoelectron band (81KOB/ARA).	217	907	29	121	69BEN/CRU	766-90-5
β-methylstyrene (trans)	(8.08) IP is onset of photoelectron band (81KOB/ARA).	(214)	(897)	28	117	69BEN/CRU	873-66-5

Table 1. Positive Ion Table – Continued

ION / Neutral	Ionization potential eV	$\Delta_f H$(Ion) kcal/mol	$\Delta_f H$(Ion) kJ/mol	$\Delta_f H$(Neutral) kcal/mol	$\Delta_f H$(Neutral) kJ/mol	Neutral reference	CAS registry number
$C_9H_{10}^+$							
α-methylstyrene (C₆H₅–C(CH₃)=CH₂)	8.19±0.02	216	903	27	113	69BEN/CRU	98-83-9
allylbenzene (C₆H₅–CH₂–CH=CH₂)	8.60 See also: 78FU/DUN.	(236)	(986)	37±2	156±8	81CHI/HYM	300-57-2
cyclopropylbenzene	8.35 IP from 78FU/DUN.	229	957	36±0.2	151±1	82FUC/HAL	873-49-4
2-methylstyrene	8.20±0.02	217	909	28	118	69BEN/CRU	611-15-4
3-methylstyrene	8.15±0.02	215	901	27	115	69BEN/CRU	100-80-1
4-methylstyrene	8.1±0.1 IP is onset of photoelectron band.	(214)	(896)	27	115	69BEN/CRU	622-97-9
indan	(8.3) IP is onset of photoelectron band.	(206)	(862)	15±0.2	61±1	80KUD/KUD	496-11-7
cuneane	(8.47)	(293)	(1225)	97±2	408±8	73ENG/AND2	452-61-9

Table 1. Positive Ion Table - Continued

ION / Neutral	Ionization potential eV	$\Delta_f H$(Ion) kcal/mol kJ/mol		$\Delta_f H$(Neutral) kcal/mol kJ/mol		Neutral reference	CAS registry number

$C_9H_{10}^+$

(8.2) (246) (1030) 57 239 *EST 766-30-3
IP is onset of photoelectron band.

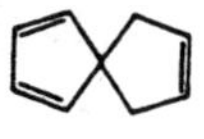

(8.2) (246) (1030) 57 239 *EST 24430-29-3
IP is onset of photoelectron band.

(8.3) (344) (1441) 153 640 *EST 55980-70-6
IP is onset of photoelectron band (82SPA/KOR).

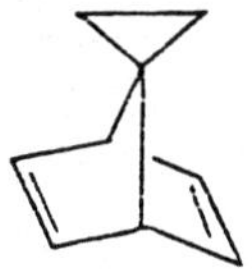

(7.9) (271) (1133) 89 371 *EST 7092-57-1
IP is onset of photoelectron band.

$C_9H_{10}Br^+$

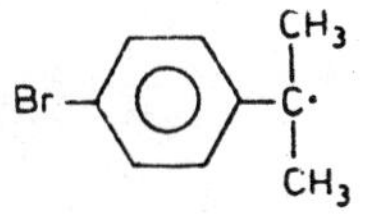

186 777
Value from appearance energy determinations (86ORL/MIS).

$C_9H_{10}BrNO^+$

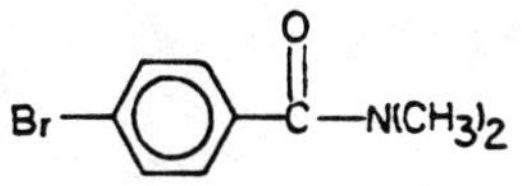

(≤9.09) (≤192) (≤803) −18 −74 *EST 18469-37-9
IP from 85GAL/GER.

$C_9H_{10}Cl^+$

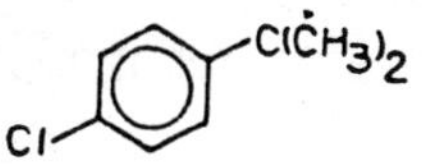

180 753
From proton affinity of 4-$ClC_6H_4C(CH_3)=CH_2$ (RN 1712-70-5). PA = 205.0 kcal/mol, 858. kJ/mol. Value from appearance energy determination (86ORL/MIS) = 171 kcal/mol, 716 kJ/mol.

Table 1. Positive Ion Table - Continued

ION / Neutral	Ionization potential eV	$\Delta_f H$(Ion) kcal/mol	$\Delta_f H$(Ion) kJ/mol	$\Delta_f H$(Neutral) kcal/mol	$\Delta_f H$(Neutral) kJ/mol	Neutral reference	CAS registry number
$C_9H_{10}ClNO^+$ Cl-C6H4-C(O)-N(CH3)2	(≤9.16) IP from 85GAL/GER.	(≤182)	(≤760)	−30	−124	*EST	14062-80-7
$C_9H_{10}F^+$ F-C6H4-C(CH3)2	From proton affinity of 4-FC6H4C(CH3)=CH2 (RN 350-40-3). PA = 206.7 kcal/mol, 865. kJ/mol. Value from appearance energy determinations (86ORL/MIS).	138	579				
$C_9H_{10}FNO^+$ F-C6H4-C(O)-N(CH3)2	(≤9.13) IP from 85GAL/GER.	(≤140)	(≤587)	−70	−294	*EST	24167-56-4
$C_9H_{10}I^+$ I-C6H4-C(CH3)2	Value from appearance energy determinations (86ORL/MIS).	199	833				
$C_9H_{10}N^+$ $(HC\equiv CCH_2)_3NH$	From proton affinity of $(HC\equiv CCH_2)_3N$ (RN 6921-29-5). PA = 220.2 kcal/mol, 921. kJ/mol.	(319)	(1336)				
$C_9H_{10}NO_2^+$ O2N-C6H4-C(CH3)2	Value from appearance energy determinations (86ORL/MIS).	189	789				
$C_9H_{10}N_2^+$ NC-C6H4-N(CH3)2	(7.60) IP is onset of photoelectron band (81MOD/DIS).	(230)	(963)	55	230	*EST	1197-19-9

Table 1. Positive Ion Table - Continued

ION / Neutral	Ionization potential eV	$\Delta_f H$(Ion) kcal/mol	$\Delta_f H$(Ion) kJ/mol	$\Delta_f H$(Neutral) kcal/mol	$\Delta_f H$(Neutral) kJ/mol	Neutral reference	CAS registry number
$C_9H_{10}N_2O_3^+$ 4-nitro-N,N-dimethylbenzamide	(≤9.46) IP from 85GAL/GER.	(≤192)	(≤803)	−26	−110	*EST	7291-01-2
$C_9H_{10}N_4^+$ 2,3,6-trimethylpyrazinopyrazine	(≤8.7) IP from 84GLE/SPA2	(≤261)	(≤1090)	60	251	*EST	6479-02-3
$C_9H_{10}O^+$ 3-phenylpropanal	(8.7±0.2) IP from 84DEN/AUD.	(182)	(763)	−17	−73	84DEN/AUD	1335-10-0
2-methylbenzaldehyde (o-tolualdehyde)	(8.5) IP from 83AUD/MIL.	(176)	(735)	−20	−85	83AUD/MIL	69380-02-5
2′-methylacetophenone	(8.92) IP is onset of photoelectron band. See also: 81RAB/HEL.	(180)	(754)	−26	−107	*EST	577-16-2
3′-methylacetophenone	(8.85) IP is onset of photoelectron band. See also: 81RAB/HEL.	(175)	(734)	−29	−120	*EST	585-74-0
4′-methylacetophenone	(8.85) IP is onset of photoelectron band. See also: 81RAB/HEL, 85GAL/GER.	(176)	(735)	−28	−119	*EST	122-00-9
propiophenone	(9.16) IP from 79MCA/TRA.	(185)	(775)	−26±0.5	−109±2	77PED/RYL	93-55-0

Table 1. Positive Ion Table – Continued

ION / Neutral	Ionization potential eV	$\Delta_f H$(Ion) kcal/mol	kJ/mol	$\Delta_f H$(Neutral) kcal/mol	kJ/mol	Neutral reference	CAS registry number

$C_9H_{10}O^+$

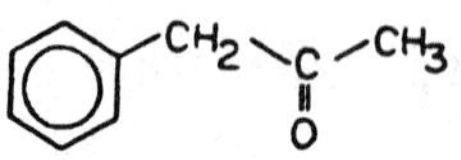	(8.7)	(177)	(741)	−23.6±0.3	−98.6±1.4	77PED/RYL	103-79-7

IP is onset of photoelectron band (78CEN/FRA).

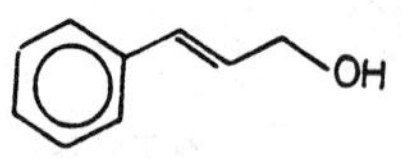	(8.4±0.2)	(186)	(779)	−7	−29	84DEN/AUD	104-54-1

IP from 84DEN/AUD.

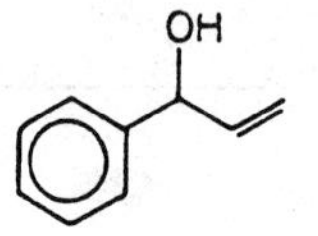	(8.6±0.2)	(192)	(802)	−6	−25	84DEN/AUD	

IP from 84DEN/AUD.

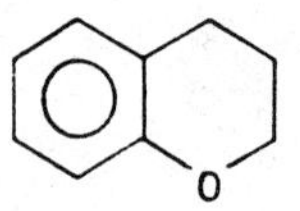	(7.93)	(161)	(673)	−22±1	−92±5	77SHA/GOL	493-08-3

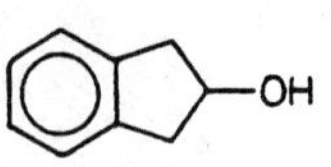	(8.6)	(167)	(697)	−32	−133	83AUD/MIL	4254-29-9

IP from 83AUD/MIL.

$C_9H_{10}O_2^+$

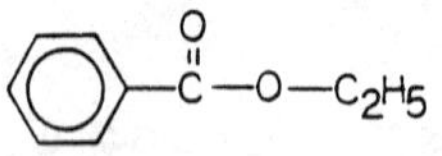	(8.9)	(128)	(537)	−77	−322	*EST	93-89-0

IP is onset of photoelectron band (81MEE/WAH).

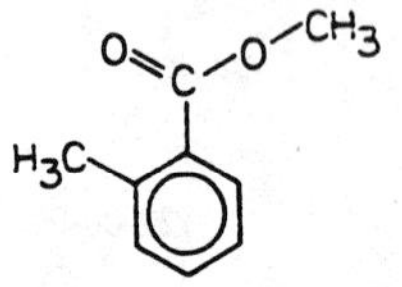	(8.6)	(123)	(514)	−75	−316	*EST	89-71-4

IP is onset of photoelectron band (81MEE/WAH).

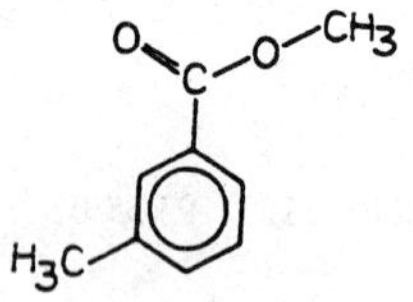	(8.5)	(119)	(499)	−77	−321	*EST	99-36-5

IP is onset of photoelectron band (81MEE/WAH).

Table 1. Positive Ion Table - Continued

ION / Neutral	Ionization potential eV	$\Delta_f H$(Ion) kcal/mol	kJ/mol	$\Delta_f H$(Neutral) kcal/mol	kJ/mol	Neutral reference	CAS registry number
$C_9H_{10}O_2{}^+$							
methyl 4-methylbenzoate	(8.4) IP is onset of photoelectron band (81MEE/WAH).	(117)	(489)	−77	−321	*EST	99-75-2
3-methylphenyl acetate	(8.98±0.2)	(132)	(553)	−75±0.5	−313±2	77PED/RYL	122-46-3
4′-methoxyacetophenone	8.2±0.1 See also: 85GAL/GER.	(132)	(552)	−57	−239	*EST	100-06-1
3′-methoxyacetophenone	(8.53±0.05)	(137)	(573)	−59.8±1	−250±4	*EST	586-37-8
2,6-dimethylbenzoic acid	(8.9) IP from 81MEE/WAH.	(124)	(517)	−81.6±0.4	−341.6±1.7	84COL/JIM	632-46-2
methyl norbornene-2-carboxylate	(≤8.92) IP from 83HOU/RON.	(≤176)	(≤737)	−30	−124	*EST	3604-36-2
bicyclic diketone	(8.2) IP is onset of photoelectron band.	(155)	(649)	−34	−142	*EST	60526-42-3
spiro diketone	(≤9.3) IP from 85GLE/JAH.	(≤191)	(≤799)	−23	−98	*EST	94499-48-6

Table 1. Positive Ion Table − Continued

ION / Neutral	Ionization potential eV	Δ_fH(Ion) kcal/mol	Δ_fH(Ion) kJ/mol	Δ_fH(Neutral) kcal/mol	Δ_fH(Neutral) kJ/mol	Neutral reference	CAS registry number
$C_9H_{10}O_2^+$							
(bicyclic diketone)	(9.14) IP is onset of photoelectron band (85GLE/JAH).	(187)	(784)	−23	−98	*EST	94595-48-9
(bicyclic diketone)	(≤8.85) IP from 78MAR/SCH.	(≤167)	(≤699)	−37	−155	*EST	67843-62-3
(bicyclic diketone)	(≤8.85) IP from 78MAR/SCH.	(≤160)	(≤668)	−44	−186	*EST	67843-61-2
(spiro diketone)	(8.4) IP is onset of photoelectron band.	(243)	(1017)	49	207	*EST	70705-73-6
$C_9H_{10}O_2S^+$							
(PhCH=CH−SO$_2$−CH$_3$)	(8.7) IP from 84CAU/FUR.	(164)	(684)	−37	−155	*EST	
$C_9H_{10}O_2Si^+$							
(methyl(H)silyl difuran)	(8.0) IP is onset of photoelectron band (83ZYK/ERC).	(156)	(651)	−29	−121	*EST	1911-24-6
(methyl(H)silyl difuran isomer)	(8.1) IP is onset of photoelectron band (83ZYK/ERC).	(157)	(661)	−29	−121	*EST	73357-16-1

Table 1. Positive Ion Table — Continued

ION / Neutral	Ionization potential eV	$\Delta_f H$(Ion) kcal/mol	$\Delta_f H$(Ion) kJ/mol	$\Delta_f H$(Neutral) kcal/mol	$\Delta_f H$(Neutral) kJ/mol	Neutral reference	CAS registry number

$C_9H_{11}{}^+$

C₆H₅–Ċ(CH₃)₂

| 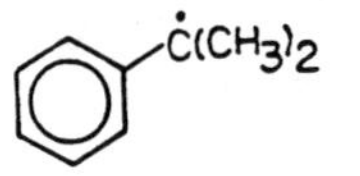 | (6.6) | (186) (196) | (777) (821) | 32.4±1.5 | 135.5±6.3 | 81ROB/STE | 16804-70-9 |

Value at 298 K from proton affinity of $C_6H_5C(CH_3)=CH_2$ (RN 98-83-9).
PA = 207.0 kcal/mol, 866. kJ/mol Value at 0 K from appearance potential measurements (83BRA/BAE, 85BUT/LER). See also: 85DOM/LAK. IP is $\Delta_f H$(Ion) - $\Delta_f H$(Neutral).

4-CH₃–C₆H₄–ĊHCH₃

| 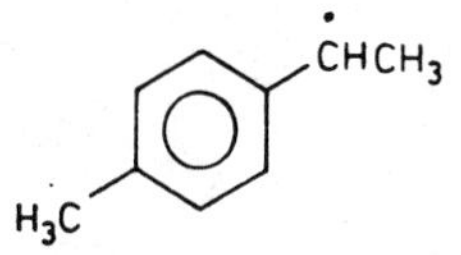 | | 186 | 780 | | | | |

From proton affinity of 4-$CH_3C_6H_4CH=CH_2$ (RN 622-97-9) (84HAR/HOU).
PA = 206.8 kcal/mol, 865. kJ/mol.

$C_9H_{11}Cl^+$

3,5-dimethylbenzyl chloride

| 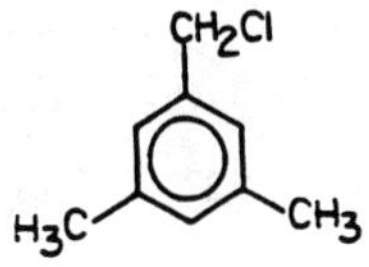 | (8.63±0.03) | (187) | (784) | –12 | –49 | *EST | 2745-54-2 |

$C_9H_{11}N^+$

N-phenylazetidine

| 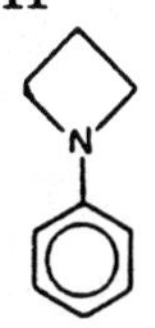 | (7.1) | (222) | (929) | 58 | 244 | *EST | 3334-89-2 |

IP is onset of photoelectron band (82ROZ/HOU2).

1-(4-methylphenyl)aziridine

|  | (≤8.0) | (≤248) | (≤1037) | 63 | 265 | *EST | 38201-24-0 |

IP from 82CRI/LIC.

5,6,7,8-tetrahydroquinoline

| 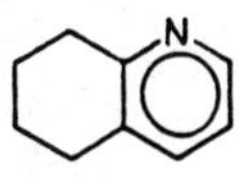 | (≤9.15) | (≤229) | (≤957) | 18 | 74 | *EST | 10500-57-9 |

IP from 79AUE/BOW.

5,6,7,8-tetrahydroisoquinoline

| 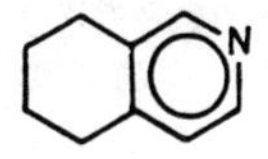 | (≤9.19) | (≤230) | (≤963) | 18 | 76 | *EST | 36556-06-6 |

IP from 79AUE/BOW.

Table 1. Positive Ion Table - Continued

ION / Neutral	Ionization potential eV	$\Delta_f H$(Ion) kcal/mol	$\Delta_f H$(Ion) kJ/mol	$\Delta_f H$(Neutral) kcal/mol	$\Delta_f H$(Neutral) kJ/mol	Neutral reference	CAS registry number
$C_9H_{11}NO^+$							
PhC(O)N(CH$_3$)$_2$	(≤9.04) IP from 85GAL/GER.	(≤186)	(≤777)	−23	−95	*EST	611-74-5
5,5-dimethyl-3-cyanocyclohex-2-enone	(≤9.72) IP from 82PFI/GER.	(≤214)	(≤896)	−10	−42	*EST	65115-71-1
4-(CH$_3$)$_2$N-C$_6$H$_4$-CHO	7.36±0.02 See also: 85GAL/GER.	(160)	(670)	−10	−40	*EST	100-10-7
1-(4-methoxyphenyl)aziridine	(≤7.6) IP from 82CRI/LIC.	(≤210)	(≤880)	35	147	*EST	27347-09-7
$C_9H_{11}NOS^+$							
2,4,6-trimethylphenyl-N=S=O	(8.2) IP is onset of photoelectron band (82LOU/VAN).	(160)	(670)	−29	−121	*EST	
$C_9H_{11}NO_2^+$							
2,4,6-trimethylnitrobenzene	(8.8) IP is onset of photoelectron band.	(200)	(836)	−3	−13	*EST	603-71-4
4-(CH$_3$)$_2$N-C$_6$H$_4$-COOH	(7.1) IP is onset of photoelectron band (81MEE/WAH).	(97)	(405)	−67	−280	*EST	619-84-1
phenylalanine (PhCH$_2$CH(NH$_2$)COOH)	8.4 See also: 83CAN/HAM.	119	497	−74.8±0.3	−312.9±1.2	77PED/RYL	150-30-1

Table 1. Positive Ion Table - Continued

ION / Neutral	Ionization potential eV	$\Delta_f H$(Ion) kcal/mol	$\Delta_f H$(Ion) kJ/mol	$\Delta_f H$(Neutral) kcal/mol	$\Delta_f H$(Neutral) kJ/mol	Neutral reference	CAS registry number
$C_9H_{11}NO_3^+$ (HO-C₆H₄-CH₂CH(NH₂)COOH)	(8.0)	(68)	(286)	−116	−486	*EST	556-03-6

IP is onset of photoelectron band(83CAN/HAM).

| $C_9H_{11}NS^+$ (PhC(=S)N(CH₃)₂) | (≤7.70) | (≤212) | (≤885) | 34 | 142 | *EST | 15482-60-7 |

IP from 82BER/HEN.

| $C_9H_{11}NSe^+$ (PhC(=Se)N(CH₃)₂) | (≤7.33) | (≤220) | (≤919) | 51 | 212 | *EST | 13120-03-1 |

IP from 82BER/HEN.

| $C_9H_{11}O^+$ (4-CH₃-C₆H₄-C(OH)CH₃) | | 128 | 535 | | | | |

From proton affinity of (4-CH₃)C₆H₄COCH₃ (RN 122-00-9). PA = 208.7 kcal/mol, 873. kJ/mol.

| (4-CH₃O-C₆H₄-ĊHCH₃) | | 150 | 628 | | | | |

From proton affinity of (4-CH₃O)C₆H₄CH=CH₂ (RN 637-69-4) (84HAR/HOU). PA = 214.4 kcal/mol, 897. kJ/mol.

| $C_9H_{12}^+$ (cyclononatetraene) | 8.43±0.02 | 228 | 954 | 34 | 141 | 76JEN | 696-86-6 |

| (PhCH₂CH₂CH₃) | 8.72±0.01 | 203 | 849 | 1.9±0.2 | 7.9±0.7 | 77PED/RYL | 103-65-1 |

Value from charge transfer equilibrium constant determinations (78LIA/AUS) is in agreement. See also: 82SEL/HEL.

| (PhCH(CH₃)₂) | 8.73±0.01 | 202 | 846 | 1.0±0.2 | 4.0±1.0 | 77PED/RYL | 98-82-8 |

Value from charge transfer equilibrium constant determinations (78LIA/AUS) is in agreement. See also: 84HOW/GON.

Table 1. Positive Ion Table - Continued

ION / Neutral	Ionization potential eV	$\Delta_f H$(Ion) kcal/mol	$\Delta_f H$(Ion) kJ/mol	$\Delta_f H$(Neutral) kcal/mol	$\Delta_f H$(Neutral) kJ/mol	Neutral reference	CAS registry number

$C_9H_{12}^+$

1,2,3-trimethylbenzene: 8.42±0.02, 192, 803, −2.3±0.2, −9.5±1.1, 77PED/RYL, 526-73-8
From charge transfer equilibrium constant determinations (78LIA/AUS). See: 84HOW/GON.

1,2,4-trimethylbenzene: 8.27±0.01, 187, 784, −3.3±0.2, −13.8±1.0, 77PED/RYL, 95-63-6
IP from 77ROS/DRA, 84HOW/GON.

1,3,5-trimethylbenzene: 8.41±0.01, 190, 795, −3.8±0.3, −15.9±1.3, 77PED/RYL, 108-67-8
Value from charge transfer equilibrium constant determinations (78LIA/AUS) is in agreement. See also: 83CET/LAP, 84HOW/GON.

(8.07), (207), (868), 21, 89, *EST, 29304-70-9
IP from 83BAL/NEU.

8.81±0.03, 229, 959, 26.1±0.3, 109±1, 72KOZ/TIM
IP from 85TUR/PAN.

(8.89), (236), (988), 31, 130, *EST
IP from 85TUR/PAN.

(8.3), (231), (965), 39, 164, *EST, 16529-82-1
IP is onset of photoelectron band.

(≤8.92±0.03), (≤252), (≤1056), 47, 195, *EST, 16529-83-2

Table 1. Positive Ion Table − Continued

ION / Neutral	Ionization potential eV	$\Delta_f H$(Ion) kcal/mol	$\Delta_f H$(Ion) kJ/mol	$\Delta_f H$(Neutral) kcal/mol	$\Delta_f H$(Neutral) kJ/mol	Neutral reference	CAS registry number

$C_9H_{12}^+$

| | (8.2) | (283) | (1185) | 94.1 | 393.7 | 81GOD/SCH | 3105-29-1 |

IP is onset of photoelectron band.

| | ≤8.10 | (≤217) | (≤910) | 31 | 128 | *EST | 766-29-0 |

IP is onset of photoelectron band.

| | (≤9.12) | (≤317) | (≤1325) | 106 | 445 | *EST | 31561-59-8 |

$C_9H_{12}BrO_2^+$

| | (7.75) | (88) | (369) | −91 | −379 | *EST | 5408-07-1 |

IP is onset of photoelectron band (81CAU/GIA).

$C_9H_{12}ClNO_2^+$

| | (≤8.03) | (≤83) | (≤346) | −103 | −429 | *EST | 58921-31-6 |

IP from 81CAU/GIA.

| | (≤7.94) | (≤81) | (≤337) | −103 | −429 | *EST | 56453-93-1 |

IP from 81CAU/GIA.

$C_9H_{12}N^+$

| | | (156) | (651) | | | | |

From proton affinity of 2,3-cyclohexenopyridine (RN 10500-57-9).
PA = (227.7) kcal/mol, (953.) kJ/mol.

| | | (156) | (653) | | | | |

From proton affinity of 3,4-cyclohexenopyridine (RN 36566-06-6).
PA = (227.7) kcal/mol, (953.) kJ/mol.

Table 1. Positive Ion Table - Continued

ION / Neutral	Ionization potential eV	$\Delta_f H$(Ion) kcal/mol	$\Delta_f H$(Ion) kJ/mol	$\Delta_f H$(Neutral) kcal/mol	$\Delta_f H$(Neutral) kJ/mol	Neutral reference	CAS registry number

$C_9H_{12}N^+$

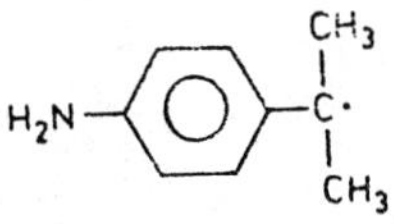

[structure: H_2N–C$_6H_4$–C(CH$_3$)$_2$·]

179   750
From appearance energy determination (86ORL/MIS).

$C_9H_{12}NO^+$

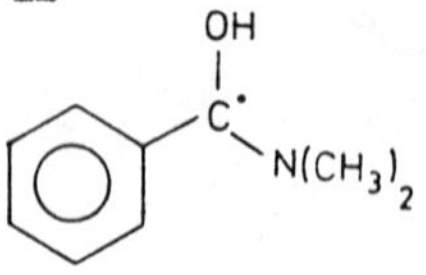

[structure: C$_6H_5$–C(OH)·–N(CH$_3$)$_2$]

(122)   (510)
From proton affinity of $C_6H_5CON(CH_3)_2$ (RN 611-74-5) (86TAF). PA = (221) kcal/mol, (925) kJ/mol.

$C_9H_{12}NO_2{}^+$

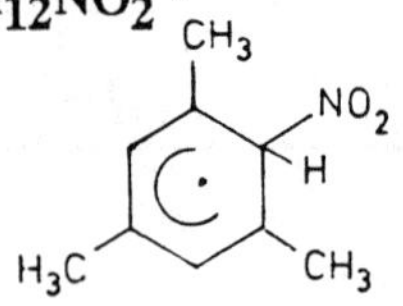

[structure: 2,4,6-trimethyl-nitrobenzene radical cation with H added]

164   687
From proton affinity of 2,4,6-$(CH_3)_3C_6H_2NO_2$ (RN 603-71-4) (84ROL/HOU). PA = 198.4 kcal/mol, 830. kJ/mol.

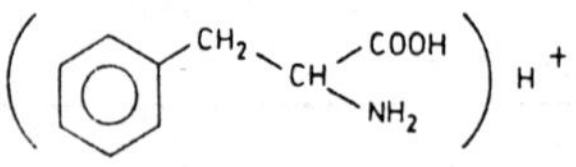

[structure: $(C_6H_5CH_2CH(NH_2)COOH)H^+$]

74   311
From proton affinity of L-$C_6H_5CH_2CH(NH_2)COOH$ (RN 150-30-1). PA = 216.5 kcal/mol, 906. kJ/mol.

$C_9H_{12}NO_3{}^+$

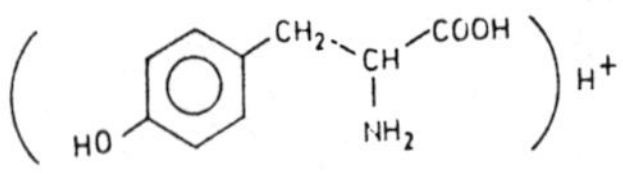

[structure: $(HO$–C_6H_4–$CH_2CH(NH_2)COOH)H^+$]

27   114
From proton affinity of L-tyrosine. PA = 222.3 kcal/mol, 930. kJ/mol.

$C_9H_{12}N_2O_4{}^+$

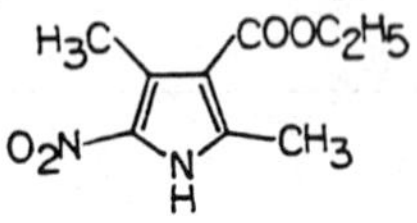

[structure: pyrrole with H$_3$C, COOC$_2$H$_5$, O$_2$N, CH$_3$ substituents]

(≤8.78)   (≤103)   (≤432)   −99   −415   *EST
IP from 81CAU/GIA.

[structure: pyrrole with O$_2$N, CH$_3$, H$_3$C, COOC$_2$H$_5$ substituents]

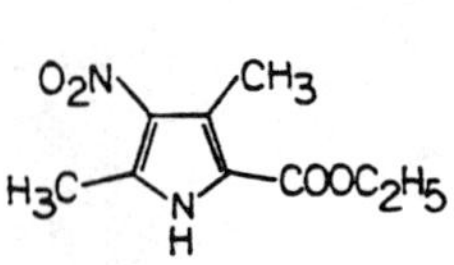

(≤8.76)   (≤103)   (≤430)   −99   −415   *EST
IP from 81CAU/GIA.

Table 1. Positive Ion Table - Continued

ION / Neutral	Ionization potential eV	$\Delta_f H$(Ion) kcal/mol	kJ/mol	$\Delta_f H$(Neutral) kcal/mol	kJ/mol	Neutral reference	CAS registry number
$C_9H_{12}N_2O_6^+$ (uridine)	(9.0)	(142)	(593)	−66	−275	*EST	58-96-8
$C_9H_{12}O^+$							
isopropyl phenyl ether	(≤8.32)	(≤159)	(≤665)	−33	−138	*EST	2741-16-4
2-methyl-1-ethoxybenzene	(8.0) IP from 81BAK/ARM.	(152)	(637)	−32	−135	*EST	614-71-1
2,6-dimethylanisole	8.10±0.02	(161)	(674)	−26	−108	*EST	1004-66-6
$C_9H_{12}OS^+$							
4-methylphenyl ethyl sulfoxide	(≤8.56) IP from 81MOH/JIA.	(≤180)	(≤752)	−18	−74	*EST	6378-07-0
$C_9H_{12}O_2^+$							
3,4-dimethoxytoluene	(≤7.95)	(≤122)	(≤511)	−61	−256	*EST	494-99-5
camphorquinone	(9.0) IP is onset of photoelectron band (80FRO/WES).	(143)	(599)	−64	−269	*EST	38476-46-9

Table 1. Positive Ion Table - Continued

ION Neutral	Ionization potential eV	$\Delta_f H$(Ion) kcal/mol	 kJ/mol	$\Delta_f H$(Neutral) kcal/mol	 kJ/mol	Neutral reference	CAS registry number
$C_9H_{12}O_2S^+$							
PhSO₂-(CH₂)₂CH₃	(9.21±0.03)	(136)	(570)	−76.3±0.5	−319±2	*EST	13596-75-3
(bicyclic sulfone)	(9.1) IP is onset of photoelectron band (84AIT/GOS).	(176)	(735)	−34	−143	*EST	
(bicyclic sulfone isomer)	(9.4) IP is onset of photoelectron band (84AIT/GOS).	(183)	(764)	−34	−143	*EST	
$C_9H_{12}S^+$							
PhS-(CH₂)₂CH₃	(7.81±0.03)	(194)	(811)	14	57	*EST	874-79-3
PhSCH(CH₃)₂	(7.9) IP is onset of photoelectron band.	(195)	(814)	12	52	*EST	3019-20-3
m-CH₃-C₆H₄-SC₂H₅	(≤7.92)	(≤193)	(≤808)	11	44	*EST	34786-24-8
p-CH₃-C₆H₄-SC₂H₅	(8.0) IP is onset of photoelectron band.	(195)	(816)	11	44	*EST	622-63-9
$C_9H_{12}Se^+$							
o-CH₃-C₆H₄-SeC₂H₅	(7.3) IP is onset of photoelectron band (81BAK/ARM).	(193)	(806)	24	102	*EST	37773-42-5

Table 1. Positive Ion Table – Continued

ION / Neutral	Ionization potential eV	$\Delta_f H$(Ion) kcal/mol	$\Delta_f H$(Ion) kJ/mol	$\Delta_f H$(Neutral) kcal/mol	$\Delta_f H$(Neutral) kJ/mol	Neutral reference	CAS registry number
$C_9H_{12}Se^+$							
CH_3–C$_6$H$_4$–SeC$_2$H$_5$	(7.1)	(187)	(784)	24	99	*EST	37773-43-6
	IP is onset of photoelectron band (81BAK/ARM).						
C$_6$H$_5$–SeCH(CH$_3$)$_2$	(≤8.3)	(≤217)	(≤908)	26	107	*EST	22233-89-2
	IP from 81BAK/ARM.						
$C_9H_{13}^+$							
1,3,5-trimethylbenzene H-adduct		161	674				
	From proton affinity of 1,3,5-(CH$_3$)$_3$C$_6$H$_3$ (RN 108-67-8). PA = 200.7 kcal/mol, 840. kJ/mol.						
n-propylbenzene H-adduct		175	733				
	From proton affinity of n-C$_3$H$_7$C$_6$H$_5$ (RN 103-65-1). PA = 192.4 kcal/mol, 805. kJ/mol.						
isopropylbenzene H-adduct		175	730				
	From proton affinity of i-C$_3$H$_7$C$_6$H$_5$ (RN 98-82-8). PA = 192.1 kcal/mol, 804. kJ/mol.						
$C_9H_{13}N^+$							
2,4,6-trimethylaniline	(7.15)	(164)	(686)	−1	−4	*EST	88-05-1
	See also: 83CET/LAP						
3-phenylpropylamine	(≤8.89±0.12)	(≤216)	(≤902)	11	44	*EST	2038-57-5
amphetamine	(8.5)	(203)	(849)	7	29	*EST	300-62-9
	IP is onset of photoelectron band.						

Table 1. Positive Ion Table – Continued

ION / Neutral	Ionization potential eV	$\Delta_f H$(Ion) kcal/mol	kJ/mol	$\Delta_f H$(Neutral) kcal/mol	kJ/mol	Neutral reference	CAS registry number
$C_9H_{13}N^+$							
C₆H₅CH₂CH₂NHCH₃	(8.4) IP is onset of photoelectron band.	(205)	(857)	11	47	*EST	589-08-2
2,6-dimethyl-N-methylaniline	(7.34)	(182)	(763)	13	55	*EST	767-71-5
C₆H₅CH₂N(CH₃)₂	7.69 See also: 81LOG/TAK, 79AUE/BOW.	(197)	(826)	20	84	*EST	103-83-3
2-methyl-N,N-dimethylaniline	7.40±0.02	(195)	(813)	24	99	*EST	609-72-3
3-methyl-N,N-dimethylaniline	7.02 IP from charge transfer equilibrium constant determinations (85LIA/JAC). Reference standard: IP ($C_6H_5N(CH_3)_2$) = 7.12 eV.	(178)	(744)	16	67	*EST	121-72-2
4-methyl-N,N-dimethylaniline	6.93 IP from charge transfer equilibrium constant determinations (85LIA/JAC, 84MAU/NEL); Reference standard: IP($C_6H_5N(CH_3)_2$) = 7.12 eV.	(177)	(739)	17	70	*EST	99-97-8
4-tert-butylpyridine	(≤9.30±0.05)	(≤222)	(≤929)	8	32	*EST	3978-81-2
$C_9H_{13}NO^+$							
4-tert-butylpyridine-N-oxide	(7.8) IP is onset of photoelectron band.	(169)	(705)	−11	−48	*EST	23569-17-7

Table 1. Positive Ion Table – Continued

ION / Neutral	Ionization potential eV	$\Delta_f H$(Ion) kcal/mol	$\Delta_f H$(Ion) kJ/mol	$\Delta_f H$(Neutral) kcal/mol	$\Delta_f H$(Neutral) kJ/mol	Neutral reference	CAS registry number
$C_9H_{13}NO_2^+$							
ethyl 3,5-dimethylpyrrole-2-carboxylate	(≤7.91) IP from 81CAU/GIA.	(≤87)	(≤363)	−96	−400	*EST	
ethyl 2,4-dimethylpyrrole-3-carboxylate	(≤7.95) IP from 81CAU/GIA.	(≤88)	(≤367)	−96	−400	*EST	
$C_9H_{13}N_2O_6^+$							
uridine · H$^+$	From proton affinity of uridine (RN 58-96-8) PA = (208) kcal/mol, (870) kJ/mol.	−66	−275				
$C_9H_{13}O_3^+$							
1,3,5-trimethoxybenzene · H$^+$	From proton affinity of 1,3,5-$C_6H_3(OCH_3)_3$ (RN 621-23-8) PA = 220.6 kcal/mol, 923. kJ/mol.	55	228				
$C_9H_{14}^+$							
1,2,3,4-tetramethylcyclopentadiene	7.8±0.1	(183)	(768)	4	15	*EST	4249-10-9
1,2,5,5-tetramethylcyclopentadiene	7.84±0.05	(183)	(765)	2	9	*EST	4249-11-0
bicyclic C9H14	(8.0) IP is onset of photoelectron band.	(195)	(817)	11	45	81MAI/SCH	17530-61-9
bicyclic C9H14	(8.7) IP is onset of photoelectron band.	(200)	(835)	−1±0.7	−4±3	83JOC/DEK	7124-86-9

Table 1. Positive Ion Table - Continued

ION / Neutral	Ionization potential eV	$\Delta_f H$(Ion) kcal/mol	kJ/mol	$\Delta_f H$(Neutral) kcal/mol	kJ/mol	Neutral reference	CAS registry number
$C_9H_{14}^+$							
(methylenebicyclic)	(≤8.87)	(≤202)	(≤847)	−2±0.7	−9±3	77PED/RYL	2972-20-5
(tricyclic)	(8.3)	(210)	(879)	19	78	*EST	81969-71-3
IP is onset of photoelectron band (82SPA/GLE).							
(tricyclic)	(8.2)	(208)	(869)	19	78	*EST	81969-72-4
IP is onset of photoelectron band (82SPA/GLE).							
(bicyclic)	(≤9.65±0.03)	(≤236)	(≤987)	13	56	73ENG/AND	16526-28-6
(bicyclic)	(8.8)	(211)	(884)	8	35	73ENG/AND	16526-27-5
IP is onset of photoelectron band.							
(spiro)	(8.73)	(208)	(872)	7	30	*EST	873-12-1
(spiro)	(8.3)	(237)	(993)	46	192	*EST	24973-90-8
IP is onset of photoelectron band (82SPA/GLE).							

$C_9H_{14}N^+$

$C_6H_5CH_2N(CH_3)_2 \cdot H^+$ (158)   (660)

From proton affinity of $C_6H_5CH_2N(CH_3)_2$ (RN 103-83-3). PA = 228.1 kcal/mol, 954. kJ/mol.

Table 1. Positive Ion Table - Continued

ION / Neutral	Ionization potential eV	$\Delta_f H$(Ion) kcal/mol	$\Delta_f H$(Ion) kJ/mol	$\Delta_f H$(Neutral) kcal/mol	$\Delta_f H$(Neutral) kJ/mol	Neutral reference	CAS registry number

$C_9H_{14}N^+$

| | | 157 | 658 | | | | |

From proton affinity of 3-$CH_3C_6H_4N(CH_3)_2$ (RN 121-72-2). PA = 224.5 kcal/mol, 939. kJ/mol.

| | | 157 | 656 | | | | |

From proton affinity of 4-$CH_3C_6H_4N(CH_3)_2$ (RN 99-97-8). PA = 225.6 kcal/mol, 944. kJ/mol.

| | | (156) | (651) | | | | |

From proton affinity of $C_6H_5N(CH_3)(C_2H_5)$ (RN 613-97-8). PA = 227.1 kcal/mol, 950. kJ/mol.

| | | (139) | (582) | | | | |

From proton affinity of 2,6-diethylpyridine (RN 935-28-4). PA = 231.1 kcal/mol, 967. kJ/mol.

| | | (145) | (607) | | | | |

From proton affinity of 2-tert-butylpyridine (RN 5944-41-2). PA = (227.4) kcal/mol, (951.) kJ/mol.

| | | (147) | (616) | | | | |

From proton affinity of 4-tert-butylpyridine (RN 3978-81-2). PA = 225.9 kcal/mol, 945. kJ/mol.

$C_9H_{14}O^+$

| | (≤9.07) | (≤160) | (≤669) | −49 | −206 | *EST | 78-59-1 |

IP from 82PFI/GER.

| | (8.6) | (144) | (603) | −54 | −227 | *EST | 13211-15-9 |

IP is onset of photoelectron band (80FRO/WES).

Table 1. Positive Ion Table - Continued

ION / Neutral	Ionization potential eV	$\Delta_f H$(Ion) kcal/mol	$\Delta_f H$(Ion) kJ/mol	$\Delta_f H$(Neutral) kcal/mol	$\Delta_f H$(Neutral) kJ/mol	Neutral reference	CAS registry number
$C_9H_{14}O^+$ (H₃C,H₃C-bicyclic ketone)	(8.75) IP is onset of photoelectron band (80FRO/WES).	(148)	(617)	−54	−227	*EST	38476-45-8
$C_9H_{14}O_2^+$ (H₃C,H₃C-cyclohexenone-OCH₃)	(≤9.35) IP from 82PFI/GER.	(≤138)	(≤576)	−78	−326	*EST	4683-45-8
$C_9H_{14}SSi^+$ (Ph-S-Si(CH₃)₃)	(8.67±0.05)	(166)	(696)	−34	−141	*EST	4551-15-9
$C_9H_{14}Si^+$ (Ph-Si(CH₃)₃)	8.22 IP is onset of photoelectron band (82TRA/RED).	(168)	(704)	−21	−89	*EST	768-32-1
$C_9H_{14}Sn^+$ (Ph-Sn(CH₃)₃)	8.83±0.05	231	965	27±1	113±5	77PED/RYL	934-56-5
$C_9H_{15}N^+$ $(CH_2=CHCH_2)_3N$	(7.5) IP is onset of photoelectron band. See also: 79AUE/BOW.	(226)	(948)	54	224	*EST	102-70-5
(N-cyclohexenyl azetidine)	(≤7.46) IP from 81MUL/PRE2.	(≤197)	(≤826)	25	106	*EST	7326-44-5
(1-cyclopentenyl pyrrolidine)	7.1 IP from 79AUE/BOW.	(164)	(686)	0.2	1	*EST	7148-07-4

Table 1. Positive Ion Table – Continued

ION / Neutral	Ionization potential eV	$\Delta_f H$(Ion) kcal/mol	$\Delta_f H$(Ion) kJ/mol	$\Delta_f H$(Neutral) kcal/mol	$\Delta_f H$(Neutral) kJ/mol	Neutral reference	CAS registry number
$C_9H_{15}N^+$	(7.57±0.02)	(165)	(692)	−9	−38	*EST	281-27-6
$C_9H_{15}NO^+$	(≤8.11) IP from 82PFI/GER.	(≤144)	(≤602)	−43	−180	*EST	701-58-6
$C_9H_{15}N_2O_6^+$		−76	−317				

From proton affinity of 5,6-dihydrouridine (RN 5627-05-4). PA = (208) kcal/mol, (870) kJ/mol.

ION / Neutral	Ionization potential eV	$\Delta_f H$(Ion) kcal/mol	$\Delta_f H$(Ion) kJ/mol	$\Delta_f H$(Neutral) kcal/mol	$\Delta_f H$(Neutral) kJ/mol	Neutral reference	CAS registry number
$C_9H_{16}^+$ (E)-n-C_5H_{11}CH=CHCH=CH_2	(8.44) IP from 81MAS/MOU.	(193)	(809)	−1	−5	*EST	56700-77-7
1-C_9H_{16}	(9.93±0.02)	(244)	(1020)	15±0.7	62±3	79ROG/DAG	3452-09-3
2-C_9H_{16}	9.30±0.02	225	941	11±1	44±3	79ROG/DAG	19447-29-1
3-C_9H_{16}	9.20±0.01	222	930	10±0.7	42±3	79ROG/DAG	20184-89-8
4-C_9H_{16}	(9.17±0.03)	(221)	(927)	10±0.7	42±3	79ROG/DAG	20184-91-2
$(CH_2)_7$(CH=CH) (Z)	(8.81±0.15)	(190)	(795)	−13	−55	78GRE/LIE	933-21-1
(cyclooctane-fused cyclopropane)	≤9.36	≤210	≤878	−6.0±0.3	−25.2±1.4	84WIB/LUP	39124-79-3
(cycloheptane-fused cyclopropane)	(≤9.4)	(≤211)	(≤884)	−5.5±0.2	−23±1	77PED/RYL	286-60-2

Table 1. Positive Ion Table – Continued

ION / Neutral	Ionization potential eV	$\Delta_f H$(Ion) kcal/mol	kJ/mol	$\Delta_f H$(Neutral) kcal/mol	kJ/mol	Neutral reference	CAS registry number
$C_9H_{16}^+$							
(cis-hydrindane)	(9.46±0.06) IP from 80MIK/ZAI.	(187)	(782)	−31±0.5	−131±2	77PED/RYL	3296-50-2
(trans-hydrindane)	(9.46±0.06) IP from 80MIK/ZAI.	(188)	(786)	−30±0.5	−127±2	77PED/RYL	4551-51-3
(bicyclic)	(9.35)	(185)	(774)	−31±1	−128±3	77PAR/STE	280-65-9
(bicyclic)	(9.0) IP is onset of photoelectron band.	(183)	(765)	−25	−103	81MAI/SCH	283-19-2
$C_9H_{16}ClN^+$							
(structure with CH$_3$, CH$_3$, CH$_3$, NCl)	(≤8.34) IP from 82NEL/GAN.	(≤179)	(≤748)	−14	−57	*EST	82666-06-6
$C_9H_{16}N^+$							
$(CH_2=CHCH_2)_3NH$		(189)	(792)				
From proton affinity of $(CH_2=CHCH_2)_3N$ (RN 102-70-5). PA = 230.0 kcal/mol, 962. kJ/mol.							
$C_9H_{16}NO_2^+$							
(tetramethyl piperidone N-oxide)	7.40±0.05	120	499	−51±2	−215±7	77PED/RYL	2896-70-0
$C_9H_{17}N^+$							
cyclohexyl-$N=C(CH_3)_2$	(8.23)	(183)	(763)	−7	−31	*EST	6407-36-9

Table 1. Positive Ion Table – Continued

ION / Neutral	Ionization potential eV	$\Delta_f H$(Ion) kcal/mol	kJ/mol	$\Delta_f H$(Neutral) kcal/mol	kJ/mol	Neutral reference	CAS registry number
$C_9H_{17}N^+$							
N-CH=C(CH₃)₂ piperidine	(≤7.93±0.03) See also: 81MUL/PRE2.	(≤172)	(≤717)	−11	−48	*EST	673-33-6
N-butenyl piperidine	≤7.46 IP from 81MUL/PRE2.	(≤160)	(≤670)	−12	−50	*EST	7182-10-7
N-butenyl pyrrolidine	(≤7.29) IP from 81MUL/PRE2.	(≤164)	(≤688)	−4	−15	*EST	13750-57-7
$C_9H_{17}NO^+$							
2,2,6,6-tetramethyl-4-piperidone	(7.74)	(113)	(474)	−65±1	−273±4	77PED/RYL	826-36-8
$C_9H_{17}NO_2^+$							
2,2,6,6-tetramethyl-1-hydroxy-4-piperidone	(8.51±0.05)	(125)	(523)	−71±1	−298±5	77PED/RYL	3637-11-4
dimethoxy azabicyclic	(≤7.9) IP from 79AUE/BOW.	(≤104)	(≤436)	−78	−326	*EST	
$C_9H_{18}^+$							
1-C_9H_{18}	(9.42±0.01)	(192)	(805)	−25±0.2	−104±1	74ROG/KAN	124-11-8
n-$C_4H_9C(CH_3)=C(CH_3)_2$	(8.14±0.01)	(157)	(655)	−31	−131	*EST	3074-64-4
(E)-$C_3H_7C(CH_3)=C(CH_3)C_2H_5$	(8.08±0.01)	(155)	(649)	−31	−130	*EST	3074-67-7
(Z)-2-C_9H_{18}	(8.90±0.01)	(179)	(748)	−26	−111	*EST	6434-77-1
(E)-2-C_9H_{18}	(8.90±0.01)	(178)	(745)	−27	−114	*EST	6434-78-2

Table 1. Positive Ion Table - Continued

ION Neutral	Ionization potential eV	$\Delta_f H$(Ion) kcal/mol	kJ/mol	$\Delta_f H$(Neutral) kcal/mol	kJ/mol	Neutral reference	CAS registry number
$C_9H_{18}^+$							
(Z)-3-C_9H_{18}	(8.84±0.01)	(178)	(743)	−26	−110	*EST	20237-46-1
(E)-3-C_9H_{18}	8.84±0.01	(177)	(739)	−27	−114	*EST	20063-92-7
(Z)-4-C_9H_{18}	(8.80±0.01)	(177)	(739)	−26	−110	*EST	10405-84-2
(E)-4-C_9H_{18}	(8.81±0.01)	(176)	(736)	−27	−114	*EST	10405-85-3
cycloheptane with two CH₃	(10.21) IP from 81HER/SIC.	(196)	(818)	−40	−167	*EST	13151-51-4
cycloheptane with two CH₃	(10.31) IP from 81HER/SIC.	(196)	(820)	−42	−175	*EST	13151-50-3
cycloheptane with two CH₃	(10.41) IP from 81HER/SIC.	(197)	(824)	−43	−180	*EST	13151-53-6
cyclohexyl-(CH₂)₂CH₃	(9.46) From charge transfer equilibrium constants (82SIE/MAU). Reference standards, IP's of fluorobenzenes.	(172)	(720)	−46.0±0.2	−192.7±0.7	77PED/RYL	1678-92-8
cyclohexyl-CH(CH₃)₂	(9.33) From charge transfer equilibrium constants (82SIE/MAU). Reference standards, IP's of fluorobenzenes. IP from photoionization threshold:9.55 eV.	(168)	(703)	−47	−197	*EST	696-29-7
cyclohexyl with C₂H₅ and CH₃	(9.34) From charge transfer equilibrium constants (82SIE/MAU). Reference standards, IP's of fluorobenzenes.	(169)	(706)	−47±0.5	−195±2	77PED/RYL	4926-90-3
cyclohexyl with C₂H₅ and CH₃	(9.32) From charge transfer equilibrium constants (82SIE/MAU). Reference standards, IP's of fluorobenzenes.	(168)	(704)	−47±0.5	−195±2	77PED/RYL	4923-78-8

Table 1. Positive Ion Table – Continued

ION / Neutral	Ionization potential eV	$\Delta_f H$(Ion) kcal/mol	$\Delta_f H$(Ion) kJ/mol	$\Delta_f H$(Neutral) kcal/mol	$\Delta_f H$(Neutral) kJ/mol	Neutral reference	CAS registry number
$C_9H_{18}^+$							
1,1,2-trimethylcyclohexane	9.39	160	671	−56.2	−235.1	69STU/WES	3073-66-3
	IP from charge transfer equilibrium constants (82SIE/MAU). Reference standards, IP's of fluorobenzenes.						
1,3,5-trimethylcyclohexane	(9.38)	(166)	(695)	−50	−210	*EST	2234-75-5
	IP from 82SIE/MAU.						
n-butylcyclopentane	(9.95±0.03)	(189)	(792)	−40	−168	71ASTM	2040-95-1
$C_9H_{18}N^+$							
(1-(N-piperidino)isobutene)H+		(128)	(534)				
	From proton affinity of 1-(N-piperidino)isobutene (RN 673-33-6). PA = (230.7) kcal/mol, (965.) kJ/mol.						
$C_9H_{18}NO^+$							
2,2,6,6-tetramethylpiperidine-N-oxide	(6.73)	(181)	(757)	26±2	108±10	*EST	2564-83-2
$C_9H_{18}NO_2^+$							
4-hydroxy-2,2,6,6-tetramethylpiperidine-N-oxide	(7.4±0.1)	(101)	(423)	−70±2	−291±9	77PED/RYL	2226-96-2
(3,3-dimethoxy-1-azabicyclo[2.2.2]octane)H+		(56)	(233)				
	From proton affinity of 3,3-dimethoxy-1-azabicyclo[2.2.2]octane. PA = (232) kcal/mol, (971) kJ/mol.						

Table 1. Positive Ion Table - Continued

| ION | Ionization potential | $\Delta_f H$(Ion) | | $\Delta_f H$(Neutral) | | Neutral | CAS registry |
Neutral	eV	kcal/mol	kJ/mol	kcal/mol	kJ/mol	reference	number
$C_9H_{18}N_2^+$							
(bicyclic diamine)	7.0	(166)	(694)	5	19	*EST	
	IP is onset of photoelectron band (85HON/YAN).						
(bicyclic diamine)	7.0	(157)	(656)	−5	−19	*EST	
	IP is onset of photoelectron band (85HON/YAN).						
(N,N′-dimethyl bicyclic diamine)	(6.8)	(164)	(685)	7	29	*EST	14789-33-4
	IP is onset of photoelectron band (81LIV/ROB).						
$C_9H_{18}O^+$							
n-$C_7H_{15}COCH_3$	(9.16)	(130)	(542)	−81±0.5	−340±2	78SEL/STR2	821-55-6
	IP from 81HOL/FIN.						
(n-C_4H_9)$_2$CO	(9.07)	(127)	(530)	−82.4±0.3	−344.9±1.2	77PED/RYL	502-56-7
	IP from 81HOL/FIN.						
(iso-C_4H_9)$_2$CO	9.04±0.03	123	515	−85.5±0.3	−357.6±1.1	77PED/RYL	108-83-8
(t-C_4H_9)$_2$CO	8.67±0.02	117	491	−82.6±0.3	−345.8±1.1	77PED/RYL	815-24-7
$C_9H_{19}^+$							
(n-C_4H_9)(n-C_3H_7)(CH_3)C		133	556			84LOS/HOL	92056-65-0
	From appearance potential measurement (84LOS/HOL).						
$C_9H_{19}N^+$							
(2,2,6,6-tetramethylpiperidine)	7.59	137	572	−38±0.7	−160±3	81SUR/HAC	768-66-1
	IP from 82ROZ/HOU, 79AUE/BOW.						
$C_9H_{19}N_2^+$							
(1,5-diazabicyclo[3.3.3]undecane)		166	696				
	From proton affinity of 1,5-diazabicyclo[3.3.3]undecane. PA = 232.4 kcal/mol, 972. kJ/mol.						

Table 1. Positive Ion Table – Continued

ION / Neutral	Ionization potential eV	$\Delta_f H$(Ion) kcal/mol	$\Delta_f H$(Ion) kJ/mol	$\Delta_f H$(Neutral) kcal/mol	$\Delta_f H$(Neutral) kJ/mol	Neutral reference	CAS registry number
$C_9H_{19}O^+$							
(tert-C_4H_9)$_2$COH		77	320				

From proton affinity of (tert-C_4H_9)$_2$CO (RN 815-24-7). PA = 206.5 kcal/mol, 864. kJ/mol.

$C_9H_{20}^+$							
n-C_9H_{20}	(9.72)	(170)	(709)	−54.5±0.1	−228.4±0.6	74SCO	111-84-2
		(182)	(761)	−42.3±0.1	−177.1±0.6		

IP from charge transfer equilibrium constants (81MAU/SIE, 82LIA). Reference standards, fluorobenzenes.

$C_9H_{20}N^+$							
2,2,6,6-tetramethylpiperidine·H⁺		(96)	(401)				

From proton affinity of 2,2,6,6-tetramethylpiperidine (RN 768-66-1). PA = (231.7) kcal/mol, (969.) kJ/mol.

$C_9H_{21}BO_3^+$							
(n-C_3H_7O)$_3$B	(10.02)	(−26)	(−109)	−257±1	−1076±5	77PED/RYL	688-71-1

$C_9H_{21}N^+$							
(n-C_3H_7)$_3$N	(7.4)	(132)	(552)	−38±0.2	−161±1	*EST	102-69-2

IP is onset of photoelectron band.

tert-C_5H_{11}(tert-C_4H_9)NH	(7.81±0.1)	(134)	(563)	−46±1	−191±4	*EST	58471-09-3

$\Delta_f H$(Ion) predicted from hydrogen affinities of secondary amines: 131 kcal/mol, 548 kJ/mol. Corresponding IP = 7.7 eV.

$C_9H_{22}N^+$							
(n-C_3H_7)$_3$NH		(93)	(390)				

From proton affinity of (n-C_3H_7)$_3$N (RN 102-69-2). PA = 234.0 kcal/mol, 979. kJ/mol.

(tert-C_4H_9)C(CH$_3$)$_2$NH(CH$_3$)$_2$		(97)	(404)				

From proton affinity of (tert-C_4H_9)C(CH$_3$)$_2$N(CH$_3$)$_2$ (RN 3733-36-6). PA = 235.1 kcal/mol, 984. kJ/mol.

(tert-C_5H_{11})(tert-C_4H_9)NH$_2$		(88)	(366)				

From proton affinity of (tert-C_5H_{11})(tert-C_4H_9)NH (RN 58471-09-3). PA = 232.5 kcal/mol, 973. kJ/mol.

$C_9H_{22}OP^+$							
(i-C_3H_7)$_3$POH		17	73				

From proton affinity of (i-C_3H_7)$_3$PO (RN 17513-58-5) (85BOL/HOU). PA = 227.5 kcal/mol, 952. kJ/mol.

Table 1. Positive Ion Table – Continued

ION / Neutral	Ionization potential eV	$\Delta_f H$(Ion) kcal/mol	$\Delta_f H$(Ion) kJ/mol	$\Delta_f H$(Neutral) kcal/mol	$\Delta_f H$(Neutral) kJ/mol	Neutral reference	CAS registry number
$C_9H_{25}N_3OP^+$ $HOP(CH_2N(CH_3)_2)_3$		51	214				

From proton affinity of $OP(CH_2N(CH_3)_2)_3$ (RN 2327-88-0) (85BOL/HOU).
PA = 235. kcal/mol, 983. kJ/mol.

ION / Neutral	IP eV	$\Delta_f H$(Ion) kcal/mol	kJ/mol	$\Delta_f H$(Neutral) kcal/mol	kJ/mol	Neutral reference	CAS registry number
$C_9H_{27}NSi_3^+$ $((CH_3)_3Si)_3N$	(≤8.60)	(≤38)	(≤160)	−160±3	−670±12	77PED/RYL	1586-73-8
$C_{10}BrCo_3O_9^+$	7.8	−81	−337	−261±2	−1090±9	82PIL/SKI	19439-14-6

IP is onset of photoelectron band (81CHE/HAL, 82COS/LLO). See also: 82GRA/TON.

$C_{10}ClCo_3O_9^+$	7.8	−76	−316	−255±2	−1069±10	82PIL/SKI	13682-02-5

IP is onset of photoelectron band (81CHE/HAL, 82GRA/TON, 82COS/LLO).

$C_{10}F_8^+$	8.85	(−88)	(−368)	−292	−1222	*EST	313-72-4

IP from 84HOH/DIS, 82LEV/LIA.

$C_{10}H_4Cl_2O_2^+$	(9.5)	(180)	(754)	−39±2	−162±10	*EST	117-80-6

IP is onset of photoelectron band (80RED/FRE).

$C_{10}H_5ClO_2^+$	(9.6)	(189)	(789)	−33	−137	*EST	1010-60-2

IP is onset of photoelectron band (80RED/FRE).

$C_{10}H_5NO_5W^+$	7.53±0.05	29	121	−145	−606	84ALT/CON2	14586-49-3

Table 1. Positive Ion Table – Continued

ION / Neutral	Ionization potential eV	$\Delta_f H$(Ion) kcal/mol	$\Delta_f H$(Ion) kJ/mol	$\Delta_f H$(Neutral) kcal/mol	$\Delta_f H$(Neutral) kJ/mol	Neutral reference	CAS registry number
$C_{10}H_6^+$							
1,2-diethynylbenzene	(8.69±0.02)	(329)	(1378)	129	540	*EST	21792-52-9
1,3-diethynylbenzene	(8.82±0.02)	(332)	(1390)	129	539	*EST	1785-61-1
1,4-diethynylbenzene	(8.58±±0.02)	(327)	(1368)	129	540	*EST	935-14-8
$C_{10}H_6Cl_2N_2^+$							
4,4'-dichloro-2,2'-bipyridine	(8.8)	(257)	(1074)	54	225	*EST	1762-41-0
	IP is onset of photoelectron band (83DOB/HIL).						
$C_{10}H_6N_2^+$							
	7.7	(309)	(1294)	132	551	*EST	
	IP is onset of photoelectron band (85YAM/HIG).						
	8.3	(323)	(1352)	132	551	*EST	
	IP is onset of photoelectron band (85YAM/HIG).						
$C_{10}H_6O_2^+$							
1,4-naphthoquinone	9.56±0.01	194	811	−27±1	−111±4	77PED/RYL	130-15-4
	See also: 80RED/FRE.						

Table 1. Positive Ion Table — Continued

ION / Neutral	Ionization potential eV	$\Delta_f H$(Ion) kcal/mol	$\Delta_f H$(Ion) kJ/mol	$\Delta_f H$(Neutral) kcal/mol	$\Delta_f H$(Neutral) kJ/mol	Neutral reference	CAS registry number
$C_{10}H_6S^+$ (naphtho-fused S ring)	(8.0) IP is onset of photoelectron band (81BOC/BRA).	(262)	(1096)	77	324	*EST	3968-63-6
$C_{10}H_6SSe^+$ (Se—S peri-naphthalene)	(≤7.14) IP from 81BOC/BRA.	(≤236)	(≤986)	71	297	*EST	64869-35-8
$C_{10}H_6S_2^+$ (S—S peri-naphthalene)	7.14 IP from 81BOC/BRA, 82LEV/LIA.	(222)	(931)	58	242	*EST	209-22-3
$C_{10}H_6Se_2^+$ (Se—Se peri-naphthalene)	(7.06) IP from 81BOC/BRA.	(247)	(1033)	84	352	*EST	36579-71-2
$C_{10}H_7Br^+$ (1-bromonaphthalene)	(8.09) IP from 83KLA/KOV.	(228)	(954)	42	174	*EST	90-11-9
$C_{10}H_7Cl^+$ (1-chloronaphthalene)	(8.13) IP from 83KLA/KOV.	(216)	(904)	29±2	120±10	77PED/RYL	90-13-1
(2-chloronaphthalene)	(8.11) IP from 83KLA/KOV.	(220)	(920)	33±2	137±10	77PED/RYL	91-58-7

Table 1. Positive Ion Table - Continued

ION / Neutral	Ionization potential eV	$\Delta_f H$(Ion) kcal/mol	$\Delta_f H$(Ion) kJ/mol	$\Delta_f H$(Neutral) kcal/mol	$\Delta_f H$(Neutral) kJ/mol	Neutral reference	CAS registry number
$C_{10}H_7F^+$							
1-fluoronaphthalene	(8.15) IP from 83KLA/KOV.	(200)	(835)	12	49	*EST	321-38-0
2-fluoronaphthalene	(8.23) IP from 83KLA/KOV.	(201)	(843)	12	49	*EST	323-09-1
$C_{10}H_7I^+$							
1-iodonaphthalene	(8.03) IP from 83KLA/KOV.	(241)	(1009)	56±2	234±9	77PED/RYL	76279-71-5
$C_{10}H_7NO_2^+$							
1-nitronaphthalene	8.60±0.01 See also: 83KLA/KOV.	234	980	36±1	150±5	77PED/RYL	86-57-7
2-nitronaphthalene	8.65±0.02 IP from 83KLA/KOV, 82LEV/LIA.	(232)	(970)	32	135	*EST	581-89-5
$C_{10}H_7NO_2S^+$							
2-phenylthiazole-4-carboxylic acid	(8.6) IP from 84DEM/SIM.	(168)	(705)	−30	−125	*EST	7113-10-2
2-phenylthiazole-5-carboxylic acid	(8.7) IP from 84DEM/SIM.	(171)	(714)	−30	−125	*EST	10058-38-5

Table 1. Positive Ion Table - Continued

ION / Neutral	Ionization potential eV	$\Delta_f H$(Ion) kcal/mol	$\Delta_f H$(Ion) kJ/mol	$\Delta_f H$(Neutral) kcal/mol	$\Delta_f H$(Neutral) kJ/mol	Neutral reference	CAS registry number
$C_{10}H_8^+$							
(structure)	(8.0)	(238)	(997)	54	225	*EST	34305-47-0
	IP is onset of photoelectron band (81GLE/GUB).						
(structure)	7.41±0.02	240	1004	69±0.7	289±3	77PED/RYL	275-51-4
(structure)	8.14±0.01	223.6	935.8	35.9±0.3	150.4±1	82COL/JIM	91-20-3
$C_{10}H_8CrO_3^+$							
(structure)	6.9±0.2	(108)	(452)	−51±2	−214±9	77PED/RYL	12125-72-3
(structure)	(6.6±0.2)	(61)	(257)	−91±1	−380±5	84ALT/CON	12083-24-8
$C_{10}H_8CrO_4^+$							
(structure)	(6.75±0.1)	(39)	(162)	−117	−489	84ALT/CON	12116-44-8
$C_{10}H_8MoO_3^+$							
(structure)	(7.0)	(111)	(466)	−50±1	−209±7	82PIL/SKI	12125-77-8
	IP is onset of photoelectron band.						

Table 1. Positive Ion Table – Continued

ION / Neutral	Ionization potential eV	$\Delta_f H$(Ion) kcal/mol	$\Delta_f H$(Ion) kJ/mol	$\Delta_f H$(Neutral) kcal/mol	$\Delta_f H$(Neutral) kJ/mol	Neutral reference	CAS registry number
$C_{10}H_8N_2^+$							
2,2'-bipyridine	8.35±0.02 See also: 83DOB/HIL.	(262)	(1095)	69.1±1.2	289.0±5.2	85FAO/AKA	366-18-7
4,4'-bipyridine	(9.10±0.02)	(283)	(1182)	73	304	*EST	553-26-4
2-phenylpyrimidine	(8.65) IP is onset of photoelectron band (84BAR/CAU).	(270)	(1131)	71	296	*EST	3438-48-0
$C_{10}H_8O^+$							
1-naphthol	7.76±0.03	172	719	−7.1±0.2	−29.9±1	77PED/RYL	90-15-3
2-naphthol	7.85±0.05 IP from 85OIK/ABE, 82LEV/LIA.	174	727	−7.2±0.3	−30.3±1.2	77PED/RYL	135-19-3
2,3-benzotropone	(7.9) IP is onset of photoelectron band (84AND/CER).	(230)	(962)	48±2	200±10	77PED/RYL	4759-11-9
$C_{10}H_8O_2^+$							
benzocyclobutenedione dimer	(9.3) IP is onset of photoelectron band (85GLE/JAH).	(241)	(1009)	27	112	*EST	87258-06-8
$C_{10}H_8S^+$							
2-phenylthiophene	(8.06)	(235)	(981)	49	203	*EST	825-55-8

Table 1. Positive Ion Table - Continued

ION / Neutral	Ionization potential eV	$\Delta_f H$(Ion) kcal/mol	$\Delta_f H$(Ion) kJ/mol	$\Delta_f H$(Neutral) kcal/mol	$\Delta_f H$(Neutral) kJ/mol	Neutral reference	CAS registry number
$C_{10}H_9^+$							
(bicyclic H₂ structure)		215	898				
From proton affinity of azulene (RN 275-51-4). PA = 220. kcal/mol, 921. kJ/mol.							
(naphthalene H₂ structure)		207	865				
From proton affinity of naphthalene (RN 91-20-3). PA = 194.7 kcal/mol, 815. kJ/mol.							
$C_{10}H_9BrO^+$							
2-Br-C₆H₄-CH=CH-C(O)CH₃	(8.7±0.05)	(202)	(843)	1	4	79SCH/GRU	
IP from 79SCH/GRU, 80GRU/SCH, 81SCH/GRO.							
3-Br-C₆H₄-CH=CH-C(O)CH₃	(8.9)	(206)	(862)	1	4	*EST	65300-30-3
IP from 81SCH/GRO.							
4-Br-C₆H₄-CH=CH-C(O)CH₃	(8.9)	(206)	(863)	1	4	*EST	3815-31-4
IP from 81SCH/GRO.							
$C_{10}H_9ClO^+$							
2-Cl-C₆H₄-CH=CH-C(O)CH₃	(8.8)	(190)	(795)	-13	-54	*EST	
IP from 80GRU/SCH, 81SCH/GRO.							
3-Cl-C₆H₄-CH=CH-C(O)CH₃	(8.9)	(192)	(805)	-13	-54	*EST	30626-02-9
IP from 81SCH/GRO.							
4-Cl-C₆H₄-CH=CH-C(O)CH₃	(8.7)	(188)	(785)	-13	-54	*EST	30626-03-0
IP from 81SCH/GRO.							

Table 1. Positive Ion Table - Continued

ION / Neutral	Ionization potential eV	$\Delta_f H$(Ion) kcal/mol	$\Delta_f H$(Ion) kJ/mol	$\Delta_f H$(Neutral) kcal/mol	$\Delta_f H$(Neutral) kJ/mol	Neutral reference	CAS registry number
$C_{10}H_9FO^+$							
(2-fluorophenyl methyl ketone structure)	(8.9) IP from 79SCH/GRU, 80GRU/SCH.	(154)	(646)	−51	−213	79SCH/GRU	2143-80-8
$C_{10}H_9IO^+$							
(2-iodobenzylideneacetone)	(8.6±0.05) IP from 81SCH/GRO. See also: 80GRU/SCH.	(214)	(895)	16	65	*EST	
(3-iodobenzylideneacetone)	(8.7±0.05) IP from 81SCH/GRO.	(214)	(893)	13	54	*EST	
(4-iodobenzylideneacetone)	(8.4±0.05) IP from 81SCH/GRO.	(207)	(864)	13	54	*EST	
$C_{10}H_9N^+$							
1-naphthylamine	(7.1) IP is onset of photoelectron band (83KLA/KOV).	(201)	(843)	38±2	158±7	77PED/RYL	134-32-7
2-naphthylamine	7.10±0.02 See also: 83KLA/KOV.	196	821	32±3	136±12	77PED/RYL	91-59-8
(1H-benzo[b]azepine-like)	7.75 IP from 84AND/CER.	(266)	(1115)	88±2	367±7	77PED/RYL	4753-55-3
$C_{10}H_9NO^+$							
1-methyl-2(1H)-quinolinone	(8.0) IP is onset of photoelectron band (81PFI/GUI).	(174)	(727)	−11	−45	*EST	606-43-9

Table 1. Positive Ion Table - Continued

ION / Neutral	Ionization potential eV	$\Delta_f H$(Ion) kcal/mol	$\Delta_f H$(Ion) kJ/mol	$\Delta_f H$(Neutral) kcal/mol	$\Delta_f H$(Neutral) kJ/mol	Neutral reference	CAS registry number
$C_{10}H_9NO_2S^+$	(9.0)	(203)	(849)	−4	−19	*EST	69957-44-4

IP is onset of photoelectron band (84CAU/FUR).

| $C_{10}H_9NO_3^+$ | (9.0) | (198) | (827) | −10 | −41 | 79SCH/GRU | 20766-40-9 |

IP from 80GRU/SCH.

| $C_{10}H_9O^+$ | | (147) | (617) | | | | 45883-76-9 |

$\Delta_f H$(Ion) from appearance potential determinations (79SCH/GRU).

| $C_{10}H_{10}^+$ | 8.15±0.04 | (237) | (990) | 49 | 204 | *EST | 2288-18-8 |

IP from 75DER/JOC, 83DAS/GRO.

| | 8.06±0.07 | (235) | (982) | 49 | 204 | *EST | 16939-57-4 |

IP from 74KOP/SCH, 83DAS/GRO.

| | (8.39) | (243) | (1017) | 50 | 208 | *EST | 31915-94-3 |

| | 8.35±0.02 | (259) | (1082) | 66 | 276 | *EST | 622-76-4 |

IP from 82LEV/LIA, 81ELB/LIE. See also: 74KOP/SCH.

| | (8.6) | (260) | (1089) | 62 | 259 | *EST | 33598-22-0 |

IP from 74KOP/SCH.

Table 1. Positive Ion Table – Continued

ION / Neutral	Ionization potential eV	$\Delta_f H$(Ion) kcal/mol	$\Delta_f H$(Ion) kJ/mol	$\Delta_f H$(Neutral) kcal/mol	$\Delta_f H$(Neutral) kJ/mol	Neutral reference	CAS registry number
$C_{10}H_{10}^+$							
PhCH₂CH₂C≡CH	(8.5) IP from 74KOP/SCH.	(263)	(1099)	67	279	*EST	16520-62-0
benzocyclobutene-CH₂	8.20±0.02 IP from 75DER/JOC, 82LEV/LIA. See also: 83DAS/GRO.	(249)	(1041)	60	250	*EST	3365-26-2
benzocyclobutene isomer	(8.42) IP from 83DAS/GRO.	(258)	(1078)	64	266	*EST	20211-64-7
1-methyl-1-phenylcyclopropane	(8.3) IP from 84BAI/DOM.	(277)	(1160)	86	359	*EST	65051-83-4
1,2-dihydronaphthalene	8.07±0.04 IP from 83DAS/GRO, 74KOP/SCH.	(214)	(897)	28	119	77PED/RYL	447-53-0
1-methylindene	(8.27) IP from 83DAS/GRO.	(226)	(945)	35	147	*EST	767-59-9
3-methylindene	8.05 IP from 83DAS/GRO, 74KOP/SCH.	(219)	(916)	33	139	*EST	767-60-2
1-methyleneindane	(8.00±0.02) See also: 83DAS/GRO.	(220)	(921)	36	149	*EST	1194-56-5

Table 1. Positive Ion Table – Continued

ION / Neutral	Ionization potential eV	$\Delta_f H$(Ion) kcal/mol	kJ/mol	$\Delta_f H$(Neutral) kcal/mol	kJ/mol	Neutral reference	CAS registry number
$C_{10}H_{10}^+$							
(2-methyleneindane)	(8.34)	(230)	(964)	38	159	*EST	68846-65-1
	See also: 83DAS/GRO.						
	(8.26)	(254)	(1065)	64	268	*EST	
	IP from 83DAS/GRO.						
	(8.6)	(252)	(1054)	53.5±1	224±4	86LIE/PAQ	6053-74-3
	IP is onset of photoelectron band.						
	(8.17)	(265)	(1107)	76	319	*EST	1610-51-1
	(8.18)	(266)	(1114)	78	325	*EST	58436-35-4
	8.09±0.05	266	1115	80±0.7	334±3	81MAN/SUN	1005-51-2
	(8.3)	(310)	(1298)	119±5	497±20	73ENG/AND	4572-17-2
	IP is onset of photoelectron band (82HON/EAT).						
$C_{10}H_{10}Br_2Ti^+$							
	≤8.8	(≤158)	(≤663)	−44	−186	*EST	1293-73-8
	IP from 82BOH. See also: 82LEV/LIA.						

Table 1. Positive Ion Table – Continued

ION / Neutral	Ionization potential eV	$\Delta_f H$(Ion) kcal/mol	$\Delta_f H$(Ion) kJ/mol	$\Delta_f H$(Neutral) kcal/mol	$\Delta_f H$(Neutral) kJ/mol	Neutral reference	CAS registry number
$C_{10}H_{10}Cl_2Hf^+$	(8.5)	(93)	(391)	−103±0.7	−429±3	82PIL/SKI	12116-66-4
	IP is onset of photoelectron band.						
$C_{10}H_{10}Cl_2Ti^+$	(8.2)	(126)	(525)	−64±2	−266±9	82PIL/SKI	1271-19-8
	IP is onset of photoelectron band. See also: 82BOH.						
$C_{10}H_{10}Co^+$	(5.2)	(193)	(809)	73±1	307±5	77PED/RYL	1277-43-6
$C_{10}H_{10}Cr^+$	5.50	184	772	58±1	241±5	77PED/RYL	1271-24-5
$C_{10}H_{10}F_3^+$		35	146				
	From proton affinity of 4-CF$_3$C$_6$H$_4$C(CH$_3$)=CH$_2$ (RN 55186-75-9). PA = 199.6 kcal/mol, 835. kJ/mol.						
$C_{10}H_{10}F_3NO^+$	(≤9.38)	(≤31)	(≤128)	−186	−777	*EST	25771-21-5
	IP from 85GAL/GER.						
$C_{10}H_{10}Fe^+$	6.747	213	893	58±0.7	242±3	77PED/RYL	102-54-5
	IP from 82BAR/HEI. See also: 86VON.						

Table 1. Positive Ion Table – Continued

ION / Neutral	Ionization potential eV	$\Delta_f H$(Ion) kcal/mol	$\Delta_f H$(Ion) kJ/mol	$\Delta_f H$(Neutral) kcal/mol	$\Delta_f H$(Neutral) kJ/mol	Neutral reference	CAS registry number
$C_{10}H_{10}Mg^+$ magnesocene	(8.11)	(218)	(913)	31±2	131±8	77PED/RYL	1284-72-6
$C_{10}H_{10}Mn^+$ manganocene	6.55	217	909	66	277	82PIL/SKI	1271-27-8
$C_{10}H_{10}N^+$ NC-C6H4-C(CH3)2		219	915				

From appearance energy determinations (86ORL/MIS).

(1-naphthalenamine)H+ : 187, 781

From proton affinity of 1-naphthalenamine (RN 134-32-7). PA = 216.9 kcal/mol, 907.5 kJ/mol.

ION / Neutral	Ionization potential eV	$\Delta_f H$(Ion) kcal/mol	$\Delta_f H$(Ion) kJ/mol	$\Delta_f H$(Neutral) kcal/mol	$\Delta_f H$(Neutral) kJ/mol	Neutral reference	CAS registry number
$C_{10}H_{10}N_2^+$ 1,5-diaminonaphthalene	(6.74±0.02)	(194)	(815)	39	165	*EST	2243-62-1
1,8-diaminonaphthalene	(6.65±0.02)	(199)	(835)	46	193	*EST	479-27-6
$C_{10}H_{10}Ni^+$ nickelocene	6.2	228	955	85±1	357±5	77PED/RYL	1271-28-9

Table 1. Positive Ion Table - Continued

ION / Neutral	Ionization potential eV	$\Delta_f H$(Ion) kcal/mol	$\Delta_f H$(Ion) kJ/mol	$\Delta_f H$(Neutral) kcal/mol	$\Delta_f H$(Neutral) kJ/mol	Neutral reference	CAS registry number
$C_{10}H_{10}O^+$ benzalacetone	(8.8±0.05) IP from 79SCH/GRU, 81SCH/GRO, 80GRU/SCH.	(197)	(824)	−6	−25	79SCH/GRU	122-57-6
$C_{10}H_{10}OS^+$ 2,3-dimethylbenzothiophene S-oxide	(≤8.40) IP from 82BEN/DUR.	(≤134)	(≤561)	−60	−249	*EST	70445-88-4
$C_{10}H_{10}O_2^+$ o-methylcinnamic acid	(8.65±0.05) IP from 84SCH.	(134)	(563)	−65	−272	84SCH	939-57-1
1,4-diacetylbenzene	(≤9.61) IP from 85GAL/GER.	(≤160)	(≤670)	−61	−257	*EST	1009-61-6
isopropylidene norbornene dione	(8.0) IP is onset of photoelectron band.	(173)	(726)	−11	−46	*EST	60526-38-7
	(≤9.25) IP from 85GLE/JAH.	(≤240)	(≤1002)	26	110	*EST	94499-49-7
	(≤9.02) IP from 85ALB/HEL.	(≤157)	(≤656)	−51	−214	*EST	72590-52-4
$C_{10}H_{10}O_3^+$ o-methoxycinnamic acid	(8.50±0.05) IP from 84SCH.	(102)	(427)	−94	−393	84SCH	1011-54-7

Table 1. Positive Ion Table – Continued

ION / Neutral	Ionization potential eV	$\Delta_f H$(Ion) kcal/mol	$\Delta_f H$(Ion) kJ/mol	$\Delta_f H$(Neutral) kcal/mol	$\Delta_f H$(Neutral) kJ/mol	Neutral reference	CAS registry number
$C_{10}H_{10}O_4^+$ (dimethyl phthalate)	(9.64±0.07)	(66)	(276)	−156.2±4	−654±17	*EST	131-11-3
$C_{10}H_{10}Pb^+$ (plumbocene)	(≤7.55) IP from 82BAX/COW, 82LEV/LIA.	(≤308)	(≤1288)	134	559	85DEW/HOL	1294-74-2
$C_{10}H_{10}Ru^+$ (ruthenocene)	(7.1) IP is onset of photoelectron band.	(102)	(425)	−62	−260	*EST	1287-13-4
$C_{10}H_{10}V^+$ (vanadocene)	(6.4) IP is onset of photoelectron band.	(196)	(822)	49±2	204±10	77PED/RYL	1277-47-0
$C_{10}H_{11}Cl^+$	(≤8.67)	(≤221)	(≤925)	21±1	88±4	*EST	63340-05-6
$C_{10}H_{11}Fe^+$		(214)	(893)				
From proton affinity of Iron, bis(η^5-cyclopentadienyl) (RN 102-54-5). PA = (210) kcal/mol, (879) kJ/mol.							
$C_{10}H_{11}NO^+$	≤8.37 IP is onset of photoelectron band.	(≤238)	(≤998)	45	190	*EST	2904-57-6

Table 1. Positive Ion Table - Continued

ION / Neutral	Ionization potential eV	$\Delta_f H$(Ion) kcal/mol	$\Delta_f H$(Ion) kJ/mol	$\Delta_f H$(Neutral) kcal/mol	$\Delta_f H$(Neutral) kJ/mol	Neutral reference	CAS registry number

$C_{10}H_{11}NO_5W^+$

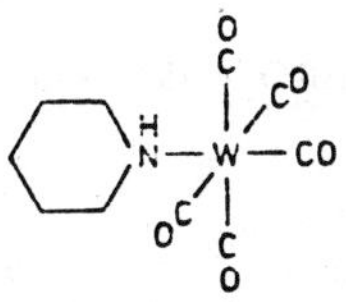

(7.0) (−33) (−140) −195 −815 84ALT/CON2 31082-68-5
IP is onset of photoelectron band.

$C_{10}H_{11}N_2^+$

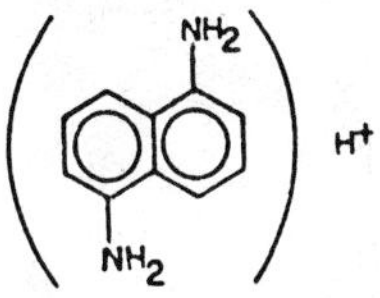

188 787
From proton affinity of 1,8-diaminonaphthalene (RN 479-27-6). PA = 223.8 kcal/mol, 936. kJ/mol.

$C_{10}H_{11}Ni^+$

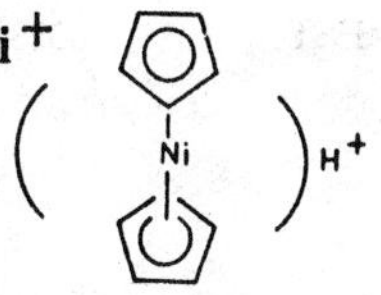

228 954
From proton affinity of Nickel, bis(η^5-cyclopentadinyl) (RN 1271-28-9). PA = 223. kcal/mol, 933. kJ/mol.

$C_{10}H_{11}Ru^+$

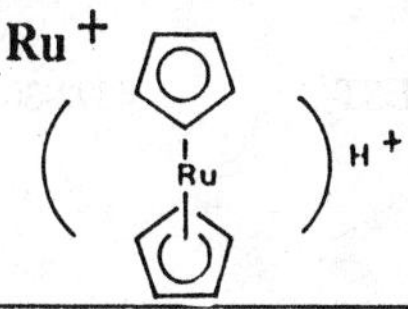

(86) (358)
From proton affinity of Ruthenium, bis(η^5-cyclopentadienyl) (RN 1287-13-4). PA = (218) kcal/mol, (912) kJ/mol.

$C_{10}H_{12}^+$

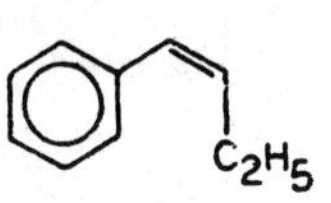

(8.15) (213) (892) 25 106 *EST 1560-09-4
IP from onset of photoelectron band (81KOB/ARA).

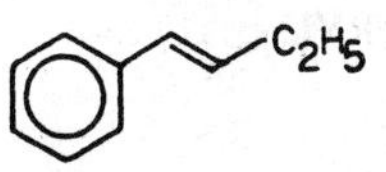

(8.0) (208) (873) 24 101 *EST 1005-64-7
IP from onset of photoelectron band (81KOB/ARA).

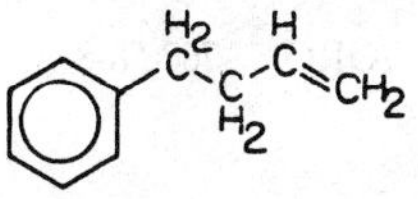

(8.6) (225) (943) 27 113 *EST 768-56-9
IP from 78FU/DUN.

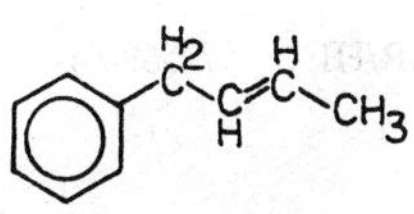

(8.48) (220) (918) 24 100 *EST 935-00-2
IP from 78FU/DUN.

Table 1. Positive Ion Table - Continued

ION Neutral	Ionization potential eV	$\Delta_f H$(Ion) kcal/mol	$\Delta_f H$(Ion) kJ/mol	$\Delta_f H$(Neutral) kcal/mol	$\Delta_f H$(Neutral) kJ/mol	Neutral reference	CAS registry number
$C_{10}H_{12}{}^+$							
(o-methyl-isopropenylbenzene)	(7.78±0.04) See also: 78FU/DUN.	(199)	(832)	19	81	85DAS/GRO	1587-04-8
(2,6-dimethylstyrene)	(8.10±0.02)	(212)	(886)	25	104	*EST	2039-90-9
(1,2,4,5-tetrasubstituted diene)	(7.4) IP from onset of photoelectron band. See also: 82DEW.	(205)	(856)	34	142	*EST	63238-49-3
(phenylcyclobutane)	(8.4) IP from onset of photoelectron band.	(226)	(946)	33	136	*EST	4392-30-7
(1-methyl-1-phenylcyclopropane)	(8.4) IP from onset of photoelectron band.	(223)	(930)	29±1	120±4	*EST	2214-14-4
(tetralin)	8.47 See also: 80MAU.	201	841	6±0.5	24±2	77PED/RYL	119-64-2
(1-methylindan)	(8.47)	(205)	(856)	9	39	85DAS/GRO	767-58-8
(bicyclic dimethylene)	≤8.98	≤268	≤1123	61	257	80MAR/HEL	72569-84-7

Table 1. Positive Ion Table – Continued

ION / Neutral	Ionization potential eV	$\Delta_f H$(Ion) kcal/mol	$\Delta_f H$(Ion) kJ/mol	$\Delta_f H$(Neutral) kcal/mol	$\Delta_f H$(Neutral) kJ/mol	Neutral reference	CAS registry number
$C_{10}H_{12}^+$							
(isopropylidene norbornadiene)	(7.97)	(249)	(1042)	65	273	*EST	36456-22-1
(dihydropentalene)	≤9.00	(≤238)	(≤996)	30.5±1	128±4	86LIE/PAQ	31678-74-7
(dihydrodicyclopentadiene)	(8.79±0.05)	(248)	(1038)	45±2	190±9	80ROT/KLA	77-73-6
	≤8.83±0.03	≤275	≤1152	72	300	80ROT/KLA	6574-77-2
	7.33±0.05	(260)	(1087)	91	380	*EST	36262-33-6
	(8.3)	(298)	(1246)	106	445	*EST	54440-40-3

IP is onset of photoelectron band (82SPA/KOR).

	(≤7.74)	(≤269)	(≤1125)	90	378	*EST	30353-70-9
$C_{10}H_{12}Mo^+$							
(MoH₂(Cp)₂)	(≤6.4±0.1)	(≤220)	(≤920)	72±1	303±6	86SIM/BEA	1291-40-3

Table 1. Positive Ion Table - Continued

ION / Neutral	Ionization potential eV	$\Delta_f H$(Ion) kcal/mol	$\Delta_f H$(Ion) kJ/mol	$\Delta_f H$(Neutral) kcal/mol	$\Delta_f H$(Neutral) kJ/mol	Neutral reference	CAS registry number
$C_{10}H_{12}N_2^+$ (tryptamine)	(7.7) IP is onset of photoelectron band.	(211)	(882)	33	139	*EST	61-54-1
$C_{10}H_{12}N_4^+$ (tetramethylpyrazine-like)	(≤8.6) IP from 84GLE/SPA2.	(≤249)	(≤1040)	50	210	*EST	6479-03-4
$C_{10}H_{12}O^+$ PhCO(CH$_2$)$_2$CH$_3$	9.06±0.02 IP is average of values from 79MCL/TRA and 81DAL/NIB.	178	746	−30.6±0.6	−128.2±2.4	77PED/RYL	495-40-9
Ph-CH(OH)-cyclopropyl	(8.31) IP from 81DAL/NIB.	(186)	(780)	−5	−22	81DAL/NIB	1007-03-0
HOCH$_2$-C(Ph)(cyclopropyl)	(8.35) IP from 81DAL/NIB.	(189)	(790)	−4	−16	81DAL/NIB	31729-66-5
$C_{10}H_{12}O_2^+$ duroquinone	(9.1) IP from 80BOC/KAI, 82LEV/LIA.	(150)	(626)	−60	−252	*EST	527-17-3
	(≤9.0) IP is onset of photoelectron band (85GLE/JAH).	(≤180)	(≤752)	−28	−116	*EST	87305-43-9
	(8.8) IP from 85GLE/JAH.	(175)	(733)	−28	−116	*EST	87305-42-8

Table 1. Positive Ion Table – Continued

ION / Neutral	Ionization potential eV	$\Delta_f H$(Ion) kcal/mol	$\Delta_f H$(Ion) kJ/mol	$\Delta_f H$(Neutral) kcal/mol	$\Delta_f H$(Neutral) kJ/mol	Neutral reference	CAS registry number
$C_{10}H_{12}O_2^+$							
(tricyclic diketone)	(≤9.06) IP from 85ALB/HEL.	(≤130)	(≤542)	−79	−332	*EST	
(spiro diketone)	(9.0±0.02) IP from 84OLI/FLE.	(216)	(904)	9	36	*EST	4893-00-9
$C_{10}H_{12}O_2S^+$							
(p-tolyl vinyl methylsulfone)	(8.3) IP is onset of photoelectron band (84CAU/FUR).	(146)	(613)	−45	−188	*EST	77355-29-4
$C_{10}H_{12}O_2Si^+$							
(dimethyldi(2-furyl)silane)	(≤8.60) IP from 83ZYK/ERC.	(≤151)	(≤633)	−47	−197	*EST	1578-44-5
$C_{10}H_{12}O_3S^+$							
(p-methoxyphenyl vinyl methylsulfone)	(≤8.52) IP from 84CAU/FUR.	(≤123)	(≤516)	−73	−306	*EST	70784-98-4
$C_{10}H_{12}Se^+$							
(2,2-dimethyl-2,3-dihydrobenzo[b]selenophene)	(7.3) IP is onset of photoelectron band (81BAK/ARM).	(144)	(603)	−24	−101	*EST	60096-27-7
$C_{10}H_{12}W^+$							
(bis(cyclopentadienyl)tungsten dihydride)	(6.35±0.2)	(221)	(924)	74±1	311±5	82PIL/SKI	1271-33-6

Table 1. Positive Ion Table - Continued

ION / Neutral	Ionization potential eV	$\Delta_f H$(Ion) kcal/mol	$\Delta_f H$(Ion) kJ/mol	$\Delta_f H$(Neutral) kcal/mol	$\Delta_f H$(Neutral) kJ/mol	Neutral reference	CAS registry number

$C_{10}H_{13}^+$

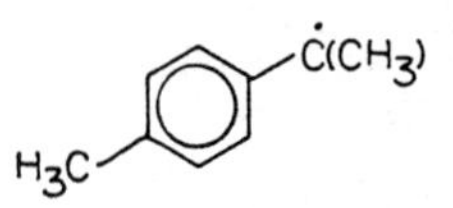

4-CH$_3$-C$_6$H$_4$-Ċ(CH$_3$)$_2$ (with H$_3$C– on ring)

(174) (727)
From proton affinity of 4-CH$_3$C$_6$H$_4$C(CH$_3$)CH$_2$ (RN 1195-32-0). PA = 211.0 kcal/mol, 883. kJ/mol and from appearance energy determination (86ORL/MIS).

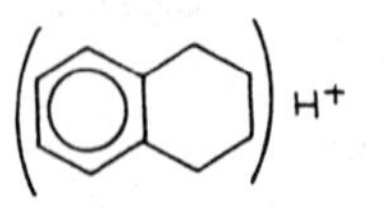

1,2,3,4-tetrahydronaphthalene·H$^+$

177   740
From proton affinity of 1,2,3,4-tetrahydronaphthalene (RN 119-64-2). PA = 194.7 kcal/mol, 815. kJ/mol.

$C_{10}H_{13}Br^+$

4-Br-C$_6$H$_4$-C(CH$_3$)$_3$

| 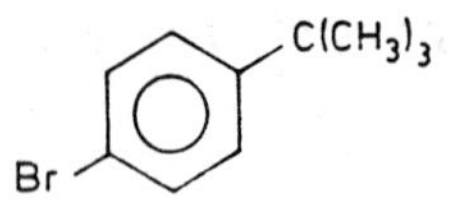 | 8.50±0.02 | (198) | (828) | 2 | 8 | 86ORL/MIS | 3972-65-4 |

IP from 86ORL/MIS, 85BAI/MIS.

$C_{10}H_{13}Cl^+$

4-Cl-C$_6$H$_4$-C(CH$_3$)$_3$

| 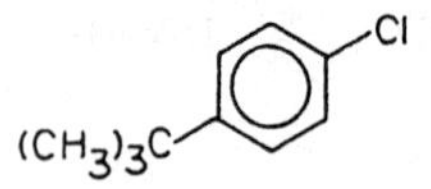 | (8.56±0.02) | (184) | (772) | −13 | −54 | 86ORL/MIS | 3972-56-3 |

IP from 86ORL/MIS. See also: 85BAI/MIS.

$C_{10}H_{13}F^+$

4-F-C$_6$H$_4$-C(CH$_3$)$_3$

| 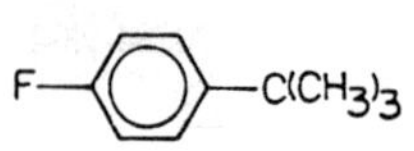 | (8.59) | (146) | (609) | −52 | −219 | 86ORL/MIS | 701-30-4 |

IP from 85ORL/MIS.

$C_{10}H_{13}I^+$

4-I-C$_6$H$_4$-C(CH$_3$)$_3$

| 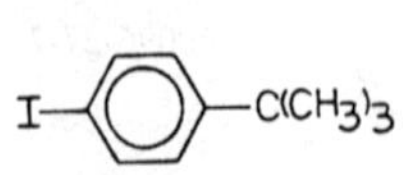 | (8.35±0.02) | (206) | (862) | 14 | 57 | 86ORL/MIS | 35779-04-5 |

IP from 86ORL/MIS. See also: 85BAI/MIS.

$C_{10}H_{13}N^+$

N-phenylpyrrolidine

| 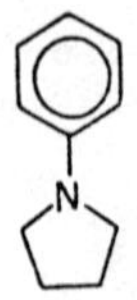 | (6.8) | (185) | (773) | 28 | 117 | *EST | 4096-21-3 |

IP is onset of photoelectron band (82ROZ/HOU2).

GAS-PHASE ION AND NEUTRAL THERMOCHEMISTRY

Table 1. Positive Ion Table – Continued

ION / Neutral	Ionization potential eV	$\Delta_f H$(Ion) kcal/mol	$\Delta_f H$(Ion) kJ/mol	$\Delta_f H$(Neutral) kcal/mol	$\Delta_f H$(Neutral) kJ/mol	Neutral reference	CAS registry number

$C_{10}H_{13}N^+$

| | (7.1) | (222) | (927) | 58 | 242 | *EST | 19198-94-8 |

IP is onset of photoelectron band (82ROZ/HOU2).

| | (≤7.80) | (≤243) | (≤1017) | 63 | 265 | *EST | 78376-89-3 |

IP from 82ROZ/HOU2.

| | (7.6) | (232) | (969) | 56 | 236 | *EST | 78376-90-6 |

IP is onset of photoelectron band (82ROZ/HOU2). See also: 82CRI/LIC.

$C_{10}H_{13}NO^+$

| | ≤7.55 | (≤157) | (≤655) | −17 | −73 | *EST | 2124-31-4 |

| | (≤8.90) | (≤175) | (≤731) | −31 | −128 | *EST | 14062-78-3 |

IP from 85GAL/GER.

$C_{10}H_{13}NO_2^+$

| | (9.2) | (203) | (850) | −9 | −38 | 85ORL/MIS | 3282-56-2 |

IP is onset of photoelectron band (85BAI/MIS2). See also: 86ORL/MIS.

| | ≤8.40 | (≤135) | (≤564) | −59 | −246 | *EST | 7291-00-1 |

IP from 85GAL/GER.

| | (≤8.01±0.06) | (≤136) | (≤570) | −49 | −203 | *EST | 51497-09-7 |

Table 1. Positive Ion Table - Continued

ION Neutral	Ionization potential eV	$\Delta_f H$(Ion) kcal/mol	kJ/mol	$\Delta_f H$(Neutral) kcal/mol	kJ/mol	Neutral reference	CAS registry number

$C_{10}H_{13}O^+$

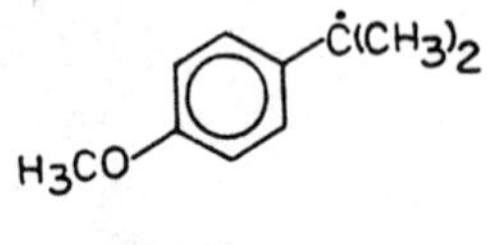

4-CH$_3$O-C$_6$H$_4$-C(CH$_3$)$_2$ 139   580

From proton affinity of 4-CH$_3$OC$_6$H$_4$(C(CH$_3$)=CH$_2$) (RN 1712-69-2).
PA = 217.4 kcal/mol, 910. kJ/mol. Value from appearance energy determination (86ORL/MIS) = 143 kcal/mol, 598 kJ/mol.

$C_{10}H_{14}^+$

Neutral	IP (eV)	kcal/mol	kJ/mol	kcal/mol	kJ/mol	Ref	CAS
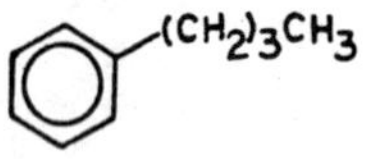 C$_6$H$_5$-(CH$_2$)$_3$CH$_3$	8.69±0.01	198	827	-3.1±0.1	-13.2±0.6	77PED/RYL	104-51-8

IP at 298 K from charge transfer equilibrium constant determinations (78LIA/AUS) is 8.71±0.01 eV.

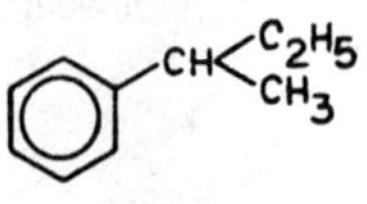 C$_6$H$_5$-CH(C$_2$H$_5$)(CH$_3$)	8.68±0.01	196	820	-4.1±0.2	-17.3±1	77PED/RYL	135-98-8
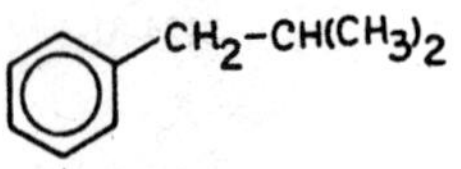 C$_6$H$_5$-CH$_2$-CH(CH$_3$)$_2$	8.68±0.01	195	816	-5.1±0.3	-21.5±1	77PED/RYL	538-93-2
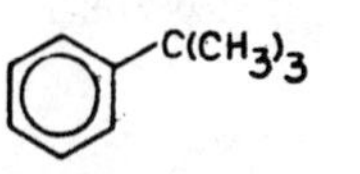 C$_6$H$_5$-C(CH$_3$)$_3$	8.64±0.02	194	812	-5.1±0.3	-21.5±1.2	77PED/RYL	98-06-6

IP is average of values from 80VAN (cited in 83BRA/BAE) and from 84HOW/GON.
IP at 298 K from charge transfer equilibrium constant determinations (78LIA/AUS) is 8.72±0.01 eV. See also: 85DOM/LAK, 85BAI/MIS.

| 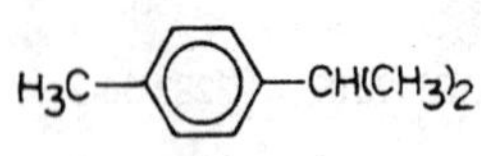 4-H$_3$C-C$_6$H$_4$-CH(CH$_3$)$_2$ | (8.29) | (184) | (772) | -7 | -28 | *EST | 99-87-6 |

IP from 84HOW/GON.

| 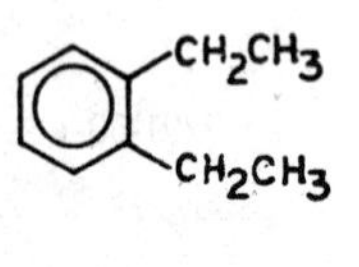 1,2-(CH$_2$CH$_3$)$_2$C$_6$H$_4$ | ≤8.51 | ≤192 | ≤804 | -4±0.2 | -17±1 | 77PED/RYL | 135-01-3 |
| 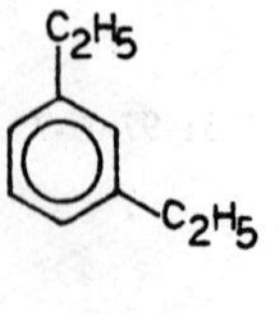 1,3-(C$_2$H$_5$)$_2$C$_6$H$_4$ | (8.49±0.01) | (191) | (798) | -5 | -21 | 77PED/RYL | 141-93-5 |

IP is 298 K value from charge transfer equilibrium constant determinations (78LIA/AUS).

Table 1. Positive Ion Table – Continued

ION / Neutral	Ionization potential eV	$\Delta_f H$(Ion) kcal/mol	$\Delta_f H$(Ion) kJ/mol	$\Delta_f H$(Neutral) kcal/mol	$\Delta_f H$(Neutral) kJ/mol	Neutral reference	CAS registry number

$C_{10}H_{14}{}^+$

1,4-diethylbenzene	8.40 See also: 80GLE/HOP.	189	790	−5±0.5	−20±2	77PED/RYL	105-05-5
1,2,3-trimethyl-...	8.16±0.02 IP from 82LEV/LIA, 84HOW/GON.	180	754	−8	−33	75GOO	488-23-3
1,2,3,5-...	(8.07) IP from 84HOW/GON.	(176)	(738)	−10	−41	75GOO	527-53-7
1,2,4,5-tetramethylbenzene	8.04±0.01 See also: 82CAB/COW, 84HOW/GON.	174	731	−11	−45	75GOO	95-93-2
bicyclic diene	(8.7) IP from 81BIS/GLE.	(248)	(1036)	47	197	*EST	77614-69-8
dispiro compound	(≤8.48)	(≤259)	(≤1085)	64	267	*EST	53143-76-3

$C_{10}H_{14}BeO_4{}^+$

Be(acac)$_2$	(8.1) IP is onset of photoelectron band.	(−90)	(−376)	−277±1	−1158±4	80TEL/RAB	10210-64-7

$C_{10}H_{14}CoO_4{}^+$

Co(acac)$_2$	7.6 IP is onset of photoelectron band (82LEV/LIA, 83KIT/MOR).	(−17)	(−70)	−192±0.5	−803±2	83KAK/GIE	14024-48-7

Table 1. Positive Ion Table - Continued

ION Neutral	Ionization potential eV	$\Delta_f H$(Ion) kcal/mol	$\Delta_f H$(Ion) kJ/mol	$\Delta_f H$(Neutral) kcal/mol	$\Delta_f H$(Neutral) kJ/mol	Neutral reference	CAS registry number
$C_{10}H_{14}CuO_4^+$	(7.2)	(5)	(20)	−161±0.5	−675±2	83KAK/GIE	13395-16-9
\multicolumn{8}{l}{IP is onset of photoelectron band (83KIT/MOR).}
$C_{10}H_{14}Fe^+$	(6.6)	(192)	(803)	40	166	*EST	74910-62-6
\multicolumn{8}{l}{IP is onset of photoelectron band (84GLE/BOH).}
$C_{10}H_{14}FeO_4^+$	(7.50±0.04)	(−25)	(−105)	−198±0.5	−829±2	83KAK/GIE	14024-17-0
$C_{10}H_{14}MnO_4^+$	(8.34±0.05)	(−37)	(−154)	−229±1	−959±4	83KAK/GIE	14024-58-9
$C_{10}H_{14}N^+$		(171)	(716)				
\multicolumn{8}{l}{From proton affinity of N-phenylpyrrolidine (RN 4096-21-3). PA = 224.7 kcal/mol, 940. kJ/mol.}
$C_{10}H_{14}N_2^+$	(≤7.1)	(≤230)	(≤965)	67	280	*EST	82027-08-5
\multicolumn{8}{l}{IP from 82CRI/LIC.}
$C_{10}H_{14}NiO_4^+$	(7.1)	(−31)	(−130)	−195±0.5	−815±2	83KAK/GIE	3264-82-2
\multicolumn{8}{l}{IP is onset of photoelectron band. See also: 83KIT/MOR.}

Table 1. Positive Ion Table - Continued

ION / Neutral	Ionization potential eV	$\Delta_f H$(Ion) kcal/mol	$\Delta_f H$(Ion) kJ/mol	$\Delta_f H$(Neutral) kcal/mol	$\Delta_f H$(Neutral) kJ/mol	Neutral reference	CAS registry number
$C_{10}H_{14}O^+$							
2-tert-butylphenol	(7.9)	(138)	(576)	−44	−186	*EST	88-18-6
	IP is onset of photoelectron band (85BAI/MIS2). See also: 83CET/LAP.						
3-tert-butylphenol	(≤8.40)	(≤145)	(≤608)	−48	−202	*EST	585-34-2
	IP from 83CET/LAP.						
4-tert-butylphenol	(7.8)	(132)	(551)	−48	−202	*EST	98-54-4
	IP is onset of photoelectron band (85BAI/MIS). See also: 83CET/LAP.						
adamantanone	8.62	(144)	(601)	−55±1	−231±5	78ARO/STE	700-58-3
	IP is onset of photoelectron band.						
$C_{10}H_{14}OS^+$							
phenyl tert-butyl sulfoxide	(≤8.50)	(≤171)	(≤717)	−25	−103	*EST	4170-71-2
	IP from 81MOH/JIA.						
$C_{10}H_{14}O_2^+$							
camphorquinone	(9.11)	(119)	(497)	−91	−382	*EST	31211-08-2
	IP is onset of photoelectron band (80FRO/WES).						
$C_{10}H_{14}O_2S^+$							
	(9.15)	(165)	(690)	−46	−192	*EST	
	IP is onset of photoelectron band (84AIT/GOS).						
phenyl tert-butyl sulfone	(≤9.7)	(145)	(607)	−78	−328	*EST	4170-72-3
	IP from 81MOH/JIA.						

Table 1. Positive Ion Table – Continued

ION / Neutral	Ionization potential eV	$\Delta_f H$(Ion) kcal/mol	$\Delta_f H$(Ion) kJ/mol	$\Delta_f H$(Neutral) kcal/mol	$\Delta_f H$(Neutral) kJ/mol	Neutral reference	CAS registry number
$C_{10}H_{14}O_2S^+$	(9.2)	(166)	(696)	−46	−192	*EST	

IP is onset of photoelectron band (84AIT/GOS).

$C_{10}H_{14}O_4Zn^+$	7.8	(−26)	(−107)	−206±2	−860±10	83KAK/GIE	14024-63-6

IP is onset of photoelectron band (83KIT/MOR, 82LEV/LIA).

$C_{10}H_{14}S^+$	8.39±0.05	(197)	(825)	4	15	*EST	3019-19-0
(m-methylphenyl isopropyl sulfide)	(≤8.38)	(≤198)	(≤828)	5	19	*EST	14905-80-7
(p-methylphenyl isopropyl sulfide)	(8.5)	(201)	(839)	5	19	*EST	14905-81-8

IP is onset of photoelectron band.

$C_{10}H_{14}Se^+$	(7.2)	(184)	(772)	18	77	*EST	78805-16-0

IP is onset of photoelectron band (81BAK/ARM).

$C_{10}H_{15}^+$		170	713				

From proton affinity of n-$C_4H_9C_6H_5$ (RN 104-51-8). PA = 192.1 kcal/mol, 804. kJ/mol.

(tert-butylbenzene)H$^+$		167	700				

From proton affinity of tert-$C_4H_9C_6H_5$ (RN 98-06-6). PA = 193.0 kcal/mol, 807. kJ/mol.

Table 1. Positive Ion Table - Continued

ION / Neutral	Ionization potential eV	$\Delta_f H$(Ion) kcal/mol	kJ/mol	$\Delta_f H$(Neutral) kcal/mol	kJ/mol	Neutral reference	CAS registry number
$C_{10}H_{15}^+$							
(1-adamantyl radical)	(6.21)	(159)	(665)	16	66	86KRU/BEA	19740-18-2

$\Delta_f H$(Ion) from chloride and hydride transfer equilibrium constant determinations (85SHA/SHA, 86KRU/BEA); $\Delta_f H$ (Adamantyl chloride) estimated as -43 kcal/mol, -180 kJ/mol.

| | (6.73) | (168) | (704) | 13 | 54 | 86KRU/BEA | |

IP from 86KRU/BEA.

| $C_{10}H_{15}Br^+$ | | | | | | | |
| (1-bromoadamantane) | 9.30±0.06 | (183) | (766) | -31 | -131 | *EST | 768-90-1 |

IP from 84ABE/DEL, 82LEV/LIA.

| (2-bromoadamantane) | (9.31±0.05) | (185) | (772) | -30 | -126 | *EST | 7314-85-4 |

| $C_{10}H_{15}Br_3Ti^+$ | | | | | | | |
| | (8.0) | (30) | (126) | -154 | -646 | *EST | 33151-84-7 |

IP is onset of photoelectron band (84TER/LOU).

| $C_{10}H_{15}Cl^+$ | | | | | | | |
| | (≤9.11) | (≤193) | (≤809) | -17 | -70 | *EST | 4017-64-5 |

IP from 81NES/BAI.

| (1-chloroadamantane) | (9.30) | (171) | (717) | -43 | -180 | *EST | 935-56-8 |

Table 1. Positive Ion Table - Continued

ION / Neutral	Ionization potential eV	$\Delta_f H$(Ion) kcal/mol	$\Delta_f H$(Ion) kJ/mol	$\Delta_f H$(Neutral) kcal/mol	$\Delta_f H$(Neutral) kJ/mol	Neutral reference	CAS registry number

$C_{10}H_{15}ClN^+$

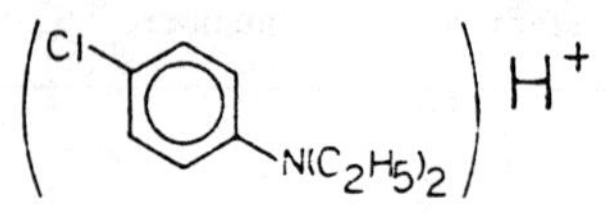

(4-ClC$_6$H$_4$N(C$_2$H$_5$)$_2$)H$^+$ — 142, 594

From proton affinity of 4-ClC$_6$H$_4$N(C$_2$H$_5$)$_2$ (RN 2873-89-4). PA = 225.6 kcal/mol, 944. kJ/mol.

$C_{10}H_{15}Cl_3Ti^+$

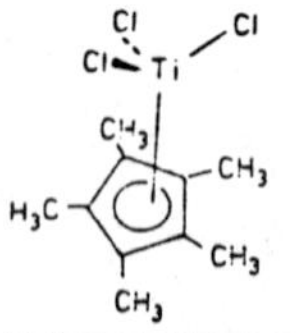

(pentamethylcyclopentadienyl)TiCl$_3$: (8.1), (7), (30), −179, −751, *EST, 12129-06-5

IP is onset of photoelectron band (84TER/LOU).

$C_{10}H_{15}F^+$

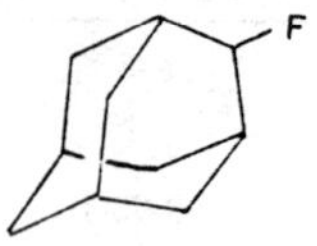

2-fluoroadamantane: (9.46), (141), (592), −77, −321, *EST, 16668-83-0

$C_{10}H_{15}I^+$

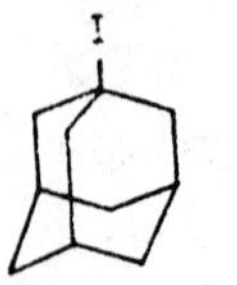

1-iodoadamantane: (8.6), (182), (760), −17, −70, *EST, 768-93-4

IP is onset of photoelectron band (84ABE/DEL).

$C_{10}H_{15}N^+$

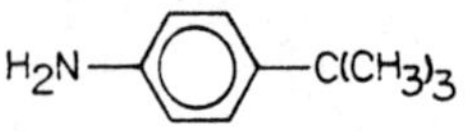

4-tert-butylaniline (H$_2$N-C$_6$H$_4$-C(CH$_3$)$_3$): (7.35±0.02), (165), (691), −4.5, −19, 85ORL/MIS, 769-92-6

IP from 85ORL/MIS. See also: 85BAI/MIS2.

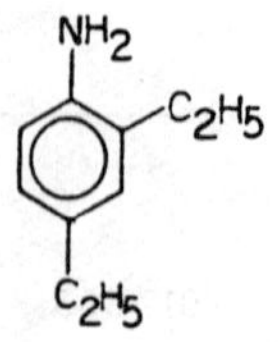

2,4-diethylaniline: (≤7.77), (≤176), (≤736), −3, −14, *EST, 579-66-8

IP from 82ROZ/HOU2.

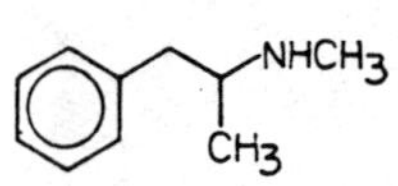

N-methylamphetamine (C$_6$H$_5$CH$_2$CH(CH$_3$)NHCH$_3$): (≤8.60±0.20), (≤199), (≤832), 0.5, 2, *EST, 7632-10-2

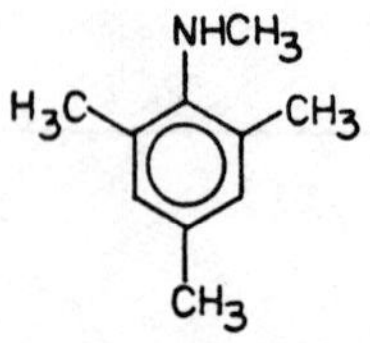

N,2,4,6-tetramethylaniline: (7.22), (171), (717), 5, 20, *EST, 13021-14-2

Table 1. Positive Ion Table – Continued

ION / Neutral	Ionization potential eV	$\Delta_f H$(Ion) kcal/mol	$\Delta_f H$(Ion) kJ/mol	$\Delta_f H$(Neutral) kcal/mol	$\Delta_f H$(Neutral) kJ/mol	Neutral reference	CAS registry number
$C_{10}H_{15}N^+$							
phenethyl-N(CH₃)₂	(7.70±0.05) See also: 81LOG/TAK.	(193)	(807)	15	64	*EST	1126-71-2
C₆H₅-N(C₂H₅)₂	6.98±0.02 IP from charge transfer equilibrium constant determinations; reference standard: IP (C₆H₅N(CH₃)₂ = 7.12eV) (84MAU/NEL, 85LIA/JAC).	(171)	(714)	9.5	40	69BEN/CRU	91-66-7
4-CH₃-C₆H₄-CH₂N(CH₃)₂	(7.61) See also: 81LOG/TAK.	(187)	(784)	12	49	*EST	4052-88-4
2,4-(CH₃)₂-C₆H₃-N(CH₃)₂	(≤7.79) IP from 82ROZ/HOU2.	(≤196)	(≤820)	16	68	*EST	769-53-9
2,6-(CH₃)₂-C₆H₃-N(CH₃)₂	(7.30±0.02) See also: 82ROZ/HOU2.	(190)	(797)	22	93	*EST	769-06-2
3,5-(CH₃)₂-C₆H₃-N(CH₃)₂	(6.95) IP from charge transfer equilibrium constant determinations; reference standard: IP (C₆H₅N(CH₃)₂ = 7.12 eV) (85LIA/JAC).	(168)	(706)	8	35	*EST	4913-13-7
$C_{10}H_{15}NO^+$							
4-CH₃O-C₆H₄-CH₂CH(NH₂)CH₃	(≤8.16±0.06)	(≤184)	(≤768)	−5	−19	*EST	23239-32-9
$C_{10}H_{15}NO_2^+$							
3,4-(CH₃O)₂-C₆H₃-CH₂CH₂NH₂	7.4 IP is onset of photoelectron band (81DOM/EAT, 82LEV/LIA).	(113)	(473)	−58	−241	*EST	120-20-7

Table 1. Positive Ion Table – Continued

ION Neutral	Ionization potential eV	$\Delta_f H$(Ion) kcal/mol	$\Delta_f H$(Ion) kJ/mol	$\Delta_f H$(Neutral) kcal/mol	$\Delta_f H$(Neutral) kJ/mol	Neutral reference	CAS registry number
$C_{10}H_{15}NO_2^+$							
(3,4-dimethyl-5-methyl pyrrole-2-carboxylate ethyl ester)	(≤7.71) IP from 81CAU/GIA.	(≤74)	(≤311)	−103	−433	*EST	2199-46-4
(2,5-dimethyl-3-ethoxycarbonyl-4-methyl pyrrole)	(7.5) IP is onset of photoelectron band (81CAU/GIA).	(69)	(290)	−103	−433	*EST	55770-78-0
(N-ethoxycarbonyl azabicyclic)	(8.0) IP is onset of photoelectron band (81CAR/GAN).	(114)	(479)	−70	−293	*EST	3693-69-4
$C_{10}H_{15}NO_3^+$							
(N-ethoxycarbonyl oxo-azabicyclic)	(8.5) IP is onset of photoelectron band (81CAR/GAN).	(53)	(220)	−143	−600	*EST	37778-51-1
$C_{10}H_{15}N_2O_5^+$							
(thymidine protonated)		(−72)	(−301)				
From proton affinity of thymidine (RN 50-89-5). PA = (208) kcal/mol, (870) kJ/mol.							
$C_{10}H_{15}O_2P^+$							
(phenyl diethylphosphonate)	(8.2) IP is onset of photoelectron band (81ARS/ZVE, 81ZVE/VIL2).	(87)	(362)	−103	−429	*EST	1638-86-4
$C_{10}H_{16}^+$							
(Z,Z)-cyclodecadiene	(≤8.68)	(≤194)	(≤813)	−6	−24	76JEN	1124-79-4
(E,E)-cyclodecadiene	(≤8.05)	(≤184)	(≤769)	−2	−8	76JEN	15840-81-0

Table 1. Positive Ion Table – Continued

ION Neutral	Ionization potential eV	$\Delta_f H$(Ion) kcal/mol	$\Delta_f H$(Ion) kJ/mol	$\Delta_f H$(Neutral) kcal/mol	$\Delta_f H$(Neutral) kJ/mol	Neutral reference	CAS registry number
$C_{10}H_{16}^+$							
(α-pinene)	(8.07)	(193)	(807)	7±0.5	28±2	77PED/RYL	80-56-8
(camphene) IP from 81NES/BAI.	(≤8.86)	(≤198)	(≤827)	−7	−28	77KOZ/BYC	79-92-5
IP is onset of photoelectron band (82SPA/GLE).	(8.5)	(219)	(915)	23	95	*EST	81969-73-5
	9.35±0.05	201.2	841.9	−14.4±1	−60.2±3	71BOY/SAN	6004-38-2
(adamantane)	9.24±0.06	181	759	−31.8±0.3	−132.7±1.3	75CLA/KNO	281-23-2
IP is onset of photoelectron band.	(8.7)	(209)	(875)	9	36	*EST	53764-10-6
	(≤9.17)	(≤211)	(≤882)	−0.7	−3	*EST	24518-94-3
IP is onset of photoelectron band (82SPA/GLE, 82LEV/LIA).	(8.5)	(231)	(967)	35	147	*EST	24029-74-1

Table 1. Positive Ion Table – Continued

ION / Neutral	Ionization potential eV	$\Delta_f H$(Ion) kcal/mol	$\Delta_f H$(Ion) kJ/mol	$\Delta_f H$(Neutral) kcal/mol	$\Delta_f H$(Neutral) kJ/mol	Neutral reference	CAS registry number

$C_{10}H_{16}N^+$

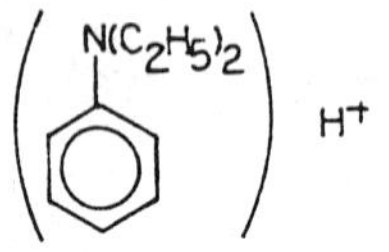

C$_6$H$_5$N(C$_2$H$_5$)$_2$ · H$^+$ — — 148 617 — — — —
From proton affinity of $C_6H_5N(C_2H_5)_2$ (RN 91-66-7). PA = 227.6 kcal/mol, 952. kJ/mol.

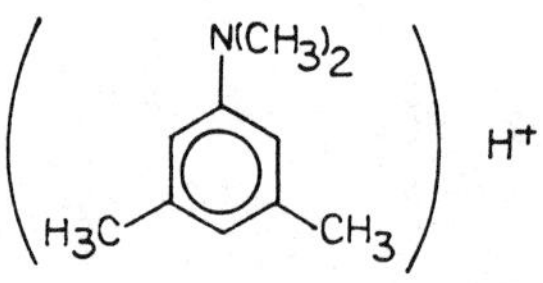

3,5-(CH$_3$)$_2$C$_6$H$_3$N(CH$_3$)$_2$ · H$^+$ — — 147 615 — — — —
From proton affinity of $3,5\text{-}(CH_3)_2C_6H_3N(CH_3)_2$ (RN 4913-13-7). PA = 227.0 kcal/mol, 950. kJ/mol.

$C_{10}H_{16}N_2^+$

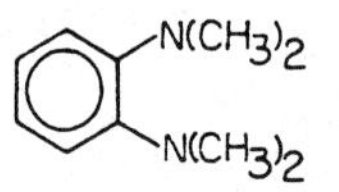

1,2-(N(CH$_3$)$_2$)$_2$C$_6$H$_4$ — (7.1) (200) (836) 36 151 *EST 704-01-8
IP is onset of photoelectron band (81NEL/GRE).

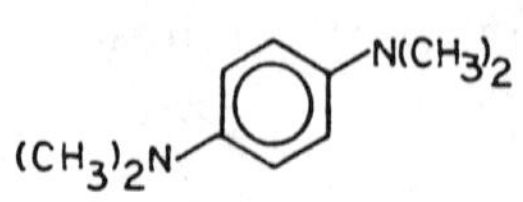

1,4-(N(CH$_3$)$_2$)$_2$C$_6$H$_4$ — 6.20±0.05 164 686 21 88 83MET/ARA 100-22-1

$C_{10}H_{16}N_6S^+$

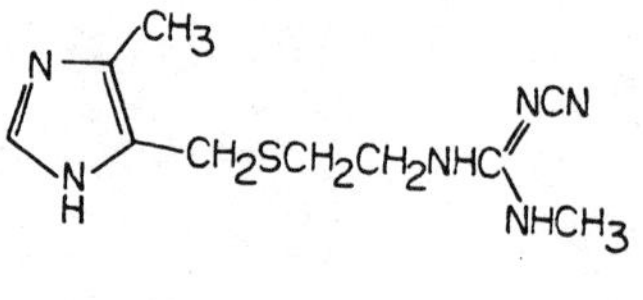

(cimetidine) — (7.7) (249) (1042) 72 300 *EST 51481-61-9
IP is onset of photoelectron band (80KLA/BUT).

$C_{10}H_{16}O^+$

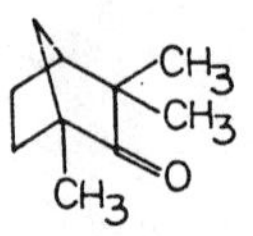

camphor isomer — (8.5) (125) (523) −71 −297 *EST 1195-79-5
IP is onset of photoelectron band (80FRO/WES).

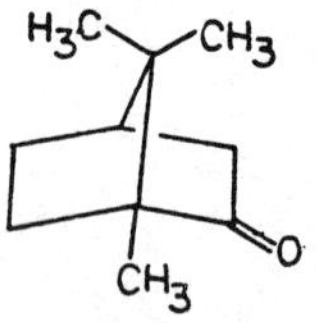

camphor — (8.76±0.03) (138) (578) −64±0.7 −267±3 77STE 76-22-2

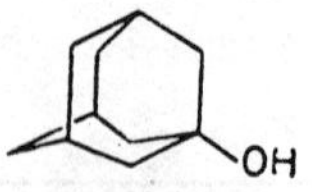

1-adamantanol — (9.09±0.05) (136) (566) −74±0.7 −311±3 78ARO/STE 768-95-6

Table 1. Positive Ion Table – Continued

ION / Neutral	Ionization potential eV	$\Delta_f H$(Ion) kcal/mol	$\Delta_f H$(Ion) kJ/mol	$\Delta_f H$(Neutral) kcal/mol	$\Delta_f H$(Neutral) kJ/mol	Neutral reference	CAS registry number
$C_{10}H_{16}O^+$	(9.09±0.07)	(139)	(578)	−71±1	−299±5	78ARO/STE	700-57-2
$C_{10}H_{16}OS^+$	(8.2) IP is onset of photoelectron band (82PFI/GER).	(147)	(613)	−43	−178	*EST	52735-49-6
$C_{10}H_{16}OSi^+$	(≤8.06) IP from 83HOU/RON.	(≤136)	(≤571)	−49	−207	*EST	68364-22-7
$C_{10}H_{16}O_2^+$	(≤8.87) IP from 82PFI/GER.	(≤117)	(≤489)	−88	−367	*EST	6267-39-6
$C_{10}H_{16}O_2S^+$	≤9.75 IP from 83JIA/MOH.	(≤185)	(≤773)	−40	−168	*EST	
$C_{10}H_{16}O_2S_3^+$	≤8.55 IP from 83JIA/MOH.	(≤152)	(≤637)	−45	−188	*EST	
$C_{10}H_{16}S^+$	≤8.40 IP from 83JIA/MOH.	(≤237)	(≤992)	43	182	*EST	

Table 1. Positive Ion Table – Continued

ION / Neutral	Ionization potential eV	$\Delta_f H$(Ion) kcal/mol	$\Delta_f H$(Ion) kJ/mol	$\Delta_f H$(Neutral) kcal/mol	$\Delta_f H$(Neutral) kJ/mol	Neutral reference	CAS registry number
$C_{10}H_{16}S^+$							
(methylene thiadecalin structure)	(8.22) IP from 80SAR/WOR.	(187)	(782)	−3	−11	*EST	77471-74-0
(methylene thiadecalin isomer)	(8.26) IP from 80SAR/WOR.	(185)	(773)	−6	−24	*EST	77471-73-9
(trimethylnorbornanethione)	(8.13) IP from 80FRO/WES. See also: 82LEV/LIA.	(167)	(697)	−21	−87	*EST	875-06-9
adamantane-SH	(8.6) IP is onset of photoelectron band.	(158)	(663)	−40	−167	*EST	34301-54-7
$C_{10}H_{16}SSi^+$							
PhS-CH$_2$-Si(CH$_3$)$_3$	(≤7.81±0.05)	(≤121)	(≤506)	−59	−248	*EST	17873-08-4
$C_{10}H_{16}S_3^+$							
(dithiolane-thiepane structure)	7.8 IP is onset of photoelectron band (83JIA/MOH).	(219)	(915)	39	162	*EST	
$C_{10}H_{16}Si^+$							
Ph-CH$_2$Si(CH$_3$)$_3$	8.35	(164)	(685)	−29	−121	*EST	770-09-2

Table 1. Positive Ion Table - Continued

ION Neutral	Ionization potential eV	$\Delta_f H$(Ion) kcal/mol kJ/mol		$\Delta_f H$(Neutral) kcal/mol kJ/mol		Neutral reference	CAS registry number
$C_{10}H_{16}Sn^+$							
PhCH₂-Sn(CH₃)₃	8.08±0.05	206	863	20±1	83±6	77PED/RYL	4314-94-7
$C_{10}H_{17}^+$							
(trimethyl-methylenecyclohexene cation)		(148)	(618)				

From proton affinity of 1,5,5-trimethyl-3-methylenecyclohexene (RN 16609-28-2).
PA = (216.1) kcal/mol, (904.) kJ/mol.

ION Neutral	IP eV	$\Delta_f H$(Ion) kcal/mol kJ/mol		$\Delta_f H$(Neutral) kcal/mol kJ/mol		Neutral reference	CAS registry number
$C_{10}H_{17}N^+$							
1-(1-cyclohexenyl)pyrrolidine	7.10	(165)	(689)	1	4	*EST	1125-99-1

See also: 81MUL/PRE2.

| | (7.0) | (138) | (580) | −23±1 | −95±4 | *EST | 1614-92-2 |

IP is onset of photoelectron band.

| | (≤8.67) | (≤198) | (≤828) | −2 | −9 | *EST | 13487-72-4 |

IP from 81NES/BAI.

| $C_{10}H_{17}NO^+$ | | | | | | | |
| | (≤7.88) | (≤143) | (≤596) | −39 | −164 | *EST | 31039-88-0 |

IP from 82PFI/GER.

| $C_{10}H_{17}NO_2^+$ | | | | | | | |
| | (7.9) | (63) | (265) | −119 | −497 | *EST | 39926-11-9 |

IP is onset of photoelectron band (81CAR/GAN).

Table 1. Positive Ion Table - Continued

ION / Neutral	Ionization potential eV	$\Delta_f H$(Ion) kcal/mol	$\Delta_f H$(Ion) kJ/mol	$\Delta_f H$(Neutral) kcal/mol	$\Delta_f H$(Neutral) kJ/mol	Neutral reference	CAS registry number

$C_{10}H_{17}N_2{}^+$

1,2-$(N(CH_3)_2)_2C_6H_4 \cdot H^+$ 167   697

From proton affinity of 1,2-$(N(CH_3)_2)_2C_6H_4$ (RN 704-01-8). PA = 235.2 kcal/mol, 984. kJ/mol.

$C_{10}H_{18}{}^+$

Neutral	IP (eV)	kcal/mol	kJ/mol	kcal/mol	kJ/mol	Ref	CAS
1-$C_{10}H_{18}$	(9.91±0.02)	(239)	(998)	10±.7	42±3	79ROG/DAG	764-93-2
2-$C_{10}H_{18}$	(9.30±0.02)	(220)	(921)	6±0.7	24±3	79ROG/DAG	2384-70-5
3-$C_{10}H_{18}$	9.19±0.01	217	909	5±0.7	22±3	79ROG/DAG	2384-85-2
4-$C_{10}H_{18}$	(9.17±0.02)	(216)	(905)	5±0.7	20±3	79ROG/DAG	2384-86-3
5-$C_{10}H_{18}$	9.13±0.03	(216)	(905)	6	24	*EST	1942-46-7
(tert-C_4H_9)C≡C(tert-C_4H_9)	(9.05±0.01)	(206)	(861)	−3	−13	*EST	17530-24-4

See also: 85ORL/BOG.

Neutral	IP	kcal/mol	kJ/mol	kcal/mol	kJ/mol	Ref	CAS
cyclodecene (E)	(8.80)	(199)	(832)	−4	−17	78GRE/LIE	2198-20-1
cyclodecene (Z)	(8.80)	(196)	(820)	−7	−29	78GRE/LIE	935-31-9
trans-decalin	9.24	170	709	−43.5±0.5	−182.1±2.3	77PED/RYL	493-02-7

From charge transfer equilibrium constant determinations (82SIE/MAU, 85AUS/LIA). Photoionization onset, 9.32 eV (80MIK/ZAI); onset of photoelectron band, 9.26 eV (77BIE/BUR).

cis-decalin	9.26	173	724	−40.4±0.5	−169.1±2.3	77PED/RYL	493-01-6

From charge transfer equilibrium constant determination (85AUS/LIA). Photoionization onset, 9.32 eV (80MIK/ZAI); onset of photoelectron band, 9.26 eV.

Table 1. Positive Ion Table – Continued

ION / Neutral	Ionization potential eV	$\Delta_f H$(Ion) kcal/mol	$\Delta_f H$(Ion) kJ/mol	$\Delta_f H$(Neutral) kcal/mol	$\Delta_f H$(Neutral) kJ/mol	Neutral reference	CAS registry number

$C_{10}H_{18}NO^+$

(cis-3-amino-2-twistanol · H$^+$)
$\Delta_f H$(Ion) = (95) kcal/mol, (396) kJ/mol.
From proton affinity of cis-3-amino-2-twistanol. PA = 224.0 kcal/mol, 937. kJ/mol.

(trans-3-amino-2-twistanol isomer 1 · H$^+$)
$\Delta_f H$(Ion) = (95) kcal/mol, (398) kJ/mol.
From proton affinity of trans-3-amino-2-twistanol (isomer 1). PA = 221.5 kcal/mol, 927. kJ/mol.

(trans-3-amino-2-twistanol isomer 2 · H$^+$)
$\Delta_f H$(Ion) = (97) kcal/mol, (405) kJ/mol.
From proton affinity of trans-3-amino-2-twistanol (isomer 2). PA = 220.0 kcal/mol, 920. kJ/mol.

$C_{10}H_{18}OSi^+$

norbornenyl-OSi(CH$_3$)$_3$

IP	$\Delta_f H$(Ion) kcal/mol	kJ/mol	$\Delta_f H$(Neutral) kcal/mol	kJ/mol	Ref.	CAS
(≤8.09)	(≤101)	(≤424)	−85	−357	*EST	57722-40-4

IP from 83HOU/RON.

$C_{10}H_{18}O_2S_3^+$

IP	$\Delta_f H$(Ion) kcal/mol	kJ/mol	$\Delta_f H$(Neutral) kcal/mol	kJ/mol	Ref.	CAS
(≤9.55)	(≤132)	(≤552)	−88	−369	*EST	

IP from 83JIA/MOH.

$C_{10}H_{18}O_4Si^+$

furyl-Si(OC$_2$H$_5$)$_3$

IP	$\Delta_f H$(Ion) kcal/mol	kJ/mol	$\Delta_f H$(Neutral) kcal/mol	kJ/mol	Ref.	CAS
(8.0)	(−26)	(−110)	−211	−882	*EST	55811-52-4

IP is onset of photoelectron band (83ZYK/ERC).

$C_{10}H_{18}S^+$

IP	$\Delta_f H$(Ion) kcal/mol	kJ/mol	$\Delta_f H$(Neutral) kcal/mol	kJ/mol	Ref.	CAS
≤8.35	(≤188)	(≤787)	−5	−19	*EST	

IP from 83JIA/MOH.

Table 1. Positive Ion Table - Continued

ION / Neutral	Ionization potential eV	$\Delta_f H$(Ion) kcal/mol	$\Delta_f H$(Ion) kJ/mol	$\Delta_f H$(Neutral) kcal/mol	$\Delta_f H$(Neutral) kJ/mol	Neutral reference	CAS registry number
$C_{10}H_{18}S_2^+$	7.65	(204)	(853)	27	115	*EST	
	IP is onset of photoelectron band (83JIA/MOH).						
$C_{10}H_{18}S_3^+$	7.8	172	719	−8	−34	*EST	
	IP is onset of photoelectron band (83JIA/MOH).						
$C_{10}H_{19}N^+$	(≤7.61)	(≤161)	(≤673)	−14	−61	*EST	21086-43-1
	IP from 81MUL/PRE2.						
	(6.94±0.09)	(166)	(695)	6	25	*EST	31023-92-4
	IP is onset of photoelectron band.						
$C_{10}H_{20}^+$							
1-$C_{10}H_{20}$	9.42±0.01	188	786	−29.5±0.5	−123.3±2	77PED/RYL	872-05-9
	See also: 81HOL/FIN.						
(Z)-$C_{10}H_{20}$	8.90±0.01	(174)	(727)	−32	−132	*EST	20348-51-0
(E)-2-$C_{10}H_{20}$	8.90±0.01	(173)	(724)	−32	−135	*EST	20063-97-2
(Z)-3-$C_{10}H_{20}$	8.83±0.01	(172)	(721)	−31	−131	*EST	19398-86-8
(E)-3-$C_{10}H_{20}$	8.83±0.01	(171)	(717)	−32	−135	*EST	19150-21-1
(Z)-4-$C_{10}H_{20}$	8.78±0.01	(171)	(716)	−31	−131	*EST	19398-88-0
(E)-4-$C_{10}H_{20}$	8.78±0.01	(170)	(712)	−32	−135	*EST	19398-89-1
(Z)-5-$C_{10}H_{20}$	8.77±0.01	(171)	(715)	−31	−131	*EST	7433-78-5
(E)-5-$C_{10}H_{20}$	8.76±0.01	(170)	(710)	−32	−135	*EST	7433-56-9
(tert-C_4H_9)$_2$C=CH$_2$	(8.79±0.01)	(164)	(688)	−38	−161	*EST	5857-68-1
n-C_5H_{11}C(CH$_3$)=C(CH$_3$)$_2$	(8.13±0.01)	(151)	(633)	−36	−152	*EST	19781-18-1

Table 1. Positive Ion Table - Continued

ION Neutral	Ionization potential eV	$\Delta_f H$(Ion) kcal/mol	kJ/mol	$\Delta_f H$(Neutral) kcal/mol	kJ/mol	Neutral reference	CAS registry number
$C_{10}H_{20}{}^+$							
$C_4H_9C(C_2H_5)=C(CH_3)_2$	(8.10±0.01)	(151)	(630)	−36	−151	*EST	19780-61-1
(tert-C_4H_9)$CH_2C(CH_3)=C(CH_3)_2$	(8.10±0.01)	(146)	(610)	−41	−172	*EST	33175-59-6
(Z)-(t-C_4H_9)CH=CH(t-C_4H_9)	8.69±0.01	(171)	(717)	−29±0.7	−121±3	*EST	692-47-7
(E)-(t-C_4H_9)CH=CH(t-C_4H_9)	8.74±0.01	162	677	−40±0.7	−166±3	79FUC/PEA	692-48-8
cyclodecane	(9.5)	(182)	(762)	−36.9±0.4	−154.3±1.5	77PED/RYL	293-96-9

IP is onset of photoelectron band (77BIE/BUR).

cyclohexyl-$(CH_2)_3CH_3$	9.41	166	695	−50.9±0.2	−213.0±1	77PED/RYL	1678-93-9

From charge transfer equilibrium constant determinations (82SIE/MAU); reference standard, fluorobenzenes. Threshold determinations give IP at 0 K of 9.57 eV.

| cyclohexyl-CH(C_2H_5)(CH_3) | 9.23 | (164) | (686) | −49 | −205 | *EST | 7058-01-7 |

From charge transfer equilibrium constant determinations (82SIE/MAU); reference standard, fluorobenenes. Threshold determinations give IP at 0 K of 9.51 eV.

| cyclohexyl-$CH_2CH(CH_3)_2$ | (9.54±0.03) | (171) | (716) | −49 | −204 | *EST | 1678-98-4 |
| 1-methyl-4-isopropylcyclohexane | 9.32 | 160 | 668 | −55±0.7 | −231±3 | 77PED/RYL | 99-82-1 |

From charge transfer equilibrium constant determinations (82SIE/MAU); reference standard fluorobenzenes.

| cyclopentyl-$(CH_2)_4CH_3$ | (9.91±0.05) | (184) | (767) | −45 | −189 | 71ASTM | 3741-00-2 |

Table 1. Positive Ion Table – Continued

ION / Neutral	Ionization potential eV	Δ_fH(Ion) kcal/mol	Δ_fH(Ion) kJ/mol	Δ_fH(Neutral) kcal/mol	Δ_fH(Neutral) kJ/mol	Neutral reference	CAS registry number

$C_{10}H_{20}N^+$

| | | (142) | (592) | | | | |

From proton affinity of 1-azabicyclo[3.3.3]undecane (RN 31023-92-4). PA = 230.1 kcal/mol, 963. kJ/mol.

$C_{10}H_{20}NO^+$

| | | 67 | 280 | | | | |

From proton affinity of 4-aminodecahydro-3-naphthalenol. PA = 222.1 kcal/mol, 929. kJ/mol.

$C_{10}H_{20}N_2^+$

| | (7.60) | (195) | (814) | 19 | 81 | *EST | 60678-75-3 |

Reported values of IP's of hydrazines determined by threshold measurements are usually significantly higher than the adiabatic value because of the large geometry change associated with ionization. See also: 84NEL.

| | (7.89) | (189) | (791) | 7 | 30 | *EST | 6130-94-5 |

See also: 84NEL.

$C_{10}H_{20}O_5^+$

| | (8.9) | (14) | (60) | −191±0.5 | −799±2 | 82BYS/MAN | 33100-27-5 |

IP is onset of photoelectron band. See also: 83BAK/ARM.

$C_{10}H_{20}SSi_2^+$

| | (7.8) | (126) | (526) | −54 | −227 | *EST | 17906-71-7 |

IP is onset of photoelectron band (83VES/HAR).

$C_{10}H_{21}N^+$

| | (7.23) | (127) | (530) | −40 | −167 | *EST | 79-55-0 |

IP from 82ROZ/HOU.

Table 1. Positive Ion Table – Continued

ION / Neutral	Ionization potential eV	$\Delta_f H$(Ion) kcal/mol	$\Delta_f H$(Ion) kJ/mol	$\Delta_f H$(Neutral) kcal/mol	$\Delta_f H$(Neutral) kJ/mol	Neutral reference	CAS registry number
$C_{10}H_{21}O_5^+$		–49	–205				

From proton affinity of 1,4,7,10,13-pentaoxacyclopentadecane (15-Crown-5) (RN 33100-27-5). PA = 223.6 kcal/mol, 936. kJ/mol.

$C_{10}H_{22}^+$							
n-$C_{10}H_{22}$	9.65	163	682	–59.6±0.2	–249.5±0.9	77PED/RYL	124-18-5
		176	*738*	*–46.1±0.2*	*–192.7±0.9*		

From charge transfer equilibrium constants (81MAU/SIE). Reference standards, fluorobenzenes.

$C_{10}H_{22}N_2O_3^+$	(≤8.4)	(≤88)	(≤369)	–105	–441	*EST	31249-95-3

IP from 83BAK/ARM.

$C_{10}H_{23}N^+$							
n-$C_{10}H_{21}NH_2$	(8.63±0.05)	(148)	(619)	–51	–214	*EST	2016-57-1

See also: 79AUE/BOW.

$C_{10}H_{23}O^+$							
(n-C_5H_{11})$_2$OH		72	304				

From proton affinity of (n-C_5H_{11})$_2$O (RN 693-65-2) (86SAN/BAL, 85HOU/ROL). PA = 203.5 kcal/mol, 851. kJ/mol.

$C_{10}H_{24}N^+$							
n-$C_{10}H_{21}NH_3$		(94)	(393)				

From proton affinity of n-$C_{10}H_{21}NH_2$. PA = (220.7) kcal/mol, (923.) kJ/mol.

$C_{10}H_{24}N_2^+$							
(n-C_3H_7)$_2$NN(C_2H_5)$_2$	(≤7.87)	(≤191)	(≤797)	9	38	*EST	52598-09-1

Reported values of IP's of hydrazines determined by threshold measurements are usually significantly higher than the adiabatic value because of the large geometry change associated with ionization. See also: 84NEL.

(n-C_4H_9)$_2$NN(CH_3)$_2$	(≤7.96)	(≤191)	(≤801)	8	33	*EST	60678-67-3

Reported values of IP's of hydrazines determined by threshold measurements are usually significantly higher than the adiabatic value because of the large geometry change associated with ionization. See also: 84NEL.

Table 1. Positive Ion Table — Continued

ION / Neutral	Ionization potential eV	$\Delta_f H$(Ion) kcal/mol	$\Delta_f H$(Ion) kJ/mol	$\Delta_f H$(Neutral) kcal/mol	$\Delta_f H$(Neutral) kJ/mol	Neutral reference	CAS registry number
$C_{10}H_{24}N_4^+$	(7.7)	(182)	(761)	4.3±0.8	18.0±3.3	83CLA/COR	295-37-4
IP is onset of photoelectron band (83BAK/ARM).							
$C_{10}H_{24}O_2Si_3^+$	(≤9.36)	(≤−70)	(≤−293)	−286	−1196	*EST	76795-95-4
IP from 81KHV/ZYK.							
$C_{10}H_{25}N_2^+$ $(CH_3)_2NH(CH_2)_6N(CH_3)_2$		106	444				
From proton affinity of $(CH_3)_2N(CH_2)_6N(CH_3)_2$ (RN 111-18-2). PA = 245. kcal/mol, 1023. kJ/mol.							
$C_{10}H_{30}N_5Ta^+$ $Ta(N(CH_3)_2)_5$	(6.5)	(93)	(390)	−57±4	−237±15	82TN270	
IP is onset of photoelectron band.							
$C_{10}H_{30}O_3Si_4^+$ $[(CH_3)_3SiOSi(CH_3)_2]_2O$	(≤10.24)	(≤−226)	(≤−947)	−462±5	−1935±23	77PED/RYL	141-62-8
IP from 82ERM/KIR.							
$C_{10}H_{30}Si_4^+$ $n\text{-}Si_4(CH_3)_{10}$	7.29±0.01	32	135	−136±6	−568±24	77PED/RYL	865-76-9
$C_{10}MnO_{10}Re^+$ $MnRe(CO)_{10}$	8.22±0.01	(−184)	(−769)	−373	−1562	*EST	14693-30-2
$C_{10}Mn_2O_{10}^+$ $Mn_2(CO)_{10}$	(7.7)	(−201)	(−842)	−379±1	−1585±5	82CON/ZAF	10170-69-1
IP is onset of photoelectron band. See also: 81MIC/SVE.							
$C_{10}O_{10}Re_2^+$ $Re_2(CO)_{10}$	(7.8)	(−193)	(−806)	−373±3	−1559±11	83ALT/CON	14285-68-8
IP is onset of photoelectron band. See also: 81MIC/SVE.							
$C_{11}H_5MnO_5^+$	(8.22±0.05)	(49)	(203)	−141±0.2	−590±1	82CON/ZAF	13985-77-8

Table 1. Positive Ion Table – Continued

ION / Neutral	Ionization potential eV	Δ_fH(Ion) kcal/mol	Δ_fH(Ion) kJ/mol	Δ_fH(Neutral) kcal/mol	Δ_fH(Neutral) kJ/mol	Neutral reference	CAS registry number
$C_{11}H_7BrO_2^+$	(9.25)	(182)	(760)	−31	−132	*EST	3129-39-3
IP is onset of photoelectron band (80RED/FRE).							
$C_{11}H_7ClF_2O_2S^+$	(≤8.90)	(≤35)	(≤146)	−170	−713	*EST	
IP from 84AND/CER.							
$C_{11}H_7ClO_2^+$	(9.4)	(180)	(754)	−37	−153	*EST	17015-99-5
IP is onset of photoelectron band (80RED/FRE).							
$C_{11}H_7N^+$ (1-naphthonitrile)	(8.59)	(244)	(1021)	46	192	*EST	86-53-3
IP from 83KLA/KOV.							
$C_{11}H_7N^+$ (2-naphthonitrile)	(8.56)	(243)	(1016)	45	190	*EST	613-46-7
IP is onset of photoelectron band (83KLA/KOV).							
$C_{11}H_8^+$	(8.03)	(289)	(1210)	104	435	73BIL/CHO	286-85-1
IP from 80SCH/SCH.							
$C_{11}H_8Br_2^+$	(7.85)	(252)	(1053)	71	296	*EST	15825-93-1
IP is onset of photoelectron band (84AND/CER).							

Table 1. Positive Ion Table - Continued

ION Neutral	Ionization potential eV	$\Delta_f H$(Ion) kcal/mol	kJ/mol	$\Delta_f H$(Neutral) kcal/mol	kJ/mol	Neutral reference	CAS registry number
$C_{11}H_8CrO_5^+$	(7.02±0.1)	(4)	(18)	−157	−659	84ALT/CON	12125-87-0
$C_{11}H_8F_2^+$	(8.19±0.03) IP from 84AND/CER.	(149)	(625)	−39	−165	*EST	61997-36-2
$C_{11}H_8FeO_3^+$	(7.3) IP is onset of photoelectron band (82LEV/LIA, 80BOH/GLE).	(132)	(554)	−36±3	−150±13	82PIL/SKI	12093-05-9
$C_{11}H_8MoO_4^+$	(7.0) IP is onset of photoelectron band.	(81)	(339)	−80±3	−336±11	82PIL/SKI	12146-37-1
$C_{11}H_8O^+$	(8.3) IP is onset of photoelectron band.	(210)	(879)	19	78	*EST	4443-91-8
	(8.33) IP from 83KLA/KOV.	(199)	(834)	7	30	*EST	66-77-3
	(8.0) IP is onset of photoelectron band (84AND/CER).	(218)	(914)	34	142	*EST	36628-80-5

Table 1. Positive Ion Table – Continued

ION / Neutral	Ionization potential eV	$\Delta_f H$(Ion) kcal/mol	$\Delta_f H$(Ion) kJ/mol	$\Delta_f H$(Neutral) kcal/mol	$\Delta_f H$(Neutral) kJ/mol	Neutral reference	CAS registry number
$C_{11}H_8O_2^+$							
2-methyl-1,4-naphthoquinone	(9.3)	(184)	(770)	−30	−127	*EST	58-27-5

IP is onset of photoelectron band (80RED/FRE).

| | (8.29) | (138) | (577) | −53.3±0.2 | −223.1±0.9 | 77PED/RYL | 86-55-5 |

1-naphthoic acid; IP from 83KLA/KOV.

| | (8.26) | (135) | (564) | −55.6±0.4 | −232.5±1.6 | 77PED/RYL | 93-09-4 |

2-naphthoic acid; IP from 83KLA/KOV.

| $C_{11}H_8S_2^+$ | (7.3) | (237) | (991) | 69 | 287 | *EST | 204-14-8 |

IP is onset of photoelectron band (81BOC/BRA).

| $C_{11}H_9^+$ | (7.35±0.1) | (229) | (962) | 60 | 253 | 82MCM/GOL | 7419-60-5 |

1-naphthylmethyl radical. Appearance potential results (see 85HON/SEG and references cited therein) lead to value for $\Delta_f H$(Ion) of ~252 kcal/mol, ~1054 kJ/mol.

| $C_{11}H_9F^+$ | (8.10±0.03) | (203) | (848) | 16 | 66 | *EST | 72791-63-0 |

IP is onset of photoelectron band (84AND/CER).

| $C_{11}H_9F_3O^+$ | (9.0±0.05) | (39) | (164) | −168 | −704 | 79SCH/GRU | 76293-37-3 |

IP from 79SCH/GRU, 80GRU/SCH, 81SCH/GRO.

| | (9.1±0.05) | (42) | (175) | −168 | −703 | *EST | |

IP from 81SCH/GRO.

Table 1. Positive Ion Table – Continued

ION / Neutral	Ionization potential eV	$\Delta_f H$(Ion) kcal/mol	kJ/mol	$\Delta_f H$(Neutral) kcal/mol	kJ/mol	Neutral reference	CAS registry number
$C_{11}H_9F_3O^+$							
(F₃C-C₆H₄-O-CH=CH-CH₃ type structure)	(9.1±0.05) IP from 81SCH/GRO.	(42)	(175)	−168	−703	*EST	
$C_{11}H_{10}^+$							
1-methylnaphthalene	7.85 IP from 82LEV/LIA, 83KLA/KOV.	208	870	27±0.5	113±2	74SAB/CHA	90-12-0
1-methyl benzocycloheptene isomer	(≤7.26±0.03)	(≤227)	(≤953)	60	253	*EST	769-31-3
1-methyl benzocycloheptene isomer	(≤7.33±0.03)	(≤229)	(≤960)	60	253	*EST	17647-77-7
2-methyl benzocycloheptene isomer	(≤7.30±0.03)	(≤227)	(≤950)	59	246	*EST	1654-55-3
methyl benzocycloheptene isomer	(≤7.34±0.03)	(≤228)	(≤954)	59	246	*EST	1654-52-0
2-methylnaphthalene	(7.8) IP is onset of photoelectron band (82LEV/LIA, 83KLA/KOV).	(206)	(864)	27±0.5	111±2	74SAB/CHA	91-57-6
benzocycloheptene	(8.1) IP is onset of photoelectron band.	(253)	(1057)	66	276	*EST	4453-90-1

Table 1. Positive Ion Table – Continued

ION Neutral	Ionization potential eV	$\Delta_f H$(Ion) kcal/mol kJ/mol		$\Delta_f H$(Neutral) kcal/mol kJ/mol		Neutral reference	CAS registry number
$C_{11}H_{10}^+$ (1-methylene-naphthalene)	(7.7) IP is onset of photoelectron band (84AND/CER).	(253)	(1058)	75±1	315±6	77PED/RYL	2443-46-1
$C_{11}H_{10}CrO_3^+$ (xylene-Cr(CO)$_3$)	(6.70±0.1) See also: 82GUI/PFI.	(54)	(224)	−101	−422	*EST	12129-29-2
$C_{11}H_{10}O^+$ (1-methoxynaphthalene)	7.70 IP from 83KLA/KOV.	(177)	(742)	−0.2	−1	*EST	2216-69-5
(2-methoxynaphthalene)	(7.44) IP is onset of photoelectron band (83KLA/KOV).	(171)	(717)	−0.2	−1	*EST	93-04-9
$C_{11}H_{10}OS^+$	(≤8.40) IP from 84GLE/BIS.	(≤201)	(≤840)	7	30	*EST	
$C_{11}H_{10}O_2^+$	(8.5) IP is onset of photoelectron band.	(145)	(607)	−51	−213	*EST	20651-88-1
	≤9.1 IP from 84MAR/KAY.	≤195	≤814	−15	−64	64COO/CRU	

Table 1. Positive Ion Table - Continued

ION Neutral	Ionization potential eV	$\Delta_f H$(Ion) kcal/mol kJ/mol	$\Delta_f H$(Neutral) kcal/mol kJ/mol	Neutral reference	CAS registry number

$C_{11}H_{11}^+$

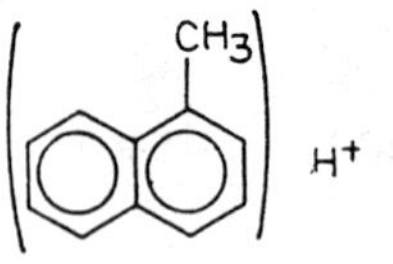

(1-methylnaphthalene·H+)

192   803

From proton affinity of 1-methylnaphthalene (RN 90-12-0). PA = 200.7 kcal/mol, 840. kJ/mol.

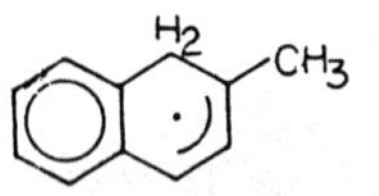

(2-methylnaphthalene protonated)

192   804

From proton affinity of 2-methylnaphthalene (RN 91-57-6). PA = 200.0 kcal/mol, 837. kJ/mol.

$C_{11}H_{11}CrNO_3^+$

| 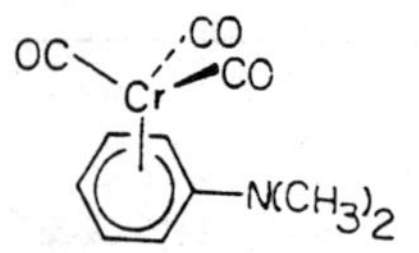 | (6.9) | (63)   (262) | −96±3   −404±13 | 84ALT/CON | 12109-10-3 |

$C_{11}H_{11}NO^+$

| 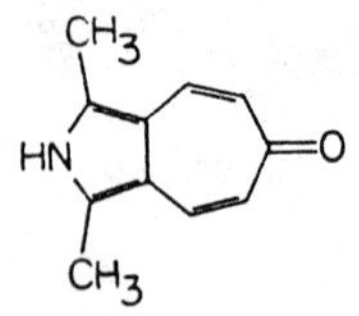 | (7.55)
IP from 84GLE/BIS. | (182)   (763) | 8   35 | *EST | |

| | (8.0)
IP is onset of photoelectron band (81PFI/GUI). | (181)   (756) | −4   −16 | *EST | 46185-83-5 |

| | (8.1)
IP is onset of photoelectron band (81PFI/GUI). | (192)   (804) | 5   23 | *EST | 13720-91-7 |

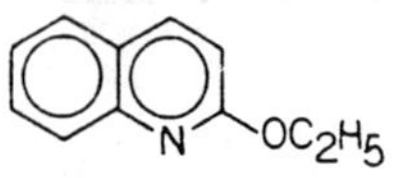

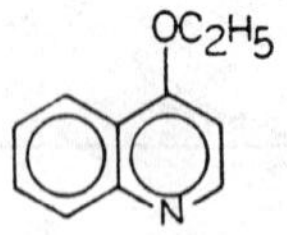

$C_{11}H_{12}^+$

| 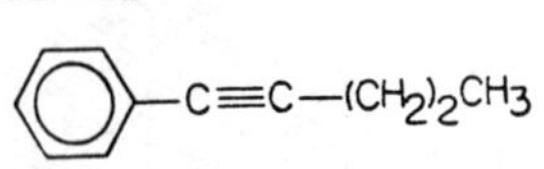 $C_6H_5-C\equiv C-(CH_2)_2CH_3$ | (≤8.29±0.02) | (≤252)   (≤1055) | 61   255 | *EST | 4250-81-1 |

| $C_6H_5-C\equiv C-CH(CH_3)_2$ | (8.35±0.08)
IP is onset of photoelectron band (81ELB/LIE). | (252)   (1053) | 59   247 | *EST | 1612-03-9 |

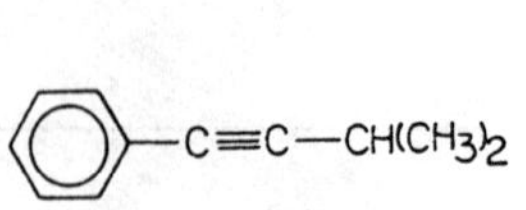

Table 1. Positive Ion Table - Continued

ION / Neutral	Ionization potential eV	$\Delta_f H$(Ion) kcal/mol	$\Delta_f H$(Ion) kJ/mol	$\Delta_f H$(Neutral) kcal/mol	$\Delta_f H$(Neutral) kJ/mol	Neutral reference	CAS registry number
$C_{11}H_{12}^+$							
2,4,6-trimethylphenylacetylene	(8.16±0.08) IP from 81ELB/LIE.	(263)	(1102)	75	315	*EST	769-26-6
1,2-dimethyl-3-phenylcyclopropene	(≤8.17) IP from 84BAI/DOM.	(≤253)	(≤1058)	65	270	*EST	23063-31-2
tricyclic C11H12	(≤8.42±0.05) IP from 82HAS/NEU, 82LEV/LIA.	(≤224)	(≤938)	30	126	*EST	4486-29-7
tricyclic C11H12	(8.05)	(228)	(956)	43	179	*EST	60582-10-7
tricyclic C11H12	(8.19)	(232)	(969)	43	179	*EST	60582-11-8
$C_{11}H_{12}N_2O_2^+$							
tryptophan	(≤7.5) See also: 83CAN/HAM.	(≤115)	(≤481)	−58	−243	*EST	54-12-6
$C_{11}H_{12}O^+$							
(E)-4-(3-methylphenyl)-3-buten-2-one	(8.6±0.05) IP from 81SCH/GRO.	(182)	(762)	−16	−68	81SCH/GRO	15753-84-1
(E)-4-(4-methylphenyl)-3-buten-2-one	(8.5±0.05) IP is onset of photoelectron band (81SCH/GRO).	(180)	(752)	−16	−68	*EST	4023-84-1

Table 1. Positive Ion Table – Continued

ION / Neutral	Ionization potential eV	$\Delta_f H$(Ion) kcal/mol	$\Delta_f H$(Ion) kJ/mol	$\Delta_f H$(Neutral) kcal/mol	$\Delta_f H$(Neutral) kJ/mol	Neutral reference	CAS registry number
$C_{11}H_{12}O^+$							
2-methylcinnamyl methyl ketone	8.5±0.05	183	766	−13	−54	79SCH/GRU	16927-82-5
	IP from 79SCH/GRU, 80GRU/SCH, 81SCH/GRO.						
2,2-dimethyl-2H-chromene	(7.8±0.05)	(170)	(711)	−10	−41	79SCH/GRU	2513-25-9
	IP from 79SCH/GRU.						
(cage ketone)	≤8.8	(≤208)	(≤871)	5	22	*EST	
	IP from 84MAR/KAY.						
$C_{11}H_{12}O_2^+$							
2-methoxycinnamyl methyl ketone	(8.2)	(146)	(612)	−43	−179	79SCH/GRU	10542-87-7
	IP from 79SCH/GRU, 80GRU/SCH.						
(cage diketone)	(8.1)	(205)	(860)	19	78	*EST	60526-44-5
	IP is onset of photoelectron band.						
$C_{11}H_{13}N^+$							
3-butylbenzonitrile	(9.77±0.1)	(254)	(1064)	29±0.2	121±1	*EST	20651-74-5
4-butylbenzonitrile	(10.08±0.1)	(261)	(1094)	29±0.2	121±1	*EST	20651-73-4
4-tert-butylbenzonitrile	(8.8)	(229)	(959)	26	110	85ORL/MIS	4210-32-6
	IP is onset of photoelectron band (85BAI/MIS2). See also: 86ORL/MIS.						

Table 1. Positive Ion Table – Continued

ION / Neutral	Ionization potential eV	$\Delta_f H$(Ion) kcal/mol	kJ/mol	$\Delta_f H$(Neutral) kcal/mol	kJ/mol	Neutral reference	CAS registry number
$C_{11}H_{13}N^+$							
(quinoline derivative)	(7.85±0.02)	(222)	(930)	41	173	*EST	4363-25-1
$C_{11}H_{13}N_2O_2^+$							
(L-tryptophan)H+		82	344				

From proton affinity of L-tryptophan (RN 54-12-6). PA = 225.4 kcal/mol, 943. kJ/mol.

$C_{11}H_{14}^+$							
(benzocycloheptane)	≤8.40±0.02	(≤198)	(≤827)	4±0.7	17±3	*EST	1075-16-7
(1,1-dimethylindane)	(8.47)	(195)	(815)	−0.5±0.2	−2±1	78OSB/SCO	4912-92-9
(2,2-dimethylindane)	(8.47)	(195)	(815)	0.5±0.2	−2±1	*EST	20836-11-7
(diethyl spiro compound)	(7.87)	(260)	(1089)	79	330	*EST	49542-94-1
(spiro compound)	(8.25)	(286)	(1196)	96	400	*EST	58738-49-1

IP is onset of photoelectron band (82SPA/KOR).

$C_{11}H_{14}N^+$							
(1,4-dihydro-1,4-ethanoquinoline)H+		175	732				

From proton affinity of 1,4-dihydro-1,4-ethanoquinoline (RN 4363-25-1). PA = 232.0 kcal/mol, 971. kJ/mol.

Table 1. Positive Ion Table — Continued

ION / Neutral	Ionization potential eV	$\Delta_f H$(Ion) kcal/mol	$\Delta_f H$(Ion) kJ/mol	$\Delta_f H$(Neutral) kcal/mol	$\Delta_f H$(Neutral) kJ/mol	Neutral reference	CAS registry number
$C_{11}H_{14}N_2^+$							
indole-3-CH$_2$N(CH$_3$)$_2$	(≤7.69±0.16)	(≤215)	(≤900)	38	158	*EST	87-52-5
indole-3-(CH$_2$)$_2$NHCH$_3$ — IP is onset of photoelectron band.	(7.7)	(206)	(864)	29	121	*EST	61-49-4
5-CH$_3$-indole-3-(CH$_2$)$_2$NH$_2$ — IP is onset of photoelectron band.	(7.6)	(201)	(839)	25	106	*EST	1821-47-2
$C_{11}H_{14}N_2O^+$							
5-H$_3$CO-indole-3-CH$_2$CH$_2$NH$_2$	(≤7.68±0.12)	(≤174)	(≤729)	−3	−12	*EST	608-07-1
$C_{11}H_{14}O^+$							
2,4,6-trimethylacetophenone — IP is onset of photoelectron band (78CEN/FRA).	(8.2)	(140)	(586)	−49.0±0.9	−204.9±3.6	77PED/RYL	1667-01-2
$C_{11}H_{14}O_2^+$							
HOOC-C$_6$H$_4$-C(CH$_3$)$_3$ — IP is onset of photoelectron band (85BAI/MIS2). See also: 86ORL/MIS.	(8.6)	(103)	(431)	−95	−399	85ORL/MIS	98-73-7
$C_{11}H_{14}O_2Si^+$							
(2-furyl)$_2$Si(CH$_3$)(C$_2$H$_5$) — IP is onset of photoelectron band (83ZYK/ERC).	(8.1)	(138)	(577)	−49	−205	*EST	

Table 1. Positive Ion Table - Continued

ION / Neutral	Ionization potential eV	$\Delta_f H$(Ion) kcal/mol	kJ/mol	$\Delta_f H$(Neutral) kcal/mol	kJ/mol	Neutral reference	CAS registry number
$C_{11}H_{15}N^+$							
1-phenylpiperidine	(7.1)	(172)	(718)	8	33	*EST	4096-20-2
	IP is onset of photoelectron band (82ROZ/HOU2).						
1-(o-tolyl)pyrrolidine	(6.8)	(184)	(771)	27	115	*EST	41378-30-7
	IP is onset of photoelectron band (82ROZ/HOU2).						
1-(2,6-dimethylphenyl)azetidine	(7.0)	(230)	(961)	68	286	*EST	19199-06-5
	IP is onset of photoelectron band (82ROZ/HOU2).						
1-(2,4-dimethylphenyl)azetidine	(≤7.48)	(≤223)	(≤933)	50	211	*EST	81506-10-7
	IP from 82ROZ/HOU2.						

$C_{11}H_{15}NO_2S^+$							
(CH₃)₂N-C₆H₄-CH=CH-SO₂-CH₃	(7.0)	(129)	(538)	−33	−137	*EST	
	IP is onset of photoelectron band (84CAU/FUR).						

$C_{11}H_{15}NO_3^+$							
pyrrole ester 1	≤8.26	(≤54)	(≤227)	−136	−570	*EST	
	IP from 81CAU/GIA.						
pyrrole ester 2	(≤8.23)	(≤54)	(≤224)	−136	−570	*EST	6314-22-3
	IP from 81CAU/GIA.						

$C_{11}H_{16}^+$							
1-methyl-3-butylbenzene	(8.42±0.1)	(184)	(768)	−11	−44	*EST	1595-04-6

Table 1. Positive Ion Table – Continued

ION Neutral	Ionization potential eV	$\Delta_f H$(Ion) kcal/mol kJ/mol		$\Delta_f H$(Neutral) kcal/mol kJ/mol		Neutral reference	CAS registry number
$C_{11}H_{16}^+$							
H₃C–C₆H₄–(CH₂)₃CH₃	(8.35±0.1)	(182)	(761)	−11	−45	*EST	1595-05-7
H₃C–C₆H₄–C(CH₃)₃	8.28 IP from 86ORL/MIS. See also: 85BAI/MIS.	(178)	(744)	−13	−55	85ORL/MIS	98-51-1
C₆H₅–CH₂–C(CH₃)₃	≤8.7	(≤187)	(≤784)	−13	−55	*EST	1007-26-7
pentamethylbenzene	7.92±0.02 See: 84HOW/GON.	(165)	(690)	−18	−74	*EST	700-12-9
$C_{11}H_{16}BrNO_2^+$							
2,4-dimethoxy-5-bromo-α-methylbenzylamine	(7.4) IP is onset of photoelectron band (81DOM/EAT).	(97)	(406)	−74	−308	*EST	60917-67-1
2,5-dimethoxy-4-bromo-α-methylbenzylamine	(7.3) IP is onset of photoelectron band (81DOM/EAT, 82LEV/LIA).	(97)	(404)	−72	−300	*EST	64638-07-9
3,4-dimethoxy-6-bromo-α-methylbenzylamine	(7.4) IP is onset of photoelectron band (81DOM/EAT).	(102)	(425)	−69	−289	*EST	32156-25-5
$C_{11}H_{16}N^+$							
1-phenylpiperidine·H⁺		154	642				
From proton affinity of 1-phenylpiperidine (RN 4096-20-2). PA = 225.8 kcal/mol, 945. kJ/mol.							

Table 1. Positive Ion Table – Continued

ION / Neutral	Ionization potential eV	$\Delta_f H$(Ion) kcal/mol	$\Delta_f H$(Ion) kJ/mol	$\Delta_f H$(Neutral) kcal/mol	$\Delta_f H$(Neutral) kJ/mol	Neutral reference	CAS registry number
$C_{11}H_{16}O^+$							
H₃CO-C₆H₄-C(CH₃)₃	(7.77) IP from 86ORL/MIS.	(138)	(576)	−41.5	−173.8	86ORL/MIS	5396-38-3
2,6-dimethylphenyl isopropyl ether	8.49	(162)	(676)	−34	−143	*EST	54350-31-1
2,4,6-trimethylphenyl ethyl ether	(≤8.28)	(≤165)	(≤692)	−26	−107	*EST	61248-63-3
$C_{11}H_{16}OS^+$							
p-tolyl isobutyl sulfoxide	(≤8.50) IP from 81MOH/JIA.	(≤163)	(≤681)	−33	−139	*EST	77919-66-5
p-tolyl tert-butyl sulfoxide	(≤8.33) IP from 81MOH/JIA.	(≤162)	(≤678)	−30	−126	*EST	49833-45-6
trimethyl thiocamphor derivative	(8.25) IP is onset of photoelectron band (80FRO/WES).	(144)	(601)	−47	−195	*EST	75503-13-8
$C_{11}H_{16}O_2^+$							
camphor-like carboxylic acid	(≤9.05) IP from 81NES/BAI.	(≤112)	(≤468)	−97	−405	*EST	10309-20-3
camphorquinone derivative	(8.86) IP is onset of photoelectron band (80FRO/WES).	(108)	(450)	−97	−405	*EST	57239-03-9

ION / Neutral	Ionization potential eV	$\Delta_f H$(Ion) kcal/mol	$\Delta_f H$(Ion) kJ/mol	$\Delta_f H$(Neutral) kcal/mol	$\Delta_f H$(Neutral) kJ/mol	Neutral reference	CAS registry number
$C_{11}H_{16}S^+$							
H3CS—⟨⟩—C(CH3)3	(≤7.83±0.05)	(≤179)	(≤747)	−2	−8	*EST	7252-86-0
[3-SC(CH3)3, CH3 benzene]	(≤8.35)	(≤188)	(≤788)	−4	−18	*EST	34786-26-0
H3C—⟨⟩—S—C(CH3)3	(≤8.31)	(≤187)	(≤784)	−4	−18	*EST	7439-10-3
$C_{11}H_{16}S_2^+$							
[camphor dithione structure]	(8.2)	(193)	(806)	4	15	*EST	75503-14-9

IP is onset of photoelectron band (80FRO/WES).

ION / Neutral	Ionization potential eV	$\Delta_f H$(Ion) kcal/mol	$\Delta_f H$(Ion) kJ/mol	$\Delta_f H$(Neutral) kcal/mol	$\Delta_f H$(Neutral) kJ/mol	Neutral reference	CAS registry number
$C_{11}H_{17}N^+$							
[4-CH3, 2,6-(CH3)2, N(CH3)2 benzene]	(7.24)	(174)	(729)	7	30	*EST	13021-15-3
H3C—⟨⟩—N(C2H5)2 (meta)	(6.90)	(160)	(670)	1	4	*EST	91-67-8

IP from charge transfer equilibrium constant determinations; reference standard: IP ($C_6H_5N(CH_3)_2$) = 7.12 eV. (85LIA/JAC).

H3C—⟨⟩—N(C2H5)2 (para)	(6.83)	(160)	(671)	3	12	*EST	613-48-9

IP from charge transfer equilibrium constant determinations; reference standard: IP ($C_6H_5N(CH_3)_2$) = 7.12 eV. (84MAU/NEL, 85LIA/JAC).

ION / Neutral	Ionization potential eV	$\Delta_f H$(Ion) kcal/mol	$\Delta_f H$(Ion) kJ/mol	$\Delta_f H$(Neutral) kcal/mol	$\Delta_f H$(Neutral) kJ/mol	Neutral reference	CAS registry number
$C_{11}H_{17}NO_2^+$							
[2,3-(OCH3)2 benzene, CH(CH3)NH2]	(≤8.30)	(≤130)	(≤544)	−61	−257	*EST	15402-81-0

IP from 81DOM/EAT.

Table 1. Positive Ion Table – Continued

ION / Neutral	Ionization potential eV	$\Delta_f H$(Ion) kcal/mol	kJ/mol	$\Delta_f H$(Neutral) kcal/mol	kJ/mol	Neutral reference	CAS registry number
$C_{11}H_{17}NO_2^+$							
4-methoxy-2-methoxy-α-methylbenzeneethanamine	(7.4)	(99)	(416)	−71	−298	*EST	23690-13-3
	IP is onset of photoelectron band (81DOM/EAT, 82LEV/LIA).						
2,5-dimethoxy-α-methylbenzeneethanamine	(7.1)	(94)	(395)	−69	−290	*EST	13641-74-2
	IP is onset of photoelectron band (81DOM/EAT, 82LEV/LIA).						
2,6-dimethoxy-α-methylbenzeneethanamine	(8.18)	(117)	(491)	−71	−298	*EST	23690-14-4
	IP from 81DOM/EAT.						
3,4-dimethoxy-α-methylbenzeneethanamine	(≤8.03±0.06)	(≤118)	(≤492)	−68	−283	*EST	120-26-3
	See also: 81DOM/GAP.						
$C_{11}H_{18}^+$							
tetramethylcycloheptyne	(8.4)	(225)	(940)	31	130	*EST	33470-40-5
	IP is onset of photoelectron band.						
1-methyladamantane	(9.17±0.02)	(170.9)	(715.0)	−40.6±0.3	−169.8±1.4	79CLA/KNO	768-91-2
2-methyladamantane	9.24	176	737	−36.9	−154	79CLA/KNO	
dispiro compound	(8.5)	(232)	(972)	36	152	*EST	52879-54-6
	IP is onset of photoelectron band (82SPA/GLE).						

Table 1. Positive Ion Table - Continued

ION / Neutral	Ionization potential eV	Δ_fH(Ion) kcal/mol	Δ_fH(Ion) kJ/mol	Δ_fH(Neutral) kcal/mol	Δ_fH(Neutral) kJ/mol	Neutral reference	CAS registry number

$C_{11}H_{18}N^+$

| | | 125 | 523 | | | | |

From proton affinity of 2,6-diisopropylpyridine (RN 6832-21-9). PA = 232.9 kcal/mol, 974. kJ/mol.

| | | 137 | 572 | | | | |

From proton affinity of 2-n-hexylpyridine (RN 1129-69-7). PA = 228.9 kcal/mol, 958. kJ/mol.

| | | 138 | 578 | | | | |

From proton affinity of 3-$CH_3C_6H_4N(C_2H_5)_2$ (RN 91-67-8). PA = 228.9 kcal/mol, 956. kJ/mol.

| | | 140 | 587 | | | | |

From proton affinity of 4-$CH_3C_6H_4N(C_2H_5)_2$ (RN 613-48-9). PA = 228.6 kcal/mol, 956. kJ/mol.

$C_{11}H_{18}O_4^+$

| | (8.7) | (46) | (190) | −155 | −649 | *EST | 75905-10-1 |

IP is onset of photoelectron band (83ZYK/ERC).

$C_{11}H_{18}S_2^+$

| | 7.65 | (203) | (848) | 26 | 110 | *EST | |

IP is onset of photoelectron band (83JIA/MOH).

$C_{11}H_{19}N^+$

| | (≤7.44±0.03) | (≤162) | (≤676) | −10 | −42 | *EST | 2981-10-4 |

Table 1. Positive Ion Table - Continued

ION / Neutral	Ionization potential eV	$\Delta_f H$(Ion) kcal/mol	kJ/mol	$\Delta_f H$(Neutral) kcal/mol	kJ/mol	Neutral reference	CAS registry number
$C_{11}H_{19}NO^+$							
5,5-dimethyl-3-(n-propylamino)cyclohex-2-enone	(≤8.03) IP from 82PFI/GER.	(≤131)	(≤548)	−54	−227	*EST	56570-54-8
5,5-dimethyl-3-(i-propylamino)cyclohex-2-enone	(≤7.94) IP from 82PFI/GER.	(≤125)	(≤525)	−58	−241	*EST	80555-73-3
$C_{11}H_{20}^+$							
$(tert-C_4H_9)_2C=C=CH_2$	(≤8.55)	(≤206)	(≤860)	8	35	*EST	22585-31-5
$(CH_3)_3CCH=C=CHC(CH_3)_3$	(8.6) IP is onset of photoelectron band (85ELS/VER).	(193)	(807)	−5	−23	*EST	42066-39-7
1-$C_{11}H_{20}$	(9.90±0.02)	(233)	(976)	5	21	*EST	2243-98-3
2-$C_{11}H_{20}$	(9.28±0.02)	(214)	(897)	0.5	2	*EST	60212-29-5
3-$C_{11}H_{20}$	(9.17±0.02)	(212)	(888)	0.8	3	*EST	60212-30-8
4-$C_{11}H_{20}$	(9.13±0.02)	(211)	(884)	0.8	3	*EST	60212-31-9
5-$C_{11}H_{20}$	(9.11±0.02)	(211)	(882)	0.8	3	*EST	2294-72-6
$C_{11}H_{20}O^+$							
di-tert-butylcyclopropanone	(≤8.45)	(≤147)	(≤613)	−48	−202	*EST	14743-58-9
$C_{11}H_{20}O_2^+$							
$(CH_3)_3C\text{-}...\text{-}C(CH_3)_3$ enol form	(7.9) Heat of formation of neutral molecule refers to enol form. IP is onset of photoelectron band.	(56)	(234)	−126±1	−528±4	81FER/RIB	1118-71-4
$C_{11}H_{21}N^+$							
1-cyclohexylpiperidine	(≤7.93±0.03)	(≤146)	(≤609)	−37	−156	*EST	3319-01-5

Table 1. Positive Ion Table - Continued

ION / Neutral	Ionization potential eV	$\Delta_f H$(Ion) kcal/mol	$\Delta_f H$(Ion) kJ/mol	$\Delta_f H$(Neutral) kcal/mol	$\Delta_f H$(Neutral) kJ/mol	Neutral reference	CAS registry number
$C_{11}H_{22}^+$							
$C_2H_5CH_2C(C_2H_5)=C(C_2H_5)_2$	(8.04±0.02)	(145)	(606)	−41	−170	*EST	50787-14-9
$C_{11}H_{24}^+$							
$n\text{-}C_{11}H_{24}$	(9.56)	(156)	(651)	−65±0.6	−271±3	77PED/RYL	1120-21-4
IP from charge transfer equilibrium constant determinations (81MAU/SIE, 82LIA).							
$n\text{-}C_8H_{17}CH(CH_3)_2$	(9.68)	(157)	(656)	−66	−278	*EST	6975-98-0
IP from charge transfer equilibrium constant determinations (81MAU/SIE, 82LIA).							
$C_{12}Co_4O_{12}^+$	7.45	(−246.2)	(−1030.1)	−418.0±3.2	−1748.9±13	82PIL/SKI	17786-31-1
IP is onset of photoelectron band. See also: 81GRE/MIN.							
$C_{12}F_8^+$	(≤9.1±0.1)	(≤−56)	(≤−234)	−266	−1112	*EST	1554-93-4
$C_{12}F_{10}^+$	(9.40±0.02)	(−115)	(−480)	−332±3	−1387±12	79PRI/SAP2	434-90-2
$C_{12}F_{12}^+$	11.14	(−211)	(−884)	−468	−1959	*EST	32937-02-3
IP is onset of photoelectron band (84HEI/WIR).							
$C_{12}F_{27}N^+$							
$(n\text{-}C_4F_9)_3N$	(11.3)	(−1067)	(−4466)	−1328±2	−5556±10	79ERA/KOL	311-89-7
IP is onset of photoelectron band (82ELB/DIE, 83MOL/PIK3).							
$C_{12}Fe_3O_{12}^+$	(7.44)	(−247)	(−1035)	−419±6	−1753±27	82PIL/SKI	17685-52-8
IP is onset of photoelectron band (82DEK/WON).							

Table 1. Positive Ion Table – Continued

ION / Neutral	Ionization potential eV	$\Delta_f H$(Ion) kcal/mol kJ/mol		$\Delta_f H$(Neutral) kcal/mol kJ/mol		Neutral reference	CAS registry number
$C_{12}H_6O_2^+$ (acenaphthenequinone)	(8.6) IP is onset of photoelectron band.	(305)	(1275)	106	445	*EST	82-86-0
$C_{12}H_8^+$ (1-ethynylnaphthalene)	(8.03) IP is onset of photoelectron band (81GLE/SCH).	(279)	(1166)	93	391	*EST	15727-65-8
(2-ethynylnaphthalene)	(8.11) IP is onset of photoelectron band (81GLE/SCH).	(280)	(1173)	93	391	*EST	2949-26-0
(acenaphthylene)	(8.22±0.04)	(252)	(1053)	62±0.2	260±1	81KUD/KUD	208-96-8
(biphenylene)	7.56±0.02 IP derived from charge transfer equilibrium constant determinations is in agreement (80MAU). See also: 85DEW/TIE.	279	1166	104±3	437±13	77PED/RYL	259-79-0
$C_{12}H_8Br_2N_2^+$ (4,4'-dibromoazobenzene)	(9.24) IP from 77NUY/MES.	(324)	(1355)	110.8	463.6	*EST	1601-98-5
$C_{12}H_8FNO^+$	9.11 IP from 80GRU/SCH. See also: 82LEV/LIA.	(222)	(927)	11	48	*EST	6238-65-9

Table 1. Positive Ion Table - Continued

ION / Neutral	Ionization potential eV	$\Delta_f H$(Ion) kcal/mol	$\Delta_f H$(Ion) kJ/mol	$\Delta_f H$(Neutral) kcal/mol	$\Delta_f H$(Neutral) kJ/mol	Neutral reference	CAS registry number
$C_{12}H_8F_2^+$							
2,2'-difluorobiphenyl	(8.35±0.02)	(147)	(616)	−45±1	−190±5	64SMI/GOV	388-82-9
3,3'-difluorobiphenyl	(8.35±0.02)	(146)	(611)	−47	−195	*EST	396-64-5
4,4'-difluorobiphenyl	(8.00±0.02)	(138)	(577)	−47±1	−195±5	64SMI/GOV	398-23-2
$C_{12}H_8F_2S_2^+$							
bis(4-fluorophenyl) disulfide	(≤8.4) IP from 82GIO/BOC.	(≤109)	(≤456)	−85	−354	*EST	405-31-2
$C_{12}H_8N_2^+$							
1,10-phenanthroline	(8.3) IP is onset of photoelectron band.	(270)	(1130)	79	329	*EST	66-71-7
4,7-phenanthroline	8.35±0.02	(269)	(1127)	77	321	*EST	230-07-9
benzo[c]cinnoline	(7.9) IP is onset of photoelectron band.	(277)	(1159)	95	397	77SCH/PET	230-17-1
phenazine	8.33±0.02	274	1148	82±0.7	344±3	80ARS	92-82-0

Table 1. Positive Ion Table – Continued

ION Neutral	Ionization potential eV	$\Delta_f H$(Ion) kcal/mol	$\Delta_f H$(Ion) kJ/mol	$\Delta_f H$(Neutral) kcal/mol	$\Delta_f H$(Neutral) kJ/mol	Neutral reference	CAS registry number
$C_{12}H_8N_2O^+$	8.00±0.02	(247)	(1036)	63	264	*EST	304-81-4
$C_{12}H_8N_2O_4S_2^+$	(≤8.98) IP from 82GIO/BOC.	(≤258)	(≤1080)	51	214	*EST	100-32-3
$C_{12}H_8N_4O_4^+$	(9.97) IP from 77NUY/MES.	(314)	(1312)	83.6	349.8	*EST	
$C_{12}H_8O^+$	7.9±0.05	202	845	20±1	83±5	77PED/RYL	132-64-9
$C_{12}H_8OS^+$	(8.1) IP is onset of photoelectron band.	(206)	(863)	19	81	*EST	1013-23-6
$C_{12}H_8O_2^+$	(7.5) IP is onset of photoelectron band.	(158)	(661)	−15	−63	82SHA	262-12-4
$C_{12}H_8O_2S^+$	(8.9) IP is onset of photoelectron band.	(171)	(714)	−35	−145	*EST	1016-05-3

Table 1. Positive Ion Table - Continued

ION / Neutral	Ionization potential eV	$\Delta_f H$(Ion) kcal/mol	kJ/mol	$\Delta_f H$(Neutral) kcal/mol	kJ/mol	Neutral reference	CAS registry number
$C_{12}H_8S^+$ (dibenzothiophene)	7.90±0.03	231	967	49±0.7	205±1	79SAB	132-65-0
$C_{12}H_8S_2^+$ (thianthrene)	(7.7) IP is onset of photoelectron band (81TRA/RED).	(201)	(840)	23±1	97±6	77PED/RYL	92-85-3
$C_{12}H_8Se^+$ (dibenzoselenophene)	(≤7.86) IP from 82TRA/ROD.	(≤243)	(≤1018)	62	260	*EST	244-95-1
$C_{12}H_8Se_2^+$	(≤7.89) IP from 82TRA/ROD.	(≤231)	(≤968)	49	207	*EST	
$C_{12}H_9^+$ (biphenylene·H⁺)		267	1116				

From proton affinity of biphenylene. (RN 259-79-0). PA = 203.4 kcal/mol, 851. kJ/mol.

ION / Neutral	Ionization potential eV	$\Delta_f H$(Ion) kcal/mol	kJ/mol	$\Delta_f H$(Neutral) kcal/mol	kJ/mol	Neutral reference	CAS registry number
$C_{12}H_9ClO_2^+$	(9.25) IP is onset of photoelectron band (80RED/FRE).	(242)	(1010)	28	118	*EST	31599-79-8
$C_{12}H_9F^+$ (2-fluorobiphenyl)	(8.20±0.02)	(185)	(774)	−4	−17	*EST	321-60-8

Table 1. Positive Ion Table - Continued

ION / Neutral	Ionization potential eV	$\Delta_f H$(Ion) kcal/mol	$\Delta_f H$(Ion) kJ/mol	$\Delta_f H$(Neutral) kcal/mol	$\Delta_f H$(Neutral) kJ/mol	Neutral reference	CAS registry number
$C_{12}H_9F^+$							
4-fluorobiphenyl	(8.00±0.02)	(180)	(755)	−4	−17	*EST	324-74-3
$C_{12}H_9N^+$							
benzonorbornadiene-2-carbonitrile	(8.5) IP is onset of photoelectron band.	(294)	(1228)	98	408	*EST	71906-57-5
benzonorbornadiene-1-carbonitrile	(8.7) IP is onset of photoelectron band.	(301)	(1259)	100	420	*EST	61346-79-0
benzonorbornadiene-6-carbonitrile	(8.7) IP is onset of photoelectron band.	(300)	(1255)	99	416	*EST	16513-60-3
carbazole	7.57±0.03	229	959	55±0.2	229±1	81KUD/KUD2	86-74-8
$C_{12}H_9NO^+$							
2-benzoylpyridine	9.06 IP from 82LEV/LIA, 80GRU/SCH.	(247)	(1032)	38	158	*EST	91-02-1
3-benzoylpyridine	(9.6±0.1)	(261)	(1090)	39	164	*EST	5424-19-1
4-benzoylpyridine	(9.6±0.1)	(261)	(1090)	39	164	*EST	14548-46-0

Table 1. Positive Ion Table – Continued

ION Neutral	Ionization potential eV	$\Delta_f H$(Ion) kcal/mol	$\Delta_f H$(Ion) kJ/mol	$\Delta_f H$(Neutral) kcal/mol	$\Delta_f H$(Neutral) kJ/mol	Neutral reference	CAS registry number
$C_{12}H_9NO_3^+$ (3,4-dimethoxy-5-methoxy amphetamine structure)	(≤8.16±0.06)	(≤90)	(≤376)	−98	−411	*EST	22199-17-3
$C_{12}H_9N_2^+$ (phenazine H)		224	938				
	From proton affinity of phenazine (RN 92-82-0). PA = 223.7 kcal/mol, 936. kJ/mol.						
$C_{12}H_{10}^+$							
phenyl-CH=CHCH=CHC≡CH	(7.9) IP from 74KOP/SCH.	(244)	(1019)	61.5	257.3	62MOM/BRA	940-50-1
biphenyl	7.95±0.02 See also: 74KOP/SCH.	226.9	949.4	43.6±0.3	182.3±1.4	77PED/RYL	92-52-4
acenaphthylene	(7.68) IP from charge transfer equilibrium constant determinations (80MAU, re-evaluated).	(214)	(896)	37±0.2	155±1	81KUD/KUD	83-32-9
1-vinylnaphthalene	(7.7) IP is onset of photoelectron band (81GLE/SCH).	(229)	(958)	51	215	*EST	826-74-4
(bicyclic structure)	(≤8.1)	(≤286)	(≤1197)	99	415	*EST	19539-78-7
(methylene dihydronaphthalene)	(7.5) IP is onset of photoelectron band (84AND/CER).	(269)	(1127)	96	403	*EST	10474-24-5

Table 1. Positive Ion Table – Continued

ION Neutral	Ionization potential eV	$\Delta_f H$(Ion) kcal/mol	$\Delta_f H$(Ion) kJ/mol	$\Delta_f H$(Neutral) kcal/mol	$\Delta_f H$(Neutral) kJ/mol	Neutral reference	CAS registry number
$C_{12}H_{10}^+$	(8.0)	(259)	(1083)	74	311	*EST	7322-47-6
	IP is onset of photoelectron band (82HAS/NEU).						
$C_{12}H_{10}Be^+$	(9.20±0.10)	(285)	(1193)	73±5	305±21	80TEL/RAB	22300-89-6
$C_{12}H_{10}Hg^+$	8.30±0.03	285	1192	93.5±0.8	391.4±3.2	77PED/RYL	587-85-9
	See also: 81FUR/PIA.						
$C_{12}H_{10}N_2^+$	(8.2)	(286)	(1195)	97±0.7	404±3	77SCH/PET	17082-12-1
	IP is onset of photoelectron band. See also: 81NAT/FRA.						
$C_{12}H_{10}N_2O^+$	7.6	(229)	(958)	54	225	*EST	20714-70-9
	IP is onset of photoelectron band (81MIL/MIL, 82LEV/LIA).						
	(8.1)	(269)	(1124)	81.7±0.6	342±2.4	86KIR/ACR	495-48-7
	IP is onset of photoelectron band (81MIL/CIL).						
$C_{12}H_{10}O^+$	(8.23)	(185)	(773)	−5±2	−21±8	*EST	941-98-0

Table 1. Positive Ion Table - Continued

ION / Neutral	Ionization potential eV	$\Delta_f H$(Ion) kcal/mol	$\Delta_f H$(Ion) kJ/mol	$\Delta_f H$(Neutral) kcal/mol	$\Delta_f H$(Neutral) kJ/mol	Neutral reference	CAS registry number

$C_{12}H_{10}O^+$

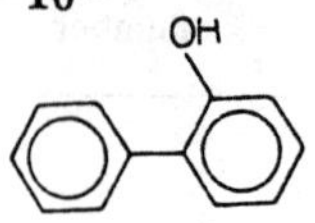	(7.80±0.02)	(181)	(756)	0.7	3	*EST	90-43-7
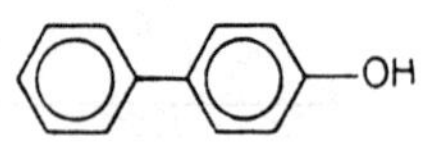	(7.78±0.03)	(180)	(754)	0.7	3	*EST	92-69-3
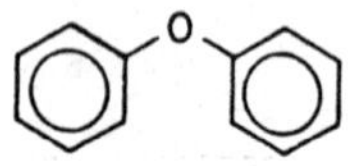	8.09±0.03	183	766	−3.6±0.4	−14.9±1.8	77PED/RYL	101-84-8

$C_{12}H_{10}OS^+$

| 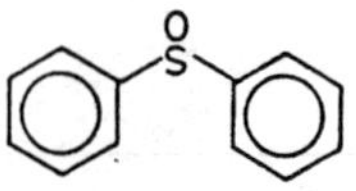 | (8.3) IP is onset of photoelectron band. | (217) | (908) | 26±0.7 | 107±3 | 77PED/RYL | 945-51-7 |

$C_{12}H_{10}O_2^+$

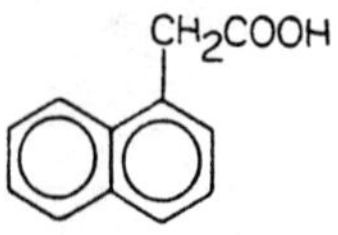

	(7.71) IP is onset of photoelectron band (83KLA/KOV).	(111)	(464)	−67	−280	*EST	86-87-3
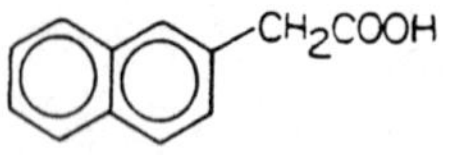	(8.05) IP from 83KLA/KOV.	(118)	(495)	−67	−282	*EST	581-96-4
	(8.5) IP is onset of photoelectron band (85ALB/HEL).	(227)	(948)	31	128	*EST	

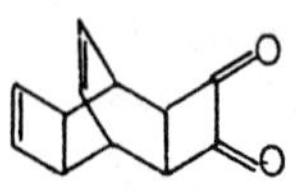

$C_{12}H_{10}O_2S^+$

| 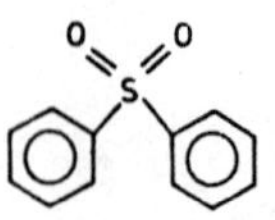 | 9.16±0.03 See: 81TRA/RED. | 183 | 765 | −28±0.7 | −119±3 | 77PED/RYL | 127-63-9 |

Table 1. Positive Ion Table - Continued

ION / Neutral	Ionization potential eV	$\Delta_f H$(Ion) kcal/mol	$\Delta_f H$(Ion) kJ/mol	$\Delta_f H$(Neutral) kcal/mol	$\Delta_f H$(Neutral) kJ/mol	Neutral reference	CAS registry number
$C_{12}H_{10}S^+$							
(diphenyl sulfide)	7.86±0.04 See also: 81TRA/RED.	236	989	55±0.7	231±3	77PED/RYL	139-66-2
(cyclic structure)	(7.91) IP is onset of photoelectron band (81GUT/BES).	(232)	(972)	50	209	*EST	
$C_{12}H_{10}S_2^+$							
(diphenyl disulfide)	≤8.3 IP from 82GIO/BOC.	≤250	≤1045	58±1	244±4	77PED/RYL	882-33-7
(cyclic structure)	(7.4) IP is onset of photoelectron band (81GUT/BES).	(223)	(931)	52	217	*EST	75574-98-0
$C_{12}H_{10}S_3^+$							
(cyclic structure)	(7.2) IP is onset of photoelectron band (81GUT/BES).	(221)	(925)	55	230	*EST	75574-99-1
$C_{12}H_{10}Se^+$							
(diphenyl selenide)	(≤7.79) IP from 82TRA/ROD.	(≤248)	(≤1038)	68.4±1.2	286.4±5.2	77PED/RYL	1132-39-4
$C_{12}H_{11}^+$							
biphenyl·H$^+$		213	892				
From proton affinity of biphenyl (RN 92-52-4). PA = 196.1 kcal/mol, 820. kJ/mol.							
acenaphthene·H$^+$		199	834				
From proton affinity of acenaphthene (RN 83-32-9). PA = 203.5 kcal/mol, 851. kJ/mol.							

ION Neutral	Ionization potential eV	$\Delta_f H$(Ion) kcal/mol	kJ/mol	$\Delta_f H$(Neutral) kcal/mol	kJ/mol	Neutral reference	CAS registry number
$C_{12}H_{11}ClO^+$	9.0 IP from 84MAR/KAY.	(204)	(853)	−4	−15	*EST	
$C_{12}H_{11}N^+$	7.16±0.04	217	910	52±0.7	219±3	78STE	122-39-4
$C_{12}H_{11}P^+$	(7.80±0.01)	(234)	(979)	54	226	*EST	829-85-6
$C_{12}H_{12}^+$	7.78±0.03	199	834	20	83	69STU/WES	571-58-4
	(9.0) IP is onset of photoelectron band.	(344)	(1441)	137	573	80BAR/STR	60323-50-4
	(≤7.18±0.03)	(≤219)	(≤915)	53	222	*EST	56594-77-5
	(≤7.29±0.03)	(≤221)	(≤924)	53	221	*EST	56594-78-6
	(≤7.20±0.03)	(≤219)	(≤916)	53	221	*EST	46030-99-3

Table 1. Positive Ion Table - Continued

ION Neutral	Ionization potential eV	$\Delta_f H$(Ion) kcal/mol	kJ/mol	$\Delta_f H$(Neutral) kcal/mol	kJ/mol	Neutral reference	CAS registry number
$C_{12}H_{12}^+$							
1,4-dimethyl (naphthalene deriv.)	(≤7.27±0.03)	(≤221)	(≤923)	53	222	*EST	7206-52-2
2,3-dimethyl	(≤7.17±0.03)	(≤218)	(≤915)	53	223	*EST	10556-12-4
2,4-dimethyl	(≤7.08±0.03)	(≤216)	(≤906)	53	223	*EST	56594-76-4
2-ethylnaphthalene	7.95 IP from 83KLA/KOV.	(203)	(853)	20	86	*EST	939-27-5
1,2-dimethyl	(≤7.86±0.03)	(≤201)	(≤840)	20	82	69STU/WES	575-41-7
1,5-dimethyl	(≤7.85±0.03)	(≤201)	(≤839)	20	82	69STU/WES	571-61-9
1,8-dimethyl	(7.5) IP is onset of photoelectron band (81GUT/BES).	(199)	(832)	26.0±0.2	108.7±1	77PED/RYL	569-41-5
2,3-dimethyl	(≤7.89±0.03)	(≤202)	(≤845)	20	84	69STU/WES	581-40-8

Table 1. Positive Ion Table – Continued

ION / Neutral	Ionization potential eV	$\Delta_f H$(Ion) kcal/mol	kJ/mol	$\Delta_f H$(Neutral) kcal/mol	kJ/mol	Neutral reference	CAS registry number
$C_{12}H_{12}^+$							
2,6-dimethylnaphthalene	(≤7.89±0.03)	(≤202)	(≤844)	20	83	69STU/WES	582-16-1
	(7.7) IP is onset of photoelectron band (81GLE/GUB).	(269)	(1125)	91	382	*EST	21657-71-6
	(8.2) IP is onset of photoelectron band (82HAS/NEU).	(235)	(984)	46	193	*EST	
	(≤8.0)	(≤257)	(≤1076)	73	304	*EST	38310-32-6
	(≤8.12±0.05)	(≤247)	(≤1033)	60	250	*EST	4897-73-8
	(8.15±0.05) IP from 81HEI/KOV.	(312)	(1306)	124	520	*EST	60323-52-6
	(7.5) IP from 84AND/CER.	(239)	(1002)	66	278	*EST	58790-01-5
$C_{12}H_{12}Cr^+$							
bis(benzene)chromium	5.40 IP from 82CAB/COW.	177	741	53±2	220±8	77PED/RYL	1271-54-1

Table 1. Positive Ion Table - Continued

| ION | Ionization potential | $\Delta_f H$(Ion) | | $\Delta_f H$(Neutral) | | Neutral | CAS registry |
Neutral	eV	kcal/mol	kJ/mol	kcal/mol	kJ/mol	reference	number
$C_{12}H_{12}Cr^+$	(5.4)	(260)	(1087)	135	566	*EST	12093-81-1
	IP is onset of photoelectron band (85DAV/GAR).						
$C_{12}H_{12}CrO_3^+$	(6.8)	(45)	(190)	−111±2	−466±10	77PED/RYL	12129-67-8
	IP is onset of photoelectron band.						
$C_{12}H_{12}Mo^+$	(≤5.52±0.05)	(≤223)	(≤935)	96±5	402±20	77PED/RYL	12129-68-9
$C_{12}H_{12}MoO_3^+$	(7.0)	(60)	(251)	−101±3	−424±13	82PIL/SKI	12089-15-5
	IP is onset of photoelectron band.						
$C_{12}H_{12}N_2^+$				78	326	69BEN/CRU	122-66-7
	A value of 7.78 eV has been reported for the adiabatic IP of this compound. Reported values of IP's of hydrazines determined by threshold measurements are usually significantly higher than the adiabatic value because of the large geometry change associated with ionization.						
	(8.2)	(241)	(1008)	52	217	*EST	1134-35-6
	IP is onset of photoelectron band (83DOB/HIL).						
$C_{12}H_{12}O^+$	(7.0)	(186)	(778)	25	103	*EST	
	IP is onset of photoelectron band (84AND/CER).						

Table 1. Positive Ion Table – Continued

ION / Neutral	Ionization potential eV	$\Delta_f H$(Ion) kcal/mol	$\Delta_f H$(Ion) kJ/mol	$\Delta_f H$(Neutral) kcal/mol	$\Delta_f H$(Neutral) kJ/mol	Neutral reference	CAS registry number
$C_{12}H_{12}O^+$	≤8.95 IP from 84MAR/KAY.	(≤206)	(≤864)	0	0	*EST	
$C_{12}H_{12}O_2^+$	(8.3) IP is onset of photoelectron band.	(185)	(775)	−6	−26	*EST	21377-44-6
	(7.60) IP is onset of photoelectron band.	(148)	(620)	−27	−113	*EST	73650-68-7
$C_{12}H_{12}O_3W^+$	(7.0) IP is onset of photoelectron band.	(74)	(309)	−87±4	−366±15	84ALT/CON2	12129-69-0
$C_{12}H_{12}S_2^+$	(7.7) IP is onset of photoelectron band (81GUT/BES).	(225)	(940)	47	197	*EST	60948-99-4
	7.4 IP is onset of photoelectron band.	(214)	(895)	43	181	*EST	10075-73-7
	(7.3) IP is onset of photoelectron band.	(212)	(885)	43	181	*EST	10075-74-8
	(7.2) IP is onset of photoelectron band	(215)	(901)	49	206	*EST	7343-31-9

Table 1. Positive Ion Table – Continued

ION / Neutral	Ionization potential eV	$\Delta_f H$(Ion) kcal/mol	kJ/mol	$\Delta_f H$(Neutral) kcal/mol	kJ/mol	Neutral reference	CAS registry number
$C_{12}H_{12}S_2^+$							
2,6-bis(methylthio)naphthalene	7.1	(207)	(866)	43	181	*EST	10075-77-1
IP is onset of photoelectron band.							
[dithia cyclophane]	(7.95)	(258)	(1079)	75	312	*EST	73650-69-8
$C_{12}H_{12}Si^+$							
diphenylsilane derivative	(8.8)	(248)	(1037)	45	188	*EST	775-12-2
IP is onset of photoelectron band.							
$C_{12}H_{13}NO^+$							
trimethyl pyrrolo-tropone	(7.3)	(176)	(734)	7	30	*EST	
IP is onset of photoelectron band (84GLE/BIS).							
$C_{12}H_{14}^+$							
PhC≡C–C(CH₃)₃	(8.32±0.08)	(244)	(1020)	52	217	*EST	4250-82-2
IP from 81ELB/LIE. See also: 85ORL/BOG.							
	(≤8.7)	(≤247)	(≤1032)	46	193	*EST	20295-17-4
	(≤8.0)	(≤229)	(≤958)	44	186	*EST	24139-33-1
	(7.94)	(193)	(809)	10	43	*EST	495-52-3

Table 1. Positive Ion Table - Continued

ION Neutral	Ionization potential eV	$\Delta_f H$(Ion) kcal/mol	kJ/mol	$\Delta_f H$(Neutral) kcal/mol	kJ/mol	Neutral reference	CAS registry number
$C_{12}H_{14}^+$							
	(8.09)	(200)	(836)	13	55	*EST	1076-17-1
	(8.2) IP from 81PAD/PAT.	(255)	(1068)	66	277	*EST	
$C_{12}H_{14}O_2^+$							
	(8.1) IP is onset of photoelectron band.	(152)	(638)	−34	−144	*EST	21377-45-7
$C_{12}H_{15}N_2^+$		181	757				
From proton affinity of N,N'-dimethyl-1,8-naphthalenediamine (RN 20734-56-9). PA = 230.0 kcal/mol, 962. kJ/mol.							
$C_{12}H_{16}^+$							
	8.29±0.04 See also: 81KOB/ARA.	(207)	(866)	16±1	66±4	77PED/RYL	3740-05-4
	7.80±0.04 See also: 81KOB/ARA.	(188)	(786)	8±2	33±9	77PED/RYL	3846-66-0
	(≤9.16) IP from 83GLE/HAI2	(≤300)	(≤1255)	88.7	371.1	83GLE/HAI2	82865-42-7
	(≤9.02) IP from 83GLE/HAI2	(≤294)	(≤1231)	86.2	360.7	83GLE/HAI2	87753-95-5

Table 1. Positive Ion Table - Continued

ION Neutral	Ionization potential eV	$\Delta_f H$(Ion) kcal/mol	$\Delta_f H$(Ion) kJ/mol	$\Delta_f H$(Neutral) kcal/mol	$\Delta_f H$(Neutral) kJ/mol	Neutral reference	CAS registry number
$C_{12}H_{16}^+$							
[(CH$_2$)$_6$-benzene]	(7.5) IP is onset of photoelectron band.	(196)	(821)	23	97	*EST	53011-74-8
	(≤8.9)	(≤223)	(≤934)	18	75	*EST	24139-32-0
	(8.7) IP is onset of photoelectron band.	(278)	(1161)	77	322	*EST	5103-78-6
	(≤8.22)	(≤326)	(≤1365)	137	572	*EST	24375-17-5
	(8.6) IP from 81PAD/PAT.	(231)	(968)	33	138	*EST	262-30-6
	(8.2) IP from 82SPA/KOR.	(331)	(1385)	142	594	*EST	64371-17-1
$C_{12}H_{16}Mo^+$							
[Cp$_2$Mo(CH$_3$)$_2$]	(≤6.1±0.1)	(≤226)	(≤943)	85±1	354±6	82PIL/SKI	39333-52-3
$C_{12}H_{16}N_2^+$							
[indole-CH$_2$CH$_2$N(CH$_3$)$_2$]	(7.3) IP is onset of photoelectron band.	(201)	(842)	33	138	*EST	61-50-7

Table 1. Positive Ion Table - Continued

ION / Neutral	Ionization potential eV	$\Delta_f H$(Ion) kcal/mol	$\Delta_f H$(Ion) kJ/mol	$\Delta_f H$(Neutral) kcal/mol	$\Delta_f H$(Neutral) kJ/mol	Neutral reference	CAS registry number
$C_{12}H_{16}O_2^+$							
(bicyclic diketone)	8.5 IP is onset of photoelectron band.	(133)	(558)	−63	−262	*EST	21377-46-8
(dispiro diketone)	(8.9±0.01) IP from 84OLI/FLE.	(161)	(675)	−44	−184	*EST	5011-61-0
$C_{12}H_{16}W^+$							
(bis-cyclopentadienyl dimethyl tungsten)	(5.8) IP is onset of photoelectron band.	(220)	(919)	86±1	359±6	82PIL/SKI	39333-53-4
$C_{12}H_{17}N^+$							
(2-methylphenyl piperidine)	(7.1) IP is onset of photoelectron band (82ROZ/HOU2).	(169)	(706)	5	21	*EST	7250-70-6
(2,4-dimethylphenyl pyrrolidine)	(≤7.60) IP from 82ROZ/HOU2.	(≤219)	(≤918)	44	185	*EST	81506-12-9
(2,6-dimethylphenyl pyrrolidine)	(7.0) IP is onset of photoelectron band (82ROZ/HOU2).	(199)	(834)	38	159	*EST	64175-53-7
$C_{12}H_{17}NO_4^+$							
(pyrrole diester)	(≤8.15) IP from 81CAU/GIA.	(≤4)	(≤15)	−184	−771	*EST	2436-79-5

Table 1. Positive Ion Table - Continued

ION / Neutral	Ionization potential eV	$\Delta_f H$(Ion) kcal/mol	$\Delta_f H$(Ion) kJ/mol	$\Delta_f H$(Neutral) kcal/mol	$\Delta_f H$(Neutral) kJ/mol	Neutral reference	CAS registry number
$C_{12}H_{17}N_2O_6^+$		(−60)	(−251)				

From proton affinity of 2',3'-O'-isopropylideneuridine (RN 362-43-6).
PA = (208) kcal/mol, (870) kJ/mol.

ION / Neutral	Ionization potential eV	$\Delta_f H$(Ion) kcal/mol	$\Delta_f H$(Ion) kJ/mol	$\Delta_f H$(Neutral) kcal/mol	$\Delta_f H$(Neutral) kJ/mol	Neutral reference	CAS registry number
$C_{12}H_{18}^+$							
n-C_4H_9C≡CC≡C(n-C_4H_9)	(8.67)	(258)	(1077)	58	241	77PED/RYL	1120-29-2
(tert-C_4H_9C≡C)$_2$	(8.61±0.02)	(249)	(1040)	50±1	209±5	77KUP/SHI	6130-98-9
1,4-di-n-propylbenzene	(≤8.31) IP from 80GLE/HOP.	(≤176)	(≤736)	−16	−66	*EST	4815-57-0
1,4-diisopropylbenzene	(8.35)	(175)	(732)	−18	−75	*EST	100-18-5
1,3,5-triethylbenzene	(8.32) IP from 84HOW/GON.	(173)	(724)	−19	−79	*EST	102-25-0
hexamethylbenzene	7.85 See also: 84HOW/GON.	160	670	−21±0.7	−87±3	77PED/RYL	87-85-4
octamethylcyclobutadiene dimer	(≤7.83)	(≤219)	(≤917)	39	162	78GRE/LIE	7641-77-2
octahydronaphthalene	(≤9.05)	(≤198)	(≤830)	−10	−43	*EST	38992-78-8

Table 1. Positive Ion Table - Continued

ION / Neutral	Ionization potential eV	$\Delta_f H$(Ion) kcal/mol	$\Delta_f H$(Ion) kJ/mol	$\Delta_f H$(Neutral) kcal/mol	$\Delta_f H$(Neutral) kJ/mol	Neutral reference	CAS registry number
$C_{12}H_{18}{}^+$							
	(≤9.50±0.03)	(≤219)	(≤916)	−0.2±1	−1±5	73ENG/AND2	53862-33-2
	(≤9.57±0.03)	(≤232)	(≤968)	11±2	45±8	73ENG/AND2	15914-95-1
	(8.3) IP is onset of photoelectron band.	(232)	(972)	41	171	*EST	40827-30-3
$C_{12}H_{18}Hg^+$ $((CH_3)_3CC{\equiv}C)_2Hg$	(9.03) IP is onset of photoelectron band (81FUR/PIA).	(285)	(1194)	77	323	*EST	73838-84-3
$C_{12}H_{18}O_4{}^+$ $(CH_3)_3C[C(=O)]_4C(CH_3)_3$	(8.5) IP from 85GLE/DOB.	(25)	(105)	−171	−715	*EST	19909-70-7
$C_{12}H_{19}{}^+$		138	576				
	From proton affinity of hexamethylbenzene (RN 87-85-4). PA = 207.3 kcal/mol, 867. kJ/mol.						
$C_{12}H_{19}N^+$							
	(≤7.82) IP from 82ROZ/HOU2.	(≤241)	(≤1007)	60	253	*EST	81506-11-8
$(CH_3)_3C{-}\bigcirc{-}N(CH_3)_2$	(6.90) IP from 86ORL/MIS. See also: 85BAI/MIS2.	(158)	(661)	−1.2	−4.9	85ORL/MIS	2909-79-7

Table 1. Positive Ion Table – Continued

ION / Neutral	Ionization potential eV	$\Delta_f H$(Ion) kcal/mol	$\Delta_f H$(Ion) kJ/mol	$\Delta_f H$(Neutral) kcal/mol	$\Delta_f H$(Neutral) kJ/mol	Neutral reference	CAS registry number
$C_{12}H_{19}N^+$ — C₆H₅N(n-C₃H₇)₂	6.93	(161)	(672)	1	3	*EST	2217-07-4

IP from charge transfer equilibrium constant determinations; reference standard: IP $C_6H_5N(CH_3)_2$ = 7.12eV. (85LIA/JAC).

$C_{12}H_{19}NO^+$	(≤7.54)	(≤138)	(≤579)	−35	−148	*EST	3357-16-2

IP from 82PFI/GER.

$C_{12}H_{19}NO_2^+$ (2,4-dimethoxy-5-methyl)	(7.2)	(87)	(366)	−79	−329	*EST	79440-50-9

IP is onset of photoelectron band (81DOM/EAT).

(2,5-dimethoxy-4-methyl)	(6.8)	(80)	(335)	−77	−321	*EST	26011-50-7

IP is onset of photoelectron band (81DOM/EAT, 82LEV/LIA).

(3,4-dimethoxy-2-methyl)	(6.9)	(85)	(356)	−74	−310	*EST	56966-33-7

IP is onset of photoelectron band (81DOM/EAT).

$C_{12}H_{19}NO_2S^+$	(6.9)	(92)	(385)	−67	−281	*EST	79440-52-1

IP is onset of photoelectron band (81DOM/EAT).

	(6.8)	(91)	(383)	−65	−273	*EST	61638-07-1

IP is onset of photoelectron band (81DOM/EAT).

	(6.9)	(94)	(393)	−65	−273	*EST	

IP is onset of photoelectron band (81DOM/EAT).

Table 1. Positive Ion Table - Continued

ION Neutral	Ionization potential eV	$\Delta_f H$(Ion) kcal/mol	kJ/mol	$\Delta_f H$(Neutral) kcal/mol	kJ/mol	Neutral reference	CAS registry number
$C_{12}H_{19}NO_3^+$							
(2,3,4-trimethoxy-α-methylphenethylamine)	(≤8.09±0.06)	(≤88)	(≤370)	−98	−411	*EST	22199-12-8
(2,4,5-trimethoxy-α-methylphenethylamine)	(7.0)	(54)	(224)	−108	−451	*EST	22199-15-1

IP is onset of photoelectron band (81DOM/EAT, 82LEV/LIA).

(2,4,6-trimethoxy-α-methylphenethylamine)	(≤7.76±0.06)	(≤67)	(≤279)	−112	−470	*EST	22199-16-2
(3,4,5-trimethoxy-N-methylphenethylamine)	(≤8.44±0.40)	(≤101)	(≤421)	−94	−393	*EST	4838-96-4

$C_{12}H_{20}^+$							
1,3-dimethyladamantane	(9.15)	(159)	(664)	−52±0.7	−219±3	77STE/WAT	702-79-4
2-ethyladamantane	(9.2)	(250)	(1049)	38±0.5	161±2	81GOD/SCH2	14451-87-7
dispiro compound	(8.6)	(233)	(976)	35	146	*EST	64601-40-7

IP is onset of photoelectron band (82SPA/GLE).

$C_{12}H_{20}N^+$							
$C_6H_5N(n-C_3H_7)_2$		138	578				

From proton affinity of $C_6H_5N(n-C_3H_7)_2$ (RN 2217-07-4). PA = 228.6 kcal/mol, 956. kJ/mol.

Table 1. Positive Ion Table – Continued

ION / Neutral	Ionization potential eV	$\Delta_f H$(Ion) kcal/mol	$\Delta_f H$(Ion) kJ/mol	$\Delta_f H$(Neutral) kcal/mol	$\Delta_f H$(Neutral) kJ/mol	Neutral reference	CAS registry number
$C_{12}H_{20}N^+$		152	634				
(2-(t-C₄H₉)C₆H₄N(CH₃)₂)H⁺	From proton affinity of 2-(t-C₄H₉)C₆H₄N(CH₃)₂ (RN 22025-87-2). 229.3 kcal/mol, 959. kJ/mol.						
$C_{12}H_{20}N_2^+$							
1,4-bis(N(CH₃)₂)-2,5-dimethylbenzene isomer	(7.3)	(196)	(822)	28	118	*EST	66102-30-5
	IP is onset of photoelectron band (81NEL/GRE).						
other isomer	(6.4)	(168)	(704)	21	86	*EST	54929-05-4
	IP is onset of photoelectron band (81NEL/GRE).						
$C_{12}H_{21}N^+$							
(CH₂=C(CH₃)CH₂)₃N	(7.8)	(208)	(869)	28	116	*EST	
	IP from 79AUE/BOW.						
$C_{12}H_{21}NO^+$							
5,5-dimethyl-3-(t-C₄H₉NH)-cyclohex-2-enone	(≤7.69)	(≤111)	(≤464)	−66	−278	*EST	27336-61-4
	IP from 82PFI/GER.						
5,5-dimethyl-3-(i-C₄H₉NH)-cyclohex-2-enone	(≤7.98)	(≤122)	(≤513)	−61	−257	*EST	82663-49-8
	IP from 82PFI/GER.						
5,5-dimethyl-3-(N(C₂H₅)₂)-cyclohex-2-enone	(7.3)	(116)	(486)	−52	−218	*EST	65115-73-3
	IP is onset of photoelectron band (82PFI/GER).						
$C_{12}H_{21}NO_2^+$							
cyclododecanone oxime	(8.99±0.03)	(132)	(552)	−75	−315	*EST	4422-06-4
	IP from 79GOL/KUL.						

Table 1. Positive Ion Table - Continued

ION / Neutral	Ionization potential eV	$\Delta_f H$(Ion) kcal/mol	$\Delta_f H$(Ion) kJ/mol	$\Delta_f H$(Neutral) kcal/mol	$\Delta_f H$(Neutral) kJ/mol	Neutral reference	CAS registry number
$C_{12}H_{21}O^+$		87	366				

From the proton affinity of 2,5-Di-t-butylfuran (RN 4789-40-6) (85HOU/ROL).
PA = 213.4 kcal/mol, 893 kJ/mol.

ION / Neutral	Ionization potential eV	$\Delta_f H$(Ion) kcal/mol	$\Delta_f H$(Ion) kJ/mol	$\Delta_f H$(Neutral) kcal/mol	$\Delta_f H$(Neutral) kJ/mol	Neutral reference	CAS registry number
$C_{12}H_{22}^+$							
1-$C_{12}H_{22}$	(9.90±0.02)	(228)	(956)	0.1	0.4	*EST	765-03-7
2-$C_{12}H_{22}$	(9.29±0.02)	(210)	(878)	-4	-18	*EST	629-49-2
3-$C_{12}H_{22}$	(9.17±0.02)	(207)	(868)	-4	-17	*EST	6790-27-8
4-$C_{12}H_{22}$	(9.14±0.03)	(207)	(865)	-4	-17	*EST	22058-01-1
5-$C_{12}H_{22}$	(9.09±0.03)	(206)	(860)	-4	-17	*EST	19780-12-2
$CH_2=C(t-C_4H_9)C(t-C_4H_9)=CH_2$	(8.5)	(179)	(750)	-17	-70	*EST	3378-20-9

IP is onset of photoelectron band (84HON/ZHO).

trans,trans-$((tert-C_4H_9)CH=CH)_2$	(8.23±0.04)	(168)	(704)	-22	-90	*EST	22430-49-5
(Z) cyclic	(8.78±0.15)	(173)	(727)	-29	-120	76JEN	1129-89-1
(E) cyclic	(8.74±0.15)	(173)	(725)	-28	-118	76JEN	1486-75-5
bicyclohexyl	(9.41)	(164.8)	(689.5)	-52.2±.7	-218.4±3.1	78MON/ROS	92-51-3

ION / Neutral	Ionization potential eV	$\Delta_f H$(Ion) kcal/mol	$\Delta_f H$(Ion) kJ/mol	$\Delta_f H$(Neutral) kcal/mol	$\Delta_f H$(Neutral) kJ/mol	Neutral reference	CAS registry number
$C_{12}H_{22}ClNO^+$							
(chlorocyclododecanone oxime)	(9.18±0.03)	(160)	(668)	-52	-218	*EST	4806-74-0

IP from 79GOL/KUL.

Table 1. Positive Ion Table - Continued

ION / Neutral	Ionization potential eV	$\Delta_f H$(Ion) kcal/mol	$\Delta_f H$(Ion) kJ/mol	$\Delta_f H$(Neutral) kcal/mol	$\Delta_f H$(Neutral) kJ/mol	Neutral reference	CAS registry number

$C_{12}H_{22}N^+$
$(CH_2=C(CH_3)CH_2)_3NH$

| | | (163) | (684) | | | | |

From proton affinity of $(CH_2=C(CH_3)CH_2)_3N$. PA = (230.7) kcal/mol, (965.) kJ/mol.

$C_{12}H_{22}NO^+$

| 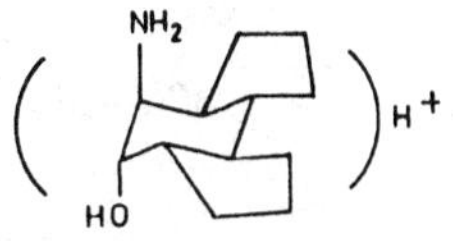 | | 83 | 347 | | | | |

From proton affinity of 3-amino-tricyclo[7.3.0.0^{4,8}] dodecan-2-ol. PA = 220.0 kcal/mol, 920. kJ/mol.

$C_{12}H_{22}O^+$

| 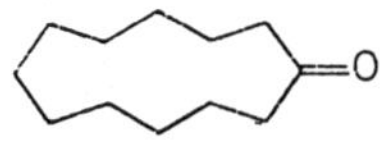 | (8.96±0.03) | (123) | (514) | −84 | −350 | *EST | 830-13-7 |

IP from 79GOL/KUL.

$C_{12}H_{22}Si_2^+$
$(CH_3)_3Si$—⌬—$Si(CH_3)_3$

| 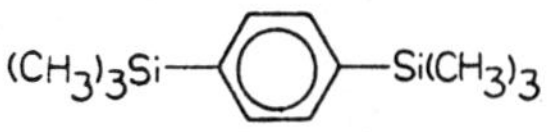 | (8.45) | (132) | (554) | −62 | −261 | *EST | 13183-70-5 |

IP is onset of photoelectron band (82TRA/RED).

$C_{12}H_{23}Cl^+$

| 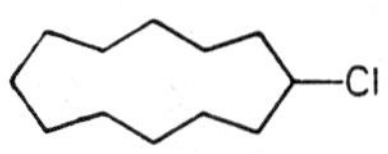 | (9.04±0.03) | (≤143) | (≤598) | −65 | −274 | *EST | 34039-83-3 |

IP from 79GOL/KUL.

$C_{12}H_{23}NO^+$

| 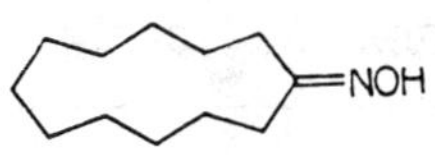 | (8.84±0.03) | (154) | (643) | −50 | −210 | *EST | 946-89-4 |

IP from 79GOL/KUL.

$C_{12}H_{24}^+$
(Z)-$(CH_3)_3CCH_2C(CH_3)=CHC(CH_3)_3$

| | (8.35±0.01) | (142) | (594) | −50 | −211 | *EST | 27656-50-4 |
| 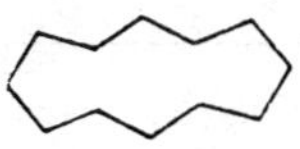 | (9.72±0.03) | (169) | (707) | −55±0.5 | −230±2 | 77PED/RYL | 294-62-2 |

IP from 79GOL/KUL.

Table 1. Positive Ion Table − Continued

ION Neutral	Ionization potential eV	$\Delta_f H$(Ion) kcal/mol kJ/mol		$\Delta_f H$(Neutral) kcal/mol kJ/mol		Neutral reference	CAS registry number
$C_{12}H_{24}O^+$ (cyclododecanol)	(9.26±0.03) IP from 79GOL/KUL.	(119)	(499)	−94	−394	*EST	1724-39-6
$C_{12}H_{24}O_6^+$ (18-crown-6)	8.9 IP is onset of photoelectron band (83BAK/ARM, 82LEV/LIA).	(−22)	(−91)	−227	−950	*EST	17455-13-9
$C_{12}H_{25}N_2^+$ (1,6-diazabicyclo[4.4.4]tetradecane·H+)		117	490				
	From proton affinity of 1,6-diazabicyclo[4.4.4]tetradecane (RN 71058-67-8). PA = 226.0 kcal/mol, 946. kJ/mol.						
$C_{12}H_{25}O_6^+$ (18-crown-6·H+)		−91	−382				
	From proton affinity of 1,4,7,10,13,16-hexaoxacyclooctadecane (18-Crown-6) (RN 17455-13-9). PA = 230. kcal/mol, 962. kJ/mol.						
$C_{12}H_{26}N_2O_4^+$	(≤8.4) IP from 83BAK/ARM.	(≤52)	(≤218)	−141	−592	*EST	23978-55-4
$C_{12}H_{27}BO_3^+$ $(n\text{-}C_4H_9O)_3B$	(≤10.72±0.74)	(≤−27)	(≤−113)	−274±1	−1147±4	77PED/RYL	688-74-4
$C_{12}H_{27}N^+$ $(n\text{-}C_4H_9)_3N$	(7.4) IP is onset of photoelectron band (82ELB/DIE), giving $\Delta_f H$(Ion) in good agreement with value predicted from hydrogen affinity of tertiary amines.	(118)	(494)	−53±0.2	−222±1	*EST	102-82-9
$C_{12}H_{27}P^+$ $(n\text{-}C_4H_9)_3P$	(7.5) IP is onset of photoelectron band.	(160)	(668)	−13±8	−56±35	77PED/RYL	998-40-3
$C_{12}H_{28}N^+$ $(n\text{-}C_4H_9)_3NH$		77	323				
	From proton affinity of $(n\text{-}C_4H_9)_3N$ (RN 102-82-9). PA = 235.4 kcal/mol, 985 kJ/mol (85BOL/HOU).						

Table 1. Positive Ion Table - Continued

ION / Neutral	Ionization potential eV	$\Delta_f H$(Ion) kcal/mol	$\Delta_f H$(Ion) kJ/mol	$\Delta_f H$(Neutral) kcal/mol	$\Delta_f H$(Neutral) kJ/mol	Neutral reference	CAS registry number
$C_{12}H_{28}N_2^+$							
$(n-C_3H_7)_2NN(n-C_3H_7)_2$	(≤7.74)	(≤197)	(≤825)	19	78	*EST	60678-69-5

Reported values of IP's of hydrazines determined by threshold measurements are usually significantly higher than the adiabatic value because of the large geometry change associated with ionization. See also: 84NEL.

$(n-C_4H_9)_2NN(C_2H_5)_2$	(≤7.77)	(≤198)	(≤828)	19	78	*EST	60678-68-4

Reported values of IP's of hydrazines determined by threshold measurements are usually significantly higher than the adiabatic value because of the large geometry change associated with ionization. See also: 84NEL.

ION / Neutral	IP eV	$\Delta_f H$(Ion) kcal/mol	kJ/mol	$\Delta_f H$(Neutral) kcal/mol	kJ/mol	Neutral reference	CAS registry number
$C_{12}H_{28}Sn^+$							
$(C_3H_7)_4Sn$	(≤8.82)	(≤168)	(≤705)	−35±1	−146±6	77PED/RYL	2176-98-9
$(iso-C_3H_7)_4Sn$	(≤8.46)	(≤166)	(≤693)	−29±2	−123±7	77PED/RYL	2949-42-0
$C_{12}H_{30}Ge_2^+$							
$((C_2H_5)_3Ge)_2$	7.48±0.01	90	375	−83±2	−347±8	80TEL/RAB	993-62-4
$C_{12}H_{30}N_3P^+$							
$P(N(C_2H_5)_2)_3$	(≤7.19)	(≤112)	(≤468)	−54±2	−226±10	77PED/RYL	2283-11-6

IP from 82WOR/HAR.

$C_{12}H_{30}Sn_2^+$							
$[(C_2H_5)_3Sn]_2$	(6.60±0.02)	(115)	(482)	−37±2	−155±10	77PED/RYL	993-63-5
$C_{12}H_{31}N_3OP^+$							
$HOP(N(C_2H_5)_2)_3$		9	37				

From proton affinity of $OP(N(C_2H_5)_2)_3$ (RN 2622-07-3) (85BOL/HOU).
PA = 230.0 kcal/mol, 962. kJ/mol.

$C_{12}H_{36}Mo_2N_6^+$							
$Mo_2((CH_3)_2N)_6$	(6.74)	(125)	(522)	−31±3	−128±13	79ADE/CAV	51956-20-8
$C_{12}H_{36}N_6W^+$							
$W(N(CH_3)_2)_6$	(6.3)	(209)	(876)	64±3	268±14	79ADE/CAV	54935-70-5

IP is onset of photoelectron band.

$C_{12}H_{36}N_9P_3^+$							
[(H₃C)₂N]₆P₃N₃ (ring)	(7.85±0.05)	(76)	(318)	−105±3	−439±13	80TEL/RAB	974-68-5
$C_{12}H_{36}Si_5^+$							
$Si(Si(CH_3)_3)_4$	(7.41±0.01)	(37)	(156)	−134±10	−559±40	77PED/RYL	4098-98-0

Table 1. Positive Ion Table - Continued

ION / Neutral	Ionization potential eV	$\Delta_f H$(Ion) kcal/mol	$\Delta_f H$(Ion) kJ/mol	$\Delta_f H$(Neutral) kcal/mol	$\Delta_f H$(Neutral) kJ/mol	Neutral reference	CAS registry number
$C_{12}O_{12}Os_3^+$	(7.6±0.3)	(−218)	(−911)	−393±7	−1644±28	80CON	15696-40-9
IP is onset of photoelectron band. See also: 81GRE/MIN, 82SHE/HAL.							
$C_{12}O_{12}Ru_3^+$	(7.3)	(−267)	(−1116)	−435±6	−1820±26	77PED/RYL	15243-33-1
IP is onset of photoelectron band. See also: 81GRE/MIN.							
$C_{13}H_7N_3O^+$	(8.44)	(290)	(1211)	95	397	*EST	59019-84-0
$C_{13}H_8O_2^+$	(8.42±0.03)	(174)	(727)	−20±2	−85±7	82JOH/KIM	90-47-1
$C_{13}H_9ClO^+$	9.64±0.04	(229)	(959)	7±2	29±8	*EST	134-85-0
$C_{13}H_9N^+$	7.8	249	1044	69±0.2	291±1	81KUD/KUD2	260-94-6
	(8.14±0.02)	(244)	(1019)	56±2	234±7	81STE/BAR	85-02-9

Table 1. Positive Ion Table – Continued

ION / Neutral	Ionization potential eV	$\Delta_f H$(Ion) kcal/mol	$\Delta_f H$(Ion) kJ/mol	$\Delta_f H$(Neutral) kcal/mol	$\Delta_f H$(Neutral) kJ/mol	Neutral reference	CAS registry number
$C_{13}H_9N^+$							
(benzoquinoline structure)	(8.04±0.02)	(240)	(1007)	55±1	231±5	81STE/BAR	230-27-3
(acridine-like structure)	(8.31±0.02)	(250)	(1046)	58±1	244±6	81STE/BAR	229-87-8
$C_{13}H_9NO^+$							
(acridine N-oxide)	(7.45±0.02)	(222)	(930)	50	211	*EST	10399-73-2
$C_{13}H_{10}^+$							
(fluorene)	7.89±0.03	227	948	45±0.2	187±1	81KUD/KUD	86-73-7
Value of IP from charge transfer equilibrium constant determinations (80MAU, re-evaluated) is in agreement.							
$C_{13}H_{10}BrN^+$							
(structure)	(8.6)	(274)	(1146)	76	316	*EST	74309-56-1
IP from 80GRU/SCH, 82LEV/LIA.							
(structure)	(8.62)	(274)	(1148)	76	316	*EST	
(structure)	(8.05)	(262)	(1098)	77	321	*EST	76293-40-8
IP from 80GRU/SCH.							
(structure)	(8.05)	(258)	(1081)	73	304	*EST	77275-12-8
IP from 80SCH/RAM.							

Table 1. Positive Ion Table - Continued

ION / Neutral	Ionization potential eV	$\Delta_f H$(Ion) kcal/mol	$\Delta_f H$(Ion) kJ/mol	$\Delta_f H$(Neutral) kcal/mol	$\Delta_f H$(Neutral) kJ/mol	Neutral reference	CAS registry number
$C_{13}H_{10}BrN^+$	(≤8.15±0.05)	(≤258)	(≤1078)	70	292	*EST	5847-71-2
$C_{13}H_{10}ClN^+$	(8.6) IP from 80GRU/SCH, 82LEV/LIA.	(262)	(1096)	64	266	*EST	74309-55-0
	(8.58)	(261)	(1094)	64	266	*EST	
	(8.07) IP from 80GRU/SCH.	(251)	(1051)	65	272	*EST	5350-12-9
	8.06±0.01 IP from 80SCH/RAM, 82LEV/LIA.	(247)	(1032)	61	254	*EST	6772-77-6
$C_{13}H_{10}FN^+$	(8.66) IP from 82LEV/LIA, 80GRU/SCH.	(223)	(931)	23	96	*EST	74309-53-8
	(8.68)	(223)	(933)	23	96	*EST	
	(≤8.1) IP from 80SCH/RAM.	(≤207)	(≤866)	20	84	*EST	77275-10-6

Table 1. Positive Ion Table – Continued

ION Neutral	Ionization potential eV	$\Delta_f H$(Ion) kcal/mol	kJ/mol	$\Delta_f H$(Neutral) kcal/mol	kJ/mol	Neutral reference	CAS registry number
$C_{13}H_{10}FN^+$	(8.18)	(213)	(890)	24	101	*EST	76293-38-4
	IP from 80GRU/SCH.						
$C_{13}H_{10}IN^+$	(8.3)	(281)	(1175)	89	374	*EST	74309-57-2
	IP from 80GRU/SCH, 82LEV/LIA.						
	(7.95)	(274)	(1147)	91	380	*EST	
	IP from 80GRU/SCH.						
	(7.95)	(270)	(1129)	86	362	*EST	6772-85-6
	IP from 80SCH/RAM.						
$C_{13}H_{10}N^+$		203	851				
	From proton affinity of acridine. (RN 260-94-6). PA = 231.9 kcal/mol, 970. kJ/mol.						
$C_{13}H_{10}N_2O_2^+$	(8.3)	(198)	(828)	6	27	*EST	37790-20-8
	IP is onset of photoelectron band.						
	(8.4)	(240)	(1005)	47	195	*EST	69173-79-1
	IP is onset of photoelectron band.						
	(8.30)	(259)	(1086)	68	285	*EST	50385-24-5
	IP from 80GRU/SCH.						

Table 1. Positive Ion Table - Continued

ION Neutral	Ionization potential eV	Δ_fH(Ion) kcal/mol	Δ_fH(Ion) kJ/mol	Δ_fH(Neutral) kcal/mol	Δ_fH(Neutral) kJ/mol	Neutral reference	CAS registry number
$C_{13}H_{10}N_2O_2^+$							
(2-nitrostyryl)pyridine	(8.3) IP from 80SCH/RAM.	(255)	(1069)	64	268	*EST	77340-84-2
$C_{13}H_{10}O^+$							
biphenyl-CHO	(8.47±0.03)	(210)	(879)	15±0.7	62±3	*EST	3218-36-8
benzophenone	9.05±0.05 IP from 78CEN/FRA, 82LEV/LIA.	221	923	12±0.7	50±3	78SAB/LAF3	119-61-9
$C_{13}H_{10}O_2^+$							
4-hydroxybenzophenone	(8.3) IP is onset of photoelectron band.	(160)	(670)	−31.2±2	−131±8	*EST	1137-42-4
phenyl benzoate	8.99±0.02	173	724	−34±0.7	−143±3	77PED/RYL	93-99-2
$C_{13}H_{10}O_3^+$							
diphenyl carbonate	(9.01±0.05)	(134)	(558)	−74±2	−311±9	77PED/RYL	102-09-0
$C_{13}H_{11}^+$							
fluorene·H+		210	880				

From proton affinity of fluorene (RN 86-73-7). PA = 200.0 kcal/mol, 837. kJ/mol.

Table 1. Positive Ion Table – Continued

ION / Neutral	Ionization potential eV	$\Delta_f H$(Ion) kcal/mol	kJ/mol	$\Delta_f H$(Neutral) kcal/mol	kJ/mol	Neutral reference	CAS registry number
$C_{13}H_{11}ClN_2O^+$							
2-hydroxy-5-methyl-(3-chlorophenylazo)benzene	(7.7) IP is onset of photoelectron band (81MIL/MIL).	(217)	(910)	40	167	*EST	19116-23-5
2-hydroxy-5-methyl-(4-chlorophenylazo)benzene	(7.7) IP is onset of photoelectron band (81MIL/MIL).	(217)	(910)	40	167	*EST	2491-56-7
$C_{13}H_{11}N^+$							
N-benzylideneaniline	7.9 IP is onset of photoelectron band.	(232)	(972)	50	210	*EST	538-51-2
2-(1-phenylvinyl)pyridine	(8.65) See also: 80GRU/SCH.	(270)	(1130)	71	295	*EST	15260-65-8
3-(1-phenylvinyl)pyridine	(8.73)	(269)	(1125)	68	283	*EST	74309-58-3
4-(1-phenylvinyl)pyridine	(8.90)	(277)	(1159)	72	300	*EST	54813-56-8
2-(2-phenylvinyl)pyridine	(8.15) IP from 80GRU/SCH.	(264)	(1105)	76	319	*EST	1519-59-1
2-styrylpyridine	(≤7.99±0.05) See also: 80SCH/RAM.	(≤252)	(≤1054)	68	283	*EST	538-49-8

Table 1. Positive Ion Table - Continued

ION / Neutral	Ionization potential eV	$\Delta_f H$(Ion) kcal/mol	kJ/mol	$\Delta_f H$(Neutral) kcal/mol	kJ/mol	Neutral reference	CAS registry number

$C_{13}H_{11}N^+$

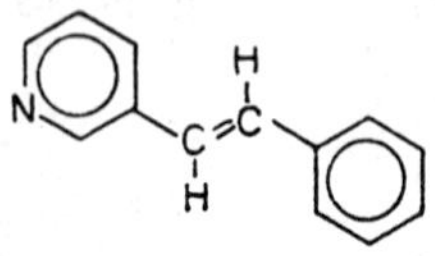

3-styrylpyridine (E) — (≤8.10±0.05) (≤256) (≤1072) 69 290 *EST 5097-91-6
See also: 80SCH/RAM.

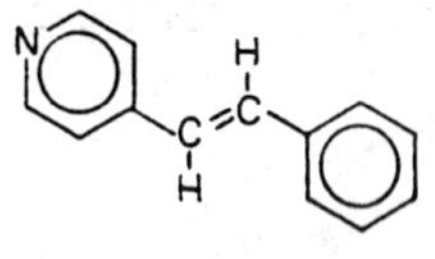

4-styrylpyridine (E) — (≤8.34±0.05) (≤261) (≤1093) 69 288 *EST 5097-93-8
See also: 80SCH/RAM.

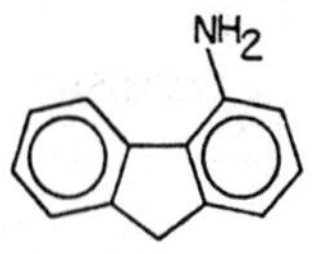

1-aminofluorene — (7.25) (216) (904) 49 205 *EST 7083-63-8
IP is onset of photoelectron band (84GLE/SCH).

$C_{13}H_{11}NO^+$

2-methylphenyl 2-pyridyl ketone — (8.72) (231) (966) 30 125 *EST
IP from 82LEV/LIA, 80GRU/SCH.

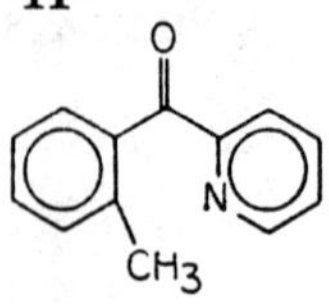

$C_{13}H_{11}N_3O_3^+$

(2-hydroxy-5-methylphenylazo)-4-nitrobenzene — (7.7) (221) (924) 43 181 *EST 1435-68-3
IP is onset of photoelectron band (81MIL/MIL).

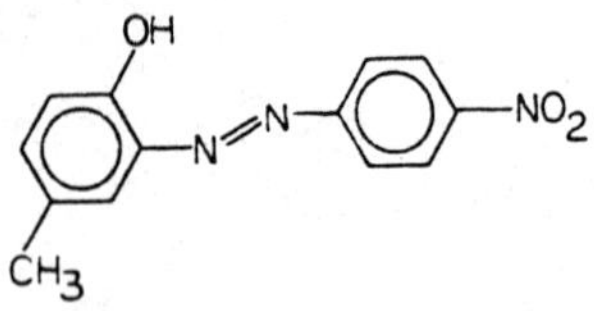

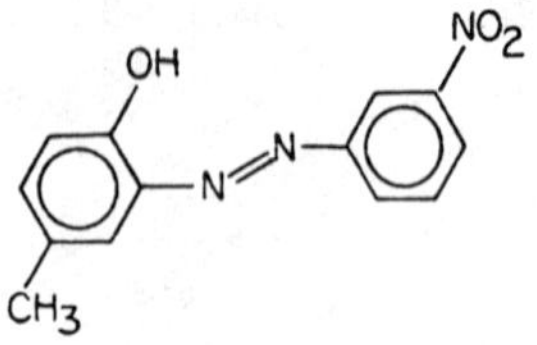

(2-hydroxy-5-methylphenylazo)-3-nitrobenzene — (≤8.19) (≤232) (≤971) 43 181 *EST 19020-84-9
IP from 81MIL/MIL.

$C_{13}H_{11}O^+$

hydroxydiphenylmethyl cation — 167 698
From proton affinity of $(C_6H_5)_2CO$ (RN 119-61-9). PA = 210.9 kcal/mol, 882. kJ/mol.

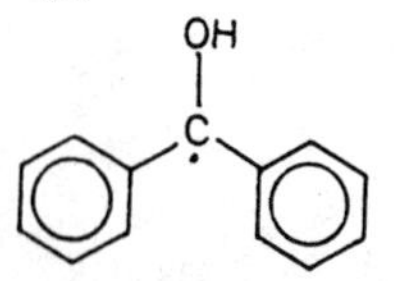

Table 1. Positive Ion Table - Continued

ION Neutral	Ionization potential eV	$\Delta_f H$(Ion) kcal/mol	$\Delta_f H$(Ion) kJ/mol	$\Delta_f H$(Neutral) kcal/mol	$\Delta_f H$(Neutral) kJ/mol	Neutral reference	CAS registry number
$C_{13}H_{12}^+$							
diphenylmethane	8.55±0.03	230	965	33±0.7	140±3	77PED/RYL	101-81-5
2-methylbiphenyl	(8.10±0.02)	(228)	(954)	41±2	172±7	77PED/RYL	643-58-3
3-methylbiphenyl	(7.95±0.02)	(219)	(917)	36±2	150±8	*EST	643-93-6
4-methylbiphenyl	(7.80±0.02)	(216)	(904)	36±2	151±8	*EST	644-08-6
phenylnorbornadiene	(≤9.06) IP from 83HOU/RON.	(≤289)	(≤1210)	79	330	*EST	74437-39-1
spiro compound	(8.0±0.1)	(266)	(1115)	82	343	*EST	29150-13-8
$C_{13}H_{12}N_2O^+$							
2-hydroxy-5-methylazobenzene	(7.4) IP is onset of photoelectron band (81MIL/MIL).	(217)	(910)	47	196	*EST	952-47-6
$C_{13}H_{12}O^+$							
2,7-dimethyltropone derivative	(8.1) IP is onset of photoelectron band.	(186)	(780)	-0.5±3	-2±11	77PED/RYL	2484-16-4

Table 1. Positive Ion Table - Continued

ION Neutral	Ionization potential eV	$\Delta_f H$(Ion) kcal/mol	kJ/mol	$\Delta_f H$(Neutral) kcal/mol	kJ/mol	Neutral reference	CAS registry number
$C_{13}H_{12}S^+$	(7.87±0.02)	(227)	(950)	46	191	*EST	831-91-4
$C_{13}H_{13}P^+$	(≤8.28±0.05) IP from 82IKU/KEB.	(≤235)	(≤984)	44	185	*EST	1486-28-8
$C_{13}H_{14}^+$	(7.10)	(209)	(873)	45	188	*EST	941-81-1
	≤8.95 IP from 84MAR/KAY.	(≤222)	(≤929)	16	65	*EST	
$C_{13}H_{14}O^+$	(7.82) IP from 81DAL/NIB.	(197)	(824)	17	70	81DAL/NIB	64353-61-3
$C_{13}H_{14}OP^+$		118	494				

From proton affinity of $(C_6H_5)_2CH_3PO$ (RN 2129-89-7) (86TRA/MUN). PA = 216. kcal/mol, 904. kJ/mol.

| $C_{13}H_{14}P^+$ | | 180 | 752 | | | | |

From proton affinity of $(C_6H_5)_2(CH_3)P$ (RN 1486-28-8). PA = 230.3 kcal/mol, 963.5 kJ/mol.

Table 1. Positive Ion Table – Continued

ION Neutral	Ionization potential eV	$\Delta_f H$(Ion) kcal/mol	$\Delta_f H$(Ion) kJ/mol	$\Delta_f H$(Neutral) kcal/mol	$\Delta_f H$(Neutral) kJ/mol	Neutral reference	CAS registry number
$C_{13}H_{14}Si^+$	(8.75±0.15)	(229)	(959)	27	115	*EST	776-76-1
$C_{13}H_{15}MnO_3^+$	(7.0) IP is onset of photoelectron band (81CAL/HUB).	(14)	(57)	−148	−618	*EST	34807-89-1
$C_{13}H_{16}^+$	(8.24±0.08) IP from 81ELB/LIE.	(239)	(1000)	49	205	*EST	
$C_{13}H_{16}N_2O_2^+$	(7.03) IP is onset of photoelectron band (83CAN/HAM).	(109)	(454)	−54	−224	*EST	
$C_{13}H_{16}O^+$	(7.85) IP from 85ORL/MIS.	(196)	(820)	15	63	85ORL/MIS	
$C_{13}H_{17}N_2^+$		78	327				

From proton affinity of N,N,N'-trimethyl-1,8-naphthalenediamine (RN 20723-57-0). PA = 235.6 kcal/mol, 986. kJ/mol.

$C_{13}H_{18}^+$	(8.0) IP is onset of photoelectron band.	(195)	(817)	11	45	*EST	3761-63-5

Table 1. Positive Ion Table - Continued

ION / Neutral	Ionization potential eV	$\Delta_f H$(Ion) kcal/mol	kJ/mol	$\Delta_f H$(Neutral) kcal/mol	kJ/mol	Neutral reference	CAS registry number
$C_{13}H_{18}N_2O^+$ (5-methoxy-N,N-dimethyltryptamine)	(≤7.61±0.14)	(≤172)	(≤721)	−3	−13	*EST	1019-45-0
$C_{13}H_{19}N^+$ (1-(2,4-dimethylphenyl)piperidine)	(≤7.70) IP from 82ROZ/HOU2.	(≤202)	(≤844)	24	101	*EST	81506-14-1
(1-(2,6-dimethylphenyl)piperidine)	(7.35) IP is onset of photoelectron band (82ROZ/HOU2).	(185)	(774)	16	65	*EST	81506-15-2
$C_{13}H_{21}NO^+$ (5,5-dimethyl-3-piperidino-2-cyclohexenone)	(≤7.67) IP from 82PFI/GER.	(≤131)	(≤546)	−46	−194	*EST	13358-76-4
$C_{13}H_{22}N^+$ (2,4-di-tert-butylpyridine H+)		115	483				

From proton affinity of 2,4-di-tert-butylpyridine (RN 29939-31-9).
PA = (231.4) kcal/mol, (968) kJ/mol.

		113	473				
(2,6-di-tert-butylpyridine H+)							

From proton affinity of 2,6-di-tert-butylpyridine (RN 585-48-4).
PA = 233.4 kcal/mol, 976. kJ/mol.

| $C_{13}H_{23}N^+$ | (6.8) IP is onset of photoelectron band (82ALD/ARR). | (184) | (770) | 27 | 114 | *EST | 84509-55-7 |

Table 1. Positive Ion Table – Continued

ION / Neutral	Ionization potential eV	$\Delta_f H$(Ion) kcal/mol	$\Delta_f H$(Ion) kJ/mol	$\Delta_f H$(Neutral) kcal/mol	$\Delta_f H$(Neutral) kJ/mol	Neutral reference	CAS registry number
$C_{13}H_{23}NO^+$							
(structure: 5,5-dimethyl-3-(n-pentylamino)cyclohex-2-enone)	(≤8.07) IP from 82PFI/GER.	(≤122)	(≤512)	−64	−267	*EST	82663-50-1
$C_{13}H_{24}^+$							
1-$C_{13}H_{24}$	(9.90±0.02)	(223)	(934)	−5	−21	*EST	26186-02-7
2-$C_{13}H_{24}$	(9.28±0.02)	(205)	(856)	−9	−39	*EST	28467-75-6
3-$C_{13}H_{24}$	(9.14±0.03)	(202)	(844)	−9	−38	*EST	60186-78-9
4-$C_{13}H_{24}$	(9.07±0.03)	(200)	(837)	−9	−38	*EST	60186-79-0
5-$C_{13}H_{24}$	(9.09±0.03)	(201)	(839)	−9	−38	*EST	60186-80-3
6-$C_{13}H_{24}$	(9.05±0.03)	(200)	(835)	−9	−38	*EST	42371-66-4
cyclohexenyl-$(CH_2)_6CH_3$	(8.37±0.02)	(232)	(969)	39±1	161±5	*EST	15232-86-7
$C_{13}H_{24}Si_2^+$							
(o-bis(trimethylsilylmethyl)benzene type: $Si(CH_3)_3$ / $CH_2Si(CH_3)_3$)	(8.26) IP is onset of photoelectron band (82TRA/RED).	(152)	(637)	−38	−160	*EST	1899-74-7
$C_{13}H_{25}N^+$							
(bicyclic amine structure)	(7.3) IP from 82ALD/ARR.	(157)	(657)	−11	−47	81ALD/ARR	
$C_{13}H_{26}^+$							
1-$C_{13}H_{26}$	(9.38) IP from 81HOL/FIN.	(172)	(719)	−44.5	−186.2	*EST	2437-56-1
$((CH_3)_3C)_2C=CHCH(CH_3)_2$	(8.31±0.01)	(136)	(569)	−56	−233	*EST	50787-12-7

Table 1. Positive Ion Table – Continued

ION / Neutral	Ionization potential eV	$\Delta_f H$(Ion) kcal/mol kJ/mol	$\Delta_f H$(Neutral) kcal/mol kJ/mol	Neutral reference	CAS registry number

$C_{13}H_{26}N^+$

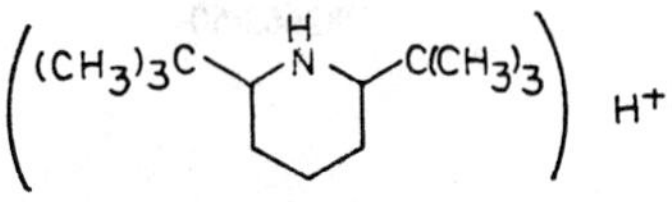

[(CH₃)₃C–NH–C(CH₃)₃ piperidine structure] H⁺
56   233
From proton affinity of 2,6-di-tert-butylpiperidine (RN 29939-31-9).
PA = 234.3 kcal/mol, 980. kJ/mol.

[bicyclic amine structure] H⁺
140   586
From proton affinity of out-6H-1-azabicyclo[4.4.4]tetradecane.
PA = 214.3 kcal/mol, 896. kJ/mol.

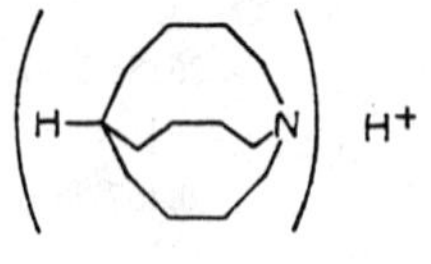

$C_{13}H_{30}N_4^+$

[tetraazamacrocycle structure]
(≤8.0)   (≤185)   (≤775)   1   3   *EST
IP from 83BAK/ARM.

$C_{14}F_{10}^+$

[perfluoroanthracene structure]
(8.28±0.05)   (−165)   (−691)   −356   −1490   *EST   1580-19-4

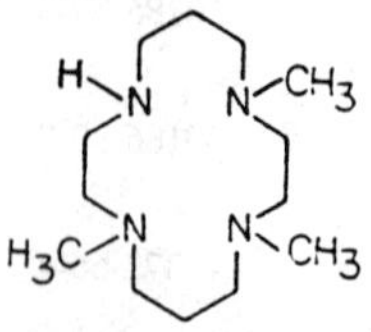

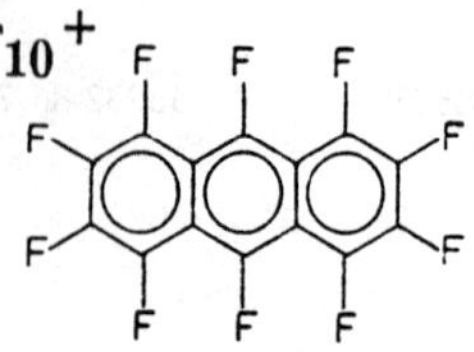

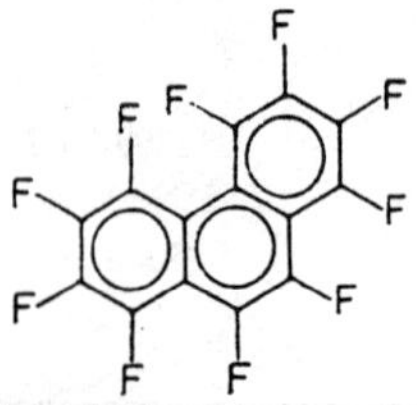

[perfluorophenanthrene structure]
(8.75±0.05)   (−160)   (−669)   −362   −1513   *EST   1580-20-7

$C_{14}H_8^+$

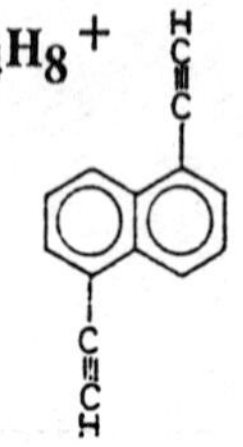

[1,5-diethynylnaphthalene structure]
(7.91)   (324)   (1357)   142   594   *EST   67665-34-3
IP from 81GLE/SCH.

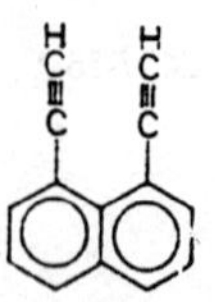

[1,8-diethynylnaphthalene structure]
(7.88)   (330)   (1381)   148   621   *EST   18067-44-2
IP from 81GLE/SCH, 84GLE/SCH.

Table 1. Positive Ion Table - Continued

ION / Neutral	Ionization potential eV	$\Delta_f H$(Ion) kcal/mol	$\Delta_f H$(Ion) kJ/mol	$\Delta_f H$(Neutral) kcal/mol	$\Delta_f H$(Neutral) kJ/mol	Neutral reference	CAS registry number
$C_{14}H_8O_2^+$ (anthraquinone)	9.25±0.03	190	797	−22.8±1.6	−95.2±6.6	77PED/RYL	84-65-1
(phenanthrenequinone)	(8.64±0.03)	(166±1)	(695±5)	−33±1	−139±5	77PED/RYL	84-11-7
$C_{14}H_9Br^+$ (9-bromoanthracene)	(7.58) IP from 83KLA/KOV, 82LEV/LIA.	(236)	(986)	61	255	*EST	1564-64-3
$C_{14}H_9Cl^+$ (9-chloroanthracene)	(7.45±0.03) IP from 82LEV/LIA, 83KLA/KOV.	(221)	(924)	49	205	*EST	716-53-0
$C_{14}H_9F^+$ (9-fluoroanthracene)	(7.46) IP from 83KLA/KOV, 82LEV/LIA.	(179)	(751)	7	31	*EST	529-85-1
$C_{14}H_9NO_2^+$ (9-nitroanthracene)	7.87±0.01 IP from 82LEV/LIA, 83KLA/KOV.	(233)	(974)	51	215	*EST	602-60-8
$C_{14}H_{10}^+$ (diphenylacetylene)	7.90±0.02 See also: 81ELB/LIE.	278	1165	96±1	403±4	82CHI/LIE	501-65-5

Table 1. Positive Ion Table - Continued

ION Neutral	Ionization potential eV	$\Delta_f H$(Ion) kcal/mol	kJ/mol	$\Delta_f H$(Neutral) kcal/mol	kJ/mol	Neutral reference	CAS registry number
$C_{14}H_{10}{}^+$							
anthracene	7.45±0.03 See also: 83KLA/KOV, 84STA/MAQ. Value of IP from charge transfer equilibrium constant determination (80MAU, re-evaluated) is in agreement.	227	949	55±0.2	230±1	79KUD/KUD4	120-12-7
phenanthrene	7.86±0.02 Value of IP from charge transfer equilibrium constant determination (80MAU, re-evaluated), 7.89 eV.	230	965	49±0.2	207±1	79KUD/KUD4	85-01-8
	(7.55) IP from 81GLE/GUB.	(293)	(1226)	119	498	*EST	40480-63-5
	(7.71) IP from 81GLE/GUB.	(247)	(1036)	70	292	*EST	77669-79-5
$C_{14}H_{10}O^+$							
diphenylketene	(7.85)	(206)	(862)	25	105	80DEM/WUL	525-06-4
	(7.45)	(207)	(866)	35±4	147±18	*EST	257-05-6
anthrone	(8.83±0.03)	(211)	(883)	7	31	78KIM/WIN	90-44-8
$C_{14}H_{10}O_2{}^+$							
benzil	(8.5) IP is onset of photoelectron band.	(183)	(764)	−13±0.7	−56±3	77PED/RYL	134-81-6

Table 1. Positive Ion Table – Continued

ION / Neutral	Ionization potential eV	$\Delta_f H$(Ion) kcal/mol	$\Delta_f H$(Ion) kJ/mol	$\Delta_f H$(Neutral) kcal/mol	$\Delta_f H$(Neutral) kJ/mol	Neutral reference	CAS registry number
$C_{14}H_{10}O_2^+$							
(dibenzodioxin-like)	(7.28±0.02) IP from 81BOU/DAG.	(153)	(639)	−15	−63	81BOU/DAG	
(2-phenyl-benzodioxin)	(7.60±0.02) IP from 81BOU/DAG.	(171)	(716)	−4	−17	81BOU/DAG	
$C_{14}H_{11}^+$							
(9,10-dihydroanthracenyl)	From proton affinity of anthracene (RN 120-12-7). PA = 207.0 kcal/mol, 866. kJ/mol.	214	894				
(dihydrophenanthrenyl)	From proton affinity of phenanthrene (RN 85-01-8). PA = 198.7 kcal/mol, 831. kJ/mol.	216	906				
$C_{14}H_{12}^+$							
(1,1-diphenylethylene)	(8.00±0.02)	(243)	(1018)	59±1	246±4	77PED/RYL	530-48-3
(trans-stilbene)	(7.80±0.02)	(240)	(1005)	60.3±0.4	252.4±1.6	77PED/RYL	645-49-8
(cis-stilbene)	7.70±0.03	234	978	56±0.7	235±3	77PED/RYL	103-30-0
(1,8-divinylnaphthalene)	(7.72) IP from GLE/SCH.	(252)	(1054)	74	309	*EST	17935-66-9

Table 1. Positive Ion Table – Continued

ION Neutral	Ionization potential eV	$\Delta_f H$(Ion) kcal/mol	$\Delta_f H$(Ion) kJ/mol	$\Delta_f H$(Neutral) kcal/mol	$\Delta_f H$(Neutral) kJ/mol	Neutral reference	CAS registry number
$C_{14}H_{12}^+$							
(phenanthrene-dihydro structure)	(7.55±0.02)	(216)	(903)	42±2	175±8	77SHA/GOL	776-35-2
(acenaphthylene-cyclobutane structure)	(7.60) IP from 82GLE/GUB.	(265)	(1107)	89	374	*EST	
$C_{14}H_{12}ClNO_3^+$							
(chloronaphthoquinone-N(COCH3)(C2H5))	(8.7) IP is onset of photoelectron band (80RED/FRE).	(120)	(504)	−80	−335	*EST	4497-72-7
$C_{14}H_{12}O^+$							
(4-methylbenzophenone)	(9.13±0.05)	(217)	(907)	6.1±1	26±4	*EST	
(deoxybenzoin, PhCH2COPh)	(8.50) IP is onset of photoelectron band (78CEN/FRA).	(201)	(842)	5±1	22±5	77PED/RYL	451-40-1
$C_{14}H_{13}^+$							
($Ph_2\dot{C}$–CH_3)		213	889				
	From proton affinity of $(C_6H_5)_2C=CH_2$ (RN 530-48-3). PA = 211.9 kcal/mol, 887. kJ/mol.						
$C_{14}H_{13}N^+$							
(o-tolyl-N=CH-Ph)	(7.7) IP is onset of photoelectron band.	(236)	(988)	59	245	*EST	5877-55-4
(Ph-N=CH-m-tolyl)	(≤8.07)	(≤245)	(≤1024)	59	245	*EST	6906-25-8

Table 1. Positive Ion Table – Continued

ION / Neutral	Ionization potential eV	$\Delta_f H$(Ion) kcal/mol	$\Delta_f H$(Ion) kJ/mol	$\Delta_f H$(Neutral) kcal/mol	$\Delta_f H$(Neutral) kJ/mol	Neutral reference	CAS registry number
$C_{14}H_{13}N^+$							
2-methylphenyl(2-pyridyl)methylene	8.55 IP from 80GRU/SCH.	(261)	(1092)	64	268	*EST	74309-54-9
3-methylphenyl(2-pyridyl)methylene	(8.48)	(258)	(1080)	63	262	*EST	
4-methylphenyl(2-pyridyl)methylene	(8.45)	(257)	(1077)	63	262	*EST	
2-methylstyryl-2-pyridine	8.01 IP from 80GRU/SCH, 80SCH/RAM.	(249)	(1040)	64	267	*EST	77275-11-7
4-methylstyryl-3-pyridine	(≤7.90±0.05)	(≤242)	(≤1012)	60	250	*EST	6892-33-7
styryl-4-pyridine methyl	(≤8.39±0.05)	(≤254)	(≤1063)	60	253	*EST	18150-12-4
$C_{14}H_{13}NO^+$							
3-methoxyphenyl(2-pyridyl)methylene	(8.27)	(225)	(942)	34	144	*EST	
4-methoxyphenyl(2-pyridyl)methylene	(8.15)	(222)	(930)	34	144	*EST	

Table 1. Positive Ion Table − Continued

ION / Neutral	Ionization potential eV	$\Delta_f H$(Ion) kcal/mol	kJ/mol	$\Delta_f H$(Neutral) kcal/mol	kJ/mol	Neutral reference	CAS registry number
C$_{14}$H$_{13}$NO$^+$							
(2-methoxyphenyl-vinyl-pyridine)	(7.87) IP from 80GRU/SCH.	(217)	(908)	36	149	*EST	62205-27-0
(3-methoxyphenyl-vinyl-pyridine)	(≤7.72±0.05)	(≤211)	(≤883)	33	138	*EST	5847-73-4
C$_{14}$H$_{13}$N$_3$O$_3^+$							
(methoxy-methyl-phenyl-azo-nitrophenyl)	(7.8) IP is onset of photoelectron band (81MIL/MIL).	(229)	(959)	49	206	*EST	
C$_{14}$H$_{14}^+$							
(dicycloheptyl)	(8.2) IP is onset of photoelectron band.	(288)	(1203)	99	412	*EST	39473-62-6
(bibenzyl)	8.7±0.1	235	982	34.2±0.4	143.0±1.8	77PED/RYL	103-29-7
(2,2'-dimethylbiphenyl)	(8.05±0.02)	(214)	(895)	28	118	*EST	605-39-0
(3,3'-dimethylbiphenyl)	(7.85±0.02)	(208)	(871)	27	114	*EST	612-75-9
(4,4'-dimethylbiphenyl)	(8.50)	(223)	(934)	27	114	*EST	613-33-2

Table 1. Positive Ion Table – Continued

ION / Neutral	Ionization potential eV	$\Delta_f H$(Ion) kcal/mol	$\Delta_f H$(Ion) kJ/mol	$\Delta_f H$(Neutral) kcal/mol	$\Delta_f H$(Neutral) kJ/mol	Neutral reference	CAS registry number
$C_{14}H_{14}^+$	(7.7)	(261)	(1094)	84	351	*EST	88635-77-2
	IP is onset of photoelectron band (84AND/CER).						
$C_{14}H_{14}Hg^+$	(7.94)	(261)	(1091)	78	325	*EST	537-64-4
	IP is onset of photoelectron band (81FUR/PIA).						
$C_{14}H_{14}N_2^+$	(8.35)	(265)	(1109)	72	303	*EST	6574-83-0
$C_{14}H_{14}N_2O^+$	(≤7.88)	(≤221)	(≤923)	39	163	*EST	19020-81-6
	IP from 81MIL/MIL.						
	(≤7.88)	(≤221)	(≤923)	39	163	*EST	17739-97-8
	IP from 81MIL/MIL.						
	(7.3)	(221)	(925)	53	221	*EST	77046-80-1
	IP is onset of photoelectron band (81MIL/MIL).						
$C_{14}H_{14}N_2O_2^+$	(≤7.85)	(≤192)	(≤802)	11	45	*EST	23375-56-6
	IP from 81MIL/MIL.						
	(≤7.76)	(≤190)	(≤794)	11	45	*EST	15096-05-6
	IP from 81MIL/MIL.						

Table 1. Positive Ion Table – Continued

ION / Neutral	Ionization potential eV	$\Delta_f H$(Ion) kcal/mol	$\Delta_f H$(Ion) kJ/mol	$\Delta_f H$(Neutral) kcal/mol	$\Delta_f H$(Neutral) kJ/mol	Neutral reference	CAS registry number
$C_{14}H_{14}N_2O_2^+$	(7.72) IP from 77NUY/MES.	(198)	(830)	20	85	*EST	501-58-6
$C_{14}H_{14}N_2O_3^+$	(≤8.06) IP from 81MIL/CIL.	(≤202)	(≤844)	16	66	*EST	1562-94-3
$C_{14}H_{14}O^+$	(≤7.78)	(≤161)	(≤674)	−18	−77	*EST	5040-51-7
$C_{14}H_{14}OS^+$	(8.1) IP is onset of photoelectron band (84GLE/BIS).	(227)	(950)	40	169	*EST	
	(≤8.45) IP from 81MOH/JIA.	(≤204)	(≤855)	10	40	*EST	
$C_{14}H_{14}OSi^+$	(8.0±0.1)	(158)	(661)	−27	−111	*EST	18414-62-5
	(~7.0) IP from 82TRA/RED.	(~57)	(~240)	−104	−435	*EST	

Table 1. Positive Ion Table – Continued

ION / Neutral	Ionization potential eV	$\Delta_f H$(Ion) kcal/mol	kJ/mol	$\Delta_f H$(Neutral) kcal/mol	kJ/mol	Neutral reference	CAS registry number
$C_{14}H_{14}O_2S^+$ (bis(4-methylphenyl) sulfone)	(8.66±0.04)	(151)	(634)	−48±0.7	−202±3	77PED/RYL	599-66-6
$C_{14}H_{14}O_2S_2^+$ (bis(4-methoxyphenyl) disulfide)	7.6 IP from 82GIO/BOC.	(161)	(674)	−14	−59	*EST	5335-87-5
$C_{14}H_{14}S^+$ (dibenzyl sulfide)	(8.05±0.02)	(232)	(969)	46±1	192±4	77PED/RYL	538-74-9
$C_{14}H_{14}SSi^+$ (5,5-dimethyldibenzosilathiin)	(7.45) IP is onset of photoelectron band (82TRA/RED). See also: 81TRA/RED.	(206)	(864)	35	145	*EST	61431-08-1
$C_{14}H_{14}S_2^+$ (bis(4-methylphenyl) disulfide)	7.5 IP is onset of photoelectron band (82GIO/BOC).	(215)	(901)	42	177	*EST	103-19-5
$C_{14}H_{14}S_2Si^+$	(8.4) IP is onset of photoelectron band (83AND/CAU).	(220)	(919)	26	109	*EST	57864-56-9
$C_{14}H_{14}Se^+$ (dibenzyl selenide)	(≤7.96) IP from 81BAK/ARM.	(≤243)	(≤1015)	59	247	*EST	1842-38-2

Table 1. Positive Ion Table – Continued

ION Neutral	Ionization potential eV	$\Delta_f H$(Ion) kcal/mol kJ/mol	$\Delta_f H$(Neutral) kcal/mol kJ/mol	Neutral reference	CAS registry number
$C_{14}H_{14}Si^+$	(7.4) IP is onset of photoelectron band.	(178) (743)	7 29	*EST	13688-68-1
$C_{14}H_{15}^+$		205 859 From proton affinity of $C_6H_5CH_2CH_2C_6H_5$ (RN 103-29-7). PA = 194.6 kcal/mol, 814. kJ/mol.			
$C_{14}H_{15}BrO^+$	(≤8.57) IP from 82PFI/GER.	(≤184) (≤770)	−14 −57	*EST	72036-54-5
$C_{14}H_{15}ClO^+$	(8.67) IP from 82PFI/GER.	(173) (724)	−27 −113	*EST	59344-32-0
$C_{14}H_{15}FO^+$	(8.90) IP from 82PFI/GER.	(124) (518)	−82 −341	*EST	72036-55-6
$C_{14}H_{15}NO_3^+$	(≤9.28) IP from 82PFI/GER.	(≤193) (≤806)	−21 −89	*EST	29339-45-5

Table 1. Positive Ion Table — Continued

ION / Neutral	Ionization potential eV	$\Delta_f H$(Ion) kcal/mol	$\Delta_f H$(Ion) kJ/mol	$\Delta_f H$(Neutral) kcal/mol	$\Delta_f H$(Neutral) kJ/mol	Neutral reference	CAS registry number
$C_{14}H_{16}^+$							
2,3,6,7-tetramethylnaphthalene	(≤7.60±0.03)	(≤180)	(≤754)	5±0.7	21±3	*EST	1134-40-3
(tricyclic structure)	(7.95±0.05) IP from 81HEI/KOV.	(241)	(1007)	57	240	*EST	54922-12-2
$C_{14}H_{16}Cr^+$							
bis(methylbenzene)chromium	(≤5.24±0.1) See also: 82CAB/COW.	(≤86)	(≤360)	−35	−146	*EST	12087-58-0
$C_{14}H_{16}O^+$							
4,4-dimethyl-6-phenylcyclohex-2-enone	(≤8.90) IP from 82PFI/GER.	(≤187)	(≤781)	−19	−78	*EST	36047-17-3
$C_{14}H_{16}Si^+$							
dimethyldiphenylsilane	(8.5) IP from 81TRA/RED.	(209)	(875)	13	55	*EST	778-24-5
$C_{14}H_{17}NO^+$							
3-(4-aminophenyl)-5,5-dimethylcyclohex-2-enone	(≤7.85) IP from 82PFI/GER.	(≤163)	(≤683)	−18	−74	*EST	72036-57-8
$C_{14}H_{18}^+$							
octahydroanthracene	(7.86) IP from charge transfer equilibrium constant determinations (80MAU).	(172)	(721)	−9±0.7	−37±3	77PED/RYL	1079-71-6

Table 1. Positive Ion Table - Continued

ION / Neutral	Ionization potential eV	$\Delta_f H$(Ion) kcal/mol	$\Delta_f H$(Ion) kJ/mol	$\Delta_f H$(Neutral) kcal/mol	$\Delta_f H$(Neutral) kJ/mol	Neutral reference	CAS registry number
$C_{14}H_{18}^+$	7.89	174	727	−8±2	−34±8	77SHA/GOL	5325-97-3

IP from charge transfer equilibrium constant determinations (80MAU).

| | (≤8.37) | (≤246) | (≤1029) | 53 | 221 | *EST | |

IP from 80GLE/HOP.

| $C_{14}H_{18}N_2^+$ | (6.70±0.02) | (200) | (839) | 46 | 193 | *EST | 10075-69-1 |
| | (6.45±0.02) | (212) | (884) | 63 | 262 | *EST | 20734-58-1 |

| $C_{14}H_{18}N_4^+$ | (7.3) | (244) | (1021) | 76 | 317 | *EST | 85698-56-2 |

IP is onset of photoelectron band (83DOB/HIL).

$C_{14}H_{19}^+$

| | | 154 | 645 | | | | |

From proton affinity of 1,2,3,4,5,6,7,8-octahydroanthracene (RN 1079-71-6).
PA = 202.6 kcal/mol, 848. kJ/mol.

| | | 153 | 640 | | | | |

From proton affinity of 1,2,3,4,5,6,7,8-octahydrophenanthrene (RN 5325-97-3).
PA = 204.7 kcal/mol, 856. kJ/mol.

Table 1. Positive Ion Table – Continued

ION / Neutral	Ionization potential eV	Δ_fH(Ion) kcal/mol	kJ/mol	Δ_fH(Neutral) kcal/mol	kJ/mol	Neutral reference	CAS registry number
$C_{14}H_{19}N_2^+$		186	780				

From proton affinity of N,N,N',N'-tetramethyl-1,8-naphthalenediamine (RN 20734-58-1). PA = 241.8 kcal/mol, 1012. kJ/mol.

ION / Neutral	Ionization potential eV	Δ_fH(Ion) kcal/mol	kJ/mol	Δ_fH(Neutral) kcal/mol	kJ/mol	Neutral reference	CAS registry number
$C_{14}H_{20}^+$							
	(≤8.17) IP from 80GLE/HOP.	(≤190)	(≤795)	2	7	*EST	4685-74-9
	(8.93)	(171.1)	(717.1)	−34.5	−144.5	79CLA/KNO	2292-79-7
$C_{14}H_{20}O_2^+$							
	9.0±0.05 IP from 84OLI/FLE.	(141)	(589)	−67	−279	*EST	950-21-0
$C_{14}H_{20}O_5^+$							
	(≤8.0) IP from 83BAK/ARM.	(≤19)	(≤80)	−165	−692	*EST	14098-44-3
$C_{14}H_{21}N^+$							
	(≤7.60) IP from 82ROZ/HOU2.	(≤208)	(≤869)	33	136	*EST	81506-13-0
$C_{14}H_{22}^+$							
	(≤8.40) IP from 80GLE/HOP. See also: 85BAI/MIS.	(≤163)	(≤681)	−31±1.4	−129±6	84NES/VER	1571-86-4

Table 1. Positive Ion Table - Continued

ION / Neutral	Ionization potential eV	$\Delta_f H$(Ion) kcal/mol	$\Delta_f H$(Ion) kJ/mol	$\Delta_f H$(Neutral) kcal/mol	$\Delta_f H$(Neutral) kJ/mol	Neutral reference	CAS registry number
$C_{14}H_{22}^+$							
1,2-di-tert-butylbenzene	(≤8.60±0.07)	(≤185)	(≤774)	−13	−56	*EST	1012-76-6
1,3-di-tert-butylbenzene	(8.71±0.07)	(171)	(713)	−30±1.4	−127±6	84NES/VER	1014-60-4
1,4-di-tert-butylbenzene	8.24±0.01	(161)	(673)	−29	−122	85ORL/MIS	1012-72-2
	IP from 82LEV/LIA, 84HOW/GON, 86ORL/MIS. See also: 85BAI/MIS.						
$C_{14}H_{22}O^+$							
2,6-di-tert-butylphenol	(7.70±0.02)	(112)	(468)	−66	−275	*EST	128-39-2
	See also: 83CET/LAP.						
3,5-di-tert-butylphenol	(7.90±0.02)	(109)	(455)	−73	−307	*EST	1138-52-9
$C_{14}H_{23}N^+$							
2,6-diethyl-N,N-diethylaniline	(≤7.77)	(≤207)	(≤867)	28	117	*EST	81506-16-3
	IP from 82ROZ/HOU2.						
$C_{14}H_{23}NO^+$							
	(≤7.75)	(≤116)	(≤486)	−63	−262	*EST	1500-76-1
	IP from 82PFI/GER.						

Table 1. Positive Ion Table - Continued

ION Neutral	Ionization potential eV	$\Delta_f H$(Ion) kcal/mol	$\Delta_f H$(Ion) kJ/mol	$\Delta_f H$(Neutral) kcal/mol	$\Delta_f H$(Neutral) kJ/mol	Neutral reference	CAS registry number
$C_{14}H_{24}{}^+$							
(trans-anti-trans perhydroanthracene)	(8.8)	(145)	(606)	−58.1±0.9	−243.2±3.8	77PED/RYL	
	IP is onset of photoelectron band (84HEI/HON).						
(perhydroanthracene isomer)	(9.0)	(158)	(660)	−50	−208	71ALL/WUE	
	IP is onset of photoelectron band (84HEI/HON).						
$C_{14}H_{24}O_4{}^+$							
(benzo-crown ether)	(≤9.2)	(≤39)	(≤162)	−174	−726	*EST	
	IP from 83BAK/ARM.						
$C_{14}H_{26}{}^+$							
1-$C_{14}H_{26}$	(9.89±0.02)	(218)	(913)	−10	−41	*EST	765-10-6
2-$C_{14}H_{26}$	(9.26±0.03)	(199)	(833)	−14	−60	*EST	638-60-8
3-$C_{14}H_{26}$	(9.17±0.02)	(197)	(826)	−14	−59	*EST	60212-32-0
4-$C_{14}H_{26}$	(9.11±0.03)	(196)	(820)	−14	−59	*EST	60212-33-1
5-$C_{14}H_{26}$	(9.10±0.03)	(196)	(819)	−14	−59	*EST	60212-34-2
6-$C_{14}H_{26}$	(9.09±0.02)	(196)	(818)	−14	−59	*EST	3730-08-3
7-$C_{14}H_{26}$	(9.03±0.04)	(194)	(812)	−14	−59	*EST	35216-11-6
$C_{14}H_{26}S_2Si_2{}^+$							
$(CH_3)_3Si-CH_2-S-C_6H_4-S-CH_2-Si(CH_3)_3$	(7.0)	(23)	(96)	−138	−579	*EST	69209-20-7
	IP is onset of photoelectron band (82TRA/RED).						
$C_{14}H_{28}{}^+$							
$((CH_3)_3C)_2C=CHC(CH_3)_3$	(8.17±0.01)	(131)	(550)	−57	−238	81HOL/FIN	28923-90-2

Table 1. Positive Ion Table - Continued

ION / Neutral	Ionization potential eV	$\Delta_f H$(Ion) kcal/mol	kJ/mol	$\Delta_f H$(Neutral) kcal/mol	kJ/mol	Neutral reference	CAS registry number
$C_{14}H_{28}N^+$ (1-methyl-2,6-di-tert-butylpiperidine·H⁺)		60	250				

From proton affinity of 1-methyl-2,6-di-tert-butylpiperidine. PA = 239.2 kcal/mol, 1001. kJ/mol.

| $C_{14}H_{32}N_4^+$ | (≤8.0) | (≤184) | (≤770) | −0.5 | −2 | *EST | |

IP from 83BAK/ARM.

| $C_{15}F_{18}^+$ | 11.3 | (−530) | (−2216) | −790 | −3306 | *EST | 33021-47-5 |

IP is onset of photoelectron band (84HEI/WIR).

| $C_{15}H_9N^+$ (9-cyanoanthracene) | (7.80±0.03) | (267) | (1114) | 87±0.2 | 362±1 | *EST | 1210-12-4 |

See also: 83KLA/KOV.

| $C_{15}H_{10}O^+$ (9-anthraldehyde) | 7.69±0.03 | (204) | (852) | 26.3±2 | 110±8 | *EST | 642-31-9 |

| (diphenylcyclopropenone) | (8.1) | (262) | (1099) | 76±2 | 318±8 | 85STE/GAM | 886-38-4 |

IP is onset of photoelectron band.

| $C_{15}H_{12}^+$ | (7.6) | (232) | (970) | 57±0.7 | 237±3 | *EST | 256-81-5 |

IP is onset of photoelectron band.

Table 1. Positive Ion Table - Continued

ION / Neutral	Ionization potential eV	$\Delta_f H$(Ion) kcal/mol	kJ/mol	$\Delta_f H$(Neutral) kcal/mol	kJ/mol	Neutral reference	CAS registry number
$C_{15}H_{12}^+$							
2-methylanthracene	(7.37)	(215)	(898)	45	187	*EST	613-12-7

IP from charge transfer equilibrium constant determinations (80MAU).

9-methylanthracene	7.24±0.03	(215)	(899)	48	201	*EST	779-02-2

See also: 80MAU, 83KLA/KOV.

1-methylphenanthrene	7.7±0.03	(217)	(907)	39±2	164±7	*EST	832-69-9
2-methylphenanthrene	(7.7)	(217)	(907)	39±2	164±7	*EST	2531-84-2
3-methylphenanthrene	(7.68±0.01)	(216)	(905)	39	164	*EST	832-71-3
4-methylphenanthrene	(7.70±0.02)	(222)	(929)	44±4	186±15	*EST	832-64-4
1,2-diphenylcyclopropene	(7.45)	(282)	(1180)	110	461	*EST	24168-52-3
methylphenanthrene	7.46±0.03	(214)	(897)	42±0.2	177±1	*EST	883-20-5

Table 1. Positive Ion Table - Continued

ION / Neutral	Ionization potential eV	$\Delta_f H$(Ion) kcal/mol	$\Delta_f H$(Ion) kJ/mol	$\Delta_f H$(Neutral) kcal/mol	$\Delta_f H$(Neutral) kJ/mol	Neutral reference	CAS registry number
$C_{15}H_{12}AlF_9O_6^+$	(8.7) IP is onset of photoelectron band.	(−580)	(−2428)	−781±3	−3267±13	80TEL/RAB	14354-59-7
$C_{15}H_{12}O_2^+$	(8.3) IP is onset of photoelectron band.	(131)	(550)	−60±0.7	−251±3	81FER/RIB	120-46-7
$C_{15}H_{13}^+$ (2-methylanthracene + H⁺)		200	837				
From proton affinity of 2-methylanthracene (RN 613-12-7). PA = 210.3 kcal/mol, 880. kJ/mol.							
(9-methylanthracene radical)		200	836				
From proton affinity of 9-methylanthracene (RN 779-02-2). PA = 213.9 kcal/mol, 895. kJ/mol.							
$C_{15}H_{14}^+$ (α-methylstilbene)	(≤8.10±0.05)	(≤236)	(≤986)	49	204	*EST	833-81-8
(trans-1,2-diphenylcyclopropane)	(8.20)	(249)	(1043)	60±0.5	252±2	77PED/RYL	1138-48-3
(cis-1,2-diphenylcyclopropane)	(8.05)	(243)	(1016)	57±0.7	239±3	77PED/RYL	1138-47-2
	(8.0) IP is onset of photoelectron band.	(351)	(1469)	167	697	*EST	73045-27-9

Table 1. Positive Ion Table – Continued

ION / Neutral	Ionization potential eV	$\Delta_f H$(Ion) kcal/mol	$\Delta_f H$(Ion) kJ/mol	$\Delta_f H$(Neutral) kcal/mol	$\Delta_f H$(Neutral) kJ/mol	Neutral reference	CAS registry number
$C_{15}H_{14}^+$	(7.6) IP is onset of photoelectron band.	(386)	(1616)	211	883	*EST	73050-58-5
$C_{15}H_{15}La^+$	(7.9±0.3)	(218)	(912)	36±2	150±7	77PED/RYL	1272-23-7
$C_{15}H_{15}N^+$	(7.1) IP is onset of photoelectron band (84GLE/SCH).	(216)	(905)	53	220	*EST	92013-89-3
$C_{15}H_{15}NO^+$	(≤9.20) IP from 82PFI/GER.	(≤226)	(≤946)	14	58	*EST	72036-56-7
$C_{15}H_{15}Pr^+$	(7.68±0.1)	(200)	(838)	23±2	97±9	77PED/RYL	11077-59-1
$C_{15}H_{15}Tm^+$	(7.43±0.1)	(186)	(779)	15±1	62±6	77PED/RYL	1272-26-0
$C_{15}H_{15}Yb^+$	(7.5±0.3)	(206)	(862)	33±1	138±6	77PED/RYL	1295-20-1

Table 1. Positive Ion Table - Continued

ION / Neutral	Ionization potential eV	$\Delta_f H$(Ion) kcal/mol	kJ/mol	$\Delta_f H$(Neutral) kcal/mol	kJ/mol	Neutral reference	CAS registry number
$C_{15}H_{16}N_2^+$	(7.50±0.05)	(253)	(1059)	80	335	*EST	63378-86-9
$C_{15}H_{16}OS^+$	(8.15)	(213)	(890)	25	104	*EST	
	IP is onset of photoelectron band (84GLE/BIS).						
$C_{15}H_{18}^+$	(7.1)	(219)	(918)	56	233	*EST	88635-76-1
	IP is onset of photoelectron band (84AND/CER).						
	(7.85±0.05)	(205)	(857)	24	100	*EST	1206-79-7
	IP from 81HEI/KOV.						
$C_{15}H_{18}CrO_3^+$	(6.35±0.1)	(10)	(42)	−136±3	−571±13	77PED/RYL	12088-11-8
$C_{15}H_{18}O^+$	(≤8.59)	(≤172)	(≤718)	−26	−111	*EST	72036-52-3
	IP from 82PFI/GER.						
$C_{15}H_{18}OP^+$				89	373		
	From proton affinity of i-$C_3H_7(C_6H_5)_2$PO (RN 2959-75-3)(86TRA/MUN). PA = 216. kcal/mol, 904. kJ/mol.						

Table 1. Positive Ion Table - Continued

ION / Neutral	Ionization potential eV	$\Delta_f H$(Ion) kcal/mol	$\Delta_f H$(Ion) kJ/mol	$\Delta_f H$(Neutral) kcal/mol	$\Delta_f H$(Neutral) kJ/mol	Neutral reference	CAS registry number
$C_{15}H_{18}O_2^+$	(≤8.26) IP from 82PFI/GER.	(≤136)	(≤568)	−55	−229	*EST	29339-44-4
$C_{15}H_{19}^+$		165	694				

From proton affinity of 1,4-dimethyl-7-isopropylazulene (RN 489-84-9). PA = 233. kcal/mol, 975. kJ/mol.

ION / Neutral	Ionization potential eV	$\Delta_f H$(Ion) kcal/mol	$\Delta_f H$(Ion) kJ/mol	$\Delta_f H$(Neutral) kcal/mol	$\Delta_f H$(Neutral) kJ/mol	Neutral reference	CAS registry number
$C_{15}H_{20}^+$	(8.29±0.08) IP from 81ELB/LIE.	(230)	(962)	39	162	*EST	80025-09-8
$C_{15}H_{21}AlO_6^+$	(7.78±0.05) IP from 81WES/REI.	(−220)	(−919)	−399±1	−1669±4	80TEL/RAB	13963-57-0
$C_{15}H_{21}CrO_6^+$	6.95±0.2 IP is onset of photoelectron band(81WES/REI).	(−182)	(−760)	−342±2	−1431±7	82PIL/SKI	21679-31-2
$C_{15}H_{21}FeO_6^+$	(7.55) IP is onset of photoelectron band. See also: 81WES/REI.	(−123)	(−515)	−297±1	−1244±6	77PED/RYL	14024-18-1
$C_{15}H_{21}MnO_6^+$	(7.58±0.05) IP from 81WES/REI.	(−135)	(−564)	−310±1	−1295±6	77PED/RYL	14284-89-0

Table 1. Positive Ion Table – Continued

ION / Neutral	Ionization potential eV	$\Delta_f H$(Ion) kcal/mol	$\Delta_f H$(Ion) kJ/mol	$\Delta_f H$(Neutral) kcal/mol	$\Delta_f H$(Neutral) kJ/mol	Neutral reference	CAS registry number
$C_{15}H_{24}^+$ 1,3,5-triisopropylbenzene	(8.24) IP from 84HOW/GON.	(158)	(661)	−32	−134	*EST	717-74-8
$C_{15}H_{24}O^+$ 2,6-di-tert-butyl-4-methylphenol	(≤7.80) IP from 83CET/LAP.	(≤107)	(≤449)	−73	−304	*EST	128-37-0
$C_{16}F_{10}^+$ decafluoropyrene	(8.36±0.05)	(−167)	(−697)	−359	−1504	*EST	1493-68-1
$C_{16}F_{16}^+$	10.1 IP is onset of photoelectron band (84HEI/WIR).	(−347)	(−1451)	−580	−2425	*EST	42858-85-5
$C_{16}H_8F_2O_4^+$	(8.7) IP is onset of photoelectron band (85GLE/DOB).	(39)	(165)	−161	−674	*EST	97245-28-8
$C_{16}H_{10}^+$ 2,2'-diethynylbiphenyl	(8.2) IP is onset of photoelectron band (81GLE/SCH).	(340)	(1421)	151	630	*EST	18442-29-0
pyrene	7.41 See also: 81CLA/ROB. IP value at 298 K from charge transfer equilibrium constant determinations (80MAU) = 7.50 eV.	222	931	52±0.2	216±1	79KUD/KUD2	129-00-0

GAS-PHASE ION AND NEUTRAL THERMOCHEMISTRY

Table 1. Positive Ion Table - Continued

ION / Neutral	Ionization potential eV	$\Delta_f H$(Ion) kcal/mol	$\Delta_f H$(Ion) kJ/mol	$\Delta_f H$(Neutral) kcal/mol	$\Delta_f H$(Neutral) kJ/mol	Neutral reference	CAS registry number
$C_{16}H_{10}^+$ (fluoranthene)	(7.95±0.04)	(253)	(1056)	69.2±0.3	289.4±1.1	81KUD/KUD	206-44-0
$C_{16}H_{10}O_4^+$ (1,2,3,4-tetraketo-1,4-diphenylbutane)	(8.5)	(130)	(544)	−66	−276	*EST	19909-44-5

IP is onset of photoelectron band (85GLE/DOB).

ION / Neutral		kcal/mol	kJ/mol				
$C_{16}H_{11}^+$ (protonated pyrene)		211	884				

From proton affinity of pyrene (RN 129-00-0). PA = 206.1 kcal/mol, 862. kJ/mol.

| | | 235 | 985 | | | | |

From proton affinity of fluoranthene (RN 206-44-0). PA = 199.3 kcal/mol, 834. kJ/mol.

ION / Neutral	Ionization potential eV	$\Delta_f H$(Ion) kcal/mol	$\Delta_f H$(Ion) kJ/mol	$\Delta_f H$(Neutral) kcal/mol	$\Delta_f H$(Neutral) kJ/mol	Neutral reference	CAS registry number
$C_{16}H_{12}^+$ (1,4-diphenyl-1-buten-3-yne)	(7.5)	(276)	(1154)	103	430	*EST	13343-79-8

IP is onset of photoelectron band (80AND/BIC).

| 1,8-bis(propynyl)naphthalene | (7.48) | (311) | (1304) | 139 | 582 | *EST | 22360-77-6 |

IP from 84GLE/SCH.

| 9,10-dimethyleneanthracene | (7.6) | (233) | (976) | 58±3 | 243±12 | *EST | 3302-51-0 |

IP is onset of photoelectron band.

| dibenzobicyclic | (7.7) | (253) | (1060) | 76 | 317 | *EST | |

IP is onset of photoelectron band (82HAS/NEU).

Table 1. Positive Ion Table - Continued

ION / Neutral	Ionization potential eV	$\Delta_f H$(Ion) kcal/mol	kJ/mol	$\Delta_f H$(Neutral) kcal/mol	kJ/mol	Neutral reference	CAS registry number
$C_{16}H_{14}^+$							
1,4-diphenyl-1,3-butadiene	7.55	237	993	63	265	69STU/WES	538-81-8
2,7-dimethylphenanthrene	7.99±0.04	218	914	34±0.5	143±2	77PED/RYL	1576-69-8
1,8-dimethylphenanthrene	7.56±0.1	220	924	46±1	194±6	77PED/RYL	3674-69-9
4,5-dimethylphenanthrene	(8.01±0.05)	(225)	(940)	40±2	167±9	77PED/RYL	604-83-1
dibenzobicyclo compound	(8.1) IP is onset of photoelectron band (82HAS/NEU).	(224)	(936)	37	155	*EST	
$C_{16}H_{16}^+$							
1,2-diphenylcyclobutane	(8.2±0.1) IP from 84GRO/CHE.	(247)	(1035)	58	244	84GRO/CHE	20071-09-4
1,2-diphenyl-1-methylcyclopropane	(7.9) IP from 81KLY/SHU.	(235)	(984)	53	222	*EST	14161-72-9
1,2-diphenyl-1-methylcyclopropane (isomer)	(7.9) IP from 81KLY/SHU.	(232)	(971)	50	209	*EST	14161-73-0

Table 1. Positive Ion Table – Continued

ION / Neutral	Ionization potential eV	$\Delta_f H$(Ion) kcal/mol	$\Delta_f H$(Ion) kJ/mol	$\Delta_f H$(Neutral) kcal/mol	$\Delta_f H$(Neutral) kJ/mol	Neutral reference	CAS registry number
$C_{16}H_{16}^+$	7.9　IP is onset of photoelectron band.	(223)	(933)	41±2	171±7	77PED/RYL	2319-97-3
	7.8±0.1　IP from 82LEV/LIA, 82GLE/ECK. See also: 81ZHO/KOV.	239	998	59±0.7	246±3	80NIS/SAK	1633-22-3
$C_{16}H_{16}BrN^+$	(≤7.04)　IP from 85CAU/FUR.	(≤200)	(≤835)	37	156	*EST	2844-19-1
$C_{16}H_{16}ClN^+$	(≤7.05)　IP from 85CAU/FUR.	(≤190)	(≤796)	28	116	*EST	69957-42-2
$C_{16}H_{16}CrO_4^+$	(≤5.77)　IP from 82CAB/COW.	(≤35)	(≤147)	−98	−410	*EST	1272-35-1
$C_{16}H_{16}FN^+$	(6.39)　IP is onset of photoelectron band (85CAU/FUR).	(160)	(671)	13	54	*EST	38695-34-0
$C_{16}H_{16}O^+$	(8.0)　IP is onset of photoelectron band.	(217)	(909)	33±3	137±12	77PED/RYL	25401-39-2

Table 1. Positive Ion Table - Continued

ION / Neutral	Ionization potential eV	$\Delta_f H$(Ion) kcal/mol	kJ/mol	$\Delta_f H$(Neutral) kcal/mol	kJ/mol	Neutral reference	CAS registry number
$C_{16}H_{16}U^+$	≤6.17±0.03	(≤247)	(≤1035)	105±3	439±13	77TEL/RAB	11079-26-8
$C_{16}H_{17}^+$		193	809				

From proton affinity of $(4-CH_3C_6H_4)_2C=CH_2$ (RN 2919-20-2). PA = 215.4 kcal/mol, 901. kJ/mol.

$C_{16}H_{18}N_2O_3^+$	(7.2)	(166)	(695)	0	0	*EST	4792-83-0

IP is onset of photoelectron band (81MIL/CIL).

$C_{16}H_{19}^+$		194	810				

From proton affinity of $C_6H_5(CH_2)_4C_6H_5$ (RN 1083-56-3). PA = 195.9 kcal/mol, 820. kJ/mol.

$C_{16}H_{20}Cr^+$	(≤5.21)	(≤105)	(≤439)	−15	−64	*EST	12092-21-6

IP from 82CAB/COW.

$C_{16}H_{20}OP^+$		83	347				

From proton affinity of $t-C_4H_9(C_6H_5)_2PO$ (RN 56598-35-7) (86TRA/MUN). PA = 216 kcal/mol, 904 kJ/mol.

$C_{16}H_{28}^+$	(9.1)	(173)	(726)	−36±3	−152±13	77PED/RYL	283-68-1

IP is onset of photoelectron band (84GLE/SPA).

Table 1. Positive Ion Table - Continued

ION / Neutral	Ionization potential eV	$\Delta_f H$(Ion) kcal/mol	kJ/mol	$\Delta_f H$(Neutral) kcal/mol	kJ/mol	Neutral reference	CAS registry number
$C_{16}H_{32}N_2O_5{}^+$	(≤7.7) IP from 83BAK/ARM.	(≤7)	(≤31)	−170	−712	*EST	31364-42-8
$C_{16}H_{34}N_2{}^+$ (E)-$((CH_3)_3CCH_2C(CH_3)_2)_2N_2$	(≤8.00)	(≤137)	(≤575)	−47±2	−197±9	80ENG	55204-43-8
$C_{16}H_{36}Sn^+$ $(C_4H_9)_4Sn$	(8.0) IP is onset of photoelectron band.	(132)	(553)	−52±1	−219±4	77PED/RYL	1461-25-2
(iso-$C_4H_9)_4Sn$	(≤8.68)	(≤165)	(≤689)	−35	−148	*EST	3531-43-9
$C_{16}H_{44}Si_4Ti^+$ $[(CH_3)_3SiCH_2]_4Ti$	(8.0) IP is onset of photoelectron band.	(−3)	(−14)	−188±8	−786±33	86SIM/BEA	33948-28-6
$C_{16}H_{44}Si_4Zr^+$ $((CH_3)_3SiCH_2)_4Zr$	(8.2) IP is onset of photoelectron band.	(−9)	(−36)	−198±8	−827±33	86SIM/BEA	32665-18-2
$C_{17}H_{12}{}^+$	(7.53) IP from 84GLE/SCH.	(349)	(1458)	(175)	(732)	*EST	32137-40-9
$C_{17}H_{16}N_2{}^+$	(≤7.31) IP from 85CAU/FUR.	(≤261)	(≤1094)	93	389	*EST	
$C_{17}H_{18}{}^+$	(7.6) IP is onset of photoelectron band (81ZHO/KOV).	(226)	(947)	51	214	*EST	24262-07-5

Table 1. Positive Ion Table - Continued

ION / Neutral	Ionization potential eV	$\Delta_f H$(Ion) kcal/mol	$\Delta_f H$(Ion) kJ/mol	$\Delta_f H$(Neutral) kcal/mol	$\Delta_f H$(Neutral) kJ/mol	Neutral reference	CAS registry number
$C_{17}H_{19}NO^+$ (CH₃)₂N-C₆H₄-CH=CH-C₆H₄-OCH₃	(6.16)	(166)	(696)	24	102	*EST	2844-24-8

IP is onset of photoelectron band (85CAU/FUR).

| $C_{17}H_{20}N_2^+$ fluorene with N(CH₃)₂ substituents | (6.7) | (226) | (945) | 71 | 299 | *EST | 86943-85-3 |

IP is onset of photoelectron band (84GLE/SCH).

| $C_{17}H_{26}O^+$ 2,6-diisopropyl-4-isopropylacetophenone | (8.0) | (104) | (437) | −80 | −335 | *EST | 2234-14-2 |

IP is onset of photoelectron band (78CEN/FRA).

| $C_{17}H_{29}N^+$ 2,4,6-tri-tert-butylpyridine | 8.20 | (133) | (558) | −56 | −233 | *EST | 20336-15-6 |

IP is onset of photoelectron band.

| $C_{18}H_{12}^+$ | 7.43±0.03 | 239 | 1001 | 68±0.2 | 284±1 | 79KUD/KUD2 | 56-55-3 |

See also: 81AKI/HAR.

| | 7.60 | 245 | 1024 | 70±0.2 | 291±1 | 79KUD/KUD2 | 195-19-7 |

| | 7.59±0.02 | 243 | 1016 | 67.8±0.2 | 283.7±0.8 | 79KUD/KUD2 | 218-01-9 |

Value of IP from charge transfer equilibrium constant determinations (80MAU) is in agreement. See also: 81SHA/AKI, 80SHU/BOY.

| | 6.97±0.02 | 229 | 956 | 68±0.2 | 284±1 | 79KUD/KUD2 | 92-24-0 |

See also: 84STA/MAQ, 80SHU/BOY.

Table 1. Positive Ion Table – Continued

ION Neutral	Ionization potential eV	$\Delta_f H$(Ion) kcal/mol kJ/mol	$\Delta_f H$(Neutral) kcal/mol kJ/mol	Neutral reference	CAS registry number
$C_{18}H_{12}^+$ (triphenylene)	7.84±0.01	245 1026	64±0.2 270±1	79KUD/KUD2	217-59-4

Value of IP from charge transfer equilibrium constant determinations (80MAU) is in agreement. See also: 80SHU/BOY.

$C_{18}H_{13}^+$					
(dihydronaphthacene radical)		216 903			

From proton affinity of naphthacene (RN 92-24-0). PA = 217.8 kcal/mol, 911. kJ/mol.

(chrysene)H$^+$		227 950			

From proton affinity of chrysene (RN 218-01-9). PA = 201.6 kcal/mol, 843. kJ/mol.

(triphenylene)H$^+$		232 970			

From proton affinity of triphenylene (RN 217-59-4). PA = 198.5 kcal/mol, 830.5 kJ/mol.

$C_{18}H_{14}^+$					
(diyne)	(7.50)	(343) (1434)	170 710	*EST	32137-39-6

IP from 84GLE/SCH.

(diphenylfulvene)	(≤7.96)	(≤280) (≤1170)	96±4 402±15	77PED/RYL	2175-90-8

(o-terphenyl)	8.0	(252) (1054)	68 283	*EST	84-15-1

IP is onset of photoelectron band (83KOB, 82LEV/LIA).

(m-terphenyl)	8.01±0.01	(252) (1056)	68 283	*EST	92-06-8

IP from 82LEV/LIA. See also: 83KOB.

Table 1. Positive Ion Table - Continued

ION Neutral	Ionization potential eV	$\Delta_f H$(Ion) kcal/mol	$\Delta_f H$(Ion) kJ/mol	$\Delta_f H$(Neutral) kcal/mol	$\Delta_f H$(Neutral) kJ/mol	Neutral reference	CAS registry number
$C_{18}H_{14}^+$	7.78±0.01	(247)	(1034)	68	283	*EST	92-94-4
$C_{18}H_{14}O_4^+$	(≤8.8) IP from 85GLE/DOB.	(≤121)	(≤507)	−82	−342	*EST	19909-64-9
$C_{18}H_{15}As^+$	7.32±0.05	266	1114	98±3	408±11	79STE	603-32-7
$C_{18}H_{15}B^+$	(8.60±0.03)	(229)	(960)	31±2	130±8	77PED/RYL	960-71-4
$C_{18}H_{15}Bi^+$	7.45±0.05	317	1328	146±2	609±10	79STE	603-33-8
$C_{18}H_{15}N^+$	6.80±0.04	176	734	19±0.2	78±1	78STE	603-34-9
$C_{18}H_{15}P^+$	7.39±0.03 IP from 82IKU/KEB, 77ROS/DRA, 82LEV/LIA.	249	1041	78±5	328±21	79STE	603-35-0

Table 1. Positive Ion Table – Continued

ION Neutral	Ionization potential eV	$\Delta_f H$(Ion) kcal/mol	$\Delta_f H$(Ion) kJ/mol	$\Delta_f H$(Neutral) kcal/mol	$\Delta_f H$(Neutral) kJ/mol	Neutral reference	CAS registry number
$C_{18}H_{15}Sb^+$ (triphenylstibine)	7.26±0.05	271	1135	104±4	435±19	79STE	603-36-1
$C_{18}H_{16}^+$	(7.4)	(275)	(1152)	105	438	*EST	

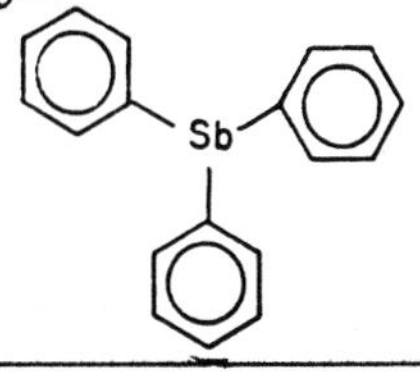

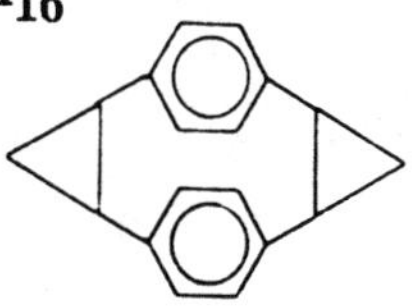

IP is onset of photoelectron band (82GLE/ECK).

$C_{18}H_{16}As^+$

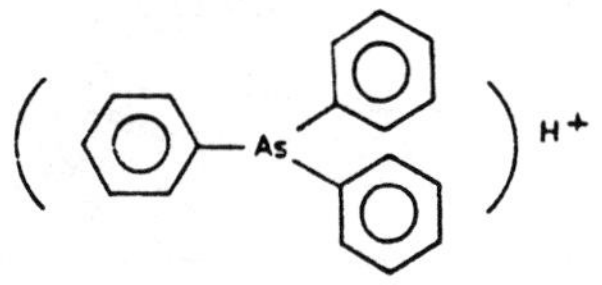

247 1034

From proton affinity of $(C_6H_5)_3$As (RN 603-32-7)(86TRA/MUN). PA = 216. kcal/mol, 904. kJ/mol.

$C_{18}H_{16}AsO^+$

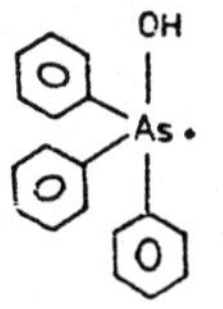

198 827

From proton affinity of $(C_6H_5)_3$AsO (RN 1153-05-5) (86TRA/MUN). PA = 216. kcal/mol, 904. kJ/mol.

$C_{18}H_{16}N^+$

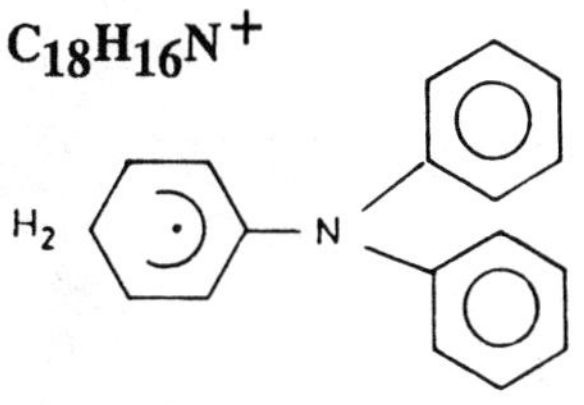

168 704

From proton affinity of $(C_6H_5)_3$N (RN 603-34-9)(86TRA/MUN). PA = 216. kcal/mol, 904. kJ/mol.

$C_{18}H_{16}OP^+$

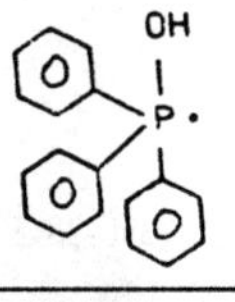

154 644

From proton affinity of $(C_6H_5)_3$PO (RN 791-28-6)(86TRA/MUN). PA = 216. kcal/mol, 904. kJ/mol.

$C_{18}H_{16}P^+$

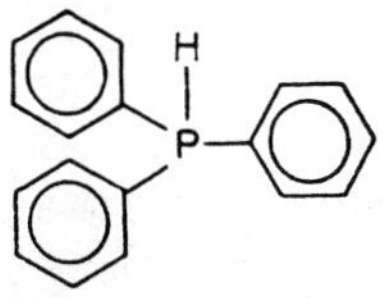

214 896

From proton affinity of $(C_6H_5)_3$P (RN 603-35-0). PA = (230) kcal/mol, (962) kJ/mol.

Table 1. Positive Ion Table – Continued

ION / Neutral	Ionization potential eV	$\Delta_f H$(Ion) kcal/mol kJ/mol	$\Delta_f H$(Neutral) kcal/mol kJ/mol	Neutral reference	CAS registry number
$C_{18}H_{16}PS^+$		206 860			
	From proton affinity of $(C_6H_5)_3PS$ (RN 3878-45-3)(86TRA/MUN). PA = 216. kcal/mol, 904. kJ/mol.				
$C_{18}H_{16}Sb^+$		267 1119			
	From proton affinity of $(C_6H_5)_3Sb$ (RN 603-36-1)(86TRA/MUN). PA = 202. kcal/mol, 846. kJ/mol.				
$C_{18}H_{16}Si^+$	(8.4)	(257) (1075)	63 265	*EST	789-25-3
	IP is onset of photoelectron band.				
$C_{18}H_{18}^+$	(6.60)	(276) (1156)	124±5 519±20	74OTH/BUN	2040-73-5
	IP from 82BAU/BUN.				
	(7.13)	(201) (843)	37 156	*EST	62337-65-9
	IP from 78KLA/KOV, 83KLA/KOV.				
	7.13	(201) (843)	37 155	*EST	13719-97-6
	IP from 83KLA/KOV.				
	(7.8±0.1)	(210) (879)	30±1 126±6	77PED/RYL	7396-38-5
	(7.5±0.1)	(211) (881)	38±1 157±6	77PED/RYL	7343-06-8

Table 1. Positive Ion Table – Continued

ION / Neutral	Ionization potential eV	$\Delta_f H$(Ion) kcal/mol	$\Delta_f H$(Ion) kJ/mol	$\Delta_f H$(Neutral) kcal/mol	$\Delta_f H$(Neutral) kJ/mol	Neutral reference	CAS registry number
$C_{18}H_{18}{}^+$							
	(7.3)	(221)	(926)	53	222	*EST	
	\multicolumn{6}{l}{IP is onset of photoelectron band (84ZHO/HEI).}	
	7.8	(222)	(931)	43	178	*EST	
	\multicolumn{6}{l}{IP is onset of photoelectron band.}	
	7.8	(236)	(987)	56	234	*EST	58002-98-5
	7.4	(212)	(886)	41	172	*EST	27165-88-4
	\multicolumn{6}{l}{IP is onset of photoelectron band.}	
$C_{18}H_{18}N_2{}^+$							
	(7.4)	(275)	(1150)	104	436	*EST	
	\multicolumn{6}{l}{IP is onset of photoelectron band (81ZHO/HEI).}	
	(7.6)	(279)	(1169)	104	436	*EST	
	\multicolumn{6}{l}{IP is onset of photoelectron band (81ZHO/HEI).}	
$C_{18}H_{20}{}^+$							
	(≤7.85±0.05)	(≤225)	(≤939)	43	182	*EST	
	\multicolumn{6}{l}{IP from 81ZHO/KOV.}	
	(7.4)	(214)	(897)	44	183	*EST	
	\multicolumn{6}{l}{IP is onset of photoelectron band (81ZHO/KOV).}	

Table 1. Positive Ion Table – Continued

ION / Neutral	Ionization potential eV	$\Delta_f H$(Ion) kcal/mol	$\Delta_f H$(Ion) kJ/mol	$\Delta_f H$(Neutral) kcal/mol	$\Delta_f H$(Neutral) kJ/mol	Neutral reference	CAS registry number
$C_{18}H_{20}{}^+$	(≤7.85±0.05) IP from 81ZHO/KOV.	(≤225)	(≤939)	43	182	*EST	
	(8.12±0.08) IP from 81ELB/LIE.	(240)	(1002)	52	219	*EST	
$C_{18}H_{20}U^+$	(≤6.08) IP from 83GRE/PAY.	(≤229)	(≤959)	89	373	*EST	41367-67-3
$C_{18}H_{22}N_2O_3{}^+$	(≤7.64) IP from 81MIL/CIL.	(≤167)	(≤697)	−10	−40	*EST	23315-55-1
$C_{18}H_{24}{}^+$	(7.70±0.05) IP from 81HEI/KOV.	(175)	(732)	−3	−11	*EST	1610-39-5
$C_{18}H_{24}Cr^+$	(≤5.04) IP from 82CAB/COW.	(≤134)	(≤562)	18	76	*EST	57820-96-9
	4.97 IP from 82CAB/COW.	130	543	15±3	64±12	82PIL/SKI	1274-07-3

Table 1. Positive Ion Table – Continued

ION / Neutral	Ionization potential eV	$\Delta_f H$(Ion) kcal/mol	$\Delta_f H$(Ion) kJ/mol	$\Delta_f H$(Neutral) kcal/mol	$\Delta_f H$(Neutral) kJ/mol	Neutral reference	CAS registry number
$C_{18}H_{29}Br^+$ (2,4,6-tri-tert-butylbromobenzene)	8.0 — IP is onset of photoelectron band (83CET/LAP).	(151)	(631)	−33	−140	*EST	3975-77-7
$C_{18}H_{29}I^+$ (2,4,6-tri-tert-butyliodobenzene)	7.5 — IP is onset of photoelectron band (83CET/LAP).	(156)	(651)	−17	−73	*EST	31039-82-4
$C_{18}H_{29}NO^+$ (2,4,6-tri-tert-butylnitrosobenzene)	(≤8.69) — IP from 83CET/LAP.	(≤184)	(≤768)	−17	−70	*EST	24973-59-9
$C_{18}H_{29}NO_2^+$ (2,4,6-tri-tert-butylnitrobenzene)	(≤8.78) — IP from 83CET/LAP.	(≤154)	(≤646)	−48	−201	*EST	3463-37-4
$C_{18}H_{30}^+$ (1,2,4-tri-tert-butylbenzene)	(≤8.60±0.07)	(≤164)	(≤687)	−34±1.4	−143±6	67ARN/SAN	1459-11-6
$C_{18}H_{30}^+$ (1,3,5-tri-tert-butylbenzene)	(8.19) — IP from 84HOW/GON. See also: 83CET/LAP.	(131)	(548)	−58±1	−242±4	77PED/RYL	1460-02-2
$C_{18}H_{30}O^+$ (2,4,6-tri-tert-butylphenol)	(7.5) — IP is onset of photoelectron band (83CET/LAP).	(80)	(335)	−93	−389	*EST	732-26-3

Table 1. Positive Ion Table – Continued

ION / Neutral	Ionization potential eV	$\Delta_f H$(Ion) kcal/mol	$\Delta_f H$(Ion) kJ/mol	$\Delta_f H$(Neutral) kcal/mol	$\Delta_f H$(Neutral) kJ/mol	Neutral reference	CAS registry number
$C_{18}H_{31}N^+$ (2,4,6-tri-tert-butylaniline)	(6.9) IP is onset of photoelectron band (83CET/LAP).	(110)	(460)	−49	−206	*EST	
$C_{18}H_{36}N_2O_6^+$	(≤7.8) IP from 83BAK/ARM.	(≤−28)	(≤−118)	−208	−871	*EST	23978-09-8
$C_{18}H_{42}N_3P^+$ $P(N(n-C_3H_7)_2)_3$	(≤7.05) IP from 82WOR/HAR.	(≤78)	(≤325)	−85	−355	*EST	5848-64-6
$C_{19}H_{14}^+$ (1-methyl)	(7.46±0.03) IP from 81SHA/AKI.	(226)	(944)	54	224	*EST	3351-28-8
(2-methyl)	(7.49±0.03) IP from 81SHA/AKI.	(226)	(947)	54	224	*EST	3351-32-4
(3-methyl)	(7.46±0.03) IP from 81SHA/AKI.	(226)	(944)	54	224	*EST	3351-31-3
(4-methyl)	(7.44±0.03) IP from 81SHA/AKI.	(230)	(963)	59	245	*EST	3351-30-2
(5-methyl)	(7.40±0.03) IP from 81SHA/AKI.	(229)	(959)	59	245	*EST	3697-24-3

Table 1. Positive Ion Table – Continued

ION / Neutral	Ionization potential eV	$\Delta_f H$(Ion) kcal/mol	kJ/mol	$\Delta_f H$(Neutral) kcal/mol	kJ/mol	Neutral reference	CAS registry number
$C_{19}H_{14}^+$	(7.44±0.03) IP from 81SHA/AKI.	(228)	(953)	57	236	*EST	1705-85-7
	(7.30) IP from 81AKI/HAR.	(224)	(938)	56	234	*EST	2498-76-2
	(7.29) IP from 81AKI/HAR.	(224)	(937)	56	234	*EST	2498-75-1
	(7.30) IP from 81AKI/HAR.	(224)	(938)	56	234	*EST	316-49-4
	(7.33) IP from 81AKI/HAR.	(225)	(941)	56	234	*EST	316-14-3
	(7.24) IP from 81AKI/HAR.	(223)	(933)	56	234	*EST	2541-69-7
	(7.33) IP from 81AKI/HAR.	(225)	(941)	56	234	*EST	2381-31-9
	(7.31) IP from 81AKI/HAR.	(224)	(939)	56	234	*EST	2381-16-0

Table 1. Positive Ion Table – Continued

ION Neutral	Ionization potential eV	$\Delta_f H$(Ion) kcal/mol kJ/mol		$\Delta_f H$(Neutral) kcal/mol kJ/mol		Neutral reference	CAS registry number

$C_{19}H_{14}{}^+$

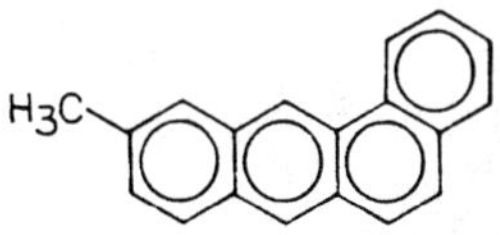

(7.30) (224) (938) 56 234 *EST 2381-15-9
IP from 81AKI/HAR.

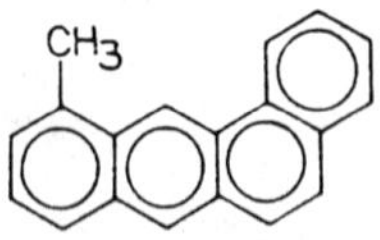

(7.30) (224) (938) 56 234 *EST 6111-78-0
IP from 81AKI/HAR.

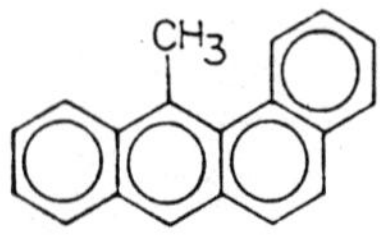

(7.27) (243) (1015) 75 314 *EST 2422-79-9
IP from 81AKI/HAR.

$C_{19}H_{16}{}^+$

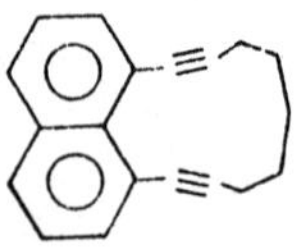

(7.48) (337) (1411) 165 690 *EST 87842-94-2
IP from 84GLE/SCH.

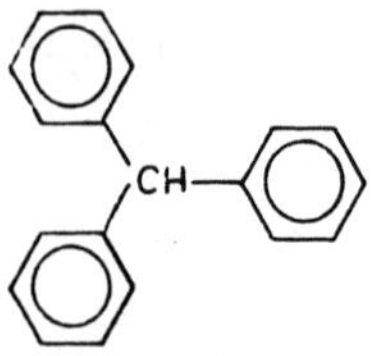

8.34±0.03 257 1076 65±1 271±4 77PED/RYL 519-73-3

$C_{19}H_{22}{}^+$

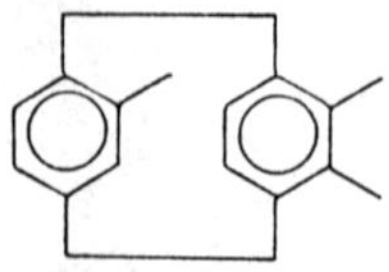

(7.3) (207) (867) 39 163 *EST
IP is onset of photoelectron band (81ZHO/KOV).

$C_{20}F_{24}{}^+$

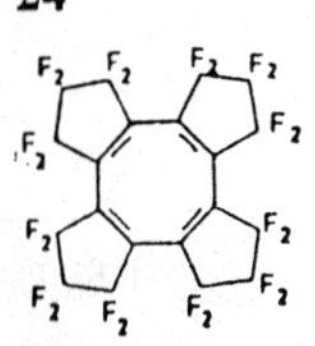

10.75 (−761) (−3183) −1009 −4220 *EST 32936-99-5
IP is onset of photoelectron band (84HEI/WIR).

Table 1. Positive Ion Table - Continued

ION Neutral	Ionization potential eV	$\Delta_f H$(Ion) kcal/mol	kJ/mol	$\Delta_f H$(Neutral) kcal/mol	kJ/mol	Neutral reference	CAS registry number
$C_{20}H_{12}^+$	7.12±0.01	233	976	69	289	77STE/GOL	50-32-8
	7.41 IP from 79CLA/SCH.	(233)	(976)	62	261	77STE/GOL	192-97-2
	6.90±0.01	233	974	74±1	308±4	77PED/RYL	198-55-0
	6.84 IP from 81SAT/SEK.	(270)	(1129)	112	469	*EST	4670-86-4
	(6.58)	(269)	(1126)	117	491	*EST	54100-60-6
	(6.76)	(273)	(1143)	117	491	*EST	6580-41-2
$C_{20}H_{12}Br_2^+$	(8.1) IP from 83MAR/MAY.	(265)	(1107)	78	326	*EST	
$C_{20}H_{13}^+$		228	954				

From proton affinity of perylene (RN 198-55-0). PA = 211.4 kcal/mol, 884. kJ/mol.

ION / Neutral	Ionization potential eV	$\Delta_f H$(Ion) kcal/mol	$\Delta_f H$(Ion) kJ/mol	$\Delta_f H$(Neutral) kcal/mol	$\Delta_f H$(Neutral) kJ/mol	Neutral reference	CAS registry number
$C_{20}H_{13}Br^+$	(7.9)	(260)	(1086)	77	324	*EST	
IP is onset of photoelectron band (83MAR/MAY).							
$C_{20}H_{14}^+$	(7.8)	(257)	(1074)	77±3	322±13	77PED/RYL	
IP is onset of photoelectron band (83MAR/MAY, 82HAS/NEU).							
$C_{20}H_{14}N_4^+$	6.6	−86.4	−361.5	−238.6±0.4	−998.3±1.7	70LON/FIN	101-60-0
IP from 80DUP/ROB.							
$C_{20}H_{14}O_2^+$	(7.08±0.02)	(172)	(721)	9	38	81BOU/DAG	75694-46-1
IP from 81BOU/DAG.							
$C_{20}H_{16}^+$	(7.9)	(354)	(1481)	172	719	*EST	
IP is onset of photoelectron band (81GLE/SCH).							
	(7.20)	(210)	(878)	43.9±0.9	183.7±3.9	77PED/RYL	316-51-8
IP from 81AKI/HAR.							
	(7.18)	(232)	(971)	66	278	*EST	35187-19-0
IP from 81AKI/HAR.							
	(7.10)	(230)	(963)	66.4±1.0	277.7±4.4	77PED/RYL	57-97-6
IP from 81AKI/HAR.							

Table 1. Positive Ion Table – Continued

ION / Neutral	Ionization potential eV	$\Delta_f H$(Ion) kcal/mol	$\Delta_f H$(Ion) kJ/mol	$\Delta_f H$(Neutral) kcal/mol	$\Delta_f H$(Neutral) kJ/mol	Neutral reference	CAS registry number
$C_{20}H_{16}ClN_2O_3^+$	(7.80±0.05) IP from 81TIM/KOR.	(157)	(656)	−23	−97	*EST	
$C_{20}H_{18}^+$	(7.4) IP is onset of photoelectron band.	(244)	(1020)	73	306	*EST	4432-72-8
$C_{20}H_{20}^+$	(7.6) IP is onset of photoelectron band.	(233)	(975)	58	242	*EST	
	(7.4) IP is onset of photoelectron band.	(226)	(944)	55	230	*EST	
	(7.35) IP is onset of photoelectron band (81ZHO/HEI).	(237)	(993)	68	284	*EST	
$C_{20}H_{20}NP^+$	(≤7.43)	(≤216)	(≤903)	44±2	186±9	77PED/RYL	47182-04-7
$C_{20}H_{20}O^+$	(≤8.88) IP from 82PFI/GER.	(≤186)	(≤778)	−19	−79	*EST	72036-53-4

Table 1. Positive Ion Table — Continued

ION / Neutral	Ionization potential eV	$\Delta_f H$(Ion) kcal/mol	$\Delta_f H$(Ion) kJ/mol	$\Delta_f H$(Neutral) kcal/mol	$\Delta_f H$(Neutral) kJ/mol	Neutral reference	CAS registry number
$C_{20}H_{20}U^+$	(≤6.02)	(≤300)	(≤1256)	161	675	*EST	70377-87-6
IP from 83GRE/PAY.							
$C_{20}H_{24}^+$	(7.2)	(200)	(838)	34	144	*EST	
IP is onset of photoelectron band (81ZHO/KOV).							
	(≤7.55±0.05)	(≤209)	(≤872)	34	144	*EST	
IP from 81ZHO/KOV.							
	≤7.60±0.05	(≤210)	(≤877)	34	144	*EST	
IP from 81ZHO/KOV.							
$C_{20}H_{24}O_6^+$	(7.5)	(1.8)	(7.6)	−171	−716	*EST	
IP is onset of photoelectron band (83BAK/ARM).							
$C_{20}H_{24}U^+$	(5.9)	(215)	(900)	79	331	*EST	37274-10-5
IP is onset of photoelectron band (83GRE/PAY).							
$C_{20}H_{26}N_2O_3^+$	(≤7.61)	(≤156)	(≤654)	−19	−80	*EST	17051-01-3
IP from 81MIL/CIL.							

Table 1. Positive Ion Table - Continued

ION / Neutral	Ionization potential eV	$\Delta_f H$(Ion) kcal/mol	kJ/mol	$\Delta_f H$(Neutral) kcal/mol	kJ/mol	Neutral reference	CAS registry number
$C_{20}H_{28}Cr^+$	(≤5.23) IP from 82CAB/COW.	(≤128)	(≤538)	8	33	*EST	51951-64-5
	(≤4.85) IP from 82CAB/COW.	(≤108)	(≤454)	−3	−14	*EST	57820-98-1
$C_{20}H_{30}Cl_2Zr^+$	7.1 IP is onset of photoelectron band (81CIL/CON).	(60)	(252)	−103±1	−433±4	82PIL/SKI	54039-38-2
$C_{20}H_{30}S_2^+$	(7.5) IP is onset of photoelectron band.	(125)	(524)	−48	−200	*EST	34895-45-9
$C_{20}H_{36}^+$	(5.9) IP is onset of photoelectron band.	(226)	(946)	90±5.5	377±23	*EST	66809-05-0
	(7.1) IP is onset of photoelectron band.	(257)	(1076)	93±5.5	391±23	*EST	66809-06-1
$C_{20}H_{36}O_6^+$	(8.6) IP is onset of photoelectron band.	(−59)	(−248)	−258	−1078	*EST	16069-36-6
$C_{20}H_{44}Hf^+$ $((CH_3)_3CCH_2)_4Hf$	(8.1) IP is onset of photoelectron band.	(132)	(554)	−54±9	−228±33	86SIM/BEA	50654-35-8

Table 1. Positive Ion Table - Continued

ION / Neutral	Ionization potential eV	$\Delta_f H$(Ion) kcal/mol	$\Delta_f H$(Ion) kJ/mol	$\Delta_f H$(Neutral) kcal/mol	$\Delta_f H$(Neutral) kJ/mol	Neutral reference	CAS registry number
$C_{20}H_{44}Ti^+$							
$((CH_3)_3CCH_2)_4Ti$	(7.7) IP is onset of photoelectron band.	(140)	(586)	−38±8	−157±33	86SIM/BEA	36945-13-8
$C_{21}H_{18}^+$							
	(7.7) IP is onset of photoelectron band (81GLE/SCH).	(345)	(1442)	167	699	*EST	
	(7.06±0.03) IP from 81AKI/HAR.	(217)	(909)	54	228	*EST	35187-24-7
$C_{21}H_{26}^+$							
	(≤7.55±0.05) IP from 81ZHO/KOV.	(≤199)	(≤831)	25	103	*EST	
$C_{21}H_{36}^+$							
	(8.17) IP from 84HOW/GON.	(111)	(466)	−77	−322	*EST	21411-39-2
$C_{22}H_{12}^+$							
	7.15 See also: 80MAU.	237	992	72	302	77STE/GOL	191-24-2
	(6.92±0.04)	(233)	(978)	74	310	77STE/GOL	191-26-4
$C_{22}H_{12}O_2^+$							
	(8.07±0.05)	(196)	(823)	10±2	44±9	77PED/RYL	3029-32-1

Table 1. Positive Ion Table – Continued

ION / Neutral	Ionization potential eV	$\Delta_f H$(Ion) kcal/mol	$\Delta_f H$(Ion) kJ/mol	$\Delta_f H$(Neutral) kcal/mol	$\Delta_f H$(Neutral) kJ/mol	Neutral reference	CAS registry number
$C_{22}H_{13}^+$		229	960				

From proton affinity of 1,12-benzoperylene (RN 191-24-2). PA = 208.5 kcal/mol, 872. kJ/mol.

ION / Neutral	Ionization potential eV	$\Delta_f H$(Ion) kcal/mol	$\Delta_f H$(Ion) kJ/mol	$\Delta_f H$(Neutral) kcal/mol	$\Delta_f H$(Neutral) kJ/mol	Neutral reference	CAS registry number
$C_{22}H_{14}^+$	6.61±0.02 See also: 84STA/MAQ.	(237)	(992)	85	354	*EST	135-48-8
	7.00 See also: 75CLA/SCH.	(244)	(1020)	82	345	*EST	226-88-0
	7.27±0.02 See also: 79CLA/SCH.	(250)	(1046)	82	345	*EST	222-93-5
	7.47±0.04 See also: 75CLA/SCH.	(269)	(1127)	97	406	*EST	188-52-3
	7.39±0.02 See also: 75CLA/SCH, 79CLA/SCH.	251	1049	80	336	77STE/GOL	215-58-7
	7.38±0.04 See also: 75CLA/SCH.	250	1048	80	336	77STE/GOL	53-70-3
	(7.40±0.02) See also: 75CLA/SCH.	(251)	(1050)	80	336	77STE/GOL	224-41-9

Table 1. Positive Ion Table – Continued

ION / Neutral	Ionization potential eV	$\Delta_f H$(Ion) kcal/mol	kJ/mol	$\Delta_f H$(Neutral) kcal/mol	kJ/mol	Neutral reference	CAS registry number
$C_{22}H_{14}^+$	7.48	(250)	(1048)	78	326	*EST	213-46-7

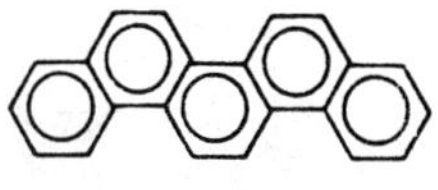

IP from charge transfer equilibrium constant determinations (80MAU), in agreement with value from 79CLA/SCH.

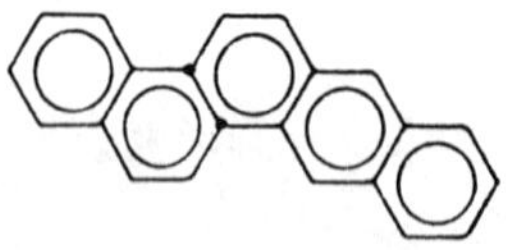	(7.14±0.04)	(245)	(1024)	80	336	*EST	214-17-5

$C_{22}H_{15}^+$

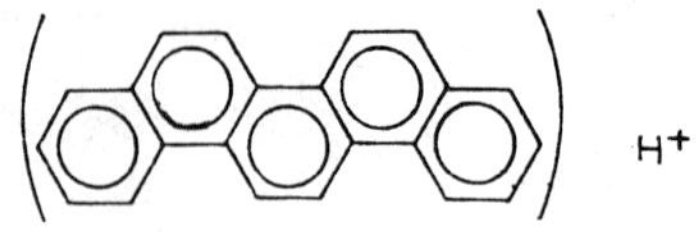

240 1005

From proton affinity of picene (RN 213-46-7). PA = 203.4 kcal/mol, 851. kJ/mol.

$C_{22}H_{22}^+$	(7.35)	(256)	(1072)	87	363	*EST	

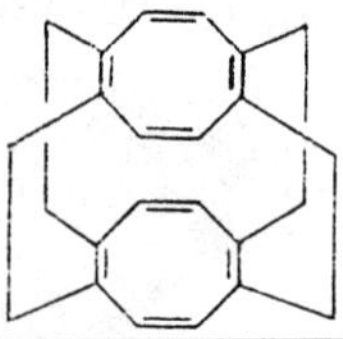

IP is onset of photoelectron band (84ZHO/HEI).

$C_{22}H_{22}O_4^+$	(≤8.6)	(≤76)	(≤318)	−122	−512	*EST	19909-65-0

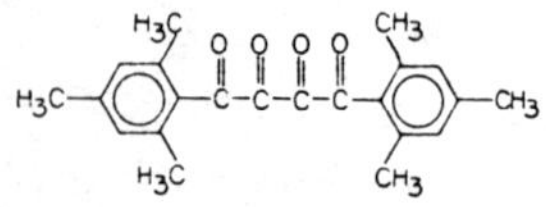

IP from 85GLE/DOB.

$C_{22}H_{28}^+$	(7.0)	(176)	(737)	15	62	*EST	

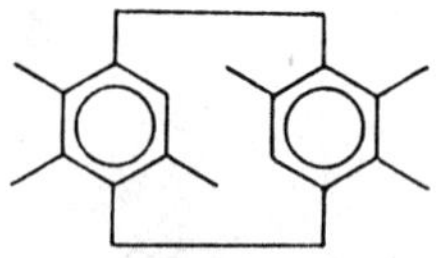

IP is onset of photoelectron band (81ZHO/KOV).

$C_{22}H_{28}O^+$	(7.9)	(137)	(574)	−45±2	−189±7	82INA/MUR	33574-11-7

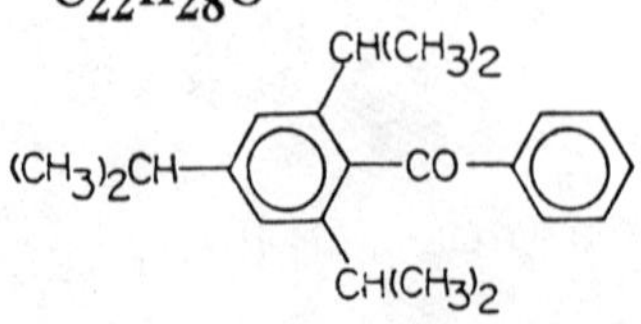

IP is onset of photoelectron band (78CEN/FRA).

Table 1. Positive Ion Table – Continued

ION / Neutral	Ionization potential eV	$\Delta_f H$(Ion) kcal/mol	$\Delta_f H$(Ion) kJ/mol	$\Delta_f H$(Neutral) kcal/mol	$\Delta_f H$(Neutral) kJ/mol	Neutral reference	CAS registry number
$C_{22}H_{30}N_2O_3{}^+$	(≤7.63) IP from 81MIL/CIL.	(≤147)	(≤616)	−29	−120	*EST	19482-05-4
$C_{23}H_{30}{}^+$	(≤7.40±0.05) IP from 81ZHO/KOV.	(≤182)	(≤763)	12	49	*EST	
$C_{23}H_{30}O^+$	(≤8.15±0.03)	(≤150)	(≤626)	−38±4	−160±15	77PED/RYL	25401-43-8
	(7.6) IP is onset of photoelectron band (78CEN/FRA).	(125)	(523)	−50	−210	*EST	78823-28-6
$C_{24}H_{12}{}^+$	7.29 IP at 298 K from charge transfer equilibria, 7.26 eV (80MAU, re-evaluated). See also: 81CLA/ROB.	245	1026	77	323	77STE/GOL	191-07-1
$C_{24}H_{13}{}^+$	From proton affinity of coronene (RN 191-07-1). PA = 205.0 kcal/mol, 858. kJ/mol.	238	995				
$C_{24}H_{14}{}^+$	(6.95) IP from 79CLA/SCH.	(243)	(1018)	83	348	77STE/GOL	189-55-9

Table 1. Positive Ion Table – Continued

ION Neutral	Ionization potential eV	$\Delta_f H$(Ion) kcal/mol	$\Delta_f H$(Ion) kJ/mol	$\Delta_f H$(Neutral) kcal/mol	$\Delta_f H$(Neutral) kJ/mol	Neutral reference	CAS registry number
$C_{24}H_{16}^+$							
	(7.48) IP from 82GLE/GUB.	(321)	(1342)	148	620	*EST	14620-98-5
	7.58 IP from 82GLE/GUB.	(323)	(1351)	148	620	*EST	15065-28-8
	(7.1) IP is onset of photoelectron band.	(305)	(1274)	141	589	*EST	43012-17-5
$C_{24}H_{20}^+$							
syn	(7.0) IP is onset of photoelectron band.	(250)	(1046)	89	371	*EST	14724-91-5
anti	(7.3) IP is onset of photoelectron band.	(257)	(1075)	89	371	*EST	17341-02-5
achiral	(6.8) IP is onset of photoelectron band.	(245)	(1027)	89	371	*EST	54835-57-3
chiral	(7.1) IP is onset of photoelectron band.	(253)	(1058)	89	373	*EST	54835-57-3
	(7.3) IP is onset of photoelectron band.	(240)	(1005)	72	301	*EST	73608-51-2

Table 1. Positive Ion Table - Continued

ION / Neutral	Ionization potential eV	$\Delta_f H$(Ion) kcal/mol	$\Delta_f H$(Ion) kJ/mol	$\Delta_f H$(Neutral) kcal/mol	$\Delta_f H$(Neutral) kJ/mol	Neutral reference	CAS registry number
$C_{24}H_{20}^+$	(7.0) IP is onset of photoelectron band.	(317)	(1325)	155	650	*EST	7130-24-7
$C_{24}H_{20}Ge^+$	(8.1) IP is onset of photoelectron band (84NOV/POT).	(293)	(1226)	(106±6)	(445±24)	77PED/RYL	1048-05-1
$C_{24}H_{20}Pb^+$	(8.0) IP is onset of photoelectron band (84NOV/POT).	(346)	(1446)	161±4	674±15	78STE	595-89-1
$C_{24}H_{20}Si^+$	(8.50±0.03) See also: 84NOV/POT.	(278)	(1162)	82±1	342±6	82PIL/SKI	1048-08-4
$C_{24}H_{20}Sn^+$	(8.34±0.03) See also: 84NOV/POT.	(329)	(1378)	137±2	573±8	77KAN/MOR	595-90-4
$C_{24}H_{24}^+$	(7.3) IP is onset of photoelectron band.	(253)	(1057)	84	353	*EST	60144-50-5
$C_{24}H_{24}Cr_2N_4O_4^+$	(6.5) IP is onset of photoelectron band.	(−41)	(−171)	−191±2	−798±9	81CAV/GAR	67634-82-6

Table 1. Positive Ion Table - Continued

ION / Neutral	Ionization potential eV	$\Delta_f H$(Ion) kcal/mol	$\Delta_f H$(Ion) kJ/mol	$\Delta_f H$(Neutral) kcal/mol	$\Delta_f H$(Neutral) kJ/mol	Neutral reference	CAS registry number
$C_{24}H_{24}Mo_2N_4O_4^+$	(5.5) IP is onset of photoelectron band.	(−16)	(−66)	−143±2	−597±9	81CAV/GAR	67634-80-4
$C_{24}H_{32}^+$	(6.9) IP is onset of photoelectron band (81ZHO/KOV).	(168)	(702)	9	36	*EST	
$C_{24}H_{32}U^+$	(≤6.05) IP from 83GRE/PAY.	(≤199)	(≤831)	59	247	*EST	37274-12-7
	(≤6.03) IP from 83GRE/PAY.	(≤193)	(≤809)	54	227	*EST	63230-70-6
$C_{24}H_{34}N_2O_3^+$	(≤7.55) IP from 81MIL/CIL.	(≤136)	(≤568)	−38	−160	*EST	2587-42-0
$C_{24}H_{36}Cr^+$	(≤4.68)	(≤87)	(≤364)	−21±3	−88±12	82PIL/SKI	12243-39-9
$C_{25}H_{16}^+$	(7.5) IP is onset of photoelectron band.	(286)	(1199)	114	475	*EST	159-66-0

Table 1. Positive Ion Table – Continued

ION / Neutral	Ionization potential eV	$\Delta_f H$(Ion) kcal/mol	kJ/mol	$\Delta_f H$(Neutral) kcal/mol	kJ/mol	Neutral reference	CAS registry number
$C_{24}H_{14}^+$							
	(6.89)	(240)	(1004)	81	339	*EST	197-70-6
	(7.35) IP from 79CLA/SCH.	(253)	(1057)	83	348	*EST	193-09-9
	7.39 IP from 79CLA/SCH.	(249)	(1042)	79	329	*EST	192-51-8
	(6.71)	(237)	(991)	82	344	*EST	191-85-5
	(6.82) IP from 79CLA/SCH.	(243)	(1015)	85	357	*EST	
	(6.82) IP from 79CLA/SCH.	(240)	(1006)	83	348	77STE/GOL	189-64-0
	(7.11) IP from 79CLA/SCH.	(245)	(1025)	81	339	*EST	
	(7.07) IP from 79CLA/SCH.	(245)	(1026)	82	344	*EST	

Table 1. Positive Ion Table - Continued

ION / Neutral	Ionization potential eV	$\Delta_f H$(Ion) kcal/mol	$\Delta_f H$(Ion) kJ/mol	$\Delta_f H$(Neutral) kcal/mol	$\Delta_f H$(Neutral) kJ/mol	Neutral reference	CAS registry number
$C_{25}H_{20}^+$	(8.0)	(280)	(1170)	95±1	398±4	77PED/RYL	630-76-2

IP is onset of photoelectron band (84NOV/POT).

$C_{26}H_{14}^+$	(7.12)	(248)	(1038)	84	351	*EST	190-95-4
	6.72±0.02	(241)	(1008)	86	360	*EST	188-96-5
	(6.99)	(247)	(1034)	86	360	*EST	5869-30-7
	(6.96)	(244)	(1022)	84	351	*EST	190-84-1
	(6.82±0.04)	(243)	(1018)	86	360	*EST	188-89-6
$C_{26}H_{16}^+$	(7.37)	(290)	(1213)	120	502	*EST	187-83-7
	(6.61±0.02)	(251)	(1050)	99	413	*EST	239-98-5

Table 1. Positive Ion Table - Continued

ION / Neutral	Ionization potential eV	$\Delta_f H$(Ion) kcal/mol	$\Delta_f H$(Ion) kJ/mol	$\Delta_f H$(Neutral) kcal/mol	$\Delta_f H$(Neutral) kJ/mol	Neutral reference	CAS registry number
$C_{26}H_{16}^+$	7.17±0.02	(267)	(1117)	102	425	*EST	217-42-5
	(7.36)	(262)	(1095)	92	385	*EST	217-37-8
	6.97±0.02 See also: 75CLA/SCH, 79CLA/SCH.	(255)	(1067)	94	394	*EST	216-00-2
	(6.99±0.02) See also: 75CLA/SCH.	(258)	(1078)	96	403	*EST	227-04-3
	(6.97±0.04)	(257)	(1076)	96	403	*EST	217-54-9
	7.20±0.02 See also: 75CLA/SCH, 79CLA/SCH.	(256)	(1072)	90	377	*EST	191-68-4
	(6.36±0.02) See also: 75CLA/SCH.	(247)	(1035)	101	422	*EST	258-31-1
	(6.92±0.02)	(258)	(1080)	99	413	*EST	222-78-6

Table 1. Positive Ion Table - Continued

ION / Neutral	Ionization potential eV	$\Delta_f H$(Ion) kcal/mol	kJ/mol	$\Delta_f H$(Neutral) kcal/mol	kJ/mol	Neutral reference	CAS registry number
$C_{26}H_{16}^+$							
	(7.19±0.02)	(253)	(1057)	87	363	*EST	220-77-9
	7.15±0.02	(258)	(1080)	93	390	*EST	196-64-5
	(6.83±0.02)	(254)	(1062)	96	403	*EST	220-82-6
	7.40±0.02 See also: 75CLA/SCH.	(263)	(1099)	92	385	*EST	215-26-9
	(7.20±0.02)	(262)	(1098)	96	403	*EST	222-54-8
$C_{26}H_{25}ClN_2O_3^+$							
	(6.94±0.05) IP from 81TIM/KOR.	(115)	(483)	−45	−187	*EST	989-38-8
$C_{26}H_{38}N_2O_3^+$							
	(≤7.57) IP from 81MIL/CIL.	(≤127)	(≤530)	−48	−200	*EST	2635-26-9
$C_{26}H_{46}^+$							
$CH_3(CH_2)_{16}-CH-CH_2CH_3$	(8.95±0.10)	(123)	(516)	−83±1.2	−348±5	77PED/RYL	72557-70-1

Table 1. Positive Ion Table – Continued

ION / Neutral	Ionization potential eV	$\Delta_f H$(Ion) kcal/mol	kJ/mol	$\Delta_f H$(Neutral) kcal/mol	kJ/mol	Neutral reference	CAS registry number
$C_{28}H_{14}^+$							
	(7.08)	(248)	(1037)	84	353	*EST	190-70-5
	(6.92±0.04)	(249)	(1040)	89	372	*EST	190-71-6
	(6.30)	(234)	(980)	89	372	*EST	190-39-6
$C_{28}H_{16}^+$							
	(6.51)	(252)	(1055)	102	426	*EST	191-87-7
	(6.64)	(247)	(1033)	94	392	*EST	191-81-1
	(6.51)	(247)	(1035)	97	406	*EST	190-36-3
	(6.96) IP from 79CLA/SCH.	(262)	(1098)	102	426	*EST	191-20-8
	(6.99) IP from 79CLA/SCH.	(256)	(1072)	95	397	*EST	192-47-2

Table 1. Positive Ion Table - Continued

ION Neutral	Ionization potential eV	$\Delta_f H$(Ion) kcal/mol	kJ/mol	$\Delta_f H$(Neutral) kcal/mol	kJ/mol	Neutral reference	CAS registry number
$C_{28}H_{16}^+$							
	(6.85)	(253)	(1058)	95	397	*EST	197-69-3
	(6.83) IP from 79CLA/SCH.	(257)	(1075)	99	416	*EST	
	(7.00) IP from 79CLA/SCH.	(252)	(1055)	91	380	*EST	
	(7.00±0.04)	(250)	(1044)	88	369	*EST	385-14-8
	(6.57) IP from 79CLA/SCH.	(253)	(1059)	102	425	*EST	196-45-2
	(6.82)	(254)	(1064)	97	406	*EST	14147-38-7
	(6.95) IP from 79CLA/SCH.	(260)	(1086)	99	416	*EST	193-11-3
	(6.86)	(253)	(1059)	95	397	*EST	197-74-0

Table 1. Positive Ion Table – Continued

ION / Neutral	Ionization potential eV	$\Delta_f H$(Ion) kcal/mol	$\Delta_f H$(Ion) kJ/mol	$\Delta_f H$(Neutral) kcal/mol	$\Delta_f H$(Neutral) kJ/mol	Neutral reference	CAS registry number
$C_{28}H_{16}^+$	(7.33±0.04) See also: 79CLA/SCH.	(264)	(1104)	95	397	*EST	192-59-6
$C_{28}H_{32}ClN_2O_3^+$	(6.70±0.05) IP from 81TIM/KOR.	(109)	(455)	−46	−191	*EST	
$C_{30}H_{14}^+$	(6.50)	(244)	(1021)	94	394	*EST	190-31-8
	(6.42±0.02)	(244)	(1022)	96	403	*EST	190-55-6
$C_{30}H_{16}^+$	(7.04)	(269)	(1125)	107	446	*EST	14258-76-5
	(6.78)	(265)	(1110)	109	455	*EST	5869-31-8
	(6.97)	(254)	(1063)	93	391	*EST	190-87-4
	(6.90±0.04)	(259)	(1086)	100	420	*EST	385-13-7

Table 1. Positive Ion Table – Continued

ION / Neutral	Ionization potential eV	$\Delta_f H$(Ion) kcal/mol	kJ/mol	$\Delta_f H$(Neutral) kcal/mol	kJ/mol	Neutral reference	CAS registry number
$C_{30}H_{16}^+$							
	(6.42±0.02)	(246)	(1029)	98	409	*EST	188-72-7
	(7.13)	(260)	(1088)	96	400	*EST	190-81-8
	(6.77)	(256)	(1072)	100	419	*EST	190-85-2
$C_{30}H_{18}^+$							
	(7.35±0.02)	(280)	(1171)	110	462	*EST	196-62-3
	(6.59±0.02)	(280)	(1172)	128	536	*EST	222-81-1
	(7.19±0.02)	(273)	(1144)	108	450	*EST	27798-46-5
	6.62±0.02 See also: 75CLA/SCH.	(263)	(1101)	110	462	*EST	216-08-0
	(6.64±0.02)	(264)	(1103)	110	462	*EST	227-09-8

Table 1. Positive Ion Table - Continued

ION Neutral	Ionization potential eV	$\Delta_f H$(Ion) kcal/mol	kJ/mol	$\Delta_f H$(Neutral) kcal/mol	kJ/mol	Neutral reference	CAS registry number
$C_{30}H_{18}^+$	(7.17±0.02)	(276)	(1154)	110	462	*EST	213-44-5
	(6.89±0.02)	(274)	(1145)	115	480	*EST	222-75-3
	(7.04±0.02)	(275)	(1150)	113	472	*EST	222-58-2
	(7.25)	(314)	(1315)	147	616	*EST	16914-68-4
	7.43±0.02 See also: 75CLA/SCH.	(275)	(1151)	104	434	*EST	215-11-2
	(6.99±0.02) See also: 75CLA/SCH.	(269)	(1127)	108	453	*EST	215-96-3
$C_{30}H_{36}ClN_2O_3^+$	(6.58±0.05) IP from 81TIM/KOR.	(99)	(416)	−52	−219	*EST	
$C_{32}H_{14}^+$	6.71 See also: 81CLA/ROB.	254	1062	99	415	77STE/GOL	190-26-1

Table 1. Positive Ion Table - Continued

ION / Neutral	Ionization potential eV	$\Delta_f H$(Ion) kcal/mol	$\Delta_f H$(Ion) kJ/mol	$\Delta_f H$(Neutral) kcal/mol	$\Delta_f H$(Neutral) kJ/mol	Neutral reference	CAS registry number
$C_{32}H_{16}^+$	(7.04)	(263)	(1101)	101	422	*EST	190-66-9
	(6.92)	(260)	(1089)	101	422	*EST	190-72-7
	(6.88)	(264)	(1104)	105	440	*EST	190-74-9
$C_{32}H_{18}^+$	(6.65) IP from 79CLA/SCH.	(269)	(1125)	115	483	*EST	189-43-5
	(6.94) IP from 79CLA/SCH.	(274)	(1145)	114	475	*EST	
	(6.91) IP from 79CLA/SCH.	(270)	(1132)	111	465	*EST	192-60-9
	(6.42) IP from 79CLA/SCH.	(264)	(1103)	115	483	*EST	
	(7.02) IP from 79CLA/SCH.	(276)	(1153)	114	476	*EST	

Table 1. Positive Ion Table – Continued

ION / Neutral	Ionization potential eV	$\Delta_f H$(Ion) kcal/mol	$\Delta_f H$(Ion) kJ/mol	$\Delta_f H$(Neutral) kcal/mol	$\Delta_f H$(Neutral) kJ/mol	Neutral reference	CAS registry number
$C_{32}H_{18}^+$	(6.99) IP from 79CLA/SCH.	(277)	(1153)	116	485	*EST	
	(6.36) IP from 79CLA/SCH.	(264)	(1107)	118	493	*EST	196-46-3
	(7.30±0.04)	(279)	(1169)	111	465	*EST	192-54-1
$C_{34}H_{16}^+$	(6.74±0.02)	(261)	(1093)	106	443	*EST	188-11-4
	6.82±0.02	(261)	(1092)	104	434	*EST	187-94-0
$C_{34}H_{18}^+$	(6.59±0.02)	(265)	(1109)	113	473	*EST	
	(6.48±0.02)	(263)	(1102)	114	477	*EST	
	(6.42±0.02)	(262)	(1097)	114	477	*EST	190-93-2

Table 1. Positive Ion Table - Continued

ION Neutral	Ionization potential eV	$\Delta_f H$(Ion) kcal/mol	kJ/mol	$\Delta_f H$(Neutral) kcal/mol	kJ/mol	Neutral reference	CAS registry number
$C_{34}H_{18}^+$	(6.59±0.02)	(265)	(1109)	113	473	*EST	191-46-8
	(6.84)	(267)	(1119)	110	459	*EST	313-63-3
	(6.27±0.02)	(256)	(1073)	112	468	*EST	191-79-7
	(6.22±0.02)	(260)	(1088)	117	488	*EST	188-13-6
	6.58	(276)	(1155)	124	520	*EST	191-53-7
$C_{34}H_{20}^+$	(7.15)	(327)	(1370)	162	680	*EST	20495-12-9
	(6.83±0.02)	(280)	(1172)	123	513	*EST	385-15-9
	(6.90±0.02)	(286)	(1196)	127	530	*EST	214-87-9

Table 1. Positive Ion Table - Continued

ION / Neutral	Ionization potential eV	$\Delta_f H$(Ion) kcal/mol	kJ/mol	$\Delta_f H$(Neutral) kcal/mol	kJ/mol	Neutral reference	CAS registry number
$C_{34}H_{20}^+$	(7.00±0.02)	(281)	(1177)	120	502	*EST	215-95-2
	(6.73±0.02)	(278)	(1162)	122	513	*EST	385-16-0
$C_{36}H_{16}^+$	(6.76±0.02)	(267)	(1117)	111	464	*EST	53086-28-5
	(6.70±0.04)	(265)	(1111)	111	464	*EST	190-47-6
$C_{36}H_{18}^+$	(≤7.10)	(≤284)	(≤1187)	120	502	*EST	188-00-1
	(6.88) IP from 79CLA/SCH.	(306)	(1282)	148	618	*EST	
	(6.88)	(271)	(1135)	113	471	*EST	313-62-2
$C_{36}H_{20}^+$	(6.68)	(284)	(1190)	130	545	*EST	197-73-9

Table 1. Positive Ion Table - Continued

ION / Neutral	Ionization potential eV	$\Delta_f H$(Ion) kcal/mol	$\Delta_f H$(Ion) kJ/mol	$\Delta_f H$(Neutral) kcal/mol	$\Delta_f H$(Neutral) kJ/mol	Neutral reference	CAS registry number
$C_{36}H_{20}^+$	(6.82)	(287)	(1202)	130	544	*EST	36474-85-8
	(6.95) IP from 79CLA/SCH.	(286)	(1195)	125	525	*EST	
	(6.74) IP from 79CLA/SCH.	(283)	(1183)	127	533	*EST	
$C_{38}H_{16}^+$	(6.81±0.02)	(271)	(1134)	114	477	*EST	41163-25-1
$C_{38}H_{18}^+$	(6.38±0.02)	(270)	(1132)	123	516	*EST	190-90-9
	(6.50±0.02)	(277)	(1158)	127	531	*EST	190-89-6
$C_{38}H_{20}^+$	(6.58) IP from 79CLA/SCH.	(282)	(1181)	130	546	*EST	
	(6.06±0.02)	(266)	(1112)	126	528	*EST	187-96-2

Table 1. Positive Ion Table – Continued

ION / Neutral	Ionization potential eV	$\Delta_f H$(Ion) kcal/mol	kJ/mol	$\Delta_f H$(Neutral) kcal/mol	kJ/mol	Neutral reference	CAS registry number
$C_{38}H_{20}^+$	(6.40±0.02)	(273)	(1144)	126	527	*EST	34814-77-2
	(6.72)	(285)	(1193)	130	545	*EST	14529-73-8
$C_{38}H_{22}^+$	(7.07)	(365)	(1527)	202	844	*EST	20495-14-1
	6.65±0.02 See also: 75CLA/SCH.	(290)	(1212)	136	570	*EST	216-07-9
$C_{40}H_{20}^+$	(6.11±0.02)	(270)	(1128)	129	539	*EST	188-73-8
$C_{42}H_{18}^+$	6.87±0.02	(280)	(1170)	121	508	*EST	190-24-9
$C_{42}H_{20}^+$	(6.72±0.02)	(287)	(1199)	132	551	*EST	34814-80-7

Table 1. Positive Ion Table - Continued

ION Neutral	Ionization potential eV	$\Delta_f H$(Ion) kcal/mol	$\Delta_f H$(Ion) kJ/mol	$\Delta_f H$(Neutral) kcal/mol	$\Delta_f H$(Neutral) kJ/mol	Neutral reference	CAS registry number
$C_{42}H_{22}^+$							
	(6.22) IP from 79CLA/SCH.	(294)	(1231)	151	631	*EST	190-09-0
	(6.71±0.02)	(283)	(1186)	129	538	*EST	190-22-7
	(6.18±0.02)	(282)	(1181)	140	585	*EST	34814-82-9
$C_{42}H_{24}^+$							
	(6.99)	(390)	(1633)	229	959	*EST	57520-29-3
	(7.52±0.02)	(356)	(1491)	183	765	*EST	190-23-8
	(6.85±0.02)	(317)	(1326)	159	665	*EST	214-77-7
$C_{42}H_{28}^+$							
	6.41 IP from 81SAT/SEK.	334	1399	187±5	781±22	77PED/RYL	517-51-1
$C_{44}H_{20}^+$							
	(6.79±0.02)	(287)	(1199)	130	544	*EST	70346-75-7

Table 1. Positive Ion Table – Continued

ION / Neutral	Ionization potential eV	$\Delta_f H$(Ion) kcal/mol	kJ/mol	$\Delta_f H$(Neutral) kcal/mol	kJ/mol	Neutral reference	CAS registry number
$C_{44}H_{22}^+$	(6.80) IP from 79CLA/SCH.	(333)	(1394)	176	738	*EST	
$C_{46}H_{26}^+$	(6.95)	(417)	(1744)	256	1073	*EST	57468-45-8
	(6.88±0.02)	(325)	(1360)	166	696	*EST	62662-49-1
$C_{48}H_{24}^+$	(6.75)	(297)	(1242)	141	590	*EST	1065-80-1
$C_{50}H_{26}^+$	(6.70) IP from 79CLA/SCH.	(329)	(1379)	175	732	*EST	72382-92-4
$C_{50}H_{28}^+$	(6.93)	(444)	(1856)	284	1187	*EST	57468-46-9
$C_{54}H_{30}^+$	(6.91)	(470)	(1968)	311	1302	*EST	24386-06-9

Table 1. Positive Ion Table - Continued

ION Neutral	Ionization potential eV	$\Delta_f H$(Ion) kcal/mol	$\Delta_f H$(Ion) kJ/mol	$\Delta_f H$(Neutral) kcal/mol	$\Delta_f H$(Neutral) kJ/mol	Neutral reference	CAS registry number
$C_{58}H_{32}^+$	(6.88)	(497)	(2080)	338	1416	*EST	57483-71-3
Ca^+							
Ca	6.11321±0.00002	183.6	768.0	42.6	178.2	82TN270	7440-70-2
		183.5	767.5	42.5	177.7		
$CaCl^+$							
CaCl	5.61±0.13	106	443	−24.7±1.2	−103.4±5.0	87GAR/PAR	15606-71-0
		106	444	−24.5±1.2	−102.7±5.0		
IP and $\Delta_f H$(Ion) derived from onset of endothermic reaction (84MEY/SCH).							
$CaCl_2^+$							
$CaCl_2$	(≤10.0)	(≤118)	(≤494)	−113	−471	82TN270	10043-52-4
		(≤118)	(≤493)	−113	−472		
See also: 82EMO/KIE, 79LEE/POT2.							
CaH^+							
CaH	(5.86±0.09)	(190)	(794)	55	229	82TN270	14452-75-6
		(190)	(795)	55	230		
Value for $\Delta_f H$(Ion) derived from onset energy of endothermic reaction is in good agreement (86ELK/ARI).							
$CaHO^+$							
CaOH	5.7	(89)	(371)	−42.0	−175.7	87GAR/PAR	12177-67-2
$\Delta_f H$(Ion) from onset of endothermic reaction (83MUR). See also: 81MUR. 0 K values.							
CaI^+							
CaI	(6.1±0.3)	(139)	(584)	−1±21	−5±84	79HUB/HER	15923-87-2
		(137)	(572)	−4	−17		
CaI_2^+							
CaI_2	(8.7)	(139)	(581)	−62±4	−258±17	85JANAF	10102-68-8
		(140)	(584)	−61±4	−255±17		
IP is onset of photoelectron band (79LEE/POT2). See also: 82EMO/KIE.							
CaO^+							
CaO	(6.9)	(166)	(693)	(6±4)	(27±17)	83PED/MAR	1305-78-8
IP from 83MUR.							
CaO_4W^+							
$CaWO_4$	(9.8)	(0)	(0)	−226	−946	76DEL/HAL	
Cd^+							
Cd	8.993	234.2	979.7	26.8	112.0	82TN270	7440-43-9
		234.2	979.8	26.8	112.1		

Table 1. Positive Ion Table – Continued

ION / Neutral	Ionization potential eV	$\Delta_f H$(Ion) kcal/mol	kJ/mol	$\Delta_f H$(Neutral) kcal/mol	kJ/mol	Neutral reference	CAS registry number
Ce⁺							
Ce	5.5387±0.0004	229	957	101	423	82TN270	7440-45-1
		229	957	101.1	423.4		
CeI₃⁺							
CeI₃	8.7	101	422	−100	−417	82TN270	
	IP is onset of photoelectron band (83RUS/GOO).						
CeO⁺							
CeO	(4.90±0.1)	(81)	(339)	−32±3	−134±12	83PED/MAR	12014-74-3
		(81)	(341)	−32	−132		
CeS⁺							
CeS	(6.0±0.6)	(170)	(710)	31	131	82TN270	12014-82-3
		(170)	(713)	32	134		
Ce₂⁺							
Ce₂	(5.6±0.4)	(273)	(1142)	144	602	82TN270	12595-88-9
		(274)	(1147)	145	607		
Cf⁺							
Cf	6.3	192	804	47	196	85KLE/WAR	7440-71-3
	See: 81CHE/GAB.						
Cl⁺							
Cl	12.967	328	1372	29.0	121.3	85JANAF	22537-15-1
		328	1371	28.6	119.6		
	See also: 81KIM/KAT.						
ClCs⁺							
CsCl	(7.84±0.05)	(122)	(510)	−59	−247	84PAR/WEX	7647-17-8
		(122)	(512)	−58.4±1.8	−244.4±7.5		
	A value of 8.32±0.1 eV has also been reported for the ionization potential.						
ClCsNa⁺							
NaCsCl	3.9±0.1	(21)	(88)	−69	−288	*EST	95860-64-3
	IP from 85KAP/RAD. 0 K values.						
ClCs₂⁺							
Cs₂Cl	3.4±0.2	−1	−4	−79±6	−332±25	85KAP/RAD	87331-16-6
	IP from 85KAP/RAD. 0 K values.						
ClCu⁺							
CuCl	(10.7±0.3)	(265)	(1110)	19	78	79HUB/HER	7758-89-6
	0 K values.						
ClF⁺							
ClF	12.65±0.01	280	1170	−12.0±0.1	−50.3±0.4	85JANAF	7790-89-8
		280	1170	−12.0±0.1	−50.2±0.4		
	See also: 84DYK/JOS.						

Table 1. Positive Ion Table - Continued

ION Neutral	Ionization potential eV	$\Delta_f H$(Ion) kcal/mol	 kJ/mol	$\Delta_f H$(Neutral) kcal/mol	 kJ/mol	Neutral reference	CAS registry number
$ClFO_2^+$ ClO_2F	(12.41±0.10) IP from 80BAL/NIK.	(278)	(1164)	−8	−33	73BAR	13637-83-7
$ClFO_2S^+$ SO_2FCl	(12.4) IP is onset of photoelectron band.	(151)	(632)	−135	−564	81WOO	13637-84-8
$ClFO_3^+$ ClO_3F	(12.945±0.005)	(293) (295)	(1225) (1234)	−6 −4	−24 −15	82TN270	7616-94-6
ClF_2^+ ClF_2	(12.77±0.05) $\Delta_f H$(Ion) derived from appearance potential (13.78±0.07 eV) in ClF_3 is 261 kcal/mol, 1091 kJ/mol.	(269)	(1127)	−25	−105	62ARM/KRI	24801-48-7
ClF_3^+ ClF_3	(12.65±0.05)	(253) (254)	(1057) (1061)	−39 −38	−163 −159	82BAU/COX	7790-91-2
ClF_5S^+ SF_5Cl	(12.335±0.005)	(34) (37)	(142) (155)	−250 −247	−1048 −1035	82TN270	13780-57-9
ClH^+ HCl	12.747 IP for formation of $HCl^+(^2\Pi_{3/2})$ from 79HUB/HER, 82NAT/PEN, 77ROS/DRA, 82LEV/LIA. IP for formation of $HCl^+(^2\Pi_{1/2})$ = 12.828 eV. See also: 82VON/ASB, 84WAN/DIL, 81KIM/KAT.	271.9 271.4	1137.6 1137.7	−22.1±0.04 −22.0±0.04	−92.3±0.2 −92.1±0.2	85JANAF	7647-01-0
ClD^+ DCl	12.754 IP for formation of $DCl(^2\Pi_{3/2})$ from 79HUB/HER, 83PEN/NAT.	271.8 271.9	1137.3 1137.6	−22.3±0.05 −22.3±0.05	−93.3±0.2 −93.1±0.2	85JANAF	7698-05-7
$ClHO^+$ HOCl	(11.12±0.01)	(238) (239)	(995) (998)	−19 −18	−78 −75	82BAU/COX	7790-92-3
ClH_2^+ H_2Cl		207	867				
	From proton affinity of HCl (RN 7647-01-0) (85MCM/KEB) re-evaluated relative to CO standard (84LIA/LIE). PA = 128.6 kcal/mol, 538 kJ/mol.						
ClH_2N^+ NH_2Cl	(9.85±0.02)	(240)	(1003)	13	53	*EST	10599-90-3
ClH_3Si^+ SiH_3Cl	11.4 IP is onset of photoelectron band.	(215)	(899)	−48	−201	81BEL/PER	13465-78-6

Table 1. Positive Ion Table – Continued

ION Neutral	Ionization potential eV	$\Delta_f H$(Ion) kcal/mol	kJ/mol	$\Delta_f H$(Neutral) kcal/mol	kJ/mol	Neutral reference	CAS registry number
ClI^+							
ICl	10.088±0.01	236.8	990.8	4.2±0.02	17.5±0.1	85JANAF	7790-99-0
		237.2	*992.4*	*4.6±0.2*	*19.1±0.1*		
	See also: 84DYK/JOS, 71POT/PRI.						
$ClIn^+$							
ClIn	(9.51)	(201)	(843)	−18	−75	82TN270	13465-10-6
		(204)	*(852)*	*−15*	*−65*		
ClK^+							
KCl	(8.0±0.4)	(133)	(557)	−51.3±0.1	−214.7±0.4	85JANAF	7447-40-7
		(134)	*(559)*	*−50.9±0.1*	*−212.9±0.4*		
$ClKNa^+$							
NaKCl	4.0±0.1	(26)	(107)	−67	−279	*EST	95860-66-5
	IP from 85KAP/RAD. 0 K values.						
ClK_2^+							
K_2Cl	3.5±0.2	*10*	*44*	*−70±4*	*−294±17*	85KAP/RAD	95386-61-1
	IP from 85KAP/RAD. 0 K values.						
$ClLi^+$							
LiCl	9.57	174	728	−47±3	−196±13	85JANAF	7447-41-8
		174	*728*	*−47±3*	*−196±13*		
$ClNO^+$							
NOCl	10.87±0.01	263	1101	12	52	82BAU/COX	2696-92-6
		264	*1103*	*13*	*54*		
	See also: 83BIN.						
$ClNO_2^+$							
$ClNO_2$	(11.84)	(276)	(1155)	3	13	82BAU/COX	13444-90-1
		(277)	*(1160)*	*4*	*18*		
ClN_3^+							
ClN_3	(10.20±0.01)	(313.9)	(1313.4)	78.7	329.3	83DEW/RZE	13973-88-1
$ClNa^+$							
NaCl	8.92±0.06	162	679	−43±0.5	−181±2	85JANAF	7647-14-5
		163	*681*	*−43±0.5*	*−180±2*		
$ClNa_2^+$							
Na_2Cl	4.1±0.1	*36*	*152*	*−58±4*	*−244±17*	85KAP/RAD	84008-89-9
	IP from 85KAP/RAD. 0 K values.						
$ClNi^+$							
NiCl	(11.4±0.5)	(306)	(1282)	43±1	182±4	85JANAF	13931-83-4
		(306)	*(1282)*	*43±1*	*182±4*		

Table 1. Positive Ion Table - Continued

ION Neutral	Ionization potential eV	$\Delta_f H$(Ion) kcal/mol	 kJ/mol	$\Delta_f H$(Neutral) kcal/mol	 kJ/mol	Neutral reference	CAS registry number
ClO^+							
ClO	10.95	277	1158	24.4	101.9	82BAU/COX	14989-30-1
		277	1158	24.3	101.8		
	IP is onset of photoelectron band.						
$ClOP^+$							
POCl	(11.5)	(205)	(859)	−60	−251	83BIN/LAK	21295-50-1
	IP from 83BIN.						
$ClOSb^+$							
SbOCl	(10.7)	(247)	(1032)	0	0	83BIN	7791-08-4
	IP from 83BIN.						
ClO_2^+							
OClO	10.36±0.02	262	1097	23±2	97±8	82BAU/COX	10049-04-4
		263	1099	24	99		
	See also: 80BAL/NIK.						
$ClRb^+$							
RbCl	(8.50±0.03)	(141)	(591)	−55	−229	82TN270	7791-11-9
		(142)	(593)	−54	−227		
$ClSr^+$							
SrCl	5.10±0.06	(88)	(368)	−30±2	−124±8	85JANAF	14989-33-4
		(88)	(370)	−29±2	−122±8		
	See also: 84MEY/SCH.						
$ClTl^+$							
TlCl	9.70±0.03	207	868	−16	−68	82TN270	7791-12-0
		207	868	−16	−68		
	See also: 83BAN/BRI.						
Cl_2^+							
Cl_2	11.480±0.005	265	1108	0	0	*DEF	7782-50-5
		265	1108	0	0		
	Cited ionization potential is for formation of $Cl_2^+ (^2\Pi_{3/2})$ (77ROS/DRA, 82LEV/LIA, 84VAN/DEL2, 84DYK/JOS)). Formation of $Cl_2^+ (^2\Pi_{1/2})$ requires 11.56 eV. See also: 81KIM/KAT.						
Cl_2Co^+							
$CoCl_2$	(10.4)	(217)	(909)	−22±2	−94±8	85JANAF	7646-79-9
		(217)	(908)	−23±2	−95±8		
	IP is onset of photoelectron band.						
Cl_2Cr^+							
$CrCl_2$	(9.4)	(186)	(779)	−31	−128	82TN270	10049-05-5
	IP is onset of photoelectron band.						

Table 1. Positive Ion Table - Continued

ION / Neutral	Ionization potential eV	$\Delta_f H$(Ion) kcal/mol	$\Delta_f H$(Ion) kJ/mol	$\Delta_f H$(Neutral) kcal/mol	$\Delta_f H$(Neutral) kJ/mol	Neutral reference	CAS registry number
$Cl_2CrO_2^+$							
Cl_2CrO_2	11.6	(139)	(581)	−129	−538	82TN270	14977-61-8
		(140)	*(585)*	*−128*	*−534*		
	IP is onset of photoelectron band.						
$Cl_2Cs_2^+$							
(Cs−Cl−Cs−Cl ring)	(≤9.15)	(≤53)	(≤223)	−158	−660	81LIN/BES	12258-95-6
		(≤54)	*(≤227)*	*−157*	*−656*		
$Cl_2F_4N_3P_3^+$							
(cyclic $P_3N_3F_4Cl_2$)	(10.97±0.3)	(−150)	(−629)	−403	−1687	*EST	29871-62-3
	IP from 81CLA/SOW.						
Cl_2Fe^+							
$FeCl_2$	(10.0)	(197)	(824)	−34	−141	85JANAF	7758-94-3
		(197)	*(823)*	*−34*	*−142*		
	IP is onset of photoelectron band.						
Cl_2Ge^+							
$GeCl_2$	(10.20±0.05)	(194)	(813)	−41±1	−171±5	79TPIS	10060-11-4
		(195)	*(814)*	*−41*	*−170*		
	IP from 82JON/VAN.						
Cl_2HN^+							
$NHCl_2$	(9.98±0.05)	(269)	(1124)	38	161	*EST	3400-09-7
$Cl_2H_2Si^+$							
SiH_2Cl_2	11.4	(183)	(765)	−80	−335	81BEL/PER	4109-96-0
	IP is onset of photoelectron band.						
Cl_2Hg^+							
$HgCl_2$	11.380±0.003	227	952	−35±1	−146±6	71JANAF	7487-94-7
	Cited ionization potential (from 83LIN/BRO) refers to formation of $HgCl_2^+$ $(^2\Pi_{3/2g})$. Ionization potential for formation of $HgCl_2^+$ $(^2\Pi_{1/2g})$ is 11.505±0.003 eV. See also: 81LEE/POT.						
$Cl_2K_2^+$							
(K−Cl−K−Cl ring)	(≤9.60)	(≤72)	(≤303)	−149	−623	82TN270	12258-97-8

Table 1. Positive Ion Table – Continued

ION / Neutral	Ionization potential eV	$\Delta_f H$(Ion) kcal/mol	kJ/mol	$\Delta_f H$(Neutral) kcal/mol	kJ/mol	Neutral reference	CAS registry number
$Cl_2Li_2^+$	10.20	93	390	−142	−594	82TN270	12345-57-2
		94	393	−141	−591		
Cl_2Mg^+ / $MgCl_2$	(8.5)	(102)	(428)	−94	−392	85JANAF	7786-30-3
		(102)	(427)	−94	−393		
IP is onset of photoelectron band. See also: 77LEE/POT2.							
Cl_2Mn^+ / $MnCl_2$	(10.8)	(186)	(778)	−63	−264	82TN270	7773-01-5
IP is onset of photoelectron band.							
$Cl_2MoO_2^+$ / MoO_2Cl_2	(11.93±0.02)	(124)	(517)	−152	−634	82TN270	13637-68-8
$Cl_2Na_2^+$	(≤10.30)	(≤102)	(≤428)	−135±2	−566±8	85JANAF	12258-98-9
		(≤103)	(≤432)	−134±2	−562±8		
Cl_2Ni^+ / $NiCl_2$	(10.8)	(231)	(968)	−18±0.1	−74±0.3	82JANAF	7718-54-9
		(231)	(968)	−18±0.1	−74±0.3		
IP is onset of photoelectron band.							
Cl_2O^+ / Cl_2O	10.94	271	1136	19	80	82BAU/COX	7791-21-1
		272	1138	20	82		
Cl_2OS^+ / $SOCl_2$	10.96	(202)	(844)	−51	−213	82TN270	7719-09-7
		(203)	(847)	−50	−210		
$Cl_2O_2S^+$ / SO_2Cl_2	12.05	193	808	−85	−355	85JANAF	7791-25-5
		195	814	−83	−349		
Cl_2Pb^+ / $PbCl_2$	(10.0)	(189)	(791)	−42±0.3	−174±1	85JANAF	7758-95-4
		(189)	(793)	−41±0.3	−172±1		
IP is onset of photoelectron band. (See: 84NOV/POT2).							

Table 1. Positive Ion Table – Continued

ION / Neutral	Ionization potential eV	$\Delta_f H$(Ion) kcal/mol	$\Delta_f H$(Ion) kJ/mol	$\Delta_f H$(Neutral) kcal/mol	$\Delta_f H$(Neutral) kJ/mol	Neutral reference	CAS registry number
$Cl_2Rb_2^+$							
Rb-Cl-Rb (cyclic)	(≤9.30)	(≤64) (≤65)	(≤269) (≤271)	−150 −150	−628 −626	82TN270	12265-61-1
Cl_2S^+							
SCl_2	9.45±0.03	214 214	894 895	−4 −4	−18 −16	85JANAF	10545-99-0
	IP from 81KAU/VAH.						
$Cl_2S_2^+$							
S_2Cl_2	(9.66±0.03)	(218) (219)	(914) (915)	−4 −4	−18 −17	82TN270	10025-67-9
	IP from 81KAU/VAH.						
Cl_2Se^+							
$SeCl_2$	9.25	(206)	(860)	−8	−32	82TN270	14457-70-6
	IP is onset of photoelectron band.						
$Cl_2Se_2^+$							
Se_2Cl_2	(9.4)	(221)	(924)	4	17	82TN270	10025-68-0
	IP is onset of photoelectron band.						
Cl_2Si^+							
$SiCl_2$	(10.93±0.10)	(212) (212)	(889) (889)	−40 −40	−166 −166	82TN270	13569-32-9
Cl_2Sn^+							
$SnCl_2$	(10.0)	(182) (183)	(762) (764)	−49 −49±2	−203 −201±10	82TPIS	7772-99-8
	IP is onset of photoelectron band (84NOV/POT2, 82LEV/LIA).						
Cl_2Sr^+							
$SrCl_2$	9.70±0.1	(115)	(481)	−109	−455	82EMO/KIE	10476-85-4
	See also: 82EMO/KIE, 79LEE/POT2. 0 K values.						
Cl_2Zn^+							
$ZnCl_2$	11.85	210	877	−64	−266	82TN270	7646-85-7
	IP is onset of photoelectron band.						
$Cl_3Cu_3^+$							
(cyclic Cu-Cl structure)	(≤9.52)	(≤158) (≤158)	(≤660) (≤660)	−62±0.5 −62±0.5	−259±2 −259±2	85JANAF	11093-65-5

Table 1. Positive Ion Table – Continued

ION / Neutral	Ionization potential eV	$\Delta_f H$(Ion) kcal/mol	$\Delta_f H$(Ion) kJ/mol	$\Delta_f H$(Neutral) kcal/mol	$\Delta_f H$(Neutral) kJ/mol	Neutral reference	CAS registry number
$Cl_3F_3N_3P_3^+$							
(structure)	(10.76±0.03) IP from 81CLA/SOW.	(−5)	(−22)	−253	−1060	*EST	25251-05-2
Cl_3Ga^+							
$GaCl_3$	11.52	159	664	−107	−448	82TN270	13450-90-3
Cl_3HSi^+							
$SiHCl_3$	(11.7) IP is onset of photoelectron band.	(155) *(156)*	(647) *(652)*	−115 *−114*	−482 *−477*	81BEL/PER	10025-78-2
Cl_3In^+							
$InCl_3$	(11.4)	(173) *(173)*	(722) *(724)*	−90 *−90±2*	−378 *−376±7*	82TPIS	10025-82-8
Cl_3La^+							
$LaCl_3$	(10.6) IP is onset of photoelectron band (83RUS/GOO).	(67)	(282)	−177	−741	82TN270	10099-58-8
$Cl_3Li_3^+$							
(structure)	(10.17)	(5) *(6)*	(19) *(26)*	−230 *−228*	−962 *−955*	82TN270	59217-69-5
Cl_3Lu^+							
$LuCl_3$	(11.5±0.5)	(110)	(461)	−155	−649	82TN270	10099-66-8
Cl_3N^+							
NCl_3	(10.12±0.1)	(297)	(1244)	64	268	*EST	10025-85-1
Cl_3NbO^+							
$NbOCl_3$	≤12.14	≤100.1 *≤100.8*	≤419.0 *≤421.7*	−179.8 *−179.1*	−752.3 *−749.6*	82TN270	13597-20-1
Cl_3OP^+							
$POCl_3$	11.36±0.02	129 *130*	538 *543*	−133 *−132*	−558 *−553*	82TN270	10025-87-3
Cl_3OV^+							
$VOCl_3$	(11.6) IP is onset of photoelectron band.	(101) *(102)*	(423) *(426)*	−166 *−166*	−696 *−693*	82TN270	7727-18-6

Table 1. Positive Ion Table - Continued

ION / Neutral	Ionization potential eV	Δ_fH(Ion) kcal/mol	Δ_fH(Ion) kJ/mol	Δ_fH(Neutral) kcal/mol	Δ_fH(Neutral) kJ/mol	Neutral reference	CAS registry number
Cl_3P^+ / PCl_3	9.91	160 / 160	667 / 671	−69 / −68	−289 / −286	85JANAF	7719-12-2
See also: 83OZG, 81CHA/FIN.							
Cl_3PS^+ / $PSCl_3$	9.71±0.03	137	574	−87	−363	71JANAF	3982-91-0
Cl_3Sb^+ / $SbCl_3$	(10.1±0.1)	(158)	(660)	−75	−314	82TN270	10025-91-9
IP is onset of photoelectron band. See also: 83OZG.							
Cl_3Si^+ / $SiCl_3$		(108)	(454)				19165-34-5
From appearance potentials, 11.91 eV in $SiHCl_3$ and 11.90 eV in CH_3SiCl_3.							
$Cl_4F_2N_3P_3^+$	(10.48±0.03)	(−53)	(−222)	−295	−1233	*EST	25251-04-1
IP from 81CLA/SOW.							
Cl_4Ge^+ / $GeCl_4$	11.68±0.05	(151) / (151)	(631) / (633)	−119 / −118	−496 / −494	82TN270	10038-98-9
Cl_4Hf^+ / $HfCl_4$	(11.7)	(59)	(246)	−211	−883	81SPE	13499-05-3
IP is onset of photoelectron band.							
Cl_4Mo^+ / $MoCl_4$	(10.5±0.1)	(152)	(636)	−90	−377	82TN270	13320-71-3
IP from 83MAK/VER.							
Cl_4Si^+ / $SiCl_4$	11.79±0.01	126 / 124	528 / 520	−146 / −148	−610 / −618	81BEL/PER	10026-04-7
Cl_4Sn^+ / $SnCl_4$	(11.88±0.05)	(161) / (162)	(674) / (677)	−113 / −112	−472 / −469	82TN270	7646-78-8
Cl_4Th^+ / $ThCl_4$	(12.7±0.3)	(62) / (62)	(259) / (260)	−231 / −230.8	−966 / −965.6	82TN270	10026-08-1
Cl_4Ti^+ / $TiCl_4$	11.65±0.15	(86) / (86)	(361) / (362)	−182 / −182	−763 / −762	85JANAF	7550-45-0

Table 1. Positive Ion Table - Continued

ION / Neutral	Ionization potential eV	$\Delta_f H$(Ion) kcal/mol	kJ/mol	$\Delta_f H$(Neutral) kcal/mol	kJ/mol	Neutral reference	CAS registry number
Cl_4U^+							
UCl_4	9.18	18	76	−193	−810	82TN270	10026-10-5
Cl_4V^+							
VCl_4	(9.2)	(86)	(362)	−126	−526	82TN270	7632-51-1
		(87)	(364)	−125	−524		
	IP is onset of photoelectron band.						
Cl_4W^+							
WCl_4	(8.0)	(104)	(436)	−80±8	−336±33	85JANAF	13470-13-8
		(104)	(436)	−80±8	−336±33		
Cl_4Zr^+							
$ZrCl_4$	(11.2)	(50)	(211)	−208	−870	82TN270	10026-11-6
		(51)	(212)	−208	−869		
	IP is onset of photoelectron band.						
Cl_5Mo^+							
$MoCl_5$	(8.7)	(94)	(392)	−107	−448	85JANAF	10241-05-1
		(94)	(393)	−106	−446		
	IP is onset of photoelectron band.						
Cl_5Nb^+							
$NbCl_5$	(10.97)	(85)	(355)	−168	−703	85JANAF	10026-12-7
		(85)	(357)	−168	−701		
Cl_5P^+							
PCl_5	10.7	(157)	(657)	−90	−375	82TN270	10026-13-8
		(158)	(662)	−88	−370		
	IP is onset of photoelectron band.						
Cl_5Re^+							
$ReCl_5$	(9.2)	(136)	(570)	−76	−318	82TN270	13596-35-5
	IP is onset of photoelectron band.						
Cl_5Sb^+							
$SbCl_5$	(10.8)	(155)	(648)	−94	−394	82TN270	7647-18-9
		(155)	(650)	−94	−392		
	IP is onset of photoelectron band (81ELB/DIE).						
Cl_5Ta^+							
$TaCl_5$	11.08	73	304	−183	−765	85JANAF	7721-01-9
		73	306	−182	−763		
Cl_5W^+							
WCl_5	(8.5)	(97)	(407)	−99±8	−413±33	85JANAF	13470-14-9
		(98)	(409)	−98±8	−411±33		
	IP is onset of photoelectron band.						

Table 1. Positive Ion Table – Continued

ION / Neutral	Ionization potential eV	$\Delta_f H$(Ion) kcal/mol	$\Delta_f H$(Ion) kJ/mol	$\Delta_f H$(Neutral) kcal/mol	$\Delta_f H$(Neutral) kJ/mol	Neutral reference	CAS registry number
$Cl_6Ga_2^+$	(11.4)	(30)	(125)	−233	−975	82TN270	15654-66-7
IP is onset of photoelectron band.							
$Cl_6N_3P_3^+$	9.8	(51)	(213)	−175	−732	69BEN/CRU	940-71-6
IP is onset of photoelectron band. See also: 81CLA/SOW.							
$Cl_6Si_2^+$ / Si_2Cl_6	(10.4)	(−4)	(−16)	−244	−1019	81BEL/PER	13465-77-5
See also: 81KHV/ZYK.							
Cl_6W^+ / WCl_6	(9.5)	(83)	(347)	−136	−570	81WOO	13283-01-7
				−136	*−570*		
$Cl_9Re_3^+$	(8.7)	(64)	(266)	−137	−573	82TN270	14973-59-2
IP is onset of photoelectron band.							
Cm^+ / Cm	6.09±0.02	233	974	92	386	85KLE/WAR	7440-51-9
See also: 81CHE/GAB.							
Co^+ / Co	7.864±0.001	283	1184	102	425	82TN270	7440-48-4
		282	*1182*	*101*	*423*		
See also: 82DYK/GRA.							
CoH^+ / CoH	(7.3±0.1)	(287)	(1203)	(119)	(496)	81ARM/BEA	14994-20-8
$\Delta_f H$(Ion) from onset of endothermic reaction (86ELK/ARM4). See also: 81ARM/HAL. IP from 81ARM/BEA. 0 K values.							
$CoHO^+$ / CoOH		*220*	*920*				12314-24-8
$\Delta_f H$(Ion) from photodissociation onset, proton affinity of CoO(84CAS/FRE). 0 K values.							
CoO^+ / CoO	8.9±0.2	(277)	(1159)	72±3	301±13	79HUB/HER	1307-96-6
$\Delta_f H$(Ion) from 81ARM/HAL, 82ARM/HAL. See also: 81KAP/STA. 0 K values.							

Table 1. Positive Ion Table - Continued

ION Neutral	Ionization potential eV	$\Delta_f H$(Ion) kcal/mol	$\Delta_f H$(Ion) kJ/mol	$\Delta_f H$(Neutral) kcal/mol	$\Delta_f H$(Neutral) kJ/mol	Neutral reference	CAS registry number
Cr^+							
Cr	6.766	250.8 *250.3*	1049.4 *1047.3*	94.8 *94.3*	396.6 *394.5*	82TN270	7440-47-3
CrF^+							
CrF	(8.4±0.3)	(199)	(831)	5	21	81WOO	13943-42-5
CrF_2^+							
CrF_2	(10.1±0.3)	(181)	(758)	−52	−216	81WOO	10049-10-2
CrF_3^+							
CrF_3	(12.2±0.3)	(124)	(517)	−158	−660	81WOO	7788-97-8
CrH^+							
CrH		(274)	(1145)				13966-79-5
	\multicolumn{6}{l	}{$\Delta_f H$(Ion) from onset of endothermic reaction (86ELK/ARM). See also: 81ARM/HAL. 0 K values.}	
CrO^+							
CrO	7.85±0.02	(233) (230)	(975) (961)	52±7 *49±3*	218±29 *203±12*	83PED/MAR	12018-00-7
	\multicolumn{6}{l	}{IP from 83DYK/GRA. $\Delta_f H$(Ion) at 0 K from 81ARM/HAL, 82ARM/HAL. See also: 81BAL/GIG, 81KAP/STA.}	
CrO_2^+							
CrO_2	(10.3±0.5)	(223)	(935)	−14	−59	82TN270	12018-01-8
	0 K values.						
CrO_2P^+							
$CrPO_2$	(8.0±0.5)	(236)	(989)	52±3	218±13	81BAL/GIG	
	IP from 81BAL/GIG. 0 K values.						
CrO_3^+							
CrO_3	(11.6±0.5)	(175)	(733)	−92	−386	82TN270	1333-82-0
Cs^+							
Cs	3.894	108.0 *108.3*	451.8 *453.3*	18.2 *18.5*	76.1 *77.6*	82TN270	7440-46-2
	See also: 84ASA/YAS, 85SCH/WEI.						
CsF^+							
CsF	(8.80±0.10)	(117) (117)	(488) (490)	−86 −85.8±1.8	−361 −359.0±7.5	84PAR/WEX	13400-13-0
$CsHO^+$							
CsOH	(7.3±0.15)	(106)	(445)	−62	−259	81LIN/BES	21351-79-1
CsH_2O^+							
$CsOH_2$		36	149				
	\multicolumn{6}{l	}{$\Delta_f H$(Ion) from equilibrium constant determination (69SEA/DZI).}	

Table 1. Positive Ion Table — Continued

ION Neutral	Ionization potential eV	$\Delta_f H$(Ion) kcal/mol	$\Delta_f H$(Ion) kJ/mol	$\Delta_f H$(Neutral) kcal/mol	$\Delta_f H$(Neutral) kJ/mol	Neutral reference	CAS registry number
CsI^+							
CsI	7.10±0.05	127	531	−37	−154	84PAR/WEX	7789-17-5
		128	*535*	*−35.9±3.4*	*−150±14*		
	See also: 82EMO/HOR, 82LEL/BAL, 84VIS/HIL.						
CsK^+							
KCs	(3.9±0.1)	(119)	(498)	(29)	(122)	79HUB/HER	
	IP from 85KAP/SCH. 0 K values.						
$CsLi^+$							
LiCs	(4.1±0.1)	(134)	(562)	(40)	(166)	79HUB/HER	12018-59-6
	IP from 85KAP/SCH. 0 K values.						
$CsNa^+$							
NaCs	(4.05±0.04)	(128)	(535)	(35)	(144)	79HUB/HER	12018-60-9
	IP from 85KAP/SCH. 0 K values.						
CsO^+							
CsO	6.22	153.6	642.8	10.2	42.7	82TPIS	24774-39-8
		154.1	*644.9*	*10.7±5*	*44.8±21*		
	IP from 84BUT/KUD.						
$CsRb^+$							
RbCs	3.7±0.1	96	401	11	44	86IGE/WED	12331-83-8
	IP from 85KAP/SCH.						
Cs_2^+							
Cs_2	3.7±0.1	(111)	(464)	26±0.1	107±0.3	85JANAF	12184-83-7
		(112)	*(469)*	*27±0.1*	*112±0.3*		
	IP from 85KAP/RAD, 85KAP/SCH. See also: 83HEL/MOL.						
$Cs_2MoO_4^+$							
Cs_2MoO_4	(7.0)	(−114)	(−479)	−276	−1154	81LIN/BES	
Cs_2O^+							
Cs_2O	4.41±0.03	(80)	(333)	−22	−92	81LIN/BES	20281-00-9
	IP from 77ROS/DRA, 84BUT/KUD.						
Cu^+							
Cu	7.72634±0.00002	<u>259.0</u>	<u>1083.8</u>	80.9	338.3	82TN270	7440-50-8
		<u>*258.8*</u>	<u>*1082.7*</u>	*80.6*	*337.2*		
CuF^+							
CuF	10.15±0.02	(235)	(984)	1	5	81WOO	13478-41-6
		(231)	*(967)*	*−3*	*−12*		
	IP from 80DYK/FAY. See also: 77EHL/WAN.						
CuF_2^+							
CuF_2	(12.7)	(229)	(958)	−64	−267	81WOO	7789-19-7
		(230)	*(960)*	*−63*	*−265*		
	IP is onset of photoelectron band (80DYK/FAY). See also: 77EHL/WAN.						

Table 1. Positive Ion Table — Continued

ION / Neutral	Ionization potential eV	$\Delta_f H$(Ion) kcal/mol	$\Delta_f H$(Ion) kJ/mol	$\Delta_f H$(Neutral) kcal/mol	$\Delta_f H$(Neutral) kJ/mol	Neutral reference	CAS registry number
CuH⁺							
CuH	(9.5)	(289)	(1208)	70	291	79HUB/HER	
	$\Delta_f H$(Ion) from onset of endothermic reaction (86ELK/ARM4). IP is $\Delta_f H$(Ion) - $\Delta_f H$(Neutral). 0 K values.						
CuO⁺							
CuO		(286±8)	(1197±33)	73±10	306±41	85JANAF	1317-38-0
	$\Delta_f H$(Ion) from (81KAP/STA). Ion/molecule bracketing results.						
CuSn⁺							
CuSn	(7.2±1.0)	(277)	(1161)	111	466	79HUB/HER	12054-11-4
	0 K values.						
Cu₂⁺							
Cu₂	7.894±0.015	298	1247	116	485	85JANAF	12190-70-4
		_298_	_1247_	_116_	_485_		
	IP from 83POW/HAN.						
D⁺							
D	13.602	<u>366.6</u>	<u>1534.0</u>	52.98	221.67	82TN270	16873-17-9
		<u>_366.2_</u>	<u>_1532.1_</u>	_52.52_	_219.76_		
DH⁺							
HD	15.44477±0.00007	<u>356.2</u>	<u>1490.5</u>	.077	.32	85JANAF	13983-20-5
		<u>_356.2_</u>	<u>_1490.5_</u>	_.079_	_.33_		
DLi⁺							
LiD	7.7±0.1	(211)	(884)	33.7	141.1	82TN270	13587-16-1
		_(211)_	_(884)_	_33.7_	_141.1_		
D₂⁺							
D₂	15.46660±0.0001	<u>356.7</u>	<u>1492.2</u>	0	0	*DEF	7782-39-0
		<u>_356.7_</u>	<u>_1492.2_</u>	_0_	_0_		
	IP from 79HUB/HER.						
D₂O⁺							
D₂O	12.635±0.007	<u>231.8</u>	<u>970.0</u>	−59.56	−249.20	85JANAF	7789-20-0
		<u>_232.5_</u>	<u>_972.8_</u>	_−58.85_	_−246.25_		
D₃O⁺							
D₃O	4.3±0.1						24847-51-6
	IP from 84GEL/POR.						
Dy⁺							
Dy	5.9390±0.0006	206	863	69	290	82TN270	7429-91-6
		_207.0_	_866.1_	_70.0_	_293.1_		
DyF⁺							
DyF	(6.0±0.3)	(101)	(422)	−38	−157	79HUB/HER	
	0 K values.						

Table 1. Positive Ion Table - Continued

ION / Neutral	Ionization potential eV	$\Delta_f H$(Ion) kcal/mol	$\Delta_f H$(Ion) kJ/mol	$\Delta_f H$(Neutral) kcal/mol	$\Delta_f H$(Neutral) kJ/mol	Neutral reference	CAS registry number
DyO$^+$ / DyO	(6.08±0.1)	(122) *(121)*	(512) *(508)*	−18±10 *−19*	−75±42 *−79*	83PED/MAR	12175-28-9
Er$^+$ / Er	6.1077±0.0006	217 *216.9*	906 *907.6*	76 *76.1*	317 *318.3*	82TN270	7440-52-0
ErF$^+$ / ErF	(6.3±0.3) 0 K values.	(105)	(441)	−40	−167	79HUB/HER	
ErF$_2$$^+$ / ErF$_2$	(7.0±0.3)	(−3)	(−11)	−164	−686	82TN270	
ErI$_3$$^+$ / ErI$_3$	9.0 IP is onset of photoelectron band (83RUS/GOO).	125	524	−82	−344	82TN270	13813-42-8
ErO$^+$ / ErO	(6.30±0.1) See also: 80MUR/HIL.	(135) *(132)*	(566) *(554)*	−10±5 *−13*	−42±21 *−54*	83PED/MAR	12280-61-4
Es$^+$ / Es	6.52±0.10	182	762	31.8±3	133±13	85KLE/WAR	7429-92-7
Eu$^+$ / Eu	5.67045±0.0003	172 *173.1*	722 *724.2*	42 *42.3*	175 *177.1*	82TN270	7440-53-1
EuO$^+$ / EuO	(6.48±0.1) See also: 81BAL/GIG, 85BAL/GIG.	(139)	(582)	−10	−43	83PED/MAR	12020-60-9
EuO$_2$V$^+$ / EuVO$_2$	(8) IP from 83BAL/GIG. 0 K values.	(108)	(450)	−77	−322	83BAL/GIG	88762-30-5
EuO$_3$Ti$^+$ / EuTiO$_3$	(6.5±0.5) IP from 85BAL/GIG.	(−62)	(−260)	−212±7	−887±28	85BAL/GIG	12020-61-0
EuO$_3$V$^+$ / EuVO$_3$	8.1±0.5 IP from 83BAL/GIG. 0 K values.	(4)	(17)	(−183)	(−764)	83BAL/GIG	39432-21-8
EuS$^+$ / EuS	(6.8±0.3)	(184) *(180)*	(769) *(751)*	27 *23*	113 *95*	82TN270	12020-65-4

Table 1. Positive Ion Table – Continued

ION / Neutral	Ionization potential eV	$\Delta_f H$(Ion) kcal/mol	$\Delta_f H$(Ion) kJ/mol	$\Delta_f H$(Neutral) kcal/mol	$\Delta_f H$(Neutral) kJ/mol	Neutral reference	CAS registry number
F^+							
F	17.422	420.7	1760.2	19.0±0.1	79.4±0.3	85JANAF	14762-94-8
		420.2	*1758.2*	*18.5±0.1*	*77.4±0.3*		
FGa^+							
GaF	(9.6±0.5)	(167)	(699)	−54	−227	79HUB/HER	13966-78-4
		(167)	*(700)*	*−54*	*−226*		
	A value of 10.7±0.6 eV has also been reported for this ionization potential.						
FGe^+							
GeF	7.46	166	694	−6	−26	81WOO	14929-46-5
		166	*694*	*−6*	*−26*		
	IP from 79HUB/HER.						
FH^+							
HF	16.044±0.003	304.9	1275.5	−65.1±0.2	−272.5±0.8	85JANAF	7664-39-3
		304.9	*1275.5*	*−65.1±0.2*	*−272.5±0.8*		
	See also: 81KIM/KAT, 81BIE/ASB.						
FHO^+							
HOF	12.71±0.01	270	1128	−23±1	−98±4	82BAU/COX	14034-79-8
FH_2^+							
H_2F		184	767				
	From proton affinity of HF (RN 7664-39-3). A value of 205 kcal/mol, 859 kJ/mol is derived from the appearance potential of this ion from (HF)$_2$. PA = 117 kcal/mol, 489.5 kJ/mol.						
FH_3Si^+							
SiH_3F	11.7	(180)	(752)	−90±5	−377±21	78JANAF	13537-33-2
	IP is onset of photoelectron band.						
FHo^+							
HoF	(6.1±0.3)	(103)	(431)	−38	−158	79HUB/HER	16087-66-4
	0 K values.						
FI^+							
IF	10.62	222.2	929.9	−22.7±0.9	−94.8±3.8	85JANAF	13873-84-2
		222.7	*931.8*	*−22.2±0.9*	*−92.9±3.8*		
	IP from 84DYK/JOS.						
FIn^+							
InF	(9.6±0.5)	(177)	(740)	−44	−186	79HUB/HER	13966-95-5
	0 K values.						
FMg^+							
MgF	(7.68)	(120.5)	(504)	−56.6±2.0	−236.8±8.4	85JANAF	14953-28-7
		(121)	*(505)*	*−56.5±2.0*	*−236.4±8.4*		
FMn^+							
MnF	(8.3±0.2)	(173)	(723)	−19	−78	81WOO	13569-25-0

Table 1. Positive Ion Table – Continued

| ION | Ionization potential | $\Delta_f H$(Ion) | | $\Delta_f H$(Neutral) | | Neutral | CAS registry |
Neutral	eV	kcal/mol	kJ/mol	kcal/mol	kJ/mol	reference	number
FMo^+							
MoF	(8.0±0.3)	(249)	(1044)	65	272	81WOO	60388-18-3
FN^+							
NF	12.26±0.01	*338*	*1415*	*55.5±0.5*	*232.2±2.1*	84BER/GRE	13967-06-1
	IP from 82DYK/JON. $\Delta_f H$(Ion) from 84BER/GRE. See also: 79DUD/BAL. 0 K values.						
FNO^+							
NOF	12.63±0.03	275	1152	−16	−67	82TN270	7789-25-5
		276	*1154*	*−16*	*−65*		
FNO_2^+							
NO_2F	(13.09)	(276)	(1154)	−26±5	−109±21	85JANAF	10022-50-1
		(277)	*(1160)*	*−25±5*	*−103±21*		
FNS^+							
NSF	11.51±0.04	260	1090	−5±0.9	−21±4	73LAR/JOH	18820-63-8
FNa_2^+							
Na_2F	4.0±0.1	*5*	*20*	*−87±3*	*−366±13*	85KAP/RAD	87331-13-3
	IP from 85KAP/RAD. 0 K values.						
FNd^+							
FNd	(5.0±0.3)	(81)	(338)	−34	−144	81WOO	
	A 298 K heat of formation of -161 kJ/mol, -38.5 kcal/mol (79HUB/HER)						
	or -159 kJ/mol, -38.0 kcal/mol (82TN270) has also been recommended for NdF.						
FO^+							
OF	12.77	320	1341	26±2	109±8	82BAU/COX	12061-70-0
		320	*1341*	*26*	*109*		
FO_2^+							
O_2F	(12.6±0.2)	(294)	(1229)	3±0.5	13±2	85JANAF	15499-23-7
		(294)	*(1230)*	*3±0.5*	*14±2*		
FP^+							
PF	(≤9.74±0.01)	(≤212)	(≤887)	−12.5±5	−52±21	85JANAF	16027-92-2
		(≤212)	*(≤888)*	*−12±5*	*−51±21*		
	$\Delta_f H$(Ion) from appearance potential determinations (84BER/GRE). IP from 82DYK/JON2.						
	See also: 75TOR/WES, 82LEV/LIA.						
FPb^+							
PbF	(7.5±0.3)	(154)	(644)	−19	−80	81WOO	14986-72-2
		(154)	*(646)*	*−19*	*−78*		
FS^+							
SF	10.09	(236)	(987)	3±1	13±6	85JANAF	16068-96-5
		(233)	*(973)*	*2.9±1.5*	*12±6*		
	$\Delta_f H$(Ion) from appearance potential determination (80GOM/HAA); corresponding IP = 9.9 eV.						
	IP from 85LOS/WIL.						

Table 1. Positive Ion Table – Continued

ION Neutral	Ionization potential eV	$\Delta_f H$(Ion) kcal/mol	kJ/mol	$\Delta_f H$(Neutral) kcal/mol	kJ/mol	Neutral reference	CAS registry number
FS$_2$$^+$							
SSF		194	811				
	From appearance potential determinations (85LOS/WIL).						
FSi$^+$							
SiF	7.28	163	682	−5±6	−20±25	83WAL	11128-24-8
		166	*680*	*−5±6*	*−22±25*		
	IP from 79HUB/HER.						
FSm$^+$							
SmF	(5.7±0.3)	(68)	(286)	−63	−264	79HUB/HER	17209-59-5
		(73)	*(307)*	*−58*	*−243*		
FSn$^+$							
SnF	(7.04)	(142)	(593)	−21	−86	81WOO	13966-74-0
FSr$^+$							
SrF	(5.0±0.3)	(45)	(188)	−70.4±2.0	−294.6±8.4	85JANAF	13569-27-2
		(45)	*(189.5)*	*−70.0±2.0*	*−292.9±8.4*		
FTl$^+$							
TlF	10.52	199	833	−43	−182	82TN270	7789-27-7
		199	*833*	*−43*	*−182*		
FW$^+$							
WF	(8.5±1)	(282)	(1180)	86	360	81WOO	51621-16-0
FXe$^+$							
XeF	(10.3)	(252)	(1057)	15.3	64.0	79HUB/HER	16757-14-5
	$\Delta_f H$(Ion) *from appearance potential determinations.*						
	IP is $\Delta_f H$(Ion)-$\Delta_f H$(Neutral). 0 K values.						
FY$^+$							
YF	(6.3±0.3)	(121)	(507)	−24	−101	79HUB/HER	13981-88-9
	0 K values.						
F$_2$$^+$							
F$_2$	15.697±0.003	362.0	1514.5	0	0	*DEF	7782-41-4
		362.0	*1514.5*				
	IP from 84VAN/DEL2. See also: 84DYK/JOS, 81KIM/KAT, 81BIE/ASB.						
F$_2$Fe$^+$							
FeF$_2$	(11.3±0.3)	(177)	(740)	−84	−350	81WOO	7789-28-8
		(177)	*(741)*	*−83*	*−349*		
F$_2$Ge$^+$							
GeF$_2$	(11.65)	(132)	(551)	−137	−573	81WOO	13940-63-1
	IP from 82JON/VAN3.						
F$_2$HN$^+$							
HNF$_2$	(11.53±0.08)	(250)	(1047)	−16±1	−65±6	69PAN/ZER	10405-27-3

Table 1. Positive Ion Table – Continued

ION / Neutral	Ionization potential eV	$\Delta_f H$(Ion) kcal/mol	$\Delta_f H$(Ion) kJ/mol	$\Delta_f H$(Neutral) kcal/mol	$\Delta_f H$(Neutral) kJ/mol	Neutral reference	CAS registry number
$F_2HO_2S^+$ / F_2SOOH		38	159				
From proton affinity of F_2SO_2 (RN 2699-79-8) (85MCM/KEB, 85MCM/KEB2) re-evaluated relative to CO standard (84LIA/LIE). PA = 146.2 kcal/mol, 612. kJ/mol.							
$F_2H_2Si^+$ / SiH_2F_2	12.2	(92) / (94)	(386) / (395)	−189±5 / −187±5	−791±21 / −782±21	85JANAF	13824-36-7
IP is onset of photoelectron band.							
F_2IP^+ / PF_2I^+		(9.8) / (84)	(350)	−142.3±1	−595.4±4.2	84BER/GRE	13819-11-9
IP is onset of photoelectron band. 0 K values.							
F_2Kr^+ / KrF_2	13.1±0.05	317	1325	14±0.7	60±3	67GUN	13773-81-4
F_2Mg^+ / MgF_2	(13.4±0.4)	(136) / (137)	(569) / (571)	−173 / −172	−724 / −722	82TN270	7783-40-6
F_2Mn^+ / MnF_2	(11.4)	(137)	(575)	−125	−525	81WOO	7782-64-1
F_2Mo^+ / MoF_2	(9.00±0.15)	(167)	(700)	−40	−168	81WOO	20205-60-1
$F_2MoO_2^+$ / MoO_2F_2	(13.0±0.3)	(56)	(236)	−243	−1018	81WOO	13824-57-2
F_2N^+ / NF_2	11.628±0.01	275 / 276.5	1153 / 1156.8	8 / 8.3	31 / 34.9	84BER/GRE	3744-07-8
IP from 84BER/GRE. See also: 79DUD/BAL.							
F_2NS^+ / NSF_2		253	1060				
From appearance potential (15.47 eV) in NSF_3.							
$F_2N_2^+$ / (E)-N_2F_2	(12.8)	(315) / (316)	(1316) / (1321)	19±1 / 21±1	81±5 / 86±5	85JANAF	13776-62-0
F_2Nd^+ / F_2Nd	(5.6±0.3)	(−29)	(−120)	−158	−660	81WOO	
F_2O^+ / OF_2	13.11±0.01	308 / 309	1290 / 1292	5.9±0.4 / 6.4±0.4	24.5±1.6 / 26.8±1.6	85JANAF	7783-41-7

Table 1. Positive Ion Table – Continued

ION Neutral	Ionization potential eV	$\Delta_f H$(Ion) kcal/mol	$\Delta_f H$(Ion) kJ/mol	$\Delta_f H$(Neutral) kcal/mol	$\Delta_f H$(Neutral) kJ/mol	Neutral reference	CAS registry number
F_2OS^+							
SOF_2	12.25	(164)	(688)	−118±8	−494±32	87HER	7783-42-8
		(166)	(693)	−117±8	−489±32		
	See also: 81COS/LLO.						
$F_2O_2S^+$							
SO_2F_2	13.04±0.01	119	499	−181±2	−759±8	87HER	2699-79-8
		121	508	−179±2	−750±8		
$F_2O_2W^+$							
WO_2F_2	(12.5±0.3)	(70)	(291)	−219	−915	81WOO	14118-73-1
	IP from 81MAL/MEL.						
F_2P^+							
PF_2	8.847±0.010	90	378.5	−115±0.5	−482±2.1	84BER/GRE	13873-52-4
		90	375	−114.4±0.5	−478.6±2.1		
	IP from 84BER/GRE. See also: 75TOR/WES, 82LEV/LIA.						
F_2Pb^+							
PbF_2	(11.5)	(162)	(677)	−103	−432	81WOO	7783-46-2
		(163)	(681)	−102	−429		
	IP is onset of photoelectron band (83NOV/POT2).						
F_2Pt^+							
PtF_2	(11.85±0.25)	(247)	(1032)	−26±6	−111±25	83KOR/BON	18820-56-9
	IP from 83KOR/BON.						
F_2S^+							
SF_2	(10.08)	(161)	(676)	−71±4	−297±17	87HER	13814-25-0
		(162)	(678)	−70±4	−295±17		
	See also: 80GOM/HAA, 85LOS/WIL.						
$F_2S_2^+$							
FSSF	10.62±0.02	176	739	−68±2	−286±10	87HER	13709-35-8
		177	742	−67±2	−283±10		
	IP from 85LOS/WIL.						
SSF_2	10.41±0.02	169	707	−71±2	−297±10	87HER	101947-30-2
	IP from 85LOS/WIL. See also: 84COO/KRO, 82LEV/LIA.						
F_2Si^+							
SiF_2	10.78±0.05	(108)	(450)	−141±2	−590±8	83WAL	13966-66-0
		(108)	(451)	−141±2	−589±8		
F_2Sn^+							
SnF_2	(11.1)	(140)	(586)	−116	−485	81WOO	7783-47-3
	IP is onset of photoelectron band (83NOV/POT2).						
F_2Ti^+							
TiF_2	(12.2±0.5)	(125)	(524)	−156	−653	81WOO	13814-20-5

Table 1. Positive Ion Table – Continued

ION / Neutral	Ionization potential eV	$\Delta_f H$(Ion) kcal/mol	$\Delta_f H$(Ion) kJ/mol	$\Delta_f H$(Neutral) kcal/mol	$\Delta_f H$(Neutral) kJ/mol	Neutral reference	CAS registry number
F_2W^+ / WF_2	(9.0±0.3)	(182)	(763)	−25	−105	81WOO	33963-15-4
F_2Xe^+ / XeF_2	12.35±0.01	259	1085	−26±0.2	−107±1	72JOH/MAL	13709-36-9
F_2Zr^+ / F_2Zr	(12.0±0.5)	(143) (144)	(600) (602)	−133±5 −133±5	−558±21 −556±21	85JANAF	13842-94-9
F_3Fe^+ / FeF_3	(12.5±0.3)	(101) (101)	(421) (424)	−188 −187	−785 −782	81WOO	7783-50-8
F_3HN^+ / F_2NFH		199	832				

From proton affinity of NF$_3$ (RN 7783-54-2) (85MCM/KEB) re-evaluated relative to CO standard (84LIA/LIE). PA = 136.9 kcal/mol, 573. kJ/mol.

F_3HOP^+ / $P(OH)F_3$		−91	−383				

From proton affinity of POF$_3$ (RN 13478-20-1). PA = 167.8 kcal/mol, 702. kJ/mol.

F_3HP^+ / HPF_3		−20	−86				

From proton affinity of PF$_3$ (RN 7783-55-3). PA = 166.5 kcal/mol, 697. kJ/mol.

F_3HSi^+ / $SiHF_3$	(14.0)	(36) (37)	(150) (157)	−287±5 −285±5	−1201±21 −1194±21	85JANAF	13465-71-9

IP is onset of photoelectron band.

$F_3H_2OSi^+$ / SiF_3OH_2		(−264)	(−1103)				

From proton affinity of SiF$_3$OH (84REE/MUJ). PA = (162) kcal/mol, (676) kJ/mol.

F_3Mn^+ / MnF_3	(12.57±0.2)	(104)	(434)	−186	−779	81WOO	7783-53-1
F_3Mo^+ / MoF_3	(9.88±0.10)	(87) (87)	(361) (364)	−141 −141	−592 −589	81WOO	20193-58-2
F_3MoS^+ / $MoSF_3$	(13.0±0.3)	(134)	(559)	−166±6	−695±27	80MAL/ALI	67374-76-9

IP from 80MAL/ALI, 80MAL/ALI2.

F_3N^+ / NF_3	13.00±0.02	268 270	1122 1128	−31±0.3 −30±0.3	−132±1 −126±1	85JANAF	7783-54-2

See also: 84BER/GRE, 84BER/GRE2, 79DUD/BAL.

Table 1. Positive Ion Table - Continued

ION / Neutral	Ionization potential eV	$\Delta_f H$(Ion) kcal/mol	$\Delta_f H$(Ion) kJ/mol	$\Delta_f H$(Neutral) kcal/mol	$\Delta_f H$(Neutral) kJ/mol	Neutral reference	CAS registry number
F_3NO^+							
NOF_3	13.26±0.01	(267)	(1116)	−39±5	−163±21	85JANAF	13847-65-9
		(269)	*(1124)*	*−37±5*	*−155±21*		
F_3NS^+							
NSF_3	(12.0)	(192)	(802)	−85±0.5	−356±2	70O'H/HUB	15930-75-3
	IP is onset of photoelectron band.						
F_3OP^+							
POF_3	12.76±0.01	(−5)	(−23)	−300±2	−1254±8	85JANAF	13478-20-1
		(−3)	*(−14)*	*−298±2*	*−1245±8*		
	See also: 83NES/MIL.						
F_3OV^+							
VOF_3	(13.88±0.05)	(25)	(105)	−295.0±7.0	−1234±29	75FLE/SVE	13709-31-4
F_3P^+							
PF_3	11.44	(35)	(146)	−229±1	−958±4	85JANAF	7783-55-3
		(36)	*(151)*	*−228±1*	*−953±4*		
	IP from 84BER/GRE. See also: 83NES/MIL, 75TOR/WES, 82LEV/LIA.						
F_3PS^+							
F_3PS	≤11.05±0.035	(≤14)	(≤57)	−241±15	−1009±63	85JANAF	2404-52-6
		(≤16)	*(≤65)*	*−239±15*	*−1001±63*		
F_3Sb^+							
SbF_3	(12.1)	(80)	(334)	−199	−833	81WOO	7783-56-4
	IP is onset of photoelectron band(83NOV/POT).						
F_3Si^+							
SiF_3	(9.3)	(−24)	(−99)	−239±5	−1000±21	83WAL	
		(−23)	*(−96)*	*−238±5*	*−996±21*		
	From appearance potential (13.33 eV) in CH_3SiF_3. IP is $\Delta_f H$(Ion) - $\Delta_f H$(Neutral).						
F_3Ti^+							
TiF_3	(10.5±0.5)	(−36)	(−151)	−278	−1164	81WOO	7783-57-5
		(−35)	*(−147)*	*−277*	*−1160*		
F_3W^+							
WF_3	(9.0±0.2)	(81)	(337)	−127	−531	81WOO	51621-17-1
F_3Xe^+							
XeF_3		234	981				
	From appearance potential (13.10 eV) in XeF_4.						
F_4Ge^+							
GeF_4	(15.5)	(73)	(306)	−284	−1190	81WOO	7783-58-6
	IP is onset of photoelectron band (75LLO/ROB).						

Table 1. Positive Ion Table - Continued

ION / Neutral	Ionization potential eV	$\Delta_f H$(Ion) kcal/mol	$\Delta_f H$(Ion) kJ/mol	$\Delta_f H$(Neutral) kcal/mol	$\Delta_f H$(Neutral) kJ/mol	Neutral reference	CAS registry number
F_4HSi^+ / SiF_3FH		−140	−588				
	From proton affinity of SiF_4 (RN 7783-61-1)(84REE/MUJ). PA = 120.2 kcal/mol, 503. kJ/mol.						
F_4Mo^+ / MoF_4	(9.9)	(0)	(1)	−228	−954	81WOO	23412-45-5
		(1)	*(4)*	*−227*	*−951*		
F_4MoO^+ / $MoOF_4$	13.8	2	6	−317	−1325	86BUR/FAW	14459-59-7
		3	*13*	*−315*	*−1318*		
	IP is onset of photoelectron band (81VOV/DUD).						
F_4MoS^+ / $MoSF_4$	(12.6±0.3)	(58)	(245)	−232±7	−971±29	80MAL/ALI	70487-60-4
	IP from 80MAL/ALI, 80MAL/ALI2.						
$F_4N_2^+$ / N_2F_4	11.94±0.03	267	1119	−8	−33	84BER/GRE	10036-47-2
		270	*1131*	*−5*	*−21*		
	IP from 84BER/GRE.						
F_4ORe^+ / $ReOF_4$	10.5	−22	−91	−264	−1104	86BUR/FAW	17026-29-8
	IP is onset of photoelectron band (81VOV/DUD).						
F_4OS^+ / SOF_4	(12.3)	(61)	(254)	−223±11	−933±44	87HER	13709-54-1
	IP is onset of photoelectron band (81COS/LLO).						
F_4OW^+ / WOF_4	13.6	−28	−119	−342	−1431	86BUR/FAW	13520-79-1
		−27	*−111*	*−340*	*−1423*		
	IP is onset of photoelectron band (81VOV/DUD).						
$F_4P_2^+$ / P_2F_4	≤9.28	≤−56	≤−235	−270	−1130	84BER/GRE	13824-74-3
	IP from 84BER/GRE, 82LEV/LIA. 0 K values.						
F_4Pb^+ / PbF_4	(10.4±0.3)	(42)	(175)	−198	−828	81WOO	7783-59-7
		(41)	*(170)*	*−197*	*−823*		
F_4Pt^+ / PtF_4	(12.83±0.28)	(171)	(714)	−125±6	−524±25	83KOR/BON	13455-15-7
	IP from 83KOR/BON.						

Table 1. Positive Ion Table - Continued

ION / Neutral	Ionization potential eV	$\Delta_f H$(Ion) kcal/mol	$\Delta_f H$(Ion) kJ/mol	$\Delta_f H$(Neutral) kcal/mol	$\Delta_f H$(Neutral) kJ/mol	Neutral reference	CAS registry number
F_4S^+							
SF_4	12.03±0.05	95	397	−182±5	−763±21	85JANAF	7783-60-0
		98	*408*	*−181±5*	*−757±21*		
	See also: 81COS/LLO.						
F_4SW^+							
WSF_4	(≤12.0±0.2)	(≤5)	(≤21)	≤−272±9	≤−1137±38	81MAL/ALI	41831-80-5
	IP from 81MAL/ALI.						
$F_4S_2^+$							
F_3SSF	(10.15±0.10)	(76)	(319)	−158±6	−660±24	87HER	27245-05-2
	IP from 80GOM/HAA.						
F_4Si^+							
SiF_4	(15.7)	(−24)	(−100)	−386.0±0.3	−1615±1	85JANAF	7783-61-1
		(−23)	*(−94)*	*−384.6±0.3*	*−1609±1*		
	IP is onset of photoelectron band. (75LLO/ROB, 82BIE/ASB, 82LEV/LIA)						
F_4U^+							
UF_4	(9.51)	(−163)	(−681)	−382	−1599	82TN270	10049-14-6
		(−162)	*(−676)*	*−381*	*−1594*		
F_4W^+							
WF_4	(9.89±0.10)	(−18)	(−75)	−246	−1029	81WOO	13766-47-7
F_4Xe^+							
XeF_4	12.65±0.1	242	1015	−49±0.2	−206±1	72JOH/MAL	13709-61-0
F_5I^+							
IF_5	12.943±0.005	106	445	−201±0.5	−840±2	85JANAF	7783-66-6
		108	*453*	*−199±0.5*	*−832±2*		
F_5Mo^+							
MoF_5	10.5±0.3	−54	−228	−297±1	−1241±4	85JANAF	13819-84-6
		−53	*−223*	*−295±1*	*−1236±4*		
	IP from 80MAL/ALI2.						
F_5ORe^+							
$ReOF_5$	(13.2±0.1)	(21)	(88)	−283	−1186	81WOO	23377-53-9
F_5P^+							
PF_5	(15.1)	(−33)	(−139)	−381	−1596	82TN270	7647-19-0
		(−30)	*(−127)*	*−379*	*−1584*		
	IP is onset of photoelectron band.						
F_5S^+							
SF_5	10.5±0.1	23	97	−219	−915.9	81BAB/STR	10546-01-7
		25	*106*	*−216*	*−906*		
	IP from charge exchange bracketing experiments (81BAB/STR);						
	$\Delta_f H$(Ion) from equilibrium: $CF_3^+ + SF_6 = SF_5^+ + CF_4$ (81BAB/STR).						

Table 1. Positive Ion Table – Continued

ION / Neutral	Ionization potential eV	$\Delta_f H$(Ion) kcal/mol	$\Delta_f H$(Ion) kJ/mol	$\Delta_f H$(Neutral) kcal/mol	$\Delta_f H$(Neutral) kJ/mol	Neutral reference	CAS registry number
F_5U^+ / UF_5	(11.4)	(−200) / (−199)	(−837) / (−832)	−463 / −462	−1937 / −1932	82TN270	13775-07-0
F_5W^+ / WF_5	(10.03±0.10)	(−103)	(−429)	−334	−1397	81WOO	19357-83-6
F_6Mo^+ / MoF_6	(14.5±0.1)	(−38) / (−36)	(−159) / (−152)	−372.4±0.2 / −370.7±0.2	−1558±1 / −1551±1	85JANAF	7783-77-9
$F_6N_3P_3^+$	11.58	(−245)	(−1024)	−512	−2141	*EST	15599-91-4

IP form 82LEV/LIA and 81CLA/SOW.

ION / Neutral	Ionization potential eV	$\Delta_f H$(Ion) kcal/mol	$\Delta_f H$(Ion) kJ/mol	$\Delta_f H$(Neutral) kcal/mol	$\Delta_f H$(Neutral) kJ/mol	Neutral reference	CAS registry number
F_6Re^+ / ReF_6	(11.0)	(−69)	(−288)	−322	−1349	84BAR/YEH	10049-17-9

IP from 80VOV/DUD.

ION / Neutral	Ionization potential eV	$\Delta_f H$(Ion) kcal/mol	$\Delta_f H$(Ion) kJ/mol	$\Delta_f H$(Neutral) kcal/mol	$\Delta_f H$(Neutral) kJ/mol	Neutral reference	CAS registry number
F_6S^+ / SF_6	15.33±0.03	62 / 65	259 / 273	−291.7±0.2 / −288.3±0.2	−1220.5±.8 / −1206.5±.8	85JANAF	2551-62-4

See also: 82BIE/ASB.

ION / Neutral	Ionization potential eV	$\Delta_f H$(Ion) kcal/mol	$\Delta_f H$(Ion) kJ/mol	$\Delta_f H$(Neutral) kcal/mol	$\Delta_f H$(Neutral) kJ/mol	Neutral reference	CAS registry number
F_6U^+ / UF_6	14.00±0.10	−190 / −189	−796 / −791	−513 / −512	−2147 / −2141	82TN270	7783-81-5
F_6Xe^+ / XeF_6	12.19±0.02	214	897	−67±0.5	−279±2	72JOH/MAL	13693-09-9
F_7Re^+ / ReF_7	(14.1±0.1)	(−16)	(−69)	−342±3	−1429±13	84BAR/YEH	17029-21-9
Fe^+ / Fe	7.870	281 / 280	1175 / 1173	99 / 99	416 / 414	82TN270	7439-89-6

See also: 82DYK/GRA.

ION / Neutral	Ionization potential eV	$\Delta_f H$(Ion) kcal/mol	$\Delta_f H$(Ion) kJ/mol	$\Delta_f H$(Neutral) kcal/mol	$\Delta_f H$(Neutral) kJ/mol	Neutral reference	CAS registry number
FeH^+ / FeH		(283)	(1184)				15600-68-7

$\Delta_f H$(Ion) from onset of endothermic reaction (86ELK/ARM3). See also: 81ARM/HAL, 84HAL/KLE.

ION / Neutral	Ionization potential eV	$\Delta_f H$(Ion) kcal/mol	$\Delta_f H$(Ion) kJ/mol	$\Delta_f H$(Neutral) kcal/mol	$\Delta_f H$(Neutral) kJ/mol	Neutral reference	CAS registry number
$FeHO^+$ / FeOH	7.9±0.2	211 / (214)	884 / (895)	32	133	80MUR	12315-09-2

IP from 80MUR. $\Delta_f H$(Ion) at 298 K from proton affinity of FeO (84CAS/FRE).

Table 1. Positive Ion Table - Continued

ION / Neutral	Ionization potential eV	$\Delta_f H$(Ion) kcal/mol	$\Delta_f H$(Ion) kJ/mol	$\Delta_f H$(Neutral) kcal/mol	$\Delta_f H$(Neutral) kJ/mol	Neutral reference	CAS registry number
FeI⁺							
FeI	(7.8±0.5)	(247)	(1033)	(67)	(280)	84GRA/ROS2	

$\Delta_f H$(Ion) from 84GRA/ROS2. Cited IP is $\Delta_f H$(Ion) - $\Delta_f H$(Neutral). See also: 85GRA/ROS. 0 K values.

FeI$_2$⁺							
FeI$_2$	9.3	(233)	(976)	(19)	(79)	84GRA/ROS2	7783-86-0

IP from 84GRA/ROS. See also: 84GRA/ROS2, 85GRA/ROS. 0 K values.

FeO⁺							
FeO	8.9±0.1	265.2	1109.7	60.0±5	251.0±21	85JANAF	1345-25-1
		265.3	1109.8	60.0±5	251.1±21		

IP from 82ARM/HAL. See also: 84JAC/JAC, 81ARM/HAL, 81KAP/STA, 80MUR.

FeV⁺							
VFe	(5.4)	(302)	(1264)	177	743	85HET/FRE	

$\Delta_f H$(Ion) and IP from 85HET/FRE. 0 K values.

Fe$_2$⁺							
Fe$_2$	6.30±0.01	325	1361	180	753	82SHI/GIN	12596-01-9

IP from 84ROH/COX. 0 K values.

Fm⁺							
Fm	6.64±0.11						7440-72-4
Ga⁺							
Ga	5.999	203	851	65.0	272.0	85JANAF	7440-55-3
		203	850	64.8	271.0		

See also: 85HIR/STR.

GaI⁺							
GaI	(9.0±0.3)	(219)	(915)	11.1	46.4	79HUB/HER	15605-68-2
		(219)	(917)	11.6	48.5		
GaI$_3$⁺							
GaI$_3$	9.40	183	765	−34	−142	82TN270	13450-91-4
GaO⁺							
GaO	(9.4±0.5)	(257)	(1074)	40±10	167±42	83PED/MAR	12024-08-7
		(257)	(1074)	40	167		
Gd⁺							
Gd	6.1502±0.0006	237	991	95	398	82TN270	7440-54-2
		237.2	992.3	95.3	398.9		
GdO⁺							
GdO	(5.75±0.1)	(116)	(486)	−16±3	−69±13	83PED/MAR	12024-77-0
		(116)	(484)	−17	−71		

See also: 80MUR/HIL.

Table 1. Positive Ion Table – Continued

ION / Neutral	Ionization potential eV	$\Delta_f H$(Ion) kcal/mol	$\Delta_f H$(Ion) kJ/mol	$\Delta_f H$(Neutral) kcal/mol	$\Delta_f H$(Neutral) kJ/mol	Neutral reference	CAS registry number
GdS^+							
GdS	(6.9±0.6)	(197)	(825)	38	159	82TN270	12134-74-6
	0 K values.						
Ge^+							
Ge	7.899	272.2	1138.7	90.0	376.6	82TN270	7440-56-4
		271.5	1135.9	89.3	373.8		
GeH_4^+							
GeH_4	11.33	283	1184	22	91	64GUN/GRE	7782-65-2
		285	1195	24	102		
GeH_5^+							
GeH_5		221	926				
	From proton affinity of GeH_4 (RN 7782-65-2) (80SEN/ABE). PA = 166.2 kcal/mol, 695. kJ/mol.						
GeI_2^+							
GeI_2	(8.9)	(216)	(906)	11.2	46.9	82TN270	13573-08-5
	IP is onset of photoelectron band (83JON/VAN).						
GeI_4^+							
GeI_4	(9.42)	(204)	(852)	−14	−57	82TN270	13450-95-8
		(205)	(857)	−12.3	−51.5		
GeO^+							
GeO	11.25±0.01	250	1044	−9.9±0.7	−41±3	84RAU/SCH	20619-16-3
		250	1044	−9.9	−41		
GeS^+							
GeS	9.98±0.02	252	1055	22	92	82TN270	12025-32-0
$GeSe^+$							
GeSe	(9.3)	(230)	(964)	23	96	77PED/RYL	12065-10-0
		(237)	(993)	23	96		
	IP is onset of photoelectron band.						
$GeSi^+$							
GeSi	8.2±0.3	315	1319	126	528	79HUB/HER	12025-36-4
	0 K values.						
Ge_2^+							
Ge_2	(7.8)	(293)	(1226)	113	473	86KIN/NAG	12596-05-3
		(293)	(1224)	113	473		
$Ge_2H_6^+$							
Ge_2H_6	(12.5±0.3)	(327)	(1368)	38.8	162	64GUN/GRE	13818-89-8
$Ge_3H_8^+$							
Ge_3H_8	(9.6±0.3)	(276)	(1153)	54.2	227	64GUN/GRE	14691-44-2

Table 1. Positive Ion Table - Continued

ION / Neutral	Ionization potential eV	$\Delta_f H$(Ion) kcal/mol	$\Delta_f H$(Ion) kJ/mol	$\Delta_f H$(Neutral) kcal/mol	$\Delta_f H$(Neutral) kJ/mol	Neutral reference	CAS registry number
H^+							
H	13.598	365.7	1530.0	52.10	217.999	85JANAF	12385-13-6
		365.2	*1528.0*	*51.63*	*216.035*		
HHe^+							
HHe		323	1352				13766-24-0

$\Delta_f H$(Ion) from 79HUB/HER. Corresponding proton affinity of He = 42.5 kcal/mol, 178. kJ/mol.

HI^+							
HI	10.386±0.001	245.8	1028.5	6.3±0.05	26.4±0.2	85JANAF	10034-85-2
		246.3	*1030.6*	*6.8±0.05*	*28.5±0.2*		

See also: 81KIM/KAT.

HK^+							
KH	(8.0±1.0)	(214)	(895)	29±3	123±15	85JANAF	7693-26-7
		(215)	*(896)*	*30±3*	*126±15*		

IP from 82FAR/SRI.

HKO^+							
KOH	(7.50±0.15)	(117)	(491)	−56	−233	81LIN/BES	1310-58-3
		(119)	*(497)*	*−54*	*−227*		

See also: 82FAR/SRI.

HKr^+							
KrH		264	1105				

From proton affinity of Kr (RN 7439-90-9). PA = 101.6 kcal/mol, 425. kJ/mol.

HLi^+							
LiH	7.7	(211)	(882)	33.3±0.01	139.2±0.04	79HUB/HER	7580-67-8
		(211)	*(882)*	*33.3±0.01*	*139.4±0.04*		

IP from 79HUB/HER.

HLi_2O^+							
Li_2OH		37	155				

From reaction enthalpies of Li_2OH^+ ions (84BUT/KUD). Corresponding proton affinity of Li_2O (RN 12057-24-8) is 289 kcal/mol, 1208 kJ/mol.

$HMgO^+$							
MgOH	7.5±0.3	(143)	(599)	−30	−125	81MUR	12141-11-6

$\Delta_f H$(Ion) from 81MUR. 0 K values.

HMn^+							
MnH	(7.8)	(242)	(1011)	(61)	(256)	79HUB/HER	14452-76-7

$\Delta_f H$(Ion) from onset of endothermic reaction (86ELK/ARM2). See also: 81ARM/HAL. IP is $\Delta_f H$(Ion) - $\Delta_f H$(Neutral). 0 K values.

HMn_2^+							
Mn_2H		(284)	(1186)				

$\Delta_f H$(Ion) from onset of endothermic reaction (86ARM). 0 K value.

Table 1. Positive Ion Table – Continued

ION / Neutral	Ionization potential eV	$\Delta_f H$(Ion) kcal/mol	$\Delta_f H$(Ion) kJ/mol	$\Delta_f H$(Neutral) kcal/mol	$\Delta_f H$(Neutral) kJ/mol	Neutral reference	CAS registry number
HMo^+ / MoH		(331)	(1385)				
	$\Delta_f H$(Ion) from onset of endothermic reaction. 0 K value.						
HN^+ / NH	13.49±0.01	401.1 / 401.1	1678.2 / 1678.1	90.0±4.0 / 90.0±4.0	376.6±16.7 / 376.5±16.7	85JANAF	13774-92-0
	$\Delta_f H$(Ion) from appearance potential determination (85GIB/GRE).						
HNO^+ / NOH		274.3 / 274.8	1147.7 / 1149.8				
	$\Delta_f H$(Ion) from appearance potential determination (82KUT/GOO).						
HNO	(10.1)	(256.3) / (256.8)	(1072.3) / (1074.4)	24	100	82BAU/COX	14332-28-6
	$\Delta_f H$(Ion) from appearance potential determination (82KUT/GOO). IP is $\Delta_f H$(Ion)-$\Delta_f H$(Neutral).						
$HNOS^+$ / HN=S=O	(11.3)	(302)	(1265)	41.7	175	82OLE/TUR	13817-04-4
	IP is onset of photoelectron band.						
HNO_2^+ / HNO_2	≤11.3	234 / ≤243	977 / ≤1018	−19 / −17	−80 / −72	82BAU/COX	7782-77-6
	$\Delta_f H$(Ion) at 298 K from proton affinity of NO_2 (RN 10102-44-0) (84POL/MUN). PA = 140 kcal/mol, 586 kJ/mol.						
HNO_3^+ / HNO_3	11.95±0.01	244 / 246	1018 / 1028	−32 / −30	−135 / −125	82BAU/COX	7697-37-2
HN_2^+ / HN_2		247.5	1035.5				
	From proton affinity of N_2; threshold determination (82LEV/LIA) gives the same value. PA = 118.2 kcal/mol, 494.5 kJ/mol.						
HN_2O^+ / HNNO		246	1031				
	From proton affinity of N_2O (RN 10024-97-2). See also: 85MCM/KEB, 85MCM/KEB2. PA = 138.8 kcal/mol, 581 kJ/mol.						
HN_3^+ / HN_3	10.72±0.025	317.5 / 318.9	1328.3 / 1334.8	70.3 / 71.8	294.1 / 300.5	82TN270	7782-79-8
HNb^+ / NbH		(330)	(1380)				
	$\Delta_f H$(Ion) from onset of endothermic reaction. 0 K value.						

Table 1. Positive Ion Table - Continued

ION / Neutral	Ionization potential eV	$\Delta_f H$(Ion) kcal/mol	$\Delta_f H$(Ion) kJ/mol	$\Delta_f H$(Neutral) kcal/mol	$\Delta_f H$(Neutral) kJ/mol	Neutral reference	CAS registry number
HNe^+							
NeH		318	1329				

$\Delta_f H$(Ion) from 68CHU/RUS. Corresponding proton affinity of Ne = 48.1 kcal/mol, 201. kJ/mol.

ION / Neutral	IP eV	$\Delta_f H$(Ion) kcal/mol	kJ/mol	$\Delta_f H$(Neutral) kcal/mol	kJ/mol	Neutral reference	CAS registry number
HNi^+							
NiH	(≤9.0)	(291)	(1216)	>(83)	>(347)	79HUB/HER	14332-32-2

$\Delta_f H$(Ion) from onset of endothermic reaction (86ELK/ARM4).
See also: 80ARM/BEA, 81ARM/HAL. IP is $\Delta_f H$(Ion) - $\Delta_f H$(Neutral). 0 K values.

ION / Neutral	IP eV	$\Delta_f H$(Ion) kcal/mol	kJ/mol	$\Delta_f H$(Neutral) kcal/mol	kJ/mol	Neutral reference	CAS registry number
HO^+							
OH	13.00	309.1	1293.3	9.3±0.3	39.0±1.2	85JANAF	3352-57-6
		309.0	1292.7	9.2±0.3	38.4±1.2		

$\Delta_f H$(Ion) from appearance potential measurements; IP derived from $\Delta_f H$(Ion) - $\Delta_f H$(Neutral) is in good agreement with the experimentally determined value of 13.01 eV. See also: 84VAN/DEL.

ION / Neutral	IP eV	$\Delta_f H$(Ion) kcal/mol	kJ/mol	$\Delta_f H$(Neutral) kcal/mol	kJ/mol	Neutral reference	CAS registry number
$HOSr^+$							
SrOH	5.1±0.2	74	309	-44	-183	83MUR	

$\Delta_f H$(Ion) from onset of endothermic reaction (83MUR);
IP is $\Delta_f H$(Ion) - $\Delta_f H$(Neutral). 0 K values.

ION / Neutral	IP eV	$\Delta_f H$(Ion) kcal/mol	kJ/mol	$\Delta_f H$(Neutral) kcal/mol	kJ/mol	Neutral reference	CAS registry number
HO_2^+							
HO_2	11.35±0.01	264.2	1105.5	2.5	10.5	82TN270	3170-83-0
		264.9	1108.5	3.2	13.4		

IP from 81DYK/JON. Value of $\Delta_f H$(Ion) from appearance potential measurements corrected to 298 K: 264.8 kcal/mol, 1107.9 kJ/mol.

ION / Neutral	IP eV	$\Delta_f H$(Ion) kcal/mol	kJ/mol	$\Delta_f H$(Neutral) kcal/mol	kJ/mol	Neutral reference	CAS registry number
HO_2S^+							
OSOH		143	597				

From proton affinity of SO_2 (RN 7446-09-5) (85MCM/KEB, 85MCM/KEB2) re-evaluated relative to CO standard (84LIA/LIE). PA = 152.1 kcal/mol, 636. kJ/mol.

ION / Neutral	IP eV	$\Delta_f H$(Ion) kcal/mol	kJ/mol	$\Delta_f H$(Neutral) kcal/mol	kJ/mol	Neutral reference	CAS registry number
HO_3S^+							
O_2SOH		(133)	(557)				

From proton affinity of SO_3 (RN 7446-11-9). PA = (138) kcal/mol, (577) kJ/mol.

ION / Neutral	IP eV	$\Delta_f H$(Ion) kcal/mol	kJ/mol	$\Delta_f H$(Neutral) kcal/mol	kJ/mol	Neutral reference	CAS registry number
HP^+							
PH	10.18±0.1	291	1218	56±2	236±8	86BER/CUR	13967-14-1
		291	1219	57±2	237±8		

$\Delta_f H$(Ion) from 79HUB/HER, 86BER/CUR. IP from 86BER/CUR.

ION / Neutral	IP eV	$\Delta_f H$(Ion) kcal/mol	kJ/mol	$\Delta_f H$(Neutral) kcal/mol	kJ/mol	Neutral reference	CAS registry number
HPd^+							
PdH		(281)	(1176)				

$\Delta_f H$(Ion) from onset of endothermic reaction (86ELK/ARM). 0 K value.

Table 1. Positive Ion Table – Continued

ION / Neutral	Ionization potential eV	$\Delta_f H$(Ion) kcal/mol	kJ/mol	$\Delta_f H$(Neutral) kcal/mol	kJ/mol	Neutral reference	CAS registry number
HS⁺ SH	10.37±0.01	272.4 / 271.8	1139.8 / 1137.0	33.3±1.2 / 32.6±1.2	139.3±5.0 / 136.5±5.0	85JANAF	13940-21-1

IP from 79DUN/DYK, $\Delta_f H$(Ion) from 83PRE/TZE, in good agreement with earlier results. See also: 81SMI/ADA.

| **HSc⁺** ScH | | 239 | 999 | | | | 33486-02-1 |

$\Delta_f H$(Ion) from onset of endothermic reaction (84TOL/BEA). See also: 87SUN/ARI. 0 K values.

| **HSe⁺** SeH | (9.79) | (258) | (1080) | (32) | (135) | 79HUB/HER | 13940-22-2 |

0 K values.

| **HSi⁺** SiH | 7.89±0.07 | 272.0 / 271.5 | 1138.0 / 1136.2 | 90.0±2.0 / 89.6±2.0 | 376.7±8.4 / 374.9±8.4 | 85JANAF | 13774-94-2 |

$\Delta_f H$(Ion) from 84ELK/ARM. IP from 87BOO/ARM.

| **HTe⁺** TeH | (9.09) | (244) | (1020) | 34 | 143 | 79HUB/HER | 13940-36-8 |

| **HTi⁺** TiH | (6.0) | (265) | (1109) | (127) | (532) | 79HUB/HER | |

$\Delta_f H$(Ion) from onset of endothermic reaction (86ELK/ARM).
IP is $\Delta_f H$(Ion) - $\Delta_f H$(Neutral). 0 K values.

| **HU⁺** UH | | 256 | 1070 | | | | |

$\Delta_f H$(Ion) from onset of endothermic reaction (77ARM/HOD).

| **HV⁺** VH | | (282) | (1179) | | | | |

$\Delta_f H$(Ion) from onset energy of endothermic reaction (84ARI/ARM, 85ELK/ARM). 0 K value.

| **HXe⁺** XeH | | 247 | 1034 | | | | |

From proton affinity of Xe (RN 7440-63-3). PA = 118.6 kcal/mol, 496. kJ/mol.

| **HY⁺** YH | | (238) | (995) | | | | |

$\Delta_f H$(Ion) from onset of endothermic reaction. 0 K value.

| **HZn⁺** ZnH | (9.4) | (241) | (1008) | (25) | (106) | 79HUB/HER | |

From proton affinity of Zn (RN 7440-66-6). IP is $\Delta_f H$(Ion) - $\Delta_f H$(Neutral).

Table 1. Positive Ion Table - Continued

ION Neutral	Ionization potential eV	$\Delta_f H$(Ion) kcal/mol	$\Delta_f H$(Ion) kJ/mol	$\Delta_f H$(Neutral) kcal/mol	$\Delta_f H$(Neutral) kJ/mol	Neutral reference	CAS registry number
HZr^+							
ZrH				123.4	516.3	85JANAF	
		(301)	(1260)	123.6	517.3		
$\Delta_f H$(Ion) from onset of endothermic reaction. 0 K value.							
H_2^+							
H_2	15.42589±0.00005	<u>355.7</u>	<u>1488.3</u>	0	0	*DEF	1333-74-0
		<u>355.7</u>	<u>1488.3</u>	0	0		
See also: 81KIM/KAT.							
H_2I^+							
H_2I		225	941				
From proton affinity of HI (RN 10034-85-2) results of 85MCM/KEB re-evaluated relative to CO standard (84LIA/LIE). PA = 147.1 kcal/mol, 615. kJ/mol.							
$H_2I_2Si^+$							
SiH_2I_2	(9.4)	(208)	(896)	−9±5	−38±20	85JANAF	13760-02-6
		(206)	(861)	−7±5	−28±20		
IP is onset of photoelectron band.							
H_2KO^+							
KOH_2		(47)	(198)				
$\Delta_f H$(Ion) from equilibrium constant determination (69SEA/DZI).							
H_2N^+							
NH_2	11.14±0.01	302.0	1263.8	45.1±0.3	188.7±1.3	85GIB/GRE	15194-15-7
		302.7	1266.4	45.8±0.3	191.6±1.3		
$\Delta_f H$(Ion) from appearance potential determination is in agreement. IP from 85GIB/GRE.							
H_2NO^+							
H_2NO		224.6	939.7				
$\Delta_f H$(Ion) from appearance potential determination (82KUT/GOO).							
$H_2N_2^+$							
(Z)-HN=NH	(9.52±0.05)	(275)	(1150)	55	232	82CAS/GOD	28647-38-3
(E)-HN=NH	(9.59±0.01)	(272)	(1137)	51	212	82CAS/GOD	3618-05-1
$H_2N_3^+$							
H_2NNN		(257)	(1075)				
From proton affinity of HN_3 (RN 7782-79-8) (84BEA/EYE). PA = 179 kcal/mol, 749 kJ/mol.							
H_2NaO^+							
$NaOH_2$		71	296				
From proton affinity of NaOH (RN 1310-73-2) (69SEA/DZI). PA = 248 kcal/mol, 1036 kJ/mol.							

Table 1. Positive Ion Table - Continued

ION / Neutral	Ionization potential eV	$\Delta_f H$(Ion) kcal/mol	$\Delta_f H$(Ion) kJ/mol	$\Delta_f H$(Neutral) kcal/mol	$\Delta_f H$(Neutral) kJ/mol	Neutral reference	CAS registry number
H_2O^+							
H_2O	12.612±0.010	<u>233.0</u> *233.7*	<u>975.0</u> *977.9*	−57.80 *−57.10*	−241.83 *−238.92*	85JANAF	7732-18-5
See also: 81KIM/KAT.							
$H_2O_2^+$							
H_2O_2	10.54	210 *212*	881 *887*	−32.6 *−31.1*	−136.3 *−130.0*	82BAU/COX	7722-84-1
See also: 77ASH/BUR, 81KIM/KAT.							
H_2P^+							
PH_2	9.824±0.002	261 *261*	1093 *1090*	33.3 *34.0±0.6*	139.5 *142.2±2.5*	86BER/CUR	
IP from 86BER/CUR. See also: 82DYK/JON2. 0 K values.							
H_2S^+							
H_2S	10.453±0.008	236 *237*	988 *991*	−4.9 *−4.2*	−20.5±0.8 *−17.6±0.8*	85JANAF	7783-06-4
IP is average of several spectroscopic and photoionization-onset determinations (77ROS/DRA, 82LEV/LIA, 84BLA/WAL, 83PRE/TZE). See also: 81SMI/ADA, 81WAL/BLA, 81KIM/KAT.							
$H_2S_2^+$							
H_2S_2	(9.3)	(218)	(913)	4	16	82TN270	13465-07-1
IP is onset of photoelectron band.							
H_2Sc^+							
HScH		(238)	(996)				13598-30-6
$\Delta_f H$(Ion) from onset of endothermic reaction (84TOL/BEA). See also: 87SUN/ARI. 0 K value.							
H_2Se^+							
H_2Se	9.882±0.001	235 *236*	983 *987*	7 *8*	30 *34*	82TN270	7783-07-5
H_2Si^+							
SiH_2	8.92±0.07	276.1	1155.2	69±2	289±8	87BOO/ARM	13825-90-6
IP and $\Delta_f H$(Ion) from 87BOO/ARM, in agreement with unpublished data of R.R. Corderman and J.L. Beauchamp. See also: 83DYK/JON2, 84CHA/HIL.							
H_2Te^+							
H_2Te	9.138±0.005	235	982	24	100	82TN270	7783-09-7
H_3^+							
H_3		264.5 *265*	1106.6 *1107*				12184-91-7
From proton affinity of H_2 (RN 1333-74-0) (84ADA/SMI). PA = 101.2 kcal/mol, 423.4 kJ/mol.							

Table 1. Positive Ion Table — Continued

ION Neutral	Ionization potential eV	$\Delta_f H$(Ion) kcal/mol	 kJ/mol	$\Delta_f H$(Neutral) kcal/mol	 kJ/mol	Neutral reference	CAS registry number
H_3ISi^+ SiH_3I	(9.5)	(219) (221)	(915) (925)	−0.5±4 *2±4*	−2±17 *8±17*	85JANAF	13598-42-0
	IP is onset of photoelectron band.						
H_3N^+ NH_3	10.16±0.01	223.2 *224.9*	934.0 *941.0*	−11.0 *−9.3*	−45.9±0.4 *−38.9±0.4*	85JANAF	7664-41-7
	See also: 81KIM/KAT, 73RAB/KAR.						
H_3NO^+ NH_2OH	10.00	(221)	(923)	−10	−42	69BEN/CRU	7803-49-8
	IP from 83KOP/MOL. See also: 81KIM/KAT, 82KUT/GOO.						
H_3O^+ H_3O		141 *143*	591 *597*				
	$\Delta_f H$(Ion) at 298 K from proton affinity of H_2O; $\Delta_f H$(Ion) at 0 K from appearance potential from $(H_2O)_2$ (77NG/TRE). PA = 166.5 kcal/mol, 697. kJ/mol.						
$H_3O_2^+$ H_2OOH		171	716				
	From proton affinity of H_2O_2 (RN 7722-84-1). PA = 162. kcal/mol, 678. kJ/mol.						
$H_3O_4S^+$ $(HO)_3SO$		(21)	(88)				
	From proton affinity of H_2SO_4 (RN 7664-93-9). PA = (169) kcal/mol, (707) kJ/mol.						
H_3P^+ PH_3	9.869±0.002	229 *231*	957 *966*	1.3±0.4 *3.1*	5.4±1.7 *13.3*	61GUN/GRE	7803-51-2
	IP from 83MAR/REI, 86BER/CUR. See also: 82COW/KEM.						
H_3S^+ H_3S		190	797				
	From proton affinity of H_2S (RN 7783-06-4). See also: 83PRE/TZE2, 84BLA/WAL, 83ERM/AKO. PA = 170.2 kcal/mol, 712. kJ/mol.						
H_3Sb^+ SbH_3	9.54±0.03	255 *257*	1066 *1074*	35 *37*	145 *153*	82TN270	7803-52-3
H_3Se^+ H_3Se		202	843				
	From proton affinity of H_2Se (RN 7783-07-5). PA = 171.3 kcal/mol, 717. kJ/mol.						
H_3Si^+ SiH_3	8.14±0.01	237.1	992	48.5±1.5	202.9±6.3	87BOO/ARM	13765-44-1
	IP from 83DYK/JON2. See also: 84CHA/HIL, 85DIN/CAS, 87BOO/ARM.						

Table 1. Positive Ion Table - Continued

ION / Neutral	Ionization potential eV	$\Delta_f H$(Ion) kcal/mol	$\Delta_f H$(Ion) kJ/mol	$\Delta_f H$(Neutral) kcal/mol	$\Delta_f H$(Neutral) kJ/mol	Neutral reference	CAS registry number
H_3Te^+ / TeH_3		214	894				

$\Delta_f H$(Ion) from proton affinity of H_2Te (RN7783-09-7)(86KAR/JAS). PA = 176 kcal/mol, 736 kJ/mol.

| H_4N^+ / NH_4 | (4.73±0.06) | (151) | (630) | | | | |

$\Delta_f H$(Ion) from proton affinity of NH_3 (RN 7664-41-7). IP from neutralized ion-beam spectroscopy data (82GEL/CLE). PA = (204.0) kcal/mol, (854.) kJ/mol.

| $H_4N_2^+$ / N_2H_4 | 8.1±0.15 | (210) | (876) | 22.8±0.2 | 95.3±0.8 | 85JANAF | 302-01-2 |
| | | (213) | (891) | 26.1±0.2 | 109.4±0.8 | | |

From charge transfer equilibrium constant determinations(84MAU/NEL). See also: 81KIM/KAT.

| $H_4N_4^+$ / (E)-$H_2NN=NNH_2$ | (≤8.99) | (≤260) | (≤1089) | 53 | 222 | 82TN270 | 54410-57-0 |

| H_4P^+ / PH_4 | | 178 | 746 | | | | |

From proton affinity of PH_3 (RN 7803-51-2). PA = 188.6 kcal/mol, 789. kJ/mol.

| $H_4P_2^+$ / P_2H_4 | 8.8±0.1 | (219) | (918) | 16 | 69 | *EST | 13445-50-6 |

IP is onset of photoelectron band.

| H_4Si^+ / SiH_4 | 11.65 | 277 | 1159 | 8 | 35 | 81BEL/PER | 7803-62-5 |
| | | 280 | 1170 | 11 | 46 | | |

| H_4Sn^+ / SnH_4 | (10.75) | (287) | (1200) | 39 | 163 | 82TN270 | 2406-52-2 |
| | | (290) | (1212) | 42 | 175 | | |

The SnH_4^+ ion has not been observed.

| $H_5N_2^+$ / NH_3NH_2 | | 184 | 770 | | | | |

From proton affinity of hydrazine (RN 302-01-2). PA = 204.7 kcal/mol, 856. kJ/mol.

| H_5Si^+ / SiH_5 | | (219) | (917) | | | | |

From proton affinity of SiH_4 (RN 7803-62-5). PA = (155) kcal/mol, (648) kJ/mol.

| $H_6Si_2^+$ / Si_2H_6 | (9.7) | (243) | (1016) | 19 | 80 | 81BEL/PER | 1590-87-0 |
| | | (247) | (1032) | 23 | 96 | | |

IP is onset of photoelectron band. See also: 84CHA/HIL.

Table 1. Positive Ion Table - Continued

ION Neutral	Ionization potential eV	$\Delta_f H$(Ion) kcal/mol	kJ/mol	$\Delta_f H$(Neutral) kcal/mol	kJ/mol	Neutral reference	CAS registry number
$H_8Si_3^+$							
Si_3H_8	(9.2)	(241)	(1009)	29	121	81BEL/PER	7783-26-8
	IP is onset of photoelectron band.						
$H_{10}Si_4^+$							
Si_4H_{10}	(8.9)	(244)	(1021)	39	162	81WAL	7783-29-1
	IP is onset of photoelectron band.						
He^+							
He	24.587	567.0	2372	0	0	*DEF	7440-59-7
		567.0	2372	0	0		
$HeNe^+$							
HeNe	20.87	481.3	2013.9	−0.028	−0.12	79HUB/HER	12162-16-2
	$\Delta_f H$(Ion) from 78DAB/HER. 0 K values.						
He_2^+							
He_2	22.223	512.4	2144.1	−0.02	−0.09	79HUB/HER	12184-98-4
	IP from 79HUB/HER. 0 K values.						
Hf^+							
Hf	6.78	304	1273	148	619	82TN270	7440-58-6
		304	1273	148	619		
	IP from 76MEG/MOO.						
HfO^+							
HfO	(7.55±0.1)	(190)	(795)	16±3	67±13	83PED/MAR	12029-22-0
		(192)	(804)	18	76		
Hg^+							
Hg	10.437	255.3	1068.3	14.7	61.3	82TN270	7439-97-6
		256.1	1071.5	15.4	64.5		
	See also: 84LIN/LIA.						
HgI_2^+							
HgI_2	9.5088±0.0022	215.2	900.3	−4.1	−17.2	82TN270	7774-29-0
		216.7	906.6	−2.6	−10.9		
	Cited ionization potential (83LIN/TZE) refers to formation of HgI_2^+ $(^2\Pi_{3/2})$. Ionization potential for formation of HgI_2^+ $(^2\Pi_{1/2})$ is 10.1953±0.0025 eV. See also: 81LEE/POT.						
Hg_2^+							
Hg_2	9.103±0.010	237	992	27	114	82HIL	12596-25-7
		239	1000	29	122		
	IP from 84LIN/LIA.						
Ho^+							
Ho	6.0216±0.0006	211	882	72	301	82TN270	7440-60-0
		211.2	883.6	72.3	302.6		

Table 1. Positive Ion Table – Continued

ION / Neutral	Ionization potential eV	$\Delta_f H$(Ion) kcal/mol	$\Delta_f H$(Ion) kJ/mol	$\Delta_f H$(Neutral) kcal/mol	$\Delta_f H$(Neutral) kJ/mol	Neutral reference	CAS registry number
HoO⁺							
HoO	(6.17±0.1)	(128)	(534)	−15±6	−61±25	83PED/MAR	12281-10-6
		(126)	*(528)*	*−16*	*−67*		
	See also: 80MUR/HIL.						
I⁺							
I	10.451	266.5	1115.2	25.5	106.8	82BAU/COX	14362-44-8
		266.6	*1115.6*	*25.6*	*107.2*		
	See also: 81HOA/CAB, 85GRA/ROS.						
IK⁺							
KI	(7.21±0.3)	(136)	(570)	−30.0±0.5	−125.5±2.1	85JANAF	7681-11-0
		(137)	*(573)*	*−29.2±0.5*	*−122.1±2.1*		
	See also: 82EMO/HOR.						
ILi⁺							
LiI	(7.5)	(151)	(633)	−21.7±2.0	−91.0±8.4	85JANAF	10377-51-2
		(152)	*(635)*	*−21.3±2.0*	*−89.1±8.4*		
	IP is onset of photoelectron band.						
INa⁺							
NaI	7.64±0.02	157	659	−18.6	−77.8	82TN270	7681-82-5
		158	*662*	*−17.9*	*−74.9*		
	See also: 82EMO/HOR, 83HIL/GIN, 84HIL, 82LEL/BAL.						
IRb⁺							
RbI	(7.12±0.1)	(132)	(554)	−32	−133	79HUB/HER	7790-29-6
		(133)	*(558)*	*−30.9*	*−129.3*		
	See also: 82EMO/HOR.						
ITl⁺							
TlI	8.47±0.02	197	824	2	7	82TN270	7790-30-9
		197	*823*	*1*	*6*		
	See: 83BAN/BRI.						
I₂⁺							
I₂	9.3995±0.0012	231.7	969.3	14.9	62.4	82BAU/COX	7553-56-2
		232.4	*972.4*	*15.7*	*65.5*		
	See also: 81HOA/CAB, 85GRA/ROS, 81KIM/KAT.						
I₂Li₂⁺							
(Li–I–Li–I ring structure)	(≤9.23±0.06)	(≤126)	(≤529)	−87±4	−362±17	85JANAF	37279-36-0
		(≤127)	*(≤532)*	*−85±4*	*−356±17*		
I₂Mg⁺							
MgI₂	(9.57±0.03)	(180)	(751)	−41	−172	82TN270	10377-58-9

Table 1. Positive Ion Table - Continued

ION / Neutral	Ionization potential eV	$\Delta_f H$(Ion) kcal/mol	kJ/mol	$\Delta_f H$(Neutral) kcal/mol	kJ/mol	Neutral reference	CAS registry number
$I_2O_2W^+$							
WO_2I_2	(10.4±0.4)	(137.5)	(575.4)	−102.3	−428.0	76DEL/HAL	14447-89-3
I_2Pb^+							
PbI_2	8.86±0.03	(205)	(856)	0.2±1	1±4	85JANAF	10101-63-0
	Onset of photoelectron band: 8.6 eV. See: 84NOV/POT2. 0 K values.						
I_2Sn^+							
SnI_2	8.83±0.1	204	854	0.5	2	82TPIS	10294-70-9
	IP from 83HIL/GIN, 84NOV/POT2.						
I_2Sr^+							
SrI_2	(8.3)	(126)	(526)	−65.7±1.5	−275±6	85JANAF	10476-86-5
		(126)	(529)	−65.0±1.5	−272±6		
	IP is onset of photoelectron band (79LEE/POT2). See also: 82EMO/KIE.						
I_3La^+							
LaI_3	8.8	119	498	−84	−351	82TN270	
	IP is onset of photoelectron band (83RUS/GOO).						
I_3Nd^+							
NdI_3	8.7	124	519	−76	−320	82TN270	13813-24-6
	IP is onset of photoelectron band (83RUS/GOO).						
I_4Ti^+							
TiI_4	(9.1)	(143)	(600)	−66±2	−278±8	85JANAF	7720-83-4
		(145)	(606)	−65±2	−272±8		
	IP is onset of photoelectron band.						
I_4Zr^+							
ZrI_4	(9.3)	(128)	(534)	−95±2	−363±8	85JANAF	13986-26-0
		(130)	(544)	−85±2	−357±8		
	IP is onset of photoelectron band.						
In^+							
In	5.786	191.7	801.9	58.2	243.7	82TN270	7440-74-6
		191.6	802.6	58.2	243.3		
	See also: 82GOM/CHA, 85KAP/LEL.						
InS^+							
InS	(7.0±0.5)	(218)	(911)	57	236	79HUB/HER	12030-14-7
	0 K values.						
$InSe^+$							
InSe	(7.1±0.5)	(218)	(913)	55	228	79HUB/HER	1312-42-1
	0 K values.						
$InTe^+$							
InTe	(7.6±0.5)	(230)	(962)	55	229	79HUB/HER	12030-19-2
	0 K values.						

Table 1. Positive Ion Table – Continued

ION Neutral	Ionization potential eV	$\Delta_f H$(Ion) kcal/mol	 kJ/mol	$\Delta_f H$(Neutral) kcal/mol	 kJ/mol	Neutral reference	CAS registry number
In_2^+							
In_2	(5.8±0.3)	(227)	(949)	93	389	79HUB/HER	61178-97-0
	0 K values.						
In_2O^+							
In_2O	8.0±0.2	(174)	(728)	−10	−43	82TPIS	12030-22-7
		(175)	(734)	−9±5	−38±20		
	IP from 85KAP/LEL, 77ROS/DRA. See also: 82GOM/CHA.						
Ir^+							
Ir	9.02	367	1535	159	665	82TN270	7439-88-5
		366.8	1534.6	158.8	664.3		
	IP from 79RAU/ACK.						
IrO^+							
IrO	(10.1)	(367)	(1535)	(134)	(561)	79HUB/HER	12030-48-7
	0 K values.						
IrO_3^+							
IrO_3	(11.9)	(276)	(1156)	2	8	82TN270	12030-50-1
K^+							
K	4.341	121.4	507.8	21.3±0.1	89.0±0.4	85JANAF	7440-09-7
		121.6	508.7	21.5±0.1	89.9±0.4		
KLi^+							
LiK	4.57±0.04	123	514	17	73	86IGE/WED	12030-83-0
	IP from 85KAP/SCH.						
KNa^+							
NaK	4.41636±0.00017	134.2	561.5	32.4	135.4	86ZGE/WED	12056-29-0
	IP from 81LEU/HOF, 85KAP/RAD. 0 K values.						
KO^+							
KO	7.09±0.1	178	745	15±5	61±21	83PED/MAR	12401-70-6
		179	747	15±5	63±21		
	IP from 82LEV/LIA, 84BUT/KUD.						
KRb^+							
KRb	(3.9±0.1)	(120)	(500)	(30)	(124)	79HUB/HER	12333-39-0
	IP from 85KAP/SCH. 0 K values.						
K_2^+							
K_2	4.0637±0.0002	124.0	518.9	30.3	126.9	79HUB/HER	25681-80-5
		124.8	522.3	31.1	130.3		
	IP from 85KAP/RAD, 85BRO/CHE, in good agreement with values from 81LEU/HOF, 78HER/SCH, and 84DAO/PET.						
K_2O^+							
K_2O	4.96±0.2	(80)	(336)	−34±4	−142±15	79BYK/ELI	12136-45-7
	IP from 84BUT/KUD. See also: 82FAR/SRI, 84DAO/PET.						

Table 1. Positive Ion Table – Continued

ION / Neutral	Ionization potential eV	$\Delta_f H$(Ion) kcal/mol	$\Delta_f H$(Ion) kJ/mol	$\Delta_f H$(Neutral) kcal/mol	$\Delta_f H$(Neutral) kJ/mol	Neutral reference	CAS registry number
$K_2O_2^+$							
K_2O_2	(5)	(44)	(184)	−71±4	−298±15	79BYK/ELI	17014-71-0
Kr^+							
Kr	13.9997±0.00001	322.8	1350.8	0	0	*DEF	7439-90-9
		322.8	*1350.8*	*0*	*0*		
	See also: 81KIM/KAT.						
$KrXe^+$							
KrXe	11.760±0.014	270.8	1132.9	−0.42	−1.77	79HUB/HER	12521-42-5
	See: 82DEH/PRA, 85PRA/DEH2. 0 K values.						
Kr_2^+							
Kr_2	12.866±0.003	296.3	1240.9	−0.36	−1.51	79HUB/HER	12596-40-6
	IP from 82PRA/DEH. 0 K values.						
La^+							
La	5.577	232	969	103	431	82TN270	7439-91-0
		231.7	*969.4*	*103.1*	*431.3*		
LaO^+							
LaO	4.90±0.1	84	352	−29±2	−121±10	83PED/MAR	12031-20-8
		85	*354*	*−28*	*−119*		
$LaPt^+$							
LaPt	(5.4±0.8)	(243)	(1018)	119±5	497±21	81NAP/GIN	12142-67-5
	IP from 81NAP/GIN.						
Li^+							
Li	5.392	<u>162.4</u>	<u>679.6</u>	38.1	159.4	82TN270	7439-93-2
		<u>*162.0*</u>	<u>*678.0*</u>	*37.7*	*157.8*		
	See also: 81NAK/ASA.						
$LiNa^+$							
LiNa	5.05±0.04	137	572	20	85	86IGE/WED	12333-49-2
	IP from 85KAP/SCH.						
LiO^+							
LiO	(8.45±0.20)	(214)	(894)	19±0.5	79±2	83PED/MAR	12142-77-7
		(214)	*(894)*	*19±0.5*	*79±2*		
	See also: 81NAK/ASA, 79WU/KUD, 84BUT/KUD.						
$LiOH_2^+$							
$LiOH_2$		69	289				
	From proton affinity of LiOH (RN 1310-58-3). PA = 241 kcal/mol, 1007 kJ/mol.						
$LiRb^+$							
LiRb	4.3±0.1	116	485	17	70	86IGE/WED	12031-70-8
	IP from 85KAP/SCH.						

Table 1. Positive Ion Table – Continued

ION / Neutral	Ionization potential eV	$\Delta_f H$(Ion) kcal/mol	kJ/mol	$\Delta_f H$(Neutral) kcal/mol	kJ/mol	Neutral reference	CAS registry number
Li_2^+							
Li_2	5.1127±0.0003	169.5	709.2	51.6±0.7	215.9±3.0	85JANAF	14452-59-6
		169.4	*708.8*	*51.5±0.7*	*215.5±3.0*		
	IP from 83MCG/SCH. See also: 82EIS/DEM.						
$Li_2MoO_4^+$							
	(9.7±0.5)	(−22)	(−94)	−246	−1030	81LIN/BES	
Li_2O^+							
Li_2O	6.19±0.20	(103)	(430)	−40	−167	81LIN/BES	12057-24-8
		(103)	*(431)*	*−40*	*−166*		
	See also: 82IKE/TAM, 81NAK/ASA, 79WU/KUD.						
$Li_2O_2^+$							
	(7.88±0.2)	(84)	(350)	−98±12	−410±50	79WU/KUD	12031-80-0
	IP from 79WU/KUD. 0 K values.						
$Li_2O_3Si^+$							
Li_2SiO_3	8.3±0.2	−99	−415	−291	−1216	81NAK/ASA	
	IP from 81NAK/ASA.						
$Li_2O_4W^+$							
Li_2WO_4	(9.2±0.5)	(−29)	(−122)	−241	−1010	81LIN/BES	
Li_3O^+							
Li_3O	(4.54±0.2)	(50)	(210)	−54±10	−228±42	79WU/KUD	69235-02-5
	IP from 79WU/KUD. 0 K values.						
Lu^+							
Lu	5.4259±0.00001	227	951	102	428	82TN270	7439-94-3
		227.4	*951.3*	*102.2*	*427.8*		
LuO^+							
LuO	(6.79±0.1)	(153)	(640)	−3.5	−14.6	82TN270	12032-02-9
		(153)	*(642)*	*−3*	*−13*		
	A value of 2±17 kJ/mol, 0.5±4 kcal/mol has also been recommended for the 298 K heat of formation of LuO (83PED/MAR). See also: 80MUR/HIL.						
Md^+							
Md	6.74±0.12						7440-11-1

Table 1. Positive Ion Table - Continued

ION Neutral	Ionization potential eV	$\Delta_f H$(Ion) kcal/mol	kJ/mol	$\Delta_f H$(Neutral) kcal/mol	kJ/mol	Neutral reference	CAS registry number
Mg^+							
Mg	7.646	<u>211.6</u>	<u>885.4</u>	35.3	147.7	82TN270	7439-95-4
		<u>211.3</u>	<u>884.2</u>	35.0	146.5		
	See also: 81SAS/HAR.						
MgO^+							
MgO	9.7	(236±8)	(997±33)	13.4	56.1	79HUB/HER	1309-48-4
		(238±8)	(997±33)	13.5	56.5		
	$\Delta_f H$(Ion) from 81KAP/STA. See also: 81MUR. IP is $\Delta_f H$(Ion) - $\Delta_f H$(Neutral).						
Mg_2H^+							
MgHMg		78	327				
	From proton affinity of Mg_2 (RN 29904-79-8). PA = (219) kcal/mol, (916) kJ/mol.						
Mn^+							
Mn	7.435	239	998	67	281	82TN270	7439-96-5
		238	996	67	279		
MnO^+							
MnO	8.65±0.2	(240)	(1005)	41	170	67CHE/BAR	1344-43-0
	IP from 82ARM/HAL. See also: 81ARM/HAL, 81KAP/STA. 0 K values.						
Mn_2^+							
Mn_2	6.9±0.4	(280)	(1172)	(121±7)	(506±29)	83ERV/LOH	12596-53-1
	IP from 83ERV/LOH. 0 K values.						
Mo^+							
Mo	7.099	321.0	1343.1	157.3	658.1	82TN270	7439-98-7
		320.6	1341.5	156.9	656.6		
$MoNa_2O_4^+$							
Na_2MoO_4	(7.2)	(−87)	(−364)	−253	−1059	82TN270	
MoO^+							
MoO	(8.0±0.6)	(267)	(1119)	83±5	347±21	83PED/MAR	12058-07-0
		(267)	(1119)	83±5	347±21		
MoO_2^+							
MoO_2	(9.2)	(213)	(890)	−2±3	−8±13	85JANAF	
		(213)	(892)	−2±3	−6±13		
MoO_3^+							
MoO_3	(11.8±0.5)	(186)	(777)	−87	−362	81WOO	1313-27-5
		(187)	(781)	−86	−358		

Table 1. Positive Ion Table – Continued

ION / Neutral	Ionization potential eV	$\Delta_f H$(Ion) kcal/mol	$\Delta_f H$(Ion) kJ/mol	$\Delta_f H$(Neutral) kcal/mol	$\Delta_f H$(Neutral) kJ/mol	Neutral reference	CAS registry number
$Mo_2O_6^+$	12.1±0.6	(201)	(841)	−78	−326	82TN270	12412-19-0
	IP from 77ROS/DRA, 85KAP/LEL.						
$Mo_3O_9^+$	(12.0±1.0)	(−174)	(−729)	−451	−1887	82TN270	12163-83-6
	See also: 85KAP/LEL.						
N^+ / N	14.534	448.2	1875.0	113.0	472.7	82TN270	17778-88-0
		447.7	1873.1	112.5	470.8		
NO^+ / NO	9.26436±0.00006	235.33	984.61	21.82	91.28	82BAU/COX	10102-43-9
		235.33	984.65	21.69	90.78		
	See: 83SEA/CHU, 84MUL/SAN, 83EBA/ANE for confirming high precision measurements. See also: 81KIM/STE, 82FAN/GIA, 81KIM/KAT.						
NO_2^+ / NO_2	9.75±0.01	233	974	7.9	33.2	82BAU/COX	10102-44-0
		233	977	8.6	36.0		
	Ionization involves a bent-linear transition with a broad Franck-Condon envelope and weak onset. Selected IP consistent with occurrence of reaction: ($NO_2^+ + C_6H_5CF_3 \rightarrow C_6H_5CF_3^+ + NO_2$)(78AUS/LIA). See also: 81KIM/KAT, 82KAT/SHI.						
NP^+ / NP	11.85	298	1248	25±1	105±5	85JANAF	17739-47-8
		299	1249	25±1	106±5		
NS^+ / NS	8.87±0.01	268	1119	63±25	264±105	85JANAF	51801-08-2
		268	1119	63±25	263±105		
	IP from 79HUB/HER.						
NTi^+ / TiN	(6)	(250)	(1045)	112	466	79HUB/HER	25583-20-4
	0 K values.						
NZr^+ / ZrN	(7.9±0.4)	(352.7)	(1475.6)	170.5	713.4	85JANAF	25658-42-8
		(352.9)	(1476.5)	170.7	714.3		

Table 1. Positive Ion Table - Continued

ION / Neutral	Ionization potential eV	$\Delta_f H$(Ion) kcal/mol	$\Delta_f H$(Ion) kJ/mol	$\Delta_f H$(Neutral) kcal/mol	$\Delta_f H$(Neutral) kJ/mol	Neutral reference	CAS registry number
N_2^+							
N_2	15.5808	359.3	1503.3	0	0	*DEF	7727-37-9
		359.3	*1503.3*	*0*	*0*		
	IP from 79HUB/HER. See also: 84STE/MAR, 81ARM/TAR, 81KIM/KAT.						
N_2O^+							
N_2O	12.886	316.8	1325.4	19.6	82.1	82BAU/COX	10024-97-2
		317.6	*1328.8*	*20.4*	*85.5*		
	See also: 81KIM/KAT.						
$N_2O_4^+$							
N_2O_4	10.8±0.2	(251)	(1051)	2	9	82BAU/COX	10544-72-6
		(254)	*(1061)*	*5*	*19*		
	See also: 82CHO/FRO.						
$N_2O_5^+$							
N_2O_5	(11.9)	(277)	(1159)	3	11	82BAU/COX	10102-03-1
		(280)	*(1173)*	*6*	*25*		
	IP is onset of photoelectron band.						
Na^+							
Na	5.139	<u>144.1</u>	<u>603.1</u>	25.6±0.2	107.3±0.7	85JANAF	7440-23-5
		<u>*144.2*</u>	<u>*603.4*</u>	*25.7±0.2*	*107.6±0.7*		
	See also: 84PET/DAO.						
NaO^+							
NaO	(7.41)	(190.9)	(798.7)	20.0±10.0	83.7±41.8	85JANAF	12401-86-4
		(191.2)	*(800.0)*	*20.3±10.0*	*85.0±41.8*		
	IP from 84BUT/KUD.						
$NaRb^+$							
NaRb	4.32±0.04	115	481	15	64	86IGE/WED	12333-61-8
	IP from 85KAP/SCH.						
Na_2^+							
Na_2	4.88898±0.00016	<u>146.7</u>	<u>613.8</u>	34.0±0.3	142.1±1.2	85JANAF	25681-79-2
		<u>*147.3*</u>	<u>*616.3*</u>	*34.6±0.3*	*144.6±1.2*		
	IP from 81LEU/HOF, in agreement with values from 82MAR/CHE, 85KAP/RAD, 84PET/DAO, 78HER/SCH. $\Delta_f H$(Ion) in agreement with that derived from data of 83WAG/ISE.						
Na_2Cl^+							
Na_2Cl	4.15±0.22	(59)	(245)	−37	−155	83PET/DAO	
	IP from 83PET/DAO. 0 K values.						
Na_2O^+							
Na_2O	(5.06±0.4)	(110)	(461)	−6	−27	83PET/DAO	1313-59-3
		(111)	*(465)*	*−5*	*−23*		
	IP from 83PET/DAO. See also: 84BUT/KUD.						

Table 1. Positive Ion Table – Continued

ION Neutral	Ionization potential eV	$\Delta_f H$(Ion) kcal/mol	$\Delta_f H$(Ion) kJ/mol	$\Delta_f H$(Neutral) kcal/mol	$\Delta_f H$(Neutral) kJ/mol	Neutral reference	CAS registry number
Nb$^+$ Nb	6.88	334 *333*	1397 *1394*	175±2 *174.5±2*	733±8 *730±8*	85JANAF	7440-03-1
NbO$^+$ NbO	(6.1)	(186±53) (187±53)	(778.5±222) (780±222)	48±5 *48±5*	200±21 *199±21*	85JANAF	12034-57-0
	$\Delta_f H$(Ion) from 81KAP/STA. IP is $\Delta_f H$(Ion) - $\Delta_f H$(Neutral).						
Nd$^+$ Nd	5.5250±0.0006	205.80 *206.04*	861.08 *862.08*	78 *78.5*	328 *328.6*	82TN270	7440-00-8
NdO$^+$ NdO	(4.97±0.1)	(84) (84)	(354) (354)	−30±3 *−30±3*	−126±12 *−126±12*	83PED/MAR	12035-20-0
Ne$^+$ Ne	21.56471±0.00001	<u>497.29</u> <u>497.29</u>	<u>2080.66</u> <u>2080.66</u>	0 *0*	0 *0*	*DEF	7440-01-9
NeKr$^+$ NeKr	(13.950±0.003)	(321.5)	(1345.3)	−0.15	−0.62	79HUB/HER	
	IP from 82PRA/DEH2. 0 K values.						
NeXe$^+$ NeXe	(12.094±0.004)	(278.7)	(1166.3)	−0.15	−0.63	79HUB/HER	58984-40-0
	IP from 82PRA/DEH2. See also: 85PRA/DEH2. 0 K values.						
Ne$_2$$^+$ Ne$_2$	20.33±0.08	*469*	*1961*	*−0.047*	*−0.195*	79HUB/HER	12185-05-6
	IP from 84TRE/POL. See also: 79HUB/HER. 0 K values.						
Ni$^+$ Ni	7.635	278.9 *278.4*	1166.8 *1164.8*	102.8 *102.3*	430.1 *428.1*	82TN270	7440-02-0
	See also: 82DYK/GRA.						
NiO$^+$ NiO	9.5±0.2	(290)	(1214)	71±4	297±17	83PED/MAR	1313-99-1
	IP from 81ARM/HAL, 82ARM/HAL, 77ROS/DRA. See also: 81KAP/STA.						
No$^+$ No	6.84±0.12						10028-14-5
Np$^+$ Np	6.2657±0.0005	256	1070	111	465	85KLE/WAR	7439-99-8
NpO$^+$ NpO	(5.7±0.1)	(130)	(546)	−1±10	−4±42	83PED/MAR	12202-03-8

Table 1. Positive Ion Table - Continued

ION / Neutral	Ionization potential eV	$\Delta_f H$(Ion) kcal/mol	$\Delta_f H$(Ion) kJ/mol	$\Delta_f H$(Neutral) kcal/mol	$\Delta_f H$(Neutral) kJ/mol	Neutral reference	CAS registry number
O^+							
O	13.618	373.6	1563.1	59.6	249.2±0.1	85JANAF	17778-80-2
		373.0	1560.7	59.0	246.8±0.1		
OP^+							
PO	8.39±0.01	186	777	−8±3	−33±13	83PED/MAR	14452-66-5
		186	778	−8	−32		
	IP from 82DYK/MOR. See also: 81BAL/GIG.						
OPb^+							
PbO	9.08±0.10	224	939	15±3	63±13	79HUB/HER	1317-36-8
		227	949	17	73		
	See also: 83SEM/RYK, 84NIK/OVC.						
OPd^+							
PdO	(9.1)	(293)	(1224)	83	346	79HUB/HER	1314-08-5
	0 K values.						
OPr^+							
PrO	(4.90±0.1)	(79)	(331)	−34±4	−142±17	82TN270	12035-81-3
		(75)	(314)	−38	−159		
OPt^+							
PtO	(10.1±0.3)	(334)	(1397)	101	423	79HUB/HER	12035-82-4
		(339)	(1417)	106	443		
ORb^+							
RbO	6.69	168.6	705.3	14.3	59.8	82TPIS	12509-27-2
		168.9	706.6	14.6±5	61.1±20		
	IP from 84BUT/KUD.						
ORb_2^+							
Rb_2O	4.63	25.8	107.8	−81.0±2.0	−338.9±8.4	82TPIS	18088-11-4
		26.7	111.6	−80.1	−335.1		
	IP from 84BUT/KUD.						
ORh^+							
RhO	(9.3)	(309)	(1294)	95±10	397±42	83PED/MAR	12137-18-7
ORu^+							
RuO	(8.7)	(290)	(1211)	89±10	372±42	83PED/MAR	12143-05-4
OS^+							
SO	10.32±0.02	239.2	1000.7	1.2±0.3	5.0±1.3	85JANAF	13827-32-2
		239.2	1000.7	1.2±0.3	5.0±1.3		
OS_2^+							
S_2O	10.54±0.04	231	965	−12±0.2	−52±1	86NIM/ELL	20901-21-7
		230	962	−13±0.2	−55±1		

Table 1. Positive Ion Table - Continued

ION Neutral	Ionization potential eV	$\Delta_f H$(Ion) kcal/mol	kJ/mol	$\Delta_f H$(Neutral) kcal/mol	kJ/mol	Neutral reference	CAS registry number
OSi⁺							
SiO	11.43	239.6	1002.4	−24.0±2	−100.4±8.4	85JANAF	10097-28-6
		239.3	1001.2	−24.3±2	−101.6±8.4		
	IP from 82LEV/LIA, 79HUB/HER. See also: 81NAK/ASA.						
OSm⁺							
SmO	5.55±0.1	100	418	−28±3	−117±12	83PED/MAR	12035-88-0
		97	*405*	*−31*	*−130*		
OSn⁺							
SnO	9.60±0.02	226	944	4.2	17.5	81LAU/BRI	21651-19-4
		226	*945*	*4.6*	*19.2*		
	IP from 82DYK/MOR2.						
OSr⁺							
SrO	7.0±0.15	(158.2)	(662.8)	−3.2±4	−13.4±16.7	85JANAF	1314-11-0
		(158.7)	*(663.9)*	*−2.7±4*	*−11.5±16.7*		
	$\Delta_f H$(Ion) from onset of endothermic reaction (83MUR); IP is $\Delta_f H$(Ion) - $\Delta_f H$(Neutral).						
OTa⁺							
TaO	(7.92±0.1)	(228.6)	(956.7)	46.0±15	192.5±62.8	85JANAF	12035-90-4
		(228.9)	*(957.9)*	*46.3±15*	*193.7±62.8*		
OTb⁺							
TbO	(5.62±0.1)	(113)	(471)	−17±3	−71±12	83PED/MAR	12035-91-5
		(111)	*(463)*	*−19*	*−79*		
OTe⁺							
TeO	8.72	218	910	16±5	69±21	83PED/MAR	13451-17-7
		218	*912*	*17*	*71*		
OTh⁺							
ThO	6.1±0.1	(133)	(557)	−7±2	−31±10	83PED/MAR	12035-93-7
		(134)	*(559)*	*−7*	*−29*		
OTi⁺							
TiO	6.56±0.03	164.3	687.3	13.0±2.0	54.4±8.4	85JANAF	12137-20-1
		164.2	*686.8*	*12.9±2.0*	*53.9±8.4*		
	IP from 84DYK/GRA. See also: 80MUR/HIL, 82BAN/CHA, 85BAL/GIG, 81KAP/STA.						
OTm⁺							
TmO	(6.44±0.1)	(130)	(542)	−19	−79	82TN270	12281-29-7
	See also: 80MUR/HIL. 0 K values.						
OU⁺							
UO	(5.65±0.2)	(136)	(570)	6±2	25±10	83PED/MAR	12035-97-1
		(136)	*(568)*	*6*	*23*		

Table 1. Positive Ion Table – Continued

ION Neutral	Ionization potential eV	$\Delta_f H$(Ion) kcal/mol	$\Delta_f H$(Ion) kJ/mol	$\Delta_f H$(Neutral) kcal/mol	$\Delta_f H$(Neutral) kJ/mol	Neutral reference	CAS registry number
OV$^+$ VO	(7.5)	(203.4) (203.5)	(851.2) (851.4)	30.5±5.0 30.5±5.0	127.6±20.9 127.8±20.9	85JANAF	12035-98-2

$\Delta_f H$(Ion) from onset energy of endothermic reaction (84ARI/ARM, 85ELK/ARM). IP is $\Delta_f H$(Ion) - $\Delta_f H$(Neutral). See also: 81KAP/STA.

ION Neutral	Ionization potential eV	$\Delta_f H$(Ion) kcal/mol	$\Delta_f H$(Ion) kJ/mol	$\Delta_f H$(Neutral) kcal/mol	$\Delta_f H$(Neutral) kJ/mol	Neutral reference	CAS registry number
OW$^+$ WO	(9.1±1)	(311.5) (311.6)	(1303.1) (1303.7)	101.6±10.0 101.7±10.0	425.1±41.8 425.7±41.8	85JANAF	12035-99-3
OY$^+$ YO	5.85±0.15	124 124	518 519	−11±2 −11	−46±10 −45	83PED/MAR	12036-00-9

See also: 80MUR/HIL.

ION Neutral	IP eV	$\Delta_f H$(Ion) kcal/mol	kJ/mol	$\Delta_f H$(Neutral) kcal/mol	kJ/mol	Neutral reference	CAS registry number
OYb$^+$ YbO	(6.55±0.1)	(147)	(615)	−4±2	−17±8	83PED/MAR	25578-79-4
OZn$^+$ ZnO		(275±8)	(1151±33)				

$\Delta_f H$(Ion) from 81KAP/STA. 0 K values.

ION Neutral	IP eV	$\Delta_f H$(Ion) kcal/mol	kJ/mol	$\Delta_f H$(Neutral) kcal/mol	kJ/mol	Neutral reference	CAS registry number
OZr$^+$ ZrO	(6.1±0.3)	(154.7) (154.9)	(647.1) (648.2)	14.0±12.0 14.2±12.0	58.6±50.2 59.6±50.2	85JANAF	12036-01-0

See also: 81KAP/STA.

ION Neutral	IP eV	$\Delta_f H$(Ion) kcal/mol	kJ/mol	$\Delta_f H$(Neutral) kcal/mol	kJ/mol	Neutral reference	CAS registry number
O$_2^+$ O$_2$	12.071±0.001	278.5 278.4	1165.3 1164.7	0 0	0 0	*DEF	7782-44-7

See also: 81KIM/KAT.

ION Neutral	IP eV	$\Delta_f H$(Ion) kcal/mol	kJ/mol	$\Delta_f H$(Neutral) kcal/mol	kJ/mol	Neutral reference	CAS registry number
O$_2$P$^+$ PO$_2$	(10.5±0.1)	(175) (176)	(733) (736)	−67 −66	−280 −277	85JANAF	12164-97-5
O$_2$Pt$^+$ PtO$_2$	(11.2±0.3)	(299)	(1253)	41	172	82TN270	1314-15-4
O$_2$Rh$^+$ RhO$_2$	(10.0)	(275)	(1149)	44	184	82TN270	12137-27-8
O$_2$S$^+$ SO$_2$	12.32±0.02	213 214	892 894	−70.9±0.1 −70.3±0.1	−296.8±0.2 −294.3±0.2	85JANAF	7446-09-5

See also: 81SMI/STE, 84ORI/SRI, 81KIM/KAT.

ION Neutral	IP eV	$\Delta_f H$(Ion) kcal/mol	kJ/mol	$\Delta_f H$(Neutral) kcal/mol	kJ/mol	Neutral reference	CAS registry number
O$_2$Sn$_2^+$ Sn$_2$O$_2$	(9.8±0.5)	(166)	(695)	−60	−251	82TN270	12534-17-7

Table 1. Positive Ion Table – Continued

ION / Neutral	Ionization potential eV	$\Delta_f H$(Ion) kcal/mol	kJ/mol	$\Delta_f H$(Neutral) kcal/mol	kJ/mol	Neutral reference	CAS registry number
O_2Th^+ ThO_2	(8.7±0.15)	(82) (82)	(341) (344)	−119 −118	−498 −495	82TN270	1314-20-1
O_2Ti^+ TiO_2	(9.54±0.1) See also: 82BAN/CHA, 85BAL/GIG.	(149) (149)	(625) (623)	(−71) (−71)	(−299) (−297)	85BAL/GIG	13463-67-7
O_2U^+ UO_2	(5.4±0.1)	(13) (14)	(55) (57)	−111±1 −111	−466±5 −464	80GRE	1344-57-6
O_2W^+ WO_2	(9.6±0.3) See also: 81BAL/GIG.	(240) (240)	(1003) (1005)	18±6 19±6	77±29 79±29	85JANAF	12036-22-5
O_2Zr^+ ZrO_2	(9.5±0.3)	(151) (150)	(631) (629)	−68±11 −68±11	−286±46 −284±46	85JANAF	1314-23-4
O_3^+ O_3	12.43 IP from 84KAT/SHI.	321 321	1342 1344	34 35	143 145	82TN270	10028-15-6
O_3Ru^+ RuO_3	(11.2)	(240)	(1003)	−19	−78	82TN270	12036-36-1
O_3S^+ SO_3	12.80±0.04 See also: 81SMI/STE.	200 202	839 845	−94.6±0.2 −93.2±0.2	−395.8±0.7 −390.0±0.7	85JANAF	7446-11-9
$O_3Sn_3^+$ Sn_3O_3	(9.8±0.5)	(100)	(419)	−126	−527	82TN270	12534-28-0
$O_3Ti_2^+$ Ti_2O_3	(8.3±0.5) IP from 85BAL/GIG2. 0 K values.	(39)	(164)	(−152)	(−636)	85BAL/GIG2	1344-54-3
O_3U^+ UO_3	(10.5±0.5)	(51)	(213)	−191±5	−800±20	80GRE	1344-58-7
O_3W^+ WO_3	(11.8±0.6) See also: 81BAL/GIG.	(202) (203)	(846) (851)	−70 −69	−293 −288	81WOO	1314-35-8

Table 1. Positive Ion Table - Continued

ION / Neutral	Ionization potential eV	Δ_fH(Ion) kcal/mol	Δ_fH(Ion) kJ/mol	Δ_fH(Neutral) kcal/mol	Δ_fH(Neutral) kJ/mol	Neutral reference	CAS registry number
O_4Os^+							
OsO_4	12.320	204	852	−81	−337	82TN270	20816-12-0
O_4Ru^+							
RuO_4	12.15±0.03	236	988	−44	−184	82TN270	20427-56-9
		238	994	−43	−178		
O_4SnW^+							
$SnWO_4$	(10.8) 0 K values.	(41)	(172)	−208	−870	82TN270	14553-36-7
$O_4Sn_4^+$							
Sn_4O_4	(9.2±0.5)	(19)	(80)	−193	−808	82TN270	
O_4SrW^+							
$SrWO_4$	(9.4)	(−33)	(−139)	−250	−1046	76DEL/HAL	
$O_4Ti_2^+$							
Ti_2O_4	(10.5±0.5) 0 K values.	(−19)	(−79)	(−261)	(−1092)	85BAL/GIG3	
$O_5Sn_2W^+$							
Sn_2WO_5	(8.4) 0 K values.	(−75)	(−315)	−269	−1125	82TN270	
$O_6P_4^+$	(9.5) IP is onset of photoelectron band.	(−293) (−288)	(−1227) (−1203)	−512±8 −507±6	−2144±33 −2120±33	85JANAF	10248-58-5
$O_6W_2^+$	(12.2±0.2)	(3) (4)	(11) (17)	−278 −277	−1164 −1158	85JANAF	12165-16-1
$O_7Re_2^+$							
Re_2O_7	(12.7±0.2)	(30)	(124)	−263	−1101	81WOO	1314-68-7
$O_9W_3^+$	(12.0±0.2)	(−191)	(−800)	−468	−1958	82TN270	12165-37-6

Table 1. Positive Ion Table — Continued

ION / Neutral	Ionization potential eV	$\Delta_f H$(Ion) kcal/mol	$\Delta_f H$(Ion) kJ/mol	$\Delta_f H$(Neutral) kcal/mol	$\Delta_f H$(Neutral) kJ/mol	Neutral reference	CAS registry number
$O_{10}P_4^+$	(13.3±0.2)	(−371) (−363)	(−1551) (−1517)	−677±2 −669±2	−2834±9 −2800±9	85JANAF	16752-60-6
$O_{12}W_4^+$	(12.0±0.2)	(−372)	(−1557)	−649	−2715	82TN270	12165-45-6
Os^+ / Os	8.28 IP from 79RAU/ACK.	380	1590	189	791	82TN270	7440-04-2
P^+ / P	10.486	317 317	1328 1328	75.6±0.2 75.4±0.2	316.4±1.0 315.6±1.0	85JANAF	7723-14-0
PS^+ / PS	(9.0)	(245) (245)	(1024) (1024)	36±1 36±1	151±4 151±4	79HUB/HER	12281-36-6
PSe^+ / PSe	(8.2) 0 K values.	(232)	(971)	43	180	79HUB/HER	12509-41-0
P_2^+ / P_2	10.53 IP from 79HUB/HER.	(277.2) (277.6)	(1159.7) (1161.5)	34.3±0.5 34.8±0.5	143.7±2.1 145.5±2.1	85JANAF	12185-09-0
P_3^+ / P_3	(7.85±0.2)	(241)	(1006)	59.4±4	249±16	74BEN/MAR	55030-78-9
P_4^+	9.08±0.05	223 225	935 942	14±0.5 16±0.5	59±2 66±2	85JANAF	12185-10-3
Pa^+ / Pa	5.89±0.12	270	1131	135	563	85KLE/WAR	7440-13-3

Table 1. Positive Ion Table – Continued

ION / Neutral	Ionization potential eV	$\Delta_f H$(Ion) kcal/mol	$\Delta_f H$(Ion) kJ/mol	$\Delta_f H$(Neutral) kcal/mol	$\Delta_f H$(Neutral) kJ/mol	Neutral reference	CAS registry number
Pb^+							
Pb	7.416	217.6	910.5	46.6	195.0	82TN270	7439-92-1
		217.8	911.1	46.8	195.6		
	See also: 83SEM/RYK, 84NIK/OVC.						
PbS^+							
PbS	(8.5±0.5)	(228)	(954)	32	134	79HUB/HER	1314-87-0
		(229)	(956)	32	136		
$PbSe^+$							
PbSe	(8.4±0.5)	(224)	(935)	30	125	79HUB/HER	12069-00-0
	0 K values.						
$PbTe^+$							
PbTe	(≤8.04)	(≤220)	(≤922)	35	146	79HUB/HER	1314-91-6
	0 K values.						
Pb_2^+							
Pb_2	(6.1±0.3)	(214)	(897)	(74)	(308)	79HUB/HER	12596-92-8
		(215)	(901)	(75)	(312)		
	IP from 82SAI/YAM.						
Pd^+							
Pd	8.34	283	1183	90	378	82TN270	7440-05-3
		282	1182	90	377		
$PdSi^+$							
PdSi	(8.4±0.5)	(318)	(1329)	124	519	79HUB/HER	12137-77-8
	0 K values.						
Pd_2^+							
Pd_2	(7.7±0.3)	(341)	(1426)	163	683	79HUB/HER	12596-93-9
	0 K values.						
Pm^+							
Pm	5.582						
Pr^+							
Pr	5.464±0.006	211	883	85	356	82TN270	7440-10-0
		211.2	883.9	85.2	356.7		
Pt^+							
Pt	8.61	334	1396	135	565	82TN270	7440-06-4
		333	1395	134.9	564.4		
	IP from 79RAU/ACK. See also: 81GUP/NAP.						
Pu^+							
Pu	6.03±0.10	222	927	82.5	345	85KLE/WAR	7440-07-5
	IP from 81CHE/GAB.						

Table 1. Positive Ion Table - Continued

ION Neutral	Ionization potential eV	$\Delta_f H$(Ion) kcal/mol	$\Delta_f H$(Ion) kJ/mol	$\Delta_f H$(Neutral) kcal/mol	$\Delta_f H$(Neutral) kJ/mol	Neutral reference	CAS registry number
Ra$^+$ Ra	5.279 IP from 70MOO.	160	668	38	159	82TN270	7440-14-4
Rb$^+$ Rb	4.177	116 *116*	484 *485*	19.3±0.1 *19.6±0.1*	80.9±0.4 *82.2±0.4*	85JANAF	7440-17-7
Rb$_2^+$ Rb$_2$	(3.9±0.1) IP from 85KAP/SCH.	(117.0) *(118.0)*	(489.6) *(493.6)*	27.1±0.6 *28.0±0.6*	113.3±2.5 *117.3±2.5*	85JANAF	
Re$^+$ Re	7.76 IP from 79RAU/ACK.	363 *363*	1519 *1518*	184 *184*	770 *769*	82TN270	7440-15-5
Rh$^+$ Rh	7.46 See also: 81HAQ/GIN.	305 *305*	1275 *1275*	133 *133*	557 *556*	82TN270	7440-16-6
RhTi$^+$ TiRh	(8.2±1.0) 0 K values.	(342)	(1431)	153	640	79HUB/HER	12600-90-7
Rh$_2^+$ Rh$_2$	(7.1±1.0) 0 K values.	(363)	(1518)	199	833	79HUB/HER	12596-98-4
Rn$^+$ Rn	10.748 IP from 70MOO.	247.9 *247.9*	1037.0 *1037.0*	0 *0*	0 *0*	*DEF	10043-92-2
Ru$^+$ Ru	(7.37)	(324) *(323)*	(1354) *(1352)*	154 *153*	643 *641*	82TN270	7440-18-8
S$^+$ S	10.360 See also: 86LIA/NG, 79DUN/DYK.	305 *304*	1275 *1272*	66.2±0.1 *65.6±0.1*	277.0±0.3 *274.7±0.3*	85JANAF	7704-34-9
SSe$^+$ SeS	(9.2±0.2) IP from 83GRA/WIE, 77LEV/LIA. 0 K values.	(243)	(1015)	30	127	83GRA/WIE	7446-34-6

Table 1. Positive Ion Table - Continued

ION / Neutral	Ionization potential eV	$\Delta_f H$(Ion) kcal/mol	kJ/mol	$\Delta_f H$(Neutral) kcal/mol	kJ/mol	Neutral reference	CAS registry number
SSn⁺ SnS	(8.8)	(231)	(968)	28	119	82TN270	1314-95-0
	IP is onset of photoelectron band.						
STi⁺ TiS	(7.1±0.3)	(237)	(990)	73	305	82TN270	12039-07-5
SY⁺ YS	(6.0)	(180) (180)	(754) (755)	42 42	175 176	82TN270	12210-79-6
S₂⁺ S₂	9.356±0.002	246.5 246.4	1031.3 1031.0	30.7±0.1 30.7±0.1	128.6±0.3 128.3±0.3	85JANAF	23550-45-0
	IP from 86LIA/NG. See also: 83ROS/GRA, 83GRA/WIE.						
S₃⁺ S₃	(9.68±0.03)	(257)	(1076)	34±2	142±8	85JANAF	12597-03-4
	See also: 83ROS/GRA.						
S₄⁺ (cyclic S₄)	(10.1)	(270)	(1131)	35±2	146±8	85JANAF	19269-85-3
	$\Delta_f H$(Ion) from appearance potential of 11.94±0.05 in S₆. IP from 83ROS/GRA.						
S₅⁺ (cyclic S₅)	(8.60±0.05)	(224)	(939)	26±2	109±8	85JANAF	12597-10-3
	See also: 83ROS/GRA.						
S₆⁺ (cyclic S₆)	(9.00±0.03)	(232)	(971)	24±2	102±8	85JANAF	13798-23-7
	See also: 83ROS/GRA.						
S₇⁺ (cyclic S₇)	(8.67±0.03)	(227)	(951)	27±2	114±8	85JANAF	21459-04-1
	See also: 83ROS/GRA.						

Table 1. Positive Ion Table - Continued

ION / Neutral	Ionization potential eV	$\Delta_f H$(Ion) kcal/mol	$\Delta_f H$(Ion) kJ/mol	$\Delta_f H$(Neutral) kcal/mol	$\Delta_f H$(Neutral) kJ/mol	Neutral reference	CAS registry number
S_8^+ / (S₈ ring)	(9.04±0.03)	(232) / (233)	(972) / (976)	24.0±0.2 / 25.0±0.2	100.4±0.6 / 104.4±0.6	85JANAF	10544-50-0

See also: 83ROS/GRA.

| Sb^+ / Sb | 8.641 | 261.9 / 261.9 | 1096.0 / 1095.7 | 62.7 / 62.6 | 262.3 / 262.0 | 82TN270 | 7440-36-0 |

It has been suggested (83MAZ) that this value of the IP is too high.

| Sb_2^+ / Sb_2 | (9.3±0.2) | (271) / (271) | (1133) / (1134) | 56 / 57 | 236 / 237 | 82TN270 | 32679-33-7 |

The cited ionization potential is from a spectroscopic determination. Threshold determinations have led to values of 8.4±0.3, 8.64±0.06, 8.7±0.3, 8.9±0.3, and 9.5±0.5 eV.

| Sb_4^+ / Sb_4 (tetrahedral) | (7.40±0.10) | (220) / (221) | (919) / (924) | 49 / 50 | 205 / 210 | 82TN270 | 12597-17-0 |

IP from 84ELB/KUD.

| Sc^+ / Sc | 6.54 | 241 / 241 | 1009 / 1007 | 90 / 90 | 378 / 376 | 82TN270 | 7440-20-2 |

See: 85DYK/GRA.

| Se^+ / Se | 9.752 | 279.2 / 279.0 | 1168.0 / 1167.3 | 54.27 / 54.11 | 227.07 / 226.40 | 82TN270 | 7782-49-2 |

| $SeSn^+$ / SeSn | (8.6) | (229) / (228) | (959) / (953) | 31 / 29 | 129 / 123 | 79HUB/HER | 1315-06-6 |

IP is onset of photoelectron band.

| $SeTe^+$ / SeTe | (8.5±0.2) | (227) | (948) | 31 | 128 | 83GRA/WIE | 12067-42-4 |

IP from 83GRA/WIE.

| SeY^+ / SeY | (6.1±1) | (90) | (376) | −51 | −213 | 79HUB/HER | 12067-44-6 |

0 K values.

Table 1. Positive Ion Table - Continued

ION Neutral	Ionization potential eV	$\Delta_f H$(Ion) kcal/mol	kJ/mol	$\Delta_f H$(Neutral) kcal/mol	kJ/mol	Neutral reference	CAS registry number
Se_2^+							
Se_2	8.70±0.05	236	985	35	146	82TN270	12185-17-0
		236	*987*	*35*	*148*		
	See also: 83POT/NOV, 83GRA/WIE.						
Si^+							
Si	8.15172±0.00003	295	1236	108±2	450±8	82TN270	7440-21-3
		295	*1233*	*106±2*	*446±8*		
Si_2^+							
Si_2	(7.4)	(311.6)	(1303.9)	141.0±3	589.9±13	85JANAF	12597-35-2
		(311.0)	*(1301.1)*	*140.3±3*	*587.1±13*		
Sm^+							
Sm	5.6437±0.0006	180	751	49.4	206.7	82TN270	7440-19-9
		179	*751*	*49.3*	*206.1*		
Sn^+							
Sn	7.344	241.5	1010.7	72.2	302.1	82TN270	7440-31-5
		241.5	*1010.6*	*72.2*	*302.0*		
Sr^+							
Sr	5.695	170	713	39±0.5	164±2	85JANAF	7440-24-6
		170	*713*	*39±0.5*	*164±2*		
Ta^+							
Ta	7.40	358	1496	187	782	85JANAF	7440-25-7
		357	*1495*	*186.7*	*781.4*		
	IP from 79RAU/ACK.						
Tb^+							
Tb	5.8639±0.0006	228	955	93	389	82TN270	7440-27-9
		228.6	*956.4*	*93.4*	*390.6*		
Tc^+							
Tc	(7.28)	(330)	(1380)	162	678	82TN270	7440-26-8
Te^+							
Te	9.009	255	1066	47	197	82TN270	22541-49-7
		255	*1066*	*47*	*197*		
TeY^+							
YTe	(6.0±1.0)	(206)	(860)	67	281	79HUB/HER	12187-04-1
	0 K values.						
Te_2^+							
Te_2	8.29±0.03	223	933	32	133	79HUB/HER	10028-16-7
		224	*936*	*32*	*136*		
	See also: 83GRA/WIE.						

Table 1. Positive Ion Table – Continued

ION Neutral	Ionization potential eV	$\Delta_f H$(Ion) kcal/mol	$\Delta_f H$(Ion) kJ/mol	$\Delta_f H$(Neutral) kcal/mol	$\Delta_f H$(Neutral) kJ/mol	Neutral reference	CAS registry number
Th$^+$							
Th	6.08	283	1184	143	597	85KLE/WAR	7440-29-1
		283	*1184*	*143*	*597*		
Ti$^+$							
Ti	6.82	270	1128	112	470	82TN270	7440-32-6
		269	*1125*	*112*	*467*		
Tl$^+$							
Tl	6.108	184.4	771.6	43.5	182.2	82TN270	7440-28-0
		184.5	*772.1*	*43.7*	*182.8*		
Tl$_2$$^+$							
Tl$_2$	(6.5±0.5)	(223)	(932)	73	305	80BAL/PIA	76939-73-6
	IP from 80BAL/PIA. 0 K values.						
Tm$^+$							
Tm	6.18	198	828	55	232	82TN270	7440-30-4
		198	*830*	*55.8*	*233.4*		
U$^+$							
U	6.1912	270	1128	127	531	85KLE/WAR	7440-61-1
		270	*1128*	*127*	*531*		
	IP from 70EME/KHO, 76SOL/MAY. See also: 81CHE/GAB.						
V$^+$							
V	6.74	278	1165	123±2	515±8	85JANAF	7440-62-2
		278	*1162*	*122±2*	*512±8*		
	See also: 85DYK/GRA.						
W$^+$							
W	7.60	379	1584	203.4±1.5	851.0±6.3	85JANAF	7440-33-7
		378	*1582*	*203.7±1.5*	*849.8±6.3*		
Xe$^+$							
Xe	12.130	279.7	1170.4	0	0	*DEF	7440-63-3
		279.7	*1170.4*	*0*	*0*		
	See also: 81KIM/KAT.						
Xe$_2$$^+$							
Xe$_2$	11.13±0.02	*256*	*1072*	*−0.53*	*−2.22*	79HUB/HER	12185-19-2
	See also: 82POL/DEH. 0 K values.						
Y$^+$							
Y	(6.22)	(244)	(1021)	101	421	82TN270	7440-65-5
		(244)	*(1021)*	*100.5*	*420.4*		
	IP from 73GAR/REE.						
Yb$^+$							
Yb	6.254	180	755	36	152	82TN270	7440-64-4
		180.7	*756.2*	*36.5*	*152.8*		

Table 1. Positive Ion Table – Continued

ION Neutral	Ionization potential eV	$\Delta_f H$(Ion) kcal/mol	kJ/mol	$\Delta_f H$(Neutral) kcal/mol	kJ/mol	Neutral reference	CAS registry number
Zn⁺							
Zn	9.394	247.8	1036.8	31.2	130.4±0.2	85JANAF	7440-66-6
		247.7	*1036.3*	*31.0*	*129.9±0.2*		
Zr⁺							
Zr	6.84	303	1270	146±2	610±8	85JANAF	7440-67-7
		302	*1262*	*144±2*	*602±8*		

Table 2. Negative Ion Table

Ion $\Delta_f H(A^-)$ $\Delta_f H(X\cdot\cdot Y^-)$	EA(A) eV	$\Delta H_{acid}(AH)$ $\Delta H_{aff}(X\cdot\cdot Y^-)$	$\Delta G_{acid}(AH)$ $\Delta G_{aff}(X\cdot\cdot Y^-)$	Method	Comment	Reference
e⁻					$\Delta_f H(AH)= 218$	82TN270
e⁻					BDE(A–H)= 1312	82TN270
* 0		1312 [f]	1308 [h]	Def		82TN270
Ag⁻						
Ag⁻					$\Delta_f H(A)= 285$	82TN270
* 159±1 [b]	1.302±0.007			LPES		85HOT/LIN
Al⁻						
Al⁻					$\Delta_f H(AH)= 259\pm1$	82TN270
					BDE(A–H)= 285±3	81KAN/MOO
* 284±5 [a]	0.441±0.010	1554±4 [e]		LPES		85HOT/LIN
AlBeF₆⁻						
BeF₂··AlF₄⁻						
−2921±21 [c]		182±10		TDAs		80NIK/SOR
AlBeF₇K⁻						
KBeF₃··AlF₄⁻						
−3522±21 [c]		192±8		TDAs		80NIK/SOR
AlBeF₇Na⁻						
NaBeF₃··AlF₄⁻						
−3497±21 [c]		192±8		TDAs		80NIK/SOR
AlF₂⁻						
AlF₂⁻					$\Delta_f H(A)= -749\pm13$	81WOO
−971±13	2.25±0.13			TDEq	EA: 111 kJ < EA(F), new EA(F) data used	74SRI/UY
AlF₄⁻						
AlF₃··F⁻						
* −1945±10 [c]		488±8		TDAs		86NIK/IGO
				Summary of literature data plus new work. Recommended average value		
−1972±21 [c]		498±7		TDAs	F⁻A: 1100K; $\Delta_f H$(AlF₄⁻): 298K	80SID/NIK
−1964±14 [c]		495±11		TDEq	F⁻A: 93±1 kJ > UF₄	79NIK/SKO
−1954±12 [c]		500±8		TDEq	F⁻A:17 kJ > ScF₃	81NIK/SID
−2092±13		628±42 [k]		TDEq	2AlF₂ + AlF₂⁻ = 2AlF + AlF₄⁻	74SRI/UY
−1949±16 [c]		496±13		TDEq	KF₂⁻ + KAlF₄ = AlF₄⁻ + 2KF	80GUS/PYA
AlF₅K⁻						
KF··AlF₄⁻						
−2397±33 [c]		120±8		TDAs		79GUS/GOR
AlF₇Mn⁻						
MnF₃··AlF₄⁻						
−2950±60				TDAs		84KOR/CHI
AlO⁻						
AlO⁻					$\Delta_f H(A)= 67\pm8$	85JANAF
−282±21 [b]	3.62±0.13			TDEq	EA: near EA(Cl)	72SRI/UY

Table 2. Negative Ion Table - Continued

Ion $\Delta_f H(X\cdot\cdot Y^-)$	$\Delta_f H(A^-)$ EA(A) eV	$\Delta H_{acid}(AH)$ $\Delta H_{aff}(X\cdot\cdot Y^-)$	$\Delta G_{acid}(AH)$ $\Delta G_{aff}(X\cdot\cdot Y^-)$	Method	Comment	Reference
AlO_2^-						
AlO_2^-					$\Delta_f H(A) = -130$	82KAS/CHE
−583±13 [b]	4.05±0.13			TDEq		72SRI/UY
				EA: 42 kJ > EA(Cl), new data for $\Delta_f H(AlO_2)$ and EA(Cl) used		
$Al_2F_7^-$						
$AlF_3\cdot\cdot AlF_4^-$						
−3394±15 [c]		204±4	175±8	TDAs		80SID/NIK
−3393±33				TDAs		79GUS/GOR
$Al_2F_8K^-$						
$KAlF_4\cdot\cdot AlF_4^-$						
−4011±42 [c]		147±6	123±10	TDAs		80SID/NIK
$Al_2F_8Na^-$						
$NaAlF_4\cdot\cdot AlF_4^-$						
−4006±42 [c]		166±9	141±13	TDAs		80SID/NIK
$ArBr^-$						
$Ar\cdot\cdot Br^-$						
−219 [c]		6		MobI		84GAT
As^-						
As^-						
* 224±5 [b]	0.81±0.03			PD	$\Delta_f H(A) = 303\pm 2$	82TN270
						85HOT/LIN
$AsBr^-$						
$AsBr^{-\cdot}$						
7	1.3			EIAP	From $AsBr_3$	76PAB/BEN
$AsBr_2^-$						
$AsBr_2^-$						
	3.5±0.1			EIAP	From $AsBr_3$	78PAB/MAR
−303	3.5			EIAP	From $AsBr_3$	76PAB/BEN
$AsCl^-$						
$AsCl^{-\cdot}$						
−9	1.3			EIAP	From $AsCl_3$	76PAB/BEN
$AsClF_3^-$						
$AsF_3\cdot\cdot Cl^-$						
* −1121±12 [c]		108±8 [g]	78±8	IMRE		85LAR/MCM
$AsCl_2^-$						
$AsCl_2^-$						
−273	2.2				$\Delta_f H(A) = 67\pm 21$	82TN270
				EIAP	From $AsCl_3$	76PAB/BEN
	2.2±0.1			EIAP	From $AsCl_3$	78PAB/MAR
AsF^-						
$AsF^{-\cdot}$						
	1.3			EIAP	From AsF_3	76PAB/BEN

Table 2. Negative Ion Table - Continued

Ion $\Delta_f H(A^-)$ $\Delta_f H(X\cdot\cdot Y^-)$	EA(A) eV	$\Delta H_{acid}(AH)$ $\Delta H_{aff}(X\cdot\cdot Y^-)$	$\Delta G_{acid}(AH)$ $\Delta G_{aff}(X\cdot\cdot Y^-)$	Method	Comment	Reference
AsF_2^-						
AsF_2^-						
−543	0.8			EIAP	From AsF_3	76PAB/BEN
	0.8±0.1			EIAP	From AsF_3	78PAB/MAR
AsF_4^-						
$AsF_3\cdot\cdot F^-$						
* −1236±13 [c]		202±8 [g]	172±8	IMRE		85LAR/MCM
AsH^-						
AsH^-						
	1.0±0.1			PD		77RAC/FEL
<167				IMRB	$As^- + AsH_3 \rightarrow$	74WYA/HOL
	<1.1			IMRB	From AsH_3	64EBI/KRA
AsH_2^-					$\Delta_f H(AH)=$ 67±1	82TN270
AsH_2^-				D-EA	BDE(A-H)= 326±33	
* 52±26 [a]		1515±26 [g]	1483±25	IMRB	Between PH_3, H_2S	74WYA/HOL
*	1.27±0.03			PD		72SMY/BRA2
<41±20 [a]	<1.1±0.5 [d]	<1505±19		EIAP	From AsH_3	64EBI/KRA
As_2^-					$\Delta_f H(A)=$ 190±3	73BEN/MAR
As_2^-						
	<0.8			PD		77FEL/RAC
180±19	0.1±0.2 [i]			EIAP	From As_4	73BEN/MAR
As_2H^-						
As_2H^-						
<288				IMRB	$As^- + AsH_3 \rightarrow As_2H^- + H_2$	74WYA/HOL
As_3^-					$\Delta_f H(A)=$ 241±16	73BEN/MAR
As_3^-						
160±18	0.8±0.4 [i]			EIAP	From As_4	73BEN/MAR
Au^-					$\Delta_f H(AH)=$ 295±2	82TN270
Au^-					BDE(A-H)= 289±4	82TN270
* 144±6 [a]	2.309	1379±4 [e]		LPD		85HOT/LIN
AuF_6^-						
AuF_6^-						
	>1.0			NBIP		80COM/REI
B^-					$\Delta_f H(AH)=$ 450±2	82TN270
B^-					BDE(A-H)= 211±10	85JANAF
* 416±13 [a]	0.277±0.010	1497±11 [e]	1468±13 [h]	LPES		85HOT/LIN
$BBrCl_2^-$						
BCl_2Br^-					$\Delta_f H(A)=$ −337±42	85JANAF
−403±61 [b]	0.7±0.2			NBIP		80ROT/MAT

Table 2. Negative Ion Table – Continued

Ion $\Delta_f H(X \cdot \cdot Y^-)$	$\Delta_f H(A^-)$ EA(A) eV	$\Delta H_{acid}(AH)$ $\Delta H_{aff}(X \cdot \cdot Y^-)$	$\Delta G_{acid}(AH)$ $\Delta G_{aff}(X \cdot \cdot Y^-)$	Method	Comment	Reference
BBr$_2$Cl$^-$						
BBr$_2$Cl$^-$·					$\Delta_f H(A) = -272 \pm 42$	85JANAF
-363 ± 61 [b]	0.9 ± 0.2			NBIP		80ROT/MAT
BBr$_3^-$						
BBr$_3^-$·					$\Delta_f H(A) = -206$	82TN270
-285 ± 20 [b]	0.8 ± 0.2			NBIP		80ROT/MAT
BClF$_3^-$						
BF$_3 \cdot \cdot$Cl$^-$						
* -1473 ± 12 [c]		109 ± 8 [g]	81 ± 8	IMRE		85LAR/MCM
BCl$_2^-$						
BCl$_2^-$					$\Delta_f H(AH) = -248 \pm 4$	71JANAF
-144 ± 109 [b]	0.6			Est2	Est: from IP, EA of isoelectronic NO$_2$, BF$_2$, AlF$_2$	82JANAF
BCl$_3^-$						
BCl$_3^-$·					$\Delta_f H(A) = -404 \pm 1$	82TN270
-436 ± 20 [b]	0.3 ± 0.2			NBIP		80ROT/MAT
BCl$_3$F$^-$						
BCl$_3 \cdot \cdot$F$^-$						
< -890		> 238 [k]		IMRB	F$^-$A: > SF$_5$	72STO/NEL
BCl$_4^-$						
BCl$_3 \cdot \cdot$Cl$^-$						
-920 ± 6		289 ± 8 [k]		Latt		77KRI/TIT
BF$_2^-$						
BF$_2^-$					$\Delta_f H(AH) = -734 \pm 3$	85JANAF
					BDE(A-H) = 362 ± 17	85JANAF
-796 ± 26 [b]	2.13 ± 0.13	1468 ± 29 [e]	1436 ± 31 [h]	IMRE	EA: 122 kJ < EA(F), new EA(F) used	74SRI/UY
BF$_2$O$^-$						
BF$_2$O$^-$					$\Delta_f H(AH) = -1092 \pm 8$	82TN270
					BDE(A-H) = 473 ± 23	85JANAF
< -1002 ± 25		< 1619 ± 33 [f]		IMRB	DO$^-$ + BF$_3$ →	72STO/NEL
BF$_3^-$						
BF$_3^-$·					$\Delta_f H(A) = -1137 \pm 2$	85JANAF
	0.0 ± 0.2			NBIP	See also: 72STO/NEL	80ROT/MAT
	2.6			SI		69PAG/GOO
BF$_4^-$						
BF$_3 \cdot \cdot$F$^-$						
* -1687 ± 25 [c]		301 ± 21 [g]	266 ± 8	IMRE		85LAR/MCM
-1716 ± 44 [c]		330 ± 40		TDEq		84PYA/GUS
-1773 ± 26		385 ± 25 [k]		Latt		84MAL/ROS
-1779 ± 21		393 ± 21 [k]		Latt		77KRI/TIT
< -1812				TDEq	BF$_3$ + BF$_2^-$ = BF$_4^-$ + BF	74SRI/UY
< -1368				IMRB	F$^-$A: > SF$_5$	72STO/NEL

Table 2. Negative Ion Table - Continued

Ion $\Delta_f H(X\cdot\cdot Y^-)$	EA(A) eV	$\Delta H_{acid}(AH)$ $\Delta H_{aff}(X\cdot\cdot Y^-)$	$\Delta G_{acid}(AH)$ $\Delta G_{aff}(X\cdot\cdot Y^-)$	Method	Comment	Reference
BH_4^-						
$BH_3\cdot\cdot H^-$						
< 197±28				IMRB	$HO^- + B_2H_6 \rightarrow$	68DUN
−96±21		341 [k]		Latt		55ALT
−85±8		322±8 [k]		Latt		77KRI/ITT
BKO_2^-						
KBO_2^-					$\Delta_f H(A) = -672\pm10$	85FAR/SRI
−785±31 [b]	1.2±0.2			EIAP	From K_2BO_2F	76SHE/ILJ
$BNaO_2^-$						
$NaBO_2^-$					$\Delta_f H(A) = -644\pm42$	82TN270
−782±63 [b]	1.4±0.2			EIAP	From Na_2BO_2F	76SHE/ILJ
BO^-						
BO^-						
−196±17 [b]	2.84±0.09			TDEq		71SRI/UY
					EA(BO) < EA(Cl) by 75 kJ, new $\Delta_f H(BO\cdot)$ and EA(Cl) used	
	> 2.48			TDEq		70JEN
BO_2^-						
BO_2^-					$\Delta_f H(AH) = -562\pm4$	82TN270
					$BDE(A-H) = 479\pm6$	82TN270
−736±18	4.51±0.21 [i]	1356±26 [e]		TDEq		83SID/RUD
−617±15 [b]	3.28±0.13			TDEq		71SRI/UY
					EA(BO_2) < EA(Cl) by 32 kJ, new $\Delta_f H(BO_2)$ and EA(Cl) used	
	3.4±0.5			EIAP	From K_2BO_2F	76SHE/ILJ
	4.19±0.31			TDEq		70JEN
BeF_3^-						
$BeF_2\cdot\cdot F^-$						
−1477±15 [c]		407±10		TDEq	F^-A: 83±7 kJ < AlF_3	80NIK/SOR
BeH^-						
BeH^-					$\Delta_f H(A) = 344$	79HUB/HER
276 [b]	0.7±0.1			PD		77RAC/FEL
$Be_2F_5^-$						
$Be_2F_4\cdot\cdot F^-$						
		464±8		TDEq	F^-A: 26±8 kJ < AlF_3	80NIK/SOR
$Be_2F_6K^-$						
$KF\cdot\cdot Be_2F_5^-$						
−617 [c]		290±10		TDAs		80NIK/SOR
$Be_2F_6Na^-$						
$NaF\cdot\cdot Be_2F_5^-$						
−564 [c]		273±10		TDAs		80NIK/SOR
$Be_3F_7^-$						
$BeF_2\cdot\cdot Be_2F_5^-$						
−969 [c]		175±10		TDAs		80NIK/SOR

Table 2. Negative Ion Table - Continued

Ion $\Delta_f H(X\cdots Y^-)$	$\Delta_f H(A^-)$ EA(A) eV	$\Delta H_{acid}(AH)$ $\Delta H_{aff}(X\cdots Y^-)$	$\Delta G_{acid}(AH)$ $\Delta G_{aff}(X\cdots Y^-)$	Method	Comment	Reference
$Be_3F_8K^-$						
$KBeF_3\cdots Be_2F_5^-$						
−1482±21 [c]		188±8		TDAs		80NIK/SOR
Bi^-					$\Delta_f H(A) = $ 207±4	82TN270
Bi^-						
* 116±5 [b]	0.946±0.010			LPES		85HOT/LIN
Br^-					$\Delta_f H(AH) = $ −36	85JANAF
Br^-					BDE(A−H) = 366	82BAU/COX
* −213±1 [a]	3.365±0.003	1354 [e]	1331±1 [h]	PLA		85HOT/LIN
		1349±9 [g]	1326±8	IMRE		86TAF
$BrClH^-$						
$HCl\cdots Br^-$						
* −387±9 [c]		82±8	54±11	TDAs		85CAL/KEB
$BrCl_2^-$						
$BrCl_2^-$						
< −464		> 251 [k]		PDis		79LEE/SMI
$BrCl_2P^-$						
$PBrCl_2^-$				Est2	$\Delta_f H(A) = $ −188±42	
−335±61 [b]	1.5±0.2			NBIP		76MAT/ROT
$BrFH^-$						
$HF\cdots Br^-$						
* −557±10 [c]		71±8		Est	Extrapolated from other bihalide data	84LAR/MCM3
$BrHI^-$						
$HBr\cdots I^-$						
* −292±9 [c]		67±8	43±11	TDAs		85CAL/KEB
$BrHNO_3^-$						
$HBr\cdots NO_3^-$						
−438±10 [c]		94±8	78±7	TDEq		77DAV/FEH
BrH_2O^-						
$HOH\cdots Br^-$						
−517 [c]		62	37	TDAs		82BUR/HAY
		53±8	29±8	TDAs		70ARS/YAM
BrI^-						
IBr^-					$\Delta_f H(A) = $ 41±1	82TN270
−205±11 [b]	2.5±0.1			NBIP		72BAE
	2.5±0.1			NBIP		73AUE/HUB
	2.7±0.2			EnCT		71CHU/BER
	1.62±0.05			NBIP	Vertical EA	76HUB/KLE

Table 2. Negative Ion Table – Continued

Ion $\Delta_f H(X \cdot \cdot Y^-)$	$\Delta_f H(A^-)$	EA(A) eV	$\Delta H_{acid}(AH)$ $\Delta H_{aff}(X \cdot \cdot Y^-)$	$\Delta G_{acid}(AH)$ $\Delta G_{aff}(X \cdot \cdot Y^-)$	Method	Comment	Reference
BrK⁻							
KBr⁻·						$\Delta_f H(A) = -180\pm2$	85JANAF
−239 [b]		0.6			Scat		79DEV/WIJ
BrKr⁻							
Kr··Br⁻							
−221 [c]			8		Mobl		84GAT
BrNa⁻							
NaBr⁻·						$\Delta_f H(A) = -143\pm8$	82TN270
−234 [b]		0.9			Scat		79DEV/WIJ
BrO⁻							
BrO⁻						$\Delta_f H(AH) = -79\pm8$	76BEN
						$BDE(A-H) = 423\pm13$	82TN270
<−20±21		>1.5±0.2 [i]	<1590±29 [f]		Endo	$Br^- + O_2 \rightarrow$	77VOG/DRE
BrO₂S⁻							
SO₂··Br⁻							
−590±10 [c]			81±8	53±11	TDAs		85CAL/KEB
BrPb⁻							
PbBr⁻		0.9±0.2			EIAP	From PbBr₂	67HAS/BLO
BrXe⁻							
Xe··Br⁻							
−227 [c]			14		Mobl		84GAT
Br₂⁻							
Br₂⁻·						$\Delta_f H(A) = 31$	82BAU/COX
*		2.5±0.1			NBIP		72BAE
		2.4			ECD	Vertical EA: 1.6 eV	81AYA/WEN
		2.5±0.1			EnCT		71CHU/BER
		2.6±0.2			NBIP		77DIS/LAC2
		2.6±0.2			EnCT		73HUG/LIF
		2.9±0.1			EIAP	From CBr₄	71DEC/FRA
		1.47±0.05			NBIP	Vertical EA	76HUB/KLE
Br₂ClP⁻							
PBr₂Cl⁻·					Est2	$\Delta_f H(A) = -152\pm42$	
−309±61 [b]		1.6±0.2			NBIP		76MAT/ROT
Br₂Ge⁻							
GeBr₂⁻·						$\Delta_f H(A) = -63\pm8$	82TN270
<−217 [b]		>1.6			EIAP	From GeBr₄	77PAB/MAR
Br₂H⁻							
HBr··Br⁻							
* −336±9 [c]			86±8	58±11	TDAs		85CAL/KEB

Table 2. Negative Ion Table – Continued

Ion $\Delta_f H(X\cdot\cdot Y^-)$	$\Delta_f H(A^-)$ EA(A) eV	$\Delta H_{acid}(AH)$ $\Delta H_{aff}(X\cdot\cdot Y^-)$	$\Delta G_{acid}(AH)$ $\Delta G_{aff}(X\cdot\cdot Y^-)$	Method	Comment	Reference
Br_2I^-						
IBr_2^-						
−251		95 [k]		Latt		77FIN/GAT
Br_2Si^-						
$SiBr_2^{-\cdot}$						
	>1.7			EIAP	From $SiBr_4$	77PAB/MAR
Br_2Sn^-						
$SnBr_2^{-\cdot}$						
−54	1.3			EIAP	From $SnBr_4$	77PAB/PER
Br_3Ge^-						
$GeBr_3^-$						
	>0.9			EIAP	From $GeBr_4$	77PAB/MAR
Br_3P^-						
$PBr_3^{-\cdot}$					$\Delta_f H(A) = -139\pm8$	82TN270
−293±23 [b]	1.6±0.2			NBIP		76MAT/ROT
Br_3Si^-						
$SiBr_3^-$					$\Delta_f H(AH) = -318\pm2$	82TN270
	>1.5±0.2			EIAP	From $SiBr_4$	77PAB/MAR
Br_3Sn^-						
$SnBr_3^-$					$\Delta_f H(AH) = -318\pm8$	82TN270
					BDE(A−H) = 349±28	77PAB/PER
	3.08±0.01			EIAP	From $SnBr_4$	78PAB/MAR
<−484	>3.1			EIAP	From $SnBr_4$	77PAB/PER
Br_3Ti^-						
$TiBr_3^-$					$\Delta_f H(A) = -377\pm42$	74BEN/PAB
	0.76±0.01			EIAP	From $TiBr_4$	78PAB/MAR
−452±15	0.8±0.3			EIAP	From $TiBr_4$	74BEN/PAB
C^-						
C^-					$\Delta_f H(AH) = 596$	82TN270
* 595±1 [a]	1.263	1529±1 [e]	1506±2 [h]	LPD	BDE(A−H) = 339±1	82TN270
						85HOT/LIN
	>1.2±1.0			EIAP	From graphite	54HON
$CBrF_3^-$						
$CF_3Br^{-\cdot}$					$\Delta_f H(A) = -652$	78KUD/KUD
−740 [b]	0.9±0.2			NBIP		78COM/REI2
CBr_3^-						
Br_3C^-					$\Delta_f H(AH) = 24\pm5$	84BIC/MIN
					BDE(A−H) = 402±7	82MCM/GOL
40±29 [b]	1.7±0.2	1546±34 [f]	1514±38 [h]	SI		69PAG/GOO
CBr_4^-						
$Br_4C^{-\cdot}$					$\Delta_f H(A) = 84\pm3$	84BIC/MIN
−115 [b]	2.1			SI		69PAG/GOO

Table 2. Negative Ion Table - Continued

Ion $\Delta_f H(A^-)$ $\Delta_f H(X \cdot \cdot Y^-)$	EA(A) eV	$\Delta H_{acid}(AH)$ $\Delta H_{aff}(X \cdot \cdot Y^-)$	$\Delta G_{acid}(AH)$ $\Delta G_{aff}(X \cdot \cdot Y^-)$	Method	Comment	Reference
CClF$_2^-$					$\Delta_f H(AH) = -484 \pm 2$	77PED/RYL
CF$_2$Cl$^-$					BDE(A-H) = 425±4	82MCM/GOL
−431±35 [a]	1.6±0.3	1583±33 [e]	1550±37 [h]	NBAP	From CF$_2$Cl$_2$	78DIS/LAC
	>1.9			EIAP	From CF$_3$Cl	79ILL/SCH
CClF$_2$O$^-$						
CF$_2$=O··Cl$^-$						
* −920±11 [c]		52±8 [g]	28±8	IMRE		85LAR/MCM
<−728±25				IMRB	ClCO$^-$ or ClF$^-$ + CF$_2$O →	76KAR/KLE
CClO$^-$						
ClCO$^-$						
<−356		>21 [k]		EIAP	From Cl$_2$CO	76KAR/KLE
CClO$_2^-$						
CO$_2$··Cl$^-$						
* −654±2 [c]		33	9	TDAs		80KEE/LEE
		32±8	9±8	TDEq		86HIR/SHO
CClS$_2^-$						
CS$_2$··Cl$^-$						
* −159±10 [c]		49±8 [g]	24±8	IMRE		85LAR/MCM
CCl$_2^-$						
CCl$_2^-$·					$\Delta_f H(AH) = 109 \pm 4$	83WEI/BEN
					BDE(A-H) = 272±17	85LIA/KAR
−10±42 [b]	1.8±0.3	1411±46 [e]		NBAP	From CCl$_4$, CFCl$_3$, CHCl$_3$	78DIS/LAC
	2.5±0.6			EIAP	From CCl$_4$, CHCl$_3$, CH$_2$Cl$_2$	80SCH/ILL
CCl$_2$F$^-$					$\Delta_f H(AH) = -281$	78KUD/KUD
CCl$_2$F$^-$					BDE(A-H) = 425±4	82MCM/GOL
	>2.4±0.2	<1506±23 [e]		EIAP	From CF$_2$Cl$_2$	79ILL/SCH
	1.1±0.3			NBAP	From CFCl$_3$	78DIS/LAC
CCl$_2$FO$^-$						
CCl$_2$=O··F$^-$						
<−590±50				IMRB	FCO$^-$ + CCl$_2$O →	76KAR/KLE
CCl$_2$F$_2^-$						
CCl$_2$F$_2^-$·					$\Delta_f H(A) = -477 \pm 5$	77PED/RYL
−516±25 [b]	0.4±0.2			NBIP		78DIS/LAC
CCl$_3^-$					$\Delta_f H(AH) = -105 \pm 2$	77PED/RYL
CCl$_3^-$					BDE(A-H) = 401±4	82MCM/GOL
* −141±28 [a]	2.3±0.3 [d]	1494±26 [g]	1461±25	IMRB	> acetone, ≤ C$_5$H$_6$	72BOH/LEE
	2.6±0.2			EIAP	From CCl$_4$	80SCH/ILL
	>1.9			EIAP	From CFCl$_3$	79ILL/SCH
	1.3±0.3			NBAP	From CHCl$_3$, CCl$_4$	78DIS/LAC
	>2.1±0.3			EIAP	From CFCl$_3$	61CUR
	1.44±0.05			SI		66GAI/KAY

Table 2. Negative Ion Table - Continued

Ion $\Delta_f H(A^-)$ $\Delta_f H(X \cdot \cdot Y^-)$	EA(A) eV	$\Delta H_{acid}(AH)$ $\Delta H_{aff}(X \cdot \cdot Y^-)$	$\Delta G_{acid}(AH)$ $\Delta G_{aff}(X \cdot \cdot Y^-)$	Method	Comment	Reference
CCl_3F^-						
$CCl_3F^-\cdot$					$\Delta_f H(A) = -268\pm8$	77PED/RYL
-374 ± 37 [b]	1.1 ± 0.3			NBIP		78DIS/LAC
CCl_3O^-						
$CCl_2=O \cdot \cdot Cl^-$						
* -498 ± 9 [c]		52 ± 8 [g]	27 ± 8	IMRE		85LAR/MCM
-460 ± 8				IMRB		76KAR/KLE
CCl_4^-						
$CCl_4^-\cdot$					$\Delta_f H(A) = -97\pm3$	77PED/RYL
-290 ± 22 [b]	2.0 ± 0.2			NBIP		83LAC/MAN
	2.0 ± 0.2			NBIP		78DIS/LAC
	2.1 ± 0.1			SI		66GAI/KAY
CCl_5^-						
$CCl_4 \cdot \cdot Cl^-$						
-384 ± 7 [c]		59 ± 3	25 ± 4	TDAs		74DOU/DAL
CF^-						
$CF^-\cdot$					$\Delta_f H(A) = 255$	85JANAF
	$>3.3\pm0.3$			EIAP	From C_2F_4	70THY/MAC2
CFN^-						
$FCN^-\cdot$					$\Delta_f H(A) = 36\pm17$	85JANAF
-318	2.9 [i]			EIAP	From CF_3NC	86HEN/ILL
	>4.0			EIAP	From PF_2CN	74HAR/RAN
CFO^-						
FCO^-				Est	$\Delta_f H(AH) = -380$	
					$BDE(A-H) = 415\pm29$	81DYK/JON2
-444 ± 10	2.7 [i]	104 [k]		EIAP	From CF_2O	70THY/MAC
-435 [a]	2.3 ± 0.5 [d]	1475 ± 19		EIAP	From $HCOF$	77KAR/KLE
	3.3			EIAP	From $(CF_3)_2CO$	70HAR/THY
$CFOS^-$						
$COS \cdot \cdot F^-$						
* -524 ± 11 [c]		133 ± 8 [g]	103 ± 8	IMRE		85LAR/MCM
CFO_2^-						
$CO_2 \cdot \cdot F^-$						
* -775 ± 11 [c]		133 ± 8 [g]	103 ± 8	IMRE		85LAR/MCM
-780 ± 15 [c]		138 ± 13		IMRE		78MCM/NOR
CFS_2^-						
$CS_2 \cdot \cdot F^-$						
* -262 ± 11 [c]		131 ± 8 [g]	101 ± 8	IMRE		85LAR/MCM
CF_2^-						
$CF_2^-\cdot$					$\Delta_f H(A) = -205\pm13$	85LIA/KAR
<-102				IMRB	$O^- + CH_2F_2 \rightarrow$	76DAW/JEN
	$<1.3\pm0.8$			EIAP	From $c\text{-}C_4F_8$	72HAR/THY2
	>0.2			EIAP	From C_2F_4	70THY/MAC2

Table 2. Negative Ion Table – Continued

Ion $\Delta_f H(X \cdot \cdot Y^-)$	$\Delta_f H(A^-)$ EA(A) eV	$\Delta H_{acid}(AH)$ $\Delta H_{aff}(X \cdot \cdot Y^-)$	$\Delta G_{acid}(AH)$ $\Delta G_{aff}(X \cdot \cdot Y^-)$	Method	Comment	Reference
CF_2^-						
$CF_2^-\cdot$					$\Delta_f H(A) = -205\pm13$	85LIA/KAR
	2.6			SI		69PAG/GOO
CF_2N^-						
CF_2N^-						
<−222				EIAP	From CF_3NC	86HEN/ILL
CF_3^-						
CF_3^-					$\Delta_f H(AH) = -695\pm1$	78KUD/KUD
					BDE(A−H) = 443±7	86TSA
* −648±10 [a]	1.84±0.16 [d]	1577±9 [g]	1545±8	IMRE		79BAR/SCO
*	2.82±0.01			PD	Vertical detachment energy	75RIC/STE4
	1.9±0.3			NBAP	From CF_4	78DIS/LAC
	>2.0±0.2			EIAP	From C_3F_8	74HAR/FRA
	>2.4±0.5			EIAP	From C_2F_6	74HAR/FRA
	2.2±0.3			EIAP	From CF_4	74HAR/FRA
−683	2.2			EIAP	From CF_4	74FRA/WAN
−651	1.9			EIAP	From CF_4	73WAN/MAR
	3.1±0.2			EIAP	From CF_4	72LIF/GRA
	2.1±0.3			EIAP	From C_2F_4	70THY/MAC2
	1.8±0.2			EIAP	From CF_3OF	70THY/MAC
	2.7±0.2			EIAP	From CF_4	70MAC/THY
	2.5			EIAP	From $(CF_3)_2CO$	70HAR/THY
	<2.6			EIAP	From C_2F_6	69MAC/THY
	2.0			EIAP	From C_3F_8	69LIF/GRA
	3.3			EIAP	From C_2F_6	63BIB/CAR
	2.0±0.2			SI		69PAG/GOO
			1539±8	IMRE[o]		79BAR/SCO
CF_3I^-						
$CF_3I^-\cdot$					$\Delta_f H(A) = -590\pm21$	78KUD/KUD
	1.6±0.2			NBIP		78COM/REI2
	1.4±0.2			NBIP		76TAN/MAT
	2.2±0.2			NBIP		73MCN/LAC
CF_3N^-						
$CF_3N^-\cdot$						
<145±39				EIAP	From CF_3NC	86HEN/ILL
CF_3NO^-						
$CF_3NO^-\cdot$				Est2	$\Delta_f H(A) = -527$	
<−720 [b]	>2.0±0.2			EIAP	From $(CF_3)_2NO$	77HAR
CF_3O^-						
$CF_2=O\cdot\cdot F^-$					$\Delta_f H(AH) = -876\pm21$	79KLO/SEP
					BDE(A−H) = 452±13	68CZA/CAS
* −1062±13 [c]	4.35±0.48 [d]	178±8 [g]	142±8	IMRE		83LAR/MCM
−1030±17 [c]		146±13		IMRE		78MCM/NOR
−937±25				IMRB		76KAR/KLE
	>1.9±0.2			EIAP	From CF_3OOCF_3	72MAC/THY
	1.9±0.1			EIAP	From CF_3OF	70THY/MAC
	1.3			SI		69PAG/GOO

Table 2. Negative Ion Table - Continued

Ion $\Delta_f H(X\cdot\cdot Y^-)$	$\Delta_f H(A^-)$ EA(A) eV	$\Delta H_{acid}(AH)$ $\Delta H_{aff}(X\cdot\cdot Y^-)$	$\Delta G_{acid}(AH)$ $\Delta G_{aff}(X\cdot\cdot Y^-)$	Method	Comment	Reference
$CF_3O_3S^-$						
$CF_3SO_3^-$						
	4.9±0.3			IMRB		86VIG
					$\Delta_{acid}G$: CF_3SO_3H < FSO_3H < H_2SO_4 < HPO_3 < HI, $\Delta_{acid}G(CF_3SO_3H)$ < 1312 kJ	
		<1312±8		EIAP	From CF_3SO_3H,anhydride	86ADA/SMI
CF_3S^-						
CF_3S^-						
	1.8			SI		69PAG/GOO
$CFeO^-$						
$Fe(CO)^-$						
*	1.260±0.022			LPES		79ENG/LIN2
68±25				EIAP	From $Fe(CO)_5$	76COM/STO
CI^-						
CI^-					$\Delta_f H(A)$ = 552	76REF/FRA2
<363 [b]	>2.0			Endo	$I^- + CO \rightarrow$	77VOG/MIS
222±21	3.4±0.2 [i]			Endo	$I^- + CO \rightarrow$	76REF/FRA2
CIO^-						
ICO^-						
−412	3.1			Endo	$I^- + COS \rightarrow$	76REF
CIO_2^-						
$CO_2\cdot\cdot I^-$						
* −605±1 [c]		23	2	TDAs		80KEE/LEE
CN^-						
CN^-					$\Delta_f H(AH)$ = 135	82TN270
					BDE(A−H) = 518±8	82MCM/GOL
* 74±9 [a]	3.74±0.17 [d]	1469±8 [g]	1438±8	IMRE		79BAR/SCO
*	3.82±0.02	1461±10 [e]		PI		69BER/CHU
74				Endo	$I^- + (CN)_2 \rightarrow$	77REF/FRA
−105±19	3.2±0.1 [i]			EIAP	From CH_3CN	71DEC/BAF
	3.2			SI		74CHA/PAG
	2.8			SI		72PAG
	2.80±0.02			SI	New DH(H−CN) used	63NAP/PAG
			1447±8	IMRE[o]		79BAR/SCO
CNO^-						
CNO^-						
142				EIAP	From $MeNO_2$	72DID/FRA
190±13				EIAP	From $MeNO_2$	69TSU/YOK2
CNO^-						
NCO^-					$\Delta_f H(AH)$ = −105±12	86SPI/PER
					BDE(A−H) = 477±26	70OKA
* −192±21 [a]	3.59±0.36 [d]	1443±9 [g]	1415±8	IMRE		80WIG/BEA
	>2.6±0.4			EIAP	From PF_2NCO	72THY

Table 2. Negative Ion Table - Continued

Ion $\Delta_f H(X \cdot \cdot Y^-)$	$\Delta_f H(A^-)$ EA(A) eV	$\Delta H_{acid}(AH)$ $\Delta H_{aff}(X \cdot \cdot Y^-)$	$\Delta G_{acid}(AH)$ $\Delta G_{aff}(X \cdot \cdot Y^-)$	Method	Comment	Reference
CNO_4^-						
$CO_2 \cdot \cdot NO_3^-$						
* -740 ± 2 [c]		39	8±1	TDAs		80KEE/LEE
CNS^-						
SCN^-					$\Delta_f H(AH) = 128 \pm 2$	82TN270
					$BDE(A-H) = 464 \pm 6$	63NAP/PAG
		1375±25 [g]	1343±21	IMRB	Acid: HNCS	84BIE/GRA
	2.0			SI		72PAG
	2.15±0.02			SI	From $(SCN)_2$	63NAP/PAG
$CNSe^-$						
$SeCN^-$						
	2.6			SI		69PAG/GOO
CN_2^-						
$CN_2^{-\cdot}$						
< 649				IMRB	$O^- + CH_2N_2$ or $(CN)_2 \rightarrow$	79DAW/NOE
$CN_3O_6^-$						
$(NO_2)_3C^-$					$\Delta_f H(AH) = -2 \pm 2$	77PED/RYL
	3.1			EIAP	From $C(NO_2)_4$	67JAE/HEN
CO^-						
$CO^{-\cdot}$					$\Delta_f H(A) = -110$	82TN270
-243	1.4			EnCT		76REF/FRA2
COS^-						
$COS^{-\cdot}$					$\Delta_f H(A) = -142 \pm 1$	77PED/RYL
-187 ± 20 [b]	0.5±0.2			NBIP		75COM/REI
	> 0.4			ECD		83CHE/WEN
CO_2^-						
$CO_2^{-\cdot}$					$\Delta_f H(A) = -394$	82TN270
						75COM/REI
CO_3^-						
$CO \cdot \cdot O_2^-$						
> -210 [c]		< 57		IMRB	$CO \cdot \cdot O_2^- + O_2 \rightarrow O_4^- + CO$	70ADA/BOH
CO_3^-						
$CO_2 \cdot \cdot O^{-\cdot}$						
-503 ± 6 [c]	3.3±0.2 [i]	218±4		PDis		80HIL/VES
-502				NBAP	From ethylene carbonate	83COM/REI
	> 3.079			LPES		79NOV/ENG
	3.3±0.1			PD		77VES/MAU
-469 ± 12 [c]		183±10		PDis		77VES/MAU
	2.7±0.1			PD		77HON/WOO
	> 2.80	> 190 [k]		IMRE	$O_3^- + CO_2 = CO_3^- + O_2$	77DOT/DAV
		174±10		PDis		76MOS/COS
	1.8±0.2			PD		72BUR
-469 [c]		183		PDis		79SMI/LEE
	3.1±0.2			CIDT		78TIE/WU

Table 2. Negative Ion Table – Continued

Ion $\Delta_f H(A^-)$ $\Delta_f H(X\cdot\cdot Y^-)$	EA(A) eV	$\Delta H_{acid}(AH)$ $\Delta H_{aff}(X\cdot\cdot Y^-)$	$\Delta G_{acid}(AH)$ $\Delta G_{aff}(X\cdot\cdot Y^-)$	Method	Comment	Reference
CO_3^-						
$CO_2\cdot\cdot O^-$						
−455 [c]		169		PDis		78SMI/LEE
−520±23 [c]		234±21 [g]	201±21	IMRE	$O_3^- + CO_2 \rightleftharpoons CO_3^- + O_2$	70ADA/BOH
CO_4^-						
$CO_2\cdot\cdot O_2^-$						
−542±20 [c]		106±19		PDis		77VES/MAU
−515±10				IMRE	$O_4^- + CO_2 \rightleftharpoons CO_4^- + O_2$	70ADA/BOH
−510±9 [c]			51±5	kine		66PAC/PHE2
CO_5S^-						
$CO_2\cdot\cdot SO_3^-$						
−981±17 [c]		27±1	1±1	TDAs		80KEE/LEE
CS^-						
$CS^{-\cdot}$					$\Delta_f H(A) = 268$	79HUB/HER
* 248 [b]	0.205±0.021			LPES		82BUR/FEI
	>1.6±0.3			EIAP	From COS	72THY
CS_2^-						
$CS_2^{-\cdot}$					$\Delta_f H(A) = 117±1$	77PED/RYL
* 68±11 [b]	0.51±0.10			TDEq		87KEB/CHO
	0.53±0.11			IMRE		85GRI/CAL
	0.895±0.200			LPES		86OAK/ELL
	0.6±0.1			ECD		83CHE/WEN
	1.0±0.2			NBIP		75COM/REI
	0.5±0.2			EnCT		73HUG/LIF
	0.9±0.3			IMRB	Between NH_2^-, C^-	61KRA/MUL
CH^-						
$CH^{-\cdot}$					$\Delta_f H(AH) = 390±8$	82TN270
					$BDE(A-H) = 423±18$	79HUB/HER
* 477±27 [a]	1.238±0.008	1616±18 [e]	1588±20 [h]	LPES		75KAS/HER2
	0.74±0.05			PD		70FEL
	2.6±0.3			EIAP	From CH_4, C_2H_2, C_2H_4	70LOC/MOM
633				EIAP	From CH_4	63TRE/NEU
$CHBrN^-$						
$HCN\cdot\cdot Br^-$						
* −145±9 [c]		67±8		Est	Extrapolated from other halide data	84LAR/MCM3
$CHClF_3^-$						
$CHF_3\cdot\cdot Cl^-$						
* −992±12 [c]		70±10 [g]	41±8	IMRE		84LAR/MCM2
$CHClN^-$						
$HCN\cdot\cdot Cl^-$						
* −180±10 [c]		88±8 [g]	58±8	IMRE		84LAR/MCM2

Table 2. Negative Ion Table - Continued

Ion $\Delta_f H(X\cdots Y^-)$	$\Delta_f H(A^-)$ EA(A) eV	$\Delta H_{acid}(AH)$ $\Delta H_{aff}(X\cdots Y^-)$	$\Delta G_{acid}(AH)$ $\Delta G_{aff}(X\cdots Y^-)$	Method	Comment	Reference
$CHCl_2^-$						
$CHCl_2^-$					$\Delta_f H(AH) = -96\pm 1$	77PED/RYL
					BDE(A-H)= 422±5	83WEI/BEN
−59±17 [a]	1.7±0.2 [d]	1567±16 [g]	1535±13	IMRB	Comparable to DMSO	72BOH/LEE
$CHCl_2F_2^-$						
$CHF_2Cl\cdots Cl^-$						
* −783±12 [c]		72±8 [g]	43±8	IMRE		84LAR/MCM2
$CHCl_3^-$						
$CHCl_3^-$					$\Delta_f H(A) = -105\pm 2$	77PED/RYL
−274±7 [b]	1.76±0.05			SI		66GAI/KAY
$CHCl_3F^-$						
$CHFCl_2\cdots Cl^-$						
* −582 [c]		74±8 [g]	45±8	IMRE		84LAR/MCM2
$CHCl_3Si^-$						
$HCSiCl_3^-$						
142±42				EIAP	From $MeSiCl_3$	68JAE/HEN
$CHCl_4^-$						
$CHCl_3\cdots Cl^-$						
* −396±12 [c]		64±8	45±8	TDAs		71YAM/KEB
		76±8 [g]	47±8	IMRE		84LAR/MCM2
−412±6 [c]		80±3	49±4	TDEq		74DOU/DAL
			43	TDEq		82FRE/IKU
CHF^-						
HCF^-					$\Delta_f H(A) = 109\pm 12$	85LIA/KAR
<116				IMRB	$O^- + CH_3F \rightarrow$	76DAW/JEN
$CHFN^-$						
$HCN\cdots F^-$						
* −279±11 [c]		165±8 [g]	138±8	IMRE		83LAR/MCM
CHF_2^-						
HCF_2^-					$\Delta_f H(AH) = -453\pm 1$	78KUD/KUD
					BDE(A-H)= 432±4	83PIC/ROD
−364±28 [a]	1.3±0.3 [d]	1618±28 [g]	1586±25	IMRB		77SUL
CHF_2O^-						
$HCF=O\cdots F^-$						
<−703 [c]		>76		IMRB	$FCO^- + HCFO \rightarrow$	77KAR/KLE
CHF_4^-						
$CF_3H\cdots F^-$						
* −1057±12 [c]		113±8 [g]	82±8	IMRE		83LAR/MCM
CHN^-						
HCN^-					$\Delta_f H(A) = 135$	82TN270
<38 [b]	>1.0			EIAP	From CH_3CN	71TSU/YOK

Table 2. Negative Ion Table - Continued

Ion $\Delta_f H(A^-)$ $\Delta_f H(X\cdot\cdot Y^-)$	EA(A) eV	ΔH_{acid}(AH) ΔH_{aff}(X$\cdot\cdot$Y$^-$)	ΔG_{acid}(AH) ΔG_{aff}(X$\cdot\cdot$Y$^-$)	Method	Comment	Reference
$CHNO_2^-$						
$CHNO_2^-\cdot$						
<59				IMRB	$O^- + CH_3NO_2 \rightarrow$	59HEN/MUC
CHN_2^-					$\Delta_f H(AH) = 230\pm17$	78VOG/WIL
CHN_2^-						
262±38 [a]		1561±22 [g]	1527±17	IMRB	Near MeCN	83DEP/SCH
CHO^-					$\Delta_f H(AH) = -109\pm1$	77PED/RYL
HCO^-					$BDE(A-H) = 364\pm3$	83MOO/SEI
* 8±4 [a]	0.313±0.005	1646±3 [e]	1613±5 [h]	LPES		86MUR/MIL
			1648±19	IMRB		75KAR/KLE
CDO^-						
DCO^-						
	0.301±0.005			LPES		86MUR/MIL
$CHOS^-$					$\Delta_f H(AH) = -182\pm8$	85KAS/DEP
$HCOS^-$						
		1435±13		IMRB		85KAS/DEP
CHO_2^-					$\Delta_f H(AH) = -379$	77PED/RYL
HCO_2^-					$BDE(A-H) = 444\pm8$	
* -464±13 [a]	3.23±0.21 [d]	1444±12 [g]	1415±8	IMRE		78CUM/KEB
		1446±12 [g]	1416±8	IMRE		81FUJ/MCI
CHO_3^-						
$CO_2\cdot\cdot OH^-$						
-897 [c]		367		Endo		84HIE/PAU
CHO_3^-				Est2	$\Delta_f H(AH) = -280\pm42$	
$HC(=O)OO^-$						
-260±46 [a]	<1.1	1551±4 [g]	<1523	IMRB		86BOW/DEP
CH_2^-					$\Delta_f H(AH) = 146\pm1$	81HEN/KNO
CH_2^-					$BDE(A-H) = 462\pm2$	82TN270
* 327±1 [b]	0.652±0.006	1712±2 [e]	1679±3 [h]	LPES	Singlet-triplet splitting of CH_2 = 37.7 kJ	85LEO/MUR
	0.670			LPES		85LEO/MUR
	0.210±0.015			LPES	Hot band problem	81ENG/COR
	0.208±0.031			LPES		76ZIT/ELL
					Hot band problem, singlet-triplet splitting = 81.6 kJ	
	<0.60±0.03			PD		77FEL/RAC
	>0.9±0.4			EIAP	From $CH_2=CH_2$	71THY/MAC
<328±38				EIAP	From ketene	70COL/LOC
<290				EIAP	From CH_4	63TRE/NEU
CD_2^-						
$CD_2^-\cdot$					$\Delta_f H(A) = 390\pm1$	82TN270
*	0.645±0.006			LPES		85LEO/MUR
	1.043±0.010			LPES		81ENG/COR

Table 2. Negative Ion Table - Continued

Ion $\Delta_f H(A^-)$ $\Delta_f H(X \cdot \cdot Y^-)$	EA(A) eV	$\Delta H_{acid}(AH)$ $\Delta H_{aff}(X \cdot \cdot Y^-)$	$\Delta G_{acid}(AH)$ $\Delta G_{aff}(X \cdot \cdot Y^-)$	Method	Comment	Reference
CH_2Br^-					$\Delta_f H(AH) = -38\pm1$	84BIC/MIN
CH_2Br^-					BDE(A-H)= 427±8	82MCM/GOL
* 75±18 [a]	1.0±0.3 [d]	1643±16 [g]	1614±13	IMRB		85ING/NIB2
	1.9			SI		69PAG/GOO
CH_2Cl^-					$\Delta_f H(AH) = -82\pm1$	79KUD/KUD
CH_2Cl^-					BDE(A-H)= 422±8	82MCM/GOL
* 45±16 [a]	0.80±0.24 [d]	1657±15 [g]	1628±13	IMRE		85ING/NIB2
			1641±17	IMRB		85HEN/HIE
$CH_2ClO_2^-$						
$HCO_2H \cdot \cdot Cl^-$						
* −721±10 [c]		115±8	84±8	TDAs		82FRE/IKU
		107±8 [g]	77±8	IMRE		84LAR/MCM2
		156±8	106±8	TDAs		71YAM/KEB
$CH_2Cl_3^-$						
$CH_2Cl_2 \cdot \cdot Cl^-$						
* −389±10 [c]		66±8 [g]	38±8	IMRE		84LAR/MCM2
		65±1	37±3	TDEq		74DOU/DAL
$CH_2FO_2^-$						
$HCO_2H \cdot \cdot F^-$						
* −817±11 [c]		190±8 [g]	159±8	IMRE		83LAR/MCM
CH_2I^-					$\Delta_f H(AH) = 15\pm1$	77PED/RYL
CH_2I^-						
102±25 [a]		1617±24 [g]	1587±20	IMRB		85ING/NIB2
$CH_2IO_2^-$						
$HCO_2H \cdot \cdot I^-$						
* −646±5 [c]		79±4	53±9	TDAs		84CAL/KEB
CH_2N^-					$\Delta_f H(AH) = 135$	78DEF/HEH
$CH_2=N^-$						
230 [a]	0.51±0.07	1625±22 [g]	1594±21	IMRB	EA: between O_2 and cyclooctatetraene	85KAS/DEP
CH_2NO^-				Est2	$\Delta_f H(AH) = 29\pm13$	
$CH_2=NO^-$						
<56		<1557 [f]		EIAP	From $MeNO_2$	72DID/FRA
CH_2NO^-					$\Delta_f H(AH) = -186$	69BEN/CRU
$HN=CHO^-$						
* −210 [a]		1506±11 [g]	1476±8	IMRE		86TAF
CH_2NO^-						
$HOH \cdot \cdot CN^-$						
* −225 [c]		58±8	33±8	TDAs		71PAY/YAM

Table 2. Negative Ion Table - Continued

Ion $\Delta_f H(X \cdot \cdot Y^-)$	$\Delta_f H(A^-)$ EA(A) eV	$\Delta H_{acid}(AH)$ $\Delta H_{aff}(X \cdot \cdot Y^-)$	$\Delta G_{acid}(AH)$ $\Delta G_{aff}(X \cdot \cdot Y^-)$	Method	Comment	Reference
$CH_2NO_2^-$						
$CH_2=NO_2^-$					$\Delta_f H(AH) = -75\pm1$	77PED/RYL
* −114±13 [a]		1491±12 [g]	1463±8	IMRE		79BAR/SCO
		1495±12 [g]	1467±8	IMRE		78CUM/KEB
	<2.36		1467±8	IMRE	EA: < NO_2	78MAC/BOH
84	0.5			EIAP	From CH_3NO_2	69TSU/YOK
			1473±8	IMRE[o]		79BAR/SCO
CH_2NS^-						
$CH_2=NS^-$			1436±15	IMRB		85KAS/DEP
CH_2NS^-						
$H_2S \cdot \cdot CN^-$						
* −29±24 [c]		83±15 [g]	52±10	IMRE		87LAR/MCM
$CH_2O_4^-$						
$HOH \cdot \cdot CO_3^-$						
* −793 [c]		48±4 [g]	28±2	IMRE		74FEH/FER
> −906 [c]		< 161		PDis		78SMI/LEE
	1.9±0.2			PD		72BUR
−792				PDis		76COS/LIN
CH_2S^-						
$CH_2=S^-$					$\Delta_f H(A) = 100\pm13$	76BEN
56±15 [b]	0.465±0.023			LPES		87MOR/ELL
CH_3^-						
CH_3^-					$\Delta_f H(A) = 147\pm5$	82MCM/GOL
* 139±8 [a]	7.8±0.030	1744±7 [e]	1710±7 [h]	LPES		78ELL/ENG
	<0.5			PD		77FEL/RAC
	<0.6 [d]	>1691 [g]	>1657	IMRB		72BOH/LEE
	1.1			SI		72PAG
	1.0			SI		69PAG/GOO
	1.1			SI		68GAI/PAG
$CH_3BF_3O^-$						
$BF_3 \cdot \cdot MeO^-$						
<−1477±13 [c]		>92±8		IMRB	$MeOH \cdot \cdot MeO^- + BF_3 \rightarrow$	73BLA/ISO
CH_3BrCl^-						
$MeBr \cdot \cdot Cl^-$						
−311±4 [c]		46±2	30±5	TDAs		74DOU/ROB
		51±13		IMRB	Anchored: 84LAR/MCM	73RIV/BRE
$CH_3Br_2^-$						
$MeBr \cdot \cdot Br^-$						
−290±4 [c]		38±2	21±3	TDAs		74DOU/ROB

Table 2. Negative Ion Table – Continued

Ion $\Delta_f H(X \cdots Y^-)$	$\Delta_f H(A^-)$ EA(A) eV	$\Delta H_{acid}(AH)$ $\Delta H_{aff}(X \cdots Y^-)$	$\Delta G_{acid}(AH)$ $\Delta G_{aff}(X \cdots Y^-)$	Method	Comment	Reference
CH_3ClF^-						
MeF$\cdots$Cl$^-$						
* −522 [c]		48±8		IMRE		84LAR/MCM2
$CH_3ClF_3Si^-$						
MeSiF$_3\cdots$Cl$^-$						
* −1532 [c]		67±8 [g]	40±8	IMRE		85LAR/MCM
CH_3ClI^-						
MeI$\cdots$Cl$^-$						
−253±3 [c]		41±1	29±5	TDAs		74DOU/ROB
$CH_3ClNO_2^-$						
MeNO$_2\cdots$Cl$^-$						
−371±14 [c]		68±13		IMRB	Anchored: 84LAR/MCM	73RIV/BRE
$CH_3Cl_2^-$						
MeCl$\cdots$Cl$^-$						
* −360±10 [c]		51±8 [g]	26±8	IMRE		84LAR/MCM2
		36±1	17±2	TDAs		74DOU/DAL
$CH_3Cl_2Si^-$					$\Delta_f H(AH)=$ −402±4	77PED/RYL
MeSiCl$_2^-$						
−105±21		1828±25 [f]		EIAP	From MeSiCl$_3$, probably ca. 300 kJ more stable	68JAE/HEN
$CH_3F_4Si^-$						
MeSiF$_3\cdots$F$^-$						
* −1697 [c]		211±8 [g]	180±8	IMRE		85LAR/MCM
		257±21		IMRB		77MUR/BEA3
CH_3I^-					$\Delta_f H(A)=$ 15±1	77PED/RYL
CH$_3$I$^-\cdot$						
−13±20 [b]	0.3±0.2			NBIP	Vertical EA	74MOU/ATE
$CH_3I_2^-$						
MeI$\cdots$I$^-$						
−210±10 [c]		38±8	17±1	TDAs		74DOU/ROB
$CH_3NO_2^-$					$\Delta_f H(A)=$ −75±1	77PED/RYL
CH$_3$NO$_2^-\cdot$						
* −121±11 [b]	0.48±0.10			TDEq		87KEB/CHO
	0.49±0.11			IMRE		85GRI/CAL
	0.45±0.05			ECD		83CHE/WEN
	0.4±0.2			NBIP		78COM/REI2
$CH_3N_2O^-$					$\Delta_f H(AH)=$ −246±2	77PED/RYL
HN=C(NH$_2$)O$^-$						
* −259±15 [a]		1517±13 [g]	1487±10	IMRE		86TAF

Table 2. Negative Ion Table - Continued

Ion $\Delta_f H(X \cdot \cdot Y^-)$	EA(A) eV	ΔH_{acid}(AH) $\Delta H_{aff}(X \cdot \cdot Y^-)$	ΔG_{acid}(AH) $\Delta G_{aff}(X \cdot \cdot Y^-)$	Method	Comment	Reference
CH_3O^-						
MeO$^-$					$\Delta_f H(AH) = -202$	77PED/RYL
					BDE(A–H) = 437±4	82MCM/GOL
* −139±10 [a]	1.62±0.14 [d]	1592±9 [g]	1565±8	IMRE		79BAR/SCO
*	1.570±0.022	1597±6 [e]		LPES		78ENG/ELL
	1.59±0.04			PD		78JAN/ZIM
	<1.59±0.04			PD		75REE/BRA
		1595±2	1569±3	TDEq		86MEO/SIE
	2.6			EIAP	From MeOMe	64TSU/HAM
	0.4			SI		69PAG/GOO
			1559±8	IMRE[o]		79BAR/SCO
CD_3O^-						
CD_3O^-						
	1.552±0.022			LPES		78ENG/ELL
$CH_3O_3^-$						
HOH··HCO$_2^-$						
−773 [c]		67±4	38±7	TDAs		86MEO/SIE2
CH_3S^-						
MeS$^-$					$\Delta_f H(AH) = -23$	77PED/RYL
					BDE(A–H) = 364±9	83SHU/BEN
* −60±13 [a]	1.90±0.22 [d]	1493±12 [g]	1467±8	IMRE		79BAR/SCO
*	1.882±0.022			LPES		78ENG/ELL
	1.861±0.004			LPD		80JAN/REE
	1.861±0.004			LPD		80JAN/BRA
	1.4			SI		69PAG/GOO
			1476±8	IMRE[o]		79BAR/SCO
CD_3S^-						
CD_3S^-						
	1.858±0.006			LPD		80JAN/BRA
CH_4ClO^-						
MeOH··Cl$^-$						
* −488±10 [c]		59±8	41±8	TDAs		71YAM/KEB
		70±8 [g]	41±8	IMRE		84LAR/MCM2
		73±8	43±11	TDAs		86YAM/FUR
			41	TDEq		82FRE/IKU
		59	41	TDAs		73YAM/PAY
CH_4FO^-						
MeOH··F$^-$						
* −574±11 [c]		124±8 [g]	95±8	IMRE		83LAR/MCM
CH_4FS^-						
MeSH··F$^-$						
* −415±11 [c]		143±8 [g]	114±8	IMRE		83LAR/MCM
CH_4IO^-						
MeOH··I$^-$						
* −437±5 [c]		47±4	25±9	TDAs		84CAL/KEB

Table 2. Negative Ion Table - Continued

Ion $\Delta_f H(A^-)$ $\Delta_f H(X \cdot \cdot Y^-)$	EA(A) eV	$\Delta H_{acid}(AH)$ $\Delta H_{aff}(X \cdot \cdot Y^-)$	$\Delta G_{acid}(AH)$ $\Delta G_{aff}(X \cdot \cdot Y^-)$	Method	Comment	Reference
CH_4N^-						
MeNH$^-$					$\Delta_f H(AH) = -23$	77PED/RYL
					BDE(A–H) = 418±10	82MCM/GOL
* 134±5 [a]	0.45±0.16 [d]	1687±5 [g]	1656±3	IMRE		76MAC/HEM
	<1.6			EIAP	From MeNH$_2$	68COL/HUB
$CH_4O_3^-$						
MeOH$\cdot\cdot$O$_2^-$						
* −324±5 [c]		80±4	52±4	TDAs		73YAM/PAY
$CH_5O_2^-$						
HOH$\cdot\cdot$MeO$^-$						
−481 [c]		100±1	71±1	TDAs		86MEO/SIE
C_2^-						
$C_2^{-\cdot}$					$\Delta_f H(AH) = 565±4$	82MCM/GOL
					BDE(A–H) = 485±5	79HUB/HER
* 505±2 [b]	3.391±0.017	1470±7 [e]		LPD		80JON/MEA
	3.54±0.05			PD		70FEL
>596±18 [a]		>1561±13 [g]	>1531±8	IMRB		75SCH/BOH
	>2.9±0.5			EIAP	From C_2H_4	71THY/MAC
	3.3±0.2			EIAP	From C_2H_2, C_2H_4	70LOC/MOM
<826±19				EIAP	From ketene	70COL/LOC
	>2.9			EIAP	From C_2H_4	63TRE/NEU
	4.0			EIAP	From graphite	54HON
$C_2ClF_4O^-$						
CF$_3$CF=O$\cdot\cdot$Cl$^-$						
* −1339±30 [c]		70±8 [g]	42±8	IMRE		85LAR/MCM
$C_2Cl_2F_3O^-$						
CF$_3$CCl=O$\cdot\cdot$Cl$^-$						
* −1143±30 [c]		74±8 [g]	47±8	IMRE		85LAR/MCM
$C_2Cl_5^-$						
$C_2Cl_5^-$						
	1.5			SI	Correct value probably 1 eV larger	66GAI/KAY
$C_2Cl_6^-$						
$C_2Cl_6^{-\cdot}$					$\Delta_f H(A) = -150±5$	83KOL/PAP
	1.48±0.10			SI		66GAI/KAY
C_2F^-						
FC≡C$^-$					$\Delta_f H(AH) = 109$	80STA/VOG
					BDE(A–H) = 552±21	
	>3.4±0.8	<1536±98 [e]	<1504±100 [h]	EIAP	From $CH_2=CF_2$	71THY/MAC
$C_2F_2^-$						
F$_2$C=C$^{-\cdot}$						
<15				IMRB	O$^-$ + CH$_2$=CF$_2$ →	76DAW/JEN
−646±58	1.7±0.2			EIAP	From CF$_3$CHO	75HAR/THY

Table 2. Negative Ion Table – Continued

Ion $\Delta_f H(A^-)$ $\Delta_f H(X\cdot\cdot Y^-)$	EA(A) eV	$\Delta H_{acid}(AH)$ $\Delta H_{aff}(X\cdot\cdot Y^-)$	$\Delta G_{acid}(AH)$ $\Delta G_{aff}(X\cdot\cdot Y^-)$	Method	Comment	Reference
$C_2F_2O^-$						
$F_2C=C=O^{-\cdot}$						
-156 ± 58	2.4 ± 0.6			EIAP	From CF_3CHO	75HAR/THY
$C_2F_3^-$					$\Delta_f H(AH)= -490\pm8$	77PED/RYL
$C_2F_3^-$					$BDE(A-H)= 516\pm17$	83SPY/SAU
-391 ± 19	2.1 ± 0.2 [i]	1630 ± 36 [e]		EIAP	From C_3F_8	83SPY/SAU
	>1.6			EIAP	From $CF_3CF=CFCF_3$	79SAU/CHR
-637 ± 58				EIAP	From CF_3CF_2CHO	75HAR/THY
	3.1 ± 0.3			EIAP	From CF_3CHO	75HAR/THY
-420 ± 42	2.0 ± 0.4			EIAP	From C_2F_4	72LIF/GRA
	2.0 ± 0.4			EIAP	From C_2F_4	70THY/MAC2
$C_2F_3O^-$						
CF_3CO^-				Est	$\Delta_f H(AH)= -800\pm13$	
					$BDE(A-H)= 368\pm17$	
$>-707\pm29$ [a]	<0.6	$>1623\pm17$ [e]		EIAP	From $(CF_3)_2CO$	70HAR/THY
$C_2F_3O_2^-$					$\Delta_f H(AH)= -1031\pm1$	77PED/RYL
$CF_3CO_2^-$					$BDE(A-H)= 444\pm8$	
* -1210 ± 18 [a]	4.20 ± 0.27 [d]	1351 ± 17 [g]	1323 ± 8	IMRE		78CUM/KEB
		1351 ± 17 [g]	1324 ± 8	IMRE		86TAF
$C_2F_3O_2^-$						
$FCOCOF\cdot\cdot F^-$						
* -1170 ± 31 [c]		191 ± 8 [g]	155 ± 8	IMRE		85LAR/MCM
$C_2F_4N^-$						
$CF_3CN\cdot\cdot F^-$						
* -871 ± 8 [c]		122 ± 8 [g]	92 ± 8	IMRE		85LAR/MCM
$C_2F_5^-$					$\Delta_f H(AH)= -1105\pm6$	82MCM/GOL
$C_2F_5^-$					$BDE(A-H)= 430\pm2$	82MCM/GOL
* -1067 ± 23 [a]	1.8 ± 0.2 [d]	1567 ± 17 [g]	1535 ± 13	IMRB	Between $tBuO^-$, F^-	76SUL/BEA
	2.2 ± 0.3			EIAP	From $n-C_4F_{10}$	73HAR/THY2
	2.1 ± 0.2			EIAP	From C_3F_8	72HAR/THY
	2.4			EIAP	From C_2F_6	69MAC/THY
	2.3			EIAP	From C_3F_8	69LIF/GRA
	>3.3			EIAP	From C_3F_8	63BIB/CAR
	$>2.2\pm0.3$			SI		69PAG/GOO
			1524 ± 11	IMRB[o]		76SUL/BEA
$C_2F_5O^-$						
$CF_3CF=O\cdot\cdot F^-$						
* -1481 ± 31 [c]		191 ± 8 [g]	156 ± 8	IMRE		85LAR/MCM
$C_2FeO_2^-$						
$Fe(CO)_2^-$						
*	1.220 ± 0.022			LPES		79ENG/LIN2
-256 ± 25				NBAP	From $Fe(CO)_5$	76COM/STO

Table 2. Negative Ion Table - Continued

Ion $\Delta_fH(X\cdots Y^-)$	$\Delta_fH(A^-)$ EA(A) eV	$\Delta H_{acid}(AH)$ $\Delta H_{aff}(X\cdots Y^-)$	$\Delta G_{acid}(AH)$ $\Delta G_{aff}(X\cdots Y^-)$	Method	Comment	Reference
C_2N^-						
C_2N^-						
< 290±19	> 2.3±0.2			EIAP	From CH_3CN	71TSU/YOK
C_2O^-						
$CCO^{-\cdot}$						
* 8±11 [b]	1.848±0.027			LPES		83OAK/JON
< 339				IMRB	O^- + cis-CHF=CHF →	79DAW/NOE
26±19				EIAP	From ketene	70COL/LOC
$C_2O_3^-$						
$C_2O_3^-$						
−554				EIAP	From maleic anhydride	73COO/COM
$C_2O_5^-$						
$CO_2\cdots CO_3^-$						
* −926±7 [c]		30	3±1	TDAs		80KEE/LEE
C_2H^-					$\Delta_fH(AH)=$ 228±1	77PED/RYL
$HC\equiv C^-$					BDE(A−H)= 552±8	85WOD/LEE
* 274±10 [a]	2.99±0.19 [d]	1576±10 [g]	1542±8	IMRE		79BAR/SCO
*	2.940±0.100			LPD	Adiabatic EA: 3.18±0.25 eV	79JAN/BRA
		1585±8	1546±8	TDEq		87MEO
	3.73±0.05			PD		70FEL
		1589±2		TDEq		86MEO/SIE
		1611±4 [g]	1577±3	IMRE		74BOH/MAC
		1572±38		Endo		73HUG/LIF
						72BOH/LEE
	> 2.3±0.7			EIAP	From C_2H_4	71THY/MAC
	2.1±0.3			EIAP	From C_2H_2, C_2H_4	70LOC/MOM
< 515±19				EIAP	From ketene	70COL/LOC
	> 2.8			EIAP	From C_2H_4	63TRE/NEU
	2.6			SI		69PAG/GOO
			1536±8	IMRE[o]		79BAR/SCO
$C_2HClF_5^-$						
$CF_3CF_2H\cdots Cl^-$						
* −1411±16 [c]		79±8 [g]	49±8	IMRE		84LAR/MCM2
$C_2HClF_5O^-$						
$CF_3OCF_2H\cdots Cl^-$						
*			51±8	IMRE		84LAR/MCM
$C_2HCl_2FN^-$						
$CHCl_2F\cdots CN^-$						
* −281 [c]		74±15 [g]	44±10	IMRE		87LAR/MCM
$C_2HCl_2O_2^-$					Est2 $\Delta_fH(AH)=$ −427±17	
$CHCl_2CO_2^-$					BDE(A−H)= 444±8	
* −499±28 [a]	3.96±0.20 [d]	1374±11 [g]	1347±8	IMRE		78CUM/KEB
−587±28 [a]		1369±11 [g]	1342±8	IMRE		81FUJ/MCI

Table 2. Negative Ion Table - Continued

Ion $\Delta_fH(A^-)$ $\Delta_fH(X\cdot\cdot Y^-)$	EA(A) eV	$\Delta H_{acid}(AH)$ $\Delta H_{aff}(X\cdot\cdot Y^-)$	$\Delta G_{acid}(AH)$ $\Delta G_{aff}(X\cdot\cdot Y^-)$	Method	Comment	Reference
$C_2HCl_3N^-$						
$CHCl_3\cdot\cdot CN^-$						
* −106±26 [c]		76±15 [g]	45±10	IMRE		87LAR/MCM
$C_2HCl_3NO^-$				Est	$\Delta_fH(AH) = -235\pm13$	
$HN=C(CCl_3)O^-$						
* −329±23 [a]		1436±11 [g]	1406±8	IMRE		86TAF
C_2HF^-						
$FCH=C^{-\cdot}$						
−139				EIAP	$O^- + FCH=CH_2 \rightarrow$	76DAW/JEN
C_2HFN^-						
$CHFCN^-$						
*		1544±11 [g]	1513±8	IMRE		86TAF
$C_2HF_2O_2^-$				Est2	$\Delta_fH(AH) = -824\pm17$	
$CHF_2CO_2^-$					$BDE(A-H) = 444\pm8$	
* −971±29 [a]	3.85±0.21 [d]	1384±12 [g]	1354±8	IMRE		78CUM/KEB
		1385±12 [g]	1355±8	IMRE		81FUJ/MCI
$C_2HF_3N^-$						
$CHF_3\cdot\cdot CN^-$						
* −692±25 [c]		71±15 [g]	40±10	IMRE		87LAR/MCM
$C_2HF_3NO^-$				Est	$\Delta_fH(AH) = -837\pm13$	
$HN=C(CF_3)O^-$						
* −928±23 [a]		1438±11 [g]	1409±8	IMRE		86TAF
$C_2HF_4^-$						
$F_2C=CFH\cdot\cdot F^-$						
* −849±19 [c]		110±8 [g]	78±8	IMRE		83LAR/MCM
−841±36 [c]		102±25		IMRB		76SUL/BEA
$C_2HF_6^-$						
$C_2F_5H\cdot\cdot F^-$						
* −1480±17 [c]		127±8 [g]	94±8	IMRE		83LAR/MCM
$C_2HF_6O^-$						
$CF_3OCF_2H\cdot\cdot F^-$						
*			113±8	IMRE		84LAR/MCM
C_2HN^-						
$HCCN^{-\cdot}$						
		1569±18 [g]	1539±13	IMRB	Between H_2O_2 and mCl–toluene	87GRA/MEL
	0.8±0.4			EIAP	From CH_3CN	86HEN/ILL2
<422				IMRB	$O^- + CH_3CN \rightarrow$	76DAW/JEN
309±19	>1.1			EIAP	From CH_3CN	71TSU/YOK

Table 2. Negative Ion Table – Continued

Ion $\Delta_f H(X\cdots Y^-)$	$\Delta_f H(A^-)$ EA(A) eV	$\Delta H_{acid}(AH)$ $\Delta H_{aff}(X\cdots Y^-)$	$\Delta G_{acid}(AH)$ $\Delta G_{aff}(X\cdots Y^-)$	Method	Comment	Reference
C_2HNO^-						
$HCCNO^-$						
502				EIAP	From $CH_2=CHNO_2$	72SHI/YAM
$C_2HN_2^-$						
$HCN\cdots CN^-$						
* 119±24 [c]		91±15 [g]	57±10	IMRE		87LAR/MCM
126±18 [c]		84±8		Est		84LAR/MCM3
C_2HO^-					$\Delta_f H(AH)= -48\pm3$	77PED/RYL
$HC\equiv CO^-$				D-EA	$BDE(A-H)= 441\pm9$	
*	2.350±0.022			LPES		83OAK/JON
* −51±13 [a]		1527±11 [g]	1497±8	IMRE	Acid: ketene	83OAK/JON
<−54±19				EIAP	From ketene	70COL/LOC
$C_2H_2^-$						
$H_2C=C^{-\cdot}$						
*	0.470±0.020			LPES		83BUR/STE
255±146				IMRB		78DAW/NIB
255±146				IMRB	$O^- + C_2H_4 \to$, $C_2H_2^- + N_2O \to CH_2CN^-$	76DAW/JEN
	<0.4			IMRB		75LIN/ALB
$C_2D_2^-$						
$D_2C=C^{-\cdot}$						
*	0.490±0.020			LPES		83BUR/STE
$C_2H_2BrO_2^-$				Est	$\Delta_f H(AH)= -395\pm6$	
$BrCH_2CO_2^-$					$BDE(A-H)= 444\pm8$	
* −528±19 [a]	3.71±0.22 [d]	1397±13 [g]	1370±8	IMRE		78CUM/KEB
$C_2H_2ClF_4O^-$						
$(CF_2H)_2O\cdots Cl^-$						
*		71±8		IMRE		84LAR/MCM
$C_2H_2ClO_2^-$					$\Delta_f H(AH)= -435\pm8$	77PED/RYL
$ClCH_2CO_2^-$					$BDE(A-H)= 444\pm8$	
* −558±21 [a]	3.61±0.21 [d]	1407±12 [g]	1376±8	IMRE		78CUM/KEB
		1407±12 [g]	1376±8	IMRE		81FUJ/MCI
$C_2H_2Cl_2N^-$						
$CH_2Cl_2\cdots CN^-$						
* −90±24 [c]		68±15 [g]	38±10	IMRE		87LAR/MCM
$C_2H_2FO^-$					$\Delta_f H(AH)= -444\pm3$	77PED/RYL
$CH_2=CFO^-$					$BDE(A-H)= 406\pm8$	
* −484±20 [a]	2.4±0.3 [d]	148±8 [k]	1460±15	IMRB	Between $MeCOCH_2F$, cyclopentadiene	80FAR/MCM
*	2.22±0.09			PD		77ZIM/REE
		148±8 [g]	115±8	IMRE		83LAR/MCM
			1459±13	IMRB[o]		80FAR/MCM

Table 2. Negative Ion Table – Continued

Ion $\Delta_f H(A^-)$ $\Delta_f H(X\cdot\cdot Y^-)$	EA(A) eV	$\Delta H_{acid}(AH)$ $\Delta H_{aff}(X\cdot\cdot Y^-)$	$\Delta G_{acid}(AH)$ $\Delta G_{aff}(X\cdot\cdot Y^-)$	Method	Comment	Reference
$C_2H_2FO_2^-$						
$FCH_2CO_2^-$				Est2	$\Delta_f H(AH) = -586\pm8$	
* -700 ± 21 [a]	3.52 ± 0.21 [d]	1416 ± 12 [g]	1385 ± 8	IMRE	BDE(A-H) = 444 ± 8	78CUM/KEB
		1418 ± 12 [g]	1386 ± 8	IMRE		81FUJ/MCI
$C_2H_2F_2O_2P^-$						
$C_2H_2F_2O_2P^-$						
<-1125				IMRB	$CH_2=CHO^- + PF_3O \rightarrow$	78SUL/BEA
$C_2H_2F_3^-$						
$CF_2=CH_2\cdot\cdot F^-$						
-697 ± 17		112 ± 21 [k]		IMRB		76SUL/BEA
$C_2H_2F_3O^-$					$\Delta_f H(AH) = -888\pm5$	77PED/RYL
$CF_3CH_2O^-$					BDE(A-H) = 436 ± 4	
* -904 ± 20 [a]	2.42 ± 0.20 [d]	1514 ± 15 [g]	1482 ± 8	IMRE		79BAR/SCO
			1493 ± 8	IMRE[o]		79BAR/SCO
$C_2H_2F_3O_2S^-$						
$CF_3SO_2CH_2^-$						
*		1452 ± 11 [g]	1422 ± 8	IMRE		86TAF
$C_2H_2F_3O_3^-$						
$HOH\cdot\cdot CF_3CO_2^-$						
-1509 [c]		57 ± 4	27 ± 7	TDAs		86MEO/SIE2
$C_2H_2F_5O^-$						
$(CHF_2)_2O\cdot\cdot F^-$						
*		151 ± 8 [g]	117 ± 8	IMRE		83LAR/MCM
$C_2H_2N^-$					$\Delta_f H(AH) = 75\pm1$	83AN/MAN
CH_2CN^-					BDE(A-H) = 389 ± 10	82MCM/GOL
* 105 ± 12 [a]	1.46 ± 0.22 [d]	1560 ± 11 [g]	1528 ± 8	IMRE		79BAR/SCO
*	1.543 ± 0.014			LPES		87MOR/ELL3
		1562 ± 11 [g]	1530 ± 8	IMRE		78CUM/KEB
	1.507 ± 0.018	1556 ± 12 [e]	1523 ± 15 [h]	LPD		77ZIM/BRA
	1.560 ± 0.006			LPD		86MAR/WET
		1534 ± 19		EIAP	From CH_3CN	86HEN/ILL2
20 ± 19	$>1.6\pm0.2$			EIAP	From CH_3CN, EtCN	71TSU/YOK
			1525 ± 8	IMRE[o]		79BAR/SCO
$C_2H_2N^-$					$\Delta_f H(AH) = 173\pm1$	77BAG/COL
CH_2NC^-						
	1.059 ± 0.024			LPES		87MOR/ELL2
$C_2D_2N^-$						
CD_2CN^-						
	1.538 ± 0.012			LPES		87MOR/ELL3

Table 2. Negative Ion Table – Continued

Ion $\Delta_f H(A^-)$ $\Delta_f H(X\cdot\cdot Y^-)$	EA(A) eV	$\Delta H_{acid}(AH)$ $\Delta H_{aff}(X\cdot\cdot Y^-)$	$\Delta G_{acid}(AH)$ $\Delta G_{aff}(X\cdot\cdot Y^-)$	Method	Comment	Reference
$C_2D_2N^-$						
CD_2NC^-	1.070±0.024			LPES		87MOR/ELL2
$C_2H_2NO_2^-$						
$H_2C=C=NO_2^-$		1515±19		EIAP	From $CH_2=CHNO_2$	72SHI/YAM
		<1563±3 [g]	<1531	IMRB		80BAR
$C_2H_2O_2^-$						
$O=CH-CH=O^{-\cdot}$					$\Delta_f H(A) = -212\pm1$	77PED/RYL
−272±25				NBAP	From ethylene carbonate	83COM/REI
$C_2H_3^-$						
$C_2H_3^-$					$\Delta_f H(AH) = 52$	77PED/RYL
					BDE(A−H) = 460±8	82MCM/GOL
* 221±9 [a]	0.8±0.2 [d]	1699		Bran		84DEP/BIE
	>0.4			IMRB		75LIN/ALB
			>1661	IMRB		86FRO/FRE
$C_2H_3BrN^-$						
$MeCN\cdot\cdot Br^-$						
* −192±10 [c]		54±8	33±8	TDAs		72YAM/KEB
$C_2H_3ClF_3^-$						
$CF_2HCH_2F\cdot\cdot Cl^-$						
* −1055±18 [c]		79±8 [g]	59±8	IMRE		84LAR/MCM2
$C_2H_3ClF_3O^-$						
$CF_3CH_2OH\cdot\cdot Cl^-$						
* −1216±15 [c]		100±8 [g]	69±8	IMRE		84LAR/MCM2
$C_2H_3ClN^-$						
$MeCN\cdot\cdot Cl^-$						
* −208±10 [c]		56±8	38±8	TDAs		72YAM/KEB
		57±8	37±11	TDAs		86YAM/FUR
		44±8 [g]	19±8	IMRE		84LAR/MCM2
$C_2H_3Cl_2O_2^-$						
$ClCO_2Me\cdot\cdot Cl^-$						
*		59±8 [g]	33±8	IMRE		85LAR/MCM
$C_2H_3FN^-$						
$MeCN\cdot\cdot F^-$						
* −240±11 [c]		67±8	50±8	TDAs		72YAM/KEB
$C_2H_3F_2^-$						
$CHF=CH_2\cdot\cdot F^-$						
−453±27 [c]		65±17		IMRB		76SUL/BEA

Table 2. Negative Ion Table — Continued

Ion $\Delta_f H(X\cdot\cdot Y^-)$	$\Delta_f H(A^-)$ EA(A) eV	$\Delta H_{acid}(AH)$ $\Delta H_{aff}(X\cdot\cdot Y^-)$	$\Delta G_{acid}(AH)$ $\Delta G_{aff}(X\cdot\cdot Y^-)$	Method	Comment	Reference
$C_2H_3F_2O^-$				Est	$\Delta_f H(AH) = -620\pm4$	
$F_2CHCH_2O^-$					$BDE(A-H) = 436\pm4$	
*	-618 ± 16 [a] 2.23 ± 0.17 [d]	1533 ± 12 [g]	1503 ± 8	IMRE		79BAR/SCO
			1505 ± 8	IMRE[o]		79BAR/SCO
$C_2H_3F_4^-$						
$CF_2HCH_2F\cdot\cdot F^-$						
*	-1108 ± 19 [c]	111 ± 8 [g]	79 ± 8	IMRE		83LAR/MCM
$C_2H_3F_4O^-$						
$CF_3CH_2OH\cdot\cdot F^-$						
*	-1300 ± 16 [c]	164 ± 8 [g]	130 ± 8	IMRE		83LAR/MCM
$C_2H_3IN^-$						
$MeCN\cdot\cdot I^-$						
*	-163 ± 10 [c]	50 ± 8	27 ± 8	TDAs		72YAM/KEB
$C_2H_3NO_2^-$						
$CH_2=CHNO_2^-\cdot$						
	>1.6			IMRB		80BAR
$C_2H_3NO_2^-$						
$MeCN\cdot\cdot O_2^-$						
*	-36 ± 6 [c]	69 ± 4	47 ± 4	TDAs		73YAM/PAY
$C_2H_3O^-$					$\Delta_f H(AH) = -166$	77PED/RYL
$CH_2=CHO^-$				D-EA	$BDE(A-H) = 394\pm15$	
*	-165 ± 13 [a]	1531 ± 12 [g]	1502 ± 8	IMRE		79BAR/SCO
*	1.817 ± 0.023			LPES		82ELL/ENG
		1533 ± 12 [g]	1505 ± 8	IMRE		78CUM/KEB
	1.81 ± 0.06			PD		77ZIM/REE
			1505 ± 8	IMRE[o]		79BAR/SCO
$C_2H_3O^-$					$\Delta_f H(AH) = -166$	77PED/RYL
CH_3CO^-					$BDE(A-H) = 360\pm3$	82MCM/GOL
*	-60 ± 11 [a] 0.4 ± 0.1 [d]	1636 ± 11 [g]	1604 ± 8	IMRB		85DEP/BIE
$C_2D_3O^-$						
$CD_2=CDO^-$						
*	1.817 ± 0.029			LPES		82ELL/ENG
$C_2H_3O_2^-$					$\Delta_f H(AH) = -356\pm1$	77PED/RYL
$HCO_2CH_2^-$						
	-249 ± 20 [a]	1637 ± 19 [g]	1607 ± 17	IMRB		85DEP/GRA
$C_2H_3O_2^-$					$\Delta_f H(AH) = -432$	78CHA/ZWO
$MeCO_2^-$					$BDE(A-H) = 443\pm8$	82MCM/GOL
*	-504 ± 13 [a] 3.07 ± 0.21 [d]	1459 ± 12 [g]	1429 ± 8	IMRE		78CUM/KEB
		1457 ± 12 [g]	1427 ± 8	IMRE		86TAF
		1459 ± 12 [g]	1430 ± 8	IMRE		81FUJ/MCI
	3.36 ± 0.05			ECD		68WEN/CHE
	3.3 ± 0.2			EIAP	From $MeCO_2Et$	64TSU/HAM

Table 2. Negative Ion Table – Continued

Ion $\Delta_f H(A^-)$ $\Delta_f H(X\cdot\cdot Y^-)$	EA(A) eV	$\Delta H_{acid}(AH)$ $\Delta H_{aff}(X\cdot\cdot Y^-)$	$\Delta G_{acid}(AH)$ $\Delta G_{aff}(X\cdot\cdot Y^-)$	Method	Comment	Reference
$C_2H_3O_4^-$ $HCO_2H\cdot\cdot HCO_2^-$ -997 ± 17 [c]		154 ± 4	105 ± 7	TDAs		86MEO/SIE2
$C_2H_3Si^-$ $H_3SiC\equiv C^-$ <322				IMRB	$HC\equiv C^- + SiH_4 \rightarrow$	76PAY/TAN
$C_2H_4B_3^-$ $1,5-C_2B_3H_4^-$		<1795		EIAP	From closo-$1,5-C_2B_3H_5$	73ONA/HOW
$C_2H_4ClF_2^-$ $MeCHF_2\cdot\cdot Cl^-$ * -787 ± 18 [c]		62 ± 8 [g]	34 ± 8	IMRE		84LAR/MCM2
$C_2H_4ClF_3N^-$ $CF_3CH_2NH_2\cdot\cdot Cl^-$ * -1004 ± 14 [c]		75 ± 8 [g]	45 ± 8	IMRE		84LAR/MCM2
$C_2H_4ClO^-$ $MeCHO\cdot\cdot Cl^-$ * -453 ± 10 [c]		60 ± 8 [g]	33 ± 8	IMRE		84LAR/MCM2
$C_2H_4ClO_2^-$ $MeCO_2H\cdot\cdot Cl^-$ * -750 ± 10 [c]		90 ± 8 100 ± 8 [g]	66 ± 8 70 ± 8	TDAs IMRE		71YAM/KEB 84LAR/MCM2
$C_2H_4Cl_2Si^-$ $HCSiMeCl_2^-$ 343 ± 21				EIAP	From Me_2SiCl_2	68JAE/HEN
$C_2H_4F^-$ $CH_2=CH_2\cdot\cdot F^-$ -221 ± 15 [c]		25 ± 13		IMRB	Structure: 85ROY/MCM	76SUL/BEA
$C_2H_4FO^-$ $FCH_2CH_2O^-$ -399 ± 25 [a]	2.1 ± 0.2 [d]	1548 ± 16 [g]	1521 ± 15 1527 ± 14 1520 ± 17	Est IMRB IMRB IMRB[o]	$\Delta_f H(AH) = -417\pm8$ $BDE(A-H) = 436\pm4$ Between HF, acetone	80CLA/MCM 77DAW/JEN 80CLA/MCM
$C_2H_4FO_2^-$ $MeCO_2H\cdot\cdot F^-$ * -865 ± 11 [c]		185 ± 8 [g]	153 ± 8	IMRE		83LAR/MCM
$C_2H_4F_4N^-$ $CF_3CH_2NH_2\cdot\cdot F^-$ * -1067 ± 19 [c]		118 ± 8 [g]	85 ± 8	IMRE		83LAR/MCM

Table 2. Negative Ion Table − Continued

Ion $\Delta_f H(X\cdots Y^-)$	$\Delta_f H(A^-)$ EA(A) eV	$\Delta H_{acid}(AH)$ $\Delta H_{aff}(X\cdots Y^-)$	$\Delta G_{acid}(AH)$ $\Delta G_{aff}(X\cdots Y^-)$	Method	Comment	Reference
$C_2H_4IO_2^-$						
$MeCO_2H\cdots I^-$						
* −691±5 [c]		71±4	44±9	TDAs		84CAL/KEB
$C_2H_4N^-$					$\Delta_f H(AH)=$ 71±8	69BEN/CRU
$CH_2=NCH_2^-$						
151±32 [a]	0.8±0.3	1610±23 [g]	1582±21	IMRB	EA: between cyclooctatetraene, SO_2	85KAS/DEP
$C_2H_4NO^-$					$\Delta_f H(AH)=$ −238±1	77PED/RYL
$HN=C(Me)O^-$						
* −339±12 [a]		1429±11 [g]	1400±8	IMRE		86TAF
$C_2H_4NO^-$					$\Delta_f H(AH)=$ −20±8	69BEN/CRU
$MeCH=NO^-$						
* −20±21 [a]		1530±12 [g]	1500±8	IMRE		79BAR/SCO
			1503±8	IMRE°		79BAR/SCO
$C_2H_4NO^-$				Est2	$\Delta_f H(AH)=$ −787±4	
$MeN=CHO^-$						
* −809±15 [a]		1508±11 [g]	1479±8	IMRE		86TAF
$C_2H_4NO^-$						
$MeOH\cdots CN^-$						
* −196±24 [c]		69±15 [g]	38±10	IMRE		87LAR/MCM
$C_2H_4NO_2^-$					$\Delta_f H(AH)=$ −391±5	77NGA/SAB
$H_2NCH_2CO_2^-$					BDE(A−H)= 444±8	
* −488±15 [a]	3.35±0.19 [d]	1433±10 [g]	1404±8	IMRE		83LOC/MCI
$C_2H_4NO_2^-$				Est	$\Delta_f H(AH)=$ −417±4	
$HN=C(OMe)O^-$						
* −433±15 [a]		1514±11 [g]	1485±8	IMRE		86TAF
$C_2H_4NO_2^-$					$\Delta_f H(AH)=$ −102	77PED/RYL
$MeCH=NO_2^-$						
* −143±13 [a]		1490±12 [g]	1462±8	IMRE		79BAR/SCO
		1496±12 [g]	1469±8	IMRE		78CUM/KEB
			1472±8	IMRE°		79BAR/SCO
$C_2H_5^-$					$\Delta_f H(AH)=$ −84	74SCO
$MeCH_2^-$					BDE(A−H)= 421±2	86BRO/LIG
* 147±9 [a]		1761±8	1725±10 [h]	Bran		84DEP/BIE
	1.0			SI		72PAG
	0.9			SI		69PAG/GOO
$C_2H_5B_4^-$						
$1,2-C_2B_4H_5^-$						
		<1409±29		EIAP	From closo−$1,2-C_2B_4H_6$	73ONA/HOW

Table 2. Negative Ion Table - Continued

Ion $\Delta_f H(A^-)$ $\Delta_f H(X \cdot \cdot Y^-)$	EA(A) eV	$\Delta H_{acid}(AH)$ $\Delta H_{aff}(X \cdot \cdot Y^-)$	$\Delta G_{acid}(AH)$ $\Delta G_{aff}(X \cdot \cdot Y^-)$	Method	Comment	Reference
$C_2H_5B_4^-$						
1,6-$C_2B_4H_5^-$						
		<1891		EIAP	From closo-1,6-$C_2B_4H_6$	73ONA/HOW
$C_2H_5Br_2^-$						
EtBr$\cdot\cdot$Br$^-$						
* −324 [c]		49	25	TDAs		74DOU
$C_2H_5ClFO^-$						
FCH$_2$CH$_2$OH$\cdot\cdot$Cl$^-$						
* −730±18 [c]		86±8 [g]	54±8	IMRE		84LAR/MCM2
$C_2H_5Cl_2^-$						
EtCl$\cdot\cdot$Cl$^-$						
−400±20 [c]		61±19		IMRB	Anchored: 84LAR/MCM	73RIV/BRE
$C_2H_5Cl_2O^-$						
ClCH$_2$CH$_2$OH$\cdot\cdot$Cl$^-$						
* −579±14 [c]		90±8 [g]	59±8	IMRE		84LAR/MCM2
$C_2H_5F_2O^-$						
FCH$_2$CH$_2$OH$\cdot\cdot$F$^-$						
* −811±19 [c]		146±8 [g]	113±8	IMRE		83LAR/MCM
$C_2H_5N^-$						
EtN$^{-\cdot}$						
*	1.9±0.2			PD		74RIC/STE2
$C_2H_5N_2O^-$					Est2 $\Delta_f H(AH) =$ 49±8	
MeN(NO)CH$_2^-$						
* 113±19 [a]		1594±11 [g]	1564±8	IMRE		85ING/NIB3
			1567±8	IMRE^o		85ING/NIB3
$C_2H_5O^-$					$\Delta_f H(AH) =$ −235	77PED/RYL
EtO$^-$					BDE(A-H) = 436±4	82MCM/GOL
* −186±10 [a]	1.75±0.14 [d]	1579±10 [g]	1551±8	IMRE		79BAR/SCO
*	1.726±0.033	1582±8 [e]		LPES		82ELL/ENG
	1.7±0.1			EIAP	From EtONO	68WIL/HAM
	>1.7			EIAP	From EtOH	63TRE/NEU
	0.6			SI		69PAG/GOO
			1546±8	IMRE^o		79BAR/SCO
$C_2H_5O^-$					$\Delta_f H(AH) =$ −184	77PED/RYL
MeOCH$_2^-$					BDE(A-H) = 389±4	82MCM/GOL
* −11±9 [a]		1703±8	1666±12 [h]	Bran		84DEP/BIE
$C_2D_5O^-$						
CD$_3$CD$_2$O$^-$						
*	1.702±0.033			LPES		82ELL/ENG

Table 2. Negative Ion Table – Continued

Ion $\Delta_f H(A^-)$ $\Delta_f H(X \cdots Y^-)$	EA(A) eV	$\Delta H_{acid}(AH)$ $\Delta H_{aff}(X \cdots Y^-)$	$\Delta G_{acid}(AH)$ $\Delta G_{aff}(X \cdots Y^-)$	Method	Comment	Reference
$C_2H_5OS^-$					$\Delta_f H(AH) = -151\pm 1$	77PED/RYL
MeSOCH$_2^-$						
* -119 ± 10 [a]		1563±10 [g]	1533±8	IMRE		79BAR/SCO
		1566±10 [g]	1536±8	IMRE		78CUM/KEB
			1530±8	IMRE[o]		79BAR/SCO
$C_2H_5O_2S^-$					$\Delta_f H(AH) = -373\pm 3$	77PED/RYL
MeSO$_2$CH$_2^-$						
* -373 ± 15 [a]		1531±12 [g]	1499±8	IMRE		79BAR/SCO
-370 ± 15 [a]		1533±12 [g]	1502±8	IMRE		78CUM/KEB
			1502±8	IMRE[o]		79BAR/SCO
$C_2H_5O_3^-$						
HOH$\cdots$MeCO$_2^-$						
* -813 [c]		67±4	39±7	TDAs		86MEO/SIE2
$C_2H_5O_3^-$						
MeOH$\cdots$HCO$_2^-$						
* -740 ± 17 [c]		74±4	44±7	TDAs		86MEO/SIE2
$C_2H_5S^-$					$\Delta_f H(AH) = -46$	77PED/RYL
EtS$^-$					$BDE(A-H) = 364\pm 9$	
* -90 ± 13 [a]	1.97±0.22 [d]	1486±12 [g]	1460±8	IMRE		79BAR/SCO
*	1.953±0.004	1488±9 [e]		LPD		80JAN/REE
	1.6			SI		69PAG/GOO
			1469±8	IMRE[o]		79BAR/SCO
$C_2H_5S^-$					$\Delta_f H(AH) = -38$	77PED/RYL
MeSCH$_2^-$						
* 77±11 [a]		1645±11 [g]	1615±8	IMRE		85ING/NIB
$C_2H_5Si^-$					$\Delta_f H(AH) = 92\pm 8$	86WAL
MeSiCH$_2^-$						
155±32 [a]		1593±23 [g]	1565±21	IMRB		86DAM/DEP2
$C_2H_6BF_2^-$						
Me$_2$BF$\cdots$F$^-$						
-773 [c]		259		IMRB		77MUR/BEA2
				F$^-$A: Et$_3$B > Me$_2$BF > MeSiF$_3$ > Me$_3$B > SF$_4$		
$C_2H_6BF_2O_2^-$						
(MeO)$_2$BF$\cdots$F$^-$						
*		218±21 [g]	190±21	IMRE		85LAR/MCM
$C_2H_6B_5^-$						
2,4-C$_2$B$_5$H$_6^-$						
		<1891		EIAP	From closo-2,4-C$_2$B$_4$H$_7$	73ONA/HOW
$C_2H_6BrOS^-$						
Me$_2$SO$\cdots$Br$^-$						
* -437 ± 6 [c]		72±4	46±9	TDAs		84MAG/CAL

Table 2. Negative Ion Table - Continued

Ion $\Delta_f H(A^-)$ $\Delta_f H(X\cdot\cdot Y^-)$	EA(A) eV	$\Delta H_{acid}(AH)$ $\Delta H_{aff}(X\cdot\cdot Y^-)$	$\Delta G_{acid}(AH)$ $\Delta G_{aff}(X\cdot\cdot Y^-)$	Method	Comment	Reference
$C_2H_6ClO^-$						
EtOH$\cdot\cdot$Cl$^-$						
* -535 ± 10 [c]		72 ± 8 [g]	44 ± 8	IMRE		84LAR/MCM2
$C_2H_6ClOS^-$						
Me$_2$SO$\cdot\cdot$Cl$^-$						
* -457 ± 6 [c]		78 ± 4	52 ± 9	TDAs		84MAG/CAL
$C_2H_6ClSi^-$						
Me$_2$SiCl$^-$						
67 ± 21				EIAP	From Me$_2$SiCl$_2$	68JAE/HEN
$C_2H_6FO^-$						
EtOH$\cdot\cdot$F$^-$						
* -615 ± 11 [c]		132 ± 8 [g]	101 ± 8	IMRE		83LAR/MCM
$C_2H_6F_3Si^-$						
Me$_2$SiF$_2$$\cdot\cdot$F$^-$						
		232 ± 21		IMRB	F$^-$A: SF$_4$ < Me$_2$SiF$_2$ < Me$_3$B	77MUR/BEA3
$C_2H_6IO^-$						
EtOH$\cdot\cdot$I$^-$						
* -474 ± 5 [c]		51 ± 4	27 ± 9	TDAs		84CAL/KEB
$C_2H_6IOS^-$						
Me$_2$SO$\cdot\cdot$I$^-$						
* -405 ± 6 [c]		66 ± 4	38 ± 9	TDAs		84MAG/CAL
$C_2H_6N^-$					$\Delta_f H(AH) = -48\pm1$	77PED/RYL
EtNH$^-$					BDE(A–H) = 423 ± 13	83MCM/GOL
* 93 ± 8 [a]	0.66 ± 0.20 [d]	1671 ± 7 [g]	1639 ± 3	IMRE		76MAC/HEM
$C_2H_6N^-$					$\Delta_f H(AH) = -18$	77PED/RYL
Me$_2$N$^-$					BDE(A–H) = 383 ± 8	82MCM/GOL
* 109 ± 7 [a]	0.39 ± 0.15 [d]	1658 ± 6 [g]	1628 ± 3	IMRE		76MAC/HEM
	1.0			SI		69PAG/GOO
$C_2H_6O_4P^-$				Est2	$\Delta_f H(AH) = -1017\pm63$	
(MeO)$_2$PO$_2^-$						
-1084 ± 149 [a]		1463 ± 86 [g]	1435 ± 84	IMRB		80HOD/SUL
$C_2H_7O_2^-$						
MeOH$\cdot\cdot$MeO$^-$						
-461 ± 11 [c]		120 ± 1	87 ± 2	TDAs		86MEO/SIE
-432 ± 18 [c]		91 ± 8	64 ± 7	TDAs		84CAL/ROZ
					The difference between 84CAL/ROZ and 86MEO/SIE2 has not been resolved.	
C_3^-						
C$_3^-$						
*	1.981 ± 0.020			LPES	From propene discharge	86OAK/ELL
	2.5 ± 1.0			EIAP	From graphite	54HON

Table 2. Negative Ion Table - Continued

Ion $\Delta_fH(X\cdots Y^-)$	EA(A) eV	$\Delta H_{acid}(AH)$ $\Delta H_{aff}(X\cdots Y^-)$	$\Delta G_{acid}(AH)$ $\Delta G_{aff}(X\cdots Y^-)$	Method	Comment	Reference
$C_3ClF_6O^-$						
$(CF_3)_2CO\cdots Cl^-$						
* -1720 ± 30 [c]		96 ± 8 [g]	68 ± 8	IMRE		85LAR/MCM
$C_3F_3^-$						
$C_3F_3^-$						
-425				EIAP	From $CF_2=CF-CF=CF_2$	79SAU/CHR
-941				EIAP	From $CF_3CF=CF_2$	72HAR/THY
$C_3F_3^-$						
$CF_3C\equiv C^-$					$\Delta_fH(AH) = -414\pm13$	86SMA
					$BDE(A-H) = 552\pm21$	
* -458 ± 21 [a]	3.92 ± 0.31 [d]	1486 ± 9 [g]	1454 ± 8	IMRE		86TAF
	<5.6			EIAP	From $CF_3C\equiv CCF_3$	79SAU/CHR
$C_3F_4O^-$						
$CF_3CFCO^{-\cdot}$						
-926 ± 58				EIAP	From CF_3CF_2CHO	75HAR/THY
$C_3F_5^-$						
$C_3F_5^-$						
	2.7 ± 0.2			EIAP	From $c-C_4F_8$	72HAR/THY2
-1052	3.0			EIAP	From $c-C_4F_8, 2-C_4F_8$	79SAU/CHR
	$>2.7\pm0.2$			EIAP	From $CF_3CF=CF_2$	72THY
-950 ± 38	2.6 ± 0.4			EIAP	From $CF_3CF=CF_2$	72LIF/GRA
	2.7 ± 0.1			EIAP	From $CF_3CF=CF_2$	72HAR/THY
$C_3F_5O^-$						
$CF_2=C(CF_3)O^-$				Est	$\Delta_fH(AH) = -1201\pm21$	
* -1318 ± 42 [a]		1413 ± 21 [g]	1384 ± 17	IMRB	Between FCH_2CO_2H, HCl; nearer to HCl	80FAR/MCM
	2.1 ± 0.3			EIAP	From $(CF_3)_2CO$	70HAR/THY
			1356 ± 10	IMRB[o]		80FAR/MCM
$C_3F_6^-$						
$(CF_3)_2C^{-\cdot}$						
* -1181 ± 17 [a]		1527 ± 17 [g]	1498 ± 17	IMRB		84MCD/CHO
	0.6			EIAP	From $(CF_3)_2CO$	70HAR/THY
$C_3F_6N^-$						
$CF_3CF_2CN\cdots F^-$						
*		126 ± 8 [g]	97 ± 8	IMRE		83LAR/MCM
$C_3F_7^-$						
$(CF_3)_2CF^-$						
	$>2.7\pm0.2$			EIAP	From $i-C_5F_{12}$	85SPY/HUN
	$>2.6\pm0.2$			EIAP	From $i-C_4F_{10}$	83SPY/SAU
$C_3F_7^-$						
$C_3F_7^-$					$\Delta_fH(A) = -1337\pm23$	*83EVA/WEE*
	$>3.4\pm0.3$			EIAP	From $neo-C_5F_{12}$	85SPY/HUN
	$>2.7\pm0.2$			EIAP	From $i-C_5F_{12}$	85SPY/HUN
	$>2.6\pm0.1$			EIAP	From $i-C_4F_{10}$	85SPY/HUN
	$>2.6\pm0.4$			EIAP	From C_3F_8	83SPY/SAU

Table 2. Negative Ion Table – Continued

Ion $\Delta_f H(A^-)$ $\Delta_f H(X \cdot \cdot Y^-)$	EA(A) eV	$\Delta H_{acid}(AH)$ $\Delta H_{aff}(X \cdot \cdot Y^-)$	$\Delta G_{acid}(AH)$ $\Delta G_{aff}(X \cdot \cdot Y^-)$	Method	Comment	Reference
$C_3F_7^-$						
$C_3F_7^-$					$\Delta_f H(A) = -1337 \pm 23$	83EVA/WEE
	>2.8±0.1			EIAP	From $n-C_6F_{14}$	83SPY/SAU
	>2.6±0.1			EIAP	From $n-C_5F_{12}$	83SPY/SAU
	>2.5±0.4			EIAP	From $n-C_4F_{10}$	83SPY/SAU
	>2.2±0.2			EIAP	From $n-C_4F_{10}$	73HAR/THY2
−1582±7	>2.3±0.2			EIAP	From C_3F_8	72HAR/THY
	>2.4			EIAP	From C_3F_8	69LIF/GRA
$C_3F_7O^-$						
$(CF_3)_2CO \cdot \cdot F^-$						
* −1854±31 ^{c}		208±8 ^{g}	174±8	IMRE		85LAR/MCM
$C_3F_7O^-$						
$CF_3CF_2CFO \cdot \cdot F^-$						
* −1919±31 ^{c}		197±8 ^{g}	162±8	IMRE		85LAR/MCM
$C_3FeO_3^-$						
$Fe(CO)_3^-$						
*	1.800±0.200			LPES		79ENG/LIN2
<−950				NBAP	From $Fe(CO)_5$	76COM/STO
C_3N^-						
$N \equiv CC \equiv C^-$					$\Delta_f H(AH) = 351$	85HAR
					$BDE(A-H) = 552 \pm 21$	
289 ^{a}	4.11±0.32 ^{d}	1468±10	1438±10	TDEq		87MEO
−365±19				EIAP	From $CH_2=CHCN$	86HEN/ILL2
−512±21				EIAP	From TCNE	72BRI/OLS
	2.4			EIAP	From EtCN	71TSU/YOK
318±29	2.4			EIAP	From $HC \equiv C-C \equiv N$	61DIB/REE
C_3O^-						
$C_3O^{-\cdot}$						
	1.340±0.150			LPES	Large geometry change on detachment	86OAK/ELL
$C_3O_2^-$						
$C_3O_2^-$						
	0.850±0.150			LPES		86OAK/ELL
C_3H^-						
HC_3^-						
	1.858±0.027			LPES	From propene discharge	86OAK/ELL
$C_3HClF_5O^-$						
$CF_3COCF_2H \cdot \cdot Cl^-$						
* −1428 ^{c}			68±8	IMRE		84LAR/MCM
$C_3HCrO_3^-$						
$(CO)_3CrH^-$						
<−287				IMRB		85LAN/SQU

Table 2. Negative Ion Table – Continued

Ion $\Delta_f H(A^-)$ $\Delta_f H(X\cdot\cdot Y^-)$	EA(A) eV	$\Delta H_{acid}(AH)$ $\Delta H_{aff}(X\cdot\cdot Y^-)$	$\Delta G_{acid}(AH)$ $\Delta G_{aff}(X\cdot\cdot Y^-)$	Method	Comment	Reference
$C_3HF_3^-$						
$CF_3CH=C^-$						
−614				EIAP	$O^- + CF_3CH=CH_2 \rightarrow$	76DAW/JEN
$C_3HF_4O^-$				Est	$\Delta_f H(AH) = -971\pm17$	
$CF_2=C(CHF_2)O^-$						
* −1071±44 [a]		1430±27 [g]	1401±23	IMRB	Between HCO_2H, FCH_2CO_2H	80FAR/MCM
			1400±25	IMRB[o]		80FAR/MCM
$C_3HF_5NO^-$						
$CF_3OCF_2H\cdot\cdot CN^-$						
*		78±15 [g]	47±10	IMRE		87LAR/MCM
$C_3HF_6^-$					$\Delta_f H(AH) = -1406\pm8$	86KOL/KOZ
$(CF_3)_2CH^-$					BDE(A-H) = 452±33	84MCD/CHO
* −1414±29 [a]	2.5±0.6 [d]	1522±21 [g]	1490±17	IMRB		84MCD/CHO
$C_3HF_6O^-$				Est	$\Delta_f H(AH) = -1536\pm8$	
$(CF_3)_2CHO^-$					BDE(A-H) = 438±4	
* −1623±19 [a]	3.19±0.16 [d]	1443±11 [g]	1415±8	IMRE		86TAF
			1424	IMRB		81KOP/PIK
C_3HN^-						
$C=CHCN^-\cdot$						
<402				IMRB	$O^- + CH_2=CHCN \rightarrow$	76DAW/JEN
C_3HN^-						
$HC\equiv C-CN^-\cdot$					$\Delta_f H(A) = 351$	85HAR
134±19				EIAP	From $CH_2=CHCN$	86HEN/ILL2
$C_3HN_2^-$					$\Delta_f H(AH) = 266\pm2$	77PED/RYL
$HC(CN)_2^-$						
		1405±11 [g]	1373±8	IMRE		81FUJ/MCI
* 141±13 [a]		1406±11 [g]	1373±8	IMRE		78CUM/KEB
$C_3H_2^-$						
$H_2C=C=C^-\cdot$						
	1.794±0.025			LPES	From propene discharge	86OAK/ELL
<191				IMRB	$O^- + $ allene $\rightarrow$	76DAW/JEN
$C_3H_2Cl^-$				Est	$\Delta_f H(AH) = 169\pm13$	
$ClCH_2C\equiv C^-$					BDE(A-H) = 552±21	
* 179±22 [a]		1540±10 [g]	1507±8	IMRE		86TAF
$C_3H_2ClF_4O^-$						
$(CF_2H)_2CO\cdot\cdot Cl^-$						
* −1198 [c]			76±8	IMRE		84LAR/MCM
$C_3H_2F_3O^-$				Est	$\Delta_f H(AH) = -811\pm13$	
$CH_2=C(CF_3)O^-$				D-EA	BDE(A-H) = 398±22	
* −880±22 [a]		1461±10 [g]	1431±8	IMRE		86TAF
*	2.6±0.1			PD		77ZIM/REE

Table 2. Negative Ion Table – Continued

Ion $\Delta_f H(A^-)$ $\Delta_f H(X \cdot \cdot Y^-)$	EA(A) eV	$\Delta H_{acid}(AH)$ $\Delta H_{aff}(X \cdot \cdot Y^-)$	$\Delta G_{acid}(AH)$ $\Delta G_{aff}(X \cdot \cdot Y^-)$	Method	Comment	Reference
$C_3H_2F_3O^-$						
$CH_2=C(CF_3)O^-$				Est	$\Delta_f H(AH) = -811\pm13$	
				D-EA	BDE(A-H) = 398±22	
		1466±15 ^{g}	1436±8	IMRE		78CUM/KEB
$C_3H_2F_3O_2^-$						
$CF_3CH_2CO_2^-$				Est	$\Delta_f H(AH) = -1085\pm8$	
					BDE(A-H) = 444±8	
* −1215±19 ^{a}	3.68±0.20 ^{d}	1401±11 ^{g}	1371±8	IMRE		86TAF
$C_3H_2F_4NO^-$						
$(CF_2H)_2O \cdot \cdot CN^-$						
*		92±15 ^{g}	63±10	IMRE		87LAR/MCM
$C_3H_2F_5O^-$						
$CF_3CF_2CH_2O^-$					$\Delta_f H(AH) = -1310\pm3$	77PED/RYL
					BDE(A-H) = 435±8	
−1354±33 ^{a}	2.7±0.4 ^{d}	1487±30 ^{g}	1459±25	IMRB	Between $(CF_3)_2CHOH$, CF_3CH_2OH	77DAW/JEN
$C_3H_2F_7O^-$						
$(CF_3)_2CHOH \cdot \cdot F^-$						
* −1889±19 ^{c}		105±8 ^{g}	185±8	IMRE		83LAR/MCM
$C_3H_2N^-$						
$CH_2=CCN^-$					$\Delta_f H(AH) = 184\pm2$	82CHU/NGU
* 207±14 ^{a}		1553±12 ^{g}	1528±8	IMRE		80BAR
		1524±19		EIAP	From $CH_2=CHCN$	86HEN/ILL2
			1523±8	IMRE^o		80BAR
$C_3H_2NO^-$						
$CH_2=C(CN)O^-$				Est2	$\Delta_f H(AH) = 22$	
					BDE(A-H) = 406±8	
* −67 ^{a}	2.87±0.20 ^{d}	1441±11 ^{g}	1413±8	IMRE		86TAF
			1432±21	IMRB		68BRA/BLA
$C_3H_2NO_2^-$						
$NCCH_2CO_2^-$				Est2	$\Delta_f H(AH) = -297\pm21$	
					BDE(A-H) = 444±8	
* −445±32 ^{a}	3.87±0.20 ^{d}	1382±11 ^{g}	1354±8	IMRE		86TAF
$C_3H_2N_2^-$						
pyrazolide$^-$						
*		1480±11 ^{g}	1449±8	IMRE		86TAF/ANV
$C_3H_3^-$						
$CH_2=C=CH^-$					$\Delta_f H(AH) = 191\pm1$	77PED/RYL
					BDE(A-H) = 367±8	82MCM/GOL
* 253±12 ^{a}	0.893±0.026	1592±11 ^{e}	1556±13 ^{h}	LPES		83OAK/ELL
	2.3			SI		69PAG/GOO
$C_3H_3^-$						
$MeC \equiv C^-$					$\Delta_f H(AH) = 187\pm2$	77PED/RYL
					BDE(A-H) = 552±21	
* 251±12 ^{a}	2.80±0.32 ^{d}	1595±10 ^{g}	1562±8	IMRE		79BAR/SCO
*	>2.602±0.043			LPES		83OAK/ELL
			1556±8	IMRE^o		79BAR/SCO

Table 2. Negative Ion Table – Continued

Ion $\Delta_f H(A^-)$ $\Delta_f H(X\cdots Y^-)$	EA(A) eV	$\Delta H_{acid}(AH)$ $\Delta H_{aff}(X\cdots Y^-)$	$\Delta G_{acid}(AH)$ $\Delta G_{aff}(X\cdots Y^-)$	Method	Comment	Reference
$C_3H_2D^-$ $CH_2=C=CD^-$ * 258±25 [a]	0.880±0.150	1601±23 [e]		LPES	$\Delta_f H(AH) = 187\pm 2$ $BDE(A-H) = 374\pm 8$	77PED/RYL 83OAK/ELL
$C_3HD_2^-$ $CD_2=C=CH^-$ *	0.907±0.023			LPES		83OAK/ELL
$C_3H_3F_2O^-$ $CF_2=C(Me)O^-$	>1.0±0.3			EIAP	From CF_3COMe	72THY
$C_3H_3F_2O^-$ $CHF=C(CH_2F)O^-$ * −625±36 [a]		1466±15 [g]	1436±13 1433±10	Est IMRB IMRB[o]	$\Delta_f H(AH) = -561\pm 21$ Between $PhCH_2CN$, CF_3COCH_3	80FAR/MCM 80FAR/MCM
$C_3H_3F_3N^-$ $CF_2HCH_2F\cdots CN^-$ *		77±15 [g]	46±10	IMRE		87LAR/MCM
$C_3H_3F_3NO^-$ $CF_3CH_2OH\cdots CN^-$ * −916±29 [c]		103±15 [g]	69±10	IMRE		87LAR/MCM
$C_3H_3N^-$ $MeCCN^-\cdot$ <401				IMRB	$O^- + EtCN \rightarrow$	76DAW/JEN
$C_3H_3N_2^-$ $CH_2=CHCNN^-$ <−435±21				IMRB	$N_2O + CH_2=CHCH_2^- \rightarrow$	77BIE/DEP
$C_3H_3N_2^-$ $MeCN\cdots CN^-$ * 81±24 [c]		69±15 [g]	38±10	IMRE		87LAR/MCM
$C_3H_3N_2^-$ imidazolide[−] *		1465±11 [g]	1434±8	IMRE		86TAF/ANV
$C_3H_3N_3^-$ sym-triazine[−]· 183 [b]	0.5			ETS	$\Delta_f H(A) = 226\pm 1$	82BYS 75NEN/SCH
$C_3H_4BrO_2^-$ $MeCHBrCO_2^-$ * −556±19 [a]		1407±11 [g]	1377±8	Est2 IMRE	$\Delta_f H(AH) = -432\pm 8$ $BDE(A-H) = 444\pm 8$	85CAL/MCM

Table 2. Negative Ion Table - Continued

Ion $\Delta_f H(A^-)$ EA(A) $\Delta H_{acid}(AH)$ $\Delta_f H(X\cdot\cdot Y^-)$ eV $\Delta H_{aff}(X\cdot\cdot Y^-)$	$\Delta G_{acid}(AH)$ $\Delta G_{aff}(X\cdot\cdot Y^-)$	Method	Comment	Reference
$C_3H_4ClO_2^-$		Est	$\Delta_f H(AH) = -481\pm4$	
ClCH$_2$CH$_2$CO$_2^-$			BDE(A-H) = 444±8	
* −585±20 [a] 3.41±0.25 [d] 1426±16 [g]	1397±8	IMRE		78CUM/KEB
$C_3H_4ClO_2^-$		Est	$\Delta_f H(AH) = -472\pm13$	
MeCHClCO$_2^-$			BDE(A-H) = 444±8	
* −594±22 [a] 3.61±0.19 [d] 1407±10 [g]	1380±8	IMRE		78CUM/KEB
$C_3H_4F^-$				
CH$_2$=CFCH$_2^-$				
* 1586±14 [g]	1559±13	IMRB		84BAR/BUR
1579±10 [g]	1551±8	IMRB		78MCM/NOR
	1558±17	IMRB[o]		84BAR/BUR
63±8 [k]	1546±13	IMRB[o]		78MCM/NOR
$C_3H_4FO^-$		Est	$\Delta_f H(AH) = -383\pm21$	
CH$_2$=C(CH$_2$F)O$^-$			BDE(A-H) = 389±8	
−381±41 [a] 1.8±0.3 [d] 1532±21 [g]	1503±17	IMRB		80CLA/MCM
$C_3H_4FO^-$		Est	$\Delta_f H(AH) = -383\pm21$	
CHF=C(Me)O$^-$				
* −416±39 [a] 1497±18 [g]	1465±15	IMRB	Between pyrrole, MeNO$_2$	80FAR/MCM
	1469±10	IMRB[o]		80FAR/MCM
$C_3H_4F_3O^-$		Est	$\Delta_f H(AH) = -905\pm8$	
CF$_3$CH(Me)O$^-$			BDE(A-H) = 438±4	
* −928±19 [a] 1507±11 [g]	1480±8	IMRE		85CAL/MCM
	1491±8	IMRE[o]		85CAL/MCM
$C_3H_4N^-$			$\Delta_f H(AH) = 51$	82CHU/NGU
MeCHCN$^-$			BDE(A-H) = 377±4	82MCM/GOL
* 90±11 [a] 1.24±0.16 [d] 1569±11 [g]	1537±8	IMRE		79BAR/SCO
	1532±8	IMRE[o]		79BAR/SCO
$C_3H_4NO^-$				
CH$_2$=C(NO)CH$_2^-$				
	1586±21	IMRB		86KAS/FIL
$C_3H_4NO^-$				
CH$_2$=CH−CH=NO$^-$				
	1504±13	IMRB		86KAS/FIL
$C_3H_4NO^-$		Est	$\Delta_f H(AH) = -35\pm8$	
MeOCHCN$^-$				
* −10±23 [a] 1556±15 [g]	1524±8	IMRE		79BAR/SCO
	1522±8	IMRE[o]		79BAR/SCO
$C_3H_4O^-$				
CH$_2$=C(CH$_2$.)O$^-$				
<132		IMRB	O$^-$ + Me$_2$CO →	79DAW/NOE2

Table 2. Negative Ion Table – Continued

Ion $\Delta_fH(A^-)$ $\Delta_fH(X\cdot\cdot Y^-)$	EA(A) eV	$\Delta H_{acid}(AH)$ $\Delta H_{aff}(X\cdot\cdot Y^-)$	$\Delta G_{acid}(AH)$ $\Delta G_{aff}(X\cdot\cdot Y^-)$	Method	Comment	Reference
$C_3H_5^-$					$\Delta_f H(AH) = 20$	77PED/RYL
$CH_2=CHCH_2^-$					BDE(A–H) = 362±6	79ROS/GOL
* 125±10 [a]	0.41±0.17 [d]	1635±10 [g]	1607±8	IMRE		79BAR/SCO
*	0.362±0.020			LPES		84OAK/ELL
	0.551±0.052			LPD		77ZIM/BRA
		1633±4 [g]	1605±2	IMRE		78MAC/LIE
$C_3H_5^-$					$\Delta_f H(AH) = 20$	77PED/RYL
$CH_2=CMe^-$						
>184±3 [a]		>1694±3 [g]	>1661	IMRB		86FRO/FRE
$C_3H_5^-$					$\Delta_f H(AH) = 20$	77PED/RYL
$MeCH=CH^-$						
>184±4 [a]		>1694±4 [g]	>1661	IMRB		86FRO/FRE
$C_3H_5^-$					$\Delta_f H(AH) = 53±1$	77PED/RYL
cyclopropanide$^-$					BDE(A–H) = 445±1	82MCM/GOL
* 247±9 [a]	0.3±0.1 [d]	1724±8	1687±11 [h]	Bran		84DEP/BIE
>213±3 [a]		>1690±3 [g]	>1654	IMRB		72BOH/LEE
			>1654	IMRB		86FRO/FRE
$C_3H_4D^-$						
$CH_2=CDCH_2^-$						
	0.373±0.020			LPES		83OAK/ELL
$C_3D_5^-$						
$CD_2=CDCD_2^-$						
	0.380±0.026			LPES		83OAK/ELL
$C_3H_5ClNO^-$						
$ClCH_2CH_2OH\cdot\cdot CN^-$						
* −275±28 [c]		88±15 [g]	56±10	IMRE		87LAR/MCM
$C_3H_5FNO^-$						
$FCH_2CH_2OH\cdot\cdot CN^-$						
* −428±32 [c]		85±15 [g]	54±10	IMRE		87LAR/MCM
$C_3H_5F_2O^-$				Est	$\Delta_f H(AH) = −620±4$	
$(FCH_2)_2CHO^-$					BDE(A–H) = 436±4	
* −628±25 [a]		1521±21 [g]	1492±17	IMRB	Between MeCHO, PhCOMe	80CLA/MCM
			1498±17	IMRB^o		80CLA/MCM
$C_3H_5F_2O^-$						
c-$CH_2(O)CHCH_2F\cdot\cdot F^-$						
* −610±15 [c]		107±8 [g]	77±8	IMRE		83LAR/MCM
$C_3H_5N_2O_2^-$				Est2	$\Delta_f H(AH) = −441±8$	
$H_2NCON=C(Me)O^-$						
*		1458±12 [g]	1427±8	IMRE	Acid: acetylurea	78CUM/KEB

Table 2. Negative Ion Table - Continued

Ion $\Delta_fH(A^-)$ $\Delta_fH(X\cdot\cdot Y^-)$	EA(A) eV	$\Delta H_{acid}(AH)$ $\Delta H_{aff}(X\cdot\cdot Y^-)$	$\Delta G_{acid}(AH)$ $\Delta G_{aff}(X\cdot\cdot Y^-)$	Method	Comment	Reference
$C_3H_5O^-$					$\Delta_fH(AH)= -217$	76CHA/ZWO
$CH_2=C(Me)O^-$					BDE(A-H)= 411±11	70SOL/GOL
* −203±11 [a]	1.86±0.23 [d]	1544±11 [g]	1514±8	IMRE		79BAR/SCO
*	1.757±0.033			LPES		82ELL/ENG
		1546±11 [g]	1516±8	IMRE		78CUM/KEB
	1.76±0.06			PD		77ZIM/REE
			1513±8	IMRE[o]		79BAR/SCO
$C_3H_5O^-$					$\Delta_fH(AH)= -187±2$	77PED/RYL
$MeCH=CHO^-$				D-EA	BDE(A-H)= 372±12	
* −189±12 [a]		1528±10 [g]	1501±8	IMRE		79BAR/SCO
*	1.611±0.023			LPES		82ELL/ENG
		1531±10 [g]	1504±8	IMRE		78CUM/KEB
	1.69±0.06			PD		77ZIM/REE
			1503±8	IMRE[o]		79BAR/SCO
$C_3H_5O_2^-$					$\Delta_fH(AH)= -410±1$	77PED/RYL
$CH_2=C(OMe)O^-$				D-EA	BDE(A-H)= 418±15	
* −384±10 [a]		1556±10 [g]	1528±8	IMRE		79BAR/SCO
*	1.80±0.06			PD		77ZIM/REE
			1524±8	IMRE[o]		79BAR/SCO
$C_3H_5O_2^-$					$\Delta_fH(AH)= -448±2$	77PED/RYL
$EtCO_2^-$					BDE(A-H)= 445±8	82MCM/GOL
* −525±14 [a]	3.15±0.21 [d]	1454±12 [g]	1424±8	IMRE		78CUM/KEB
$C_3H_5O_3^-$				Est2	$\Delta_fH(AH)= -556±17$	
$MeOCH_2CO_2^-$					BDE(A-H)= 444±8	
* −657±28 [a]	3.38±0.20 [d]	1429±11 [g]	1402±8	IMRE		86TAF
$C_3H_6ClF_2O^-$						
$(FCH_2)_2CHOH\cdot\cdot Cl^-$						
* −946±14 [c]		99±8 [g]	67±8	IMRE		84LAR/MCM2
$C_3H_6ClO^-$						
$Me_2CO\cdot\cdot Cl^-$						
* −504±10 [c]		59±8 [g]	34±8	IMRE		84LAR/MCM2
		57±8	33±8	TDAs		82FRE/IKU
$C_3H_6F_3O^-$						
$(FCH_2)_2CHOH\cdot\cdot F^-$						
* −1026±15 [c]		158±8 [g]	125±8	IMRE		83LAR/MCM
$C_3H_6IO_2^-$						
$EtCO_2H\cdot\cdot I^-$						
* −706±7 [c]		69±4	44±9	TDAs		84CAL/KEB
$C_3H_6NO^-$						
$EtOH\cdot\cdot CN^-$						
* −233±24 [c]		73±15 [g]	42±10	IMRE		87LAR/MCM

Table 2. Negative Ion Table - Continued

Ion $\Delta_f H(A^-)$ $\Delta_f H(X \cdot \cdot Y^-)$	EA(A) eV	$\Delta H_{acid}(AH)$ $\Delta H_{aff}(X \cdot \cdot Y^-)$	$\Delta G_{acid}(AH)$ $\Delta G_{aff}(X \cdot \cdot Y^-)$	Method	Comment	Reference
$C_3H_6NO^-$					$\Delta_f H(AH) = -192\pm2$	77PED/RYL
HCON(Me)CH$_2^-$						
* -52 ± 21 [a]		1670 ± 19 [g]	1640 ± 17	IMRB		85DEP/GRA
$C_3H_6NO^-$					Est2 $\Delta_f H(AH) = -63\pm13$	
Me$_2$C=NO$^-$						
* -61 ± 25 [a]		1532 ± 12 [g]	1502 ± 8	IMRE		79BAR/SCO
			1505 ± 8	IMRE^o		79BAR/SCO
$C_3H_6NO^-$						
Me$_2$CO$\cdot\cdot$CN$^-$						
* -204 ± 24 [c]		62 ± 15 [g]	33 ± 10	IMRE		87LAR/MCM
$C_3H_6NO_2^-$					$\Delta_f H(AH) = -414\pm4$	77NGA/SAB
H$_2$NCH(Me)CO$_2^-$					BDE(A-H) = 444 ± 8	
* -519 ± 14 [a]	3.42±0.19 [d]	1425 ± 10 [g]	1396 ± 8	IMRE		83LOC/MCI
$C_3H_6NO_2^-$					$\Delta_f H(AH) = -446\pm8$	75BER/BOU
HN=C(OEt)O$^-$						
* -462 ± 20 [a]		1514 ± 12 [g]	1485 ± 9	IMRE		86TAF
$C_3H_6NO_2^-$					$\Delta_f H(AH) = -139\pm1$	77PED/RYL
Me$_2$C=NO$_2^-$						
* -179 ± 13 [a]		1490 ± 12 [g]	1464 ± 8	IMRE		79BAR/SCO
		1491 ± 12 [g]	1466 ± 8	IMRE		78CUM/KEB
			1474 ± 8	IMRE^o		79BAR/SCO
$C_3H_6NO_2^-$					$\Delta_f H(AH) = -368\pm1$	77SAB/LAF
MeNHCH$_2$CO$_2^-$					BDE(A-H) = 444 ± 8	
* -469 ± 10 [a]	3.39±0.19 [d]	1429 ± 10 [g]	1400 ± 8	IMRE		83LOC/MCI
$C_3H_6NS^-$						
HCSN(Me)CH$_2^-$						
*		1587 ± 11 [g]	1558 ± 8	IMRE		85ING/NIB3
			1561 ± 8	IMRE^o		85ING/NIB3
$C_3H_7^-$					$\Delta_f H(AH) = -105$	74SCO
Me$_2$CH$^-$					BDE(A-H) = 398 ± 4	82MCM/GOL
* 118 ± 9 [a]		1753 ± 8	1719 ± 10 [h]	Bran		84DEP/BIE
	0.7			SI		69PAG/GOO
$C_3H_7Br_2^-$						
iPrBr$\cdot\cdot$Br$^-$						
		51	26	TDAs		74DOU
$C_3H_7Br_2^-$						
nPrBr$\cdot\cdot$Br$^-$						
		49	24	TDAs		74DOU

Table 2. Negative Ion Table - Continued

Ion $\Delta_f H(A^-)$ $\Delta_f H(X\cdots Y^-)$	EA(A) eV	$\Delta H_{acid}(AH)$ $\Delta H_{aff}(X\cdots Y^-)$	$\Delta G_{acid}(AH)$ $\Delta G_{aff}(X\cdots Y^-)$	Method	Comment	Reference
$C_3H_7ClSi^-$						
HCSiMe$_2$Cl$^-$						
−93±21				EIAP	From Me$_3$SiCl	68JAE/HEN
$C_3H_7N_2O^-$						
HN=C(NMe$_2$)O$^-$				Est2	$\Delta_f H(AH) = -243\pm13$	
* −259±25 [a]		1514±13 [g]	1484±10	IMRE		86TAF
$C_3H_7O^-$					$\Delta_f H(AH) = -273$	77PED/RYL
iPrO$^-$					BDE(A-H) = 438±4	82MCM/GOL
* −232±10 [a]	1.86±0.14 [d]	1571±10 [g]	1543±8	IMRE		79BAR/SCO
*	1.839±0.029			LPES		82ELL/ENG
	1.7±0.1			EIAP	From iPrONO	68WIL/HAM
	>1.7			EIAP	From iPrOH	63TRE/NEU
	0.7			SI		69PAG/GOO
			1538±8	IMRE[o]		79BAR/SCO
$C_3H_7O^-$					$\Delta_f H(AH) = -255\pm1$	77PED/RYL
nPrO$^-$					BDE(A-H) = 433±4	82MCM/GOL
* −212±10 [a]	1.78±0.14 [d]	1573±9 [g]	1546±8	IMRE		79BAR/SCO
*	1.789±0.033			LPES		82ELL/ENG
	1.9±0.1			EIAP	From nPrONO	68WIL/HAM
	>1.8			EIAP	From nPrOH	63TRE/NEU
			1540±8	IMRE[o]		79BAR/SCO
$C_3H_7O_2^-$					$\Delta_f H(AH) = -366\pm4$	
MeOCH$_2$CH$_2$O$^-$				Est	BDE(A-H) = 436±4	
* −332±16 [a]	1.90±0.17 [d]	1564±12 [g]	1535±8	IMRE		79BAR/SCO
			1530±8	IMRE[o]		79BAR/SCO
$C_3H_7S^-$					$\Delta_f H(AH) = -76\pm1$	77PED/RYL
iPrS$^-$					BDE(A-H) = 364±9	
* −128±13 [a]	2.05±0.22 [d]	1479±12 [g]	1452±8	IMRE		79BAR/SCO
*	2.020±0.020			LPD		80JAN/REE
			1461±8	IMRE[o]		79BAR/SCO
$C_3H_7S^-$					$\Delta_f H(AH) = -68$	77PED/RYL
nPrS$^-$					BDE(A-H) = 364±9	
* −116±13 [a]	2.02±0.22 [d]	1482±12 [g]	1456±8	IMRE		79BAR/SCO
*	2.000±0.020			LPD		80JAN/REE
			1465±8	IMRE[o]		79BAR/SCO
$C_3H_7Si^-$					$\Delta_f H(AH) = 21\pm17$	86WAL
CH$_2$=Si(Me)CH$_2^-$						
* 104±41 [a]		1613±25 [g]	1586±21	IMRB		86DAM/DEP
$C_3H_8B^-$					$\Delta_f H(AH) = -123\pm10$	77PED/RYL
Me$_2$BCH$_2^-$					BDE(A-H) = 397±21	71BEL/PLA
−120±39 [a]	1.8±0.5 [d]	1532±29 [g]	1502±25	IMRB	Between AsH$_3$, PH$_3$	76MUR/BEA
			1492±20	IMRB[o]		76MUR/BEA

Ion $\Delta_f H(X \cdot \cdot Y^-)$	EA(A) eV	ΔH_{acid}(AH) $\Delta H_{aff}(X \cdot \cdot Y^-)$	ΔG_{acid}(AH) $\Delta G_{aff}(X \cdot \cdot Y^-)$	Method	Comment	Reference
$C_3H_8ClO^-$ iPrOH$\cdot\cdot$Cl$^-$						
* −574±10 [c]		74±8 [g]	45±8	IMRE		84LAR/MCM2
$C_3H_8ClO^-$ nPrOH$\cdot\cdot$Cl$^-$						
* −556±10 [c]		74±8 [g]	45±8	IMRE		84LAR/MCM2
$C_3H_8FO^-$ iPrOH$\cdot\cdot$F$^-$						
* −657±11 [c]		135±8 [g]	103±8	IMRE		83LAR/MCM
$C_3H_8FO^-$ nPrOH$\cdot\cdot$F$^-$						
* −639±11 [c]		135±8 [g]	103±8	IMRE		83LAR/MCM
$C_3H_8IO^-$ iPrOH$\cdot\cdot$I$^-$						
* −512±5 [c]		51±4	27±9	TDAs		84CAL/KEB
$C_3H_8N^-$ Et(Me)N$^-$				Est	$\Delta_f H(AH) = -46±4$ BDE(A–H) = 383±8	82MCM/GOL
* 77±15 [a]	0.43±0.20 [d]	1653±11 [g]	1621±8	IMRE		85ING/NIB2
$C_3H_8N^-$ Me$_2$NCH$_2^-$					$\Delta_f H(AH) = -24$ BDE(A–H) = 351±8	77PED/RYL 82MCM/GOL
		>1700 [g]	>1665	IMRB		78MAC/BOH2
$C_3H_8N^-$ iPrNH$^-$					$\Delta_f H(AH) = -84±1$ BDE(A–H) = 423±13	77PED/RYL
49±17 [a]	0.8±0.3 [d]	1662±16 [g]	1631±13	IMRB		71BRA/BLA
$C_3H_8N^-$ nPrNH$^-$					$\Delta_f H(AH) = -70$ BDE(A–H) = 423±13	77PED/RYL
67±17 [a]	0.7±0.3 [d]	1667±16 [g]	1636±13	IMRB		71BRA/BLA
$C_3H_8NO^-$ iPrOH$\cdot\cdot$CN$^-$						
* −274±24 [c]		76±15 [g]	45±10	IMRE		87LAR/MCM
$C_3H_8P^-$ Me$_2$PCH$_2^-$					$\Delta_f H(AH) = -101±5$	77PED/RYL
* 5±16 [a]		1636±11 [g]	1606±8	IMRE		85ING/NIB2
$C_3H_9BF^-$ Me$_3$B$\cdot\cdot$F$^-$						
* −569±21 [c]		197±8 [g]	166±8	IMRE		85LAR/MCM
−616 [c]		245		IMRB	F$^-$A: MeSiF$_3$ > Me$_3$B > SF$_4$	77MUR/BEA2

Table 2. Negative Ion Table - Continued

Ion $\Delta_f H(X \cdot \cdot Y^-)$	$\Delta_f H(A^-)$ EA(A) eV	$\Delta H_{acid}(AH)$ $\Delta H_{aff}(X \cdot \cdot Y^-)$	$\Delta G_{acid}(AH)$ $\Delta G_{aff}(X \cdot \cdot Y^-)$	Method	Comment	Reference
$C_3H_9BFO_3^-$						
(MeO)$_3$B$\cdot\cdot$F$^-$						
* −1324±21 [c]		176±17 [g]	142±13	IMRB		85LAR/MCM
$C_3H_9F_2Si^-$						
Me$_3$SiF$\cdot\cdot$F$^-$						
*		160±8 [g]	132±8	IMRE		85LAR/MCM
		< 226±42		IMRB		77MUR/BEA3
$C_3H_9O_2^-$						
EtOH$\cdot\cdot$MeO$^-$						
−459±20 [c]		85±10 [g]	57±8	IMRE		84CAL/ROZ
$C_3H_9Si^-$					$\Delta_f H(AH) = -163\pm8$	81WAL
Me$_3$Si$^-$					BDE(A−H) = 378±17	81WAL
−98±23 [a]	1.0±0.3 [d]	1595±15 [g]	1565±13	IMRB		87THO/BAR
$C_3H_{10}NSi^-$						
Me$_3$SiNH$^-$						
		1585±15 [g]	1552±13	IMRB		87THO/BAR
$C_4CoO_4^-$						
Co(CO)$_4^-$						
			< 1294±8	IMRB		87STE/BEA
$C_4F_4O_3^-$						
tetrafluorosuccinic anhydride$^{-\cdot}$						
	0.5±0.2			NBIP		74COO/COM
$C_4F_5^-$						
$C_4F_5^-$						
−685	2.0			EIAP	From c−C_4F_6	79SAU/CHR
$C_4F_6O^-$						
CF$_3$CF$_2$CFCO$^{-\cdot}$						
−1331±58				EIAP	From CF$_3$CF$_2$CF$_2$CHO	75HAR/THY
$C_4F_7^-$						
$C_4F_7^-$					$\Delta_f H(A) = -1167\pm29$	83SPY/SAU
−1457±73 [b]	3.0±0.5			EIAP	From n−C_6F_{14}	83SPY/SAU
	0.9±0.2			EIAP	From CF$_3$CF=CFCF$_3$	72LIF/GRA
	2.7			SI		69PAG/GOO
$C_4F_8^-$						
$C_4F_8^{-\cdot}$						
	> 0.7±0.4			EIAP	From n−C_5F_{12}	83SPY/SAU
$C_4F_8^-$						
CF$_3$CF=CFCF$_3^{-\cdot}$					$\Delta_f H(A) = -1602$	70BEN/O'N
< −1670 [b]	> 0.7±0.3			EnCT		73LIF/TIE

Table 2. Negative Ion Table - Continued

Ion $\Delta_f H(X \cdot \cdot Y^-)$	$\Delta_f H(A^-)$	EA(A) eV	$\Delta H_{acid}(AH)$ $\Delta H_{aff}(X \cdot \cdot Y^-)$	$\Delta G_{acid}(AH)$ $\Delta G_{aff}(X \cdot \cdot Y^-)$	Method	Comment	Reference
$C_4F_8^-$							
c-$C_4F_8^-$·						$\Delta_f H(A) = -1543 \pm 10$	77PED/RYL
	<-1581±39 [b]	>0.4±0.3			EnCT		73LIF/TIE
$C_4F_8N^-$							
$CF_3CF_2CF_2CN \cdot \cdot F^-$							
*			129±8 [g]	99±8	IMRE		85LAR/MCM
$C_4F_9^-$							
$(CF_3)_2CFCF_2^-$							
		3.5±0.5			EIAP	From i-C_4F_{10}	85SPY/HUN
		3.5±0.5			EIAP	From i-C_4F_{10}	83SPY/SAU
$C_4F_9^-$							
$(CF_3)_3C^-$					Est	$\Delta_f H(A) = -1820$	
		3.4±0.1			EIAP	From $(CF_3)_3CF$	85SPY/HUN
		3.4±0.2			EIAP	From $(CF_3)_3CF$	83SPY/SAU
$C_4F_9^-$							
$C_4F_9^-$							
		>4.0±0.2			EIAP	From n-C_4F_{10}	83SPY/SAU
		>2.9±0.1			EIAP	From n-C_5F_{12}	83SPY/SAU
		3.2±0.3			EIAP	From n-C_4F_{10}	73HAR/THY2
$C_4F_9^-$							
$CF_3CF_2CF(CF_3)^-$							
		>3.2±0.1			EIAP	From i-C_5F_{12}	85SPY/HUN
$C_4F_9O^-$							
$(CF_3)_3CO^-$					Est2	$\Delta_f H(AH) = -2297 \pm 21$	
						BDE(A-H) = 439±8	
*	-2439±33 [a]	3.77±0.21 [d]	1388±12 [g]	1356±8	IMRE		86TAF
	-2442 [a]			1352±21	IMRB		81KOP/PIK
	-2451 [a]			1345±21	IMRB		80CLA/MCM
$C_4FeO_4^-$							
$Fe(CO)_4^-$						$\Delta_f H(A) = -414 \pm 23$	81SMI/LAI
*	-646±52 [b]	2.398±0.300			LPES		79ENG/LIN2
		2.1±0.3			EIAP		76COM/STO
						$Fe(CO)_5 + e^- \rightarrow Fe(CO)_4^- + CO$ "near thermoneutral". BDE from 81SMI/LAI	
C_4O^-							
C_4O^-·							
		2.050±0.150			LPES		86OAK/ELL
$C_4HF_5NO^-$							
$CF_3COCF_2H \cdot \cdot CN^-$							
*	-1234±44 [c]		108±15 [g]	75±10	IMRE		87LAR/MCM
$C_4HF_{10}O^-$							
$(CF_3)_3COH \cdot \cdot F^-$							
*	-2617±31 [c]		71±8 [g]	151±8	IMRE		83LAR/MCM

Table 2. Negative Ion Table - Continued

Ion $\Delta_f H(X \cdot \cdot Y^-)$	$\Delta_f H(A^-)$ EA(A) eV	$\Delta H_{acid}(AH)$ $\Delta H_{aff}(X \cdot \cdot Y^-)$	$\Delta G_{acid}(AH)$ $\Delta G_{aff}(X \cdot \cdot Y^-)$	Method	Comment	Reference
$C_4HFeO_4^-$						
$Fe(CO)_4H^-$			1313±23	IMRB		87STE/BEA
$C_4H_2F_6NO^-$						
$(CF_3)_2CHOH \cdot \cdot CN^-$						
*	−1566±32 [c]	105±15 [g]	70±10	IMRE		87LAR/MCM
$C_4H_2F_7O^-$				Est2	$\Delta_f H(AH) = -1561±21$	
$CF_3CF_2CF_2CH_2O^-$					BDE(A–H) = 435±8	
	−1626±51 [a] 2.9±0.4 [d]	1465±30 [g]	1437±25	IMRB	Between $(CF_3)_2CHOH, CF_3CH_2OH$	77DAW/JEN
$C_4H_2NO_2^-$				Est2	$\Delta_f H(AH) = -287±8$	
maleimidate$^-$						
		1360±19		EIAP	From maleimide	73COO/COM
$C_4H_2N_2^-$						
fumaronitrile$^{-\cdot}$					$\Delta_f H(A) = 339$	82CHU/NGU
*	219 [b] 1.24±0.10			TDEq		87KEB/CHO
	1.25±0.09			TDEq		86CHO/KEB
	0.8±0.1			SI		67FAR/PAG
$C_4H_2O_3^-$						
maleic anhydride$^{-\cdot}$					$\Delta_f H(A) = -397±4$	77PED/RYL
*	−536±14 [b] 1.44±0.10			TDEq		87KEB/CHO
	1.41±0.11			IMRE		85GRI/CAL
	1.38±0.05			IMRE		85FUK/MCI
	1.4±0.2			NBIP		74COM/REI
$C_4H_3F_3NO^-$						
$CH_3COCF_3 \cdot \cdot CN^-$						
*	−822±36 [c]	85±15 [g]	54±10	IMRE		87LAR/MCM
$C_4H_3F_6O^-$				Est	$\Delta_f H(AH) = -1576±4$	
$(CF_3)_2C(Me)O^-$					BDE(A–H) = 440±4	
*	−1648±14 [a]	1457±10 [g]	1425±8	IMRE		85CAL/MCM
			1431±8	IMRE^o		85CAL/MCM
$C_4H_3N_2^-$					$\Delta_f H(AH) = 197±1$	77PED/RYL
pyrimidinide$^-$						
*	272±9 [a]	1606±8	1569±8	TDEq		87MEO
$C_4H_3N_2O_3^-$					$\Delta_f H(AH) = -554±8$	72DOM
barbiturate$^-$						
*	−680±12 [a]	1402±12 [g]	1369±8	IMRE	Acid: barbituric acid	78CUM/KEB
$C_4H_3O^-$						
$CH_2=CHC \equiv CO^-$						
	< 35			IMRB	$CH_2=CHCH_2^- + CF_2=O \rightarrow$	79DAW/NOE

Table 2. Negative Ion Table — Continued

Ion $\Delta_f H(A^-)$ $\Delta_f H(X\cdots Y^-)$	EA(A) eV	$\Delta H_{acid}(AH)$ $\Delta H_{aff}(X\cdots Y^-)$	$\Delta G_{acid}(AH)$ $\Delta G_{aff}(X\cdots Y^-)$	Method	Comment	Reference
$C_4H_3O^-$				Est2	$\Delta_f H(AH) = 67\pm13$	
MeCOC≡C$^-$					BDE(A-H)= 552±21	
* 44±23 [a]		1507±10 [g]	1474±9	IMRE		86TAF
$C_4H_3O_2^-$				Est2	$\Delta_f H(AH) = -142\pm13$	
MeOCOC≡C$^-$					BDE(A-H)= 552±21	
* −171±22 [a]		1501±10 [g]	1469±8	IMRE		86TAF
$C_4H_4F_3^-$				Est	$\Delta_f H(AH) = -649\pm13$	
$CH_2=C(CF_3)CH_2^-$						
* −615±23 [a]		1565±10 [g]	1537±8	IMRE		84BAR/BUR
			1532±8	IMRE^o		84BAR/BUR
$C_4H_4F_3O_2S^-$				Est2	$\Delta_f H(AH) = -929\pm13$	
$CF_3SO_2CH=CHCH_2^-$						
* −1023±23 [a]		1436±11 [g]	1407±8	IMRE		86TAF
$C_4H_4F_7O^-$						
$(CF_3)_2C(Me)OH\cdots F^-$						
* −1933±15 [c]		109±8 [g]	189±8	IMRE		83LAR/MCM
$C_4H_4N^-$					$\Delta_f H(AH) = 130$	80WIL/BAE
$CH_2=C(CN)CH_2^-$						
* 151 [a]		1551±10 [g]	1523±8	IMRE		84BAR/BUR
			1523±8	IMRE^o		84BAR/BUR
$C_4H_4N^-$						
$CH_2=CHCH=C=N^-$						
			<1527±8	IMRB	Acid: $CH_2=CHCH_2CN$	80DAW/NIB
$C_4H_4N^-$					$\Delta_f H(AH) = 184\pm1$	82FUC/HAL
$c-(CH_2)_2CCN^-$						
* 225±13 [a]		1571±12 [g]	1539±8	IMRE	Acid:cyanocyclopropane	79BAR/SCO
			1533±8	IMRE^o		79BAR/SCO
$C_4H_4N^-$					$\Delta_f H(AH) = 108$	77PED/RYL
pyrrolide$^-$				D-EA	BDE(A-H)= 419±25	
* 79±13 [a]		1501±12 [g]	1468±8	IMRE		79BAR/SCO
*	2.4±0.1			PD		75RIC/STE3
83±13 [a]		1505±12 [g]	1472±8	IMRE		78CUM/KEB
			1477±8	IMRE^o		79BAR/SCO
$C_4H_4NO_2^-$					$\Delta_f H(AH) = -360\pm8$	69BEN/CRU
succinimidate$^-$						
* −445±18 [a]		1445±10 [g]	1414±8	IMRE		78CUM/KEB
			1379±19	EIAP		73COO/COM
$C_4H_4NS^-$						
2-(thiofuryl)-NH$^-$						
*		1472±11 [g]	1441±8	IMRE		86TAF

Table 2. Negative Ion Table – Continued

Ion $\Delta_f H(A^-)$ $\Delta_f H(X \cdot \cdot Y^-)$	EA(A) eV	$\Delta H_{acid}(AH)$ $\Delta H_{aff}(X \cdot \cdot Y^-)$	$\Delta G_{acid}(AH)$ $\Delta G_{aff}(X \cdot \cdot Y^-)$	Method	Comment	Reference
$C_4H_4N_2^-$						
pyrazine$^-$·					$\Delta_f H(A) = 196 \pm 1$	77PED/RYL
157 [b]	0.4			ETS		75NEN/SCH
$C_4H_4N_2^-$						
pyridazine$^-$·					$\Delta_f H(A) = 278 \pm 1$	77PED/RYL
254 [b]	0.3			ETS		75NEN/SCH
$C_4H_4N_2^-$						
pyrimidine$^-$·					$\Delta_f H(A) = 197 \pm 1$	77PED/RYL
	0.0			ETS		75NEN/SCH
$C_4H_5ClN^-$						
pyrrole··Cl$^-$						
* -198 ± 10 [c]		79±8 [g]	49±8	IMRE		84LAR/MCM2
			59	TDEq		82FRE/IKU
$C_4H_5FN^-$						
pyrrole··F$^-$						
* -283 ± 11 [c]		143±8 [g]	111±8	IMRE		83LAR/MCM
$C_4H_5N^-$						
EtCCN$^-$·						
<381				IMRB	O$^-$ + nPrCN →	76DAW/JEN
$C_4H_5N_2^-$						
3-Me-pyrazolide$^-$						
*		1485±11 [g]	1452±8	IMRE		86TAF
$C_4H_5N_2^-$						
4-Me-pyrazolide$^-$						
*		1484±11 [g]	1454±8	IMRE		86TAF
$C_4H_5O^-$						
$CH_2=C(CH=CH_2)O^-$					$\Delta_f H(AH) = -138 \pm 8$	79VAJ/HAR
* -148 ± 19 [a]		1520±11 [g]	1492±8	IMRE		86BAR/KIP
			1500±10	IMRE^o		86BAR/KIP
$C_4H_5O^-$						
$CH_2=C(CHO)CH_2^-$						
*		1578±16 [g]	1549±13	IMRB		84BAR/BUR
$C_4H_5O^-$						
$CH_2=CHCH=CHO^-$					$\Delta_f H(AH) = -104 \pm 2$	77PED/RYL
* -149 ± 11 [a]		1484±10 [g]	1456±8	IMRE		86BAR/KIP
			1466±10	IMRE^o		86BAR/KIP
$C_4H_5O^-$						
cyclobutanone enolate$^-$				Est2	$\Delta_f H(AH) = -88 \pm 4$	
*	1.84±0.07			PD		78ZIM/JAC

Table 2. Negative Ion Table – Continued

Ion $\Delta_f H(X\cdots Y^-)$	$\Delta_f H(A^-)$ EA(A) eV	$\Delta H_{acid}(AH)$ $\Delta H_{aff}(X\cdots Y^-)$	$\Delta G_{acid}(AH)$ $\Delta G_{aff}(X\cdots Y^-)$	Method	Comment	Reference
$C_4H_6BrO_2^-$				Est2	$\Delta_f H(AH) = -477\pm13$	
EtCHBrCO$_2^-$					BDE(A–H) = 444±8	
* −600±23 [a]		1407±11 [g]	1378±8	IMRE		85CAL/MCM
$C_4H_6ClO_2^-$				Est	$\Delta_f H(AH) = -501\pm4$	
Cl(CH$_2$)$_3$CO$_2^-$					BDE(A–H) = 444±8	
* −586±20 [a]	3.22±0.25 [d]	1445±16 [g]	1416±8	IMRE		78CUM/KEB
$C_4H_6ClO_2^-$				Est	$\Delta_f H(AH) = -492\pm13$	
EtCHClCO$_2^-$					BDE(A–H) = 444±8	
* −610±22 [a]	3.56±0.19 [d]	1412±10 [g]	1384±8	IMRE		78CUM/KEB
$C_4H_6ClO_2^-$				Est	$\Delta_f H(AH) = -516\pm4$	
MeCHClCH$_2$CO$_2^-$					BDE(A–H) = 444±8	
* −616±20 [a]	3.37±0.25 [d]	1431±16 [g]	1401±8	IMRE		78CUM/KEB
$C_4H_6F_2NO^-$						
(CH$_2$F)$_2$CHOH$\cdots$CN$^-$						
* −654±28 [c]		109±15 [g]	66±10	IMRE		87LAR/MCM
$C_4H_6F_3O^-$				Est	$\Delta_f H(AH) = -905\pm4$	
CF$_3$C(Me)$_2$O$^-$					BDE(A–H) = 440±4	
* −928±14 [a]	2.54±0.14 [d]	1507±10 [g]	1479±8	IMRE		85CAL/MCM
			1490±8	IMRE[o]		85CAL/MCM
$C_4H_6N^-$					$\Delta_f H(AH) = 25\pm1$	77PED/RYL
Me$_2$CCN$^-$					BDE(A–H) = 362±8	82MCM/GOL
* 64±13 [a]	1.08±0.21 [d]	1570±12 [g]	1539±8	IMRE		79BAR/SCO
			1534±8	IMRE[o]		79BAR/SCO
$C_4H_6NO_2^-$					$\Delta_f H(AH) = -430\pm4$	69BEN/CRU
MeCON=C(Me)O$^-$						
* −509±19 [a]		1451±15 [g]	1422±8	IMRE		78CUM/KEB
$C_4H_6NO_3^-$						
HN=C(CO$_2$Et)O$^-$						
*		1472±11 [g]	1442±8	IMRE		86TAF
$C_4H_6O_2^-$						
2,3-butanedione$^{-\cdot}$					$\Delta_f H(A) = -327\pm1$	77PED/RYL
* −394±11 [b]	0.69±0.10			TDEq		87KEB/CHO
	0.70±0.11			IMRE		85GRI/CAL
	1.1			ES		66COM/CHR
$C_4H_7^-$					$\Delta_f H(AH) = -17\pm1$	77PED/RYL
CH$_2$=C(Me)CH$_2^-$					BDE(A–H) = 356±1	77LIA/AUS
* 86±11 [a]	0.36±0.12 [d]	1633±10 [g]	1602±9	IMRE		84BAR/BUR
$C_4H_7O^-$					$\Delta_f H(AH) = -241$	77PED/RYL
CH$_2$=C(Et)O$^-$					BDE(A–H) = 406±8	
* −222±14 [a]	1.75±0.06	1549±14 [e]	1520±18 [h]	PD		77ZIM/REE

Table 2. Negative Ion Table - Continued

Ion $\Delta_f H(A^-)$ $\Delta_f H(X \cdot \cdot Y^-)$	EA(A) eV	$\Delta H_{acid}(AH)$ $\Delta H_{aff}(X \cdot \cdot Y^-)$	$\Delta G_{acid}(AH)$ $\Delta G_{aff}(X \cdot \cdot Y^-)$	Method	Comment	Reference
$C_4H_7O^-$ $CH_2=C(OMe)CH_2^-$ -60 ± 30 [a]		1614±26 [g]	1586±23	Est IMRB	$\Delta_f H(AH) = -144\pm4$	84BAR/BUR
$C_4H_7O^-$ $EtCH=CHO^-$ * -206 ± 19 [a]	1.67±0.05	1532±18 [e]	1504±22 [h]	PD	$\Delta_f H(AH) = -208\pm2$ $BDE(A-H) = 381\pm13$	77PED/RYL 77ZIM/REE
$C_4H_7O^-$ $MeCH=C(Me)O^-$ -231 ± 13 [a] *	1.64±0.19 [d] 1.67±0.05	1540±12 [g]	1512±8	IMRE PD	$\Delta_f H(AH) = -241$ $BDE(A-H) = 386\pm6$	77PED/RYL 82MCM/GOL 78CUM/KEB 77ZIM/REE
$C_4H_7O_2^-$ $iPrCO_2^-$ * -562 ± 15 [a]	3.17±0.24 [d]	1449±11 [g]	1420±8	Est IMRE	$\Delta_f H(AH) = -482\pm4$ $BDE(A-H) = 444\pm13$	86TAF
$C_4H_7O_2^-$ $nPrCO_2^-$ * -553 ± 16 [a]	3.17±0.21 [d]	1450±12 [g]	1420±8	IMRE	$\Delta_f H(AH) = -473\pm4$ $BDE(A-H) = 444\pm8$	82BUT/FRA 78CUM/KEB
$C_4H_7O_4^-$ $MeCO_2H \cdot \cdot MeCO_2^-$ -1059 ± 17 [c]		123±4	85±7	TDAs		86MEO/SIE2
$C_4H_8ClO^-$ $EtCOMe \cdot \cdot Cl^-$ * -530 ± 10 [c]		62±8 [g]	36±8	IMRE		84LAR/MCM2
$C_4H_8IO_2^-$ $iPrCO_2H \cdot \cdot I^-$ * -740 ± 9 [c]		70±4	44±9	TDAs		84CAL/KEB
$C_4H_8NO^-$ $CH_2=C(NMe_2)O^-$ * -196 [a]		1569±21 [g]	1540±8 1535±8	IMRE IMRE[o]	$\Delta_f H(AH) = -234$	78BEA/LEE 79BAR/SCO 79BAR/SCO
$C_4H_8NO^-$ $Me_2C(NO)CH_2^-$ 40±34 [a]		1613±28 [g]	1586±25	IMRB	$\Delta_f H(AH) = -43\pm6$	74CHO/MEN 80NOE/NIB
$C_4H_9^-$ Me_3C^- * 67±9 [a]	0.7 0.6	1732±8	1701±10 [h]	Bran SI SI	$\Delta_f H(AH) = -135$ $BDE(A-H) = 390\pm8$	74SCO 82MCM/GOL 84DEP/BIE 72PAG 69PAG/GOO
$C_4H_9Br_2^-$ $iBuBr \cdot \cdot Br^-$ -374 [c]		54	27	TDAs		74DOU

Table 2. Negative Ion Table - Continued

Ion / $\Delta_f H(X\cdot\cdot Y^-)$	EA(A) eV	$\Delta H_{acid}(AH)$ / $\Delta H_{aff}(X\cdot\cdot Y^-)$	$\Delta G_{acid}(AH)$ / $\Delta G_{aff}(X\cdot\cdot Y^-)$	Method	Comment	Reference
$C_4H_9Br_2^-$ tBuBr··Br$^-$						
−397 [c]		52	28	TDAs		74DOU
$C_4H_9ClF^-$ tBuF··Cl$^-$						
* −614±18 [c]		56±8 [g]	30±8	IMRE		84LAR/MCM2
$C_4H_9Cl_2^-$ tBuCl··Cl$^-$						
* −469±11 [c]		60±8 [g]	33±8	IMRE		84LAR/MCM2
$C_4H_9F_2^-$ tBuF··F$^-$						
* −673±15 [c]		93±8 [g]	64±8	IMRE		83LAR/MCM
$C_4H_9O^-$ iBuO$^-$					$\Delta_f H(AH) = -284\pm2$	77PED/RYL
					BDE(A−H) = 436±6	
* −246±11 [a]	1.87±0.16 [d]	1568±9 [g]	1540±8	IMRE		79BAR/SCO
			1535±8	IMRE^o		79BAR/SCO
$C_4H_9O^-$ nBuO$^-$					$\Delta_f H(AH) = -275$	77PED/RYL
					BDE(A−H) = 431±5	82MCM/GOL
* −234±10 [a]	1.78±0.15 [d]	1571±10 [g]	1543±8	IMRE		79BAR/SCO
		1569±12	1541±13 [h]	CIDC		83BOA/HOU
	1.9±0.1			EIAP	From nBuONO	68WIL/HAM
	0.9			SI		69PAG/GOO
			1537±8	IMRE^o		79BAR/SCO
$C_4H_9O^-$ sBuO$^-$					$\Delta_f H(AH) = -295$	77PED/RYL
					BDE(A−H) = 441±4	82MCM/GOL
* −259±10 [a]	1.95±0.14 [d]	1566±10 [g]	1538±8	IMRE		86TAF
		1565±11	1538±13 [h]	CIDC		83BOA/HOU
			1533±8	IMRE^o		79BAR/SCO
$C_4H_9O^-$ tBuO$^-$					$\Delta_f H(AH) = -313\pm3$	77PED/RYL
					BDE(A−H) = 440±4	82MCM/GOL
* −275±12 [a]	1.91±0.14 [d]	1567±9 [g]	1540±8	IMRE		79BAR/SCO
*	1.912±0.054			LPES		82ELL/ENG
	1.87±0.01			PD		78JAN/ZIM
	<1.87±0.04			PD		75REE/BRA
			1534±8	IMRE^o		79BAR/SCO
$C_4H_9O_3^-$ EtOH··MeCO$_2^-$						
		87±4	50±7	TDAs		86MEO/SIE2
$C_4H_9O_3^-$ HOH··iPrCO$_2^-$						
		66±4	37±7	TDAs		86MEO/SIE2

Table 2. Negative Ion Table – Continued

Ion $\Delta_f H(A^-)$ $\Delta_f H(X\cdot\cdot Y^-)$	EA(A) eV	$\Delta H_{acid}(AH)$ $\Delta H_{aff}(X\cdot\cdot Y^-)$	$\Delta G_{acid}(AH)$ $\Delta G_{aff}(X\cdot\cdot Y^-)$	Method	Comment	Reference
$C_4H_9S^-$ iBuS$^-$					$\Delta_f H(AH) = -97\pm1$ $BDE(A-H) = 364\pm10$	77PED/RYL
* -149 ± 13 [a]	2.06±0.23 [d]	1477±12 [g]	1451±8	IMRE		86TAF
$C_4H_9S^-$ nBuS$^-$					$\Delta_f H(AH) = -88\pm1$ $BDE(A-H) = 364\pm10$	77PED/RYL
* -138 ± 13 [a]	2.04±0.23 [d]	1480±12 [g]	1454±8	IMRE		86TAF
*	2.030±0.020			LPD		80JAN/REE
$C_4H_9S^-$ tBuS$^-$					$\Delta_f H(AH) = -110\pm1$ $BDE(A-H) = 364\pm9$	77PED/RYL
* -165 ± 13 [a]	2.09±0.22 [d]	1475±12 [g]	1449±8	IMRE		79BAR/SCO
*	2.070±0.020			LPD		80JAN/REE
			1458±8	IMRE[o]		79BAR/SCO
$C_4H_{10}BF_2^-$ $Et_2BF\cdot\cdot F^-$						
* -740 ± 44 [c]		243±21 [g]	215±21	IMRE		85LAR/MCM
-765 [c]		268		IMRB	F^-: $iPr_3B > Et_2BF > Et_3B$	77MUR/BEA2
$C_4H_{10}ClO^-$ nBuOH$\cdot\cdot$Cl$^-$						
* -576 ± 10 [c]		74±8 [g]	45±8	IMRE		84LAR/MCM2
$C_4H_{10}ClO^-$ tBuOH$\cdot\cdot$Cl$^-$						
* -599 ± 12 [c]		59±8	46±8	TDAs		71YAM/KEB
		76±8 [g]	46±8	IMRE		84LAR/MCM2
$C_4H_{10}FO^-$ nBuOH$\cdot\cdot$F$^-$						
* -658 ± 11 [c]		135±8 [g]	103±8	IMRE		83LAR/MCM
$C_4H_{10}FO^-$ tBuOH$\cdot\cdot$F$^-$						
* -701 ± 13 [c]		139±8 [g]	107±8	IMRE		83LAR/MCM
$C_4H_{10}IO^-$ tBuOH$\cdot\cdot$I$^-$						
*		51±4	27±9	TDAs		84CAL/KEB
$C_4H_{10}NO^-$ Et_2NO^-				Est	$\Delta_f H(AH) = -36\pm13$ $BDE(A-H) = 291\pm8$	78CAC/LIS
* -15 ± 23 [a]	0.54±0.20 [d]	1551±11 [g]	1523±8	IMRE		83BAR/BAS
			1520±8	IMRE[o]		83BAR/BAS
$C_4H_{11}O_2^-$ EtOH$\cdot\cdot$EtO$^-$						
		115±4	82±7	TDEq		86MEO/SIE2
-507 ± 21 [c]		86±10 [g]	59±7	IMRE		84CAL/ROZ

The difference between 84CAL/ROZ and 86MEO/SIE2 has not been resolved.

Table 2. Negative Ion Table – Continued

Ion $\Delta_f H(X \cdots Y^-)$	$\Delta_f H(A^-)$ eV	EA(A) $\Delta H_{aff}(X \cdots Y^-)$	$\Delta H_{acid}(AH)$ $\Delta G_{aff}(X \cdots Y^-)$	$\Delta G_{acid}(AH)$	Method	Comment	Reference
$C_4H_{11}O_2^-$							
MeOH$\cdots$nPrO$^-$							
	−496±21 [c]		83±10 [g]	55±8	IMRE		84CAL/ROZ
$C_4H_{11}Si^-$							
Me$_3$SiCH$_2^-$						$\Delta_f H(AH) = -233\pm3$	83STE
						BDE(A−H) = 415±8	83STE2
	−102±26 [a]	0.7±0.3 [d]	1661±23 [g]	1635±21	IMRB		84DEP/DAM
$C_4H_{12}FSi^-$							
Me$_4$Si$\cdots$F$^-$							
*	−607±13 [c]		125±8 [g]	99±8	IMRE		85LAR/MCM
$C_5ClFeO_5^-$							
Fe(CO)$_5\cdots$Cl$^-$							
	−1053±16 [c]		58±13 [g]	33±13	IMRB		85LAN/SAL
$C_5CrO_5^-$							
Cr(CO)$_5^-$							
		>2.3			IMRB		85SAL/LAN
$C_5FFeO_5^-$							
Fe(CO)$_5\cdots$F$^-$							
	−1188±13 [c]		171±8 [g]	144±8	IMRE		85LAN/SAL
$C_5F_6O_3^-$							
hexafluoroglutaric anhydride$^{-\cdot}$							
		1.5±0.2			NBIP		74COO/COM
$C_5F_9^-$							
$C_5F_9^-$						$\Delta_f H(A) = -1573\pm29$	83SPY/SAU
	−2017±73 [b]	4.6±0.5			EIAP	From n-C_6F_{14}	83SPY/SAU
		>3.1±0.3			EIAP	From c-$C_4F_6(CF_3)_2$	72THY
		3.1			EIAP	From c-$C_4F_6(CF_3)_2$	70LIF/PEE
$C_5F_9O_2^-$							
FCOCF$_2$CF$_2$CF$_2$CFO$\cdots$F$^-$							
*				192±19	IMRE		84LAR/MCM
$C_5F_{10}^-$							
$C_5F_{10}^{-\cdot}$						$\Delta_f H(A) = -2007\pm21$	83SPY/SAU
	<−2508±64 [b]	5.2±0.5			EIAP	From n-C_5F_{12}	83SPY/SAU
$C_5F_{11}^-$							
(CF$_3$)$_3$CCF$_2^-$							
		4.7±0.3			EIAP	From neo-C_5F_{12}	85SPY/HUN
$C_5F_{11}^-$							
C$_2$F$_5$(CF$_3$)$_2$C$^-$							
		>4.2±0.3			EIAP	From i-C_5F_{12}	85SPY/HUN

Table 2. Negative Ion Table – Continued

Ion $\Delta_f H(A^-)$ $\Delta_f H(X\cdot\cdot Y^-)$	EA(A) eV	$\Delta H_{acid}(AH)$ $\Delta H_{aff}(X\cdot\cdot Y^-)$	$\Delta G_{acid}(AH)$ $\Delta G_{aff}(X\cdot\cdot Y^-)$	Method	Comment	Reference
$C_5F_{11}^-$						
$C_5F_{11}^-$	>4.5±0.2			EIAP	From n-C_5F_{12}	83SPY/SAU
$C_5MnO_5^-$						
$Mn(CO)_5^-$					$\Delta_f H(A) = -740\pm10$	82CON/ZAF
			1309±17	IMRB		87STE/BEA
C_5N^-						
N≡CC≡CC≡C$^-$				Est2	$\Delta_f H(AH) = 577\pm21$ BDE(A–H) = 552±21	
682	2.3	1643±21 ^{e}		EIAP	From HC≡C-(C≡C)$_2$-C≡N	61DIB/REE
$C_5N_3^-$						
$(NC)_2C=CCN^-$	3.8±0.5			EIAP	From tetracyanoethylene	72BRI/OLS
$C_5HFeO_5^-$						
$Fe(CO)_5\cdot\cdot H^-$						
−858 ^{c}		235±13		IMRB		85LAN/SAL
$C_5HFeO_6^-$						
$Fe(CO)_5\cdot\cdot OH^-$						
−1142 ^{c}		237±17 ^{g}	196±17	IMRB		85LAN/SAL
<−1075				IMRB		84LAN/LEE
$C_5H_3F_2^-$						
difluorocyclopentadienide$^-$						
<9				IMRB	$CH_2=CHCH_2^- + C_2F_4 \rightarrow$	79DAW/NOE
$C_5H_4^-$						
cyclopentadienylide$^-\cdot$				D–EA	$\Delta_f H(AH) = 217\pm10$ BDE(A–H) = 466±46	82MCM/GOL
274±27 ^{a}		1587±16 ^{g}	1556±13	IMRB		80MCD/CHO
<243±19				EIAP		72DID/HAR
			1546±13	IMRB^o		80MCD/CHO
$C_5H_4F_3O_2^-$						
$CF_3COCH=C(Me)O^-$					$\Delta_f H(AH) = -1003\pm4$	84ERA/KOL
		1374±17 ^{g}	1347±8	IMRE		81FUJ/MCI
−1130±21 ^{a}		1374±17 ^{g}	1348±8	IMRE		78CUM/KEB
$C_5H_4F_6NO^-$						
$(CF_3)_2C(Me)OH\cdot\cdot CN^-$						
* −1609±28 ^{c}		108±15 ^{g}	74±10	IMRE		87LAR/MCM
$C_5H_4N^-$						
pyridinide$^-$					$\Delta_f H(AH) = 140\pm1$	79KUD/KUD
* 250±3 ^{a}		1640±2	1602±2	TDEq		87MEO
			<1574±8	IMRB	O$^-$ deprotonates	78BRU/FER
	2.41±0.03			SI		76FAI/JOY

Table 2. Negative Ion Table – Continued

Ion $\Delta_fH(A^-)$ $\Delta_fH(X\cdots Y^-)$	EA(A) eV	$\Delta H_{acid}(AH)$ $\Delta H_{aff}(X\cdots Y^-)$	$\Delta G_{acid}(AH)$ $\Delta G_{aff}(X\cdots Y^-)$	Method	Comment	Reference
$C_5H_4O^-$						
$C_5H_4O^{-\cdot}$				Est2	$\Delta_f H(A)= -35\pm35$	
84±21				NBAP		75COO/NAF
			From benzoquinone. Possibly cyclopentadienone$^{-\cdot}$?			
$C_5H_5^-$					$\Delta_f H(AH)= 131\pm4$	77PED/RYL
cyclopentadienide$^-$					BDE(A–H)= 329±8	82MCM/GOL
* 82±16 ^{a}	1.67±0.21 ^{d}	1481±12 ^{g}	1455±8	IMRE		79BAR/SCO
*	1.786±0.020			LPES		77ENG/LIN2
		1485±12 ^{g}	1459±8	IMRE		78CUM/KEB
	1.839±0.030			LPD		73RIC/STE
79±8	<2.2±0.3			EIAP	From cyclopentadiene	72DID/HAR
			1464±8	IMRE^o		79BAR/SCO
$C_5H_5N_2^-$						
pyrrole$\cdots$CN$^-$						
* 101±24 ^{c}		82±15 ^{g}	51±10	IMRE		87LAR/MCM
$C_5H_5N_2O_2^-$						
EtOCOCN$\cdots$CN$^-$						
*		73±15 ^{g}	42±10	IMRE		87LAR/MCM
$C_5H_6Cl^-$						
cyclopentadiene$\cdots$Cl$^-$						
			<10	TDEq		82FRE/IKU
$C_5H_6NO^-$				Est2	$\Delta_f H(AH)= 21\pm13$	
Me$_2$NCOC≡C$^-$					BDE(A–H)= 552±21	
* 8±22 ^{a}		1517±10 ^{g}	1484±8	IMRE		86TAF
$C_5H_7^-$					$\Delta_f H(AH)= 75\pm1$	77PED/RYL
CH$_2$=C(CH=CH$_2$)CH$_2^-$						
159±24 ^{a}		1614±23 ^{g}	1586±21	IMRB	Acid: isoprene	79BAR/MCI
$C_5H_7^-$					$\Delta_f H(AH)= 144\pm4$	79ROG/DAG
nPrC≡C$^-$					BDE(A–H)= 552±21	
* 203±19 ^{a}	2.85±0.37 ^{d}	1589±15 ^{g}	1556±8	IMRE		79BAR/SCO
			1551±8	IMRE^o		79BAR/SCO
$C_5H_7^-$					$\Delta_f H(AH)= 106$	77PED/RYL
pentadienide$^-$					BDE(A–H)= 318±13	82MCM/GOL
* 118±16 ^{a}	0.91±0.03	1542±15 ^{e}	1522±22 ^{h}	PD	Acid: 1,4-pentadiene	78ZIM/GYG
$C_5H_7N_2^-$						
3,5-diMe-pyrazolide$^-$						
*		1481±11 ^{g}	1450±8	IMRE		86TAF
$C_5H_7O^-$					$\Delta_f H(AH)= -194\pm2$	77PED/RYL
cyclopentanone enolate$^-$						
*	1.62±0.06			PD		78ZIM/JAC

Table 2. Negative Ion Table – Continued

Ion $\Delta_fH(A^-)$ $\Delta_fH(X\cdot\cdot Y^-)$	EA(A) eV	$\Delta H_{acid}(AH)$ $\Delta H_{aff}(X\cdot\cdot Y^-)$	$\Delta G_{acid}(AH)$ $\Delta G_{aff}(X\cdot\cdot Y^-)$	Method	Comment	Reference
$C_5H_7O_2^-$					$\Delta_fH(AH)= -384\pm2$	79HAC/PIL
MeCOCH=C(Me)O$^-$						
* -472 ± 11 [a]		1438±10 [g]	1408±8	IMRE		78CUM/KEB
		1438±10 [g]	1409±8	IMRE		86TAF
$C_5H_7O_3^-$				Est2	$\Delta_fH(AH)= -573\pm13$	
MeCO$_2$CH=C(Me)O$^-$					BDE(A-H)= 377±8	
* -638 ± 25 [a]		1466±12 [g]	1436±8	IMRE		78CUM/KEB
$C_5H_8Cl^-$						
CH$_2$=CHCH$_2$CH=CH$_2\cdot\cdot$Cl$^-$						
			15	TDEq		82FRE/IKU
$C_5H_8ClO_2^-$						
MeCOCH$_2$COMe$\cdot\cdot$Cl$^-$						
			56	TDEq		82FRE/IKU
$C_5H_9O^-$				Est	$\Delta_fH(AH)= -244\pm4$	
Me$_2$C(CHO)CH$_2^-$						
-153 ± 25 [a]		1621±21 [g]	1594±17	IMRB		80NOE/NIB
$C_5H_9O^-$					$\Delta_fH(AH)= -262\pm1$	77PED/RYL
Me$_2$C=C(Me)O$^-$					BDE(A-H)= 364±13	
* -257 ± 13 [a]	1.46±0.26 [d]	1535±12 [g]	1508±8	IMRE		78CUM/KEB
$C_5H_9O^-$					$\Delta_fH(AH)= -259\pm1$	77PED/RYL
MeCH=C(Et)O$^-$					BDE(A-H)= 390±17	
* -246 ± 13 [a]	1.65±0.30 [d]	1542±12 [g]	1512±8	IMRE		78CUM/KEB
*	1.68±0.05			PD		77ZIM/REE
$C_5H_9O_2^-$					$\Delta_fH(AH)= -515\pm6$	77PED/RYL
iBuCO$_2^-$					BDE(A-H)= 444±8	
* -596 ± 17 [a]	3.17±0.20 [d]	1449±11 [g]	1420±8	IMRE		86TAF
$C_5H_9O_2^-$					$\Delta_fH(AH)= -490\pm2$	77PED/RYL
nBuCO$_2^-$					BDE(A-H)= 444±8	
* -572 ± 11 [a]	3.2±0.2 [d]	1449±10	1419±12 [h]	CIDC		81MCL/CAM
$C_5H_9O_2^-$				Est	$\Delta_fH(AH)= -512\pm4$	
tBuCO$_2^-$					BDE(A-H)= 444±8	
* -600 ± 15 [a]	3.25±0.20 [d]	1442±11 [g]	1412±8	IMRE		86TAF
$C_5H_{10}ClO^-$						
Et$_2$CO$\cdot\cdot$Cl$^-$						
* -545 ± 10 [c]		59±8 [g]	34±8	IMRE		84LAR/MCM2
$C_5H_{10}ClO^-$						
tBuCHO$\cdot\cdot$Cl$^-$						
* -534 ± 14 [c]		63±8 [g]	35±8	IMRE		84LAR/MCM2

Table 2. Negative Ion Table – Continued

Ion $\Delta_f H(X\cdot\cdot Y^-)$	$\Delta_f H(A^-)$ EA(A) eV	$\Delta H_{acid}(AH)$ $\Delta H_{aff}(X\cdot\cdot Y^-)$	$\Delta G_{acid}(AH)$ $\Delta G_{aff}(X\cdot\cdot Y^-)$	Method	Comment	Reference
$C_5H_{10}FO^-$						
tBuCHO··F$^-$						
*	−596±15 [c]	103±8 [g]	70±8	IMRE		83LAR/MCM
$C_5H_{10}IO_2^-$						
tBuCO$_2$H··I$^-$						
*	−765±9 [c]	64±4	37±9	TDAs		84CAL/KEB
$C_5H_{10}NO^-$						
HN=C(tBu)O$^-$					Est2	$\Delta_f H(AH) = -322\pm13$
*	−354±23 [a]	1499±11 [g]	1469±8	IMRE		86TAF
$C_5H_{10}NO^-$						
tBuCH=NO$^-$					Est	$\Delta_f H(AH) = -135\pm8$
*	−147±23 [a]	1518±14 [g]	1489±10	IMRE		79BAR/SCO
			1497±8	IMRE^o		79BAR/SCO
$C_5H_{10}NO^-$						
tBuOH··CN$^-$						
*	−314±26 [c]	76±15 [g]	45±10	IMRE		87LAR/MCM
$C_5H_{10}NO_2^-$						
tBuCH=NO$_2^-$					Est	$\Delta_f H(AH) = -189\pm4$
*	−233±16 [a]	1486±12 [g]	1458±8	IMRE		79BAR/SCO
			1467±8	IMRE^o		79BAR/SCO
$C_5H_{11}Br_2^-$						
tBuCH$_2$Br··Br$^-$						
	−418 [c]	60	29	TDAs		74DOU
$C_5H_{11}O^-$						
Et$_2$CHO$^-$					$\Delta_f H(AH) = -316\pm1$	77PED/RYL
					BDE(A−H) = 438±4	
*	−286±12 [a] 2.0±0.2 [d]	1559±11	1532±13 [h]	CIDC		83BOA/HOU
		1556±10		CIDC^o		83BOA/HOU
$C_5H_{11}O^-$						
iPrCH(Me)O$^-$					$\Delta_f H(AH) = -316\pm1$	77PED/RYL
					BDE(A−H) = 438±4	
*	−285±13 [a] 2.0±0.2 [d]	1561±11	1533±13 [h]	CIDC		83BOA/HOU
		1556±10		CIDC^o		83BOA/HOU
$C_5H_{11}O^-$						
iPrCH$_2$CH$_2$O$^-$					Est $\Delta_f H(AH) = -306\pm4$	
					BDE(A−H) = 436±4	
*	−274±15 [a] 1.9±0.2 [d]	1563±11	1535±13 [h]	CIDC		83BOA/HOU
		1559±10	1531±12 [h]	CIDC^o		83BOA/HOU
$C_5H_{11}O^-$						
nC$_5$H$_{11}$O$^-$					$\Delta_f H(AH) = -297\pm2$	77PED/RYL
					BDE(A−H) = 436±4	
*	−262±13 [a] 1.9±0.2 [d]	1564±11	1537±13 [h]	CIDC		83BOA/HOU
		1560±10		CIDC^o		83BOA/HOU

Table 2. Negative Ion Table - Continued

Ion $\Delta_f H(A^-)$ $\Delta_f H(X \cdots Y^-)$	EA(A) eV	$\Delta H_{acid}(AH)$ $\Delta H_{aff}(X \cdots Y^-)$	$\Delta G_{acid}(AH)$ $\Delta G_{aff}(X \cdots Y^-)$	Method	Comment	Reference
$C_5H_{11}O^-$ tBuCH$_2$O$^-$				Est	$\Delta_f H(AH) = -318\pm2$ BDE(A-H)= 428$\pm$6	82MCM/GOL
* -290 ± 14 [a]	1.88$\pm$0.19 [d]	1559$\pm$12 [g]	1531$\pm$8	IMRE		79BAR/SCO
*	1.93$\pm$0.05			PD		78JAN/ZIM
	<1.93$\pm$0.06			PD		75REE/BRA
			1528$\pm$8	IMRE[o]		79BAR/SCO
$C_5H_{11}O^-$ tPnO$^-$					$\Delta_f H(AH) = -331\pm1$ BDE(A-H)= 440$\pm$4	77PED/RYL
* -300 ± 13 [a]	2.0$\pm$0.2 [d]	1561$\pm$11	1533$\pm$13 [h]	CIDC		83BOA/HOU
		1556$\pm$10		CIDC[o]		83BOA/HOU
$C_5H_{11}S^-$ nC$_5$H$_{11}$S$^-$					$\Delta_f H(AH) = -110\pm1$ BDE(A-H)= 364$\pm$10	77PED/RYL
* -165 ± 13 [a]	2.090$\pm$0.020	1475 [e]		LPD		80JAN/REE
$C_5H_{11}S^-$ tBuCH$_2$S$^-$					$\Delta_f H(AH) = -129\pm1$ BDE(A-H)= 364$\pm$10	77PED/RYL
* -188 ± 13 [a]	2.13$\pm$0.23 [d]	1472$\pm$12 [g]	1445$\pm$8	IMRE		86TAF
$C_5H_{12}FSi^-$ c-(CH$_2$)$_3$Si(Me)$_2 \cdots$F$^-$ -544 ± 23 [c]		158$\pm$9 [g]	130$\pm$9	IMRE		81SUL/DEP
$C_5H_{13}O_2^-$ EtOH$\cdots$nPrO$^-$ -531 ± 21 [c]		85$\pm$10 [g]	57$\pm$8	IMRE		84CAL/ROZ
$C_5H_{13}O_2^-$ MeOH$\cdots$tBuO$^-$		107$\pm$4	72$\pm$7	TDEq		86MEO/SIE2
-556 ± 23 [c]		79$\pm$10 [g]	51$\pm$7	IMRE		84CAL/ROZ
$C_5H_{15}Si^-$ nPnSiH$_3 \cdots$H$^-$		45$\pm$23		IMRB		86HAJ/SQU
$C_6Br_4O_2^-$ bromanil$^{-\cdot}$ -218 ± 40 [b]	2.4$\pm$0.2			Est NBIP	$\Delta_f H(A) = 18\pm21$	78COO/FRE
$C_6Cl_4O_2^-$ chloranil$^{-\cdot}$					$\Delta_f H(A) = -186\pm12$	77PED/RYL
* -454 ± 21 [b]	2.78$\pm$0.10			TDEq		87KEB/CHO
	2.68$\pm$0.11			IMRE		85GRI/CAL
	2.67$\pm$0.05			IMRE		85FUK/MCI
	2.8$\pm$0.2			NBIP		78COO/FRE
	2.5$\pm$0.3			SI		66FAR/PAG

Table 2. Negative Ion Table - Continued

Ion $\Delta_f H(X\cdot\cdot Y^-)$	$\Delta_f H(A^-)$ EA(A) eV	$\Delta H_{acid}(AH)$ $\Delta H_{aff}(X\cdot\cdot Y^-)$	$\Delta G_{acid}(AH)$ $\Delta G_{aff}(X\cdot\cdot Y^-)$	Method	Comment	Reference
$C_6Cl_5^-$					$\Delta_f H(AH) = -40\pm9$	85PLA/SIM2
$C_6Cl_5^-$					$BDE(A-H) = 464\pm13$	
	2.8	1510 ± 13 e		SI		69PAG/GOO
$C_6F_4O_2^-$						
fluoranil$^-\cdot$				Est	$\Delta_f H(A) = -816\pm41$	
* -1076 ± 51 b	2.70 ± 0.10			TDEq		87KEB/CHO
-1043 ± 46 b	2.36 ± 0.05			IMRE		85FUK/MCI
	2.9 ± 0.2			NBIP		78COO/FRE
	2.3			SI		69PAG/GOO
$C_6F_5^-$					$\Delta_f H(AH) = -806\pm7$	77PED/RYL
$C_6F_5^-$					$BDE(A-H) = 487\pm8$	82MCM/GOL
-797 ± 34 b	2.7 ± 0.2	1539 ± 28 e	1506 ± 29 h	NBAP	From perfluorobenzene	82COM/REI
-464				Endo	$I^- + C_6F_6 \rightarrow$	73LIF/TIE
	2.7			SI		69PAG/GOO
$C_6F_5O^-$					$\Delta_f H(AH) = -957\pm2$	77PED/RYL
pentafluorophenoxide$^-$						
	3.06 ± 0.09			ECD		84HER/WEN
$<-857\pm8$		$<1630\pm10$ f		IMRB	$HO^- + C_6F_6 \rightarrow$, acidity probably ca. 1340 kJ	75BRI/RIV
$C_6F_6^-$						
$C_6F_6^-\cdot$					$\Delta_f H(A) = -946\pm8$	79PRI/SAP
* -996 ± 18 b	0.52 ± 0.10			TDEq		87KEB/CHO
	0.52 ± 0.10			TDEq		86CHO/GRI
	1.8 ± 0.3			EnCT		73LIF/TIE
	1.20 ± 0.07			SI		69PAG/GOO
$C_6F_{10}^-$						
perfluorocyclohexene$^-\cdot$					$\Delta_f H(A) = -2369\pm8$	79PRI/SAP
$<-2504\pm37$ b	1.4 ± 0.3			EnCT		73LIF/TIE
$C_6F_{11}^-$						
$C_6F_{11}^-$						
	$>4.2\pm0.2$			EIAP	From c-$C_4F_6(CF_3)_2$	72THY
	3.5			EIAP	From c-C_6F_{12}	70LIF/PEE
$C_6F_{13}^-$						
$C_6F_{13}^-$						
	$>4.6\pm0.2$			EIAP	From n-C_6F_{14}	83SPY/SAU
$C_6N_4^-$						
tetracyanoethylene$^-\cdot$					$\Delta_f H(A) = 705\pm6$	77PED/RYL
* 400 ± 25 b	3.17 ± 0.20			TDEq		87KEB/CHO
	3.17 ± 0.20			TDEq		86CHO/KEB
	2.300 ± 0.300			LPD		76LYO/PAL
	2.03 ± 0.05			PD		73LYO/PAL
	1.700 ± 0.300			LPD		75LYO/PAL
	2.88 ± 0.06			SI		67FAR/PAG

Table 2. Negative Ion Table - Continued

Ion $\Delta_f H(A^-)$ $\Delta_f H(X \cdot \cdot Y^-)$	EA(A) eV	$\Delta H_{acid}(AH)$ $\Delta H_{aff}(X \cdot \cdot Y^-)$	$\Delta G_{acid}(AH)$ $\Delta G_{aff}(X \cdot \cdot Y^-)$	Method	Comment	Reference
$C_6HCl_3O_2^-$						
triCl-benzoquinone$^-$·				Est2	$\Delta_f H(A) = -180 \pm 13$	
* -423 ± 17 [b]	2.52 ± 0.05			IMRE		85FUK/MCI
$C_6HF_4O^-$						
2,3,5,6-tetrafluorophenoxide$^-$				Est2	$\Delta_f H(AH) = -764 \pm 13$	
					$BDE(A-H) = 385 \pm 17$	
	2.75 ± 0.09			ECD		84HER/WEN
$C_6H_2Cl_2O_2^-$						
2,5-diCl-benzoquinone$^-$·				Est2	$\Delta_f H(A) = -174 \pm 13$	
* -409 ± 22 [b]	2.43 ± 0.10			TDEq		87KEB/CHO
	2.29 ± 0.05			IMRE		85FUK/MCI
$C_6H_2Cl_2O_2^-$						
2,6-diCl-benzoquinone$^-$·					$\Delta_f H(A) = -174 \pm 12$	77PED/RYL
* -414 ± 21 [b]	2.48 ± 0.10			TDEq		87KEB/CHO
	2.39 ± 0.11			IMRE		85GRI/CAL
	2.40 ± 0.05			IMRE		85FUK/MCI
$C_6H_2Cl_3O^-$						
3,4,5-triCl-phenoxide$^-$				Est	$\Delta_f H(AH) = -164 \pm 8$	
					$BDE(A-H) = 362 \pm 13$	
* -310 ± 21 [a]	3.00 ± 0.26 [d]	1384 ± 12 [g]	1355 ± 8	IMRE		81FUJ/MCI
$C_6H_2FO_2^-$						
fluorobenzoquinonide$^-$				Est2	$\Delta_f H(AH) = -387 \pm 13$	
	2.4 ± 0.1			SI		66FAR/PAG
$C_6H_2N_3O_7^-$						
2,4,6-triNO$_2$-phenoxide$^-$				Est2	$\Delta_f H(AH) = -159 \pm 21$	
					$BDE(A-H) = 381 \pm 17$	
$< -365 \pm 25$ [a]		$< 1324 \pm 4$ [g]	< 1293	IMRB	I$^-$ deprotonates	74DZI/CAR
$C_6H_3ClNO_3^-$						
2-Cl-4-NO$_2$-phenoxide$^-$				Est2	$\Delta_f H(AH) = -151 \pm 17$	
					$BDE(A-H) = 381 \pm 17$	
* -328 ± 28 [a]		1353 ± 11 [g]	1323 ± 8	IMRE		86TAF
$C_6H_3Cl_2NO_2^-$						
2,3-diCl-nitrobenzene$^-$·				Est2	$\Delta_f H(A) = 3 \pm 8$	
* -116 ± 13 [b]	1.23 ± 0.05			IMRE		85FUK/MCI
$C_6H_3Cl_2NO_2^-$						
3,4-diCl-nitrobenzene$^-$·				Est	$\Delta_f H(A) = 8 \pm 8$	
* -125 ± 13 [b]	1.38 ± 0.05			IMRE		85FUK/MCI
$C_6H_3Cl_2O^-$						
3,5-diCl-phenoxide$^-$				Est	$\Delta_f H(AH) = -153 \pm 8$	
					$BDE(A-H) = 362 \pm 13$	
* -284 ± 19 [a]	2.85 ± 0.24 [d]	1399 ± 11 [g]	1370 ± 8	IMRE		81FUJ/MCI
$C_6H_3FO_2^-$						
fluorobenzoquinone$^-$·				Est2	$\Delta_f H(A) = -387 \pm 13$	
	1.5 ± 0.2			SI		66FAR/PAG

Table 2. Negative Ion Table - Continued

Ion $\Delta_f H(A^-)$ $\Delta_f H(X\cdot\cdot Y^-)$	EA(A) eV	$\Delta H_{acid}(AH)$ $\Delta H_{aff}(X\cdot\cdot Y^-)$	$\Delta G_{acid}(AH)$ $\Delta G_{aff}(X\cdot\cdot Y^-)$	Method	Comment	Reference
$C_6H_3F_2^-$ m-difluorophenide$^-$					$\Delta_f H(AH) = -309\pm1$	77PED/RYL
$<-264\pm3$ [a]		$<1576\pm1$ [g]	<1543	IMRB	$<$ iPrOH	75BRI/RIV
$C_6H_3F_2^-$ o-difluorophenide$^-$					$\Delta_f H(AH) = -294\pm1$ BDE(A–H) = 460 ± 13	77PED/RYL
-242 ± 18 [a]	2.0 ± 0.3 [d]	1582 ± 16 [g]	1547 ± 13	IMRB	Between EtO$^-$, iPrO$^-$	75BRI/RIV
$C_6H_3F_2^-$ p-difluorophenide$^-$					$\Delta_f H(AH) = -307\pm1$ BDE(A–H) = 460 ± 13	77PED/RYL
-247 ± 16 [a]	1.9 ± 0.3 [d]	1590 ± 15 [g]	1555 ± 13	IMRB	$<$ MeOH, $\leq$ EtOH	75BRI/RIV
$C_6H_3FeO_6^-$ Fe(CO)$_5\cdot\cdot$OMe$^-$						
-1095 ± 37 [c]		188 ± 25 [g]	149 ± 25	IMRB		85LAN/SAL
$C_6H_3N_3O_6^-$ 1,3,5-trinitrobenzene$^-\cdot$					$\Delta_f H(A) = 62\pm2$	77PED/RYL
-191 [b]	2.6			SI		69PAG/GOO
$C_6H_3O_2^-$ benzoquinonide$^-$					$\Delta_f H(AH) = -123\pm3$	77PED/RYL
			<1607	IMRB		87JOH/SPE
	2.00 ± 0.04			SI		66FAR/PAG
$C_6H_4^-$ o-benzyne$^-\cdot$					$\Delta_f H(A) = 494\pm21$	80POL/HEH
* 440 ± 22 [b]	0.560 ± 0.010			LPES		86LEO/MIL
<433				IMRB	O$^-$ + C$_6$H$_6$ →, D label indicates ortho loss	78BRU/FER
$C_6D_4^-$ o-benzyne-d$_4^-\cdot$						
*	0.551 ± 0.010			LPES		86LEO/MIL
$C_6H_4BrNO_2^-$ mBr–nitrobenzene$^-\cdot$				Est	$\Delta_f H(A) = 90\pm4$	
* -38 ± 14 [b]	1.32 ± 0.10			TDEq		87KEB/CHO
$C_6H_4BrNO_2^-$ oBr–nitrobenzene$^-\cdot$				Est2	$\Delta_f H(A) = 92\pm8$	
* -21 ± 18 [b]	1.17 ± 0.10			TDEq		87KEB/CHO
$C_6H_4BrNO_2^-$ pBr–nitrobenzene$^-\cdot$				Est	$\Delta_f H(A) = 90\pm4$	
* -35 ± 14 [b]	1.29 ± 0.10			TDEq		87KEB/CHO
$C_6H_4Cl^-$ chlorophenide$^-$					$\Delta_f H(AH) = 54\pm1$ BDE(A–H) = 460 ± 13	85PLA/SIM
144 ± 24 [a]	1.6 ± 0.4 [d]	1620 ± 23 [g]	1586 ± 21	IMRB		79BAR/MCI

Table 2. Negative Ion Table - Continued

Ion $\Delta_f H(A^-)$ $\Delta_f H(X \cdot \cdot Y^-)$	EA(A) eV	$\Delta H_{acid}(AH)$ $\Delta H_{aff}(X \cdot \cdot Y^-)$	$\Delta G_{acid}(AH)$ $\Delta G_{aff}(X \cdot \cdot Y^-)$	Method	Comment	Reference
$C_6H_4ClF_2^-$						
m-$C_6H_4F_2 \cdot \cdot Cl^-$						
* −598±11 [c]		61±8 [g]	33±8	IMRE		84LAR/MCM2
			32±4	TDEq		82FRE/IKU
$C_6H_4ClF_2^-$						
o-$C_6H_4F_2 \cdot \cdot Cl^-$						
* −581±11 [c]		60±8 [g]	33±8	IMRE		84LAR/MCM2
$C_6H_4ClF_2^-$						
p-$C_6H_4F_2 \cdot \cdot Cl^-$						
* −592±11 [c]		58±8 [g]	31±8	IMRE		84LAR/MCM2
$C_6H_4ClNO_2^-$						
mCl-nitrobenzene$^-\cdot$				Est	$\Delta_f H(A) = 38 \pm 8$	
* −85±18 [b]	1.28±0.10			TDEq		87KEB/CHO
	1.22±0.11			IMRE		85GRI/CAL
	1.20±0.05			IMRE		85FUK/MCI
$C_6H_4ClNO_2^-$						
oCl-nitrobenzene$^-\cdot$				Est	$\Delta_f H(A) = 42 \pm 4$	
* −68±14 [b]	1.14±0.10			TDEq		87KEB/CHO
	1.08±0.11			IMRE		85GRI/CAL
	1.05±0.05			IMRE		85FUK/MCI
$C_6H_4ClNO_2^-$						
pCl-nitrobenzene$^-\cdot$				Est	$\Delta_f H(A) = 38 \pm 8$	
* −84±18 [b]	1.26±0.10			TDEq		87KEB/CHO
	1.19±0.11			IMRE		85GRI/CAL
	1.17±0.05			IMRE		85FUK/MCI
$C_6H_4ClO^-$					$\Delta_f H(AH) = -146 \pm 8$	77PED/RYL
mCl-phenoxide$^-$					BDE(A−H) = 362±8	
* −245±29 [a]	2.52±0.30 [d]	1431±21 [g]	1402±8	IMRE		81FUJ/MCI
		1433±21 [g]	1404±8	IMRE		77MCM/KEB
$C_6H_4ClO^-$				Est2	$\Delta_f H(AH) = -173 \pm 17$	
oCl-phenoxide$^-$					BDE(A−H) = 402±17	
* −266±30 [a]	2.87±0.31 [d]	1437±13 [g]	1410±8	IMRE		77MCM/KEB
*	<2.58±0.08			PD		75RIC/STE2
$C_6H_4ClO^-$					$\Delta_f H(AH) = -153 \pm 8$	77PED/RYL
pCl-phenoxide$^-$					BDE(A−H) = 362±13	
* −248±18 [a]	2.47±0.23 [d]	1436±10 [g]	1407±8	IMRE		81FUJ/MCI
		1438±10 [g]	1409±8	IMRE		77MCM/KEB
$C_6H_4Cl_2^-$					$\Delta_f H(A) = 33 \pm 2$	85PLA/SIM
o-dichlorobenzene$^-\cdot$						
24 [b]	9.4			ECD		69STE/WEN

Table 2. Negative Ion Table – Continued

Ion $\Delta_f H(X\cdot\cdot Y^-)$	$\Delta_f H(A^-)$ EA(A) eV	$\Delta H_{acid}(AH)$ $\Delta H_{aff}(X\cdot\cdot Y^-)$	$\Delta G_{acid}(AH)$ $\Delta G_{aff}(X\cdot\cdot Y^-)$	Method	Comment	Reference
$C_6H_4F^-$ fluorophenide$^-$					$\Delta_f H(AH) = -116\pm1$ $BDE(A-H) = 460\pm13$	77PED/RYL
	-26 ± 26 [a] 1.6±0.4 [d]	1620±25 [g]	1586±22	IMRB		75BRI/RIV
$C_6H_4FNO_2^-$ mF–nitrobenzene$^{-\cdot}$				Est	$\Delta_f H(A) = -126\pm8$	
*	-245 ± 18 [b] 1.23±0.10			TDEq		87KEB/CHO
	1.18±0.11			IMRE		85GRI/CAL
	1.15±0.05			IMRE		85FUK/MCI
$C_6H_4FNO_2^-$ oF–nitrobenzene$^{-\cdot}$				Est	$\Delta_f H(A) = -118\pm8$	
*	-221 ± 18 [b] 1.07±0.10			TDEq		87KEB/CHO
	1.02±0.11			IMRE		85GRI/CAL
	1.04±0.05			IMRE		85FUK/MCI
$C_6H_4FNO_2^-$ pF–nitrobenzene$^{-\cdot}$				Est	$\Delta_f H(A) = -131\pm8$	
*	-239 ± 18 [b] 1.12±0.10			TDEq		87KEB/CHO
	1.05±0.11			IMRE		85GRI/CAL
	1.04±0.05			IMRE		85FUK/MCI
$C_6H_4FO^-$ mF–phenoxide$^-$				Est	$\Delta_f H(AH) = -297\pm8$ $BDE(A-H) = 362\pm8$	
*	-389 ± 18 [a] 2.45±0.19 [d]	1438±10 [g]	1409±8	IMRE		81FUJ/MCI
		1441±10 [g]	1413±8	IMRE		77MCM/KEB
	2.61±0.09	1422±17 [e]	1393±18 [h]	ECD		84HER/WEN
$C_6H_4FO^-$ oF–phenoxide$^-$				Est2	$\Delta_f H(AH) = -285$	
*		1445±12 [g]	1418±8	IMRE		81FUJ/MCI
		1447±12 [g]	1420±8	IMRE		77MCM/KEB
$C_6H_4FO^-$ pF–phenoxide$^-$				Est	$\Delta_f H(AH) = -291\pm8$ $BDE(A-H) = 362\pm13$	
*	-370 ± 18 [a] 2.31±0.23 [d]	1451±10 [g]	1422±8	IMRE		81FUJ/MCI
		1455±10 [g]	1426±8	IMRE		77MCM/KEB
$C_6H_4F_2N^-$ 2,4–diF–anilide$^-$				Est	$\Delta_f H(AH) = -478\pm13$	
*	-497 ± 25 [a]	1510±12 [g]	1480±8	IMRE		79BAR/SCO
			1480±8	IMRE^o		79BAR/SCO
$C_6H_4NO_2^-$ pNO–phenoxide$^-$				Est	$\Delta_f H(AH) = -91\pm8$	
*	-246 ± 19 [a]	1376±11 [g]	1345±8	IMRE		86TAF
$C_6H_4NO_3^-$ mNO$_2$–phenoxide$^-$				Est	$\Delta_f H(AH) = -113\pm8$ $BDE(A-H) = 362\pm8$	
*	-244 ± 19 [a] 2.85±0.20 [d]	1399±11 [g]	1370±8	IMRE		81FUJ/MCI
		1400±11 [g]	1371±8	IMRE		77MCM/KEB

Table 2. Negative Ion Table – Continued

Ion $\Delta_f H(X\cdot\cdot Y^-)$	$\Delta_f H(A^-)$ EA(A) eV	$\Delta H_{acid}(AH)$ $\Delta H_{aff}(X\cdot\cdot Y^-)$	$\Delta G_{acid}(AH)$ $\Delta G_{aff}(X\cdot\cdot Y^-)$	Method	Comment	Reference
$C_6H_4NO_3^-$ oNO_2–phenoxide$^-$				Est2	$\Delta_f H(AH) = -105\pm13$	
*			1379±8	IMRE		77MCM/KEB
$C_6H_4NO_3^-$ pNO_2–phenoxide$^-$				Est	$\Delta_f H(AH) = -117\pm8$	
* −276±19 [a]		1372±11 [g]	1343±8	IMRE		81FUJ/MCI
$C_6H_4N_2O_4^-$ mNO_2–nitrobenzene$^{-\cdot}$					$\Delta_f H(A) = 59\pm1$	76FER/PIA
* −101±11 [b]	1.65±0.10			TDEq		87KEB/CHO
	1.57±0.11			IMRE		85GRI/CAL
−93±5 [b]	1.57±0.05			IMRE		85FUK/MCI
$C_6H_4N_2O_4^-$ oNO_2–nitrobenzene$^{-\cdot}$				Est2	$\Delta_f H(A) = 84\pm8$	
* −76±18 [b]	1.65±0.10			TDEq		87KEB/CHO
$C_6H_4N_2O_4^-$ pNO_2–nitrobenzene$^{-\cdot}$					$\Delta_f H(A) = 57\pm3$	76FER/PIA
* −136±13 [b]	2.00±0.10			TDEq		87KEB/CHO
	1.89±0.11			IMRE		85GRI/CAL
	1.89±0.05			IMRE		85FUK/MCI
$C_6H_4N_3^-$ benzotriazolide$^-$						
*		1413±11 [g]	1382±8	IMRE		86TAF
$C_6H_4O_2^-$ o–benzoquinone$^{-\cdot}$				Est2	$\Delta_f H(A) = -121\pm21$	
	1.620±0.048			LPD		85MAR/COM
$C_6H_4O_2^-$ p–benzoquinone$^{-\cdot}$					$\Delta_f H(A) = -123\pm3$	77PED/RYL
* −307±13 [b]	1.91±0.10			TDEq		87KEB/CHO
	1.81±0.11			IMRE		85GRI/CAL
	1.990±0.048			LPD		85MAR/COM
	1.83±0.05			IMRE		85FUK/MCI
	1.9±0.3			NBIP		75COO/NAF
	>0.0			ES		70COL/CHR
	1.37±0.08			SI		66FAR/PAG
$C_6H_5^-$ phenide$^-$					$\Delta_f H(AH) = 83$	77PED/RYL
					$BDE(A-H) = 464\pm8$	82MCM/GOL
* 229±3 [a]	1.03±0.11 [d]	1677±2	1636±3	TDEq		86MEO/SIE
			1632±27	IMRB		79BAR/MCI
341±29				EIAP	From benzonitrile	86HEN/ILL2
	1.1±0.3 [d]	1665±25 [g]	1628±23	IMRB		71BOH/YOU
	2.36±0.04			SI		76FAI/JOY
	2.2			SI		72PAG

Table 2. Negative Ion Table — Continued

Ion $\Delta_f H(X\cdots Y^-)$	$\Delta_f H(A^-)$ EA(A) eV	$\Delta H_{acid}(AH)$ $\Delta H_{aff}(X\cdots Y^-)$	$\Delta G_{acid}(AH)$ $\Delta G_{aff}(X\cdots Y^-)$	Method	Comment	Reference
$C_6H_5BrCl^-$ PhBr$\cdots$Cl$^-$			28	TDEq		82FRE/IKU
$C_6H_5ClF^-$ PhF$\cdots$Cl$^-$			25	TDEq		82FRE/IKU
$C_6H_5ClFO^-$ pF-C_6H_4OH$\cdots$Cl$^-$ * -629 ± 18 [c]		110 ± 8	81 ± 8	TDEq		77CUM/FRE
$C_6H_5ClI^-$ PhI$\cdots$Cl$^-$			30	TDEq		82FRE/IKU
$C_6H_5ClN^-$ mCl-anilide$^-$ * 26 ± 18 [a]		1502 ± 10 [g]	1471 ± 8 1480 ± 8	Est IMRE IMRE^o	$\Delta_f H(AH)= 55\pm8$ BDE(A-H)= 368 ± 13	79BAR/SCO 79BAR/SCO
$C_6H_5ClN^-$ pCl-anilide$^-$ * 33 ± 18 [a]		1508 ± 10 [g]	1477 ± 8 1482 ± 8	Est IMRE IMRE^o	$\Delta_f H(AH)= 55\pm8$ BDE(A-H)= 368 ± 13	79BAR/SCO 79BAR/SCO
$C_6H_5ClNO_2^-$ PhNO$_2\cdots$Cl$^-$			30	TDEq		82FRE/IKU
$C_6H_5Cl_2^-$ PhCl$\cdots$Cl$^-$ * -230 ± 10 [c]		57 ± 8 [g] 57 ± 4 [g]	29 ± 8 29 ± 4 27	IMRE IMRE TDEq		84LAR/MCM2 84LAR/MCM4 82FRE/IKU
$C_6H_5Cl_2O^-$ pCl-C_6H_4OH$\cdots$Cl$^-$ * -498 ± 18 [c]		118 ± 8	87 ± 8	TDEq		77CUM/FRE
$C_6H_5FN^-$ mF-anilide$^-$ * -132 ± 19 [a]		1511 ± 11 [g]	1481 ± 8 1489 ± 8	Est IMRE IMRE^o	$\Delta_f H(AH)= -113\pm8$ BDE(A-H)= 368 ± 13	79BAR/SCO 79BAR/SCO
$C_6H_5FN^-$ oF-anilide$^-$ * -143 ± 29 [a]	1.91 ± 0.30 [d]	1517 ± 12 [g]	1487 ± 8 1495 ± 8	Est2 IMRE IMRE^o	$\Delta_f H(AH)= -130\pm17$ BDE(A-H)= 389 ± 17	79BAR/SCO 79BAR/SCO

Table 2. Negative Ion Table - Continued

Ion $\Delta_f H(X\cdot\cdot Y^-)$	$\Delta_f H(A^-)$ EA(A) eV	$\Delta H_{acid}(AH)$ $\Delta H_{aff}(X\cdot\cdot Y^-)$	$\Delta G_{acid}(AH)$ $\Delta G_{aff}(X\cdot\cdot Y^-)$	Method	Comment	Reference
$C_6H_5FN^-$ pF–anilide$^-$				Est	$\Delta_f H(AH)= -109\pm 8$ $BDE(A-H)= 368\pm 13$	
*	-115 ± 19 [a] 1.62 ± 0.24 [d]	1524 ± 11 [g]	1494 ± 8	IMRE		79BAR/SCO
			1499 ± 8	IMRE^o		79BAR/SCO
$C_6H_5F_5NS^-$ mSF$_5$–anilide$^-$					$BDE(A-H)= 368\pm 13$	
*	2.76 ± 0.24 [d]	1414 ± 11 [g]	1383 ± 8	IMRE		86TAF
$C_6H_5F_5NS^-$ pSF$_5$–anilide$^-$					$BDE(A-H)= 368\pm 13$	
*	2.92 ± 0.24 [d]	1399 ± 11 [g]	1368 ± 8	IMRE		86TAF
$C_6H_5N^-$ PhN$^{-\cdot}$						
*	263 ± 26 [a]	1556 ± 16 [g]	1527 ± 13	IMRB	Acidity near MeCN	81MCD/CHO
*	1.461 ± 0.013			LPD		84DRZ/BRA
			1532 ± 13	IMRB^o		81MCD/CHO
$C_6H_5NO_2^-$ nitrobenzene$^{-\cdot}$					$\Delta_f H(A)= 67\pm 1$	77PED/RYL
*	-30 ± 11 [b] 1.01 ± 0.10			TDEq		87KEB/CHO
	0.96 ± 0.11			IMRE		85GRI/CAL
	0.97 ± 0.05			IMRE		85FUK/MCI
	$> 0.7\pm 0.2$			EnCT		73LIF/TIE
	> 0.4			ES		66COM/CHR
	< 1.1			IMRB	EA: $< SO_2$	59HEN/MUC
$C_6H_5N_2O^-$ PhN=NO$^-$						
$< 308\pm 25$				IMRB	Ph$^-$ + $N_2O \rightarrow$; thermochemical limit	77BIE/DEP
$C_6H_5N_2O_2^-$ mNO$_2$–anilide$^-$					$\Delta_f H(AH)= 62\pm 2$ $BDE(A-H)= 368\pm 13$	83NIS/SAK
*	6 ± 13 [a] 2.14 ± 0.24 [d]	1474 ± 11 [g]	1443 ± 8	IMRE		86TAF
$C_6H_5N_2O_2^-$ pNO$_2$–anilide$^-$					$\Delta_f H(AH)= 55\pm 2$	83NIS/SAK
*	-38 ± 13 [a]	1437 ± 11 [g]	1407 ± 8	IMRE		86TAF
$C_6H_5O^-$ phenoxide$^-$					$\Delta_f H(AH)= -96\pm 1$ $BDE(A-H)= 362\pm 8$	77PED/RYL 82MCM/GOL
*	-165 ± 10 [a] 2.21 ± 0.19 [d]	1461 ± 10 [g]	1432 ± 8	IMRE		81FUJ/MCI
*	$< 2.36\pm 0.06$			PD		75RIC/STE2
		1466 ± 10 [g]	1437 ± 8	IMRE		78CUM/KEB
					86SHI/VOR: tautomer acidities $\Delta_{acid}H$(ortho) = 1439 ± 13 kJ, (para) = 1423 ± 8 kJ	
			1441 ± 8	IMRE^o		79BAR/SCO
$C_6H_5O_2^-$ mOH–phenoxide$^-$					$\Delta_f H(AH)= -274\pm 2$ $BDE(A-H)= 362\pm 8$	79KUD/KUD
*	-354 ± 13 [a] 2.32 ± 0.20 [d]	1451 ± 11 [g]	1422 ± 8	IMRE		81FUJ/MCI
		1444 ± 11 [g]	1415 ± 8	IMRE		77MCM/KEB

Table 2. Negative Ion Table – Continued

Ion $\Delta_f H(X\cdot\cdot Y^-)$	EA(A) eV	$\Delta H_{acid}(AH)$ $\Delta H_{aff}(X\cdot\cdot Y^-)$	$\Delta G_{acid}(AH)$ $\Delta G_{aff}(X\cdot\cdot Y^-)$	Method	Comment	Reference
$C_6H_5O_2^-$ oOH–phenoxide$^-$					$\Delta_f H(AH) = -272\pm4$	79KUD/KUD
*		1421±11 ^{g}	1392±8	IMRE		81FUJ/MCI
		1422±11 ^{g}	1393±8	IMRE		77MCM/KEB
$C_6H_5O_2^-$ pOH–phenoxide$^-$					$\Delta_f H(AH) = -264\pm2$	79KUD/KUD
* −328±13 ^{a}		1466±11 ^{g}	1436±8	IMRE		81FUJ/MCI
$C_6H_5S^-$ thiophenoxide$^-$					$\Delta_f H(AH) = 113\pm1$	77PED/RYL
					BDE(A–H) = 335±9	82MCM/GOL
*	<2.47±0.06	>1409±15 ^{e}		PD		75RIC/STE2
$C_6H_6Cl^-$ $C_6H_6\cdot\cdot Cl^-$						
*		41 ^{g}	20±8	IMRE		84LAR/MCM2
			16	TDEq		82FRE/IKU
$C_6H_6ClO^-$ PhOH$\cdot\cdot$Cl$^-$						
−432 ^{c}		109	72	TDAs		82FRE/IKU
−426±10 ^{c}		103±8	83±8	TDEq		77CUM/FRE
		81±8	62±8	TDAs		71YAM/KEB
$C_6H_6FO^-$ PhOH$\cdot\cdot$F$^-$						
* −518±11 ^{c}		173±8 ^{g}	140±8	IMRE		83LAR/MCM
$C_6H_6N^-$ anilide$^-$					$\Delta_f H(AH) = 87\pm1$	77PED/RYL
					BDE(A–H) = 368±8	82MCM/GOL
* 90±12 ^{a}	1.53±0.20 ^{d}	1533±11 ^{g}	1502±8	IMRE		79BAR/SCO
	1.704±0.030			LPD		84DRZ/BRA2
			1505±8	IMRE^o		79BAR/SCO
$C_6H_6NO^-$ mNH$_2$–phenoxide$^-$					$\Delta_f H(AH) = -90\pm2$	86NUN/BAR
					BDE(A–H) = 362±8	
* −153±11 ^{a}	2.15±0.19 ^{d}	1467±10 ^{g}	1438±8	IMRE		81FUJ/MCI
		1469±10 ^{g}	1441±8	IMRE		77MCM/KEB
$C_6H_6NO^-$ oNH$_2$–phenoxide$^-$				Est2	$\Delta_f H(AH) = -105\pm17$	
					BDE(A–H) = 391±17	
*			1428±8	IMRE		77MCM/KEB
$C_6H_6NO^-$ pNH$_2$–phenoxide$^-$					$\Delta_f H(AH) = -82\pm2$	86NUN/BAR
					BDE(A–H) = 368±13	
* −137±11 ^{a}		1475±10 ^{g}	1446±8	IMRE		81FUJ/MCI
		1483±10 ^{g}	1454±8	IMRE		77MCM/KEB
$C_6H_6N_2O_2^-$ mNH$_2$–nitrobenzene$^-$					$\Delta_f H(A) = 59\pm1$	77PED/RYL
* −33±11 ^{b}	0.95±0.10			TDEq		87KEB/CHO

Table 2. Negative Ion Table – Continued

Ion $\Delta_f H(X \cdot \cdot Y^-)$	$\Delta_f H(A^-)$ EA(A) eV	$\Delta H_{acid}(AH)$ $\Delta H_{aff}(X \cdot \cdot Y^-)$	$\Delta G_{acid}(AH)$ $\Delta G_{aff}(X \cdot \cdot Y^-)$	Method	Comment	Reference
$C_6H_7^-$ 1,3-cyclohexadienide$^-$ 138±21 [a] 134±75	0.6±0.4 [d]	1562±21 [g]	1531±17	IMRB IMRB	$\Delta_f H(AH)=$ 106 BDE(A-H)= 305±21 Between SiH_4, tBuOH	77PED/RYL 82MCM/GOL 86LEE/SQU 78DEP/BIE
$C_6H_7^-$ 1-methylcyclopentadienide$^-$ *	1.670±0.039			Est LPD	$\Delta_f H(AH)=$ 96±4	73RIC/STE
$C_6H_7FN^-$ $PhNH_2 \cdot \cdot F^-$ * −292±11 [c]		131±8 [g]	98±8	IMRE		83LAR/MCM
$C_6H_7O^-$ cyclohexenone-4-enolate$^-$ * −150±22 [a]		1496±10 [g]	1464±8 1473±8	Est2 IMRE IMRE^o	$\Delta_f H(AH)=$ −116±13	86BAR/KIP 86BAR/KIP
$C_6H_7O_2^-$ $HOH \cdot \cdot PhO^-$ −471±14 [c]		64±4	34±7	TDAs		86MEO/SIE2
$C_6H_8B^-$ $MeB(CH=CH)_2CH^-$ 17±31 [a]		1402±18 [g]	1370±17	Est IMRB	$\Delta_f H(AH)=$ 146±13 Acid: 3-methyl-3-bora-1,4-cyclohexadiene	77SUL
$C_6H_9^-$ cyclohexenide$^-$ 82±25 [a]		1617±25 [g]	1586±21	IMRB	$\Delta_f H(AH)=$ −5	77PED/RYL 86LEE/SQU
$C_6H_9^-$ $tBuC \equiv C^-$ * 157±15 [a]	2.93±0.34 [d]	1582±12 [g]	1549±8 1544±8	IMRE IMRE^o	$\Delta_f H(AH)=$ 106±3 BDE(A-H)= 552±21	77KUP/SHI 79BAR/SCO 79BAR/SCO
$C_6H_9O^-$ cyclohexanone enolate$^-$ *	1.55±0.05			PD	$\Delta_f H(AH)=$ −226±2	77PED/RYL 78ZIM/JAC
$C_6H_{11}^-$ cyclohexanide$^-$ >37±4 [a]		1690±4 [g]	>1665	IMRB	$\Delta_f H(AH)=$ −123 BDE(A-H)= 400±4	77PED/RYL 82MCM/GOL 72BOH/LEE
$C_6H_{11}O^-$ $CH_2=C(tBu)O^-$ * −280±15 [a]	1.84±0.07	1540±15 [e]	1512±18 [h]	PD	$\Delta_f H(AH)=$ −290±1 BDE(A-H)= 406±8	77PED/RYL 77ZIM/REE
$C_6H_{11}O^-$ $tBuCH=CHO^-$ * −282±21 [a]	1.82±0.06	1517±18 [e]	1490±23 [h]	Est PD	$\Delta_f H(AH)=$ −269±2 BDE(A-H)= 381±13	77ZIM/REE

Table 2. Negative Ion Table - Continued

Ion $\Delta_f H(A^-)$ $\Delta_f H(X \cdot \cdot Y^-)$	EA(A) eV	$\Delta H_{acid}(AH)$ $\Delta H_{aff}(X \cdot \cdot Y^-)$	$\Delta G_{acid}(AH)$ $\Delta G_{aff}(X \cdot \cdot Y^-)$	Method	Comment	Reference
$C_6H_{11}O_2^-$ nPnCO$_2^-$					$\Delta_f H(AH) = -514 \pm 2$ BDE(A-H) = 444±8	77PED/RYL
* −597±11 [a]	3.2±0.2 [d]	1447±10	1418±12 [h]	CIDC		81MCL/CAM
$C_6H_{11}O_2^-$ tBuCH$_2$CO$_2^-$				Est	$\Delta_f H(AH) = -538 \pm 4$ BDE(A-H) = 444±8	
* −623±15 [a]		1444±11 [g]	1415±8	IMRE		86TAF
$C_6H_{11}S_2^-$ 5,5-dimethyl-1,3-dithianide$^-$				Est	$\Delta_f H(AH) = -59 \pm 17$	
* −24±28 [a]		1566±11 [g]	1535±8 1530±8	IMRE IMRE^o		81BAR/HAY 81BAR/HAY
$C_6H_{13}O^-$ Et$_2$C(Me)O$^-$				Est	$\Delta_f H(AH) = -356 \pm 4$ BDE(A-H) = 440±4	
* −330±15 [a]	2.0±0.2 [d]	1556±11 1553±10	1528±13 [h]	CIDC CIDC^o		83BOA/HOU 83BOA/HOU
$C_6H_{13}O^-$ iPrCH(Et)O$^-$				Est	$\Delta_f H(AH) = -342 \pm 4$ BDE(A-H) = 438±4	
* −318±15 [a]	2.0±0.2 [d]	1554±11 1551±10	1527±13 [h]	CIDC CIDC^o		83BOA/HOU 83BOA/HOU
$C_6H_{13}O^-$ iPrCH$_2$CH$_2$CH$_2$O$^-$				Est	$\Delta_f H(AH) = -327 \pm 4$ BDE(A-H) = 436±4	
* −296±14 [a]	1.9±0.1 [d]	1561±10 1557±10	1533±11 [h]	CIDC CIDC^o		83BOA/HOU 83BOA/HOU
$C_6H_{13}O^-$ nC$_6$H$_{13}$O$^-$					$\Delta_f H(AH) = -315 \pm 1$ BDE(A-H) = 436±4	77PED/RYL
* −284±12 [a]	1.9±0.2 [d]	1561±11 1557±10	1533±13 [h]	CIDC CIDC^o		83BOA/HOU 83BOA/HOU
$C_6H_{13}O^-$ nPrC(Me)$_2$O$^-$				Est	$\Delta_f H(AH) = -352 \pm 4$ BDE(A-H) = 440±4	
* −326±15 [a]	2.0±0.2 [d]	1557±11 1554±10	1529±13 [h]	CIDC CIDC^o		83BOA/HOU 83BOA/HOU
$C_6H_{13}O^-$ tBuCH(Me)O$^-$				Est	$\Delta_f H(AH) = -351 \pm 4$ BDE(A-H) = 438±4	
* −328±16 [a]	2.05±0.17 [d]	1553±12 [g]	1525±8 1523±8	IMRE IMRE^o		79BAR/SCO 79BAR/SCO
$C_6H_{13}O^-$ tBuCH$_2$CH$_2$O$^-$				Est	$\Delta_f H(AH) = -332 \pm 4$ BDE(A-H) = 436±4	
* −304±15 [a]	2.0±0.2 [d]	1559±11 1555±10	1531±13 [h]	CIDC CIDC^o		83BOA/HOU 83BOA/HOU
$C_6H_{13}O_2^-$ nPrOH$\cdot\cdot$CH$_2$=C(Me)O$^-$ −518±23 [c]		61±10 [g]	33±8	IMRE		84CAL/ROZ

Table 2. Negative Ion Table – Continued

Ion $\Delta_f H(A^-)$ $\Delta_f H(X \cdot \cdot Y^-)$	EA(A) eV	$\Delta H_{acid}(AH)$ $\Delta H_{aff}(X \cdot \cdot Y^-)$	$\Delta G_{acid}(AH)$ $\Delta G_{aff}(X \cdot \cdot Y^-)$	Method	Comment	Reference
$C_6H_{14}BF_2^-$						
iPr$_2$BF··F$^-$						
< −817 [c]		278		IMRB	F$^-$A: SiF$_4$ > iPr$_2$BF > iPr$_3$B	77MUR/BEA2
$C_6H_{15}BCl^-$						
Et$_3$B··Cl$^-$						
* −476±15 [c]		100±8 [g]	72±8	IMRE		85LAR/MCM
$C_6H_{15}BF^-$						
Et$_3$B··F$^-$						
* −611±16 [c]		213±8 [g]	182±8	IMRE		85LAR/MCM
		259		IMRB	F$^-$A: iPr$_3$B > Et$_3$B > MeSiF$_3$	77MUR/BEA2
$C_6H_{15}BFO_3^-$						
(EtO)$_3$B··F$^-$						
* −1434±17 [c]		184±13 [g]	153±8	IMRB		85LAR/MCM
$C_6H_{15}OSi^-$						
Et$_3$SiO$^-$				Est2	$\Delta_f H(AH)$ = −559±8	
−580±19 [a]		1508±11 [g]	1479±8	IMRE		87THO/BAR
$C_6H_{15}O_2^-$						
EtOH··tBuO$^-$						
−592±23 [c]		82±10 [g]	54±8	IMRE		84CAL/ROZ
$C_6H_{15}O_2^-$						
MeOH··tBuCH$_2$O$^-$						
−569±25 [c]		78±10 [g]	50±8	IMRE		84CAL/ROZ
$C_6H_{15}O_2^-$						
nPrOH··nPrO$^-$						
−554±21 [c]		88±10 [g]	60±8	IMRE		84CAL/ROZ
$C_6H_{17}Si^-$						
Et$_3$SiH··H$^-$						
−98 [c]		43±23		IMRB		86HAJ/SQU
$C_6H_{18}NSi_2^-$						
(Me$_3$Si)$_2$N$^-$					$\Delta_f H(AH)$ = −477±6	77PED/RYL
					BDE(A−H) = > 421	78ROB/WIN
−497±15 [a]	2.32 [d]	1509±10 [g]	1477±8	IMRE		87THO/BAR
$C_7F_5N^-$						
$C_6F_5CN^{-\cdot}$				Est	$\Delta_f H(A)$ = −746±13	
* −852±22 [b]	1.10±0.10			TDEq		87KEB/CHO
	1.10±0.10			TDEq		86CHO/GRI
$C_7F_8^-$						
perfluorotoluene$^{-\cdot}$					$\Delta_f H(A)$ = −1187±8	77PED/RYL
* −1278±17 [b]	0.94±0.10			TDEq		87KEB/CHO
	0.91±0.10			IMRE		86CHO/GRI
	> 1.7±0.3			EnCT		73LIF/TIE

Table 2. Negative Ion Table – Continued

Ion $\Delta_f H(A^-)$ $\Delta_f H(X \cdot \cdot Y^-)$	EA(A) eV	$\Delta H_{acid}(AH)$ $\Delta H_{aff}(X \cdot \cdot Y^-)$	$\Delta G_{acid}(AH)$ $\Delta G_{aff}(X \cdot \cdot Y^-)$	Method	Comment	Reference
$C_7F_{13}^-$				Est	$\Delta_f H(AH) = -2705 \pm 21$	
perfluoromethylcyclohexanide$^-$						
-3063 [b]	3.9			EIAP	From c-$C_6F_{11}(CF_3)$	70LIF/PEE
$C_7F_{14}^-$					$\Delta_f H(A) = -2900 \pm 1$	77PED/RYL
perfluoromethylcyclohexane$^-\cdot$						
* -3002 ± 11 [b]	1.06 ± 0.10			TDEq		85GRI/CHO
	<1.6			IMRB		85GRI/CAL
$C_7H_3Cl_2N^-$				Est2	$\Delta_f H(A) = 156 \pm 13$	
2,6–diCl–benzonitrile$^-\cdot$						
* 87 ± 22 [b]	0.72 ± 0.10			TDEq		87KEB/CHO
	0.70 ± 0.09			TDEq		86CHO/KEB
$C_7H_3Cl_3O_2^-$				Est2	$\Delta_f H(A) = -212 \pm 17$	
Me–triCl–benzoquinone$^-\cdot$						
* -449 ± 21 [b]	2.46 ± 0.05			IMRE		85FUK/MCI
$C_7H_3F_5O^-$				Est2	$\Delta_f H(A) = -937 \pm 8$	
pentafluoroanisole$^-\cdot$						
-990 ± 17 [b]	0.54 ± 0.09			ECD		84HER/WEN
$C_7H_3N_3O_4^-$				Est	$\Delta_f H(A) = 188 \pm 4$	
3–NO_2–5–CN–nitrobenzene$^-\cdot$						
* -20 ± 14 [b]	2.16 ± 0.10			TDEq		87KEB/CHO
$C_7H_4ClO_2^-$					$\Delta_f H(AH) = -342 \pm 4$	77PED/RYL
mCl–benzoate$^-$					$BDE(A-H) = 444 \pm 13$	
* -473 ± 15 [a]	3.69 ± 0.24 [d]	1400 ± 11 [g]	1368 ± 8	IMRE		77MCM/KEB
$C_7H_4ClO_2^-$					$\Delta_f H(AH) = -325 \pm 3$	77PED/RYL
oCl–benzoate$^-$					$BDE(A-H) = 444 \pm 13$	
* -454 ± 14 [a]	3.67 ± 0.24 [d]	1401 ± 11 [g]	1372 ± 8	IMRE		77MCM/KEB
$C_7H_4ClO_2^-$					$\Delta_f H(AH) = -341 \pm 3$	77PED/RYL
pCl–benzoate$^-$					$BDE(A-H) = 444 \pm 13$	
* -472 ± 14 [a]	3.69 ± 0.24 [d]	1399 ± 11 [g]	1369 ± 8	IMRE		77MCM/KEB
$C_7H_4FO_2^-$				Est	$\Delta_f H(AH) = -490 \pm 4$	
mF–benzoate$^-$					$BDE(A-H) = 444 \pm 13$	
* -617 ± 15 [a]	3.65 ± 0.24 [d]	1403 ± 11 [g]	1372 ± 8	IMRE		77MCM/KEB
$C_7H_4FO_2^-$				Est2	$\Delta_f H(AH) = -502 \pm 13$	
oF–benzoate$^-$					$BDE(A-H) = 460 \pm 17$	
* -623 ± 25 [a]	3.76 ± 0.30 [d]	1410 ± 12 [g]	1378 ± 8	IMRE		77MCM/KEB
$C_7H_4FO_2^-$					$\Delta_f H(AH) = -495 \pm 3$	77PED/RYL
pF–benzoate$^-$					$BDE(A-H) = 444 \pm 13$	
* -620 ± 14 [a]	3.63 ± 0.24 [d]	1405 ± 11 [g]	1376 ± 8	IMRE		77MCM/KEB

Table 2. Negative Ion Table - Continued

Ion $\Delta_fH(A^-)$ $\Delta_fH(X\cdot\cdot Y^-)$	EA(A) eV	$\Delta H_{acid}(AH)$ $\Delta H_{aff}(X\cdot\cdot Y^-)$	$\Delta G_{acid}(AH)$ $\Delta G_{aff}(X\cdot\cdot Y^-)$	Method	Comment	Reference
$C_7H_4F_3^-$					$\Delta_fH(AH) = -599\pm1$	77PED/RYL
CF_3–phenide$^-$					$BDE(A-H) = 460\pm13$	
-511 ± 24 [a]	1.6 ± 0.4 [d]	1618 ± 23 [g]	1586 ± 21	IMRB		79BAR/MCI
$C_7H_4F_3NO_2^-$				Est	$\Delta_fH(A) = -604\pm8$	
mCF$_3$–nitrobenzene$^{-\cdot}$						
* -740 ± 18 [b]	1.41 ± 0.10			TDEq		87KEB/CHO
	1.34 ± 0.11			IMRE		85GRI/CAL
	1.33 ± 0.05			IMRE		85FUK/MCI
$C_7H_4F_3NO_2^-$				Est	$\Delta_fH(A) = -604\pm4$	
oCF$_3$–nitrobenzene$^{-\cdot}$						
* -732 ± 14 [b]	1.33 ± 0.10			TDEq		87KEB/CHO
$C_7H_4F_3NO_2^-$				Est	$\Delta_fH(A) = -604\pm4$	
pCF$_3$–nitrobenzene$^{-\cdot}$						
* -746 ± 14 [b]	1.47 ± 0.10			TDEq		87KEB/CHO
$C_7H_4F_3O^-$				Est	$\Delta_fH(AH) = -765\pm8$	
mCF$_3$–phenoxide$^-$					$BDE(A-H) = 362\pm8$	
* -875 ± 18 [a]	2.64 ± 0.19 [d]	1420 ± 10 [g]	1391 ± 8	IMRE		81FUJ/MCI
$C_7H_4F_3O^-$				Est	$\Delta_fH(AH) = -765\pm8$	
pCF$_3$–phenoxide$^-$					$BDE(A-H) = 362\pm13$	
* -885 ± 19 [a]	2.74 ± 0.24 [d]	1410 ± 11 [g]	1381 ± 8	IMRE		81FUJ/MCI
$C_7H_4F_3OS^-$					$BDE(A-H) = 362\pm8$	
mSCF$_3$–phenoxide$^-$						
*	2.72 ± 0.20 [d]	1411 ± 11 [g]	1382 ± 8	IMRE		86TAF
$C_7H_4F_3OS^-$					$BDE(A-H) = 362\pm13$	
pSCF$_3$–phenoxide$^-$						
*	2.81 ± 0.23 [d]	1403 ± 10 [g]	1374 ± 8	IMRE		86TAF
$C_7H_4F_3O_3S^-$					$BDE(A-H) = 362\pm8$	
mSO$_2$CF$_3$–phenoxide$^-$						
*	3.06 ± 0.20 [d]	1379 ± 11 [g]	1350 ± 8	IMRE		86TAF
$C_7H_4F_3O_3S^-$					$BDE(A-H) = 362\pm13$	
pSO$_2$CF$_3$–phenoxide$^-$						
*	3.36 ± 0.24 [d]	1350 ± 11 [g]	1321 ± 8	IMRE		86TAF
$C_7H_4F_4O^-$				Est	$\Delta_fH(A) = -845\pm4$	
2,3,5,6–tetrafluoroanisole$^{-\cdot}$						
-866 ± 13 [b]	0.22 ± 0.09			ECD		84HER/WEN
$C_7H_4NO^-$				Est	$\Delta_fH(AH) = 43\pm8$	
mCN–phenoxide$^-$					$BDE(A-H) = 362\pm8$	
* -82 ± 18 [a]	2.79 ± 0.19 [d]	1405 ± 10 [g]	1376 ± 8	IMRE		81FUJ/MCI
		1405 ± 10 [g]	1377 ± 8	IMRE		77MCM/KEB

Table 2. Negative Ion Table – Continued

Ion $\Delta_f H(X\cdot\cdot Y^-)$	$\Delta_f H(A^-)$ EA(A) eV	$\Delta H_{acid}(AH)$ $\Delta H_{aff}(X\cdot\cdot Y^-)$	$\Delta G_{acid}(AH)$ $\Delta G_{aff}(X\cdot\cdot Y^-)$	Method	Comment	Reference
$C_7H_4NO^-$						
oCN-phenoxide$^-$				Est2	$\Delta_f H(AH)= 25\pm13$	
					BDE(A–H)= 378±17	
*	−105±25 [a] 3.00±0.30 [d]	1400±12 [g]	1369±8	IMRE		81FUJ/MCI
		1400±12 [g]	1369±8	IMRE		77MCM/KEB
$C_7H_4NO^-$						
pCN-phenoxide$^-$				Est	$\Delta_f H(AH)= 43\pm8$	
*	−97±19 [a]	1390±11 [g]	1361±8	IMRE		81FUJ/MCI
		1392±11 [g]	1363±8	IMRE		77MCM/KEB
$C_7H_4NO_4^-$						
mNO$_2$-benzoate$^-$				Est	$\Delta_f H(AH)= -310\pm8$	
					BDE(A–H)= 444±13	
*	−458±19 [a] 3.88±0.24 [d]	1382±11 [g]	1350±8	IMRE		77MCM/KEB
		1379±11 [g]	1347±8	IMRE		86TAF
$C_7H_4N_2O_2^-$						
mCN-nitrobenzene$^{-\cdot}$				Est	$\Delta_f H(A)= 204\pm8$	
*	53±18 [b] 1.56±0.10			TDEq		87KEB/CHO
	1.48±0.11			IMRE		85GRI/CAL
	1.49±0.05			IMRE		85FUK/MCI
$C_7H_4N_2O_2^-$						
oCN-nitrobenzene$^{-\cdot}$				Est	$\Delta_f H(A)= 204\pm4$	
*	48±14 [b] 1.61±0.10			TDEq		87KEB/CHO
$C_7H_4N_2O_2^-$						
pCN-nitrobenzene$^{-\cdot}$				Est	$\Delta_f H(A)= 202\pm4$	
*	36±14 [b] 1.72±0.10			TDEq		87KEB/CHO
	1.65±0.11			IMRE		85GRI/CAL
$C_7H_4N_3O_6^-$					$\Delta_f H(AH)= 39\pm2$	77PEL
2,4,6-triNO$_2$-C$_6$H$_2$CH$_2^-$						
	−112±27 [a]	1379±25 [g]	1351±21	IMRB		74DZI/CAR
$C_7H_5ClNO^-$						
pCN-C$_6$H$_4$OH$\cdot\cdot$Cl$^-$						
		141±8	109±8	TDEq		77CUM/FRE
$C_7H_5ClO_2^-$						
2-Cl-5-Me-benzoquinone$^{-\cdot}$				Est2	$\Delta_f H(A)= -180\pm17$	
*	−375±21 [b] 2.02±0.05			IMRE		85FUK/MCI
$C_7H_5FO^-$						
mF-benzaldehyde$^{-\cdot}$				Est	$\Delta_f H(A)= -230\pm8$	
	−295±13 [b] 0.67±0.05			ECD		75WEN/KAO
$C_7H_5FO^-$						
oF-benzaldehyde$^{-\cdot}$				Est	$\Delta_f H(A)= -230\pm21$	
	−292±25 [b] 0.64±0.04			ECD		75WEN/KAO

Table 2. Negative Ion Table — Continued

Ion $\Delta_f H(X\cdot\cdot Y^-)$	$\Delta_f H(A^-)$	EA(A) eV	$\Delta H_{acid}(AH)$ $\Delta H_{aff}(X\cdot\cdot Y^-)$	$\Delta G_{acid}(AH)$ $\Delta G_{aff}(X\cdot\cdot Y^-)$	Method	Comment	Reference
$C_7H_5FO^-$							
pF–benzaldehyde$^-\cdot$					Est	$\Delta_f H(A) = -226\pm8$	
	-273 ± 10 [b]	0.49 ± 0.02			ECD		75WEN/KAO
$C_7H_5F_3N^-$							
mCF$_3$–anilide$^-$					Est	$\Delta_f H(AH) = -585\pm8$	
						$BDE(A-H) = 368\pm13$	
*	-621 ± 18 [a]		1493 ± 10 [g]	1463 ± 8	IMRE		79BAR/SCO
				1472 ± 8	IMRE^o		79BAR/SCO
$C_7H_5F_3N^-$							
pCF$_3$–anilide$^-$					Est	$\Delta_f H(AH) = -585\pm10$	
*	-636 ± 19 [a]		1479 ± 10 [g]	1448 ± 8	IMRE		79BAR/SCO
				1457 ± 8	IMRE^o		79BAR/SCO
$C_7H_5F_3NO_2S^-$							
mSO$_2$CF$_3$–anilide$^-$						$BDE(A-H) = 368\pm13$	
*		2.37 ± 0.24 [d]	1451 ± 11 [g]	1421 ± 8	IMRE		86TAF
$C_7H_5F_3NO_2S^-$							
pSO$_2$CF$_3$–anilide$^-$						$BDE(A-H) = 368\pm13$	
*		2.73 ± 0.24 [d]	1417 ± 11 [g]	1386 ± 8	IMRE		86TAF
$C_7H_5F_3NS^-$							
mSCF$_3$–anilide$^-$						$BDE(A-H) = 368\pm13$	
*		2.01 ± 0.24 [d]	1487 ± 11 [g]	1456 ± 8	IMRE		86TAF
$C_7H_5F_3NS^-$							
pSCF$_3$–anilide$^-$						$BDE(A-H) = 368\pm13$	
*		2.19 ± 0.24 [d]	1469 ± 11 [g]	1438 ± 8	IMRE		86TAF
$C_7H_5N^-$							
benzonitrile$^-\cdot$						$\Delta_f H(A) = 219\pm2$	82CHU/NGU
	194 ± 4 [b]	0.26 ± 0.02			ECD		75WEN/KAO
		0.3 ± 0.1			ECD		83ZLA/LEE
$C_7H_5NO_3^-$							
mCHO–nitrobenzene$^-\cdot$					Est	$\Delta_f H(A) = -52\pm4$	
*	-188 ± 14 [b]	1.41 ± 0.10			TDEq		87KEB/CHO
$C_7H_5NO_3^-$							
oCHO–nitrobenzene$^-\cdot$					Est	$\Delta_f H(A) = -52\pm4$	
*	-198 ± 14 [b]	1.51 ± 0.10			TDEq		87KEB/CHO
$C_7H_5NO_3^-$							
pCHO–nitrobenzene$^-\cdot$					Est	$\Delta_f H(A) = -52\pm4$	
*	-213 ± 14 [b]	1.67 ± 0.10			TDEq		87KEB/CHO
$C_7H_5N_2^-$							
indazolide$^-$							
*			1456 ± 11 [g]	1424 ± 8	IMRE		86TAF

Table 2. Negative Ion Table − Continued

Ion $\Delta_fH(X\cdot\cdot Y^-)$	$\Delta_fH(A^-)$ EA(A) eV	$\Delta H_{acid}(AH)$ $\Delta H_{aff}(X\cdot\cdot Y^-)$	$\Delta G_{acid}(AH)$ $\Delta G_{aff}(X\cdot\cdot Y^-)$	Method	Comment	Reference
$C_7H_5N_2^-$ mCN−anilide$^-$				Est	$\Delta_f H(AH)= 223\pm4$ BDE(A−H)= 368 ± 13	
*	170 ± 14 [a] 2.11 ± 0.23 [d]	1477 ± 10 [g]	1446 ± 8	IMRE		86TAF
$C_7H_5N_2^-$ pCN−anilide$^-$				Est	$\Delta_f H(AH)= 216\pm4$	
*	146 ± 14 [a]	1460 ± 10 [g]	1429 ± 8	IMRE		86TAF
$C_7H_5O_2^-$ benzoate$^-$					$\Delta_f H(AH)= -294\pm2$ BDE(A−H)= 444 ± 13	77PED/RYL
*	-407 ± 14 [a]	1418 ± 12 [g]	1388 ± 8	IMRE		78CUM/KEB
		1423 ± 12 [g]	1393 ± 8	IMRE		81FUJ/MCI
$C_7H_5O_2^-$ mCHO−phenoxide$^-$				Est	$\Delta_f H(AH)= -213\pm8$ BDE(A−H)= 362 ± 8	
*	-319 ± 18 [a] 2.58 ± 0.19 [d]	1425 ± 10 [g]	1396 ± 8	IMRE		81FUJ/MCI
$C_7H_5O_2^-$ pCHO−phenoxide$^-$				Est	$\Delta_f H(AH)= -213\pm8$	
*	-350 ± 19 [a]	1393 ± 11 [g]	1364 ± 8	IMRE		81FUJ/MCI
$C_7H_5O_3^-$ mOH−benzoate$^-$				Est	$\Delta_f H(AH)= -470\pm8$ BDE(A−H)= 444 ± 13	
*	-587 ± 19 [a] 3.54 ± 0.24 [d]	1414 ± 11 [g]	1382 ± 8	IMRE		77MCM/KEB
$C_7H_5O_3^-$ oOH−benzoate$^-$					$\Delta_f H(AH)= -495$	77PED/RYL
*	-660 ± 13 [a]	1365 ± 12 [g]	1332 ± 8	IMRE		77MCM/KEB
$C_7H_5O_3^-$ pOH−benzoate$^-$				Est	$\Delta_f H(AH)= -470\pm8$ BDE(A−H)= 444 ± 13	
*	-598 ± 19 [a] 3.66 ± 0.24 [d]	1402 ± 11 [g]	1371 ± 8	IMRE		77MCM/KEB
$C_7H_6Cl^-$ mCl−$C_6H_4CH_2^-$				Est	$\Delta_f H(AH)= 18\pm8$ BDE(A−H)= 356 ± 8	80PRY
*	53 ± 19 [a] 1.07 ± 0.20 [d]	1565 ± 11 [g]	1535 ± 8	IMRE		83CAL/BAR
$C_7H_6Cl^-$ pCl−$C_6H_4CH_2^-$				Est	$\Delta_f H(AH)= 18\pm8$ BDE(A−H)= 360 ± 8	80PRY
*	53 ± 19 [a] 1.11 ± 0.20 [d]	1565 ± 11 [g]	1535 ± 8	IMRE		83CAL/BAR
$C_7H_6F^-$ mF−$C_6H_4CH_2^-$				Est	$\Delta_f H(AH)= -150\pm8$ BDE(A−H)= 358 ± 8	
*	-109 ± 19 [a] 1.03 ± 0.20 [d]	1571 ± 11 [g]	1541 ± 8	IMRE		83CAL/BAR
$C_7H_6F^-$ pF−$C_6H_4CH_2^-$					$\Delta_f H(AH)= -148\pm1$ BDE(A−H)= 360 ± 13	77PED/RYL
*	-90 ± 12 [a] 0.87 ± 0.24 [d]	1588 ± 11 [g]	1558 ± 8	IMRE		83CAL/BAR

Table 2. Negative Ion Table – Continued

Ion $\Delta_f H(A^-)$ EA(A) $\Delta_f H(X \cdot\cdot Y^-)$ eV	$\Delta H_{acid}(AH)$ $\Delta H_{aff}(X \cdot\cdot Y^-)$	$\Delta G_{acid}(AH)$ $\Delta G_{aff}(X \cdot\cdot Y^-)$	Method	Comment	Reference
$C_7H_6FNO_2^-$					
2-Me-4-F-nitrobenzene$^-$·			Est2	$\Delta_f H(A) = -155\pm17$	
* −246±21 [b] 0.95±0.05			IMRE		85FUK/MCI
$C_7H_6FO^-$					
mF−C$_6$H$_3$OMe$^-$			Est	$\Delta_f H(AH) = -267\pm8$	
* −208±23 [a]	1589±15 [g]	1556±13	IMRB		83ING/NIB
$C_7H_6FO^-$					
oF−C$_6$H$_3$OMe$^-$			Est	$\Delta_f H(AH) = -264\pm8$	
−175±32 [a]	1618±23 [g]	1586±21	IMRB		83ING/NIB
$C_7H_6FO^-$					
pF−C$_6$H$_3$OMe$^-$			Est	$\Delta_f H(AH) = -267\pm8$	
−178±32 [a]	1618±23 [g]	1586±21	IMRB		83ING/NIB
$C_7H_6NO^-$					
HN=C(Ph)O$^-$				$\Delta_f H(AH) = -101\pm13$	82TOR/SAB2
* −149±23 [a]	1482±11 [g]	1452±8	IMRE		86TAF
$C_7H_6NO^-$					
PhCH=NO$^-$			Est	$\Delta_f H(AH) = 108\pm8$	
* 54±28 [a]	1477±20 [g]	1447±8	IMRE		79BAR/SCO
		1453±8	IMRE^o		79BAR/SCO
$C_7H_6NO^-$					
mNO−C$_6$H$_4$CH$_2^-$			Est	$\Delta_f H(AH) = 55\pm4$ $BDE(A-H) = 360\pm13$	
* 64±15 [a] 1.38±0.24 [d]	1539±11 [g]	1511±8	IMRE		86TAF
$C_7H_6NO^-$					
pCHO−anilide$^-$			Est	$\Delta_f H(AH) = -34\pm4$	
* −101±15 [a]	1463±11 [g]	1432±8	IMRE		86TAF
$C_7H_6NO^-$					
pNO−C$_6$H$_4$CH$_2^-$			Est	$\Delta_f H(AH) = 55\pm4$	
* −3±15 [a]	1472±11 [g]	1444±8	IMRE		86TAF
$C_7H_6NO_2^-$					
mNH$_2$−benzoate$^-$				$\Delta_f H(AH) = -289\pm4$ $BDE(A-H) = 444\pm13$	77NAB/SAB
* −393±15 [a] 3.42±0.24 [d]	1426±11 [g]	1395±8	IMRE		77MCM/KEB
$C_7H_6NO_2^-$					
mNO$_2$−C$_6$H$_4$CH$_2^-$				$\Delta_f H(AH) = 31\pm4$ $BDE(A-H) = 360\pm13$	77PED/RYL
* 19±15 [a]	1518±11 [g]	1488±8	IMRE		83CAL/BAR
$C_7H_6NO_2^-$					
oNH$_2$−benzoate$^-$				$\Delta_f H(AH) = -298\pm2$	77NAB/SAB
* −422±14 [a]	1406±12 [g]	1377±8	IMRE		77MCM/KEB

Table 2. Negative Ion Table — Continued

Ion $\Delta_f H(X \cdots Y^-)$	EA(A) eV	$\Delta H_{acid}(AH)$ $\Delta H_{aff}(X \cdots Y^-)$	$\Delta G_{acid}(AH)$ $\Delta G_{aff}(X \cdots Y^-)$	Method	Comment	Reference
$C_7H_6NO_2^-$						
oNO_2-$C_6H_4CH_2^-$				Est2	$\Delta_f H(AH) = 53\pm13$	
* 13±23 [a]		1490±11 [g]	1459±8	IMRE		86TAF
$C_7H_6NO_2^-$						
pNH_2-benzoate$^-$					$\Delta_f H(AH) = -294\pm4$	77NAB/SAB
					BDE(A-H) = 444±13	
* -397±15 [a] 3.40±0.24 [d]		1427±11 [g]	1397±8	IMRE		77MCM/KEB
$C_7H_6NO_2^-$						
pNO_2-$C_6H_4CH_2^-$					$\Delta_f H(AH) = 30\pm4$	77PED/RYL
* -25±14 [a]		1475±10 [g]	1445±8	IMRE		86TAF
-23±14 [a]		1477±10 [g]	1447±8	IMRE		78CUM/KEB
$C_7H_6NO_3^-$						
2-Me-4-NO_2-phenoxide$^-$				Est	$\Delta_f H(AH) = -142\pm8$	
* -297±21 [a]		1375±12 [g]	1343±8	IMRE		81FUJ/MCI
$C_7H_6N_2O_4^-$						
2-Me-3-NO_2-nitrobenzene$^-$·				Est2	$\Delta_f H(A) = 203\pm13$	
* 69±17 [b] 1.39±0.05				IMRE		85FUK/MCI
$C_7H_6O^-$						
benzaldehyde$^-$·					$\Delta_f H(A) = -37\pm2$	77PED/RYL
-78±3 [b] 0.429±0.009				ECD		75WEN/KAO
0.39±0.05				ECD		83ZLA/LEE
0.42±0.01				ECD		67WEN/CHE
$C_7H_6O_2^-$						
methylbenzoquinone$^-$·				Est	$\Delta_f H(A) = -155\pm8$	
* -334±18 [b] 1.85±0.10				TDEq		87KEB/CHO
1.75±0.11				IMRE		85GRI/CAL
1.76±0.05				IMRE		85FUK/MCI
$C_7H_7^-$						
$PhCH_2^-$					$\Delta_f H(AH) = 50$	77PED/RYL
					BDE(A-H) = 368±4	82MCM/GOL
* 113±10 [a] 0.90±0.15 [d]		1593±10 [g]	1564±8	IMRE		79BAR/SCO
* 0.863±0.013				LPD		84DRZ/BRA2
0.885±0.065				LPD		75RIC/STE
		1609±31 [g]	1579±29	IMRB		71BOH/YOU
2.35±0.07				SI		76FAI/JOY
1.1				SI		72PAG
0.8				SI		69PAG/GOO
0.8				SI		68GAI/PAG
			1558±8	IMRE^o		79BAR/SCO
$C_7H_7^-$						
cycloheptatrienide$^-$					$\Delta_f H(AH) = 183\pm1$	77PED/RYL
					BDE(A-H) = 305±8	82MCM/GOL
* 223±13 [a] 0.49±0.21 [d]		1570±12 [g]	1545±8	IMRE		79BAR/SCO
			1539±8	IMRE^o		79BAR/SCO

Table 2. Negative Ion Table – Continued

Ion $\Delta_f H(A^-)$ $\Delta_f H(X\cdot\cdot Y^-)$	EA(A) eV	ΔH_{acid}(AH) $\Delta H_{aff}(X\cdot\cdot Y^-)$	ΔG_{acid}(AH) $\Delta G_{aff}(X\cdot\cdot Y^-)$	Method	Comment	Reference
$C_7H_7^-$					$\Delta_f H(AH) = 238\pm4$	80ROG/CHO
norbornadienide$^-$						
* 380±14 [a]		1672±10 [g]	1637±6	IMRB	Between $EtNH_2$, $nPrNH_2$	86LEE/SQU
			1628±21	IMRB		81WRI/BEA
$C_7H_7ClNO_2^-$						
pNO_2-$C_6H_4CH_3\cdot\cdot Cl^-$						
			31	TDEq		82FRE/IKU
$C_7H_7F_2^-$						
$PhCH_2F\cdot\cdot F^-$						
* −230 [c]		102±8 [g]	69±8	IMRE		83LAR/MCM
$C_7H_7NO_2^-$						
mMe-nitrobenzene$^{-\cdot}$				Est	$\Delta_f H(A) = 31\pm4$	
* −65±14 [b]	0.99±0.10			TDEq		87KEB/CHO
	0.93±0.11			IMRE		85GRI/CAL
	0.92±0.05			IMRE		85FUK/MCI
	0.8±0.1			ECD		83ZLA/LEE
$C_7H_7NO_2^-$						
oMe-nitrobenzene$^{-\cdot}$					$\Delta_f H(A) = 53\pm8$	77PED/RYL
* −36±18 [b]	0.92±0.10			TDEq		87KEB/CHO
	0.87±0.11			IMRE		85GRI/CAL
	0.89±0.05			IMRE		85FUK/MCI
$C_7H_7NO_2^-$						
pMe-nitrobenzene$^{-\cdot}$					$\Delta_f H(A) = 31\pm4$	77PED/RYL
* −61±13 [b]	0.95±0.10			TDEq		87KEB/CHO
	0.89±0.11			IMRE		85GRI/CAL
	0.91±0.05			IMRE		85FUK/MCI
$C_7H_7NO_3^-$						
3-Me-4-NO_2-phenoxide$^-$				Est	$\Delta_f H(AH) = -142\pm17$	
* −292±28 [a]		1380±11 [g]	1350±8	IMRE		81FUJ/MCI
$C_7H_7NO_3^-$						
mOMe-nitrobenzene$^{-\cdot}$				Est	$\Delta_f H(A) = -90\pm4$	
* −191±14 [b]	1.04±0.10			TDEq		87KEB/CHO
	0.98±0.11			IMRE		85GRI/CAL
$C_7H_7NO_3^-$						
pOMe-nitrobenzene$^{-\cdot}$				Est	$\Delta_f H(A) = -90\pm4$	
* −178±14 [b]	0.91±0.10			TDEq		87KEB/CHO
	0.85±0.11			IMRE		85GRI/CAL
$C_7H_7O^-$					$\Delta_f H(AH) = -100\pm1$	77PED/RYL
$PhCH_2O^-$					BDE(A-H) = 436±4	
* −82±13 [a]	2.07±0.17 [d]	1548±12 [g]	1520±8	IMRE		79BAR/SCO
*	2.142±0.013			LPD		85MOY/DOD
			1519±8	IMRE^o		79BAR/SCO

Table 2. Negative Ion Table – Continued

Ion $\Delta_fH(X\cdots Y^-)$	$\Delta_fH(A^-)$	EA(A) eV	$\Delta H_{acid}(AH)$ $\Delta H_{aff}(X\cdots Y^-)$	$\Delta G_{acid}(AH)$ $\Delta G_{aff}(X\cdots Y^-)$	Method	Comment	Reference
$C_7H_7O^-$						$\Delta_f H(AH) = -132\pm1$	79KUD/KUD
mMe–phenoxide$^-$						BDE(A–H) = 362±8	
*	−200±11 [a]	2.19±0.19 [d]	1463±10 [g]	1434±8	IMRE		81FUJ/MCI
			1467±10 [g]	1438±8	IMRE		77MCM/KEB
$C_7H_7O^-$						$\Delta_f H(AH) = -124\pm1$	79KUD/KUD
oMe–phenoxide$^-$						BDE(A–H) = 362±13	
*	−192±13 [a]	2.19±0.26 [d]	1462±12 [g]	1431±8	IMRE		81FUJ/MCI
*		<2.36±0.06			PD		75RIC/STE2
			1465±12 [g]	1434±8	IMRE		77MCM/KEB
$C_7H_7O^-$						$\Delta_f H(AH) = -125\pm2$	79KUD/KUD
pMe–phenoxide$^-$						BDE(A–H) = 362±13	
*	−190±11 [a]	2.16±0.23 [d]	1466±10 [g]	1437±8	IMRE		81FUJ/MCI
			1466±10 [g]	1437±8	IMRE		79BAR/SCO
			1471±10 [g]	1442±8	IMRE		77MCM/KEB
$C_7H_7O_2^-$					Est	$\Delta_f H(AH) = -250\pm8$	
mOMe–phenoxide$^-$						BDE(A–H) = 362±8	
*	−324±18 [a]	2.26±0.19 [d]	1456±10 [g]	1427±8	IMRE		81FUJ/MCI
			1459±10 [g]	1431±8	IMRE		77MCM/KEB
$C_7H_7O_2^-$					Est2	$\Delta_f H(AH) = -264\pm17$	
oOMe–phenoxide$^-$							
*				1433±8	IMRE		77MCM/KEB
$C_7H_7O_2^-$					Est	$\Delta_f H(AH) = -242\pm8$	
pOMe–phenoxide$^-$						BDE(A–H) = 362±13	
*	−306±18 [a]	2.15±0.23 [d]	1466±10 [g]	1437±8	IMRE		81FUJ/MCI
			1469±10 [g]	1440±8	IMRE		77MCM/KEB
$C_7H_7O_2S^-$						$\Delta_f H(AH) = -254\pm3$	77PED/RYL
PhSO$_2$CH$_2^-$							
*	−266±13 [a]		1518±10 [g]	1487±8	IMRE		78CUM/KEB
$C_7H_7O_2S^-$					Est	$\Delta_f H(AH) = -194\pm8$	
mSOMe–phenoxide$^-$						BDE(A–H) = 362±8	
*	−297±18 [a]	2.55±0.19 [d]	1428±10 [g]	1399±8	IMRE		81FUJ/MCI
$C_7H_7O_2S^-$					Est	$\Delta_f H(AH) = -194\pm8$	
pSOMe–phenoxide$^-$							
*	−312±19 [a]		1412±11 [g]	1383±8	IMRE		81FUJ/MCI
$C_7H_7O_3S^-$					Est	$\Delta_f H(AH) = -443\pm8$	
mSO$_2$Me–phenoxide$^-$						BDE(A–H) = 362±8	
*	−567±18 [a]	2.77±0.19 [d]	1406±10 [g]	1377±8	IMRE		81FUJ/MCI
$C_7H_7O_3S^-$					Est	$\Delta_f H(AH) = -443\pm8$	
pSO$_2$Me–phenoxide$^-$							
*	−587±19 [a]		1385±11 [g]	1356±8	IMRE		81FUJ/MCI

Table 2. Negative Ion Table - Continued

Ion $\Delta_f H(A^-)$ $\Delta_f H(X\cdots Y^-)$	EA(A) eV	$\Delta H_{acid}(AH)$ $\Delta H_{aff}(X\cdots Y^-)$	$\Delta G_{acid}(AH)$ $\Delta G_{aff}(X\cdots Y^-)$	Method	Comment	Reference
$C_7H_7S^-$ MeSC$_6$H$_4^-$					$\Delta_f H(AH)=$ 98±1 BDE(A-H)= 460±13	77PED/RYL
185±25 [a]		1617±23 [g]	1586±21 1583±33	IMRB IMRB[o]		85ING/NIB 85ING/NIB
$C_7H_7S^-$ PhSCH$_2^-$					$\Delta_f H(AH)=$ 98±1	77PED/RYL
* 164±12 [a]		1597±11 [g]	1566±8 1560±8	IMRE IMRE[o]		85ING/NIB 85ING/NIB
$C_7H_8Cl^-$ PhMe$\cdots$Cl$^-$			17	TDEq		82FRE/IKU
$C_7H_8ClO^-$ PhOMe$\cdots$Cl$^-$			31	TDEq		82FRE/IKU
$C_7H_8ClO^-$ pMe-C$_6$H$_4$OH$\cdots$Cl$^-$						
* −453±11 [c]		101±8	69±8	TDEq		77CUM/FRE
$C_7H_8N^-$ PhNMe$^-$					$\Delta_f H(AH)=$ 85±4 BDE(A-H)= 366±8	78COL/BEN 82MCM/GOL
* 81±15 [a]	1.57±0.20 [d]	1526±11 [g]	1496±8	IMRE		86TAF
$C_7H_8N^-$ mMe-anilide$^-$				Est	$\Delta_f H(AH)=$ 54±8 BDE(A-H)= 368±13	
* 59±18 [a]	1.51±0.23 [d]	1535±10 [g]	1505±8 1507±8	IMRE IMRE[o]		79BAR/SCO 79BAR/SCO
$C_7H_8N^-$ pMe-anilide$^-$				Est	$\Delta_f H(AH)=$ 59±4 BDE(A-H)= 368±13	
* 65±15 [a]	1.49±0.24 [d]	1537±11 [g]	1507±8 1510±8	IMRE IMRE[o]		79BAR/SCO 79BAR/SCO
$C_7H_8NO^-$ pOMe-anilide$^-$				Est	$\Delta_f H(AH)=$ −59±8 BDE(A-H)= 368±13	
* −53±18 [a]	1.50±0.23 [d]	1536±10 [g]	1505±8 1509±8	IMRE IMRE[o]		79BAR/SCO 79BAR/SCO
$C_7H_8NO_2S^-$ mSO$_2$Me-anilide$^-$				Est	$\Delta_f H(AH)=$ −236±4 BDE(A-H)= 368±13	
* −291±15 [a]	2.13±0.24 [d]	1475±11 [g]	1445±8	IMRE		86TAF
$C_7H_8NO_2S^-$ pSO$_2$Me-anilide$^-$				Est	$\Delta_f H(AH)=$ −236±4 BDE(A-H)= 368±13	
* −312±15 [a]	2.34±0.24 [d]	1455±11 [g]	1424±8	IMRE		86TAF

Table 2. Negative Ion Table – Continued

Ion $\Delta_fH(A^-)$ $\Delta_fH(X\cdot\cdot Y^-)$	EA(A) eV	ΔH_{acid}(AH) $\Delta H_{aff}(X\cdot\cdot Y^-)$	ΔG_{acid}(AH) $\Delta G_{aff}(X\cdot\cdot Y^-)$	Method	Comment	Reference
$C_7H_8NS^-$ mSMe–anilide$^-$				Est	$\Delta_fH(AH) = 104\pm8$ BDE(A–H) = 368 ± 13	
* 89 ± 18 [a]	1.71 ± 0.23 [d]	1515 ± 10 [g]	1484 ± 8	IMRE		79BAR/SCO
			1492 ± 8	IMRE^o		79BAR/SCO
$C_7H_9^-$ heptatrienide$^-$				Est	$\Delta_fH(AH) = 133\pm4$	
*	1.27 ± 0.03			PD		78ZIM/GYG
$C_7H_9^-$ norbornenide$^-$					$\Delta_fH(AH) = 90\pm4$	80ROG/CHO
242 ± 19 [a]		1682 ± 15 [g]	1648 ± 13	IMRB	between NH_3, $EtNH_2$	86LEE/SQU
$C_7H_9O^-$ 2–norbornanone enolate$^-$					$\Delta_fH(AH) = -168\pm3$	78STE
*	1.61 ± 0.05			PD		78ZIM/JAC
$C_7H_{11}O^-$ 2,5–diMe–cyclopentanone enolate$^-$				Est	$\Delta_fH(AH) = -272\pm4$	
*	1.49 ± 0.04			PD		78ZIM/JAC
$C_7H_{11}O^-$ cycloheptanone enolate$^-$					$\Delta_fH(AH) = -248\pm2$	77PED/RYL
*	1.48 ± 0.04			PD		78ZIM/JAC
$C_7H_{11}O_4^-$ $HC(CO_2Et)_2^-$				Est	$\Delta_fH(AH) = -839\pm2$	
* -912 ± 12 [a]		1457 ± 10 [g]	1432 ± 8	IMRE		78CUM/KEB
$C_7H_{13}O^-$ $EtCH=C(nPr)O^-$				Est	$\Delta_fH(AH) = -301\pm4$ BDE(A–H) = 389 ± 8	
* -296 ± 18 [a]	1.72 ± 0.06	1535 ± 14 [e]		PD		77ZIM/REE
$C_7H_{13}O^-$ $Me_2C=C(iPr)O^-$					$\Delta_fH(AH) = -311\pm1$ BDE(A–H) = 364 ± 13	77PED/RYL
* -307 ± 19 [a]	1.47 ± 0.05	1535 ± 18 [e]	1505 ± 23 [h]	PD		77ZIM/REE
$C_7H_{13}O^-$ c-C_6H_{11}–CH_2O^-				Est	$\Delta_fH(AH) = -305\pm4$ BDE(A–H) = 435 ± 8	
* -271 ± 14 [a]	1.90 ± 0.19 [d]	1564 ± 10 [g]	1536 ± 8	IMRE		86TAF
$C_7H_{13}S^-$ c-C_6H_{11}–CH_2S^-				Est	$\Delta_fH(AH) = -116\pm4$ BDE(A–H) = 364 ± 10	
* -171 ± 16 [a]	2.09 ± 0.23 [d]	1475 ± 12 [g]	1449 ± 8	IMRE		86TAF
$C_7H_{15}O^-$ $(iPr)_2CHO^-$				Est	$\Delta_fH(AH) = -369\pm4$ BDE(A–H) = 438 ± 4	
* -348 ± 15 [a]	2.1 ± 0.2 [d]	1551 ± 11	1523 ± 13 [h]	CIDC		83BOA/HOU
		1549 ± 10		CIDC^o		83BOA/HOU

Table 2. Negative Ion Table – Continued

Ion $\Delta_f H(X \cdots Y^-)$	$\Delta_f H(A^-)$	EA(A) eV	$\Delta H_{acid}(AH)$ $\Delta H_{aff}(X \cdots Y^-)$	$\Delta G_{acid}(AH)$ $\Delta G_{aff}(X \cdots Y^-)$	Method	Comment	Reference
$C_7H_{15}O^-$							
Et$_3$CO$^-$					Est	$\Delta_f H(AH)= -366\pm4$	
						BDE(A–H)= 440±4	
*	−344±15 [a]	2.1±0.2 [d]	1552±11	1524±13 [h]	CIDC		83BOA/HOU
			1549±10		CIDC^o		83BOA/HOU
$C_7H_{15}O^-$							
nBuC(Me)$_2$O$^-$					Est	$\Delta_f H(AH)= -373\pm4$	
						BDE(A–H)= 440±4	
*	−348±15 [a]	2.0±0.2 [d]	1555±11	1527±13 [h]	CIDC		83BOA/HOU
			1552±10		CIDC^o		83BOA/HOU
$C_7H_{15}O^-$							
nC$_7$H$_{15}$O$^-$						$\Delta_f H(AH)= -336\pm2$	77PED/RYL
						BDE(A–H)= 436±4	
*	−307±13 [a]	2.0±0.2 [d]	1559±11	1531±13 [h]	CIDC		83BOA/HOU
			1555±10		CIDC^o		83BOA/HOU
$C_7H_{15}O^-$							
tBuCH(Et)O$^-$					Est	$\Delta_f H(AH)= -371\pm4$	
						BDE(A–H)= 438±4	
*	−353±16 [a]	2.10±0.17 [d]	1548±12 [g]	1520±8	IMRE		79BAR/SCO
				1519±8	IMRE^o		79BAR/SCO
$C_7H_{15}OS_2^-$							
MeOH··5,5-diMe-1,3-dithianide$^-$							
	−287±38 [c]		62±10 [g]	34±7	IMRE		84CAL/ROZ
$C_7H_{17}O_2^-$							
EtOH··tBuCH$_2$O$^-$							
	−605±24 [c]		80±10 [g]	53±8	IMRE		84CAL/ROZ
$C_7H_{17}O_2^-$							
nPrOH··tBuO$^-$							
	−615±23 [c]		85±10 [g]	57±8	IMRE		84CAL/ROZ
$C_8F_4N_2^-$							
pCN-perfluorobenzonitrile$^{-\cdot}$					Est	$\Delta_f H(A)= -417\pm17$	
*	−599±26 [b]	1.89±0.10			TDEq		87KEB/CHO
		1.89±0.10			IMRE		86CHO/GRI
$C_8HN_2O_2^-$							
2,3-diCN-benzoquinonide$^-$							
		1.82±0.09			SI		66FAR/PAG
$C_8H_3F_5O^-$							
C$_6$F$_5$COCH$_3^{-\cdot}$					Est	$\Delta_f H(A)= -1052\pm17$	
*	−1143±26 [b]	0.94±0.10			TDEq		87KEB/CHO
		0.94±0.10			IMRE		86CHO/GRI
$C_8H_3F_6NO_2^-$							
3,5-diCF$_3$-nitrobenzene$^{-\cdot}$					Est	$\Delta_f H(A)= -1276\pm4$	
*	−1449±14 [b]	1.79±0.10			TDEq		87KEB/CHO

Table 2. Negative Ion Table – Continued

Ion $\Delta_fH(A^-)$ $\Delta_fH(X\cdot\cdot Y^-)$	EA(A) eV	$\Delta H_{acid}(AH)$ $\Delta H_{aff}(X\cdot\cdot Y^-)$	$\Delta G_{acid}(AH)$ $\Delta G_{aff}(X\cdot\cdot Y^-)$	Method	Comment	Reference
$C_8H_3F_6O^-$						
3,5–diCF$_3$–phenoxide$^-$				Est	$\Delta_fH(AH) = -1485\pm17$	
					BDE(A–H)= 362±13	
* −1636±28 [a]	3.05±0.24 [d]	1380±11 [g]	1351±8	IMRE		86TAF
$C_8H_4F_3N^-$						
mCF$_3$–benzonitrile$^{-\cdot}$				Est	$\Delta_fH(A) = -434\pm8$	
* −499±18 [b]	0.67±0.10			TDEq		87KEB/CHO
	0.67±0.09			TDEq		86CHO/KEB
$C_8H_4F_3N^-$						
oCF$_3$–benzonitrile$^{-\cdot}$				Est	$\Delta_fH(A) = -452\pm4$	
* −519±14 [b]	0.70±0.10			TDEq		87KEB/CHO
$C_8H_4F_3N^-$						
pCF$_3$–benzonitrile$^{-\cdot}$				Est	$\Delta_fH(A) = -452\pm4$	
* −525±14 [b]	0.76±0.10			TDEq		87KEB/CHO
$C_8H_4F_3O_2^-$						
mCF$_3$–benzoate$^-$				Est	$\Delta_fH(AH) = -976\pm8$	
					BDE(A–H)= 444±13	
* −1114±19 [a]	3.77±0.24 [d]	1392±11 [g]	1361±8	IMRE		86TAF
$C_8H_4F_3O_2^-$						
pCF$_3$–benzoate$^-$				Est	$\Delta_fH(AH) = -976\pm8$	
					BDE(A–H)= 444±13	
* −1115±19 [a]	3.78±0.24 [d]	1391±11 [g]	1361±8	IMRE		86TAF
$C_8H_4F_6N^-$						
3,5–diCF$_3$–anilide$^-$				Est	$\Delta_fH(AH) = -1302\pm8$	
					BDE(A–H)= 368±13	
* −1377±19 [a]	2.33±0.24 [d]	1456±11 [g]	1425±8	IMRE		86TAF
$C_8H_4NO_2^-$						
mCN–benzoate$^-$				Est	$\Delta_fH(AH) = -158\pm13$	
					BDE(A–H)= 444±13	
* −309±23 [a]	3.90±0.24 [d]	1379±11 [g]	1348±8	IMRE		77MCM/KEB
$C_8H_4NO_2^-$						
pCN–benzoate$^-$				Est	$\Delta_fH(AH) = -158\pm13$	
					BDE(A–H)= 444±13	
* −314±23 [a]	3.95±0.24 [d]	1374±11 [g]	1345±8	IMRE		77MCM/KEB
$C_8H_4N_2^-$						
mCN–benzonitrile$^{-\cdot}$					$\Delta_fH(A) = 363\pm2$	80SAT/SAK
* 275±12 [b]	0.91±0.10			TDEq		87KEB/CHO
	0.91±0.09			TDEq		86CHO/KEB
$C_8H_4N_2^-$						
o-CN–benzonitrile$^{-\cdot}$				Est2	$\Delta_fH(A) = 363\pm13$	
* 271±22 [b]	0.95±0.10			TDEq		87KEB/CHO
	0.95±0.09			TDEq		86CHO/KEB
	1.1±0.1			SI		67FAR/PAG
$C_8H_4N_2^-$						
p-CN–benzonitrile$^{-\cdot}$				Est2	$\Delta_fH(A) = 363\pm8$	
* 257±18 [b]	1.10±0.10			TDEq		87KEB/CHO
	1.10±0.09			TDEq		86CHO/KEB

Table 2. Negative Ion Table - Continued

Ion $\Delta_f H(A^-)$ $\Delta_f H(X\cdot\cdot Y^-)$	EA(A) eV	$\Delta H_{acid}(AH)$ $\Delta H_{aff}(X\cdot\cdot Y^-)$	$\Delta G_{acid}(AH)$ $\Delta G_{aff}(X\cdot\cdot Y^-)$	Method	Comment	Reference
$C_8H_4O_3^-$ phthalic anhydride$^-\cdot$						
* −487±12 [b]	1.21±0.10			TDEq		87KEB/CHO
*	1.20±0.05			IMRE		85FUK/MCI
$C_8H_5^-$ PhC≡C$^-$					$\Delta_f H(AH) = 306\pm2$ BDE(A−H) = 552±21	85DAV/ALL
* 327±15 [a]	3.25±0.36 [d]	1551±13 [g]	1518±8	IMRE		79BAR/SCO
			1518±8	IMRE^o		79BAR/SCO
$C_8H_5ClN^-$ mCl−C$_6$H$_4$CHCN$^-$				Est	$\Delta_f H(AH) = 156\pm4$	
* 68±18 [a]		1441±13 [g]	1412±8	IMRE		81FUJ/MCI
$C_8H_5ClN^-$ pCl−C$_6$H$_4$CHCN$^-$				Est	$\Delta_f H(AH) = 156\pm4$	
* 70±18 [a]		1444±13 [g]	1416±8	IMRE		81FUJ/MCI
$C_8H_5FN^-$ mF−C$_6$H$_4$CHCN$^-$				Est	$\Delta_f H(AH) = -7\pm4$	
* −70±19 [a]		1467±15 [g]	1439±8	IMRE		86TAF
$C_8H_5FN^-$ pF−C$_6$H$_4$CHCN$^-$				Est	$\Delta_f H(AH) = -7\pm4$	
* −77±15 [a]		1460±11 [g]	1433±8	IMRE		86TAF
$C_8H_5F_3NO^-$ PhN=C(CF$_3$)O$^-$				Est2	$\Delta_f H(AH) = -706\pm13$	
* −841±23 [a]		1395±11 [g]	1366±8	IMRE		86TAF
$C_8H_5NO^-$ mCHO−benzonitrile$^-\cdot$				Est	$\Delta_f H(A) = 99\pm4$	
* 2±14 [b]	1.00±0.10			TDEq		87KEB/CHO
	1.01±0.09			TDEq		86CHO/KEB
$C_8H_5NO^-$ pCHO−benzonitrile$^-\cdot$				Est	$\Delta_f H(A) = 99\pm4$	
* −19±14 [b]	1.22±0.10			TDEq		87KEB/CHO
	1.22±0.09			TDEq		86CHO/KEB
$C_8H_5N_2O_2^-$ mNO$_2$−C$_6$H$_4$CHCN$^-$				Est	$\Delta_f H(AH) = 171\pm4$	
* 53±19 [a]		1412±15 [g]	1384±8	IMRE		86TAF
$C_8H_5N_2O_2^-$ pNO$_2$−C$_6$H$_4$CHCN$^-$				Est	$\Delta_f H(AH) = 171\pm4$	
* 19±18 [a]		1378±13 [g]	1350±8	IMRE		81FUJ/MCI
$C_8H_5O_3^-$ pCHO−benzoate$^-$				Est	$\Delta_f H(AH) = -414\pm8$ BDE(A−H) = 444±13	
* −550±19 [a]	3.74±0.24 [d]	1395±11 [g]	1363±8	IMRE		86TAF

Table 2. Negative Ion Table — Continued

Ion $\Delta_f H(X \cdots Y^-)$	$\Delta_f H(A^-)$ EA(A) eV	$\Delta H_{acid}(AH)$ $\Delta H_{aff}(X \cdots Y^-)$	$\Delta G_{acid}(AH)$ $\Delta G_{aff}(X \cdots Y^-)$	Method	Comment	Reference
$C_8H_6ClO^-$				Est	$\Delta_f H(AH) = -116\pm 8$	
mCl-C_6H_4C(=CH_2)O^-						
*	-152 ± 18 [a]	1495 ± 10 [g]	1466 ± 8	IMRE		79BAR/SCO
$C_8H_6Cl_2O_2^-$						
2,5-diCl-3,6-diMe-benzoquinone$^-\cdot$				Est2	$\Delta_f H(A) = -230\pm 17$	
*	-437 ± 21 [b] 2.14 ± 0.05			IMRE		85FUK/MCI
$C_8H_6F_3^-$				Est	$\Delta_f H(AH) = -622\pm 8$	
mCF$_3$-C_6H_4CH$_2^-$						
*	-608 ± 18 [a]	1545 ± 10 [g]	1515 ± 8	IMRE		83CAL/BAR
$C_8H_6F_3^-$				Est	$\Delta_f H(AH) = -622\pm 8$	
pCF$_3$-C_6H_4CH$_2^-$						
*	-617 ± 18 [a]	1536 ± 10 [g]	1505 ± 8	IMRE		83CAL/BAR
$C_8H_6F_3O_2^-$						
pSO$_2$CF$_3$-C_6H_4CH$_2^-$						
*		1454 ± 11 [g]	1425 ± 8	IMRE		86TAF
$C_8H_6N^-$				Est	$\Delta_f H(AH) = 186\pm 4$	
PhCHCN$^-$						
*	123 ± 18 [a]	1467 ± 13 [g]	1440 ± 8	IMRE		81FUJ/MCI
		1471 ± 13 [g]	1443 ± 8	IMRE		78CUM/KEB
			1451 ± 8	IMRE^o		79BAR/SCO
$C_8H_6N^-$					$\Delta_f H(AH) = 157\pm 5$	77PED/RYL
indolide$^-$						
*	89 ± 15 [a]	1461 ± 11 [g]	1431 ± 8	IMRE		86TAF
$C_8H_6N^-$				Est	$\Delta_f H(AH) = 183\pm 8$	
mCN-C_6H_4CH$_2^-$						
*	198 ± 18 [a]	1545 ± 10 [g]	1515 ± 8	IMRE		83CAL/BAR
$C_8H_6N^-$				Est	$\Delta_f H(AH) = 182\pm 8$	
pCN-C_6H_4CH$_2^-$						
*	162 ± 19 [a]	1510 ± 11 [g]	1479 ± 10	IMRE		83CAL/BAR
$C_8H_6O_2^-$				Est	$\Delta_f H(A) = -157\pm 8$	
p-CHO-benzaldehyde$^-\cdot$						
	-211 [b] 0.6			ECD		68KUH/LEV
$C_8H_7ClO^-$				Est	$\Delta_f H(A) = -117\pm 8$	
mCl-acetophenone$^-\cdot$						
	-173 ± 9 [b] 0.583 ± 0.006			ECD		69STE/WEN
$C_8H_7ClO^-$				Est	$\Delta_f H(A) = -117\pm 8$	
pCl-acetophenone$^-\cdot$						
	-172 ± 9 [b] 0.567 ± 0.005			ECD		69STE/WEN

Table 2. Negative Ion Table — Continued

Ion $\Delta_f H(A^-)$ $\Delta_f H(X \cdot \cdot Y^-)$	EA(A) eV	$\Delta H_{acid}(AH)$ $\Delta H_{aff}(X \cdot \cdot Y^-)$	$\Delta G_{acid}(AH)$ $\Delta G_{aff}(X \cdot \cdot Y^-)$	Method	Comment	Reference
$C_8H_7ClO_2^-$						
2-Cl-3,6-diMe-benzoquinone$^-\cdot$				Est2	$\Delta_f H(A) = -212\pm17$	
* -398 ± 21 [b]	1.93 ± 0.05			IMRE		85FUK/MCI
$C_8H_7FO^-$						
mF-acetophenone$^-\cdot$				Est	$\Delta_f H(A) = -280\pm8$	
-336 ± 11 [b]	0.58 ± 0.03			ECD		75WEN/KAO
$C_8H_7FO^-$						
oF-acetophenone$^-\cdot$				Est	$\Delta_f H(A) = -280\pm21$	
-323 ± 22 [b]	0.442 ± 0.009			ECD		75WEN/KAO
$C_8H_7FO^-$						
pF-acetophenone$^-\cdot$				Est	$\Delta_f H(A) = -280\pm8$	
-318 ± 10 [b]	0.40 ± 0.01			ECD		75WEN/KAO
$C_8H_7N^-$						
oMe-benzonitrile$^-\cdot$				Est	$\Delta_f H(A) = 178\pm1$	
* 110 ± 11 [b]	0.70 ± 0.10			TDEq		87KEB/CHO
110 ± 9 [b]	0.70 ± 0.09			TDEq		86CHO/KEB
$C_8H_7N^-$						
pMe-benzonitrile$^-\cdot$				Est	$\Delta_f H(A) = 182\pm1$	
* 109 ± 9 [b]	0.76 ± 0.09			TDEq		86CHO/KEB
$C_8H_7NO_3^-$						
mCOMe-nitrobenzene$^-\cdot$				Est	$\Delta_f H(A) = -103\pm4$	
* -229 ± 14 [b]	1.31 ± 0.10			TDEq		87KEB/CHO
$C_8H_7NO_3^-$						
oCOMe-nitrobenzene$^-\cdot$				Est2	$\Delta_f H(A) = -84\pm8$	
* -217 ± 18 [b]	1.38 ± 0.10			TDEq		87KEB/CHO
$C_8H_7NO_3^-$						
pCOMe-nitrobenzene$^-\cdot$				Est	$\Delta_f H(A) = -103\pm4$	
* -252 ± 14 [b]	1.55 ± 0.10			TDEq		87KEB/CHO
$C_8H_7O^-$					$\Delta_f H(AH) = -87\pm2$	77PED/RYL
$CH_2=C(Ph)O^-$				D-EA	BDE(A-H) = 399 ± 18	
* -105 ± 13 [a]		1512 ± 11 [g]	1483 ± 8	IMRE		79BAR/SCO
*	2.06 ± 0.08			PD		77ZIM/REE
-101 ± 13 [a]		1516 ± 11 [g]	1487 ± 8	IMRE		78CUM/KEB
			1491 ± 8	IMRE[o]		79BAR/SCO
$C_8H_7O^-$						
PhCH=CHO$^-$				Est	$\Delta_f H(AH) = -53\pm4$	
*	2.10 ± 0.08			PD		77ZIM/REE
$C_8H_7O^-$						
mCHO-$C_6H_4CH_2^-$				Est	$\Delta_f H(AH) = -71\pm8$	
* -47 ± 19 [a]		1554 ± 11 [g]	1524 ± 8	IMRE		83CAL/BAR

Table 2. Negative Ion Table - Continued

Ion $\Delta_f H(X\cdot\cdot Y^-)$	$\Delta_f H(A^-)$ EA(A) eV $\Delta H_{aff}(X\cdot\cdot Y^-)$	$\Delta H_{acid}(AH)$ $\Delta G_{aff}(X\cdot\cdot Y^-)$	$\Delta G_{acid}(AH)$	Method	Comment	Reference
$C_8H_7O^-$						
pCHO-$C_6H_4CH_2^-$				Est	$\Delta_f H(AH) = -75\pm8$	
*	-100 ± 21 [a]	1505±12 [g]	1475±10	IMRE		86TAF
$C_8H_7O_2^-$						
PhCH$_2$CO$_2^-$				Est	$\Delta_f H(AH) = -320\pm4$	
					BDE(A-H) = 444±8	
*	-423 ± 15 [a] 3.40±0.20 [d]	1428±11 [g]	1398±8	IMRE		86TAF
$C_8H_7O_2^-$						
mCOMe-phenoxide$^-$				Est	$\Delta_f H(AH) = -264\pm8$	
					BDE(A-H) = 362±8	
*	-361 ± 18 [a] 2.50±0.19 [d]	1433±10 [g]	1404±8	IMRE		81FUJ/MCI
$C_8H_7O_2^-$						
mMe-benzoate$^-$					$\Delta_f H(AH) = -329\pm1$	76COL/JIM
					BDE(A-H) = 444±13	
*	-437 ± 12 [a] 3.46±0.24 [d]	1422±11 [g]	1391±8	IMRE		77MCM/KEB
$C_8H_7O_2^-$						
oMe-benzoate$^-$					$\Delta_f H(AH) = -320\pm1$	76COL/JIM
*	-436 ± 13 [a]	1415±12 [g]	1384±8	IMRE		77MCM/KEB
$C_8H_7O_2^-$						
pCOMe-phenoxide$^-$				Est	$\Delta_f H(AH) = -264\pm8$	
*	-390 ± 19 [a]	1404±11 [g]	1375±8	IMRE		81FUJ/MCI
$C_8H_7O_2^-$						
pMe-benzoate$^-$					$\Delta_f H(AH) = -332\pm1$	76COL/JIM
					BDE(A-H) = 444±13	
*	-440 ± 12 [a] 3.46±0.24 [d]	1422±11 [g]	1392±8	IMRE		77MCM/KEB
$C_8H_7O_3^-$						
mCO$_2$Me-phenoxide$^-$				Est	$\Delta_f H(AH) = -468\pm8$	
					BDE(A-H) = 362±8	
*	-559 ± 18 [a] 2.44±0.19 [d]	1439±10 [g]	1410±8	IMRE		81FUJ/MCI
$C_8H_7O_3^-$						
mOMe-benzoate$^-$					$\Delta_f H(AH) = -446\pm1$	78COL/JIM
					BDE(A-H) = 444±13	
*	-559 ± 12 [a] 3.51±0.24 [d]	1417±11 [g]	1386±8	IMRE		77MCM/KEB
$C_8H_7O_3^-$						
oOMe-benzoate$^-$				Est	$\Delta_f H(AH) = -452\pm8$	
*	-567 ± 19 [a]	1415±11 [g]	1386±8	IMRE		77MCM/KEB
$C_8H_7O_3^-$						
pCO$_2$Me-phenoxide$^-$				Est	$\Delta_f H(AH) = -468\pm8$	
*	-587 ± 19 [a]	1411±11 [g]	1382±8	IMRE		81FUJ/MCI
$C_8H_8^-$						
cyclooctatetraene$^-\cdot$					$\Delta_f H(A) = 297\pm1$	77PED/RYL
242±5 [b]	0.58±0.04			ECD		69WEN/RIS
	<0.8			PD		79GYG/PET

Table 2. Negative Ion Table – Continued

Ion $\Delta_fH(A^-)$ $\Delta_fH(X\cdot\cdot Y^-)$	EA(A) eV	$\Delta H_{acid}(AH)$ $\Delta H_{aff}(X\cdot\cdot Y^-)$	$\Delta G_{acid}(AH)$ $\Delta G_{aff}(X\cdot\cdot Y^-)$	Method	Comment	Reference
$C_8H_8ClO^-$						
PhCOMe$\cdot\cdot$Cl$^-$			40	TDEq		82FRE/IKU
$C_8H_8NO^-$					$\Delta_fH(AH) = -129\pm1$	77PED/RYL
PhN=C(Me)O$^-$						
* -205 ± 11 [a]		1454±10 [g]	1425±8	IMRE		86TAF
		1476±10 [g]	1447±8	IMRE		78CUM/KEB
$C_8H_8NO^-$				Est	$\Delta_fH(AH) = -100\pm4$	
mCOMe–anilide$^-$					BDE(A–H) = 368±13	
* -125 ± 15 [a]	1.82±0.24 [d]	1505±11 [g]	1474±8	IMRE		86TAF
$C_8H_8NO^-$				Est2	$\Delta_fH(AH) = -88\pm4$	
pCOMe–anilide$^-$						
* -148 ± 15 [a]		1470±11 [g]	1439±8	IMRE		86TAF
$C_8H_8NO_2^-$				Est	$\Delta_fH(AH) = -300\pm4$	
mCO$_2$Me–anilide$^-$					BDE(A–H) = 368±13	
* -322 ± 15 [a]	1.78±0.24 [d]	1509±11 [g]	1478±8	IMRE		86TAF
$C_8H_8NO_2^-$				Est	$\Delta_fH(AH) = -300\pm4$	
pCO$_2$Me–anilide$^-$						
* -356 ± 15 [a]		1475±11 [g]	1444±8	IMRE		86TAF
$C_8H_8O^-$					$\Delta_fH(A) = -87\pm2$	77PED/RYL
acetophenone$^{-\cdot}$						
-119 ± 2 [b]	0.334±0.004			ECD		75WEN/KAO
	0.334±0.004			ECD		67WEN/CHE
$C_8H_8O^-$				Est	$\Delta_fH(A) = -71\pm8$	
mMe–benzaldehyde$^{-\cdot}$						
-110 ± 10 [b]	0.41±0.01			ECD		75WEN/KAO
$C_8H_8O^-$				Est	$\Delta_fH(A) = -75\pm8$	
pMe–benzaldehyde$^{-\cdot}$						
-111 ± 10 [b]	0.37±0.02			ECD		75WEN/KAO
$C_8H_8O_2^-$				Est2	$\Delta_fH(A) = -187\pm8$	
2,5–diMe–benzoquinone$^{-\cdot}$						
* -358 ± 18 [b]	1.77±0.10			TDEq		87KEB/CHO
	1.72±0.11			IMRE		85GRI/CAL
$C_8H_8O_2^-$				Est	$\Delta_fH(A) = -187\pm8$	
2,6–diMe–benzoquinone$^-$						
* -359 ± 18 [b]	1.78±0.10			TDEq		87KEB/CHO
	1.67±0.05			IMRE		85FUK/MCI
$C_8H_8O_2^-$				Est	$\Delta_fH(A) = -182\pm8$	
mOMe–benzaldehyde$^{-\cdot}$						
-224 ± 13 [b]	0.43±0.04			ECD		75WEN/KAO

Table 2. Negative Ion Table − Continued

Ion $\Delta_f H(X\cdot\cdot Y^-)$	$\Delta_f H(A^-)$ EA(A) eV	$\Delta H_{acid}(AH)$ $\Delta H_{aff}(X\cdot\cdot Y^-)$	$\Delta G_{acid}(AH)$ $\Delta G_{aff}(X\cdot\cdot Y^-)$	Method	Comment	Reference
$C_8H_8O_2^-$						
methyl benzoate$^{-\cdot}$					$\Delta_f H(A) = -288\pm7$	77PED/RYL
	-305^b 0.2			ECD		68KUH/LEV
$C_8H_8O_2^-$						
oOH–acetophenone$^{-\cdot}$				Est2	$\Delta_f H(A) = -100\pm13$	
*	-184 ± 17^b 0.86±0.05			IMRE		85FUK/MCI
$C_8H_8O_4^-$						
2,6–diMeO–benzoquinone$^{-\cdot}$						
*	1.73±0.10			TDEq		87KEB/CHO
$C_8H_9^-$						
2-methylenenorborn-5-en-3-ide$^-$						
*		1632±10 ^{g}	1603±8	IMRB		86LEE/SQU
$C_8H_9^-$						
PhCHMe$^-$					$\Delta_f H(AH) = 29$	77PED/RYL
					BDE(A–H) = 354±8	81ROB/STE
*	88±10 ^{a} 0.80±0.19 ^{d}	1589±10 ^{g}	1562±8	IMRE		79BAR/SCO
			1556±8	IMRE^o		79BAR/SCO
$C_8H_9^-$						
bicyclo[3.2.1]octa-2,6-dien-4-ide$^-$						
*		1588±11 ^{g}	1559±8	IMRE		86LEE/SQU
$C_8H_9^-$						
mMe–$C_6H_4CH_2^-$					$\Delta_f H(AH) = 17$	77PED/RYL
					BDE(A–H) = 368±9	86HAY/KRU
*	82±12 ^{a} 0.89±0.22 ^{d}	1595±12 ^{g}	1564±10	IMRE		83CAL/BAR
$C_8H_9^-$						
pMe–$C_6H_4CH_2^-$					$\Delta_f H(AH) = 18\pm1$	77PED/RYL
					BDE(A–H) = 367±10	86HAY/KRU
*	86±12 ^{a} 0.84±0.22 ^{d}	1598±11 ^{g}	1568±10	IMRE		79BAR/SCO
$C_8H_9NO_2^-$						
1,2–diMe–3–nitrobenzene$^{-\cdot}$				Est2	$\Delta_f H(A) = 13\pm13$	
*	-70 ± 22^b 0.86±0.10			TDEq		87KEB/CHO
	0.81±0.11			IMRE		85GRI/CAL
	0.86±0.05			IMRE		85FUK/MCI
$C_8H_9NO_2^-$						
1,2–diMe–4–nitrobenzene$^{-\cdot}$				Est	$\Delta_f H(A) = -1\pm8$	
*	-85 ± 13^b 0.87±0.05			IMRE		85FUK/MCI
$C_8H_9NO_2^-$						
1,3–diMe–2–nitrobenzene$^{-\cdot}$				Est	$\Delta_f H(A) = 40\pm13$	
*	-33 ± 17^b 0.76±0.05			IMRE		85FUK/MCI
$C_8H_9NO_2^-$						
1,3–diMe–4–nitrobenzene$^{-\cdot}$				Est	$\Delta_f H(A) = 20\pm8$	
*	-60 ± 13^b 0.83±0.05			IMRE		85FUK/MCI

Table 2. Negative Ion Table - Continued

Ion $\Delta_fH(A^-)$ $\Delta_fH(X\cdot\cdot Y^-)$	EA(A) eV	$\Delta H_{acid}(AH)$ $\Delta H_{aff}(X\cdot\cdot Y^-)$	$\Delta G_{acid}(AH)$ $\Delta G_{aff}(X\cdot\cdot Y^-)$	Method	Comment	Reference
$C_8H_9O^-$ mEt-phenoxide$^-$					$\Delta_fH(AH) = -146\pm2$ BDE(A–H) = 362±8	77PED/RYL
* -215 ± 11 [a]	2.20±0.19 [d]	1461±10 [g]	1433±8	IMRE		81FUJ/MCI
$C_8H_9O^-$ pEt-phenoxide$^-$					$\Delta_fH(AH) = -144\pm1$ BDE(A–H) = 362±8	77PED/RYL
* -210 ± 10 [a]	2.18±0.19 [d]	1464±10 [g]	1435±8	IMRE		81FUJ/MCI
$C_8H_9OS^-$ pSOMe-$C_6H_4CH_2^-$				Est	$\Delta_fH(AH) = -32\pm8$	
* -31 ± 19 [a]		1531±11 [g]	1503±8	IMRE		86TAF
$C_8H_9O_2S^-$ PhSO$_2$CHMe$^-$				Est	$\Delta_fH(AH) = -280\pm4$	
* -283 ± 13 [a]		1527±8 [g]	1495±8	IMRE		78CUM/KEB
$C_8H_9O_2S^-$ pSO$_2$Me-$C_6H_4CH_2^-$					$\Delta_fH(AH) = -273\pm3$	77PED/RYL
* -302 ± 14 [a]		1501±11 [g]	1473±8	IMRE		86TAF
$C_8H_9O_3^-$ PhOH$\cdot\cdot$MeCO$_2^-$						
		109±4	*79±7*	TDAs		86MEO/SIE2
$C_8H_{10}Cl^-$ PhEt$\cdot\cdot$Cl$^-$						
			21	TDEq		82FRE/IKU
$C_8H_{10}Cl^-$ m-xylene$\cdot\cdot$Cl$^-$						
			16	TDEq		82FRE/IKU
$C_8H_{10}Cl^-$ p-xylene$\cdot\cdot$Cl$^-$						
			16	TDEq		82FRE/IKU
$C_8H_{10}N^-$ PhNEt$^-$					$\Delta_fH(AH) = 56\pm6$ BDE(A–H) = 366±8	77PED/RYL
* 50 ± 17 [a]	1.60±0.20 [d]	1523±11 [g]	1493±8	IMRE		86TAF
$C_8H_{10}NO^-$ mNMe$_2$-phenoxide$^-$				Est	$\Delta_fH(AH) = -84\pm8$ BDE(A–H) = 362±8	
* -148 ± 18 [a]	2.15±0.19 [d]	1466±10 [g]	1437±8	IMRE		81FUJ/MCI
$C_8H_{10}NO^-$ pNMe$_2$-phenoxide$^-$				Est	$\Delta_fH(AH) = -84\pm8$	
* -144 ± 18 [a]		1470±10 [g]	1441±8	IMRE		81FUJ/MCI
$C_8H_{10}N_2O_2^-$ mNMe$_2$-nitrobenzene$^-\cdot$					$\Delta_fH(A) = 67\pm2$	84FUR/MUR
* -21 ± 6 [b]	0.92±0.05			IMRE		85FUK/MCI

Table 2. Negative Ion Table – Continued

Ion $\Delta_f H(A^-)$ $\Delta_f H(X \cdot \cdot Y^-)$	EA(A) eV	$\Delta H_{acid}(AH)$ $\Delta H_{aff}(X \cdot \cdot Y^-)$	$\Delta G_{acid}(AH)$ $\Delta G_{aff}(X \cdot \cdot Y^-)$	Method	Comment	Reference
$C_8H_{11}^-$ 2-methylenenorbornan-3-ide$^-$				Est2	$\Delta_f H(AH) = 39 \pm 13$	
* 138±18 ^{a}		1629±5 ^{g}	1600±3	IMRE		86LEE/SQU
$C_8H_{11}^-$ bicyclo[3.2.1]oct-2-en-4-ide$^-$				Est2	$\Delta_f H(AH) = 13 \pm 17$	
* 117±22 ^{a}		1635±5 ^{g}	1604±3	IMRE		86LEE/SQU
$C_8H_{11}^-$ cyclooctadienide$^-$				Est2	$\Delta_f H(AH) = 42 \pm 13$	
88±29 ^{a}		1576±16 ^{g}	1548±13	IMRB	between EtOH, nPrOH	86LEE/SQU
$C_8H_{11}O^-$ 4,4-diMe-cyclohexenone-6-enolate$^-$				Est2	$\Delta_f H(AH) = -180 \pm 13$	
* -181±22 ^{a}		1529±10 ^{g}	1497±8	IMRE		86BAR/KIP
			1500±8	IMRE^o		86BAR/KIP
$C_8H_{11}O_2^-$ 5,5-diMe-1,3-cyclohexandion-2-ide$^-$				Est	$\Delta_f H(AH) = -287 \pm 13$	
* -399±22 ^{a}		1418±10 ^{g}	1385±8	IMRE	Acid: dimedone	78CUM/KEB
$C_8H_{11}O_2^-$ EtOH··PhO$^-$						
		81±4	47±7	TDAs		86MEO/SIE2
$C_8H_{12}B^-$ $Me_2C(CH=CH)_2BCH_2^-$				Est	$\Delta_f H(AH) = 86 \pm 13$	
100±32 ^{a}		1544±19 ^{g}	1515±17	IMRB		77SUL
$C_8H_{13}^-$ cyclooctenide$^-$					$\Delta_f H(AH) = -27 \pm 1$	77PED/RYL
60±26 ^{a}		1617±25 ^{g}	1586±21	IMRB	Between EtOH, nPrOH	86LEE/SQU
$C_8H_{13}O^-$ cycloctanone enolate$^-$					$\Delta_f H(AH) = -272 \pm 5$	77PED/RYL
*	1.63±0.06			PD		78ZIM/JAC
$C_8H_{13}O_2^-$ $cC_6H_{11}-CH_2CO_2^-$				Est	$\Delta_f H(AH) = -523 \pm 8$ $BDE(A-H) = 444 \pm 8$	
* -609±19 ^{a}	3.23±0.20 ^{d}	1444±11 ^{g}	1415±8	IMRE		86TAF
$C_8H_{15}O_4^-$ iPrCO$_2$H··iPrCO$_2^-$						
		125±4	83±7	TDAs		86MEO/SIE2
$C_8H_{17}O^-$ nC$_8$H$_{17}$O$^-$					$\Delta_f H(AH) = -355 \pm 1$ $BDE(A-H) = 436 \pm 4$	77PED/RYL
* -330±12 ^{a}	2.0±0.2 ^{d}	1556±11	1528±13 ^{h}	CIDC		83BOA/HOU
		1553±10		CIDC^o		83BOA/HOU

Table 2. Negative Ion Table – Continued

Ion $\Delta_f H(X \cdot \cdot Y^-)$	EA(A) eV	$\Delta H_{acid}(AH)$ $\Delta H_{aff}(X \cdot \cdot Y^-)$	$\Delta G_{acid}(AH)$ $\Delta G_{aff}(X \cdot \cdot Y^-)$	Method	Comment	Reference
$C_8H_{17}O^-$				Est	$\Delta_f H(AH) = -392 \pm 4$	
tBuCH(iPr)O$^-$					BDE(A-H) = 438±4	
* −379±16 [a]	2.15±0.17 [d]	1543±12 [g]	1515±8	IMRE		79BAR/SCO
			1514±8	IMRE[o]		79BAR/SCO
$C_8H_{17}O_5^-$						
MeO(CH$_2$CH$_2$O)$_2$Me··MeCO$_2^-$						
		63±4	40±7	TDAs		86MEO/SIE2
$C_8H_{19}O_2^-$						
nPrOH··tBuCH$_2$O$^-$						
−627±25 [c]		83±10 [g]	55±8	IMRE		84CAL/ROZ
$C_8H_{19}O_2^-$						
tBuOH··tBuO$^-$						
−673±26 [c]		85±10 [g]	58±8	IMRE		84CAL/ROZ
$C_9HN_5^-$						
2,3,5,6-tetracyanopyridine$^-$·				Est	$\Delta_f H(A) = 669 \pm 17$	
	2.17±0.07			SI		67FAR/PAG
$C_9H_3F_6N^-$						
3,5-diCF$_3$-benzonitrile$^-$·				Est	$\Delta_f H(A) = -1125 \pm 4$	
* −1235±14 [b]	1.14±0.10			TDEq		87KEB/CHO
$C_9H_3F_6O_2^-$				Est	$\Delta_f H(AH) = -1637 \pm 8$	
3,5-diCF$_3$-benzoate$^-$					BDE(A-H) = 444±13	
* −1810±19 [a]	4.13±0.24 [d]	1357±11 [g]	1328±8	IMRE		86TAF
$C_9H_4N^-$				Est	$\Delta_f H(AH) = 443 \pm 8$	
pCN-C$_6$H$_4$C≡C$^-$					BDE(A-H) = 552±21	
* 383±18 [a]	4.08±0.32 [d]	1471±10 [g]	1438±8	IMRE		86TAF
$C_9H_5CrO_3^-$					$\Delta_f H(AH) = -350 \pm 9$	77PED/RYL
(CO)$_3$CrC$_6$H$_5^-$						
−326±30 [a]		1554±21		IMRB		85LAN/SQU
$C_9H_5F_3N^-$				Est	$\Delta_f H(AH) = -485 \pm 4$	
mCF$_3$-C$_6$H$_4$CHCN$^-$						
* −585±19 [a]		1431±15 [g]	1403±8	IMRE		86TAF
$C_9H_5F_3N^-$				Est	$\Delta_f H(AH) = -485 \pm 4$	
pCF$_3$-C$_6$H$_4$CHCN$^-$						
* −595±19 [a]		1420±15 [g]	1393±8	IMRE		86TAF
$C_9H_5F_6^-$				Est	$\Delta_f H(AH) = -1320 \pm 8$	
3,5-diCF$_3$-C$_6$H$_3$CH$_2^-$					BDE(A-H) = 368±13	
* −1340±19 [a]	1.76±0.24 [d]	1510±11 [g]	1482±8	IMRE		86TAF

Table 2. Negative Ion Table – Continued

Ion $\Delta_f H(A^-)$ $\Delta_f H(X\cdots Y^-)$	EA(A) eV	$\Delta H_{acid}(AH)$ $\Delta H_{aff}(X\cdots Y^-)$	$\Delta G_{acid}(AH)$ $\Delta G_{aff}(X\cdots Y^-)$	Method	Comment	Reference
$C_9H_5N_2^-$ Ph–C(CN)$_2^-$ *		1348±11 [g]	1317±8	IMRE		86TAF
$C_9H_5N_2^-$ mCN–C$_6$H$_4$CHCN$^-$ * 211±18 [a]		1419±13 [g]	1390±8	Est IMRE	$\Delta_f H(AH)= 322\pm4$	81FUJ/MCI
$C_9H_5N_2^-$ pCN–C$_6$H$_4$CHCN$^-$ * 192±18 [a]		1400±13 [g]	1372±8	Est IMRE	$\Delta_f H(AH)= 322\pm4$	81FUJ/MCI
$C_9H_6BrO_2^-$ 4-Br-cubyl-CO$_2^-$ *	3.61±0.21 [d]	1407±12 [g]	1378±8	IMRE	$BDE(A-H)= 444\pm8$	86TAF
$C_9H_6F_3O^-$ pCOCF$_3$–C$_6$H$_4$CH$_2^-$ * –776±15 [a]		1470±11 [g]	1439±8	Est IMRE	$\Delta_f H(AH)= -715\pm4$	86TAF
$C_9H_6N^-$ quinolinide$^-$ * 289±9 [a]		1608±8	1572±8	TDEq	$\Delta_f H(AH)= 211\pm1$	79VIS 87MEO
$C_9H_6NO^-$ pCOCN–C$_6$H$_4$CH$_2^-$ * –69±23 [a]		1446±11 [g]	1418±8	Est2 IMRE	$\Delta_f H(AH)= 15\pm13$	86TAF
$C_9H_7^-$ indenide$^-$ * 106±12 [a]	1.98±0.24 [d]	1473±11 [g]	1442±8	IMRE	$\Delta_f H(AH)= 163\pm1$ $BDE(A-H)= 351\pm13$	80KUD/KUD 82MCM/GOL 86TAF
$C_9H_7F_3O^-$ mCF$_3$–acetophenone$^{-\cdot}$ –869±9 [b]	0.663±0.009			Est ECD	$\Delta_f H(A)= -805\pm8$	75WEN/KAO
$C_9H_7F_3O^-$ oCF$_3$–acetophenone$^{-\cdot}$ –867±9 [b]	0.642±0.009			Est ECD	$\Delta_f H(A)= -805\pm8$	75WEN/KAO
$C_9H_7F_3O^-$ pCF$_3$–acetophenone$^{-\cdot}$ –867±9 [b]	0.642±0.009			Est ECD	$\Delta_f H(A)= -805\pm8$	75WEN/KAO
$C_9H_7NO^-$ pCOMe–benzonitrile$^{-\cdot}$ * –61±14 [b]	1.13±0.10 1.12±0.09			Est TDEq TDEq	$\Delta_f H(A)= 49\pm4$	87KEB/CHO 86CHO/KEB

Table 2. Negative Ion Table - Continued

Ion $\Delta_f H(A^-)$ $\Delta_f H(X\cdot\cdot Y^-)$	EA(A) eV	$\Delta H_{acid}(AH)$ $\Delta H_{aff}(X\cdot\cdot Y^-)$	$\Delta G_{acid}(AH)$ $\Delta G_{aff}(X\cdot\cdot Y^-)$	Method	Comment	Reference
$C_9H_7O_2^-$ cubyl–CO_2^-				Est2	$\Delta_f H(AH)= 238\pm21$ $BDE(A-H)= 444\pm8$	
* 136±33 [a]	3.40±0.21 [d]	1428±12 [g]	1398±8	IMRE		86TAF
$C_9H_7O_3^-$ pCOMe-benzoate$^-$				Est	$\Delta_f H(AH)= -464\pm4$ $BDE(A-H)= 444\pm13$	
* −595±15 [a]	3.69±0.24 [d]	1399±11 [g]	1369±8	IMRE		86TAF
$C_9H_8^-$ indene$^-\cdot$					$\Delta_f H(A)= 163\pm1$	80KUD/KUD
146±3 [b]	0.17±0.03			ECD		81WOJ/FOL
$C_9H_8N^-$ pMe-C_6H_4CHCN$^-$				Est	$\Delta_f H(AH)= 153\pm8$	
* 94±23 [a]		1471±15 [g]	1443±8	IMRE		86TAF
$C_9H_8NO^-$ pOMe-C_6H_4CHCN$^-$				Est	$\Delta_f H(AH)= 30\pm4$	
* −29±19 [a]		1471±15 [g]	1443±8	IMRE		86TAF
$C_9H_8O^-$ PhCH=CHCHO$^-\cdot$				Est	$\Delta_f H(A)= 21\pm8$	
−59±13 [b]	0.82±0.04			ECD		67WEN/CHE
$C_9H_9^-$ 1-phenylcyclopropanide$^-$					$\Delta_f H(AH)= 151\pm1$	82FUC/HAL
260±17 [a]		1639±16 [g]	1607±13	IMRB		84AND/DEP
$C_9H_9^-$ $CH_2=C(Ph)CH_2^-$					$\Delta_f H(AH)= 113\pm4$	69BEN/CRU
196±31 [a]		1613±27 [g]	1586±23	IMRB		84BAR/BUR
$C_9H_9ClO_2^-$ Cl-triMe-benzoquinone$^-\cdot$				Est2	$\Delta_f H(A)= -243\pm17$	
* −423±21 [b]	1.86±0.05			IMRE		85FUK/MCI
$C_9H_9N^-$ 3,5-diMe-benzonitrile$^-\cdot$				Est2	$\Delta_f H(A)= 149\pm13$	
* 39±21 [b]	1.14±0.09			TDEq		86CHO/KEB
$C_9H_9O^-$ MeCH=C(Ph)O$^-$					$\Delta_f H(AH)= -109\pm2$ $BDE(A-H)= 389\pm8$	77PED/RYL
* −131±23 [a]		1508±21 [g]	1481±8	IMRE		79BAR/SCO
		1509±21 [g]	1482±8	IMRE		78CUM/KEB
			1483±8	IMRE^o		79BAR/SCO
$C_9H_9O^-$ MeOH$\cdot\cdot$PhC≡C$^-$						
70±26 [c]		56±10 [g]	32±8	IMRE		84CAL/ROZ

Table 2. Negative Ion Table – Continued

Ion $\Delta_f H(A^-)$ $\Delta_f H(X \cdot \cdot Y^-)$	EA(A) eV	$\Delta H_{acid}(AH)$ $\Delta H_{aff}(X \cdot \cdot Y^-)$	$\Delta G_{acid}(AH)$ $\Delta G_{aff}(X \cdot \cdot Y^-)$	Method	Comment	Reference
$C_9H_9O^-$					$\Delta_f H(AH) = -98 \pm 2$	77PED/RYL
PhCH=C(Me)O$^-$						
* -163 ± 16 [a]		1465 ± 15 [g]	1441 ± 8	IMRE		79BAR/SCO
		1469 ± 15 [g]	1445 ± 8	IMRE		78CUM/KEB
			1451 ± 8	IMRE[o]		79BAR/SCO
$C_9H_9O^-$				Est	$\Delta_f H(AH) = -119 \pm 4$	
pCOMe–C$_6$H$_4$CH$_2^-$						
* -136 ± 15 [a]		1513 ± 11 [g]	1485 ± 8	IMRE		86TAF
$C_9H_9O_2^-$				Est	$\Delta_f H(AH) = -244 \pm 4$	
mOMe–C$_6$H$_4$C(=CH$_2$)O$^-$						
* -264 ± 15 [a]		1509 ± 11 [g]	1481 ± 8	IMRE		79BAR/SCO
			1490 ± 8	IMRE[o]		79BAR/SCO
$C_9H_9O_2^-$				Est	$\Delta_f H(AH) = -320 \pm 4$	
pCO$_2$Me–C$_6$H$_4$CH$_2^-$						
* -336 ± 15 [a]		1515 ± 11 [g]	1487 ± 8	IMRE		86TAF
$C_9H_9O_2S^-$				Est	$\Delta_f H(AH) = -161 \pm 4$	
PhSO$_2$–cyclopropanide$^-$						
* -179 ± 14 [a]		1512 ± 10 [g]	1485 ± 8	IMRE		78CUM/KEB
$C_9H_9O_3^-$				Est	$\Delta_f H(AH) = -502 \pm 4$	
mCO$_2$Et–phenoxide$^-$					BDE(A–H) = 362 ± 8	
* -593 ± 14 [a]	2.44 ± 0.19 [d]	1439 ± 10 [g]	1410 ± 8	IMRE		81FUJ/MCI
$C_9H_{10}ClO^-$						
PhCH$_2$COMe$\cdot\cdot$Cl$^-$						
			45	TDEq		82FRE/IKU
$C_9H_{10}ClO_2^-$				Est2	$\Delta_f H(AH) = -410 \pm 13$	
4-Cl-bicyclo[2.2.2]octene-CO$_2^-$					BDE(A–H) = 444 ± 8	
* -535 ± 25 [a]	3.63 ± 0.21 [d]	1405 ± 12 [g]	1376 ± 8	IMRE		86TAF
$C_9H_{10}O^-$					$\Delta_f H(A) = -109 \pm 2$	77PED/RYL
propiophenone$^{-\cdot}$						
-143 ± 3 [b]	0.351 ± 0.004			ECD		75WEN/KAO
$C_9H_{10}O_2^-$				Est	$\Delta_f H(A) = -313 \pm 8$	
benzyl acetate$^{-\cdot}$						
-328 ± 18 [b]	0.1 ± 0.1			ECD		83ZLA/LEE
$C_9H_{10}O_2^-$				Est2	$\Delta_f H(A) = -220 \pm 8$	
triMe-benzoquinone$^{-\cdot}$						
* -374 ± 13 [b]	1.60 ± 0.05			IMRE		85FUK/MCI
$C_9H_{10}O_4^-$						
2,3-diMeO-5-Me-benzoquinone$^{-\cdot}$						
*	1.86 ± 0.10			TDEq		87KEB/CHO

Table 2. Negative Ion Table - Continued

Ion $\Delta_f H(A^-)$ $\Delta_f H(X\cdot\cdot Y^-)$	EA(A) eV	$\Delta H_{acid}(AH)$ $\Delta H_{aff}(X\cdot\cdot Y^-)$	$\Delta G_{acid}(AH)$ $\Delta G_{aff}(X\cdot\cdot Y^-)$	Method	Comment	Reference
$C_9H_{11}^-$					$\Delta_f H(AH)= 4\pm1$	77PED/RYL
PhCMe$_2^-$					BDE(A-H)= 350±7	81ROB/STE
* 59±11 [a]	0.79±0.18 [d]	1586±10 [g]	1560±8	IMRE		79BAR/SCO
			1554±8	IMRE[o]		79BAR/SCO
$C_9H_{11}NO_2^-$				Est2	$\Delta_f H(A)= -17\pm13$	
2,4,6-triMe-nitrobenzene$^-$						
* -84±22 [b]	0.70±0.10			TDEq		87KEB/CHO
	0.67±0.11			IMRE		85GRI/CAL
	0.72±0.05			IMRE		85FUK/MCI
$C_9H_{11}O^-$					$\Delta_f H(AH)= -195\pm13$	77PED/RYL
miPr-phenoxide$^-$					BDE(A-H)= 362±8	
* -264±22 [a]	2.21±0.19 [d]	1461±10 [g]	1432±8	IMRE		81FUJ/MCI
$C_9H_{11}O^-$					$\Delta_f H(AH)= -182\pm13$	77PED/RYL
oiPr-phenoxide$^-$						
* -258±25 [a]		1454±12 [g]	1423±8	IMRE		81FUJ/MCI
$C_9H_{11}O^-$					$\Delta_f H(AH)= -209\pm13$	77PED/RYL
piPr-phenoxide$^-$					BDE(A-H)= 362±13	
* -278±22 [a]	2.20±0.23 [d]	1461±10 [g]	1433±8	IMRE		81FUJ/MCI
$C_9H_{11}O_2^-$				Est2	$\Delta_f H(AH)= -363\pm13$	
bicyclo[2.2.2]octene-CO$_2^-$					BDE(A-H)= 444±8	
* -460±25 [a]	3.35±0.21 [d]	1433±12 [g]	1403±8	IMRE		86TAF
$C_9H_{11}O_2S^-$				Est	$\Delta_f H(AH)= -319\pm2$	
PhSO$_2$CHEt$^-$						
* -326±10 [a]		1523±8 [g]	1491±8	IMRE		78CUM/KEB
$C_9H_{12}BrO_2^-$				Est2	$\Delta_f H(AH)= -480\pm13$	
4-Br-bicyclo[2.2.2]octane-CO$_2^-$					BDE(A-H)= 444±8	
* -598±25 [a]	3.56±0.21 [d]	1412±12 [g]	1382±8	IMRE		86TAF
$C_9H_{12}Cl^-$						
1,3,5-triMe-benzene$\cdot\cdot$Cl$^-$						
		19		TDEq		82FRE/IKU
$C_9H_{12}Cl^-$						
PhiPr$\cdot\cdot$Cl$^-$						
		23		TDEq		82FRE/IKU
$C_9H_{12}Cl^-$						
PhnPr$\cdot\cdot$Cl$^-$						
		21		TDEq		82FRE/IKU
$C_9H_{12}ClO_2^-$				Est2	$\Delta_f H(AH)= -523\pm13$	
3-Cl-bicyclo[2.2.2]octane-CO$_2^-$					BDE(A-H)= 444±8	
* -629±25 [a]	3.44±0.21 [d]	1423±12 [g]	1394±8	IMRE		86TAF

Table 2. Negative Ion Table – Continued

Ion $\Delta_f H(A^-)$ $\Delta_f H(X \cdot \cdot Y^-)$	EA(A) eV	$\Delta H_{acid}(AH)$ $\Delta H_{aff}(X \cdot \cdot Y^-)$	$\Delta G_{acid}(AH)$ $\Delta G_{aff}(X \cdot \cdot Y^-)$	Method	Comment	Reference
$C_9H_{12}ClO_2^-$ 4-Cl-bicyclo[2.2.2]octane-CO_2^-				Est2	$\Delta_f H(AH) = -530\pm13$ $BDE(A-H) = 444\pm8$	
* -645 ± 25 [a]	3.53 ± 0.21 [d]	1415 ± 12 [g]	1385 ± 8	IMRE		86TAF
$C_9H_{12}FO_2^-$ 4-F-bicyclo[2.2.2]octane-CO_2^-				Est2	$\Delta_f H(AH) = -677\pm13$ $BDE(A-H) = 444\pm8$	
* -790 ± 25 [a]	3.51 ± 0.21 [d]	1417 ± 12 [g]	1387 ± 8	IMRE		86TAF
$C_9H_{12}N^-$ mNMe$_2$-$C_6H_4CH_2^-$				Est	$\Delta_f H(AH) = 67\pm8$	
134 ± 32 [a]		1597 ± 23 [g]	1569 ± 21	IMRB		83CAL/BAR
$C_9H_{12}N^-$ pNMe$_2$-$C_6H_4CH_2^-$				Est	$\Delta_f H(AH) = 71\pm8$	
155 ± 32 [a]		1614 ± 23 [g]	1586 ± 21	IMRB		83CAL/BAR
$C_9H_{12}NO_4^-$ 4-NO$_2$-bicyclo[2.2.2]octane-CO_2^-				Est2	$\Delta_f H(AH) = -537\pm13$ $BDE(A-H) = 444\pm8$	
* -664 ± 25 [a]	3.65 ± 0.21 [d]	1403 ± 12 [g]	1374 ± 8	IMRE		86TAF
$C_9H_{13}O_2^-$ bicyclo[2.2.2]octane-CO_2^-				Est2	$\Delta_f H(AH) = 8\pm13$ $BDE(A-H) = 444\pm8$	
* -82 ± 23 [a]	3.27 ± 0.20 [d]	1440 ± 11 [g]	1411 ± 8	IMRE		86TAF
$C_9H_{15}O^-$ cyclononanone enolate$^-$				Est	$\Delta_f H(AH) = -279\pm8$	
*	1.69 ± 0.06			PD		78ZIM/JAC
$C_9H_{19}O^-$ (tBu)$_2$CHO$^-$				Est	$\Delta_f H(AH) = -415\pm4$ $BDE(A-H) = 438\pm4$	
* -412 ± 16 [a]	2.25 ± 0.17 [d]	1533 ± 12 [g]	1505 ± 8 1509 ± 8	IMRE IMRE^o		79BAR/SCO 79BAR/SCO
$C_9H_{19}O^-$ nC$_9$H$_{19}$O$^-$					$\Delta_f H(AH) = -376\pm2$ $BDE(A-H) = 436\pm4$	77PED/RYL
* -353 ± 13 [a]	2.0 ± 0.2 [d]	1553 ± 11 1551 ± 10	1525 ± 13 [h]	CIDC CIDC^o		83BOA/HOU 83BOA/HOU
$C_9H_{21}BF^-$ iPr$_3$B$\cdot\cdot$F$^-$ -773 [c]		272		IMRB	F$^-$A: iPr$_2$BF > iPr$_3$B > Et$_2$BF > Et$_3$B	77MUR/BEA2
$C_9H_{21}O_2^-$ tBuOH$\cdot\cdot$tBuCH$_2$O$^-$ -687 ± 27 [c]		85 ± 10 [g]	57 ± 8	IMRE		84CAL/ROZ
$C_{10}N_6^-$ hexacyanobutadiene$^-$·				Est	$\Delta_f H(A) = 586\pm42$	
	3.3 ± 0.1			SI		69PAG/GOO
	3.3 ± 0.1			SI		67FAR/PAG

Table 2. Negative Ion Table - Continued

Ion $\Delta_f H(A^-)$ $\Delta_f H(X\cdot\cdot Y^-)$	EA(A) eV	$\Delta H_{acid}(AH)$ $\Delta H_{aff}(X\cdot\cdot Y^-)$	$\Delta G_{acid}(AH)$ $\Delta G_{aff}(X\cdot\cdot Y^-)$	Method	Comment	Reference
$C_{10}HN_4^-$ 2,3,5,6-tetracyanophenide$^-$	2.41±0.04			SI		67FAR/PAG
$C_{10}H_2F_{12}O_6U^-$ $UO_2\cdot(hexafluoroAcAc)_2^-$	1.9±0.3			NBIP		82YOK/QUI
$C_{10}H_2N_4^-$ 1,2,4,5-tetracyanobenzene$^-\cdot$	2.2±0.2			Est2 SI	$\Delta_f H(A) = 627\pm13$	67FAR/PAG
$C_{10}H_4Cl_2O_2^-$ 2,3-diCl-1,4-naphthoquinone$^-\cdot$ * −374±20 ^{b}	2.19±0.10 2.08±0.11			Est2 TDEq IMRE	$\Delta_f H(A) = -162\pm10$	87KEB/CHO 85GRI/CAL
$C_{10}H_5O_2^-$ 1,4-naphthoquinonide$^-$		1641±3 ^{g}	<1607	IMRB	$\Delta_f H(AH) = -111\pm4$	77PED/RYL 87JOH/SPE
$C_{10}H_6Cl_4O_4^-$ dimethyl tetrachloroterephthalate$^-\cdot$ 711 ^{b}	0.8			Est2 ECD	$\Delta_f H(A) = 785\pm13$	68KUH/LEV
$C_{10}H_6N_2O_4^-$ 1,3-diNO$_2$-naphthalene$^-\cdot$ * −52±14 ^{b}	1.78±0.10			Est TDEq	$\Delta_f H(A) = 120\pm4$	87KEB/CHO
$C_{10}H_6N_2O_4^-$ 1,5-diNO$_2$-naphthalene$^-\cdot$ * −51±14 ^{b}	1.77±0.10			Est TDEq	$\Delta_f H(A) = 120\pm4$	87KEB/CHO
$C_{10}H_6O_2^-$ 1,4-naphthoquinone$^-\cdot$ * −286±14 ^{b}	1.81±0.10 1.71±0.11 1.71±0.05 >0.8 >0.6			TDEq IMRE IMRE ECD ES	$\Delta_f H(A) = -111\pm4$	77PED/RYL 87KEB/CHO 85GRI/CAL 85FUK/MCI 83CHE/WEN 70COL/CHR
$C_{10}H_7^-$ naphthalenide$^-$ * 272±6 ^{a}		1651±5	1611±5	TDEq	$\Delta_f H(AH) = 150\pm1$	82COL/JIM 87MEO
$C_{10}H_7Cl^-$ 1-Cl-naphthalene$^-\cdot$ 93±10 ^{b}	0.277±0.003			ECD	$\Delta_f H(A) = 120\pm10$	77PED/RYL 69STE/WEN

Table 2. Negative Ion Table – Continued

Ion $\Delta_fH(A^-)$ $\Delta_fH(X\cdot\cdot Y^-)$	EA(A) eV	$\Delta H_{acid}(AH)$ $\Delta H_{aff}(X\cdot\cdot Y^-)$	$\Delta G_{acid}(AH)$ $\Delta G_{aff}(X\cdot\cdot Y^-)$	Method	Comment	Reference
$C_{10}H_7NO_2^-$						
1-NO_2-naphthalene$^-\cdot$					$\Delta_fH(A)=$ 150±2	77PED/RYL
* 31±12 [b]	1.23±0.10			TDEq		87KEB/CHO
$C_{10}H_7NO_2^-$						
2-NO_2-naphthalene$^-\cdot$				Est2	$\Delta_fH(A)=$ 150±8	
* 36±18 [b]	1.18±0.10			TDEq		87KEB/CHO
$C_{10}H_7N_2^-$						
pMe-C_6H_4-C(CN)$_2^-$						
*		1354±12 [g]	1323±8	IMRE		86TAF
$C_{10}H_7O^-$						
2-naphthoxide$^-$					$\Delta_fH(AH)=$ -30±1	77PED/RYL
* -122±11 [a]		1438±10 [g]	1408±8	IMRE		86TAF
$C_{10}H_8^-$						
azulene$^-\cdot$					$\Delta_fH(A)=$ 289±3	77PED/RYL
* 223±13 [b]	0.69±0.10			TDEq		87KEB/CHO
	0.75±0.11			IMRE		85GRI/CAL
	0.68±0.04			Kine		85GRI/CHO2
	0.52±0.01			ECD		81WOJ/FOL
	>0.5			ES		70CHA/CHR
	0.656±0.008			ECD		66BEC/CHE
$C_{10}H_8^-$						
naphthalene$^-\cdot$					$\Delta_fH(A)=$ 150±1	82COL/JIM
137±6 [b]	0.14±0.05			ECD		83ZLA/LEE
	0.13±0.04			ECD		81WOJ/FOL
	0.148±0.006			ECD		66BEC/CHE
$C_{10}H_9BrCl_2O_2^-$						
2,6-diCl-Br-tBu-benzoquinone$^-\cdot$						
*	2.42±0.05			IMRE		85FUK/MCI
$C_{10}H_9N_2^-$						
1,5-diaminonaphthalenide$^-$				Est	$\Delta_fH(AH)=$ 164±13	
* 127±22 [a]		1493±10 [g]	1463±8	IMRE		82ARN/VEN
			1472±8	IMRE^o		82ARN/VEN
$C_{10}H_9N_2^-$						
1,8-diaminonaphthalenide$^-$				Est2	$\Delta_fH(AH)=$ 192±8	
*			1441±8	IMRE		82ARN/VEN
			1450±8	IMRE^o		82ARN/VEN
$C_{10}H_9O_2^-$						
PhCOCH=C(Me)O$^-$				Est	$\Delta_fH(AH)=$ -250±2	
* -358±12 [a]		1422±10 [g]	1393±8	IMRE		78CUM/KEB

Table 2. Negative Ion Table – Continued

Ion $\Delta_f H(A^-)$ $\Delta_f H(X \cdot \cdot Y^-)$	EA(A) eV	$\Delta H_{acid}(AH)$ $\Delta H_{aff}(X \cdot \cdot Y^-)$	$\Delta G_{acid}(AH)$ $\Delta G_{aff}(X \cdot \cdot Y^-)$	Method	Comment	Reference
$C_{10}H_{10}Cl_2O_2^-$ 2,3-diCl-tBu-benzoquinone⁻·						
*	2.25±0.05			IMRE		85FUK/MCI
$C_{10}H_{10}F_3O_2^-$ 4-CF₃-bicyclo[2.2.2]octene-CO₂⁻				Est2	$\Delta_f H(AH)= -1028±13$ BDE(A–H)= 444±8	
* −1153±25 [a]	3.63±0.21 [d]	1405±12 [g]	1376±8	IMRE		86TAF
$C_{10}H_{10}NO_2^-$ 4-CN-bicyclo[2.2.2]octene-CO₂⁻				Est2	$\Delta_f H(AH)= -231±13$ BDE(A–H)= 444±8	
* −367±25 [a]	3.75±0.21 [d]	1394±12 [g]	1365±8	IMRE		86TAF
$C_{10}H_{10}O_4^-$ dimethyl isophthalate⁻·				Est2	$\Delta_f H(A)= -681±8$	
−734 [b]	0.6			ECD		68KUH/LEV
$C_{10}H_{10}O_4^-$ dimethyl phthalate⁻·				Est	$\Delta_f H(A)= -654±17$	
−707 [b]	0.6			ECD		68KUH/LEV
$C_{10}H_{10}O_4^-$ dimethyl terephthalate⁻·				Est2	$\Delta_f H(A)= -681±8$	
−743 [b]	0.6			ECD		68KUH/LEV
$C_{10}H_{11}ClO_2^-$ 2-Cl-5-tBu-benzoquinone⁻·						
*	2.06±0.05			IMRE		85FUK/MCI
$C_{10}H_{11}N_2^-$ pNMe₂-C₆H₄CHCN⁻				Est	$\Delta_f H(AH)= 195±8$	
* 143±23 [a]		1478±15 [g]	1450±8	IMRE		86TAF
$C_{10}H_{11}O_2^-$ triMe-benzoquinone-CH₂⁻				Est	$\Delta_f H(AH)= -252±8$	
	0.80±0.09			SI		67FAR/PAG
$C_{10}H_{12}F_3O_2^-$ 4-CF₃-bicyclo[2.2.2]octane-CO₂⁻				Est2	$\Delta_f H(AH)= -1148±13$ BDE(A–H)= 444±8	
* −1264±25 [a]	3.55±0.21 [d]	1413±12 [g]	1384±8	IMRE		86TAF
$C_{10}H_{12}NO^-$ mCONMe₂-C₆H₄CH₂⁻				Est2	$\Delta_f H(AH)= -130±8$	
* −95±19 [a]		1564±11 [g]	1536±8	IMRE		86TAF
$C_{10}H_{12}NO^-$ pCONMe₂-C₆H₄CH₂⁻				Est2	$\Delta_f H(AH)= -130±8$	
* −131±19 [a]		1529±11 [g]	1501±8	IMRE		86TAF
$C_{10}H_{12}NO_2^-$ 2-CN-bicyclo[2.2.2]octane-CO₂⁻				Est2	$\Delta_f H(AH)= -354±13$ BDE(A–H)= 444±8	
* −478±25 [a]	3.63±0.21 [d]	1405±12 [g]	1376±8	IMRE		86TAF

Table 2. Negative Ion Table – Continued

Ion $\Delta_f H(A^-)$ $\Delta_f H(X\cdot\cdot Y^-)$	EA(A) eV	$\Delta H_{acid}(AH)$ $\Delta H_{aff}(X\cdot\cdot Y^-)$	$\Delta G_{acid}(AH)$ $\Delta G_{aff}(X\cdot\cdot Y^-)$	Method	Comment	Reference
$C_{10}H_{12}NO_2^-$ 3-CN-bicyclo[2.2.2]octane-CO_2^-				Est2	$\Delta_f H(AH)= -354\pm13$ BDE(A-H)= 444 ± 8	
* -470 ± 25 [a]	3.55 ± 0.21 [d]	1413 ± 12 [g]	1384 ± 8	IMRE		86TAF
$C_{10}H_{12}NO_2^-$ 4-CN-bicyclo[2.2.2]octane-CO_2^-				Est2	$\Delta_f H(AH)= -350\pm13$ BDE(A-H)= 444 ± 8	
* -476 ± 25 [a]	3.64 ± 0.21 [d]	1405 ± 12 [g]	1375 ± 8	IMRE		86TAF
$C_{10}H_{12}O^-$ 2,4,6-triMe-benzaldehyde$^-\cdot$				Est2	$\Delta_f H(A)= -138\pm13$	
-180 ± 17 [b]	0.44 ± 0.04			ECD		69WEN/RIS
$C_{10}H_{12}O_2^-$ 2-iPr-5-Me-benzoquinone$^-\cdot$						
*	1.79 ± 0.10			TDEq		87KEB/CHO
$C_{10}H_{12}O_2^-$ tetraMe-benzoquinone$^-\cdot$				Est	$\Delta_f H(A)= -252\pm8$	
* -405 ± 18 [b]	1.59 ± 0.10 1.52 ± 0.05			TDEq IMRE		87KEB/CHO 85FUK/MCI
$C_{10}H_{13}O^-$ mtBu-phenoxide$^-$				Est	$\Delta_f H(AH)= -202\pm8$ BDE(A-H)= 362 ± 8	
* -274 ± 18 [a]	2.23 ± 0.19 [d]	1459 ± 10 [g]	1430 ± 8	IMRE		81FUJ/MCI
$C_{10}H_{13}O^-$ otBu-phenoxide$^-$				Est2	$\Delta_f H(AH)= -186\pm13$	
* -270 ± 25 [a]		1447 ± 12 [g]	1415 ± 8	IMRE		81FUJ/MCI
$C_{10}H_{13}O^-$ ptBu-phenoxide$^-$				Est	$\Delta_f H(AH)= -202\pm8$ BDE(A-H)= 362 ± 13	
* -274 ± 18 [a]	2.24 ± 0.23 [d]	1458 ± 10 [g]	1429 ± 8	IMRE		81FUJ/MCI
$C_{10}H_{13}O_2^-$ 4-Me-bicyclo[2.2.2]octene-CO_2^-				Est2	$\Delta_f H(AH)= -395\pm13$ BDE(A-H)= 444 ± 8	
* -497 ± 25 [a]	3.39 ± 0.21 [d]	1428 ± 12 [g]	1399 ± 8	IMRE		86TAF
$C_{10}H_{13}O_2S^-$ $PhSO_2CHiPr^-$				Est	$\Delta_f H(AH)= -349\pm2$	
* -362 ± 12 [a]		1517 ± 10 [g]	1487 ± 8	IMRE		78CUM/KEB
$C_{10}H_{14}^-$ 1,2,3,5-tetramethylbenzene$^-\cdot$					$\Delta_f H(A)= -42\pm8$	75GOO
-52 ± 10 [b]	0.11 ± 0.01			ECD		81WOJ/FOL
$C_{10}H_{14}^-$ 1,2,4,5-tetramethylbenzene$^-\cdot$					$\Delta_f H(A)= -46\pm8$	75GOO
-51 ± 10 [b]	4.80 ± 0.02			ECD		81WOJ/FOL

Table 2. Negative Ion Table - Continued

Ion $\Delta_f H(A^-)$ $\Delta_f H(X \cdot \cdot Y^-)$	EA(A) eV	$\Delta H_{acid}(AH)$ $\Delta H_{aff}(X \cdot \cdot Y^-)$	$\Delta G_{acid}(AH)$ $\Delta G_{aff}(X \cdot \cdot Y^-)$	Method	Comment	Reference
$C_{10}H_{15}^-$				Est2	$\Delta_f H(AH) = -33 \pm 17$	
pentaMe-cyclopentadienide$^-$						
* -54 ± 29 [a]		1510 ± 12 [g]	1485 ± 8	IMRE		86TAF
$C_{10}H_{15}O_2^-$				Est2	$\Delta_f H(AH) = -515 \pm 13$	
4-Me-bicyclo[2.2.2]octane-CO_2^-					BDE(A-H) = 444 ± 8	
* -609 ± 25 [a]	3.31 ± 0.21 [d]	1436 ± 12 [g]	1407 ± 8	IMRE		86TAF
$C_{10}H_{15}O_3^-$				Est2	$\Delta_f H(AH) = -628 \pm 13$	
3-OMe-bicyclo[2.2.2]octane-CO_2^-					BDE(A-H) = 444 ± 8	
* -720 ± 25 [a]	3.30 ± 0.21 [d]	1438 ± 12 [g]	1408 ± 8	IMRE		86TAF
$C_{10}H_{15}O_3^-$				Est2	$\Delta_f H(AH) = -631 \pm 13$	
4-OMe-bicyclo[2.2.2]octane-CO_2^-					BDE(A-H) = 444 ± 8	
* -732 ± 25 [a]	3.38 ± 0.21 [d]	1430 ± 12 [g]	1400 ± 8	IMRE		86TAF
$C_{10}H_{17}O^-$				Est	$\Delta_f H(AH) = -304 \pm 4$	
cyclodecanone enolate$^-$						
*	1.83 ± 0.07			PD		78ZIM/JAC
$C_{10}H_{23}O_2^-$						
$tBuCH_2OH \cdot \cdot tBuCH_2O^-$						
-698 ± 26 [c]		90 ± 10 [g]	62 ± 8	IMRE		84CAL/ROZ
$C_{11}H_7N^-$						
1-naphthonitrile$^{-\cdot}$				Est2	$\Delta_f H(A) = 286 \pm 13$	
* 221 ± 22 [b]	0.68 ± 0.10			TDEq		87KEB/CHO
	0.68 ± 0.09			TDEq		86CHO/KEB
$C_{11}H_7N^-$						
2-naphthonitrile$^{-\cdot}$				Est2	$\Delta_f H(A) = 286 \pm 13$	
* 223 ± 22 [b]	0.65 ± 0.10			TDEq		87KEB/CHO
	0.65 ± 0.09			TDEq		86CHO/KEB
$C_{11}H_8O^-$						
1-naphthaldehyde$^{-\cdot}$				Est	$\Delta_f H(A) = 31 \pm 8$	
* -37 ± 18 [b]	0.70 ± 0.10			TDEq		87KEB/CHO
	0.68 ± 0.02			ECD		75WEN/KAO
	0.74 ± 0.07			ECD		67WEN/CHE
$C_{11}H_8O^-$						
2-naphthaldehyde$^{-\cdot}$				Est	$\Delta_f H(A) = 31 \pm 8$	
* -32 ± 18 [b]	0.65 ± 0.10			TDEq		87KEB/CHO
	0.62 ± 0.02			ECD		75WEN/KAO
	0.62 ± 0.04			ECD		67WEN/CHE
$C_{11}H_8O_2^-$						
2-Me-1,4-naphthoquinone$^{-\cdot}$				Est	$\Delta_f H(A) = -127 \pm 8$	
* -295 ± 18 [b]	1.74 ± 0.10			TDEq		87KEB/CHO
	1.66 ± 0.05			IMRE		85FUK/MCI

Table 2. Negative Ion Table – Continued

Ion $\Delta_f H(A^-)$ $\Delta_f H(X\cdots Y^-)$	EA(A) eV	$\Delta H_{acid}(AH)$ $\Delta H_{aff}(X\cdots Y^-)$	$\Delta G_{acid}(AH)$ $\Delta G_{aff}(X\cdots Y^-)$	Method	Comment	Reference
$C_{11}H_9NO_2^-$						
2-Me-1-NO_2-naphthalene$^-\cdot$				Est	$\Delta_f H(A)= 117\pm 4$	
* 18±14 [b]	1.03±0.10			TDEq		87KEB/CHO
$C_{11}H_9NO_3^-$						
4-MeO-1-NO_2-naphthalene$^-\cdot$				Est	$\Delta_f H(A)= -21\pm 4$	
* −127±14 [b]	1.10±0.10			TDEq		87KEB/CHO
$C_{11}H_9O_4^-$						
4-CO_2Me-cubyl-CO_2^-					BDE(A-H)= 444±8	
*	3.55±0.21 [d]	1413±12 [g]	1384±8	IMRE		86TAF
$C_{11}H_{10}^-$						
1-Me-naphthalene$^-\cdot$					$\Delta_f H(A)= 113\pm 2$	74SAB/CHA
97±13 [b]	0.2±0.1			ECD		81WOJ/FOL
$C_{11}H_{10}^-$						
2-Me-naphthalene$^-\cdot$					$\Delta_f H(A)= 111\pm 2$	74SAB/CHA
97±9 [b]	0.14±0.07			ECD		81WOJ/FOL
$C_{11}H_{13}O^-$						
nPrOH$\cdots$PhC≡C$^-$						
8±26 [c]		64±10 [g]	37±8	IMRE		84CAL/ROZ
$C_{11}H_{14}ClO_2^-$						
3-Cl-1-adamantyl-CO_2^-				Est2	$\Delta_f H(AH)= -577\pm 13$	
					BDE(A-H)= 444±8	
* −692±23 [a]		1416±11 [g]	1387±8	IMRE		86TAF
$C_{11}H_{14}O^-$						
2,4,6-triMe-acetophenone$^-\cdot$					$\Delta_f H(A)= -205\pm 4$	77PED/RYL
−252±8 [b]	0.49±0.04			ECD		69WEN/RIS
$C_{11}H_{15}NO_2^-$						
p-t-amyl-nitrobenzene$^-\cdot$				Est2	$\Delta_f H(A)= -97\pm 13$	
−306±29 [b]	2.2±0.2			CIDC		84BUR/FUK
$C_{11}H_{15}O_2^-$						
1-adamantyl-CO_2^-				Est2	$\Delta_f H(AH)= -532\pm 13$	
					BDE(A-H)= 444±8	
* −624±23 [a]		1438±11 [g]	1408±8	IMRE		86TAF
$C_{11}H_{16}^-$						
pentamethylbenzene$^-\cdot$				Est2	$\Delta_f H(A)= -75\pm 8$	
−93±10 [b]	0.18±0.01			ECD		81WOJ/FOL
$C_{11}H_{25}O_2^-$						
tBuCH$_2$OH$\cdots$tBuCH(Me)O$^-$						
−736±28 [c]		89±10 [g]	62±8	IMRE		84CAL/ROZ
$C_{12}F_{10}^-$						
C_6F_5-$C_6F_5^-\cdot$				Est2	$\Delta_f H(A)= -785\pm 13$	
* −873±22 [b]	0.91±0.10			TDEq		87KEB/CHO
	0.91±0.10			IMRE		86CHO/GRI

Table 2. Negative Ion Table - Continued

Ion $\Delta_f H(X\cdot\cdot Y^-)$	$\Delta_f H(A^-)$ EA(A) eV	$\Delta H_{acid}(AH)$ $\Delta H_{aff}(X\cdot\cdot Y^-)$	$\Delta G_{acid}(AH)$ $\Delta G_{aff}(X\cdot\cdot Y^-)$	Method	Comment	Reference
$C_{12}N_6^-$						
hexacyanobenzene$^-\cdot$				Est	$\Delta_f H(A) = 900\pm21$	
2.5±0.1				SI		67FAR/PAG
$C_{12}H_4N_4^-$						
tetracyanoquinodimethane$^-\cdot$					$\Delta_f H(A) = 770\pm10$	77PED/RYL
* 500±19 [b] 2.8±0.1				NBIP		74KLO/COM
2.8±0.3				NBIP		77COM/COO
2.8±0.1				SI		79NAZ/POK
2.9±0.2				SI		67FAR/PAG
$C_{12}H_8^-$						
acenaphthylene$^-\cdot$					$\Delta_f H(A) = 260$	81KUD/KUD
221±3 [b] 0.40±0.03				ECD		81WOJ/FOL
$C_{12}H_8N^-$						
carbazolide$^-$					$\Delta_f H(AH) = 229\pm4$	81KUD/KUD2
* 143±15 [a]		1444±11 [g]	1412±8	IMRE		86TAF
$C_{12}H_8O_2^-$						
2-Ph-benzoquinone$^-\cdot$						
* 2.04±0.10				TDEq		87KEB/CHO
$C_{12}H_9NO_2^-$						
mPh-nitrobenzene$^-\cdot$				Est2	$\Delta_f H(A) = 167\pm8$	
* 58±18 [b] 1.13±0.10				TDEq		87KEB/CHO
$C_{12}H_9NO_2^-$						
oPh-nitrobenzene$^-\cdot$				Est2	$\Delta_f H(A) = 188\pm8$	
* 85±18 [b] 1.07±0.10				TDEq		87KEB/CHO
$C_{12}H_9NO_2^-$						
pPh-nitrobenzene$^-\cdot$				Est2	$\Delta_f H(A) = 167\pm8$	
* 52±18 [b] 1.20±0.10				TDEq		87KEB/CHO
$C_{12}H_{10}^-$						
biphenyl$^-\cdot$					$\Delta_f H(A) = 182\pm1$	77PED/RYL
170±5 [b] 0.13±0.04				ECD		81WOJ/FOL
$C_{12}H_{10}N^-$						
Ph_2N^-					$\Delta_f H(AH) = 219\pm3$	78STE
* 157±14 [a]		1468±11 [g]	1438±8	IMRE		86TAF
$C_{12}H_{10}O^-$						
1-acetonaphthone$^-\cdot$				Est	$\Delta_f H(A) = -21\pm8$	
−79±11 [b] 0.60±0.03				ECD		75WEN/KAO
$C_{12}H_{12}^-$						
1,4-diMe-naphthalene$^-\cdot$					$\Delta_f H(A) = 83\pm8$	69STU/WES
59±16 [b] 0.25±0.08				ECD		81WOJ/FOL

Table 2. Negative Ion Table - Continued

Ion $\Delta_fH(A^-)$ $\Delta_fH(X\cdot\cdot Y^-)$	EA(A) eV	$\Delta H_{acid}(AH)$ $\Delta H_{aff}(X\cdot\cdot Y^-)$	$\Delta G_{acid}(AH)$ $\Delta G_{aff}(X\cdot\cdot Y^-)$	Method	Comment	Reference
$C_{12}H_{12}^-$						
1-Et-naphthalene$^{-\cdot}$				Est	$\Delta_fH(A) = 96\pm8$	
82±14 ^{b}	0.15±0.06			ECD		81WOJ/FOL
$C_{12}H_{12}^-$						
2,3-diMe-naphthalene$^{-\cdot}$					$\Delta_fH(A) = 84\pm8$	69STU/WES
67±21 ^{b}	0.2±0.1			ECD		81WOJ/FOL
$C_{12}H_{12}^-$						
2,6-diMe-naphthalene$^{-\cdot}$				Est	$\Delta_fH(A) = 84\pm4$	
68±11 ^{b}	0.16±0.07			ECD		81WOJ/FOL
$C_{12}H_{12}^-$						
2-Et-naphthalene$^{-\cdot}$				Est	$\Delta_fH(A) = 86\pm8$	
67±14 ^{b}	0.20±0.06			ECD		81WOJ/FOL
$C_{12}H_{14}O_4^-$						
diethyl phthalate$^{-\cdot}$					$\Delta_fH(A) = -688\pm12$	77PED/RYL
-740 ^{b}	0.5			ECD		68KUH/LEV
$C_{12}H_{15}O_4^-$				Est2	$\Delta_fH(AH) = -753\pm17$	
4-CO_2Et-bicyclo[2.2.2]octene-CO_2^-					BDE(A-H) = 444±8	
* -865±28 ^{a}	3.50±0.20 ^{d}	1418±11 ^{g}	1389±8	IMRE		86TAF
$C_{12}H_{18}^-$						
hexamethylbenzene$^{-\cdot}$					$\Delta_fH(A) = -87\pm3$	77PED/RYL
-98±4 ^{b}	0.12±0.02			ECD		81WOJ/FOL
$C_{12}H_{21}O^-$				Est	$\Delta_fH(AH) = -350\pm8$	
cyclododecanone enolate$^-$						
*	1.90±0.07			PD		78ZIM/JAC
$C_{12}H_{27}O_2^-$						
tBuCH(Me)OH$\cdot\cdot$tBuCH(Me)O$^-$						
-768±31 ^{c}		90±10 ^{g}	62±8	IMRE		84CAL/ROZ
$C_{13}F_{10}O^-$						
$(C_6F_5)_2CO^{-\cdot}$				Est	$\Delta_fH(A) = -1868\pm21$	
* -2023±31 ^{b}	1.61±0.10			TDEq		87KEB/CHO
	1.61±0.10			IMRE		85GRI/CAL
$C_{13}H_8F_2O^-$						
p,p'-diF-benzophenone$^{-\cdot}$				Est	$\Delta_fH(A) = -327\pm8$	
* -403±13 ^{b}	0.79±0.05			IMRE		85FUK/MCI
$C_{13}H_9^-$					$\Delta_fH(AH) = 187\pm1$	81KUD/KUD
fluorenide$^-$					BDE(A-H) = 339±13	70TRO/BAZ
* 129±12 ^{a}	1.86±0.24 ^{d}	1472±11 ^{g}	1439±8	IMRE		86TAF
		1478±11 ^{g}	1446±8	IMRE		78CUM/KEB

Table 2. Negative Ion Table – Continued

Ion $\Delta_fH(A^-)$ $\Delta_fH(X\cdot\cdot Y^-)$	EA(A) eV	$\Delta H_{acid}(AH)$ $\Delta H_{aff}(X\cdot\cdot Y^-)$	$\Delta G_{acid}(AH)$ $\Delta G_{aff}(X\cdot\cdot Y^-)$	Method	Comment	Reference
$C_{13}H_9^-$						
perinaphthalenide$^-$				Est2	$\Delta_f H(AH) = 226 \pm 13$	
*	1.1±0.1			PD		79GYG/PET
$C_{13}H_9ClO^-$						
pCl-benzophenone$^{-\cdot}$				Est	$\Delta_f H(A) = 29 \pm 8$	
* −53±13 ^{b}	0.85±0.05			IMRE		85FUK/MCI
$C_{13}H_9FO^-$						
pF-benzophenone$^{-\cdot}$				Est	$\Delta_f H(A) = -134 \pm 8$	
* −196±18 ^{b}	0.64±0.10			TDEq		87KEB/CHO
	0.74±0.05			IMRE		85FUK/MCI
$C_{13}H_9O_2^-$						
mCOPh-phenoxide$^-$				Est	$\Delta_f H(AH) = -131 \pm 8$	
					BDE(A−H) = 362±8	
* −232±18 ^{a}	2.54±0.19 ^{d}	1428±10 ^{g}	1400±8	IMRE		81FUJ/MCI
$C_{13}H_9O_2^-$						
pCOPh-phenoxide$^-$				Est	$\Delta_f H(AH) = -131 \pm 8$	
* −268±19 ^{a}		1393±11 ^{g}	1364±8	IMRE		81FUJ/MCI
$C_{13}H_{10}^-$						
fluorene$^{-\cdot}$					$\Delta_f H(A) = 188 \pm 1$	81KUD/KUD
162±3 ^{b}	0.28±0.03			ECD		81WOJ/FOL
$C_{13}H_{10}Cl^-$						
mCl-C$_6$H$_4$-CH(Ph)$^-$				Est	$\Delta_f H(AH) = 110 \pm 4$	
* 85±16 ^{a}		1505±12 ^{g}	1482±8	IMRE		86TAF
$C_{13}H_{10}F^-$						
mF-C$_6$H$_4$CH(Ph)$^-$				Est	$\Delta_f H(AH) = -53 \pm 8$	
* −76±21 ^{a}		1507±12 ^{g}	1479±8	IMRE		86TAF
$C_{13}H_{10}O^-$						
benzophenone$^{-\cdot}$					$\Delta_f H(A) = 50 \pm 3$	78SAB/LAF3
* −10±13 ^{b}	0.62±0.10			TDEq		87KEB/CHO
	0.61±0.11			IMRE		85GRI/CAL
	0.69±0.05			IMRE		85FUK/MCI
	0.64±0.05			ECD		83CHE/WEN
$C_{13}H_{11}^-$						
Ph$_2$CH$^-$					$\Delta_f H(AH) = 140 \pm 3$	77PED/RYL
					BDE(A−H) = 351±4	82MCM/GOL
* 131±13 ^{a}	1.47±0.14 ^{d}	1521±10 ^{g}	1499±8	IMRE		79BAR/SCO
		1512±10 ^{g}	1489±8	IMRE		78CUM/KEB
	0.8±0.3			SI		68GAI/PAG
			1502±8	IMRE^o		79BAR/SCO
$C_{13}H_{11}FO^-$						
mF-C$_6$H$_4$CH$_2$OPh$^{-\cdot}$				Est	$\Delta_f H(A) = -166 \pm 4$	
	0.28±0.09			ECD		84HER/WEN

Ion $\Delta_f H(A^-)$ $\Delta_f H(X \cdot \cdot Y^-)$	EA(A) eV	$\Delta H_{acid}(AH)$ $\Delta H_{aff}(X \cdot \cdot Y^-)$	$\Delta G_{acid}(AH)$ $\Delta G_{aff}(X \cdot \cdot Y^-)$	Method	Comment	Reference
$C_{13}H_{11}F_{12}PUO_{10}^-$						
$UO_2 \cdot (hexafluoroAcAc)_2 \cdot OP(OMe)_3^-$						
	1.5±0.3			NBIP		82YOK/QUI
$C_{13}H_{11}O_2S^-$						
$pSO_2Ph-C_6H_4CH_2^-$				Est2	$\Delta_f H(AH) = -160 \pm 13$	
* −187±23 [a]		1504±11 [g]	1473±8	IMRE		86TAF
$C_{13}H_{12}^-$						
$Ph_2CH_2^{-\cdot}$						
125±7 [b]	0.16±0.04			ECD		81WOJ/FOL
$C_{13}H_{12}Cl^-$						
$Ph_2CH_2 \cdot \cdot Cl^-$						
			31	TDEq		82FRE/IKU
$C_{13}H_{15}O^-$						
$tBuOH \cdot \cdot PhC\equiv C^-$						
−57±28 [c]		72±10 [g]	44±8	IMRE		84CAL/ROZ
$C_{13}H_{21}O_2^-$						
$tBuCH(Me)OH \cdot \cdot PhCH_2O^-$						
−523±27 [c]		90±10 [g]	63±8	IMRE		84CAL/ROZ
$C_{14}H_7ClO_2^-$						
1-Cl-9,10-anthraquinone$^{-\cdot}$				Est2	$\Delta_f H(A) = -125 \pm 13$	
* −290±22 [b]	1.71±0.10			TDEq		87KEB/CHO
$C_{14}H_7O_2^-$						
9,10-anthraquinonide$^-$					$\Delta_f H(AH) = -95 \pm 7$	77PED/RYL
			1607±17	IMRB		87JOH/SPE
$C_{14}H_8O_2^-$						
9,10-anthraquinone$^{-\cdot}$					$\Delta_f H(A) = -95 \pm 7$	77PED/RYL
−249±16 [b]	1.59±0.10			TDEq		87KEB/CHO
	1.1±0.1			SI		69PAG/GOO
$C_{14}H_9Cl^-$						
1-Cl-anthracene$^{-\cdot}$				Est	$\Delta_f H(A) = 201 \pm 4$	
* 126±14 [b]	0.78±0.10			TDEq		87KEB/CHO
$C_{14}H_9Cl^-$						
2-Cl-anthracene$^{-\cdot}$				Est	$\Delta_f H(A) = 201 \pm 4$	
* 128±14 [b]	0.75±0.10			TDEq		87KEB/CHO
$C_{14}H_9Cl^-$						
9-Cl-anthracene$^{-\cdot}$				Est	$\Delta_f H(A) = 201 \pm 4$	
* 118±14 [b]	0.86±0.10			TDEq		87KEB/CHO

Table 2. Negative Ion Table – Continued

Ion $\Delta_f H(A^-)$ $\Delta_f H(X\cdot\cdot Y^-)$	EA(A) eV	$\Delta H_{acid}(AH)$ $\Delta H_{aff}(X\cdot\cdot Y^-)$	$\Delta G_{acid}(AH)$ $\Delta G_{aff}(X\cdot\cdot Y^-)$	Method	Comment	Reference
$C_{14}H_9NO_2^-$						
9-NO_2-anthracene$^-\cdot$				Est	$\Delta_f H(A) = 213\pm4$	
* 75±14 [b]	1.43±0.10			TDEq		87KEB/CHO
$C_{14}H_{10}^-$						
PhC≡CPh$^-\cdot$					$\Delta_f H(A) = 402\pm4$	82CHI/LIE
371±11 [b]	0.32±0.07			ECD		81WOJ/FOL
$C_{14}H_{10}^-$						
anthracene$^-\cdot$					$\Delta_f H(A) = 230\pm1$	79KUD/KUD4
* 172±11 [b]	0.60±0.10			TDEq		87KEB/CHO
	0.48±0.04			ECD		81WOJ/FOL
	0.57±0.02			ECD		68LYO/MOR
	0.556±0.008			ECD		66BEC/CHE
$C_{14}H_{10}^-$						
phenanthrene$^-\cdot$					$\Delta_f H(A) = 207\pm1$	79KUD/KUD4
181±4 [b]	0.27±0.04			ECD		81WOJ/FOL
	0.307±0.007			ECD		66BEC/CHE
$C_{14}H_{10}F_3^-$						
mCF_3-C_6H_4-CH(Ph)$^-$				Est	$\Delta_f H(AH) = -528\pm4$	
* -574±14 [a]		1484±10 [g]	1462±8	IMRE		86TAF
$C_{14}H_{10}F_{12}O_7U^-$						
UO_2·(hexafluoroAcAc)$_2$·THF$^-$						
1.6±0.2				NBIP		82YOK/QUI
$C_{14}H_{10}N^-$						
mCN-C_6H_4-CH(Ph)$^-$				Est	$\Delta_f H(AH) = 276\pm4$	
* 216±14 [a]		1470±10 [g]	1448±8	IMRE		86TAF
$C_{14}H_{11}^-$						
2-Me-fluorenide$^-$				Est2	$\Delta_f H(AH) = 155\pm8$	
* 100±21 [a]		1475±12 [g]	1443±8	IMRE		86TAF
$C_{14}H_{11}^-$						
9-Me-fluorenide$^-$				Est2	$\Delta_f H(AH) = 109\pm13$	
* 47±23 [a]		1468±11 [g]	1437±8	IMRE		86TAF
$C_{14}H_{11}O^-$						
pCOPh-$C_6H_4CH_2^-$				Est	$\Delta_f H(AH) = 26\pm4$	
* 3±15 [a]		1507±11 [g]	1479±8	IMRE		86TAF
$C_{14}H_{11}O_2S^-$						
9-SO_2Me-fluorenide$^-$				Est2	$\Delta_f H(AH) = -141\pm13$	
* -287±23 [a]		1384±11 [g]	1351±8	IMRE		86TAF
$C_{14}H_{12}^-$						
(E)-PhCH=CHPh$^-\cdot$					$\Delta_f H(A) = 235\pm3$	77PED/RYL
197±9 [b]	0.39±0.06			ECD		81WOJ/FOL

Table 2. Negative Ion Table — Continued

Ion $\Delta_f H(A^-)$ $\Delta_f H(X \cdots Y^-)$	EA(A) eV	$\Delta H_{acid}(AH)$ $\Delta H_{aff}(X \cdots Y^-)$	$\Delta G_{acid}(AH)$ $\Delta G_{aff}(X \cdots Y^-)$	Method	Comment	Reference
$C_{14}H_{12}^-$ $Ph_2C=CH_2^-\cdot$ 208±10 [b]	0.39±0.06			ECD		81WOJ/FOL
$C_{14}H_{15}O_2^-$ $PhCH_2OH \cdots PhCH_2O^-$ −276±18 [c]		93±4	66±7	TDAs		84CAL/ROZ
$C_{14}H_{20}O_2^-$ 2,6-di-tBu-benzoquinone$^-\cdot$ * −516±22 [b]	1.88±0.10			Est2 TDEq	$\Delta_f H(A) = -335\pm13$	87KEB/CHO
$C_{15}H_9N^-$ 9-CN-anthracene$^-\cdot$ * 244±14 [b]	1.27±0.10			Est TDEq	$\Delta_f H(A) = 366\pm4$	87KEB/CHO
$C_{15}H_{10}O^-$ 9-anthraldehyde$^-\cdot$ * −16±18 [b]	1.31±0.10 1.0±0.1			Est2 TDEq ECD	$\Delta_f H(A) = 110\pm8$	87KEB/CHO 67WEN/CHE
$C_{15}H_{10}O^-$ 9-phenanthraldehyde$^-\cdot$ 0±9 [b]	0.724±0.009 0.7±0.1			Est2 ECD ECD	$\Delta_f H(A) = 70\pm8$	75WEN/KAO 67WEN/CHE
$C_{15}H_{13}^-$ 9-Et-fluorenide$^-$ * 27±23 [a]		1469±11 [g]	1437±8	Est2 IMRE	$\Delta_f H(AH) = 88\pm13$	86TAF
$C_{15}H_{13}O^-$ $PhCH_2OH \cdots PhC \equiv C^-$ 145±26 [c]		82±10 [g]	54±8	IMRE		84CAL/ROZ
$C_{16}H_{10}^-$ fluoranthene$^-\cdot$ 228 [b]	0.6			ECD	$\Delta_f H(A) = 289\pm1$	81KUD/KUD 69MIC
$C_{16}H_{10}^-$ pyrene$^-\cdot$ 168±4 [b]	0.50±0.03 0.591±0.008			ECD ECD	$\Delta_f H(A) = 216\pm1$	79KUD/KUD2 68LYO/MOR 66BEC/CHE
$C_{16}H_{12}O^-$ 9-COMe-anthracene$^-\cdot$ * −34±14 [b]	0.97±0.10			Est TDEq	$\Delta_f H(A) = 60\pm4$	87KEB/CHO
$C_{16}H_{12}O_2^-$ 2-Et-9,10-anthraquinone$^-\cdot$ * −299±14 [b]	1.56±0.10			Est TDEq	$\Delta_f H(A) = -149\pm4$	87KEB/CHO

Table 2. Negative Ion Table - Continued

Ion $\Delta_fH(X\cdot\cdot Y^-)$	$\Delta_fH(A^-)$ EA(A) eV	$\Delta H_{acid}(AH)$ $\Delta H_{aff}(X\cdot\cdot Y^-)$	$\Delta G_{acid}(AH)$ $\Delta G_{aff}(X\cdot\cdot Y^-)$	Method	Comment	Reference
$C_{16}H_{15}^-$ 9-iPr-fluorenide$^-$				Est2	$\Delta_fH(AH)=$ 59±13	
*	−2±23 [a]	1470±11 [g]	1437±8	IMRE		86TAF
$C_{17}H_{12}Cl^-$ 2-Ph-5-pCl-C_6H_4-cyclopentadienide$^-$				Est2	$\Delta_fH(AH)=$ 293±13	
*	170±23 [a]	1407±11 [g]	1376±8	IMRE		86TAF
$C_{17}H_{13}^-$ 1,4-diphenylcyclopentadienide$^-$				Est	$\Delta_fH(AH)=$ 322±8	
*	205±18 [a]	1413±10 [g]	1383±8	IMRE		86TAF
$C_{17}H_{17}^-$ 9-iBu-fluorenide$^-$				Est2	$\Delta_fH(AH)=$ 42±13	
*	−21±23 [a]	1468±11 [g]	1435±8	IMRE		86TAF
$C_{17}H_{17}^-$ 9-tBu-fluorenide$^-$				Est2	$\Delta_fH(AH)=$ 25±17	
*	−36±28 [a]	1469±11 [g]	1438±8	IMRE		86TAF
$C_{18}H_{12}^-$ benz[a]anthracene$^{-\cdot}$					$\Delta_fH(A)=$ 285±1	79KUD/KUD2
	224±2 [b] 0.630±0.008			ECD		66BEC/CHE
$C_{18}H_{12}^-$ benzo[c]phenanthrene$^{-\cdot}$					$\Delta_fH(A)=$ 293±1	79KUD/KUD2
	240±2 [b] 0.545±0.008			ECD		66BEC/CHE
$C_{18}H_{12}^-$ chrysene$^{-\cdot}$					$\Delta_fH(A)=$ 284±1	79KUD/KUD2
	246±2 [b] 0.397±0.008			ECD		66BEC/CHE
$C_{18}H_{12}^-$ naphthacene$^{-\cdot}$					$\Delta_fH(A)=$ 284±1	79KUD/KUD2
	199±5 [b] 0.88±0.04			ECD		68LYO/MOR
$C_{18}H_{12}^-$ triphenylene$^{-\cdot}$					$\Delta_fH(A)=$ 270±1	79KUD/KUD2
	242±2 [b] 0.285±0.008			ECD		66BEC/CHE
$C_{18}H_{15}^-$ 2-Ph-5-p-tolyl-cyclopentadienide$^-$				Est	$\Delta_fH(AH)=$ 288±8	
*	171±19 [a]	1413±11 [g]	1381±8	IMRE		86TAF
$C_{18}H_{16}O_2^-$ 2-tBu-9,10-anthraquinone$^{-\cdot}$				Est	$\Delta_fH(A)=$ −202±4	
*	−353±14 [b] 1.56±0.10			TDEq		87KEB/CHO
$C_{18}H_{19}^-$ 9-tBuCH$_2$-fluorenide$^-$				Est	$\Delta_fH(AH)=$ 4±17	
*	−74±28 [a]	1452±11 [g]	1419±8	IMRE		86TAF

Table 2. Negative Ion Table – Continued

Ion $\Delta_f H(A^-)$ $\Delta_f H(X \cdot \cdot Y^-)$	EA(A) eV	$\Delta H_{acid}(AH)$ $\Delta H_{aff}(X \cdot \cdot Y^-)$	$\Delta G_{acid}(AH)$ $\Delta G_{aff}(X \cdot \cdot Y^-)$	Method	Comment	Reference
$C_{19}H_{11}^-$						
fluoradenide$^-$						
*		1391±10 ^{g}	1359±8	IMRE		86TAF
$C_{19}H_{13}^-$						
9-Ph-fluorenide$^-$				Est2	$\Delta_f H(AH)=$ 318±13	
* 224±23 ^{a}		1436±11 ^{g}	1404±8	IMRE		86TAF
$C_{19}H_{15}^-$						
Ph_3C^-					$\Delta_f H(AH)=$ 271±4	77PED/RYL
242±16 ^{a}		1501±12 ^{g}	1467±8	IMRE		86TAF
		1510±13 ^{g}	1476±10	IMRE		84BAR
	2.56			IMRE	Solution equilibrium + solvation cycle	30BEN
	0.8			SI	From hexaphenylethane	68GAI/PAG
$C_{19}H_{16}Cl^-$						
$Ph_3CH \cdot \cdot Cl^-$						
			17	TDEq		82FRE/IKU
$C_{20}H_{12}^-$						
benz[a]pyrene$^-\cdot$					$\Delta_f H(A)=$ 289±4	77STE/GOL
	0.680±0.008			ECD		66BEC/CHE
$C_{20}H_{12}^-$						
benz[e]pyrene$^-\cdot$				Est	$\Delta_f H(A)=$ 261±4	
210±5 ^{b}	0.534±0.008			ECD		66BEC/CHE
$C_{21}H_{15}^-$						
1,3-diphenylindenide$^-$				Est	$\Delta_f H(AH)=$ 371±8	
* 244±18 ^{a}		1403±10 ^{g}	1376±8	IMRE		86TAF
$C_{22}H_{14}^-$						
dibenz[a,h]anthracene$^-\cdot$					$\Delta_f H(A)=$ 336±4	77STE/GOL
279±5 ^{b}	0.595±0.008			ECD		66BEC/CHE
$C_{22}H_{14}^-$						
dibenz[a,j]anthracene$^-\cdot$				Est	$\Delta_f H(A)=$ 336±4	
279±5 ^{b}	0.591±0.008			ECD		66BEC/CHE
$C_{22}H_{14}^-$						
picene$^-\cdot$				Est	$\Delta_f H(A)=$ 326±8	
274±9 ^{b}	0.542±0.008			ECD		66BEC/CHE
$C_{27}H_{19}^-$						
1,2,3-triPh-indenide$^-$						
*		1404±11 ^{g}	1373±8	IMRE		86TAF
CaH^-						
CaH^-					$\Delta_f H(A)=$ 229±42	82TN270
* 139±47 ^{b}	0.93±0.05			PD		77RAC/FEL

Table 2. Negative Ion Table – Continued

Ion $\Delta_fH(X\cdot\cdot Y^-)$	$\Delta_fH(A^-)$	EA(A) eV	$\Delta H_{acid}(AH)$ $\Delta H_{aff}(X\cdot\cdot Y^-)$	$\Delta G_{acid}(AH)$ $\Delta G_{aff}(X\cdot\cdot Y^-)$	Method	Comment	Reference
CeF_4^-							
$CeF_3\cdot\cdot F^-$	−2005±29	3.60±0.30 [i]	459±29 [k]		TDEq		81SID/SOR
CeI^-							
CeI^-		>0.3±0.3			EIAP	From CeI_3	76CHA
CeI_2^-							
CeI_2^-	<−221 [b]	>0.3±0.2			EIAP	$\Delta_fH(A)=$ −192 From CeI_3	76CHA 76CHA
CeI_3^-							
CeI_3^-	<−368 [b]	>0.3			IMRB	$\Delta_fH(A)=$ −339 $CeI_2^- + CeI_3 \rightarrow$	76CHA 76CHA
CeI_4^-							
CeI_4^-	−808 [c]		280±33	245±42	TDEq		76CHA
Cl^-							
Cl^- *	−227±1 [a]	3.617±0.003	1395±1 [e] 1396±9 [g]	1372±1 [h] 1374±8	LOG IMRE	$\Delta_fH(A)=$ 122	85JANAF 85HOT/LIN 81FUJ/MCI
$ClCrO^-$							
$CrOCl^-$	−231±48	1.2±0.1			EIAP	$\Delta_fH(A)=$ −116±48 From CrO_2Cl_2	69FLE/WHI 69FLE/WHI
$ClCrO_2^-$							
CrO_2Cl^-	−531±48	2.4±0.4			EIAP	$\Delta_fH(A)=$ −309±48 From CrO_2Cl_2	69FLE/WHI 69FLE/WHI
ClF^-							
ClF^-	−195±29 [b]	1.5±0.3 >1.5±0.2 2.9±0.2 >1.5±0.4			NBIP EIAP EIAP EIAP	$\Delta_fH(A)=$ −50 From CF_2Cl_2 From $CFCl_3$ From ClF_3 From SF_5Cl	85JANAF 78DIS/LAC 79ILL/SCH 79DUD/GOR 72THY
$ClFH^-$							
$HF\cdot\cdot Cl^-$ *	−591±10 [c]		91±8 [g]	63±8	IMRE		84LAR/MCM2
$ClFO^-$							
$ClOF^-$		>2.0±0.2			Est2 EIAP	$\Delta_fH(A)=$ 54±21	80BAL/NIK2
$ClFO_2^-$							
ClO_2F^-	−255 [b]	>2.3			EIAP	$\Delta_fH(A)=$ −33 From ClO_3F	73BAR 83ALE/FED

Table 2. Negative Ion Table — Continued

Ion $\Delta_f H(X \cdot \cdot Y^-)$	$\Delta_f H(A^-)$ EA(A) eV	$\Delta H_{acid}(AH)$ $\Delta H_{aff}(X \cdot \cdot Y^-)$	$\Delta G_{acid}(AH)$ $\Delta G_{aff}(X \cdot \cdot Y^-)$	Method	Comment	Reference
ClF_2^-						
$\quad ClF_2^-$						
	>3.2±0.2			EIAP	From ClF_5	80BAL/NIK
	>0.9±0.2			EIAP	From ClF_3	79DUD/GOR
ClF_2OS^-						
$\quad F_2SO \cdot \cdot Cl^-$						
$\quad * \;-851\pm30$ c		72±8 g	43±8	IMRE		85LAR/MCM
ClF_3^-						
$\quad ClF_3^-$					$\Delta_f H(A) = -163\pm2$	82BAU/COX
	>2.4±0.1			EIAP	From ClF_5	80BAL/NIK
ClF_3OP^-						
$\quad PF_3O \cdot \cdot Cl^-$						
$\quad * \;-1497\pm12$ c		58±8 g	32±8	IMRE		85LAR/MCM
ClF_3P^-						
$\quad PF_3 \cdot \cdot Cl^-$						
$\quad * \;-1211\pm12$ c		65±8 g	38±8	IMRE		85LAR/MCM
ClF_4Si^-						
$\quad SiF_4 \cdot \cdot Cl^-$						
$\quad * \;-1940\pm12$ c		98±8 g	70±8	IMRE		85LAR/MCM
$ClHI^-$						
$\quad HCl \cdot \cdot I^-$						
$\quad * \;-343\pm9$ c		62±8	37±11	TDAs		85CAL/KEB
ClH_2O^-						
$\quad HOH \cdot \cdot Cl^-$						
$\quad * \;-532$ c		62±1	38±6	TDAs		80KEE/CAS2
		62±8	38±11	TDAs		86YAM/FUR
		60±8 g	35±8	IMRE		84LAR/MCM2
		62	37	TDAs		82BUR/HAY
		55±8	30±8	TDAs		71YAM/KEB
$ClH_2O_2^-$						
$\quad HOOH \cdot \cdot Cl^-$						
$\quad -456\pm6$ c		92±4	65±4	TDEq	Relative to $HOH \cdot \cdot Cl^-$, 80KEE/LEE	84BOH/FAH
$ClH_2O_4S^-$						
$\quad HCl \cdot \cdot HSO_4^-$						
		66±4	47±4	TDEq	Relative to $HOH \cdot \cdot HSO_4^-$, 84BOH/FAH	84BOH/FAH
ClH_3N^-						
$\quad NH_3 \cdot \cdot Cl^-$						
$\quad * \;-317\pm18$ c		44±17 g	19±8	IMRE		84LAR/MCM2

Table 2. Negative Ion Table - Continued

Ion $\Delta_fH(A^-)$ $\Delta_fH(X\cdot\cdot Y^-)$	EA(A) eV	$\Delta H_{acid}(AH)$ $\Delta H_{aff}(X\cdot\cdot Y^-)$	$\Delta G_{acid}(AH)$ $\Delta G_{aff}(X\cdot\cdot Y^-)$	Method	Comment	Reference
ClI⁻						
ICl⁻·					$\Delta_fH(A)=\ 18$	85JANAF
-215 ± 10 [b]	2.4 ± 0.1			NBIP		73AUE/HUB
-155	1.8 [i]			Endo	$I^- + NOCl \rightarrow$	77REF/FRA
	1.48 ± 0.05			NBIP	Vertical EA	76HUB/KLE
ClK⁻						
KCl⁻·					$\Delta_fH(A)=\ -215$	85JANAF
-276 [b]	0.6			Scat		79DEV/WIJ
	>1.3			EIAP	From (KCl)$_2$	64EBI
ClLi⁻						
LiCl⁻·					$\Delta_fH(A)=\ -196\pm8$	85JANAF
-255 ± 10 [b]	0.610 ± 0.020			LPES		76CAR/PET
	>1.3			EIAP	From (LiCl)$_2$	64EBI
ClNa⁻						
NaCl⁻·					$\Delta_fH(A)=\ -181\pm8$	85JANAF
-255 [b]	0.8			Scat		79DEV/WIJ
	>1.3			EIAP	From (NaCl)$_2$	64EBI
ClO⁻						
ClO⁻					$\Delta_fH(AH)=\ -79\pm8$	82BAU/COX
					BDE(A-H)= 399 ± 9	82TN270
* -108 ± 18 [a]	2.170	1502 ± 9 [e]	1474 ± 10 [h]	LPD		79LEE/SMI
	2.4 ± 0.2			EIAP	From Cl$_2$O	80BAL/NIK2
	1.9 ± 0.3			IMRB		78DOT/ALB
$<-54\pm21$	$>1.6\pm0.2$ [i]			Endo	$Cl^- + O_2 \rightarrow$	77VOG/DRE
ClOV⁻						
VOCl⁻						
-310 ± 48	1.4 ± 0.4			EIAP	From VOCl$_3$	75FLE/SVE
ClO$_2$⁻						
OClO⁻					$\Delta_fH(A)=\ 97\pm8$	82BAU/COX
-29 ± 50 [b]	1.3 ± 0.4			ECD		81WEC/CHR
	1.8 ± 0.2			EIAP	From FClO$_3$	80BAL/NIK2
ClO$_2$S⁻						
SO$_2\cdot\cdot$Cl⁻						
* -617 ± 11 [c]		93 ± 8	66 ± 8	TDAs		85CAL/KEB
		93 ± 8	63 ± 7	TDEq	Relative to HOH$\cdot\cdot$Cl⁻ in 80KEE/LEE	84BOH/FAH
		91 ± 1	62 ± 1	TDAs		80KEE/LEE
		87 ± 8 [g]	62 ± 8	IMRE		85LAR/MCM
<-565				IMRB		79ROB/FRA
-326				IMRB		78SUL/BEA2
ClO$_3$⁻						
ClO$_3$⁻					$\Delta_fH(A)=\ 126\pm21$	82TN270
-183 ± 21 [b]	>3.2			EIAP	From ClO$_3$F	83ALE/FED

Table 2. Negative Ion Table - Continued

Ion $\Delta_fH(A^-)$ $\Delta_fH(X\cdot\cdot Y^-)$	EA(A) eV	$\Delta H_{acid}(AH)$ $\Delta H_{aff}(X\cdot\cdot Y^-)$	$\Delta G_{acid}(AH)$ $\Delta G_{aff}(X\cdot\cdot Y^-)$	Method	Comment	Reference
ClO_3S^-						
$SO_3\cdot\cdot Cl^-$						
		<1312±8		EIAP	From $ClSO_3H$ (Appearance Potential = 0 eV)	86ADA/SMI
$ClO_4S_2^-$						
$SO_2\cdot\cdot SO_2Cl^-$						
−982				IMRE		80KEE/CAS
<−920				IMRB		79ROB/FRA
$ClPb^-$						
$PbCl^-$						
	1.0±0.2			EIAP	From $PbCl_2$	67HAS/BLO
$ClRb^-$						
$RbCl^-\cdot$					$\Delta_fH(A)=$ −229	82TN270
	>1.5			EIAP	From $(RbCl)_2$	64EBI
$ClXe^-$						
$Xe\cdot\cdot Cl^-$						
		13		MobI		84GAT
		13		MobI		80THA/EIS
		<13		MobI		79DEV/WIJ2
Cl_2^-						
$Cl_2^-\cdot$						
* −232±19 [b]	2.4±0.2			NBIP		77DIS/LAC2
	2.3			ECD	Vertical EA: 1.02 eV	81AYA/WEN
	2.3±0.1			EnCT		73HUG/LIF
	2.5±0.1			IMRB		72DUN/FEH
	2.5±0.1			NBIP		72BAE
	2.5±0.2			EIAP	From CCl_4	71DEC/FRA
	1.02±0.05			NBIP	Vertical EA	76HUB/KLE
	2.4±0.1			EnCT		71CHU/BER
	3.2±0.2			NBIP		70LAC/HER
Cl_2CrO^-						
$CrOCl_2^-$					$\Delta_fH(A)=$ −309±48	69FLE/WHI
−550±48	2.5±0.1			EIAP	From CrO_2Cl_2	69FLE/WHI
Cl_2Ge^-						
$GeCl_2^-\cdot$					$\Delta_fH(A)=$ −172±4	79TPIS
−418 [b]	2.6			EIAP	From $GeCl_4$	77PAB/MAR
Cl_2H^-						
$HCl\cdot\cdot Cl^-$						
* −419±10 [c]		100±8	72±11	TDAs		85CAL/KEB
		97±8 [g]	67±8	IMRE		84LAR/MCM2
		99±1	70±1	TDAs		74YAM/KEB
<−521±48				EIAP	From $CHCl_3$	80SCH/ILL

Table 2. Negative Ion Table - Continued

Ion $\Delta_f H(A^-)$ $\Delta_f H(X\cdot\cdot Y^-)$	EA(A) eV	$\Delta H_{acid}(AH)$ $\Delta H_{aff}(X\cdot\cdot Y^-)$	$\Delta G_{acid}(AH)$ $\Delta G_{aff}(X\cdot\cdot Y^-)$	Method	Comment	Reference
Cl_2I^-						
ICl_2^-						
−605		377 ^{k}		Latt		77FIN/GAT
Cl_2O^-						
$Cl_2O^{-\cdot}$					$\Delta_f H(A) = 105\pm2$	82TN270
< −109 ^{b}	> 2.2			ECD		81WEC/CHR
Cl_2OP^-						
Cl_2PO^-						
	3.8±0.3			NBAP	From $POCl_3$	76MAT/ROT
Cl_2OV^-						
$VOCl_2^-$						
−590±48	3.2±0.5			EIAP	From $VOCl_3$	75FLE/SVE
$Cl_2O_2S^-$						
$SO_2Cl_2^{-\cdot}$					$\Delta_f H(A) = -364\pm2$	82TN270
< −598 ^{b}	> 2.4			IMRB	EA: > Cl_2^-	79ROB/FRA
Cl_2P^-						
PCl_2^-						
	0.9±0.1			EIAP	From PCl_3	78PAB/MAR
< −891±19				EIAP	From $POCl_3$	74HAL/KLE
Cl_2Si^-						
$SiCl_2^{-\cdot}$					$\Delta_f H(A) = -166$	82TN270
	0.8±0.1			EIAP	From $SiCl_4$	77PAB/MAR
−228±21	> 2.5			EIAP	From $SiCl_4$	68JAE/HEN
Cl_2Sn^-						
$SnCl_2^{-\cdot}$					$\Delta_f H(A) = -203\pm4$	82TPIS
−95	1.0			EIAP	From $SnCl_4$	77PAB/PER
Cl_2V^-						
VCl_2^-					$\Delta_f H(A) = -1073\pm8$	82TN270
−1189±28 ^{b}	1.2±0.2			EIAP	From $VOCl_3$	75FLE/SVE
Cl_3^-						
Cl_3^-						
−300		70 ^{k}		IMRE		79ROB/FRA2
−300±21	> 4.3±0.2 ^{i}			IMRB		79ROB/FRA
> −410 ^{c}			< 182	PDis		79LEE/SMI
Cl_3Ge^-						
$GeCl_3^-$						
	> 2.6			NBAP	From $GeCl_4$	79MAT/ROT
	1.8±0.1			EIAP	From $GeCl_4$	78PAB/MAR
	1.8			EIAP	From $GeCl_4$	77PAB/MAR

Table 2. Negative Ion Table – Continued

Ion $\Delta_f H(\text{X}\cdots\text{Y}^-)$	EA(A) eV	ΔH_{acid}(AH) ΔH_{aff}(X$\cdots$Y$^-$)	ΔG_{acid}(AH) ΔG_{aff}(X$\cdots$Y$^-$)	Method	Comment	Reference
Cl_3OP^-						
$\text{Cl}_3\text{PO}^{-\cdot}$					$\Delta_f H(A) = -558\pm1$	82TN270
-694 ± 20 [b]	1.4 ± 0.2			NBIP		76MAT/ROT
Cl_3OV^-						
$\text{VOCl}_3^{-\cdot}$					$\Delta_f H(A) = -696$	82TN270
$<-1043\pm49$ [b]	3.6 ± 0.5			IMRB	EA: > Cl$^-$	75FLE/SVE
$\text{Cl}_3\text{O}_2\text{S}^-$						
$\text{SO}_2\text{Cl}_2\cdots\text{Cl}^-$						
$<-644\pm21$				IMRB	Cl$^-$A: > Cl$_2$, SO$_2$	79ROB/FRA
Cl_3P^-						
$\text{PCl}_3^{-\cdot}$					$\Delta_f H(A) = -289\pm2$	85JANAF
-368 ± 12 [b]	0.8 ± 0.1			NBIP		76MAT/ROT
	>3.6			IMRB	From PCl$_5$	74HAL/KLE
Cl_3Si^-						
SiCl_3^-					$\Delta_f H(AH) = -481\pm8$	81BEL/PER
					BDE(A–H) = 382 ± 4	81WAL
$<-510\pm13$ [a]	>2.0	<1501 [e]		EIAP	From SiCl$_4$	77PAB/MAR
-589 ± 21	3.5 ± 0.4			EIAP	From SiCl$_4$	68JAE/HEN
Cl_3Sn^-						
SnCl_3^-						
	3.4 ± 0.2			NBAP	From SnCl$_4$	83LAC/MAN
	3.7 ± 0.5			NBAP	From SnCl$_4$	79MAT/ROT
	2.53 ± 0.01			EIAP	From SnCl$_4$	78PAB/MAR
-583	2.5			EIAP	From SnCl$_4$	77PAB/PER
Cl_3Ti^-						
TiCl_3^-					$\Delta_f H(A) = -542\pm2$	82TN270
-601 ± 18 [b]	0.6 ± 0.2			NBAP	From TiCl$_4$	79MAT/ROT
	0.6 ± 0.1			EIAP	From TiCl$_4$	78PAB/MAR
-597 ± 13	0.6 ± 0.2			EIAP	From TiCl$_4$	74BEN/PAB
Cl_3V^-						
VCl_3^-						
-569 ± 48	2.2 ± 0.5			EIAP	From VOCl$_3$	75FLE/SVE
Cl_4I^-						
ICl_4^-						
-631				Latt		77FIN/GAT
Cl_4Nb^-						
NbCl_4^-					$\Delta_f H(A) = -561\pm2$	82TN270
<-696 [b]	>1.4			EIAP	From NbCl$_5$	75BEN/MAR
Cl_4Sn^-						
$\text{SnCl}_4^{-\cdot}$					$\Delta_f H(A) = -472\pm2$	82TN270
-684 ± 21 [b]	2.2 ± 0.2			NBIP		83LAC/MAN
	2.5 ± 0.2			NBIP		79MAT/ROT

Table 2. Negative Ion Table - Continued

Ion $\Delta_f H(A^-)$ $\Delta_f H(X\cdot\cdot Y^-)$	EA(A) eV	$\Delta H_{acid}(AH)$ $\Delta H_{aff}(X\cdot\cdot Y^-)$	$\Delta G_{acid}(AH)$ $\Delta G_{aff}(X\cdot\cdot Y^-)$	Method	Comment	Reference
Cl_4Ta^-						
$TaCl_4^-$					$\Delta_f H(A) = -561\pm2$	82TN270
<-696 [b]	>1.4			EIAP	From $TaCl_5$	75BEN/MAR
Cl_4Ti^-						
$TiCl_4^-$					$\Delta_f H(A) = -763\pm2$	85JANAF
-1041 ± 17 [b]	2.9 ± 0.2			NBIP		79MAT/ROT
Cl_5Si^-						
$SiCl_4\cdot\cdot Cl^-$						
* -986 ± 12 [c]		101 ± 8 [g]	74 ± 8	IMRE		85LAR/MCM
Co^-						
Co^-					$\Delta_f H(A) = 425\pm2$	82TN270
* 361 ± 2 [b]	0.662 ± 0.003	1437 ± 5 [e]		LPES		86LEO/LIN
372 [a]			1395 ± 13	IMRB		85SAL/LAN
CoH^-						
CoH^-					$\Delta_f H(A) = 477\pm13$	81ARM/BEA
* 412 ± 14 [b]	0.671 ± 0.010			LPES		87MIL/FEI
CoH_2^-						
CoH_2^-						
*	1.450 ± 0.014			LPES		86MIL/FEI
CoD_2^-						
CoD_2^-						
*	1.465 ± 0.013			LPES		86MIL/FEI
Co_2^-						
Co_2^-					$\Delta_f H(A) = 683\pm8$	82TN270
* 576 ± 9 [b]	1.110 ± 0.008			LPES		86LEO/LIN
Cr^-						
Cr^-					$\Delta_f H(A) = 397\pm2$	82TN270
* 332 ± 3 [b]	0.666 ± 0.012			LPES		85HOT/LIN
			1389 ± 13	IMRB		85SAL/LAN
$CrCl^-$						
$CrCl^-$					$\Delta_f H(A) = 48\pm48$	69FLE/WHI
-145 ± 48	1.1 ± 0.2			EIAP	From CrO_2Cl_2	69FLE/WHI
$CrCl_2^-$						
$CrCl_2^-$					$\Delta_f H(A) = -128\pm2$	82TN270
-309 ± 48	1.7 ± 0.2			EIAP	From CrO_2Cl_2	69FLE/WHI
CrF^-						
CrF^-					$\Delta_f H(A) = 21$	81WOO
-67 ± 48	1.0 ± 0.4			EIAP	From CrO_2F_2	69FLE/WHI

Table 2. Negative Ion Table – Continued

Ion $\Delta_fH(X\cdot\cdot Y^-)$	EA(A) eV	ΔH_{acid}(AH) $\Delta H_{aff}(X\cdot\cdot Y^-)$	ΔG_{acid}(AH) $\Delta G_{aff}(X\cdot\cdot Y^-)$	Method	Comment	Reference
CrFO⁻						
CrOF⁻·					$\Delta_fH(A) = -309\pm48$	69FLE/WHI
−367±48	0.7±0.2			EIAP	From CrO_2F_2	69FLE/WHI
CrFO$_2^-$						
CrO$_2$F⁻					$\Delta_fH(A) = -473\pm48$	69FLE/WHI
−724±48	2.5±0.2			EIAP	From CrO_2F_2	69FLE/WHI
CrF$_2^-$						
CrF$_2^-$					$\Delta_fH(A) = -216$	81WOO
−540±48	1.5±0.4			EIAP	From CrO_2F_2	69FLE/WHI
CrF$_2$O⁻						
CrOF$_2^-$					$\Delta_fH(A) = -618\pm48$	69FLE/WHI
−820±48	2.1±0.1			EIAP	From CrO_2F_2	69FLE/WHI
CrH⁻						
CrH⁻						
*	0.563±0.010			LPES		87MIL/FEI
CrHO$_3^-$						
HCrO$_3^-$						
−1132±40	2.37±0.42 [i]			TDEq		72MIL
CrH$_2^-$						
CrH$_2^-$						
	>2.500			LPES		86MIL/FEI
CrKO$_4^-$						
KCrO$_4^-$						
−1000±16				TDEq		85RUD/SID
CrO⁻						
CrO⁻					$\Delta_fH(A) = 218\pm29$	83PED/MAR
183±48	1.3±0.7			EIAP	From CrO_2F_2	69FLE/WHI
CrO$_2^-$						
CrO$_2^-$					$\Delta_fH(A) = -59\pm21$	82TN270
<−594±42				IMRB		72MIL
−280±48	2.3±0.7			EIAP	From CrO_2F_2	69FLE/WHI
CrO$_3^-$						
CrO$_3^-$·					$\Delta_fH(A) = -386\pm2$	82TN270
−674±27	3.70±0.30 [i]			TDEq		85RUD/SID
−838±82 [a]	4.04±0.42 [i]	1437±40		TDEq		72MIL
CrO$_4^-$						
CrO$_4^-$						
−785±30				TDEq		85RUD/SID

Table 2. Negative Ion Table – Continued

Ion $\Delta_f H(A^-)$ $\Delta_f H(X \cdot \cdot Y^-)$	EA(A) eV	$\Delta H_{acid}(AH)$ $\Delta H_{aff}(X \cdot \cdot Y^-)$	$\Delta G_{acid}(AH)$ $\Delta G_{aff}(X \cdot \cdot Y^-)$	Method	Comment	Reference
$Cr_2O_6^-$						
$Cr_2O_6^-$·	1.6±0.3			EIAP	From $(CrO_3)_3$	75WAN/MAR
$Cr_3O_9^-$						
$Cr_3O_9^-$·	1.8			EIAP	From $(CrO_3)_5$	75WAN/MAR
Cs^-					$\Delta_f H(A) =$ 76	82TN270
Cs^- * 31±5 [a]	0.472	1445±3 [e]		LPD		85HOT/LIN
CsI_2^-						
$CsI \cdot \cdot I^-$ −492±5 [c]		151±5		TDAs		79GUS/GOR
$Cs_2I_3^-$						
$Cs_2I_2 \cdot \cdot I^-$ −766±13		115±13 [k]		TDAs		79GUS/GOR
Cu^-					$\Delta_f H(A) =$ 338	82TN270
Cu^- * 220±1 [b]	1.228±0.010	1459±22 [f]		LPES		85HOT/LIN
Cu_7^-						
Cu_7^-	1.870±0.080			LPES		86ZHE/KAR
Cu_8^-						
Cu_8^-	< 1.440			LPES		86ZHE/KAR
Cu_9^-						
Cu_9^-	2.270±0.060			LPES		86ZHE/KAR
Cu_{10}^-						
Cu_{10}^-	2.010±0.060			LPES		86ZHE/KAR
Cu_{11}^-						
Cu_{11}^-	2.380±0.060			LPES		86ZHE/KAR
Cu_{12}^-						
Cu_{12}^-	2.140±0.070			LPES		86ZHE/KAR
Cu_{13}^-						
Cu_{13}^-	2.605±0.175			LPES		86ZHE/KAR

Ion $\Delta_f H(A^-)$ $\Delta_f H(X\cdots Y^-)$	EA(A) eV	$\Delta H_{acid}(AH)$ $\Delta H_{aff}(X\cdots Y^-)$	$\Delta G_{acid}(AH)$ $\Delta G_{aff}(X\cdots Y^-)$	Method	Comment	Reference
Cu_{14}^-						
Cu_{14}^-						
	2.075±0.025			LPES		86ZHE/KAR
Cu_{15}^-						
Cu_{15}^-						
	2.575±0.135			LPES		86ZHE/KAR
Cu_{16}^-						
Cu_{16}^-						
	2.325±0.115			LPES		86ZHE/KAR
Cu_{17}^-						
Cu_{17}^-						
	<2.720			LPES		86ZHE/KAR
Cu_{18}^-						
Cu_{18}^-						
	2.570±0.130			LPES		86ZHE/KAR
Cu_{19}^-						
Cu_{19}^-						
	2.705±0.265			LPES		86ZHE/KAR
F^-						
F^-						
* −249±2 [a]	3.399±0.003	1554±1 [e]	1530±2 [h]	PLA	$\Delta_f H(A) =$ 79	85JANAF
			1530±8	IMRE[o]		85HOT/LIN
						79BAR/SCO
FHI^-						
$HF\cdots I^-$						
* −524±10 [c]		63±8		Est	Extrapolated from other bihalide data	84LAR/MCM3
FH_2O^-						
$HOH\cdots F^-$						
−588 [c]		97±8	76±8	TDAs		70ARS/YAM
FH_2S^-						
$HSH\cdots F^-$						
* −414±11 [c]		145±8 [g]	121±8	IMRE		83LAR/MCM
FK^-						
$KF^-\cdot$						
−427±22 [b]	1.0±0.2			EIAP	$\Delta_f H(A) =$ −327±2	85JANAF
	<1.50			IMRE	From K_2BO_2F	76SHE/ILJ
	0.2			Scat		80SID/SKO
	>1.3			EIAP	From $(KF)_2$	79DEV/WIJ
						64EBI
FLi^-						
$LiF^-\cdot$						
	>1.4			EIAP	$\Delta_f H(A) =$ −340 From $(LiF)_2$	82TN270
						64EBI

Table 2. Negative Ion Table - Continued

Ion $\Delta_f H(A^-)$ $\Delta_f H(X\cdots Y^-)$	EA(A) eV	$\Delta H_{acid}(AH)$ $\Delta H_{aff}(X\cdots Y^-)$	$\Delta G_{acid}(AH)$ $\Delta G_{aff}(X\cdots Y^-)$	Method	Comment	Reference
FN⁻						
FN⁻·					$\Delta_f H(A) = 232\pm 2$	84BER/GRE
184±2 [b]	0.5			EIAP		82SID
FNP⁻						
NPF⁻						
< −285				IMRB	$NH_2^- + PF_3 \rightarrow$	78SUL/BEA
FNa⁻						
NaF⁻·					$\Delta_f H(A) = -291$	82TN270
−399±20 [b]	1.1±0.2			EIAP	From Na_2BO_2F	76SHE/ILJ
	0.4			Scat		79DEV/WIJ
	> 1.4			EIAP	From $(NaF)_2$	64EBI
FNa₂⁻						
Na_2F^-						
−300±42				EIAP	From Na_2BO_2F	76SHE/ILJ
FO⁻						
FO⁻					$\Delta_f H(AH) = -96\pm 4$	82BAU/COX
					$BDE(A-H) = 412\pm 13$	82BAU/COX
−89±13 [b]	2.05±0.08			EIAP	From F_2O	84ALE/VOL
	> 1.4±0.5			EIAP	From CF_3OF	70THY/MAC
FOV⁻						
VOF⁻						
−473±48	1.2±0.4			EIAP	From VOF_3	75FLE/SVE
FO₂S⁻						
$SO_2\cdots F^-$						
* −729±12 [c]		183±8 [g]	154±8	IMRE		83LAR/MCM
< −595				EIAP	From SO_2F_2	80WAN/FRA
−511				IMRB		78SUL/BEA2
	2.8			SI		69PAG/GOO
−715				EIAP	From SO_2F_2	58REE/DIB
FO₃S⁻						
$SO_3\cdots F^-$						
* −971±45 [c]	4.6±0.6 [d]	326±42 [g]	297±42	IMRB		85LAR/MCM
< −971±13 [a]		< 1312±8		EIAP	From FSO_3H (Appearance Potential = 0 eV)	86ADA/SMI
FS⁻						
FS⁻					$\Delta_f H(A) = 13\pm 6$	85JANAF
−180±55 [b]	2.0±0.5			Est	From trends in EA of SF_x	82JANAF
FXe⁻						
$Xe\cdots F^-$						
−276 [c]		27±4		Mobl		79DEV/WIJ2
F₂⁻						
F_2^-·						
−297 [b]	3.1			ECD	Vertical EA: 1.24 eV	81AYA/WEN
	2.9±0.2			EIAP	From NF_3	74HAR/FRA

Table 2. Negative Ion Table – Continued

Ion $\Delta_f H(X \cdot \cdot Y^-)$	$\Delta_f H(A^-)$ EA(A) eV	$\Delta H_{acid}(AH)$ $\Delta H_{aff}(X \cdot \cdot Y^-)$	$\Delta G_{acid}(AH)$ $\Delta G_{aff}(X \cdot \cdot Y^-)$	Method	Comment	Reference
F_2^-						
$F_2^-\cdot$						
	2.9±0.2			EIAP	From BF_3	71DEC/FRA
	3.2			EIAP	From SO_2F_2	80WAN/FRA
	>2.8±0.3			EIAP	From CF_2O	72THY
	3.1±0.1			EnCT		71CHU/BER
	>3.0			EIAP	From SO_2F_2	58REE/DIB
F_2Ge^-						
$GeF_2^-\cdot$					$\Delta_f H(A) = -573$	81WOO
−695±29	>1.3±0.3			EIAP	From GeF_4	72HAR/CRA
F_2H^-						
$FH \cdot \cdot F^-$						
* −683±11 c		162±8 g	134±8	IMRE		83LAR/MCM
<−666±19		>145±19 k		EIAP	From $CHF=CHF$	85HEN/ILL
F_2HNOP^-						
$HNOPF_2^-$						
<−1079				IMRB	$NH_2^- + OPF_3 \rightarrow HNOPF_2^- + HF$; $HNOPF_2^- + OPF_3 \rightarrow (F_3PO)_2N^- + HF$	78SUL/BEA
F_2HNP^-						
$HNPF_2^-$						
<−556				IMRB	$NH_2^- + PF_3 \rightarrow$	78SUL/BEA
F_2K^-						
$KF \cdot \cdot F^-$						
−806±11 c		224±3		TDAs		81NIK/SID
−790±6 c		200±4		TDEq	F^-A: 1100K; $\Delta Hf(KF_2^-)$: 298K	80SID/NIK
<−803±21						79GUS/GOR
F_2Mn^-						
$MnF_2^-\cdot$					$\Delta_f H(A) = -525$	81WOO
−943±15 b	4.36±0.15			TDEq		82SID/GUB
F_2N^-						
NF_2^-					$\Delta_f H(AH) = -65±6$	69PAN/ZER
					$BDE(A-H) = 314±10$	84BER/GRE
* −93±15 a	1.28±0.20 d	1502±10 g	1473±8	IMRE		86TAF
			1477	IMRE		81KOP/PIK
−123±31	1.7±0.2			EIAP	From NF_3	74HAR/FRA
<−45±19	>0.7±0.2			EIAP	From NF_3	79DUD/BAL
	>0.4±0.1			EIAP	From N_2F_4	78DUD/BAL
	3.0			SI		69PAG/GOO
F_2NOP^-						
$ONPF_2^-\cdot$						
<−582				IMRB	$HNO^- + PF_3 \rightarrow NOPF_2^- + HF$	78SUL/BEA

Table 2. Negative Ion Table - Continued

Ion / $\Delta_f H(X \cdot \cdot Y^-)$	$\Delta_f H(A^-)$	EA(A) eV	$\Delta H_{acid}(AH)$ / $\Delta H_{aff}(X \cdot \cdot Y^-)$	$\Delta G_{acid}(AH)$ / $\Delta G_{aff}(X \cdot \cdot Y^-)$	Method	Comment	Reference
F_2OP^-							
F_2PO^-							
	<−962				IMRB	$HNO^- + OPF_3 \rightarrow$	78SUL/BEA
	−448±19	3.4±0.2			EIAP	From F_3PO	71RHY/DIL
F_2OPS^-							
F_2POS^-							
	<−1033				IMRB	$HS^- + OPF_3 \rightarrow$	78SUL/BEA
F_2OV^-							
VOF_2^-							
	−925±48	2.8±0.5			EIAP	From VOF_3	75FLE/SVE
$F_2O_2P^-$							
$F_2PO_2^-$							
	<−1167				IMRB	HO^- or $EtO^- + OPF_3 \rightarrow$	78SUL/BEA
$F_2O_2S^-$							
$SO_2F_2^-$							$\Delta_f H(A) = -759\pm8$	87HER
		<3.1			IMRB	EA: < F_2	78GAL/FAI
$F_2O_2U^-$							
$UO_2F_2^-$							
		3.36±0.52			TDEq		84GOR/PYA
F_2P^-							
PF_2^-						$\Delta_f H(A) = -482\pm2$	84BER/GRE
	−636±51 [b]	1.6±0.5			EIAP	From PF_2NCS	72THY
		>1.6±0.5			SI		69PAG/GOO
		1.5±0.5			Est2		82JANAF
F_2PS^-							
F_2PS^-							
		2.6±1.0			EIAP	From PF_3S	71RHY/DIL
F_2V^-							
VF_2^-							
	−703±48	0.4±0.5			EIAP	From VOF_3	75FLE/SVE
F_3Cr^-							
$CrF_2 \cdot \cdot F^-$							
	−1124±15				TDEq		83IGO
F_3Cu^-							
$CuF_2 \cdot \cdot F^-$							
		>5.26 [i]	351±17		TDEq	Anchor: $F^-A(FeF_3)$ 84CHI/KOR	86KUZ/KOR
F_3Fe^-							
$FeF_2 \cdot \cdot F^-$							
	−1069±12 [c]	3.62±0.13 [i]	359±9		TDEq		86SID/BOR
						Corrections to 81SOR/SID, better neutral pressure determination	
			374±17		TDEq		86KUZ/KOR

Table 2. Negative Ion Table — Continued

Ion $\Delta_f H(X \cdot \cdot Y^-)$	$\Delta_f H(A^-)$ EA(A) eV	$\Delta H_{acid}(AH)$ $\Delta H_{aff}(X \cdot \cdot Y^-)$	$\Delta G_{acid}(AH)$ $\Delta G_{aff}(X \cdot \cdot Y^-)$	Method	Comment	Reference
F_3Fe^-						
$FeF_2 \cdot \cdot F^-$						
−1138±14 ^{c}	4.30±0.20 ^{i}	441±14		TDEq	F^-A: 64±5 kJ < AlF_3	81SOR/SID
F_3Ge^-						
GeF_3^-						
−860±21	1.1±0.4			EIAP	From GeF_4	74WAN/MAR
−858	1.6			EIAP	From GeF_4	74FRA/WAN
	3.1±0.1			EIAP	From GeF_4	72HAR/CRA
F_3Mn^-						
$MnF_2 \cdot \cdot F^-$						
−1213 ^{c}	4.36 ^{i}	430		TDEq		81SID/SOR
F_3Ni^-						
$NiF_2 \cdot \cdot F^-$						
		338±15		TDEq	Reanalyzed literature data, 150 kJ < AlF_3	86NIK/IGO
F_3OS^-						
$F_2SO \cdot \cdot F^-$						
* −904±42 ^{c}		156±8 ^{g}	126±8	IMRE		83LAR/MCM
F_3OV^-						
VOF_3^-					$\Delta_f H(A) = -1234±29$	75FLE/SVE
	3.1±0.4			IMRB	EA: > VOF_2^-, < F^-	75FLE/SVE
F_3OW^-						
WOF_3^-						
	>0.3			EIAP	From WOF_4	77HIL
$F_3O_2S^-$						
$SO_2F_2 \cdot \cdot F^-$						
* −1157±19 ^{c}		150±8 ^{g}	115±8	IMRE		83LAR/MCM
−1284±21				IMRB		78GAL/FAI
F_3Pb^-						
PbF_3^-					$\Delta_f H(A) = -510±54$	75BEN/WAN
−867±54	3.7			EIAP	From PbF_4	75BEN/WAN
−887	4.3			EIAP	From PbF_4	74FRA/WAN
F_3S^-						
SF_3^-					$\Delta_f H(A) = -488±25$	87HER
−785±44 ^{b}	3.1±0.2			NBAP	From SF_6	78COM/REI
	2.9±0.1			EIAP	From SF_4	71HAR/THY
	2.7±0.7			Est	Reanalysis: 71HAR/THY	82JANAF
	2.7			SI		69PAG/GOO
F_3Se^-						
SeF_3^-						
−774				EIAP	From SeF_6	69BRI

Table 2. Negative Ion Table - Continued

Ion $\Delta_f H(X\cdot\cdot Y^-)$	$\Delta_f H(A^-)$	EA(A) eV	$\Delta H_{acid}(AH)$ $\Delta H_{aff}(X\cdot\cdot Y^-)$	$\Delta G_{acid}(AH)$ $\Delta G_{aff}(X\cdot\cdot Y^-)$	Method	Comment	Reference
F_3Si^-							
SiF_3^-						$\Delta_f H(AH) = -1201\pm21$	85JANAF
						BDE(A-H) = 419±4	81WAL
*	−1284±35 [a]	2.9±0.1	1446±14 [e]	1414±15 [h]	PD		75RIC/STE4
	−1176	2.0			EIAP	From SiF_4	74FRA/WAN
	−1176	2.0			EIAP	From SiF_4	73WAN/MAR
		3.7			EIAP	From SiF_4	70MAC/THY
		3.4			SI		69PAG/GOO
F_3Sn^-							
SnF_3^-							
		>1.2			EIAP	From SnF_4	77PAB/PER
	−632	>1.2			EIAP	From SnF_4	75BEN/WAN
	−887	2.6			EIAP	From SnF_4	74FRA/WAN
F_3V^-							
VF_3^-							
	−1033±48	1.6±0.4			EIAP	From VOF_3	75FLE/SVE
F_4Cr^-							
$CrF_3\cdot\cdot F^-$							
	−1467±15				TDEq		83IGO
						$FeF_3^- + CrF_4^- \rightleftharpoons FeF_4^- + CrF_3^-$, $\Delta_{rxn}H = 9$ kJ	
F_4Fe^-							
$FeF_3\cdot\cdot F^-$							
	−1423±18 [c]		451±10		TDEq	F⁻A: 92.5 kJ > FeF_2	86SID/BOR
	−1490 [c]		456±14		TDEq	F⁻A: 37 kJ < AlF_3	84CHI/KOR
	−1412±14 [c]	5.45±0.20 [i]	439±14		TDEq	F⁻A: 62 kJ < AlF_3	81SOR/SID
$F_4Ge_2^-$							
$Ge_2F_4^-$							
	<−121				IMRB		72HAR/CRA
F_4La^-							
$LaF_3\cdot\cdot F^-$							
	−2004±33				TDEq		79GUS/GOR
F_4Mn^-							
$MnF_3\cdot\cdot F^-$							
	−1463±60 [c]		421±13		TDEq	F⁻A: 72±3 kJ < AlF_3	84CHI/KOR
	−1466±60	5.23±0.03 [i]			TDEq	F⁻A: 79 kJ < AlF_3	84KOR/CHI
F_4OP^-							
$F_3PO\cdot\cdot F^-$							
*	−1660±13 [c]		200±8 [g]	168±8	IMRE		85LAR/MCM
	−1594±46 [c]		134±42		IMRB	F⁻A: SF_4 > F_3PO > SF_5	71RHY/DIL
F_4OU^-							
$UOF_3\cdot\cdot F^-$							
		3.80±0.43			TDEq		84GOR/PYA

Ion $\Delta_fH(A^-)$ $\Delta_fH(X\cdot\cdot Y^-)$	EA(A) eV	$\Delta H_{acid}(AH)$ $\Delta H_{aff}(X\cdot\cdot Y^-)$	$\Delta G_{acid}(AH)$ $\Delta G_{aff}(X\cdot\cdot Y^-)$	Method	Comment	Reference
F_4P^-						
$PF_3\cdot\cdot F^-$						
* -1336 ± 13 ^{c}		168 ± 8 ^{g}	136 ± 8	IMRE		83LAR/MCM
		209 ± 21		IMRB	$F^-A:$ < OPF_3, > F, SF_4, Me_3SiF, HCN, SO_2	78SUL/BEA
F_4PS^-						
$F_3PS\cdot\cdot F^-$						
-1374 ± 106 ^{c}		134 ± 42		IMRB	$F^-A:$ between SF_4, SF_5	71RHY/DIL
F_4Pt^-						
PtF_4^-					$\Delta_fH(A) = -524\pm25$	83KOR/BON
	5.20 ± 0.16			TDEq	EA: 2.5 kJ > MnF_4	84KOR/CHI
F_4Rh^-						
RhF_4^-						
	5.00 ± 0.20 ^{i}	401 ± 14		TDEq	$F^-A:$ 22 kJ < MnF_3	84CHI/KOR
F_4S^-						
$SF_4^{-\cdot}$					$\Delta_fH(A) = -763\pm21$	85JANAF
* -990 ± 31 ^{b}	2.4 ± 0.1			IMRB	EA: between NO_2^-, HS^-	81BAB/STR2
	0.8 ± 0.2			NBIP		78COM/REI
	1.3 ± 0.1			ES		74DON/HAR
F_4Sc^-						
$ScF_3\cdot\cdot F^-$						
-2013 ± 13 ^{c}		495 ± 10		TDEq	$F^-A:$ 10 kJ < AlF_3	81SKO/NIK
-2009 ± 13 ^{c}		487 ± 10		TDEq	$F^-A:$ 17 kJ < AlF_3	81NIK/SID
		470 ± 10		TDEq	Reanalyzed data, 18 kJ < AlF_3	86NIK/IGO
F_4Se^-						
$SeF_4^{-\cdot}$						
	1.7 ± 0.1			EIAP	From SeF_6	73HAR/THY
-795 ± 42				EIAP	From SeF_6	69BRI
F_4Te^-						
$TeF_4^{-\cdot}$						
	2.2 ± 0.1			EIAP	From TeF_6	73HAR/THY
-895 ± 42				EIAP		69BRI
F_4Ti^-						
$TiF_4^{-\cdot}$					$\Delta_fH(A) = -1552\pm2$	82TN270
	> 0.0			EIAP		74BEN/PAB
F_4U^-						
UF_4^-					$\Delta_fH(A) = -1599\pm2$	82TN270
* -1725 ± 30	1.24 ± 0.36 ^{i}	415 ± 42 ^{k}		TDEq	Critical review	84PYA/GUS
	< 1.8			IMRB		80SID/SKO
F_4W^-						
$WF_4^{-\cdot}$					$\Delta_fH(A) = -1029$	81WOO
-1280 ^{b}	2.6			EIAP	From WF_6	77DEW/NEU
	> 2.3 ± 0.1			EIAP	From WF_6	73THY/HAR2

Table 2. Negative Ion Table - Continued

Ion $\Delta_fH(A^-)$ $\Delta_fH(X\cdot\cdot Y^-)$	EA(A) eV	$\Delta H_{acid}(AH)$ $\Delta H_{aff}(X\cdot\cdot Y^-)$	$\Delta G_{acid}(AH)$ $\Delta G_{aff}(X\cdot\cdot Y^-)$	Method	Comment	Reference
F_4W^-						
WF_4^-					$\Delta_fH(A) = -1029$	81WOO
	>1.0			EIAP	From WF_6	77HIL
F_5Cr^-						
$CrF_4\cdot\cdot F^-$						
-1753 ± 15				TDEq		83IGO
					$FeF_3^- + CrF_5^- = FeF_4^- + CrF_4^-$, $\Delta_{rxn}H = -48$ kJ	
$F_5Fe_2^-$						
$FeF_2\cdot\cdot FeF_3^-$						
* -1740 ± 43 c	3.80 ± 0.40 i	202 ± 37		TDEq		86SID/BOR
-1769 ± 17 c		201 ± 4		TDAs	$\Delta_fH(A^-)$ at 0K	81SOR/SID
F_5Ge^-						
$GeF_4\cdot\cdot F^-$						
-1856 ± 26		418 ± 29 k		Latt		84MAL/ROS
<-2038 c		>405		IMRB		72HAR/CRA
F_5Hf^-						
HfF_5^-						
-2386 ± 17 c		429 ± 17		TDEq	Reanalyzed literature data, 59 kJ < AlF_3	86NIK/IGO
		405 ± 9		TDEq	F^-A: 84 kJ < AlF_3	80NIK/SOR
F_5Mn^-						
MnF_5^-						
-1565 ± 84		348 ± 84		TDEq	F^-A: 73 kJ < MnF_3	84KOR/CHI
F_5Mo^-						
MoF_5^-					$\Delta_fH(A) = -1241$	85JANAF
	>3.5			NBAP	From MoF_6	78COM/REI
	$>3.3\pm0.4$			NBAP	From MoF_6	77MAT/ROT
F_5Pt^-						
PtF_5^-						
	6.50			TDEq		79SID/NIK
F_5S^-						
SF_5^-						
* -1195 ± 31 c	3.01 ± 0.29 i	183 ± 8 g	151 ± 8	IMRE		83LAR/MCM
$<-1263\pm33$	$>3.7\pm0.3$ i			IMRB	F^-A: $SF_4 > SF_5$	81BAB/STR2
-1251 ± 25				NBAP	From SF_6	74LEF/TAN
-1269 ± 33 b	3.7 ± 0.2			Est	Literature average	82JANAF
	2.7 ± 0.2			NBAP	From SF_6	78COM/REI
	$>2.9\pm0.1$			NBAP	From SF_6	75HUB/LOS
	$>2.8\pm0.1$			EnCT		73LIF/TIE
	$>2.8\pm0.2$			NBAP	From SF_6	73COM/COO
	3.2 ± 0.2			EIAP	From SF_6, new EA(F^-)	61CUR2
	3.66 ± 0.04			SI		64KAY/PAG

Ion $\Delta_fH(A^-)$ $\Delta_fH(X\cdot\cdot Y^-)$	EA(A) eV	$\Delta H_{acid}(AH)$ $\Delta H_{aff}(X\cdot\cdot Y^-)$	$\Delta G_{acid}(AH)$ $\Delta G_{aff}(X\cdot\cdot Y^-)$	Method	Comment	Reference
F_5Se^-						
SeF_5^-					$\Delta_fH(A) = -476\pm42$	69BRI
-1385 ± 40	$>5.1^i$			NBAP	From SeF_6	78COM/REI
	3.3 ± 0.1			EIAP	From SeF_6	73HAR/THY
<-1197				EIAP	From SeF_6	69BRI
F_5Si^-						
$SiF_4\cdot\cdot F^-$						
* -2115 ± 19^c		251 ± 17^g	226 ± 17	IMRE		85LAR/MCM
		285 ± 21		IMRB	$F^-A: <BF_3, >iPr_2BF$	77MUR/BEA3
<-2318				IMRB		70MAC/THY
F_5Te^-						
TeF_5^-					$\Delta_fH(A) = -586\pm42$	69BRI
	4.5			NBAP	From TeF_6	78COM/REI
	4.2 ± 0.1			EIAP	From TeF_6	73HAR/THY
<-1397				EIAP	From TeF_6	69BRI
F_5Th^-						
$ThF_4\cdot\cdot F^-$						
-2432 ± 13		436 ± 15^k		TDEq	$F^-A: 88\ kJ < AlF_3, 15\ kJ < ZrF_4$	83SID/ZHU
F_5U^-						
UF_5^-						
-2275 ± 19^c	2.99 ± 0.20^i	427 ± 15		TDEq	Reanalyzed literature data, 61 kJ < AlF_3	86NIK/IGO
* -2322 ± 15	3.47 ± 0.26^i	424^k		TDEq	Critical review, other literature data corrected	84PYA/GUS
-2256 ± 4^c	3.30 ± 0.16^i	410 ± 1		TDEq	$F^-A: 93\ kJ < AlF_3$	80SID/SKO
-2297 ± 33	3.78 ± 0.40^i	448 ± 36^k		TDEq		80PYA/GUS
-2297 ± 33				TDEq		79GUS/GOR
-2297 ± 33	$>1.9\pm0.4^i$			NBAP	From UF_6	77MAT/ROT
-2265 ± 14	4.0 ± 0.4^i			NBAP	From UF_6	77COM
F_5W^-						
WF_5^-					$\Delta_fH(A) = -1397$	81WOO
>-1631	<3.5			IMRB	EA: $WF_5 < WF_6$	79GEO/BEA
	$>1.8\pm0.3$			NBAP	From WF_6	78COM/REI
$<-1338\pm25$	$>0.4\pm0.2$			EIAP	From WF_6	77HIL
	1.2 ± 0.3			NBAP	From WF_6	77DIS/LAC
	1.3 ± 0.2			EIAP	From WF_6	77DEW/NEU
-1409 ± 29	0.8 ± 0.2	270^k		EIAP	From WF_6	73THY/HAR2
F_5Zr^-						
$ZrF_4\cdot\cdot F^-$						
-2338 ± 31^c		415 ± 8		TDEq	$F^-A: 92\pm3\ kJ < AlF_3$	82SKO/SOR
-2343 ± 17^c		403 ± 4		TDEq	$F^-A: 97\ kJ < AlF_3$	81SKO/NIK
$F_6Fe_2^-$						
$Fe_2F_6^-$						
-2071 ± 38	4.45 ± 0.24^i			TDEq		86SID/BOR

Table 2. Negative Ion Table - Continued

Ion $\Delta_f H(A^-)$ $\Delta_f H(X\cdot\cdot Y^-)$	EA(A) eV	$\Delta H_{acid}(AH)$ $\Delta H_{aff}(X\cdot\cdot Y^-)$	$\Delta G_{acid}(AH)$ $\Delta G_{aff}(X\cdot\cdot Y^-)$	Method	Comment	Reference
$F_6Ge_2^-$						
$Ge_2F_6^-$						
<-117				IMRB		72HAR/CRA
F_6Ir^-						
$IrF_6^-\cdot$					$\Delta_f H(A) = -544 \pm 21$	82TN270
	$>5.1\pm0.5$			NBIP		78COM/REI
F_6Mo^-						
$MoF_6^-\cdot$					$\Delta_f H(A) = -1558 \pm 1$	85JANAF
	$>5.1\pm0.5$			NBIP		78COM/REI
	$>4.5\pm0.4$			NBIP		77MAT/ROT
F_6P^-						
$PF_5\cdot\cdot F^-$						
* -2200 ± 46 [c]		356 ± 42 [g]	308 ± 42	IMRE		85LAR/MCM
		423 ± 33		latt		84MAL/ROS
F_6Pt^-						
$PtF_6^-\cdot$					$\Delta_f H(A) = -676 \pm 28$	86KOR/NIK
* -1448 ± 57 [b]	8.00 ± 0.30			TDEq	EA: 272 kJ > PtF_4	81NIK/SID2
	$>5.1\pm0.5$			NBIP		78COM/REI
F_6Re^-						
$ReF_6^-\cdot$					$\Delta_f H(A) = -1349$	84BAR/YEH
	$>5.1\pm0.5$			NBIP		78COM/REI
F_6S^-						
$SF_6^-\cdot$					$\Delta_f H(A) = -1221 \pm 1$	85JANAF
* -1322 ± 10 [b]	1.05 ± 0.10	159 ± 15 [k]		TDEq		85GRI/CHO
	0.542			LPD		82DRZ/BRA
	0.8			Kine		83LIF
				Review: literature consistent with $\Delta S^\ddagger$ for detachment = -59 J/mol-K		
	0.5 ± 0.2			NBIP		78COM/REI
	1.4 ± 0.1			Kine		83HEN/BEN
	>0.7			ECD		83CHE/WEN
	1.2 ± 0.3			Est	Literature average	82JANAF
<-1310				CIDT		78REF/FRA
	0.3 ± 0.1			NBIP		75HUB/LOS
	0.8 ± 0.1			NBIP		74LEF/TAN
	$>0.6\pm0.1$			EnCT		73LIF/TIE
	0.5 ± 0.1			NBIP		73COM/COO2
	0.5 ± 0.2			NBIP		73COM/COO
	0.9 ± 0.5			IMRB		71FEH
	0.4			IMRB		70LIF/HUG
	>0.7			ECD		68CHE/GEO
	1.1			ES		66COM/CHR
	1.5 ± 0.2			SI		64KAY/PAG

Table 2. Negative Ion Table – Continued

Ion $\Delta_f H(X\cdot\cdot Y^-)$	$\Delta_f H(A^-)$ $\Delta H_{aff}(X\cdot\cdot Y^-)$	EA(A) eV	$\Delta H_{acid}(AH)$	$\Delta G_{acid}(AH)$ $\Delta G_{aff}(X\cdot\cdot Y^-)$	Method	Comment	Reference
F_6Sb^-							
$SbF_5\cdot\cdot F^-$		>6.0			NBAP	From Sb_2F_{10}	80COM/REI
F_6Se^-							
SeF_6^-						$\Delta_f H(A) = -1117\pm21$	82TN270
	-1397 ± 40 [b]	2.9 ± 0.2			NBIP		78COM/REI
F_6Te^-							
TeF_6^-						$\Delta_f H(A) = -1318\pm21$	82TN270
*	-1636 ± 31 [b]	3.3 ± 0.1			NBIP		78COM/REI
		3.3 ± 0.2			NBIP		73COM/COO2
		3.3 ± 0.2			NBIP		73COM/COO
F_6U^-							
UF_6^-						$\Delta_f H(A) = -2147\pm2$	82TN270
*	-2680 ± 25	5.58 ± 0.31 [i]			TDEq	Critical review	84PYA/GUS
	-2649 ± 30	5.20 ± 0.34 [i]			TDEq	$F^-A: 55\pm8$ kJ > UF_4	83SKO/SOR
	-2628 ± 24 [c]	4.89 ± 0.25 [i]		424 ± 17	TDEq	$F^-A:(1100K)$ 14 ± 1 kJ > UF_4. $\Delta_f H(A^-):298K$	80SID/SKO
		6.33 ± 0.50			TDEq		80PYA/GUS
	-2724 ± 42	5.8 ± 0.3 [i]			Latt		84MAL/ROS
		>3.6			IMRB		80STR/NEW
		>5.5			IMRB		80ANN/STO
		>4.3 ± 0.4			NBIP		77MAT/ROT
		>5.1			NBIP		77COM
		4.9 ± 0.5			IMRB	Endo F^- transfer to BF_3 at 1.5 eV observed	76BEA
		2.9			SI		69PAG/GOO
F_6W^-							
WF_6^-						$\Delta_f H(A) = -1722\pm8$	82TN270
	-2046 ± 28 [b]	3.4 ± 0.2			IMRB		85VIG/PAU
	-2061 ± 25	3.5 ± 0.1			IMRB	EA: > F^-, < Cl^-	79GEO/BEA
		>5.1 ± 0.5			NBIP		78COM/REI
		>4.9 ± 0.4			NBIP		77MAT/ROT
		3.7 ± 0.2			NBIP		77DIS/LAC
		2.7			SI		69PAG/GOO
$F_7Fe_2^-$							
$FeF_3\cdot\cdot FeF_4^-$							
	-2379 ± 37 [c]	4.5 ± 0.2 [i]	189 ± 24		TDAs		86SID/BOR
	-2280 ± 18		204 ± 4		TDAs	$\Delta_f H(A^-)$ at 0K	81SOR/SID
F_7MnPt^-							
$MnF_3\cdot\cdot PtF_4^-$							
	-2054 ± 105				TDEq		84KOR/CHI
$F_7Mn_2^-$							
$MnF_3\cdot\cdot MnF_4^-$							
	-2517 ± 84				TDAs		84KOR/CHI

Table 2. Negative Ion Table – Continued

Ion $\Delta_f H(X\cdots Y^-)$	$\Delta_f H(A^-)$ EA(A) eV	$\Delta H_{acid}(AH)$ $\Delta H_{aff}(X\cdots Y^-)$	$\Delta G_{acid}(AH)$ $\Delta G_{aff}(X\cdots Y^-)$	Method	Comment	Reference
$F_7Sc_2^-$						
$ScF_3\cdots ScF_4^-$		228±1	199±1	TDAs		81NIK/SID
F_7U^-						
$UF_6\cdots F^-$						
−2630±30		237±30 [k]		TDEq	Critical review	84PYA/GUS
−2588±46 [c]		192±42		IMRB		76BEA
F_7W^-						
$WF_6\cdots F^-$						
−2266±24	<6.5	289±21 [k]		IMRB	F^-A: $SiF_4 < WF_6 < BF_3$	79GEO/BEA
$F_8Ge_2^-$						
$Ge_2F_8^-$						
<−151				IMRB		72HAR/CRA
$F_8KSc_2^-$						
$KScF_4\cdots ScF_4^-$		144±3	120±4	TDAs		81NIK/SID
$F_8U_2^-$						
$U_2F_8^-$						
>−3598±100	2.30 [i]			TDEq		84PYA/GOR
$F_9U_2^-$						
$U_2F_9^-$						
−4130±30	4.30±0.52	500±50 [k]		TDEq		84PYA/GOR
−4138±33				TDEq		80PYA/GUS
$F_9Zr_2^-$						
$ZrF_4\cdots ZrF_5^-$						
−4228±15 [c]		214±4		TDAs		82SKO/SOR
$F_{10}U_2^-$						
$U_2F_{10}^-$						
−4490±30	4.50±0.40 [i]	520±50 [k]		TDEq		84PYA/GOR
$F_{11}U_2^-$						
$U_2F_{11}^-$						
−4850±40	6.10±0.70 [i]	540±50 [k]		TDEq		84PYA/GOR
$F_{12}U_2^-$						
$U_2F_{12}^-$						
>−5200±79	7.90±0.80 [i]			TDEq		84PYA/GOR
Fe^-					$\Delta_f H(AH) = 471\pm29$	79DEN/VAN
Fe^-					BDE(A−H) = 163±29	79DEN/VAN
* 402±1 [b]	0.151±0.003	1461±30 [e]		LPES		86LEO/LIN
*		1420±13 [g]	1389±13	IMRB		85SAL/LAN
	0.163±0.035			LPES		85HOT/LIN
>361±42 [a]	<0.3±0.2	1420±13 [e]		EIAP	From $Fe(CO)_5$	76COM/STO

Table 2. Negative Ion Table – Continued

Ion $\Delta_f H(X\cdot\cdot Y^-)$	$\Delta_f H(A^-)$ EA(A) eV	$\Delta H_{acid}(AH)$ $\Delta H_{aff}(X\cdot\cdot Y^-)$	$\Delta G_{acid}(AH)$ $\Delta G_{aff}(X\cdot\cdot Y^-)$	Method	Comment	Reference
FeH⁻						
FeH⁻						
*	0.934±0.010			LPES		83STE/FEI
FeH₂⁻						
FeH₂⁻						
*	1.049±0.014			LPES		86MIL/FEI
FeD₂⁻						
FeD₂⁻						
*	1.038±0.013			LPES		86MIL/FEI
FeO⁻					$\Delta_f H(AH)=$ 133±17	80MUR
FeO⁻					BDE(A–H)= 336±38	85JANAF
* 107±56 [a]	1.492±0.020	1504±40 [e]		LPES		77ENG/LIN
Fe₂⁻						
Fe₂⁻						
*	0.902±0.008			LPES		86LEO/LIN
Ga⁻				DH	$\Delta_f H(AH)=$ 220±13	
Ga⁻					BDE(A–H)= 262±8	81KAN/MOO
236±36 [a]	0.3±0.1	1546±23 [e]		PD		85HOT/LIN
Ge⁻					$\Delta_f H(A)=$ 377±2	82TN270
Ge⁻						
* 258±2 [b]	1.233±0.003			LPES		86MIL/MIL
GeH₃⁻					$\Delta_f H(AH)=$ 91±2	82TN270
GeH₃⁻					BDE(A–H)= 345±10	83NOB/WAL
* 50±17 [a]	1.739±0.043	1490±15 [e]	1455±15 [h]	LPD		74REE/BRA
H⁻					BDE(A–H)= 436	85JANAF
H⁻						
* 145 [a]	0.8	1675 [e]	1649 [h]	Calc	Given: 0.754209(3) eV	85HOT/LIN
	0.78±0.02			PD		70FEL
HIS⁻					$\Delta_f H(A)=$ 105	76REF
ISH⁻·						
–48	1.1			Endo	I⁻ + H₂S →	76REF
HI₂⁻						
HI··I⁻						
* –233±9 [c]		71±8	41±11	TDAs		85CAL/KEB
HK₂O⁻						
K₂OH⁻						
–345±12				TDEq		84BUR/KUD

Table 2. Negative Ion Table – Continued

Ion $\Delta_f H(X \cdot \cdot Y^-)$	$\Delta_f H(A^-)$ EA(A) eV	$\Delta H_{acid}(AH)$ $\Delta H_{aff}(X \cdot \cdot Y^-)$	$\Delta G_{acid}(AH)$ $\Delta G_{aff}(X \cdot \cdot Y^-)$	Method	Comment	Reference
HMg⁻						
MgH⁻						
*	1.05±0.06			PD		77RAC/FEL
HMn⁻						
MnH⁻					$\Delta_f H(A) = 256$	79HUB/HER
* 172 [b]	0.869±0.010			LPES		83STE/FEI
HMoO₄⁻						
HMoO₄⁻					$\Delta_f H(AH) = -887±21$	82TN270
−1055±61 [a]		1362±40		TDEq	e⁻ + H₂MoO₄ = HMoO₄⁻ + H	79MIL
HN⁻						
NH⁻·					$\Delta_f H(AH) = 189±1$	85GIB/GRE
					BDE(A−H) = 406±18	85JANAF
* 340±21 [a]	0.381±0.014	1682±20 [e]	1653±21 [h]	LPES	See also 85NEU/LYK	76ENG/LIN
	0.380±0.030			LPES		74CEL/BEN
HNO⁻						
HNO⁻·					$\Delta_f H(A) = 100±4$	82BAU/COX
* 68±6 [b]	0.338±0.015			LPES		83ELL/ELL
			>1498	IMRB		77SUL
DNO⁻						
DNO⁻·						
*	0.330±0.015			LPES		83ELL/ELL
HNO₃⁻						
HNO₃⁻·					$\Delta_f H(A) = -135$	82TN270
−190±15 [b]	0.6±0.1			NBIP		76MAT/ROT2
	0.6±0.2			EnCT		82PAU/DAL
HN₂O⁻						
HN=NO⁻						
<247				IMRB	RONO + NH₂⁻ →	81KIN/MAR
<130±21				IMRB	CH₂=N⁻ + N₂O →	85KAS/DEP
HN₂O₄⁻						
HONO··NO₂⁻						
* −405±22 [c]		136±4		TDAs		80LEE/KEE
HN₂O₆⁻						
HNO₃··NO₃⁻						
* −545±10 [c]		103±8	87±7	TDEq		77DAV/FEH
HNi⁻						
NiH⁻						
*	0.481±0.007			LPES		87MIL/FEI
HO⁻						
HO⁻					$\Delta_f H(AH) = -242$	82TN270
					BDE(A−H) = 499	85JANAF
* −137 [a]	1.828	1635 [e]	1607±1 [h]	LPD	Given: 1.827670(21) eV	82SCH/MEA
	1.825±0.002			LPD		74HOT/PAT

Table 2. Negative Ion Table – Continued

Ion $\Delta_f H(X\cdot\cdot Y^-)$	$\Delta_f H(A^-)$ EA(A) eV	$\Delta H_{acid}(AH)$ $\Delta H_{aff}(X\cdot\cdot Y^-)$	$\Delta G_{acid}(AH)$ $\Delta G_{aff}(X\cdot\cdot Y^-)$	Method	Comment	Reference
HO⁻					$\Delta_f H(AH) = -242$	82TN270
HO⁻					BDE(A–H) = 499	85JANAF
	1.829±0.010			LPES		74CEL/BEN
	1.83±0.04			PD		66BRA
	1.8±0.2			EIAP	From MeOH, EtOH, nPrOH	64TSU/HAM
	1.9±0.1			SI		69PAG/GOO
DO⁻					$\Delta_f H(AH) = -249$	82TN270
DO⁻					BDE(A–H) = 504±1	82TN270
−139±1 ᵃ	1.826	1640±1 ᵉ	1615±1 ʰ	LPD	Given: 1.822549(37) eV	82SCH/MEA
	1.823±0.002			LPD		74HOT/PAT
HO₂⁻					$\Delta_f H(AH) = -136\pm1$	82TN270
HOO⁻					BDE(A–H) = 365±3	82TN270
* −94±10 ᵃ	1.08±0.12 ᵈ	1573±9 ᵍ	1542±8	IMRE		81BIE/SCH
*	1.078±0.017			LPES		85OAK/HAR
	1.9±0.1			Ther	From a solution phase thermodynamic cycle	80BEN/NAN
	1.19±0.01		1536±12	IMRE°		81BIE/SCH
DO₂⁻						
DOO⁻						
*	1.089±0.017			LPES		85OAK/HAR
HO₂S⁻						
HSO₂⁻						
−415 ᶜ		264±67 ᵍ	238±67	IMRB		85LAH/HAY
HO₃S⁻						
SO₂··OH⁻						
< −802 ᶜ		> 368		IMRB	CO₂··HO⁻ + SO₂ →	84HIE/PAU
HO₄S⁻					$\Delta_f H(AH) = -735\pm8$	85JANAF
HSO₄⁻						
< −953±17 ᵃ		< 1312±8	< 1281±10 ʰ	EIAP	From H₂SO₄ (Appearance Potential = 0eV)	86ADA/SMI
	4.5 ᵈ	< 1320 ᵍ	< 1289	IMRB	I⁻ + H₂SO₄ →	80VIG/PER
HO₄W⁻					$\Delta_f H(AH) = -906\pm4$	85JANAF
HWO₄⁻						
−1084±46 ᵃ		1352±41	1322±48 ʰ	TDEq	H₂WO₄ + e⁻ = HWO₄⁻ + H measured	70JEN/MIL
HP⁻					$\Delta_f H(AH) = 139\pm3$	86BER/CUR
PH⁻·					BDE(A–H) = 315±11	86BER/CUR
* 137±12 ᵃ	1.028±0.010	1528±9 ᵉ		LPES		76ZIT/LIN
	1.00±0.06			PD		77RAC/FEL
218±18	> 0.5±0.2			EIAP	From PH₃	69HAL/PLA
	< 1.1			IMRB		64EBI/KRA
HS⁻					$\Delta_f H(AH) = -21\pm1$	82TN270
HS⁻					BDE(A–H) = 381±1	82TN270
* −81±10 ᵃ	2.32±0.10 ᵈ	1469±9 ᵍ	1443±8	IMRE		79BAR/SCO
*	2.310±0.010	1470±2 ᵉ	1443±3 ʰ	LPD		80JAN/REE
		1473±9 ᵍ	1446±8	IMRE		78CUM/KEB

Table 2. Negative Ion Table - Continued

Ion $\Delta_f H(X\cdots Y^-)$	$\Delta_f H(A^-)$	EA(A) eV	$\Delta H_{acid}(AH)$ $\Delta H_{aff}(X\cdots Y^-)$	$\Delta G_{acid}(AH)$ $\Delta G_{aff}(X\cdots Y^-)$	Method	Comment	Reference
HS⁻						$\Delta_f H(AH) = -21\pm 1$	82TN270
HS⁻						BDE(A-H)= 381±1	82TN270
		2.302±0.001			LPD		74EYL/ATK
		2.32±0.01			PD		68STE
	−69	2.2 ^{i}			Endo		76REF
		2.30±0.04			SI		69PAG/GOO
				1453±8	IMRE^o		79BAR/SCO
HSe⁻						$\Delta_f H(AH) = 30\pm 8$	82TN270
HSe⁻						BDE(A-H)= 368±19	72DON/LIT
*	−34±28 ^{a}	2.213	1466±19 ^{e}	1440±19 ^{h}	LPD		86STO/LAR
		2.21±0.03			PD		72SMY/BRA3
			1434±38 ^{g}	1407±38	IMRB	Between H$_2$S, HCl	72DIX/HOL
HSi⁻						$\Delta_f H(AH) = 237\pm 16$	81DON/WAL
SiH⁻						BDE(A-H)= 353±8	81DON/WAL
*	249±3 ^{b}	1.277±0.009			LPES		75KAS/HER
HTe⁻						$\Delta_f H(AH) = 100\pm 2$	82TN270
TeH⁻							
*		2.102±0.015			LPES		86FRE/SNO
HZn⁻							
ZnH⁻							
		<0.9			PD		77RAC/FEL
H$_2$IO⁻							
HOH··I⁻							
*	−472 ^{c}		42±4	23±9	TDAs		84CAL/KEB
			46	22±1	TDAs		80KEE/CAS2
			43±8	23±8	TDAs		70ARS/YAM
H$_2$Mn⁻							
MnH$_2$⁻							
*		0.444±0.016			LPES		86MIL/FEI
D$_2$Mn⁻							
MnD$_2$⁻							
*		0.465±0.014			LPES		86MIL/FEI
H$_2$N⁻						$\Delta_f H(AH) = -46$	82TN270
NH$_2$⁻						BDE(A-H)= 449±3	82TN270
*	113±4 ^{a}	0.75±0.06 ^{d}	1689±3 ^{g}	1657±3	IMRE		76MAC/HEM
*		0.776±0.037			LPES		74CEL/BEN
		0.744±0.022			LPD		72SMY/BRA2
		0.740±0.030			LPD		71SMY/MCI
		0.76±0.04			PD		71FEL
	49±19				EIAP	From NH$_3$	68COL/HUB
		1.1			SI		69PAG/GOO

Ion $\Delta_fH(X\cdots Y^-)$	EA(A) eV	$\Delta H_{acid}(AH)$ $\Delta H_{aff}(X\cdots Y^-)$	$\Delta G_{acid}(AH)$ $\Delta G_{aff}(X\cdots Y^-)$	Method	Comment	Reference
$H_2NO_3^-$						
$HOH\cdots NO_2^-$						
* −494 [c]		64	34±1	TDAs		80LEE/KEE
		60±8	33±8	TDAs		71PAY/YAM
			34±24	Endo		82PAU/DAL
−431 [c]	2.850			LPD		79SMI/LEE2
$H_2NO_4^-$						
$HOH\cdots NO_3^-$						
* −610 [c]		61±1	30±1	TDAs		80LEE/KEE
		52±8	28±8	TDAs		71PAY/YAM
$H_2NO_4^-$						
$HOOH\cdots NO_2^-$						
−410±15 [c]		85±4	60±4	TDEq	Relative to $HOH\cdots NO_2^-$, 80KEE/LEE	84BOH/FAH
$H_2NO_5^-$						
$HOOH\cdots NO_3^-$						
* −524±6 [c]		80±4	54±4	TDEq	Relative to $HOH\cdots NO_3^-$, 80KEE/LEE	84BOH/FAH
H_2NS^-						
H_2NS^-						
		1493±16 [g]	1467±13	IMRB		81DEP/BIE
					Between CF_3CH_2OH and H_2S, comparable to MeSH	
			1480±13	IMRB	$NH_2^- + COS \rightarrow$	84BIE/GRA
			1476±13	IMRB[o]		81DEP/BIE
H_2Ni^-						
NiH_2^-						
*	1.934±0.008			LPES		86MIL/FEI
D_2Ni^-						
NiD_2^-						
*	1.926±0.007			LPES		86MIL/FEI
H_2O^-						
$HO\cdots H^-$						
−34±17		287 [k]		IMRB		84DEK/NIB
$H_2O_3^-$						
$HOH\cdots O_2^-$						
* −361 [c]		77±8	52±8	TDAs		70ARS/KEB
			49±8	IMRE		71PAR
H_2P^-						
PH_2^-					$\Delta_fH(AH) = 5\pm2$	61GUN/GRE
					$BDE(A-H) = 354\pm5$	86BER/CUR
* 27±10 [a]	1.19±0.14 [d]	1552±8 [g]	1520±8	IMRE		79BAR/SCO
*	1.271±0.010	1544±6 [e]		LPES		76ZIT/LIN
	1.25±0.03			PD		72SMY/BRA
	1.300±0.030			LPD		71SMY/MCI
		1524±19		EIAP		69HAL/PLA
<9±21 [a]	<1.4±0.3 [d]	<1534±19		EIAP		64EBI/KRA

Table 2. Negative Ion Table – Continued

Ion $\Delta_f H(A^-)$ $\Delta_f H(X \cdots Y^-)$	EA(A) eV	$\Delta H_{acid}(AH)$ $\Delta H_{aff}(X \cdots Y^-)$	$\Delta G_{acid}(AH)$ $\Delta G_{aff}(X \cdots Y^-)$	Method	Comment	Reference
H_2P^-					$\Delta_f H(AH) = 5\pm2$	61GUN/GRE
PH_2^-					BDE(A–H) = 354±5	86BER/CUR
	1.6			SI		69PAG/GOO
			1519±8	IMRE°		79BAR/SCO
H_2Si^-					$\Delta_f H(AH) = 203\pm6$	87BOO/ARM
SiH_2^-					BDE(A–H) = 304±15	87BOO/ARM
* 181±10 [b]	1.123±0.022	1508±17 [e]		LPES		75KAS/HER
H_3O^-						
$HOH \cdots H^-$						
−169±17		72±21 [k]		Endo	$HOH \cdots HO^- + H_2 \rightarrow$	84PAU/HEN
−199±49				IMRB	$H^- + HCO_2H \rightarrow$	83KLE/NIB
H_3OSi^-						
H_3SiO^-						
<−107				IMRB	$HO^- + SiH_4 \rightarrow$	76PAY/TAN
$H_3O_2^-$						
$HOH \cdots OH^-$						
* −479 [c]		100±8	78±8	TDAs		71PAY/YAM
*	2.9±0.2			PD		68GOL/STE
		112±4	84±7	TDEq		86MEO/SIE2
		94±8	71±8	TDAs		70ARS/KEB
		149±29		CIDT		70DEP/GIA
$D_3O_2^-$						
$DOD \cdots OD^-$						
−491 [c]		112±3	84±5	TDAs		86MEO/SIE
$H_3O_5S^-$						
$HOH \cdots HSO_4^-$						
		50±4	25±4	TDAs		84BOH/FAH
$H_3O_6S^-$						
$HOOH \cdots HSO_4^-$						
−1156±22 [c]		67±4	45±4	TDEq	Relative to $HOH \cdots HSO_4^-$, 84BOH/FAH	84BOH/FAH
$H_3P_2^-$						
$P_2H_3^-$						
<66				IMRB	$PH_2^- + PH_3 \rightarrow$	72SMY/BRA
H_3Si^-					$\Delta_f H(AH) = 35\pm2$	81BEL/PER
SiH_3^-					BDE(A–H) = 386±8	87BOO/ARM
* 63±10 [a]	1.45±0.17 [d]	1558±8 [g]	1522±8	IMRE		79BAR/SCO
*	1.406±0.014	1562±10 [e]		LPES		86NIM/ELL2
	<1.440±0.030			LPD		74REE/BRA
486±10				EIAP		64EBI/KRA
			1519±8	IMRE°		79BAR/SCO

Table 2. Negative Ion Table – Continued

Ion $\Delta_f H(X \cdots Y^-)$	$\Delta_f H(A^-)$	EA(A) eV	$\Delta H_{acid}(AH)$ $\Delta H_{aff}(X \cdots Y^-)$	$\Delta G_{acid}(AH)$ $\Delta G_{aff}(X \cdots Y^-)$	Method	Comment	Reference
D_3Si^-							
SiD_3^-		1.386±0.022			LPES		86NIM/ELL2
H_4N^-							
$NH_3 \cdots H^-$		1.110±0.019			LPES		87SNO/COE3
		1.110±0.019			LPES		85COE/SNO
$H_5N_2^-$							
$NH_3 \cdots NH_2^-$	16 [c]		50		PDis		87SNO/COE2
H_5Si^-							
$SiH_4 \cdots H^-$	86 [c]		94±19		IMRE		86HAJ/SQU
$H_7N_2^-$							
$(NH_3)_2 \cdots H^-$	−114 [c]	1.460±0.019			LPES		87SNO/COE3
$H_8N_3^-$							
$(NH_3)_2 \cdots NH_2^-$		1.780±0.019			LPES		87SNO/COE2
I^-							
I^-						$\Delta_f H(A) = 107$	82BAU/COX
*	−188±1 [a]	3.059	1315 [e]	1294±1 [h]	LOG		83WEB/MCD
IK_2^-							
K_2I^-	−244±11				TDEq		84BUR/KUD
ILi^-							
LiI^-						$\Delta_f H(A) = -91±8$	85JANAF
	<−199 [b]	>1.1			EIAP	From $(LiI)_2$	64EBI
IN^-							
IN^-						$\Delta_f H(A) = 215$	76REF2
	96±21	1.3±0.2			Endo	$I^- + NO_2 \rightarrow$	76REF2
IO^-							
IO^-	<−66	>2.5 [i]			Endo	$I^- + CO \rightarrow$	77VOG/MIS
	−42±35	>2.1±0.3 [i]			Endo	$I^- + O_2 \rightarrow$	77VOG/DRE
	−79±21	2.6 [i]			Endo	$I^- + O_2 \rightarrow$	76REF/FRA2
	−48	2.3 [i]			Endo	$I^- + SO_2 \rightarrow$	76REF/FRA
	<−147	>3.3 [i]			IMRB	$O^- + I_2 \rightarrow$	59HEN/MUC

Table 2. Negative Ion Table – Continued

Ion $\Delta_f H(X\cdot\cdot Y^-)$	$\Delta_f H(A^-)$	EA(A) eV	$\Delta H_{acid}(AH)$ $\Delta H_{aff}(X\cdot\cdot Y^-)$	$\Delta G_{acid}(AH)$ $\Delta G_{aff}(X\cdot\cdot Y^-)$	Method	Comment	Reference
IOS⁻							
ISO⁻							
−67					Endo	I⁻ + SO₂ →	76REF/FRA
IO₂S⁻							
SO₂··I⁻							
* −545±10 ᶜ			60±8	38±11	TDAs		85CAL/KEB
−539±2 ᶜ			54	37±1	TDAs		80KEE/LEE
IS⁻							
IS⁻						$\Delta_f H(A) = 310$	76REF/FRA
47±29		2.7±0.3 ⁱ			Endo	I⁻ + H₂S and CS₂ →	76REF
I₂⁻							
I₂⁻·						$\Delta_f H(A) = 62$	82BAU/COX
* −181 ᵇ		2.5±0.1			NBIP		73BAE/AUE
		1.72±0.05			NBIP	Vertical EA	76HUB/KLE
		2.3			ECD	Vertical EA: 1.7 eV	81AYA/WEN
		2.4±0.2			EnCT		73HUG/LIF
		2.4±0.1			NBIP		71MOU/ATE
		2.6±0.1			EIAP	From CHI₃	71DEC/FRA
		2.6±0.1			EnCT		71CHU/BER
I₂K⁻							
KI··I⁻							
−483±8					TDEq		84BUR/KUD
I₂Sn⁻							
SnI₂⁻·							
		1.7			EIAP	From SnI₄	77PAB/PER
I₃⁻							
I₃⁻							
−482			356 ᵏ		Latt		77FIN/GAT
<−207					IMRB		28HOG/HAR
						I₂⁻ + I₂ →; First negative ion/molecule reaction reported.	
I₃K₂⁻							
K₂I₃⁻							
−760±15					TDEq		84BUR/KUD
I₃Sn⁻							
SnI₃⁻							
		3.21±0.01			EIAP	From SnI₄	78PAB/MAR
		3.2			EIAP	From SnI₄	77PAB/PER
I₃Ti⁻							
TiI₃⁻						$\Delta_f H(A) = -150±33$	85JANAF
<−240±18		>0.9			EIAP	From TiI₄	74BEN/PAB

Table 2. Negative Ion Table – Continued

Ion $\Delta_fH(X\cdot\cdot Y^-)$	$\Delta_fH(A^-)$ EA(A) eV	$\Delta H_{acid}(AH)$ $\Delta H_{aff}(X\cdot\cdot Y^-)$	$\Delta G_{acid}(AH)$ $\Delta G_{aff}(X\cdot\cdot Y^-)$	Method	Comment	Reference
In⁻						
In⁻					$\Delta_f H(A) = 244$	82TN270
* 215±36 [a]	0.3±0.2	1508±28 [e]		PD		85HOT/LIN
	0.8±0.2			EIAP	From InBr	80BRU/COT
Ir⁻						
Ir⁻					$\Delta_f H(A) = 665\pm2$	82TN270
* 514±3 [b]	1.565±0.008			LPES		85HOT/LIN
K⁻						
K⁻					$\Delta_f H(A) = 89$	82TN270
* 41 [b]	0.501	1448±15 [e]	1428±17 [h]	LPD		85HOT/LIN
KO₄S⁻						
KSO₄⁻						
−992±11				TDEq		85RUD/SID2
Li⁻						
Li⁻					$\Delta_f H(A) = 161$	82TN270
* 101 [a]	0.618±0.001	1492 [e]	1470±1 [h]	LPD		85HOT/LIN
Mo⁻						
Mo⁻					$\Delta_f H(A) = 658\pm2$	82TN270
* 586±3 [b]	0.746±0.010			LPES		85HOT/LIN
			1402±13	IMRB		85SAL/LAN
MoO₃⁻						
MoO₃⁻					$\Delta_f H(A) = -362$	81WOO
−655±40	2.58±0.41 [i]			TDEq	H + HMoO₄⁻ = H₂O + MoO₃⁻	79MIL
NO⁻						
NO⁻					$\Delta_f H(A) = 91$	82BAU/COX
* 89±18 [a]	2.4±0.010	1519±9 [e]	1492±10 [h]	LPES		72SIE/CEL
	0.1±0.1			ECD		83CHE/WEN
	2.0±0.1			CIDT		78TIE/WU
	0.0±0.1			NBIP		77DUR/PAR
	0.7±0.2			Endo		76REF2
	2.500±0.007			ETS		74BUR
	>0.1±0.1			NBIP		73NAL/COM
	1.5±0.1			EnCT		73HUG/LIF
	2.60±0.02			Kine		72PAR/SUG
	>6.0±0.1			EnCT		71CHA
	>9.0			EnCT		71BER/CHU
	0.0±0.2			NBIP		70LAC/HER
	>0.7±0.1			EIAP	From NO₂	69STO/COM
	0.8±0.1			EIAP	From EtONO, nBuONO	68WIL/HAM
	0.8			SI		69PAG/GOO
	0.9			SI		64FAR/PAG

Table 2. Negative Ion Table — Continued

Ion $\Delta_f H(A^-)$ $\Delta_f H(X\cdot\cdot Y^-)$	EA(A) eV	ΔH_{acid}(AH) $\Delta H_{aff}(X\cdot\cdot Y^-)$	ΔG_{acid}(AH) $\Delta G_{aff}(X\cdot\cdot Y^-)$	Method	Comment	Reference
NOS⁻						
NSO⁻						
<−142			1414±21	IMRB	$NH_2^- + SO_2 \rightarrow$	84BIE/GRA
NO₂⁻					$\Delta_f H(AH) = -80\pm8$	82BAU/COX
NO₂⁻					BDE(A−H) = 331±9	82BAU/COX
* −189±10 [b]	2.30±0.10	1421±18 [e]	1389±18 [h]	TDEq		87KEB/CHO
	2.359±0.100			LPES		74HER/PAT
	2.31±0.11			IMRE		85GRI/CAL
	2.1±0.2			ECD		83CHE/WEN
	2.350±0.100			LPD		79SMI/LEE2
	2.800±0.050			LPD		74RIC/STE
	<2.6			IMRB		72FER/DUN
	2.4±0.1			CIDT		78TIE/WU
	2.1			EnCT		76REF2
	>2.5±0.1			NBIP		73NAL/COM
	2.50±0.05			NBIP		73LEF/JAC
	2.3±0.1			IMRB		73HUG/LIF
	2.38±0.06			IMRB		72DUN/FEH
	2.5±0.1			NBIP		72BAE
	1.8±0.2			NBIP		77DUR/PAR
	<3.9			PD		71MIL/JAC
	2.0			EnCT		71BER/CHU
	2.3±0.1			EnCT		70LIF/HUG
	2.1±0.2			IMRB		69VOG
9±29				IMRE	$CO_3^- + NO \rightarrow$ [isomer?]	70ADA/BOH
	3.10±0.05			PD		69WAR
	3.9±0.2			EIAP	From MeNO₂, EtNO₂	64TSU/HAM
	>3.8			IMRB		62CUR
	1.800±0.050			LPD		74RIC/STE
	4.0			SI		64FAR/PAG
NO₃⁻					$\Delta_f H(AH) = -135$	82BAU/COX
NO₃⁻					BDE(A−H) = 424±21	77DAV/FEH
* −307±1 [a]	3.92±0.24 [i]	1358±1	1330±1	TDEq		77DAV/FEH
			Relative to HBr, reevaluated with current HBr acidity			
		1358±2		TDEq		72FER/DUN
		1371±24		Endo	$I^- + HNO_3 \rightarrow$	76REF/FRA3
		1380±20		NBAP	From HNO₃	76MAT/ROT2
	3.70±0.20			IMRE	$NO_3^- + NO = NO_2^- + NO_2$	72MCF/DUN
		1491		Endo		71BER/CHU
<−10				IMRB	$O_4^- + NO \rightarrow NO_3^- + O_2$; isomer?	70ADA/BOH
−135±21 [c]		276±21		PDis		78SMI/LEE
		<193		PDis	isomer: $O_4^- + NO \rightarrow$	79SMI/LEE2
NO₄S⁻						
$SO_2\cdot\cdot NO_2^-$						
* −594±12 [c]		108±1	62±1	TDAs		80KEE/LEE
		102±4	62±4	TDEq	Relative to $HOH\cdot\cdot NO_2^-$, 80KEE/LEE	84BOH/FAH

Table 2. Negative Ion Table - Continued

Ion $\Delta_f H(X\cdot\cdot Y^-)$	$\Delta_f H(A^-)$	EA(A) eV	$\Delta H_{acid}(AH)$ $\Delta H_{aff}(X\cdot\cdot Y^-)$	$\Delta G_{acid}(AH)$ $\Delta G_{aff}(X\cdot\cdot Y^-)$	Method	Comment	Reference
NO_5S^-							
$SO_2\cdot\cdot NO_3^-$							
*	-676 ± 11 [c]		72 ± 8	40 ± 8	TDEq	Relative to $HOH\cdot\cdot NO_3^-$, 80KEE/LEE	84BOH/FAH
			76 ± 5	37 ± 4	TDAs		83WLO/LUC
NS^-							
NS^-							
*		1.194 ± 0.011			LPES		82BUR/FEI
N_2O^-							
N_2O^-						$\Delta_f H(A) = 82$	82BAU/COX
	61 ± 10 [b]	0.2 ± 0.1	47 ± 12 [k]		CIDT		78TIE/WU
	67 ± 12 [c]	0.2 ± 0.1 [i]	41 ± 10		CIDT	Vertical detachment: -2.23 ± 0.20 eV	76HOP/WAH
							73NAL/COM
		0.3 ± 0.2			ECD		71WEN/CHE
		0.760 ± 0.100			LPES	Vertical detachment	86COE/SNO
$N_2O_2^-$							
$N_2\cdot\cdot O_2^-$							
	>-99 [c]		<57		IMRB	$N_2\cdot\cdot O_2^- + O_2 \to O_4^-$	70ADA/BOH
$N_2O_3^-$							
$N_2O\cdot\cdot O_2^-$							
	>-17 [c]		<57		IMRB	$N_2O\cdot\cdot O_2^- + O_2 \to O_4^- + N_2O$	70ADA/BOH
N_3^-							
N_3^-						$\Delta_f H(AH) = 294\pm2$	82TN270
*					D-EA	$BDE(A-H) = 387\pm21$	
*		2.762 ± 0.043			LPD		85ILL/COM
*	203 ± 15 [a]	2.7 ± 0.1	1439 ± 13 [g]	1414 ± 12	IMRB	Acidity near HCO_2H	81PEL/JAC
		>2.540			LPES		76ENG/LIN
	199 ± 29	3.1 ± 0.3 [i]	1418 ± 21 [f]		EIAP	From MeN_3 and HN_3	58FRA/DIB
$N_3O_2^-$							
$N_2O\cdot\cdot NO^-$							
	151 ± 18 [b]	0.258 ± 0.009	19 [k]		LPES		87COE/SNO
$N_4O_2^-$							
$(N_2O)_2^-$							
		0.950 ± 0.100			LPES		86COE/SNO
$N_5O_3^-$							
$(N_2O)_2\cdot\cdot NO^-$							
	213 ± 18 [c]	0.513 ± 0.022	19 [k]		LPES		87COE/SNO
Na^-							
Na^-						$\Delta_f H(AH) = 130$	82TN270
						$BDE(A-H) = 195\pm1$	85JANAF
*	54 ± 1 [b]	0.548	1455 ± 1 [e]	1434 ± 3 [h]	LPD		85HOT/LIN
Nb^-							
Nb^-						$\Delta_f H(A) = 733\pm8$	85JANAF
*	647 ± 11 [b]	0.893 ± 0.025			LPES		85HOT/LIN

Table 2. Negative Ion Table – Continued

Ion $\Delta_f H(A^-)$ $\Delta_f H(X\cdot\cdot Y^-)$	EA(A) eV	$\Delta H_{acid}(AH)$ $\Delta H_{aff}(X\cdot\cdot Y^-)$	$\Delta G_{acid}(AH)$ $\Delta G_{aff}(X\cdot\cdot Y^-)$	Method	Comment	Reference
Ni⁻						
Ni⁻					$\Delta_f H(A) = 430\pm2$	82TN270
* 318±3 [b]	1.156±0.010			LPES		85HOT/LIN
O⁻						
O⁻					$\Delta_f H(AH) = 39\pm1$	85JANAF
					$BDE(A-H) = 428\pm1$	85JANAF
* 108±2 [a]	1.461	1599±1 [e]	1574±2 [h]	LPD	Given: 1.461122(3) eV	85NEU/LYK
	1.462			LPD		85HOT/LIN
OP⁻						
OP⁻					$\Delta_f H(A) = -33\pm13$	83PED/MAR
* −139±14 [b]	1.092±0.010			LPES		76ZIT/LIN
OS⁻						
SO⁻·					$\Delta_f H(A) = 5\pm1$	85JANAF
* −100±6 [b]	1.09±0.05			PD		70FEL
−111	1.12±0.01 [i]			Endo	I⁻ + SO₂ →	76REF/FRA
	1.1			EIAP	From SO₂	73HAR/FRA
	>1.2±0.1			EIAP	From SO₂	72THY
	<1.1			IMRB		61KRA/MUL
	<1.1			IMRB	EA: < SO₂	59HEN/MUC
−100	1.2			EIAP	From SO₂	58REE/DIB
OS₂⁻						
S₂O⁻					$\Delta_f H(A) = -53$	86NIM/ELL
* −234±1 [b]	1.877±0.008			LPES		86NIM/ELL
OSe⁻						
SeO⁻					$\Delta_f H(A) = 53$	82TN270
* −87±2 [b]	1.456±0.020			LPES		86COE/SNO2
OTe⁻						
TeO⁻					$\Delta_f H(A) = 69\pm21$	83PED/MAR
* −95±23 [b]	1.697±0.022			LPES		86FRE/COE
O₂⁻						
O₂⁻·					$\Delta_f H(AH) = 10\pm8$	82TN270
					$BDE(A-H) = 206\pm8$	82TN270
* −42±1 [b]	0.440±0.008	1476±9 [e]	1449±9 [h]	LPES		72CEL/BEN
	0.430±0.030			LPES		71CEL/BEN
	0.45±0.05			ECD		83CHE/WEN
	0.4±0.1			CIDT	From O₂⁻	78TIE/WU
	0.4±0.1			NBIP		77DUR/PAR
	0.45±0.02			ETS		74BUR
	0.5±0.1			NBIP		72BAE
	>0.5±0.1			EnCT		71TIE/HUG
	0.46±0.05			NBIP		71NAL/COM
	>0.6±0.1			EnCT		71CHA
	>0.5			EnCT		71BER/CHU
	1.12±0.07			IMRB		70VOG/HAU
	0.5±0.2			NBIP		70LAC/HER
	>1.3±0.2			EnCT		70BAI/MAH
	>1.1±0.1			EIAP	From NO₂	69STO/COM

Table 2. Negative Ion Table – Continued

Ion $\Delta_f H(A^-)$ $\Delta_f H(X\cdot\cdot Y^-)$	EA(A) eV	$\Delta H_{acid}(AH)$ $\Delta H_{aff}(X\cdot\cdot Y^-)$	$\Delta G_{acid}(AH)$ $\Delta G_{aff}(X\cdot\cdot Y^-)$	Method	Comment	Reference
O_2^-						
$O_2^{-\cdot}$					$\Delta_f H(AH)=$ 10±8	82TN270
					BDE(A–H)= 206±8	82TN270
	0.43±0.02			Kine		66PAC/PHE
	0.15±0.05			PD		58BUR/SMI
O_2P^-						
PO_2^-					$\Delta_f H(A)=$ −280±2	85JANAF
−645±18	3.80±0.22 [i]			TDEq		86RUD/VOV
−569 [b]	3.00			IMRE		79WOR/KOB
O_2S^-						
$SO_2^{-\cdot}$					$\Delta_f H(A)=$ −297±1	85JANAF
* −403±2 [b]	1.107±0.008			LPES		86NIM/ELL
	1.097±0.036			LPES		74CEL/BEN
	1.00±0.05			PD		70FEL
	1.1			EnCT		76REF/FRA
	1.1±0.2			NBIP		75ROT/TAN
	1.0±0.1			EnCT		73HUG/LIF
	1.1±0.1			IMRB	Between NH_2^-, C^-	61KRA/MUL
O_2Se^-						
SeO_2^-						
*	1.823±0.040			LPES		87SNO/COE
O_2Te^-						
TeO_2^-						
	> 2.200			LPES		87SNO/COE
O_3^-						
O_3^-					$\Delta_f H(A)=$ 143±2	82TN270
* −60±2 [b]	2.103±0.003			LPES		79NOV/ENG
	1.9±0.1			PD		71WON/VOR
−66 [c]	2.2±0.4 [i]	174±19		PDis		78SMI/LEE
−66 [c]		174±5		CIDT		78LIF/WU
> −99 [c]	2.06±0.06 [i]	< 207		PDis		78COS/MOS
−66 [c]	2.2 [i]	174±10		CIDT	Excited state: 81 kJ up	77WU/TIE
	> 1.8			IMRB		77DOT/DAV
	2.1±0.2			NBIP		75ROT/TAN
	> 2.0			EnCT	$I^- + O_3 \to$	71BER/CHU
O_3P^-						
PO_3^-					$\Delta_f H(AH)=$ −565±63	85HEN/VIG
					BDE(A–H)= 456±167	85HEN/VIG
−943±16	4.49±0.53 [i]			TDEq		86RUD/VOV
−993±23				TDEq		83SID/RUD
< −772±78 [a]	> 4.6 [d]	< 1323±15 [g]	< 1293±13	IMRB		85HEN/VIG
−795	3.5			IMRB		79WOR/KOB
O_3Re^-						
$ReO_3^{-\cdot}$					$\Delta_f H(A)=$ −284±21	75GOU/MIL
−574±40	3.01±0.43 [i]			TDEq		75GOU/MIL
	> 2.5			IMRB		72CEN

Table 2. Negative Ion Table – Continued

Ion $\Delta_f H(A^-)$ $\Delta_f H(X\cdot\cdot Y^-)$	EA(A) eV	$\Delta H_{acid}(AH)$ $\Delta H_{aff}(X\cdot\cdot Y^-)$	$\Delta G_{acid}(AH)$ $\Delta G_{aff}(X\cdot\cdot Y^-)$	Method	Comment	Reference
O_3S^-						
$SO_3^-\cdot$					$\Delta_f H(A) = -396\pm 1$	82TN270
-560 ± 15 [b]	1.7 ± 0.2			NBIP		75ROT/TAN
-601 ± 8				TDEq		85RUD/SID2
O_3W^-						
$WO_3^-\cdot$					$\Delta_f H(A) = -293$	81WOO
-698 ± 40	3.64 ± 0.41 [i]			TDEq	$HWO_4^- + H = WO_3^- + H_2O$	70JEN/MIL
	>2.5			IMRB		72CEN
O_4^-						
$O_2\cdot\cdot O_2^-$						
-194 [c]	2.0 ± 0.2 [i]	151 ± 19		PDis		78SMI/LEE
	1.9 ± 0.2			PD		72BUR2
-99 [c]		57 ± 1	17 ± 1	TDAs		68CON/NES
			17 ± 2	IMRE		71PAR
		$<77\pm 8$		IMRB		70ADA/BOH
					$O_4^- + H_2O \rightarrow O_2^-\cdot\cdot H_2O + O_2$, anchored on 70ARS/KEB	
O_4Re^-						
ReO_4^-					$\Delta_f H(AH) = -665\pm 42$	82TN270
-976 ± 30				TDEq		83SID/RUD
-867 ± 82 [a]	4.46 ± 0.52 [i]	1328 ± 40		TDEq		75GOU/MIL
	>2.5			IMRB		72CEN
O_4S^-						
$SO_4^-\cdot$						
-744 ± 10				TDEq		85RUD/SID2
$O_4S_2^-$						
$SO_2\cdot\cdot SO_2^-$						
-801 ± 4 [c]		100 ± 1	58 ± 2	TDAs		80KEE/LEE
$O_5S_2^-$						
$SO_2\cdot\cdot SO_3^-$						
-912 ± 17 [c]		56	32 ± 1	TDAs		80KEE/LEE
P^-						
P^-					$\Delta_f H(AH) = 236\pm 8$	86BER/CUR
					$BDE(A-H) = 298\pm 10$	85JANAF
* 244 ± 1 [b]	0.747	1538 ± 10 [e]	1514 ± 10 [h]	LPD		85HOT/LIN
	0.77 ± 0.05			EIAP	From P_4	74BEN/MAR
P_2^-						
P_2^-					$\Delta_f H(A) = 144\pm 2$	85JANAF
* 88 ± 5 [b]	0.589 ± 0.025			LPES		85SNO/COE
	<0.7			PD		77FEL/RAC
156 ± 20	0.2 ± 0.2			EIAP	From P_4	74BEN/MAR
P_3^-						
P_3^-					$\Delta_f H(A) = 249\pm 17$	74BEN/MAR
160 ± 19	0.9 ± 0.4			EIAP	From P_4	74BEN/MAR

Table 2. Negative Ion Table - Continued

Ion $\Delta_f H(X\cdot\cdot Y^-)$	$\Delta_f H(A^-)$ EA(A) eV $\Delta H_{aff}(X\cdot\cdot Y^-)$	$\Delta H_{acid}(AH)$ $\Delta G_{aff}(X\cdot\cdot Y^-)$	$\Delta G_{acid}(AH)$	Method	Comment	Reference
Pb^-						
Pb^-					$\Delta_f H(A) = 195\pm 2$	82TN270
* 160±3 [b]	0.364±0.008			LPES		85HOT/LIN
Pd^-						
Pd^-					$\Delta_f H(A) = 378\pm 2$	82TN270
* 325±3 [b]	0.557±0.008			LPES		85HOT/LIN
Pt^-						
Pt^-					$\Delta_f H(A) = 565\pm 2$	82TN270
* 360±2 [b]	2.128±0.002			LPD		85HOT/LIN
Rb^-						
Rb^-					$\Delta_f H(A) = 81$	82TN270
* 34 [b]	0.486			LPD		85HOT/LIN
Re_2^-						
Re_2^-						
*	1.571±0.008			LPES		86LEO/MIL2
Rh^-						
Rh^-					$\Delta_f H(A) = 557\pm 2$	82TN270
* 447±3 [b]	1.137±0.008			LPES		85HOT/LIN
S^-					$\Delta_f H(AH) = 139\pm 5$	85JANAF
S^-					$BDE(A-H) = 356\pm 5$	85JANAF
* 77 [b]	2.077	1467±5 [e]	1444±6 [h]	LPD		85HOT/LIN
S_2^-						
S_2^-					$\Delta_f H(A) = 129\pm 1$	85JANAF
* −32±5 [b]	1.663±0.040			LPES		74CEL/BEN
< 46±10	> 0.8±0.1 [i]			IMRB	$S^- + COS \rightarrow S_2^- + CO$. Also $S_2^- + COS \rightarrow S_3^- + CO$, etc. to n = 6	68DIL/FRA
	> 2.5±0.8			EIAP	From CS_2	72THY
S_3^-						
S_3^-					$\Delta_f H(A) = 142\pm 8$	85JANAF
* −60±11 [b]	2.093±0.025			LPES		86NIM/ELL
	2.0±0.1			PD		77FEL/RAC
Sb^-						
Sb^-					$\Delta_f H(A) = 262\pm 2$	82TN270
* 159±7 [b]	1.07±0.05			PD		85HOT/LIN
Sc^-						
Sc^-					$\Delta_f H(A) = 378\pm 4$	82TN270
* 360±6 [b]	0.188±0.020			LPES		85HOT/LIN
Se^-						
Se^-					$\Delta_f H(A) = 227$	82TN270
* 32 [b]	2.021			LPD		85HOT/LIN

Table 2. Negative Ion Table - Continued

Ion $\Delta_f H(X\cdot\cdot Y^-)$	$\Delta_f H(A^-)$ EA(A) eV	$\Delta H_{acid}(AH)$ $\Delta H_{aff}(X\cdot\cdot Y^-)$	$\Delta G_{acid}(AH)$ $\Delta G_{aff}(X\cdot\cdot Y^-)$	Method	Comment	Reference
Se_2^-						
Se_2^-					$\Delta_f H(A) = 146\pm8$	82TN270
* −41±15 [b]	1.940±0.070			LPES		87SNO/COE
Se_3^-						
Se_3^-						
	>2.200			LPES		87SNO/COE
Si^-						
Si^-					$\Delta_f H(AH) = 377\pm8$	85JANAF
					BDE(A−H) = 297±10	82TN270
* 322±3 [b]	1.385±0.005	1475±11 [e]	1453±12 [h]	LPES		75KAS/HER
Sn^-						
Sn^-					$\Delta_f H(A) = 302\pm2$	82TN270
* 195±4 [b]	1.113±0.020			LPES		86MIL/MIL
	1.1±0.1			PD		85HOT/LIN
Ta^-						
Ta^-					$\Delta_f H(A) = 782$	82TN270
* 751±1 [b]	0.322±0.012			LPES		85HOT/LIN
Te^-						
Te^-					$\Delta_f H(AH) = 143$	79HUB/HER
* 6 [b]	1.971			LPD		85HOT/LIN
Te_2^-						
Te_2^-					$\Delta_f H(A) = 168\pm8$	82TN270
* −17±15 [b]	1.920±0.070			LPES		87SNO/COE
Te_3^-						
Te_3^-						
	<2.700			LPES		87SNO/COE
Ti^-						
Ti^-					$\Delta_f H(AH) = 532$	79HUB/HER
* 462±3 [b]	7.9±0.014	1460 [f]		LPES		85HOT/LIN
Tl^-						
Tl^-					$\Delta_f H(A) = 182\pm1$	82TN270
* 163±20 [b]	0.2±0.2			PD		85HOT/LIN
	1.1±0.2			EIAP	From TlBr	80BRU/COT
V^-						
V^-					$\Delta_f H(A) = 515\pm8$	85JANAF
* 464±10 [b]	0.525±0.012			LPES		85HOT/LIN
			1389±13	IMRB		85SAL/LAN
W^-						
W^-					$\Delta_f H(A) = 851\pm6$	85JANAF
* 772±7 [b]	0.815±0.008			LPES		85HOT/LIN

Table 2. Negative Ion Table - Continued

Ion $\Delta_f H(A^-)$ $\Delta_f H(X\cdot\cdot Y^-)$	EA(A) eV	$\Delta H_{acid}(AH)$ $\Delta H_{aff}(X\cdot\cdot Y^-)$	$\Delta G_{acid}(AH)$ $\Delta G_{aff}(X\cdot\cdot Y^-)$	Method	Comment	Reference
Y⁻						
Y⁻					$\Delta_f H(A) = 421\pm2$	82TN270
* 392±3 [b]	0.307±0.012			LPES		85HOT/LIN
Zr⁻						
Zr⁻					$\Delta_f H(A) = 610\pm8$	85JANAF
* 569±10 [b]	0.426±0.014			LPES		85HOT/LIN

References to Tables 1 and 2

28HOG/HAR
T.R. Hogness and R.W. Harkness, "The Ionization Processes of Iodine Interpreted by the Mass Spectrograph," Phys. Rev. **32**, 784 (1928).

29ROT/MUE
W.A. Roth and F. Mueller, Ber. Deut. Chem. Ges. **62**, 1188 (1929).

30BEN
H.E. Bent, "The Electron Affinity of Triphenylmethyl," J. Am. Chem. Soc. **52**, 1498 (1930).

47KAP/MAK
A.F. Kaputinskii, I.A. Makalkin and L.I. Krishtalik, Russ. J. Phys. Chem. **21**, 125 (1947).

51COL/GIL
L.G. Cole and E.C. Gilbert, J. Am. Chem. Soc. **73**, 5423 (1951).

54HON
R.E. Honig, "Mass Spectrometric Study of the Molecular Sublimation of Graphite," J. Chem. Phys. **22**, 126 (1954).

55ALT
A.P. Altschuller, "Lattice Energies and Related Thermodynamic Properties of the Alkali Metal Borohydrides and of the Borohydride Ion," J. Am. Chem. Soc. **77**, 5455 (1955).

56BRO/GIN
H.C. Brown and D. Gintis, J. Am. Chem. Soc. **78**, 5378 (1956).

58BEN/BUS
S.W. Benson and J.H. Buss, J. Chem. Phys. **29**, 546 (1958).

58BUR/SMI
D.S. Burch, S.J. Smith and L.M. Branscomb, "Photodetachment of O_2^-," Phys. Rev. **112**, 171 (1958).

58FRA/DIB
J.L. Franklin, V.H. Dibeler, R.M. Reese and M. Krauss, "Ionization and Dissociation of Hydrazoic Acid and Methyl Azide by Electron Impact," J. Am. Chem. Soc. **80**, 298 (1958).

59HEN/MUC
A. Henglein and G.A. Muccini, "Negative Ion-Molecule Reactions," J. Chem. Phys. **31**, 1426 (1959).

58REE/DIB
R.M. Reese, V.H. Dibeler, J.L. Franklin, "Electron Impact Studies of Sulfur Dioxide and Sulfuryl Fluoride," J. Chem. Phys. **29**, 880 (1958).

61CUR
R.K. Curran, "Positive and Negative Ion Formation in CCl_3F," J. Chem. Phys. **34**, 1069 (1961).

61CUR2
R.K. Curran, "Low Energy Process for F^- Formation in SF_6," J. Chem. Phys. **34**, 2007 (1961).

61DIB/REE
V.H. Dibeler, R.H. Reese and J.L. Franklin, "Mass Spectrometric Study of Cyanogen and Cyanoacetylenes," J. Am. Chem. Soc. **83**, 1813 (1961).

61GOW/JON
B.G. Gowenlock, P.P. Jones and J.R. Majer, Trans. Farad. Soc. **57**, 23 (1961).

61GUN/GRE
S.R. Gunn and L.G. Green, J. Phys. Chem. **65**, 779 (1961).

61KRA/MUL
K. Kraus, W. Muller-Duysing and H. Neuert, "Uber Stosse Langsamer Negativer Ionen mit Ladungsubertragung," Z. Naturfor. **16A**, 1385 (1961).

61ZIM/GEI
H. Zimmerman and H. Geisenfelder, Z. Elektrochem. **65**, 368 (1961).

62ARM/KRI
G.T. Armstrong and L.A. Krieger, "Progress of International Research on Thermodynamic and Transport Properties" (ed. J.F. Masi and D.H. Tsai, Academic Press, New York, 1962).

62CUR
R.K. Curran, "Formation of NO_2^- by Charge Transfer at Very Low Energies," Phys. Rev. **125**, 910 (1962).

62MOM/BRA
J. Momigny, L. Brakier and L. D'Or, Bull. Classe Sci. Acad. Roy. Belg. **48**, 1002 (1962).

63BIB/CAR
M.M. Bibby and G. Carter, "Ionization and Dissociation in Some Fluorocarbon Gases," Trans. Farad. Soc. **59**, 2455 (1963).

63NAP/PAG
R. Napper and F.M. Page, "Determination of Electron Affinities. Part 5. Cyanide and Thiocyanate Radicals," Trans. Farad. Soc. **59**, 1086 (1963).

63TRE/NEU
L. V. Trepka and H. Neuert, "Uber die Entstehenung von Negativen Ionen aus einigen Kohlenwasserstoffen und Alkoholen durch Elektronenstoss," Z. Naturfor. **18A**, 1295 (1963).

64COO/CRU
R.C. Cookson, E. Crundwell, R.R. Hill and J. Hudec, J. Chem. Soc. 3062 (1964).

64EBI
H.Z. Ebinghaus, "Negative Ionen aus Alkalihalogeniden und Electronenaffinitaten der Alkalimetalle und Alkalihalogenide," Z. Naturfor. **19A**, 727 (1964).

64EBI/KRA
H. Ebinghaus, K. Kraus, H. Neuert and W. Muller-Duysing, "Negative Ionen durch Elecktronenresonanzeinfang in PH_3, AsH_3, und SiH_4," Z. Naturfor. **19A**, 732 (1964).

64FAR/PAG
A.L. Farragher, F.M. Page and R.C. Wheeler, "Electron Affinities of the Nitrogen Oxides," Disc. Faraday Soc. **37**, 203 (1964).

64GUN
S.R. Gunn, J. Phys. Chem. **68**, 949 (1964).

64GUN/GRE
S.R. Gunn and L.G. Green, J. Phys. Chem. **68**, 946 (1964).

64KAY/PAG
J. Kay and F.M. Page, "Determination of Electron Affinities. Part 7.- Sulphur Hexafluoride and Disulphur Decafluoride," Trans. Farad. Soc. **60**, 1042 (1964).

64SMI/GOV
N.K. Smith, G. Govid, W.D. Good and J.P. McCollough, J. Phys. Chem. **68**, 940 (1964).

64TSU/HAM
S. Tsuda and W.H. Hamill, "Ionization Efficiency Measurements by the Retarding Potential Difference Method," Adv. Mass Spectrom. **3**, 249 (1964).

65BAC/BET
R.A. Back and J. Betts, Can. J. Chem. **43**, 2157 (1965).

66BEC/CHE
R.S. Becker and E. Chen, "Extension of Electron Affinities and Ionization Potentials of Aromatic Hydrocarbons," J. Chem. Phys. **45**, 2403 (1966).

66BRA
L.M. Branscomb, "Photodetachment Cross Section, Electron Affinity, and Structure of the Negative Hydroxyl Ion," Phys. Rev. **148**, 11 (1966).

66COM/CHR
R.N. Compton, L.G. Christophorou, G.S. Hurst and P.W. Reinhardt, "Nondissociative Electron Capture in Complex Molecules and Negative Ion Lifetimes," J. Chem. Phys. **45**, 4634 (1966).

66FAR/PAG
A.L. Farragher and F.M. Page, "Experimental Determination of Electron Affinities. Part 9. - Benzoquinone and Chloranil and Related Compounds," Trans. Farad. Soc. **62**, 3072 (1966).

66GAI/KAY
A.F. Gaines, J. Kay and F.M. Page, "Determination of Electron Affinities. Part 8. - CCl_4, $CHCl_3$, and CH_2Cl_2," J. Chem. Soc. Faraday Trans. **62**, 874 (1966).

66PAC/PHE
J.L. Pack and A.V. Phelps, "Electron Attachment and Detachment. I. Pure O_2 at Low Energy," J. Chem. Phys. **44**, 1870 (1966).

66PAC/PHE2
J.L. Pack and A.V. Phelps, "Electron Attachment and Detachment. II. Mixtures of O_2 and CO_2 and of O_2 and H_2O," J. Chem. Phys. **45**, 4316 (1966).

66WAD
I. Wadso, Acta Chem. Scand. **20**, 544 (1966).

67ARN/SAN
E.M. Arnett, J.C. Sanda, J.M. Bollinger and M. Barber, J. Am. Chem. Soc. **89**, 5389 (1967).

67BID/MCI
D.R. Bidinosti and N.S. McIntyre, Can. J. Chem. **45**, 641 (1967).

67CHE/BAR
C.J. Cheetam and R.F. Barrow, Adv. High Temp. Chem. **1**, 7 (1967).

67COL/HUB
J.E. Collin, M.J. Hubin-Franskin and L. D'Or, "Negative Ions Produced by Electron Impact in Ammonia, Methylamine, and Deuterated Methylamine-Nd_2," Adv. Mass Spectrom. **4**, 713 (1967).

67FAR/PAG
A.L. Farragher and F.M. Page, "Experimental Determination of Electron Affinities. Part 11. - Electron Capture by Some Cyanocarbons and Related Compounds," Trans. Farad. Soc. **63**, 2369 (1967).

67GUN
S.R. Gunn, J. Phys. Chem. **71**, 2934 (1967).

67HAS/BLO
J.W. Hastie, H. Bloom and J.D. Morrison, "Electron Impact Studies of $PbCl_2$, $PbBr_2$, and $PbBrCl$," J. Chem. Phys. **47**, 158 (1967).

67HIR
J.A. Hirsch, Top. Stereochem. **1**, 199 (1967).

67JAE/HEN
K. Jaeger and A. Henglein, "Negative Ionen durch Elektronenstoss aus Organischen Nitroverbindungen. Athylnitrit und Athylnitrat," Z. Naturfor. **22A**, 700 (1967).

67KOR/PEP
B.L. Korsunskii, V.I. Pepekin, Yu.A. Lebedev and A.Ya. Apin, Bull. Acad. Sci. USSR Div. Chem. Sci. 509 (1967).

67LOU/LAI
L.F. Loucks and K.J. Laidler, Can. J. Chem. **45**, 2785 (1967).

67MAN/KOE
A. Mannschreck and O. Koelle, Tetrahedron Lett. 863 (1967).

67SHV/TAY
Y.H. Shvo, E.C. Taylor and J. Bartulin, Tetrahedron Lett. 3259 (1967).

67WEN/CHE
W.E. Wentworth and E. Chen, "Experimental Determination of the Electron Affinity of Several Aromatic Aldehydes and Ketones," J. Phys. Chem. **71**, 1929 (1967).

68BOU/CHA
R. Bougon, J. Chatelet, J.P. Desmolin and P. Plurien, Compt. Rend. Acad. Sci. **266C**, 176 (1968).

68BRA/BLA
J.I. Brauman and L.K. Blair, "Gas Phase Acidities of Carbon Acids," J. Am. Chem. Soc. **90**, 5636 (1968).

68CHE/GEO
E.C.M. Chen, R.D. George and W.E. Wentworth, "Experimental Determination of Rate Constants for Thermal Electron Attachment to Gaseous SF_6 and C_7F_{14}," J. Chem. Phys. **49**, 1973 (1968).

68CHU/RUS
W.A. Chupka and M.E. Russell, J. Chem. Phys. **49**, 5426 (1968).

68COL/HUB
J.E. Collin, M.J. Hubin-Franskin, L. D'Or, "Negative Ions Produced by Electron Impact in Ammonia, Methylamine, and Deuterated Methylamine-Nd_2," Adv. Mass Spectrom. **4**, 713 (1968).

68CON/NES
D.C. Conway, L.E. Nesbit, "Stability of O_4^-," J. Chem. Phys. **48**, 509 (1968).

68CZA/CAS
J. Czarnowski, E. Castellano and H. Schumacher, "The Energy of the O-F Bond in CF_3OF," Chem. Comm., 1255 (1968).

68DIL/FRA
J.G. Dillard and J.L. Franklin, "Ion-Molecule Reactions of Negative Ions. I. Negative Ions of Sulfur," J. Chem. Phys. **48**, 2349 (1968).

68DUN
R.C. Dunbar, "Ion-Molecule Chemistry of Diborane by Ion Cyclotron Resonance," J. Am. Chem. Soc. **90**, 5676 (1968).

68GAI/PAG
A.F. Gaines and F.M. Page, "The Stabilities of Negative Ions. I. The Methyl-, Diphenylmethyl, and Triphenylmethyl Negative Ions," Int. J. Mass Spectrom. Ion Phys. **1**, 315 (1968).

68GOL/STE
S. Golub and B. Steiner, "Photodetachment of $[OH(H_2O)]^-$," J. Chem. Phys. **49**, 5191 (1968).

68JAE/HEN
K. Jaeger and A. Henglein, "Die Bildung Negativer Ionen aus $SiCl_4$ und Organischen Siliciumchloriden durch Elektronenstoss," Z. Naturfor. **23A**, 1122 (1968).

68KUH/LEV
W.F. Kuhn, R.J. Levins and A.C. Lilly, Jr., "Electron Affinities and Ionization Potentials of Phthalate Compounds," J. Chem. Phys. **49**, 5550 (1968).

68LYO/MOR
L.E. Lyons, G.C. Morris and L.J. Warren, "Electron Affinites and the Electron Capture Method for Aromatic Hydrocarbons," J. Phys. Chem. **72**, 3677 (1968).

68LAC/SKI
J.R. Lacher and H.A. Skinner, J. Chem. Soc. A 1034 (1968).

68LOW
J.P. Lowe, Prog. Phys. Org. Chem. **6**, 1 (1968).

68STE
B. Steiner, "Photodetachment of Electrons From SH^-," J. Chem. Phys. **49**, 5097 (1968).

68WEN/CHE
W.E. Wentworth, E. Chen and J.C. Steelhammer, "Determination of Electron Affinities of Radicals and Bond Dissociation Energies by Electron Attachment Studies at Thermal Energies - Electron Affinity of the Acetate Radical," J. Phys. Chem. **72**, 2671 (1968).

68TUR/GOE
R.B. Turner, P. Goebel, B.J. Mallon, W. von E. Doering, J.F. Coburn, Jr. and M. Pomerantz, J. Am. Chem. Soc. **90**, 4315 (1968).

68WAL/PAP
C. Walling and C.G. Papaioannou, J. Phys. Chem. **72**, 2260 (1968).

68WIL/HAM
J.M. Williams and W.H. Hamill, "Ionization Potentials of Molecules and Free Radicals and Appearance Potentials by Electron Impact in the Mass Spectrometer," J. Chem. Phys. **49**, 4467 (1968).

69BEN/CRU
S.W. Benson, F.R. Cruickshank, D.M. Golden, G.R. Haugen, H.E. O'Neal, A.S. Rogers, R. Shaw and R. Walsh, "Additivity Rules for the Estimation of Thermochemical Properties," Chem. Rev. **69**, 279 (1969).

69BER/CHU
J. Berkowitz, W.A. Chupka and T.A. Walter, "Photoionization of HCN: The Electron Affinity and Heat of Formation of CN," J. Chem. Phys. **50**, 1497 (1969).

69BOG/GRI
G.M. Bogolyubov, N.N. Grishin and A.A. Petrov, "Organic Derivatives of Group V and Group VI Elements. VIII. Mass Spectra of Phosphines and Diphosphines," Zh. Obs. Khim. **39**, 1808 (1969).

69BRI
C.E. Brion, "Negative Ion Formation in the Hexafluorides of Sulphur, Selenium, and Tellurium," Int. J. Mass Spectrom. Ion Phys. **3**, 197 (1969).

69FLE/WHI
G.D. Flesch, R.M. White and H.J. Svec, "The Positive and Negative Ion Mass Spectra of Chromyl Chloride and Chromyl Fluoride," Int. J. Mass Spectrom. Ion Phys. **3**, 339 (1969).

69GOL/BEN
D.M. Golden and S.W. Benson, Chem. Rev. **69**, 125 (1969).

69HAL/PLA
M. Halmann and I. Platzner, "Negative Ions Produced by Electron Capture in Phosphine," J. Phys. Chem. **73**, 4376 (1969).

69LIF/GRA
C. Lifshitz and R. Grajower, "Dissociative Electron Capture and Dissociative Ionization in Perfluoropropane," Int. J. Mass Spectrom. Ion Phys. **3**, 211 (1969).

69MAC/THY
K.A.G. MacNeil and J.C.J. Thynne, "Ionization and Dissociation of Hexafluoroethane, and of 1,1,1-Trifluoroethane and Fluoroform, by Electron Impact," Int. J. Mass Spectrom. Ion Phys. **2**, 1 (1969).

69MAC/THY2
K.A.G. MacNeil and J.C.J. Thynne, "The Deconvolution of Negation Ion Data," Int. J. Mass Spectrom. Ion Phys. **3**, 35 (1969).

69MIC
J. Michl, "Electronic Spectrum of Fluoranthene," J. Mol. Spectrosc. **30**, 66 (1969).

69OKA/MEL
H. Okabe and A. Mele, J. Chem. Phys. **51**, 2100 (1969).

69PAG/GOO
F.M. Page and G.C. Goode, "Negative Ions and the Magnetron," Wiley, NY 1969.

69PAN/ZER
A.V. Pankratov, Z.N. Zercheninov, V.I. Chesnokov and N.N. Zhadanaova, Russ. J. Phys. Chem. **43**, 212 (1969).

69SEA/DZI
S.K. Searles, I. Dzidic and P. Kebarle, "Proton Affinities of the Alkali Hydroxides," J. Am. Chem. Soc. **91**, 281 (1969).

69STE/WEN
J.C. Steelhammer and W.E. Wentworth, "Correlation of Electron Beam and Thermal Electron Attachment Studies for Some Chloro, Bromo, Iodo Aromatic Compounds," J. Chem. Phys. **51**, 1802 (1969).

69STO/COM
J.A.D. Stockdale, R.N. Compton, G.S. Hurst and P.W. Reinhardt, "Collisions of Monoenergetic Electrons with NO_2: Possible Lower Limits to the Electron Affinities of O_2 and NO," J. Chem. Phys. **50**, 2176 (1969).

69STU/WES
D.R. Stull, E.F. Westrum, Jr. and G.C. Sinke, "The Chemical Thermodynamics of Organic Compounds," (John Wiley & Sons, New York, 1969).

69TSU/YOK
S. Tsuda, A. Yokohata and M. Kawai, "Measurement of Negative Ions Formed by Electron Impact. II. The Ionization Efficiency Curves of Negative Nitro, Oxygen Atoms, and Nitromethylene," Bull. Chem. Soc. Japan **42**, 614 (1969).

69TSU/YOK2
S. Tsuda, A. Yokohata and M. Kawai, "Measurement of Negative Ions Formed by Electron Impact. III. The Ionization Efficiency Curves of Negative Ions of M/E 26 and 42 From Nitroalkanes." Bull Chem. Soc. Japan **42**, 1515 (1969).

69VOG
D. Vogt, "Uber die Energieanhangigkeit und den Mechanismus von Reaktionen bei Stossen Langsamer Negativer Ionen auf Molekule," Int. J. Mass Spectrom. Ion Phys. **3**, 81 (1969).

69WAR
P. Warneck, "Photodetachment of NO_2^-," Chem. Phys. Lett. **3**, 532 (1969).

69WEN/RIS
W.E. Wentworth and W. Ristau, "Thermal Electron Attachment Involving a Change in Molecular Geometry," J. Phys. Chem. **73**, 2126 (1969).

70ADA/BOH
N. Adams, D.K. Bohme, D.B. Dukin, D. Fehsenfeld and E.E. Ferguson, "Flowing Afterglow Studies of Formation and Reactions of Cluster Ions of O_2^+, O_2^-, and O^-," J. Chem. Phys. **52**, 3133 (1970).

70ARS/KEB
M. Arshadi and P. Kebarle, "Hydration of OH^- and O_2^- in the Gas Phase. Comparative Solvation of OH^- by Water and the Hydrogen Halides. Effect of Acidity," J. Phys. Chem. **74**, 1483 (1970).

70ARS/YAM
M. Arshadi, R. Yamdagni and P. Kebarle, "Hydration of Halide Negative Ions in the Gas Phase. II. Comparision of Hydration Energies for the Alkali Positive and Halide Negative Ions," J. Phys. Chem. **74**, 1475 (1970).

70BAI/MAH
T.L. Bailey and P. Mahadevan, "Electron Transfer and Detachment in Collisions of Low Energy Negative Ions with O_2," J. Chem. Phys. **52**, 179 (1970).

70BEN/O'N
S.W. Benson and H.E. O'Neal, "Kinetic Data on Gas Phase Unimolecular Reactions," NSRDS-NBS **21**, (1970).

70CHA/CHR
E.L. Chaney, L.G. Christophorou, P.M. Collins and J.C. Carter, "Electron Attachment in the Field of the Ground and Excited States of the Azulene Molecule," J. Chem. Phys. **52**, 4413 (1970).

70COL/CHR
P.M. Collins, L.G. Christophorou, E.L. Chaney and J.G. Carter, "Energy Dependence of the Electron Attachment Cross Section and the Transient Negative Ion Lifetime for p-Benzoquinone and 1,4-Naphthoquinone," Chem. Phys. Lett. **4**, 646 (1970).

70COL/LOC
J.E. Collin and R. Locht, "Positive and Negative Ion Formation in Ketene by Electron Impact," Int. J. Mass Spectrom. Ion Phys. **3**, 465 (1970).

70DEP/GIA
M. De Paz, A.G. Giardini, L. Friedman, "Tandem-Mass Spectrometer Study of Solvated Derivatives of OD^-. Total Hydration Energy of the Proton," J. Chem. Phys. **52**, 687 (1970).

70EME/KHO
A.M. Emel'yanov, Y.S. Khodeev and L.N. Gorokhov, "Determination of the Ionization Potentials of Atomic Uranium by an Electron Impact Method. I. Measurement of the First Ionization Potential of Uranium," Teplofiz. Vys. Temp. **8**, 296 (1970).

70FEL
D. Feldman, "Photoablosung von Electronen bei einigen Stabilen Negativen Ionen," Z. Naturfor. **25A**, 621 (1970).

70FIN/GAR
A. Finch and P.J. Gardner, "Progress in Boron Chemistry," Vol. 3 (ed. R. Brotherton and H. Steinberg, Pergamon, New York, 1970).

70FUR/GOL
S. Furayama, D.M. Golden and S.W. Benson, Int. J. Chem. Kinet. 2, 93 (1970).

70HAR/THY
P.W. Harland and J.C.J. Thynne, "Positive and Negative Ion Formation in Hexafluoroacetone by Electron Impact," J. Phys. Chem. 74, 52 (1970).

70HEH/DIT
W.J. Hehre, R. Ditchfield, L. Radom and J.A. Pople, J. Am. Chem. Soc. 92, 4796 (1970).

70JEN
D.E. Jensen, "Electron Attachment and Compound Formation in Flames. II. Mass Spectrometry of Boron-Containing Flames," J. Chem. Phys. 52, 3305 (1970).

70JEN/MIL
D.E. Jensen and W.J. Miller, "Electron Attachment and Compound Formation in Flames. III. Negative Ion and Compound Formation in Flames Containing Tungsten and Potassium," J. Chem. Phys. 53, 3287 (1970).

70KLO/PAS
E. Kloster-Jensen, C. Pascual and J. Vogt, Helv. Chim Acta 53, 2109 (1970).

70LAC/HER
K. Lacmann and D.R. Herschbach, "Collisional Excitation and Ionization of K Atoms by Diatomic Molecules: Role of Ion-pair States," Chem. Phys. Lett. 6, 106 (1970).

70LIF/HUG
C. Lifshitz, B.M. Hughes and T.O. Tiernan, "Electron Affinites for Endothermic Negative Ion Charge Transfer Reactions. NO_2 and SF_6," Chem. Phys. Lett. 7, 469 (1970).

70LIF/PEE
C. Lifshitz, A.M. Peers, R. Grajower and M. Weiss, "Breakdown Curves for Polyatomic Negative Ions," J. Chem. Phys. 53, 4605 (1970).

70LOC/MOM
R. Locht and J. Momigny, "Mass Spectrometric Determination of the Electron Affinities of Radicals," Chem. Phys. Lett. 6, 273 (1970).

70LON/FIN
F.R. Longo, J.D. Finarelli, E. Schmalzbach and A.D. Adler, J. Phys. Chem. 74, 3297 (1970).

70MAC/THY
K.A.G. MacNeil and J.C.J. Thynne, "The Formation of Negative Ions by Electron Impact on Silicon Tetrafluoride and Carbon Tetrafluoride," Int. J. Mass Spectrom. Ion Phys. 3, 455 (1970).

70MOO
C.E. Moore, "Ionization Potentials and Ionization Limits Derived from the Analyses of Optical Spectra," Nat. Stand. Ref. Data Ser., Nat. Bur. Stand. (U.S.) 34, (1970).

70O'H/HUB
P.A.G. O'Hare, W.N. Hubbard, O. Glemser and J. Wegener, J. Chem. Thermodyn. 2, 71 (1970).

70OKA
H. Okabe, J. Chem. Phys. 53, 3507 (1970).

70SOL/GOL
R.K. Solly, D.M. Golden and S.W. Benson, "Kinetics of the Gas Phase Reaction of Acetone with Iodine: Heat of formation of the Acetonyl Radical," Int. J. Chem. Kinet. 2, 11 (1970).

70THY/MAC
J.C.J. Thynne and K.A.G. MacNeil, "Ionisation and Dissociation of Carbonyl Fluoride and Trifluoromethyl Hypofluorite by Electron Impact," Int. J. Mass Spectrom. Ion Phys. 5, 95 (1970).

70THY/MAC2
J.C.J. Thynne and K.A.G. MacNeil, "Ionisation of Tetrafluoroethylene by Electron Impact," Int. J. Mass Spectrom. Ion Phys. 5, 329 (1970).

70VOG/HAU
D. Vogt, B. Hauffle and H. Neuert, "Ladungsaustausch-Reaktionen Einiger Negativer Ionen mit O_2 und die Elektronenaffinitat des O_2," Z. Phys. 232, 439 (1970).

71ALL/WUE
N.L. Allinger and M.T. Wuesthoff, J. Org. Chem. 36, 2051 (1971).

71ASTM
"Physical Constants of Hydrocarbons C_1 to C_{10}," ASTM Data Series for Testing and Materials, TM DS 4A (Philadelphia, 1971).

71BEL/PLA
T.N. Bell and A.E. Platt, "The Reactions of CF_3 and CD_3 Radicals with Boron Trimethyl," Int. J. Chem. Kinet. 3, 307 (1971).

71BER/CHU
J. Berkowitz, W.A. Chupka and D. Gutman, "Electron Affinities of O_2, O_3, NO, NO_2, NO_3 by Endothermic Charge Transfer," J. Chem. Phys. 55, 2733 (1971).

71BOH/LEE
D.K. Bohme, E. Lee-Ruff and L.B. Young, "A Standard Acidity Scale. The pKa of Alcohols in the Gas Phase," J. Am. Chem. Soc. 93, 4608 (1971).

71BOH/YOU
D.K. Bohme and L.B. Young, "Electron Affinities from Thermal Proton Transfer Reactions: C_6H_5 and $C_6H_5CH_2$," Can. J. Chem. 49, 2918 (1971).

71BOY/SAN
R.H. Boyd, S.N. Sanwal, S. Shary-Tehrany and D. McNally, J. Phys. Chem. 75, 1264 (1971).

71BRA/BLA
J.I. Brauman and L.K. Blair, "Gas Phase Acidities of Amines," J. Am. Chem. Soc. 93, 3911 (1971).

71CEL/BEN
R.J. Celotta, R.A. Bennett, J.L. Hall, J. Levine and M.W. Siegel, "Electron Affinity of O_2 by Laser Photodetachment," Bull. Am. Phys. Soc. 16, 212 (1971).

71CHA
P.J. Chantry, "Doppler Broadening in Beam Experiments," J. Chem. Phys. 55, 2746 (1971).

71CHU/BER
W.A. Chupka, J. Berkowitz and D. Gutman, "Electron Affinities of Halogen Diatomic Molecules as Determined by Endoergic Charge Exchange," J. Chem. Phys. 55, 2724 (1971).

71DEC/BAF
J.J. DeCorpo, D.A. Bafus and J.L. Franklin, "Correlation of Excess Energies of Dissociative Electron Attachment Processes with the Translational Energies of Their Products," J. Chem. Phys. 54, 1592 (1971).

71DEC/FRA
J.J. DeCorpo and J.L. Franklin, "Electron Affinities of the Halogen Molecules by Dissociative Electron Attachment," J. Chem. Phys. 54, 1885 (1971).

71FEH
F.C. Fehsenfeld, "Ion Chemistry of SF_6," J. Chem. Phys. 54, 438 (1971).

71FEL
D. Feldman, "Photoablosung von Elektronen bei Si^- und NH_2^-," Z. Naturfor. 26A, 1100 (1971).

71HAR/THY
P.W. Harland and J.C.J. Thynne, "Autodetachment Lifetimes, Attachment Cross Sections, and Negative Ions Formed by Sulfur Hexafluoride and Sulfur Tetrafluoride," J. Phys. Chem. 75, 3517 (1971).

71JANAF
D.R. Stull and H. Prophet, "JANAF Thermochemical Tables," NSRDS-NBS 37, U.S. Gov't. Print. Off., Washington, DC, 1971.

71KIN/GOL
K.D. King, D.M. Golden and S.W. Benson, "Thermochemistry of the Equilibrium $CH_3COCH_3 + Br_2 = CH_3COCH_2Br + HBr$," J. Chem. Therm. **3**, 129 (1971).

71MOU/ATE
A.M.C. Moutinho, J.A. Aten and J. Los, "Temperature Dependence of the Total Cross Section for Chemi-Ionization in Alkali Halide-Halogen Collisions," Physica **53**, 471 (1971).

71NAL/COM
S.J. Nalley and R.N. Compton, "Collisional Ionization of Cesium by Oxygen: the Electron Affinity of O_2," Chem. Phys. Lett. **9**, 529 (1971).

71NUT/LAU
R.L. Nuttall, A.H. Laufer and M.V. Kilday, J. Chem. Thermodyn. **3**, 107 (1971).

71PAR
D.A. Parkes, "Electron Attachment and Negative Ion-Molecule Reactions in Pure O_2," Trans. Farad. Soc. **97**, 711 (1971).

71PAY/YAM
J.D. Payzant, R. Yamdagni and P. Kebarle, "Hydration of CN^-, NO_2^-, NO_3^-, and HO^- in the Gas Phase," Can. J. Chem. **49**, 3308 (1971).

71POT/PRI
A.W. Potts and W.C. Price, "Photoelectron Spectra of the Halogens and Mixed Halides, ICl and IBr," Trans. Faraday Soc. **67**, 1242 (1971).

71RAP/WES
N.J. Rapport, E.F. Westrum, Jr. and J.T.J. Andrews, J. Am. Chem. Soc. **93**, 4363 (1971).

71RHY/DIL
T.C. Rhyne and J.G. Dillard, "Reactions of Gaseous Inorganic Negative Ions: III. SF_6^- with POF_3 and PSF_3," Int. J. Mass Spectrom. Ion Phys. **7**, 371 (1971).

71SEL
P. Sellers, Acta Chem. Scand. **25**, 2194 (1971).

71SMY/MCI
K.C. Smyth, R.T. McIver, J.I. Brauman and R.W. Wallace, "Photodetachment of Negative Ions Using a Continuously Tunable Laser and an ICR Spectrometer," J. Chem. Phys. **54**, 2758 (1971).

71SRI/UY
R.D. Srivastava, O.M. Uy and M. Farber, "Effusion Mass Spectrometric Study of Thermodynamic Properties of BO^- and BO_2^-," Trans. Farad. Soc. **67**, 2941 (1971).

71THY/MAC
J.C.J. Thynne and K.A.G. MacNiel, "Negative Ion Formation by Ethylene and 1,1-difluoroethylene," J. Phys. Chem. **75**, 2584 (1971).

71TIE/HUG
T.O. Tiernan, B.M. Hughes and C. Lifschitz, "Electron Affinities from Endothermic Negative Ion Charge Transfer Reactions. II. O_2," J. Chem. Phys. **55**, 5692 (1971).

71TSU/YOK
S. Tsuda, A. Yokohata and T. Umaba, "Measurement of Negative Ions formed by Electron Impact. VIII. Ionization Efficiency Curves of Negative Ions from Methyl and Ethyl Cyanides," Bull. Chem. Soc. Jpn. **44**, 1486 (1971).

71WEN/CHE
W.E. Wentworth, E. Chen and R. Freeman, "Thermal Electron Attachment to N_2O," J. Chem. Phys. **55**, 2075 (1971).

71WIL/ZWO
R.C. Wilhoit and B.J. Zwolinski, "Handbook of Vapor Pressures and Heats of Vaporization of Hydrocarbons and Related Compounds" (Thermodynamics Research Center, College Station, Texas, 1971).

71WON/VOR
S.F. Wong, T.V. Vorburger and S.V. Woo, "Photodetachment of O_3^-," Bull. Am. Phys. Soc. **16**, 213 (1971).

71YAM/KEB
R. Yamdagni and P. Kebarle, "Hydrogen Bonding Energies to Negative Ions from Gas Phase Measurements of Ionic Equilibria," J. Am. Chem. Soc. **93**, 7139 (1971).

72BAE
A.P.M. Baeda, "The Adiabatic Electron Affinities of Cl_2, Br_2, I_2, IBr, NO_2, and O_2," Physica **59**, 541 (1972).

72BOH/LEE
D.K. Bohme, E. Lee-Ruff and L.B. Young, "Acidity Order of Selected Bronsted Acids in the Gas Phase at 300K," J. Am. Chem. Soc. **94**, 5153 (1972).

72BRI/OLS
C.E. Brion and L.A.R. Olsen, "Negative Ion Formation in Tetracyanoethylene," Int. J. Mass Spectrom. Ion Phys. **9**, 413 (1972).

72BUR
J.A. Burt, "Photodetachment Cross Sections for CO_3^- and Its First Hydrate," J. Chem. Phys. **57**, 4649 (1972).

72BUR2
J.A. Burt, "Measurement of the Photodetachment Cross Section for O_4^- at High Pressure," J. Geophys. Res. **77**, 6280 (1972).

72CEL/BEN
R.J. Celotta, R.A. Bennett, J.L. Hall, M.W. Siegel and J. Levine, "Molecular Photodetachment Spectrometry. II. The Electron Affinity of O_2 and the Structure of O_2^-," Phys. Rev. **6A**, 631 (1972).

72CEN
R.E. Center, "Ion-Molecule Experiments Involving Negative Ions of Tungsten and Rhenium Oxides," J. Chem. Phys. **56**, 371 (1972).

72CON/COL
G. Conde-Caprace and J.E. Collin, "Electron Impact Induced Fragmentation of 1,3,6-Dioxathiocane," Org. Mass Spectrom. **6**, 341 (1972).

72DID/FRA
A. DiDomenico and J.L. Franklin, "Negative Ions in the Mass Spectrum of Nitromethane," Int. J. Mass Spectrom. Ion Phys. **9**, 171 (1972).

72DID/HAR
A. DiDomenico, P.W. Harland and J.L. Franklin, "Negative Ion Formation and Negative Ion-Molecule Reactions in Cyclopentadiene," J. Chem. Phys. **56**, 5299 (1972).

72DIX/HOL
D.A. Dixon, D. Holtz and J.L. Beauchamp, "Acidity, Basicity, and Gas-Phase Ion Chemistry of Hydrogen Selenide by ICR Spectroscopy," Inorg. Chem. **11**, 960 (1972).

72DOM
E.S. Domalski, J. Phys. Chem. Ref. Data **1**, 221 (1972).

72DON/LIT
R.J. Donovan, D.J. Little, J. Konstantatos, "Vacuum Ultraviolet Spectra of Transient Molecules and Radicals," J. Chem. Soc. Farad. Trans. II **68**, 1812 (1972).

72DUN/FEH
D.B. Dunkin, F.C. Fehsenfeld and E.E. Ferguson, "Thermal Energy Rate Constants for the Reactions $NO_2^- + Cl_2 \rightarrow Cl_2^-$, $Cl_2^- + NO_2 \rightarrow Cl^-$, $HS^- + NO_2 \rightarrow NO_2^-$, $HS^- + Cl_2 \rightarrow Cl_2^-$, and $S^- + NO_2 \rightarrow NO_2^-$," Chem. Phys. Lett. **15**, 257 (1972).

72FER/DUN
E.E. Ferguson, D.B. Dunkin and F.C. Fehsenfeld, "Reactions of NO_2^- and NO_3^- with HCl and HBr," J. Chem. Phys. **57**, 1459 (1972).

72GAF
"M-PYROL: N-Methylpyrrolidone" (GAF Corporation, New York, 1972).

72GEI/RAU
G. Geiseler and H.J. Rauh, Z. Phys. Chem. (Leipzig) **249**, 376 (1972).

72GOR
A.S. Gordon, Int. J. Chem. Kinet. **4**, 541 (1972).

72GRE
A. Greenberg, J. Chem. Ed. **49**, 575 (1972).

72GRO
M.L. Gross, "An Ion Cyclotron Resonance Study of the Structure of $C_3H_6^+$ and the Mechanism of Its Reaction with Ammonia," J. Am. Chem. Soc. **94**, 3744 (1972).

72HAR/CRA
P.W. Harland, S. Cradock and J.C.J. Thynne, "Positive- and Negative-Ion Formation Due to the Electron Bombardment of Germanium Tetrafluoride," Int. J. Mass Spectrom. Ion Phys. **10**, 169 (1972).

72HAR/THY
P.W. Harland and J.C.J. Thynne, "Dissociative Electron Capture in Perfluoropropylene and Perfluoropropane," Int. J. Mass Spectrom. Ion Phys. **9**, 253 (1972).

72HAR/THY2
P.W. Harland and J.C.J. Thynne, "Ionisation of Perfluorocyclobutane by Electron Impact," Int. J. Mass Spectrom. Ion Phys. **10**, 11 (1972).

72HEH/RAD
W.J. Hehre, L.A. Radom and J.A. Pople, J. Am. Chem. Soc. **94**, 1496 (1972).

72JOH/MAL
G.K. Johnson, J.G. Malm and W.N. Hubbard, J. Chem. Thermodyn. **4**, 879 (1972).

72KOZ/TIM
M.P. Kozina, L.P. Timofeeva, S.M. Pinenova, V.A. Aleshna, N.A. Belikova, A.A. Bobyleva and A.F. Plate, Russ. J. Phys. Chem. **46**, 1689 (1972).

72LAU/OKA
A.H. Laufer and H. Okabe, J. Phys. Chem. **76**, 3504 (1972).

72LIF/GRA
C. Lifshitz and R. Grajower, "Dissociative Electron Capture and Dissociative Ionization in Perfluorocyclobutane," Int. J. Mass Spectrom. Ion Phys. **10**, 25 (1972).

72MAC/THY
K.A.G. MacNeil and J.C.J. Thynne, "Negative Ion Formation at Low Electron Energies by Hexafluorodimethyl Peroxide," Int. J. Mass Spectrom. Ion Phys. **9**, 135 (1972).

72MCF/DUN
M. McFarland, D.B. Dunkin, F.C. Fehsenfeld, A.L. Schmeltekopf and E.E. Ferguson, "Collisional Detachment Studies of NO^-," J. Chem. Phys. **56**, 2358 (1972).

72MIL
E.S. Miller, "Electron Attachment and Compound Formation in Flames. V. Negative Ion Formation in Flames Containing Chromium and Potassium," J. Chem. Phys. **57**, 2354 (1972).

72PAG
Page, F.M., "Experimental Determination of the Electron Affinities of Inorganic Radicals," Adv. Chem. Ser. **36**, 68 (1972).

72PAR/SUG
D.A. Parkes and T.M. Sugden, "Electron Attachment and Detachment in Nitric Oxide," J. Chem. Soc. Faraday II **68**, 600 (1972).

72PIL
G. Pilcher MTP Review of Science, Series 1, Vol. 10 (ed. H.A. Skinner, Butterworths, London, 1972).

72POT/SOR
V.K. Potapov and V.V. Sorokin, "Kinetic Energies of Products of Dissociative Photoionization of Molecules. 1. Aliphatic Ketones and Alcohols," Khim. Vys. Energ. **6**, 387 (1972).

72SHA
R. Shaw, Int. J. Chem. Kinet. **5**, 261 (1972).

72SHI/YAM
T. Shiga, H. Yamaoka, K. Arakawa and T. Suguira, "A Negative Ion-Molecule Reaction in Nitroethylene," Bull. Chem. Soc. Jpn. **45**, 2065 (1972).

72SIE/CEL
M.W. Siegel, R.J. Celotta, F.L. Hall, J. Levine and R.A. Bennett, "Molecular Photodetachment Spectroscopy. I. The Electron Affinity of Nitric Oxide and the Molecular Constants of NO^-," Phys. Rev. A **6**, 607 (1972).

72SMY/BRA
K.C. Smyth and J.I. Brauman, "Photodetachment of Electrons from Phosphide Ion; the Electron Affinity of PH_2^-," J. Chem. Phys. **56**, 1132 (1972).

72SMY/BRA2
K.C. Smyth and J.I. Brauman, "Photodetachment of Electrons from Amide and Arsenide Ions: the Electron Affinities of $NH_2 \cdot$ and $AsH_2 \cdot$," J. Chem. Phys. **56**, 4620 (1972).

72SMY/BRA3
K.C. Smyth and J.I. Brauman, "Photodetachment of an Electron from Selenide Ion; The Electron Affinity and Spin-Orbit Coupling Constant for SeH," J. Chem. Phys. **56**, 5993 (1972).

72SRI/UY
R.D. Srivastava, O.M. Uy and M. Farber, "Effusion Mass Spectrometric Study of the Thermodynamic Properties of AlO^- and AlO_2^-," J. Chem. Soc. Faraday Trans. II **1**, 1388 (1972).

72STO/NEL
J.A.D. Stockdale, D.R. Nelson, F.J. Davis and R.N. Compton, "Studies of Electron Impact Excitation, Negative Ion Formation, and Negative Ion-Molecule Reactions in Boron Trifluoride and Boron Trichloride," J. Chem. Phys. **56**, 3336 (1972).

72THY
J.C.J. Thynne, Dyn. Mass Spectrom. **3**, 67 (1972).

72TRI/ALL
M.T. Tribble and N.L. Allinger, Tetrahedron **28**, 2147 (1972).

72WAL
L.C. Walker, J. Chem. Thermodyn. **4**, 219 (1972).

72YAM/KEB
R. Yamdagni and P. Kebarle, "Solvation of Negative Ions by Protic and Aprotic Solvents. Gas Phase Solvation of Halide Ions by Acetonitrile and Water Molecules," J. Am. Chem. Soc. **94**, 2940 (1972).

73ALF/GOL
A.B. Alfassi, D.M. Golden and S.W. Benson, J. Chem. Thermodyn. **5**, 511 (1973).

73ARS/SHA
M.R. Arshadi and M. Shabrang, J. Chem. Soc. Perkins II, 1732 (1973).

73AUE/HUB
D.J. Auerbach, M.M. Hubers, A.P.M. Baeda and J. Los, "Chemi-Ionization in Alkali-Heteronuclear Halogen Collisions: Role of Excited Molecular Ion States," Chem. Phys. **2**, 107 (1973).

73BAE/AUE
A.P.M. Baeda, J. Auerbach, and D.J. Los, "Fragmentation of Negative Ions Formed in Collisions of Alkali Atoms and Halogen Molecules," Physica **64**, 134 (1973).

73BAR
P. Barbieri, Inform. Sci. Tech, Commis. Energ. At. **55**, 180 (1973). CA: 79:58336m (1973).

73BAT/MIL
L. Batt and R.T. Milne, Int. J. Chem. Kinet. **5**, 1067 (1973).

73BEN/MAR
S.L. Bennett, J.L. Margrave, J.L. Franklin and J.E. Hudson, "High Temperature Negative Ions: Electron Impact of As_4 Vapor," J. Chem. Phys. **59**, 5814 (1973).

73BIL/CHO
W.E. Billups, W.Y. Chong, K.H. Leavell, E.S. Lewis, J.L. Margrave, R.L. Sass, J.J. Shieh, P.G. Werness and J.L. Wood, J. Am. Chem. Soc. **95**, 7878 (1973).

73BLA/ISO
L.K. Blair, P.C. Isolani and J.M. Riveros, "Formation, Reactivity, and Relative Stability of Clustered Alkoxide Ions by ICR Spectroscopy," J. Am. Chem. Soc. **95**, 1057 (1973).

73COM/COO
R.N. Compton and C.D. Cooper, "Molecular Electron Affinities from Collisional Ionization of Cesium. II. SF_6 and TeF_6," J. Chem. Phys. 59, 4140 (1973).

73COM/COO2
R.N. Compton, R.D. Cooper, W.T. Divver and P.W. Reinhardt, "Molecular Electron Affinities from Collisional Ionization of Cesium: SF_6," Bull. Am. Phys. Soc. 18, 810 (1973).

73COO/COM
C.D. Cooper and R.N. Compton, "Electron Attachment and Cesium Collisional Ionization Studies of Tetrafluorosuccinic and Hexafluoroglutaric Anhydrides: Molecular Electron Affinities," J. Chem. Phys. 59, 3550 (1973).

73COW/JOH
S.A. Cowling and R.A.W. Johnstone, J. Electron Spectrosc. Relat. Phenom. 2, 161 (1973).

73EGG/COC
K.W. Egger and A.T. Cocks, "The Chemistry of the Carbon-Halogen Bond," S. Patai, Ed., Wiley, NY, 1973, Ch. 10.

73ENG/AND
E.M. Engler, J.D. Andose and P. von R. Schleyer, J. Am. Chem. Soc. 95, 8003 (1973).

73GAR/REE
W.R.S. Garton, E.M. Reeves, F.S. Tomkins and B. Ercoli, "Rydberg Series and Autoionization Resonances in the Y I Absorption Spectrum," Proc. R. Soc. Lond. A333, 17 (1973).

73GOL/KOR
I.V. Gol'denfel'd, I.Z. Korostyshevskii, B.G. Mischanchuk and V.A. Pokrovskii, "Determination of Ionization Potentials of Atoms and Molecules Using a Field Mass Spectrometer Equipped with an Energy Analyzer," Dokl. Akad. Nauk SSSR, 213, 626 (1973).

73HAA/MCD
J.C. Haartz and D.H. McDaniel, "Fluoride Ion Affinity of Some Lewis Acids," J. Am. Chem. Soc. 95, 8562 (1973).

73HAR/FRA
P.W. Harland, J.L. Franklin and D.E. Carter, "Use of Translational Energy Measurements in the Evaluation of the Energetics for Dissociative Attachment Processes," J. Chem. Phys. 58, 1430 (1973).

73HAR/THY
P.W. Harland and J.C.J. Thynne, "Comparision of Negative Ion Formation by the Hexafluorides of Sulphur, Selenium, Tellurium, and Tungsten," Inorg. Nucl. Chem. Lett. 9, 265 (1973).

73HAR/THY2
P.W. Harland and J.C.J. Thynne, "Negative Ion Formation by Perfluoro-n-butane as the Result of Low Energy Electron Impact," Int. J. Mass Spectrom. Ion Phys. 11, 445 (1973).

73HUG/LIF
B.M. Hughes, C. Lifschitz and T.O. Tiernan, "Electron Affinities from Endothermic Negative-ion Charge-Transfer Reactions. III. NO, NO_2, S_2, CS_2, Cl_2, Br_2, I_2, and C_2H," J. Chem. Phys. 59, 3162 (1973).

73LAR/JOH
J.W. Larson, G.K. Johnson, P.A.G. O'Hare and O. Glemser, J. Chem. Thermodyn. 5, 689 (1973).

73LAT/RAD
W.A. Lathan, L. Radom, P.C. Hariharan, W.J. Hehre and J.A. Pople, Top. Curr. Chem. 40, 1 (1973).

73LEF/JAC
C.B. Leffert, W.M. Jackson and E.W. Rothe, "Measurement of the Electron Affinity of NO_2," J. Chem. Phys. 58, 5801 (1973).

73LIF/TIE
C. Lifshitz, T.O. Tiernan and B.M. Hughes, "Electron Affinities from Endothermic Negative-Ion Charge Transfer Reactions. IV. SF_6, Selected Fluorocarbons, and other Polyatomic Molecules," J. Chem. Phys. 59, 3182 (1973).

73LYO/PAL
L.E. Lyons and L.D. Palmer, "Photodetachment of Electrons from Tetracyanoethylene Negative Ions," Chem. Phys. Lett. 21, 442 (1973).

73MCI/SCO
R.T. McIver, Jr., J.A. Scott and J.M. Riveros, "Effect of Solvation on the Intrinsic Relative Acidity of Methanol and Ethanol," J. Am. Chem. Soc. 95, 2706 (1973).

73MCN/LAC
P.E. McNamee, K. Lacmann and D.R. Herschbach, Faraday Disc. Chem. Soc. 55, 318 (1973).

73NAL/COM
S.J. Nalley, R.N. Compton, H.C. Schweinler and V.E. Anderson, "Molecular Electron Affinities from Collisional Ionization of Cesium. I. NO, NO_2, and N_2O," J. Chem. Phys. 59, 4125 (1973).

73ONA/HOW
T. Onak, J. Howard and C. Brown, "Negative Ion Mass Spectrometry of closo-Carboranes," J. Chem. Soc. Dalton 76, (1973).

73PEP/GAF
V.I. Pepekin, R.G. Gafurov, Yu.A. Lebedev, L.T. Eremenko, E.M. Soyomonyan and A. Ya. Apin, Bull. Acad. Sci. USSR, Div. Chem. Sci. 22, 304 (1973).

73RAB/KAR
J.W. Rabalais, L. Karlsson, L.O. Werme, T. Bergmark and K. Siegbahn, "Analysis of Vibrational Structure and Jahn-Teller Effects in the Electron Spectrum of Ammonia," J. Chem. Phys. 58, 3370 (1973).

73RAD/LAT
L. Radom, W.A. Lathan, W.J. Hehre and J.A. Pople, J. Am. Chem. Soc. 95, 693 (1973).

73RIC/STE
J.H. Richardson, L.M. Stephenson and J.I. Brauman, "Photodetachment of Electrons from Large Molecular Systems: Cyclopentadienide and Methylcyclopentadienide Ions. An Upper Limit to the Electron Affinities of C_5H_5· and $CH_3C_5H_4$," J. Chem. Phys. 59, 5068 (1973).

73RIV/BRE
J.M. Riveros, A.C. Breda and L.K. Blair, "Formation and Relative Stability of Chloride Ion Clusters in the Gas Phase by ICR Spectroscopy," J. Am. Chem. Soc. 95, 4066 (1973).

73SEN/FRA
D.K. SenSharma and J.L. Franklin, "Heat of Formation of Free Radicals by Mass Spectrometry," J. Am. Chem. Soc. 95, 6562 (1973).

73THY/HAR
T.C.J. Thynne and P.W. Harland, Int. J. Mass Spectrom. Ion Phys. 11, 399 (1973).

73THY/HAR2
J.C.J. Thynne and P.W. Harland, "Negative Ion Formation by Tungsten Fluoride," Int. J. Mass Spectrom. Ion Phys. 11, 137 (1973).

73WAN/MAR
J.L.-F. Wang, J.L. Margrave and J.L. Franklin, "Interpretation of Dissociative Electron Attachment Processes for Carbon and Silicon Tetrafluorides," J. Chem. Phys. 58, 5417 (1973).

73YAM/PAY
R. Yamdagni, J.D. Payzant and P. Kebarle, "Solvation of Cl- and O_2^- with H_2O, CH_3OH, and CH_3CN in the Gas Phase," Can. J. Chem. 51, 2507 (1973).

74BAT/CHR
L. Batt, K. Christie, R.T. Milne and A.J. Summers, Int. J. Chem. Kinet. 6, 877 (1974).

74BEA
J.L. Beauchamp, "Chemical Applications of New Developments in Ion Cyclotron Resonance Spectroscopy," Adv. Mass Spectrom. **6**, 717 (1974).

74BEA/MUE
P. Beak, D.S. Mueller and J. Lee, J. Am. Chem. Soc. **96**, 3867 (1974).

74BEN/MAR
S.L. Bennett, J.L. Margrave and J.L. Franklin, "High Temperature Negative Ions. Electron Impact Study of Tetratomic Phosphorous Vapor," J. Chem. Phys. **61**, 1647 (1974).

74BEN/PAB
S.L. Bennett, S.E. Pabst, J.L. Margrave and J.L. Franklin, "Negative Ion Electron Impact Studies of Titanium Tetrahalides," Int. J. Mass Spectrom. Ion Phys. **15**, 451 (1974).

74BET/BAK
D. Betteridge, A.D. Baker, P. Bye, S.K. Hasannudin, N.R. Kemp and M. Thompson, "A Cheap Versatile Ultraviolet Photoelectron Spectrometer," J. Electron Spectrosc. Rel. Phenom. **4**, 163 (1974).

74BLI/MCM
R.J. Blint, T.B. McMahon and J.L. Beauchamp, "Gas Phase Ion Chemistry of Fluoromethanes by Ion Cyclotron Resonance Spectroscopy. New Techniques for the Determination of Carbonium Ion Stabilities," J. Am. Chem. Soc. **96**, 1269 (1974).

74BOH/MAC
D.K. Bohme, G.I. MacKay, H.I. Schiff and R.S. Hemsworth, "Equilibrium $OH^- + C_2H_2 = C_2H^- + H_2O$ and the Determination of $\Delta H_{f298}(C_2H^-)$," J. Chem. Phys. **61**, 2175 (1974).

74BUR
P.D. Burrow, "Temporary Negative Ion Formation in NO and O_2," Chem. Phys. Lett. **26**, 265 (1974).

74BUR/HAI
J. Burgess, I. Haigh and R.D. Peacock, J. Chem. Soc. Dalton Trans. 1062 (1974).

74CEL/BEN
R.J. Celotta, R.A. Bennett and J.L. Hall, "Laser Photodetachment Determination of the Electron Affinities of OH, NH_2, NH, SO_2, and S_2," J. Chem. Phys. **60**, 1740 (1974).

74CHA/PAG
A.T. Chamberlin, F.M. Page and M.R. Painter, "A Study of the Negative Ions Produced during Surface Ionization on Hot Metal Filaments," Adv. Mass Spectrom. **6**, 311 (1974).

74CHA/ROD
J. Chao, A.S. Rodgers, R.C. Wilhoit and B.J. Zwolinski, J. Phys. Chem. Ref. Data **3**, 141 (1974).

74CHO/MEN
K.Y. Choo, G.D. Mendenhall, D.M. Golden and S.W. Benson, "The Pyrolysis of Nitrosoisobutane and the Bond Dissociation Energies of Nitroso Compounds," Int. J. Chem. Kinet. **6**, 813 (1974).

74COM/REI
R.N. Compton, P.W. Reinhardt and C.D. Cooper, "Mass Spectrometry Utilizing Collisional Ionization of Cesium: Maleic Anhydride and Succinic Anhydride," J. Chem. Phys. **60**, 2953 (1974).

74COO/COM
C.D. Cooper and R.N. Compton, "Electron Attachment and Collisional Ionization Studies of Tetrafluorosuccinic and Hexafluoroglutaric Anhydrides: Molecular Electron Affinities," J. Chem. Phys. **60**, 2424 (1974).

74DON/HAR
R.J. Donovan, P.W. Harland, J.H. Knox, J.A. Makowski and J.C.J. Thynne, "Electron Affinity of SF_4," Int. J. Mass Spectrom. Ion Phys. **13**, 464 (1974).

74DOU/DAL
R.C. Dougherty, J. Dalton and J.D. Roberts, "S_N2 Reactions in the Gas Phase: Structure of the Transition State," Org. Mass Spectrom. **8**, 77 (1974).

74DOU
R.C. Dougherty, "S_N2 Reactions in the Gas Phase. Alkyl Group Structural Effects," Org. Mass Spectrom. **8**, 85 (1974).

74DOU/ROB
R.C. Dougherty and J.D. Roberts, "S_N2 Reactions in the Gas Phase. Nucleophilicity Effects," Org. Mass Spectrom. **8**, 81 (1984).

74DZI/CAR
I. Dzidic, D.I. Carroll, R.N. Stillwell and E.C. Horning, "Gas Phase Reactions. Ionization by Proton Transfer to Superoxide Anions," J. Am. Chem. Soc. **96**, 5258 (1974).

74EYL/ATK
J.R. Eyler and G.H. Atkinson, "Dye Laser-induced Photodetachment of Electrons from SH^- Studied by ICR Spectroscopy," Chem. Phys. Lett. **28**, 217 (1974).

74FEH/FER
F.C. Fehsenfeld and E.E. Ferguson, "Laboratory Studies of Negative Ion Reactions with Atmospheric Trace Constituents," J. Chem. Phys. **61**, 3181 (1974).

74FRA/WAN
J.L. Franklin, J.L.-F. Wang, S.L. Bennett, P.W. Harland and J.L. Margrave, "Studies of the Energies of Negative Ions at High Temperatures," Adv. Mass Spectrom. **6**, 319 (1974).

74HAL/KLE
M. Halmann and Y. Klein, "Positive and Negative Ion Mass Spectra of Phosphorous Compounds," Adv. Mass Spectrom. **3**, 267 (1974).

74HAR/FRA
P.W. Harland and J.L. Franklin, "Partitioning of Excess Energy in Dissociative Resonance Capture Processes," J. Chem. Phys. **61**, 1621 (1974).

74HAR/RAN
P.W. Harland, D.W.H. Rankin and J.C.J. Thynne, "Ionisation by Electron Impact of Phosphorus Trifluoride and Difluorocyanophosphine," Int. J. Mass Spectrom. Ion Phys. **13**, 395 (1974).

74HER/PAT
E. Herbst, T.A. Patterson and W.C. Lineberger, "Laser Photodetachment of NO_2^-," J. Chem. Phys. **61**, 1300 (1974).

74HOT/PAT
H. Hotop, T.A. Patterson and W.C. Lineberger, "High Resolution Photodetachment Study of OH^- and OD^- in the Threshold Region 7000-6450 Å," J. Chem. Phys. **60**, 1806 (1974).

74JANAF
M.W. Chase, J.L. Curnutt, A.T. Hu, H. Prophet, A.N. Syverud and L.C. Walker, "JANAF Thermochemical Tables, 1974 Supplement," J. Phys. Chem. Ref. Data **3**, 311 (1974).

74KIM/SET
K.C. Kim, D.W. Setser and C.M. Bogan, "HF Infrared Chemiluminescence and Energy Partioning, and $D(H-GeH_3)$ from the Reaction of F Atoms with Germane," J. Chem. Phys. **60**, 1837 (1974).

74KOP/SCH
C. Koppel, H. Schwarz and F. Bohlmann, "Elektronenstossinduzierte Fragmentierung von Acetylenverbindungen," Org. Mass Spectrom. **9**, 324 (1974).

74LAT/CUR
W.A. Lathan, L.A. Curtiss, W.J. Hehre, J.B. Lisle and J.A. Pople, Prog. Phys. Org. Chem. **11**, 175 (1974).

74LEF/TAN
C.B. Leffert, S.Y. Tang, E.W. Rothe and T.C. Cheng, "Collisional Ionization of Cs with SF_6," J. Chem. Phys. **61**, 4929 (1974).

74LIE/GRE
J.F. Liebman and A. Greenberg, Biophys. Chem. **1**, 222 (1974).

74MCA
T. McAllister, Int. J. Mass Spectrom. Ion Phys. **15**, 303 (1974).

74MOU/ATE
A.M.C. Moutinho, J.A. Aten and J. Los, "Chemi-Ionization in Alkali-Methylhalogen Collisions," Chem. Phys. **5**, 84 (1974).

74OTH/BUN
J.F.M. Oth, J.-C. Bunzli and Y. de Julien de Zelicourt, Helv. Chim. Acta **57**, 2276 (1974).

74PAL/KEN
M.H. Palmer and S.M.F. Kennedy, J. Chem. Soc. Perkin II 1893 (1974).

74PEA/SCH
P.K. Pearson, H.F. Schaefer,III, J.H. Richardson, L.M. Stephenson and J.I. Brauman, "Three Isomers of the NO_2^- Ion," J. Am. Chem. Soc. **96**, 6778 (1974).

74PIH/TAS
K. Pihlaja and E. Taskinen, "Physical Methods in Heterocyclic Chemistry," Vol. 6 (ed. A.R. Katritzky, Academic Press, New York, 1974).

74REE/BRA
K.J. Reed and J.I. Brauman, "Photodetachment of Electrons from Group IVa Binary Hydride Anions: The Electron Affinities of the SiH_3 and GeH_3 Radicals," J. Chem. Phys. **61**, 4830 (1974).

74RIC/STE
J.H. Richardson, L.M. Stephenson and J.I. Brauman, "Photodetachment of NO_2^-: Experimental Evidence for a New Isomer," Chem. Phys. Lett. **25**, 318 (1974).

74RIC/STE2
J.H. Richardson, L.M. Stephenson and J.I. Brauman, "Photodetachment of Electrons from Phenoxides and Thiophenoxide," Chem. Phys. Lett. **25**, 321 (1974).

74RID/BEA
D.P. Ridge and J.L. Beauchamp, "Chemical Consequences of Strong Hydrogen Bonding in the Reactions of Organic Ions in the Gas Phase. Base Induced Elimination Reactions," J. Am. Chem. Soc. **96**, 637 (1974).

74ROG/KAN
D.W. Rogers and S. Kanupong, J. Phys. Chem. **78**, 2569 (1974).

74SAB/CHA
R. Sabbah, R. Chastel and M. Laffitte, Thermochim. Acta **10**, 353 (1974).

74SCO
D.W. Scott, "Chemical Thermodynamic Properties of Hydrocarbons and Related Substances: Properties of Alkane Hydrocarbons C_1 through C_{10}," APIRP62 Report 39, (U.S. Dept. of Interior, Bureau of Mines, 1974).

74SRI/UY
R.D. Srivastava, O.M. Uy and M. Farber, "Experimental Determination of Heats of Formation of Negative Ions and Electron Affinities of Several Boron and Aluminum Fluorides," J. Chem. Soc. Faraday Trans. I **70**, 1033 (1974).

74WAN/MAR
J.L.-F. Wang, J.L. Margrave and J.L. Franklin, "Enthalpy of Formation of Germanium Trifluoride," J. Chem. Phys. **60**, 2158 (1974).

74WAN/MAR2
J.L.-F. Wang, J.L. Margrave and J.L. Franklin, "Interpretation of Dissociative-Electron Attachment Processes for Silicon Tetrachloride," J. Chem. Phys. **61**, 1357 (1974).

74WYA/HOL
R.H. Wyatt, D. Holtz, T.B. McMahon and J.L. Beauchamp, "Acidity, Basicity, and Ion-Molecule Reactions of Arsine in the Gas Phase by ICR Spectroscopy," Inorg. Chem **13**, 1511 (1974).

74YAM/KEB
R. Yamdagni and P. Kebarle, "The Hydrogen Bond Energies in $ClHCl^-$ and $Cl^-(HCl)_n$," Can. J. Chem. **52**, 2449 (1974).

75ALF/GOL
Z. Alfassi, D.M. Golden and S.W. Benson, J. Chem. Thermodyn. **5**, 411 (1975).

75ALL/MEY
N.L. Allinger and A.Y. Meyer, Tetrahedron **31**, 1897 (1975).

75ASU/BLA
O.I. Asubiojo, L.K. Blair and J.I. Brauman, "Tetrahedral Intermediates in Gas Phase Ionic Displacement Reactions at Carbonyl Carbons," J. Am. Chem. Soc. **97**, 6685 (1975).

75BAR/PIL
D.S. Barnes and G. Pilcher, J. Chem. Thermodyn. **7**, 377 (1975).

75BEN/MAR
S.L. Bennett, J.L. Margrave and J.L. Franklin, "Negative Ion Electron Impact Studies of Inorganic Halides. Niobium and Tantalum Pentachlorides," J. Inorg. Nucl. Chem. **37**, 937 (1975).

75BEN/WAN
S.L. Bennett, J.L. Wang, J.L. Margrave and J.L. Franklin, "High Temperature Negative Ions. The Enthalpies of Formation of Gaseous PbF_3 and SnF_3 from Low-Energy Electron Impact Studies," High Temp. Sci. **7**, 142 (1975).

75BER/BOU
M.A. Bernardi, Y. Boukari and F. Busnot, Thermochim. Acta **16**, 2677 (1975).

75BRI/RIV
S.M.J. Briscese and J.M. Riveros, "Gas Phase Nucleophilic Reactions of Aromatic Systems," J. Am. Chem. Soc. **97**, 230 (1975).

75CHE/ROD
S.S. Chen, A.S. Rodgers, J. Chao, R.C. Wilhoit and B.J. Zwolinski, J. Phys. Chem. Ref. Data **4**, 441 (1975).

75CHI
J.S. Chickos, J. Chem. Ed. **52**, 134 (1975).

75CHO/GOL
K.Y. Choo, D.M. Golden and S.W. Benson, Int. J. Chem. Kinet. **7**, 713 (1975).

75CLA/KNO
T. Clark, T. McO. Knox, H. Mackle, M.A. McKervey and J.J. Rooney, J. Am. Chem. Soc. **97**, 3835 (1975).

75CLA/SCH
E. Clar and W. Schmidt, "Correlations Between Photoelectron and Ultraviolet Absorption Spectra of Polycyclic Hydrocarbons and the Number of Aromatic Sextets," Tetrahedron **31**, 2263 (1975).

75COM
F. Compernolle, Org. Mass. Spectrom. **10**, 289 (1975).

75COM/DES
F. Compernolle and F. DeSchryver, J. Am. Chem. Soc. **97**, 3909 (1975).

75COM/REI
R.N. Compton, P.W. Reinhardt and C.D. Cooper, "Collisional Ionization of Na, K, and Cs by CO_2, COS, and CS_2: Molecular Electron Affinities," J. Chem. Phys. **63**, 3821 (1975).

75COO/NAF
C.D. Cooper, W.T. Naff and R.N. Compton, "Negative Ion Properties of p-Benzoquinone: Electron Affinity and Compound States," J. Chem. Phys. **63**, 2752 (1975).

75DER/JOC
J.-L. Derocque and M. Jochem, "Studies in Mass Spectrometry. III. Formation of a Common Intermediate in the Primary Fragmentation Process of 1-Phenylcyclobutene and of 2-Phenyl-1,3-butadiene," Org. Mass Spectrom. **10**, 935 (1975).

75DIE/FRA
H. tom Dieck, K.-D. Franz and W. Majunke, "Darstellung und Eigenschaften von Diacetylbis(methylimin)," Z. Naturforsch. **30b**, 922 (1975).

75FER
L.N. Ferguson, "Organic Molecular Structure," (Willard Grant Press, Boston, 1975).

75FLE/SVE
G.D. Flesch and H.J. Svec, "Thermochemistry Of Vanadium Oxytrichloride and Vanadium Oxytrifluoride by Mass Spectrometry," Inorg. Chem. **14**, 1817 (1975).

75GAL/WIL
L. Galyer, G. Wilkinson and D.R. Lloyd, "The Photoelectron Spectra of Hexamethyltungsten and Pentamethyltantalum," J. Chem. Soc. Chem. Commun. 497 (1975).

75GOO
W.D. Good, J. Chem. Thermodyn. 7, 49 (1975).

75GOU/MIL
B.K. Gould and W.J. Miller, "Electron Attachment and Compound Formation in Flames. VI. Negative Ion and Compound Formation in Flames Containing Rhenium and Potassium," J. Chem. Phys. 62, 644 (1975).

75HAR/THY
P.W. Harland and J.C.J. Thynne, "Dissociative Electron Capture in Trifluoroacetaldehyde, Pentafluoropropionaldehyde, and Heptafluorobutyraldehyde," Int. J. Mass Spectrom. Ion Phys. 18, 73 (1975).

75HEH/POP
W.J. Hehre and J.A. Pople, J. Am. Chem. Soc. 97, 6941 (1975).

75HOT/LIN
H. Hotop and W.C. Lineberger, "Binding Energies of Atomic Negative Ions," J. Phys. Chem. Ref. Data 4, 539 (1975).

75HUB/LOS
M.M. Hubers and J. Los, "Ion Pair Formation in Alkali-SF_6 Collisions: Dependence on Collisional and Vibrational Energy," Chem. Phys. 10, 235 (1975).

75JANAF
M.W. Chase, J.L. Curnutt, H. Prophet, R.A. McDonald and A.N. Syverud, "JANAF Thermochemical Tables, 1975 Supplement," J. Phys. Chem. Ref. Data 4, 1 (1975).

75KAR/KLE
Z. Karpas and F.S. Klein, "Negative Ion-Molecule Reactions in a Mixture of Ammonia-Formaldehyde - An ICR Mass Spectrometry Study," Int. J. Mass Spectrom. Ion Phys. 18, 65 (1975).

75KAS/HER
A. Kasdan, E. Herbst and W.C. Lineberger, "Laser Photoelectron Spectrometry of the Negative Ions of Silicon and its Hydrides," J. Chem. Phys. 62, 541 (1975).

75KAS/HER2
A. Kasdan, E. Herbst and W.C. Lineberger, "Laser Photoelectron Spectrometry of CH_2^-," Chem. Phys. Lett. 31, 78 (1975).

75KAS/HER2
A. Kasdan, E. Herbst and W.C. Lineberger, "Laser Photoelectron Spectrometry of the Negative Ions of Silicon and Its Hydrides," J. Chem. Phys. 62, 541 (1975).

75KIN/GOD
K.D. King and R.D. Goddard, "Very-Low-Pressure Pyrolysis of Alkyl Cyanides. II. n-Propyl Cyanide and n-Butyl Cyanide. The Heat of Formation of the Cyanomethyl Radical," Int. J. Chem. Kinet. 7, 837 (1975).

75KOL/MCK
P. Kollman, J. McKelvey, A. Johansson and S. Rothenberg, J. Am. Chem. Soc. 97, 855 (1975).

75LEB/MIR
V.P. Lebedev, E. Miroshnickenko, Y.N. Matyushin, V.P. Larionov, V.S. Romanov, V.E. Bukolov, G.M. Denisov, A.A. Balepin and Y.A. Lebedev, Russ. J. Phys. Chem. 49, 1133 (1975).

75LIN/ALB
W. Lindinger, A.L. Albritton, F.C. Fehsenfeld and E.E. Ferguson, "Reactions of O^- with N_2, N_2O, SO_2, NH_3, CH_4, C_2H_4, and $C_2H_2^-$ with O_2 from 300K to Relative Kinetic Energies of 2 eV," J. Chem. Phys. 63, 3238 (1975).

75LLO/ROB
D.R. Lloyd and P.J. Roberts, "Photoelectron Spectra of Halides. VII. Variable Temperature He(I) and He(II) Studies of CF_4, SiF_4, and GeF_4," J. Electron Spectrosc. Rel. Phenom. 7, 325 (1975).

75LYO/PAL
L.E. Lyons and L.D. Palmer, "A Surface Ionization Source and Quadrupole Mass Filter for Photodetachment Studies," Int. J. Mass Spectrom. Ion Phys. 16, 431 (1975).

75MCE/SAN
D.M. McEachern, O. Sandoval and J.C. Iniguez, J. Chem. Thermodyn. 7, 299 (1975).

75MOS/PRI
G.M. Moselby and H.O. Pritchard, J. Chem. Thermodyn. 7, 977 (1975).

75NEN/SCH
I. Nenner and G.J. Schultz, "Temporary Negative Ions and Electron Affinities of Benzene and N-Heterocyclic Molecules: Pyridine, Pyridazine, Pyrimidine, Pyrazine, and s-Triazine," J. Chem. Phys. 62, 1747 (1975).

75OKA
H. Okabe, J. Chem. Phys. 62, 2782 (1975).

75OKA/WHI
E.N. Okafo and E. Whittle, Int. J. Chem. Kinet. 7, 213 (1975).

75REE/BRA
K.J. Reed and J.I. Brauman, "Electron Affinities of Alkoxy Radicals and the Bond Dissociation Energies in Aliphatic Alcohols," J. Am. Chem. Soc. 97, 1625 (1975).

75RIC/STE
J.H. Richardson, L.M. Stephenson and J.I. Brauman, "Photodetachment of Electrons from Large Molecular Systems: Benzyl Anion. An Upper Limit to the Electron Affinity of $C_6H_5CH_2$," J. Chem. Phys. 63, 74 (1975).

75RIC/STE2
J.H. Richardson, L.M. Stephenson and J.I. Brauman, "Photodetachment of Electrons from Phenoxides and Thiophenoxide," J. Am. Chem. Soc. 97, 2967 (1975).

75RIC/STE3
J.H. Richardson, L.M. Stephenson and J.I. Brauman, "Photodetachment of Electrons from Large Molecular Systems. Pyrrolate Ion. Electron Affinity of C_4H_4N," J. Am. Chem. Soc. 97, 1160 (1975).

75RIC/STE4
J.H. Richardson, L.M. Stephenson and J.I. Brauman, "Photodetachment of Electrons from Trifluoromethyl and Trifluorosilyl Ions; The Electron Affinities of CF_3 and SiF_3," Chem. Phys. Lett. 30, 17 (1975).

75ROT/TAN
E.W. Rothe, S.Y. Tang and G.P. Reck, "Measurement of Electron Affinities of O_3, SO_2, and SO_3 by Collisional Ionization," J. Chem. Phys. 62, 3829 (1975).

75SCH/BOH
H.I. Schiff and D.K. Bohme, "Flowing Afterglow Studies at York University," Int. J. Mass Spectrom. Ion Phys. 16, 167 (1975).

75SOL/FIE
J.J. Solomon and F.H. Field, "Reversible Reactions of Gaseous Ions. IX. The Stability of C_4-C_7 Tertiary Alkyl Carbonium Ions," J. Am. Chem. Soc. 97, 2625 (1975).

75SUB/ZWO
D.J. Subach and B.J. Zwolinski, J. Chem. Eng. Data 20, 232 (1975).

75TOR/WES
D.F. Torgerson and J.B. Westmore, "Energetics of the Ionization and Fragmentation of Phosphorus Trifluoride by Electron Impact," Can. J. Chem. 53, 933 (1975).

75TRC
Selected Values of Properties of Chemical Compounds. Thermodynamic Research Center, Texas A & M (Table compiled 1975).

75VAN/RIN
A.J. Vanderwielen, M.A. Ring and H.E. O'Neal, J. Am. Chem. Soc. 97, 993 (1975).

75WAN/MAR
J.L.-F. Wang, J.L. Margrave and J.L. Franklin, "Low Energy Electron Attachment to Gaseous Chromium Oxides," J. Inorg. Nucl. Chem. 37, 1107 (1975).

75WEN/KAO
W.E. Wentworth, L.W. Kao and R.S. Becker, "Electron Affinities of Substituted Aromatic Compounds," J. Phys. Chem. **79**, 1161 (1975).

76ALL
N.L. Allinger, Advan. Phys. Org. Chem. **13**, 1 (1976).

76ANT/CAR
M.E. Anthoney, A.S. Carson, P.G. Carson, P.G. Laye and M. Yurckli, J. Chem. Thermodyn. **8**, 1009 (1976).

76ASH
S.J. Ashcroft, J. Chem. Eng. Data **21**, 397 (1976).

76ASH/BUR
A.J. Ashe III, F. Burger, M.Y. El-Sheik, E. Heilbronner, J.P. Maier and J.-F. Muller, "202. Angular- and Energy-Dependence of Band Intensities in the Photoelectron Spectra of Phosphabenzene and Arsabenzene," Helv. Chim. Acta **59**, 1944 (1976).

76AUD/FET
H.E. Audiek, M. Fetizon, Y. Henry and T. Prange, Org. Mass Spectrom. **11**, 1047 (1976).

76BAE/TSA
T. Baer, B.P. Tsai, D. Smith and P.T. Murray, "Absolute Unimolecular Decay Rates of Energy Selected Metastable Halobenzene Ions," J. Chem. Phys. **64**, 2460 (1976).

76BEA
J.L. Beauchamp, "Ion Cyclotron Resonance Studies of Endothermic Reactions of UF_6^- Generated by Surface Ionization," J. Chem. Phys. **64**, 929 (1976).

76BEN
S.W. Benson, "Thermochemical Kinetics," 2nd Ed., Wiley, NY, 1976.

76BOB/BAR
M.V. Bobetic and J.A. Barker, J. Chem. Phys. **64**, 2367 (1976).

76BOW/STA
J.H. Bowie and B.J. Stapleton, "Electron Impact Studies. C. Doubly Charged Negative Ions," J. Am. Chem. Soc. **98**, 6480 (1976).

76CAR/PET
J.L. Carlstein, J.R. Peterson and W.C. Lineberger, "Binding of an Electron by the Field of a Molecular Dipole - $LiCl^-$," Chem. Phys. Lett. **37**, 5 (1976).

76CHA
P.J. Chantry, "Negative Ion Formation in Cerium Triiodide," J. Chem. Phys. **65**, 4412 (1976).

76CHA/ZWO
J. Chao and B.J. Zwolinski, J. Phys. Chem. Ref. Data **5**, 319 (1976).

76COL/JIM
M. Colomina, P. Jimenez, R. Perez-Ossario and C. Turrion, J. Chem. Thermodyn. **8**, 439 (1976).

76COM/STO
R.N. Compton and J.A.D. Stockdale, "Formation of Gas Phase Negative Ions in $Fe(CO)_5$ and $Ni(CO)_4$," Int. J. Mass Spectrom. Ion Phys. **22**, 47 (1976).

76COS/LIN
P.C. Cosby, J.H. Ling, J.R. Peterson and J.T. Moseley, "Photodissociation and Photodetachment of Molecular Negative Ions. III. Ions Formed in $CO_2.O_2.H_2O$ Mixtures," J. Chem. Phys. **65**, 5267 (1976).

76DAW/JEN
J.H.J. Dawson and K.R. Jennings, "Production of Gas Phase Radical Anions by Reaction of O^- Ions with Organic Substrates," J. Chem. Soc. Faraday Trans. II **72**, 700 (1976).

76DEL/HAL
I. Dellienl, F.M. Hall and L.G. Hepler, Chem. Rev. **76**, 283 (1976).

76ENG/LIN
P.C. Engleking and W.C. Lineberger, "Laser Photoelectron Spectrometry of NH^-: Electron Affinity and Intercombination Energy Difference in NH," J. Chem. Phys. **65**, 4323 (1976).

76FAI/JOY
R.L. Failes, J.T. Joyce and E.C. Walton, "The Behaviour of Some Dimethyl and Trimethyl Substituted Pyridines in the Magnetron," J. Phys., D **9**, 1543 (1976).

76FER/PIA
D. Ferro, V. Piacente, R. Gigli and G. D'Ascenzo, J. Chem. Thermodyn. **8**, 1137 (1976).

76GOR/MUN
A. Goren and B. Munson, "Thermochemistry of Alkyl Ions," J. Phys. Chem. **80**, 2848 (1976).

76GUY/CHU
P.M. Guyon, W.A. Chupka and J. Berkowitz, "Photoionization Mass Spectrometric Study of Formaldehyde H_2CO, HDCO, and D_2CO," J. Chem. Phys. **65** 1419 (1976).

76HAM/THO
W.S. Hamilton, P. Thompson and S. Pustejovsky, J. Chem. Eng. Data **21**, 428 (1976).

76HOP/BOS
H.P. Hopkins, Jr., D. Bostwick and C.J. Alexander, J. Am. Chem. Soc. **98**, 1355 (1976).

76HOP/WAH
D.G. Hopper, A.C. Wahl, R.L.C. Wu and T.O. Tiernan, "Theoretical and Experimental Studies of the N_2O^- and N_2O Ground State Potential Energy Surface. Implications for the $O^- + N_2 \rightarrow N_2O + e^-$ and Other Processes," J. Chem. Phys. **65**, 5474 (1976).

76HUB/KLE
M.M. Hubers, A.W. Kleyn and J. Los, "Ion Pair Formation in Alkali-Halogen Collisions at High Velocities," Chem. Phys. **17**, 303 (1976).

76JEN
J.L. Jensen, Prog. Phys. Org. Chem. **12**, 189 (1976).

76KAR/KLE
Z. Karpas and F.S. Klein, "ICR Study of the Gas Phase Ion Chemistry of the Carbonyl Halides: Cl_2CO, F_2CO and $ClFCO$," Int. J. Mass Spectrom. Ion Phys. **22**, 189 (1976).

76KEB
P. Kebarle, "Ion Thermochemistry and Solvation from Gas Phase Ion Equilibria," Ann. Rev. Phys. Chem. **28**, 445 (1977).

76LIA/AUS
S.G. Lias, P. Ausloos and Z. Horvath, "Charge Transfer Reactions in Alkane and Cycloalkane Systems. Estimated Ionization Potentials," Int. J. Chem. Kinet. **8**, 725 (1976).

76LIN
H.J. Lindner, Tetrahedron **32**, 753 (1976).

76LOS/TRA
F.P. Lossing and J.C. Traeger, Int. J. Mass Spectrom. Ion Phys. **19**, 9 (1976).

76LYO/PAL
L.E. Lyons and L.D. Palmer, "The Electron Affinity of Tetracyanoethylene and Other Organic Electron Acceptors," Aust. J. Chem. **29**, 1919 (1976).

76MAC/HEM
G.J. MacKay, R.S. Hemsworth and D.K. Bohme, "Absolute Gas-Phase Acidities of CH_3NH_2, $C_2H_5NH_2$, $(CH_3)_2NH$, and $(CH_3)_3N$," Can. J. Chem. **54**, 1624 (1976).

76MAS
H. Massey, "Negative Ions," 3rd. Ed., Cambridge Univ. Press, 1976.

76MAT/ROT
B.P. Mathur, E.W. Rothe, S.Y. Tang and G.P Reck, "Negative Ions from Phosphorus Halides Due to Cesium Charge Exchange," J. Chem. Phys. **64**, 565 (1976).

76MAT/ROT2
B.P. Mathur, E.W. Rothe, S.Y. Tang, K. Mahajan and G.P. Reck, "Negative Gaseous Ions from Nitric Acid," J. Chem. Phys. **64**, 1247 (1976).

76MAU/SOL
M. Mautner (Meot-Ner), J.J. Solomon and F.H. Field, "Stability of Some C_7 Tertiary Carbonium Ions," J. Am. Chem. Soc. **98**, 1025 (1976).

76MEG/MOO
W.F. Meggers and C.E. Moore, "The First Spectrum of Hafnium (Hf I)," Nat. Bur. Stand. (U.S) Monogr. 153 (1976).

76MEY/HOT
E.F. Meyer and C.A. Hotz, J. Chem. Eng. Data **21**, 274 (1976).

76MOS/COS
J.T. Moseley, P.C. Cosby and J.R. Peterson, "Photodissociation Spectroscopy of CO_3^-," J. Chem. Phys. **65**, 2512 (1976).

76MUR/BEA
M.K. Murphy and J.L. Beauchamp, "Acid-Base Properties and Gas-Phase Ion Chemistry of $(CH_3)_3B$," J. Am. Chem. Soc. **98**, 1433 (1976).

76NUG/WU
W.A. Nugent, M.M.-H. Wu, T.P. Fehlner and J.K. Kochi, "Enhanced Reactivity of exo-Norbornyl Derivatives. Evidence for σ-Participation in the Absence of Steric Effects," J. Chem. Soc. Chem. Commun. 456 (1976).

76PAB/BEN
R.E. Pabst, S.L. Bennett, J.L. Franklin and J.L. Margrave, "Negative Ion Electron Impact Studies of Arsenic Trihalides: AsF_3, $AsCl_3$, and $AsBr_3$," J. Chem. Phys. **64**, 1550 (1976).

76PAL/KEN
M.H. Palmer and S.M.F. Kennedy, J. Chem. Soc. Perkin II 81 (1976).

76PAY/TAN
J.D. Payzant, K. Tanaka, K.D. Betowski and D.K. Bohme, "Gas Phase S_N2 Reactions at Silicon and Carbon Centers. An Experimental Appraisal of Theory," J. Am. Chem. Soc. **98**, 894 (1976).

76POP
D. Poppinger, Aust. J. Chem. **29**, 465 (1976).

76REF
K.M.A. Refaey, "Endoergic Ion-Molecule-Collision Processes of Negative Ions. II. Collisions of I^- on H_2S, CS_2, and COS," J. Chem. Phys. **65**, 2002 (1976).

76REF2
K.M.A. Refaey, "Endoergic Ion-Molecule-Collision Processes of Negative Ions. IV. Collisions of I^- on NO_2, N_2O and NO," Int. J. Mass Spectrom. Ion Phys. **21**, 21 (1976).

76REF/FRA
K.M.A. Refaey and J.L. Franklin, "Endoergic Ion-Molecule-Collision Processes of Negative Ions. V. Collision of I^- on HNO_3. The Electron Affinity of NO_3," J. Chem. Phys. **64**, 4810 (1976).

76REF/FRA2
K.M.A. Refaey and J.L. Franklin, "Endoergic Ion-Molecule-Collision Processes of Negative Ions. I. Collision of I^- on SO_2," J. Chem. Phys. **65**, 1994 (1976).

76REF/FRA3
K.M.A. Refaey and J.L. Franklin, "Endoergic Ion-Molecule-Collision Processes of Negative Ions, III. Collisions of I^- on O_2, CO and CO_2," Int. J. Mass Spectrom. Ion Phys. **20**, 19 (1976).

76ROD/CHA
H.J. Rodriguez, J.-C. Chang and T.F. Thomas, J. Am. Chem. Soc. **98**, 2027 (1976).

76ROS
F.D. Rossini, J. Chem. Thermodyn. **87**, 651 (1976).

76SHE/ILJ
V.E. Shevchenko, M.K. Iljin, O.K. Nikitin and L.N. Sidorov, "Mass Spectrometric Study of Mixed Dimers M_2BO_2F," Int. J. Mass Spectrom. Ion Phys. **21**, 279 (1976).

76SOL/FIE
J.J. Solomon and F.H. Field, "Reversible Reactions of Gaseous Ions. X. The Intrinsic Stability of the Norbornyl Cation," J. Am. Chem. Soc. **98**, 1567 (1976).

76SOL/MAY
R.W. Solarz, C.A. May, L.R. Carlson, E.F. Worden, S.A. Johnson, J.A. Paisner and L.J. Radziemski, Jr., Phys. Ref. **A14**, 1129 (1976).

76SUL/BEA
S.A. Sullivan and J.L. Beauchamp, "Competition Between Proton Transfer and Elimination in the Reactions of Strong Bases with Fluoroethanes in the Gas Phase. Influence of Base Strength on Reactivity," J. Am. Chem. Soc. **98**, 1160 (1976).

76TAN/MAT
S.Y. Tang, B.P. Mathur, E.W. Roth and G.P. Reck, "Negative Ion Formation in Halocarbons by Charge Exchange with Cesium," J. Chem. Phys. **64**, 1270 (1976).

76WHA/WEI
D.L. Whalen, J.F. Weimaster, A.M. Ross and R. Radhe, J. Am. Chem. Soc. **98**, 7319 (1976).

76WIL/LEB
A.D. Williamson, P.R. LeBreton and J.L. Beauchamp, J. Am. Chem. Soc. **98**, 2705 (1976).

76ZIT/ELL
P.F. Zittel, G.B. Ellison, S.V. O'Neil, E. Herbst, W.C. Lineberger and W.P. Reinhardt, "Laser Photoelectron Spectrometry of CH_2^-. Singlet-Triplet Splitting and Electron Affinity of CH_2^1," J. Am. Chem. Soc. **98**, 3731 (1976).

76ZIT/LIN
P.F. Zittel and W.C. Lineberger, "Laser Photoelectron Spectrometry of PO^-, PH^-, and PH_2^-," J. Chem. Phys. **65**, 1236 (1976).

77ALL/KLO
M. Allan, E. Kloster-Jensen and J.P. Maier, "Emission Spectra of $Cl-C\equiv C-H^+$, $Br-C\equiv C-H^+$ and $I-C\equiv C-H^+$ Radical Cations: $A^2\Pi \to X^2\Pi$ Band Systems and the Decay of the $A^2\Pi$ States," J. Chem. Soc., Faraday Trans. II **73**, 1406 (1977).

77ARM/HOD
P. Armentrout, R. Hodges and J.L. Beauchamp, "Metal Atoms as Superbases: The Gas Phase Proton Affinity of Uranium," J. Am. Chem. Soc. **99**, 3162 (1977).

77ARN/CHA
E.M. Arnett, B. Chawla, L. Bell, M. Taagepera, W.J. Hehre and R.W. Taft, "Solvation and Hydrogen Bonding of Pyridinium Ions," J. Am. Chem. Soc. **99**, 5729 (1977).

77ASH/BUR
F.S. Ashmore and A.R. Burgess, "Study of Some Medium Size Alcohols and Hydroperoxides by Photoelectron Spectroscopy," J. Chem. Soc., Faraday Trans. II **73**, 1247 (1977).

77BAG/COL
M.H. Baghal-Vayjooee, J.L. Collister and H.O. Pritchard, Can. J. Chem. **55**, 2634 (1977).

77BEC/LIP
K.H. Becker, H. Lippmann and U. Schurath, Ber. Bunsenges. Phys. Chem. **81**, 567 (1977).

77BIE/BUR
G. Bieri, F. Burger, E. Heilbronner and J.P. Maier, "Valence Ionization Energies of Hydrocarbons," Helv. Chim. Acta **60**, 2213 (1977).

77BIE/DEP
V.M. Bierbaum, C.H. DePuy and R.J. Shapiro, "Gas Phase Reactions of Anions with Nitrous Oxide and Carbon Dioxide," J. Am. Chem. Soc. **99**, 5800 (1977).

77CAR/LAY
J.A.S. Carson, P.G. Laye and M. Yureali, J. Chem. Thermodyn. **9**, 827 (1977).

77CIM/PER
R. Cimiraglia, M. Persico and J. Tomasi, J. Phys. Chem. **81**, 1876 (1977).

77COM
R.N. Compton, "On the Formation of Positive and Negative Ions in Gaseous UF_6," J. Chem. Phys. **66**, 4478 (1977).

77COM/COO
R.N. Compton and C.D. Cooper, "Negative Ion Properties of Tetracyanoquinodimethane: Electron Affinity and Compound States," J. Chem. Phys. **66**, 4325 (1977).

77COW/GOO
A.H. Cowley, D.W. Goodman, N.A. Kuebler, M. Sanchez and J.G. Verkade, "Molecular Photoelectron Spectroscopic Investigation of Some Caged Phosphorus Compounds and Related Acyclic Species," Inorg. Chem. **16**, 854 (1977).

77CUM/FRE
J.B. Cummings, M.A. French and P. Kebarle, "Effect of Charge Delocalization on Hydrogen Bonding to Negative Ions and Solvation of Negative Ions. Substituted Phenols and Phenoxide Ions," J. Am. Chem. Soc. **99**, 6999 (1977).

77DAV/FEH
J.A. Davidson, F.C. Fehsenfeld and C.J. Howard, "The Heats of Formation of NO_3^- and NO_3^- Association Complexes with HNO_3 and HBr," Int. J. Chem. Kinet. **9**, 17 (1977).

77DAW/JEN
J.H.J. Dawson and K.R. Jennings, "Relative Gas Phase Acidities of Some Fluoroalcohols," Int. J. Mass Spectrom. Ion Phys. **25**, 47 (1977).

77DEW/NEU
R. De Wall and H. Neuert, "Die Bildung Negativer Ionen bei Elektronenstoss auf WF_6," Z. Naturfor. **32A**, 1968 (1977).

77DIS/LAC
H. Dispert and K. Lacmann, "Formation of WF_6^- and Its Dissociative Products by Collisional Ionization," Chem Phys. Lett. **45**, 311 (1977).

77DIS/LAC2
H. Dispert and K. Lacmann, "Chemiionization in Alkali-Halogen Reactions: Evidence for Ion Formation By Alkali Dimers," Chem. Phys. Lett. **47**, 533 (1977).

77DON/WAL
A.M. Doncaster and R. Walsh, "Kinetic Determination of the BDE $D(Me_3Ge-H)$ and Its Implication for Bond Strengths in Germanes," J. Chem. Soc. Chem. Comm. 446 (1977).

77DOT/DAV
I. Dotan, J.A. Davidson, G.E. Streit, D.L. Albritton and F.C. Fehsenfeld, "A Study of the Reaction $O_3^- + CO_2 = CO_3^- + O_2$ and Its Implication on the Thermochemistry of CO_3 and O_3 and Their Negative Ions," J. Chem. Phys. **67**, 2874 (1977).

77DUR/PAR
M. Durup, G. Parlant, J. Appell, J. Durup and J.-B. Ozenne, "Translational Spectroscopy of Neutralization-Reionization Double Collision Processes of Ar^+ Ions at keV Energies," Chem. Phys. **25**, 245 (1977).

77EFR/HUA
A. Efraty, M.H.A. Huang and C.A. Weston, "Mass Spectra of Organometallic Compounds. 4. Electron-Impact Study of Some Cyclopentadienylmetal Carbonyl Dimers," Inorg. Chem. **16**, 79 (1977).

77EHL/WAN
T.C. Ehlert and J.S. Wang, "Thermochemistry of the Copper Fluorides," J. Phys. Chem. **81**, 2069 (1977).

77ENG/LIN
P.C. Engelking and W.C. Lineberger, "Laser Photoelecton Spectrometry of FeO^-: Electron Affinity, Electronic State Separations, and Ground State Vibrations of Iron Oxide, and a New Ground State Assignment," J. Chem. Phys. **66**, 5054 (1977).

77ENG/LIN2
P.C. Engelking and W.C. Lineberger, "Laser Photoelectron Spectrometry of $C_5H_5^-$: A Determination of the Electron Affinity and Jahn-Teller Coupling in Cyclopentadienyl," J. Chem. Phys. **67**, 1412 (1977).

77FEL/RAC
D. Feldman, R. Rackwitz, H.J. Kaiser and E. Heincke, "Photodetachment bei einigen Neagtiven Molekulionen: P_2^-, As_2^-, CH_2^-, CH_3^-, S_3^-," Z. Naturfor. **32A**, 600 (1977).

77FIN/GAT
A. Finch, P.N. Gates and S.J. Peake, "Thermochemistry of Polyhalides. III. Cesium and Rubidium Tetrachloroiodates," J. Inorg. Nucl. Chem. **39**, 2135 (1977).

77FRO/MCD
D.C. Frost, C.A. McDowell and N.P.C. Westwood, "The Photoelectron Spectrum of Formyl Chloride," Chem. Phys. Lett. **51**, 607 (1977).

77HAR
P.W. Harland, "Electron Attachment to the Stable Free Radical Bis-trifluoromethylnitroxide in the Gas Phase," Int. J. Mass Spectrom. Ion Phys. **25**, 61 (1977).

77HIL
D.L. Hildebrand, "Studies of Some Negative Ion Processes Involving the Tungsten Fluorides," Int. J. Mass Spectrom. Ion Phys. **25**, 121 (1977).

77HIR/KEB
K. Hiraoka and P. Kebarle, "Condensation Reactions Involving Carbonium Ions in the Gas Phase Synthesis of Protonated Acids in Gaseous Methane Containing Carbon Monoxide and Water Vapor," J. Am. Chem. Soc. **99**, 366 (1977).

77HON/WOO
S.P. Hong, S.B. Woo and E.M. Helmy, "Photodetachment of Thermally Relaxed CO_3^-," Phys. Rev. A **15**, 1563 (1977).

77KAN/MOR
A.S. Kana'an and T.I. Morrison, J. Chem. Thermodyn. **9**, 423 (1977).

77KAR/JAD
L. Karlsson, R. Jadrny, L. Mattsson, F.T. Chau and K. Siegbahn, Phys. Scr. **16**, 225 (1977).

77KAR/KLE
Z. Karpas and F.S. Klein, "The Gas Phase Ion Chemistry of Carbonyl Compounds: Formyl Fluoride and a Binary Mixture of H_2CO-F_2CO or H_2CO-Cl_2CO," Int. J. Mass Spectrom. Ion Phys. **24**, 137 (1977).

77KOZ/BYC
M.P. Kozina, L.V. Bychikhina and G.L. Gal'chenko, Russ. J. Phys. Chem. **51**, 1258 (1977).

77KRE/PRI
M.J. Krech, S.J.W. Price and H.P. Sapiano, Can. J. Chem. **55**, 4222 (1977).

77KRI/TIT
N.V. Krivtsov, K.V. Titova, V.Ya. Rosolovskii, "Thermochemical Study of Complex Borates," Russ. J. Inorg. Chem. **22**, 374 (1977).

77KUP/SHI
A.I. Kupreev and G.S. Shimonaev, Russ. J. Phys. Chem. **49**, 1133 (1977).

77LEB/RYA
N.D. Lebedeva, V.L. Ryadnenko, N.N. Kiseleva and L.F. Nazarova, Vses. Konf. Kalorim. (Rasshir. Tezisy Dokl.) 7th, **1**, 91 (1977) (CA 93:75617q (1980).)

77LIA/AUS
S.G. Lias and P. Ausloos, "Ion-Molecule Reactions Involving Halomethyl Ions; Heats of Formation of Halomethyl Ions," Int. J. Mass Spectrom. Ion Phys. **23**, 273 (1977).

77LIU/LOU
M.T.H. Liu, L.F. Loucks and D.G. Hooper, "Pyrolysis of Trifluoroacetaldehyde," Int. J. Chem. Kinet. **9**, 589 (1977).

77MAT/ROT
B.P. Mathur, R.W. Rothe and G.P. Reck, "Ionization Reactions of Metal Hexafluorides with Alkali Atoms and Dimers," J. Chem. Phys. **67**, 377 (1977).

77MCM/KEB
T.B. McMahon and P. Kebarle, "Intrinsic Acidities of Substituted Phenols and Benzoic Acids Determined by Gas Phase Proton Transfer Equilibria," J. Am. Chem. Soc. **99**, 2222 (1977).

77MOF
J.B. Moffat, J. Mol. Struct. **42**, 251 (1977).

77MUR/BEA
M.K. Murphy and J.L. Beauchamp, J. Am. Chem. Soc. **99**, 2085 (1977).

77MUR/BEA2
M.K. Murphy and J.L. Beauchamp, "Fluorine and Alkyl Substituent Effects on Gas-Phase Lewis Acidities of Boranes by ICR Spectroscopy," Inorg. Chem. **16**, 2437 (1977).

77MUR/BEA3
M.K. Murphy and J.L. Beauchamp, "Methyl and Fluorine Substituent Effects on the Gas-Phase Lewis Acidities of Silanes by ICR Spectroscopy," J. Am. Chem. Soc. **99**, 4992 (1977).

77NAB/SAB
M. Nabavian, R. Sabbah, R. Chastel and M. Laffitte, J. Chim. Phys. **74**, 115 (1977).

77NGA/SAB
S.N. Ngauv, R. Sabbah and M. Laffitte, Thermochim. Acta **20**, 371 (1977).

77NUY/MES
O. Nuyken and K. Messmer, "Massenspektrometrische Untersuchungen an Azoverbindungen. II- Ermittlung thermodynamischer Grossen," Org. Mass Spectrom. **12**, 106 (1977).

77OTH/OLS
J.F.M. Oth, J. Olsen and J.P. Snyder, J. Am. Chem. Soc. **99**, 8504 (1977).

77PAB/MAR
R.E. Pabst, J.L. Margrave and J.L. Franklin, "Electron Impact Studies of the Tetrachlorides and Tetrabromides of Silicon and Germanium," Int. J. Mass Spectrom. Ion Phys. **25**, 361 (1977).

77PAB/PER
R.E. Pabst, D.L. Perry, J.L. Margrave and J.L. Franklin, "Electron Impact Studies of Tin Tetrahalides $SnCl_4$, $SnBr_4$ and SnI_4," Int. J. Mass Spectrom. Ion Phys. **24**, 323 (1977).

77PAR/STE
W. Parker, W.V. Steele and I. Watt, J. Chem. Thermodyn. **9**, 307 (1977).

77PED/RYL
J.B. Pedley and J. Rylance, "Sussex-N.P.L. Computer Analysed Thermochemical Data: Organic and Organometallic Compounds," University of Sussex (1977).

77PEL
P.A. Pella, J. Chem. Thermodyn. **9**, 301 (1977).

77PIC/ROD
J.M. Pickard and A.S. Rodgers, Int. J. Chem. Kinet. **9**, 759 (1977).

77POL/HEH
S.K. Pollack and W.J. Hehre, J. Am. Chem. Soc. **99**, 4845 (1977).

77POP/RAD
D. Poppinger, L. Radom and J.A. Pople, J. Am. Chem. Soc. **99**, 7806 (1977).

77PRA/HUB
M.-T. Praet, M.-J. Hubin-Franskin, J.P. Delwiche and R. Schoos, Org. Mass Spectrom. **12**, 297 (1977).

77RAC/FEL
R. Rackwitz, D. Feldman, H.J. Kaiser and E. Heincke, "Photodetachment bei einigen Zweiatomigen Negativen Hydridionen: BeH^-, MgH^-, CaH^-, ZnH^-, PH^-, AsH^-," Z. Naturfor. **32A**, 594 (1977).

77REF/FRA
K.M.A. Refaey and J.L. Franklin, "Endoergic Ion-Molecule Collision Processes of Negative Ions. VI. Collisions of I^- on $(CN)_2$ and NOCl," Int. J. Mass Spectrom. Ion Phys. **23**, 13 (1977).

77REI/PRA
R.C. Reid, J.M. Prausnitz and T.K. Sherwood "The Properties of Gases and Liquids" 3rd Edition, McGraw Hill, New York, (1977).

77ROS/DRA
H.M. Rosenstock, K. Draxl, B.W. Steiner and J.T. Herron, "Energetics of Gaseous Ions," J. Phys. Chem. Ref. Data **6**, Supp. 1 (1977).

77ROS/SOL
P. Rosmus, B. Solouki and H. Bock, "Ground and Excited States of Thioketene Radical Cation, H_2CCS^+," Chem. Phys. **22**, 453 (1977).

77SAB/LAF
R. Sabbah and M. Laffitte, J. Chem. Thermo. **9**, 1107 (1977).

77SAL/YOU
P.P.S. Saluga, T.M. Young, R.F. Rodewald, F.H. Fuchs, D. Kohli and R. Fuchs, J. Am. Chem. Soc. **99**, 2949 (1977).

77SCH/PET
F.W. Schulte, H.-J. Petrick, H.K. Cammenga and H. Klinge, Z. Phys. Chem. (Frankfurt) **107**, 1 (1977).

77SCH/SCH
H. Schmidt, A. Schweig, W. Thiel and M. Jones, Jr., Chem. Ber. **111**, 1958 (1977).

77SHA/GOL
R. Shaw, D.M. Golden and S.W. Benson, J. Phys. Chem. **81**, 1716 (1977).

77SLA/LIN
J. Slater and W.C. Linberger, "High Resolution Photodetachment Study of P^- and Te^-," Phys. Rev. A **15**, 2277 (1977).

77STA/WIE
R.H. Staley, R.D. Wieting and J.L. Beauchamp, "Carbenium Ion Stabilities in the Gas Phase and Solution. An Ion Cyclotron Resonance Study of Bromide Transfer Reactions Involving Alkali Ions, Alkyl Carbenium Ions, Acyl Cations and Cyclic Halonium Ions," J. Am. Chem. Soc. **99**, 5964 (1977).

77STE
W.V. Steele, J. Chem. Thermodyn. **9**, 311 (1977).

77STE/GOL
S.E. Stein, D.M. Golden and S.W. Benson, J. Phys. Chem. **81**, 314 (1977).

77STE/WAT
W.V. Steele and I. Watt, J. Chem. Thermodyn. **9**, 843 (1977).

77SUL
S.A. Sullivan California Institute of Technology Phd. thesis, 1977.

77TEL/RAB
V.I. Tel'noi and I.B. Rabinovich, Russ. Chem. Rev. **46**, 689 (1977).

77VES/MAU
M.L. Vestal and G.H. Mauclaire, "Photodissociaton of Negative Ions Formed in CO_2 and CO_2/O_2 Mixtures," J. Chem. Phys. **67**, 3758 (1977).

77VOG/DRE
D. Vogt, W. Dreves and J. Mischke, "Energy Dependence of Differential Cross Sections in Endoergic Ion-Molecule Collision Processes of Negative Ions," Int. J. Mass Spectrom. Ion Phys. **24**, 285 (1977).

77VOG/MIS
D. Vogt and J. Mischke, "Endoergic Ion-Molecule Collision Processes of Negative Ions in Collisions of I^- on CO," Phys. Lett. **60A**, 19 (1977).

77WU/TIE
R.L.C. Wu, T.O. Tiernan and C. Lifschitz, "A Long-Lived Excited State of O_3^-: Evidence From Collision Induced Dissociation," Chem Phys. Lett. **51**, 211 (1977).

77ZIM/BRA
A.H. Zimmerman and J.I. Brauman, "Electron Photodetachment from Negative Ions of C_{2v} Symmetry. Electron Affinities of Allyl and Cyanomethyl Radicals," J. Am. Chem. Soc. **99**, 3565 (1977).

77ZIM/REE
A.H. Zimmerman, K.J. Reed and J.I. Brauman, "Photodetachment of Electrons from Enolate Anions. Gas Phase Electron Affinities of Enolate Radicals," J. Am. Chem. Soc. **99**, 7203 (1977).

78ADA/VOG
A.W. Adamson, A. Vogler, H. Kunkely and R. Wachter, J. Am. Chem. Soc. **100**, 1298 (1978).

78ARO/STE
M. Arova and W.V. Steele, J. Chem. Thermodyn. **10**, 403 (1978).

78AUS/LIA
P. Ausloos and S.G. Lias, "Reactions of NO_2^+ and Solvated NO_2^+ Ions with Aromatic Compounds and Alkanes," Int. J. Chem. Kinetics **10**, 657 (1978).

78BEA/LEE
P. Beak, J.K. Lee and J.M. Ziegler, J. Org. Chem. **43**, 1536 (1978).

78BEN
S.W. Benson, Chem. Rev. **78**, 23 (1978).

78BIE/JON
G. Bieri and B.-O. Jonsson, "HNC^+ Radical Cation Studied by Charge-Exchange Mass Spectrometry," Chem. Phys. Lett. **56**, 446 (1978).

78BRU/FER
A.P. Bruins, A.J. Ferrer-Correia, A.G. Harrison, K.R. Jennings and R.K. Mithcum, "Negative Ion Chemical Ionization Mass Spectrometry of Some Aromatic Compounds Using $O^-·$ as the Reagent Ion," Adv. Mass Spectrom. **7A**, 355 (1978).

78CAC/LIS
T. Caceres, E.A. Lissi and E. Sanhueza, "Autooxidation of Diethylhydroxylamine," Int. J. Chem. Kinet. **10**, 1167 (1978).

78CEN/FRA
G. Centineo, I. Fragala, G. Bruno and S. Spampinato, "Photoelectron Spectroscopy of Benzophenone, Acetophenone and Their ortho-Alkyl Derivatives," J. Molec. Struct. **44**, 203 (1978).

78CHA/ZWO
J. Chao and B.J. Zwolinski, J. Phys. Chem. Ref. Data **7**, 363 (1978).

78COL/BEN
A.J. Colussi and S.W. Benson, Int. J. Chem. Kinet. **10**, 1139 (1978).

78COL/JIM
M. Colomina, P. Jimenez, M.V. Roux and C. Turrion, J. Chem. Thermodyn. **10**, 661 (1978).

78COM/REI
R.N. Compton, P.W. Reinhardt and C.D. Cooper, "Collisional Ionization between Fast Alkali Atoms and Selected Hexafluoride Molecules," J. Chem. Phys. **68**, 2023 (1978).

78COM/REI2
R.N. Compton, P.W. Reinhardt and C.D. Cooper, "Collisional Ionization Between Alkali Atoms and Some Methane Derivatives: Electron Affinities for CH_3NO_2, CF_3I, and CF_3Br," J. Chem. Phys. **68**, 4360 (1978).

78COO/FRE
C.D. Cooper, W.F. Frey and R.N. Compton, "Negative Ion Properties of Fluoranil, Chloranil, and Bromanil: Electron Affinities," J. Chem. Phys. **69**, 2367 (1978).

78COS/MOS
P.C. Cosby, J.T. Moseley, J.R. Peterson and J.H. Ling, "Photodissociation Spectroscopy of O_3^-," J. Chem. Phys. **69**, 2771 (1978).

78CUM/KEB
J.B. Cumming and P. Kebarle, "Summary of Gas Phase Measurements involving Acids AH. Entropy Changes in Proton Transfer Reactions involving Negative Ions. Bond Dissociation Energies D(A-H) and Electron Affinities EA(A)," Can. J. Chem. **56**, 1 (1978).

78DAB/HER
I. Dabrowski and G. Herzberg, "The Spectrum of $HeNe^+$," J. Molec. Spectrosc. **73**, 183 (1978).

78DAW/NIB
J.H.J. Dawson and N.M.M. Nibbering, "Concerning $CH_2=C^-·$ and Its Reaction with $^{14}N^{15}NO$," J. Am. Chem. Soc. **100**, 1928 (1978).

78DEF/HEH
D.J. DeFrees and W.J. Hehre, J. Phys. Chem. **82**, 391 (1978).

78DEP/BIE
C.H. DePuy, V.M. Bierbaum, R.J. Schmitt and R.H. Shapiro, "Gas Phase Oxidation and Reduction Reactions with $C_6H_7^-$, HNO^-, and HO_2^-," J. Am. Chem. Soc. **100**, 2970 (1978).

78DIS/LAC
H. Dispert and K. Lacmann, "Negative Ion Formation in Collisions between Potassium and Fluoro- and Chloromethanes: Electron Affinities and Bond Dissociation Energies," Int. J. Mass Spectrom. Ion Phys. **28**, 49 (1978).

78DOT/ALB
I. Dotan, D.L. Albritton, F.C. Fehsenfeld, G.E. Streit and E.E. Ferguson, "Rate Constants for the Reactions of O^-, O_2^-, NO_2^-, CO_3^-, and CO_4^- with HCl and ClO^- with NO, NO_2, SO_2, and CO_2 at 300K," J. Chem. Phys. **68**, 5414 (1978).

78DUD/BAL
A.V. Dudin, A.V. Balaev and L.N. Gorokhov, "Mass Spectrometric Study of Tetrafluorohydrazine and the Products Resulting from Its Breakdown Under Electron Impact," Izv. Akad. Nauk SSSR, Ser. Khim. 1306 (1978).

78ELL/ENG
G.B. Ellison, P.C. Engelking and W.C. Lineberger, "An Experimental Determination of the Geometry and Electron Affinity of CH_3," J. Am. Chem. Soc. **100**, 2556 (1978).

78ENG/ELL
P.C. Engleking, G.B. Ellison and W.C. Lineberger, "Laser Photodetachment Electron Spectrometry of Methoxide, Deuteromethoxide, and Thiomethoxide: Electron Affinities and Vibrational Structure of CH_3O, and CH_3S," J. Chem. Phys. **69**, 1826 (1978).

78FU/DUN
E.W. Fu and R.C. Dunbar, "Photodissociation Spectroscopy and Structural Rearrangements in Ions of Cyclooctatetraene, Styrene and Related Molecules," J. Am. Chem. Soc. **100**, 2283 (1978).

78GAL/FAI
S.E. Galembeck, J.F.G. Faigle and J.M. Riveros, An. Acad. Brasil Cienc. **50**, 1 (1978).

78GAN/PEE
T.H. Gan, J.B. Peel and G.D. Willett, "Photoelectron Spectra of the Gauche and Trans Conformers of 1,2-Dibromoethane," J. Molec. Struct. **44**, 211 (1978).

78GRE/LIE
A. Greenberg and J.F. Liebman, "Strained Organic Molecules" (Academic Press, New York, 1978).

78GUN/HEA
H.A. Gundry and A.J. Head, J. Chem. Thermodyn. **10**, 195 (1978).

78HAR/HEA
D. Harrop and A.J. Head, J. Chem. Thermodyn. **10**, 705 (1978).

78HAV/MON
J.J. Havel, R.L. Montgomery, C.-C. Lau and M. Grissom, J. Chem. Eng. Data **23**, 132 (1978).

78HEA/HEF
G.A. Heath, G.T. Hefter and W.V. Steele, J. Chem. Thermodyn. **10**, 395 (1978).

78HER/SCH
A. Herrmann, E. Schumacher and L. Woste, "Preparation and Photoionization Potentials of Molecules of Sodium, Potassium and Mixed Atoms," J. Chem. Phys. **68**, 2327 (1978).

78JANAF
M.W. Chase, J.L. Curnutt, R.A. McDonald and A.N. Syverud, "JANAF Thermochemical Tables, 1978 Supplement," J. Phys. Chem. Ref. Data **7**, 793 (1978).

78JAN/ZIM
B.K. Janousek, A.H. Zimmerman, K.J. Reed and J.I. Brauman, "Electron Detachment from Aliphatic Molecular Anions. Gas Phase Electron Affinites of Methoxyl, tert-Butoxyl, and Neopentoxyl Radicals," J. Am. Chem. Soc. 100, 6142 (1978).

78JOH/RAD
I.G. John and L. Radom, J. Am. Chem. Soc. 100, 3981 (1978).

78JOR/BUR
K.D. Jordan and P.D. Burrow, "Studies of the Temporary Anion States of Unsaturated Hydrocarbons by Electron Transmission Spectroscopy," Acc. Chem. Res. 11, 341 (1978).

78KAO/RAD
J. Kao and L. Radom, J. Am. Chem. Soc. 100, 760 (1978).

78KIM/WIN
K.Y. Kim, R.E. Winans, W.N. Hubbard and C.E. Johnson, J. Phys. Chem. 82, 402 (1978).

78KUD/KUD
S.A. Kudchadker, A.P. Kudchadker, R.C. Wilhoit and B.J. Zwolinski, J. Phys. Chem. Ref. Data 7, 417 (1978).

78KUD/KUD2
S.A. Kudchadker and A.P. Kudchadker, J. Phys. Chem. Ref. Data 7, 1285 (1978).

78LEB/TSV
B.V. Lebedev, L.Y. Tsvetkova and I.B. Rabinovich, J. Chem. Thermodyn. 10, 809 (1978).

78LEU/WIR
W. Leupin and J. Wirz, Helv. Chim. Acta 61, 1663 (1978).

78LIA/AUS
S.G. Lias and P. Ausloos, "Ionization Energies of Organic Compounds by Equilibrium Measurements," J. Am. Chem. Soc. 100, 6027 (1978).

78LIF/WU
C. Lifshitz, R.L.C. Wu, T.O. Tiernan and T.E. Terwilliger, "Negative Ion-Molecule Reactions of Ozone and Their Implications on the Thermochemistry of O_2^-," J. Chem. Phys. 68, 247 (1978).

78LUC/WLO
Z. Luczynski, S. Wlodek and H. Wincel, "Stabilities of $HCOO^- \cdot (HCOOH)_n$ and $Cl^- \cdot (HCOOH)_n$ Clusters," Int. J. Mass Spectrom. Ion Phys. 26, 103 (1978).

78MAC/BOH
G.I. MacKay and D.K. Bohme, "Proton-Transfer Reactions in Nitromethane at 297K," Int. J. Mass Spectrom. Ion Phys. 26, 327 (1978).

78MAC/BOH2
G.I. Mackay and D.K. Bohme, "Bridging the Gap Between the Gas Phase and Solution: Transition in the Relative Acidity of Water and Methanol at 296±2 K," J. Am. Chem. Soc. 100, 327 (1978).

78MAC/LIE
G.I. Mackay, M.H. Lien, A.C. Hopkinson and D.K. Bohme, "Experimental and Theoretical Studies of Proton Removal from Propene," Can. J. Chem. 56, 131 (1978).

78MAR/SCH
H.-D. Martin, H.-J. Schiwek, J. Spanget-Larsen and R. Gleiter, "Synthese, spektroskopische Eigenschaften und transannulare Wechselwirkungen tricyclischer 1,2-Cyclobutandione," Chem. Ber. 111, 2557 (1978).

78MCC/FRE
D.A. McCrery and B.S. Freiser, "Gas Phase Photodissociation of $C_7H_7^+$," J. Am. Chem. Soc. 100, 2902 (1978).

78MCC/HAM
D.G. McCormick and W.S. Hamilton, J. Chem. Thermodyn. 10, 275 (1978).

78MCM/NOR
T.B. McMahon and C.J. Northcott, "The Fluoroformate Ion FCO_2^-: An ICR Study of the Gas Phase Lewis Acidity of Carbon Dioxide and Related Isoelectronic Species," Can. J. Chem. 56, 1068 (1978).

78MOF
J.B. Moffat, J. Mol. Struct. 44, 637 (1978).

78MON/ROS
R.L. Montgomery and F.D. Rossini, J. Chem. Eng. Data 23, 125 (1978).

78OLS/HOW
J.F. Olsen and J.M. Howell, Theor. Chim. Acta 47, 39 (1978).

78OSB/SCO
A.G. Osborn and D.W. Scott, J. Chem. Thermodyn. 10, 619 (1978).

78PAB/MAR
R.E. Pabst, J.L. Margrave and J.L. Franklin, "Energy Distribution in the Products of Ionic Decomposition," Adv. Mass Spectrom. 7B, 1217 (1978).

78PAL/KEN
M.H. Palmer and S.M.F. Kennedy, J. Mol. Struct. 43, 203 (1978).

78PAP/KOL
T.S. Papina and V.P Kolesov, Vestn. Mosk. Univ. Ser. 2 Khim. 19, 500 (1978).

78PAU/KIM
J.K. Pau, J.K. Kim and M.C. Caserio, "Mechanisms of Ionic Reactions in the Gas Phase. Displacement Reactions at Carbonyl Carbon," J. Am. Chem. Soc. 100, 3831 (1978).

78POP/RAD
D. Poppinger and L. Radom, J. Am. Chem. Soc. 100, 3674 (1978).

78RAI/MOO
L.J. Rains, H.E. Moore and R.T. McIver, Jr., "Equilibrium Electron-Transfer Reactions in the Gas Phase Involving Long-Lived Negative Ion Radicals," J. Chem. Phys. 68, 3309 (1978).

78REF/FRA
K.M.A. Refaey and J.L. Franklin, "Collisional Decomposition of SF_6^-," Int. J. Mass Spectrom. Ion Phys. 26, 125 (1978).

78ROB/WIN
B.P. Roberts and J.N. Winter, "Generation and Some Reactions of the Bis(trimethylsilyl)aminyl Radical," Chem. Comm. 545 (1978).

78ROG/VON
D.W. Rogers, H. von Voithenberg and N.L. Allinger, J. Org. Chem. 43, 360 (1978) and personal communication from D.W. Rogers to the authors.

78ROT/BIE
W.R. Roth, M. Biermann, H. Dekker, R. Jochem, C. Mosselman and H. Hermann, Chem. Ber. 111, 3872 (1978).

78SAB/LAF
R. Sabbah and M. Laffitte, J. Chem. Thermodyn. 10, 101 (1978).

78SAB/LAF2
R. Sabbah and M. Laffitte, Bull. Soc. Chim. Fr. 1, 50 (1978).

78SAB/LAF3
R. Sabbah and M. Laffitte, Thermochim. Acta 23, 196 (1978).

78SEL/STR
P. Sellers, G. Stridh and S. Sunner, J. Chem. Eng. Data 23, 3 (1978).

78SEL/STR2
P. Sellers, G. Stridh and S. Sunner, J. Chem. Eng. Data 23, 250 (1978).

78SHA
R. Shaw, "The Chemistry of the Carbon-Carbon Triple Bond" Part 1 (ed. S. Patai, John Wiley & Sons, New York, 1978).

78SMI/LEE
G.P. Smith, L.C. Lee, P.C. Cosby, J.R. Peterson and J.T. Moseley, "Photodissociation and Photodetachment of Molecular Negative Ions. V. Atmospheric Ions from 7000 to 8400 A[a]," J. Chem. Phys. 68, 3818 (1978).

78STE
W.V. Steele, J. Chem. Thermodyn. 10, 441 (1978).

78STE2
W.V. Steele, J. Chem. Thermodyn. **10**, 445 (1978).
78STE3
W.V. Steele, J. Chem. Thermodyn. **10**, 585 (1978).
78SUL/BEA
S.A. Sullivan and J.L. Beauchamp, "Nucleophilic Reactions of Anions with PF_3 and OPF_3 in the Gas Phase by ICR Spectroscopy," Inorg. Chem **17**, 1589 (1978).
78SUL/BEA2
S.A. Sullivan and J.L. Beauchamp, "Positive and Negative Ion Chemistry of Sulfuryl Halides," Int. J. Mass Spectrom. Ion Phys. **28**, 69 (1978).
78TAF/TAA
R.W. Taft, M. Taagepera, J.L.M. Abboud, J.F. Wolf, D.J. DeFrees, W.J. Hehre, J.E. Bartmess and R.T. McIver, Jr., "Regarding the Separation of Polarizability and Inductive Effects in Gas- and Solution-Phase Proton Transfer Equilibria," J. Am. Chem. Soc. **100**, 7765 (1978).
78TIE/WU
T.O. Tiernan and R.L.C. Wu, "Thermochemical Data for Molecular Negative Ions from Collisional Dissociation Thresholds," Adv. Mass Spectrom. **7A**, 136 (1978).
78TPIS
L.V. Gurvich, I.V. Veits, V.A. Medvedev, G.A. Khachkuruzov, V.S. Yungman and G.A. Bergman, et. al., "Termodinamicheskie Svoistva Individual'nykh Veshchestv" (Thermodynamic Properties of Individual Substances); Glushko, V.P., gen. ed., Vol. 1, parts 1 and 2 (1978).
78TRA/MCL
J.C. Traeger and R.G. McLoughlin, "A Photoionization Study of the Energetics of $C_7H_7^+$ Ion Formed from C_7H_8 Precursors," Int. J. Mass Spectrom. Ion Phys. **27**, 319 (1978).
78TRC
Selected Values of Properties of Chemical Compounds. Thermodynamic Research Center, Texas A & M (Table compiled 1978).
78VAN/OSK
H. Van Dam and A. Oskam, "He(I) and He(II) Photoelectron Spectra of Some Substituted Ethylenes," J. Electron Spectrosc. Rel. Phenom. **13**, 273 (1978).
78VOG/WIL
J. Vogt, A.D. Williamson and J.L. Beauchamp, J. Am. Chem. Soc. **100**, 3478 (1978).
78ZAB/BEN
F. Zabel, S.W. Benson and D.M. Golden, Int. J. Chem. Kinet. **10**, 295 (1978).
78ZIM/GYG
A.H. Zimmerman, R. Gygax and J.I. Brauman, "Electron Photodetachment Spectroscopy of Polyene Anions. Electron Affinities of Pentadienyl and Heptatrienyl Radicals," J. Am. Chem. Soc. **100**, 5595 (1978).
78ZIM/JAC
A.H. Zimmerman, R.L. Jackson, B.K. Janousek and J.J. Brauman, "Electron Photodetachment from Cyclic Enolate Anions in the Gas Phase: Electron Affinities of Cyclic Enolate Radicals," J. Am. Chem. Soc. **100**, 4674 (1978).
79ADE/CAV
F.A. Adedeji, K.J. Cavell, S. Cavell, J.A. Connor, H.A. Skinner and M.T. Zafarani-Moattar, J. Chem. Soc. Faraday Trans. I **75**, 603 (1979).
79AND/KOL
G.M. Anderson, III, P.A. Kollman, L.N. Domelsmith and K.N. Houk, J. Am. Chem. Soc. **101**, 2344 (1979).
79AUE/BOW
D.H. Aue and M.T. Bowers, "Stabilities of Positive Ions from Equilibrium Gas-Phase Basicity Measurements,"in "Gas Phase Ion Chemistry," M.T. Bowers Editor, Vol. 2, pp. 1-51 Academic Press, New York (1979).

79BAG/NIK
N.V. Bagarat'yan and O.T. Nikitin, "Electron Ionization of Vapor over Boron Oxide," Vest. Mosk. Univ. Khim. **34**, 539 (1979).
79BAR/MCI
J.E. Bartmess and R.T. McIver, Jr., "The Gas Phase Acidity Scale," in "Gas Phase Ion Chemistry," V. 2, M.T. Bowers, Ed., Academic Press, NY, 1979, Ch. 11.
79BAR/SCO
J.E. Bartmess, J.A. Scott and R.T. McIver, Jr., "The Gas Phase Acidity Scale from Methanol to Phenol," J. Am. Chem. Soc. **101**, 6047 (1979).
79BRE/ENG
E.J. Bredford and F. Engelke, J. Chem. Phys. **71**, 1994 (1979).
79BUC/VOG
U. Buchler and J. Vogt, Org. Mass Spectrom. **14**, 503 (1979).
79BYK/ELI
H.J. Byker, I. Eliezer, R.C. Howard and T.C. Ehlert, High Temp. Sci. **11**, 153 (1979).
79CAR/MOU
P. Carlier and G. Mouvier, "Etude par Spectrometrie de Photoelectrons de la Structure Electronique des Ynals et des Ynones Conjugues," J. Electron Spectrosc. Rel. Phenom. **17**, 169 (1979).
79CLA/KNO
T. Clark, T. McO. Knox, M.A. McKervey, H. Mackle, J.J. Rooney, J. Am. Chem. Soc. **101**, 2404 (1979).
79CLA/SCH
E. Clar and W. Schmidt, "Correlations between Photoelectron and UV Absorption Spectra of Polycyclic Hydrocarbons. The Pyrene Series," Tetrahedron **35**, 1027 (1979).
79COR
M. Corval, "Elimination sous Impact Electronique de HCN et H a partir de l'Indole. Comparaison avec l'Indolizine," Org. Mass Spectrom. **14**, 213 (1979).
79COR/ENG
R.R. Corderman, P.C. Engelking and W.C. Lineberger, "Laser Photoelectron Spectrometry of Co^- and Ni^-," J. Chem. Phys. **70**, 4474 (1979).
79DAW/NOE
J.H.J. Dawson, A.J. Noest and N.M.M. Nibbering, "The Gas Phase Allyl Anion," Int. J. Mass Spectrom. Ion Phys. **29**, 205 (1979).
79DAW/NOE2
J.H.J. Dawson, A.J. Noest and N.M.M. Nibbering, "1,1 and 1,3 Eliminations of Water from the Reaction Complex of $O^-\cdot$ with 1,1,1,-Trideuterioacetone," Int. J. Mass Spectrom. Ion Phys. **30**, 189 (1979).
79DEK/OON
C.G. DeKruif and H.A.J. Oonk, J. Chem. Thermodyn. **11**, 2877 (1979).
79DEK/VOO
C.G. DeKruif, J. Voogd and J.C.A. Offringa, J. Chem. Thermodyn. **11**, 651 (1979).
79DEL
J.E. Del Bene, J. Am. Chem. Soc. **101**, 6184 (1979) and personal communication of the results of unpublished ab-initio calculations.
79DEN/VAN
R.J. Dendramas, R.J. Van Zee, W. Weltner, J. Astrophys. **231**, 632 (1979).
79DEV/WIJ
C. De Vrengd, R.W. Wijnaendts van Resandt, J. Los and B. Smith, "Differential Cross Sections for Collisions of Negative Halogen Ions and Alkali Atoms," Chem. Phys. **42**, 305 (1979).
79DEV/WIJ2
C. De Vrengd, R.W. Wijnaendts van Resandt and J. Los, "The Well Depths of XeF^- and $XeCl^-$ from Differential Scattering Measurements," Chem. Phys. Lett. **65**, 93 (1979).
79DIL/GRE
J.D. Dill, A. Greenberg and J.F. Liebman, J. Am. Chem. Soc. **101**, 6814 (1979).

79DIL/MCL
J.D. Dill and F.W. McLafferty, "Collisional Activation and Theoretical Studies of Gaseous CSH_3^+ Ions," J. Am. Chem. Soc. **101**, 6526 (1979).

79DRA/GLA
J.E. Drake, B.M. Glavincevski and K. Gorzelska, "The Photoelectron Spectra of Methylgermane, Trifluoro- and Trichloro-methylgermane," J. Electron Spectrosc. Rel. Phenom. **17**, 73 (1979).

79DRA/GLA2
J.E. Drake, B.M. Glavincevski and K. Gorzelska, "The Photoelectron Spectra of Trimethylgermane, Chloro- and Fluoro-Trimethylgermane," J. Electron Spectrosc. Rel. Phenom. **16**, 331 (1979).

79DUD/BAL
A.V. Dudin, A.V. Baluev and L.N. Gorokhov, "A Mass Spectrometric Investigation of Nitrogen Trifluoride by the Electron Shock Method," Bull. Acad. Sci. USSR, Div. Chem. Sci. (Engl. Trans.) **28**, 1996 (1979).

79DUD/GOR
A.V. Dudin, L.N. Gorokhov and A.V. Balaev, "A Study of the Electron Impact Ionization of Chlorine Trifluoride and Its Decomposition Products by Mass Spectrometry," Izv. Akad. Nauk SSSR, Ser. Khim., 2408 (1979).

79DUN/DYK
S. Dunlavey, J. Dyke, N. Fayad, N. Jonathan and A. Morris, "Vacuum Ultraviolet Photoelectron Spectroscopy of Transient Species. Part 10. The $SH(X_2\Pi i)$ Radical and the $S(^3P)$ Atom," Mol. Phys. **38**, 729 (1979).

79ELL/EAD
M.R. Ellenberger, R.A. Eades, M.W. Thomsen, W.E. Farneth and D.A. Dixon, J. Am. Chem. Soc. **101**, 7151 (1979).

79ENG/LIN
P.C. Engelking and W.C. Lineberger, Phys. Rev. A **19**, 149 (1979).

79ENG/LIN2
P.C. Engelking and W.C. Lineberger, "Laser Photoelectron Spectrometry of the Negative Ions of Iron and Iron Carbonyls. Electron Affinity Determination for the Series $Fe(CO)_n$, n = 0,1,2,3,4," J. Am. Chem. Soc. **101**, 5569 (1979).

79ERA/KOL
P.A. Erastov and V.P. Kolesov, Russ. J. Gen. Chem. **49**, 1186 (1979).

79FUC/PEA
R. Fuchs and L.A. Peacock, Can. J. Chem. **57**, 2302 (1979).

79FUC/PEA2
R. Fuchs and L.A. Peacock, J. Phys. Chem. **83**, 1975 (1979).

79GEO/BEA
P.M. George and J.L. Beauchamp, "The Electron and Fluoride Affinites of Tungsten Hexafluoride by ICR Spectroscopy," Chem. Phys. **36**, 345 (1979).

79GOL/KUL
A.E. Golubitskii, N.S. Kulikov, A.M. Zyakun, V.A. Valovoi, A.M. Alekseev and V.N. Volkov, "Photoionization Mass Spectra of Alicyclic Compounds with Various Substituents, and Their Ionization Energies and Appearance Energies," Izvest. Akad. Nauk SSSR, Seriya Khimicheskaya **11**, 2602 (1979).

79GUS/GOR
A.V. Gusarov, L.N. Gorokhov, A.T. Pyatenko and I.V. Sidorova, "Negative Ions in the Vapors of Inorganic Compounds," Adv. Mass Spectrom. **8A**, 262 (1979).

79GYG/PET
R. Gygax, H.L. Peters and J.I. Brauman, "Photodetachment of Electrons from Anions of High Symmetry. Electron Photodetachment Spectra of the Cycloctatetraenyl and Perinaphthenyl Anions," J. Am. Chem. Soc. **101**, 2567 (1979).

79HA
T.-K. Ha, J. Mol. Struct. **51**, 87 (1979).

79HAC/PIL
J.M. Hacking and G. Pilcher, J. Chem. Thermodyn. **11**, 1015 (1979).

79HOL/LOS
J.L. Holmes and F.P. Lossing, Org. Mass Spectrom. **14**, 572 (1979).

79HOL/TER
J.L. Holmes and J.K. Terlouw, "Structures of $[C_4H_4O]^+$ Ions Produced from 2- and 4-Pyrone," J. Am. Chem. Soc. **101**, 4973 (1979).

79HOU
F.A. Houle Ph. D. Thesis, California Institute of Technology (1979).

79HUB/HER
K.P. Huber and G. Herzberg, "Molecular Spectra and Molecular Structure. IV. Constants of Diatomic Molecules," Van Nostrand Reinhold Co. (1979).

79ILL/SCH
T. Illenberger, H. Scheunemann and H. Baumgartel, "Negative Ion Formation in CF_2Cl_2, CF_3Cl, and $CFCl_3$ Following Low Energy (0-10eV) Impact with Near Monoenergetic Electrons," Chem. Phys. **37**, 21 (1979).

79JAN/BRA
B.K. Janousek, J.I.Brauman and J. Simons, "An Experimental and Theoretical Determination of the Electron Affinity of the Ethynyl Radical HC_2," J. Chem. Phys. **71**, 2057 (1979).

79JAN/BRA2
B. Janousek and J.I. Brauman, "Electron Affinities," in "Gas Phase Ion Chemistry," V. 2, M.T. Bowers, Ed., Academic Press, NY, 1979, Chapter 10.

79JOC/LOH
H.W. Jochims, W. Lohr and H. Baumgartel, "Photoreactions of Small Organic Molecules. VI. Photoionization Processes of Difluoroethylenes," Nouv. J. Chim. **3**, 109 (1979).

79JOS
R.M. Joshi, J. Macromol. Sci. Chem. **A13**, 1015 (1979).

79KAO/RAD
J. Kao and L. Radom, J. Am. Chem. Soc. **101**, 311 (1979).

79KLO/SEP
G. Kloter and K. Sepplet, "Trifluoromethanol (CF_3OH) and Trifluoromethylamine (CF_3NH_2)," J. Am. Chem. Soc. **101**, 347 (1979).

79KUD/KUD
S.A. Kudchadker, A.P. Kudchadker, R.C. Wilhoit and B.J. Zwolinski, Thermochim. Acta **30**, 319 (1979).

79KUD/KUD2
A.P. Kudchadker, S.A. Kudchadker and R.C. Wilhoit, "Four-Ring Condensed Aromatic Compounds," API Monograph 709-79, American Petroleum Institute, Washington, D.C. (1979).

79KUD/KUD3
A.P. Kudchadker and S.A. Kudchadker, "Pyridine and Phenylpyridines," API Monograph 710-79, American Petroleum Institute, Washington, D.C. (1979).

79KUD/KUD4
S.A. Kudchadker, A.P. Kudchadker and B.J. Zwolinski, J. Chem. Thermodyn. **11**, 1051 (1979).

79LEE/POT
E.P.F. Lee and A. W,. Potts, "The HeII α Photoelectron Spectra of the Barium Halides," Chem. Phys. Lett. **63**, 61 (1979).

79LEE/POT2
E.P.F. Lee and A.W. Potts, "An Investigation of the Valence Shell Electronic Structure of Alkaline Earth Halides by Using Ab Initio S. C. F. Calculations and Photoelectron Spectroscopy," Proc. Roy. Soc. Lond. A **365**, 395 (1979).

79LEE/SMI
L.C. Lee, G.P. Smith, J.T. Moseley, P.C. Cosby and J.A. Guest, "Photodissociation and Photodetachment of Cl_2^-, ClO^-, Cl_3^-, and $BrCl_2^-$," J. Chem. Phys. **70**, 3237 (1979).

79LEI
J. Leitch, Int. J. Chem. Kinet. **11**, 1249 (1979).

79MAJ/SVO
V. Majer, V. Svoboda, J. Koubeck and J. Pick, Collect. Czech. Chem. Commun. **44**, 3521 (1979).

79MAR/KUN
H.-D. Martin, M. Kunze and J.D. Beckhaus, Tetrahedron Lett. 3069 (1979).

79MAT/ROT
E.P. Mathur, E.W. Rothe and G.P. Reck, "Negative Ions from the Reactions of Alkalis with $SnCl_4$, $GeCl_4$, and $TiCl_4$," Int. J. Mass Spectrom. Ion Phys. **31**, 77 (1979).

79MCL/TRA
R.G. McLoughlin and J.C. Traeger, "A Photoionization Study of Some Benzoyl Compounds - Thermochemistry of $[C_7H_5O]^+$ Formation," Org. Mass Spectrom. **14**, 434 (1979).

79MIL
W.J. Miller, "The Use of Flames as Media for the Study of Ion-Molecule Thermochemistry," in, "Characterization of High Temperature Vapors and Gases," NBS Spec. Pub. **561/1**, 443 (1979).

79NAZ/POK
V.A. Nazarenko and V.D. Pokhodenko, "The Formation of Negative Ions in High Electric Fields," Int. J. Mass Spectrom. Ion Phys. **31**, 381 (1979).

79NEL/KES
S.F. Nelsen, C.R. Kessel and H.N. Brace, "Twisted and Bent Hydrazine Radical Cations," J. Am. Chem. Soc. **101**, 1874 (1979).

79NIK/SKO
M.I. Nikitin, E.V. Skokan, I.D. Sorokin and L.N. Sidirov, Dokl. Akad. Nauk SSSR **247**, 151 (1979).

79NOV/ENG
S.E. Novich, P.C. Engelking, P.L. Jones, J.H. Futrell and W.C. Lineberger, "Laser Photoelectron, Photodetachment, and Photodestruction Spectra of O_3^-," J. Chem. Phys. **70**, 2652 (1979).

79OLS
J.F. Olsen, J. Mol. Struct. **57**, 245 (1979).

79OSA
E. Osawa, J. Am. Chem. Soc. **101**, 5523 (1979).

79PET/MAJ
L. Petros, V. Majer, J. Koubeck, V. Svoboda and J. Pick, Collect. Czech. Chem. Commun. **44**, 3533 (1979).

79PRI/SAP
S.J.W. Price and H.J. Sapiano, Can. J. Chem. **57**, 685 (1979).

79PRI/SAP2
S.J.W. Price and H.J. Sapiano, Can. J. Chem. **57**, 1468 (1979).

79RAU/ACK
E.G. Rauh and R.J. Ackermann, "The First Ionization Potentials of the Transition Metals," J. Chem. Phys. **70**, 1004 (1979).

79ROB/FRA
R. Robbiani and J.L. Franklin, "Formation of the Trihalide Ion Cl_3^- in the Gas Phase," J. Am. Chem. Soc. **101**, 764 (1979).

79ROB/FRA2
R. Robbiani and J.L. Franklin, "Negative Ion-Molecule Reaction in Sulfuryl Halides," J. Am. Chem. Soc. **101**, 3709 (1979).

79ROG/DAG
D.W. Rogers, O.A. Dagdagan and N.L. Allinger, J. Am. Chem. Soc. **101**, 671 (1979).

79ROS/GOL
M. Rossi and D.M. Golden, "Absolute Rate Constants for the Metathesis Reactions of Allyl and Benzyl Radicals with HI(DI). Heat of Formation of Allyl and Benzyl Radicals," J. Am. Chem. Soc. **101**, 1230 (1979).

79SAB
R. Sabbah, Bull. Soc. Chim. Fr. I-434 (1979).

79SAL/PEA
P.P.S. Saluja, L.A. Peacock and R. Fuchs, J. Am. Chem. Soc. **101**, 1958 (1979).

79SAN/EPS
D.J. Sandman, A.J. Epstein, J.S. Chickos, J. Ketchum and H.A. Scheraga, J. Chem. Phys. **70**, 305 (1979).

79SAU/CHR
I. Sauers, J.G. Christophorou and J.G. Carter, "Electron Attachment to Perfluorocarbon Compounds. III. Fragmentation of Aliphatic Perfluorocarbons of Interest to Gaseous Dielectrics," J. Chem. Phys. **71**, 3016 (1979).

79SCH/BIE
R.J. Schmitt, V.M. Bierbaum and C.H. DePuy, "Gas Phase Reactions of Carbanions with Triplet and Singlet Molecular Oxygen," J. Am. Chem. Soc. **101**, 6443 (1979).

79SCH/GRU
B. Schaldach and H.F. Grutzmacher, "Kinetics Energy Release and Position of the Transition State during the Intramolecular Substitution of Ionized Benzalacetones," Int. J. Mass Spectrom. Ion Phys. **31**, 271 (1979).

79SCH/SCH
R. Schulz and A. Schweig, "Elucidation of Thermal Reactions by Variable Temperature Photoelectron Spectral Detection of Reactive Intermediates. The UV Photoelectron Spectra of Transient Fulveneketene, Fulvenethioketene, a Ketoketene, and Thiobenzpropiolactone," Tetrahedron Lett. 59 (1979).

79SCH/THI
A. Schweig and W. Thiel, J. Am. Chem. Soc. **101**, 4742 (1979).

79SCH/THO
A. Schweig, N. Thon and H. Vermeer, "On the Use of Photoelectron Spectroscopy in Studying Rotational Isomerism in Tetramethyldiphosphine," J. Am. Chem. Soc. **101**, 80 (1979).

79SID/NIK
L.N. Sidirov, M.I. Nikitin and V.M. Korobov, "Determination of the Electron Affinity of Platinum Fluorides and Manganese Tetrafluoride by an Effusion Method," Dokl. Akad. Nauk SSSR, Ser. Khim. **248**, 1387 (1979).

79SMI/LEE
G.P. Smith, L.C. Lee and P.C. Cosby, "Photodissociation and Photodetachment of Molecular Negative Ions. VII. Ions Formed in $CO_2/O_2/H_2O$ Mixtures, 3500-5300 Å," J. Chem. Phys. **71**, 4464 (1979).

79SMI/LEE2
G.P. Smith, L.C. Lee and J.T. Moseley, "Photodissociation and Photodetachment of Molecular Negative Ions. VIII. Nitrogen Oxides and Hydrates, 3500-8250 Å," J. Chem. Phys. **71**, 4034 (1979).

79STE
W.V. Steele, J. Chem. Thermodyn. **11**, 1185 (1979).

79SUN/SVE
S. Sunner, C. Svenson and A.S. Zelepuga, J. Chem. Thermodyn. **11**, 491 (1979).

79TER/BUR
J.K. Terlouw, P.C. Burgers and J.L. Holmes, "Thermochemistry and Generation of Vinylketene," J. Am. Chem. Soc. **101**, 225 (1979).

79TPIS
L.V. Gurvich, I.V. Veits, V.A. Medvedev, G.A. Khachkuruzov, V.S. Yungman and G.A. Bergman, et. al., "Termodinamicheskie Svoistva Individual'nykh Veshchestv" (Thermodynamic Properties of Individual Substances); Glushko, V.P., gen. ed., Vol. 2, parts 1 and 2(1979). Izdatel'stvo"Nauka"Moscow.

79VAJ/HAR
J.H. Vajda and A.G. Harrison, Int. J. Mass Spectrom. Ion Phys. **30**, 293 (1979).

79VIS
D.S. Viswanath, "Quinoline," **API Monograph 711-79**, American Petroleum Institute, Washington, D.C. (1979).

79VIS/WIL
D.S. Viswanath and R.C. Wilhoit, "Isoquinoline," **API Monograph 712-79**, American Petroleum Institute, Washington, D.C. (1979).

79WIB/SQU
K.B. Wiberg and R.R. Squires, J. Chem. Thermodyn. 11, 773 (1979).

79WIB/SQU2
K.B. Wiberg and R.R. Squires, J. Am. Chem. Soc. 101, 5512 (1979).

79WIL/WAT
S.R. Wilson and I.D. Watson, J. Chem. Thermodyn. 11, 911 (1979).

79WOL/HOL
P. Wolkoff and J.L. Holmes, "Isomeric Cyclic $[C_6H_{10}]^+$ Ions. The Energy Barrier to Ring Opening," Can. J. Chem. 57, 348 (1979).

79WOR/KOB
J.C. Wormhoudt and C.E. Kobb, "MS Determination of Negative and Positive Ion Concentrations in Coal Fired MHD Plasmas," in Proc. 10th Materials Res. Symp. on Characterization of High Temp. Vapors," NBS Spec. Pub. No. 561/1, 457 (1979).

79WU/KUD
C.H. Wu, H. Kudo and H.R. Ihle, "Thermochemical Properties of Gaseous Li_3O and Li_2O_2," J. Chem. Phys. 70, 1815 (1979).

80ADE/BOU
P. Adeney, W.J. Bouma, L. Radom and W.R. Rodwell, J. Am. Chem. Soc. 102, 4069 (1980).

80ALI/STE
A.S. Alikhanyan, A.V. Steblevskii, V.B. Lazarev, V.T. Kalinnikov, Y.K. Grinberg, E.G. Zhukov, L.M. Agamirova and V.I. Gorgoraki, "Thermodynamic Properties of Gaseous Arsenic Iodides," Izv. Akad. Nauk SSSR, Neorganisch. Mat. 16, 73 (1980).

80ALL/YUH
N.L. Allinger, Y. Yuh and J.T. Sprague, J. Comput. Chem. 1, 30 (1980).

80AND/BAL
G.D. Andrews, J.E. Baldwin and K.E. Gilbert, J. Org. Chem. 45, 1523 (1980).

80AND/BIC
M.V. Andreocci, P. Bicev, C. Cauletti and M.N. Piancastelli, "The Electronic Structure of the Π-Systems of Acetylenic Oligomers and Related Substances: An UPS Study of Diphenylbutadiyne and Diphenylbutenyne," Gazz. Chim. Ital. 110, 31 (1980).

80AND/BOS
M.V. Andreocci, M. Bossa, V. di Castro, C. Furlani, G. Mattogno and H.W. Roesky, "Electronic Structure of S_3N_2 Ring Derivatives: A Photoelectron Spectroscopy Study," Gazz. Chim. Ital. 110, 1 (1980).

80AND/DEV
M.V. Andreocci, F.A. Devillanova, C. Furlani, G. Mattogno, G. Verani and R. Zanoni, "Structural Characterization of Some Substituted Azolidine Molecules: UPS Photoelectron Spectroscopic Studies," J. Molec. Str. 69, 151 (1980).

80ANN/STO
B.K. Annis and J.A.D. Stockdale, "Internal Excitation of UF_6^- Ions in Collisions with Argon Atoms," Chem. Phys. Lett. 74, 365 (1980).

80ARM/BEA
P.B. Armentrout and J.L. Beauchamp, "Endothermic Reactions of Ni^+ with H_2, HD and D_2," Chem. Phys. 50, 37 (1980).

80ARN/PIE
E.M. Arnett and N.J. Pienta, J. Am. Chem. Soc. 102, 3239 (1980).

80ARS
M.R. Arshadi, J. Chem. Thermodyn. 12, 903 (1980).

80BAC/MOU
M. Bachiri, G. Mouvier, P. Carlier and J.E. Dubois, "Evaluation Quantitative des Effets de Substituants sur les Premiers Potentiels d'Ionisation de Composes Monofonctionnels Aliphatiques," J. Chim. Phys. 77, 899 (1980).

80BAE
T. Baer, "Gas Phase Heats of Formation of $C_2H_5^+$ and $C_3H_7^+$," J. Am. Chem. Soc. 102, 2482 (1980).

80BAL/LEB
A.A. Balepin, V.P. Lebedev, A.A. Kuzsnetsova, K. Venters, M. Trusule, D. Lola and Y.A. Lebedev, Izv. Akad. Nauk. SSSR, Ser. Khim. 848 (1980).

80BAL/NIK
A.V. Baluev, I.M. Nikitin, L.I. Fedorova and V.Ya. Rossolovskii, "Mass Spectrometric Study of Chlorine Pentafluoride Ionization by Electron Impact," Izv. Akad. Nauk SSSR, Ser. Khim., 497 (1980).

80BAL/NIK2
A.V. Baluev, Z.K. Nikitina, L.I. Fedorova and V.Ya. Rosolovskii, "Mass Spectrometric Investigation of Electron-Impact Induced Ionization of Chlorine Dioxide and Chloryl Fluoride Molecules," Izv. Akad. Nauk. SSSR, Ser. Khim. 1963 (1980).

80BAL/PIA
G. Balducci and V. Piacente, "Dissociation Energy of the $Tl_2(g)$ Molecule," J. Chem. Soc. Chem. Comm. 1287 (1980).

80BAR
J.E. Bartmess, "Solvent Effects on Ion-Molecule Reactions. Vinyl Anions vs. Conjugate Addition," J. Am. Chem. Soc. 102, 2483 (1980).

80BAR/STR
A. Barkovich, E.S. Strauss and K.P.C. Vollhardt, Isr. J. Chem. 20, 225 (1980).

80BEN/NAN
S.W. Benson and P.S. Nangia, "Electron Affinity of HO_2· and HO_x Radicals," J. Am. Chem. Soc. 102, 2843 (1980).

80BOC/AYG
H. Bock, S. Aygen, P. Rosmus and B. Solouki, "Analyse und Optimierung von Gasphasen-Reaktionen. XVII. Selenoketen," Chem. Ber. 113, 3187 (1980).

80BOC/KAI
H. Bock, W. Kaim, P.L. Timms and P. Hawker, "Durosemiquinone and its BF Analogue - Detection of 1,4-Diborine as an Unexpected Elimination Product," Chem. Ber. 113, 3196 (1980).

80BOC/STE
H. Bock, U. Stein and A. Semkov, "1,2-Dithiolan - Bindungsmodell fur α-Liponsaure," Chem. Ber. 113, 3208 (1980).

80BOH/CAR
M.C. Bohm, R.V.C. Carr, R. Gleiter and L.A. Paquette, "Electronic Control of Stereoselectivity. 4. Effects of Neighboring Fused Bicyclic Frameworks on the Stereochemical Outcome of Diels-Alder Cycloadditions to Cyclopentadiene Rings," J. Am. Chem. Soc. 102, 7218 (1980).

80BOH/DAU
M.C. Bohm, J. Daub, R. Gleiter, P. Hofmann, M.F. Lappert and K. Ofele, "Die He(I) Photoelektronenspektren von Tetracarbonyleisen(O)-Komplexen mit Carbenen," Chem. Ber. 113, 3629 (1980).

80BOH/GLE
M.C. Bohm and R. Gleiter, "The Electronic Structure and the He(I) Photoelectron Spectrum of Tricarbonylcyclooctatetraene-iron," Z. Naturforsch. 35b, 1028 (1980).

80BOU/RAD
W.J. Bouma, L. Radom and W.R. Rodwell, Theor. Chim. Acta 56, 149 (1980).

80BRU/COT
A. Brunot, M. Cottin, M.H. Donnart and J.C. Muller, "Mesure de L'electroaffinite du Thallium et de l'Indium par Attachement Electronique Dissociatif sur les Bromures et les Iodures de Thallium et d'Indium," Int. J. Mass Spectrom. Ion Phys. 33, 417 (1980).

80CAR/COP
T.A. Carslon, J. Copley, N. Duric, N. Elander, Perman, M. Larsson and M. Lyyra, "The Oscillator Strengths and the Dissociation Energy of SiH^+ as Determined From Time Resolved Precision Spectroscopy," Astron. Astrophys. **83**, 238 (1980).

80CLA/MCM
R.L. Clair and T.B. McMahon, "An Ion Cyclotron Resonance Study of Base-Induced Elimination Reactions of Fluorinated Alcohols and Unimolecular Loss of HF from Chemically Activated Fluoroalkoxide Ions," Int. J. Mass Spectrom. Ion Phys. **33**, 21 (1980).

80COM/REI
R.W. Compton and P.W. Reinhardt, "Reactions of Fast Cesium Atoms with Polymers of Antimony Pentafluoride and Gold Pentafluoride," J. Chem. Phys. **72**, 4655 (1980).

80CON
J.A. Connor, "Transition Metal Clusters" (ed. B.F.G. Johnson, John Wiley & Sons, New York, 1980).

80CRA/SNY
D.C. Crans and J.P. Snyder, Chem. Ber. **113**, 1201 (1980).

80DAV/FIN
R.H. Davies, A. Finch and P.J. Gardner, J. Chem. Thermodyn. **12**, 291 (1980).

80DAW/NIB
J.H.J. Dawson and N.M.M. Nibbering, "The Gas Phase Anionic Chemistry of Saturated and Unsaturated Aliphatic Nitriles," Int. J. Mass Spectrom. Ion Phys. **33**, 3 (1980).

80DEF/MCI
D.J. DeFrees, R.T. McIver, Jr. and W.J. Hehre, "Heats of Formation of Gaseous Free Radicals via Ion Cyclotron Double Resonance Spectroscopy," J. Am. Chem. Soc. **102**, 3334 (1980).

80DEL/HUB
J. Delwiche, M.-J. Hubin-Franskin, G. Caprace, P. Natalis and D. Roy, "On the He(I) and Ne(I) Photoelectron Spectra of OCS," J. Electron Spectrosc. Rel. Phenom. **21**, 205 (1980).

80DEM/WUL
R.L. Deming and C.A. Wulff *The Chemistry of Ketenes, Allenes and Related Compounds*, S. Patai, Editor, part 1, pp. 155-164 J. Wiley and Sons, New York (1980).

80DEP/BIE
C.H. DePuy, V.M. Bierbaum, L.A. Flippin, J.J. Brabowski, G.K. King, R.J. Schmidt and S.A. Sullivan, "Gas Phase Reactions of Anions with Substituted Silanes," J. Am. Chem. Soc. **102**, 5012 (1980).

80DEW/DAV
M.J.S. Dewar and D.E. David, "Ultraviolet Photoelectron Spectrum of the Phenoxy Radical," J. Am. Chem. Soc. **102**, 7387 (1980).

80DUP/ROB
P. Dupuis, R. Roberge and C. Sandorfy, "The Very Low Ionization Potentials of Porphyrins and the Possible Role of Rydberg States in Photosynthesis," Chem. Phys. Lett. **75**, 434 (1980).

80DYK/FAY
J.M. Dyke, N.K. Fayad, G.D. Josland and A. Morris, "Study by High-temperature Photoelectron Spectroscopy of the Electronic Structure of the Transition Metal Difluorides, CuF_2 and ZnF_2," J. Chem. Soc. Faraday Trans. II **76**, 1672 (1980).

80DYK/JON
J.M. Dyke, N. Jonathan, A. Morris and M.J. Winter, "The First Ionization Potential of the Formyl Radical, HCO (X^2A), Studied Using Photoelectron Spectroscopy," Molec. Phys. **39**, 629 (1980).

80EME/KOM
D.P. Emerick, L. Komorowski, J. Lipinski, F.C. Nahm and K. Niedenzu, "Experimental and Theoretical Studies on Monomeric Iminoboranes," Z. Anorg. Allg. Chem. **468**, 44 (1980).

80ENG
P.S. Engel, Chem. Rev. **80**, 99 (1980).

80FAR/MCM
R. Farid and T.B. McMahon, "The Gas Phase Acidities of Fluorinated Acetones. An ICR Investigation of the Role of Fluorine Substituents in the Stabilization of Planar Carbanions," Can. J. Chem. **58**, 2307 (1980).

80FRO/WES
D.C. Frost, N.P.C. Westwood and N.H. Werstiuk, "Ultraviolet Photoelectron Spectra of 2-Norbornanone, 2,5-Norbornanedione, Their Alkyl Derivatives and Thio-Analogues. An Investigation of Transannular Interactions by Photoelectron Spectroscopy," Can. J. Chem. **58**, 1659 (1980).

80FUC/PEA
R. Fuchs and L.A. Peacock, Can. J. Chem. **58**, 2796 (1980).

80GAJ
J.J. Gajewski, "Hydrocarbon Thermal Rearrangements" (Academic Press, New York, 1980).

80GLE/HOP
R. Gleiter, H. Hopf, M. Eckert-Maksic and K.-L. Noble, "Photoelektronenspektren von [8]Paracyclophan und [8]Paracyclophan-4-en. Eine Ermittlung des induktiven und hyperkonjugativen Effekts fur [n]Paracyclophane," Chem. Ber. **113**, 3401 (1980).

80GOF/YAR
M.M. Gofman, V.G. Yarzhemsky and V.I. Nefedov, "Relative Intensities in the He(I) and He(II) Photoelectron Spectra of Benzoyl Chloride," J. Electron Spectrosc. Rel. Phenom. **21**, 171 (1980).

80GOM/HAA
W. Gombler, A. Haas and H. Willner, "Chalkogenfluoride in niedrigen Oxydationsstufen. V. Die ungewohnlichen chemischen Gleichgewichte $F_3S-SF = 2\ SF_2$ und $CF_3SF_2-SCF_3 = 2\ CF_3SF$," Z. Anorg. Allg. Chem. **469**, 135 (1980).

80GOR
M.S. Gordon, J. Am. Chem. Soc. **102**, 7419 (1980).

80GRE
D.W. Green, Int. J. Thermophys. **1**, 61 (1980).

80GRE/SED
J.C. Green and E.A. Seddon, "UV Photoelectron Studies of $Cr(\eta-C_3H_5)_3$, $Cr_2(\eta-C_3H_5)_4$ and $Mo_2(\eta-C_3H_5)_4$," J. Organometall. Chem. **198**, C61 (1980).

80GRU/SCH
H.-F. Grutzmacher, B. Schaldach, R. Schubert and D.V. Ramana, "Ion Kinetic Energy Release as a Transition State Probe in Intramolecular Aromatic Substitutions," Adv. Mass Spectrom. **8A**, 795 (1980).

80GUS/PYA
A.V. Gusarov, A.T. Pyatenko and L.N. Gorokhov, "Tetrafluoroaluminate (AlF_4^-) and Fluoroaluminate ($Al_2F_7^-$) Ions in Aluminum Fluoride Vapors," Teplofiz. Vys. Temperatiur. **18**, 961. CA: 94, 10584y (1980).

80HIL/VES
J.F. Hiller and M.L. Vestal, "Tandem Quadrupole Study of Laser Photodissociation of CO_3^-," J. Chem. Phys. **72**, 4713 (1980).

80HOD/SUL
R.V. Hodges, S.A. Sullivan and J.L. Beauchamp, "Nucleophilic Reactions of Anions with Trimethyl Phosphate in the Gas Phase by ICR Spectroscopy," J. Am. Chem. Soc. **102**, 935 (1980).

80HOL/LOS
J.L. Holmes and F.P. Lossing, J. Am. Chem. Soc. **102**, 1591 (1980).

80HOL/LOS2
J.L. Holmes and F.P. Lossing, J. Am. Chem. Soc. **102**, 3732 (1980).

80HOL/TER
J.L. Holmes, J.K. Terlouw and P.C. Burgers, Org. Mass Spectrom. **15**, 140 (1980).

80HOT/NEI
A. Hotzel, R. Neidlein, R. Schulz and A. Schweig, "Direct Detection of Dicyanoketene in the Gas Phase," Angew. Chem. Int. Ed. **19**, 739 (1980).

80HOU/SCH
R. Houriet, H. Schwarz and W. Zummack, "Proton and Hydrogen Affinity of Furan and the Site of Protonation in the Gas Phase," Angew. Chem. Int. Ed. **19**, 905 (1980).

80HUN/SET
D.F. Hunt and S.K. Sethi, "Gas Phase Ion/Molecule Isotope Exchange Reactions: Methodology for Counting Hydrogen Atoms in Specific Organic Structural Environments by Chemical Ionization Mass Spectrometry," J. Am. Chem. Soc. **102**, 6953 (1980).

80ING/HAN
M.G. Inghram, G.R. Hanson and R. Stockbauer, "The Fragmentation of C_2F_6," Int. J. Mass Spectrom. Ion Phys. **33**, 253 (1980).

80JAN/BRA
B.K. Janousek and J.I. Brauman, "Electron Photodetachment of Thiomethoxyl and Deuterothiomethoxyl Anions: Electron Affinities, Vibrational Frequencies, and Spin-Orbit Splitting in CH_3S^- and CD_3S^-," J. Chem. Phys. **72**, 694 (1980).

80JAN/REE
B.K. Janousek, K.J. Reed and J.I. Brauman, "Electron Photodetachment from Mercaptyl Anions (RS^-). Electron Affinities of Mercaptyl Radicals and the S-H Bond Strength in Mercaptans," J. Am. Chem. Soc. **102**, 3125 (1980).

80JON/MEA
P.L. Jones, R.D. Mead, B.E. Kohler, S.D. Rosner and W.C. Lineberger, "Photodetachment Spectroscopy of C_2^- Autodetaching Resonances," J. Chem. Phys. **73**, 4419 (1980).

80JOR/CAR
F.S. Jorgensen, L. Carlsen and F. Duus, "The Electronic Structure of Propyl 3-Mercaptocrotonate Studied by Photoelectron Spectroscopy," Acta Chem. Scand. **B34**, 695 (1980).

80KAI/TES
W. Kaim, H. Tesmann and H. Bock, "Me_3C-, Me_3Si-, Me_3Ge-, Me_3Sn- und Me_3Pb-substituierte Benzol- und Naphthalin-Derivate und ihre Radikalanionen," Chem. Ber. **113**, 3221 (1980).

80KEE/CAS
R.G. Keesee and A.W. Castleman, Jr., "Heats of Formation of SO_2Cl^- and $(SO_2)_2Cl^-$," J. Am. Chem. Soc. **102**, 1446 (1980).

80KEE/CAS2
R.G. Keesee and A.W. Castleman, Jr., "Gas Phase Studies of Hydration Complexes of Cl^- and I^- and Comparison to Electrostatic Calculations in the Gas Phase," Chem. Phys. Lett. **74**, 139 (1980).

80KEE/LEE
R.G. Keesee, N. Lee and A.W. Castleman, Jr., "Properties of Clusters in the Gas Phase: V. Complexes of Neutral Molecules onto Negative Ions," J. Chem. Phys. **73**, 2195 (1980).

80KLA/BUT
L. Klasinc, V. Butkovic, I. Novak, M. Mihalic, R. Toso and V. Sunjic, "Application of Photoelectron Spectroscopy to Biologically Active Molecules and Their Constituent Parts. VII. N-Cyanoazomethines," Gazz. Chim. Ital. **110**, 287 (1980).

80KOL
H. Kollmar, J. Am. Chem. Soc. **102**, 2617 (1980).

80KOP/COM
I. Koppel and M.B. Comisarow, "Ab Initio SCF LCAO MO Calculations of Molecules. I. Calculation of Proton Affinities. General Comparison with Experiment," Organic Reactivity (Tartu State University), Engl. Ed. XVII, 495 (1980).

80KRA
M.O. Krause, "Photoionization of Atomic Silver between 17 and 41 eV," J. Chem. Phys. **72**, 6474 (1980).

80KUD/KUD
A.P. Kudchadker and S.A. Kudchadker, "Indan and Indenes" API Monograph 714-80 (American Petroleum Institute, Washington, DC, 1980).

80LEB/MAS
N.D. Lebedeva, T.N. Masalitinova, V.L. Ryadnenko and O.N. Mon'yakova, Zh. Prikl. Khim. **53**, 2444 (1980).

80LEE/KEE
N. Lee, R.G. Keesee and A.W. Castleman, Jr., "The Properties of Clusters in the Gas Phase. IV. Complexes of H_2O and HNO_x Clustering on NO_x^-," J. Chem. Phys. **72**, 1089 (1980).

80LEU/HEI
W. Leupin, E. Heilbronner and J. Wirz, "The Photoelectron Spectrum of 2-Methylbenzotriazole," J. Molec. Str. **68**, 329 (1980).

80LLO/AGO
J.R. Lloyd, W.C. Agosta and F.H. Field, "Gaseous Anion Chemistry. Hydrogen-Deuterium Exchange in Mono- and Dialcohol Alkoxide Ions: Ionization Reactions in Dialcohols," J. Org. Chem. **45**, 3483 (1980).

80MAI/THO
J.P. Maier and F. Thommen, "Radiative and Nonradiative Decay Rates of State Selected $H-(C\equiv C)-_2H^+$, $D-(C\equiv C)-_2D^+$, $A^2\Pi_u$, Determined by a Photoelectron-Photoion Coincidence Technique," J. Chem. Phys. **73**, 5616 (1980).

80MAJ/SVA
V. Majer, L. Svab and V. Svoboda, J. Chem. Thermodyn. **12**, 843 (1980).

80MAJ/WAG
V. Majer, Z. Wagner, V. Svoboda and V. Cadek, J. Chem. Thermodyn. **12**, 387 (1980).

80MAL/ALI
I.P. Malkerova, A.S. Alikhanyan and V.I. Gorgoraki, "Heats of Formation of Molybdenum Sulphide Fluorides $MoSF_3$ and $MoSF_4$," Zh. Neorganich. Khim. **25**, 3181 (1980); Engl. Trans., Russ. J. Inorg. Chem. **25**, 1742 (1980).

80MAL/ALI2
I.P. Malkerova, A.S. Alikhanyan, V.S. Pervov, V.D. Butskii and V.I. Gorgoraki, "Composition of the Gas Phase over Molybdenum Thiofluoride $MoSF_3$ [Molybdenum Sulphide Trifluoride]," Zh. Neorganich. Khim. **25**, 2067 (1980); Engl. Trans., Russ. J. Inorg. Chem. **25**, 1145 (1980).

80MAR/HEL
H.-D. Martin, G. Heller, B. Mayer and H.-D. Beckhaus, Chem. Ber. **113**, 258 (1980).

80MAU
M. Meot-Ner (Mautner), "Ion Thermochemistry of Low Volatility Compounds in the Gas Phase. 3. Polycyclic Aromatics: Ionization Energies, Proton, and Hydrogen Affinities. Extrapolations to Graphite," J. Phys. Chem. **84**, 2716 (1980).

80MCD/CHO
R.N. McDonald, A.K. Chowdhury and D.W. Setser, "Gas Phase Generation of Phenylnitrene Anion Radical: Proton Affinity and Heat of Formation of $PhN^{-\cdot}$ and Its Clustering with ROH Molecules," J. Am. Chem. Soc. **103**, 6599 (1981).

80MCD/CHO2
R.N. McDonald, A.K. Chowdhury and D.W. Setser, "Hypovalent Radicals. 4. Gas Phase Studies of the Ion-Molecule Reactions of Cyclopentadienylidene Anion Radical in a Flowing Afterglow," J. Am. Chem. Soc. **102**, 6491 (1980).

80MCL/MCG
F.W. McLafferty and D.C. McGilvery, "Gaseous HCN^+, HNC^+ and $HCNH^+$ Ions," J. Am. Chem. Soc. **102**, 6189 (1980).

80MEI/HSI
G.G. Meisels, T. Hsieh, and J.P. Gilman, "Ion Fragmentation from Noninterconverting Electronic States," J. Chem. Phys. **73**, 4126 (1980).

80MIK/ZAI
A.I. Mikaya and V.G. Zaikin, "Determination of the Difference in Enthalpies of Formation of the cis- and trans-Isomers of Bicyclo[4.3.0]Nonane and Bicyclo[4.4.0]Decane Using Appearance Potentials," Izvest. Akad. Nauk SSSR, Ser. Khim. **6**, 1286 (1980).

80MOF
J.B. Moffat, J. Mol. Struct. **62**, 213 (1980).

80MUR
E. Murad, "Thermochemical Properties of Gaseous FeO and FeOH," J. Chem. Phys. **73**, 1381 (1980).

80MUR/HIL
E. Murad and D.L. Hildenbrand, "Dissociation Energies of GdO, HoO, ErO, TmO, and LuO. Correlation of Results for the Lanthanide Monoxide Series," J. Chem. Phys. **73**, 4005 (1980).

80NAN/BEN
P.S. Nangia and S.W. Benson, J. Am. Chem. Soc. **102**, 3105 (1980).

80NEL/KES
S.F. Nelsen, C.R. Kessel, L.A. Grezzo and D.J. Steffek, "Thermodynamic Destabilization of N-Centered Radical Cations by a γ-Keto Group," J. Am. Chem. Soc. **102**, 5482 (1980).

80NIK/SOR
M.I. Nikitin, I.D. Sorokin, E.V. Skokan and L.N. Sidirov, "Negative Ions in the Saturated Vapors of the Potassium Fluoride - Hafnium Tetrafluoride and Potassium Fluoride - Beryllium Difluoride Systems," Russ. J. Phys. Chem. **54**, Russ:1337 (1980).

80NIS/SAK
K. Nishiyama, M. Sakiyama, S. Seki, H. Horita, T. Otsubo and S. Misumi, Bull. Chem. Soc. Jpn. **53**, 869 (1980).

80NOE/NIB
A.J. Noest and N.M.M. Nibbering, "Homoconjugation vs. Charge Dipole Stabilization Interaction Effects in the Stabilization of Carbanions in the Gas Phase," J. Am. Chem. Soc. **102**, 6427 (1980).

80PAL/NIS
M.H. Palmer and J.D. Nisbet, "The Molecular and Electronic Structure of Homoaromatic Compounds: cis,cis,cis-Cyclonona-1,4,7-triene and 1,4,7-Trioxonin; A Study by Photoelectron Spectroscopy and Ab Initio Molecular Orbital Methods," J. Molec. Str. **67**, 65 (1980).

80POL/HEH
S.K. Pollack and W.J. Hehre, Tetrahedron Lett. **21**, 2483 (1980).

80PRY
W.A. Pryor, "Frontiers of Free Radical Chemistry," Academic Press, NY, 1980.

80PYA/GUS
A.T. Pyatenko, A.V. Gusarov and L.N. Gorokhov, "Thermochemical Properties of Negative Ions in Vapor over UF_4," Teplofiz. Vys. Temperatur. **18**, 1154. CA: 92, 7246p (1980).

80RED/FRE
V.V. Redchenko, Y.F. Freimanis and Y.Y. Dregeris, "Photoelectron Spectroscopy of 2,3-Disubstituted Naphthoquinones," Zh. Obsh. Khim. **50**, 1847 (1980); English trans.: J. Gen. Chem. USSR **50**, 1507 (1980).

80ROG/CHO
D.W. Rogers, L.S. Choi, R.S. Girellini, T.J. Holmes and N.L. Allinger, J. Phys. Chem. **84**, 1810 (1980).

80ROS/STO
H.M. Rosenstock, R. Stockbauer and A.C. Parr, "Photoelectron-photoion Coincidence Study of the Bromobenzene Ion," J. Chem. Phys. **73**, 773 (1980).

80ROS/STO2
H.M. Rosenstock, R. Stockbauer and A.C. Parr, "Photoelectron-photoion Coincidence Study of Benzonitrile," J. Chim. Phys. **77**, 745 (1980).

80ROT/KLA
W.R. Roth, F.-G. Klarner and H.W. Lennart, Chem. Ber. **113**, 1818 (1980).

80ROT/MAT
E.W. Rothe, B.P. Mathur and G.P. Reck, "Measurement of Boron Trihalide Electron Affinities: Correlation with Boron-Nitrogen Adduct Strengths," Inorg. Chem. **19**, 829 (1980).

80SAB
R. Sabbah, Thermochim. Acta **41**, 33 (1980).

80SAB2
R. Sabbah, Thermochim. Acta **35**, 73 (1980).

80SAB/SKO
R. Sabbah and S. Skoulika, Thermochim. Acta **36**, 179 (1980).

80SAR/WOR
R. Sarneel, C.W. Worrell, P. Pasman, J.W. Verhoeven and G.F. Mes, "The Photoelectron Spectra of 4-Methylene Thiacyclohexane Derivatives Through-Bond Interaction," Tetrahedron **36**, 3241 (1980).

80SAT/SAK
T. Sato-Toshima, M. Sakiyama and S. Seki, Bull. Chem. Soc. Jpn. **53**, 2462 (1980).

80SCH/ILL
H.U. Scheunemann, E. Illenberger and H. Baumgartel, "Dissociative Electron Attachment to CCl_4, $CHCl_3$, CH_2Cl_2, and CH_3Cl," Ber. Bunsenges Phys. Chem. **84**, 580 (1980).

80SCH/RAM
R. Schubert, D.V. Ramana and H.-F. Grutzmacher, "Freisetzung kinetischer Energie und Hammond-Postulat bei der intramolekularen aromatischen Substitution in 2-Stilbazol-Ionen," Chem. Ber. **113**, 3758 (1980).

80SCH/SCH
R. Schulz, A. Schweig, C. Wentrup and H.-W. Winter, "2-Vinylidene-2H-indene," Angew. Chem. Int. Ed. **19**, 821 (1980).

80SCH/SCH2
R. Schulz and A. Schweig, "Direct Detection of Dicyanothioketene in the Gas Phase," Angew. Chem. Int. Ed. **19**, 740 (1980).

80SCH/THI
A. Schweig and W. Thiel, J. Comput. Chem. **1**, 129 (1980).

80SCH/THO
A. Schweig, N. Thon, S.F. Nelsen and L.A. Grezzo, "Conformational Study of 1,2-Dimethylhexahydropyridazine by Variable-Temperature Photoelectron Spectroscopy," J. Am. Chem. Soc. **102**, 7438 (1980).

80SEN/ABE
S.N. Senzer, R.N. Abernathy and F.W. Lampe, "GeH_5^+ and the Proton Affinity of Monogermane," J. Phys. Chem. **84**, 3066 (1980).

80SHU/BOY
B. Shushan and R.K. Boyd, "Unimolecular and Collision Induced Fragmentations of Molecular Ions of Polycyclic Aromatic Hydrocarbons," Org. Mass Spectrom. **15**, 445 (1980).

80SID/NIK
L.N. Sidorov, M.I. Nikitin, E.V. Skokan and I.D. Sorokin, "Mass-Spectrometric Determination of Enthalpies of Dissociation of Gaseous Complex Fluorides into Neutral and Charged Particles. II. Heats of Formation of AlF_4^- and KF_2^-," Int. J. Mass Spectrom. Ion Phys. **35**, 203 (1980).

80SID/SKO
L.N. Sidorov, E.V. Skokan, M.I. Nitikin and I.D. Sorokin, "Mass Spectrometric Determination of Enthalpies of Dissociation of Gaseous Complex Fluorides into Neutral and Charged Particles. III. Heat of Formation of UF_5^- and Electron Affinity of UF_5," Int. J. Mass Spectrom. Ion Phys. **35**, 215 (1980).

80STA/VOG
J.P. Stadelmann and J. Vogt, Int. J. Mass Spectrom. Ion Phys. **35**, 83 (1980).

80STR/NEW
G.E. Streit and T.W. Newton, "Negative Ion-Uranium Hexafluoride Charge Transfer Reactions," J. Chem. Phys. **73**, 3178 (1980).

80SVO/UCH
V. Svoboda, V. Uchytilova, V. Majer and J. Pick, Collect. Czech. Chem. Commun. **45**, 3233 (1980).

80TED/VID
J.M. Tedder and P.H. Vidaud, "Charge Exchange Mass Spectra of Thiophene, Pyrrole and Furan," J. Chem. Soc. Faraday Trans. II **76**, 1516 (1980).

80TEL/RAB
V.I. Tel'noi and I.B. Rabinovich, Russ. Chem. Rev. **49**, 603 (1980).

80TEP/YAN
A.B. Teplitsky, I.K. Yanson, O.T. Glukhova, A. Zielenkiewicz, W. Zielenkiewicz and K.L. Wierzchowski, Biophys. Chem. **11**, 17 (1980).

80TER/HEE
J.K. Terlouw, W. Heerma, J.L. Holmes and P.C. Burgers, "Structure and Formation of Gaseous $[C_4H_6O]^+$ Ions. 1-The Enolic Ions $[CH_2=C(OH)-CH=CH_2]^+$ and $[CH_2=CH-CH=CH(OH)]^+$ and Their Relationship with Their Keto Counterparts," Org. Mass Spectrom. **15**, 582 (1980).

80THA/EIS
M.G. Thackston, F.L. Eisele, W.M. Pope, H.W. Ellis, E.W. McDaniel and I.R. Gatland, "Mobility of Cl⁻ Ions in Xe Gas and the Cl⁻-Xe Interaction Potential," J. Chem. Phys. **73**, 3183 (1980).

80TRA
J.C. Traeger, Int. J. Mass Spectrom. Ion Phys. **32**, 309 (1980).

80TRE
A.B. Trentwith, J. Chem. Soc. Trans. Farad. I **76**, 166 (1980).

80TSV/ALE
V.G. Tsvetkov, V.A. Aleksandrov, V.N. Glushakova, N.A. Skorodumora and G.M. Kol'yakova, Russ. J. Gen. Chem. **50**, 198 (1980).

80VAN
J. Van der Greef Ph. D. Thesis, Univ. Amsterdam (1980).

80VAN/TER
H. Van Dam, A. Terpstra, D.J. Stufkens and A. Oskam, "UV Photoelectron Spectroscopic Studies of the Metal-Olefin Bond. 2. Bonding in (β-Diketonato)rhodium(I) and -iridium(I) Carbonyl and Olefin Complexes," Inorg. Chem. **19**, 3448 (1980).

80VER/SAL
A.N. Vereshchagin, A.M. Salikhova, V.V. Zverev, F.G. Saitkulova and Y.Y. Villem, "Physical Properties, Conformations and Intramolecular Interactions of α,α-Dichlorodimethyl Ether," Izv. Akad. Nauk SSSR, Ser. Khim. 997 (1980); Engl. trans., Bull. Acad. Sci. USSR, Div. Chem. Sci. **29**, 706 (1980).

80VIG/PER
A.A. Vigiano, R.A. Perry, D.L. Albritton, E.E. Ferguson and F.C. Fehsenfeld, "The Role of H_2SO_4 in Stratospheric Negative Ion Chemistry," J. Geophys. Res. **85**, 4551 (1980).

80VIL/PER
R. Vilcu and S. Perisanu, Rev. Roum. Chim. **25**, 619 (1980).

80VON/BIE
W. Von Niessen, G. Bieri and L. Asbrink, "30.4 nm He(II) Photoelectron Spectra of Organic Molecules. Part III. Oxo-compounds (C, H, O)," J. Electron Spectrosc. Rel. Phenom. **21**, 175 (1980).

80VOV/DUD
V.I. Vovna, A.S. Dudin, S.N. Lopatin and E.G. Rakov, "Photoelectronic Spectra of Hexafluorides of Transition Metals with Open Shells (ReF_6 and OsF_6)," Koord. Khim. **6**, 1580 (1980).

80WAN/FRA
J.-S.Wang and J.L. Franklin, "Reactions and Energy Distributions in Dissociative Electron Capture Processes in Sulfuryl Halides," Int. J. Mass Spectrom. Ion Phys. **36**, 233 (1980).

80WIG/BEA
C.A. Wight and J.L. Beauchamp, "Acidity, Basicity, and Ion/Molecule Reactions of Isocyanic Acid in the Gas Phase by ICR Spectroscopy," J. Phys. Chem. **84**, 2503 (1980).

80WIL/BAE
G.D. Willett and T. Baer, J. Am. Chem. Soc. **102**, 6774 (1980).

80WLO/LUC
S. Wlodek, Z. Luczynski and H. Wincel, "Stabilities of Gas-Phase $NO_3^-\cdot(HNO_3)_n$, $n \leq 6$, Clusters," Int. J. Mass Spectrom. Ion Phys. **35**, 39 (1980).

80WOL/HOL
P. Wolkoff, J.L. Holmes and F.P. Lossing, "Ubiquitous [Cyclopentenium]$^+$ Formation from C_6H_{10} Molecular Ions by Methyl Loss, and from Higher Homologues," Adv. Mass Spectrom. **8A**, 743 (1980).

80ZVE/VIL
V.V. Zverev and Y.Y. Villem, "Ionization Potentials of Phosphoryl Compounds," Zh. Strukt. Khim. **21**, 30 (1980); English trans., J. Struct. Chem. (USSR), **21**, 22 (1980).

81AJO/CAS
Flexibility of the Dehydroalanine Derivatives: Molecular and Electronic Structure of (Z)-N-Acetyldehydrophenylalanine," Tetrahedron **37**, 3507 (1981).

81AJO/CAS2
D. Ajo, M. Casarin, G. Granozzi and I. Fragala, "UV Photoelectron Spectra of 5- and 6-Azauracil," Chem. Phys. Lett. **80**, 188 (1981).

81AKI/HAR
I. Akiyama, R.G. Harvey and P.R. LeBreton, "Ultraviolet Photoelectron Studies of Methyl-Substituted Benz[a]anthracenes," J. Am. Chem. Soc. **103**, 6330 (1981).

81ALD/ARR
R.W. Alder, R.J. Arrowsmith, A. Casson, R.B. Sessions, E. Heilbronner, B. Kovac, H. Huber and M. Taagepera, J. Am. Chem. Soc. **103**, 6137 (1981).

81ALL/GLA
N.L. Allinger, J.A. Glaser, H.E. Davis and D.W. Rogers, J. Org. Chem. **46**, 658 (1981).

81ALL/MIG
S.H. Allam, M.D. Migahed and A. El Khodary, "Electron Impact Study of Nitrobenzene and Nitromethane," Int. J. Mass Spectrom. Ion Phys. **39**, 117 (1981).

81AND/DEK
E.L. Andersen, R.L. DeKock and T.P. Fehlner, "Electronic Structure of Diiron Ferraboranes," Inorg. Chem. **20**, 3291 (1981).

81ARI/ARM
N. Aristov and P. Armentrout, "Bond Energy-Bond Order Relations in Transition-Metal Bonds: Vanadium," J. Am. Chem. Soc. **106**, 4065 (1984).

81ARM/BEA
P.B. Armentrout and J.L. Beauchamp, "Ion Beam Studies of the Reactions of Atomic Cobalt Ions with Alkanes: Determination of Metal-Hydrogen and Metal-Carbon Bond Energies and an Examination of the Mechanism by which Transition Metals Cleave Carbon-Carbon Bonds," J. Am. Chem. Soc. **103**, 784 (1981).

81ARM/BEA2
P. Armentrout and J. Beauchamp, "Cobalt Carbene Ion: Reactions of Co$^+$ with C_2H_4, cyclo-C_3H_6, and cyclo-C_2H_4O," J. Chem. Phys. **74**, 2819 (1981).

81ARM/HAL
P. B. Armentrout, L. F. Halle and J. L. Beauchamp, "Periodic Trends in Transition Metal-Hydrogen, Metal-Carbon, and Metal-Oxygen Bond Dissociation Energies. Correlation with Reactivity and Electronic Structure," J. Am. Chem. Soc. **103**, 6501 (1981).

81ARM/TAR
P. B. Armentrout, S. M. Tarr, A. Dori and R. S. Freund, "Electron Impact Ionization Cross Section of Metastable N_2 ($A^2\Sigma_u^+$)," J. Chem. Phys. **75**, 2788 (1981).

81ARS/ZVE
R. P. Arshinova, V. V. Zverev, Y. Y. Villem and N. V. Villem, "Ionization of Potentials, Electron Structures, and Steric Structures of Tervalent-Phosphorus Di- and Tri-Esters," Zh. Obs. Khim. **51**, 1757 (1980); English translation, J. Gen. Chem. (USSR) **51**, 1503 (1982).

81ASB/SVE
L. Asbrink, A. Svensson, W. Von Niessen and G. Bieri, "30.4 nm He(II) Photoelectron Spectra of Organic Molecules," J. Electron Spectrosc. Rel. Phenom. **24**, 293 (1981).

81AUE/PED
D. Aue, M. Pedley, and M.T. Bowers, unpublished result cited in: A. J. Illies, S. Liu and M. T. Bowers, "Formation and Structure of $C_2H_4N^+$. Effect of Pressure and Reaction Exothermicity on Collision-Induced Dissociation Spectra," J. Am. Chem. Soc. **103**, 5674 (1981).

81AUS
P. Ausloos, J. Am. Chem. Soc. **103**, 3931 (1981).

81AYA/WEN
J.A. Ayala, W.E. Wentworth and E.C.M. Chen, "Electron Attachment to Halogens," J. Phys. Chem. **85**, 768 (1981).

81BAB/STR
L.M. Babcock and G.E. Streit, "Ion-Molecule Reactions of SF_6: Determination of I. P. (SF_6), A. P.(SF_5^+/SF_6), and D(SF_5-F)," J. Chem. Phys. **74**, 5700 (1981).

81BAB/STR2
L.M. Babcock and G.E. Streit, "Negative Ion-Molecule Reactions of SF_4," J. Chem. Phys. **75**, 3864 (1981).

81BAI/CHI
V.N. Baidin, Y.V. Chizhov, M.M. Timoshenko, Y.A. Ustynyuk and I.I. Kritskaya, "He(I) Photoelectronic Spectra of Organic Compounds with a Mercury Atom Attached to an sp^2 Hybridized Carbon," Izv. Akad. Nauk SSSR, Ser. Khim. **12**, 2831 (1981).

81BAI/CHI2
V.N. Baidin, Y.V. Chizhov, M.M. Timoshenko, O.K. Sokolikova, Y.K. Grishin and Y.A. Ustynyuk, "The Photoelectron Spectra of Alkylmercury Chlorides," Zh. Strukt. Khim. **22**, 164 (1981).

81BAK/ARM
A.D. Baker, G.H. Armen and Y. Guang-di, "Photoelectron Spectra of Alkyl Aryl Selenides. Electronic and Steric Factors in the Observation of Rotamers," J. Org. Chem. **46**, 4127 (1981).

81BAL/GIG
G. Balducci, G. Gigli and M. Guido, "Dissociation Energies of the Molecules $CrPO_2$(g) and CoO(g) by High-temperature Mass Spectrometry," J. Chem. Soc. Faraday Trans. II **77**, 1107 (1981).

81BAL/GIG2
G. Balducci, G. Gigli and M. Guido, "Thermodynamic Study of Gaseous Ternary Oxide Molecules. The Europium-Vanadium-Oxygen System," J. Chem. Phys. **79**, 5623 (1981).

81BAR/HAY
J.E. Bartmess, R.L. Hays, H.N. Khatri, R.N. Misra and S.W. Wilson, "Elimination, Fragmentation and Proton Transfer in 1,3-Dithianes and 1,3-Dithiolanes in the Gas Phase," J. Am. Chem. Soc. **103**, 4746 (1981).

81BEC/HOF
E. Beck, P. Hofmann and A. Sieber, "Zur Elektronenstruktur Vicinaler Triketone: Bicyclo[3.1.0]hexan-2,3,4-trione," Tetrahedron Lett. **22**, 4683 (1981).

81BEL/PER
T.N. Bell, K.A. Perkins and P.G. Perkins, J. Chem. Soc. Faraday Trans. I **77**, 1779 (1981).

81BER/BEA
D.W. Berman, J.L. Beauchamp and L.R. Thorne, "Ion Cyclotron Resonance and Photoionization Investigations of the Thermochemistry and Reactions of Ions Derived from CF_3I," Int. J. Mass Spectrom. Ion Phys. **39**, 47 (1981).

81BER/BOM
D.W. Berman, D.S. Bomse and J.L. Beauchamp, "Photoionization Threshold Measurements for CF_2 Loss from Perfluoropropylene, Perfluorocyclopropane, and Trifluoromethylbenzene. The Heat of Formation of CF_2 and the Potential Energy Surface for C_3F_6 Neutrals and Ions," Int. J. Mass Spectrom. Ion Phys. **39**, 263 (1981).

81BER/GAR
M. Berry, C.D. Garner, I.H. Hillier and A.A. MacDowell, "Electronic Structure and Photoelectron Spectrum of Tris(π-allyl)chromium, Cr($\eta3$-C_3H_5)$_3$," Inorg. Chem. **20**, 1962 (1981).

81BEV/SAN
J.W. Bevan, C. Sandorfy, F. Pang and J.E. Bogg, "The Photoelectron Spectrum of Methylisocyanide-borane," Spectrochimica Acta **37A**, 601 (1981).

81BIA/LIF
S.E. Biali, C. Lifshitz and Z. Rappoport, "Thermochemistry and Unimolecular Reactions of Ionized 1,2-Dimesityl-2-phenylethanone and 2,2-Dimesityl-1-phenylethanone and Their Enols and Enol Acetates in the Gas Phase," J. Am. Chem. Soc. **103**, 2896 (1981).

81BIE/ASB
G. Bieri, L. Asbrink and W. Von Niessen, "30.4 nm He(II) Photoelectron Spectra of Organic Molecules. Part IV. Fluoro-compounds (C, H, F)," J. Electron Spectrosc. Rel. Phenom. **23**, 281 (1981).

81BIE/SCH
V.M. Bierbaum, R.J. Schmidt, C.H. DePuy, R.H. Mead, P.A. Schulz and W.C. Lineberger, "Reactions of Carbanions with Triplet and Singlet Molecular Oxygen," J. Am. Chem. Soc. **103**, 6262 (1981).

81BIE/VON
G. Bieri, W. Von Niessen, L. Asbrink and A. Svensson, "The He(II) Photoelectron Spectra of the Fluorosubstituted Ethylenes and Their Analysis by the Green's Function Method," Chem. Phys. **60**, 61 (1981).

81BIS/COL
P. Biscarini, F.P. Colonna, M. Guerra and G. Distefano, "Mercury-Sulphur Bonding in Some Di(alkylthio)mercury(II) Compounds Studied by Means of Ultraviolet Photoelectron Spectroscopy," Inorg. Chim. Acta **50**, 243 (1981).

81BIS/GLE
P. Bischof, R. Gleiter, K. Gubernator, R. Haider, H. Musso, W. Schwarz, W. Trautmann and H. Hopf, "Photoelectronen-spektroskopische Untersuchungen an Divinylcyclobutanen," Chem. Ber. **114**, 994 (1981).

81BOC/BRA
H. Bock, G. Brahler, D. Dauplaise and J. Meinwald, "One-Electron Oxidation of 1,8-Chalcogen-Bridged Naphthalenes," Chem. Ber. **114**, 2622 (1981).

81BOC/DAM
H. Bock, R. Dammel and L. Horner, "Die Pyrolyse von Methylazid," Chem. Ber. **114**, 220 (1981).

81BOC/ECK
M.C. Bohm, M. Eckert-Maksic, R. Gleiter, J. Grobe and D. Le Van, "Die He(I)-Photoelektronenspektren von $(CH_3)_2PSCH_3$, $(CH_3)_2AsSCH_3$, $(CH_3)_2AsSeCH_3$ und $(CH_3)_2PSeCH_3$," Chem. Ber. **114**, 2300 (1981).

81BOC/HIR
H. Bock, T. Hirabayashi and S. Mohmand, "Thermische Erzeugung von Alkyl- und Halogenketenen," Chem. Ber. **114**, 2595 (1981).

81BOC/RIE
H. Bock, W. Ried and U. Stein, "Analyse und Optimierung von Gasphasen-Reaktionen, 19. Pyrolyse von Cyclobuten-1,2-dionen zu Acetylenen," Chem. Ber. **114**, 673 (1981).

81BOC/SCH
H. Bock, W. Schulz and M. Schmidt, "P. E. Spektren und Molekuleigenschaften. 89. Ionissationsmuster und Konformation von Cyclo-Polythianen $(H_2CS)_n$," Z. Anorg. Allg. Chem. **474**, 199 (1981).

81BOC/SCH2
H. Bock, W. Schulz and U. Stein, "Radikalionen, 47. Notiz: Die Strukturanderung wahrend der Einelektronen-Oxidation von Bis(dimethylamino)disulfid," Chem. Ber. **114**, 2632 (1981).

81BOH/ECK
M.C. Bohm, M. Eckert-Maksic, R. Gleiter, J. Grobe and D. Le Van, "Die He(I)-Photoelektronenspektren von $(CH_3)_2PSCH_3$, $(CH_3)_2AsSCH_3$, $(CH_3)_2AsSeCH_3$ und $(CH_3)_2PSeCH_3$," Chem. Ber. **114**, 2300 (1981).

81BOM/BER
D.S. Bomse, D.W. Berman and J.L. Beauchamp, J. Am. Chem. Soc. **103**, 3967 (1981).

81BOM/DAN
R. Bombach, J. Dannacher, J.-P. Stadelmann and J. Vogt, "The Fragmentation of Formaldehyde Molecular Cations: The Lifetime of CD_2O^+ (A^2B_1)," Chem. Phys. Lett. **77**, 399 (1981).

81BOU/DAG
G. Bouchoux and J. Dagaut, "Mechanisms of Formation of $[M-HCO]^+$ and $[M-C_6H_5CO]^+$ Ions from Isomers of 1,4-Benzodioxin Derivatives," Org. Mass Spectrom. **16**, 246 (1981).

81BOU/HOP
G. Bouchoux and Y. Hoppilliard, "Fragmentation Mechanisms of Isoxazole," Org. Mass Spectrom. **16**, 459 (1981).

81BRU/CIL
G. Bruno, E. Ciliberto, I. Fragala and G. Granozzi, "The Electronic Structure of Hydrotris(1-pyrazolyl)borate Ligand by He-I and He-II Photoelectron Spectroscopy," Inorg. Chim. Acta **48**, 61 (1981).

81BUC/FOR
G. Buckley, W.G.F. Ford and A.S. Rodgers, Thermochim. Acta **49**, 199 (1981).

81BUF/PAR
R.D. Buff, A.C. Parr and A.J. Jason, "The Photoionization of Allyl Chloride from Onset to 20 eV," Int. J. Mass Spectrom. Ion Phys. **40**, 31 (1981).

81BUR/JEN
B.E. Bursten, J.R. Jensen, D.J. Gordon, P.M. Treichel and R.F. Fenske, "Electronic Structure of Transition-Metal Nitrosyls. $X(\alpha)$-SW and Configuration Interaction Calculations of the Valence Ionization Potentials of $Co(CO)_3NO$ and $Mn(CO)_4NO$," J. Am. Chem. Soc. **103**, 5226 (1981).

81CAB/COW
D.E. Cabelli, A.H. Cowley and M.J.S. Dewar, "UPE Studies of Conjugation Involving Group 5A Elements. 2. Substituted tert-Butylacetylenes," J. Am. Chem. Soc. **103**, 3290 (1981).

81CAB/COW2
D.E. Cabelli, A.H. Cowley and M.J.S. Dewar, "UPE Studies of Conjugation Involving Group 5A Elements. 1. Phenylphosphines," J. Am. Chem. Soc. **103**, 3286 (1981).

81CAL/HUB
D.C. Calabro, J.L. Hubbard, C.H. Blevins II, A.C. Campbell and D.L. Lichtenberger, "The Effects of Methyl Group Substitution on Metal-Coordinated Cyclopentadienyl Rings. The Core and Valence Ionizations of Methylated Tricarbonyl(η^5-cyclopentadienyl)metal Complexes," J. Am. Chem. Soc. **103**, 6839 (1981).

81CAL/LIC
D.C. Calabro and D.L. Lichtenberger, "Valence Ionizations of Olefins Coordinated to Metals. Olefin Dicarbonyl(η^5-(methyl and pentamethyl)cyclopentadienyl)manganese Complexes," J. Am. Chem. Soc. **103**, 6846 (1981).

81CAR/GAN
F. Carnovale, R.-H. Gan, J.B. Peel and A.B. Holmes, "Photoelectron Spectroscopic Studies of Some 2-Azabicyclo[2.2.2]octan-5-one and Bicyclo[2.2.2]octanone Derivatives," J. Chem. Soc. Perkin Trans. II **7**, 991 (1981).

81CAU/GIA
C. Cauletti, C. Giancaspro, A. Monaci, M.N. Piancastelli, "Free Energy Relationships of Ionization Energies Measured by Ultraviolet Photoelectron Spectroscopy in Substituted Pyrroles," J. Chem. Soc. Perkin Trans. II **7**, 656 (1981).

81CAV/CON
K.J. Cavell, J.A. Connor, G. Pilcher, M.A.V. Ribeiro da Silva, D.M.C. Ribeiro da Silva, Y. Vipmani and M.T. Zafarani-Moattar, J. Chem. Soc. Faraday Trans. I **77**, 1585 (1981).

81CAV/GAR
K.J. Cavell, C.D. Garner, J.A. Martinho-Simoes, G. Pilcher, H. Al-Samman, H.A. Skinner, G. Al-Tekhin, I.B. Walton and M.T. Zafarani-Moattar, J. Chem. Soc. Faraday Trans. I **77**, 2927 (1981).

81CHA/FIN
S. Chattorpadhyay, G.L. Findley and S.P. McGlynn, "Photoelectron Spectroscopy of Phosphites and Phosphates," J. Electron Spectrosc. Rel. Phenom. **24**, 27 (1981).

81CHE/GAB
A.P. Chetverikov, V.Y. Gabeskiriya and V.V. Puchkov, "Ionization of Uranium, Plutonium, Americium, Rhenium, Curium, and Californium on a Rhenium Surface," Sov. Phys. Tech. Phys. **26**, 73 (1981).

81CHE/HAL
P.T. Chesky and M.B. Hall, "Electronic Structure of Metal Clusters. 1. Photoelectron Spectra and Molecular Orbital Calculations on (Alkylidyne)tricobalt Nonacarbonyl Clusters," Inorg. Chem. **20**, 4419 (1981).

81CHI/HYM
J.S. Chickos, A.S. Hyman, L.H. Ladon and J.F. Liebman, J. Org. Chem. **46**, 4294 (1981).

81CHO/KIR
D.P. Chong, C. Kirby, W.M. Lau, T. Minato and N.P.C. Westwood, "Difluoroborane, HBF_2. A Study by HeI Photoelectron Spectroscopy, and Ab Initio Methods Including Perturbation Corrections to Koopmans' Theorem," Chem. Phys. **59**, 75 (1981).

81CIL/CON
E. Ciliberto, G. Condorelli, P.J. Fagan, J.M. Manriquez, I. Fragala and T. J. Marks, "Photoelectron Spectroscopy of f-Element Organometallic Complexes. 4. Comparative Studies of Bis(pentamethylcyclopentadienyl)Dichloride and Dimethyl Complexes of Uranium(IV), Thorium(IV), and Zirconium(IV)," J. Am. Chem. Soc. **103**, 4755 (1981).

81CLA/ROB
E. Clar, J.M. Robertson, R. Schlogl and W. Schmidt, "Photoelectron Spectra of Polynuclear Aromatics. 6. Application to Structural Elucidation: 'Circumanthracene'," J. Am. Chem. Soc. **103**, 1320 (1981).

81CLA/SOW
P. Clare and D.B. Sowerby, "Electron Impact Ionisation Energies of Some Halo-cyclotriphosphazenes," J. Inorg. Nucl. Chem. **43**, 477 (1981).

81COL/FRO
D. Colbourne, D.C. Frost, C.A. McDowell and N.P.C. Westwood, "The He(I) Photoelectron Spectra of the Alkyl Hypochlorites, ROCl (R = Me, Et and t-Bu)," J. Electron Spectrosc. Rel. Phenom. **23**, 109 (1981).

81COS/LLO
N.C.V. Costa, D.R. Lloyd, P.J. Roberts, D.W.J. Cruickshank, E. Avramides, A. Chablo, G.A.D. Collins, B. Dobson and I.H. Hillier, "Experimental and Theoretical Study of the Electronic Structures of Thionyl Fluoride, Sulphur Tetrafluoride and Sulphur Tetrafluoride Oxide," J. Chem. Soc. Faraday Trans. II **77**, 899 (1981).

81DAB/HER
I. Dabrowski and G. Herzberg, "The Spectrum of $HeAr^+$," J. Molec. Spectrosc. **89**, 491 (1981).

81DAL/NIB
J.W. Dallinga, N.M.M. Nibbering and G.J. Louter, "Formation and Structure of $[C_8H_8O]^+$ Ions, Generated from Gas Phase Ions of Phenylcyclopropylcarbinol and 1-Phenyl-1-(hydroxymethyl)cyclopropane," Org. Mass Spectrom. **16**, 4 (1981).

81DEH/POL
P.M. Dehmer and E.D. Poliakoff, "Photoionization of the Ar_2 Dimer," Chem. Phys. Lett. **77**, 326 (1981).

81DEP/BIE
C.H. DePuy and V.M. Bierbaum, "Gas Phase Sulfur Anions: Synthesis and Reactions of H_2NS^- and Related Ions," Tetrahedron Lett. **22**, 5129 (1981).

81DOM/EAT
L.N. Domelsmith, T.A. Eaton, K.N. Houk, G.M. Anderson III, R.A. Glennon, A.T. Shulgin, N. Castagnoli, Jr. and P.A. Kollman, "Photoelectron Spectra of Psychotropic Drugs. 6. Relationships between Physical Properties and Pharmacological Actions of Amphetamine Analogues," J. Med. Chem. **24**, 1414 (1981).

81DON/WAL
A.M. Doncaster and R. Walsh, "Kinetics of the Gas Phase Reaction between Iodine and Monosilane and the Bond Dissociation Energy $D(H_3Si-H)$," Int. J. Chem. Kinet. **13**, 503 (1981).

81DRA/GOR
J. E. Drake and K. Gorzelska, "The Photoelectron Spectra of Methyl(bromo)germanes," J. Electron Spectrosc. Rel. Phenom. **21**, 365 (1981).

81DRE/BEC
C. Dreier, J. Becher, E. G. Frandsen and L. Henriksen, "Pyridinethiones - V. Spectroscopic Investigation and Electronic Structure of 3-Formyl-2(1H)-pyridones, -thiones and -selones," Tetrahedron **37**, 2663 (1981).

81DUM/DUP
J.-M. Dumas, P. Dupuis, G. Pfister-Guillouzo and C. Sandorfy, "Ionization Potentials and Ultraviolet Absorption Spectra of Fluorocarbon Anesthetics," Can. J. Spectrosc. **26**, 102 (1981).

81DYK/JON
J. M. Dyke, N. B. H. Jonathan, A. Morris and M. J. Winters, "Vacuum Ultraviolet Photoelectron Spectroscopy of Transient Species. Part 13. Observation of the X^3A'' State of HO_2," Molec. Phys. **44**, 1059 (1981).

81DYK/JON2
J. Dyke, N. Jonathan, A. Morris and M. Winter, "First Ionization Potential of the FCO (X^2A') Radical Studied Using Photoelectron Spectroscopy," J. Chem. Soc. Faraday Trans. II **77**, 667 (1981).

81EAD/WEI
R.A. Eades, D.A. Weil, M.R. Ellenberger, D.A. Dixon and C.H. Douglass, Jr., J. Am. Chem. Soc. **103**, 5372 (1981).

81EIC/HEY
K. Eichler and H. Heydtmann, Int. J. Chem. Kinet. **13**, 1107 (1981).

81ELB/DIE
S. Elbel and H. tom Dieck, "Die Stiborane Me_3SbX_2 (X = Me, Cl, Br, I) und $SbCl_5$ - im Vergleich mit Nebengruppenanaloga $TaMe_5$, $TaCl_5$ und $NbCl_5$," Z. Anorg. Allg. Chem. **483**, 33 (1981).

81ELB/LIE
S. Elbel, K. Lienert, A. Krebs and H. tom Dieck, "Phenylethin - Mustersonde fur Substituenteneffekte," Liebigs Ann. Chem. 1785 (1981).

81ELL/DIX
M.R. Ellenberger, D.A. Dixon and W.E. Farneth, J. Am. Chem. Soc. **103** 5377 (1981).

81ELS/ALL
T. M. El-Sherbini, S. H. Allam, M. D. Migahed and A. M. Dawoud, "Mass Spectrometric Investigation of Aliphatic Aldehydes," Z. Naturforsch. **36a**, 1334 (1981).

81ENG/COR
P.E. Engelking, R.R. Corderman, J.J. Wenddoski, G.B. Ellison, V.S. O'Niel and W.C. Lineberger, "Laser Photoelectron Spectroscopy of CH_2^-, and the Singlet-Triplet Splitting in Methylene," J. Chem. Phys. **74**, 5460 (1981).

81ERA/KOL
P.A. Erastov, V.P. Kolesov, L.N. Dityat'eva and Y.G. Golovanova, J. Chem. Thermodyn. **13**, 663 (1981).

81FAR/SRI
M. Farber and R. D. Srivastava, "Electron Impact Ionization of $Ba(OH)_2$ (g)," J. Chem. Phys. **74**, 2160 (1981).

81FEI/COR
C.S. Feigerle, R.R. Corderman, S.V. Bobashev and W.C. Lineberger, "Binding Energies and Structure of Transition Metal Negative Ions," J. Chem. Phys. **74**, 1580 (1981). [Superceded: 85HOT/LIN].

81FER/RIB
M.L.C.C.H. Ferrao, M.A.V. Ribeiro de Silva, S. Suradi, G. Pilcher and H.A. Skinner, J. Chem. Thermodyn. **13**, 567 (1981).

81FOR/MAI
P. Forster, J. P. Maier and F. Thommen, "Radiative and Non-Radiative Decay Rates of Alkyl Substituted Diacetylene Cations at Selected Energies within their 2A States Determined via Photoelectron-Photoion Coincidence Measurements," Chem. Phys. **59**, 85 (1981).

81FRO/KIR
D.C. Frost, C. Kirby, C.A. McDowell and N.P.C. Westwood, "Preparation and HeI Photoelectron Spectra of the Dihaloboranes, HBX_2 (X = Cl and Br)," J. Am. Chem. Soc. **103**, 4428 (1981).

81FRO/MAC
D.C. Frost, C.B. MacDonald, C.A. McDowell and N.P.C. Westwood, "Preparation and HeI Photoelectron Spectra of the Halogen Thiocyanates, XSCN (X = Cl and Br)," J. Am. Chem. Soc. **103**, 4423 (1981).

81FUJ/MCI
M. Fujio, R.T. McIver, Jr. and R.W. Taft, "Effects on the Acidities of Phenols from Specific Substituent-Solvent Interactions. Inherent Substituent Parameters from Gas Phase Acidities," J. Am. Chem. Soc. **103**, 4017 (1981).

81FUR/PIA
C. Furlani, M.N. Piancastelli, C. Cauletti, F. Faticanti and G. Ortaggi, "He(I) and He(II) Photoelectron Spectra of Some Organomercury Compounds with Carbon π-Systems," J. Electron Spectrosc. Rel. Phenom. **22**, 309 (1981).

81FUS/NOT
H. Fussstetter and H. Noth, "Zur Darstellung von 1,1-Bis(diorganylboryl)-2,2-dimethylhydrazinen," Liebigs Ann. Chem. 633 (1981).

81GAL/KLA
V. Galasso, L. Klasinc, A. Sabluic, N. Trinajstic, G. C. Pappalardo and W. Steglich, "Conformation and Photoelectron Spectra of 2-(2-Furyl)pyrrole and 2-(2-Thienyl)pyrrole," J. Chem. Soc. Perkins II, 127 (1981).

81GIN/PEL
K.A. Gingerich, M. Pelino and R. Haque, High Temp. Sci. **14**, 137 (1981).

81GLE/BAR
R. Gleiter and R. Bartetzko, "The Structures of S_4N, $S_3N_2O_2$, and S_4N_3," Z. Naturforsch. **36b**, 492 (1981).

81GLE/BOH
R. Gleiter, M. C. Bohm and M. Baudler, "Photoelektronenspektroskopische Untersuchungen an Phosphor-Drei- und -Vierring-Systemen," Chem. Ber. **114**, 1004 (1981).

81GLE/GUB
R. Gleiter, K. Gubernator, M. Eckert-Maksic, J. Spanget-Larsen, B. Bianco, G. Gandillon and U. Berger, "120. The Electronic Structure of Phenylene and Naphthylene Bicyclobutanes. Photoelectron Spectroscopy and Model Calculations," Helv. Chim. Acta **64**, 1312 (1981).

81GLE/GUB2
R. Gleiter, K. Gubernator and W. Grimme, "Evidence for a Strong Through-Bond Interaction in anti-Tricyclo[6.4.0.0^{2,7}]dodecatetraene," J. Org. Chem. **46**, 1247 (1981).

81GLE/SCH
R. Gleiter, W. Schafer and M. Eckert-Maksic, "Transannulare Wechselwirkungen zwischen Acetylenen - Photoelektronenspektroskopische Untersuchungen an 1,8-Diethinylnaphthalin und cyclischen Derivaten von 2,2'-Diethinylbiphenyl," Chem. Ber. **114**, 2309 (1981).

81GOD/SCH
S.A. Godleski, P. von R. Schleyer, E. Osawa and W.T. Wipke, Prog. Phys. Org. Chem. **13**, 67 (1981).

81GRA/TON
G. Granozzi, E. Tondello, M. Casarin and D. Ajo, "Electronic Structure of μ-Methylene-Bis-[Dicarbonyl (η^5-Cyclopentadienyl)- Manganese] by UV Photoelectron Spectroscopy," Inorg. Chim. Acta **48**, 73 (1981).

81GRE/MIN
J. C. Green, D. M. P. Mingos and E. A. Seddon, "Ultraviolet Photoelectron Studies on Bonding in Some Metal Carbonyl and Metal Hydrido Carbonyl Clusters," Inorg. Chem. **20**, 2595 (1981).

81GRI/LOS
D. Griller and F. P. Lossing, "On the Thermochemistry of α-Aminoalkyl Radicals," J. Am. Chem. Soc. **103**, 1586 (1981).

81GRO/SCH
G. Gross, R. Schulz, A. Schweig and C. Wentrup, "Isobenzofulvene," Angew. Chem. Int. Ed. **20**, 1021 (1981).

81GRU
H.-F. Grutzmacher, "The Loss of ortho Halogeno Substituents from Substituted Thiobenzamide Ions," Org. Mass Spectrom. **16**, 448 (1981).

81GUP/NAP
S. K. Gupta, B. M. Nappi and K. A. Gingerich, "Mass Spectrometric Study of the Stabilities of the Gaseous Molecules Pt$_2$ and PtY," Inorg. Chem. **20**, 966 (1981).

81GUS/VOL
L. E. Gusel'nikov, V. V. Volkova, V. G. Zaikin, N. A. Tarasenko, A. A. Tishenkov, N. S. Nametkin, M. G. Voronkov and S. V. Kirpichenko, "Mass Spectra of 3,3-Dimethyl-3-silathietane and 3,3-Diethyl-2,4-dimethyl-3-silathietane. First Observation of Silathione Ions and Calculation of Their Heats of Formation," J. Organometall. Chem. **215**, 9 (1981).

81GUS/VOL2
L. E. Gusel'nikov, V. V. Volkova, N. A. Tarasenko, A. A. Tishenkov, V. G. Zaikin, E. I. Eremina and N. S. Nametkin, "Deuterium Labelling and Thermochemical Studies of Dissociative Ionization of Methyl Substituted Monosilacyclobutanes. Ring Expansion in the Molecular Ion of 1,1,3-Trimethyl-1-silacyclobutane," Org. Mass Spectrom. **16**, 242 (1981).

81GUT/BES
H. G. Guttenberger, H. J. Bestmann, F. L. Dickert, F. S. Jorgensen and J. P. Snyder, "Sulfur-Bridged peri-Naphthalenes: Synthesis, Conformational Analysis, and Photoelectron Spectroscopy of the Mono-, Di-, and Trisulfides of 1,8-Dimethylnaphthalene," J. Am. Chem. Soc. **103**, 159 (1981).

81HAL/ARM
L. F. Halle, P. B. Armentrout and J. L. Beauchamp, "Formation of Chromium Carbene Ions by Reaction of Electronically Excited Chromium Ions with Methane in the Gas Phase," J. Am. Chem. Soc. **103**, 962 (1981).

81HAQ/GIN
R. Haque and K. A. Gingerich, "Identification and Atomization Energies of Gaseous Molecules ScC$_2$, ScC$_3$, ScC$_4$, ScC$_5$, and ScC$_6$ by High Temperature Mass Spectrometry," J. Chem. Phys. **74**, 6407 (1981).

81HEI/KOV
E. Heilbronner, B. Kovac, W. Nutakul, A. D. Taggart and R. P. Thummel, "Trisannelated Benzenes. Preparation, Properties, and Photoelectron Spectra," J. Org. Chem. **46**, 5279 (1981).

81HEN/ISA
L. Henriksen, R. Isaksson, T. Liljefors and J. Sandstrom, "Ultraviolet Absorption and Photoelectron Spectra of Some Cyclic and Open-Chain Mono- and Dithiooxamides," Acta Chem. Scand. B **35**, 489 (1981).

81HEN/KNO
S.P. Henegan, P.A. Knoot and S.W. Benson, Int. J. Chem. Kinet. **13**, 677 (1981).

81HER/SIC
R. Herzschuh and A. Sicker, "Stereochemische Einflusse auf die Ionisations- und Auftrittsenergien cis/trans-isomerer Dimethylcycloalkane," Z. Chem. **21**, 409 (1981).

81HOA/CAB
A. Hoareau, B. Cabaud and P. Melinon, "Time-of-Flight Mass Spectroscopy of Supersonic Beam of Metallic Vapours: Intensities and Appearance Potentials of M_x Aggregates," Surface Sci. **106**, 195 (1981).

81HOL/BUR
J.L. Holmes, P.C. Burgers and J.K. Terlouw, "Water Elimination from the Keto and Enol Tautomers of Ionised Ethylacetate," Can. J. Chem. **59**, 1805 (1981).

81HOL/FIN
J.L. Holmes, M. Fingas and F.P. Lossing, "Towards a General Scheme for Estimating the Heats of Formation of Organic Ions in the Gas Phase. Part I. Odd-Electron Cations," Can. J. Chem. **59**, 80 (1981).

81HOT
K. Hottmann, "Uber einige Zusammenhange zwischen massenspektrometrischen Ionenhaufigkeiten und Molekuleigenschaften an element-organischen Verbindungen der Gruppe IVb," J. f. Prakt. Chemie **323**, 399 (1981).

81JAC/PEL
R.L. Jackson, M.J. Pellerite and J.I. Brauman, "Photodetachment of the Azide Ion in the Gas Phase. Electron Affinity of the Azide Radical," J. Am. Chem. Soc. **103**, 1802 (1981).

81JEN/RAN
W.B. Jennings, D. Randall, S.D. Worley and J.H. Hargis, "Conformation and Stereodynamics of 2-Dialkylamino-1,3-dimethyl-2,3-dihydro-1H-1,3,2-benzodiaza-phospholes. An Experimental Nuclear Magnetic Resonance, Ultraviolet Photoelectron, and Theoretical MNDO Investigation," J. Chem. Soc. Perkin Trans. II, 1411 (1981).

81JON/MOO
G. Jonkers, R. Mooyman and C.A. De Lange, "Ultraviolet Photoelectron Spectroscopy of Unstable Species: Nitrosyl Cyanide (ONCN)," Chem. Phys. **57**, 97 (1981).

81JOR
F.S. Jorgensen, "Photoelectron Spectrum and Molecular Orbital (MNDO and PRDDO) Study of Dimethoxymethane," J. Chem. Res. 212 (1981).

81JOR/CAR
F.S. Jorgensen, L. Carlsen and F. Duus, "The Electronic Structure of β-Thioxoketones. A Photoelectron Spectroscopic Study of the Enol-Enethiol Tautomerism of Thioacetylacetone and Related Compounds," J. Am. Chem. Soc. 103, 1350 (1981).

81JOR/NOR
F.S. Jorgensen, L. Norskov-Lauritsen, R.B. Jensen and G. Schroll, "Polyethers. Structural Analysis of the 1,4,5,8-Tetraoxadecalins and 2,2'-bis(1,3-Dioxolane) by Photoelectron Spectroscopy, Molecular Mechanics and Molecular Orbital Calculations," Tetrahedron 37, 3671 (1981).

81KAI
W. Kaim, "Organometal-Stabilized 1,4-Dihydropyrazines: Extremely Electron-Rich Heterocycles," Angew. Chem. Int. Ed. 20, 600 (1981).

81KAN/MOO
A. Kant and K.A. Moon, "Mass Spectrometric Determination of the Dissociation Energies of Gaseous AlH, GaH, InH, ScH, CoH and Estimation of the Maximum Dissociation Energies of TiH, CrH, MnH and FeH," High Temp. Sci. 14, 23 (1981).

81KAP/STA
M.M. Kappes and R.H. Staley, "Oxidation of Transition-Metal Cations in the Gas Phase. Oxygen Bond Dissociation Energies and Formation of an Excited State Product," J. Phys. Chem. 85, 942 (1981).

81KAU/VAH
R. Kaufel, G. Vahl, R. Minkwitz and H. Baumgartel, "Die Photoionenspektren von SCl_2, S_2Cl_2 und S_2Br_2," Z. Anorg. Allg. Chem. 481, 207 (1981).

81KHV/ZYK
V.I. Khvostenko, B.G. Zykov, V.P. Yuriev, V.F. Mironov, G.I. Kovel'zon, A.A. Panasenko, V.D. Sheludyakov and I.A. Gailyunas, "Study of $d(\pi)$-$p(\pi)$ Interaction in Vinyl- and Alkylsilicon-Containing Compounds by Photoelectron Spectroscopy," J. Organometall. Chem. 218, 155 (1981).

81KIM/KAT
K. Kimura, S. Katsumata, Y. Achiba, T. Yamazaki and S. Iwata, "Ionization Energies, Ab Initio Assignments and Valence Electronic Structure for 200 Molecules," Handbook of HeI Photoelectron Spectra of Fundamental Organic Compounds, Japan Scientific Soc. Press, Tokyo (1981) and Halsted Press, New York (1981).

81KIM/STE
Y.B. Kim, K. Stephan, E. Mark and T.D. Mark, "Single and Double Ionization of Nitric Oxide by Electron Impact from Threshold up to 180 eV," J. Chem. Phys. 74, 6771 (1981).

81KIN/MAR
G.K. King, M.M. Maricq, V.M. Bierbaum and C.H. DePuy, "Gas Phase Reaction of Negative Ions with Alkyl Nitrites," J. Am. Chem. Soc. 103, 7133 (1981).

81KLY/SHU
N.A. Klyuev, Y.V. Shurukhhin, I.I. Grandberg, I.K.81pad Yakushchenko and A.E. Bolubitskii, "Stereospecific Fragmentation of 1-Methyl-1,2-Diarylcyclopropanes," Z. Org. Khim. 17, 556 (1981).

81KOB/ARA
T. Kobayashi, T. Arai, H. Sakuragi, K. Tokumaru and C. Utsunomiya, "A New Method for Conformational Analysis by Photoelectron Spectroscopy with Application to Alkyl-Substituted Styrenes," Bull. Chem. Soc. Jpn. 54, 1658 (1981).

81KOE/MCK
T. Koenig and W. McKenna, "First Ionization Band of 1,1-Dimethylsilaethylene by Transient Photoelectron Spectroscopy," J. Am. Chem. Soc. 103, 1212 (1981).

81KOM/DYK
A. Komornicki, C.E. Dykstra, M.A. Vincent and L. Radom, J. Am. Chem. Soc. 103, 1652 (1981).

81KOP/PIK
I. Koppel, R. Pikver, A. Sugis, E. Suurmaa and E. Lippmaa, Org. Reac. 18, 3 (1981).

81KUD/KUD
A.P. Kudchadker, S.A. Kudchadker, R.C. Wilhoit and S.K. Gupta, "Acenaphthylene, Acenaphthene, Fluorene, and Fluoranthene," **API Monograph**, 715-81, American Petroleum Institute, Washington, D.C. (1981).

81KUD/KUD2
A.P. Kudchadker, S.A. Kudchadker, R.C. Wilhoit and S.K. Gupta, "Carbazole, 9-Methylcarbazole and Acridine," **API Monograph**, 716-81, American Petroleum Institute, Washington, D.C. (1981).

81KUD/KUD3
A.P. Kudchadker, S.A. Kudchadker, R.C. Wilhoit and S.K. Gupta, "Thiophene, 2,3- and 2,5-Dihydrothiophene and Tetrahydrothiophene," **API Monograph** 717-81, American Petroleum Institute, Washington, D.C. (1981).

81LAU/BRI
K.H. Lau, R.D. Brittain and D.L. Hildenbrand, Chem. Phys. Lett. 81, 227 (1981).

81LEB/YEV
B.D. Lebedev, A.A. Yevstropov and Y.G. Kiparisova, Int. J. Chem. Kinet. 13, 1185 (1981).

81LEE/POT
E.P.F. Lee and A.W. Potts, "Fine Structure in the He(I)/He(II) Photoelectron Spectra of the Metal Valence (d) Shells of the Group IIB Dihalides," J. Electron Spectrosc. Rel. Phenom. 22, 247 (1981).

81LEU/HOF
S. Leutwyler, M. Hofmann, H.-P. Harri and E. Schumacher, "The Adiabatic Ionization Potentials of the Alkali Dimers Na_2, NaK and K_2," Chem. Phys. Lett. 77, 257 (1981).

81LIF/TZI
C. Lifshitz and E. Tzidony, "Kinetic Energy Release Distributions for $C_3H_6O^+$ Ion Dissociations: A Further Test of the Applicability of the Energy Randomization Hypothesis to Unimolecular Fragmentations," Int. J. Mass Spectrom. Ion Phys. 39, 181 (1981).

81LIN/BES
T.B. Lindemer, T.M. Bessman and C.E. Johnson, J. Nucl. Mater. 100, 178 (1981).

81LIV/ROB
P. Livant, K.A. Roberts, M.D. Eggers and S.D. Worley, "The Gas Phase Conformation of 3,7-Dimethyl-3,7-Diazabicyclo[3.3.1]nonane," Tetrahedron 37, 1853 (1981).

81LOG/TAK
Y. Loguinov, V.V. Takhistov and L.P. Vatlina, "Photoionization Studies of Substituted Trimethylamines," Org. Mass Spec. 16, 239 (1981).

81LOS/LAM
F.P. Lossing, Y.-T. Lam and A. Maccoll, "Gas Phase Heats of Formation of Alkyl Immonium Ions," Can. J. Chem. 59, 2228 (1981).

81MAI
J.P. Maier, "Structure and Decay of Gaseous Organic Radical Cations Studied by Their Radiative Decay, Exemplified by the 1,3-Pentadiyne Cation," Angew. Chem. Int. Ed. Engl. 20, 638 (1981).

81MAI/MIS
J.P. Maier, L. Misev and F. Thommen, "191. Laser-Induced Fluorescence and Photoelectron-Photon Coincidence Studies of 3,5-Octadiyne Cation," Helv. Chim. Acta 64, 1985 (1981).

81MAI/SCH
W.F. Maier and P. von R. Schleyer, J. Am. Chem. Soc. 103, 1891 (1981).

81MAI/THO
J.P. Maier and F. Thommen, "Fluorescence Quantum Yields and Lifetimes of Fluorobenzene Cations in Selected Levels of Their B and C States Determined by Photoelectron-Photoion Coincidence Spectroscopy," Chem. Phys. 57, 319 (1981).

81MAI/THO2
J.P. Maier and F. Thommen, "Photoelectron-photon coincidence Measurements of the Fluorescence quantum Yields of cis-1,2-Difluoroethylene Cation in Selected Levels of the A^2A_1 State," J. Chem. Soc. Faraday Trans. II **77**, 845 (1981).

81MAL/ALI
I.P. Malkerova, A.S. Alikhanyan, V.D. Butskii, V.S. Pervov and V.I. Gorkoraki, "The Behavior of Tungsten Sulphide Tetrafluoride WSF_4 When Heated," Zh. Neorganich. Khim. **26**, 1955 (1981). Engl. Trans.: Russ. J. Inorg. Chem. **26**, 1055 (1981).

81MAL/MEL
I.P. Malkerova, E.I. Mel'nichenko, A.S. Alikhanyan, E.G. Rakov and V.I. Gorgoraki, "Thermal Decomposition of the Tungsten Oxide Fluorides $W_2O_4F.O.2(NOF)$ and W_2O_4F," Zh. Neorganich. Khim. **26**, 17 (1981); Engl. Trans.: Russ. J. Inorg. Chem. **26**, 9 (1981).

81MAN/SUN
M. Mansson and S. Sunner, J. Chem. Thermodyn. **13**, 671 (1981).

81MAS/MOU
P. Masclet, G. Mouvier and J.F. Bocquet, "Effets Electroniques et Effets Steriques dus a la Substitution Alcoyle dans les Dienes Conjugues," J. Chim. Phys. **78**, 99 (1981).

81MAU/SIE
M. Meot-Ner (Mautner), L.W. Sieck and P. Ausloos, "Ionization of Normal Alkanes: Enthalpy, Entropy, Structural, and Isotope Effects," J. Am. Chem. Soc. **103**, 5342 (1981).

81MCD/CHO
R.N. McDonald, A.K. Chowdhury and D.W. Setser, "Gas Phase Generation of Phenylnitrene Anion Radical - Proton Affinity and Heat of Formation of $PhN^{-\cdot}$ and Its Clustering with ROH Molecules," J. Am. Chem. Soc. **103**, 6599 (1981).

81MCL/CAM
S.A. McLuckey, D. Cameron and R.G. Cooks, "Proton Affinities from the Dissociation of Proton Bound Dimers," J. Am. Chem. Soc. **103**, 1313 (1981).

81MEE/WAH
J. Meeks, A. Wahlborg and S.P. McGlynn, "Photoelectron Spectroscopy of Carbonyls: Benzoic Acid and Its Derivatives," J. Elec. Spectrosc. Rel. Phenom. **22**, 43 (1981).

81MIC/SVE
G.D. Michels and H.J. Svec, "Characterization of $MnTc(CO)_{10}$ and $TcRe(CO)_{10}$," Inorg. Chem. **20**, 3445 (1981).

81MIL/CIL
S. Millefiori, E. Ciliberto, A. Millefiori and M.A. Zerbo, "Gas Phase U. V. Photoelectron Investigation of Azoxybenzene and 4,4'-di(n-alkoxy)azoxybenzenes," Spectromchim. Acta **37A**, 605 (1981).

81MIL/MIL
S. Millefiori and A. Millefiori, "Spectroscopic and Electrochemical Properties of Intramolecularly Hydrogen-Bonded Compounds. Ortho-Hydroxyazobenzenes," Can. J. Chem. **59**, 821 (1981).

81MOD/DIS
A. Modelli and G. Distefano, "L. C. B. O.: An Easy Method to Predict Valence Ionization Energies. Application to Substituted Benzenes," Z. Naturforsch. **36a**, 1344 (1981).

81MOD/DIS2
A. Modelli and G. Distefano, "He(I) Photoelectron Spectra of Chloro-, Vinyl- and Acetyl-Pyridines," J. Elec. Spectrosc. Rel. Phenom. **23**, 323 (1981).

81MOH/HIR
S. Mohmand, T. Hirabayashi and H. Bock, "Gasphasen-Reaktionen, 22. Thermische Erzeugung von C_4H_4O: Vinylketen und Ethylidenketen," Chem. Ber. **114**, 1609 (1981).

81MOH/JIA
M. Mohraz, W. Jian-qi, E. Heilbronner, A. Solladie-Cavallo and F. Matloubi-Moghadam, "11. Some Comments on the Conformations of Methyl Phenyl Sulfides, Sulfoxides and Sulfones," Helv. Chim. Acta **64**, 97 (1981).

81MOR/KOL
B.J. Morris-Sherwood, B.W.S. Kolthammer and M.B. Hall, "Photoelectron Spectra of and Molecular Orbital Calculations on(η^5-Cyclopentadienyl)dinitrosylhalochromium and -Tungsten," Inorg. Chem. **20**, 2771 (1981).

81MUL/PRE
K. Muller and F. Previdoli, "247. Enamines. III. A Theoretical and Photoelectron Spectroscopic Study of the Molecular and Electronic Structures of Aziridine Enamines," Helv. Chim. Acta **64**, 2508 (1981).

81MUL/PRE2
K. Muller, F. Previdoli and H. Desilvestro, "246. Enamines. II. A Theoretical and Photoelectron Spectroscopic Study of the Molecular and Electronic Structure of Aliphatic Enamines," Helv. Chim. Acta **64**, 2497 (1981).

81MUR
E. Murad, "Thermochemical Properties of the Gaseous Alkaline Earth Monohydroxides," J. Chem. Phys. **75**, 4080 (1981).

81NAK/ASA
H. Nakagawa, M. Asano and K. Kubo, "Mass Spectrometric Study of the Vaporization of Lithium Metasilicate," J. Nucl. Mat. **102**, 292 (1981).

81NAP/GIN
B.M. Nappi and K.A. Gingerich, "Dissociation Energy and Standard Heat of Formation of Gaseous LaPt," Inorg. Chem. **20**, 522 (1981).

81NAT/FRA
P. Natalis and J.L. Franklin, "Ionization and Dissociation of Diphenyl and Condensed-Ring Aromatics by Electron Impact. III. Azobenzene," Int. J. Mass Spectrom. Ion Phys. **40**, 35 (1981).

81NEL/GRE
S.F. Nelsen, L.A. Grezzo and W.C. Hollinsed, "Effects of Structure on the Ease of Electron Removal from o-Phenylenediamines. 2. Photoelectron Spectra of o-Phenylenediamines," J. Org. Chem. **46**, 283 (1981).

81NES/BAI
A.N. Nesmeyanov, V.N. Baiden, Y.V. Chizhov, M.M. Timoshenko, Y.S. Nekrasov and I.I. Kritskaya, "He(I) Photoelectron Investigation of Functionally Substituted Camphene Derivatives," Dokl. Akad. Nauk SSSR **256**, 121 (1981).

81NIK/SID
M.I. Nikitin, L.N. Sidorov, E.V. Skokan and I.D. Sorokin, "Mass Spectrometric Determination of the Heats of Formation of ScF_4^- and KF_2^-," Russ. J. Phys. Chem. **55**, 1107 (1981).

81NIK/SID2
M.I. Nikitin, L.N. Sidorov and M.V. Korobov, "The Electron Affinity of Platinum Hexafluoride," Int. J. Mass Spectrom. Ion Proc. **37**, 13 (1981).

81NOV/CVI
I. Novak, T. Cvitas and L. Klasinc, "Photoelectron Spectrum of Tetravinylstannane, $Sn(CH=CH_2)_4$," J. Organometall. Chem. **220**, 145 (1981).

81NOV/CVI2
I. Novak, T. Cvitas and L. Klasinc, "Photoelectron Spectrum of Tetraiodomethane," Chem. Phys. Lett. **79**, 154 (1981).

81NOV/CVI3
I. Novak, T. Cvitas, L. Klasinc and H. Gusten, "Photoelectron Spectra of Some Halogenomethanes," J. Chem. Soc. Faraday Trans. II **77**, 2049 (1981).

81ONO/OSU
Y. Ono, E.A. Osuch and C.Y. Ng, "Molecular Beam Photoionization Study of OCS, (OCS)$_2$, (OCS)$_3$, and OCS·CS$_2$," J. Chem. Phys. **74**, 1645 (1981).

81PAD/PAT
M.N. Paddon-Row, H.K. Patney, R.S. Brown and K.N. Houk, "Observation of a Very Large Orbital Interaction through Four Bonds. An Alternative Model of Orbital Interactions through Bonds," J. Am. Chem. Soc. **103**, 5575 (1981).

81PAL/SIM
M.H. Palmer, I. Simpson and J.R. Wheeler, "Gas Phase Tautomerism in the Triazoles and Tetrazoles: A Study by Photoelectron Spectroscopy and ab Initio Molecular Orbital Calculations," Z. Naturforsch. **36a**, 1246 (1981).

81PAP/ERA
T. Papina, P.A. Erastov and V.P. Kolesov, J. Chem. Thermodyn. **13**, 683 (1981).

81PAQ/HER
L.A. Paquette, L.W. Hertel, R. Gleiter, M.C. Bohm, M.A. Beno and G.G. Christoph, "Electronic Control of Stereoselectivity. 8. The Stereochemical Course of Electrophilic Additions to Aryl-Substituted 9-Isopropylidenebenzonorbornenes," J. Am. Chem. Soc. **103**, 7106 (1981).

81PEL/JAC
M.J. Pellerite, R.L. Jackson and J.I. Brauman, "Proton Affinity of the Gaseous Azide Ion. The N-H Bond Dissociation Enegry in HN$_3$," J. Phys. Chem. **85**, 1624 (1981).

81PFI/GUI
G. Pfister-Guillouzo, C. Guimon, J. Frank, J. Ellison and A.R. Katritzky, "Tautomeric Pyridines, 26. A Photoelectron Spectral Study of the Vapour Phase Tautomerism of 2- and 4-Quinolone," Liebigs Ann. Chem. 366 (1981).

81PLE/VIL
V.V. Plemenkov, Y.Y. Villem, N.V. Villem, I.G. Bolesov, L.S. Surmina, N.I. Yakushkina and A.A. Formanovskii, "Photoelectron Spectra of Polyalkylcyclopropenes and Polyalkylcyclopropanes," Zh. Obshchei. Khim. **51**, 2076 (1981).

81POL/RAI
S.K. Pollack, B.C. Raine and W.J. Hehre, "Determination of the Heats of Formation of the Isomeric Xylylenes by Ion Cyclotron Resonance Spectroscopy," J. Am. Chem. Soc. **103**, 6308 (1981).

81PRA/CHU
S.T. Pratt and W.A. Chupka, "Photoionization Study of the Kinetics of Unimolecular Decomposition of Halobenzene Ions," Chem. Phys. **62**, 153 (1981).

81PRO/RAD
A. Pross and L. Radom, Prog. Phys. Org. Chem. **13**, 1 (1981).

81RAB/HEL
M.A. Rabbih, A.I. Helal and M.A. Fahmey, "Mass Spectrometric Studies of Methylacetophenone Isomers by Electron Impact," Indian J. Pure Appl. Phys. **19**, 335 (1981).

81RAN/WRI
D.W.H. Rankin and J.G. Wright, "The Preparation and Properties of 1-Difluorophosphino-pyrrole," J. Fluorine Chem. **17**, 469 (1981).

81RID/RAY
D.M. Rider, G.W. Ray, E.J. Darland and G.E. Leroi, "A Photoionization Mass Spectrometric Investigation of CH$_3$CN and CD$_3$CN," J. Chem. Phys. **74**, 1652 (1981).

81ROB/STE
D.A. Robaugh and S.E. Stein, Int. J. Chem. Kinet. **13**, 445 (1981).

81ROT/SCH
W.R. Roth and B.P. Scholz, Chem. Ber. **114**, 3741 (1981).

81RUS/KLA
B. Ruscic, L. Klasinc, A. Wolf and J.V. Knop, "Photoelectron Spectra of and Ab Initio Calculations on Chlorobenzenes. 3. Hexachlorobenzene," J. Phys. Chem. **85**, 1495 (1981).

81RUS/KLA2
B. Ruscic, L. Klasinc, A. Wolf and J.V. Knop, "Photoelectron Spectra of and Ab Initio Calculations on Chlorobenzenes. 1. Chlorobenzene and Dichlorobenzenes," J. Phys. Chem. **85**, 1486 (1981).

81RUS/KLA3
B. Ruscic, L. Klasinc, A. Wolf and J.V. Knop, "Photoelectron Spectra of and Ab Initio Calculations on Chlorobenzenes. 2. Trichlorobenzenes, Tetrachlorobenzenes, and Pentachlorobenzene," J. Phys. Chem. **85**, 1490 (1981).

81SAB/MIN
R. Sabbah and C. Mindakis, Thermochim. Acta **43**, 269 (1981).

81SAS/HAR
T. Sasamoto, H. Hara and T. Sata, "Mass Spectrometric Study of the Vaporization of Magnesium Oxide from Magnesium Aluminate Spinel," Bull. Chem. Soc. Jpn. **54**, 3327 (1981).

81SAT/SEK
N. Sato, K. Seki and H. Inokuchi, "Polarization Energies of Organic Solids Determined by Ultraviolet Photoelectron Spectroscopy," J. Chem. Soc. Faraday Trans. II **77**, 1621 (1981).

81SCH/GRO
B. Schaldach, B. Grotemeyer, J. Grotemeyer and H.-F. Grutzmacher, "Kinetic and Thermodynamic Effects on Intramolecular Aromatic Substitution in meta and para Substituted Benzalacetones," Org. Mass Spectrom. **16**, 410 (1981).

81SCH/SCH
R. Schulz and A. Schweig, "Cyclopentadienethione," Angew. Chem. Int. Ed. **20**, 570 (1981).

81SEN/KEB
D.K. Sen Sharma and P. Kebarle, "Stability and Reactivity of the Benzyl and Tropylium Cations in the Gas Phase," Can. J. Chem. **59**, 1592 (1981).

81SHA/AKI
M. Shahbaz, I. Akiyama and P. LeBreton, "Ultraviolet Photoelectron Studies of Methyl Substituted Chrysenes," Biochemical and Biophysical Research Communications **103**, 25 (1981).

81SID/SOR
L.N. Sidorov, I.D. Sorokin, N.I. Nitikin and E.V. Skokan, "Effusion Method for Determining the Electron Affinity and Heat of Formation of Negative Ions," Int. J. Mass Spectrom. Ion Phys. **39**, 311 (1981).

81SKO/NIK
E.V. Skokan, M.I. Nikitin, I.D. Sorokin, A.V. Gusarov and L.N. Sidirov , "Determination of the Heat of Formation of the Tetrafluoroscandate and Pentfluorozirconate Ions by the Effusion Method," Russ. J. Phys. Chem. **55**, 1062 (1981).

81SMI/ADA
D. Smith, N.G. Adams and W. Lindinger, "Reactions of the H$_n$S Ions (n = 0 to 3) with Several Molecular Gases at Thermal Energies," J. Chem. Phys. **75**, 3365 (1981).

81SMI/LAI
G.P. Smith and R.M. Laine, "Organometallic Bond Dissociation Energies. Laser Pyrolysis of Fe(CO)$_5$," J. Phys. Chem. **85**, 1620 (1981).

81SMI/STE
O.I. Smith and J.S. Stevenson, "Determination of Cross Sections for Formation of Parent and Fragment Ions by Electron Impact from SO$_2$ and SO$_3$," J. Chem. Phys. **74**, 6777 (1981).

81SOR/SID
I.D. Sorokin, L.N. Sidorov,M.I. Nikitin and E.V. Skokan, "Mass-Spectrometric Determination of the Enthalpies of Dissociation of Gaseous Complex Fluorides into Neutral and Charged Particles. V. Heats of Formation of FeF$_3^-$ and FeF$_4^-$," Int. J. Mass Spectrom. Ion Phys. **41**, 45 (1981).

81SPE
P.J. Spencer, "Hafnium: Physicochemical Properties of its compounds and Alloys" ("Atomic Energy Review Special Issue 8," ed. K.L. Komarek, IAEA, Vienna, 1981).

81STE/BAR
S.E. Stein and B.D. Barton, Thermochim. Acta **44**, 265 (1981).

81SUL/DEP
S.A. Sullivan, C.H. DePuy and R. Damrauer, "Gas Phase Reactions of Cyclic Silanes," J. Am. Chem. Soc. **103**, 480 (1981).

81SUR/HAC
S. Suradi, J.M. Hacking, G. Pilcher, I. Gumrukcu and M.F. Lappert, J. Chem. Thermodyn. **13**, 857 (1981).

81SZE/KOR
L. Szepes, T. Koranyi, G. Naray-Szabo, A. Modelli and G. Distefano, "Ultraviolet Photoelectron Spectra of Group IV Hexamethyl Derivatives Containing a Metal-Metal Bond," J. Organometall. Chem. **217**, 35 (1981).

81TAA/SUM
M. Taagepera, K.D. Summerhays, W.J. Hehre, R.D. Topsom, A. Pross, L. Radom and R.W. Taft, J. Org. Chem. **46**, 891 (1981).

81TER/HEE
J.K. Terlouw, W. Heerma and G. Dijkstra, "On the Structure of the Odd Electron $[C_2H_6O]^+$ Ions in the Mass Spectrum of [1,3-Propanediol]$^+$," Org. Mass Spectrom. **16**, 326 (1981).

81TIM/KOR
M.M. Timoshenko, I.V. Korkoshko, V.T. Kleimenov, N.E. Petrachenko, Y.V. Chizhov, V.V. Ryl'kov and M.E. Akopyan, "Ionization Potentials of Rhodamine Dyes," Dokl. Akad. SSSR **260**, 138 (1981).

81TPIS
L.V. Gurvich, I.V. Veits, V.A. Medvedev, G.A. Khachkuruzov, V.S. Yungman and G.A. Bergman, et al., "Termodinamicheskie Svoistva Individual'nykh Veshchestv" (Thermodynamic Properties of Individual Substances); Glushko, V.P., gen. ed., Vol. 3, parts 1 and 2(1981), Izdatel'stvo"Nauka"Moscow.

81TRA
J.C. Traeger, "Heat of Formation of sec-Butyl Cation in the Gas Phase," Org. Mass Spectrom. **16**, 193 (1981).

81TRA/MCL
J.C. Traeger and R.G. McLoughlin, "Absolute Heats of Formation for Gas Phase Cations," J. Am. Chem. Soc. **103**, 3647 (1981).

81TRA/RED
V.F. Traven', V.V. Redchenko, M.Y. Eismont and B.I. Stepanov, "Photoelectron Spectra and Electronic and Steric Structures of Silicon and Sulfur-Containing Analogs of 9,10-Dihydroanthracene," Zh. Obs. Khim. **51**, 1297 (1981); English Trans.: J. Gen. Chem. (USSR) **51**, 1099 (1981).

81TRA/RED2
F. Traven', V.V. Redchenko and B.I. Stepanov, "Photoelectron Spectrum of Thianthrene," Zh. Obs. Khim. **51**, 1293 (1981); English Trans.: J. Gen. Chem. (USSR) **51**, 1094 (1981).

81TRO/NED
B.A. Trofimov, N.A. Nedolya, N.B. Lebedev, V.L. Ryadnenko, T.N. Masalitinova, S.L. Dobychin, R.K. Zacheslavskaya and G.N. Petrov, Bull. Acad. Sci. USSR Div. Chem. Sci. 537 (1981).

81TSA
W. Tsang, "Shock Tubes in Chemistry," (A. Lifshitz, Editor; Dekker, 1981), p. 59.

81VAN/TER
H. Van Dam, A. Terpstra, A. Oskam and J.H. Teuben, "UV Photoelectron Spectra of Some Bent Bis(η5-cyclopentadienyl)Niobium and Tantalum Complexes," Z. Naturforsch. **36b**, 420 (1981).

81VOV/DUD
V.I. Vovna, A.S. Dudin, A.M. Kleshchevnikov, S.N. Lopatin and E.G. Rakov, "Photoelectron Spectra and Electronic Structure of Molybdenum, Tungsten, Rhenium, and Osmium Oxotetrafluorides," Koord. Khim. **7**, 575 (1981).

81WAL
R. Walsh, "Bond Dissociation Energy Values in Silicon-Containing Compounds and Some of Their Implications," Acc. Chem. Res. **14**, 246 (1981).

81WAL/BLA
E.A. Walters and N.C. Blais, "Molecular Beam Photoionization of $(H_2S)_n$, n = 1 - 7," J. Chem. Phys. **75**, 4208 (1981).

81WEC/CHR
D. Wecker, A.A. Christodoulides and R.N. Schnidler, "Studies by the Electron Cyclotron Resonance (ECR) Technique. XV. Interactions of Thermal-Energy Electrons with ClO_2 and Cl_2O," Int. J. Mass Spectrom. Ion Phys. **38**, 391 (1981).

81WES/REI
J.B. Westmore, M.L.J. Reimer and C. Reichert, "Ionization Energies of Metal Chelates. Acetylacetonates, Trifluoroacetylacetonates, and Hexafluoroacetylacetonates of Trivalent Metals of the First Transition Series," Can. J. Chem. **59**, 1797 (1981).

81WHI/FRI
R.A. Whiteside, M.J. Frisch, J.S. Binkley, D.J. DeFrees, B. Schlegel, K. Raghavachari and J.A. Pople, "Carnegie-Mellon Quantum Chemistry Archive" (2nd Edn., Pittsburgh, 1981).

81WIB/SQU
K.B. Wiberg and R.R. Squires, J. Am. Chem. Soc. **103**, 4473 (1981).

81WIB/WAS
K.B. Wiberg and D.J. Wasserman, J. Am. Chem. Soc. **103**, 6563 (1981).

81WOJ/FOL
L. Wojnarovits and G. Foldiak, "Electron Capture Detection of Aromatic Hydrocarbons," J. Chromatogr. **206**, 511 (1981).

81WON/DUT
K.S. Wong, T.L. Dutta and T.P. Fehlner, "The Proton as a Probe of Cluster Bonding. The UV Photoelectron Spectra of Two Hydrido Transition Metal Clusters," J. Organometall. Chem. **215**, C48 (1981).

81WOO
A.A. Woolf, Adv. Inorg. Chem. Radiochem. **24**, 1 (1981).

81WOR/GIB
S.D. Worley, D.H. Gibson and W.-L. Hsu, "Electronic Structures of Some η^3-Allyl Transition Metal Complexes," Inorg. Chem. **20**, 1327 (1981).

81WRI/BEA
C.A. Wright and J.L. Beauchamp, "Infrared Spectra of Gas Phase Ions and Their Use in Elucidating Reaction Mechanisms. Identification of $C_7H_7^-$ Structural Isomers by Multiphoton Electron Detachment Using a Low-Powered Laser," J. Am. Chem. Soc. **103**, 6499 (1981).

81YU/ODO
C. Yu, T.J. O'Donnell and P.R. LeBreton, "Ultraviolet Photoelectron Studies of Volatile Nucleoside Models. Vertical Ionization Potential Measurements of Methylated Uridine, Thymidine, Cytidine, and Adenosine," J. Phys. Chem. **85**, 3851 (1981).

81ZHO/HEI
Y. Zhong-zhi, E. Heilbronner, H.C. Kang and V. Boekelheide, "The Photoelectron Spectra of 4,13-Diaza- and 4,16-Diaza[2,4](1,2,4,5)cyclophanes" Helv. Chim. Acta **64**, 2029 (1981).

81ZHO/KOV
Y. Zhong-zhi, B. Kovak, E. Heilbronner, S. Eltamany and H. Hopf, "192. Ionization Energies of Methyl-substituted [2.2] Paracyclophanes," Helv. Chim. Acta **64**, 1991 (1981).

81ZVE/ERM
V.V. Zverev and L.V. Ermolaeva, "Ionization Potentials and Intramolecular Charge Transfer. II. The Photoelectron Spectrum and Electronic Structure of Trichloromethylbenzene," Zh. Strukt. Khim. **22**, 22 (1981).

81ZVE/VIL
V.V. Zverev, Y.Y. Villem, N.V. Villem, B.G. Liorber and Y.P. Kitaev, "Photoelectron Spectra of Some Unsaturated Three- and Four-Coordinate Phosphorus Compounds," Zh. Obs. Khim. **51**, 303 (1981); English trans.: J. Gen. Chem.(USSR), **51**, 242 (1981).

81ZVE/VIL2
V.V. Zverev, Y.Y. Villem and R.P. Arshinova, "Photoelectron Spectra of Di- and Triesters of Trivalent Phosphorus," Dokl. Akad. Nauk, SSSR **256**, 1412 (1981).

81ZYK/KHV
B.G. Zykov, V.I. Khvostenko, M.G. Voronkov, V.P. Yur'ev, G.S. Lomakin and E.N. Suslova, "Photoelectron Spectra of Si-Substituted Chloromethylsilanes," Dokl. Akad. Nauk SSSR **258**, 135 (1981).

82ALD/ARR
R.W. Alder, R.J. Arrowsmith, C.S.J. Boothby, E. Heilbronner and Y. Zhong-zhi, "1-Azabicyclo[4.4.4]tetradec-5-ene," J. Chem. Soc. Chem. Commun. 940 (1982).

82ALL/DOD
N.L. Allinger, H. Dodziuk, D.W. Rogers and S.N. Naik, Tetrahedron **38**, 1593 (1982).

82ALL/MIG
S.H. Allam, M.D. Migahed and A. El-Khodary, "Electron Impact Ionization and Dissociation of Deuterated and non-Deuterated Methanol, Methyl Cyanide, Nitromethane and Nitrobenzene," Egypt. J. Phys. **13**, 167 (1982).

82ARM/HAL
P.B. Armentrout, L.F. Halle and J.L. Beauchamp, "Reaction of Cr^+, Mn^+, Fe^+, Co^+, and Ni^+ with O_2 and N_2O. Examination of the Translational Energy Dependence of the Cross Sections of Endothermic Reactions," J. Chem. Phys. **76**, 2449 (1982).

82ARN/VEN
E.M. Arnett, K.G. Venkatasubaramanian, R.T. McIver, E.K. Fukuda, F.G. Bordwell and F.D. Press, "Stabilization of the Monoanion of 1,8-Diaminonaphthalene by Intramolecular Hydrogen Bonding. A Novel Case of Anion Homoconjugation in Superbase Solution," J. Am. Chem. Soc. **104**, 325 (1982).

82AUD/BOU
H.E. Audier, G. Bouchoux, Y. Hoppilliard and A. Milliet, "The Mechanism of Formation of $[C_4H_9O]^+$ Ions from Isobutyl Ethyl Ether," Org. Mass Spectrom. **17**, 382 (1982).

82BAI/CON
M.A. Baig, J.P. Connerade and J. Hormes, "Autoionisation Resonances in the $4p(\pi)$ Spectrum of Methyl Bromide," J. Phys. B: At. Mol. Phys. **15**, L5 (1982).

82BAL/CAR
M.A. Baldwin, D.M. Carter and J. Gilmore, "Loss of Hydroxyl Radical from Isomeric Ethylnitrobenzenes," Org. Mass Spectrom. **17**, 45 (1982).

82BAN/CHA
S. Banon, C. Chatillon and M. Allibert, "High Temperature Mass Spectrometric Study of Ionization and Fragmentation of TiO and TiO_2 Gas Under Electron Impact," High Temp. Sci. **15**, 17 (1982).

82BAN/CHA2
G.M. Bancroft, T. Chan, R.J. Puddephatt and J.S. Tse, "Role of the Au 5d Orbitals in Bonding: Photoelectron Spectra of $[AuMe(PMe_3)]$," Inorg. Chem. **21**, 2946 (1982).

82BAN/PEL
G.M. Bancroft, E. Pellach, A.P. Sattelberger and K.W. McLaughlin, "The Photoelectron Spectrum of Quadruply Bonded $W_2(O_2CCF_3)_4$," J. Chem. Soc. Chem. Commun. 752 (1982).

82BAR
J.E. Bartmess, "Gas Phase Ion Chemistry of 5-Methylene-1,3-cyclohexadiene (o-Isotoluene) and 3-Methylene-1,4-cyclohexadiene (p-Isotoluene)," J. Am. Chem. Soc. **104**, 335 (1982).

82BAR/CAU
V. Barone, C. Cauletti, F. Lelu, M.N. Piancastelli and N. Russo, "Relative Ordering and Spacing of n and π Levels in Isomeric Bipyrimidines. A Theoretical and Gas-Phase UV Photoelectron Spectroscopic Study," J. Am. Chem. Soc. **104**, 4571 (1982).

82BAR/HEI
R. Bar, T. Heinis, C. Nager and M. Jungen, "Photoionization of Ferrocene," Chem. Phys. Lett. **91**, 440 (1982).

82BAU/BUN
H. Baumann, J.-C. Bunzli and J.F.M. Oth, "58. The Photoelectron Spectrum of [18]Annulene," Helv. Chim. Acta **65**, 582 (1982).

82BAU/COX
D.L. Baulch, R.A. Cox, P.J. Crutzen, R.F. Hampson, Jr., J.A. Kerr, J. Troe and R.T. Watson, J. Phys. Chem. Ref. Data **11**, 327 (1982).

82BAX/COW
S.G. Baxter, A.H. Cowley, J.G. Lasch, M. Lattman, W.P. Sharum and C.A. Stewart, "Electronic Structures of Bent-Sandwich Compounds of the Main-Group Elements: A Molecular Orbital and UV Photoelectron Spectroscopic Study of Bis(cyclopentadienyl)tin and Related Compounds," J. Am. Chem. Soc. **104**, 4064 (1982).

82BEN/DUR
A. Bened, R. Durand, D. Pioch, P. Geneste, J.-P. Declercq, G. Germain, J. Rambaud, R. Roques, C. Guimon and G. Pfister-Guillouzo, "Isoxazolines by Cycloadditions of Mesitonitrile Oxide with Benzo[b]thiophene S-Oxide and S,S-Dioxide. Structural Studies, Theoretical Explanations, and Kinetics," J. Org. Chem. **47**, 2461 (1982).

82BER/HEN
U. Berg, L. Henriksen, K.A. Lerstrup and J. Sandstrom, "The Torsional Barrier of the Dimethylamino Group in N,N-Dimethyltellurobenzamide. A Comparison with N,N-Dimethylbenzamide and its Thio and Seleno Analogues," Acta Chem. Scand. B **36**, 19 (1982).

82BIE/ASB
G. Bieri, L. Asbrink and W. Von Niessen, "30.4-nm He(II) Photoelectron Spectra of Organic Molecules," J. Electron Spectrosc. Rel. Phenom. **27**, 129 (1982).

82BLO/COR
E. Block, E.R. Corey, R.E. Penn, T.L. Renken, P.F. Sherwin, H. Bock, T. Hirarayashi, S. Mohmand and B. Solouki, "Synthesis and Thermal Decomposition of 1,3-Dithetane and Its S-Oxides," J. Am. Chem. Soc. **104**, 3119 (1982).

82BOC/MOH
H. Bock, S. Mohmand, T. Hirabayashi and A. Semkow, "Thioacrolein," J. Am. Chem. Soc. **104**, 312 (1982).

82BOC/MOH2
H. Bock, S. Mohmand, T. Hirabayashi and A. Semkow, "Thioacrolein: Das stabilste C_3H_4S-Isomers und sein PE-spektroskopischer Nachweis in der Gasphase," Chem. Ber. **115**, 1339 (1982).

82BOC/WIT
H. Bock, J. Wittmann, J. Mintzer and J. Russow, "Ni/Pd-Katalysierte Gasphasen-Bromierung von Trifluormethan," Chem. Ber. **115**, 2346 (1982).

82BOH
M.C. Bohm, "The Photoelectron Spectra of Bis(cyclopentadienyl)titanium Derivatives - a Green's Function Approach," Inorg. Chim. Acta **62**, 171 (1982).

82BOH/ECK
M.C. Bohm, M. Eckert-Maksic, R.D. Ernst, D.R. Wilson and R. Gleiter, "Electronic Structure of Bis(pentadienyl)iron. Semiempirical Calculations and Photoelectron Spectra," J. Am. Chem. Soc. 104, 2699 (1982).

82BOH/GLE
M.C. Bohm, R. Gleiter and W. Petz, "The He(I) Photoelectron Spectrum of Fe(CO)$_4$CS," Inorg. Chim. Acta 59, 255 (1982).

82BOH/GLE2
M.C. Bohm and R. Gleiter, "The Electronic Structure and the He(I) Photoelectron Spectrum of Bis(π-Pentadienyl)dinickel," Chem. Phys. 64, 183 (1982).

82BOM/DAN
R. Bombach, J. Dannacher, J.-P. Stadelmann, J. Vogt, L.R. Thorne and J.L. Beauchamp, "Photoelectron-Photoion Coincidence Study of CF$_3$I. Implications for the CW IR Laser Multiphoton Dissociation of CF$_3$I$^+$," Chem. Phys. 66, 403 (1982).

82BRE/SCH
M. Breitenstein, R. Schulz and A. Schweig, "Photoelectron Spectrum and Infrared Spectrum of Thermally Generated Transient Benzodithiete," J. Org. Chem. 47, 1979 (1982).

82BRO/NYB
A.G. Brook, S.C. Nyburg, F. Abdesaken, B. Gutekunst, G. Gutekunst, R.K.M. R. Kallury, Y.C. Poon, Y.-M. Chang and W. Wong-Ng, "Stable Solid Silaethylenes," J. Am. Chem. Soc. 104, 5667 (1982).

82BRU/CIL
G. Bruno, E. Ciliberto, R.D. Fischer, I. Fragala and A.W. Spieg, "Photoelectron Spectroscopy of f-Element Organometallic Complexes. 5. Comparative Study of Ring-Substituted Uranocenes," Organometall. 1, 1060 (1982).

82BUR/FEI
S.M. Burnett, C.S. Feigerle, A.E. Stevens and C.W. Lineberger, "Photoelectron Spectroscopy of CS$^-$ and NS$^-$," J. Phys. Chem. 86, 4486 (1982).

82BUR/HAY
N.A. Burdett and A.N. Hayhurst, "Hydration of Gas Phase Ions and the Measurement of Boundary Layer Cooling During Flame Sampling into a Mass Spectrometer. J. Chem. Soc. Farad. I 78, 2997 (1982).

82BUR/HOL
P.C. Burgers, J.L. Holmes, F.P. Lossing, A.A. Mommers, F.R. Povel and J.K. Terlouw, "Isomeric and Tautomeric [C$_4$H$_4$O]$^+$ Ions. Their Thermochemistry and Collisionally Induced Fragmentation Characteristics," Can. J. Chem. 60, 2246 (1982).

82BUR/HOL2
P.C. Burgers and J.L. Holmes, "Metastable Ion Studies. XIII. The Measurement of Appearance Energies of Metastable Peaks," Org. Mass Spectrom. 17, 123 (1982).

82BUR/PAW
H. Burger, G. Pawelke, R. Dammel and H. Bock, "Effects of Fluorine Substitution on Methyl Amines," J. Fluorine Chem. 19, 565 (1982).

82BUR/TER
P.C. Burgers, J.K. Terlouw and K. Levsen, "Gaseous[C$_7$H$_8$$^+$]Ions: [Methylene Cyclohexadiene]$^+$, a Stable Species in the Gas Phase," Org. Mass Spectrom. 17, 295 (1982).

82BUR/TER2
P.C. Burgers, J.K. Terlouw and J.L. Holmes, "The Vinyloxonium Cation, CH$_2$=CH-OH$_2$$^+$, a Stable [C$_2H_5$O]$^+$ Species in the Gas Phase," Org. Mass Spectrom. 17, 369 (1982).

82BUS/WEI
B. Busse and K.G. Weil, "Mass Spectrometric Studies on the Vapour Phase Composition over Solid and Fused Cs$_3$Sb," Ber. Bunsenges. Phys. Chem. 86, 93 (1982).

82BUT/BAE
J.J. Butler and T. Baer, "Photoionization Study of the Heat of Formation of HCS$^+$," J. Am. Chem. Soc. 104, 5016 (1982).

82BUT/FRA
J.J. Butler, M.L. Fraser-Monteiro, L. Fraser-Monteiro, T. Baer and J.R. Hass, "Thermochemistry and Dissociation Dynamics of State-Selected C$_4$H$_8$O$_2$$^+$ Ions. 2. Butanoic Acid," J. Phys. Chem. 86, 747 (1982).

82BYS
K. Bystrom, J. Chem. Thermodyn. 14, 865 (1982).

82BYS/MAN
K. Bystrom and M. Mansson, J. Chem. Soc. Perkins Trans. II, 505 (1982).

82CAB/COW
D.E. Cabelli, A.H. Cowley and J.J. Lagowski, "The Bonding in Some Bis(arene)Chromium Compounds as Indicated by U. V. Photoelectron Spectroscopy," Inorg. Chim. Acta 57, 195 (1982).

82CAR/KIB
F. Carnovale, M.H. Kibel, G.L. Nyberg and J.B. Peel, "Photoelectron Spectroscopic Assignment of the p-States of Benzenethiol," J. Electron Spectrosc. Rel. Phenom. 25, 171 (1982).

82CAS/CIL
M. Casarin, E. Ciliberto, I. Fragala and G. Granozzi, "Photoelectron Spectroscopy of f-Element Coordination Compounds. 2. He-II Spectra of β-Diketonate Complexes of Uranium(IV), Thorium(IV), Zirconium(IV) and Dioxouranium(VI)," Inorg. Chim. Acta 64, L247 (1982).

82CAS/GOD
C.J. Casewitt and W.A. Goddard, III, J. Am. Chem. Soc. 104, 3280 (1982).

82CHE/LAP
E.K. Chess, R.L. Lapp and M.L. Gross, "The Question of Tautomerism of Alkylnitrile and Isonitrile Radical Cations," Org. Mass Spectrom. 17, 475 (1982).

82CHI/LIE
J.S. Chickos and J.F. Liebman unpublished result.

82CHO/FRO
D.P. Chong, D.C. Frost, W.M. Lau and C.A. McDowell, "Shake-Up Satellites in HeI Photoelectron Spectra: N$_2$O$_4$ and CH$_3$NO," Chem. Phys. Lett. 90, 332 (1982).

82CHU/NGU
J.Y. Chu, T.T. Nguyen and K.D. King, J. Phys. Chem. 86, 443 (1982).

82COL/JIM
M. Colomina, P. Jimenez and C. Turrion, J. Chem. Thermodyn. 14, 779 (1982).

82COM/REI
R.N. Compton and P.W. Reinhardt, "Collisional Ionization between Fast Alkali Atoms and Hexafluorobenzene," Chem. Phys. Lett. 91, 268 (1982).

82CON/ZAF
J.A. Connor, M.T. Zafarani-Moattar, J. Bickerton, N.I. El-Saied, S. Suradi, R. Carson, G. Al Takkhin and H.A. Skinner, Organometallics 1, 1166 (1982).

82COS/LLO
N.C.V. Costa, D.R. Lloyd, P. Brint, W.K. Pelin and T.R. Spalding, "The Photoelectron Spectra of Enneacarbonyl-η^3-methylidyne- tricobalt and Some Derivatives," J. Chem. Soc. Dalton Trans. 201 (1982).

82COW/KEM
A.H. Cowley, R.A. Kemp, M. Lattman and M.L. McKee, "Lewis Base Behavior of Methylated and Fluorinated Phosphines. A Photoelectron Spectroscopic Investigation," Inorg. Chem. 21, 85 (1982).

82COW/LAT
A.H. Cowley, M. Lattman, P.M. Stricklen and J.G. Verkade, "UV Photoelectron Spectroscopic Investigation of Some Polycyclic Group 5A Compounds and Related Acyclic Species. 1. Free and Coordinated Aminophosphines and Related Compounds," Inorg. Chem. 21, 543 (1982).

82CRE
D. Cremer, J. Comput. Chem. **3**, 165 (1982).

82CRI/LIC
K. Crimaldi, R.L. Lichter and A.D. Baker, "Nitrogen-15 Nuclear Magnetic Resonance and Photoelectron Spectroscopy of Substituted N-Phenylaziridines," J. Org. Chem. **47**, 3524 (1982).

82DEH/PRA
P.M. Dehmer and S.T. Pratt, "Photoionization of ArKr, ArXe, and KrXe and Bond Dissociation Energies of the Rare Gas Dimer Ions," J. Chem. Phys. **77**, 4804 (1982).

82DEH/PRA2
P.M. Dehmer and S.T. Pratt, "Photoionization of Argon Clusters," J. Chem. Phys. **76**, 843 (1982).

82DEK/WON
R.L. DeKock, K.S. Wong and T.P. Fehlner, "Effects of Bridging Hydrogens on Metal-Metal Bonds. 2. UV Photoelectron and UV-Visible Spectra and Quantum Chemical Calculations for $Fe_3(\mu-H)_3(CO)_9(\mu_3-CCH_3)$ and $Co_3(CO)_9(\mu_3-CCH_3)$," Inorg. Chem. **21**, 3203 (1982).

82DES/DUT
P. Deshmukh, T.K. Dutta, J.L.-S. Hwang, C.E. Housecroft and T.P. Fehlner, "Photoelectron Spectroscopic Measurements of the Relative Charge on Carbyne Fragments Bound to Polynuclear Cobalt Carbonyl Clusters," J. Am. Chem. Soc. **104**, 1740 (1982).

82DEW
M.J.S. Dewar, "Ionization Energies of p-Quinodimethane and 2,5-Dimethyl-p-quinodimethane," J. Am. Chem. Soc. **104**, 1447 (1982).

82DOL/MED
W.R. Dolbier, Jr., K.S. Medinger, A. Greenberg and J.F. Liebman, Tetrahedron **38**, 2415 (1982).

82DRA/EUJ
J.E. Drake, R. Eujen and K. Gorzelska, "ESCA and UV Photoelectron Spectra of Methyl(trifluoromethyl)germanes, $(CF_3)_{4-n}Ge(CH_3)_n$ (n = 1-3), and Tetrakis(trifluoromethyl)germane, $(CF_3)_4Ge$," Inorg. Chem. **21**, 1784 (1982).

82DRA/GOR
J.E. Drake, K. Gorzelska, G.S. White and R. Eujen, "Photoelectron Spectra of Trifluoromethyl(bromo)- and Trifluoromethyl(chloro)-Germanes $(CF_3)_{4-n}GeX_n$ (X = Br, Cl; n = 1-3)," J. Electron Spectrosc. Rel. Phenom. **26**, 1 (1982).

82DRA/GOR2
J.E. Drake, K. Gorzelska, R. Helbing and R. Eujen, "UV and X-Ray Excited Photoelectron Spectra of Trifluoromethylgermanes $(CF_3)_{4-n}GeH_n$ (n = 1-3)," J. Electron Spectrosc. Rel. Phenom. **26**, 19 (1982).

82DRZ/BRA
P.S. Drzaic and J.I. Brauman, "Electron Photodetachment of Sulfur Hexafluoride Anion. Comments on the Structure of SF_6^-," J. Am. Chem. Soc. **104**, 13 (1982).

82DYK/GRA
J.M. Dyke, B.W.J. Gravenor, R.A. Lewis and A. Morris, "Gas-Phase High Temperature Photoelectron Spectroscopy: An Investigation of the Transition Metals Iron, Cobalt, and Nickel," J. Phys. B: At. Mol. Phys. **15**, 4523 (1982).

82DYK/JON
J.M. Dyke, N. Jonathan, A.E. Lewis and A. Morris, "Vacuum Ultraviolet Photoelectron Spectroscopy of Transient Species. Part 14. A Study of the Ground State of NF^+ via the Ionization Processes $NF^+(X\ ^2\Pi) \leftarrow NF(X^3\Sigma^-, a^1\Delta)$," J. Chem. Soc. Faraday Trans. II **78**, 1445 (1982).

82DYK/JON2
J.M. Dyke, N. Jonathan and A. Morris, "Recent Progress in the Study of Transient Species with Vacuum Ultraviolet Photoelectron Spectroscopy," Int. Rev. Phys. Chem. **2**, 3 (1982).

82DYK/JOS
J.M. Dyke, G.D. Josland, R.A. Lewis and A. Morris, "Improved First Ionization Potential of the Dimethylsilaethylene Molecule Obtained with High-Temperature Photoelectron Spectroscopy," J. Phys. Chem. **86**, 2913 (1982).

82DYK/MOR
J.M. Dyke, A. Morris and A. Ridha, "Study of the Ground State of PO^+ Using Photoelectron Spectroscopy," J. Chem. Soc. Faraday Trans. II **78**, 2077 (1982).

82DYK/MOR2
J.M. Dyke, A. Morris, A.M.A. Ridha and J.G. Snijders, "Gas Phase High Temperature Photoelectron Spectroscopy: The Tin Monoxide Molecule," Chem. Phys. **67**, 245 (1982).

82EIS/DEM
D. Eisel and W. Demtroder, "Accurate Ionization Potential of Li_2 from Resonant Two-Photon Ionization," Chem. Phys. Lett. **88**, 481 (1982).

82ELB/DIE
S. Elbel, H.T. Dieck and R. Demuth, "Photoelectron Spectra of Group V Compounds. IX. The Relative Perfluoroalkyl Substituent Effect," J. Fluorine Chem. **19**, 349 (1982).

82ELL/ENG
G.B. Ellison, P.C. Engleking and W.C. Lineberger, "Photoelectron Spectroscopy of Alkoxide and Enolate Negative Ions," J. Phys. Chem. **86**, 4873 (1982).

82EMO/HOR
H.-H. Emons, W. Horlbeck and D. Kiessling, "Massenspektrometrische Untersuchung der Gasphase uber Alkalimetalliodiden," Z. Anorg. Allg. Chem. **488**, 212 (1982).

82EMO/KIE
H.-H. Emons, D. Kiessling and W. Horlbeck, "Dampfdruckmessungen und massenspektrometrische Untersuchungen der Gasphase uber Erdalkalimetallhalogeniden," Z. Anorg. Allg. Chem. **488**, 219 (1982).

82ENG/SOL
P.S. Engel, L.R. Soltero, S.A. Baughman, C.J. Nalepa, P.A. Cahill and R.B. Weisman, J. Am. Chem. Soc. **104**, 1698 (1982).

82ERA/KOL
P.A. Erastov and V.P. Kolesov, J. Chem. Thermodyn. **14**, 103 (1982).

82ERM/KIR
A.I. Ermakov, E.A. Kirichenko, N.I. Pimkin, Y.V. Chizhov and V.I. Kleimenov, "Photoelectronic Spectra and Electronic Structure of Organotri- and Organotetrasiloxanes of Linear and Cyclic Structure," Zh. Strukt. Khim. **23**, 61 (1982).

82FAN/GIA
R. Fantoni, A. Giardini-Guidoni and R. Tiribelli, "(e,2e) Spectroscopy of Valence States of the NO Molecule," J. Electron Spectrosc. Rel. Phenom. **26**, 99 (1982).

82FAR/SRI
M. Farber, R.D. Srivastava and J.W. Moyer, "Mass Spectrometric Determination of the Thermodynamics of Potassium Hydroxide and Minor Potassium-Containing Species Required in Magnetohydrodynamic Power Systems," J. Chem. Thermodyn. **14**, 1103 (1982).

82FRA/FRA
M.L. Fraser-Monteiro, L. Fraser-Monteiro, J.J. Butler, T. Baer and J.R. Hass, "Thermochemistry and Dissociation Dynamics of State-Selected $C_4H_8O_2^+$ Ions. 1. 1,4-Dioxane," J. Phys. Chem. **86**, 739 (1982).

82FRA/FRA2
L. Fraser-Monteiro, M.L. Fraser-Monteiro, J.J. Butler and T. Baer, "Thermochemistry and Dissociation Dynamics of State-Selected $C_4H_8O_2^+$ Ions. 3. Ethyl Acetate," J. Phys. Chem. **86**, 752 (1982).

82FRE/IKU
M.A. French, S. Ikuta and P. Kebarle, "Hydrogen Bonding of O-H and C-H Hydrogen Donors to Cl^-. Results from Mass Spectrometric Measurement of the Ion-Molecule Equilibria RH + Cl^- = $RHCl^-$," Can. J. Chem. **60**, 1907 (1982).

82FRO/LAU
D.C. Frost, W.M. Lau, C.A. McDowell and N.P.C. Westwood, "A Study by He I Photoelectron Spectroscopy of Monomeric Nitrosomethane, the Cis and Trans Dimers, and Formaldoxime," J. Phys. Chem. **86**, 3577 (1982).

82FUC
R. Fuchs, personal communication of unpublished heat of vaporization data.

82FUC/HAL
R. Fuchs, J.H. Hallman and M.O. Perlman, Can. J. Chem. **60**, 1832 (1982).

82FUC/PEA
R. Fuchs, L.A. Peacock and W.K. Stephenson, Can. J. Chem. **60**, 1953 (1982).

82FUR/SAK
J. Furukawa, M. Sakiyama, S. Seki, Y. Saito and K. Kusano, Bull. Chem. Soc. Jpn. **55**, 3329 (1982).

82GEL/CLE
G. Gellene, D. Cleary and R. Porter, "Stability of the Ammonium and Methylammonium Radicals from Neutralized Ion-Beam Spectroscopy," J. Chem. Phys. **77**, 3471 (1982).

82GIO/BOC
J. Giordon and H. Bock, "Radical Ions, 51. Oxidative Rearrangement of Diphenyl Disulfides to Thianthrenes," Chem. Ber. **115**, 2548 (1982).

82GLE/DOB
R. Gleiter, W. Dobler and M. Eckert-Maksic, "The Electronic Structure of o-Tropoquinone, p-Tropoquinone, and Cyclopentene-1,2,3-trione - PE Spectroscopic Investigations," Nouv. J. Chim. **6**, 123 (1982).

82GLE/ECK
R. Gleiter, M. Eckert-Maksic, W. Schafer and E.A. Truesdale, "Quest for a Strong Through Bond Interaction in [2.2]Paracyclophane," Chem. Ber. **115**, 2009 (1982).

82GLE/GUB
C.R. Gleiter and K. Gubernator, "Through-Bond- und Through-Space-Wechselwirkungen bei den Photodimeren von Acenaphthylen," Chem. Ber. **115**, 3811 (1982).

82GOM/CHA
M. Gomez, C. Chatillon and M. Allibert, "Thermodynamics of Gaseous and Condensed Indium Oxides by Mass Spectrometry with Controlled Oxygen Pressure," J. Chem. Thermodyn. **14**, 447 (1982).

82GRA/AJO
G. Granozzi, D. Ajo, C. Boschi and R. Roulet, "UV Photoelectron Spectra of Iron Tricarbonyl Complexes of 2,3,5,6-Tetrakis(methylene)-7-oxabicyclo[2.2.2]heptane," J. Organometall. Chem. **224**, 147 (1982).

82GRA/CAS
G. Granozzi, M. Casarin, D. Ajo and D. Osella, "Electron Structure of [{Ni(η^5-C$_5$H$_5$)(μ-CO)}$_2$] by He(I) and He(II) Photoelectron Spectroscopy," J. Chem. Soc. Dalton Trans. 2047 (1982).

82GRA/TON
G. Granozzi, E. Tondello, D. Ajo, M. Casarin, S. Aime and D. Osella, "Gas Phase Helium I Photoelectron Spectra of Methinyltricobalt Enneacarbonyl Clusters," Inorg. Chem. **21**, 1081 (1982).

82GRE/KEL
J.C. Green, M.R. Kelly, P.D. Grebenik, C.E. Briant, N.A. McEvoy and D.M.P. Mingos, "UV Photoelectron Spectral and Theoretical Studies on Tris(butadiene)-Molybdenum and -Tungsten," J. Organometall. Chem. **228**, 239 (1982).

82GRE/LIE
A. Greenberg and J.F. Liebman, J. Org. Chem. **47**, 2084 (1982).

82GRE/MCC
M.M. Green, R.J. McCluskey and J. Vogt, "A Comparison between the Stereoselective Thermal-Induced and Ionization-Induced Elimination of Acetic Acid from 2-Butyl Acetate," J. Am. Chem. Soc. **104**, 2262 (1982).

82GRE/PAY
J.C. Green, M. Payne, E.A. Seddon and R.A. Andersen, "He-I and He-II Photoelectron Studies of Bonding in Metal Silylamido-complexes, M[N(SiMe$_3$)$_2$]$_n$ (n = 1, 2, or 3)," J. Chem. Soc. Dalton Trans. 887 (1982).

82GUI/KHA
C. Guimon, S. Khayar, G. Pfister-Guillouzo, R.M. Claramunt and J. Elguero, "A Direct Photoelectron Spectroscopy Study of the 1-Azidopyridine Pyrolysis," Spectrosc. Letters **15**, 435 (1982).

82GUI/PFI
C. Guimon, G. Pfister-Guillouzo and E. Rose, "Applications de la Spectroscopie Photoelectronique aux Proprietes Moleculaires. X. Influence de la Conformation des Arenes Chrome Tricarbonyle ortho Disubstitues sue Leur Structure Electronique et Leur Reactivite Nucleophile: Etude par Spectroscopie Photo-electronique UV(He(I), He(II)) et Calculs EHT," J. Organometall. Chem. **224**, 125 (1982).

82HA/NGU
T.-K. Ha and M.T. Nguyen, Theochem. **4**, 355 (1982).

82HAS/NEU
E. Haselbach, L. Neuhaus, R.P. Johnson, K.N. Houk and M.N. Paddon-Row, "π-Orbital Interactions in Mobius-Type Molecules as Studied by Photoelectron Spectroscopy," Helv. Chim. Acta **65**, 1743 (1982).

82HAY/IWA
T. Hayaishi, S. Iwata, M. Sasanuma, E. Ishiguro, Y. Morioka, Y. Iida and M. Nakamura, "Photoionisation Mass Spectrometric Study of Acetylene in the VUV Region," J. Phys. B: At. Mol. Phys. **15**, 79 (1982).

82HEP/TRE
J.W. Hepburn, D.J. Trevor, J.E. Pollard, D.A. Shirley and Y.T. Lee, "Multiphoton Ionization Photoelectron Spectroscopy of CCl$_2$F$_2$ and CCl$_3$F," J. Chem. Phys. **76**, 4287 (1982).

82HIL
K. Hilpert, J. Chem. Phys. **77**, 1425 (1982).

82HIR/MOH
T. Hirabayashi, S. Mohmand and H. Bock, "Thermische Zersetzung ofenkettiger kialkyl-Sulfide, -disulfide und -diselenide," Chem. Ber. **115**, 483 (1982).

82HIT/HAO
A.P. Hitchcock, N. Hao, N.H. Werstiuk, M.J. McGlinchey and T. Ziegler, "Electronic Structure of Zr(BH$_4$)$_4$ and Hf(BH$_4$)$_4$ Studied by Photoelectron Spectroscopy and LCAO-HFS Calculations," Inorg. Chem. **21**, 793 (1982).

82HOL/BUR
J.L. Holmes, P.C. Burgers and Y.A. Mollah, "Alkane Elimination from Ionized Alkanols," Org. Mass Spectrom. **17**, 127 (1982).

82HOL/LOS
J.L. Holmes, F.P. Lossing, J.K. Terlouw and P.C. Burgers, "The Radical Cation [CH$_2$OH$_2$]$^+$ and Related Stable Gas Phase Ion-Dipole Complexes," J. Am. Chem. Soc. **104**, 2931 (1982).

82HOL/LOS2
J.L. Holmes and F.P. Lossing, "Towards a General Scheme for Estimating the Heats of Formation of Organic Ions in the Gas Phase. Part II. The Effect of Substitution at Charge-Bearing Sites," Can. J. Chem. **60**, 2365 (1982).

82HOL/LOS3
J.L. Holmes and F.P. Lossing, "Heats of Formation of the Ionic and Neutral Enols of Acetaldehyde and Acetone," J. Am. Chem. Soc. **104**, 2648 (1982).

82HOL/SMI
J.B. Holbrook, B.C. Smith, C.E. Housecroft and K. Wade, Polyhedron **1**, 701 (1982).

82HON/EAT
E. Honegger, P.E. Eaton, B.K. Ravi Shankar and E. Heilbronner, "195. The Electronic Structure of Pentaprismane (C$_{10}$H$_{10}$) as Revealed by its Photoelectron Spectrum," Helv. Chim. Acta **65**, 1982 (1982).

82HUB/LIC
J.L. Hubbard and D.L. Lichtenberger, "Vibrational Fine Structure in the Valence Ionizations of Transition-Metal Hexacarbonyls: New Experimental Indication of Metal-to-Carbonyl π Bonding," J. Am. Chem. Soc. **104**, 2132 (1982).

82IKE/TAM
Y. Ikeda, M. Tamaki, G. Matsumoto, K. Amioka and T. Mizuno, "Mass Spectrometric Studies of Lithium-Containing Oxides at High Temperatures," Spectrochim. Acta **37B**, 647 (1982).

82IKU/KEB
S. Ikuta, P. Kebarle, G.M. Bancroft, T. Chan and R.J. Puddephatt, "Basicities of Methyl-, Methylphenyl-, and Phenylphosphines in the Gas Phase," J. Am. Chem. Soc. **104**, 5899 (1982).

82INA/MUR
S. Inagaki, S. Murata, M. Sakiyama, Y. Ito, Y. Umihara, T. Hijiya and T. Matsura, Bull. Chem. Soc. Jpn. **55**, 2803 (1982).

82INA/MUR2
S. Inagaki, S. Murata and M. Sakiyama, Bull. Chem. Soc. Jpn. **55**, 2808 (1982).

82JANAF
M.J. Chase, Jr., J.L. Curnutt, J.R. Downy Jr., R.A. McDonald, A.N. Syverud and E.A. Valenzuela, "JANAF Thermochemical Tables 1982 Supplement," J. Phys. Chem. Ref. Data **11**, 695 (1982).

82JOH/KIM
C.E. Johnson, K.Y. Kim and M. Mansson, Personal communication.

82JOH/POW
K. Johnson, I. Powis and C.J. Danby, "A Photoelectron-Photoion Coincidence Study of Acetaldehyde and Ethylene Oxide Molecular Ions," Chem. Phys. **70**, 329 (1982).

82JON/DEL
G. Jonkers, C.A. De Lange and J.G. Snijders, "Effects of Relativity in the He(I) Photoelectron Spectrum of CI_4," Chem. Phys. **69**, 109 (1982).

82JON/GRA
G. Jonkers, O. Grabandt, R. Mooyman and C.A. De Lange, "He(I) Photoelectron Spectroscopy of Transient Species: Fluorothiocyanate (FSCN)," J. Electron Spectrosc. Rel. Phenom. **26**, 147 (1982).

82JON/VAN
G. Jonkers, S.M. Van Der Kerk and C.A. De Lange, "He(I) Photoelectron Spectroscopy of Transient Species: Germanium Dichloride and Germanium Dibromide," Chem. Phys. **70**, 69 (1982).

82JON/VAN2
G. Jonkers, S.M. Van Der Kerk, R. Mooyman, C.A. De Lange and J.G. Snijders, "He(I) Photoelectron Spectroscopy of Tetraiodoethylene (C_2I_4)," Chem. Phys. **69**, 115 (1982).

82JON/VAN3
G. Jonkers, S.M. Van Der Kerk, R. Mooyman and C.A. De Lange, "UV Photoelectron Spectroscopy of Transient Species: Germanium Difluoride (GeF_2)," Chem. Phys. Lett. **90**, 252 (1982).

82JOS
R.M. Joshi, J. Macromol. Sci. Chem. **A18**, 861 (1982).

82KAS/CHE
O.E. Kashireninov, A.D. Chervonnyi and V.A. Piven, High Temp. Sci. **15**, 79 (1982).

82KAT/SHI
S. Katsumata, H. Shiromaru, K. Mitani, S. Iwata and K. Kimura, "Photoelectron Angular Distribution and Assignments of Photoelectron Spectra of Nitrogen Dioxide, Nitromethane and Nitrobenzene," Chem. Phys. **69**, 423 (1982).

82KLA/SAB
L. Klasinc, A. Sabljic, G. Kluge, J. Rieger and M. Scholz, "Chemistry of Excited States. Part 13. Assignment of Lowest π-Ionizations in Photoelectron Spectra of Thiophen, Furan, and Pyrrole," J. Chem. Soc. Perkin Trans. II 539 (1982).

82KOB/KUB
T. Kobayashi, T. Kubota, K. Ezumi and C. Utsunomiya, "Photoelectron Angular Distribution Study of Some Isoxazoles Combined with Perturbation Theoretic Approach," Bull. Chem. Soc. Jpn. **55**, 3915 (1982).

82KOZ/MAS
M.P. Kozina, V.S. Mastryunov and E.M. Mil'vitshaya, Russ. Chem. Rev. **1**, 765 (1982).

82KRE/SCH
J. Kreile, A. Schweig and W. Thiel, "Experimental and Theoretical Investigation of the Photoionization of Hydrogen Cyanide," Chem. Phys. Lett. **87**, 473 (1982).

82KUT/EDW
R. Kutina, A. Edwards, G. Goodman and J. Berkowitz, "Photoionization Mass Spectrometry of CH_3SH, CD_3SH, and CH_3SD: Heats of formation of CH_3S^+ (CH_2SH^+), CH_2S^+, CH_2S, and HCS^+," J. Chem. Phys. **77**, 5508 (1982).

82KUT/GOO
R.E. Kutina, G.L. Goodman and J. Berkowitz, "Photoionization Mass Spectrometry of NH_2OH: Heats of Formation of HNO^+ and NOH^+," J. Chem. Phys. **77**, 1664 (1982).

82LEL/BAL
L. Lelik, V.K. Balthazarne, O.E. Kaposi and G. Sajo, "Homo- es heterokomplexek kepzodesenek magashomersekletu tomegspektrometrias vizsgalata NaI/CsI rendszer egyensulyi goztereben, I.," Magyar Kem. Fol. **88**, 513 (1982).

82LEV/LIA
R. Levin and S.G. Lias, "Ionization Potential and Appearance Potential Measurements, 1971-1981," Nat. Stand. Ref. Data Ser., Nat. Bur. Stand. (U.S.) **71**, (1982).

82LIA
S. Lias, "Thermochemical Information from Ion-Molecule Rate Constants," Ion-Cyclotron Resonance Spectrometry II (H. Hartmann and K.-P. Wanczek, editors), Springer-Verlag, Berlin (1982), p. 409.

82LIF
C. Lifshitz, "Time-Dependent Mass Spectra and Breakdown Graphs. 2. The Kinetic Shift in Pyridine," J. Phys. Chem. **86**, 606 (1982).

82LIF2
C. Lifshitz, "A Surprisal Analysis of the Dissociation Dynamics of $C_3H_6O^+$ Cations," Int. J. Mass Spectrom. Ion Phys. **43**, 179 (1982).

82LOU/AND
J.N. Louwen, R.R. Andrea, D.J. Stufkens and A. Oskam, "He(I) and He(II) Photoelectron Spectra of $M[Co(CO)_4]_2$ and $M[Mn(CO)_5]_2$ Complexes (M = Zn, Cd, and Hg)," Z. Naturforsch. **37b**, 711 (1982).

82LOU/HAR
J.N. Louwen, J. Hart, D.J. Stufkens and A. Oskam, "The HeI and HeII Photoelectron Spectra of [Fe η^3-$C_3H_5(CO)_3X$] and Fe η^3-$C_4H_7(CO)_3X$] (X = Cl, Br, I) and [$CoC_3H_5(CO)_3$]," Z. Naturforsch. **37b**, 179 (1982).

82LOU/VAN
J.N. Louwen, H. Van Dam, D.J. Stufkens, A. Oskam and H.H. Jaffe, "The Electronic Structures of Some Aromatic Sulfinylamines," J. Electron Spectrosc. Rel. Phenom. **26**, 235 (1982).

82MAC
A. Maccoll, "Ion Enthalpies and Their Application in Mass Spectrometry," Org. Mass Spectrom. **17**, 1 (1982).

82MAI/MIS
J.P. Maier, L. Misev and F. Thommen, "Dicyanoacetylene Cation. Laser-Induced Fluorescence and Photoelectron-Photon Coincidence Studies," J. Phys. Chem. **86**, 514 (1982).

82MAI/THO
J.P. Maier and F. Thommen, "Relaxation of Dihaloacetylene Cations in Their A and B States Studied by Photoelectron-Photoion Coincidence Spectroscopy," Chem. Phys. **70**, 325 (1982).

82MAI/THO2
J.P. Maier and F. Thommen, "Photoelectron-Photoion Coincidence Studies of Halobenzene Cations in Their Excited Electronic States," J. Chem. Phys. **77**, 4427 (1982).

82MAR/CHE
S. Martin, J. Chevaleyre, S. Valignat, J.P. Perrot, M. Broyer, B. Cabaud and A. Hoareau, "Autoionizing Rydberg States of the Na_2 Molecule," Chem. Phys. Lett. **87**, 235 (1982).

82MAR/THR
D.S. Marynick, L. Throckmorton and R. Backquet, J. Am. Chem. Soc. **104**, 1 (1982).

82MAS/BOH
R.S. Mason, D.K. Bohme and K.R. Jennings, "Gas Phase Basicities of Halogenotoluenes," J. Chem. Soc. Faraday Trans. I **78**, 1943 (1982).

82MCI/FUK
R.T. McIver, Jr. and E.K. Fukuda, "Equilibrium Electron Affinities," Lec. Notes in Chem. **31** 165. Data are anchored to $EA(SO_2)$ Ref. 74CEL/BEN.

82MCM/GOL
D.F. McMillen and D.M. Golden, "Hydrocarbon Bond Dissociation Energies," Ann. Rev. Phys. Chem. **33**, 493 (1982).

82MEI/HAN
H. Meier, N. Hanold and H. Kolshorn, Angew. Chem. Int. Ed. **21**, 66 (1982).

82MIK/TRU
A.I. Mikaya, E.A. Trusova, V.G. Zaikin, E.N. Karaulova and L.M. Petrova, "Ionization Energy and Appearance Energy in Organic Chemistry. Communication 5. Energy Differences of Stereoisomers of 2-Methyl-1-Thiadecalin," Izv. Akad. Nauk SSSR, Ser. Khim. 1479 (1982); English trans.: Bull. Acad. Sci. USSR Div. Chem. Sci., 1319 (1982).

82MIN/SAB
C. Mindakis and R. Sabbah, Thermochim. Acta **55**, 147 (1982).

82MIS/POK
B.G. Mishchanchuk, V.A. Pokrovskii, V.P. Shabel'nikov and E.N. Korol, "Mass Spectrometric Study of Energy Characteristics of Methanol and Ethanol Ions During Ionization by a Strong Electric Field," Teor. Eks. Khim. **18**, 307 (1982).

82MOR/MER
J.-P. Morizur, J. Mercier and M. Sarraf, "2-Substituted-2,3-dihydro-4H-pyrans: Competition between 'Retro Diels-Alder' Fragmentation and Substituent Loss," Org. Mass Spectrom. **17**, 327 (1982).

82NAT/PEN
P. Natalis, P. Pennetreau, L. Longton and J.E. Collin, "Ionisation Energy Values for the Vibronic Transitions from HCl $X^1\Sigma^+$ ($v'' = 0$) to HCl^+ Ionic States $X^2\Pi$ ($v' = 0$-13) and $A^2\Sigma^+$ ($v' = 0$-12), Determined by Photoelectron Spectroscopy," J. Electron Spectrosc. Rel. Phenom. **27**, 267 (1982).

82NEL/GAN
S.F. Nelsen and P.M. Gannett, "The 3,3-Dimethyl-2-azabicyclo[2.2.2]octyl System as a Bredt's Rule Kinetically Stabilized Dialkylamino Group in Electron Transfer Studies," J. Am. Chem. Soc. **104**, 5292 (1982).

82NIS/SHI
N. Nishi, H. Shinohara and I. Hanazaki, J. Chem. Phys. **77**, 246 (1982).

82OLE/TUR
J.J. Oleksik and A.G. Turner, Inorg. Chim. Acta **55**, 165 (1984).

82PAD/PAT
M.N. Paddon-Row, H.K. Patney and R.S. Brown, "Orbital Interactions. XI. Application of Photoelectron Spectroscopy to the Study of Orbital Interactions in Some 2- and 9-Substituted Octahydrodimethanonaphthalenes," Aust. J. Chem. **35**, 293 (1982).

82PAM/ROG
M. Pamidimukkala, D. Rogers and G.B. Skinner, J. Phys. Chem. Ref. Data **11**, 83 (1982).

82PAP/KOL
T.S. Papina and V.P. Kolesov, Russ. J. Phys. Chem. **56**, 675 (1982).

82PAU/DAL
J.F. Paulson and J. Dale, "Reactions of $OH^-·H_2O$ with NO_2," J. Chem. Phys. **77**, 4006 (1982).

82PAU/HEH
C.F. Pau and W.J. Hehre, J. Phys. Chem. **86**, 321 (1982).

82PAU/HEH2
C.F. Pau and W.J. Hehre, J. Phys. Chem. **86**, 1282 (1982).

82PFI/GER
G. Pfister-Guillouzo, S. Geribaldi and J.-F. Gal, "Spectres Photoelectroniques de Cyclohexene-2-ones-1 Diversement Substituees en Position 3. Correlations avec la Reactivite," Can. J. Chem. **60**, 1163 (1982).

82PIE/HEH
W.J. Pietro and W.J. Hehre, J. Am. Chem. Soc. **104**, 4329 (1982).

82PIL/SKI
G. Pilcher and H.A. Skinner, "The Chemistry of the Metal-Carbon Bond" (ed. F.R. Hartley and S. Patai, John Wiley & Sons, New York, 1982).

82POL/DEH
E.D. Poliakoff, P.M. Dehmer, J.L. Dehmer and R. Stockbauer, "Photoelectron-photoion Coincidence Spectroscopy of Gas-Phase Clusters," J. Chem. Phys. **76**, 5214 (1982).

82PRA/DEH
S.T. Pratt and P.M. Dehmer, "Photoionization of the Kr_2 Dimer," Chem. Phys. Lett. **87**, 533 (1982).

82PRA/DEH2
S.T. Pratt and P.M. Dehmer, "Photoionization of the Neon-Rare Gas Dimers NeAr, NeKr, and NeXe," J. Chem. Phys. **76**, 3433 (1982).

82ROG
D.W. Rogers, Am. Lab., p. 15, et. seq. (Jan. 1982).

82ROS/BUF
H.M. Rosenstock, R. Buff, M.A.A. Ferreira, S.G. Lias, A.C. Parr, R.L. Stockbauer and J.L. Holmes, "Fragmentation Mechanism and Energetics of Some Alkyl Halide Ions," J. Am. Chem. Soc. **104**, 2337 (1982).

82ROS/DAN
H.M. Rosenstock, J. Dannacher and J.F. Liebman, "The Role of Excited Electronic States in Ion Fragmentation: $C_6H_6^+$," Radiat. Phys. Chem. **20**, 7 (1982).

82ROY/MCM
M. Roy and T.B. McMahon, Org. Mass Spectrom. **17**, 392 (1982).

82ROZ/HOU
M.D. Rozeboom and K.N. Houk, "Stereospecific Alkyl Group Effects on Amine Lone-Pair Ionization Potentials: Photoelectron Spectra of Alkylpiperidines," J. Am. Chem. Soc. **104**, 1189 (1982).

82ROZ/HOU2
M.D. Rozeboom, K.N. Houk, S. Searles and S.E. Seyedrezai, "Photoelectron Spectroscopy of N-Aryl Cyclic Amines. Variable Conformations and Relationships to Gas- and Solution-Phase Basicities," J. Am. Chem. Soc. **104**, 3448 (1982).

82SAB/GOM
R. Sabbah and L.A.T. Gomez, Thermochim. Acta **52**, 285 (1982).

82SAI/YAM
Y. Saito, K. Yamauchi, K. Mihama and T. Noda, "Formation and Ionization Potentials of Lead Clusters," Japanese J. Appl. Phys. 21, L396 (1982).

82SCH/MEA
P.A. Schulz, R.D. Mead, P.L. Jones and W.C. Lineberger, "OH$^-$ and OD$^-$ Threshold Photodetachment," J. Chem. Phys. 77, 1153 (1982).

82SCH/SCH
R. Schulz and A. Schweig, "Photoelectron Spectra of Thermally Generated Unstable Organic Compounds - 2-Propene-1-imine," J. Elec. Spectros. Rel. Phenom. 28, 33 (1982).

82SCO/ERD
L.T. Scott, I. Erden, W.R. Brunsvold, T.H. Schultz, K.N. Houk and M.N. Paddon-Row, "Competitive [6 + 2], [4 + 2], and [2 + 2] Cycloadditions. Experimental Classification of Two-Electron Cycloaddends," J. Am. Chem. Soc. 104, 3659 (1982).

82SEL/HEL
E.T.M. Selim and A.I. Helal, "The Study of C_1-C_3 Monosubstituted Alkyl Benzenes by the Inverse Convolution of First Differential Ionization Efficiency Curves," Org. Mass Spectrom. 17, 539 (1982).

82SHA
W.M. Shaub, Thermochim. Acta 55, 59 (1982).

82SHE/HAL
D.E. Sherwood, Jr. and M.B. Hall, "Electronic Structure of Metal Clusters. 2. Photoelectron Spectrum and Molecular Orbital Calculations of Decacarbonyldihydridotriosmium," Inorg. Chem. 21, 3458 (1982).

82SHI/GIN
I. Shim and K.A. Gingerich, J. Chem. Phys. 77, 2490 (1982).

82SID
L.N. Sidirov, "Molecules With A High Electron Affinity," Russ. Chem. Rev. 51, 356 (1982).

82SID/GUB
L.N. Sidirov and G.D. Gubarevich, "Dissociation of the Gaseous Complex Fluorides. Alkali Metal Trifluoromanganates and Tetrafluoromanganates," Koord. Khim. 8, 463. CA: 97, 12708c (1982).

82SIE/MAU
L.W. Sieck and M. Mautner (Meot-Ner), "Ionization Energies and Entropies of Cycloalkanes. Kinetics of Free Energy Controlled Charge-Transfer Reactions," J. Phys. Chem. 86, 3646 (1982).

82SKO/SOR
E.V. Skokan, I.D. Sorokin, M.I. Nikitin, N.S. Chilingarov and L.N. Sidirov, "The Electron Affinity of UF_6," Russ. J. Phys. Chem. 57, 1745 (1983).

82SOL/BOC
B. Solouki, H. Bock, R. Appel, A. Westerhaus, G. Becker and G. Uhl, "Photoelektronen-Spektren von Methylidinphosphanen R-CP," Chem. Ber. 115, 3747 (1982).

82SPA/GLE
J. Spanget-Larsen, R. Gleiter, K. Gubernator, R.J. Ternansky and L.A. Paquette, "Electronic and Molecular Structure of Simple Bicyclopropyls. Photoelectron Spectroscopy and Model Calculations," J. Org. Chem. 47, 3082 (1982).

82SPA/KOR
J. Spanget-Larsen, C. de Korswagen, M. Eckert-Maksic and R. Gleiter, "90. Electronic and Molecular Structure of Simple 3,3'-Bicyclopropenyls. Photoelectron Spectroscopy and Model Calculations," Helv. Chim. Acta 65, 968 (1982).

82SPL/CAL
J.S. Splitter and M. Calvin, "Conformational Dependence in the Mass Spectrum of Cyclohexanecarboxaldehyde," J. Org. Chem. 47, 4545 (1982).

82SQU/DEP
R.R. Squires and C.H. DePuy, "Flowing Afterglow Studies of the Reactions Between Negative Ions and Trimethylsilyl Enol Ethers. Regiospecific Generation of Gas Phase Enolate Ions," Org. Mass Spectrom. 17, 187 (1982).

82SUR/ELS
S. Suradi, N. El-Saiad, G. Pilcher and H.A. Skinner, J. Chem. Thermodyn. 14, 45 (1982).

82TN270
D.D. Wagman, W.H. Evans, V.B. Parker, R.H. Schumm, I. Halow, S.M. Bailey, K.L. Churney, R.L. Nuttall, "The NBS Tables of Chemical Thermodynamic Properties (NBS Tech Note 270)," J. Phys. Chem. Ref. Data 11, Supl. 1 (1982).

82TOR/SAB
L.A.F. Torres Gomez and R. Sabbah, Thermochim. Acta 57, 67 (1982).

82TOR/SAB2
L.A.F. Torres Gomez and R. Sabbah, Thermochim. Acta 58, 311 (1982).

82TPIS
L.V. Gurvich, I.V. Veits, V.A. Medvedev, G.A. Khachkuruzov, V.S. Yungman and G.A. Bergman, et al., "Termodinamicheskie Svoistva Individual'nykh Veshchestv'" (Thermodynamic Properties of Individual Substances); Glushko, V.P., gen. ed., Vol. 4, parts 1 and 2(1982), Izdatel'stvo"Nauka"Moscow.

82TRA/MCL
J.C. Trager, R.G. McLouglin and A.J.C. Nicholson, "Heat of Formation for Acetyl Cation in the Gas Phase," J. Am. Chem. Soc. 104, 5318 (1982).

82TRA/RED
V.F. Traven', V.V. Redchenko and B.I. Stepanov, "Parameterization of Quantum Chemical Calculations of Organic Compounds of Silicon by Means of Photoelectron Spectroscopy and the Electronic Spectroscopy of CTC," Zh. Obs. Khim. 52, 2262 (1982); English trans.: J. Gen. Chem. (USSR) 52, 2015 (1982).

82TRA/RED2
V.F. Traven', V.V. Redchenko, V.Y. Bartenev and B.I. Stepanov, "Photoelectron Spectra of Permethyl-di-, -tri-, and -tetra-germanes," Zh. Obs. Khim. 52, 358 (1982). English trans.: J. Gen. Chem. (USSR) 52, 310 (1982).

82TRA/ROD
V.F. Traven', O.G. Rodin, V.V. Redchenko, T.A. Chibisova and B.I. Stepanov, "Photoelectron Spectra of Selenanthrene and Dibenzoselenophene," Zh. Obs. Khim. 52, 2650 (1982); English trans.: J. Gen. Chem. (USSR) 52, 2345 (1982).

82VON/ASB
W. Von Niessen, L. Asbrink and G. Bieri, "30.4 nm He(II) Photoelectron Spectra of Organic Molecules. Part VI. Halogeno-Compounds (C, H, X: X = Cl, Br, I)," J. Electron Spectrosc. Rel. Phenom. 26, 173 (1982).

82WAR/PEA
P.M. Warner and S. Peacock, J. Comput. Chem. 3, 417 (1982).

82WIB/WEN
K.B. Wiberg and J.J. Wendolowski, J. Am. Chem. Soc. 104, 5679 (1982).

82WOR/HAR
S.D. Worley, J.H. Hargis, L. Chang, G.A. Mattson and W.B. Jennings, "The UPS of Some Compounds Containing the Heteroatoms Phosphorus, Nitrogen and Oxygen," J. Electron Spectrosc. Rel. Phenom. 25, 135 (1982).

82WOR/WEB
S.D. Worley, T.R. Webb and T.Y. Ou, "He(I) Photoelectron Spectra of Three Novel Ruthenium Tricarbonyl π Complexes," J. Electron Spectrosc. Rel. Phenom. 28, 129 (1982).

82YOK/QUI
A. Yokozeki, E.L. Quitevis and D.R. Herschbach, "Electron Attachment to Volatile Uranyl Molecules," J. Phys. Chem. 86, 617 (1982).

82ZVE/ASH
V.V. Zverev, L.K. Ashrafullina, Y.Y. Villem, N.V. Villem and R.R. Shagidullin, "Photoelectron Spectrum and Electronic and Steric Structure of o-Aminothiophenol," Izv. Akad. Nauk SSSR, Ser. Khim. 2165 (1982).

82ZVE/VIL
V.V. Zverev, Y.Y. Villem, N.V. Villem, E.N. Klimovitskii and B.A. Arbuzov, "Photoelectron Spectra and Intramolecular Interactions of Dimethoxymethane and 4,7-Dihydro-1,3-dioxepin," Zh. Obsh. Khim. 52, 1888 (1982); Engl. trans.: J. Gen. Chem. USSR 52, 1775 (1982).

83ALE/FED
V.I. Alekseev, L.I. Fedorova and A.V. Baluev, "Mass Spectrometric Study of Thermochemical Characteristics of Perchloryl Fluoride and its Decomposition Product Chlorosyl Fluoride," Izv. Akad. Nauk SSR, Ser. Khim. 1084 (1983).

83ALT/CON
G. Al-Takhin, J.A. Connor and H.A. Skinner, J. Organomet. Chem. 259, 313 (1983).

83AN/MAN
X.-W. An and M. Mansson, J. Chem. Thermodyn. 15, 287 (1983).

83AND/CAU
E. Andoni, C. Cauletti and C. Furlani, "Electronic Structure and Bonding in 2,2-Diphenyl-1,3-dithiacyclopentanes of IV A Group Elements Studied by UV Photoelectron Spectroscopy," Inorg. Chim. Acta 76, L35 (1983).

83AUD/MIL
H.E. Audier, A. Milliet and J.-P. Denhez, "Mecanismes d'Isomerisation des Indanols-2 en Spectrometrie de Masse," Bull. Soc. Chim. France II-202 (1983).

83BAK/ARM
A.D. Baker, G.H. Armen and S. Funaro, "Oral Levels of Crown Ethers and Related Macrocycles Studies by Ultraviolet Photoelectron Spectroscopy: Relationship to Complexation Studies," J. Chem. Soc. Dalton Trans., 2519 (1983).

83BAL/GIG
G. Balducci, G. Gigli and M. Guido, "Thermodynamic Study of Gaseous Ternary Oxide Molecules. The Europium-Vanadium-Oxygen System," J. Chem. Phys. 79, 5623 (1983).

83BAL/NEU
T. Bally, L. Neuhaus, S. Nitsche, E. Haselbach, J. Janssen and W. Luttke, "Cross Conjugated Polyenes Derived from 2-Vinylbutadiene: Electronic States of Their Radical Cations and Triplet Energy," Helv. Chim. Acta 66, 1288 (1983).

83BAN/BRI
G.M. Bancroft and D.J. Bristow, "High Resolution HeI and HeII Photoelectron Spectra of the Thallium Halides: Valence Bands and Tl 5d Ligand Field Splittings," Can. J. Chem. 61, 2669 (1983).

83BAN/DAV
J.A. Bandy, C.E. Davies, J.C. Green, M.L.H. Green, K. Prout and D.P.S. Rodgers, "Synthesis, Crystal Structures, and Bonding of the Molybdenum Cubane Compounds $[Mo(\mu-C_5H_4Pr^i)(\mu^3-S)]_4^{n+}$, where n = 0, 1, and 2," J. Chem. Soc. Chem. Commun. 1395 (1983).

83BAR/BAS
J.E. Bartmess, T. Basso and R.M. Georgiadis, "The Electron Affinity of a Nitroxide Radical," J. Phys. Chem. 87, 912 (1983).

83BIE/MOR
H.W. Biermann and T.H. Morton, "Reversible Tautomerization of Radical Cations. Photoionization of 2-Methoxyethanol and 3-Methoxy-1-propanol," J. Am. Chem. Soc. 105, 5025 (1983).

83BIN
M. Binnewies, "Bildung und Stabilitat von gasformigem AsOCl und SbOCl Massenspektrometrische Untersuchungen," Z. Anorg. Allg. Chem. 505, 32 (1983).

83BIN/LAK
M. Binnewies, M. Lakenbrink and H. Schnockel, Z. Anorg. Allg. Chem. 497, 7 (1983).

83BOA/HOU
G. Boand, R. Houriet and T. Baumann, "The Gas Phase Acidity of Aliphatic Alcohols," J. Am. Chem. Soc. 105, 2203 (1983).

83BOC/MOH
H. Bock, S. Mohmand, T. Hirabayashi, G. Maier and H.P. Reisenauer, "Photoelektronen-spektroskopischer Nachweis und Matrix-Isolierung von Thio-para-benzochinonen," Chem. Ber. 116, 273 (1983).

83BOC/ROT
H. Bock and B. Roth, "Radical Ions. 49. Redox Reactions of Some Thiophene Derivatives," Phosphorus and Sulfur 14, 211 (1983).

83BOH/GLE2
M.C. Bohm, R. Gleiter, T.A. Albright and V. Sriyunyongwat, "The Low-Lying Cationic Hole-States of η3-Allyl Tetracarbonyl Complexes of Mn and Re. Photoelectron Spectra and Green's Function Calculations," Molec. Phys. 50, 113 (1983).

83BOM/DAN
R. Bombach, J. Dannacher and J.-P. Stadelmann, "The Rate-Energy Functions for the Formation of Tropylium and Benzylium Ions from Toluene Molecular Cations," Chem. Phys. Lett. 95, 259 (1983).

83BOM/DAN2
R. Bombach, J. Dannacher and J.-P. Stadelmann, "Energy and Time Dependence of the Decay Processes of Toluene Molecular Cations," J. Am. Chem. Soc. 105, 4205 (1983).

83BOM/DAN3
R. Bombach, J. Dannacher, J.-P. Stadelmann and R. Neier, "Fundamental Aspects of Ionic Dissociations: The Fragmentation Pathways of Excited Bicyclobutane Cations," Helv. Chim. Acta 66, 701 (1983).

83BOM/DAN4
R. Bombach, J. Dannacher, E. Honegger, J.-P. Stadelmann and R. Neier, "Unimolecular Dissociations of Excited $C_3H_6^+$: A Photoelectron-Photoion Coincidence Study of Cyclopropanol and Allyl Alcohol," Chem. Phys. 82, 459 (1983).

83BRA/BAE
W.A. Brand and T. Baer, "Unimolecular Dissociation of Energy-Selected t-Butylbenzene Ions and Effect of Thermal Energy on Data Analysis," Int. J. Mass Spectrom. Ion Phys. 49, 103 (1983).

83BRA/BAE2
W.A. Brand, T. Baer and C.E. Klots, "Kinetic Energy Release Distributions in the Fragmentation of Energy-Selected Iodopropane Ions," Chem. Phys. 76, 111 (1983).

83BRO/BUS
R.S. Brown, J.M. Buschek, K.R. Kopecky and A.J. Miller, "Photoelectron Spectra of syn- and anti-Sesquinorbornene. Evidence for Vertical Σ-π Delocalization in Bicyclo[2.2.1]heptene," J. Org. Chem. 48, 3692 (1983).

83BUR/CAS
T.J. Burkey, A.L. Castelhano, D. Griller and F.P. Lossing, "Heats of Formation and Ionization Potentials of Some α-Aminoalkyl Radicals," J. Am. Chem. Soc. 105, 4701 (1983).

83BUR/HOL
P.C. Burgers, J.L. Holmes, A.A. Mommers and J.E. Szulejko, "The Collisionally Induced Dissociation of Allyl and 2-Propenyl Cations," Org. Mass Spectrom. 18, 596 (1983).

83BUR/HOL2
P.C. Burgers, J.L. Holmes, J.E. Szulejko, A.A. Mommers and J.K. Terlouw, "The Gas Phase Ion Chemistry of the Acetyl Cation and Isomeric $[C_2H_3O]^+$ Ions. On the Structure of the $[C_2H_3O]^+$ Daughter Ions Generated from the Enol of Acetone Radical Cation," Org. Mass Spectrom. 18, 254 (1983).

83BUR/HOL3
P.C. Burgers, J.L. Holmes, F.P. Lossing, F.R. Povel and J.K. Terlouw, "The Role of Charge-site Location in Fragmenting Ions. 1- $[CH_3CHXCOOCH_3]^+$ and $[CH_2XCH_2COOCH_3]^+$ Ions and the Structures of Daughter Ions Derived from the Loss of X(X = I, Br, Cl and CH_3)," Org. Mass Spectrom. 18, 335 (1983).

83BUR/MOM
P.C. Burgers, A.A. Mommers and J.L. Holmes, "Ionized Oxycarbenes: $[COH]^+$, $[HCOH]^+$, $[C(OH)_2]^+$, $[HCO_2]^+$, and $[COOH]^+$, Their Generation, Identification, Heat of Formation, and Dissociation Characteristics," J. Am. Chem. Soc. 105, 5976 (1983).

83BUR/STE
S.M. Burnett, A.E. Stevens, C.S. Feigerle and W.C. Lineberger, "Observation of X^1A_1 Vinylidene by Photoelectron Spectroscopy of the $C_2H_2^-$ Anion," Chem. Phys. Lett. 100, 124 (1983).

83BUT/BAE
J.J. Butler, T. Baer and S.A. Evans, Jr., "Energetics and Structures of Organosulfur Ions: $CH_3SSCH_3^+$, CH_3SS^+, $C_2H_5S^+$, and CH_2SH^+," J. Am. Chem. Soc. 105, 3451 (1983).

83BUT/BAE2
J.J. Butler and T. Baer, "A Photoionization Study of Organosulfur Ring Compounds: Thiirane, Thietane and Tetrahydrothiophene," Org. Mass Spectrom. 18, 248 (1983).

83BYS
K. Bystrom, J. Comput. Chem. 4, 308 (1983).

83CAL
W.L. Calhoun, J. Chem. Eng. Data 28, 147 (1983).

83CAL/BAR
G. Caldwell and J.E. Bartmess, unpublished results.

83CHE/WEN
E.C.M. Chen and W.E. Wentworth, "Determination of Molecular Electron Affinities Using the Electron Capture Detector in the Pulse Sampling Mode at Steady State," J. Phys. Chem. 87, 45 (1983).

83CAM/CIU
R. Cambi, G. Ciullo, A. Sgamellotti, F. Tarantelli, R. Fantoni, A. Giardini-Guidoni, I.E. McCarthy and V. di Martino, "An (e, 2e) Spectroscopic Investigation and a Green's Function Study of the Ionization of Chloro- and Bromoethylene," Chem. Phys. Lett. 101, 477 (1983).

83CAN/HAM
P.H. Cannington and N.S. Ham, "He(I) and He(II) Photoelectron Spectra of Glycine and Related Molecules," J. Electron Spectrosc. Rel. Phenom. 32, 139 (1983).

83CAR/LIV
F. Carnovale, M.K. Livett and J.B. Peel, "Identification of the Gas Phase Trimer $(CH_3)_2S\cdot(HF)_2$ by Photoelectron Spectroscopy," J. Am. Chem. Soc. 105, 6788 (1983).

83CAS/AJO
M. Casarin, D. Ajo, G. Granozzi, E. Tondello and S. Aime, "Gas-Phase Ultraviolet Photoelectron Spectra of $[\{Ni(\eta-C_5H_5)\}_2(\mu-C_2R_2)]$ (R = H or CF_3) Complexes," J. Chem. Soc. Dalton Trans., 869 (1983).

83CAS/KIM
M.C. Caserio and J.K. Kim, "Thioacylium Ions. Gas Phase Ion-Molecule Reactions of Thioic and Dithioic Acid Derivatives," J. Am. Chem. Soc. 105, 6896 (1983).

83CAT/ELG
J. Catalan, J. Elguero, R. Flammang and A. Maquestiau, "The Relative Basicities of Imidazole and Benzimidazole," Angew. Chem. Int. Ed. 22, 323 (1983).

83CET/LAP
B. Cetinkaya, M.F. Lappert and R.J. Suffolk, "Photoelectron Spectra of Some Sterically Hindered Phenols and Related Compounds," J. Chem. Res. (S), 316 (1983).

83CET/LAP2
B. Cetinkaya, M.F. Lappert, J.G. Stamper and R.J. Suffolk, "The He(I) and He(II) Photoelectron Spectra of bis(2,4,6-Tri-t-butylphenyl)-diphosphene," J. Electron Spectrosc. Rel. Phenom. 32, 133 (1983).

83CLA/COR
R.M. Clay, S. Corr, G. Keenan and W.V. Steele, J. Am. Chem. Soc. 105, 2071 (1983).

83COM/REI
R.N. Compton, P.W. Reinhardt and H.C. Schweinler, "Formation of Gas-Phase Negative Ions in Vinylene Carbonate," Int. J. Mass Spectrom. Ion Phys. 49, 113 (1983).

83DAM/BOC
R. Dammel, H. Bock and J.-M. Denis, "The Photoelectron Spectrum of 1-Azetine," Chem. Phys. Lett. 102, 239 (1983).

83DAN/ROS
J. Dannacher, H.M. Rosenstock, R. Buff, A.C. Parr, R.L. Stockbauer, R. Bombach and J.-P. Stadelmann, "Benchmark Measurement of Iodobenzene Ion Fragmentation Rates," Chem. Phys. 75, 23 (1983).

83DAS/GRO
C. Dass and M.L. Gross, "Electrocyclic Ring Opening of 1-Phenylcyclobutene and 3-Phenylcyclobutene Radical Cations," J. Am. Chem. Soc. 105, 5724 (1983).

83DEK/DES
R.L. DeKock, P. Deshmukh, T.P. Fehlner, C.E. Housecroft, J.S. Plotkin and S.G. Shore, "UV Photoelectron Spectra and Electronic Structure of $(\eta 5-C_5H_5)(CO)_2FeB_2H_5$. Comparison of the Fe-B Bonding with the Fe-C Bonding in $(CO)_4FeC_2H_4$," J. Am. Chem. Soc. 105, 815 (1983).

83DEP/SCH
C.H. Depuy and R. Schmitt, Personal Communication.

83ELL/ELL
H.B. Ellis Jr. and G.B. Ellison, "Photoelectron Spectroscopy of HNO^- and DNO^-," J. Chem. Phys. 78, 6541 (1983).

83DEW/HEA
M.J.S. Dewar and E. Healy, J. Comput. Chem. 4, 542 (1983).

83DEW/RZE
M.J.S. Dewar and H.S. Rzepa, J. Comput. Chem. 4, 158 (1983).

83DIE/BRU
H. tom Dieck, B. Bruder and K.-D. Franz, "Synthese offenkettiger und cyclischer, silylierter 1,2-Ethendiamine," Chem. Ber. 116, 136 (1983).

83DOB/HIL
B. Dobson, I.H. Hillier, J.A. Connor, D. Moncrieff, M.L. Scanlan and C.D. Garner, "Electronic Structure and Low-energy Photoelectron Spectra of 4,4'-Disubstituted 2,2'-Bipyridines," J. Chem. Soc. Faraday Trans. II 79, 295 (1983).

83DUD/GRE
N. Dudeney, J.C. Green, P. Grebenik and O.N. Kirchner, "Synthesis and Structural Characterization of the Electron Rich Complexes $Co(\eta-C_5Me_5)(R_2PCH_2CH_2PR_2)$ (R = Me, Ph). Photoelectron Spectroscopic Studies of Some Pentamethylcyclopentadienylphosphinecobalt Complexes," J. Organometall. Chem. 252, 221 (1983).

83DYK/GRA
J.M. Dyke, B.W.J. Gravenor, R.A. Lewis and A. Morris, "A Study of the First Ionization Potential of the CrO $(X^5\Pi)$ Molecule with High-temperature Photoelectron Spectroscopy," J. Chem. Soc., Faraday Trans. II 79, 1083 (1983).

83DYK/JON
J.M. Dyke, N. Jonathan, A.E. Lewis, J.D. Mills and A. Morris, "Vacuum Ultraviolet Photoelectron Spectroscopy of Transient Species. Part 16. The NCO $(X^2\Pi)$ Radical," Molec. Phys. 50, 77 (1983).

83DYK/JON2
J.M. Dyke, N. Jonathan, A. Morris, A. Ridha and M.J. Winter, "Vacuum Ultraviolet Photoelectron Spectroscopy of Transient Species. XVII. The SiH_3 (X^2A_1) Radical," Chem. Phys. 81, 481 (1983).

83DYK/KIR
J.M. Dyke, C. Kirby and A. Morris, "Study of the Ionization Process $BF^+(X^2\Sigma^+) \leftarrow BF(X^1\Sigma^+)$ by High-temperature Photoelectron Spectroscopy," J. Chem. Soc. Faraday Trans. II **79**, 483 (1983).

83EBA/ANE
T. Ebata, Y. Anezaki, M. Fujii, N. Mikami and M. Ito, "High Rydberg States of NO Studied by Two-Color Multiphoton Spectroscopy," J. Phys. Chem. **87**, 4773 (1983).

83EDM
R.S. Edmundson, "Cyclic Organophosphorus Compounds. XVIII-The Mass Spectroscopy of Some 2-Amino-1,3,2-dioxaphosphorinans, Cyclic Phosphorodiamidates and Phosphorodiamidothionates," Org. Mass Spectrom. **18**, 150 (1983).

83ELL/ELL
H.B. Ellis, Jr. and G.B. Ellison, "Photoelectron Spectroscopy of HNO^- and DNO^-," J. Chem. Phys. **78**, 6541 (1983).

83ERM/AKO
A.I. Ermolenko, M.E. Akopyan and Y.L. Sergeev, "Decomposition of Dimethyl Sulfide Molecular Ions. Randomization of States during Photoionization Dissociation of Molecules," Khim. Vys. Ener. **17**, 25 (1983); English trans.: High Energy **17**, 19 (1983).

83ERV/LOH
K. Ervin, S.K. Loh, N. Aristov and P.B. Armentrout, "Metal Cluster Ions: The Bond Energy of Mn_2^+," J. Phys. Chem. **87**, 3593 (1983).

83EVA/WEE
B.S. Evans, S.I. Weeks and E. Whittle, "Bromination of Fluoroalkanes. Part 5. Kinetics of Forward and Reverse Reactions in the System $Br_2 + i-C_3F_7H = HBr + i-C_3F_7Br$," J. Chem. Soc. Faraday Trans. I **79**, 1471 (1983).

83FUC/HAL
R. Fuchs and J.H. Hallman, Can. J. Chem. **61**, 503 (1983).

83FUC/SMI
R. Fuchs and N. Smith, Personal communication of unpublished heat of formation and heat of vaporization data.

83GAU/HOU
T. Gaumann, R. Houriet, D. Stahl, J.-C. Tabet, N. Heinrich and H. Schwarz, "Further Examples of Skeletal Rerrangement of the Wagner-Meerwein Type in Chemical Ionization Mass Spectrometry: the Case of $[C_6H_9^+]$ Ions," Org. Mass Spectrom. **18**, 215 (1983).

83GIL/HSI
J.P. Gilman, T. Hsieh and G.G. Meisels, "Competition between Isomerization and Fragmentation of Gaseous Ions. II. Nitromethane and Methylnitrite Ions," J. Chem. Phys. **78**, 1174 (1983).

83GIL/HSI2
J.P. Gilman, T. Hsieh and G.G. Meisels, "The Unimolecular Decomposition Rates of Energy Selected Methylnitrite and Deuterated Methylnitrite Ions," J. Chem. Phys. **78**, 3767 (1983).

83GLE/BOH
R. Gleiter, M.C. Bohm, A. de Meijere and T. Preuss, "Electronic Structure and Reactivity of Homobarrelene Derivatives," J. Org. Chem. **48**, 796 (1983).

83GLE/BOH2
R. Gleiter, M.C. Bohm, M. Eckert-Maksic, W. Schafer, M. Baudler, Y. Aktalay, G. Fritz and K.-D. Hoppe, "The Electronic Structure of Phosphorus Cages with the Nortricyclane Skeleton. Model Calculations and Photoelectron Spectroscopic Investigations," Chem. Ber. **116**, 2972 (1983).

83GLE/GOO
R. Gleiter, W.D. Goodmann, W. Schafer, J. Grobe and J. Apel, "He(I)-PE Spektren der Verbindungen $(CH_3)_nE(CF_3)_{3-n}$ fur $E = P, As, Sb$ und $n = 0 - 3$," Chem. Ber. **116**, 3745 (1983).

83GLE/HAI
R. Gleiter, R. Haider, P. Bischof and J.-J. Lindner, "Zur Konformation von Tetravinyl- und Trivinylmethan - Vergleich er PE-Spektren von Tetravinylmethan mit trans,trans,trans-1,2,3,4-Tetravinylcyclobutan," Chem. Ber. **116**, 3736 (1983).

83GLE/HAI2
R. Gleiter, R. Haider, K. Gubernator and P. Bischof, "cis,trans,cis- and trans,trans,trans-1,2,3,4-Tetravinylcyclobutane - Preparation and Some Spectroscopic Properties," Chem. Ber. **116**, 2983 (1983).

83GLE/SAA
R. Gleiter, R.W. Saalfrank, W. Paul, D.O. Cowan and M. Eckert-Maksic, "Das Photoelektronenspektrum von 1,1-Diethoxy-3,3-bis(trifluormethyl)allen. Der Effekt von Trifluormethylgruppen auf kumulierte Systeme," Chem. Ber. **116**, 2888 (1983).

83GLE/SPA
R. Gleiter, J. Spanget-Larsen, R. Bartetzko, H. Neunhoeffer and M. Clausen, "Photoelectron Spectra of 1,2,3-Triazine and Its Methyl Derivatives," Chem. Phys. Lett. **97**, 94 (1983).

83GON/PFI
D. Gonbeau, G. Pfister-Guillouzo, J. Escudie, C. Couret and J. Satge, "Application de la Spectroscopie Moleculaire aux Proprietes Moleculaires. XVII. Etude Structurale de Diphosphenes par Spectroscopie Photoelectronique," J. Organometall. Chem. **247**, C17 (1983).

83GOR/BOU
M.S. Gordon, P. Boudjouk and F. Anwari, J. Am. Chem. Soc. **105**, 4972 (1983).

83GRA/WIE
M. Grade, J. Wienecke, W. Rosinger and W. Hirschwald, "Electron Impact Investigation of the Molecules SeS(g) and TeSe(g) under High-Temperature Equilibrium Conditions," Ber. Bunsenges. Phys. Chem. **87**, 355 (1983).

83GRE/PAY
J.C. Green, M.P. Payne and A. Streitwieser, Jr., "He I and He II Photoelectron Spectral Studies of Alkyluranocenes," Organometall. **2**, 1707 (1983).

83GRE/TOM
A. Greenberg, R.P.T. Tomkins, M. Dobrovolny and J.F. Liebman, J. Am. Chem. Soc. **105**, 6855 (1983).

83GUI/PFI
C. Guimon, G. Pfister-Guillouzo and M. Begtrup, "Tautomerism of Pyrazoline-5-thione and Trazoline-5-thione Studied by Variable Temperature Photoelectron Spectroscopy," Can. J. Chem. **61**, 1197 (1983).

83GUI/PFI2
G. Guimon, G. Pfister-Guillouzo, H. Lavayssiere, G. Dousse, J. Barrau and J. Satge, "Generation of Dimethylgermathione and Dimethylsilathione and Their Detection in the Gas Phase by Photoelectron Spectroscopy," J. Organomet. Chem. **249**, C17 (1983).

83HAR/OHN
Y. Harada, K. Ohno and H. Mutoh, "Penning Ionization Electron Spectroscopy of CO and $Fe(CO)_5$. Study of Electronic Structure of $Fe(CO)_5$ from Electron Distribution of Individual Molecular Orbitals," J. Chem. Phys. **79**, 3251 (1983).

83HEL/MOL
H. Helm and R. Moller, "Bound-Free Spectroscopy of Cs_2^+," Phys. Rev. A **27**, 2493 (1983).

83HEN/BEN
S.P. Heneghan and S.W. Benson, "Kinetics and Thermochemistry of Electron Attachment to SF_6," Int. J. Chem. Kinet. **15**, 109 (1983).

83HIL
K. Hilpert, Ber. Buns. Gesell. Phys. Chem. **87**, 161 (1983).

83HIL/GIN
K. Hilpert and K.A. Gingerich, "Mass Spectrometric Study on the Evaporation of Phases of the System $NaI-SnI_2$," Int. J. Mass Spectrom. Ion Phys. **47**, 247 (1983).

83HOL
J.L. Holmes, Unpublished result.

83HOL/BUR
J.L. Holmes, P.C. Burgers, J.K. Terlouw, H. Schwarz, B. Ciommer and H. Halim, "Stable $C_2H_5X^+$ (X = Cl,Br) Radical Cations of Structure $[CH_3CHXH^+]$: Their Energetics and Dissociation Characteristics," Org. Mass Spectrom. **18**, 208 (1983).

83HOL/LOS
J.L. Holmes and F.P. Lossing, "The Need for Adequate Thermochemical Data for the Interpretation of Fragmentation Mechanisms and Ion Structure Assignments," Int. J. Mass Spectrom. Ion Phys. **47**, 133 (1983).

83HOL/LOS2
J.L. Holmes, F.P. Lossing, J.K. Terlouw and P.C. Burgers, "Novel Gas-Phase Ions. The Radical Cations $[CH_2XH]^{+\cdot}$ (X = F, Cl, Br, I, OH, NH_2, SH) and $[CH_2CH_2NH_3]^{+\cdot}$," Can. J. Chem. **61**, 2305 (1983).

83HOU/RON
K.N. Houk, N.G. Rondan, M.N. Paddon-Row, C.W. Jefford, P.T. Huy, P.D. Burrow and K.D. Jordan, "Ionization Potentials, Electron Affinities, and Molecular Orbitals of 2-Substituted Norbornadienes. Theory of 1,2 and Homo-1,4 Carbene Cycloaddition Selectivities," J. Am. Chem. Soc. **105**, 5563 (1983).

83ING/NIB
S. Ingemann and N.M.M. Nibbering, "Gas Phase Reactions of Anions with 2-, 3-, and 4-Fluoroanisole," J. Org. Chem. **48**, 183 (1983).

83JIA/MOH
W. Jian-qi, M. Mohraz, E. Heilbronner, A. Krebs, K. Schutz, J. Voss and B. Kopke, "79. The He(Iα) Photoelectron Spectra of Substituted 1,2-Dithietes," Helv. Chim. Acta **66**, 801 (1983).

83JOC/DEK
R. Jochem, H. Dekker, C. Mosselman and G. Soumen, J. Chem. Thermodyn. **15**, 95 (1983).

83JON/VAN
G. Jonkers, S.M. Van Der Kerk, R. Mooyman, C.A. De Lange and J.G. Snijders, "UV Photoelectron Spectroscopy of Transient Species: Germanium Diiodide (GeI_2)," Chem. Phys. Lett. **94**, 585 (1983).

83JOR/CAR
F.S. Jorgensen and L. Carlsen, "1,2-Oxathiolane - A Photoelectron Spectroscopic Study," Chem. Ber. **116**, 2374 (1983).

83JOR/MCC
F.S. Jorgensen and P.H. McCabe, "Cis-Disulfides. Photoelectron Spectrum of a 6,7-Dithiabicyclo[3.2.1]octane," Tetrahedron Lett. **24**, 319 (1983).

83JOR/PAD
F.S. Jorgensen, M.N. Paddon-Row and H.K. Patney, "Photoelectron Spectra of Some Decahydrotrimethanoanthracenes: Observation of Large π Orbital Interactions through Six Bonds and an Apparent Violation of the trans Rule," J. Chem. Soc. Chem. Commun. 573 (1983).

83KAG/UJS
N.D. Kagramanov, K. Ujszaszy, J. Tamas, A.K. Maltsev and O.M. Nefedov, "Mass Spectrometric Detection of Allylic and Perfluoroallylic Free Radicals and the Determination of Their Ionization Potentials," Izv. Akad. Nauk SSSR, Ser. Khim. **7**, 1683 (1983); English trans.: Bull. Acad. Sci. USSR Div. Chem. Sci. **7**, 1531 (1984).

83KAK/GIE
W. Kakolowicz and E. Giera, J. Chem. Thermodyn. **15**, 203 (1983).

83KIR/DOM
D.B. Kirklin and E.S. Domalski, J. Chem. Thermodyn. **15**, 941 (1983).

83KIT/MOR
S. Kitagawa, I. Morishima and K. Yoshikawa, "UV Photoelectron Spectra of Some Transition Metal(II) Acetylacetonates," Polyhedron **2**, 43 (1983).

83KLA/KOV
L. Klasinc, B. Kovac and H. Gusten, "Photoelectron Spectra of Acenes. Electronic Structure and Substituent Effects," Pure & Appl. Chem. **55**, 289 (1983).

83KLA/MAI
D. Klapstein, J.P. Maier and W. Zambach, "Emission Spectra of Rotationally Cooled Dihaloacetylene Cations in the Gas Phase: $A2\Pi_{(\Omega,g)} \to x2\Pi_{(\Omega,u)}$ Band Systems," Chem. Phys. **77**, 463 (1983).

83KLE/NIB
J.C. Kleingeld and N.M.M. Nibbering, "The Long-lived H_3O^- Ion in the Gas Phase: Its Formation, Structure, and Reactions," Int. J. Mass Spectrom. Ion Phys. **49**, 311 (1983).

83KOB
T. Kobayashi, "Conformational Analysis of Terphenyls by Photoelectron Spectroscopy," Bull. Chem. Soc. Jpn. **56**, 3224 (1983).

83KOL/PAP
V.P. Kolesov and T.S. Papina, Russ. Chem. Rev. **52**, 754 (1983).

83KOP/MOL
I.A. Koppel, U.H. Molder and R.J. Pikver, "Photoelectron Spectra of Molecules. I. Alcohols," Org. Reactivity **20**, 45 (1983).

83KOR/BON
M.V. Korobov, A.A. Bondarenko, L.N. Sidorov and V.V. Nikulin, "Enthalpies of Formation of the Gaseous Platinum Fluorides, PtF_2 and PtF_4," High Temp. Sci. **16**, 411 (1983).

83LAC/MAN
K. Lacmann, M.J.P. Maneira, A.M.C. Moutinho and U. Weigman, "Total and Double Differential Cross Sections of Ion- Pair Formations in Collisions of K Atoms with $SnCl_4$ and CCl_4," J. Chem. Phys. **78**, 1767 (1983).

83LAR/MCM
J.W. Larson and T.B. McMahon, "Strong Hydrogen Bonding in Gas-Phase Anions. An Ion Cyclotron Resonance Determination of Fluoride Binding Energetics to Bronsted Acids from Gas-Phase Fluoride Exchange Equilibria Measurements," J. Am. Chem. Soc. **105**, 2944 (1983).

83LIE
J.F. Liebman, "The Cyclophanes" (ed. P.M. Keehn and S. Rosenfeld, Academic Press, New York, 1983).

83LIF
C. Lifshitz, "Energy-Entropy Trade-offs in the Unimolecular Decompositions of SF_6^-," J. Phys. Chem. **87**, 3474 (1983).

83LIF/BER
C. Lifshitz, P. Berger and E. Tzidony, "Kinetic Energy Release Distributions (KERDs) for the Dissociation of Metastable Enol Ions," Chem. Phys. Lett. **95**, 109 (1983).

83LIF/EAT
C. Lifshitz and P.E. Eaton, "Time-Dependent Mass Spectra and Breakdown Graphs. III. The Cubane Cation Complete or Partial Instability," Int. J. Mass Spectrom. Ion Phys. **49**, 337 (1983).

83LIN/BRO
S.H. Linn, J.M. Brom, Jr., W.-B. Tzeng and C.Y. Ng, "Molecular Beam Photoionization Study of $HgCl_2$," J. Chem. Phys. **78**, 37 (1983).

83LIN/TZE
S.H. Linn, W.-B. Tzeng, J.M. Brom, Jr. and C.Y. Ng, "Molecular Beam Photoionization Study of $HgBr_2$ and HgI_2," J. Chem. Phys. **78**, 50 (1983).

83LOC/MCI
M.J. Locke and R.T. McIver, Jr., "Effect of Solvation on the Acid/Base Properties of Glycine," J. Am. Chem. Soc. **105**, 4226 (1983).

83MAK/VER
A.V. Makarov, E.N. Verkhoturov and O.T. Nikitin, "Mass Spectrometric Study of the Processes of Ionization of the Vapor above Molybdenum Dichloride," Vest. Mosk. Univ. Khim. **38**, 350 (1983); English trans.: Moscow Univ. Chem. Bull. **38**, 42 (1983).

83MAL/MIL
W.G. Mallard, J.H. Miller and K.C. Smyth, "The ns Rydberg Series of 1,3-trans-Butadiene Observed Using Multiphoton Ionization," J. Chem. Phys. **79**, 5900 (1983).

83MAR/MAY
H.-D. Martin, B. Mayer, R. Gleiter, W. Schafer and F. Vogtle, "Photoelektronenspektroskopische Untersuchung transanularer π-, σ- und n-Wechselwirkungen in bruckenkopfsubstituierten Triptycenen," Chem. Ber. **116**, 2546 (1983).

83MAR/REI
R. Maripuu, I. Reineck, H. Agren, W. Nian-Zu, J. Rong, H. Veenhuizen, S. Al-Shamma, L. Karlsson and K. Siegbahn, "The HeI Excited Electron Spectrum of Phosphine. An Experimental and Theoretical Study," Molec. Phys. **48**, 1255 (1983).

83MAU
M. Meot-Ner (Mautner), Personal communication.

83MAZ
M. Mazzoni, "^2P Photoionizatiion Cross Section of Sb I," Phys. Lett. **97A**, 381 (1983).

83MCA/HUD
D.J. McAdoo and C.E. Hudson, "The Decompositions of Metastable $[C_4H_8O]^+$ Ions and the $[C_4H_8O]^+$ Potential Surface," Org. Mass Spectrom. **18**, 466 (1983).

83MCG/SCH
M.W. McGeogh and R.E. Schlier, "Autoionizing Rydberg States of the Li_2 Molecule: Molecular Constants for Li_2^+," Chem. Phys. Lett. **99**, 347 (1983).

83MET/ARA
R.M. Metzger and E.S. Arafat, J. Chem. Phys. **78**, 2696 (1983).

83MOL/PIK
U.H. Molder, R.J. Pikver and I.A. Koppel, "Photoelectron Spectra of Molecules. 2. Ethers," Org. Reactivity **20**, 208 (1983).

83MOL/PIK2
U.H. Molder, R.J. Pikver and I.A. Koppel, "Photoelectron Spectra of Molecules. 3. Nitriles," Org. Reactivity **20**, 230 (1983).

83MOL/PIK3
U.H. Molder, R.J. Pikver and I.A. Koppel, "Photoelectron Spectra of Molecules. 4. Amines," Org. Reactivity **20**, 355 (1983).

83MOO/SEI
G.K. Moortgart, W. Seiler and P. Warnek, "Photodissociation of HCHO in Air: CO and H_2 Quantum Yields at 220 and 300K," J. Chem. Phys. **78**, 1185 (1983).

83MUR
E. Murad, "Abstraction Reactions of Ca^+ and Sr^+ Ions," J. Chem. Phys. **78**, 6611 (1983).

83NES/MIL
O. Neskovic, M. Miletic, M. Veljkovic, D. Golobocantin and K.F. Zmbov, "Ionization and Fragmentation of Phosphorous Oxyfluoride by Electron Impact," Int. J. Mass Spectrom. Ion Proc. **47**, 141 (1983).

83NIS/SAK
K. Nishiyama, M. Sakiyama and S. Seki, Bull. Chem. Soc. Jpn. **56**, 3171 (1983).

83NOB/WAL
P.N. Noble and R. Walsh, "Kinetics of the Gas Phase Reaction between Iodine and Monogermane and the Bond Dissociation Energy $D(H_3Ge-H)$," Int. J. Chem. Kinet. **15**, 547 (1983).

83NOV/POT
I. Novak and A.W. Potts, "The Ultraviolet Photoelectron Spectra of Gas Phase and Condensed Bismuth Halides and Antimony Trifluoride," J. Chem. Soc. Dalton Trans., 635 (1983).

83NOV/POT2
I. Novak and A.W. Potts, "The Ultraviolet Photoelectron Spectra and Electron Structure of Gas Phase and Condensed SnF_2 and PbF_2," J. Chem. Soc. Dalton Trans., 2211 (1983).

83OAK/ELL
J.M. Oakes and B.G. Ellison, "Photoelectron Spectroscopy of the Allenyl Anion $CH_2=C=CH^-$," J. Am. Chem. Soc. **105**, 2969 (1983).

83OAK/JON
J.M. Oakes, M.E. Jones, V.M. Bierbaum and G.B. Ellison, "Photoelectron Spectroscopy of CCO^- and $HCCO^-$," J. Phys. Chem. **87**, 4810 (1983).

83OGD/SHA
I.K. Ogden, N. Shaw, C.J. Danby and I. Powis, "Competing Dissociation Channels of Nitromethane and Methyl Nitrite Ions and the Role of Electronic and Internal Modes of Excitation," Int. J. Mass Spectrom. Ion Proc. **54**, 41 (1983).

83OHN/IMA
K. Ohno, K. Imai, S. Matsumoto and Y. Harada, "Penning Ionization Electron Spectroscopy of C_2H_5X ($X = NH_2$, OH, H, Cl, I). Relative Reactivity of Orbital Localizing on Functional Groups upon Electrophilic Attack by Metastable Helium Atoms," J. Phys. Chem. **87**, 4346 (1983).

83OZG
T. Ozgen, "Mass Spectrometric Determination of the Appearance Potentials of PCl_3, $AsCl_3$, $SbCl_3$, $BiCl_3$ and Their Fragments," Int. J. Mass Spectrom. Ion Proc. **48**, 427 (1983).

83PED/MAR
J.B. Pedley and E.M. Marshall, J. Phys. Chem. Ref. Data **12**, 957 (1983).

83PEN/NAT
P. Pennetreau, P. Natalis, L. Longton and J.E. Collin, "Ionization Energies for the Vibronic Transitions from DCl $X^1\Sigma^+$ ($v'' = 0$) to DCl^+ $X^2\Pi$ ($V' = 0$-18) and $A^2\Sigma^+$ ($v' = 0$-17) Determined by Photoelectron Spectroscopy," J. Electron Spectrosc. Rel. Phenom. **28**, 295 (1983).

83PET/DAO
K.I. Peterson, P.D. Dao and A.W. Castleman, Jr., "Photoionization Studies of Na_2Cl and Na_2O and Reactions of Metal Clusters," J. Chem. Phys. **79**, 777 (1983).

83PIA/KEL
M.N. Piancastelli, P.R. Keller, J.W. Taylor, F.A. Grimm and T.A. Carlson, "Angular Distribution Parameter as a Function of Photon Energy for Some Mono- and Diazabenzenes and Its Use for Orbital Assignment," J. Am. Chem. Soc. **105**, 4235 (1983).

83PIC/ROD
J.M. Pickard and A.S. Rodgers, "Kinetics of the Gas Phase Reaction $CH_3F + I_2 = CH_3FI + HI$: The C-H Bond Dissociation Energy in Methyl and Methylene Fluorides," Int. J. Chem. Kinet. **15**, 569 (1983).

83PLA/SIM
V.A. Platonov and Y.N. Simulin, Russ. J. Phys. Chem. **57**, 840 (1983).

83PLE/MAR
P. Plessis, P. Marmet and R. Dutil, "Ionization and Appearance Potentials of CH_4 by Electron Impact," J. Phys. B: At. Mol. Phys. **16**, 1283 (1983).

83POT/NOV
A.W. Potts and I. Novak, "Ultraviolet Photoelectron Spectra of Selenium and Tellurium," J. Electron Spectrosc. Rel. Phenom. **28a**, 267 (1983).

83POT/NOV2
A.W. Potts, I. Novak and M.L. Lyus, "The Valence Shell Electronic Structure and UV Photoelectron Spectra of the Tetrahaloethylenes," J. Electron Spectrosc. Rel. Phenom. **31**, 57 (1983).

83POW
I. Powis, "The Unimolecular Dissociation of Electronic State-Selected Methyl Iodide Cations," Chem. Phys. 74, 421 (1983).

83POW/HAN
D.E. Powers, S.G. Hansen, M.E. Geusic, D.L. Michalopoulos and R.E. Smalley, "Supersonic Copper Clusters," J. Chem. Phys. 78, 2866 (1983).

83PRE/TZE
H.F. Prest, W.-B. Tzeng, J.M. Brom, Jr. and C.Y. Ng, "Molecular Beam Photoionization Study of H_2S," Int. J. Mass Spectrom. Ion Proc. 50, 315 (1983).

83PRE/TZE2
H.F. Prest, W.-B. Tzeng, J.M. Brom, Jr. and C.Y. Ng, "Photoionization Study of $(H_2S)_2$ and $(H_2S)_3$," J. Am. Chem. Soc. 105, 7531 (1983).

83RAB/SEL
M.A. Rabbih and E.T.M. Selim, "A Mass Spectrometric Appearance Energies Study of Cyclohexanol," Egypt. J. Phys. 14, 243 (1983).

83RAK/BOH
A.B. Rakshit and D.K. Bohme, Int. J. Mass Spectrom. Ion Proc. 49, 275 (1983).

83REI/NOH
I. Reineck, C. Nohre, P. Lodin, R. Maripuu, B. Lindberg, L. Karlsson, K. Siegbahn, A.-B. Hornfeldt and S. Gronowitz, "Electronic and Vibrational Structure of 2-Substituted Selenophenes Studied by He(I) Photoelectron Spectroscopy," Chem. Scripta 22, 209 (1983).

83ROS/GRA
W. Rosinger, M. Grade and W. Hirschwald, "Detection of Ion States of S_2 to S_8 by Electron Impact," Int. J. Mass Spectrom. Ion Proc. 47, 239 (1983).

83RUS/FRE
D.H. Russell, B.S. Freiser, E.H. McBay and D.C. Canada, "The Structure of Decomposing $[C_7H_7O]^+$ Ions: Benzyl versus Tropylium Ion Structures," Org. Mass Spectrom. 18, 474 (1983).

83RUS/GOO
B. Ruscic, G.L. Goodman and J. Berkowitz, "Photoelectron Spectra of the Lanthanide Trihalides and Their Interpretation," J. Chem. Phys. 78, 5443 (1983).

83SCH/BAL
W. Schmidt, H.-J. Ballschmidt, M. Klessinger, A. Heesing and W. Herdering, "MINDO/3-Rechnungen und PE-Untersuchungen zur Reaktionsweise von Azabicyclen," Chem. Ber. 116, 1097 (1983).

83SCH/SCH
R. Schulz, A. Schweig, K. Hartke and J. Koster, "Variable Temperature Photoelectron Spectral Study of 1,3-Dithiol-2-one and 4,5-Disubstituted 1,3-Dithiol-2-ones. Thermal Generation of 1,2-Dithiete, 3,4-Disubstituted 1,2-Dithietes, and Dialkyl Tetrathiooxalates" J. Am. Chem. Soc. 105, 4519 (1983).

83SEA/CHU
M. Seaver, W.A. Chupka, S.D. Colson and D. Gauyacq, "Double Resonance Multiphoton Ionization Studies of High Rydberg States in NO," J. Phys. Chem. 87, 2226 (1983).

83SEM/RYK
V.I. Semenikhin, A.N. Rykov and L.N. Sidorov, "Mass Spectrometric Study of the Evaporation of Lead Monoxide," Zh. Fiz. Khim. 57, 1663 (1983); Engl. trans.: Russ. J. Phys. Chem. 57, 1008 (1983).

83SHU/BEN
L.G.S. Shum and S.W. Benson, "Thermochemistry and Kinetics of the Reaction of Methyl Mercaptan with Iodine," Int. J. Chem. Kinet. 15, 433 (1983).

83SID/RUD
L.N. Sidirov, E.B. Rudnyi, M.I. Nikitin and I.D. Sorokin, "Gas Phase Anion Exchange Reactions and the Determination of the Heats of Formation of Metaphosphate (PO_3-), metaborate (BO_2-), and perrhennate (ReO_4-)," Dokl. Akad. Nauk SSSR, Ser. Khim. 272, 1172 (1983).

83SID/ZHU
L.N. Sidirov, L.V. Zhuravlena, M.V. Varkov, E.V. Skokan, I.D. Sorokin, Yu. M. Koronev and P.A. Akishima, "Mass-Spectrometric Determination of Enthalpies of Dissociation of Gaseous Complex Fluorides into Neutral and Charged Particles. VII. $MF-ThF_4$ Systems," Int. J. Mass Spectrom. Ion Proc. 51, 291 (1983).

83SKO/SAB
S. Skoulika and R. Sabbah, Thermochim. Acta 61, 203 (1983).

83SKO/SOR
E.V. Skokan, I.D. Sorokin, M.I. Nikitin, N.S. Chilingarov and L.N. Sidirov, "The Electron Affinity of UF_6," Russ. J. Phys. Chem. 57, 1745 (1983).

83SMI
O.I. Smith, "Cross Sections for Formation of Parent and Fragment Ions by Electron Impact from C_2N_2," Int. J. Mass Spectrom. Ion Proc. 54, 55 (1983).

83SPY/SAU
S.M. Spyrou, I. Sauers and L.G. Christophorou, "Electron Attachment to the Perfluoroalkanes n-C_nF_{2n+2} (n = 1-6) and i-C_4F_{10}," J. Chem. Phys. 78, 7200 (1983).

83STE
S.E. Stein, personal communciation to the authors.

83STE/FEI
A.E. Stevens, C.S. Feigerle and W.C. Lineberger, "Laser Photoelectron Spectroscopy of MnH- and FeH-: Electronic Structures of the Metal Hydrides, Identification of a Low Spin Excited State of MnH," J. Chem. Phys. 78, 5420 (1983).

83STE2
W.V. Steele, J. Chem. Thermodyn. 15, 595 (1983).

83TER/HOL
J.K. Terlouw, J.L. Holmes and F.P. Lossing, "Ionized Ethylidene Ketene and Its Homologue Methylene Ketene," Can. J. Chem. 61, 1722 (1983).

83TER/WEZ
J.K. Terlouw, J. Wezenberg, P.C. Burgers and J.L. Holmes, "New Stable Isomers of $[C_2H_4O]^+$ and $[C_2H_4O_2]^+$, the Radical Cations $[CH_2COH]^+$ and $[CH_3OCOH]^+$," J. Chem. Soc. Chem. Commun. 1121 (1983).

83THO/GLI
C. Thomson and C. Glidewell, J. Comput. Chem. 4, 1 (1983).

83TOM/AMM
G.M.R. Tombo, H.J. Ammann, K. Muller and C. Ganter, "5. Nucleophilic Addition to C,C-Double Bonds. VII. Study of Proximity Effects in Olefinic Alcohols and Amines by Photoelectron Spectroscopy," Helv. Chim. Acta 66, 50 (1983).

83TUR/HAN
F. Turecek and V. Hanus, "Stereoelectronic Control of Ion Fragmentations: Loss of Hydrogen from Cyclic Ethers during Electron Impact Spectrometry," Tetrahedron 39, 1499 (1983).

83VES/HAR
T. Veszpremi, Y. Harada, K. Ohno and H. Mutoh, "Photoelectron and Penning Ionization Electron Spectroscopic Investigation of Trimethylsilyl- and t-Butyl-thiophenes," J. Organometall. Chem. 252, 121 (1983).

83WAG/ISE
G. Wagner and N.R. Isenor, "Formation and Dissociation of Na_2^+ by Ruby Laser Radiation," Can. J. Phys. 61, 40 (1983).

83WAL
R. Walsh, "Thermochemistry of Silicon-containing Compounds," J. Chem. Soc., Faraday Trans. I 79, 2233 (1983).

83WAN/LER
F.C.-Y. Wang and G.E. Leroi, "Photoionization and Fragmentation of Halogenated Methanes," Ann. Israel Phys. Soc. 6, 210 (1983).

83WEB/MCD
C.R. Webster, I.S. McDermid and C.T. Rettner, "Laser Optogalvanic Photodetachment spectroscopy: A new technique for studying photodetachment thresholds with application to I$^-$," J. Chem. Phys. **78**, 646 (1983).

83WEI/BEN
M. Weissman and S.W. Benson, J. Phys. Chem. **87**, 243 (1983).

83WLO/LUC
S. Wlodek, Z. Luczynski and H. Wincel, "Gas Phase Complexes of NO_2^- and NO_3^- with SO_2," Int. J. Mass Spectrom. Ion Proc. **49**, 301 (1983).

83ZLA/LEE
A. Zlatkis, C.K. Lee, W.E. Wentworth and E.C.M. Chen, "Constant Current Linearization for Determination of Electron Capture Mechanisms," Anal. Chem. **55**, 1596 (1983).

83ZVE/BAZ
V.V. Zverev, Z.G. Bazhanova, N.V. Villem and Y.Y. Villem, "Photoelectron Spectra and Electronic Structure of Organophosphorus Compounds of Tricoordinated Phosphorus with a Phosphorus-Sulfur Bond," Zh. Obs. Khim. **53**, 1968 (1983); Engl. trans.: J. Gen. Chem. (USSR) **53**, 1775 (1983).

83ZYK/ERC
B.G. Zykov, N.P. Erchak, V.I. Khvostenko, E. Lukevits, V.F. Matorykina and N.L. Asfandiarov, "Photoelectron Spectra of Furylsilanes and Their Carbon Analogs," J. Organometall. Chem. **253**, 301 (1983).

84ABE/DEL
R.S. Abeywickrema, E.W. Della, P.E. Pigou, M.K. Livett and J.B. Peel, "Orbital Interactions in Some Polycycloalkyl Halides: A Photoelectron Spectroscopic Study," J. Am. Chem. Soc. **106**, 732 (1984).

84ADA/SMI
N.G. Adams and D. Smith, "A Further Study of the Near-Thermoneutral Reaction $O_2H^+ + H_2 = H_3^+ + O_2$," Chem. Phys. Lett. **105**, 604 (1984).

84AIT/GOS
R.A. Aitken, I. Gosney, H. Farries, M.H. Palmer, I. Simpson, J.I.G. Cadogan and E.J. Tinley, "Chemical Repercussions of Orbital Interactions through Bond and through Space. The Reactivity of the Double Bond in Unsaturated Cyclic Sulphones towards Aziridine Formation and Epoxidation," Tetrahedron **40**, 2487 (1984).

84AJO/CAS
D. Ajo, M. Casarin, G. Granozzi, H.C.J. Ottenheijm and R. Plate, "An Investigation of the Electronic Structure of α,β-Unsaturated Acetylamino Acid Ethyl Esters Using He(I) and He(II) Photoelectron Spectroscopy," Recueil J. Royal Neth. Chem. Soc. **103**, 365 (1984).

84ALA/RYE
M. Alai and R.T.B. Rye, "Fragmentation of Selected $C_6H_{10}O$ Isomers: Evidence for a Common $[C_5H_7O]^+$ Ion Generated by Methyl Loss from Cyclohexene Oxide and 5,6-Dihydro-4-methyl-2H-pyran," Org. Mass Spectrom. **19**, 506 (1984).

84ALB/ALL
B. Albrecht, M. Allan, E. Haselbach, L. Neuhaus and P.-A. Carrupt, "26. Molecular Ions of Transient Species: Vinyl-Alcohol Cation," Helv. Chim. Acta **67**, 216 (1984).

84ALB/ALL2
B. Albercht, M. Allan, E. Haselbach, L. Neuhaus and P.-A. Carrupt, "27. Molecular Ions of Transient Species: Vinylamine-Cation," Helv. Chim. Acta **67**, 220 (1984).

84ALE/VOL
V.I. Alekseev, V.M. Volkov, L.I. Fedorova and A.V. Baluev, "Mass Spectrometric Study of the Ionization of an Oxygen Difluoride Molecule," Izv. Akad. Nauk SSR, Ser. Khim 1302 (1984).

84ALT/CON
G. Al-Takhin, J.A. Connor, H.A. Skinner and M.T. Zaharani-Moettar, J. Organomet. Chem. **260**, 189 (1984).

84ALT/CON2
G. Al-Takhin, J.A. Connor, G. Pilcher and H.A. Skinner, J. Organomet. Chem. **265**, 263 (1984).

84AND/CER
R.R. Andrea, H. Cerfontain, H.J.A. Lamberchts, J.N. Louwen and A. Oskam, "He I and He II Photoelectron Spectra and CNDO/S and MNDO MO Calculations of Some Bridged [10] Annulenes," J. Am. Chem. Soc. **106**, 2531 (1984).

84AND/DEP
A.H. Andrist, C.H. DePuy and R.R. Squires, "Structures of Isomeric Anions in the Gas Phase: Arylallyl and Arylcyclopropyl Anions," J. Am. Chem. Soc. **106**, 845 (1984).

84AND/DYK
L. Andrews, J.M. Dyke, N. Jonathan, N. Keddar, A. Morris and A. Ridha, "A Photoelectron Spectroscopic Study of the Ground States of CH_2F^+ and CD_2F^+," J. Phys. Chem. **88**, 2364 (1984).

84AND/DYK2
L. Andrews, J.M. Dyke, N. Jonathan, N. Keddar and A. Morris, "Photoelectron Spectroscopic Study of the Ground States of CH_2Cl^+, $CHCl_2^+$, and $CHFCl^+$," J. Am. Chem. Soc. **106**, 299 (1984).

84AND/DYK3
L. Andrews, J.M. Dyke, N. Jonathan, N. Keddar and A. Morris, "The First Bands in the Photoelectron Spectra of the CH_2Br, CD_2Br, $CHBr_2$, and CH_2I Free Radicals," J. Phys. Chem. **88**, 1950 (1984).

84ARI/YOS
M. Arimura and Y. Yoshikawa, "Ionization Efficiency and Ionization Energy of Cyclic Compounds by Electron Impact," Mass Spectrosc. **32**, 375 (1984).

84ASA/YAS
M. Asano, Y. Yasue and K. Kubo, "Mass Spectrometric Study of Ions Formed from Cesium Metaborate Vapor under Electron Impact," J. Nucl. Sci. Tecn. **21**, 614 (1984).

84ASF/ZYK
N.L. Asfandiarov and B.C. Zykov, "Photoelectron Spectra of Methyl-Substituted 1,3-Dioxanes," Izv. Akad. Nauk SSSR, Ser. Khim. 2293 (1983). English trans.: Bull. Acad. Sci. USSR Div. Chem. Sci. 2069 (1983).

84BAI/DOM
V.N. Baidin, I.N. Domnin, O.A. Prokhorenko, S. Elbel and A. de Meijere, "Photoelectron Spectra of Phenyl Substituted Cyclopropene Derivatives," J. Electron Spectrosc. Rel. Phenom. **34**, 103 (1984).

84BAN/YAT
G.M. Bancroft, B.W. Yates, K.H. Tan and L.L. Coatsworth, "High Resolution Gas Phase Photoelectron Spectra Using Synchrotron Radiation. Selective Enhancement of the I 5p Cross Section in CF_3I Due to Photoexcitation of I 4d Electrons," J. Chem. Soc. Chem. Commun. 1613 (1984).

84BAR
J.E. Bartmess, "The Gas Phase Thermochemistry of Ph_3C^-, $Ph_3C\cdot$, and Ph_3C^+," 32nd Ann. Conf. on Mass Spectrom. Allied Topics, San Antonio TX 27 May - 1 June, 1984. Abstracts p. 472.

84BAR/BUR
J.E. Bartmess and R. Burnham, "Effect of Central Substituents on the Gas Phase Acidities of Propenes," J. Org. Chem. **49**, 1382 (1984).

84BAR/CAU
V. Barone, C. Cauletti, L. Commisso, F. Lelj, M.N. Piancastelli and N. Russo, "Quantum-mechanical and Ultraviolet Photoelectron Spectroscopic Studies of Azabiphenyls. The Case of 4-Phenylpyridine" J. Chem. Research (S) 338 (1984).

84BAR/YEH
N. Bartlett, S. Yeh, K. Kourtakis and T. Mallouk, J. Fluor. Chem. **26**, 97 (1984).

84BEA/EYE
D.B. Beach, C.J. Eyermann, S.P. Smit, S.F. Xiang and W.L. Jolly, "Applications of the Equivalent Cores Approximation. The Determination of Proton Affinities and Isocyanide-to-Nitrile Isomerization Energies from Core Binding Energies," J. Am. Chem. Soc. **106**, 536 (1984).

84BER/GRE
J. Berkowitz, J.P. Greene, J. Foropoulos, Jr. and O.M. Neskovic, "Bonding and Ionization Energies of N-F and P-F Compounds," J. Chem. Phys. **81**, 6166 (1984).

84BER/GRE2
J. Berkowitz and J.P. Greene, "The Barrier to Inversion in NF_3^+," J. Chem. Phys. **81**, 3383 (1984).

84BIC/MIN
J. Bickerton, M.E. Minas da Piedade and G. Pilcher, J. Chem. Thermodyn. **16**, 661 (1984).

84BIC/PIL
J. Bickerton, G. Pilcher and G. Al-Takhin, J. Chem. Thermodyn. **16**, 373 (1984).

84BIE/GRA
V.M. Bierbaum, J.J. Grabowski and C.H. DePuy, "Gas-Phase Synthesis and Reactions of Nitrogen- and Sulfur-Containing Anions," J. Phys. Chem. **88**, 1389 (1984).

84BLA/WAL
E.A. Walters and N.C. Blais, "Molecular Beam Photoionization and Fragmentation of D_2S, $(H_2S)_2$, $(D_2S)_2$, and $H_2S \cdot H_2O$," J. Chem. Phys. **80**, 3501 (1984).

84BOC/AYG
H. Bock, S. Aygen, P. Rosmus, B. Solouki and E. Weissflog, "Gasphasen-Reaktionen, 40. Selenoformaldehyd: hochkorrelierte Wellenfunktion und photoelektronenspektroskopischer Nachweis," Chem. Ber. **117**, 187 (1984).

84BOC/ROS
H. Bock, P. Rosmus, B. Solouki and G. Maier, "Gas Phase Reactions. XXXXVI. Silabenzene: Photoelectron Spectrum from 1-Sila-2,5-hexadiene Pyrolysis and Assignment of Valence Ionisation Energies," J. Organometall. Chem. **271**, 145 (1984).

84BOH/FAH
H. Bohringer, D.W. Fahey, F.C. Fehsenfeld and E.E. Ferguson, "Bond Energies of the Molecules H_2O, SO_2, H_2O_2, and HCl to Various Atmospheric Negative Ions," J. Chem. Phys. **81**, 2805 (1984).

84BOL/HOU
J.-C. Bollinger, R. Houriet and T. Yvernault, "Gas Phase Basicity of Hexamethylphosphotriamide (HMPT) Phosphinoxide Derivatives," Phosphorus and Sulfur **19**, 379 (1984).

84BOU/BRA
C. Bousquet, N. Bras and Y. Majdi, J. Phys. B **17**, 1831 (1984).

84BOU/DAG
G. Bouchoux and J. Dagaut, "The Loss of Br from $[(CH_3)_2CBrCOCH_3]^+$," Org. Mass Spectrom. **19**, 291 (1984).

84BOU/FLA
G. Bouchoux, R. Flammang, Y. Hoppilliard, P. Jaudon, A. Maquestiau and P. Meyrant, "Mecanismes de Formation des Ions $[C_5H_9O]^+$ a Partir des Cetones $[CH_3COC_4H_9]^+$," Int. J. Spectrosc. **3**, 1 (1984).

84BOU/HOP
G. Bouchoux, Y. Hoppilliard, P. Jaudon and R. Houriet, "The Heats of Formation of Some Protonated Olefinic Carbonyl Compounds: $[C_5H_9O]^+$ and $[C_4H_7O_2]^+$ Ions," Org. Mass Spectrom. **19**, 394 (1984).

84BOU/PFI
J.P. Boutique, G. Pfister-Guillouzo, J. Riga, J.J. Verbist, J.G. Fripiat, J. Delhalle, R.C. Haddon and M.L. Kaplan, "Gas Phase UPS Study of Naphtho[1,8-cd:4,5-c'd']bis[1,2,6]thiadiazine," J. Electron Spectrosc. Rel. Phenom. **34**, 199 (1984).

84BOU/VER
J.P. Boutique, J.J. Verbist, J.G. Fripiat, J. Delhalle, G. Pfister-Guillouzo and G.J. Ashwell, "3,5,11,13-Tetraazacycl[3.3.3]azine: Theoretical (ab-Initio) and Experimental (X-ray and Ultraviolet Photoelectron Spectroscopy) Studies of the Electronic Structure," J. Am. Chem. Soc. **106**, 4374 (1984).

84BOW/MAC
R.D. Bowen and A. Maccoll, "Low Energy, Low Temperature Mass Spectra," Org. Mass Spectrom. **19**, 379 (1984).

84BRA/BAE
W.A. Brand and T. Baer, "Dissociation Dynamics of Energy-Selected $C_5H_{10}^+$ Ions," J. Am. Chem. Soc. **106**, 3154 (1984).

84BUR/FUK
D.J. Burinsky, E.K. Fukuda and J.E. Campana, "Electron Affinities from Dissociations of Mixed Negative Ion Dimers," J. Am. Chem. Soc. **106**, 2270 (1984).

84BUR/HOL
P.C. Burgers, J.L. Holmes and J.K. Terlouw, "Gaseous $[H_2, C, N]^+$ and $[H_3, C, N]^+$ Ions. Generation of Formation, and Dissociation Characteristics of $[H_2CN]^+$, $[HCNH]^+$, $[CNH_2]^+$, $[H_2CNH]^+$, and $[HCN]^+$," J. Am. Chem. Soc. **106**, 2762 (1984).

84BUR/HOL2
P.C. Burgers and J.L. Holmes, "The Generation of Triplet Methoxy Cations," Org. Mass Spectrom. **19**, 452 (1984).

84BUR/HOL3
P.C. Burgers and J.L. Holmes, "Fragmentation Rate Constants and Appearance Energies for Reactions Having a Large Kinetic Shift and the Energy Partitioning in Their Metastable Decomposition," Int. J. Mass Spectrom. Ion Proc. **58**, 15 (1984).

84BUR/KUD
G.G. Burdukovskaya, L.S. Kudin, M.F. Butman and K.S. Krasnov, "Ionic Forms in the Vapour over Potassium Iodide," Zh. Neorgan. Khim. **29**, 3020 (1984).

84BUT/HOL
J.J. Butler, D.M.P. Holland, A.C. Parr and R. Stockbauer, "A Threshold Photoelectron-Photoion Coincidence Spectrometric Study of Dimethyl Ether (CH_3OCH_3)," Int. J. Mass Spectrom. Ion Proc. **58**, 1 (1984).

84BUT/KUD
M.F. Butman, L.S. Kudin and K.S. Krasnov, "The Mass Spectrometric Determination of the Proton Affinity of the Molecules M_2O (M = Na, K, Rb, Cs)," Zh. Neorgan. Khim. **29**, 2150 (1984); English trans.: Russ. J. Inorg. Chem. **29**, 1228 (1984).

84CAL/KEB
G. Caldwell and P. Kebarle, "Binding Energies and Structural Effects in Halide Anion-ROH and -RCOOH Complexes from Gas Phase Equilibria Measurements," J. Am. Chem. Soc. **106**, 967 (1984).

84CAL/ROZ
G. Caldwell, M.D. Rozeboom, J.P. Kiplinger and J.E. Bartmess, "Anion-Alcohol Hydrogen Bond Strengths in the Gas Phase," J. Am. Chem. Soc. **106**, 4660 (1984).

84CAO/BAC
J.-R. Cao and M.H. Back, Int. J. Chem. Kinet. **16**, 961 (1984).

84CAR/FAH
T.A. Carlson, A. Fahlman, W.A. Svensson, M.O. Krause, T.A. Whitley, F.A. Grimm, M.N. Piancastelli and J.W. Taylor, "Angle-Resolved Photoelectron Cross Section of CF_4," J. Chem. Phys. **81**, 3828 (1984).

84CAS/FRE
C.J. Cassady and B.S. Freiser, "Determination of the Fe^+-OH and Co^+-OH Bond Energies by Deprotonation Reactions and by Photodissociation," J. Am. Chem. Soc. **106**, 6176 (1984).

84CAT/PAZ
J. Catalan, J.L.G. de Paz, M. Yanez and J. Elguero, "Relationship between Substituent-Induced Energy and Charge Effects in Proton-Transfer Equilibria Involving Heteroaromatic Nitrogen Systems. The "Lone Pair Charge" Approach," J. Am. Chem. Soc. **106**, 6552 (1984).

84CAU/FUR
C. Cauletti, C. Furlani, G. Nicotra, K.-D. Schleinitz and W. Wegener, "Substituent Effects on the Electronic Structure of Some Styryl Methyl Sulphones Studied by Ultraviolet Photoelectron Spectroscopy," J. Chem. Soc. Perkin Trans. II 533 (1984).

84CHA/HIL
H. Chatham, D. Hils, R. Robertson and A. Gallagher, "Total and Partial Electron Collisional Ionization Cross Sections for CH_4, C_2H_6, SiH_4, and Si_2H_6," J. Chem. Phys. 81, 1770 (1984).

84CHE/HAL
P.T. Chesky and M.B. Hall, "Electronic Structure of Triple-Decker Sandwiches. Photoelectron Spectra and Molecular Orbital Calculations of Bis(η5-cyclopentadienyl)(μ,η6-benzene)divanadium and Bis(η5-cyclopentadienyl)(μ,η6-mesitylene)divanadium," J. Am. Chem. Soc. 106, 5186 (1984).

84CHI/KOR
N.S. Chilingarov, M.V. Korobov, L.N. Sidirov, V.N. Mitkin, V.A. Shipachev and S.V. Zemskov, "Electron Affinity of Rhodium Tetrafluoride," J. Chem. Therm. 16, 965 (1984).

84CIL/DOR
E. Ciliberto, K.A. Doris, W.J. Pietro, G.M. Reisner, D.E. Ellis, I. Fragala, F.H. Herbstein, M.A. Ratner and T.J. Marks, "π-π Interactions and Bandwidths in 'Molecular Metals'. A Chemical, Structural, Photoelectron Spectroscopic, and Hartree-Fock-Slater Study of Monomeric and Cofacially Joined Dimeric Silicon Phthalocyanines," J. Am. Chem. Soc. 106, 7748 (1984).

84COL/JIM
M. Colomina, P. Jimenez, M.V. Roux and C. Turrion, J. Chem. Thermodyn. 16, 1121 (1984).

84COO/KRO
T.A. Cooper, H.W. Kroto, C. Kirby and N.P.C. Westwood, "A Photoelectron Spectroscopic Study of the $(FBS)_n$ System (n = 1-3)," J. Chem. Soc. Dalton Trans. 1047 (1984).

84CZI/TAM
G. Czira, J. Tamas and G. Kalaus, "Effects of Stereoisomerism on the Electron Impact Fragmentation of Some Compounds with an Eburnane Skeleton," Org. Mass Spectrom. 19, 555 (1984).

84DAO/PET
P.D. Dao, K.I. Peterson and A.W. Castleman, Jr., "The Photoionization of Oxidized Metal Clusters," J. Chem. Phys. 80, 563 (1984).

84DEH/PAR
J.L. Dehmer, A.C. Parr, S.H. Southworth and D.M.P. Holland, "Angle-Resolved Photoelectron Study of the Valence Levels of BF_3 in the Range $17 < h\nu < 28$ eV," Phys. Rev. A 30, 1783 (1984).

84DEK/NIB
L.J. de Koening and N.M.M. Nibbering, "Formation of the Long-Lived H_2O^- Ion in the Gas Phase," J. Am. Chem. Soc. 106, 7971 (1984).

84DEL/ABE
E.W. Della, R.S. Abeywickrema, M.K. Livett and J.B. Peel, "The Photoelectron Spectra of Some 1-Halogenobicycloalkanes," J. Chem. Soc. Perkin Trans. II 1653 (1984).

84DEL/PIG
E.W. Della, P.E. Pigou, M.K. Livett and J.B. Peel, "The Photoelectron Spectrum and Molecular Geometry of Bicyclo[2.1.1]Hexane," J. Elec. Spectrosc. Rel. Phenom. 33, 163 (1984).

84DEM/SIM
H. Demian, I. Simiti and N. Palibroda, "Contributions to the Study of Some Heterocycles. 58-Mass Spectra of 2-Phenyl-4-carboxy- and 5-Carboxy-thiazoles," Org. Mass Spectrom. 19, 196 (1984).

84DEN/AUD
J.P. Denhez and H.E. Audier, "Isomerization of $[C_6H_5-C_3H_5O]^+$ Ions: The Case of 1-Phenylpropenol," Org. Mass Spectrom. 19, 407 (1984).

84DEP/BIE
C.H. DePuy, V.M. Bierbaum and R. Damrauer, "Relative Gas-Phase Acidities of the Alkanes," J. Am. Chem. Soc. 106, 4051 (1984).

84DEP/DAM
C.H. DePuy and R. Damrauer, "Reactions of Organosilane Anionic Species with Nitrous Oxide, Organomet. 3, 362 (1984).

84DEW/HEA
M.J.S. Dewar, E.F. Healy and J.J.P. Stewart, J. Comput. Chem. 5, 4 (1984).

84DIX/KOM
D.A. Dixon, A. Komornicki and W.P. Kraemer, "Energetics of the Protonation of CO: Implications for the Observation of HOC^+ in Dense Interstellar Clouds," J. Chem. Phys. 81, 3603 (1984).

84DOG/POU
J.P. Dognon, C. Pouchan, A. Dargelos and J.P. Flament, "Ab Initio CI Study and Vibronic Analysis of the Photoelectron Spectra of Formaldoxime," Chem. Phys. Lett. 109, 492 (1984).

84DRZ/BRA
P.S. Drzaic and J.I. Brauman, "A Determination of the Singlet-Triplet Splitting in Phenylnitrene via Photoelectron Detachment," J. Am. Chem. Soc. 106, 3443 (1984).

84DRZ/BRA2
P.S. Drzaic and J.I. Brauman, "A Determination of the Singlet-Triplet Splitting in Phenylnitrene via Photoelectron Detachment," J. Phys. Chem. 88, 5285 (1984).

84DRZ/MAR
P.S. Drzaic, J. Marks and J.I. Brauman, "Electron Photodetachment from Gas Phase Molecular Anions," in "Gas Phase Ion Chemistry," V. 3, M.T. Bowers, Ed., Academic Press, NY, 1984, Ch. 21.

84DUD/GRE
N. Dudeney, J.C. Green, O.N. Kirchner and F.S.J. Smallwood, "A Study of the Electronic Structure of the Dimers $[Co_2(\eta-C_5Me_5)_2(CO)_2]$, $[Rh_2(\eta-C_5Me_5)_2]$, $[Co_2(\eta-C_5Me_5)_2(NO)_2]$ and $[Co_2(\eta-C_5Me_5)_2(CO)(NO)]$ by He-I and He-II Photoelectron Spectroscopy," J. Chem. Soc. Dalton Trans. 1883 (1984).

84DUD/KIR
N. Dudeney, O.N. Kirchner, J.C. Green and P. Maitlis, "Electronic Structure and Reactivity of Pentamethylcyclopentadienyl Complexes of Cobalt, Rhodium, and Iridium: He-I and He-II Photoelectron Spectroscopic Investigation," J. Chem. Soc. Dalton Trans. 1877 (1984).

84DUN/HON
R.C. Dunbar and J.P. Honovich, "Threshold Ion Photodissociation. Bromobenzene and Iodobenzene Ions," Int. J. Mass Spectrom. Ion Proc. 58, 25 (1984).

84DYK/ELL
J.M. Dyke, A.R. Ellis, N. Keddar and A. Morris, "A Reinvestigation of the First Band in the Photoelectron Spectrum of the Ethyl Radical," J. Phys. Chem. 88, 2565 (1984).

84DYK/ELL2
J.M. Dyke, A.R. Ellis, N. Jonathan, N. Keddar and A. Morris, "Observation of the CH_2OH Radical in the Gas Phase by Vacuum Ultraviolet Photoelectron Spectroscopy," Chem. Phys. Lett. 111, 207 (1984).

84DYK/GRA
J.M. Dyke, B.W.J. Gravenor, G.D. Josland, R.A. Lewis and A. Morris, "A Gas Phase Investigation of Titanium Monoxide and Atomic Titanium Using High Temperature Photoelectron Spectroscopy," Molec. Phys. 53, 465 (1984).

84DYK/JOS
J.M. Dyke, G. D. Josland, J. G. Snijders and P.M. Boerrigter, "Ionization Energies of the Diatomic Halogens and Interhalogens Studied with Relativistic Hartree-Fock-Slater Calculations," Chem. Phys. 91, 419 (1984).

84DYK/KIR
J.M. Dyke, C. Kirby, A. Morris, B.W.J. Gravenor, R. Klein and P. Rosmus, "A Study of Aluminium Monofluoride and Aluminium Trifluoride by High-Temperature Photoelectron Spectroscopy," Chem. Phys. 88, 289 (1984).

84DYK/LEW
J.M. Dyke, A.E. Lewis and A. Morris, "A Photoelectron Spectroscopic Study of the Ground State of CF^+ via the Ionization Process $CF^+(X^1\Sigma^+) \leftarrow CF(X^2\Pi)$," J. Chem. Phys. 80, 1382 (1984).

84ELB/KUD
S. Elbel, J. Kudnig, M. Grodzicki and H.J. Lempka, "Photoelectron Spectra of Group V Compounds. The Elements: Sb_4," Chem. Phys. Lett. 109, 312 (1984).

84ELK/ARM
J.L. Elkind and P.B. Armentrout, "Threshold Behavior for Chemical Reactions: Line-of-Centers Cross Section for $Si^+(^2P) + H_2 \rightarrow SiH^+ + H$," J. Phys. Chem. 88, 5454 (1984).

84ERA/KOL
P.A. Erastov, V.P. Kolesov and I.K. Igumenov, Russ. J. Phys. Chem. 58, 1311 (1984).

84FAR/SRI
M. Farber and R.D. Srivastava, "Electron and Thermal Dissociation of $BF_3(g)$," J. Chem. Phys. 81, 241 (1984).

84FLA/MAQ
R. Flammang, A. Maquestiau, J. Catalan, P. Periz and J. Elguero, "Basicity of Azoles. Experimental Gas Phase Basicities Determined by Mass Spectrometry Towards ab initio Calculated Protonation Energies," Org. Mass Spectrom. 19, 627 (1984).

84FRA/FRA
M.L. Fraser-Monteiro, L. Fraser-Monteiro, J. de Wit and T. Baer, "Dissociation Dynamics of Energy-Selected Phenol Ions," J. Phys. Chem. 88, 3622 (1984).

84FUC/HAL
R. Fuchs and J.H. Hallman Unpublished results, personal communication to the authors.

84FUK/YOS
K. Fuke, H. Yoshiuchi, K. Kaya, Y. Achiba, K. Sato and K. Kimura, "Multiphoton Ionization Photoelectron Spectroscopy and Two-Color Multiphoton Ionization Threshold Spectroscopy on the Hydrogen Bonded Phenol and 7-Azaindole in a Supersonic Jet," Chem. Phys. Lett. 108, 179 (1984).

84FUR/MUR
J. Furukawa, S. Murata, M. Sakiyama and S. Seki, Bull. Chem. Soc. Jpn. 57, 3058 (1984).

84GAN/LIV
T.H. Gan, M.K. Livett and J.B. Peel, "Comparative He I and He II Photoelectron Spectroscopic Studies of the Benzoyl Halides," J. Chem. Soc. Faraday Trans. II 80, 1281 (1984).

84GAT
I.R. Gatland, "Swarms of Ions and Electrons In Gases," W. Lindinger, Ed., Springer-Verlag NY 1984. pg. 44.

84GEF/LIF
S. Gefen and C. Lifshitz, "Time-Dependent Mass Spectra and Breakdown Graphs. V. The Kinetic Shift in Iodobenzene," Int. J. Mass Spectrom. Ion Proc. 58, 251 (1984).

84GEL/POR
G.I. Gellene and R.F. Porter, "Experimental Evidence for Metastable States of D_3O and Its Monohydrate by Neutralized Ion Beam Spectroscopy," J. Chem. Phys. 81, 5570 (1984).

84GLE/BAR
R. Gleiter, R. Bartetzko and D. Cremer, "Electronic Structure of 1,5-Dithia-2,4,6,8-tetrazocine. Model Calculations and Spectroscopic Investigations," J. Am. Chem. Soc. 106, 3437 (1984).

84GLE/BIS
R. Gleiter, P. Bischof, M.C. Bohm, R. Guilard and H. Yamaguchi, "The Electronic Structure of Heterotropones. Photoelectron Spectra and Molecular Orbital Calculations," Bull. Chem. Soc. Jpn. 57, 856 (1984).

84GLE/BOH
R. Gleiter, M.C. Bohm and R.D. Ernst, "The He(I) Photoelectron Spectrum of Bis(pentadienyl)-iron: A Comparison with the Ferrocene Spectrum," J. Electron Spectrosc. Rel. Phenom. 33, 269 (1984).

84GLE/DOB
R. Gleiter, W. Dobler, M. Eckert-Maksic, A.J. Bloodworth, H.J. Eggelte and D. Cremer, "Photoelectron Spectra of Dioxabicyclo[n.2.1]alkanes," J. Org. Chem. 49, 3716 (1984).

84GLE/FRI
R. Gleiter, G. Friedrich, M. Yoshifuji, K. Shibayama and N. Inamoto, "Photoelectron Spectra of Diaryldiphosphenes," Chem. Lett. 313 (1984).

84GLE/HAI
R. Gleiter, R. Haider, P. Bischof, N.S. Zefirov and A.M. Boganov, "Electronic Structure of the Tricyclo[2.1.0.0^{2,5}]pentane System. Photoelectron Spectroscopic Investigations of 1,5-Dimethyl-3-exo-methylenetricyclo[2.1.0.0^{2,5}]pentane and 1,5-Dimethyltricyclo[2.1.0.0^{2,5}]pentan-3-one," J. Org. Chem. 49, 375 (1984).

84GLE/SCH
R. Gleiter, W. Schafer and A. Flatow, "Interaction between Triple Bonds in 1,8-Diethynylnaphthalenes," J. Org. Chem. 49, 372 (1984).

84GLE/SCH2
R. Gleiter, W. Schafer, H.A. Staab and T. Saupe, "Electronic Structure of 4,5-Bis(dimethylamine)fluorene. PE Spectroscopic Investigations," J. Org. Chem. 49, 4463 (1984).

84GLE/SPA
R. Gleiter, J. Spanget-Larsen, H. Hopf and C. Mlynek, "Photoelectron Spectra of Some Reduction Products of [2.2]Paracyclophane," Chem. Ber. 117, 1987 (1984).

84GLE/SPA2
R. Gleiter, J. Spanget-Larsen and W.L.F. Armarego, "Through-bond Effects in Pyrazino[2,3-b]pyrazine. Photoelectron Spectroscopy and Model Calculations," J. Chem. Soc. Perkin Trans. II 1517 (1984).

84GOR/PYA
L.N. Gorokhov, A.T. Pyatenko, I.V. Sidorova and V.K. Smirnov, "Thermochemistry of Molecules and Negative Ions in a Uranium-Oxygen-Fluorine System", Probl. Kalorim. Khim. Termodin. Dokl. Vses. Konf. 2, 66 (1984). CA 104, 11261c.

84GRA/ROS
M. Grade, W. Rosinger and P.A. Dowben, "Core and Valence Electron Binding Energies of FeI_2 and Stabilities of Gas Phase Species," Ber. Bunsenges. Phys. Chem. 88, 65 (1984).

84GRA/ROS2
M. Grade and W. Rosinger, "A Mass Spectrometric Investigation of Iron(II)-Iodide," Ber. Bunsenges. Phys. Chem. 88, 767 (1984).

84GRE/POW
J.C. Green, P. Powell and J.E. van Tilborg, "He I and He II Photoelectron Spectroscopic Studies of the Bonding in Cobalt, Rhodium, and Iridium Cyclopentadienyl Diene Complexes," Organometall. 3, 211 (1984).

84GRE/STE
A. Greenberg, S.E. Stein and R.L. Brown, Sci. Totl. Env. 40, 219 (1984).

84GRO/CHE
G.S. Groenwold, E.K. Chess and M.L. Gross, "Structure of the Intermediate Formed in the Reaction of the Styrene Radical Cation and Neutral Styrene," J. Am. Chem. Soc. 106, 539 (1984).

84GRO/GRO
G.S. Groenwold and M.L. Gross, "Cation Radical Diels-Alder Reaction of 1,3-Butadiene: A Two-Step Cycloaddition," J. Am. Chem. Soc. **106**, 6569 (1984).

84GRU/WHE
S.G. Grubb, R.L. Whetten, A.C. Albrecht and E.R. Grant, "A Precise Determination of the First Ionization Potential of Benzene," Chem. Phys. Lett. **108**, 420 (1984).

84GUB/GER
A.I. Gubareva, P.A. Gerasimov and V.V. Beregovykh, Zh. Prikl. Khim. **57**, 2297 (1984).

84HAL/KLE
L.F. Halle, F.S. Klein and J.L. Beauchamp, "Properties and Reactions of Organometallic Fragments in the Gas Phase. Ion Beam Studies of FeH^+," J. Am. Chem. Soc. **106**, 2543 (1984).

84HAR/HOU
A.G. Harrison, R. Houriet and T.T. Tidwell, "Gas Phase Basicities of Substituted Styrenes. Comparison of Gas Phase and Solution Reactivities," J. Org. Chem. **49**, 1302 (1984).

84HEI/BAR
T. Heinis, R. Bar, K. Borlin and M. Jungen, "Photoionization of 1,1-Difluoroethane: The Structure of the $C_2H_3F_2^+$ Ions," Chem. Phys. Lett. **105**, 327 (1984).

84HEI/HON
E. Heilbronner, E. Honegger, W. Zambach, P. Schmitt and H. Gunther, "The Persistence of Ribbon Orbitals in Polycyclic Alkanes," Helv. Chim. Acta **67**, 1681 (1984).

84HEI/WIR
E. Heilbronner, J. Wirz and R.L. Soulen, "6. The He(Iα) Photoelectron Spectra of the Perfluoroderivatives of Trisannelated Benzenes and Tetrakisannelated Cyclooctatetraenes," Helv. Chim. Acta **67**, 47 (1984).

84HER/WEN
N. Hernandez-Gill, W.E. Wentworth and E.C.M. Chen, "Electron Affinities of Fluorinated Phenoxy Radicals," J. Phys. Chem. **88**, 6181 (1984).

84HIE/PAU
P.M. Hierl and J.F. Paulson, "Translational Energy Dependence of Cross Sections for Reactions of $OH^-(H_2O)_n$ with CO_2 and SO_2," J. Chem. Phys. **80**, 4890 (1984).

84HIL
K. Hilpert, "Vaporization of Sodium Iodide and Thermochemistry of $(NaI)_2(g)$ and $(NaI)_3(g)$: An Experimental and Theoretical Study," Ber. Bunsenges. Phys. Chem. **88**, 132 (1984).

84HOH/DIS
G. Hohlneicher, D. Distler, M. Muller and H.-J. Freund, "Identification of Shake-Up Satellites in Valence Photoelectron Spectra of Organic Compounds by Comparison with Electronic Absorption Spectra of Radical Cations. Case Study: Octafluoronaphthalene," Chem. Phys. Lett. **111**, 151 (1984).

84HOL/LOS
J.L. Holmes and F.P. Lossing, Int. J. Mass Spectrosc. Ion Proc. **58**, 113 (1984).

84HOL/MOM
J.L. Holmes, A.A. Mommers, J.E. Szulejko and J.K. Terlouw, "Two New Stable $[C_3H_8O]^+$ Isomers: the Radical Cations $[C_3H_6OH_2]^+$," J. Chem. Soc. Chem. Commun. 165 (1984).

84HOL/SZU
J.L. Holmes and J.E. Szulejko, "The Generation and Identification of the Transient Vinylidene Cation," Chem. Phys. Lett. **107**, 301 (1984).

84HON/HEI
E. Honegger, E. Heilbronner, A. Dratva and C.A. Grob, "197. 'Lone Pair' and 'CI Bond' Ionization Energies of exo- and endo-2-Norbornyl Iodides," Helv. Chim. Acta **67**, 1691 (1984).

84HON/ZHO
E. Honegger, Y. Zhong-zhi, E. Heilbronner, W.v.E. Doering and J.C. Schmidhauser, "Photoelectron-Spectroscopic Characterization of 3,4-Dimethyl-2,4-hexadienes," Helv. Chim. Acta **67**, 640 (1984).

84HOP/JAH
H.P. Hopkins, Jr., D.V. Jahagirdar, P.S. Moulik, D.H. Aue, H.M. Webb, W.R. Davidson and M.D. Pedley, "Basicities of the 2-, 4-, 2,4-Di and 2,6-Disubstituted t-Butyl Pryidines in the Gas Phase and Aqueous Phase: Steric Effects in the Solvation of tert-Butyl-Substituted Pyridines and Pyridinium Cations," J. Am. Chem. Soc. **106**, 4341 (1984).

84HOW/GON
J.O. Howell, J.M. Goncalves, C. Amatore, L. Klasinc, R.M. Wightman and J.K. Kochi, "Electron Transfer from Aromatic Hydrocarbons and Their π-Complexes with Metals. Comparison of the Standard Oxidation Potentials and Vertical Ionization Potentials," J. Am. Chem. Soc. **106**, 3968 (1984).

84JAC/JAC
T.C. Jackson, D.B. Jacobson and B.S. Freiser, "Gas Phase Reactions of FeO^+ with Hydrocarbons," J. Am. Chem. Soc. **106**, 1252 (1984).

84JEN/MOR
H.D.B. Jenkins and D.F.C. Morris, "Proton Affinity of Gaseous Ammonia," J. Chem. Soc. Faraday Trans. II **80**, 1167 (1984).

84JOR/THO
F.S. Jorgensen and T. Thomsen, "Synthesis and Structural Analysis of the Bridged peri-Naphthalene: 1,3-Dihydro-2-phenalenone," Acta Chem. Scan. **B38**, 113 (1984).

84KAT/SHI
S. Katsumata, H. Shiromaru and T. Kimura, "Photoelectron Angular Distribution and Assignment of Photoelectron Spectrum of Ozone," Bull. Chem. Soc. Jpn. **57**, 1784 (1984).

84KIN/KRO
M.A. King and H.W. Kroto, "He I Photoelectron Study of Cyanogen Isothiocyanate, NCNCS, Produced by Thermal Isomerization of Sulfur Dicyanide, $S(CN)_2$," J. Am. Chem. Soc. **106**, 7347 (1984).

84KIR/POP
K. Kirste, R. Poppek and P. Rademacher, "Photoelektronenspektren und Konformationsverhalten von Azinen," Chem. Ber. **117**, 1061 (1984).

84KLA/KUH
D. Klapstein, R. Kuhn, J.P. Maier, L. Misev and M. Ochsner, "138. Spectroscopic Characterization of Open-Shell Cations: Emission and Laser Excitation Spectra of Rotationally Cooled $CH_3(-C=C-)_2X^+$, X = Cl, Br," Helv. Chim. Acta **67**, 1222 (1984).

84KLA/MAI
D. Klapstein, J.P. Maier, M. Ochsner and W. Zambach, "Emission and Laser Excitation Spectra of the $A^2\Pi = X^2\Pi$ Transition of Rotationally Cooled Bromochloroacetylene Cation in the Gas Phase," J. Electron Spectrosc. Rel. Phenom. **34**, 161 (1984).

84KOB
T. Kobayashi, "Angle-Resolved Photoelectron Spectroscopy of Intramolecular Hydrogen Bond Systems: 2-Chloroethanol and 2-Bromoethanol," Phys. Lett. **103A**, 424 (1984).

84KOB/YOS
T. Kobayashi, Z. Yoshida, H. Awaji, T. Kawase and S. Yoneda, "Intramolecular Orbital Interaction in 6,6'-Bi(1,4-dithiafulvenyl) Studied by Photoelectron Spectroscopy," Bull. Chem. Soc. Jpn. **57**, 2591 (1984).

84KOR/CHI
M.V. Korobov, N.S. Chilingarov, N.A. Igolkina, M.I. Nikitin and L.N. Sidorov, "Molecules with a High Electron Affinity. Negative Ions in the Saturated Vapor of the Platinum-Manganese Trifluoride System," Russ. J. Phys. Chem. **58**, 1368 (1984).

84KUH/MAI
R. Kuhn, J.P. Maier and F. Thommen, "Fluorescence Quantum Yields and Lifetimes of Fluorobenzene Cations in Selected Levels of Their B and C States Determined by Photoelectron-Photon Coincidence Spectroscopy," Chem. Phys. **57**, 319 (1981).

84LAN/LEE
K.R. Lane, R.E. Lee, L. Sallans and R.R. Squires, "Formation and Reactivity of $Fe(CO)_4COOH^-$ in the Gas Phase. Implication for the $Fe(CO)_5$ Catalyzed Water Gas Shift Reaction," J. Am. Chem. Soc. **106**, 5767 (1984).

84LAR/MCM
J.W. Larson and T.B. McMahon, "Fluoride and Chloride Affinities of Main Group Oxides, Fluorides, Oxofluorides, and Alkyls. Quantitative Scales of Lewis Acidities from Ion Cyclotron Resonance Halide-Exchange Equilibria," J. Phys. Chem. **88**, 1083 (1984).

84LAR/MCM2
J.W. Larson and T.B. McMahon, "Hydrogen Bonding in Gas Phase Anions. An Experimental Investigation of the Interaction between Chloride Ion and Bronsted Acids from ICR Chloride Exchange Equilibria," J. Am. Chem. Soc. **106**, 517 (1984).

84LAR/MCM3
J.W. Larson and T.B. McMahon, "Gas Phase Bihalide and Pseudohalide Ions. An ICR Determination of Hydrogen Bond Energies in XHY^- Species (X,Y = F, Cl, Br, CN)," Inorg. Chem. **23**, 2029 (1984).

84LAR/MCM4
J.W. Larson and T.B. McMahon, "Gas Phase Negative Ion Chemistry of Alkylchloroformates," Can. J. Chem. **62**, 675 (1984).

84LEB/GUT
N.D. Lebedeva, N.M. Gutner, Y.A. Katin, N.M. Kozlova, N.N. Kiseleva, E.F. Makhina and S.K. Dobychin, Zh. Prikl. Khim. **57**, 2297 (1984).

84LEW/GOL
K.E. Lewis, D.M. Golden and G.P. Smith, "Organometallic Bond Dissociation Energies: Laser Pyrolysis of $Fe(CO)_5$, $Cr(CO)_6$, $Mo(CO)_6$, and $W(CO)_6$," J. Am. Chem. Soc. **106**, 3905 (1984).

84LIA/BUC
S.G. Lias and T.J. Buckley, "Structures and Reactions of $C_3H_6^+$ Ions Generated in Cyclopropane," Int. J. Mass Spectrom. Ion Proc. **56**, 123 (1984).

84LIA/LIE
S.G. Lias, J.F. Liebman and R.D. Levin, "Evaluated Gas Phase Basicities and Proton Affinities of Molecules; Heats of Formation of Protonated Molecules," J. Phys. Chem. Ref. Data **13**, 695 (1984).

84LIC/BLE
D.L. Lichtenberger and C.H. Blevins II, "Contribution of a Σ-Orbital Electron to a Quadruple Metal-Metal Bond. A Direct Experimental Measure from Vibrational Fine Structure in the Σ Ionization of $Mo_2(O_2CCH_3)_4$," J. Am. Chem. Soc. **106**, 1636 (1984).

84LIC/CAL
D.L. Lichtenberger, D.C. Calabro and G.E. Kellogg, "Electronic Structure and Bonding Characteristics of Cyclopentadienyl d^8 Metal-Ligand Complexes. Core and Valence Ionization Study of $CpM(CO)_2$ Where M = Co and Rh and Cp = η^5-C_5H_5 and η^5-$C_5(CH_3)_5$," Organometall. **3**, 1623 (1984).

84LIF/MAL
C. Lifshitz and Y. Malinovich, "Time Resolved Photoionization Mass Spectrometry in the Millisecond Range," Int. J. Mass Spec. Ion Proc. **60**, 99 (1984).

84LIN/LIA
S.H. Linn, C.L. Liao, C.X. Liao, J.M. Brom, Jr. and C.Y. Ng, "Photoionization Study of Hg_2," Chem. Phys. Lett. **105**, 645 (1984).

84LOS/HOL
F.P. Lossing and J.L. Holmes, "Stabilization Energy and Ion Size in Carbocations in the Gas Phase," J. Am. Chem. Soc. **106**, 6917 (1984).

84LOU/HEN
J.N. Louwen, R. Hengelmolen, D.M. Grove, A. Oskam and R.L. DeKock, "Ultraviolet Photoelectron Spectra of Square-Planar Complexes of Nickel Triad Metals. 3. He I and He II Spectra of trans-$[(PEt_3)_2MXY]$ (M = Pd, Pt. X = Y = C≡CH, C≡CCH_3, C≡N. X = Cl, Y = C≡N) and Hartree-Fock-Slater Calculations on Model Compounds," Organometall. **3**, 908 (1984).

84LOU/STU
J.N. Louwen, D.J. Stufkens and A. Oskam, "He(I) and He(II) Photoelectron Spectra of Some Organozinc and Organoaluminium Radicals Containing 1,2-Bis(t-butylimino)ethane," J. Chem. Soc. Dalton Trans. 2683 (1984).

84MAG/CAL
T.F. Magnera, G. Caldwell, J. Sumner, S. Ikuta and P. Kebarle, "Solvation of the Halide Anions in Dimethyl Sulfoxide. Factors Involved in Enhanced Reactivity of Negative Ions in Dipolar Aprotic Solvents," J. Am. Chem. Soc. **106**, 6140 (1984).

84MAI/THO
J.P. Maier and F. Thommen, "Relaxation Dynamics of Open-Shell Cations Studied by Photoelectron-Photon Coincidence Spectroscopy" Gas Phase Ion Chemistry, Vol. 3 (M. T. Bowers, editor), Academic Press, Inc., p. 357 (1984).

84MAL/ROS
T.E. Mallouk, G.L. Rosenthal, G. Muller, R. Brusasco and N. Bartlett, "Fluoride Ion Affinities of GeF_4 and BF_4 from Thermodynamic and Structural Data for $(SF_2)_2GeF_6$, ClO_2GeF_5, and ClO_2BF_4," Inorg. Chem. **23**, 3167 (1984).

84MAR/KAY
A.P. Marchand, R. Kaya and A.D. Baker, "A Photoelectron Spectroscopic Study of Proximity Effects in 8,11-Disubstituted Pentacyclo(5.4.0.0^{2,6}.0^{3,10}.0^{5,9})undecanes," Tetrahedron Lett. **25**, 795 (1984).

84MAU/NEL
M. Meot-Ner (Mautner), S.F. Nelsen, M.R. Willi and T.B. Frigo, "Special Effects of an Unusually Large Neutral to Radical Cation Geometry Change. Adiabatic Ionization Energies and Proton Affinities of Alkylhydrazines," J. Am. Chem. Soc. **106**, 7384 (1984).

84MCA/HUD
D.J. McAdoo, C.E. Hudson, F.W. McLafferty and T.E. Parks, "The Reactions of Metastable $[C_5H_{10}O]^+$ Ions with the Oxygen on the Second Carbon," Org. Mass Spectrom. **19**, 353 (1984).

84MCD/CHO
R.N. McDonald, A.K. Chowdhury and W.D. McGhee, "Gas-Phase Generation of 1,1,1,3,3,3-Hexafluoroisopropylidene Anion Radical: Proton Affinity and Heat of Formation of $(CF_3)_2C^-$ and $(CF_3)_2CH^-$," J. Am. Chem. Soc. **106**, 4112 (1984).

84MCD/CHO2
R.N. McDonald, A.K. Chodhury and P.L. Schell, "Generations and Reactions of $(OC)_3Fe^-$ in a Flowing Afterglow Apparatus," J. Am. Chem. Soc. **106**, 6095 (1984).

84MCM/HAL
J.E. McMurry, G.J. Haley, J.R. Matz, J.C. Clardy and G. Van Duyne, "Tetracyclo[8.2.2.2^{2,5}.2^{6,9}]octadeca-1,5,9-triene," J. Am. Chem. Soc. **106**, 5018 (1984).

84MEA/STE
R.D. Mead, A.E. Stevens and W.C. Lineberger, "Photodetachment in Negative Ion Beams," Gas Phase Ion Chemistry, Vol. 3 (M.T. Bowers, editor), Academic Press, NY, (1984), Ch. 22.

84MEY/SCH
H.-J. Meyer, T. Schulze and U. Ross, "Molecular Beam Study of the Chemi-Ionization in the Reactive Scattering of Ca and Sr with Cl_2 and Br_2 at Collision Energies C(c.m.) < 4.5 eV," Chem. Phys. **90**, 185 (1984).

84MIL/BAE
B.E. Miller and T. Baer, "Kinetic Energy Release Distribution in the Fragmentation of Energy-Selected Vinyl and Ethyl Bromide Ions," Chem. Phys. **85**, 39 (1984).

84MOM/BUR
A.A. Mommers, P.C. Burgers, J.L. Holmes and J.K. Terlouw, "Isomeric $[C_3H_4]^+$ Ions: Their Identification and Generation in Dissociative Ionizations," Org. Mass Spectrom. **19**, 7 (1984).

84MOR/POW
B.J. Morris-Sherwood, C.B. Powell and M.B. Hall, "Photoelectron Spectra and Molecular Orbital Calculations on Bis(cyclopentadienyldicarbonylchromium, -molybdenum, and -tungsten): Nature of the Bonding of Linear Semibridging Carbonyls," J. Am. Chem. Soc. **106**, 5079 (1984).

84MOS/MOS
J. Moskal, A. Moskal and K. Nagraba, "Conjugated Schiff's Bases. 16 - Substituent Effect on Electron Impact Fragmentation of Some 1-Oxa-4-azabutadienes," Org. Mass Spectrom. **19**, 87 (1984).

84MOY/BRA
C.R. Moyland and J.I. Brauman, "Bond Dissociation Energies in Alcohols: Kinetic and Photochemical Evidence Regarding Ion Thermochemistry," J. Phys. Chem. **88**, 3175 (1984).

84MUL/SAN
K. Muller-Dethlefs, M. Sander and E.W. Schlag, "Two-Colour Photoionization Resonance Spectroscopy of NO: Complete Separation of Rotational Levels of NO^+ at the Ionization Threshold," Chem. Phys. Lett. **112**, 291 (1984).

84NAD/REI
I. Nadler, H. Reisler, M. Noble and C. Wittig, Chem. Phys. Lett. **108**, 115 (1984).

84NEL
S.F. Nelsen, "Ionization from Nitrogen and Oxygen Lone Pairs: A Comparison of Trialkylamine, Dialkyl Ether, Tetraalkylhydrazine, and Dialkyl Peroxide Photoelectron Spectroscopic Ionization Potentials," J. Org. Chem. **49**, 1891 (1984).

84NES/VER
T.N. Nesterova, S.P. Verekin, S.Y. Karaseva, A.M. Rozhnov and V.F. Tsyetkov, Russ. J. Phys. Chem. **58**, 491 (1984).

84NIK/OVC
E.N. Nikolaev, K.V. Ovchinnikov and G.A. Semenov, "Composition of Vapor over Lead Molybdate and Tungstate," Zh. Obs. Khim. **54**, 977 (1984). English trans.: J. Gen. Chem. (USSR) **54**, 869 (1984).

84NOV/POT
I. Novak and A.W. Potts, "The UV Gas-Phase Photoelectron Spectra of Group IVB Tetraphenyl Derivatives," J. Organometall. Chem. **262**, 17 (1984).

84NOV/POT2
I. Novak and A.W. Potts, "Ultraviolet Photoelectron Spectra of Gas Phase and Condensed Tin and Lead Dihalides (MX_2, M = Sn, Pb; X = Cl, Br, I)" J. Electron Spectrosc. Rel. Phenom. **33**, 1 (1984).

84OAK/ELL
J.M. Oakes and G.B. Ellison, "Photoelectron Spectroscopy of the Allylic Anion, J. Am. Chem. Soc. **106**, 7734 (1984).

84OHN/MAT
K. Ohno, S. Matumoto, K. Imai and Y. Haraa, "Penning Ionization Electron Spectroscopy of Nitriles," J. Phys. Chem. **88**, 206 (1984).

84OLI/FLE
J.A. Olivares, G.D. Flesch and H.J. Svec, "Mass Spectrometry of Five Ketene Dimers," Int. J. Mass Spectrom. Ion Proc. **56**, 293 (1984).

84OLI/GUE
P.R. Olivato, S.A. Guerrero, A. Modelli, G. Granozzi, D. Jones and G. Distefano, "Electronic Interaction in Heterosubstituted Acetones Studied by Means of Ultraviolet Photoelectron and Electron Transmission Spectroscopy," J. Chem. Soc. Perkin Trans. II 1505 (1984).

84ORI/SRI
O.J. Orient and S.K. Srivastava, "Mass Spectrometric Determination of Partial and Total Electron Impact Ionization Cross Sections of SO_2 from Threshold up to 200 eV," J. Chem. Phys. **80**, 140 (1984).

84PAN/BAE
M. Panczel and T. Baer, "A Photoelectron Photoion Coincidence (PEPICO) Study of Fragmentation Rates and Kinetic Energy Release Distributions in Nitrobenzene," Int. J. Mass Spectrom. Ion Proc. **58**, 43 (1984).

84PAQ/DAN
L.A. Paquette, R.G. Daniels and R. Gleiter, "Synthesis, Reactivity, and Electronic Structure of (2-(Trimethylsilyl)-1,3-cyclohexadiene)iron Tricarbonyl Complexes," Organometall. **3**, 560 (1984).

84PAR/WEX
E.K. Parks and S. Wexler, J. Phys. Chem. **88**, 4492 (1984).

84PAU/HEN
J.F. Paulson and M.J. Henchman, "On the Formation of H_3O^- in an Ion-Molecule Reaction," in "Ionic Processes in the Gas Phase," M.A. Almoster Ferreira, Ed., Reidel, Dordrecht, 1984, p.331.

84PED/UND
A.H. Pedersen and K. Undheim, "N-Quaternary Compounds. Part LIX. Facile Synthesis of 3-Vinyl-4(3H)-pyrimidinethiones," J. Heterocyc. Chem. **21**, 1149 (1984).

84PET/DAO
K.I. Peterson, P.D. Dao, R.W. Farley and A.W. Castleman, Jr., "Photoionization of Sodium Clusters," J. Chem. Phys. **80**, 1780 (1984).

84PLA/SIM
V.A. Platonov and Y.N. Simulin, Russ. J. Phys. Chem. **58**, 1630 (1984).

84POL/MUN
C.W. Polley, Jr. and B. Munson, "The Proton Affinity of Nitrogen Dioxide," Int. J. Mass Spectrom. Ion Proc. **59**, 333 (1984).

84POL/TRE
J.E. Pollard, D.J. Trevor, J.E. Reutt, Y.T. Lee and D.A. Shirley, "Torsional Potential and Intramolecular Dynamics in the $C_2H_4^+$ Photoelectron Spectra," J. Chem. Phys. **81**, 5302 (1984).

84PYA/GOR
A.T. Pyatenko and L.N. Gorokhov, "Electron Affinities of the U_2F_n Molecules (8 < n < 12)," Chem. Phys. Lett. **105**, 205 (1984). [Duplicates, Russ. J. Phys. Chem. **58**, 1624 (1984).]

84PYA/GUS
A.T. Pyatenko, A.V. Gusarov and L.N. Gorokhov, "Thermochemistry of Negative Ions in the U-F System," Russ. J. Phys. Chem. **58**, 1 (1984).

84RAU/SCH
H. Rau and E. Schnedler, J. Chem. Thermodyn. **16**, 673 (1984).

84REE/MUJ
W.D. Reents, Jr. and A.M. Mujsce, "Ion/Molecule Reactions of Silicon Tetrafluoride," Int. J. Mass Spectrom. Ion Proc. **59**, 65 (1984).

84ROH/COX
E.A. Rohlfing, D.M. Cox and A. Kaldor, "Production and Characterization of Supersonic Carbon Cluster Beams," J. Chem. Phys. **81**, 3322 (1984).

84ROH/COX2
E.A. Rohlfing, D.M. Cox, A. Kaldor and K.H. Johnson, "Photoionization Spectra and Electronic Structure of Small Iron Clusters," J. Chem. Phys. **81**, 3846 (1984).

84ROL/HOU
E. Rolli and R. Houriet, "Basicite en Phase Gaseuse et Site de Protonation des p-Nitroanilines $R_2NC_6H_4NO_2$ (R = H, CH_3)," Int. J. Spectrosc. **3**, 177 (1984).

84ROT
W.R. Roth, Personal communication.

84RUS/CUR
B.M. Ruscic, L.A. Curtiss and J. Berkowitz, "Photoelectron Spectrum and Structure of B_2O_2," J. Chem. Phys. **80**, 3962 (1984).

84SCH
B. Schaldach, "Chemistry of Gaseous Ions. Part VIII. Bond Strength and Mass Spectrometric Fragmentation of 2-Methoxycinnamic Acid," Int. J. Mass Spectrom. Ion Proc. **56**, 237 (1984).

84SCH/HOU
J.C. Schultz, F.A. Houle and J.L. Beauchamp, "Photoelectron Spectroscopy of 1-Propyl, 1-Butyl, Isobutyl, Neopentyl and 2-Butyl Radicals: Free Radical Precursors to High Energy Carbonium Ion Isomers," J. Am. Chem. Soc. **106**, 3917 (1984).

84SCH/HOU2
J.C. Schultz, F.A. Houle and J.L. Beauchamp, "Photoelectron Spectroscopy of Isomeric C_4H_7 Radicals. Implications for the Thermochemistry and Structures of the Radicals and Their Corresponding Carbonium Ions," J. Am. Chem. Soc. **106**, 7336 (1984).

84SHA/URA
M. Shahbaz, S. Urano, P.R. LeBreton, M.A. Rossman, R.S. Hosmane and N.J. Leonard, "Tri-s-triazine: Synthesis, Chemical Behavior and Spectroscopic and Theoretical Probes of Valence Orbital Structure," J. Am. Chem. Soc. **106**, 2805 (1984).

84SHI/GIN
I. Shin and K.A. Gingerich, J. Chem. Phys. **81**, 5937 (1984).

84SMI/ADA
D. Smith, N.G. Adams and E.E. Ferguson, "The Heat of Formation of $C_3H_2^+$," Int. J. Mass Spectrom Ion Proc. **61**, 15 (1984).

84SMI/HAG
M.A. Smith, J.W. Hager and S.C. Wallace, "Two Color Photoionization Spectroscopy of Jet Cooled Aniline: Vibrational Frequencies of the Aniline X^2B_1 Radical Cation," J. Chem. Phys. **80**, 3097 (1984).

84SMI/HAG2
M.A. Smith, J.W. Hager and S.C. Wallace, "Two-Color Laser Photoionization Spectroscopy in a Collisionless Free-Jet Expansion: Spectroscopy and Excited-State Dynamics of Diazabicyclooctane," J. Phys. Chem. **88**, 2250 (1984).

84STA/MAQ
D. Stahl and F. Maquin, "Charge-Stripping Mass Spectrometry of Molecular Ions from Polyacenes and Molecular Orbital Theory," Chem. Phys. Lett. **108**, 613 (1984).

84STE/MAR
K. Stephen, T.D. Mark, J.H. Futrell and H. Helm, "Electron Impact Ionization of $(N_2)_2$: Appearance Energies of N_3^+ and N_4^+," J. Chem. Phys. **80**, 3185 (1984).

84STO/SPL
J.A. Stone and D.E. Splinter, "A High-Pressure Mass Spectrometric Study of the Binding of $(CH_3)_3Sn^+$ to Lewis Bases in the Gas Phase," Int. J. Mass Spectrom. Ion Proc. **59**, 169 (1984).

84SZE/BAE
L. Szepes and T. Baer, "Dissociation Dynamics of Energy Selected Hexamethyldisilane Ions and the Heats of Formation of $(CH_3)_3Si^+$ and $(CH_3)_3Si$," J. Am. Chem. Soc. **106**, 273 (1984).

84SZE/BAE2
L. Szepes and T. Baer, "$(CH_3)_3SiX$ tipusu vegyuletek vizsgalata fotoelectron-fotoion koincidenciaval, I. Meghatarozott belso energiaju hexametil-diszilan-ionok disszociaciojanak dinamikaja," Mag. Kem. Foly. **90**, 104 (1984).

84TER/LOU
A. Terpstra, J.N. Louwen, A. Oskam and J.H. Teuben, "The He(I) and He(II) Photoelectron Spectra of Some $\eta 5$-Cyclopentadienyl-Titanium, -Zirconium and -Hafnium Trihalide Complexes," J. Organometall. Chem. **260**, 207 (1984).

84TOB/TAJ
S. Tobita, S. Tajima and T. Tsuchiya, "The Substituent Effect on the Single and Double Hydrogen Atom Transfer Reactions in para-Substituted Benzoic Acid Isobutyl Esters," Org. Mass Spectrom. **19**, 326 (1984).

84TOL/BEA
M.A. Tolbert and J.L. Beauchamp, "Activation of Carbon-Hydrogen and Carbon-Carbon Bonds by transition-Metal Ions in the Gas Phase. Exhibition of Unique Reactivity by Scandium Ions," J. Am. Chem. Soc. **106**, 8117 (1984).

84TRA
J.C. Traeger, "A Study of the Allyl Cation Thermochemistry by Photoionization Mass Spectrometry," Int. J. Mass Spectrom. Ion Proc. **58**, 259 (1984).

84TRE/POL
D.J. Trevor, J.E. Pollard, W.D. Brewer, S.H. Southworth, C.M. Truesdale, D.A. Shirley and Y.T. Lee, "Photoionization Mass Spectrometry of Ne Dimers," J. Chem. Phys. **80**, 6083 (1984).

84TUM/FOS
W. Tumas, R.F. Foster and J.I. Brauman, "Unimolecular Decompositions of Gas-Phase Alkoxide Anions," J. Am. Chem. Soc. **106**, 4053 (184).

84TUR
F. Turecek, "2-Hydroxybutadiene: Preparation, Ionization Energy and Heat of Formation," Tetrahedron Lett. **25**, 5133 (1984).

84TUR2
F. Turecek, "(E)- and (Z)-Prop-1-en-ol: Gas Phase Generation and Determination of Heats of Formation by Mass Spectrometry," J. Chem. Soc. Chem. Commun. 1374 (1984).

84TUR/HAN
F. Turecek and V. Hanus, "Loss of Methyl from $[H_2C=C(OH)-CH_3]^+$ Ions Prepared by Electron Impact Ionization of Unstable 2-Hydroxypropene," Org. Mass Spectrom. **19**, 631 (1984).

84VAN/DEL
H. Van Lonkhuyzen and C.A. De Lange, "U. V. Photoelectron Spectroscopy of OH and OD Radicals," Molec. Phys. **51**, 551 (1984).

84VAN/DEL2
H. Van Lonkhuyzen and C.A. De Lange, "High-Resolution UV Photoelectron Spectroscopy of Diatomic Halogens," Chem. Phys. **89**, 313 (1984).

84VES/HAR
T. Veszpremi, Y. Harada, K. Ohno and H. Mutoh, Jr., "Photoelectron and Penning Electron Spectroscopic Investigation of Phenylhalosilanes," Organometall. Chem. **266**, 9 (1984).

84VIS/HIL
R. Viswanathan and K. Hilpert, "Mass Spectrometric Study of the Vaporization of Cesium Iodide and Thermochemistry of $(CsI)_2(g)$ and $(CsI)_3(g)$," Ber. Bunsenges. Phys. Chem. **88**, 125 (1984).

84WAN/CAP
H. Wankenne, G. Caprace and J. Momigny, "Unimolecular Decay of Metastable Ions in Formaldehyde," Int. J. Mass Spectrom. Ion Proc. **57**, 149 (1984).

84WAN/DIL
R.-G. Wang, M.A. Dillon and D. Spence, "Electron Spectroscopy of Hydrogen Chloride from 5 to 19 eV," J. Chem. Phys. **80**, 63 (1984).

84WIB/LUP
K.B. Wiberg, E.C. Lupton, D.J. Wasserman, A. de Meijere and S.R. Kass, J. Am. Chem. Soc. **106**, 1740 (1984).

84WIB/WAS
K.B. Wiberg, D.J. Wasserman and E. Martin, J. Phys. Chem. **88**, 3684 (1984).

84ZHO/HEI
Y. Zhong-Zhi, E. Heilbronner, V. Boekelheide and J. Garbe, "The He(Ia) PE Spectra of Cyclophanes Containing a Cyclooctatetraene Ring," Int. J. Mass Spectrom. Ion Proc. **58**, 233 (1984).

84ZWI/HAR
J.J. Zwinselman and A.G. Harrison, "An Energy-resolved Study of the Fragmentation of Ionized 1-Penten-3-ol" Org. Mass Spectrom. **19**, 573 (1984).

85ADA/SMI
N.G. Adams and D. Smith, "A Study of the Nearly Thermoneutral Reactions of N^+ with N_2, HD and D_2," Chem. Phys. Lett. **117**, 67 (1985).

85AJO/CAS
D. Ajo, M. Casarin, R. Bertoncello, V. Busetti, H.C.J. Ottenheijm and R. Plate, "Molecular and Electronic Structure of the Dehydroalanine Derivatives: The Cyclic Dipeptide of Dehydrophenylalanine," Tetrahedron **41**, 5543 (1985).

85ALA/ATT
M. Alai, G.G. Attardo and R.T.B. Rye, "Formation Threshold Structures of Some $[C_5H_7O]^+$ Ions: Use of General Schemes for Estimation of Heats of Formation of Gas Phase Ions," Can. J. Chem. **63**, 833 (1985).

85ALB/GEH
R.A. Alberty and C.A. Gehrig, J. Phys. Chem. Ref. Data **14**, 803 (1985).

85ALB/HEL
B. Albert, C. Heller, R. Iden, G. Martin, H.-D. Martin, B. Mayer and A. Oftring, "Design and Synthesis of α-Diketones. The Cyclobutane-1,2-dione Chromophore: Synthesis, Dienophilic Reactivity and Electronic Properties of Cyclobutenedione and Polycyclic Cyclobutanediones," Israel J. Chem. **25**, 74 (1985).

85AUD/MIL
H. Audier, A. Milliet and G. Sozzi, "Isomerisation des Cation Radicaux Acides Pentanoique et Methyl-3-butanoique in Phase Gazeuse," Bull. Soc. Chim. France **5**, 833 (1985).

85AUS/LIA
P. Ausloos and S.G. Lias, unpublished results.

85BAI/MIS
V.N. Baidin, A.D. Misharev and V.V. Takhistov, "Effect of Alkyl Substituents on the Ionization Potentials of Halogenobenzenes," Zh. Org. Khim. **21**, 817 (1985).

85BAI/MIS2
V.N. Baidin, A.D. Misharev and V.V. Takhistov, "Investigation of Substituted tert-Butylbenzenes by Photoelectron Spectroscopy," Zh. Org. Khim. **21**, 1237 (1985).

85BAJ/HUM
M. Bajic, K. Humski, L. Klasinc and B. Ruscic, "Substitution Effects on Electronic Structure of Thiophene," Z. Naturforsch. **40b**, 1214 (1985).

85BAK/KIN
J. Baker, E.E. Kingston, W.J. Bouma, A.G. Brenton and L. Radom, "Is the Methylenemethonium Radical Cation $(CH_2CH_4^{+\cdot})$ a Stable Species?" J. Chem. Soc. Chem. Commun. 1625 (1985).

85BAL/GIG
G. Balducci, G. Gigli and M. Guido, "Mass Spectrometric Study of the Thermochemistry of Gaseous $EuTiO_3$ and TiO_2," J. Chem. Phys. **83**, 1909 (1985).

85BAL/GIG2
G. Balducci, G. Gigli and M. Guido, "Identification and Stability Determinations for the Gaseous Titanium Oxide Molecules Ti_2O_3 and Ti_2O_4," J. Chem. Phys. **83**, 1913 (1985).

85BAL/HAS
T. Bally, D. Hasselmann and K. Loosen, "41. The Molecular Ion of 5-Methylene-1,3-cyclohexadiene: Electronic Absorption Spectrum and Revised Enthalpy of Formation," Helv. Chim. Acta **68**, 345 (1985).

85BAN/MTE
J.A. Bandy, V.S.B. Mtetwa, K. Prout, J.C. Green, C.E. Davies, M.L.H. Green, N.J. Hazel, A. Izquierdo and J.J. Martin-Polo, "Synthesis, Structure, and Bonding of Fulvene Complexes of Titanium, Molybdenum, and Tungsten," J. Chem. Soc. Dalton Trans. 2037 (1985).

85BIN/GRO
M. Binnewies, J. Grosse and D. Le Van, "Reaktive $E=C(p-p)\pi$-Systeme II: Massenspektrometrische Untersuchun von $F_3CP=CF_2$, $F_3CAs=CF_2$, $S=CF_2$ und $Se=CF_2$," Phosphorus and Sulfur **21**, 349 (1985).

85BIS/GLE
P. Bischof, R. Gleiter, R. Haider and C.W. Rees, "The Photoelectron Spectrum of 7b-Methyl-7bH-cyclopent[cd]indene," J. Chem. Soc. Perkin Trans. II 1001 (1985).

85BOL/HOU
J.C. Bollinger, R. Houriet, C.W. Kern, D. Perret, J. Weber and Y. Yvernault, "Experimental and Theoretical Studies of the Gas Phase Protonation of Aliphatic Phosphine Oxides and Phosphoramides," J. Am. Chem. Soc. **107**, 5352 (1985).

85BRO/CHE
M. Broyer, J. Chevaleyre, G. Delacretaz, P. Fayet and L. Woste, "One- and Two-Photon Ionization of Alkaline Clusters," Surface Sci. **156**, 342 (1985).

85BRO/COX
M. Brookhart, K. Cox, F.G.N. Cloke, J.C. Green, M.L.H. Green, P.M. Hare, J. Bashkin, A.E. Derome and P.D. Grebenik, "Hexakis(trimethylphosphine)molybdenum Chemistry: Dinitrogen, Ethylene, Butadiene, η-Cyclopentadienyl, and Related Derivatives," J. Chem. Soc. Dalton Trans. 423 (1985).

85BUR
P.C. Burgers, "Isotope Effects Associated With the Unimolecular Fragmentation of D-Labeled Formic Acid Radical Cations," Org. Mass Spectrom. **20**, 426 (1985).

85BUR/HOL
P.C. Burgers, J.L. Holmes, J.K. Terlouw and B. van Baar, "Three New Isomers of $[C_2H_6O]^{+\cdot}$: The Radical Cations $[CH_3O(H)CH_2]^{+\cdot}$, $[CH_3CHOH_2]^{+\cdot}$ and a Low-energy Isomer of Unassigned Structure," Org. Mass Spectrom. **20**, 202 (1985).

85BUT/LER
J.J. Butler, G.E. Leroi, A.C. Parr and R. Stockbauer, "The Rate Versus Energy Dependence of CH_3 Loss from t-Butylbenzene Cation," to be submitted.

85CAL/KEB
G. Caldwell and P. Kebarle, "The Hydrogen Bond Energies of the Bihalide Ions XHX^- and YHX^-," Can. J. Chem. **63**, 1399 (1985).

85CAL/MCM
G. Caldwell, T.B. McMahon, P. Kebarle, J.E. Bartmess and J.P. Kiplinger, "Methyl Substituent Effects in the Gas Phase Acidities of Halosubstituted Oxygen Acids. A Realignment with Substituent Effects in Solution," J. Am. Chem. Soc. **107**, 80 (1985).

85CAN/HAM
P.H. Cannington and N.S. Ham, "He(II) Photoelectron Spectra of Esters," J. Electron Spectrosc. Rel. Phenom. **36**, 203 (1985).

85CAU/FUR
C. Cauletti, C. Furlani, A. Palma, M.N. Piancastelli, K.D. Schleinitz and D. Gloyna, "Electronic Structure and Free-Energy Relationships for Some 4'-Substituted 4-Dimethylamino trans-Stilbenes by U. V. Photoelectron Spectroscopy," J. Prakt. Chem. **327**, 829 (1985).

85CLE/MUN
D. Clemens and B. Munson, "Selective Reagents in Chemical Ionization Mass Spectrometry: Trimethylsilyl Adduct Ions," Anal. Chem. **57**, 2022 (1985).

85COE/SNO
J.V. Coe, J.T. Snodgrass, C.B. Friedhoff, K.M. McHugh and K.H. Bowen, "Negative Ion Photoelectron Spectroscopy of the negative ion $H^-(NH_3)$," J. Chem. Phys. **83**, 3169 (1985).

85DAS/GRO
C. Dass and M.L. Gross, "The Question of Cyclic Versus Acyclic Ions: The Structure of $[C_6H_{10}]^+$ Gas Phase Ions," Org. Mass Spectrom. **20**, 34 (1985).

85DAS/NIS
P.R. Das, T. Nishimura and G.G. Meisels, "Fragmentation of Energy-Selected Hexacarbonylchromium Ion," J. Phys. Chem. **89**, 2808 (1985).

85DAV/ALL
H.E. Davis, N.L. Allinger and D.W. Rogers, J. Org. Chem. **50**, 3601 (1985).

85DAV/GAR
C.E. Davies, I.M. Gardiner, J.C. Green, M.L.H. Green, N.J. Hazel, P.D. Grebenik, V.S.B. Mtetwa and K. Prout, "Mono-η-cycloheptatrienyltitanium Chemistry: Synthesis, Molecular and Electronic Structures, and Reactivity of the Complexes $[Ti(\eta-C_7H_7)L_2X]$ (L = Tertiary Phosphine, O- or N-Donor Ligand. X = Cl or Alkyl)," J. Chem. Soc. Dalton Trans. 669 (1985).

85DEL/PIG
E.W. Della, P.E. Pigou, M.K. Livett and J.B. Peel, "The Photoelectron Spectrum of 1-Bromotricyclene," Aust. J. Chem. **38**, 69 (1985).

85DEP/BIE
C.H. DePuy, V.M. Bierbaum, R. Damrauer and J.A. Soderquist, "Gas-Phase Reactions of the Acetyl Anion," J. Am. Chem. Soc. **107**, 3385 (1985).

85DEP/GRA
C.H. DePuy, J.J. Grabowski, V.M. Bierbaum, S. Ingemann and N.M.M. Nibbering, , "Gas-Phase Reactions of Anions with Methyl Formate and N,N-Dimethylformamide," J. Am. Chem. Soc. **107**, 1093 (1985).

85DEW/GRA
M.J.S. Dewar, G.L. Grady, K.M. Merz, Jr. and J.J.P. Stewart, Organometallics **4**, 1964 (1985).

85DEW/HOL
M.J.S. Dewar, M.K. Hollowar, G.L. Grady and J.J.P. Stewart, Organometallics **4**, 1973 (1985).

85DEW/MER
M.J.S. Dewar and K.M. Merz, Jr., J. Am. Chem. Soc. **107**, 6175 (1985).

85DEW/TIE
M.J.S. Dewar and T.-P. Tien, "Photoelectron Spectrum of Benzyne," J. Chem. Soc. Chem. Commun. 1243 (1985).

85DIN/CAS
A. Ding, R. Cassidy, L. Cordis and F. Lampe, "The Photoionization Spectra of Effusing and Supersonic Molecular Beams of Monosilane," J. Chem. Phys. **83**, 3426 (1985).

85DIS/GIU
G. Distefano, A.G. Giumanini, A. Modelli and G. Poggi, "Reinvestigation of the Formaldehyde-Aniline Condensation. Part 4. Ultraviolet Photoelectron and Electron transmission Spectra of N-Methyleneaniline and its Symmetric Dimethyl Ring-Substituted Homologues and Semiempirical Theoretical Evaluation," J. Chem. Soc. Perkin Trans. II, 1623 (1985).

85DOM/LAK
I.N. Domnin, A.M. Lakshin, A.D. Misharev, V.M. Orlov and V.V. Takhistov, "Thermochemical Investigation of Some Hydrocarbon Ions Generated By Photoionization," Zh. Org. Khim. **21**, 1262 (1985).

85DUN
R. Dunbar, "Collisional Quenching of Iodobenzene Ion One-Photon Photofragmentation," Chem. Phys. Lett. **155**, 349 (1985).

85DYK/ELL
J. Dyke, A. Ellis, N. Jonathan and A. Morris, "Vacuum Ultraviolet Photoelectron Spectroscopy of Transient Species. Part 18. The Cyclopropyl, Isopropyl, an n-Propyl Radicals," J. Chem. Soc. Faraday II, **81**, 1573 (1985).

85DYK/GRA
J.M. Dyke, B.W.J. Gravenor, M.P. Hastings, G.D. Josland and A. Morris, "Gas Phase High Temperature Photoelectron Spectroscopy: An Investigation of the Transition Metals Scandium and Vanadium," J. Electron Spectrosc. Rel. Phenom. **35**, 65 (1985).

85ELB/ELL
S. Elbel, A. Ellis, E. Niecke, H. Egsgaard and L. Carlsen, "A Photoelectron Spectroscopic Study of Di-t-butylphosphazene," J. Chem. Soc. Dalton Trans. 879 (1985).

85ELK/ARM
J. Elkind and P. Armentrout, "Effect of Kinetic and Electronic Energy on the Reaction of V^+ with H_2, HD and D_2," J. Phys. Chem. **89**, 5626 (1985).

85ELS/VER
C.J. Elsevier, P. Vermeer, A. Gedanken and W. Runge, "Excited States of the Allene Chromophore: Photoelectron, Circular Dichroism, and Absorption Spectroscopy of Alkyl- and Halogenoallenes," J. Am. Chem. Soc. **107**, 2537 (1985).

85FAO/AKA
M. Faour and T.S. Akasheh, J. Chem. Soc. Perkin Trans. II 311 (1985).

85FAR/SRI
M. Farber and R.D. Srivastava, "Electron Impact and Thermodynamic Studies of Potassium Metaborate," J. Chem. Soc. Faraday Trans. I **81**, 913 (1985).

85FUC
R. Fuchs, Unpublished data, personal communication.

85FUK/MCI
E.K. Fukuda and R.T. McIver, Jr., "Relative Electron Affinities of Substituted Benzophenones, Nitrobenzenes, and Quinones. [Anchored to $EA(SO_2)$ from 74CEL/BEN]," J. Am. Chem. Soc. **107**, 2291 (1985).

85GAD/GUB
S.N. Gadzhiev, A.I. Gubareva and V.I. Khun, Izv. Vyssh. Uchebn. Zabed. Khim. Khim. Technol. **28**, 48 (1984) CA 103:130117z (1985).

85GAL/GER
J.-F. Gal, S. Geribaldi, G. Pfister-Guillouzo and D.G. Morris, "Basicity of the Carbonyl Group. Part 12. Correlations between Ionization Potentials and Lewis Basicities in Aromatic Carbonyl Compounds," J. Chem. Soc. Perkin Trans. II 103 (1985).

85GAL/TAM
G.L. Gal'chenko, N. Tamm, E.P. Brykina, D.B. Bekker, A.B. Petrunin and A.F. Zhigach, Russ. J. Phys. Chem. **59**, 1610 (1985).

85GAR/GON
J.-L. Garcia, D. Gonbeau, G. Pfister-Guillouzo, M. Roch and J. Weber, "Germathione - silathione spectres photoelectroniques et structures electroniques par la methode MS Xα," Can. J. Chem. **63**, 1518 (1985).

85GIB/GRE
S. Gibson, J. Greene and J. Berkowitz, "Photoionization of the Amidogen Radical," J. Chem. Phys. **83**, 4319 (1985).

85GLE/DOB
R. Gleiter and W. Dobler, "Die Elektronenstruktur von 1,4-disubstituierten Butantetronen," Chem. Ber. **118**, 1917 (1985).

85GLE/JAH
R. Gleiter, G. Jahne, M. Oda and M. Iyoda, "Effect of Through Bond Interaction via Strained Σ Bonds in Cyclohexane-1,4-dione Derivatives," J. Org. Chem. **50**, 678 (1985).

85GLE/KRE
R. Gleiter, G. Krennrich, D. Cremer, K. Yamamoto and I. Murata, "Electronic Structure and Thermal Stability of Thiepins. Photoelectron Spectroscopic Investigations," J. Am. Chem. Soc. **107**, 6874 (1985).

85GLE/SCH
R. Gleiter, P. Schang, M. Bloch, E. Heilbronner, J.-C. Bunzli, D.C. Frost and L. Weiler, "The He(Iα) PE Spectra and Electronic Absorption Spectra of Hexafluorocyclobutanone and of Tetrafluoro-1,2-cyclobutanedione," Chem. Ber. **118**, 2127 (1985).

85GLE/ZIM
R. Gleiter, H. Zimmermann, W.-D. Fessner and H. Prinzbach, "Dominance of Through-Bond Interaction in a syn-Tricyclo[6.4.0.0^{2,7}]dodecatetraene Moiety," Chem. Ber. **118**, 3856 (1985).

85GRA/BER
G. Granozzi, R. Bertoncello, E. Tondello and D. Ajo, "He(I)/He(II) Sn 5p Photoionization Cross Sections: Definitive Evidence from the Spectra of $Sn_2(CH_3)_6$," J. Electron Spectrosc. Rel. Phenom. **36**, 207 (1985).

85GRA/ROS
M. Grade and W. Rosinger, "Correlation of Electronic Structures and Stabilities of Gaseous FeI_2, Fe_2I_2 and Fe_2I_4 Molecules, Solid $[FeI_2]$, and Iodine Adsorbed on [Fe]," Surface Sci. **156**, 920 (1985).

85GRE/PAZ
J.C. Green, M. Paz-Sandoval and P. Powell, "He I and He II Photoelectron Spectra of Open-chain Pentadienyl Complexes of Manganese and Rhenium," J. Chem. Soc. Dalton Trans. 2677 (1985).

85GRI/CAL
E. Grimsrud, G. Caldwell and P. Kebarle, "Electron Affinities from Electron Transfer Equilibria: $A^- + B = A + B^-$," J. Am. Chem. Soc. **107**, 4627 (1985).

85GRI/CHO
E.P. Grimsrud, S. Chowdhury and P. Kebarle, "Electron Affinity of SF_6 and Perfluoromethylcyclohexane. The Unusual Kinetics of Electron Transfer Reactions $A^- + B^- + A$, where $A = SF_6$ or Perfluorinated Cycloalkanes," J. Chem. Phys. **83**, 1059 (1985).

85GRI/CHO2
E.P. Grimsrud, S. Chowdhury and P. Kebarle, "Thermal Energy Electron Detachment Rate Constants. The Electron Detachment from Azulene$^-$ and the Electron Affinity of Azulene," J. Chem. Phys. **83**, 3983 (1985).

85GRU/SPI
H.-F. Grutzmacher and R. Spilker, "Loss of CO from 4,6-Dimethyl-2-pyrone and 2,6-Dimethyl-4-pyrone Radical Cations," Org. Mass Spectrom. **20**, 258 (1985).

85GUI/PFI
C. Guimon, G. Pfister-Guillouzo, B. Chaudret and R. Poilblanc, "Application of Photoelectron Spectroscopy to Molecular Properties. Part 19. Electronic Structure of Tris(α-di-imino) Complexes of Ruthenium(0)," J. Chem. Soc. Dalton Trans. 43 (1985).

85GUI/PFI2
G. Guimon, G. Pfister-Guillouzo, G. Rima, M. El Amine and J. Barrau, "Generation, Detection and Electronic Structure of Dimethyl Germanone by Photoelectron Spectroscopy and Quantum Calculations," Spectrosc. Lett. **18**, 7 (1985).

85GUI/PFI3
C. Guimon, G. Pfister-Guillouzo, J. Dubac, A. Laporterie, G. Manuel and H. Iloughmane, "Electronic Structure of Group 14 (η_4-Metallole)tricarbonyliron Complexes," Organometall. **4**, 636 (1985).

85HAG/IVA
J. Hager, M. Ivanco, M.A. Smith and S.C. Wallace, "Solvation Effects in Jet-Cooled Van der Waals Clusters: Two-Color Threshold Photoionization Spectroscopy of Indole, Indole-Argon, Indole-Methane, Indole-Water and Indole-Methanol," Chem. Phys. Lett. **113**, 503 (1985).

85HAG/SMI
J. Hager, M. Smith and S. Wallace, "Autoionizing Rydberg Structure Observed in the Vibrationally Selective, Two-Color Threshold Photoionization Spectrum of Jet-Cooled Aniline," J. Chem. Phys. **83**, 4820 (1985).

85HAR
P.W. Harland, unpublished results, cited in B.S. Knight, C.G. Freeman, M.J. McEwan, N.G. Adams and D. Smith, Int. J. Mass Spectrom. Ion Proc. **67**, 317 (1985).

85HAR/MCI
P.W. Harland and B.J. McIntosh, "Enthalpies of Formation for the Isomeric Ions H_xCCN^+ and H_xCNC^+ ($x = 0$-3) by, "Monochromatic" Electron Impact on C_2N_2, CH_3CN and CH_3NC," Int. J. Mass Spectrom. Ion Proc. **67**, 29 (1985).

85HEI/BAR
T. Heinis, R. Bar, K. Borlin and M. Jungen, "Photoionization Mass Spectrometry of 1,1-Difluoroethane," Chem. Phys. **94**, 235 (1985).

85HEN/HIE
M. Henchman, P.M. Hierl and J.F. Paulson, "Nucleophilic Displacement vs. Proton Transfer: The System $OH^-\cdot(H_2O)_{0,1,2} + CH_3Cl$ in the Relative Energy Range 0.03-5 eV," J. Am. Chem. Soc. **107**, 2812 (1985).

85HEN/ILL
M. Heni and E. Illenberger, "The Stability of the Bifluoride Ion (HF_2^-) in the Gas Phase," J. Chem. Phys. **83**, 6056 (1985).

85HEN/VIG
M. Henchman, A.A. Viggiano, J.F. Paulson, A. Freedman and J. Wormhoudt, "Thermodynamic and Kinetic Properties of the Metaphosphate Anion, PO_3^-, in the Gas Phase," J. Am. Chem. Soc. **107**, 1453 (1985).

85HET/FRE
R. Hettich and B. Freiser, "Heteronuclear Transition-Metal Cluster Ions in the Gas Phase. Photodissociation and Reactivity of VFe^+," J. Am. Chem. Soc. **107**, 6222 (1985).

85HIL/BEN
K. Hilpert, L. Bencivenni and B. Saha, "Thermochemistry of the Molecule $(ZnI_2)_2(g)$ and the Vaporization of $ZnI_2(s)$," J. Chem. Phys. **83**, 5227 (1985).

85HIR/STR
C. Hirayama, R.D. Straw and H.M. Hobgood, "Equilibria Over GaAs in the Knudsen Cell Range," J. of the Less-Common Metals **109**, 331 (1985).

85HOD/BEA
R.V. Hodges, J.L. Beauchamp, A.J. Ashe, III and W.-T. Chan, "Proton Affinities of Pyridine, Phosphabenzene and Arsabenzene," Organometall. **4**, 457 (1985).

85HOL/MOM
J. Holmes, A. Mommers, C. DeKoster, W. Heerma and J. Terlouw, "Four Isomeric $[C, H_3, O_2]$ Ions," Chem. Phys. Lett. **115**, 437 (1985).

85HON/HEI
E. Honegger, E. Heilbronner, T. Urbanek and H.-D. Martin, "Inverted Hyperconjugation in Symmetrical 1,4-Dihalocubanes," Helv. Chim. Acta **68**, 23 (1985).

85HON/HEI2
E. Honegger, E. Heilbronner, N. Hess and H.-D. Martin, "Photoelectron Spectra of Symmetrical 1,4-Dihalonorbornanes," Chem. Ber. **118**, 2927 (1985).

85HON/HUB
E. Honegger, H. Huber, E. Heilbronner, W.P. Dailey and K.B. Wiberg, "Photoelectron Spectrum of [1.1.1]Propellane: Evidence for a Nonbonding MO?," J. Am. Chem. Soc. **107**, 7172 (1985).

85HON/SEG
J. Honovich, J. Segall and R. Dunbar, "Fragmentation Thermochemistry of Gas-Phase Ions by Threshold Photodissociation and Charge-Exchange Ionization. Methylnaphthalene and Methylstyrene Ions," J. Phys. Chem. **89**, 3617 (1985).

85HON/YAN
E. Honegger, Z.-Z. Yang and E. Heilbronner, "Lone-Pair Ionization Energies of Diazabicycloalkanes," J. Electron Spectrosc. Rel. Phenom. **36**, 297 (1985).

85HOT/LIN
H. Hotop and W.C. Lineberger, "Binding Energies in Atomic Negative Ions. II," J. Phys. Chem. Ref. Data **14**, 731 (1985).

85HOU/ROL
R. Houriet, E. Rolli, G. Bouchoux and Y. Hoppilliard, "215. Gas-Phase Basicities of Furan Compounds. The Role of Alkyl Substitution on Proton Affinity and on the Site of Protonation," Helv. Chim. Acta **68**, 2037 (1985).

85HOU/SCO
K.N. Houk, L.T. Scott, N.G. Rondan, D.C. Spellmeyer, G. Reinhardt, J.L. Hyun, G.J. DeCicco, R. Weiss, M.H.M. Chen, L.S. Bass, J. Clardy, F.S. Jorgensen, T.A. Eaton, V. Sarkozi, C.M. Petit, L. Ng and K.D. Jordan, "Pericyclynes:, 'Exploded Cycloalkanes' with Unusual Orbital Interactions and Conformational Properties. MM2 and STO-3G Calculations, X-ray Crystal Structures, Photoelectron Spectra, and Electron Transmission Spectra," J. Am. Chem. Soc. **107**, 6556 (1985).

85ILL/COM
E. Illenberger, P. Comita, J.I. Brauman, H.-P. Fenzlaff, M. Heni, N. Heinrich, W. Koch and G. Frenking, "Experimental and Theoretical Investigation of the Azide Anion (N_3^-) in the Gas Phase," Ber. Bunsen. **89**, 1026 (1985).

85ING/NIB
S. Ingemann and N.M.M. Nibbering, "Gas Phase Chemistry of Alpha-Thio Carbanions," Can. J. Chem. **62**, 2273 (1985).

85ING/NIB2
S. Ingemann and N.M.M. Nibbering, "Gas-Phase Acidity of CH_3X [X = $P(CH_3)_2$, SCH_3, F, Cl, Br, I] Compounds," J. Chem. Soc. Perkin Trans. II 837 (1985).

85ING/NIB3
S. Ingemann and N.M.M. Nibbering, "Gas Phase Chemistry of Dipole Stabilized Carbanions Derived From N,N-Dimethylthioformamide and N,N-Dimethylnitrosamine," Acta Chem. Scand. B **39**, 697 (1985).

85JANAF
M.W. Chase, Jr., C.A. Davies, J.R. Downey, Jr., D.J. Frurip, R.A. McDonald and A.N. Syverud, "JANAF Thermochemical Tables (Third Edition) Suppl. 1," J. Phys. Chem. Ref. Data **14**, (1985).

85JEO/RAK
S. Jeon, A. Raksit and G. Gellene, "Formation of Hypervalent Ammoniated Radicals by Neutralized Ion Beam Techniques," J. Am. Chem. Soc. **197**, 4129 (1985).

85JOH/WIL
C.L. Johlman and C.L. Wilkins, "Gas-Phase Reactions of Nucleophiles with Methyl Formate," J. Am. Chem. Soc. **107**, 327 (1985).

85JOR/GAJ
F.S. Jorgensen, M. Gajhede and B. Frei, "227. Cyclic Acetals. Structural Analysis of 1,3-Dioxepine and Related Compounds," Helv. Chim. Acta **68**, 2148 (1985).

85KAI
W. Kaim, "Electronic Structure of 1,4-Dihydro-1,2,4,5-tetrazines and of Related 1,4-Dihydroaromatic Compounds," J. Chem. Soc. Perkin Trans. II 1633 (1985).

85KAP/LEL
O. Kaposi, L. Lelik, G.A. Semenov and E.N. Nikolajev, "Gazfazisu indium-molibdenat kepzodeshojenek tomegspektrometrias meghatarozasa," Magy. Kem. Foly. **91**, 31 (1985).

85KAP/RAD
M.M. Kappes, P. Radi, M. Schar and E. Schumacher, "Photoionization Measurements on Dialkali Monohalides Generated in Supersonic Nozzle Beams," Chem. Phys. Lett. **113**, 243 (1985).

85KAP/RAD2
M.M. Kappes, P. Radi, M. Schar and E. Schumacher, "Probes for Electronic and Geometrical Shell Structure Effects in Alkali-Metal Clusters. Photoionization Measurements on K_xLi, K_xMg and $K_xZn(x<25)$," Chem. Phys. Lett. **119**, 11 (1985).

85KAP/SCH
M.M. Kappes and E. Schumacher, "Generation, Spectroscopic and Chemical Characterization of Metal Clusters (M_x, x < 65), A Progress Report," Surface Sci. **156**, 1 (1985).

85KAR
Z. Karpas, "The Proton Affinity of H_2Se, $SeCO$ and H_2CSe and Reactions of Positive Ions with H_2Se," Chem. Phys. Lett. **120**, 53 (1985).

85KAR/STE
Z. Karpas, W.J. Stevens, T.J. Buckley and R. Metz, "The Proton Affinity and Gas Phase Ion Chemistry of Methyl Isocyanate, Methyl Isothiocyanate, and Methyl Thiocyanate," J. Phys. Chem. **89**, 5274 (1985).

85KAS/DEP
S.R. Kass and C.H. DePuy, "Gas Phase Ion Chemistry of Azides. The Generation of $CH=N^-$ and $CH_2=NCH_2^-$," J. Org. Chem. **50**, 2874 (1985).

85KIE/WEI
J.H. Kiefer, H.C. Wei, R.D. Kern and C.H. Wu, Int. J. Chem. Kinet. **17**, 225 (1985).

85KIS/MOR
W. Kischlat and H. Morgner, "Comparative Study of $He(2^3S)$-Penning Ionization and He(I) Photoionization of CF_4, CCl_4, and the Chlorofluoromethanes by Electron-Ion Coincidence," J. Electron Spectrosc. Rel. Phenom. **35**, 273 (1985).

85KLE/WAR
P.D. Kleinschmidt, J.W. Ward, G.M. Matlack and R.G. Haire, High Temp. Sci. **19**, 267 (1985).

85KNI/FRE
J.S. Knight, C.G. Freeman and M.J. McEwan, "Selected-Ion Flow Tube Studies of HC_3N," Int. J. Mass Spectrom. Ion Phys. **67**, 317 (1985).

85KOL/MEI
H. Kolshornand and H. Meier, Chem. Ber. **118**, 176 (1985).

85KRO/MCN
H.W. Kroto and D. McNaughton, "Photoelectron Spectra of the Aminodifluoroboranes NH_2BF_2, $NHMeBF_2$, and NMe_2BF_2," J. Chem. Soc. Dalton Trans. 1767 (1985).

85LAD/HAR
K.R. Laderoute and A.G. Harrison, "Cyclopropane Intermediates in the Rearrangement and Fragmentation of Olefinic Molecular Ions," Org. Mass. Spectrom. **20**, 624 (1985).

85LAH/HAY
J. Lahnstein, R.N. Hayes and J.H. Bowie, "Gas Phase Ion Chemistry of Ambident Nucleophiles. Reactions of Alkoxide and Thiomethoxide Negative Ions with Hydrogen Free Molecules," Nouv. J. Chim. **9**, 205 (1985).

85LAN/SAL
K.R. Lane, L. Sallans and R.R. Squires, "Anion Affinities of Transition Metal Carbonyls. A Thermochemical Correlation for Iron Tetracarbonyl Acyl Negative Ions," J. Am. Chem. Soc. **107**, 5369 (1985).

85LAN/SQU
K.R. Lane and R.R. Squires, "Formation of $HCr(CO)_3^-$ from the Remarkable Reaction of Hydride Ion with Benzenechromium Tricarbonyl," J. Am. Chem. Soc. **107**, 6403 (1985).

85LAR/MCM
J.W. Larson and T.B. McMahon, "Fluoride and Chloride Affinities of the Main Group Oxides, Fluorides, Oxofluorides, and Alkyls. Quantitative Scales of Lewis Acidities from ICR Halide Exchange Equilibria," J. Am. Chem. Soc. **107**, 766 (1985).

85LAU/BRI
K.H. Lau, R.D. Brittain and D.L. Hildenbrand, J. Phys. Chem. **89**, 4369 (1985).

85LAU/WES
W.M. Lau, N.P.C. Westwood and M.H. Palmer, "A Photoelectron/Photoionisation and Ab Initio Study of the S_3N_3 Radical Produced by Vaporisation of $(SN)_x$," J. Chem. Soc. Chem. Commun. 752 (1985).

85LEE/LIV
K.-J. Lee, P.D. Livant, M.L. McKee and S.D. Worley, "Photoelectron, Infrared, and Theoretical Study of 1-Aza-5-boratricyclo[3.3.3.0^{1,5}]undecane and Related Compounds," J. Am. Chem. Soc. **107**, 5901 (1985).

85LEO/MUR
D.G. Leopold, K.K. Murray, A.E.S. Miller and W.C. Lineberger, "Methylene: A Study of the X^3B_1 and the $^1A_1$ States by Photoelectron Spectroscopy of CH_2^- and CD_2^-," J. Chem. Phys. **83**, 4849 (1985).

85LIA/AUS
S.G. Lias and P. Ausloos, "Structures of $C_6H_7^+$ Ions Formed in Unimolecular and Bimolecular Reactions," J. Chem. Phys. **82**, 3613 (1985).

85LIA/JAC
S.G. Lias, J.-A.A. Jackson, H. Argentar and J.F. Liebman, "Substituted N,N-Dialkylanilines: Relative Ionization Energies and Proton Affinities through Determinations of Ion-Molecule Reaction Equilibrium Constants," J. Org. Chem. **50**, 333 (1985).

85LIA/KAR
S.G. Lias, Z. Karpas and J.F. Liebman, "Halomethylenes: Effects of Halogen Substitution on Absolute Heats of Formation," J. Am. Chem. Soc. **107**, 6089 (1985).

85LIN/BRO
S.H. Linn, J.M. Brom, Jr., W.-B. Tzeng and C.Y. Ng, "Photoionization Study of HgAr," J. Chem. Phys. **82**, 648 (1985).

85LOS/WIL
O. Losking and H. Willner, "Thermochemische Daten und Photoionisations-Massenspektren von SSF_2, FSSF, SF_3SF und SF_3SSF," Z. Anorg. Allg. Chem. **530**, 169 (1985).

85MAL/ARA
Y. Malinovich, R. Arakawa, G. Haase and C. Lifshitz, "Time-Dependent Mass Spectra and Breakdown Graphs. VI. Slow Unimolecular Dissociation of Bromobenzene Ions at Near Threshold Energies," J. Phys. Chem. **89**, 2253 (1985).

85MAR/COM
J. Marks, P.B. Comita and J.I. Brauman, "Threshold Resonances in Electron Photodetachment Spectra. Structural Evidence for Dipole-Supported States," J. Am. Chem. Soc. **107**, 3718 (1985).

85MAR/MAN
K.N. Marsh and M. Mansson, J. Chem. Thermodyn. **17**, 995 (1985).

85MAR/MAY
H.-D. Martin, B. Mayer, R.W. Hoffmann, A. Riemann and P. Rademacher, "PE- und ^{13}C-NMR-spektroskopische Untersuchungen zur Homokonjugation in 7-Alkylidennorbornadienen," Chem. Ber. **118**, 2514 (1985).

85MAR/MOD
F. Marcuzzi, G Modena and C. Paradisi, "Gas Phase Basicity of Ring-Substituted Phenylacetylenes," J. Org. Chem. **50**, 4973 (1985).

85MCM/KEB
T.B. McMahon and P. Kebarle, "Bridging the Gap. A Continuous Scale of Gas Phase Basicities from Methane to Water from Pulsed Electron Beam High Pressure Mass Spectrometric Equilibria Measurements," J. Am. Chem. Soc. **107**, 2612 (1985).

85MCM/KEB2
T.B. McMahon and P. Kebarle, "The Formyl and Isoformyl Cations. A Pulsed Electron Beam High Pressure Mass Spectrometric Study of the Energetics of HCO^+ and HOC^+," J. Chem. Phys. **83**, 3919 (1985).

85MCM/KEB3
T.B. McMahon and P. Kebarle, "Proton Affinities of the Hydrogen, Methyl and Trifluoromethyl Halides from Pulsed Electron Beam High Pressure Mass Spectrometric Equilibria Measurements," Can. J. Chem. **63**, 3160 (1985).

85MCN/SUF
D. McNaughton and R.J. Suffolk, "The Production and Photoelectron Spectrum of Propa-1,2-dien-3-one, C_3H_2O," J. Chem. Res. 32 (1985).

85MEA/HEF
R.D. Mead, U. Hefter, P.A. Schulz and W.C. Lineberger, "Ultrahigh Resolution Spectroscopy of C_2^-: The $A^2\Pi_u$ State Characterized by Depertubation Methods," J. Chem. Phys. **82**, 1723 (1985).

85MEE/SEK
J.T. Meek, E. Sekreta, W. Wilson, K.S. Viswanathan and J.P. Reilly, "The Laser Photoelectron Spectrum of Gas Phase Aniline," J. Chem. Phys. **82**, 1741 (1985).

85MEI/KON
H. Meier, P. Konig, T. Molz, R. Gleiter and W. Schafer, "Untersuchungen zur Konformation und elektronischen Struktur von Cyclooctadieninen," Chem. Ber. **118**, 210 (1985).

85MIC/GIU
H.A. Michelsen, R.P. Giugliano and J.J. BelBruno, "Photochemistry and Photophysics of Small Heterocyclic Molecules: 1. Multiphoton Ionization and Dissociation of N-Isopropyldimethyloxaziridine," J. Phys. Chem. **89**, 3034 (1985).

85MOC/WOR
K. Mochida, S. Worley and J. Kochi, "UV Photoelectron Spectra of Peralkylated Catenates of Group 4B Elements (Silicon, Germanium, and Tin)," Bull. Chem. Soc. Jpn. **58**, 3389 (1985).

85MOY/DOD
C.R. Moylan, J.A. Dodd and J.I. Brauman, "Electron Photodetachment Spectroscopy of Solvated Anions. A Probe of Structure and Energetics, Chem. Phys. Lett. **118**, 38 (1985).

85NAC/PRO
E. Nachbaur and P. Prossegger, "HeI-Photoelektronen-Spektrum von Cl-NSO," Mon. Chem. **116**, 1385 (1985).

85NEU
A. Neubert, "Investigation of Gaseous LiBO by Knudsen Effusion Mass Spectrometry," J. Chem. Phys. **82**, 939 (1985).

85NEU/LYK
D.M. Neumark, K.R. Lykke, T. Andersen and W.C. Lineberger, "Laser Photodetachment Measurement of the Electron Affinity of Atomic Oxygen," Phys. Rev. A **32**, 1890 (1985).

85NOV/POT
I. Novak, A.W. Potts, F. Quinn, G.V. Marr, B. Dobson, I.H. Hillier and J.B. West, "Photoelectron Asymmetry Measurements for CHF_3 and CF_4 in the Photon Energy Range 19 to 80 eV," J. Phys. B: At. Mol. Phys. **18**, 1581 (1985).

85OAK/HAR
J.M. Oakes, L.B. Harding and G.B. Ellison, "The Photoelectron Spectroscopy of HO_2^-," J. Chem. Phys. **83**, 5400 (1985).

85OHN/IMA
K. Ohno, K. Imai and Y. Harada, "Variations in Reactivity of Lone-Pair Electrons due to Intramolecular Hydrogen Bonding as Observed by Penning Ionization Electron Spectroscopy," J. Am. Chem. Soc. 107, 8078 (1985).

85OHN/ISH
K. Ohno, T. Ishide, Y. Naitoh and Y. Izumi, "Study of Stereochemical Properties of Molecular Orbitals by Penning Ionization Electron Spectroscopy," J. Am. Chem. Soc. 107, 8082 (1985).

85OIK/ABE
A. Oikawa, H. Abe, N. Mikami and M. Ito, "Electronic Spectra and Ionization Potentials of Rotational Isomers of Several Disubstituted Benzenes," Chem. Phys. Letters 116, 50 (1985).

85OKU/ITO
J. Okubo, H. Ito, T. Hishi and T. Kobayashi, "Intramolecular Orbital Interactions in and Conformation of N,N'-Diphenylcarbodiimide Studied by Photoelectron Spectroscopy," Tetrahedron Lett. 26, 643 (1985).

85ORL/BOG
V.M. Orlov, A.M. Boganov, T.V. Siretskaya, V.V. Takhistov, "Thermochemical Characteristics of the Molecular and Fragmentation Ions of Substituted tert-Butylacetylenes," Izv. Akad. Nauk SSSR Ser. Khim. 12, 2795 (1985).

85PAN/BAE
M. Panczel and T. Baer, "A nitro-benzol bomlasanak vizsgalata fotoelektron-fotoion koincidenciaval, I. A bomlas dinamikaja," Magy. Kem. Foly. 91, 136 (1985).

85PAN/BAE2
M. Panczel and T. Baer, "A nitro-benzol bomlasanak vizsgalata fotoelektron-fotoion koincidenciaval, II. A bomlas termokimiaja," Magy. Kem. Foly. 91, 153 (1985).

85PAP/KOL
T.S. Papina and V.P. Kolesov, Zh. Fiz. Khim. 59, 2169 (1985).

85PFI/GUI
G. Pfister-Guillouzo and C. Guimon, "Studies by P.E.S. of Highly Reactive Sulfur Species," Phosph. and Sulfur 23, 197 (1985).

85PIM/NES
A.A. Pimerzin, T.N. Nesterova and A.M. Rozhnov, J. Chem. Thermodyn. 17, 641 (1985).

85PLA/SIM
V.A. Platonov and Y.N. Simulin, Russ. J. Phys. Chem. 59, 179 (1985).

85PLA/SIM2
V.A. Platonov, Y. N. Simulin and M.M. Rozenberg, Russ. J. Phys. Chem. 59, 814 (1985).

85PRA/DEH
S. Pratt, P. Dehmer and J. Dehmer, "The Photoelectron Spectrum of ArXe Obtained Using Resonantly Enhanced Multiphoton Ionization," J. Chem. Phys. 82, 5758 (1985).

85PRA/DEH2
S. Pratt, P. Dehmer and J. Dehmer, "Electron Spectra of NeXe, ArXe, and KrXe Using Resonantly Enhanced Multiphoton Ionization," J. Chem. Phys. 83, 5380 (1985).

85ROD/CHI
A.A. Rodin, A.B. Chistyakov, Y.S. Sarkisov, Y.L. Sergeev, K.A. V'yunov and A.V. Golovin, "Electronic Structure and Geometric Structure of Three-Member Heterocycles. I. Photoelectron Spectra of Glycidyl and Thioglycidyl Ethers," Zh. Fiz. Khim. 59, 764 (1985); English trans.: Russ. J. Phys. Chem. 59, 444 (1985).

85ROS/LEO
M.A. Rossman, N.J. Leonard, S. Urano and P.R. LeBreton, "Synthesis and Valence Orbital Structures of Azacycl[3.3.3]azines in a Systematic Series," J. Am. Chem. Soc. 107, 3884 (1985).

85ROT/BOC
B. Roth, H. Bock and H. Gotthardt, "Radikalionen 66. Thioparabansaure-Derivate: Ionisation zum Radikalkation und Reduktion zum Radikalanion," Phosphorus and Sulfur 22, 109 (1985).

85RUD/SID
E.B. Rudny, L.N. Sidirov, L.A. Kuligina and G.A. Semenov, "Heterolytic Dissociation of Potassium Chromate in the Gas Phase and the Electron Affinity of Chromium Oxides," Int. J. Mass Spectrom. Ion Phys. 64, 95 (1985).

85RUD/SID2
E.B. Rudny, L.N. Sidirov and O.M. Voyk, "Heterolytic Dissociation of Potassium Sulfate in the Gas Phase and Heats of Formation for Trioxosulfate(1-), Tetraoxosulfate(1-), and Potassium Sulfate (KSO_4^-) Ions," Teplofiz. Vys. Temp. 23, 291 (1985).

85SAL/LAN
L. Sallans, K.R. Lane, R.R. Squires and B.S. Freiser, "Generation and Reactions of Atomic Metal Anions in the Gas Phase. Determination of the Heterolytic and Homolytic Bond Energies of VH, CrH, FeH, CoH, and MoH," J. Am. Chem. Soc. 107, 4379 (1985).

85SCH/WEI
T. Scheuring and K.G. Weil, "Intermetallic Species in the Vapour above Alkali Metal-Antimony Mixtures," Surface Sci. 156, 457 (1985).

85SEE/MOL
R. Seefeldt, W. Moller and M. Schmidt, "Zur Elektronenstossionisierung des Hexamethyldisiloxans (HMDS)," Z. Phys. Chemie, Leipzig 266, 797 (1985).

85SHA/HOJ
D.K.S. Sharma, S.M. De Hojer and P. Kebarle, "Stabilities of Halonium Ions from a Study of Gas Phase Equilibria $R^+ + XR' = (RXR')^+$," J. Am. Chem. Soc. 107, 3557 (1985).

85SHA/SHA
R.B. Sharma, D.K.S. Sharma, K. Hiraoka and P. Kebarle, "Kinetics and Equilibria of Chloride Transfer Reactions. Stabilities of Carbocations Based on Chloride and Hydride Transfer Equilibria Measurements," J. Am. Chem. Soc. 107, 3747 (1985).

85SHU/BEN
L.G.S. Shum and S.W. Benson, Int. J. Chem. Kinet. 17, 749 (1985).

85SMI/ADA
D. Smith and N.G. Adams, "The Proton Affinity of CS," J. Phys. Chem. 89, 3964 (1985).

85SNO/COE
J.T. Snodgrass, J.V. Coe, C.B. Freidhoff, K.M. McHugh and K.H. Bowen, "Negative Ion Photoelectron Spectroscopy of P_2^-," Chem Phys. Lett. 122, 352 (1985).

85SPY/HUN
S.M. Spyrou, S.R. Hunter and L.G. Christophorou, "A Study of the Isomeric Dependence of Low-Energy (<10 eV) Electron Attachment: Perfluoroalkanes," J. Chem. Phys. 83, 641 (1985).

85STE/FAH
S.E. Stein and A. Fahr, J. Phys. Chem. 89, 3714 (1985).

85STE/GAM
W.V. Steele, B.E. Gammon, N.K. Smith, J.S. Chickos, A. Greenberg and J.F. Liebman, J. Chem. Thermodyn. 14, 505 (1985).

85SVY/IOF
V.A. Svyatkin, A.I. Ioffe and D.M. Nefedov, Izv. Akad. Nauk, SSSR Ser. Khim. 578 (1985).

85TAJ/TOB
S. Tajima, S. Tobita and T. Tsuchiya, "A Kinetic Energy Release Study of CO Loss from $C_6H_5CO^+$ Ions Generated from Benzoic Acid Alkyl Esters," Mass Spectrosc. 33, 39 (1985).

85TRA
J.C. Traeger, "Heat of Formation for the Propanoyl Cation by Photoionization Mass Spectrometry," Org. Mass Spectrom. 20, 223 (1985).

85TRA2
J.C. Traeger, "Heat of Formation for the Formyl Cation by Photoionization Mass Spectrometry," Int. J. Mass Spectrom. and Ion Proc. **66**, 271 (1985).

85TRE/RAD
L. Treschanke and P. Rademacher, "Electronic Structure and Conformational Properties of the Amide Linkage," J. Molec. Str. (Theochem) **122**, 47 (1985).

85TSA
W. Tsang, "The Stability of Alkyl Radicals," J. Am. Chem. Soc. **107**, 2872 (1985).

85TUR/PAN
F. Turecek, J. Pancir, D. Stahl and T. Gaumann, "Stereoelectronic Effects on the Retro-Diels-Alder Fragmentation of Ionized Bicyclo[4.3.0]nona-3,7-dienes," Org. Mass Spectrom. **20**, 360 (1985).

85VAN/LEA
V.J. Vandiver, C.S. Leasure and G.A. Eiceman, "Proton Affinity for Polycyclic Aromatic Hydrocarbons at Atmospheric Pressure in Ion Mobility Spectrometry," Int. J. Mass Spectrom. Ion Proc. **66**, 223 (1985).

85VEK/TAM
K. Vekey, J. Tamas, E. Berenyi and P. Benko, "Mass Spectrometric Study on 2-Amino-as-triazino[6,5-c]quinoline and Some of Its Derivatives," Org. Mass Spectrom. **20**, 416 (1985).

85VIG/PAU
A.A. Viggiano, J.F. Paulson, F. Dale, M. Henchman, N.G. Adams and D. Smith, "Ion Chemistry and Electon Affinity of WF_6," J. Phys. Chem. **89**, 2264 (1985).

85WAG/KEM
W. Wagner-Redeker, P.R. Kemper, M.F. Jarrold and M.T. Bowers, "The Formation and Reactivity of HOC^+: Interstellar Implications," J. Chem. Phys. **83**, 1121 (1985).

85WEI/PLA
D.A. Weil, I. Platzner, L.L. Miller and D.A. Dixon, "Positive Ion-Molecule Reactions in OCS/Hydrocarbon Mixtures," Org. Mass Specrom. **20**, 115 (1985).

85WIB/DAI
K.B. Wiberg, W.P. Dailey, F.H. Walker, S.T. Waddell, L.S. Crocker and M. Newton, J. Am. Chem. Soc. **107**, 7247 (1985).

85WIB/WAS
K.B. Wiberg, D.V. Wasserman, E.J. Martin and M.A. Murcko, J. Am. Chem. Soc. **107**, 6019 (1985).

85WOD/LEE
A.M. Wodtke and Y.T. Lee, "Photodissociation of Acetylene at 193.3 nm," J. Phys. Chem. **89**, 4744 (1985).

85YAM/HIG
H. Yamaguchi, M. Higashi, J.A.H. MacBride and R. Gleiter, "Photoelectron Spectra of Diazabiphenylenes," J. Chem. Soc. Faraday Trans. II **81**, 1831 (1985).

85ZAY/PER
A.Yu. Zayats, A.A. Perov and A.P. Simonov, "Formation of Long-lived Rydberg Atoms Upon Excitation of NF_3 and CF_2Cl_2 Molecules by Electron Impact," Sov. J. Chem. Phys. **2**, 1906 (1985).

86ADA/SMI
N.G. Adams, D. Smith, A.A. Viggiano, J.F. Paulson and M.J. Henchman, "Dissociative Attachment Reactions of Electron with Strong Acid Molecules," J. Chem. Phys. **84**, 6728 (1986).

86AND/TER
R.R. Andrea, A. Terpstra, A. Oskam, P. Bruin and J.H. Teuben, "He(I) and He(II) Photoelectron Spectra of Some Mixed Sandwich Compounds of Titanium, Zirconium and Hafnium," J. Organomet. Chem. **307**, 307 (1986).

86ARI/ARM
N. Aristov and P. Armentrout, "Reaction Mechanisms and Thermochemistry of $V^+ + C_2H_p$ (p = 1-3)," J. Am. Chem. Soc. **108**, 1806 (1986).

86ARM
P. Armentrout, "Laser Application in Chemistry and Biochemistry," Proc. SPIE **620**, 38 (1986).

86BAA/WEI
B. Van Baar, T. Weiske, J. Terlouw and H. Schwarz, "Hydroxyacetylene: Generation and Characterization of the Neutral Molecule, Radical Cation and Dication in the Gas Phase," Angew. Chem. Int. Ed. **25**, 282 (1986).

86BAL/JON
R.E. Ballard, J. Jones, E. Sutherland, D. Read and A. Inchley, "The He(I) Photoelectron Spectrum of Benzyl Alcohol - Liquid Surface and Gas Phase," Chem. Phys. Lett. **126**, 311 (1986).

86BAR/KIP
J.E. Bartmess and J.P. Kiplinger, "'Kinetic' vs. Thermodynamic Acidities of Enones in the Gas Phase," J. Org. Chem. **51**, 2173 (1986).

86BEC/HUN
K. Beck, S. Hunig, R. Poppek, F. Prokschy and P. Rademacher, "Photoelektronenspektroscopische Untersuchungen an Hexahydro-1,3,5-triazinen," Chem. Ber. **119**, 554 (1986).

86BEC/HUN2
K. Beck, S. Hunig, G. Kleefeld, H.-D. Martin, K. Peters, F. Prokschy and H.G. von Schnering, "Photoelectron and UV Spectroscopic Investigations of Homoconjugative Interactions between Parallel C=C and N=N Bonds," Chem. Ber. **119**, 543 (1986).

86BER/CUR
J. Berkowitz, L. Curtiss, S. Gibson, J. Greene, G. Hillhouse and J. Pople, "Photoionization Mass Spectrometric Study and Ab Initio Calculation of Ionization and Bonding in P-H Compounds. Heats of Formation, Bond Energies, and the $^3B_1$-$^1A_1$ Separation in $PH_2{}^+$," J. Chem. Phys. **84**, 375 (1986).

86BOC/BAN
H. Bock and M. Bankmann, "H_3C-P = CH_2: An Ylide with Two-Coordinate Phosphorus?" Angew. Chem. Int. Ed. **25**, 265 (1986).

86BOU/DJA
G. Bouchoux, F. Djazi, Y. Hoppilliard, R. Houriet and E. Rolli, "Gas Phase Protonation of Unsaturated Ethers - Experimental and Theoretical Study of 2,3-and 2,5-Dihydrofuran and Related Compounds," Org. Mass Spectrom. **21**, 209 (1986).

86BOU/HAN
G. Bouchoux, I. Hanna, R. Houriet and E. Rolli, "Gas Phase Basicity of Dihydropyran and Dihydro-1,4-dioxin," Can. J. Chem. **64**, 1345 (1986).

86BOW/DEP
J.H. Bowie, C.H. DePuy, S.A. Sullivan and V.M. Bierbaum, "Gas Phase Reactions of the Hydroperoxide and Peroxyformate Anions," Can. J. Chem. **64**, 1046 (1986).

86BRO/LIG
M. Brouard, P.D. Lightfoot and M.J. Pilling, "Observation of Equilibration in the System $H + C_2H_4 = C_2H_5$. The Determination of the Heat of Formation of C_2H_5," J. Phys. Chem. **90**, 445 (1986).

86BUD/KRA
P.H.M. Budzelaar, E. Kraka, D. Cremer and P.v.R. Schleyer, J. Am. Chem. Soc. **108**, 561 (1986).

86BUR/FAW
J. Burgess, J. Fawcett and R.D. Peacock, J. Fluor. Chem. **31**, 25 (1986).

86BUR/HOL
P.C. Burgers, J.L. Holmes, C.E.C.A. Hop and J.K. Terlouw, "Gas Phase Ion Chemistry of Methyl Acetate, Methyl Propanoate and Their Enolic Tautomers," Org. Mass Spectrom. **21**, 549 (1986).

86CAS/KEE
A.W. Castleman, Jr. and R.G. Keesee, "Ionic Clusters," Chem. Rev. **86**, 589 (1986).

86CAU/DIV
C. Cauletti, M.L. Di Vona, P. Gargano, F. Grandinetti, C. Galli and C. Lillocci, "Ring-size Effects on the Ionization Potentials of N-Substituted Azacycloalkanes," J. Chem. Soc. Perkin Trans. II 667 (1986).

86CHI/ANN
J.S. Chickos, R. Annunziata, L.H. Ladon, A.S. Hyman and J.F. Liebman, J. Org. Chem. 51, 4311 (1986).

86CHO/GRI
S. Chowdury, E.P. Grimsrud, T. Heinis and P. Kebarle, "Electron Affinities of Perfluorobenzene and Perfluorophenyl Compounds," J. Am. Chem. Soc. 108, 3630 (1986).

86CHO/KEB
S. Chowdhury and P. Kebarle, "Electron Affinities of Di- and Tetracyanoethylene and Cyanobenzenes Based on Measurements of Gas-Phase Electron Transfer Equilibria," J. Am. Chem. Soc. 108, 5453 (1986).

86COE/SNO
J.V. Coe, J.T. Snodgrass, C.B. Freidhoff, K.M. McHugh and K.H. Bowen, "Negative Ion Photoelectron Spectroscopy of N_2O^- and $(N_2O)_2^-$," Chem. Phys. Lett. 124, 274 (1986).

86COE/SNO2
J.V. Coe, J.T. Snodgrass, C.B. Freidhoff, K.M. McHugh and K.H. Bowen, "Photoelectron Spectroscopy of the Negative Ion SeO^-," J. Chem. Phys. 84, 618 (1986).

86DAM/DEP
R. Damrauer, C.H. DePuy, I.M.T. Davidson and K.J. Hughes, "Gas Phase Ion Chemistry of Dimethylsilene," Organomet. 5, 2050 (1986).

86DAM/DEP2
R. Damrauer, C.H. DePuy, I.M.T. Davidson and K.J. Hughes, "Gas Phase Ion Chemistry of Dimethylsilylene," Organomet. 5, 2054 (1986).

86DAS/GIL
P.R. Das, J.P. Gilman and G.G. Meisels, "Unimolecular Decomposition of Energy-Selected Anisole Ions. Breakdown Graph and Metastable Decay Rates," Int. J. Mass Spectrom. Ion Proc. 68, 155 (1986).

86DON/WAL
A.M. Doncaster and R. Walsh, J. Chem. Soc. Faraday Trans. II 82, 707 (1986).

86ECK/GLE
M. Eckert-Maksic and R. Gleiter, "Photoelectron Spectra of N-substituted 1,4-Dihydro-4,4-dimethylpyridines," Chem. Ber. 119, 2381 (1986).

86ELK/ARI
J. Elkind, N. Aristov, R. Georgiadis, L. Sunderlin and P. Armentrout to be published. Referred to in, "Structure, Reactivity and Thermochemistry of Ions" (P. Ausloos and S.G. Lias, editors), D. Reidel Publ. Co. (1986).

86ELK/ARM
J. Elkind and P. Armentrout, "Transition-Metal Hydride Bond Energies: First and Second Row," Inorg. Chem. 25, 1078 (1986).

86ELK/ARM2
J. Elkind and P. Armentrout, "Effect of Kinetic and Electronic Energy on the Reactions of Mn^+ with H_2, HD, and D_2," J. Chem. Phys. 84, 4862 (1986).

86ELK/ARM3
J. Elkind and P. Armentrout, "Effect of Kinetic and Electronic Energy on the Reactions of Fe^+ with H_2, HD, and D_2: State-Specific Cross Sections for $Fe^+(^6D)$ and $Fe^+(^4F)$," J. Phys. Chem. 90, 5736 (1986).

86ELK/ARM4
J. Elkind and P. Armentrout, "Effect of Kinetic and Electronic Energy on the Reactions of Co^+, Ni^+, and Cu^+ with H_2, HD, and D_2," J. Phys. Chem. 90, 6576 (1986).

86FRE/COE
C.B. Freidhoff, J.V. Coe, J.T. Snodgrass, K.M. McHugh and K.H. Bowen, "Negative Ion Photoelectron Spectroscopy of TeO^-," Chem Phys. Lett. 124, 268 (1986).

86FRE/SNO
C.B. Freidhoff, J.T. Snodgrass, J.V. Coe, K.M. McHugh and K.H. Bowen, "Negative Ion Photoelectron Spectroscopy of TeH^-," J. Chem. Phys. 84, 1051 (1986).

86FRO/FRE
S.W. Froelicher, B.S. Freiser and R.R. Squires, "The $C_3H_5^-$ Isomers. Experimental and Theoretical Studies of the Tautomeric Propenyl Ions and the Cyclopropyl Anion in the Gas Phase," J. Am. Chem. Soc. 108, 2853 (1986).

86FUJ/OHN
S. Fujisawa, K. Ohno, S. Masuda and Y. Harada, "Penning Ionization Electron Spectroscopy of Monohalogenobenzenes: C_6H_5F, C_6H_5Cl, C_6H_5Br, and C_6H_5I," J. Am. Chem. Soc. 108, 6505 (1986).

86GEO/ARM
R. Georgiadis and P. Armentrout, "Neutral and Ionic Metal Methyl Bond Energies: Zn," J. Am. Chem. Soc. 108, 2119 (1986).

86GLE/BIS
R. Gleiter, P. Bischof and M. Christl, "Electronic Structure of Octavalene. Photoelectron Spectroscopic Investigations," J. Org. Chem. 51, 2895 (1986).

86GLE/KRE
R. Gleiter, G. Krennrich and U.H. Brinker, "Electronic Structure of Spiropentane and Some Derivatives," J. Org. Chem. 51, 2899 (1986).

86GLE/KRE2
R. Gleiter, G. Krennrich, P. Bischof, T. Tsuji and S. Nishida, "103. PE Spectra of Dewar Benzenes, Bridged by a Cyclohexadiene or a Butadiene Unit," Helv. Chim. Acta 69, 962 (1986).

86GLE/USC
R. Gleiter, J. Uschmann and M. Baudler, "The Electronic Structure of Substituted 1,2,4,5-Tetraphosphaspiro[2.2]pentanes and 1,2,4,5-Tetraphospha-3-silaspiro[2.2]pentanes," J. Chem. Soc. Dalton Trans. 1659 (1986).

86GLE/USC2
R. Gleiter and J. Uschmann, "Electronic Structure of Heterospirenes - PE Spectroscopic Investigations," J. Org. Chem. 51, 370 (1986).

86HAJ/SQU
D.J. Hajdasz and R.R. Squires, "Hypervalent Silicon Hydrides: SiH_5^-," J. Am. Chem. Soc. 108, 3139 (1986).

86HAW/GRI
J.A. Hawari, D. Griller and F.P. Lossing, "Thermochemistry of Perthiyl Radicals," J. Am. Chem. Soc. 108, 3273 (1986).

86HAY/KRU
K. Hayashibara, G.H. Kruppa and J.L. Beauchamp, "Photoelectron Spectroscopy of the o-, m-, and p-Methylbenzyl Radicals. Implications for the Thermochemistry of the Radicals and Ions," J. Am. Chem. Soc. 108, 5441 (1986).

86HEN/ILL
M. Heni, E. Illenberger and D. Lentz, "The Isomers CF_3CN and CF_3NC. Formation and Dissociation of the Anions Formed on Electron Attachment," Int. J. Mass Spectrom. Ion Proc. 71, 199 (1986).

86HEN/ILL2
M. Heni and E. Illenberger, "Electron Attachment by Saturated Nitriles. Acrylonitrile (CH_2H_3CN), and Benzonitrile (C_6H_5CN)," Int. J. Mass Spectrom. Ion Phys. 73, 127 (1986).

86HET/FRE
R.L. Hettich and B.S. Freiser, "Gas-Phase Photodissociation of $FeCH_2^+$ and $CoCH_2^+$: Determination of the Carbide, Carbyne, and Carbene Bond Energies," J. Am. Chem Soc. 108, 2537 (1986).

86HIR/SHO
K. Hiraoka, T. Shoda, K. Morise, S. Yamabe, E. Kawai and K. Hirao, "Stability and Structure of Cluster Ions in the Gas Phase: Carbon Dioxide with Cl^-, H_3O^+, HCO_2^+ and HCO^+," J. Chem. Phys. 84, 2091 (1986).

86HOL/LOS
J.L. Holmes and F.P. Lossing, Unpublished result.

86HOU/SCH
R. Houriet, T. Schwitzguebel, P.-A. Carrupt and P. Vogel, "Experimental and Theoretical Studies on the Homoconjugation in the Bicyclic Carbenium and Oxonium Ions in the Gas Phase," Tetrahedron Lett. **27**, 37 (1986).

86HOV/MCM
J.K. Hovey and T.B. McMahon, "C-Xe Bond Strength in the Methylxenonium Cation Determined from Ion Cyclotron Resonance Methyl Cation Exchange Equilibria," J. Am. Chem. Soc. **108**, 528 (1986).

86HUS/WIL
N.S. Hush, G.D. Willett, M.N. Paddon-Row, H.K. Patney and J.B. Peel, "Orbital Interactions. Part 13. The Observation of Through-bond Orbital Interactions between Benzene and Double Bonds in Some Dimethanoanthracenes," J. Chem. Soc. Perkin Trans. II 827 (1986).

86IGE/WED
G. Igel-Mann, U. Wedig, P. Fuentealba and H. Stoll, J. Chem. Phys. **84**, 5007 (1986).

86KAM/BOS
J. Kamphuis, H.J.T. Bos, C.W. Worrell and W. Runge, "The Molecular Structure of Allenes and Ketenes. Part 19. Photoelectron Spectra and Conformations of Donor-substituted Allenes," J. Chem. Soc. Perkin Trans. II 1509 (1986).

86KAM/YOU
A. Kamar, A.B. Young and R.E. March, "Experimentally Determined Proton Affinities of 4-Methyl-3-Penten-2-one, 2-Propyl Ethanoate and 4-Hydroxy-4-methyl-2-pentanone in the Gas Phase," Can. J. Chem., in press.

86KAR/JAS
Z. Karpas and P. Jasien, "The Proton Affinity of Hydrogen Telluride," Int. J. Mass Spectrom. Ion Proc. **69**, 115 (1986).

86KAS/FIL
S.R. Kass, J. Filley, J.M. Van Doren and C.H. DePuy, "Nitrous Oxide in Gas-Phase Ion-Molecule Chemistry: A Versatile Reagent for the Determination of Carbanion Structure," J. Am. Chem. Soc. **108**, 2849 (1986).

86KAT/ELI
A. Katrib, B.D. El-Issa and A.W. Potts, "The He(I) and X-Ray Photoelectron Spectra of p-N,N-dimethylaminobenzalmalonitrile," Can. J. Chem. **64**, 528 (1986).

86KEE/CAS
R.G. Keesee and A.W. Castleman, Jr., "Thermochemical Data on Gas-Phase Ion-Molecule Association and Clustering Reactions," J. Phys. Chem. Ref. Data **15**, 1011 (1986).

86KIN/NAG
J.E. Kingcade, H.M. Nagarathna-Naik, I. Shim and K.A. Gingerich, J. Phys. Chem. **90**, 2830 (1986).

86KIR/ACR
J.E. Kirchner, W.E. Acree, Jr., G. Pilcher and L. Shofeng, J. Chem. Thermodyn. **18**, 793 (1986).

86KNI/FRE
J.S. Knight, C.G. Freeman and M.J. McEwan, "Isomers of $C_2H_4N^+$ and the Proton Affinities of CH_3CN and CH_3NC," J. Am. Chem. Soc. **108**, 1404 (1986).

86KOB/YOS
T. Kobayashi, Z. Yoshida, Y. Asako, S. Miki and S. Kato, "Avoided Crossing Between the Ground and First Excited $^2A'$ Cation States of Dicyanobicycloalkadiene Series Revealed by Photoelectron Spectroscopy," Chem. Phys. Lett. **125**, 586 (1986).

86KOL/KOZ
V.P. Kolesov and M.P. Kozina, "Thermochemistry of Organic and Organohalogen Compounds" Russian Chem. Revs. **55**, 912 (1986).

86KOR/NIK
M.V. Korobov, V.V. Nikulin, N.S. Chilingarov, L.N. Sidorov, J. Chem. Thermo. **18**, 235 (1986).

86KRU/BEA
G.H. Kruppa and J.L. Beauchamp, "Energetics and Structure of the 1- and 2-Adamantyl Radicals and Their Corresponding Carbonium Ions by Photoelectron Spectroscopy," J. Am. Chem. Soc. **108**, 2162 (1986).

86KUZ/KOR
S.V. Kuznetsov, M.V. Korobov, L.N. Savinova and L.N. Sidirov, "Enthalpy of the Addition of the F^- Ion to Copper and Iron Difluorides," Russ. J. Phys. Chem. **60**, 766 (1986).

86LAF/GON
C. Lafon, D. Gonbeau, G.Pfister-Guillouzo, M. Lasne, J. Ripoll and J. Denis, "Etheneamine: Spectre Photoelectronique," Nouv. J. Chem./New J. Chem. **10**, 70 (1986).

86LAN/SAL
K.R. Lane, L. Sallans and R.R. Squires, "Gas-Phase Nucleophilic Addition Reactions of Negative Ions with Transition Metal Carbonyls," J. Am. Chem. Soc. **108**, 4368 (1986).

86LAU/WES
W.M. Lau, N.P.C. Westwood and M.H. Palmer, "Vaporization of $(SN)_x$: He I Photoelectron Spectrum and ab Initio Calculations for the S_3N_3 Radical," J. Am. Chem. Soc. **108**, 3229 (1986).

86LEB/URA
P.R. LeBreton, S. Urano, M. Shahbaz, S.L. Emery and J.A. Morrison, "He I Photoelectron Spectra, Valence Electronic Structure, and Back Bonding in the Deltahedral Boron Chlorides, B_4Cl_4, B_8Cl_8, and B_9Cl_9," J. Am. Chem. Soc. **108**, 3937 (1986).

86LEE/SQU
R.E. Lee and R.R. Squires, "Anionic Homoaromaticity: a Gas Phase Experimental Study," J. Am. Chem. Soc. **105**, 5078 (1986).

86LEO/LIN
D.G. Leopold and W.C. Lineberger, "A Study of the Low-Lying Electronic States of Fe_2 and Co_2 by Negative Ion Photoelectron Spectroscopy," J. Chem. Phys. **85**, 51 (1986).

86LEO/MIL
D.G. Leopold, A.G. Miller and W.C. Lineberger, "Determination of the Singlet-Triplet Splitting and Electron Affinity of, o-Benzyne by Negative Ion Photoelectron Spectroscopy," J. Am. Chem. Soc. **108**, 1379 (1986).

86LEO/MIL2
D.G. Leopold, T.M. Miller and W.C. Lineberger, "Flowing Afterglow Negative Ion Photoelectron Spectroscopy of Dirhenium: Evidence for Multiple Bonding in Re_2 and Re_2^-," J. Am. Chem. Soc. **108**, 178 (1986).

86LEU/MAG
W. Leupin, D. Magde, G. Persy and J. Wirz, "1,4,7-Triazacycl[3.3.3]azine: Basicity, Photoelectron Spectrum, Photophysical Properties," J. Am. Chem. Soc. **108**, 17 (1986).

86LIA/NG
C. Liao and C. Ng, "Molecular Beam Photoionization Study of S_2," J. Chem. Phys. **84**, 788 (1986).

86LIC/KEL
D.L. Lichtenberger and G.E. Kellogg, "Electronic Structure Factors of Carbon-Hydrogen Bond Activation. The Photoelectron Spectroscopy of (Cyclohexenyl)manganese Tricarbonyl," J. Am. Chem. Soc. **108**, 2560 (1986).

86LIE/PAQ
J.F. Liebman, L.A. Paquette, J.L. Peterson and D.W. Rogers, J. Am. Chem. Soc. **108**, 8267 (1986).

86MAI/OLE
J. Main-Bobo, S. Loesik, W. Gase, T. Baer, A. Mommers and J. Holmes, "The Thermochemistry and Dissociation Dynamics of Internal-Energy Selected Pyrazole and Imidazole Ions," J. Am. Chem. Soc. **108**, 677 (1986).

86MAL/LIF
Y. Malinovich and C. Lifshitz, "Time-Dependent Mass Spectra and Breakdown Graphs. 7. Time-Resolved Photoionization Mass Spectrometry of Iodobenzene. The Heat of Formation of $C_6H_5^+$," J. Phys. Chem. **90**, 2200 (1986).

86MAR/TOP
S. Marriott, R.D. Topsom, C.B. Lebrilla, I. Koppel, M. Mishima and R.W. Taft, "Proton Affinities of Substituted Cyanides," J. Molec. Str. (Theochem) 137, 133 (1986).

86MAR/WET
J. Marks, D.M. Wetzel, P.B. Comita and J.I. Brauman, "A Dipole Supported State in Cyanomethyl Anion, the Conjugate Base of Acetonitrile. Rotational Band Assignments in the Electron Photodetachment Spectrum of -CH_2CN," J. Chem. Phys. 84, 5284 (1986).

86MAT/AKA
H. Matsumoto, K. Akaiwa, Y. Nagai, K. Ohno, K. Imai, S. Masuda and Y. Harada, "Analysis of Stereochemical Properties of Molecular Orbitals of (Trimethylsilyl)acetylenes by Penning Ionization Electron Spectroscopy," Organomet. 5, 1526 (1986).

86MAU
M. Meot-Ner (Mautner), Personal communication.

86MAU/KAR
M. Meot-Ner (Mautner), Z. Karpas and C.A. Deakyne, "Ion Chemistry of Cyanides and Isocyanides. I. The Carbon Lone Pair as Proton Acceptor: Proton Affinities of Isocyanides," J. Am. Chem. Soc., in press.

86MAU/LIE
M. Meot-Ner (Mautner), J.F. Liebman and J.E. Del Bene, "Proton Affinities of Azoles. Experimental and Theoretical Studies," J. Org. Chem., in press.

86MCE/ALL
S.W. McElvaney and J. Allison, "Gas-Phase Chemistry of Transition-Metal-Containing Anions with Alcohols, Chloroalkanes, and Bifunctional Organic Molecules," Organomet. 5, 416 (1986).

86MCM/HAL
J.E. McMurry, G.J. Haley, J.R. Matz, J.C. Clardy, G. Van Duyne, R. Gleiter, W. Schafer and D.H. White, "Synthesis and Chemistry of Tetracyclo[$8.2.2.2^{2,5}.2^{2,9}$]-1,5,9-octadecatriene," J. Am. Chem. Soc. 108, 2932 (1986).

86MCM/KEB
T.B. McMahon and P. Kebarle, "Strong Hydrogen Bonding in Gas-Phase Ions: A High Pressure Mass Spectrometric Study of Formation and Energetics of Methyl Fluoride Proton Bound Dimer," J. Am. Chem. Soc. 108, 6502 (1986).

86MEO/SIE
M. Meot-ner and L.W. Sieck, "Relative Acidities of Water and Methanol, and the Stabilities of the Dimer Adducts," J. Phys. Chem. 90, 6687 (1986).

86MEO/SIE2
M. Meot-ner and L.W. Sieck, "The Ionic Hydrogen Bond and Ion Solvation. 5. $OH \cdots O^-$ Bonds. Gas Phase Solvation and Clustering of Alkoxide and Carboxylate Anions," J. Am. Chem. Soc. 108, 7525 (1986).

86MIL/FEI
A.E.S. Miller, C.S. Feigerle and W.C. Lineberger, "Laser Photoelectron Spectrocopy of MnH_2^-, FeH_2^-, CoH_2^-, and NiH_2^-: Determination of the Electron Affinities for the Metal Dihydrides," J. Chem. Phys. 84, 4127 (1986).

86MIL/FEI2
A.E.S. Miller, C.S. Feigerle and W.C. Lineberger, "Laser Photoelectron Spectroscopy of CrH^-, CoH^-, and NiH^-: Periodic Trends in the Electronic Structure of the Transition-Metal Hydrides," J. Chem. Phys. 84, (1986).

86MIL/MIL
T.M. Miller, A.E.S. Miller and W.C. Lineberger, "Electron Affinities of Ge and Sn," Phys. Rev. A, Spring 1986.

86MUR/MIL
K.K. Murray, T.M. Miller, D.G. Leopold and W.C. Lineberger, "Laser Photoelectron Spectroscopy of the Formyl Anion," J. Chem. Phys. 84, 2520 (1986).

86NIK/IGO
M.I. Nikitin, N.A. Igolkina, E.V. Skokan, I.D. Sorokin and L.N. Sidirov, "Enthalpies of Formation of the AlF_4^- Ion," Russ. J. Phys. Chem. 60, 22 (1986).

86NIM/ELL
M.R. Nimlos and G.B. Ellison, "Photoelectron Spectroscopy of SO_2^-, S_3^-, and S_2O^-," J. Phys. Chem. 90, 2574 (1986).

86NIM/ELL2
M.R. Nimlos and G.B. Ellison, "Photoelectron Spectroscopy of SiH_3^- and SiD_3^-," J. Am. Chem. Soc. 108, 6522 (1986).

86NIS/DAS
T. Nishimura, P.R. Das and G.G. Meisels, "On the Dissociation Dynamics of Energy-Selected Nitrobenzene Ion," J. Chem. Phys. 84, 6190 (1986).

86NOT/PRI
H. Noth and H. Prigge, "Kernresonanz- und He(I)-Photoelektronenspektroskopische Untersuchung an Diisopropyl- und Di-tert-butylboranen," Chem. Ber. 119, 338 (1986).

86NUN/BAR
L. Nunez, L. Barral, S.G. Largo and S. Pilcher, J. Chem. Thermo. 18, 575 (1986).

86OAK/ELL
J.M. Oakes and G.B. Ellison, "Photoelectron Spectroscopy of Radical Anions," Tetrahedron 42, 6263 (1986).

86ORL/MIS
V. Orlov, A. Misharev and V. Takhistox, "Determination of the Enthalpy of Formation of para-Substituted α,α-Dimethyl Cations in the Gas Phase," Izv. Akad. Nauk SSSR, Ser. Khim. 9, 2006 (1986).

86POS/RUT
R. Postma, P. Ruttink, J. Terlouw and J. Holmes, "The Ketene-Water Radical Cation Dipole Complex $[CH_2CO \cdot H_2O]^+$," J. Chem. Soc. Chem. Commun. 683 (1986).

86REU/WAN
J.E. Reutt, L.S. Wang, Y.T. Lee and D.A. Shirley, "Molecular Beam Photoelectron Spectroscopy of $Ni(CO)_4$," Chem. Phys. Lett. 126, 399 (1986).

86ROT/LEN
W.R. Roth, H.W. Lennartz, I. Vogel, M. Leiendecker, M. Oda, Chem. Ber. 19, 837 (1986).

86RUD/VOV
E.B. Rudnyi, O.M. Vovk, L.N. Sidirov, I.D. Sorokin and A.S. Alikhanyan, "Enthalpy of Formation of PO_2^-, PO_3^-, and $NaPO_2$," High Temp. 24, 56 (1986).

86RUM
D. Rumack, Personal communication.

86SAN/BAL
I. Santos, D.W. Balogh, C.W. Doecke, A.G. Marshall and L.A. Paquette, "Gas-Phase Basicities of Cubane, Dodecahedrane, Methyl- and 1,16-Dimethyldodecahedrane as Measured by Fourier Transform Ion Cyclotron Resonance Mass Spectrometry," J. Am. Chem. Soc. 108, 8183 (1986).

86SHI/BEA
S.K. Shin and J.L. Beauchamp, "Proton Affinity and Heat of Formation of Silylene," J. Phys. Chem. 90, 1507 (1986).

86SHI/VOR
C.S. Shiner, P.E. Vorner and S.R. Kass, "Gas Phase Acidities and Heats of Formation of 2,4- and 2,5- Cyclohexadien-1-one, the Keto Tautomers of Phenol," J. Am. Chem. Soc. 108, 5699 (1986).

86SID/BOR
L.N. Sidirov, A.Ya. Borshchevsky, O.V. Boltalina, I.D. Sorokin and E.V. Skokan, "Electron Affinities of Gaseous Iron Fluorides and Dimers," Int. J. Mass Spectrom. Ion Proc. 73, 1 (1986).

86SIM/BEA
J.A. Martinho-Simoes and J.L. Beauchamp, Chem. Rev. review article in preparation.

86SMA
B. Smart, in "Molecular Structures and Energetics" Vol. 3 (ed. J.F. Liebman and A. Greenberg, VCH Publishers, Deerfield Beach, FL. 1986).

86SPA/RAD
G. Spanka and P. Rademacher, "Transannular Interactions in Difunctional Medium Rings. 1. n/π Interactions in Cyclic Amino Ketones and Aminoalkenes Studied by Photoelectron Spectroscopy," J. Org. Chem. **51**, 592 (1986).

86SPI/GRU
R. Spilker and H.-F. Grutzmacher, "Isomerization and Fragmentation of Methylfuran Ions and Pyran Ions in the Gas Phase," Org. Mass. Spectrom. **21**, 459 (1986).

86SPI/PER
T.A. Spiglanin, R.A. Perry and D.W. Chandler, J. Phys. Chem. **90**, 6184 (1986).

86STE/BEA
A.E. Stevens and J.L. Beauchamp, "Gas-Phase Acidities of $(CO)_5MnH$, $(CO)_4FeH_2$, and $(CO)_4CoH$," J. Am. Chem. Soc., in press.

86STO/LAR
R.C. Stoneman and D.J. Larson, "Photodetachment Spectroscopy of SeH^- in a Magnetic Field," J. Phys. B **19**, L405 (1986).

86TAF
R.W. Taft, Personal communication of unpublished data, 1986.

86TAF/ANV
R.W. Taft, F. Anvia, M. Taagepera, J. Catalan and J. Elgueroy, "Electrostatic Proximity Effects in the Relative Basicities of Pyrazole, Imidazole, Pyridazine, and Pyrimidine," J. Am. Chem. Soc. **108**, 3237 (1986).

86TAF/GAL
R.W. Taft, J.-F. Gal, S. Geribaldi and P.-C. Maria, "Unique Basicity Properties of Conjugated Amino Cyclohexenone Derivatives. The Effects of Molecular Structure on the Disparate Basicities toward H Acids," J. Am. Chem. Soc. **108**, 861 (1986).

86TRA
J.C. Traeger, "Heat of Formation for the 1-Methylallyl Cation," by Photoionization Mass Spectrometry," J. Phys. Chem. **90**, 4114 (1986).

86TRA/MCA
J.C. Traeger and D.J. McAdoo, "Decomposition Thresholds and Associated Translational Energy Releases for Eight $C_4H_8O^+$· Isomers," Int. J. Mass Spectrom. Ion Proc. **68**, 35 (1986).

86TRA/MUN
V.T. Tran and B. Munson, "Proton Affinities by Reactant Ion Monitoring: Triphenyl Group Va Compounds," Org. Mass Spectrom. **21**, 41 (1986).

86TSA
W. Tsang, "Single Pulse Shock Tube Study on the Stability of Perfluorobromomethane" to be published.

86TUR/HAV
F. Turecek, Z. Havlas, F. Maquin, N. Hill and T. Gaumann, "(E)- and (Z)-1-Hydroxy-1,3-butadiene: New Kinetically Unstable C_4H_6O Isomers," J. Org. Chem. **51**, 4061 (1986).

86TUR/HAV2
F. Turecek, Z. Havlas, F. Maquin and T. Gaumann, "72. The Mass Spectra of Organic Compounds 1-Buten-3-yn-2-ol. A New Kinetically Unstable C_4H_4O Isomer," Helv. Chim. Acta **69**, 683 (1986).

86TUR/HAV3
F. Turecek and Z. Havlas, "Energy Barriers to the Diels-Alder Cycloadditions and Cycloreversions of Cation-radicals in the Gas Phase," J. Chem. Soc. Perkin Trans. II 1011 (1986).

86VIG
A.A. Viggiano, Personal communication (1986).

86VON
T. Vondrak, "Electronic Structure of Ferrocene Derivatives Studied by He(I) Photoelectron Spectroscopy and CNDO/2 Method," J. Organomet. Chem. **306**, 89 (1986).

86VOR/BRO
M.G. Voronkov, E.I. Brodskaya, V.V. Belyaeva, D.D. Chuvashev, D.D. Toryashinova, A.F. Ermikov and V.P. Baryshok, "Through-Bond Interaction in Compounds Containing an Si-O-C-C-N Group," J. Organomet. Chem. **311**, 9 (1986).

86WAL
R. Walsh, "Thermochemical Kinetics: A Success Story," J. Phys. Chem. **90**, 389 (1986).

86WER
N.H. Werstiuk, "Thermolysis of N-alkylated Ethylenediamines: An Ultraviolet Photoelectron Spectroscopy Study," Can. J. Chem. **64**, 2175 (1986).

86YAM/FUR
S. Yamabe, Y. Furumiya, K. Hiraoka and K. Morise, "Theoretical Van't Hoff Plots of Gas Phase Ion Equilibria of Cl^- Ion in Water, Methanol and Acetonitrile," Chem Phys. Lett. **131**, 261 (1986).

86ZHE/KAR
L.-S. Zheng, C.M. Karner, P.J. Brucat, S.H. Yang, C.L. Pettiette, M.J. Craycraft and R.E. Smalley, "Photodetachment Studies of Metal Clusters: Electron Affinity Measurements for Cu_x," J. Chem. Phys. **85**, 1681 (1986).

87BOO/ARM
B.H. Boo and P.B. Armentrout, "Reaction of Silicon Ion (^2P) with Silane (SiH_4, SiD_4). Heats of Formation of SiH_n, SiH_n^+ ($n=1,2,3$), and $Si_2H_n^+$ ($n=0,1,2,3$). Remarkable Isotope Exchange Reaction Involving Four Hydrogen Shifts," J. Am. Chem. Soc. **109**, 3549 (1987).

87CHI
J.S. Chickos, "Molecular Structure and Energetics," Vol. 2 (ed. J.F. Liebman and A. Greenberg, VCH Publishers, Inc. Deerfield Beach, FL, 1987).

87COE/SNO
J.V. Coe, J.T. Snodgrass, C.B. Freidhoff, K.M. McHugh and K.H. Bowen, "Photoelectron Spectroscopy of the Negative Cluster Ions, $NO^-(N_2O)n=1,2$," J. Chem. Phys. **87**, 4302 (1987).

87DEA/MAU
C.A. Deakyne, M. Meot-Ner (Mautner), T.J. Buckley and R. Metz, "Proton Affinities of Diacetylene, Cyanoacetylene, and Cyanogen," J. Chem. Phys. **86**, 2334 (1987).

87FER/RON
E.E. Ferguson, J. Roncin and L. Bonazzola, "Heats of Formation and Bond Energies of H_3CO^+ and H_3COOH^+ Ions," Int. J. Mass Spectrom. Ion Proc., **79**, 215 (1987).

87GAR/PAR
D. Garvin, V.B. Parker and H.J. White, Jr., "CODATA Thermodynamic Tables: Selections for Some Compounds of Calcium and Related Mixtures: A Prototype Set of Tables" Hemisphere Publ. Corp. (1987).

87GRA/MEL
J.J. Grabowski and S.J. Melly, "Formation of Carbene Radical Anions: Gas Phase Reaction of the Atomic Oxygen Anion with Organic Neutrals," Int. J. Mass Spectrom. Ion Proc. xx,xxx (1987).

87HER
J.T. Herron, "Thermochemical Data on Gas Phase Compounds of Sulfur, Fluorine, and Oxygen Related to Pyrolysis and Oxidation of Sulfur Hexafluoride," J. Phys. Chem. Ref Data **16**, 1 (1987).

87JOH/SPE
C.L. Johlman, L. Spencer, D.T. Sawyer and C.L. Wilkins, "Hydroxide Initiated Gas Phase Chemistry of Anthraquinone and Related Quinones," J. Org. Chem. **52**, 3027 (1987).

87KEB/CHO
P. Kebarle and S. Chowdhury, "Electron Affinities and Electron Transfer Reactions," Chem. Rev. **87**, 513 (1987).

87LAR/MCM
J.W. Larson and T.B. McMahon, "Hydrogen Bonding in Gas Phase Anions. The Energetics of Interaction Between Cyanide Ion and Bronsted Acids," J. Am. Chem. Soc. **109**, 6230 (1987).

87LIA/AUS
S.G. Lias and P. Ausloos, "Structures and Heats of Formation of $C_4H_7^+$ Ions in the Gas Phase," Int. J. Mass Spectrom. Ion Proc., in press.

87MAS/FER
R. Mason, M.T. Fernandez and K.R. Jennings, J. Chem. Soc. Faraday Trans. II **83**, 89 (1987).

87MEO
M. Meot-ner, Personal communication of unpublished results.

87MIL/FEI
A.E.S. Miller, C.S. Feigerle and W.C. Lineberger, "Laser Photoelectron Spectroscopy of CrH^-, CoH^-, and NiH^-: Periodic Trends in the Electronic Structure of the Transition-Metal Hydrides," J. Chem. Phys. **86**, 1549 (1987).

87MOR/ELL
S. Moran and G.B. Ellison, "Electron Spectroscopy of CH_2S^-," Int. J. Mass Spectrom. Ion Proc. **xx**, xxx (1987).

87MOR/ELL2
S. Moran, H.B. Ellis, Jr., D.J. DeFrees, A.D. McLean, S.E. Paulson and G.B. Ellison, "Carbanion Spectroscopy: CH_2NC^-," J. Am. Chem. Soc. **109**, xxxx (1987).

87MOR/ELL3
S. Moran, H.B. Ellis, Jr., D.J. DeFrees, A.D. McLean and G.B. Ellison, "Carbanion Spectroscopy: CH_2CN^-," J. Am. Chem. Soc. **109**, xxxx (1987).

87SNO/COE
J.T. Snodgrass, J.V. Coe, K.M. McHugh, C.B. Freidhoff and K.H. Bowen, "Photoelectron Spectroscopy of the Selenium and Tellurium Containing Negative Ions: SeO_2^-, Se_2^- and Te_2^-," Chem. Phys. **87**, xxxx (1987).

87SNO/COE2
J.T. Snodgrass, J.V. Coe, C.B. Freidhoff, K.M. McHugh and K.H. Bowen, "Photoelectron Spectroscopy of the Negative Cluster Ions, $NH_2^-(NH_3)n=1,2$," J. Chem. Phys. **87**, xxxx (1987).

87SNO/COE3
J.T. Snodgrass, J.V. Coe, C.B. Freidhoff, K.M. McHugh and K.H. Bowen, "The Negative Ion Photoelectron Spectroscopy of $H^-(NH_3)$, $D^-(ND_3)$, and $H^-(NH_3)_2$," J. Chem. Phys. **87**, xxxx (1987).

87STA/NOR
S.W. Staley and T.D. Norden, Personal communication.

87STE/BEA
A.E. Stevens and J.L. Beauchamp, "Gas Phase Acidities of $(CO)_5MnH$, $(CO)_4FeH_2$, and $(CO)_4CoH$," J. Am. Chem. Soc. **109**, xxxx (1987).

87SUN/ARI
L. Sunderlin, N. Aristov and P. Armentrout, "Reaction of Scandium Ions with Ethane. First and Second Hydride-Scandium Ion Bond Energies," J. Am. Chem. Soc. **109**, 78 (1987).

87THO/BAR
D. Thomas and J.E. Bartmess, Unpublished work.

Journal of Physical and Chemical Reference Data
Cumulative Listing of Reprints and Supplements

Reprints from Volume 1

1. Gaseous Diffusion Coefficients, *T.R. Marrero and E.A. Mason,* Vol. 1, No. 1, pp. 1–118 (1972) — $7.00
2. Selected Values of Critical Supersaturation for Nucleation of Liquids from the Vapor, *G.M. Pound,* Vol. 1, No. 1, pp. 119–134 (1972) — $3.00
3. Selected Values of Evaporation and Condensation Coefficients for Simple Substances, *G.M. Pound,* Vol. 1, No. 1, pp. 135–146 (1972) — $3.00
4. Atlas of the Observed Absorption Spectrum of Carbon Monoxide between 1060 and 1900 Å, *S.G. Tilford and J.D. Simmons,* Vol. 1, No. 1, pp. 147–188 (1972) — $4.50
5. Tables of Molecular Vibrational Frequencies, Part 5, *T. Shimanouchi,* Vol. 1, No. 1, pp. 189–216 (1972) (superseded by No.103) — $4.00
6. Selected Values of Heats of Combustion and Heats of Formation of Organic Compounds Containing the Elements C, H, N, O, P, and S, *Eugene S. Domalski,* Vol. 1, No. 2, pp. 221–278 (1972) — $5.00
7. Thermal Conductivity of the Elements, *C.Y. Ho, R.W. Powell, and P.E. Liley,* Vol. 1, No. 2, pp. 279–422 (1972) — $7.50
8. The Spectrum of Molecular Oxygen, *Paul H. Krupenie,* Vol. 1, No. 2, pp. 423–534 (1972) — $6.50
9. A Critical Review of the Gas-Phase Reaction Kinetics of the Hydroxyl Radical, *Wm. E. Wilson, Jr.,* Vol. 1, No. 2, pp. 535–574 (1972) — $4.50
10. Molten Salts: Volume 3, Nitrates, Nitrites, and Mixtures, Electrical Conductance, Density, Viscosity, and Surface Tension Data, *G.J. Janz, Ursula Krebs, H.F. Siegenthaler, and R.P.T. Tomkins,* Vol. 1, No. 3, pp. 581–746 (1972) — $8.50
11. High Temperature Properties and Decomposition of Inorganic Salts—Part 3. Nitrates and Nitrites, *Kurt H. Stern,* Vol. 1, No. 3, pp. 747–772 (1972) — $4.00
12. High-Pressure Calibration: A Critical Review, *D.L. Decker, W.A. Bassett, L. Merrill, H.T. Hall, and J.D. Barnett,* Vol. 1, No. 3, pp. 773–836 (1972) — $5.00
13. The Surface Tension of Pure Liquid Compounds, *Joseph J. Jasper,* Vol. 1, No. 4, pp. 841–1009 (1972) — $8.50
14. Microwave Spectra of Molecules of Astrophysical Interest, I. Formaldehyde, Formamide, and Thioformaldehyde, *Donald R. Johnson, Frank J. Lovas, and William H. Kirchhoff,* Vol. 1, No. 4, pp. 1011–1046 (1972) — $4.50
15. Osmotic Coefficients and Mean Activity Coefficients of Uni-univalent Electrolytes in Water at 25° C, *Walter J. Hamer and Yung-Chi Wu,* Vol. 1, No. 4, pp. 1047–1099 (1972) — $5.00
16. The Viscosity and Thermal Conductivity Coefficients of Gaseous and Liquid Fluorine, *H.J.M. Hanley and R. Prydz,* Vol. 1, No. 4, pp. 1101–1113 (1972) — $3.00

Reprints from Volume 2

17. Microwave Spectra of Molecules of Astrophysical Interest, II. Methylenimine, *William H. Kirchhoff, Donald R. Johnson, and Frank J. Lovas,* Vol. 2, No. 1, pp. 1-10 (1973) — $3.00
18. Analysis of Specific Heat Data in the Critical Region of Magnetic Solids, *F.J. Cook,* Vol. 2, No. 1, pp. 11–24 (1973) — $3.00
19. Evaluated Chemical Kinetic Rate Constants for Various Gas Phase Reactions, *Keith Schofield,* Vol. 2, No. 1, pp. 25–84 (1973) — $5.00
20. Atomic Transition Probabilities for Forbidden Lines of the Iron Group Elements. (A Critical Data Compilation for Selected Lines), *M.W. Smith and W.L. Wiese,* Vol. 2, No. 1, pp. 85–120 (1973) — $4.50
21. Tables of Molecular Vibrational Frequencies, Part 6, *T. Shimanouchi,* Vol. 2, No. 1, pp. 121–162 (1973) (superseded by No. 103) — $4.50
22. Compilation of Energy Band Gaps in Elemental and Binary Compound Semiconductors and Insulators, *W.H. Strehlow and E.L. Cook,* Vol. 2, No. 1, pp. 163–200 (1973) — $4.50
23. Microwave Spectra of Molecules of Astrophysical Interest, III. Methanol, *R.M. Lees, F.J. Lovas, W.H. Kirchhoff, and D.R. Johnson,* Vol. 2, No. 2, pp. 205–214 (1973) — $3.00
24. Microwave Spectra of Molecules of Astrophysical Interest, IV. Hydrogen Sulfide, *Paul Helminger, Frank C. De Lucia, and William H. Kirchhoff,* Vol. 2, No. 2, pp. 215–224 (1973) — $3.00

Journal of Physical and Chemical Reference Data
Reprint and Supplement Orders

To: American Chemical Society
Distribution Office
1155 Sixteenth Street, N.W.
Washington, DC 20036

Name:_____

Title: _____

Organization:_____

Address:_____

City:_____ State: _____

Country: _____ Zip: _____

I am a member of _____
(ACS, AIP, or Affiliated Society)

ORDERS FOR REPRINTS AND SUPPLEMENTS MUST BE PREPAID. *Foreign orders for Reprints, add $2.50 for each reprint for postage and handling. Foreign orders for Reprint Packages, add $5.00 for each Reprint Package for postage and handling. Make checks payable to the American Chemical Society.

BULK RATES: Subtract 20% from the listed price for orders of 50 or more of any one item.

Please ship the following reprints and supplements:

Reprint No./Package _____, _____ copies $ _____
Reprint No./Package _____, _____ copies $ _____
Reprint No./Package _____, _____ copies $ _____

Vol. 2, Suppl. 1 ☐ Hardcover ☐ Softcover _____ copies $ _____
Vol. 3, Suppl. 1 ☐ Hardcover ☐ Softcover _____ copies $ _____
Vol. 6, Suppl. 1 ☐ Hardcover ☐ Softcover _____ copies $ _____
Vol. 10, Suppl. 1 ☐ Hardcover _____ copies $ _____
Vol. 11, Suppl. 1 ☐ Hardcover _____ copies $ _____
Vol. 11, Suppl. 2 ☐ Hardcover _____ copies $ _____
Vol. 13, Suppl. 1 ☐ Hardcover _____ copies $ _____
Vol. 14, Suppl. 1 ☐ Hardcover _____ copies $ _____
Vol. 14, Suppl. 2 ☐ Hardcover _____ copies $ _____
Vol. 16, Suppl. 1 ☐ Hardcover _____ copies $ _____
Other Suppl.: _____ _____ copies $ _____

Total Enclosed $ _____

(Continuation of Cumulative Listing of Reprints)

25. Tables of Molecular Vibrational Frequencies, Part 7, *T. Shimanouchi*, Vol. 2, No. 2, pp. 225–256 (1973) (superseded by No. 103) — $4.00

26. Energy Levels of Neutral Helium (^{4}He I), *W.C. Martin*, Vol. 2, No. 2, pp. 257–266 (1973) — $3.00

27. Survey of Photochemical and Rate Data for Twenty-eight Reactions of Interest in Atmospheric Chemistry, *R.F. Hampson, Editor, W. Braun, R.L. Brown, D. Garvin, J.T. Herron, R.E. Huie, M.J. Kurylo, A.H. Laufer, J.D. McKinley, H. Okabe, M.D. Scheer, W. Tsang, and D.H. Stedman*, Vol. 2, No. 2, pp. 267–312 (1973) — $4.50

28. Compilation of the Static Dielectric Constant of Inorganic Solids, *K.F. Young and H.P.R. Frederikse*, Vol. 2, No. 2, pp. 313–410 (1973) — $6.50

29. Soft X-Ray Emission Spectra of Metallic Solids: Critical Review of Selected Systems, *A.J. McAlister, R.C. Dobbyn, J.R. Cuthill, and M.L. Williams*, Vol. 2, No. 2, pp. 411–426 (1973) — $3.00

30. Ideal Gas Thermodynamic Properties of Ethane and Propane, *J. Chao, R.C. Wilhoit, and B.J. Zwolinski*, Vol. 2, No. 2, pp. 427–438 (1973) — $3.00

31. An Analysis of Coexistence Curve Data for Several Binary Liquid Mixtures Near Their Critical Points, *A. Stein and G.F. Allen*, Vol. 2, No. 3, pp. 443–466 (1973) — $4.00

32. Rate Constants for the Reactions of Atomic Oxygen (O ^{3}P) with Organic Compounds in the Gas Phase, *John T. Herron and Robert E. Huie*, Vol. 2, No. 3, pp. 467–518 (1973) — $5.00

33. First Spectra of Neon, Argon, and Xenon 136 in the 1.2–4.0 μm Region, *Curtis J. Humphreys*, Vol. 2, No. 3, pp. 519–530 (1973) — $3.00

34. Elastic Properties of Metals and Alloys, I. Iron, Nickel, and Iron-Nickel Alloys, *H.M. Ledbetter and R.P. Reed*, Vol. 2, No. 3, pp. 531–618 (1973) — $6.00

35. The Viscosity and Thermal Conductivity Coefficients of Dilute Argon, Krypton, and Xenon, *H.J.M. Hanley*, Vol. 2, No. 3, pp. 619–642 (1973) — $4.00

36. Diffusion in Copper and Copper Alloys, Part I. Volume and Surface Self-Diffusion in Copper, *Daniel B. Butrymowicz, John R. Manning, and Michael E. Read*, Vol. 2, No. 3, pp. 643–656 (1973) — $3.00

37. The 1973 Least-Squares Adjustment of the Fundamental Constants, *E. Richard Cohen and B.N. Taylor*, Vol. 2, No. 4, pp. 663–734 (1973) — $5.50

38. The Viscosity and Thermal Conductivity Coefficients of Dilute Nitrogen and Oxygen, *H.J.M. Hanley and James F. Ely*, Vol. 2, No. 4, pp. 735–756 (1973) — $4.00

39. Thermodynamic Properties of Nitrogen Including Liquid and Vapor Phases from 63 K to 2000 K with Pressures to 10,000 Bar, *Richard T. Jacobsen and Richard B. Stewart*, Vol. 2, No. 4, pp. 757–922 (1973) — $8.50

40. Thermodynamic Properties of Helium 4 from 2 to 1500 K at Pressures to 10^8 Pa, *Robert T. McCarty*, Vol. 2, No. 4, pp. 923–1042 (1973) — $7.00

Reprints from Volume 3

41. Molten Salts: Volume 4, Part 1, Fluorides and Mixtures, Electrical Conductance, Density, Viscosity, and Surface Tension Data, *G.J. Janz, G.L. Gardner, Ursula Krebs, and R.P.T. Tomkins*, Vol. 3, No. 1, pp. 1–115 (1974) — $7.00

42. Ideal Gas Thermodynamic Properties of Eight Chloro- and Fluoromethanes, *A.S. Rodgers, J. Chao, R. C. Wilhoit, and B.J. Zwolinski*, Vol. 3, No. 1, pp. 117–140 (1974) — $4.00

43. Ideal Gas Thermodynamic Properties of Six Chloroethanes, *J. Chao, A.S. Rodgers, R.C. Wilhoit, and B.J. Zwolinski*, Vol. 3, No. 1, pp. 141–162 (1974) — $4.00

44. Critical Analysis of Heat-Capacity Data and Evaluation of Thermodynamic Properties of Ruthenium, Rhodium, Palladium, Iridium, and Platinum from 0 to 300 K. A Survey of the Literature Data on Osmium, *George T. Furukawa, Martin L. Reilly, and John S. Gallagher*, Vol. 3, No. 1, pp. 163–209 (1974) — $4.50

45. Microwave Spectra of Molecules of Astrophysical Interest, V. Water Vapor, *Frank C. De Lucia, Paul Helminger, and William H. Kirchhoff*, Vol. 3, No. 1, pp. 211–219 (1974) — $3.00

46. Microwave Spectra of Molecules of Astrophysical Interest, VI. Carbonyl Sulfide and Hydrogen Cyanide, *Arthur G. Maki*, Vol. 3, No. 1, pp. 221–244 (1974) — $4.00

47. Microwave Spectra of Molecules of Astrophysical Interest, VII. Carbon Monoxide, Carbon Monosulfide, and Silicon Monoxide, *Frank J. Lovas and Paul H. Krupenie*, Vol. 3, No. 1, pp. 245–257 (1974) — $3.00

48. Microwave Spectra of Molecules of Astrophysical Interest, VIII. Sulfur Monoxide, *Eberhard Tiemann*, Vol. 3, No. 1, pp. 259–268 (1974) — $3.00

49. Tables of Molecular Vibrational Frequencies, Part 8, *T. Shimanouchi*, Vol. 3, No. 1, pp. 269–308 (1974) (superseded by No. 103) — $4.50

50. JANAF Thermochemical Tables, 1974 Supplement, *M.W. Chase, J.L. Curnutt, A.T. Hu, H. Prophet, A.N. Syverud, and L.C. Walker*, Vol. 3, No. 2, pp. 311–480 (1974) — $8.50

51. High Temperature Properties and Decomposition of Inorganic Salts, Part 4. Oxy-Salts of the Halogens, *Kurt H. Stern*, Vol. 3, No. 2, pp. 481–526 (1974) — $4.50

52. Diffusion in Copper and Copper Alloys, Part II. Copper-Silver and Copper-Gold Systems, *Daniel B. Butrymowicz, John R. Manning, and Michael E. Read*, Vol. 3, No. 2, pp. 527–602 (1974) — $5.50

53. Microwave Spectral Tables I. Diatomic Molecules, *Frank J. Lovas and Eberhard Tiemann*, Vol. 3, No. 3, pp. 609–770 (1974) — $8.50

54. Ground Levels and Ionization Potentials for Lanthanide and Actinide Atoms and Ions, *W.C. Martin, Lucy Hagan, Joseph Reader, and Jack Sugar*, Vol. 3, No. 3, pp. 771–780 (1974) — $3.00

55. Behavior of the Elements at High Pressures, *John Francis Cannon*, Vol. 3, No. 3, pp. 781–824 (1974) — $4.50

56. Reference Wavelengths from Atomic Spectra in the Range 15 Å to 25000 Å, *Victor Kaufman and Bengt Edlén*, Vol. 3, No. 4, pp. 825–895 (1974) — $5.50

57. Elastic Properties of Metals and Alloys. II. Copper, *H.M. Ledbetter and E.R. Naimon*, Vol. 3, No. 4, pp. 897–935 (1974) — $4.50

58. A Critical Review of H-Atom Transfer in the Liquid Phase: Chlorine Atom, Alkyl, Trichloromethyl, Alkoxy, and Alkylperoxy Radicals, *D.G. Hendry, T. Mill, L. Piszkiewicz, J.A. Howard, and H.K. Eigenmann*, Vol. 3, No. 4, pp. 937–978 (1974) — $4.50

59. The Viscosity and Thermal Conductivity Coefficients for Dense Gaseous and Liquid Argon, Krypton, Xenon, Nitrogen, and Oxygen, *H.J.M. Hanley, R.D. McCarty, and W.M. Haynes*, Vol. 3, No. 4, pp. 979–1017 (1974) — $4.50

Reprints from Volume 4

60. JANAF Thermochemical Tables, 1975 Supplement, *M.W. Chase, J.L. Curnutt, H. Prophet, R.A. McDonald, and A.N. Syverud*, Vol. 4, No. 1, pp. 1–175 (1975) — $8.50

61. Diffusion in Copper and Copper Alloys, Part III. Diffusion in Systems Involving Elements of the Groups IA, IIA, IIIB, IVB, VB, VIB, and VIIB, *Daniel B. Butrymowicz, John R. Manning, and Michael E. Read*, Vol. 4, No. 1, pp. 177–249 (1975) — $6.00

(Continuation of Cumulative Listing of Reprints)

62. Ideal Gas Thermodynamic Properties of Ethylene and Propylene, *Jing Chao and Bruno J. Zwolinski*, Vol. 4, No. 1, pp. 251–261 (1975) — $3.00

63. Atomic Transition Probabilities for Scandium and Titanium (A Critical Data Compilation of Allowed Lines), *W.L. Wiese and J.R. Fuhr*, Vol. 4, No. 2, pp. 263–352 (1975) — $6.00

64. Energy Levels of Iron, Fe I through Fe XXVI, *Joseph Reader and Jack Sugar*, Vol. 4, No. 2, pp. 353–440 (1975) — $6.00

65. Ideal Gas Thermodynamic Properties of Six Fluoroethanes, *S.S. Chen, A.S. Rodgers, J. Chao, R.C. Wilhoit, and B.J. Zwolinski*, Vol. 4, No. 2, pp. 441–456 (1975) — $3.00

66. Ideal Gas Thermodynamic Properties of the Eight Bromo- and Iodomethanes, *S.A. Kudchadker and A.P. Kudchadker*, Vol. 4, No. 2, pp. 457–470 (1975) — $3.00

67. Atomic Form Factors, Incoherent Scattering Functions, and Photon Scattering Cross Sections, *J.H. Hubbell, Wm.J. Veigele, E.A. Briggs, R.T. Brown, D.T. Cromer, and R.J. Howerton*, Vol. 4, No. 3, pp. 471–538 (1975) — $5.50

68. Binding Energies in Atomic Negative Ions, *H. Hotop and W.C. Lineberger*, Vol. 4, No. 3, pp. 539–576 (1975) — $4.50

69. A Survey of Electron Swarm Data, *J. Dutton*, Vol. 4, No. 3, pp. 577–856 (1975) — $12.00

70. Ideal Gas Thermodynamic Properties and Isomerization of n-Butane and Isobutane, *S.S. Chen, R.C. Wilhoit, and B.J. Zwolinski*, Vol. 4, No. 4, pp. 859–869 (1975) — $3.00

71. Molten Salts: Volume 4, Part 2, Chlorides and Mixtures, Electrical Conductance, Density, Viscosity, and Surface Tension Data, *G.J. Janz, R.P.T. Tomkins, C.B. Allen, J.R. Downey, Jr., G.L. Gardner, U. Krebs, and S.K. Singer*, Vol. 4, No. 4, pp. 871–1178 (1975) — $13.00

72. Property Index to Volumes 1–4 (1972–1975), Vol. 4, No. 4, pp. 1179–1192 (1975) — $3.00

Reprints from Volume 5

73. Scaled Equation of State Parameters for Gases in the Critical Region, *J.M.H. Levelt Sengers, W.L. Greer, and J.V. Sengers*, Vol. 5, No. 1, pp. 1–51 (1976) — $5.00

74. Microwave Spectra of Molecules of Astrophysical Interest, IX. Acetaldehyde, *A. Bauder, F.J. Lovas, and D.R. Johnson*, Vol. 5, No. 1, pp. 53–77 (1976) — $4.00

75. Microwave Spectra of Molecules of Astrophysical Interest, X. Isocyanic Acid, *G. Winnewisser, W.H. Hocking, and M.C.L. Gerry*, Vol. 5, No. 1, pp. 79–101 (1976) — $4.00

76. Diffusion in Copper and Copper Alloys, Part IV. Diffusion in Systems Involving Elements of Group VIII, *Daniel B. Butrymowicz, John R. Manning, and Michael E. Read*, Vol. 5, No. 1, pp. 103–200 (1976) — $6.50

77. A Critical Review of the Stark Widths and Shifts of Spectral Lines from Non-Hydrogenic Atoms, *N. Konjevic and J.R. Roberts*, Vol. 5, No. 2, pp. 209–257 (1976) — $5.00

78. Experimental Stark Widths and Shifts for Non-Hydrogenic Spectral Lines of Ionized Atoms (A Critical Review and Tabulation of Selected Data), *N. Konjevic and W.L. Wiese*, Vol. 5, No. 2, pp. 259–308 (1976) — $5.00

79. Atlas of the Absorption Spectrum of Nitric Oxide (NO) between 1420 and 1250 Å, *E. Miescher and F. Alberti*, Vol. 5, No. 2, pp. 309–317 (1976) — $3.00

80. Ideal Gas Thermodynamic Properties of Propanone and 2-Butanone, *Jing Chao and Bruno J. Zwolinski*, Vol. 5, No. 2, pp. 319–328 (1976) — $3.00

81. Refractive Index of Alkali Halides and Its Wavelength and Temperature Derivatives, *H.H. Li*, Vol. 5, No. 2, pp. 329–528 (1976) — $9.50

82. Tables of Critically Evaluated Oscillator Strengths for the Lithium Isoelectronic Sequence, *G.A. Martin and W.L. Wiese*, Vol. 5, No. 3, pp. 537–570 (1976) — $4.50

83. Ideal Gas Thermodynamic Properties of Six Chlorofluoromethanes, *S.S. Chen, R.C. Wilhoit, and B.J. Zwolinski*, Vol. 5, No. 3, pp. 571–580 (1976) — $3.00

84. Survey of Superconductive Materials and Critical Evaluation of Selected Properties, *B.W. Roberts*, Vol. 5, No. 3, pp. 581–821 (1976) — $12.50

85. Nuclear Spins and Moments, *Gladys H. Fuller*, Vol. 5, No. 4, pp. 835–1092 (1976) — $11.50

86. Nuclear Moments and Moment Ratios as Determined by Mössbauer Spectroscopy, *J.G. Stevens and B.D. Dunlap*, Vol. 5, No. 4, pp. 1093–1121 (1976) — $4.00

87. Rate Coefficients for Ion-Molecule Reactions, I. Ions Containing C and H, *L. Wayne Sieck and Sharon G. Lias*, Vol. 5, No. 4, pp. 1123–1146 (1976) — $4.00

88. Microwave Spectra of Molecules of Astrophysical Interest, XI. Silicon Sulfide, *Eberhard Tiemann*, Vol. 5, No. 4, pp. 1147–1156 (1976) — $3.00

89. Property Index and Author Index to Volumes 1–5 (1972–1976), Vol. 5, No. 4, pp. 1161–1183 — $4.00

Reprints from Volume 6

90. Diffusion in Copper and Copper Alloys, Part V. Diffusion in Systems Involving Elements of Group VA, *Daniel B. Butrymowicz, John R. Manning, and Michael E. Read*, Vol. 6, No. 1, pp. 1–50 (1977) — $5.00

91. The Calculated Thermodynamic Properties of Superfluid Helium-4, *James S. Brooks and Russell J. Donnelly*, Vol. 6, No. 1, pp. 51–104 (1977) — $5.00

92. Thermodynamic Properties of Normal and Deuterated Methanols, *S.S. Chen, R.C. Wilhoit, and B.J. Zwolinski*, Vol. 6, No. 1, pp. 105–112 (1977) — $3.00

93. The Spectrum of Molecular Nitrogen, *Alf Lofthus and Paul H. Krupenie*, Vol. 6, No. 1, pp. 113–307 (1977) — $9.50

94. Energy Levels of Chromium, Cr I through Cr XXIV, *Jack Sugar and Charles Corliss*, Vol. 6, No. 2, pp. 317–383 (1977) — $5.50

95. The Activity and Osmotic Coefficients of Aqueous Calcium Chloride at 298.15 K, *Bert R. Staples and Ralph L. Nuttall*, Vol. 6, No. 2, pp. 385–407 (1977) — $4.00

96. Molten Salts: Volume 4, Part 3, Bromides and Mixtures; Iodides and Mixtures–Electrical Conductance, Density, Viscosity, and Surface Tension Data, *G.J. Janz, R.P.T. Tomkins, C.B. Allen, J.R. Downey, Jr., and S.K. Singer*, Vol. 6, No. 2, pp. 409–596 (1977) — $9.00

97. The Viscosity and Thermal Conductivity Coefficients for Dense Gaseous and Liquid Methane, *H.J.M. Hanley, W.M. Haynes, and R.D. McCarty*, Vol. 6, No. 2, pp. 597–609 (1977) — $3.00

98. Phase Diagrams and Thermodynamic Properties of Ternary Copper-Silver Systems, *Y. Austin Chang, Daniel Goldberg, and Joachim P. Neumann*, Vol. 6, No. 3, pp. 621–673 (1977) — $5.00

99. Crystal Data Space-Group Tables, *Alan D. Mighell, Helen M. Ondik, and Bettijoyce Breen Molino*, Vol. 6, No. 3, pp. 675–829 (1977) — $8.00

100. Energy Levels of One-Electron Atoms, *Glen W. Erickson*, Vol. 6, No. 3, pp. 831–869 (1977) — $4.50

101. Rate Constants for Reactions of ClO_x of Atmospheric Interest, *R.T. Watson*, Vol. 6, No. 3, pp. 871–917 (1977) — $4.50

102. NMR Spectral Data: A Compilation of Aromatic Proton Chemical Shifts in Mono- and Di-Substituted Benzenes, *B.L. Shapiro and L.E. Mohrmann*, Vol. 6, No. 3, pp. 919–991 (1977) — $5.50

(Continuation of Cumulative Listing of Reprints)

103. Tables of Molecular Vibrational Frequencies. Consolidated Volume II. *T. Shimanouchi*, Vol. 6, No. 3, pp. 993–1102 (1977) (supersedes Nos. 5, 21, 25, 49) ... $6.50

104. Effects of Isotopic Composition, Temperature, Pressure, and Dissolved Gases on the Density of Liquid Water, *George S. Kell*, Vol. 6, No. 4, pp. 1109–1131 (1977) ... $4.00

105. Viscosity of Water Substance–New International Formulation and Its Background, *A. Nagashima*, Vol. 6, No. 4, pp. 1133–1166 (1977) ... $4.50

106. A Correlation of the Existing Viscosity and Thermal Conductivity Data of Gaseous and Liquid Ethane, *H.J.M. Hanley, K.E. Gubbins, and S. Murad*, Vol. 6, No. 4, pp. 1167–1180 (1977) ... $3.00

107. Elastic Properties of Zinc: A Compilation and a Review, *H.M. Ledbetter*, Vol. 6, No. 4, pp. 1181–1203 (1977) ... $4.00

108. Behavior of the AB-Type Compounds at High Pressures and High Temperatures, *Leo Merrill*, Vol. 6, No. 4, pp. 1205–1252 (1977) ... $4.50

109. Energy Levels of Manganese, Mn I through Mn XXV, *Charles Corliss and Jack Sugar*, Vol. 6, No. 4, pp. 1253–1329 (1977) ... $5.50

Reprints from Volume 7

110. Tables of Atomic Spectral Lines for the 10 000 Å to 40 000 Å Region, *Michael Outred*, Vol. 7, No. 1, pp. 1–262 (1978) ... $11.50

111. Evaluated Activity and Osmotic Coefficients for Aqueous Solutions: The Alkaline Earth Metal Halides, *R.N. Goldberg and R.L. Nuttall*, Vol. 7, No. 1, pp. 263–310 (1978) ... $4.50

112. Microwave Spectra of Molecules of Astrophysical Interest XII. Hydroxyl Radical, *Robert A. Beaudet and Robert L. Poynter*, Vol. 7, No. 1, pp. 311–362 (1978) ... $5.00

113. Ideal Gas Thermodynamic Properties of Methanoic and Ethanoic Acids, *Jing Chao and Bruno J. Zwolinski*, Vol. 7, No. 1, pp. 363–377 (1978) ... $3.00

114. Critical Review of Hydrolysis of Organic Compounds in Water Under Environmental Conditions, *W. Mabey and T. Mill*, Vol. 7, No. 2, pp. 383–415 (1978) ... $4.50

115. Ideal Gas Thermodynamic Properties of Phenol and Creosols, *S.A. Kudchadker, A.P. Kudchadker, R.C. Wilhoit, and B.J. Zwolinski*, Vol. 7, No. 2, pp. 417–423 (1978) ... $3.00

116. Densities of Liquid $CH_{4-a}X_a$ ($X = Br, I$) and $CH_{4-(a+b+c+d)}F_aCl_bBr_cI_d$ Halomethanes, *A.P. Kudchadker, S.A. Kudchadker, P.R. Patnaik, and P.P. Mishra*, Vol. 7, No. 2, pp. 425–439 (1978) ... $3.00

117. Microwave Spectra of Molecules of Astrophysical Interest XIII. Cyanoacetylene, *W.J. Lafferty and F.J. Lovas*, Vol. 7, No. 2, pp. 441–493 (1978) ... $5.00

118. Atomic Transition Probabilities for Vanadium, Chromium, and Manganese (A Critical Data Compilation of Allowed Lines), *S.M. Younger, J.R. Fuhr, G.A. Martin, and W.L. Wiese*, Vol. 7, No. 2, pp. 495–629 (1978) ... $7.50

119. Thermodynamic Properties of Ammonia, *Lester Haar and John S. Gallagher*, Vol. 7, No. 3, pp. 635–792 (1978) ... $8.00

120. JANAF Thermochemical Tables, 1978 Supplement, *M.W. Chase, Jr., J.L. Curnutt, R.A. McDonald, and A.N. Syverud*, Vol. 7, No. 3, pp. 793–940 (1978) ... $8.00

121. Viscosity of Liquid Water in the Range $-8\,°C$ to $150\,°C$, *Joseph Kestin, Mordechai Sokolov, and William A. Wakeham*, Vol. 7, No. 3, pp. 941–948 (1978) ... $3.00

122. The Molar Volume (Density) of Solid Oxygen in Equilibrium with Vapor, *H.M. Roder*, Vol. 7, No. 3, pp. 949–957 (1978) ... $3.00

123. Thermal Conductivity of Ten Selected Binary Alloy Systems, *C.Y. Ho, M.W. Ackerman, K.Y. Wu, S.G. Oh, and T.N. Havill*, Vol. 7, No. 3, pp. 959–1177 (1978) ... $10.00

124. Semi-Empirical Extrapolation and Estimation of Rate Constants for Abstraction of H from Methane by H, O, HO, and O_2, *Robert Shaw*, Vol. 7, No. 3, pp. 1179–1190 (1978) ... $3.00

125. Energy Levels of Vanadium, V I through V XXIII, *Jack Sugar and Charles Corliss*, Vol. 7, No. 3, pp. 1191–1262 (1978) ... $5.50

126. Recommended Atomic Electron Binding Energies, $1s$ to $6p_{3/2}$, for the Heavy Elements, $Z = 84$ to 103, *F.T. Porter and M.S. Freedman*, Vol. 7, No. 4, pp. 1267–1284 (1978) ... $4.00

127. Ideal Gas Thermodynamic Properties of $CH_{4-(a+b+c+d)}F_aCl_bBr_cI_d$ Halomethanes, *Shanti A. Kudchadker and Arvind P. Kudchadker*, Vol. 7, No. 4, pp. 1285–1307 (1978) ... $4.00

128. Critical Review of Vibrational Data and Force Field Constants for Polyethylene, *John Barnes and Bruno Fanconi*, Vol. 7, No. 4, pp. 1309–1321 (1978) ... $3.00

129. Tables of Molecular Vibrational Frequencies, Part 9, *Takehiko Shimanouchi, Hiroatsu Matsuura, Yoshiki Ogawa, and Issei Harada*, Vol. 7, No. 4, pp. 1323–1443 (1978) ... $7.00

130. Microwave Spectral Tables. II. Triatomic Molecules, *Frank J. Lovas*, Vol. 7, No. 4, pp. 1445–1750 (1978) ... $13.00

Reprints from Volume 8

131. Energy Levels of Titanium, Ti I through Ti XXII, *Charles Corliss and Jack Sugar*, Vol. 8, No. 1, pp. 1–62 (1979) ... $5.00

132. The Spectrum and Energy Levels of the Neutral Atom of Boron (B I), *G.A. Odintzova and A.R. Striganov*, Vol. 8, No. 1, pp. 63–67 (1979) ... $3.00

133. Relativistic Atomic Form Factors and Photon Coherent Scattering Cross Sections, *J.H. Hubbell and I. Øverbø*, Vol. 8, No. 1, pp. 69–105 (1979) ... $4.50

134. Microwave Spectra of Molecules of Astrophysical Interest. XIV. Vinyl Cyanide (Acrylonitrile), *M.C.L. Gerry, K. Yamada, and G. Winnewisser*, Vol. 8, No. 1, pp. 107–123 (1979) ... $4.00

135. Molten Salts: Volume 4, Part 4, Mixed Halide Melts. Electrical Conductance, Density, Viscosity, and Surface Tension Data, *G.J. Janz, R.P.T. Tomkins, and C.B. Allen*, Vol. 8, No. 1, pp. 125–302 (1979) ... $9.00

136. Atomic Radiative and Radiationless Yields for K and L Shells, *M.O. Krause*, Vol. 8, No. 2, pp. 307–327 (1979) ... $4.00

137. Natural Widths of Atomic K and L Levels, $K\alpha$ X-ray Lines and Several KLL Auger Lines, *M.O. Krause and J.H. Oliver*, Vol. 8, No. 2, pp. 329–338 (1979) ... $3.00

138. Electrical Resistivity of Alkali Elements, *T.C. Chi*, Vol. 8, No. 2, pp. 339–438 (1979) ... $6.50

139. Electrical Resistivity of Alkaline Earth Elements, *T.C. Chi*, Vol. 8, No. 2, pp. 439–497 (1979) ... $5.00

140. Vapor Pressures and Boiling Points of Selected Halomethanes, *A.P. Kudchadker, S.A. Kudchadker, R.P. Shukla, and P.R. Patnaik*, Vol. 8, No. 2, pp. 499–517 (1979) ... $4.00

141. Ideal Gas Thermodynamic Properties of Selected Bromoethanes and Iodoethane, *S.A. Kudchadker and A.P. Kudchadker*, Vol. 8, No. 2, pp. 519–526 (1979) ... $3.00

142. Thermodynamic Properties of Normal and Deuterated Naphthalenes, *S.S. Chen, S.A. Kudchadker, and R.C. Wilhoit*, Vol. 8, No. 2, pp. 527–535 (1979) ... $3.00

(Continuation of Cumulative Listing of Reprints)

143. Microwave Spectra of Molecules of Astrophysical Interest. XV. Propyne, *A. Bauer, D. Boucher, J. Burie, J. Demaison, and A. Dubrulle*, Vol. 8, No. 2, pp. 537–558 (1979) — $4.00

144. A Correlation of the Viscosity and Thermal Conductivity Data of Gaseous and Liquid Propane, *P.M. Holland, H.J.M. Hanley, K.E. Gubbins, and J.M. Haile*, Vol. 8, No. 2, pp. 559–575 (1979) — $4.00

145. Microwave Spectra of Molecules of Astrophysical Interest. XVI. Methyl Formate, *A. Bauder*, Vol. 8, No. 3, pp. 583–618 (1979) — $4.50

146. Molecular Structures of Gas-Phase Polyatomic Molecules Determined by Spectroscopic Methods, *Marlin D. Harmony, Victor W. Laurie, Robert L. Kuczkowski, R.H. Schwendeman, D.A. Ramsay, Frank J. Lovas, Walter J. Lafferty, and Arthur G. Maki*, Vol. 8, No. 3, pp. 619–721 (1979) — $6.50

147. Critically Evaluated Rate Constants for Gaseous Reactions of Several Electronically Excited Species, *Keith Schofield*, Vol. 8, No. 3, pp. 723–798 (1979) — $5.50

148. A Review, Evaluation, and Correlation of the Phase Equilibria, Heat of Mixing, and Change in Volume on Mixing for Liquid Mixtures of Methane + Ethane, *M.J. Hiza, R.C. Miller, and A.J. Kidnay*, Vol. 8, No. 3, pp. 799–816 (1979) — $4.00

149. Energy Levels of Aluminum, Al I through Al XIII, *W.C. Martin and Romuald Zalubas*, Vol. 8, No. 3, pp. 817–864 (1979) — $4.50

150. Energy Levels of Calcium, Ca I through Ca XX, *Jack Sugar and Charles Corliss*, Vol. 8, No. 3, pp. 865–916 (1979) — $5.00

151. Evaluated Activity and Osmotic Coefficients for Aqueous Solutions: Iron Chloride and the Bi-univalent Compounds of Nickel and Cobalt, *R.N. Goldberg, R.L. Nutall, and B.R. Staples*, Vol. 8, No. 4, pp. 923–1003 (1979) — $6.00

152. Evaluated Activity and Osmotic Coefficients for Aqueous Solutions: Bi-univalent Compounds of Lead, Copper, Manganese, and Uranium, *R.N. Goldberg*, Vol. 8, No. 4, pp. 1005–1050 (1979) — $4.50

153. Microwave Spectra of Molecules of Astrophysical Interest. XVII. Dimethyl Ether, *F.J. Lovas, H. Lutz, and H. Dreizler*, Vol. 8, No. 4, pp. 1051–1107 (1979) — $5.00

154. Energy Levels of Potassium, K I through K XIX, *Charles Corliss and Jack Sugar*, Vol. 8, No. 4, pp. 1109–1145 (1979) — $4.50

155. Electrical Resistivity of Copper, Gold, Palladium, and Silver, *R.A. Matula*, Vol. 8, No. 4, pp. 1147–1298 (1979) — $8.00

Reprints from Volume 9

156. Energy Levels of Magnesium, Mg I through Mg XII, *W.C. Martin and Romuald Zalubas*, Vol 9, No. 1, pp. 1–58 (1980) — $6.00

157. Microwave Spectra of Molecules of Astrophysical Interest. XVIII. Formic Acid, *Edmond Willemot, Didier Dangoisse, Nicole Monnanteuil, and Jean Bellet*, Vol. 9, No. 1, pp. 59–160 (1980) — $7.50

158. Refractive Index of Alkaline Earth Halides and Its Wavelength and Temperature Derivatives, *H.H. Li*, Vol. 9, No. 1, pp. 161–289 (1980). — $8.50

159. Evaluated Kinetic and Photochemical Data for Atmospheric Chemistry, *D.L. Baulch, R.A. Cox, R.F. Hampson, Jr., J.A. Kerr, J. Troe, and R.L. Watson*, Vol. 9, No. 2, pp. 295–471 (1980) — $10.00

160. Energy Levels of Scandium, Sc I through Sc XXII, *Jack Sugar and Charles Corliss*, Vol. 9, No. 2, pp. 473–511 (1980) — $5.50

161. A Compilation of Kinetic Parameters for the Thermal Degradation of n-Alkane Molecules, *D.L. Allara and Robert Shaw*, Vol. 9, No. 3, pp. 523–559 (1980) — $5.50

162. Refractive Index of Silicon and Germanium and Its Wavelength and Temperature Derivatives, *H.H. Li*, Vol. 9, No. 3, pp. 561–658 (1980) — $7.50

163. Microwave Spectra of Molecules of Astrophysical Interest XIX. Methyl Cyanide, *D. Boucher, J. Burie, A. Bauer, A. Dubrulle, and J. Demaison*, Vol. 9, No. 3, pp. 659–719 (1980). — $6.00

164. A Review, Evaluation, and Correlation of the Phase Equilibria, Heat of Mixing, and Change in Volume on Mixing for Liquid Mixtures of Methane + Propane, *R.C. Miller, A.J. Kidnay, and M.J. Hiza*, Vol. 9, No. 3, pp. 721–734 (1980) — $4.00

165. Saturation States of Heavy Water, *P.G. Hill and R.D. Chris MacMillan*, Vol. 9, No. 3, pp. 735–749 (1980) — $4.00

166. The Solubility of Some Sparingly Soluble Lead Salts: An Evaluation of the Solubility in Water and Aqueous Electrolyte Solution, *H. Lawrence Clever and Francis J. Johnston*, Vol. 9, No. 3, pp. 751–784 (1980) — $5.50

167. Molten Salts Data as Reference Standards for Density, Surface Tension, Viscosity, and Electrical Conductance: KNO_3 and NaCl, *George J. Janz*, Vol. 9, No. 4, pp. 791–829 (1980) — $5.50

168. Molten Salts: Volume 5, Part 1, Additional Single and Multi-Component Salt Systems. Electrical Conductance, Density, Viscosity, and Surface Tension Data, *G.J. Janz and R.P. Tomkins*, Vol. 9, No. 4, pp. 831–1021 (1980) — $10.50

169. Pair, Triplet, and Total Atomic Cross Sections (and Mass Attenuation Coefficients) for 1 MeV–100 GeV Photons in Elements $Z = 1$ to 100, *J.H. Hubbell, H.A. Gimm, and I. Øverbø*, Vol. 9, No. 4, pp. 1023–1147 (1980) — $8.00

170. Tables of Molecular Vibrational Frequencies, Part 10, *Takehiko Shimanouchi, Hiroatsu Matsuura, Yoshiki Ogawa, and Issei Harada*, Vol. 9, No. 4, pp. 1149–1254 (1980) — $7.50

171. An Improved Representative Equation for the Dynamic Viscosity of Water Substance, *J.T.R. Watson, R.S. Basu, and J.V. Sengers*, Vol. 9, No. 4, pp. 1255–1290 (1980) — $5.50

172. Static Dielectric Constant of Water and Steam, *M. Uematsu and E. U. Franck*, Vol. 9, No. 4, pp. 1291–1306 (1980) — $4.00

173. Compilation and Evaluation of Solubility Data in the Mercury (I) Chloride-Water System, *Y. Marcus*, Vol. 9, No. 4, pp. 1307–1329 (1980) — $5.00

Reprints from Volume 10

174. Evaluated Activity and Osmotic Coefficients for Aqueous Solutions: Bi-Univalent Compounds of Zinc, Cadmium, and Ethylene Bis(Trimethylammonium) Chloride and Iodide, *R. N. Goldberg*, Vol. 10, No. 1, pp. 1–55 (1981) — $6.00

175. Tables of the Dynamic and Kinematic Viscosity of Aqueous KCl Solutions in the Temperature Range 25–150 °C and the Pressure Range 0.1–35 MPa, *Joseph Kestin, H. Ezzat Khalifa, and Robert J. Correia*, Vol. 10, No. 1, pp. 57–70 (1981) — $4.00

176. Tables of the Dynamic and Kinematic Viscosity of Aqueous NaCl Solutions in the Temperature Range 20–150 °C and the Pressure Range 0.1–35 MPa, *Joseph Kestin, H. Ezzat Khalifa, and Robert J. Correia*, Vol. 10, No. 1, pp. 71–87 (1981) — $5.00

177. Heat Capacity and Other Thermodynamic Properties of Linear Macromolecules. I. Selenium, *Umesh Gaur, Hua-Cheng Shu, Aspy Mehta, and Bernhard Wunderlich*, Vol. 10, No. 1, pp. 89–117 (1981) — $5.00

(Continuation of Cumulative Listing of Reprints)

178. Heat Capacity and Other Thermodynamic Properties of Linear Macromolecules. II. Polyethylene, *Umesh Gaur and Bernhard Wunderlich*, Vol. 10, No. 1, pp. 119–152 (1981) ... $5.50

179. Energy Levels of Sodium, Na I through Na XI, *W. C. Martin and Romuald Zalubas*, Vol. 10, No. 1, pp. 153–195 (1981) ... $5.50

180. Energy Levels of Nickel, Ni I through Ni XXVIII, *Charles Corliss and Jack Sugar*, Vol. 10, No. 1, pp. 197–289 (1981) ... $7.00

181. Ion Product of Water Substance, 0–1000 °C, 1–10,000 bars New International Formulation and Its Background, *William L. Marshall and E. U. Franck*, Vol. 10, No. 2, pp. 295–304 (1981) ... $4.00

182. Atomic Transition Probabilities for Iron, Cobalt, and Nickel (A Critical Data Compilation of Allowed Lines), *J. R. Fuhr, G. A. Martin, W. L. Wiese, and S. M. Younger*, Vol. 10, No. 2, pp. 305–565 (1981) ... $12.50

183. Thermodynamic Tabulations for Selected Phases in the System $CaO-Al_2O_3-SiO_2-H_2O$ at 101.325 kPa (1 atm) between 273.15 and 1800 K, *John L. Haas, Jr., Gilpin R. Robinson, Jr., and Bruce S. Hemingway*, Vol. 10, No. 3, pp. 575–669 (1981) ... $7.00

184. Evaluated Activity and Osmotic Coefficients for Aqueous Solutions: Thirty-Six Uni-Bivalent Electrolytes, *R. N. Goldberg*, Vol. 10, No. 3, pp. 671–764 (1981) ... $7.00

185. Activity and Osmotic Coefficients of Aqueous Alkali Metal Nitrites, *Bert R. Staples*, Vol. 10, No. 3, pp. 765–778 (1981) ... $4.00

186. Activity and Osmotic Coefficients of Aqueous Sulfuric Acid at 298.15 K, *Bert R. Staples*, Vol. 10, No. 3, pp. 779–798 (1981) ... $5.00

187. Rate Constants for the Decay and Reactions of the Lowest Electronically Excited Singlet State of Molecular Oxygen in Solution, *Francis Wilkinson and James G. Brummer*, Vol. 10, No. 4, pp. 809–999 (1981) ... $10.00

188. Heat Capacity and Other Thermodynamic Properties of Linear Macromolecules. III. Polyoxides, *Umesh Gaur and Bernhard Wunderlich*, Vol. 10, No. 4, pp. 1001–1049 (1981) ... $5.50

189. Heat Capacity and Other Thermodynamic Properties of Linear Macromolecules. IV. Polypropylene, *Umesh Gaur and Bernhard Wunderlich*, Vol. 10, No. 4, pp. 1051–1064 (1981) ... $4.00

190. Tables of N_2O Absorption Lines for the Calibration of Tunable Infrared Lasers from 522 cm^{-1} to 657 cm^{-1} and from 1115 cm^{-1} to 1340 cm^{-1}, *W. B. Olson, A. G. Maki, and W. J. Lafferty*, Vol. 10, No. 4, pp. 1065–1084 (1981) ... $5.00

191. Microwave Spectra of Molecules of Astrophysical Interest. XX. Methane, *I. Ozier, M. C. L. Gerry, and A. G. Robiette*, Vol. 10, No. 4, pp. 1085–1095 (1981) ... $4.00

192. Energy Levels of Cobalt, Co I through Co XXVII, *Jack Sugar and Charles Corliss*, Vol. 10, No. 4, pp. 1097–1174 (1981) ... $6.50

193. A Critical Review of Henry's Law Constants for Chemicals of Environmental Interest, *Donald Mackay and Wan Ying Shiu*, Vol. 10, No. 4, pp. 1175–1199 (1981) ... $5.00

194. Property, Materials, and Author Indexes to the Journal of Physical and Chemical Reference Data, Vol. 1–10, pp. 1205–1225 (1972–1981) ... $5.00

Reprints from Volume 11

195. A Fundamental Equation of State for Heavy Water, *P. G. Hill, R. D. Chris MacMillan, and V. Lee*, Vol. 11, No. 1, pp. 1–14 (1982) ... $5.00

196. Volumetric Properties of Aqueous Sodium Chloride Solutions, *P. S. Z. Rogers and Kenneth S. Pitzer*, Vol. 11, No. 1, pp. 15–81 (1982) ... $9.00

197. Ideal Gas Thermodynamic Properties of CH_3, CD_3, CD_4, C_2D_2, C_2D_4, C_2D_6, C_2H_6, $CH_3N_2CH_3$, and $CD_3N_2CD_3$, *Krishna M. Pamidimukkala, David Rogers, and Gordon B. Skinner*, Vol. 11, No. 1, pp. 83–99 (1982) ... $6.00

198. Peak Absorption Coefficients of Microwave Absorption Lines of Carbonyl Sulphide, *Z. Kisiel and D. J. Millen*, Vol. 11, No. 1, pp. 99–116 (1982) ... $6.00

199. Vibrational Contributions to Molecular Dipole Polarizabilities, *David M. Bishop and Lap M. Cheung*, Vol. 11, No. 1, pp. 119–133 (1982) ... $5.00

200. Energy Levels of Iron, Fe I through Fe XXVI, *Charles Corliss and Jack Sugar*, Vol. 11, No. 1, pp. 135–241 (1982) ... $11.00

201. Microwave Spectra of Molecules of Astrophysical Interest. XXI. Ethanol(C_2H_5OH) and Propionitrile (C_2H_5CN), *Frank J. Lovas*, Vol. 11, No. 2, pp. 251–312 (1982) ... $8.00

202. Heat Capacity and Other Thermodynamic Properties of Linear Macromolecules, V. Polystyrene, *Umesh Gaur and Bernhard Wunderlich*, Vol. 11, No. 2, pp. 313–325 (1982) ... $5.00

203. Evaluated Kinetic and Photochemical Data for Atmospheric Chemistry: Supplement 1, CODATA Task Group on Chemical Kinetics, *D. L. Baulch, R. A. Cox, P. J. Crutzen, R. F. Hampson, Jr., J. A. Kerr (Chairman), J. Troe, and R. T. Watson*, Vol. 11, No. 2, pp. 327–496 (1982) ... $15.00

204. Molten Salts Data: Diffusion Coefficients in Single and Multi-Component Salt Systems, *G. J. Janz and N. P. Bansal*, Vol. 11, No. 3, pp. 505–693 (1982) ... $16.00

205. JANAF Thermochemical Tables, 1982 Supplement, *M. W. Chase, Jr., J. L. Curnutt, J. R. Downey, Jr., R. A. McDonald, A. N. Syverud, and E. A. Valenzuela*, Vol. 11, No. 3, pp. 695–940 (1982) ... $20.00

206. Critical Evaluation of Vapor-Liquid Equilibrium, Heat of Mixing, and Volume Change of Mixing Data. General Procedures, *Buford D. Smith, Ol Muthu, Ashok Dewan, and Matthew Gierlach*, Vol. 11, No. 3, pp. 941–951 (1982) ... $5.00

207. Rate Coefficients for Vibrational Energy Transfer Involving the Hydrogen Halides, *Stephen R. Leone*, Vol. 11, No. 3, pp. 953–996 (1982) ... $7.00

208. Behavior of the AB_2-Type Compounds at High Pressures and High Temperatures, *Leo Merrill*, Vol. 11, No. 4, pp. 1005–1064 (1982) ... $8.00

209. Heat Capacity and Other Thermodynamic Properties of Linear Macromolecules. VI. Acrylic Polymers, *Umesh Gaur, Suk-fai Lau, Brent B. Wunderlich, and Bernhard Wunderlich*, Vol. 11, No. 4, pp. 1065–1089 (1982) ... $6.00

210. Molecular Form Factors and Photon Coherent Scattering Cross Sections of Water, *L. R. M. Morin*, Vol. 11, No. 4, pp. 1091–1098 (1982) ... $5.00

211. Evaluation of Binary *PTxy* Vapor–Liquid Equilibrium Data for C_6 Hydrocarbons. Benzene + Cyclohexane, *Buford D. Smith, Ol Muthu, Ashok Dewan, and Matthew Gierlach*, Vol. 11, No. 4, pp. 1099–1126 (1982) ... $6.00

212. Evaluation of Binary Excess Enthalpy Data for C_6 Hydrocarbons. Benzene + Cyclohexane, *Buford D. Smith, Ol Muthu, Ashok Dewan, and Matthew Gierlach*, Vol. 11, No. 4, pp. 1127–1149 (1982) ... $6.00

213. Evaluation of Binary Excess Volume Data for C_6 Hydrocarbons. Benzene + Cyclohexane, *Buford D. Smith, Ol Muthu, Ashok Dewan, and Matthew Gierlach*, Vol. 11, No. 4, pp. 1151–1169 (1982) ... $6.00

Reprints from Volume 12

214. Thermodynamic Properties of Steam in the Critical Region, *J. M. H. Levelt Sengers, B. Kamgar-Parsi, F. W. Balfour, and J. V. Sengers*, Vol. 12, No. 1, pp. 1–28 (1983) ... $6.00

(Continuation of Cumulative Listing of Reprints)

215. Heat Capacity and Other Thermodynamic Properties of Linear Macromolecules. VII. Other Carbon Backbone Polymers, *Umesh Gaur, Brent B. Wunderlich, and Bernhard Wunderlich*, Vol. 12, No. 1, pp. 29–63 (1983) ... $7.00

216. Heat Capacity and Other Thermodynamic Properties of Linear Macromolecules. VIII. Polyesters and Polyamides, *Umesh Gaur, Suk-fai Lau, Brent B. Wunderlich, and Bernhard Wunderlich*, Vol. 12, No. 1, pp. 65–89 (1983) ... $6.00

217. Heat Capacity and Other Thermodynamic Properties of Linear Macromolecules. IX. Final Group of Aromatic and Inorganic Polymers, *Umesh Gaur, Suk-fai Lau, and Bernhard Wunderlich*, Vol. 12, No. 1, pp. 91–108 (1983) ... $6.00

218. An Annotated Compilation and Appraisal of Electron Swarm Data in Electronegative Gases, *J. W. Gallagher, E. C. Beaty, J. Dutton, and L. C. Pitchford*, Vol. 12, No. 1, pp. 109–152 (1983) ... $7.00

219. The Solubility of Oxygen and Ozone in Liquids, *Rubin Battino, Timothy R. Rettich, and Toshihiro Tominaga*, Vol. 12, No. 2, pp. 163–178 (1983) ... $5.00

220. Recommended Values for the Thermal Expansivity of Silicon from 0 to 1000 K, *C. A. Swenson*, Vol. 12, No. 2, pp. 179–182 (1983) ... $5.00

221. Electrical Resistivity of Ten Selected Binary Alloy Systems, *C. Y. Ho, M. W. Ackerman, K. Y. Wu, T. N. Havill, R. H. Bogaard, R. A. Matula, S. G. Oh, and H. M. James*, Vol. 12, No. 2, pp. 183–322 (1983) ... $13.00

222. Energy Levels of Silicon, Si I through Si XIV, *W. C. Martin and Romuald Zalubas*, Vol. 12, No. 2, pp. 323–380 (1983) ... $8.00

223. Evaluation of Binary $PTxy$ Vapor–Liquid Equilibrium Data for C_6 Hydrocarbons. Benzene + Hexane, *Buford D. Smith, Ol Muthu, and Ashok Dewan*, Vol. 12, No. 2, pp. 381–387 (1983) ... $5.00

224. Evaluation of Binary Excess Enthalpy Data for C_6 Hydrocarbons. Benzene + Hexane, *Buford D. Smith, Ol Muthu, and Ashok Dewan*, Vol. 12, No. 2, pp. 389–393 (1983) ... $5.00

225. Evaluation of Binary Excess Volume Data for C_6 Hydrocarbons. Benzene + Hexane, *Buford D. Smith, Ol Muthu, and Ashok Dewan*, Vol. 12, No. 2, pp. 395–401 (1983) ... $5.00

226. Atlas of the High-Temperature Water Vapor Spectrum in the 3000 to 4000 cm^{-1} Region, *A. S. Pine, M. J. Coulombe, C. Camy-Peyret, and J-M. Flaud*, Vol. 12, No. 3, pp. 413–465 (1983) ... $8.00

227. Small-Angle Rayleigh Scattering of Photons at High Energies: Tabulations of Relativistic HFS Modified Atomic Form Factors, *D. Schaupp, M. Schumacher, F. Smend, P. Rullhusen, and J. H. Hubbell*, Vol. 12, No. 3, pp. 467–512 (1983) ... $7.00

228. Thermodynamic Properties of D_2O in the Critical Region, *B. Kamgar-Parsi, J. M. H. Levelt Sengers, and J. V. Sengers*, Vol. 12, No. 3, pp. 513–529 (1983) ... $6.00

229. Chemical Kinetic Data Sheets for High-Temperature Chemical Reactions, *N. Cohen and K. R. Westberg*, Vol. 12, No. 3, pp. 531–590 (1983) ... $8.00

230. Molten Salts: Volume 5, Part 2. Additional Single and Multi-Component Salt Systems. Electrical Conductance, Density, Viscosity and Surface Tension Data, *G. J. Janz and R. P. T. Tomkins*, Vol. 12, No. 3, pp. 591–815 (1983) ... $19.00

231. International Tables of the Surface Tension of Water, *N. B. Vargaftik, B. N. Volkov, and L. D. Voljak*, Vol. 12, No. 3, pp. 817–820 (1983) ... $5.00

232. Evaluated Theoretical Cross Section Data for Charge Exchange of Multiply Charged Ions with Atoms. I. Hydrogen Atom-Fully Stripped Ion Systems, *R. K. Janev, B. H. Bransden, and J. W. Gallagher*, Vol. 12, No. 4, pp. 829–872 (1983) ... $7.00

233. Evaluated Theoretical Cross Section Data for Charge Exchange of Multiply Charged Ions with Atoms. II. Hydrogen Atom-Partially Stripped Ion Systems, *J. W. Gallagher, B. H. Bransden, and R. K. Janev*, Vol. 12, No. 4, pp. 873–890 (1983) ... $6.00

234. Recommended Data on the Electron Impact Ionization of Light Atoms and Ions, *K. L. Bell, H. B. Gilbody, J. G. Hughes, A. E. Kingston, and F. J. Smith*, Vol. 12, No. 4, pp. 891–916 (1983) ... $6.00

235. A Correlation of the Viscosity and Thermal Conductivity Data of Gaseous and Liquid Ethylene, *P. M. Holland, B. E. Eaton, and H. J. M. Hanley*, Vol. 12, No. 4, pp. 917–932 (1983) ... $5.00

236. Transport Properties of Liquid and Gaseous D_2O over a Wide Range of Temperature and Pressure, *N. Matsunaga and A. Nagashima*, Vol. 12, No. 4, pp. 933–966 (1983) ... $7.00

237. Thermochemical Data for Gaseous Monoxides, *J. B. Pedley and E. M. Marshall*, Vol. 12, No. 4, pp. 967–1031 (1983) ... $9.00

238. Vapor Pressure of Coal Chemicals, *J. Chao, C. T. Lin, and T. H. Chung*, Vol. 12, No. 4, pp. 1033–1063 (1983) ... $6.00

Reprints from Volume 13

239. Thermodynamic Properties of Aqueous Sodium Chloride Solutions, *Kenneth S. Pitzer, J. Christopher Peiper, and R. H. Busey*, Vol. 13, No. 1, pp. 1–102 (1984) ... $11.00

240. Refractive Index of ZnS, ZnSe, and ZnTe and Its Wavelength and Temperature Derivatives, *H. H. Li*, Vol. 13, No. 1, pp. 103–150 (1984) ... $7.00

241. High Temperature Vaporization Behavior of Oxides. I. Alkali Metal Binary Oxides, *R. H. Lamoreaux and D. L. Hildenbrand*, Vol. 13, No. 1, pp. 151–173 (1984) ... $6.00

242. Thermophysical Properties of Fluid H_2O, *J. Kestin, J. V. Sengers, B. Kamgar-Parsi, and J. M. H. Levelt Sengers*, Vol. 13, No. 1, pp. 175–183 (1984) ... $5.00

243. Representative Equations for the Viscosity of Water Substance, *J. V. Sengers and B. Kamgar-Parsi*, Vol. 13, No. 1, pp. 185–205 (1984) ... $6.00

244. Atlas of the Schumann–Runge Absorption Bands of O_2 in the Wavelength Region 175–205 nm, *K. Yoshino, D. E. Freeman, and W. H. Parkinson*, Vol. 13, No. 1, pp. 207–227 (1984) ... $6.00

245. Equilibrium and Transport Properties of the Noble Gases and Their Mixtures at Low Density, *J. Kestin, K. Knierim, E. A. Mason, B. Najafi, S. T. Ro, and M. Waldman*, Vol. 13, No. 1, pp. 229–303 (1984) ... $9.00

246. Evaluation of Kinetic and Mechanistic Data For Modeling of Photochemical Smog, *Roger Atkinson and Alan C. Lloyd*, Vol. 13, No. 2, pp. 315–444 (1984) ... $13.00

247. Rate Data for Inelastic Collision Processes in the Diatomic Halogen Molecules, *J. I. Steinfeld*, Vol. 13, No. 2, pp. 445–553 (1984) ... $11.00

248. Water Solubilities of Polynuclear Aromatic and Heteroaromatic Compounds, *Robert S. Pearlman, Samuel H. Yalkowsky, and Sujit Banerjee*, Vol. 13, No. 2, pp. 555–562 (1984) ... $5.00

249. The Solubility of Nitrogen and Air in Liquids, *Rubin Battino, Timothy R. Rettich, and Toshihiro Tominaga*, Vol. 13, No. 2, pp. 563–600 (1984) ... $7.00

250. Thermophysical Properties of Fluid D_2O, *J. Kestin, J. V. Sengers, B. Kamgar-Parsi, and J. M. H. Levelt Sengers*, Vol. 13, No. 2, pp. 601–609 (1984) ... $5.00

251. Experimental Stark Widths and Shifts for Spectral Lines of Neutral Atoms (A Critical Review of Selected Data for the Period 1976 to 1982), *N. Konjević, M. S. Dimitrijević, and W. L. Wiese*, Vol. 13, No. 3, pp. 619–647 (1984) ... $6.00

(Continuation of Cumulative Listing of Reprints)

252. Experimental Stark Widths and Shifts for Spectral Lines of Positive Ions (A Critical Review and Tabulation of Selected Data for the Period 1976 to 1982), *N. Konjević, M. S. Dimitrijević, and W. L. Wiese*, Vol. 13, No. 3, pp. 649–686 (1984) ... $7.00

253. A Review of Deuterium Triple-Point Temperatures, *L. A. Schwalbe and E. R. Grilly*, Vol. 13, No. 3, pp. 687–693 (1984) ... $5.00

254. Evaluated Gas Phase Basicities and Proton Affinities of Molecules; Heats of Formation of Protonated Molecules, *Sharon G. Lias, Joel F. Liebman, and Rhoda D. Levin*, Vol. 13, No. 3, pp. 695–808 (1984) ... $12.00

255. Isotopic Abundances and Atomic Weights of the Elements, *Paul De Bièvre, Marc Gallet, Norman E. Holden, and I. Lynus Barnes*, Vol. 13, No. 3, pp. 809–891 (1984) ... $10.00

256. Representative Equations for the Thermal Conductivity of Water Substance, *J. V. Sengers, J. T. R. Watson, R. S. Basu, B. Kamgar-Parsi, and R. C. Hendricks*, Vol. 13, No. 3, pp. 893–933 (1984) ... $7.00

257. Ground-State Vibrational Energy Levels of Polyatomic Transient Molecules, *Marilyn E. Jacox*, Vol. 13, No. 4, pp. 945–1068 (1984) ... $12.00

258. Electrical Resistivity of Selected Elements, *P. D. Desai, T. K. Chu, H. M. James, and C. Y. Ho*, Vol. 13, No. 4, pp. 1069–1096 (1984) ... $6.00

259. Electrical Resistivity of Vanadium and Zirconium, *P. D. Desai, H. M. James, and C. Y. Ho*, Vol. 13, No. 4, pp. 1097–1130 (1984) ... $7.00

260. Electrical Resistivity of Aluminum and Manganese, *P. D. Desai, H. M. James, and C. Y. Ho*, Vol. 13, No. 4, pp. 1131–1172 (1984) ... $7.00

261. Standard Chemical Thermodynamic Properties of Alkane Isomer Groups, *Robert A. Alberty and Catherine A. Gehrig*, Vol. 13, No. 4, pp. 1173–1197 (1984) ... $6.00

262. Evaluated Theoretical Cross-Section Data for Charge Exchange of Multiply Charged Ions with Atoms. III. Nonhydrogenic Target Atoms, *R. K. Janev and J. W. Gallagher*, Vol. 13, No. 4, pp. 1199–1249 (1984) ... $8.00

263. Heat Capacity of Reference Materials: Cu and W, *G. K. White and S. J. Collocott*, Vol. 13, No. 4, pp. 1251–1257 (1984) ... $5.00

264. Evaluated Kinetic and Photochemical Data for Atmospheric Chemistry: Supplement II. CODATA Task Group on Gas Phase Chemical Kinetics, *D. L. Baulch, R. A. Cox, R. F. Hampson, Jr., J. A. Kerr (Chairman), J. Troe, and R. T. Watson*, Vol. 13, No. 4, pp. 1259–1380 (1984) ... $12.00

Reprints from Volume 14

265. Thermodynamic Properties of Key Organic Oxygen Compounds in the Carbon Range C_1 to C_4. Part 1. Properties of Condensed Phases, *Randolph C. Wilhoit, Jing Chao, and Kenneth R. Hall*, Vol. 14, No. 1, pp. 1–175 (1985) ... $15.00

266. Standard Chemical Thermodynamic Properties of Alkylbenzene Isomer Groups, *Robert A. Alberty*, Vol. 14, No. 1, pp. 177–192 (1985) ... $5.00

267. Assessment of Critical Parameter Values for H_2O and D_2O, *J. M. H. Levelt Sengers, J. Straub, K. Watanabe, and P. G. Hill*, Vol. 14, No. 1, pp. 193–207 (1985) ... $5.00

268. The Viscosity of Nitrogen, Oxygen, and Their Binary Mixtures in the Limit of Zero Density, *Wendy A. Cole and William A. Wakeham*, Vol. 14, No. 1, pp. 209–226 (1985) ... $6.00

269. The Thermal Conductivity of Fluid Air, *K. Stephan and A. Laesecke*, Vol. 14, No. 1, pp. 227–234 (1985) ... $5.00

270. The Electronic Spectrum and Energy Levels of the Deuterium Molecule, *Robert S. Freund, James A. Schiavone, and H. M. Crosswhite*, Vol. 14, No. 1, pp. 235–383 (1985) ... $14.00

271. Microwave Spectra of Molecules of Astrophysical Interest. XXII. Sulfur Dioxide (SO_2), *F. J. Lovas*, Vol. 14, No. 2, pp. 395–488 (1985) ... $10.00

272. Evaluation of the Thermodynamic Functions for Aqueous Sodium Chloride from Equilibrium and Calorimetric Measurements below 154 °C, *E. Colin W. Clarke and David N. Glew*, Vol. 14, No. 2, pp. 489–610 (1985) ... $12.00

273. The Mark–Houwink–Sakurada Equation for the Viscosity of Linear Polyethylene, *Herman L. Wagner*, Vol. 14, No. 2, pp. 611–617 (1985) ... $5.00

274. The Solubility of Mercury and Some Sparingly Soluble Mercury Salts in Water and Aqueous Electrolyte Solutions, *H. Lawrence Clever, Susan A. Johnson, and M. Elizabeth Derrick*, Vol. 14, No. 3, pp. 631–680 (1985) ... $8.00

275. A Review and Evaluation of the Phase Equilibria, Liquid-Phase Heats of Mixing and Excess Volumes, and Gas-Phase PVT Measurements for Nitrogen + Methane, *A. J. Kidnay, R. C. Miller, E. D. Sloan, and M. J. Hiza*, Vol. 14, No. 3, pp. 681–694 (1985) ... $5.00

276. The Homogeneous Nucleation Limits of Liquids, *C. T. Avedisian*, Vol. 14, No. 3, pp. 695–729 (1985) ... $7.00

277. Binding Energies in Atomic Negative Ions: II, *H. Hotop and W. C. Lineberger*, Vol. 14, No. 3, pp. 731–750 (1985) ... $6.00

278. Energy Levels of Phosphorus, P I through P XV, *W. C. Martin, Romuald Zalubas, and Arlene Musgrove*, Vol. 14, No. 3, pp. 751–802 (1985) ... $8.00

279. Standard Chemical Thermodynamic Properties of Alkene Isomer Groups, *Robert A. Alberty and Catherine A. Gehrig*, Vol. 14, No. 3, pp. 803–820 (1985) ... $6.00

280. Standard Chemical Thermodynamic Properties of Alkylnaphthalene Isomer Groups, *Robert A. Alberty and Theodore M. Bloomstein*, Vol. 14, No. 3, pp. 821–837 (1985) ... $6.00

281. Carbon Monoxide Thermophysical Properties from 68 to 1000 K at Pressures to 100 MPa, *Robert D. Goodwin*, Vol. 14, No. 4, pp. 849–932 (1985) ... $10.00

282. Refractive Index of Water and Its Dependence on Wavelength, Temperature, and Density, *I. Thormählen, J. Straub, and U. Grigull*, Vol. 14, No. 4, pp. 933–945 (1985) ... $5.00

283. Viscosity and Thermal Conductivity of Dry Air in the Gaseous Phase, *K. Kadoya, N. Matsunaga, and A. Nagashima*, Vol. 14, No. 4, pp. 947–970 (1985) ... $6.00

284. Charge Transfer of Hydrogen Ions and Atoms in Metal Vapors, *T. J. Morgan, R. E. Olson, A. S. Schlachter, and J. W. Gallagher*, Vol. 14, No. 4, pp. 971–1040 (1985) ... $9.00

285. Reactivity of HO_2/O_2^- Radicals in Aqueous Solution, *Benon H. J. Bielski, Diane E. Cabelli, Ravindra L. Arudi, and Alberta B. Ross*, Vol. 14, No. 4, pp. 1041–1100 (1985) ... $8.00

286. The Mark–Houwink–Sakurada Equation for the Viscosity of Atactic Polystyrene, *Herman L. Wagner*, Vol. 14, No. 4, pp. 1101–1106 (1985) ... $5.00

287. Standard Chemical Thermodynamic Properties of Alkylcyclopentane Isomer Groups, Alkylcyclohexane Isomer Groups, and Combined Isomer Groups, *Robert A. Alberty and Young S. Ha*, Vol. 14, No. 4, pp. 1107–1132 (1985) ... $6.00

Reprints from Volume 15

288. Triplet–Triplet Absorption Spectra of Organic Molecules in Condensed Phases, *Ian Carmichael and Gordon L. Hug*, Vol. 15, No. 1, pp. 1–250 (1986) ... $20.00

289. Recommended Rest Frequencies for Observed Interstellar Molecular Microwave Transitions—1985 Revision, *F. J. Lovas*, Vol. 15, No. 1, pp. 251–303 (1986) ... $8.00

(Continuation of Cumulative Listing of Reprints)

290. New International Formulations for the Thermodynamic Properties of Light and Heavy Water, *J. Kestin and J. V. Sengers,* Vol. 15, No. 1, pp. 305–320 (1986) — $5.00

291. Forbidden Lines in ns^2np^k Ground Configurations and $nsnp$ Excited Configurations of Beryllium through Molybdenum Atoms and Ions, *Victor Kaufman and Jack Sugar,* Vol. 15, No. 1, pp. 321–426 (1986) — $11.00

292. Thermodynamic Properties of Twenty-One Monocyclic Hydrocarbons, *O. V. Dorofeeva, L. V. Gurvich, and V. S. Jorish,* Vol. 15, No. 2, pp. 437–464 (1986) — $6.00

293. Evaluated Kinetic Data for High-Temperature Reactions. Volume 5. Part 1. Homogeneous Gas Phase Reactions of the Hydroxyl Radical with Alkanes, *D. L. Baulch, M. Bowers, D. G. Malcolm, and R. T. Tuckerman,* Vol. 15, No. 2, pp. 465–592 (1986) — $12.00

294. Thermodynamic Properties of Ethylene from the Freezing Line to 450 K at Pressures to 260 MPa, *Majid Jahangiri, Richard T Jacobsen, Richard B. Stewart, and Robert D. McCarty,* Vol. 15, No. 2, pp. 593–734 (1986) — $13.00

295. Thermodynamic Properties of Nitrogen from the Freezing Line to 2000 K at Pressures to 1000 MPa, *Richard T Jacobsen, Richard B. Stewart, and Majid Jahangiri,* Vol. 15, No. 2, pp. 735–909 (1986) — $15.00

296. A Critical Review of Aqueous Solubilities, Vapor Pressures, Henry's Law Constants, and Octanol–Water Partition Coefficients of the Polychlorinated Biphenyls, *Wan Ying Shiu and Donald Mackay,* Vol. 15, No. 2, pp. 911–929 (1986) — $6.00

297. Computer Methods Applied to the Assessment of Thermochemical Data. Part I. The Establishment of a Computerized Thermochemical Data Base Illustrated by Data for $TiCl_4(g)$, $TiCl_4(l)$, $TiCl_3(cr)$, and $TiCl_2(cr)$, *S. P. Kirby, E. M. Marshall, and J. B. Pedley,* Vol. 15, No. 3, pp. 943–965 (1986) — $6.00

298. Thermodynamic Properties of Iron and Silicon, *P. D. Desai,* Vol. 15, No. 3, pp. 967–983 (1986) — $6.00

299. Cross Sections for Collisions of Electrons and Photons with Nitrogen Molecules, *Y. Itikawa, M. Hayashi, A. Ichimura, K. Onda, K. Sakimoto, K. Takayanagi, M. Nakamura, H. Nishimura, and T. Takayanagi,* Vol. 15, No. 3, pp. 985–1010 (1986) — $6.00

300. Thermochemical Data on Gas-Phase Ion-Molecule Association and Clustering Reactions, *R. G. Keesee and A. W. Castleman, Jr.,* Vol. 15, No. 3, pp. 1011–1071 (1986) — $8.00

301. Standard Reference Data for the Thermal Conductivity of Liquids, *C. A. Nieto de Castro, S. F. Y. Li, A. Nagashima, R. D. Trengove, and W. A. Wakeham,* Vol. 15, No. 3, pp. 1073–1086 (1986) — $5.00

302. Chemical Kinetic Data Base for Combustion Chemistry. Part I. Methane and Related Compounds, *W. Tsang and R. F. Hampson,* Vol. 15, No. 3, pp. 1087–1279 (1986) — $17.00

303. Improved International Formulations for the Viscosity and Thermal Conductivity of Water Substance, *J. V. Sengers and J. T. R. Watson,* Vol. 15, No. 4, pp. 1291–1314 (1986) — $6.00

304. The Viscosity and Thermal Conductivity of Normal Hydrogen in the Limit of Zero Density, *M. J. Assael, S. Mixafendi, and W. A. Wakeham,* Vol. 15, No. 4, pp. 1315–1322 (1986) — $5.00

305. The Viscosity and Thermal Conductivity Coefficients of Gaseous and Liquid Argon, *B. A. Younglove and H. J. M. Hanley,* Vol. 15, No. 4, pp. 1323–1337 (1986) — $5.00

306. Standard Chemical Thermodynamic Properties of Alkyne Isomer Groups, *Robert A. Alberty and Ellen Burmenko,* Vol. 15, No. 4, pp. 1339–1349 (1986) — $5.00

307. Recent Progress in Deuterium Triple-Point Measurements, *L. A. Schwalbe,* Vol. 15, No. 4, pp. 1351–1356 (1986) — $5.00

308. Rate Constants for Reactions of Radiation-Produced Transients in Aqueous Solutions of Actinides, *S. Gordon, J. C. Sullivan, and Alberta B. Ross,* Vol. 15, No. 4, pp. 1357–1367 (1986) — $5.00

309. Thermodynamic Properties of Key Organic Oxygen Compounds in the Carbon Range C_1 to C_4. Part 2. Ideal Gas Properties, *Jing Chao, Kenneth R. Hall, Kenneth N. Marsh, and Randolph C. Wilhoit,* Vol. 15, No. 4, pp. 1369–1436 (1986) — $9.00

Reprints from Volume 16

310. Thermochemical Data on Gas Phase Compounds of Sulfur, Fluorine, Oxygen, and Hydrogen Related to Pyrolysis and Oxidation of Sulfur Hexafluoride, *John T. Herron,* Vol. 16, No. 1, pp. 1–6 (1987) — $5.00

311. The Thermochemical Measurements on Rubidium Compounds: A Comparison of Measured Values with Those Predicted from the NBS Tables of Chemical and Thermodynamic Properties, *V. B. Parker, W. H. Evans, and R. L. Nuttall,* Vol. 16, No. 1, pp. 7–59 (1987) — $8.00

312. Standard Thermodynamic Functions of Gaseous Polyatomic Ions at 100–1000 K, *Aharon Loewenschuss and Yitzhak Marcus,* Vol. 16, No. 1, pp. 61–89 (1987) — $6.00

313. Thermodynamic Properties of Manganese and Molybdenum, *P. D. Desai,* Vol. 16, No. 1, pp. 91–108 (1987) — $6.00

314. Thermodynamic Properties of Selected Binary Aluminum Alloy Systems, *P. D. Desai,* Vol. 16, No. 1, pp. 109–124 (1987) — $5.00

315. ^{13}C Chemical Shielding in Solids, *T. M. Duncan,* Vol. 16, No. 1, pp. 125–151 (1987) — $6.00

316. The Mark–Houwink–Sakurada Relation for Poly(Methyl Methacrylate), *Herman L. Wagner,* Vol. 16, No. 2, pp. 165–173 (1987) — $5.00

317. The Viscosity of Carbon Dioxide, Methane, and Sulfur Hexafluoride in the Limit of Zero Density, *R. D. Trengove and W. A. Wakeham,* Vol. 16, No. 2, pp. 175–187 (1987) — $5.00

318. The Viscosity of Normal Deuterium in the Limit of Zero Density, *M. J. Assael, S. Mixafendi, and W. A. Wakeham,* Vol. 16, No. 2, pp. 189–192 (1987) — $5.00

319. Standard Chemical Thermodynamic Properties of Alkanethiol Isomer Groups, *Robert A. Alberty, Ellen Burmenko, Tae H. Kang, and Michael B. Chung,* Vol. 16, No. 2, pp. 193–208 (1987) — $5.00

320. Evaluation of Binary Excess Volume Data for the Methanol + Hydrocarbon Systems, *R. Srivastava and B. D. Smith,* Vol. 16, No. 2, pp. 209–218 (1987) — $5.00

321. Evaluation of Binary Excess Enthalpy Data for the Methanol + Hydrocarbon Systems, *R. Srivastava and B. D. Smith,* Vol. 16, No. 2, pp. 219–237 (1987) — $6.00

322. Extinction Coefficients of Triplet–Triplet Absorption Spectra of Organic Molecules in Condensed Phases: A Least-Squares Analysis, *Ian Carmichael, W. P. Helman, and G. L. Hug,* Vol. 16, No. 2, pp. 239–260 (1987) — $6.00

323. Evaluated Chemical Kinetic Data for the Reactions of Atomic Oxygen $O(^3P)$ with Unsaturated Hydrocarbons, *R. J. Cvetanović,* Vol. 16, No. 2, pp. 261–326 (1987) — $9.00

324. Spectral Data for Molybdenum Ions, Mo VI–Mo XLII, *Toshizo Shirai, Yohta Nakai, Kunio Ozawa, Keishi Ishii, Jack Sugar, and Kazuo Mori,* Vol. 16, No. 2, pp. 327–377 (1987) — $8.00

(Continuation of Cumulative Listing of Reprints)

325. Standard Chemical Thermodynamic Properties of Alkanol Isomer Groups, *Robert A. Alberty, Michael B. Chung, and Theresa M. Flood,* Vol. 16, No. 3, pp. 391–417 (1987) ... $6.00

326. High-Temperature Vaporization Behavior of Oxides II. Oxides of Be, Mg, Ca, Sr, Ba, B, Al, Ga, In, Tl, Si, Ge, Sn, Pb, Zn, Cd, and Hg, *R. H. Lamoreaux, D. L. Hildenbrand, and L. Brewer,* Vol. 16, No. 3, pp. 419–443 (1987) ... $6.00

327. Equilibrium and Transport Properties of Eleven Polyatomic Gases at Low Density, *A. Boushehri, J. Bzowski, J. Kestin, and E. A. Mason,* Vol. 16, No. 3, pp. 445–466 (1987) ... $6.00

328. The Thermochemistry of Inorganic Solids IV. Enthalpies of Formation of Compounds of the Formula MX_aY_b, *Mohamed W. M. Hisham and Sidney W. Benson,* Vol. 16, No. 3, pp. 467–470 (1987) ... $5.00

329. Chemical Kinetic Data Base for Combustion Chemistry. Part 2. Methanol, *Wing Tsang,* Vol. 16, No. 3, pp. 471–508 (1987) ... $7.00

330. Phase Diagrams and Thermodynamic Properties of the 70 Binary Alkali Halide Systems Having Common Ions, *James Sangster and Arthur D. Pelton,* Vol. 16, No. 3, pp. 509–561 (1987) ... $8.00

331. Thermophysical Properties of Fluids. II. Methane, Ethane, Propane, Isobutane, and Normal Butane, *B. A. Younglove and J. F. Ely,* Vol. 16, No. 4, pp. 577–798 (1987) ... $18.00

332. Methanol Thermodynamic Properties from 176 to 673 K at Pressures to 700 Bar, *Robert D. Goodwin,* Vol. 16, No. 4, pp. 799–892 (1987) ... $10.00

333. International Equations for the Saturation Properties of Ordinary Water Substance, *A. Saul and W. Wagner,* Vol. 16, No. 4, pp. 893–901 (1987) ... $5.00

334. Rate Data for Inelastic Collision Processes in the Diatomic Halogen Molecules. 1986 Supplement, *J. I. Steinfeld,* Vol. 16, No. 4, pp. 903–910 (1987) ... $5.00

335. Critical Survey of Data on the Spectroscopy and Kinetics of Ozone in the Mesosphere and Thermosphere, *Jeffrey I. Steinfeld, Steven M. Adler-Golden, and Jean W. Gallagher,* Vol. 16, No. 4, pp. 911–951 (1987) ... $7.00

336. Critical Compilation of Surface Structures Determined by Low-Energy Electron Diffraction Crystallography, *Philip R. Watson,* Vol. 16, No. 4, pp. 953–992 (1987) ... $7.00

337. Viscosity and Thermal Conductivity of Nitrogen for a Wide Range of Fluid States, *K. Stephan, R. Krauss, and A. Laesecke,* Vol. 16, No. 4, pp. 993–1023 (1987) ... $6.00

Reprints from Volume 17

338. Pressure and Density Series Equations of State for Steam as Derived from the Haar–Gallagher–Kell Formulation, *R. A. Dobbins, K. Mohammed, and D. A. Sullivan,* Vol. 17, No. 1, pp. 1–8 (1988) ... $5.00

339. Absolute Cross Sections for Molecular Photoabsorption, Partial Photoionization, and Ionic Photofragmentation Processes, *J. W. Gallagher, C. E. Brion, J. A. R. Samson, and P. W. Langhoff,* Vol. 17, No. 1, pp. 9–153 (1988) ... $14.00

340. Energy Levels of Molybdenum, Mo I through Mo XLII, *Jack Sugar and Arlene Musgrove,* Vol. 17, No. 1, pp. 155–239 (1988) ... $10.00

341. Standard Chemical Thermodynamic Properties of Polycyclic Aromatic Hydrocarbons and Their Isomer Groups I. Benzene Series, *Robert A. Alberty and Andrea K. Reif,* Vol. 17, No. 1, pp. 241–253 (1988) ... $5.00

Special Reprints Packages

These special reprints packages offer selected articles in specific subject areas from the JOURNAL OF PHYSICAL AND CHEMICAL REFERENCE DATA, and they are offered at a better rate than when purchased individually. You will have available a complete library of literature for your specific requirements at a fraction of the cost of purchasing back issues of the journal.

Look over the reprints packages available—they are listed by subject area. In the Cumulative Listing of Reprints you will find the titles corresponding to the reprint numbers. You are sure to find building your information bank in this manner to be thorough and economical.

Package C1 (5 Parts) MOLECULAR VIBRATIONAL FREQUENCIES. Consisting of Reprint Nos. 103, 129, 170, 257, NSRD 39.
If purchased individually: $ 33.00
Special package price: **$ 26.00**

Package C2 (22 Parts) ATOMIC ENERGY LEVELS. Consisting of Reprint Nos. 26, 54, 64, 68, 94, 100, 109, 125, 126, 131, 132, 149, 150, 154, 156, 160, 179, 180, 192, 200, 222, 278.
If purchased individually: $121.00
Special package price: **$ 96.00**

Package C3 (6 Parts) ATOMIC SPECTRA. Consisting of Reprint Nos. 33, 56, 77, 78, 110, 132.
If purchased individually: $ 33.00
Special package price: **$ 27.00**

Package C4 (5 Parts) ATOMIC TRANSITION PROBABILITIES. Consisting of Reprint Nos. 20, 63, 82, 118, 182.
If purchased individually: $ 35.00
Special package price: **$ 28.00**

Package C5 (7 Parts) MOLECULAR SPECTRA. Consisting of Reprint Nos. 4, 8, 53, 79, 93, 130, 146.
If purchased individually: $ 51.50
Special package price: **$ 41.00**

Package C6 (9 Parts) THERMODYNAMIC PROPERTIES OF ELECTROLYTE SOLUTIONS. Consisting of Reprint Nos. 15, 95, 111, 151, 152, 174, 184, 185, 186.
If purchased individually: $ 46.00
Special package price: **$ 37.00**

Package C7 (12 Parts) IDEAL GAS THERMODYNAMIC PROPERTIES. Consisting of Reprint Nos. 30, 42, 43, 62, 65, 66, 70, 80, 83, 113, 115, 141.
If purchased individually: $ 38.00
Special package price: **$ 31.00**

Package C8 (7 Parts) RESISTIVITY. Consisting of Reprint Nos. 138, 139, 155, 221, 258, 259, 260.
If purchased individually: $ 47.50
Special package price: **$ 39.00**

Package C9 (7 Parts) MOLTEN SALTS. Consisting of Reprint Nos. 10, 41, 71, 96, 135, 167, 168.
If purchased individually: $ 62.50
Special package price: **$ 44.00**

Package C10 (4 Parts) REFRACTIVE INDEX. Consisting of Reprint Nos. 81, 158, 162, 240.
If purchased individually: $ 32.50
Special package price: **$ 26.00**

Supplements to JPCRD

When the topic demands it, and the quality of the data justifies it, the JOURNAL OF PHYSICAL AND CHEMICAL REFERENCE DATA issues a special Supplement. Each Supplement is a monograph—collected tables of highly significant physical or chemical property data in one complete volume. Listed below are the special Supplements to JPCRD that have been published. Each is a valuable resource for the physical chemist and chemical physicist.

ATOMIC AND IONIC SPECTRUM LINES BELOW 2000 ANGSTROMS: HYDROGEN THROUGH KRYPTON, by Raymond L. Kelly. (Supplement No. 1 to Volume 16) 1987, 1689 pages, 3 volumes. Hardcover.
U.S. & Canada: $75.00
Abroad: $90.00

ATOMIC ENERGY LEVELS OF THE IRON-PERIOD ELEMENTS: POTASSIUM THROUGH NICKEL by J. Sugar and C. Corliss. (Supplement No. 2 to Volume 14) 1985, 664 pages. Hardcover.
U.S. & Canada: $50.00
Abroad: $58.00

JANAF THERMOCHEMICAL TABLES, Third Edition by M. W. Chase, Jr., C. A. Davies, J. R. Downey, Jr., D. J. Frurip, R. A. McDonald, and A. N. Syverud. (Supplement No. 1 to Volume 14) 1985, 1896 pages, 2 volumes. Hardcover.
U.S. & Canada: $130.00
Abroad: $156.00

HEAT CAPACITIES AND ENTROPIES OF ORGANIC COMPOUNDS IN THE CONDENSED PHASE by E.S. Domalski, W.H. Evans, and E.D. Hearing. (Supplement No. 1 to Volume 13) 1984, 288 pages. Hardcover.
U.S. & Canada: $40.00
Abroad: $48.00

THE NBS TABLES OF CHEMICAL THERMODYNAMIC PROPERTIES. SELECTED VALUES FOR INORGANIC AND C_1 AND C_2 ORGANIC SUBSTANCES IN SI UNITS by D.D. Wagman, W.H. Evans, V.B. Parker, R.H. Schumm, I. Halow, S.M. Bailey, K.L. Churney, and R.L. Nuttall. (Supplement No. 2 to Volume 11) 1982, 394 pages. Hardcover.
U.S. & Canada: $40.00
Abroad: $48.00

THERMOPHYSICAL PROPERTIES OF FLUIDS. 1. ARGON, ETHYLENE, PARAHYDROGEN, NITROGEN, NITROGEN TRIFLUORIDE, AND OXYGEN by B.A. Younglove. (Supplement No. 1 to Volume 11) 1982, 368 pages. Hardcover.
U.S. & Canada: $40.00
Abroad: $48.00

EVALUATED KINETIC DATA FOR HIGH TEMPERATURE REACTIONS: VOLUME 4, HOMOGENEOUS GAS PHASE REACTIONS OF HALOGEN- AND CYANIDE-CONTAINING SPECIES by D.L. Baulch, J. Duxbury, S.J. Grant, and D.C. Montague. (Supplement No. 1 to Volume 10) 1981, 721 pages. Hardcover.
U.S. & Canada: $80.00
Abroad: $96.00

THERMAL CONDUCTIVITY OF THE ELEMENTS: A COMPREHENSIVE REVIEW by C.Y. Ho, R.W. Powell, and P.E. Liley. (Supplement No. 1 to Volume 3) 1974, 796 pages.*
U.S. & Canada: $60/$55
Abroad: $72/$66

PHYSICAL AND THERMODYNAMIC PROPERTIES OF ALIPHATIC ALCOHOLS by R.C. Wilhoit and B.J. Zwolinski. (Supplement No. 1 to Volume 2) 1973, 420 pages.*
U.S. & Canada: $33/$30
Abroad: $40/$36

*Prices are for hardcover/softcover.

JANAF THERMOCHEMICAL TABLES
Third Edition

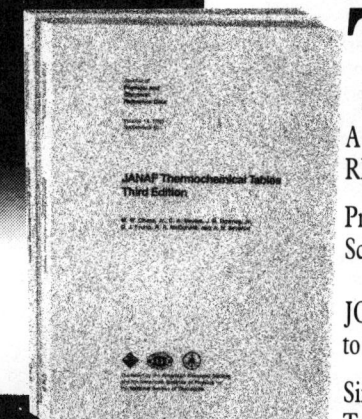

A Major Supplement from JOURNAL OF PHYSICAL AND CHEMICAL REFERENCE DATA

Presenting Reliable Data Utilized by Chemists, Chemical Engineers, and Materials Scientists from Around the World for Over 25 Years

JOURNAL OF PHYSICAL AND CHEMICAL REFERENCE DATA is very pleased to publish the Third Edition of the JANAF THERMOCHEMICAL TABLES.

Since the first version appeared 25 years ago, the JANAF THERMOCHEMICAL TABLES have been among the most widely used data tables in science and engineering. You'll find:

- Reliable tables of thermodynamic properties of substances of wide interest
- A highly professional approach with critical evaluations of the world's thermochemical and spectroscopic literature
- A concise and easy-to-use format

This Third Edition presents an extensive set of tables including thermodynamic properties of more than 1800 substances, expressed in SI units. The notation has been made consistent with current international recommendations.

There is no other reference source of thermodynamic data that satisfies the needs of such a broad base of users.

Order your 2-volume set of the JANAF THERMOCHEMICAL TABLES today! You'll get over 1890 pages of valuable information that is crucial to your research—in two hardback volumes.

SUBSCRIPTION INFORMATION

The JANAF THERMOCHEMICAL TABLES, THIRD EDITION is a two-volume supplement of *Journal of Physical and Chemical Reference Data*.

1896 pages, 2 volumes, hardcover
ISBN 0-88318-473-7
Supplement Number 1 to Volume 14, 1985

U.S. & Canada	**$130.00**
All Other Countries	**$156.00**
(Postage included.)	

All orders for supplements must be prepaid.

Foreign payment must be made in U.S. currency by international money order, UNESCO coupons, U.S. bank draft, or order through your subscription agency. For rates in Japan, contact Maruzen Co., Ltd. Please allow four to six weeks for your copy to be mailed.

For more information, write **American Chemical Society,** Marketing Communications Department, 1155 Sixteenth Street, NW, Washington, DC 20036.

In a hurry? Call TOLL FREE **800-227-5558** and charge your order!

 Published by the **American Chemical Society** and the **American Institute of Physics** for the **National Bureau of Standards**

Editors:
M.W. Chase, Jr.
Nat'l Bureau of Standards
C.A. Davies
Dow Chemical U.S.A.
J.R. Downey, Jr.
Dow Chemical U.S.A.
D.J. Frurip
Dow Chemical U.S.A.
R.A. McDonald
Dow Chemical U.S.A.
A.N. Syverud
Dow Chemical U.S.A.

The Best Source of Quantitative Numerical Data of Physics and Chemistry Published Today!

JOURNAL OF PHYSICAL AND CHEMICAL REFERENCE DATA

Editor, David R. Lide
National Bureau of Standards

Published quarterly by the American Chemical Society and the American Institute of Physics, the *JOURNAL OF PHYSICAL AND CHEMICAL REFERENCE DATA* provides you with compilations and reviews produced under the National Standard Reference Data System (NSRDS) of the National Bureau of Standards.

Chemists, physicists, materials scientists, engineers, and information specialists can all benefit from the reliable information available in this journal. You'll find data on:

- *Atomic and Molecular Science*
- *Chemical Kinetics*
- *Spectroscopy*
- *Thermodynamics*
- *Transport Phenomena*
- *Crystallography*
- *Materials Science*
- *And much more!*

The *JOURNAL OF PHYSICAL AND CHEMICAL REFERENCE DATA* contains recommended values, uncertainty limits, critical commentary on methods of measurement, and full references to the original papers.

Join the thousands of professionals who rely on the *JOURNAL OF PHYSICAL AND CHEMICAL REFERENCE DATA* as a working tool for their research.

Backed by the ACS Guarantee, the *JOURNAL OF PHYSICAL AND CHEMICAL REFERENCE DATA* is guaranteed to be a reliable, up-to-date reference source—you won't want to miss a single issue!

1988 SUBSCRIPTION INFORMATION

JOURNAL OF PHYSICAL AND CHEMICAL REFERENCE DATA is published quarterly, one volume per year.
Volume 17 (1988), ISSN: 0074-2689

	U.S.	Canada & Mexico	Europe, Mideast & N. Africa*	Asia & Oceania*
Members (ACS, AIP, and Affiliated Societies)	☐ $60	☐ $70	☐ $80	☐ $80
Nonmembers	☐ $265	☐ $275	☐ $285	☐ $285

*Surface rates are $70 (members) and $275 (nonmembers) to all countries. Member rates are for personal use only. *Air service included.*

To order your *JOURNAL OF PHYSICAL AND CHEMICAL REFERENCE DATA* subscription, call TOLL FREE 800-227-5558 and charge your order! (U.S. Only) In D.C. or outside the U.S. call (202) 872-4363, or write: American Chemical Society, 1155 Sixteenth Street, NW, Washington, DC 20036, U.S.A.

QC 702 .G37 1988

Gas-phase ion and neutral
 thermochemistry

MAR 3 1 1989